INTERNATIONAL PUBLIC HEALTH:
DISEASES, PROGRAMS, SYSTEMS, AND POLICIES

SECOND EDITION

EDITED BY

MICHAEL H. MERSON, MD
ANNA M. R. LAUDER PROFESSOR OF PUBLIC HEALTH
DEPARTMENT OF EPIDEMIOLOGY AND PUBLIC HEALTH
YALE UNIVERSITY SCHOOL OF MEDICINE

ROBERT E. BLACK, MD, MPH
EDGAR BERMAN PROFESSOR AND CHAIR
DEPARTMENT OF INTERNATIONAL HEALTH
BLOOMBERG SCHOOL OF PUBLIC HEALTH
JOHNS HOPKINS UNIVERSITY

ANNE J. MILLS, MA, DHSA, PHD
PROFESSOR OF HEALTH ECONOMICS AND POLICY
DEPARTMENT OF PUBLIC HEALTH AND POLICY
LONDON SCHOOL OF HYGIENE AND TROPICAL MEDICINE

JONES AND BARTLETT PUBLISHERS
Sudbury, Massachusetts
BOSTON   TORONTO   LONDON   SINGAPORE

Jones and Bartlett Publishers
World Headquarters
40 Tall Pine Drive
Sudbury, MA 01776
978-443-5000
info@jbpub.com
www.jbpub.com

Jones and Bartlett Publishers Canada
6339 Ormindale Way
Mississauga, Ontario L5V 1J2
Canada

Jones and Bartlett Publishers
International
Barb House, Barb Mews
London W6 7PA
United Kingdom

Jones and Bartlett's books and products are available through most bookstores and online booksellers. To contact Jones and Bartlett Publishers directly, call 800-832-0034, fax 978-443-8000, or visit our website www.jbpub.com.

Substantial discounts on bulk quantities of Jones and Bartlett's publications are available to corporations, professional associations, and other qualified organizations. For details and specific discount information, contact the special sales department at Jones and Bartlett via the above contact information or send an email to specialsales@jbpub.com.

Production Credits

Chief Executive Officer: Clayton E. Jones
Chief Operating Officer: Donald W. Jones, Jr.
President, Higher Education and Professional
  Publishing: Robert W. Holland, Jr.
V.P., Sales and Marketing: William J. Kane
V.P., Production and Design: Anne Spencer
V.P., Manufacturing and Inventory Control:
  Therese Connell
Publisher: Michael Brown

Associate Editor: Kylah McNeill
Production Editor: Jenny L. McIsaac
Associate Marketing Manager: Marissa Hederson
Interior Design: Anne Spencer
Cover Design: Timothy Dziewit
Composition: Graphic World
Cover Images: © Alexis Puentes/ShutterStock, Inc.
Text Printing and Binding: Malloy
Cover Printing: Malloy

ISBN-13: 978-0-7637-2967-7
ISBN-10: 0-7637-2967-1

Library of Congress Cataloging-in-Publication Data

International public health : diseases, programs, systems and
  policies / [edited by] Michael H. Merson, Robert E. Black, Anne
J. Mills. — 2nd ed.
    p. ; cm.
  Includes bibliographical references and index.
  ISBN-13: 978-0-7637-2967-7 (hardcover)
  1. World health.   2. Public health—International cooperation.
I. Merson, Michael H.   II. Black, Robert E.   III. Mills, Anne.
  [DNLM: 1. Public Health.   2. World Health.   3. International
Cooperation.   4. Public Health Administration.   WA 530.1 I6105
2006]
  RA441.I578 2006
  362.1—dc22   2005013182

6048
Printed in the United States of America
10 09 08 07 06   10 9 8 7 6 5 4 3

Contents

Chapter 11   The Design of Health Systems   *Anne J. Mills and M. Kent Ranson*   **513**

Chapter 12   Management and Planning for Public Health   *Andrew Green and Charles Collins*   **553**

Chapter 13   Health and the Economy   *Jennifer Prah Ruger, Dean T. Jamison, David E. Bloom, and David Canning*   **601**

Chapter 14   Global Cooperation in International Public Health
Gill Walt and Kent Buse   **649**

Chapter 15   Globalization and Health   *Kelley Lee and Derek Yach*   **681**

Contributors

Robert E. Black, MD, MPH
Edgar Berman Professor and Chair
Department of International Health
Bloomberg School of Public Health
Johns Hopkins University
Baltimore, MD

David E. Bloom, PhD, MA
Professor of Economics and Demography
Harvard School of Public Health
Boston, MA

Kent Buse, PhD, MSc
Research Fellow
Overseas Development Institute, London
London, U.K.

Benjamin Caballero, MD, PhD
Professor and Director
Center for Human Nutrition
Bloomberg School of Public Health
Johns Hopkins University
Baltimore, MD

David Canning, PhD
Professor
Harvard School of Public Health
Boston, MA

Alex Cohen, PhD
Assistant Professor, Department of Social Medicine
Harvard Medical School
Boston, MA

Charles Collins, PhD, MSoc Sc.
Nuffield Centre for International Health and
    Development
University of Leeds
Leeds, U.K.

JoAnne E. Epping-Jordan, PhD
Senior Programme Adviser
Department of Chronic Diseases and Health Promotion
World Health Organization
Geneva, Switzerland

Alan John Flisher, MB ChB, PhD, MSc, MMed, MPhil, FCPsych (SA), DCH
Professor and Head, Division of Child and
    Adolescent Psychiatry
University of Cape Town and Red Cross War Memorial
    Children's Hospital
Cape Town, South Africa

William H. Foege, MD, MPH
Emeritus Presidential Distinguished Professor of
    International Health
Rollins School of Public Health, Emory
University and Fellow, Bill and Melinda
    Gates Foundation
Vashon, WA

Andrew Green, PhD, MA
Professor, Nuffield Centre for International
    Health and Development
University of Leeds
Leeds, U.K.

Gopalakrishna Gururaj, MD, MB
Professor and Head, Department of Epidemiology
National Institute of Mental Health and Neurosciences
Bangalore, India

Corinna Hawkes, PhD
Research Fellow
International Food Policy Research Institute (IFPRI)
Washington, DC

Adnan A. Hyder, MD, PhD, MPH
Assistant Professor and Leon Robertson Chair
Department of International Health, and
Department of Health Policy and Management
Bloomberg School of Public Heath
Johns Hopkins University
Baltimore, MD

Dean T. Jamison, PhD, MS
Professor
UCSF Global Health Sciences
University of California, San Francisco
San Francisco, CA

Tord Kjellstrom, MedDr, MMEng
Professor, National Institute of Public Health
Stockholm, Sweden, and Visiting Fellow
National Centre for Epidemiology
    and Population Health
Australian National University, Canberra, Australia

Kelley Lee, DPhil, MPA, MA
Reader in Global Health
Centre on Global Change and Health
London School of Hygiene and Tropical Medicine
London, U.K.

Anthony J. McMichael, PhD, MB
Professor and Director, National Centre for
    Epidemiology and Population Health
Australian National University
Canberra, Australia

Jane Menken, PhD, MSc
Distinguished Professor of Sociology
Director, Institute of Behavioral Science
University of Colorado at Boulder
Boulder, CO

Michael H. Merson, MD
Anna M. R. Lauder Professor of Public Health
Department of Epidemiology and Public Health
Yale University School of Medicine
New Haven, CT

Anne J. Mills, MA, DHSA, PHD
Professor of Health Economics and Policy
Department of Public Health and Policy
London School of Hygiene and Tropical Medicine
London, U.K.

Richard H. Morrow, MD, MPH, FACP
Professor, Department of International Health
Health Systems Program
Bloomberg School of Public Health
Johns Hopkins University
Baltimore, MD

Robyn Norton, PhD, MPH, MA
Professor and Principal Director
The George Institute for International Health
The University of Sydney
Sydney, Australia

Vikram Patel, PhD, MBBS, MSc, MRCPsych
Reader in International Mental Health
London School of Hygiene and Tropical Medicine
London, U.K.

Christina R. Phares, PhD, MPH
Centers for Disease Control and Prevention
Atlanta, GA

M. Omar Rahman, MD, DSc, MPH
Professor of Demography
Executive Director, Centre for Health, Population and
    Development
Independent University, Bangladesh
Dhaka, Bangladesh
Adjunct Associate Professor of Demography and
    Epidemiology
Harvard School of Public Health
Boston, MA

M. Kent Ranson, MD, PhD, MPH
Clinical Lecturer
Health Policy Unit
London School of Hygiene and Tropical Medicine
London, U.K.

Arthur L. Reingold, MD
Professor and Head, Epidemiology Division
University of CA-Berkeley School of Public Health
Berkeley, CA

Jennifer Prah Ruger, PhD, MSc, MA
Assistant Professor, Division of Global Health
Co-Director, Yale/WHO Collaborating Centre
Yale School of Public Health
New Haven, CT

Susan C. Scrimshaw, PhD
Dean and Professor, School of Public Health
University of Illinois at Chicago
Chicago, IL

Kirk R. Smith, PhD, MPH
Professor, Division of Environmental Health Sciences
School of Public Health
University of California, Berkeley
Berkeley, CA

Krisela Steyn, MD, MSc, NGD
Medical Research Council
Medicina Campus
Tygerberg, South Africa

Michael J. Toole, MB
Head, Centre for International Health
Burnet Institute
Melbourne, Australia

Ronald Waldman, MD, MPH
Professor of Clinical Population and Family Health
Mailman School of Public Health
Columbia University
New York, New York

Gill Walt, PhD
Professor of Health Policy
Head, Department of Public Health and Policy
London School of Hygiene and Tropical Medicine
London, U.K.

Keith P. West, Jr., DrPH, RD
Professor, Department of International Health
Bloomberg School of Public Health
Johns Hopkins University
Baltimore, MD

Derek Yach, MBChB, MPH
Professor and Head, Division of Global Health
Associate Director, Rudd Center for Food
    Policy and Obesity
Yale School of Public Health
New Haven, CT

**Anthony B. Zwi, PhD, MB BCh, MSc, DOH,
DTMandH, FFPHM, AFPHM**
Professor and Head of School
School of Public Health and Community Medicine
The University of New South Wales
Sydney, Australia

Foreword

WILLIAM H. FOEGE

As a child, I was intrigued by a gift of magnets in the form of a white and a black dog. If placed in one orientation they moved apart; turn them around and they bonded. The mystery, for me, was that I could see no difference in their appearance when they repelled or attracted.

If we could assemble the unnecessary suffering, the premature death, and the unmet potential in the world on one of those magnets and all of the knowledge, the tools, the resources, and the interest in correcting these problems on the other magnet, we would find that through most of history the magnets were aligned in such a way that they rejected each other, unseen.

There are a few examples to the contrary, going all the way back to Sumerian assistance with famine relief for another country, but for most of history the story has been one of separation. The resources did not bond to the needs. In fact, they seemed to exist in entirely different worlds. To benefit from the accumulated knowledge acquired over hundreds and thousands of years came down to chance alone based on where you happened to have been born. While it was blatantly unfair, few noticed, and even fewer cared.

Knowledge gathered in a single community or a single country did get shared, of course, but not always in a rapid or consistent fashion. A thousand years ago, many of the health leaders in the world were Muslim scientists who were serious students of the science acquired in other areas, especially in Greece. Later, colonial governments were important conduits of health knowledge to Africa, Asia, and the Americas. A case in point is the speed with which Edward Jenner's discovery of the protective effect of cowpox in preventing smallpox was shared globally within a few years.

Finally, in the middle of the 19th century, responses became more organized. Religious organizations sent medical missionaries to areas of need in Africa, Asia, and the Americas, supplementing the efforts of colonial governments. Information flowed back regarding the problems, and resources slowly increased. But it remained a story of a grossly inadequate response, and as late as the 1940s it was common for the world to ignore even acute problems such as famine.

The last half century has witnessed a revolutionary change. Religious organizations have continued to operate in direct programs, but they have also encouraged their members to seek employment in secular organizations working in global health. During or after the Second World War many international agencies were formed, and they have sought to harness the skills and resources of the world in more coordinated approaches for the relief of health and nutrition needs. Many industrialized governments have developed large and effective bilateral programs that include direct health programs or programs that target education, literacy, development, family planning, or environmental improvement and indirectly improve health. Universities in many countries, including some in the developing world, began operating medical and public health research and delivery programs around the world. They are useful in training students and maintaining faculty with diverse interests.

Nongovernmental organizations have proliferated, now number in the thousands and can be found most everywhere. Service organizations have expanded their portfolios to include global health programs with incredible influence, as exemplified by Rotary International's catalytic role in poliomyelitis eradication efforts. Corporations are sponsoring critical work, not only to develop new tools but also, as in the case of Merck and GlaxoSmithKline, sponsoring programs to reduce the toll of onchocerciasis and lymphatic filariasis. The world has reached a point where, in the absence of political or military obstacles, it has become unacceptable to ignore a famine anyplace. It is hoped that social norms will change to the point where all inequities in health will be unacceptable.

While inequities still abound, it is heartening to see childhood immunization programs improving in many developing countries, as well as serious efforts to combat malnutrition and infectious diseases. Increasingly, university programs are undertaking cutting-edge research and providing health care in Africa and Asia. Vaccine production and low-cost drug production programs in developing countries are becoming commonplace. And it is now possible to measure declines in the HIV rates in Uganda,

Cambodia, and Brazil. New approaches, such as health and agricultural franchise programs, bring hope for future improvements.

In recent years the century-old work of the Rockefeller Foundation in global health has been broadened to include other foundations and funds. The global health community received new hope 5 years ago when Bill and Melinda Gates formed a foundation to provide resources for global health. New interest, research, tools, training, and applications are attracting talent and other resources to the field.

The increase in resources is being matched by an improvement in the tools available. My interest in global health precedes the availability of oral polio, measles, hepatitis, *H. influenza* b, and the other vaccines we now take for granted. Drugs are now available that can be used on a mass public health basis, and diagnostic techniques will soon make it possible to determine with accuracy the problems and progress of patients even in remote health facilities without the usual laboratory services. A few decades ago it was possible to be very isolated in many parts of the world. Now it is possible to keep up on medical developments as the result of computers, cell phones, and rapid communications.

Two major barriers to improved health in poor countries persist. One is the actual delivery of the improved skills and knowledge now available. Basic management capacity is often lacking to bring the abilities and resources to bear on the needs. Often lumped together into the category of infrastructure, this area includes the organization of health services, the selection of goals, logistics, evaluation, incentives, and all of the ingredients that are taken for granted in busi-

ness if one is to make a profit while selling a product. An illustration of this deficiency is seen in immunization programs, where the world has decades of experience as well as the demonstration of good returns on investment, and yet there are countries that can't offer their children even a 50-50 chance of getting life-saving measles vaccine. These errors of omission, which hurt millions, would constitute malpractice if there were a way to compare them to the errors of commission that result in lawsuits throughout the world if a single person is hurt.

There is no shortage of people and experiences to make programs work in global health, but public health programs have trouble competing for people who can make higher incomes in the commercial sector. Global health programs simply have to solve this problem if the tools are to be exploited.

The other major barrier is training a workforce to apply those skills in public health. To prepare for work in global health was once synonymous with training in tropical medicine. Few training facilities were available, and those in the field found that the traditional tropical diseases were far too narrow a focus for the problems faced by poor countries in the tropics. Merson, Black, and Mills have helped to define what needs to be included in the field of global health. They have assembled a thorough textbook to help students understand the breadth of the field, the health conditions they will confront, and the resources and programs they can look to in becoming global health practitioners. Their first edition is used widely in training, and this updated version is a welcome addition to the improved effectiveness of global health.

Introduction

MICHAEL H. MERSON, ROBERT E. BLACK, AND ANNE J. MILLS

The three of us are privileged to be faculty at schools that provide graduate education to students who plan to enter into or have already begun careers in public health. Many of them wish to learn about the public health problems and challenges facing low- and middle-income countries, often referred to as developing countries. Most are committed to teaching, to public health practice or administration, or to undertaking research in these countries or in international settings. This textbook is written for these students and those who teach and mentor them. In this introduction, we define international public health, provide a brief history of the field, and summarize the many challenges currently before it. We then explain how we put this textbook together and how we think it can best be used.

What Is International Public Health?

The term *public health* evokes different ideas and images. Is it a profession, a discipline, or a system? Is it concerned primarily with the health care of the poor? Does it mean working in an urban clinic, or providing clean water and sanitation? C.-E. A. Winslow (1920), often regarded as the founder of modern public health in the United States, defined public health as

> the science and art of preventing disease, prolonging life and promoting physical health and efficiency through organized community efforts for the sanitation of the environment, the control of communicable infections, the education of the individual in personal hygiene, the organization of medical and nursing services for the early diagnosis and preventive treatment of disease, and the development of the social machinery which will ensure to every individual a standard of living adequate for the maintenance of health; organizing these benefits in such a fashion as to enable every citizen to realize his birthright of health and longevity.

The unique features of public health (Exhibit I-1) were aptly defined in 1994 by an Essential Public Health Services Working Group of the Core Public Health Functions Steering Committee of the United States Public Health Service and further elaborated by Turnock (2004). Its most distinguishing feature is its focus on prevention. This can mean prevention of illness, deaths, hospital admissions, days lost from school or work, or consumption of unnecessary human or fiscal resources. Unfortunately, prevention efforts are often difficult; their successes are usually not visible, and most programs lack sufficient priority and resources to achieve their maximum impact. In all countries, much greater attention and budgets are directed toward the provision of medical care, including the purchase of drugs.

One of the most outstanding characteristics of public health is its grounding in a multitude of sciences. These include the quantitative sciences of epidemiology and biostatistics; the biological sciences concerned with humans, microorganisms, and vectors; and the social and behavioral sciences, including economics, psychology, anthropology, and sociology. The latter have received more attention in recent years, as greater importance has been placed on defining and directing prevention efforts toward the economic, social, and behavioral determinants of illness and not only at individuals deemed at high risk for a particular public health problem (Ashton & Seymour, 1988). A similar growth in those trained in the managerial sciences in public health stems from the current debates on the organization and financing of health services in countries rich and poor. With the human genome now fully cloned, public health efforts in the future will seek to apply the recent advances in genetics toward prevention of illness and disease, while being sure to protect the confidentiality rights of individuals. It is evident that the multidisciplinary and interdisciplinary nature of public health requires partnerships among those with diverse experiences and perspectives.

Social justice is the central pillar of public health. Its basis is that the knowledge obtained about how to ensure a healthy population must be extended equally to all groups in any society, even when the burden of disease and ill health within that society is distributed

Exhibit I-1	Selected Unique Features of Public Health

- Use of prevention as a prime intervention strategy
- Grounded in a broad array of sciences
- Basis in social justice philosophy
- Link with government and public policy

Exhibit I-2	Some Differences Between Public Health and Medicine

Public Health

- Primary focus on population
- Public service ethic, tempered by concerns for the individual
- Emphasis on health promotion and disease prevention
- Reliance on many sectors

Medicine

- Primary focus on individual
- Personal service ethic, conditioned by awareness of social responsibilities
- Emphasis on diagnosis and treatment; care for the whole patient
- Reliance on health care system

unequally. Often this fair distribution of benefits is impeded by differences in gender, social class, ethnicity, and race. A critical challenge for public health is overcoming those barriers that prevent the application of the broad array of available prevention approaches and tools.

Although many public health activities are carried out by nongovernmental organizations (NGOs) and the private sector, governments play a crucial role in at least two ways. First, they design and implement public policies that bear on social and environmental conditions, such as employment, housing, and pollution control. Second, they provide specific programs and services, usually to populations with the greatest disadvantages, in an effort to ensure equity in access and in health status. Because of its link to government and its social justice underpinnings, public health is a profession that often stimulates political debate and controversy: as an example, witness the difficulties in almost all countries in obtaining government support for needle exchange programs, despite their proven efficacy in reducing the transmission of the human immunodeficiency virus (HIV) (Hurley, Jolley, & Kaldor, 1997).

One is often asked to explain the differences between public health and medicine (Exhibit I-2). These have been nicely summarized by Feinberg (1994). Those working in public health are concerned with the health of populations, have a public service ethic tempered by concerns for the individual, and place their emphasis on health promotion and disease prevention. Those working in medicine are more interested in the well-being of individuals, have a personal service ethic conditioned by awareness of social responsibilities, and focus their efforts on diagnosis of disease and treatment of patients. Those working in public health require knowledge and input from many sectors—health, environment, social welfare, and education, to name but a few—whereas those practicing medicine rely primarily on the services of the health care system. Of course, these differences are not always so sharp, and efforts are under way around the world to enhance collaboration between public health and

medicine. Nevertheless, they help to illustrate what is meant by public health.

We define *international public health* as the application of the principles of public health to health problems and challenges that affect low- and middle-income countries and to the complex array of global and local forces that influence them. Today, these global forces include urbanization, migration, and an explosion in information technology and expanding global markets. Most of the attention in international public health is focused on low- and middle-income countries, as they have the greatest mortality and morbidity and inadequate health systems to meet the needs of their most vulnerable populations. Improving the health status of these populations requires an understanding of their social, cultural, and economic characteristics. In the study of international public health, much can be learned by comparing the approaches used by different countries in addressing their main public health problems.

What are some of the problems and issues that today's student of international public health needs to understand?

- The main causes of mortality and morbidity in the world today and also in the future, in view of the demographic transition, i.e., the transition from high to low fertility rates and mortality rates, faced by many countries

- The cultural diversity of population groups within countries and regions, and their values, belief systems, and responses to illness and death

- The causes and consequences of human population growth and the beneficial effects for women and children of reproductive health programs

- The complex relationship between nutritional status and disease patterns, including the importance of specific micronutrient deficiencies
- The main infectious agents and vectors responsible for communicable diseases, the increasing rates of noncommunicable (or chronic) diseases, and the social, economic, behavioral, and environmental factors responsible for these diseases
- The increasing burden of mortality and morbidity attributable to nonintentional and intentional injuries
- The various approaches to the design, financing, organization, and management of preventive and curative services in the public and private sectors in countries with diverse economies and resources
- The appropriate responses to complex humanitarian emergencies, especially those that involve large displacements of populations within a country and between neighboring countries
- The importance of health for the economic development of a nation and the productivity of its population, and the reciprocal impact of development, as reflected by such factors as educational levels and economic growth, on health status
- The roles of national, regional, international, and intergovernmental development agencies, as well as nongovernmental and private voluntary agencies in delivery of preventive and care services

This textbook contains chapters dedicated to these and related topics. More detail will be provided about these later, after first offering a brief history of international public health and a summary of the main challenges facing those seeking careers in this field today.

A Brief History of International Public Health

The history of international public health can be viewed as a history of how populations experience health and illness; how social, economic, and political systems create the possibilities for healthy or un-

healthy lives; how societies create the preconditions for the production and transmission of disease; and how people, both as individuals and as social groups, attempt to promote their own health or avoid illness (Rosen, 1993). A number of authors have documented this history (Arnold, 1988; Basch, 1999; Leff & Leff, 1957; Rosen, 1993; Winslow & Hallock, 1949). A brief history is presented here primarily to provide a perspective for the challenges that face us today (Exhibit I-3).

It is difficult to select a date for the origins of the field of public health. Some would begin with Hippocrates, whose book *Airs, Waters and Places*, published around 400 BC, was the first systematic effort to present the causal relations between environmental factors and disease and to offer a theoretical basis for an understanding of endemic and epidemic diseases. Others would cite the introduction of public sanitation and an organized water supply system by the Romans in the first century. Many would select the bubonic plague (or Black Death) epidemic of the fourteenth century, which began in Central Asia, was carried on ships to Constantinople, Genoa, and other European ports, and then spread to the interior, killing 25 million persons in Europe alone. Believing that plague was introduced by ships, port cities such as Venice and Marseilles adopted a 40-day quarantine period for entering vessels and established a cordon sanitaire, an approach that was to be used to control other infectious diseases in subsequent centuries.

The Middle Ages was also the period when many cities in Europe, particularly through the formation of guilds, took an active part in founding hospitals and other institutions to provide medical care and social assistance. It was also a time when many European countries expanded their horizons abroad, exploring and colonizing new lands. They brought some diseases with them (e.g., influenza, measles, and smallpox), and those who settled were forced to confront diseases that had never been seen in Europe (such as syphilis, dysentery, malaria, and sleeping sickness). European explorers also brought new pathogens from one part of Africa to another and from one area of the globe to another (e.g., from Africa to North America through the slave trade). On long voyages, however, the greatest enemy of the sailor was often scurvy, until 1875, when the British government issued its famous order that all men-of-war should carry a supply of lemon juice.

The Age of Enlightenment (1750–1830) was a pivotal period in the evolution of international public health. It was a time of social action in relation to health, as reflected by the new interest taken in the

Exhibit I-3	A Summarized History of International Public Health
400 BC	Hippocrates presents causal relation between environment and disease
1st century AD	Romans introduce public sanitation and organized water supply system
14th century	Black Death leads to quarantine and cordon sanitaire
Middle Ages	Colonial expansion spreads infectious diseases around the world
1750–1850	Industrial Revolution results in extensive health and social improvements in cities in Europe and the United States
1850–1910	Great expansion of knowledge about the causes and transmission of communicable diseases
1910–1945	Reductions in child mortality; establishment of schools of public health and international foundations and intergovernmental agencies interested in public health
1945–1990	Creation of World Bank and other UN agencies; WHO eradicates smallpox; HIV/AIDS pandemic begins; Alma Ata Conference gives emphasis to primary health care; UNICEF leads efforts for universal childhood immunization; greater attention to chronic diseases
1990–2005	Priority given to health sector reform, equity, health and development, impact of and responses to globalization, cost-effectiveness, public-private partnerships in health, and use of information and communications technologies

health problems of specific population groups. During this period, rapid advances in technology led to the development of factories. In England and elsewhere, this was paralleled by expansion of the coal mines. The Industrial Revolution had arrived. As a result, the populations of the cities of England and other industrialized nations grew enormously, creating many unsanitary conditions that caused outbreaks of cholera and other epidemic diseases that resulted in high rates of child mortality. Near the end of this period, significant efforts were made to address these problems. Improvements were made in urban water supplies and sewerage, municipal hospitals arose throughout cities in Europe and the East coast of the United States, laws were enacted limiting the work of children, and data on deaths and births began to be systematically collected in many places.

However, as industrialization continued, more efforts to protect the health of the public were needed. These occurred first in England, often regarded as the first modern industrial country, through the efforts of Edwin Chadwick. Beginning in 1832, he headed up the royal Poor Law Commission, which undertook an extensive survey of health and sanitation conditions throughout the country. The work of this commission led in 1848 to the Public Health Act, which created a General Board of Health that was empowered to appoint local boards of health and medical officers of health to deal effectively with public health problems. The impact of these developments was felt throughout Europe and especially in the United States, where

it stimulated creation of health departments in many cities and states.

Cholera, which in the first half of the nineteenth century spread in waves from South Asia to the Middle East and then to Europe and the United States, did the most to stimulate the formal internationalization of public health. The policy of establishing a cordon sanitaire, applied by many European nations in an effort to control the disease, had become a major influence on trade, necessitating an international agreement. In 1851 the First International Sanitary Conference was convened in Paris to discuss the role of quarantine in the control of cholera as well as plague and yellow fever, which were causing epidemics throughout Europe. Although no real agreement was reached, the conference laid the foundations for international cooperation in health.

The main development in international public health in the latter part of the nineteenth century was the enormous growth of knowledge in the area of microbiology, as exemplified by Louis Pasteur's proof of the germ theory of disease, Robert Koch's discovery of the tubercle bacillus, and Walter Reed's demonstration of the role of the mosquito in transmitting yellow fever. Between 1880 and 1910, the etiological cause and means of transmission of most communicable diseases were discovered in laboratories in North America and Europe. This was paralleled by related discoveries in the sciences of physiology, metabolism, endocrinology, and nutrition. Dramatic decreases soon were seen in child and adult mortality through improvements in social and economic conditions, discovery of vaccines, and implementation of programs in health education. The way was now clear for the development of public health administration based on a scientific understanding of the elements involved in the transmission of communicable diseases.

The first two decades of the twentieth century witnessed the establishment of three formal intergovernmental public health bodies: the International Sanitary Bureau to serve nations in the Western hemisphere (in 1904); L'office Internationale d'Hygiene Public in Paris, concerned with prevention and control of the main quarantinable diseases (in 1909); and the League of Nations Health Office (LNHO) in Geneva, which provided assistance to member states on technical matters related to health (in 1920). In 1926 the LNHO started publication of the *Weekly Epidemiological Record,* which has continued as the weekly publication of the World Health Organization (WHO). It also established many scientific and technical commissions, issued reports on the status of many infectious and chronic diseases, and sent its staff around the world to assist national governments in dealing with their health problems.

In North America and countries in Europe, the explosion of scientific knowledge in the latter part of the nineteenth century and the belief that social problems could be solved stimulated medical schools, such as Johns Hopkins University, to establish schools of public health. In France, public subscriptions helped to fund the Institut Pasteur (in honor of Louis Pasteur) in Paris, which subsequently developed a network of institutes throughout the francophone world that produced sera and vaccines and conducted research on a wide variety of tropical diseases. Another significant development during this period was the founding of the Rockefeller Foundation (in 1909) and its International Health Commission (in 1913). During its 38 years of operation, the commission cooperated with many governments in campaigns against endemic diseases such as hookworm, malaria, and yellow fever. The Foundation also provided essential financial support to help establish medical schools in China, Thailand, and elsewhere, and later supported international health programs in a number of American and European schools of medicine and public health. All these developments were paralleled by the development and strengthening of competencies in public health among the militaries of the United States and the countries of Europe, stimulated in great part by the buildup to and realities of World War I. Following the war, there was increasing recognition that much ill health in the colonial world was not easily solvable with medical interventions and was intractably linked to malnutrition and poverty.

Most historians would date the beginning of our current era of international public health to the end of World War II. The need to reconstruct the economies of America and the countries of Western Europe, and the rapid emergence of newly independent countries in Africa and Asia, led to the establishment of many new intergovernmental organizations. The United Nations Monetary and Financial Conference, held in Bretton Woods, New Hampshire, and attended by representatives from 43 countries, led to the establishment of the International Bank for Reconstruction and Development (or World Bank) and the International Monetary Fund. The former initially lent money to countries only at prevailing market interest rates, but beginning in 1960 also provided loans to poorer countries at much lower interest rates and with far better terms through its International Development Association. It was not until the early 1980s that the World Bank began to accelerate greatly its provisions of loans to countries for programs in health and education, but by the end of the decade these loans were the greatest source of foreign assistance to low- and middle-income countries (Ruger, 2005). In the decade after World War II, many other United Nations organizations (e.g., the United Nations Children's Fund, or UNICEF) and specialized agencies (such as WHO) were formed to assist countries in strengthening their health and other social sectors. In addition, most of the wealthier industrialized countries established agencies or bureaus that funded bilateral projects in specific low- and middle-income countries. For the former major colonial powers, such assistance was most often provided to their former colonies.

Many of the international public health efforts in the 1960s and 1970s were dedicated to the control of specific diseases. A global effort to control malaria was hampered by a number of operational and technical difficulties, including the vector's increasing resistance to insecticides and the parasite's resistance to available antimalarial drugs. However, the campaign to eradicate smallpox, led by WHO, successfully eliminated the disease in 1981 and stimulated the establishment of the Expanded Program on Immunization, which focused on the delivery of effective vaccines to infants. Also, during the 1970s, two large international research programs were initiated under the cosponsorship of various United Nations agencies: the Special Program for Research on Human Reproduction (focusing on development and testing of new contraceptive technologies) and the Tropical Disease Research Program (providing support for the development of better means of diagnosis, treatment, and prevention of six tropical diseases, including malaria). Greater attention also was given to chronic diseases, such as cardiovascular and cerebrovascular diseases and cancer.

In 1978 WHO organized a conference in Alma Ata in the then Soviet Union that gave priority to the delivery of primary health care services and the goal of health for all by the year 2000. Rather than focusing only on control of specific diseases, this conference called for international public health efforts to strengthen the capacities of low- and middle-income countries to extend their health services to populations with poor access to prevention and care. The concerns of tropical medicine, which were concentrated on the infectious diseases of warm climates, were being replaced by an emphasis on the provision of health services to reduce morbidity and premature mortality in resource-poor settings (DeCock, Lucas, Mabey, & Parry, 1995). Given the limited financial and managerial capacities of many governments, increased attention was paid to the role of NGOs in providing these services. As a result, many mission hospitals, particularly in sub-Saharan Africa, expanded their activities in their local communities, the number of local NGOs began to increase, and a number of international NGOs (e.g., Save the Children, Oxfam, Medecins sans Frontières) greatly expanded their services, often with support of bilateral agencies. Disease-specific efforts, most notably UNICEF's Child Survival Program, with its acronym GOBI (growth charts, oral rehydration, breastfeeding, immunization) and its goal of universal childhood immunization by the year 1990, were seen by many as programs that both focused on specific health problems and provided an excellent means of strengthening health systems.

The emergence of what is sometimes called "the new public health" was heralded by the Ottawa Charter of 1986, which was meant to provide a plan of action to achieve the Health for All targets set forth at Alma Ata. The Ottawa Charter pioneered the definition of health as a *resource* for development, not merely a desirable outcome of development. The prerequisites for health that were outlined in the charter were diverse and included peace, shelter, education, food, income, a stable ecosystem, sustainable resources, social justice, and equity. The charter emphasized the importance of structural factors that affect health on a societal level, rather than focusing only on the risk behaviors of individuals. It called on the worldwide public health community to address health disparities by engaging and enabling people to take charge of their health at community- and policy-making levels. This shift from a "risk behavior" focus to one of "risk

environment" continues to resonate in contemporary public health practice and research.

The one new and unexpected development in the 1980s was the arrival of the HIV/AIDS pandemic. By the time a simple laboratory test to detect HIV was discovered in 1985, more than 2 million persons in sub-Saharan Africa had been infected. In 1987, WHO formed the Global Program on AIDS, which within 2 years became the largest international public health effort ever established, with an annual budget of $90 million and 500 staff working in Geneva and in more than 80 low- and middle-income countries and regions. In 1995, with some 20 million persons (mostly living in these lower-income countries) infected with HIV, and with the understanding that the epidemic could only be brought under control through a true multisectoral effort, the program was transformed into a joint effort of UN agencies known as UNAIDS.

At the turn of the century, after more than 20 million persons had died from AIDS, particularly in sub-Saharan Africa, the pandemic finally began to receive the attention it deserved from governments and international organizations. In June 2001, the United Nations General Assembly convened a Special Session on HIV/AIDS (UNGASS), which adopted the Declaration of Commitment on HIV/AIDS emphasizing the importance of strong leadership, universal access to treatment and care for HIV-positive persons, and strengthening of prevention programs. The following year, the Global Fund for AIDS, Tuberculosis, and Malaria (GFATM) was established as an independent financial instrument for developing countries to obtain the needed resources to combat these three diseases. In 2003, the United States pledged $15 billion over a 5-year period (known as the President's Emergency Plan for AIDS Relief, or PEPFAR) to reduce the burden of HIV/AIDS in 15 high-prevalence countries. Shortly thereafter, the World Health Organization launched an initiative to treat 3 million HIV-positive people in developing countries by the end of 2005 with generic fixed-dose combination antiretroviral medications. Despite these and other efforts, the pandemic continues to expand and now promises to be the most devastating global pandemic since the Black Death of the Middle Ages.

In the last decade of the twentieth century, changes well beyond the health sector had a marked impact on its style of operation. Major shifts in political and economic ideologies led to a reconsideration of the role of governments and how they should finance and deliver public services. Much greater attention was given to focusing government's role more narrowly and to making greater use of the private sector. Indeed, international public health in the last decade of the twentieth century and the first decade of the twenty-first century can be characterized by its emphasis on health sector reform, cost-effectiveness as an important principle in the choice of interventions in the public sector, and public-private partnerships in health, paralleled by a rapid expansion of information and communications technologies.

Although rising incomes have been known for a long time to improve health status, during the past decade there has been increased attention to the importance of a healthy population for economic development. Participation of sectors other than the health sector is now viewed as essential for achieving a healthy population. More and more countries, experiencing the demographic transition from societies in which most persons are young to societies with rapidly increasing numbers of middle-aged and older adults, have had to provide preventive and care services that address health problems of both the poor and wealthy simultaneously. Witness the fact that India now has the largest middle class in the world, with high rates of cardiovascular and other noncommunicable diseases. Not surprisingly, issues regarding equity in the availability of drugs and vaccines and in access to other technological advances, and regarding the ethics of international research, have gained greater attention. Healthy populations are now viewed as essential for domestic security as well as economic development. The challenges of international public health have never been greater.

Current Challenges in International Public Health

We have witnessed major improvements in the health of populations over the past century, with the pace of change increasing rapidly in low- and middle-income countries since the Bretton Woods Conference. Public health—and, more broadly, an improved understanding of how social, behavioral, economic, and environmental factors influence the health of populations—has contributed to these improvements to an extent far greater than access to medical care. However, these improvements have not been universal. For example, at the beginning of the twenty-first century, the following facts are true:

- Nearly 11 million children below age 5 die each year from preventable causes such as pneumonia, diarrhea, malaria, malnutrition, measles, and HIV/AIDS; 98% of these deaths occur in developing countries.

- More than 120 million women want to space or limit childbearing, but do not have access to modern contraceptives.

- Nearly 600,000 women die annually from complications of pregnancy and childbirth, and another 30 million suffer pregnancy-related health problems that can be permanently disabling.

- Each year 13 million persons die from infectious diseases, most of which are preventable or curable; half of these deaths are in adults and are due to tuberculosis, malaria, or HIV/AIDS.

- Worldwide, 1.2 billion people do not have access to clean water.

- More than 300 million adults worldwide are obese, putting them at significantly increased risk for cardiovascular diseases, diabetes, hypertension, cancer, stroke, and musculoskeletal disorders.

There is a broad consensus that poverty is the most important underlying cause of preventable death, disease, and disability. Unfortunately, more people live in poverty today than 20 years ago. Literacy, access to housing, safe water, sanitation, food supplies, and urbanization are determinants of health status that interact with poverty. Economic globalization, driven by increasing world trade, greater openness of national economies to world markets, and the vast expansion of information technology, has contributed to uneven economic growth, increased economic inequality, and concerns about subordination of human and labor rights (Ahmad, 1999).

Numerous dynamic challenges face public health in the twenty-first century. Infectious diseases, once thought to have been vanquished as major killers, have emerged or reemerged around the world as top threats to health and well-being. Some of these are caused by more virulent variations of familiar, well-understood microbial agents (e.g., multidrug resistant tuberculosis), whereas others have traveled from endemic regions to previously unaffected areas (e.g., West Nile virus), and still others have yet to be fully characterized or understood (e.g., the coronavirus responsible for severe acute respiratory syndrome, or SARS) or they are threatening on the horizon (e.g., avian influenza). The underlying causes for many emerging infectious diseases can be traced to human-initiated social and environmental changes, including climatic and ecosystem disturbances, trends in food and meat consumption and production, and unsafe medical practices (Kuiken et al., 2003).

Noncommunicable or chronic diseases were once considered the problem of industrialized nations that had achieved long life expectancies. Today, millions of people in low- and middle-income countries suffer from chronic conditions such as poor nutrition (including the burden of overnutrition or obesity), cardiovascular disease, hypertension, and diabetes (Yach, Leeder, Bell & Kistnasomy, 2005). Globalizing forces that have imported Western lifestyle habits, such as tobacco smoking and increased consumption of processed foods, have hastened these disease trends. Mental illnesses, and depressive disorders in particular, remain a largely ignored and major source of death and disability worldwide.

In the first decade of the twenty-first century, we have also witnessed the addition of multifaceted and complex issues to the list of public health challenges, among them human migration and displacement, bioterrorism, and disaster preparedness.

It is within this context that the United Nations General Assembly adopted the Millennium Declaration in September 2000 as a set of guiding principles and key objectives for international cooperation. The declaration underscored the need to address inequities that have been created or worsened by globalization and to form new international linkages to achieve and protect peace, disarmament, poverty eradication, gender equality, the environment, human rights, and good governance. The goals dealing specifically with development and poverty eradication have become known as the Millennium Development Goals (MDGs), three of which explicitly refer to health (shown in bold in Exhibit I-4). All 191 member states of the UN have pledged to meet the MDGs by 2015.

The resources required to achieve the MDGs were initially spelt out by a WHO Commission on Macroeconomics and Health (WHO, 2001) and have subsequently been refined (Sachs & McArthur, 2005). Meeting them will require new forms of international and intersectoral cooperation between UN agencies with an established health role, other international bodies such as the World Trade Organization, regional bodies such as the European Union, bilateral agencies, NGOs, foundations, and the private sector, including pharmaceutical companies. It also must include the new philanthropists in international health—people such as Bill and Melinda Gates, George Soros, and Ted Turner—who bring not only significant amounts of funds into the global system but also a new, more informal and personal style of operations. Ensuring the ideal formation and effective functioning of this global health system will itself be an enormous challenge for the next decade of international public health.

Exhibit I-4	Millennium Development Goals

- Halve extreme poverty and hunger
- Achieve universal primary education
- Promote gender equality and empower women
- **Reduce under-5 mortality by two-thirds**
- **Reduce maternal mortality by three-quarters**
- **Reverse the spread of HIV/AIDS, malaria, tuberculosis, and other major diseases**
- Ensure environmental sustainability
- Develop a global partnership for development, with targets for aid, trade, and debt relief

Use and Content of This Textbook

This textbook has been prepared with these challenges foremost in mind. Its focus is on diseases, programs, health systems, and health policies in low- and middle-income (or developing) countries, making reference to and using examples from the United States, Western Europe, and other high-income countries as appropriate.[1] The individual chapters present information on health problems and issues that transcend national boundaries and are of concern to many nations.

Our intent has been, first and foremost, to provide a textbook for graduate students in various disciplines who are studying international public health. Given its broad range of content, the book as a whole may serve as the main source for an introductory graduate course on international public health or global health. Experience with the first edition has shown that the textbook also can be used as a reference text for undergraduate courses in public health or global health. Alternatively, some chapters (or parts of chapters) can be used in graduate or undergraduate courses dedicated to more specific subjects and topics. Students who use the textbook in this way will hopefully be stimulated to explore other chapters once they have read the ones they have been assigned. We believe the textbook can also be a useful reference for those already working in the field of international public health in government agencies, as well as those employed by international health and development agencies, NGOs, or the private sector.

Because of the many dynamic areas and subjects we wanted to cover, we chose to prepare an edited textbook. We selected content experts for each chapter rather than presuming to have the expertise to write the entire book ourselves. We recognize that an edited textbook has its shortcomings,

---

[1] A classification of countries can be found on the World Bank website: http://www.worldbank.org/data/countryclass/countryclass.html.

such as some inconsistency in style and presentation and occasional overlap in chapter contents. We have done our best to limit these, and hope the reader will agree that those that remain are a small price to pay for fulfilling our goal of providing the reader with the highest-quality content.

Another consequence of the dynamic nature of international public health is the occasional difficulty in providing the most up-to-date epidemiologic information on all causes of mortality and morbidity. One obvious example of this is the rapidly evolving HIV/AIDS situation in Africa and Asia. To assist the reader in obtaining this information, we have provided references in various chapters, including Internet resources.

This is the second edition of the textbook. In planning its preparation, we sought advice on how to improve it from many of those who prepared chapters in the first edition, as well as from faculty in various countries who were using the textbook in their courses.

The textbook has 15 chapters. The first two chapters set the background. Chapter 1 reviews the importance of using quantitative indicators for decision making in health. It presents the latest developments in the measurement of health status and disease burden, including the increasing use of composite measures of health that combine the effects of disease-specific morbidity and mortality on populations. It then reviews current estimates and future trends in selected countries and regions, as well as the global burden of disease. Chapter 2 examines the social, cultural, and behavioral parameters that are essential to understanding public health efforts. It does this by describing key concepts in the field of anthropology, particularly as they relate to health belief systems, and by presenting theories of health behavior that are relevant to behavior change and examples of specific national and community programs in various areas of health. The importance of combining qualitative and quantitative methodologies in measuring and assessing health status and programs is emphasized.

The next three chapters are devoted to the three greatest public health challenges traditionally faced by low-income countries: reproductive health, infectious diseases, and nutrition. Reproductive health has long been addressed primarily through family planning programs directly intended to reduce fertility. Chapter 3 presents more current views of reproductive health that broaden this concept to include empowerment of women in decisions about health and fertility. It provides information on population growth and demographic changes around the world and reviews how women control their fertility and indexes the effects of various social and biological determinants of fertility. It then examines the impact of family planning services and programs on the reduction of fertility and unwanted pregnancies and on the health of children and women.

Collectively, infectious diseases have undoubtedly been the most important causes of premature mortality and morbidity in low- and middle-income countries. Chapter 4 presents the descriptive epidemiologic features and available prevention and control strategies for the communicable diseases that are of greatest public health significance in these countries today. These include the vaccine-preventable diseases; diarrhea and acute respiratory infections in children; tuberculosis, malaria, and other parasitic diseases; HIV/AIDS and other sexually transmitted diseases in adults; and the emerging infectious diseases. Examples of successful programs using one or more of the available control approaches—preventing exposure, immunization, drug prophylaxis, and treatment—are described, as are the challenges and obstacles that confront low- and middle-income countries in successfully controlling these diseases.

Nutritional concerns in low- and middle-income countries are diverse, ranging from deprivation and hunger and consequent deficiencies in health, survival, and quality of life to obesity and chronic diseases in some regions. Chapter 5 focuses on several spheres of nutrition that are of utmost concern in these countries. These include undernutrition and its components of protein malnutrition and micronutrient deficiencies (particularly vitamin A, zinc, iron, and iodine) at various stages of life; food insecurity; the interaction of nutrition and infections; the role of breastfeeding and complementary feeding in ensuring healthy children; and the nutrition transition observed in more affluent segments of populations in rapidly developing countries.

The book's subsequent four chapters address public health priorities that have been associated with higher-income countries but are gaining importance in resource-poor countries as they become more developed economically and their populations live longer and progress through the demographic transition. These are chronic diseases, injury, mental health, and environmental health.

Chronic diseases, frequently called *noncommunicable* or *degenerative diseases*, are generally characterized by a long latency period, prolonged course of illness, noncontagious origin, functional impairment or disability, and incurability. Chapter 6 provides an overview of chronic diseases in low- and middle-income countries, with particular attention given to cardiovascular diseases (mainly coronary artery disease and stroke), common cancers, chronic respiratory diseases, and diabetes. The descriptive epidemiology and economic implication of these diseases, the behavioral risk factors that serve as determinants, and the main approaches, programs, and policy responses required to adequately prevent and manage these diseases at national and global levels are presented.

The subject of injuries is covered in a separate chapter (Chapter 7) in this second edition, reflecting the greater importance and recognition of this problem during the past decade. The subject includes unintentional injuries (ones for which there is no evidence of predetermined intent, such as road accidents and occupational injuries) and intentional injuries or violence that is planned or intended (including injuries related to self-directed, interpersonal, and collective violence). The chapter provides an overview of the global burden of injuries, outlines the causes and risk factors for them, describes interventions that can reduce their impact, and considers the opportunities and challenges that can move forward an injury prevention agenda at a global level.

It is only recently that mental health has received attention commensurate with its great importance to the disability and disease burden in low- and middle-income countries. Chapter 8 charts the historical development of public mental health; considers various concepts and classifications of mental disorders, taking into account the influence of cultural factors in the development of psychiatric classifications; and reviews what is known about the epidemiology and etiology of the more common disorders, particularly mood and anxiety disorders, schizophrenia, and substance abuse. Lastly, the chapter reviews the status of national efforts to date in resource-limited countries regarding primary, secondary, and tertiary prevention programs for the major mental disorders and concludes with a discussion of the ten mental health priorities for low- and middle-income countries put forth by the 2001 World Health Report.

Chapter 9 provides a comprehensive review of environmental health issues and problems in low- and middle-income countries. It begins with a summary of conceptual and methodological issues that constitute the important area of risk assessment and monitoring, and then reviews the profiles of environmental health hazards within the household (e.g., water and sanitation), in the workplace (e.g., on farms, in mines, and factories), in the community (e.g., outdoor air pollution), and at regional and global levels. The latter includes such controversial topics as climate change, ozone de-

pletion, and biodiversity. The chapter concludes with a discussion of the issues and projects that bear on the future of environmental health research and policy.

Chapter 10 focuses on the public health challenges that *characterize complex emergencies (CEs)*. These conflicts occur within and across state boundaries, have political antecedents, are protracted in duration, and are embedded in existing social, political, economic, and cultural structures and cleavages. At the start of 2004 there were an estimated 4.4 million internally displaced persons and 10 million refugees seeking asylum across international borders, the vast majority fleeing conflict zones. The chapter considers the causes of CEs (particularly the political causes) and their impact on populations and health systems, and reviews the technical interventions that can limit their adverse effects on the health of populations. Attention is drawn to the importance of an effective and efficient early response in influencing the long-term survival of populations and health systems and the nature of any postconflict society that is established. The chapter also reviews the impact of one natural disaster, the destructive tsunami that occurred off the coast of Indonesia in late 2004, because it has many elements of a CE.

The next two chapters are concerned with the development and implementation of effective health systems, which have a crucial influence on the ability of countries to address their disease burden and improve the health of their populations. Chapter 11 focuses on the design of health systems considered largely from an economic perspective. It provides a conceptual map of the health system along with its key elements; addresses the fundamental and often controversial question as to the role of the state; and then considers the key functions of any health system, which include regulation, financing, resource allocation, and provision. It concludes by reviewing current trends in health system reform. Four country examples are used throughout the chapter to illustrate key differences in health systems across the world.

As multipurpose and multidisciplinary endeavors, health systems require coordination among numerous individuals and units. Thus, they require effective and efficient *management*. Chapter 12 is dedicated to this topic, which is defined as the process of making decisions as to how resources will be generated, developed, and used in pursuit of particular organizational objectives. It details the important aspects of the political, social, and economic context in which a management process must operate; discusses the organizational structures under which health care systems may be organized; examines the critical process of planning and priority setting; looks at issues in the management of resources, focusing on finance, staffing, transport, and information; and concludes by discussing some cross-cutting themes, such as management style, accountability, and sustainability.

Health and health systems interrelate with a nation's economy in two main ways. The first, as noted earlier, comprises the bidirectional relationships between health status and national income and development. For example, health affects income through its impact on labor productivity, saving rates, and age structure, while a higher income improves health by increasing the capacity to produce food and to have adequate housing and education, and through incentives for fertility limitation. The second concerns linkages between health care delivery institutions, health financing (including insurance) policies, and economic outcomes. Chapter 13 reviews information available on both these challenging and closely related topics that are critical to government policy makers seeking the best ways to improve the quality of life of their populations, particularly in those countries that carry the heaviest burden of disease and poverty.

Chapter 14 presents the current state of affairs regarding global cooperation in international public health. It begins by explaining why countries seek this cooperation, the processes by which it occurs, and the institutions and actors involved. The remaining part reviews the important shift that has taken place in the overall framework of international cooperation since the establishment of the United Nations system in the late 1940s, from one characterized by vertical relationships between states and international and intergovernmental organizations, to one of horizontal, cooperative participation resulting in partnerships and alliances among nation states, UN agencies, the private sector, and NGOs. This shift has great significance for the formation of future international public health policies and programs and for approaches to global governance in the area of international health.

The final chapter provides an overview of how globalization is affecting international health at the start of the twenty-first century. It begins by seeking to define the term *globalization* and its key causes (or drivers) and explores how the many changes it is causing are having positive and negative impacts on human societies. A discussion of the links between globalization and shifting patterns of infectious and chronic diseases follows. The chapter then explores the impact of globalization on health care financing and service provision, using as examples the migration of health workers, the restructuring of the pharmaceutical industry, and the global spread of health sector reforms. It concludes by suggesting ways in which the international public health community can promote and protect health in the era of globalization.

The reader will note that there are many case studies presented in exhibits scattered throughout the text. These have been written to provide concrete examples and illustrations of key points and concepts covered in each chapter. At the conclusion of each chapter is a list of questions that can help course instructors stimulate classroom discussions about important issues covered in the chapter. The editors recognize that the book could include separate chapters on additional topics—maternal and child health, women's health, health and human rights, and demography, to name but a few. We have opted instead to provide in-depth information on the core subjects that were selected, although we did our best to cover some aspects of all of the subjects just listed in one or more of the chapters.

In many ways, international public health is at an important crossroad. Its greatest challenge is to confront global forces while at the same time promoting local, evidence-based, cost-effective, public health programs that deal with disease-specific problems and more general issues, such as poverty and gender inequality. Public health–related research is essential to gain a better understanding of the determinants of illness and of innovative approaches to prevention and care and to find means of improving the efficiency and coverage of health systems. Whether as a practitioner, policy maker, or researcher, international public health professionals can make an enormous difference by being well trained in their discipline and highly sensitive to the beliefs, culture, and value systems of the populations with whom they collaborate or serve. We hope this textbook will aid in this process.

● ● ● **References**

Ahmad, K. (1999, September). World Bank predicts development for next century. *Lancet, 354,* 1005.

Arnold, D. (1988). Introduction: Disease, medicine and empire. In D. Arnold (Ed.), *Imperial medicine and indigenous societies* (pp. 1–26). Manchester, England: Manchester University Press.

Ashton, J., & Seymour, H. (1988). The new public health: The Liverpool experience. Philadelphia: Open University Press.

Basch, P. F. (1999). *Textbook of international health* (2nd ed.). New York: Oxford University Press.

DeCock, K. M., Lucas, S. B., Mabey, D., & Parry, E. (1995, September). Tropical medicine for the 21st century. *British Medical Journal, 311,* 860–862.

Feinberg, H. V. (1994). Ethical approaches to health and development. In K. Aoki (Ed.), *Ethical dilemmas in health and development* (pp. 3–13). Tokyo: Japan Science Society Press.

Hurley, S. F., Jolley, D. J., & Kaldor, J. M. (1997). Effectiveness of needle-exchange programmes for prevention of HIV infection. *Lancet, 349,* 1797–1800.

Kuiken, T., Fouchier, R., Rimmelzwaan, G., et al. (2003). Emerging viral infections in a rapidly changing world. *Current Opinion in Biotechnology, 14,* 641–646.

Leff, S., & Leff, V. (1957). *From witchcraft to world health.* New York: Macmillan.

Rosen, G. (1993). *A history of public health* (Expanded ed.). Baltimore, MD: Johns Hopkins University Press.

Ruger, J. P. (2005). The changing role of the World Bank in global health. *American Journal of Public Health, 95,* 60–70.

Sachs, J. D., & McArthur, J. W. (2005). The Millenium Project: A plan for meeting the Millennium Development Goals. *Lancet, 365,* 347–353.

Turnock, B. J. (2004). *Public health: What it is and how it works* (3rd ed.). Sudbury, MA: Jones and Bartlett.

Winslow, C.-E. A. (1920, March). The untilled fields of public health. *Modern Medicine, 2*(3), 183–191.

Winslow, C.-E. A., & Hallock, G.T. (1949). *Health through the ages.* New York: Metropolitan Life Insurance Company.

World Health Organization. (2001). *Macroeconomics and health: Investing in health for economic development.* Geneva, Switzerland: Author.

Yach, D., Leeder, S. R., Bell J., & Kistnasomy, B. (2005). Global chronic diseases. *Science, 307,* 317.

1

Measures of Health and Disease in Populations

ADNAN ALI HYDER AND RICHARD H. MORROW

In its 1948 charter, the World Health Organization (WHO) defined health as "a state of complete physical, mental and social well-being and not merely the absence of disease or infirmity." Although this is an important ideological conceptualization, for most practical purposes, objectives of health programs are more readily defined in terms of prevention or treatment of disease.

Disease has been defined in many ways. For example, distinctions may be made between sickness and illness, but for purposes of defining and measuring disease burden a general definition will be used here. *Disease* is anything that a population (or an individual) experiences that causes, literally, "dis-ease"; that is, anything that leads to discomfort, pain, distress of all sorts, disability of any kind, or death, constitutes disease from whatever cause, including injuries or psychiatric disabilities.

It is also important to be able to diagnose and classify specific diseases to the extent that such classification aids in determining which health intervention programs would be most useful. Thus, understanding the pathogenesis of the disease process and defining disease are critical for understanding and classifying causes in order to determine the most effective prevention and treatment strategies for reducing the effects of a disease or risk factor. Just as the purpose of diagnosis of a disease in an individual patient is to provide the right treatment, the major purpose of working through a burden of disease analysis in a population is to provide the basis for the most effective mix of health and social program interventions.

Recent developments in the measurement of population health status and disease burden include the increasing use of summary, composite measures of health that combine the mortality and morbidity effects of diseases into a single indicator; the availability of results of the Global Burden of Disease (GBD) studies making use of summary indicators; and developments in the measurement of disability and risk factors. The more traditional approaches to measuring health are widely available in other public health textbooks and will be used for illustrative and comparative purposes here.

This chapter has four sections: The first discusses the reasons for and approaches to measuring disease burden, the reasons for using quantitative indicators, and the importance of using data for decision making in health. The second section is a critical review of methods for developing and using composite measures combining the mortality and morbidity from diseases in populations at national and regional levels. It explores the potential utility of these measures and discusses their limitations and implications. The third section demonstrates the application of these methods for measurement of health status and assessment of global health trends. It reviews current estimates and future trends of selected countries and regions, as well as the global burden of disease. The fourth section reviews important underlying risk factors of disease and discusses recent efforts to measure the prevalence of major risk factors and to determine their contributions to regional and global disease burdens.

Acknowledgments: The authors acknowledge Omar H. Amach for his assistance in the preparation of this chapter and for updating the necessary data and examples.

Reasons and Approaches for Measuring Health and Disease

Rationale

The many reasons for obtaining health-related information all hinge on the need for data to guide efforts toward reducing the consequences of disease and enhancing the benefits of good health. These include the need to identify which interventions would have the greatest effect, to identify emerging trends and anticipate future needs, to assist in determining priorities for expenditures, to provide information for education to the public, and to help in setting health research agendas. The primary information requirement is for understanding and assessing the health status of a population and its changes with time. In recent years, much has been made of the importance of evidence-based decisions in health. There is little reason to doubt that evidence is better than intuition, but that depends on how the evidence is used (Exhibit 1-1). This chapter examines evidence—the facts of health and disease—and demonstrates how to assemble this evidence so that it can best be used in assisting better decisions concerning health and disease.

Measuring Health and Disease

The relative importance (burden) of different diseases in a population depends on their frequency (incidence or prevalence), severity (the mortality and extent of serious morbidity), consequences (health, social, economic), and the type of people affected (gender, age).

Counting Disease

The first task in measuring disease in a population is to count its occurrence. Counting disease frequency can be done in several ways, and it is important to understand what these different methods of counting actually mean. The most useful way depends on the nature of the disease and the purpose for which it is being counted. There are three commonly used measures of disease occurrence: cumulative incidence, incidence density, and prevalence.

Cumulative incidence, or *incidence proportion*, is the number of new cases of a disease that occur in a population at risk for developing the disease during a specified period of time. It is the proportion of people who develop new disease in a specific period of time. For this to have meaning, three components are necessary: a definition of the onset of the event, a defined population, and a particular period of time. The critical point is *new cases* of disease—the disease must develop in a person who did not have the disease pre-

viously. The numerator is the number of new cases of disease (the event), and the denominator is the number of people at risk for developing the disease. Everyone included in the denominator must have the potential to become part of the group that is counted in the numerator. For example, to calculate the incidence of prostate cancer, the denominator must include only men, because women are not at risk for prostate cancer. The third component is the period of time. Any time unit can be used as long as all those counted in the denominator are followed for a period comparable with those who are counted as new cases in the numerator. The most common time denominator is 1 year.

Incidence density, or often simply *incidence rate*, is the occurrence of new cases of disease per unit of person-time. This directly incorporates time into the denominator and is generally the most useful measure of disease frequency, often expressed as new events per person-year or per 1,000 person-years. Incidence is a measure of events (in this case, the transition from a nondiseased to a diseased state) and can be considered a measure of risk. This risk can be looked at in any population group, defined by age, sex, place, time, sociodemographic characteristics, occupation, or by exposure to a toxin or any suspected causal factor.

Prevalence is a measure of present status rather than of newly occurring disease. It measures the proportion of people who have defined disease at a specific time. Thus, it is a composite measure made up of two factors—the incidence of the disease that has occurred in the past and its continuation to the present or to some specified point in time. That is, prevalence equals incidence rate of the disease multiplied by the average duration of the disease. For most chronic diseases, prevalence rates are more commonly available than are incidence rates.

Severity of Disease

To understand the burden of disease in a population, it is important to consider not only the frequency of the disease but also its severity, as indicated by the morbidity and premature mortality that it causes. *Premature mortality* is defined as death before the age of death had the disease not occurred. *Morbidity* is a statement of the extent of disability that a person suffers as a consequence of the disease over time and can be measured by a number of indicators, as discussed later in this chapter.

Mortality

Traditionally, mortality has been the most important indicator of the health status of a population. John

Exhibit 1-1	Assessing a Health System with Data: Historical Example

A well-documented historical example of the relationship between decision making and data can be seen in an assessment of the health status in Ghana in the mid-1970s. This case illustrates how able people with good intentions made decisions using established health system approaches, yet ignored good evidence gathered at the same time. A major reason for the failure to use available evidence was that it was not put forward in a form helpful to decision makers.

Assessment of the health status in Ghana in the late 1970s indicated that despite the remarkable increase in resources going into the health sector, the general health status of the population was still low. In the previous 10 years there had been little improvement in infant mortality rate, maternal mortality rate, and rate of communicable disease. That situation is strikingly illustrated in the accompanying figure. It shows how the financial resources of the nation were being allocated in reverse proportion to the numbers of people in need. The health system of Ghana could be likened to a pyramid, with the teaching hospital in Accra at the top and a network of health posts and dressing stations at the bottom. This was a system based on service delivery points and focused on buildings rather than on health services for the people. Such an emphasis on facilities creates false needs among the people for more facilities. Good health becomes synonymous with the availability of a doctor and a hospital rather than the enjoyment of a disease-free environment.

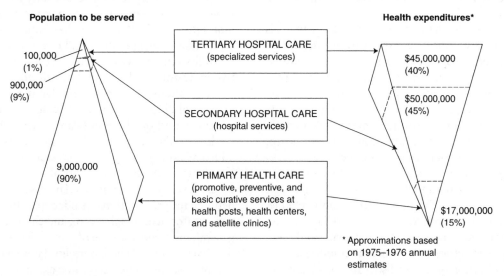

The health care dilemma in Ghana. The distribution of funds and personnel for primary health care compared with costly hospital-based care is in inverse proportion to the numbers of people that need to be reached. The health care pyramid for Ghana is upside down!

In response to this dilemma, the Health Planning Unit of the Ghana Ministry of Health developed a quantitative method for assessing the health impact of different diseases and for assisting in determining priorities for allocation of resources to alternative health programs. They used available data that were put in terms that had meaning for the decision makers—the gain in healthy life per dollar expended. This method was the first use of a common composite indicator that combined morbidity and mortality and could examine the gains in total healthy life per dollar expended on alternate health programs. At that time, the Ghana Ministry of Health had just developed the 1977–1981 health plan, which called for expanding and extending existing hospital and health center services. However, when the evidence was examined, an alternative community-based primary health care strategy that required equivalent expenditures was found to provide 20 times as much healthy life per dollar. This finding greatly strengthened the rationale for introducing a community-based primary health system in place of the hospital-centered system.

Source: Ministry of Health, Republic of Ghana, *A Primary Health Care Strategy for Ghana* (Accra, Republic of Ghana: National Health Planning Unit, 1978). Reprinted with permission.

Graunt developed the first known systematic collection of data on mortality with the Bills of Mortality in the early 1600s in London. He described the age pattern of deaths, categorized them by cause as understood at the time, and demonstrated variation from place to place and from year to year. Mortality rates according to age, sex, place, and cause continue to be central information about a population's health status and a crucial input for understanding and measuring the burden of disease. Considerable literature exists on the use of mortality to indicate health status and its application to national and subnational levels (Murray & Chen, 1992), and paradigms such as the demographic transition are based largely on the decline of mortality in the under-five age group (Mosley et al., 1993; Omran, 1971).

The *fact* of death by age, sex, and place, which is required by law in most countries through *death registration*, and *cause of death*, as required by law in many countries through *death certification*, both provide essential information. Although death is a cardinal event and generally the most widely available kind of health information, in many low-income countries the fact of death, let alone cause of death, frequently is still not reliably available.

In high-income countries, vital statistics (i.e., the registration of births and deaths, usually by age, sex, and place) are routinely collected and highly reliable. In most middle-income countries their reliability and completeness have been steadily improving and often are fairly satisfactory. In low-income countries, however, the collection of vital statistics remains highly incomplete, although improving. An analysis of death registration in the Global Burden of Disease 2000 study showed that complete or incomplete vital registration data together with sample registration systems cover 74% of global mortality. Survey data and indirect demographic techniques provide information on levels of child and adult mortality for the remaining 26% of estimated global mortality (Murray et al., 2001). Even in these countries, increasing use of survey methods provides estimates of the under-five and other mortality rates.

However, obtaining information about cause of death remains difficult even in many middle-income countries; most information depends on special surveys or studies of select populations under specific circumstances. Verbal autopsies have been used increasingly for judging likely cause of death. These can be quite useful for causes of death such as neonatal tetanus and severe diarrhea, but it has been found that sensitivity and specificity are limited for many diseases whose symptoms are variable and nonspecific (such as malaria).

Age-specific mortality profiles are a prerequisite for a burden of disease analysis. Although extensive work has been done to document and analyze child mortality in low- and middle-income countries, less has been done for adult mortality (Feachem & Kjellstrom, 1992). Developing countries have higher rates of adult mortality than the high-income nations (Lopez et al., 2002; Murray & Chen, 1992), and mortality rates are higher for both women and men at every age when compared with the high-income world. In Africa, the enormous increase in AIDS deaths in young and middle-aged women and men has had a profound impact on mortality and survival (see Exhibit 1-2).

Traditional indicators of mortality have been the standard for assessing population health status. *Infant mortality rates* (*IMR*, deaths of live-born infants before 12 months of age per thousand live births) and child mortality (under 5 years of age) are considered sensitive indicators of the overall health of nations. The United Nations Children's Fund (UNICEF) publishes an annual global report that includes a ranking of nations based on these indicators (United Nations Children's Fund, 2004). These indicators have the added advantage of having been studied for their relationships with other indicators of the social and economic development of nations. There is a clear relation between the gross national product (GNP) per capita, an indicator of national wealth, and child mortality. In general, the higher the level of economic development, the lower the rate of child mortality. However, there are exceptions, and these need to be examined carefully. For example, Sri Lanka and the Indian state of Kerala are both low-income regions that have low mortality rates. These examples demonstrate that the relationship between mortality and poverty is complex and needs in-depth investigation.

There continue to be major deficiencies in cause-specific mortality data in low- and most middle-income countries. Preston (1976) analyzed life tables for 43 national populations, including 9 developing countries, to develop cause-specific mortality profiles. In keeping with the demographic and epidemiologic transitions (see Exhibit 1-3, later in this chapter), the pattern of cause-specific mortality changes at different levels of total mortality, with a general trend of decreasing infectious and parasitic disease cause-specific mortality with declining total mortality. Indeed, mortality from these communicable causes is a major reason for the difference between high- and low-mortality populations (Murray & Chen, 1992).

The cause of death certification system based on the WHO International Classification of Diseases

Exhibit 1-2	Trends of the HIV/AIDS Epidemic

Acquired immunodeficiency syndrome (AIDS) is the leading infectious cause of adult death in the world. Untreated disease caused by the human immunodeficiency virus (HIV) has a case fatality rate that approaches 100% (World Health Organization, 2003). Unknown a quarter of a century ago, today, an estimated 36 to 44 million people are living with HIV/AIDS (UNAIDS, 2004). The most heavily burdened continent is Africa, which in 2004 was home to two-thirds of the world's people living with HIV/AIDS. However, the incidence of new infections is rising most rapidly in selected Asian countries (e.g., China, India, Vietnam, and Indonesia) and in eastern Europe (e.g., Estonia, Latvia, Ukraine, and the Russian Federation (UNAIDS, 2004).

Of the leading causes of disease burden among men and women aged 15 years and over, HIV/AIDS was the number one cause for males and the second leading cause for females, accounting for around 6% of the global burden of disease (see accompanying table). The mortality from AIDS has been so great in South Africa and Botswana that starting in 1990–1995, it has caused a dramatic decline in the life expectancy in both countries (see Figure below) (WHO, 2003).

Global Summary of HIV and AIDS Epidemic in 2004			
Number of People Living with HIV	**Total**	**39.4 million**	**[35.9–44.3 million]**
	Adults	37.2 million	[33.8–41.7 million]
	Women	17.6 million	[16.3–19.5 million]
	Children	2.2 million	[2.0–2.6 million]
Number Newly Infected with HIV	**Total**	**4.9 million**	**[4.3–4.6 million]**
	Adults	4.3 million	[3.7–5.7 million]
	Children	640,000	[570,000–750,000]
AIDS Deaths	**Total**	**3.1 million**	**[2.8–3.5 million]**
	Adults	2.6 million	[2.3–2.9 million]
	Children	510,000	[460,000–600,000]

Source: From Joint United Nations Programme on HIV/AIDS, *Global Summary of AIDS December 2004* (Geneva, Switzerland: UNAIDS, 2003). Reprinted with permission.

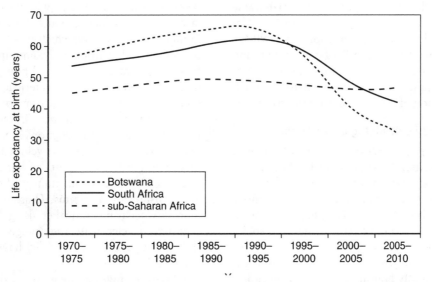

Trends in Life Expectancy in sub-Saharan Africa and Selected Countries, 1970–2010.

Source: United Nations Population Division, *World Population Prospects: The 2002 Revision Population Database,* http://esa.un.org/unpp. Reprinted with permission.

(ICD) has been used widely in many countries (WHO, 1992). Despite a standardized process for categorizing deaths, variations in the reliability of these data occur because of variations in the training and expertise of people coding cause of death, as well as the supervision and feedback provided. There have been steady improvements in many countries, however, and these kinds of data provide some of the best information available on major causes of mortality.

Mortality can be expressed in two important quantitative measures. The *mortality rate* is a form of incidence and is expressed as the number of deaths in a defined population in a defined time period. The numerator can be total deaths, age- or sex-specific deaths, or cause-specific deaths; the denominator is the number of persons at risk of dying in the stated category as defined earlier for incidence. The *case fatality ratio* (CFR) is the proportion of those with a given disease who die of that disease (at any time, unless specified). The mortality rate is equal to the case fatality ratio multiplied by the incidence rate of the disease in the population.

The distinction between the *proportion* of deaths attributable to a set of causes versus the *probability* of death from these causes is important to understand. For example, the probability of death from noncommunicable causes (indeed, from virtually all causes) is higher in low- and middle-income regions than in the high-income world. However, the proportion of deaths attributable to these chronic causes is less than those attributed to infectious causes. The risk of death and the rates of death by these causes do not increase; rather, the proportion of attributable deaths increases as the communicable proportion declines with development. For example, in 1990 the risk of dying from cancer was 50% greater in low- and middle-income countries than in high-income countries, even though cancer accounted for a much smaller proportion of total deaths in those countries.

Demographic and Epidemiologic Transitions

The term *demographic transition* was first used by F. W. Notestein in 1945 to describe the changes in birth and death rates that historically have accompanied the shift from a traditional to a modern society (Exhibit 1-3) (see also Chapter 3). With modernization (a complex term indicating social and economic development), sharp declines in mortality have been followed by a reduction in fertility, although usually lagging by years or decades. The term *transition* refers to the shift away from a stable, high-stationary stage of population in which very high birth rates are balanced by very high death rates and there is little or no population

growth. As a society undergoes modernization, there is a transition with falling mortality, especially in the under-five age group, but with continuing high birth rates leading to explosive population growth. Birth rates then tend to drop, and a new, low-stationary stage is reached in which birth and death rates are low and balance resumes. The end results are a striking change in the age structure of the population, with a decreased proportion of children and an aging population. These changes in the population age distributions are reflected in the shift from a wide-based pyramid, reflecting larger numbers in the younger age groups, to a structure with a narrow base, nearly rectangular configuration, and nearly equal percentages in each age group (see Exhibit 1-3).

Historically, all countries that have undergone modernization with a marked drop in under-five mortality have had rapid population growth. In the past, this population growth was always followed by falling fertility rates, but the reasons for the drop are not entirely clear. Maurice King has pointed to a potential major problem that may arise, termed the *demographic trap*, in which fertility rates do not drop (King, 1990). This situation would lead to the classic Malthusian scenario in which massive starvation and epidemic diseases overtake the population. King points out that there is no guarantee that there will be a drop in birth rate in all countries undergoing modernization and that changes in fertility depend very much on social and cultural characteristics.

In 1971 Omran described the underlying reasons for the demographic transition and used the term *epidemiologic transition* to explain the changing causal factors of disease that accounted for the dramatic drop in under-five mortality, which was largely due to reduction in malnutrition and communicable diseases. It is important to note that although high rates of maternal mortality are characteristic of the low- and middle-income world, reductions of maternal mortality occur in a different time frame from those of under-five mortality. Reductions in maternal mortality require a much better developed infrastructure, including ready availability of surgical and blood transfusion capacity plus improved communication and transportation systems. Thus, drops in maternal mortality occur much further along the road toward economic development, and changes occur only after shifts in the under-five mortality have been seen (see Chapter 3).

Major changes in the patterns and causes of injury are also likely to occur with modernization. For example, road traffic injuries tend to increase as countries go through the stage of development in which there is a great increase in vehicles and the speeds at which they are operated before improved roads and law enforcement are in place (Crooper & Kopits, 2003). There may also be important shifts in the nature of violence and toward whom it is directed, related to crime patterns, civil unrest, ethnic conflicts, and intrafamily tensions (WHO, 2002b). The profound impact of the HIV/AIDS epidemic was discussed earlier in Exhibit 1-2.

Morbidity and Disability

Measures of mortality have been the principal indicators of population health status for a long time. Their relative ease of observation, presence of data, and history of use make them suitable for assessing health status and consequent changes. However, the problem with mortality-based indicators is that they "note the dead and ignore the living" (Kaplan, 1990). Measurements of morbidity, on the other hand, are much more problematic because there is no clearly defined endpoint, such as death provides. In addition, several components of morbidity and disability need to be assessed: duration, severity, and consequences.

Concepts that distinguish among disease, illness, and sickness have been present in the literature for half a century, from the description of the sick role in 1929 to the development of a disability framework in the 1960s. This framework considered *disease* as an organic-level disorder confined to the individual, *illness* as a subjective state of dysfunction from the disorder at the individual level, and *sickness* as a social dysfunction within a society that goes beyond the individual. The International Classification of Impairments, Disabilities, and Handicaps (ICIDH) was developed by WHO to classify nonfatal health outcomes (WHO, 1980). This assessment was based

on a progression from disease to handicap and was analogous to the ICD series. ICIDH categories included impairment (loss or abnormality of psychological, physiological, or anatomical structure or function), disability (restriction or lack of ability to perform an activity considered normal), and handicap (disadvantage from a disability or impairment for a given individual based on the inability to fulfill a normal role as defined by age, sex, or sociocultural factors). These distinctions clarified more than just processes and helped define the contribution of medical services, rehabilitation facilities, and social welfare to the reduction of sickness. Recently, WHO has built on the ICIDH and developed the International Classification of Functioning, Disability and Health (ICF), which is a classification of health that describes body functions and structures, activities, and participation (WHO, 2002a).

Using such classifications, indicators for disability, such as impairment-, disability-, and handicap-free life expectancies, have been developed. These in turn have been used to estimate health-adjusted life expectancies using severity and preference weights for time spent in states of less-than-perfect health.

Hospital inpatient discharge records—when they are based on good clinical evidence and coded by staff well trained in coding procedures—can provide high-quality data on the major causes of morbidity serious enough to require hospitalization. They also can provide good cause of death data for those hospitalized, and some sense of the outcome status of those with serious conditions. Hospital data are generally improving in quality, especially in middle-income countries and in selected sentinel, usually tertiary care, teaching hospitals in low-income countries. Such information

---

Exhibit 1-3 **The Demographic and Epidemiologic Transitions**

Changes in the pattern of disease proceed in two steps. The first is the demographic transition, when mortality from infectious disease and undernutrition decline with a marked drop in under-five mortality plus a reduction in fertility; the second is the epidemiologic transition, with a change in disease pattern. The population grows older, and noninfectious diseases become the main causes of ill health. Health patterns in the developing world over the next three decades will be profoundly influenced by these transitions.

It is commonly assumed that when a country is going through its demographic transition, the changes in its health indicators are primarily a function of declines in mortality. In fact, both the age structure and the cause of death structure are strongly influenced by the rapid decline in fertility. When fertility is high, the age structure of a population is heavily skewed toward the young. Because birth rates remain high and larger numbers of women enter the reproductive ages every year, the base of the population is continually expanding. When birth rates start to fall rapidly, the absolute number of babies born each year may remain unchanged or even decline. The graphs that follow show the shape of the age structure of the population on the left and the percentage of total deaths in each age group on the right. The age structure for both England and Wales and for Latin America and the Caribbean shifted from a broad base and narrow top to a fairly uniform rectangular shape. At the same time there was a marked shift in the percentage of deaths by age from under-fives to the elderly.

(continued)

Exhibit 1-3   Continued

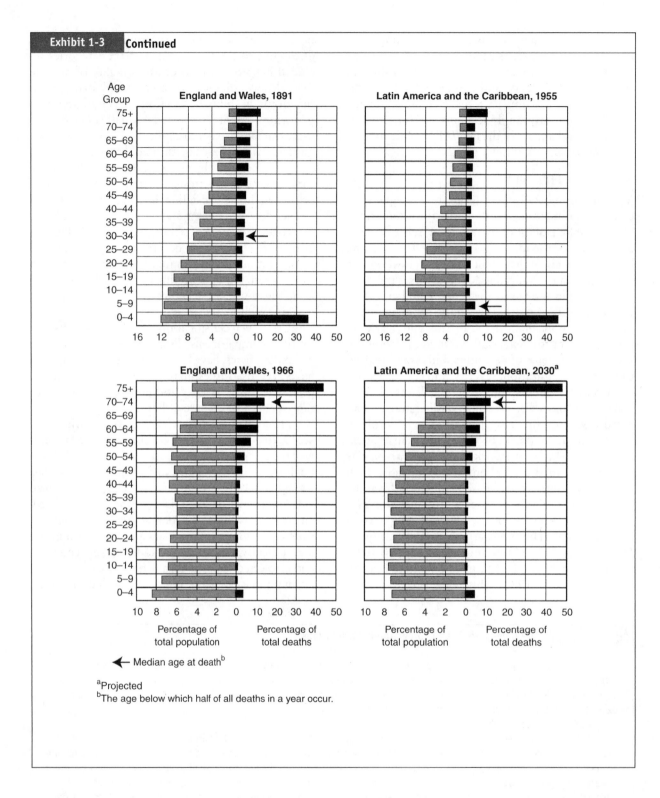

Age Group

England and Wales, 1891

Latin America and the Caribbean, 1955

England and Wales, 1966

Latin America and the Caribbean, 2030[a]

Percentage of total population   Percentage of total deaths

Percentage of total population   Percentage of total deaths

◄— Median age at death[b]

[a]Projected
[b]The age below which half of all deaths in a year occur.

is biased because of the highly skewed distribution of those using such hospitals, but in many situations it is possible to have a good understanding of those biases and make appropriate adjustments to draw useful conclusions.

Generally, outpatient records in most of the world are highly deficient in terms of diagnosis and often provide only the patient's chief complaint and probably the treatment dispensed. The main value of most such records is limited to establishing the fact of using a facility. There are usually strong biases in terms of those who use outpatient facilities because of access factors (distance and cost of use), nature and severity of the disease problem, and opportunity for using alternate services.

Visits to health care facilities, functional disability (measures of activity that is less than usual), and time spent away from work (absenteeism, work days lost) have been used to assess the magnitude of morbidity from various conditions. A common approach to evaluating morbidity in a population has been the assessment of the impact on social roles or functional performance, such as days missed from work or spent in bed (Kaplan, 1990). There is considerable literature on a wide variety of instruments used to measure such functional capacity, especially in clinical medical literature, that is not directly useful for population-based morbidity assessment.

Data about morbidity presented in the literature are often based on self-perceived or observed assessments, and frequently from survey-based interview information. The perception of morbidity and its reporting, the observation of morbidity and its impact, and other factors are responsible for the wide variation between reported and measured prevalences of conditions (Murray & Chen, 1992). This has resulted in an underestimation of the presence and impact of morbidity in both low- and middle-income as compared with high-income nations. This situation also underscores the variation in morbidity data, often interpreted to indicate that wealthy individuals and low-mortality populations *report* higher rates of morbidity (Murray & Lopez, 1996a).

Measurement of individual preferences for different health states in order to determine relative severity of disability has been done by a variety of methods (Kaplan, 1990; Murray et al., 2002; Torrence, 1986). Factors that influence preference include the type of respondent, the type of instrument used to measure the response, and the time from entry into the disabled state. Individuals who are in a particular state, healthy individuals, health care providers, caretakers, and family members have all been interviewed in studies. Adaptation, conditioning, development of special skills, and vocational training can all change the response of individuals over time within a particular health state and thus affect the value of that state to the individual. Healthy people may have different valuations for health states than people who are disabled, and the valuation by the disabled may change depending on time and adaptive processes. The value placed on a year of life by a paraplegic soon after entering that health state would be different from that obtained after several years of adjustment to that state (Murray & Lopez, 1994b).

Instruments used to extract such preferences involve visual and interview techniques (Murray & Lopez, 1996a; Torrence, 1986). Two alternative scenarios are often presented to the subject and the point of indifference sought (as in standard gamble techniques). Despite much work, there is no consensus or accepted standard method. Measurement of health-related quality of life has also been discussed in the medical literature for decades. *Health-related quality of life* refers to how well an individual functions in daily life and his or her perception of well-being. Various domains of quality have been defined, such as health perception, functional status, and opportunity, and several instruments have been developed to evaluate them. Both disease-specific and general instruments exist, abounding in fields dealing with chronic disabled states such as psychiatry, neurology, and counseling. These scales are often dependent on self-reported information, although some incorporate observational data as well. There has been repeated concern about their reliability and validity. These measures are not discussed further, because they have been primarily used in clinical assessments and do not directly relate to measures of population health.

Measuring Disability

If all the various forms of disability—physical, functional, mental, and social—are to be compared with mortality, they must be measured in an equivalent manner for use in health assessments. To do so, measurement of disability must quantify the duration and severity of this complex phenomenon. A defined process is needed that rates the severity of disability as compared with mortality, measures the duration of time spent in a disabled state, and converts disability from various causes into a common scale. General measures of disability without regard to cause (often carried out by special surveys) are useful to determine the proportion of the population that is disabled and unable to carry out normal activities, but are not much help for expressing extent of disability.

In general, three components of morbidity need to be assessed. The first component is the *case disability ratio (CDR)*, the proportion of those diagnosed with the disease who have disability. For most diseases that are diagnosed clinically, the CDR will be 1 since, by the definition of disease given earlier, they will have signs or symptoms. However, when the diagnosis is based on, for example, infection rather than disease (such as tuberculosis) or on a genetic marker rather than the physical manifestation (such as sickle trait), the CDR is likely to be less than 1.

The second component is the extent or severity of disability—how incapacitated the person is as a result of the disease. The extent of disability is expressed on a scale, usually from 0, which means no disability, to 1, which is equivalent to death. The assessment of severity can be quite subjective, particularly because there are so many different types and dimensions of disability. A number of methods have been tried to achieve comparability and obtain consensus (Murray et al., 2002). Severity of disability scales have been developed by group consensus using community surveys (Kaplan, 1990), a mixture of community and expert groups (Ghana Health Assessment Team, 1981), experts only (World Bank, 1993), and population surveys (Murray et al., 2002). These scales usually compare perfect health states to death on a scale of 0 to 1 (Table 1-1). In the Global Burden of Disease 1990 study, the disability severity estimates were based on expert opinion. Twenty-two indicator conditions were selected and used to construct seven disability classes (see Table 1-1). Outcomes from all other health conditions were categorized within these

seven classes (with special categories for treated and untreated groups). Generally, for most conditions a reasonable degree of consensus can be reached within broad categories (e.g., 25% disabled as compared with 50%), but efforts to go to much finer distinctions have been equivocal. The need to become more refined for purposes of health program decisions is a national or local decision.

The third component is the duration of the disability. The duration is generally counted from onset until cure and recovery or death. Sometimes there is continuing permanent disability after the acute phase is completed, and thus the duration would be the remaining life expectancy from the time of onset of disease.

Data for Decisions

In the collection and assessment of information, the level of precision required is an important feature. This level of precision needs to be guided by the purpose of collecting the information. The ultimate reason for data is to guide decision making—to make it better and more efficient at helping reduce the burden of disease on populations. The level of precision

Table 1-1	Examples of Disability Classification Systems	
Ghana Health Assessment Team 1981		
Class	**Severity**	**Equivalent to (max)**
1	0	Normal health
2	0.01–0.25	Loss of one limb's function
3	0.26–0.50	Loss of two limbs' function
4	0.51–0.75	Loss of three limbs' function
5	0.76–0.99	Loss of four limbs' function
6	1	Equivalent to death
Global Burden of Disease Study, 1990		
Disability Class	**Severity Weight**	**Indicator Conditions**
1	0.00–0.02	Vitiligo, height, weight
2	0.02–0.12	Acute watery diarrhea, sore throat, severe anemia
3	0.12–0.24	Radius fracture, infertility, erectile dysfunction, rheumatoid arthritis, angina
4	0.24–0.36	Below-knee amputation, deafness
5	0.36–0.50	Rectovaginal fistula, major mental retardation, Down's syndrome
6	0.50–0.70	Major depression, blindness, paraplegia
7	0.70–1.00	Psychosis, dementia, migraine, quadriplegia

Source: Data from Ghana Health Assessment Team, "A Quantitative Method for Assessing the Health Impact of Different Diseases in Less Developed Countries," 1981, *International Journal of Epidemiology, 10,* pp. 73–80; and C. J. L. Murray and A. Lopez (Eds.), *The Global Burden of Disease* (Geneva, Switzerland: World Health Organization, 1996).

depends on the decisions to be taken; even rough estimates may be helpful. Though disconcerting to some, the time, human, and monetary cost of further precision needs to be justified by its potential impact on decision making. Low- and middle-income countries, with their scarce resources, need timely and appropriate information to plan and implement health interventions that maximize the health of their populations. Methods, indicators, and assessments of disease must support and contribute to this primary purpose of health systems.

Composite Summary Measures of Population Health

This section focuses on the main approaches used for composite measures of population health status that summarize mortality and morbidity occurring in a population through the use of a single number. It discusses the rationale for composite measures, reviews the origins of each approach, examines methodological differences, makes explicit the value choices that each entails, and outlines the advantages and limitations of each.

Rationale for Composite Measures

Rationing of health care resources is a fact of life everywhere; choices about the best use of funds for health must be made (Hyder, Rotlland, & Morrow, 1998; World Bank, 1993;). The global scarcity of resources for health care is a challenge for every country, rich and poor (Evans, Hall, & Warford, 1981; World Bank, 1993), but the realities in low- and middle-income countries make the issue of choice that much starker. It is even more important for poor countries to choose carefully how to optimize health expenditures to obtain the most health in the most equitable fashion from these expenditures. Important tools under development to assist in making better choices for health spending are based on measures of the effectiveness of health interventions in improving health status in relation to their cost.

In most sectors, decisions on resource allocation are based on perceived value for money, but the health sector has had no coherent basis for determining the comparative value of different health outcomes. To make decisions about whether to put money into programs that reduce mortality in under-fives, as compared with those that reduce disabling conditions in adults, a common denominator is needed. In recent years, work has been carried out to develop composite indicators combining morbidity and mortality into a single measure that may serve as a common denominator. The common unit of measure is time lost from healthy life.

The most important reason for attempting to capture the complex mix of incommensurable consequences resulting from disease into a single number is the need to weigh the benefits of health interventions against their costs. Costs of health programs are expressed in a unidimensional measure, such as U.S. dollars; therefore, the benefits to be achieved from their expenditure must also be so expressed. *Healthy lifetime* is a unidimensional measure that can be used to compress health benefits and losses into a single time dimension. An explicit, objective, quantitative approach should enable better budgetary decisions and permit resource allocation in the health sector to be undertaken in a more effective and equitable fashion.

Note that a composite indicator is simply a tool to be used to assist decision makers in resource allocation. Like any tool, it can be misused. Conclusions that are reached on the basis of the use of these indicators must be carefully examined and looked at from all viewpoints. Not only are there problems of trying to put so many dimensions together, which inevitably leads to distortion, but also there are serious issues concerning the reliability and validity of the information on which these are based. Thus, all the problems associated with determining cause of death, counting the number of cases of disease, and assessing the extent of disability from a condition will lead to great uncertainties when they are added and multiplied together. The development of a single indicator with a specific number provides deceptive substantiality to what may be composed of fragile data. Continuing vigilance in how data are obtained, compiled, and used is critical, and those responsible for using the tool must have a clear technical understanding of what is behind the numbers and what underlying assumptions and limitations are associated with these approaches. But with all these caveats, alternative approaches to improved decision making leave even more to be desired.

Uses of Composite Indicators

Measures of health status that combine mortality and morbidity facilitate comparisons within and across populations. They can estimate the quantitative health benefits from interventions and serve as tools to assist in the allocation of resources. The development of such measures entails two major processes: the measurement of life, including losses of time from premature mortality and disability; and the valuing of life, which incorporates issues of duration, age, extent of future life, productivity, dependency, and equity (Morrow & Bryant, 1995). The purpose of developing such measures and the need for refining them become clear if the following objectives are to be achieved:

- The use of such methods at the country level for evaluating the impact of diseases
- Their use in the allocation of resources within the health sector
- The generation of more relevant and useful data for policy makers

Precursors of composite indicators have been discussed in the literature for decades and generally were developed to assist prioritization of health issues. Usually these were based on the measurement of losses of time, losses of productive time, income forgone, or other costs incurred as a result of diseases. The earlier indicators generally focused on economic losses and estimated time loss due to disease and converted this to a dollar value. These measures are thus more economic measures than disease-burden measures.

Types of Composite Summary Measures

Two types of composite summary measures have been developed: *health gaps* (healthy life lost), such as healthy life years (HeaLY) or disability-adjusted life years (DALY), and *health expectancies*, such as disability-free life expectancy (DFLE) or health-adjusted life expectancy (HALE). Both types use healthy lifetime lost through disability and death as a common measure of the impact of mortality and nonfatal health outcomes. These two types of measures are complementary (Figure 1-1).

In Figure 1-1, the bold line is the survivorship curve based on a standard hypothetical life table population that demonstrates the proportion (*y*-axis) of an initial birth cohort that remains alive at any age (*x*-axis). The area A + B is the total life expectancy at birth of this cohort. A part of this life is spent in full health; the thin line is the survivor curve of those in full health to each age *n*.

Thus, area A represents time lived in full health, whereas area B is time lived in suboptimal health (with disability). Area C represents time lost due to mortality. The area of the complete rectangle (A + B + C) represents the ideal survivorship curve—the theoretical maximum of healthy life for a cohort who lived in full health until age *n*, when all died.

Health expectancies are summary measures that estimate expectancy of life in a defined state of health. Examples include DFLE, active life expectancy, and HALE. These extend the concept of life expectancy to

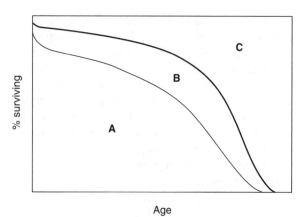

Figure 1-1 Survivorship Curve of a Hypothetical Population, Showing the Areas of Health Expectancies. *Source:* C. J. L. Murray et al., *Summary Measures of Population Health* (Geneva, Switzerland: World Health Organization, 1999). Reprinted with permission.

expectations of various states of health, not just of life per se. Health expectancies assign lower weights to life lived in less than full health on a scale of 0 to 1, in which full health is rated 1. In Figure 1-1, health expectancy is given by the following equation:

$$\text{Health Expectancy} = A + f(B)$$

where $f(\ )$ is some function that assigns weights to years lived in suboptimal health. (Full health has a weight of 1.)

Health gaps (healthy life lost) are summary measures that estimate the *difference* between actual population health and some specified norm or goal. In Figure 1-1 that difference is indicated by area C (loss due to mortality) plus some function of area B, that is, survivorship with disability:

$$\text{Health gap (healthy life lost)} = C + g(B)$$

where $g(\ )$ is some function that assigns weights to health states lived during time B. Weights are between 0, or no disability (full health), and 1, or complete disability (equivalent of death). Note that this is equivalent to healthy life lost based on the natural history of disease in a population as discussed in the section "Healthy Life Year" later in this chapter.

A major advantage of healthy life lost summary measures as compared with health expectancies is that they provide a common denominator for population health and for the outcomes in randomized trials and cohort and other health services studies, as well as for economic evaluations of interventions and monitoring of health system outcomes.

Composite Indicators

A number of composite summary indicators for burden of disease assessment have been developed. We shall focus on four: three of the health gap type—the healthy life year (HeaLY), the disability-adjusted life year (DALY), and the quality-adjusted life year (QALY)—and one of the health expectancy type, namely, HALE.

In addition to measures of morbidity and mortality per se, these composite indicators all incorporate several social value choices either explicitly or implicitly: the choice of life expectancy tables, valuing future life as compared with present, valuing life lived at different ages, valuing social or economic productivity, and valuing equity in relation to cost-effectiveness. These social value choices are discussed later in this chapter (see the section "Valuing Life"), but because some social value choices are integral to the calculations of some composite indicators, they are briefly mentioned in this section.

Healthy Life Year

The *healthy life year (HeaLY)* is a composite measure that combines the amount of healthy life lost due to morbidity with that lost due to death (loss of life expected had the disease not occurred) (Hyder, Rotllant, & Morrow, 1998). We discuss the healthy life year first because it is conceptually straightforward, serves as a prototype for other health gap indicators, and was the first of the composite measures to be used as a tool in national health planning (Ghana Health Assessment Team, 1981). The HeaLY approach is a direct derivative of the work done in Ghana incorporating several additional features.

The measure of loss from death is based on the years of life that would have been expected had the disease not occurred. The information needed in addition to the incidence rate and case fatality ratio is the age of disease onset, the age of death, and the expectation of life at these ages. All of this information is objective in nature and potentially available in every country. The main issue centers on what choice to make for the basis of life expectation. (See also the section "Expectation of Life" later in this chapter.) The original Ghana work was based on expectation-of-life tables specific for Ghana, but considerations of equity as well as those concerning comparability across countries made it preferable to use the best possible life expectation—that of the female population in Japan.

Measuring the loss of healthy life from disability is much more challenging than measuring that from

death, and many approaches have been used (Murray & Lopez, 1994b). In order for a measure to be used in a composite measure, it must have comparable dimensions to that for life lost due to death. The HeaLY includes three components: case disability ratio (CDR, comparable to the case fatality ratio), extent of disability, and duration of disability. The CDR and duration can be determined objectively, but assessment of the extent, which ranges from 0 to 1 (from no disability to that equivalent to death), has a substantial subjective element (Morrow & Bryant, 1995).

The healthy life approach focuses on knowledge of the pathogenesis and natural history of disease (Last, 2000) as the conceptual framework for assessing morbidity and mortality and for interpreting the effects of various interventions (Figure 1-2). For the purpose of estimating healthy life lost or gained, disease is defined as in the introduction of this chapter: anything that an individual (or population) experiences that causes, literally, "dis-ease"—anything that leads to discomfort, pain, distress, disability of any kind, or death, including injuries and psychiatric disabilities. With some exceptions, those with infection or some biological characteristic (such as AS hemoglobin) are considered healthy unless they have specific identifiable symptoms or signs. Preclinical or subclinical disease is not generally counted. However, the diagnostic criteria for some conditions such as hypertension, HIV infection, or onchocerciasis (diagnosed by skin snip), include individuals without signs or symptoms. Such criteria (for example, indicators of infection, high blood pressure, or genetic markers) are appropriate when they serve as the basis for intervention programs. Interventions may also be directed at reducing identifiable risk factors, such as tobacco smoking or risky sexual behavior. To the extent that risk reduction can be translated into disease reduction, the approach to measuring the benefits and costs of a risk reduction intervention program remains the same.

The onset of disease usually will be dated from the start of symptoms or signs, as determined by the individual afflicted, a family member, a medical practitioner, or as the result of a lab test. There are several different patterns of disease evolution; Figure 1-3 illustrates healthy life lost from disability and premature death due to typical cases of cirrhosis, polio, and multiple sclerosis in terms of onset, extent and duration of disability, and termination. The conclusion of the disease process depends on the natural history of the disease as modified by possible interventions. The possible outcomes include clinical recovery (the complete disappearance of clinical signs and symptoms),

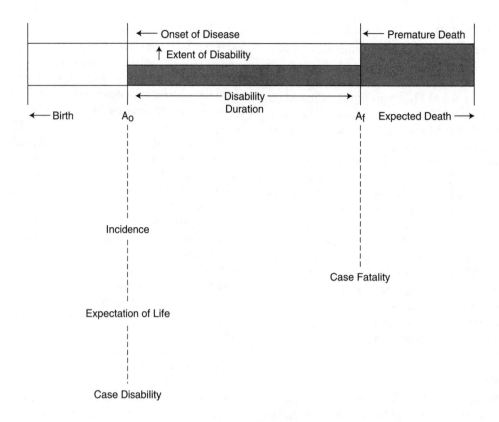

Note: A_O = average age at onset; A_f = average age at death; ■ = healthy life lost.

Figure 1-2 The HeaLY Model: Loss of Healthy Life from Disability and Death.

progression to another disease state (such as chronic hepatitis progressing to cirrhosis), and death. The latter includes death directly caused by the disease and death indirectly brought on by the disease as a result of disability.

The definition of variables and formulas to calculate HeaLYs are described later in this section and summarized in Table 1-2. Each disease will have a distribution of ages at which onset or death may occur, but for most diseases the average age will provide a satisfactory approximation for a population. In view of the limitations of data, this is the starting assumption for the application of the HeaLY method in countries. However, like other choices in this method, if sensitivity testing indicates that the average age is not satisfactory, then estimates may be based on age distributions instead. Similarly, if the natural history of a disease or response to interventions is different in different age groups, then the disease can be specifically classified by age (e.g., neonatal tetanus as compared with adult tetanus, and childhood pneumonia as compared with adult pneumonia).

In recurrent diseases or diseases with multiple episodes (e.g., diarrhea), age at onset denotes the av-

erage age at first episode. For some diseases, such as malaria, which is characterized by recurrent episodes, and schistosomiasis, in which reinfection occurs at frequent intervals, it may be useful to view them as single lifetime diseases. For example, malaria in Africa may be considered for each individual as a single, lifelong disease with chronic, usually asymptomatic, parasitemia but with intermittent severe clinical attacks (which result in high mortality in late infancy and early childhood while immunity is being acquired), followed by recurring, nonfatal clinical episodes after age 10.

The expectation of life in HeaLYs (like DALYs) is based on normative expectations of what should be achieved under optimal circumstances. Women in Japan, who have the highest global expectation of life, approximate this expectation, taken from the West model with an expectation of life at birth of 82.5 years for females (level 26) (Coale & Demeney, 1983; Coale & Guo, 1989).

The definition of disease (*dis-ease*) makes the value of the case disability ratio 1 by default for most disease states because all cases are disabled (to varying degrees and duration) if they have been labeled as diseased.

Healthy Life Lost (Cirrhosis)

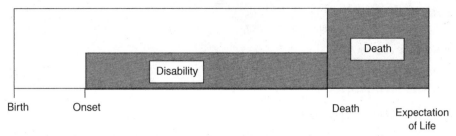

Healthy Life Lost (Polio)

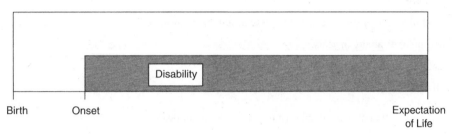

Healthy Life Lost (Multiple Sclerosis)

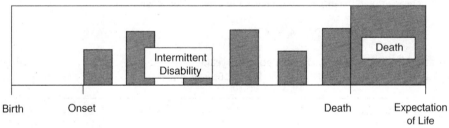

Figure 1-3 Different Patterns of Healthy Life Lost. *Source:* A. A. Hyder, G. Rotllant, and R. H. Morrow, "Measuring the Burden of Disease: Healthy Life Years," 1998, *American Journal of Public Health, 88,* pp. 196–202. Reprinted with permission.

However, there are some conditions, such as sickle cell trait or HIV positivity, and risk factors for which cases may not be considered diseased by definition, but the condition nonetheless needs to be assessed.

The duration of disability can be either temporary or permanent. If the disability is temporary, then D_t is the duration of that disability until recovery (see Table 1-2). If the disability is permanent and the disease does not affect life expectation, then D_t is the expectation of life at age of onset of disease [$D_t = E(A_o)$]. On the other hand, if the disability is permanent and the disease does reduce life expectation, then D_t is the expectation of life at age of onset reduced by the difference between ages of fatality and onset [$D_t = E(A_o) - (A_f - A_o)$].

A disability severity scale needs to be used to estimate severity (see Table 1-1). These scores represent an estimate of the *average* disability suffered by typical cases of the specific disease over its course. The Ghana scale, for example (see Table 1-1), is simple and has been used for HeaLY calculations; similar scales may be developed in countries interested in doing burden of disease studies.

The healthy life years lost from death and from disability are added and expressed as the total years of life lost per 1,000 population per year; the loss is attributed to the year in which disease onset occurs and includes the stream of life lost from disability and death at any time after onset, even if these events happen many years later. This is a prospective view of

Table 1-2	Variables for Estimating Healthy Life Years	
Symbol	**Explanation**	**Expression**
I	Incidence rate per 1,000 population per year.	/1,000/year
A_o	Average age at onset.	years
A_f	Average age at death.	years
$E(A_o)$	Expectation of life at age of onset.	years
$E(A_f)$	Expectation of life at age of death.	years
CFR	Case fatality ratio: proportion of those developing the disease who die from the disease.	0.00–1.00
CDR	Case disability ratio: proportion of those developing the disease who have disability from the disease.	0.00–1.00
D_e	Extent of disability (from none to complete disability, equivalent to death).	0.00–1.00
D_t	Duration of disability in years.	years
	Disability can be either permanent or temporary.	
	If temporary, then	
	D_t = duration of that disability(i.e., until recovery or death)	
	If permanent and disease does not affect life expectation, then	
	$D_t = E(A_o)$	
	If permanent and the disease does reduce life expectation, then	
	$D_t = A_f - A_o$	
HeaLY	Healthy life years lost per 1,000 population per year: $= I \times \{[CFR \times \{E(A_o) - [A_f - A_o]\}] + [CDR \times D_e \times D_t]\}$	HeaLYs per 1,000 per year

the event (disease onset) and its consequences because cases are followed over time.

The health status of a population can be considered as the amount of healthy life it achieves as a proportion of the total amount that the people could achieve under optimum conditions. A cohort of 1,000 newborns with an expectation of life of 82.5 years has potential of 82,500 years of healthy life. In a steady state, a random sample of 1,000 from such a population has the potential of 41,250 years of healthy life (Hyder, Rotllant, & Morrow, 1998; Morrow & Bryant, 1995). Each year this population would experience events leading to 1,000 years of healthy life lost attributable to mortality, with a distribution of age at death equivalent to that which leads to a life expectation of 82.5. Any disease that leads to disability or to death earlier than that set by this age-at-death distribution would increase the amount of healthy life lost beyond this minimum. This formulation is equivalent

to the health gap, as indicated in Figure 1-1. Discounting future life or adding productivity, dependency, or age weighting would affect these denominator numbers.

HeaLYs measure the *gap or loss* between the current situation in a country and an ideal or standard, as defined by the selected expectation of life. In recent work the standard used is based on the life expectation approximated in Japan. Thus, if exactly the same method were used to estimate the HeaLY losses for females in Japan, they would amount to 0 per 1,000 people for loss due to mortality; only that due to disability would be counted. In other words, because the population under study is the ideal, and assuming stability of the population, constancy of mortality rates, and no disability, there would be no gap to measure. This does not mean that the population is not having a loss of healthy life, but only that such loss is the minimum as defined by the structure of the population and the expectation of life, as described previously. Any country that is experiencing losses greater than this minimum, either as a result of excess mortality or disability, will have a gap that can be measured; that gap is what the HeaLYs register.

An important benefit of the HeaLY formulation in its spreadsheet form is that the effects of different kinds of interventions can be readily explored to determine their expected gains in healthy life. Interventions may usefully be divided into two broad categories: those that are used to prevent the initiation of the disease process and those that are used to treat a disease process already under way. Some interventions fall into both categories. The primary effect of preventive strategies is to reduce the incidence of new cases of disease. The main effects of treatment strategies are to interfere with the natural history of the disease process, thereby reducing the case fatality and/or case disability ratios or extending life, providing a later age at death for conditions such as diabetes and AIDS. The spreadsheet, available upon request to the authors, also incorporates the proportion of the population that are or will be covered by an intervention and allows for different levels of coverage for different segments of the population for each intervention.

Disability-Adjusted Life Year

The *disability-adjusted life year (DALY)* is a health gap population summary measure that combines time lost due to disability with that due to death (life that would have been expected had the disease not occurred) in a manner similar to the healthy life year measure. It first appeared in the World Development Report of 1993 (World Bank, 1993) and has become the most widely used composite measure of population health (Murray & Lopez, 1994a, 1994b, 1996a, 1999; Murray et al, 2002).

DALYs are calculated as two separate components and directly include three social value choices. The two components are (1) the loss of life from death, assessed by evaluating all deaths in a year for life expectancy at the time of death to estimate years of life lost (YLL) for each disease category, plus (2) the loss of healthy life from disability, estimated using years of life lived with disability (YLD) based on the incidence, the average duration of the condition (to remission or death), and a severity weight using an average health state weight. Thus,

$$\text{DALY} = \text{YLL} + \text{YLD}$$

The social value choices include life expectation tables, discount rates for future life, and weighting for life lived at different ages, as discussed later. The

DALY is described in detail in Murray and Lopez (1996a). DALYs, with their separate components of YLLs and YLDs, were estimated for three disease categories, both sexes, five age groups, and eight regions of the world and published in the Global Burden of Disease study for the year 1990 (Murray & Lopez, 1996a) and for the year 2000 (Murray et al., 2001). Some of these figures are presented in the section entitled "Comparisons and Trends in Disease Burden."

The calculation for YLL uses the age distribution of deaths by cause for a year to estimate standard expected years of life for each disease. The loss of life is obtained by comparison with a model life table based on best achievable low levels of mortality, such as in Japan, reflecting high life expectation at birth of more than 80 years (Coale & Guo, 1989).

For disability, the DALY uses estimates of incidence, duration, and severity to calculate the time lived with disability across age groups. This information is based on the expectation of a proportion of cases in most conditions experiencing some form of disability over time. The onset of this disability, an estimate of severity at each stage, and the period of time spent in each stage are used to generate YLDs. A description of the severity scale used in one version of DALYs has been given previously in the section on measurement of disability (see Table 1-1).

Note that an important difference between the HeaLY and DALY is that the starting point for the HeaLY is the onset of disease; the loss of healthy life is based on the natural history of the disease (as modified by interventions), as illustrated in Figures 1-1 and 1-2. This is true for the YLD component of the DALY, but the YLL is based on mortality in the current year. In a steady state there is no difference, but when there is an increasing incidence, such as with HIV in many parts of the globe, the DALY approach can greatly understate the true situation (Hyder & Morrow, 1999).

Once the years of life lost to mortality and morbidity have been estimated, they are discounted, usually at 3% per annum. This social time preference has been used for most estimates; recently, DALY results discounted at 0% have also become available.

DALYs are age-weighted according to an arbitrary exponential curve designed to give the most value to life lived as a young adult (Hyder, Rotllant, & Morrow, 1998; World Bank, 1993). Weighting by age was the most controversial component of the DALY and caused great dissent from other health professionals. See the section "Valuing Life Lived at Different Ages" later in this chapter. Recent DALY listings of GBD studies also include results with no age weighting (all years equally valued). It has been argued that age weighting of DALYs does not affect the final result, but this depends on the purpose for making the estimates and has been challenged (Anand & Ranaan-Eliya, 1996; Barendregt, Bonneux, & Van Der Maas, 1996; Barker & Green, 1996; Hyder, Rotllant, & Morrow, 1998).

The calculation for DALYs can be expressed in the form of an integral that was first published in the World Bank literature (Murray & Lopez, 1994a). This single equation incorporating all technical and value choices has the advantage of standardization to ensure comparability of the multiple calculations undertaken in the GBD studies, and it has certainly greatly facilitated the actual computations. However, for national and local priority setting, it may be preferable to use an indicator constructed such that the social value choices can be adjusted to suit the national and local preferences (Bobadilla, 1998; Hyder, Rotllant, & Morrow, 1998; Morrow & Bryant, 1995). Recent DALY formulations allow for this.

Quality-Adjusted Life Year

The quality-adjusted life year (QALY) was introduced in 1976 to provide a guiding principle for selecting among alternative tertiary health care interventions (Zeckhauser & Shephard, 1976). The idea was to develop a single measure of quality of life in order to compare expected outcomes from different interventions—a measure that relies on weighting the range of possible health states and the duration of time spent in each state to compute their equivalency with healthy life.

Since its introduction, a variety of QALY measures have been developed, along with a voluminous literature on alternative methods incorporating a range of disability domains and a diversity of methods to assign weights to generate and use QALYs (Kaplan, 1990; Nord, 1993). A central notion behind the QALY is that a year of life spent in one health state may be preferred over a year spent in another. Measures that focus exclusively on duration of life fail to reflect these types of value choices. Multiplying time spent in a particular health state with the value given to that state forms the basis of comparing outcomes from treatment options.

In general a quality-adjusted life year takes into account both quantity (duration or amount of time) and the quality of life generated by health care interventions. It is the arithmetic product of life expectancy and a measure of the quality of the remaining life years. A QALY places a weight on time in different health states. A year of perfect health is worth 1, whereas a year of less than perfect health is worth less than 1. Death is considered to be equivalent to 0; however, some health states may be considered worse than death and have negative scores. QALYs provide a common currency to assess the extent of the benefits gained from a variety of interventions in terms of health-related quality of life and survival for the patient. When combined with the costs of providing the interventions, cost-utility ratios can be constructed; these indicate the additional costs required to generate a year of perfect health (one QALY). Comparisons can be made among interventions, and priorities can be established based on those interventions that provide the most QALYs per net expenditure.

Particular effort has gone into researching ways in which an overall health index might be constructed to locate a specific health state on a continuum between 0 (death) and 1 (perfect health). It has been especially useful in distinguishing different types and levels of disability, impairment, and handicap. The use of QALYs is exemplified in the QALY Toolkit (Gudex & Kind, 1988) in which eight degrees of disability are combined with four levels of distress to categorize patients into one of 29 possible health states, with a weight assigned to each health state. Each is valued and compared with others, and QALYs are derived by summing the time and value product for the progress of an individual through these states as treatment is given. The nature of this construct allows the use of QALYs for individual decision making, with potential for application in policy decisions.

The QALY was not originally developed as an indicator of disease burden in a population but rather as a differentiating indicator for individual choices among tertiary health care procedures. It was used for assessment of individual preferences for different health outcomes from alternative interventions (Morrow & Bryant, 1995). But the idea has generated many alternative formulations and methods for assessment and has been put to a variety of purposes.

Perhaps the most important use of QALYs has been as a common denominator to measure utility in cost-utility analysis to assist in resource allocation among alternative health interventions (Kaplan, 1990; Nord, 1992; Torrence, 1986). *Cost-utility analysis*, in this instance, has been considered as a special form of cost-effectiveness analysis with a common unit of measure, the QALY, for gains by alternative health interventions (Torrence, 1986). Interventions can be ranked in terms of cost *per QALY*, and money can be allocated to those that have the lowest result. In general this approach is acceptable to and understood by health policy makers, though there are notable exceptions (Exhibit 1-4).

Health-Adjusted Life Expectancy

Health-adjusted life expectancy (HALE) is a composite summary measure of population health status that belongs to the family of health expectancies; it summarizes the expected number of years to be lived in what might be termed the equivalent of "full health." Some consider the HALE to provide the best available summary measure for measuring the overall level of health for populations (Mathers et al., 2001). WHO has used it as the measure of the average level of health of the populations of member states in its *World Health Reports* (WHR) for annual reporting on population health (WHO, 2000).

During the 1990s, DFLE and related measures were calculated for many countries (Mathers et al., 2001; Robine et al, 1994). However, these measures incorporate a dichotomous weighting scheme in which time spent in any health state categorized as disabled is as-signed arbitrarily a weight of zero (equivalent to death). Thus, DFLE is not sensitive to differences in the severity distribution of disability in populations. In contrast, the disability-adjusted life expectancy (DALE) adds up expectation of life for different health states with adjustment for severity weights. The term disability-adjusted-life year, or DALY, was replaced by HALE for the WHR 2001 and will be used henceforth.

Health expectancy indices combine the mortality experience of a population with the disability experience. The HALE is calculated using the prevalence of disability at each age to divide the years of life expected at each age according to a life table cohort into years with and without disability. Mortality is captured by using a life table method, while the disability component is expressed by additions of prevalence of various disabilities within the life table. This indicator allows an assessment of the proportion of life spent in disabled states. When compared with the total expectation of life, this translates to a measure of the total disability burden in a population. Comparison of the

---

Exhibit 1-4	**Oregon: Application of the Quality-Adjusted Life Year**

The best-known application of the QALY approach for allocation of health resources occurred in the state of Oregon (Blumstein, 1997). In 1988 Oregon faced a budgetary shortfall for its Medicaid program, and coverage for organ transplants was denied. In an effort to prioritize its health services, Oregon undertook one of the first attempts worldwide to explicitly ration health services. A coalition including consumers, health care providers, insurers, and business and labor representatives launched a broad and bold reform. It began with a series of experiments in which the decision-making process was based on a cost-effectiveness approach using QALYs for comparing the outcomes of treatment options among people.

The initial list, published in 1990, consisted of 1,600 condition/treatment pairs drawn up as follows:

Cost-effectiveness ratio = cost of services / (health gain x duration)

Cost of services = Charges for treatment, including all services and drugs

Quality of well-being (QWB) = sum of QWB weight (W) × each QWB state × probability that symptoms of that QWB state would occur

Health gain = QWB with treatment − QWB without treatment

From the beginning, there was great opposition to the very notion of rationing; consequent denial of services to those who had conditions that did not make the list contributed to the rancor. There were also unfortunate technical blunders in the generation of the first list.

For example, treatment for thumb sucking ranked above hospitalization for starvation, and crooked teeth ranked above early treatment for Hodgkin's disease. Such inconsistencies together with objections raised by groups advocating for the disabled gave rise to alternative approaches for establishing rankings. Though enormous public effort went into the reform and much was accomplished, the explicit cost-effectiveness approach with QALYs as the outcome measure was dropped (Blumstein, 1997; Eddy, 1991; Morrow & Bryant, 1995; Nord, 1993).

The lack of success in developing a satisfactory list of services based on the QALY in Oregon was largely due to two factors: aggregation of scores appropriate for individual choices rather than using a population base, as for HeaLYs and DALYs, and a poorly tested quality of well-being scale. The result was the ranking of many conditions and their treatment much lower than the public as well as public health experts considered appropriate. Although unsuccessful in Oregon, such a method has the potential to be converted to a population-based approach.

various methods and specific indicators is available in the literature (Robine, 1994). Alternative methods are given in the National Burden of Disease Studies manual (Mathers et al., 2001).

As originally designed, this measure does not relate to specific diseases but rather to the average extent of disability among that proportion in each age group that is disabled. The lack of correlation between a condition or disease entity and the measure makes it less valuable for resource allocation and cost-effectiveness calculations. It is possible to convert health gap measures for specific diseases or interventions and risk factors into HALEs, but it is not clear what would be gained.

Although the HALE is conceptually interesting and is now being calculated and included regularly in the WHO annual reports, it must be asked what additional information the HALE provides beyond the standard life expectancy data. At a national level, the amount of healthy life lost due to disability very closely parallels and is closely proportional to that lost due to death. The relative ranking of countries by health expectancy (HALE) is virtually identical with that of life expectation at birth.

Summary

Table 1-3 summarizes the main differences among these four summary measures in terms of origin, purpose, level of use, sources of data, and the disciplinary background of the measure's originators.

Valuing Life: Social Value Issues

The very idea of valuing some lives more than others is jarring, yet these notions are regularly reflected in our actions. The value of life is often implicit in the way resource allocation decisions are made; therefore, as much as possible such decisions should be explicit, open, and transparent. Many thoughtful people have serious reservations about assigning a single number to such a complex multidimensional phenomenon as health. But what is the alternative for use as a measure of utility or effectiveness in economic analyses? Outcome measures must be expressed as a unidimensional measure in order to be comparable to unidimensional monetary expenditure units for costs.

To construct composite measures of population health, important social value choices must be made. Choices must be made about what expectation for life should be used and about valuing life lived at different ages, valuing future life as compared with the present, valuing life in terms of economic and social productivity, and valuing equity in relation to efficiency; these choices raise major ethical concerns.

Expectation of Life

Years of life lost due to death and to chronic disability are based on life expected had the disease not

Table 1-3	Comparisons of Composite Summary Measures of Population Health			
	Healthy Life Years (HeaLY)	Disability-Adjusted Life Years (DALY)	Quality-Adjusted Life Years (QALY)	Health-Adjusted Life Expectancy (HALE)
Origin	Ghana Ministry of Health, 1981	World Bank Development Report, 1993	North America, 1976	World Health Organization Report, 2000
Purpose	Assist in resource allocation decisions	Compare disease burdens in many different populations on a comparable basis	Assess individual preferences for various outcomes from complex interventions	Compare national disease burdens
Level of use	National and district-level decisions	Broad policy decisions	Personal decisions	Global comparisons
Data	National and local data from multiple sources; expert review	Global data and expert opinion	Tertiary hospital data and personal interviews	Global data and expert opinion
Discipline Base	Epidemiologists, clinicians, national planners	Economists, statisticians	Economists, clinicians	Demographers, economists, statisticians
Social Values Incorporated	Future life discounted	Age weighting; future life discounted	Generally not included	Not relevant

occurred. To estimate the expectation of life in a population, a choice must be made between using a national or a model life table. This choice should be determined by the purpose of the study. For assisting in national and local decision making, it may be more suitable to use national life tables based on the mortality and fertility of the population in question than model life tables. On the other hand, a model life table can be selected to reflect the best health state possible, such as the West model. This selection allows a fair comparison with other countries. For example, from a global perspective it would be unfair to use national life tables to compare gains that could be achieved in Ghana from a particular intervention with those in the United Kingdom, even if both costs and lives saved were the same in each country. The reason for this is that those lives saved in Ghana would have a lower life expectancy than those in the United Kingdom, resulting in less healthy life saved for the same expenditure. From the global view point in this example, the priority would be to fund the intervention in the United Kingdom because it would produce more healthy life per expenditure than for Ghana.

Model life tables in common use are the United Nations model life tables and the Coale and Demeney life tables (1983). The latter have been revised (Coale & Guo, 1989) and have been used in the GBD study and for HeaLYs (Hyder, Rotllant, & Morrow, 1998; Murray & Lopez, 1996a). The West model life table does not refer to any geographical entity but is considered to represent a mortality pattern typical of the most technologically advanced countries. Level 26 has a female life expectancy at birth of 82.5 years, as actually experienced by women in Japan; therefore, it represents a level that should be achievable elsewhere.

The choice of life table in a burden of disease analysis should be determined by the objective of the exercise, and the impact of the choice on the results can be explored in each situation.

Valuing Life Lived at Different Ages

Age weighting refers to the valuing of a year of life according to the age at which it is lived. This immediately raises questions as to the basis for valuing human life. Is a day of anyone's life of the same value as that of anyone else? Does the value vary with age, economic productivity, or social status? Should life itself be valued separately from what is done with that life?

The Ghana Health Assessment Team (1981) judged that all human life was intrinsically valuable and that a given duration of any life was equal to that of any other life. The valuing of a year of life equally,

irrespective of age, has been considered egalitarian (Busschbach, Hesing, & de Charro, 1993; Morrow & Bryant, 1995). But the healthy life approach values individuals in direct proportion to their expectation of life at their current age. Therefore the loss of a healthy child is regarded as costing society more than the loss of a healthy adult.

Disability-adjusted life years assign an exponential function to provide a value chosen so that life lived as a dependent (e.g., infants, children, and the elderly) is given less value than that lived during the productive years. The intrinsic value of life in this system increases from 0 at birth to a maximum at age 25 and declines thereafter, so that a day of life of a 50-year-old is worth about 25% of that of a 25-year-old. Paradoxically, the age weighting used in the DALY integral leads to higher valuation of life lived at under age 15 than does the HeaLY formulation, in which life lived at all ages is valued equally. Current formulations of the DALY leave age weighting as an option, and it is not used with the HALE.

Age-related valuing has been justified by showing that individuals value their own life lived at different ages differently. Such values have been reported in the literature for decades, and recent studies report that they are consistent across respondents of different ages (Busschbach, Hesing, & de Charro, 1993). Murray reports studies from many countries that reveal a preference for saving younger lives as compared with older ones (Murray & Lopez, 1994a). But it was not clear how much of the differential valuing of life at different ages was related to an underlying appreciation that economic and social productivity varies at different ages.

If it is decided that healthy life should be valued according to economic and social productivity, then it would be better to explicitly add a productivity factor (or subtract for the societal costs of dependents, such as education) rather than subsuming it under age weighting. See the section "Valuing Life for Its Economic and Social Productivity."

Valuing Future Life Compared with Present Life: Discounting

Discounting is the process of determining the present value of future events. Social time preference takes into account the phenomenon that people value events at present more highly than those in the future (independent of inflation and of uncertainty). For investments in other sectors, time preference is normally taken into account by discounting future returns and costs by some appropriate discount rate. It can be considered the inverse of an interest rate.

This concept has been applied in the health sector because both the losses from a disease and the benefits from a health intervention often occur in the future. An intervention today may not produce immediate benefits (such as in immunization), or it may result in benefits being sustained over a long time (such as in supplementary nutrition). The costs for these activities must be borne now, but benefits take place in the future and are worth less than if they could occur now. This is equivalent to investing money now in order to obtain more in the future. A healthy life year in the present has greater intrinsic value to an individual or community than one in the future (Gold et al., 1996; Weinstein et al., 1996).

The rate at which society is supposed to discount has been termed the *social discount rate* (SDR), which is a numeric reflection of societal values regarding intertemporal allocation of current resources. There is no consensus on the choice of a discount rate in health, but most agree that it should be lower than that in the private sector. The WDR in 1993 and the GBD studies discounted at 3% a year; in lieu of other information, this rate has come to be used in most international health cost-effectiveness studies. However, the impact of using a range of different discount rates, including zero, should be explored with each study.

The main issue concerning discounting in relation to composite summary measures is whether discounting life itself is appropriate. There seems little problem about the usefulness of discounting the future value of what is produced by healthy life, but should the life itself be discounted (Morrow & Bryant, 1995)?

Valuing Life for Its Economic and Social Productivity

Whether and how to value economic and social productivity for purposes of health care decision making is highly contentious; to a large extent, the age weighting incorporated in the original DALY formulation was considered by many to be a proxy for productivity. The consensus now seems to be that any such valuations should be considered separately, made explicit, and very much depend on the purpose of the valuations.

In general, productivity may be attributed to adults aged 15 to 64, and those in these age groups could be given a higher value. Those under age 15 and over 65 may be considered as dependents and given a lower value. There are many variations for differential valuing, including type of employment. People at different socioeconomic levels in a society are expected to have different capacities for productivity, yet to value life according to income levels or social class would not seem fair and generally would not be ac-

ceptable. In poor countries the value of marginal wages for subsistence agriculture is negligible, but the value of the workers' lives certainly is not. A fundamental question is whether to consider adding a productivity component to the summary measure. Health issues do not readily conform to the requirements of market economics; information is inadequate, and misinformation is rife on the part of the providers as well as the public. Externalities from good health are generally large. Demand for costly services is largely determined by the health care provider rather than by the consumers. Competitive market forces have not worked well for those in greatest need. In the private sector, demand for services is clearly related to productivity and willingness (and ability) to pay. If left to market forces alone, inequitable distribution would be inevitable.

Economic arguments in terms of productivity have been put forward for valuing life according to productivity. Claims have been made that human life cannot be expressed in economic terms for decision-making purposes; however, efforts to avoid such expression nevertheless result in implicit valuation of life. Barnum has argued for adding productivity to the valuing of human life, stating that it has been ignored in health policy, is easily quantifiable, and does not ignore the welfare of children because the whole population is dependent on adult productivity for quality and sustenance (Barnum, 1987). Such economic appraisal of human life is often based on the net transfer of resources from the "producers" to the "consumers" and the consequent interdependence of people. Of interest in this regard is that in the report of the Commission on Macroeconomics and Health (WHO, 2001), a DALY gained was stated to be worth at least an average annual income per head. Though the basis for such a valuation was not adequately justified, the basic notion seems right. More work on explicit valuations of human life and what it produces are needed and will certainly affect health-related cost-effectiveness decisions.

Valuing Equity in Relation to Efficiency

Decisions based on cost-effectiveness (e.g., cost per healthy life year) may not accord well with concerns about equity. These calculations are generally indifferent to equity; they are designed to steer interventions to what is efficient, whatever the differential needs may be.

In terms of social justice, equity has to do with a fair distribution of benefits from social and economic development. *Equity* is used in different conceptual senses: equal access to health services for all (opportunity equality), equal resources expended for each individual (supply equality), equal resources expended on each case of a particular condition (equality of resource use to meet biological need), equal healthy life gained per dollar expended (cost-effectiveness), care according to willingness to pay (economic-demand equality, which will certainly not lead to an equitable distribution in any other sense), care according to biological or socioeconomic need; and, finally, equal health states for all.

Evaluation of the disease burden in low- and middle-income nations reveals the persistence of infectious, childhood, and maternal conditions. These and other conditions of childhood predominate in low- and middle-income countries, and their impact on the poor is severe. Cost-effective interventions, such as immunization, exist for these conditions, and yet effective delivery has not been achieved. UNICEF reports that half the world's poor are children. They are paying an excessively high price for the failures of adults, while diseases and wars continue to threaten the lives of millions of children. It is estimated that more babies are being born into poverty than ever before. Poverty means that a child born in Malawi or Uganda will likely live only half as long as one born in Sweden or Singapore. It also means that one in three babies born in Niger or Sierra Leone will not live to see his or her fifth birthday.

Equity must go beyond equality of access to health care and must entail a balance so that health system responses are in accord with equity as well as efficiency. Provided that health information is available according to socioeconomic and vulnerable groups, use of these summary indicators as tools for equity by calculating healthy life per dollar to be gained by all socioeconomic and vulnerable groups could readily be undertaken. It would be straightforward to assess the impact of specific health decisions to ensure that they enhance equity.

Composite summary measures such as HeaLYs and DALYS should be used not only to guide allocation of resources based on cost-effectiveness criteria, but also to ensure equitable distribution of those resources so as to reach those most in need. Cost-effectiveness by itself does not provide adequate guidance; equity should be an associated criterion to govern the distribution of societal benefits.

Data for Composite Measures

Types of Data

The data needs for estimating the burden of disease in a region or country are extensive, and obtaining even reasonable estimates in low- and middle-income countries has been a source of concern (Anand & Ranaan-

Eliya, 1996; Barker & Green, 1996; Bobadilla, 1998; Murray et al., 2002). Brief descriptions of the types of data required follow; available data need to be carefully reviewed and optimally utilized.

Demographic Data. Population data are integral to burden of disease estimations as both denominators and consistency checks. In a national setting, a recent census is useful for providing population counts by age, sex, and geographic location. Particularly helpful, when there is inadequate death registration, is to have a 1-year postcensus follow-up on a sample of enumeration areas in order to obtain robust age, sex, and place mortality. The age and sex distribution of the population is critical and often is a major factor that determines the nature of the disease burden. A good vital registration system is a key asset, providing birth and death numbers. Underreporting, age misreporting, and other bias in data may have to be addressed (using standard demographic methods) prior to use in burden of disease estimation.

Mortality. Mortality data are required for any burden of disease analysis; age, sex, and place mortality rates greatly assist the analysis by defining the contribution of mortality to the pattern of disease burden. They also serve as an essential framework that constrains estimates obtained from a variety of special studies that fill important information gaps but may be incomplete or biased in the populations covered. Reporting errors, such as underreporting of deaths and reporting of age at death, need to be carefully examined. Information has to be particularly evaluated for deficiencies in the under-five years and older ages. For the youngest ages, the probabilities of deaths in the first year ($1q0$) and in the next four years ($4q1$) provide better estimates of the risk of death than do overall mortality rates. Methods such as the Brass method for indirect estimates of mortality provide useful ways to assess age-specific mortality data for potential errors (Hill, 2001).

For burden of disease studies, cause of death data are required for all ages, but reliable cause of death records are rarely available in low- and middle-income countries, especially for deaths that do not occur in health care facilities. Even if available, the classification system used may be outdated rather than ICD-based, and the reliability of coding may vary by the type and location of the hospital. Young adult deaths may be better recorded than infants and the elderly. Especially in low-income countries, it can be helpful to cross-check with other information, using postmortem interviews and hospital registers to assist in defining causes of death or extrapolate from other data or other regions to assist in the estimates.

Morbidity. Meaningful data on disability are even more difficult to find and interpret. Often morbidity information is institution-based or restricted to one or two sources, such as hospital inpatient and clinic outpatient records. Representativeness of small studies and the range and types of morbidity covered in any survey need careful evaluation. National disability surveys or regional studies conducted for the evaluation of disabled people may be available. These are useful in providing some estimate of the prevalence of serious disabilities and their age and sex distribution. However, linkage between disability and disease is often not available, and attributing one type of disability to specific causes is difficult. For example, because many conditions, such as diabetes, hypertension, injuries, trachoma, and cataracts, can lead to blindness, the attribution of proportions of blindness in a population to its cause can be problematic.

Information on the duration of disability may be found in specialized studies and the experience of institutions. The severity of disability will have to be rated on a scale; the various methods used in the literature were described earlier. Although scales used in other studies may be helpful in making estimates, generally each group will have to construct its own de novo. The process used to construct a severity scale, the type of people participating, and the nature of the condition may all affect the final scale.

Variables

The types of data just described need to be processed in the form of specific disease-based estimates. The key variables are defined in Table 1-2. The incidence rate (usually expressed per 1,000 general population per year) is central to the natural history of disease concept. Although incidence is a basic epidemiologic indicator, it is usually not found in routine data collection systems. Special studies, prospective surveys, or calculations based on the prevalence (more commonly available than incidence) and knowledge of the average duration of the disease can be helpful.

The CFR is the proportion of those developing the disease who die from it at any time. It is expressed as a decimal between 0 (for nonfatal conditions) and 1 (for universally lethal conditions such as AIDS). The case disability ratio (analogous with the CFR) is the proportion of those diagnosed with a disease who have signs or symptoms, and is usually 1, as discussed earlier.

Age is required in various formats. Age at onset is when disease onset occurs in a population; age at fatality denotes the age at death as a result of the disease. The expectation of life at age of onset is that expected at that age had the disease not occurred.

Similarly, expectation of life at fatality is that expected at that age had the death not occurred.

Checking Data

Data used for generation of indicators need to be evaluated for validity, reliability, and consistency, using qualitative and quantitative criteria determined a priori. For example, large population-based studies may be given preference over smaller sample-based work if both were available and the quality of data comparable. Better conclusions may be possible by cross-checking with different sources of data. Community-based studies, which may be representative of the population but have limited diagnostic validity, may be compared with hospital-based work, in which diagnosis may be valid but would be from a biased population sample. The following are simple checks for data quality.

Comparison of Total Numbers. Cross-checks should be done to compare total numbers. It is essential to check that the number of deaths in a year in a region is the same as the sum of all deaths from all causes in the same region. Similarly, program-based data can be compared with data from other sources to ensure better estimates of causes of death. The comparison of totals allows one to work within a frame of mortality and avoids double counting of one death. However, it does not assist in the distribution of deaths within that frame.

Relationship Between Variables. Checks based on the epidemiologic relationship between parameters refer to the application of simple, yet vital, relationships such as the following:

- Prevalence (point) = incidence × average duration of disease
- Cause-specific mortality rate = incidence × case fatality rate

These checks allow estimates from different sources to be compared for internal consistency. These relationships can also be used to derive one of the estimates in the equations when the others are known.

Sensitivity Analysis. Sensitivity analysis is a useful tool to determine whether data that are more precise are required for the purposes of a particular decision. A one-way sensitivity analysis (Petiti, 1994) evaluates the effect of manipulating one variable at a time on the dependent variable. The outcome is often most sensitive to one or more variables, making their precision more important in the estimation.

Disease Groups: Classification

Murray and Chen (1992) introduced a disease group system based on the WHO ICD classification system.

Group I includes conditions characteristic of low-income countries: communicable, infectious, maternal, perinatal, and nutritional diseases. This group declines at rates faster than overall mortality rates as socioeconomic conditions improve; it contributes a relatively small share of deaths in the high-income world. Group II, noncommunicable and chronic diseases, accounts for most loss of healthy life in the high-income countries and proportionately increases with the epidemiologic transition (see Exhibit 1–3). Group III consists of injuries, both intentional and nonintentional.

The distribution of the disease burden among these three groups is one indicator of the type of disease burden and the level of epidemiologic transition in a country. The group I to group II ratios vary from 1:1 in the low- and middle-income world to 1:2 in Latin America, 1:5 in China, and 1:17 in the high-income world (Murray & Lopez, 1994a). Group III comprises 5% to 15% of the total burden, indicating that injuries are an important cause of death and disability everywhere. It is important to distinguish between the proportions of deaths attributed to these groups as opposed to the risk of dying from the conditions in these groups. For example, the proportion of deaths attributable to group II causes increases as one moves from high- to low-mortality countries (or to an older age structure of the population); however, the risk of death from group II conditions is higher in high-mortality countries.

Implementing a Burden of Disease Study

Generic steps for a national burden of disease study include the following:

- Assessing demographic information, including a census with age, sex, geographic (urban/rural), and selected socioeconomic status information distributions and vital statistics with births and deaths

- Collecting cause of death information for all deaths in a year by age, sex, geographic location, and socioeconomic status as possible according to the WHO International Classification of Disease system

- Defining disability by cause/disease and developing a severity scale using expert and community input

- Collating information by disease from all sources and assessing reliability/validity, using expert opinion when needed for defining variables for a spreadsheet

- Defining social preferences such as age weighting, discounting, economic and social produc-

tivity, and expectation of life and deciding on their usage

- Estimating healthy life lost for each disease condition and by disease groups

- Performing a sensitivity analysis to check robustness of results to critical variables and assumptions

- Considering other variations, including assessment of losses by risk factors; regional, age, and sex breakdowns; and future projections

- Reviewing policy implications on overall mortality and morbidity in the country and for each cause; feeding into cost-effectiveness analysis and further research

- Including other modifications as appropriate to the country setting

To go further and use summary measures to assist in health planning and resource allocation decisions, additional steps would include the following:

- Estimating the effectiveness (gains of healthy life) of each intervention under consideration in terms of expected coverage and reductions in incidence and/or case fatality or case disability ratios.

- Working out the costs of the interventions.

- Developing cost-effectiveness ratios to plan what combination of interventions targeted to which groups will provide a maximum return of healthy life per expenditure for the funds allocated to health.

- Reviewing the expected gains of healthy life according to age, sex, geographic area, and socioeconomic and vulnerable groups to ensure that all are better off (or at least none are worse off) and adjusting as necessary. (Note that currently no country is assessing its health planning decisions on the basis of equity as proposed in this step.)

These steps may be carried out simultaneously or in some sequence, depending on the specific national situation.

Modifications will likely be needed depending on the availability of data (Exhibit 1-5). An actual study requires careful planning on the part of those responsible for its conduct and may require many further steps that are beyond the scope of this chapter.

These steps summarize the essentials of applying the burden of disease methods to a country. A very important consideration in this process is time. The national studies in Mexico and the state of Andhra Pradesh in India have taken upwards of three years,

Exhibit 1-5	The Burden of Disease in Pakistan, 1990

Pakistan is a developing country in South Asia with a population of 112 million in 1990. A study was undertaken to estimate the burden of disease in Pakistan for 1990 and to calculate the loss of healthy life from a spectrum of common conditions (Hyder & Morrow, 2000). Nearly 200 data sources were evaluated, including national surveys, population-based studies, sentinel survey systems, and disease-specific studies.

Overall, 456 discounted HeaLYs per 1,000 people were lost due to new cases of diseases in 1990, and diarrhea and pneumonia in children caused the greatest loss of healthy life. Sixty-three percent of healthy life was lost from mortality, and 37 percent was lost due to disability. Hypertension and injuries were the leading causes of healthy life lost from disability. Nearly half the healthy life was lost in the under-five age group, demonstrating a great burden on infants and children.

Though communicable diseases dominate the burden of disease in Pakistan, noncommunicable diseases also take a heavy toll, as evident from a review of the top conditions responsible for loss of healthy life (see accompanying figure and table), and the proportion of loss from noncommunicable conditions can be expected to increase. Injuries need to be recognized as a major public health problem in the country. According to these estimates, Pakistan has a lower overall burden of disease than most countries in sub-Saharan Africa but a higher burden than most in Latin America.

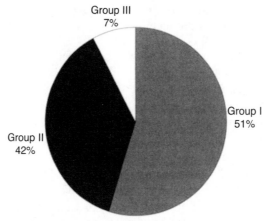

Distribution of Disease Burden in Pakistan, 1990

Loss of Healthy Life in Pakistan: Top 10 Conditions for 1990

Premature Mortality Only		Disability Only	
Rank	Disease	Rank	Disease
1	Diarrhea	1	Hypertension
2	Childhood pneumonia	2	Injuries
3	Tuberculosis	3	Eye diseases
4	Rheumatic heart disease	4	Malnutrition
5	Chronic liver disease	5	Birth diseases
6	Congenital malformations	6	Congenital malformations
7	Birth diseases	7	Dental diseases
8	Ischemic heart disease	8	Ischemic heart disease
9	Child septicemia	9	Adult female anemia
10	Other respiratory	10	Mental retardation

with two to three fulltime people. The conduct and analysis of such studies must be timely for use by policy makers and useful for resource allocation decisions. The precision and comprehensive nature of the study must be balanced by the need for timely results. Hope lies in better definition of the exact data needed for the decisions and in automated collection systems combined with computerization to provide the right data at the right time.

Comparisons and Trends in Disease Burden

This section reviews a number of country-based burden of disease studies in order to compare and assess trends in disease burden from place to place and over time.

Comparative Disease Burden Assessments

Comparing the burden of disease across populations, time, and place is an important aspect of national bur-

den of disease studies. This subsection uses examples from recent burden of disease studies to illustrate how disaggregated data can help in understanding the distribution of ill health in a country.

The Andhra Pradesh Burden of Disease Study, 2001

The regional distribution (urban/rural, state, district) of the disease burden is important to explore in a national burden of disease study. Andhra Pradesh, a state in India, was the focus of a meticulous burden of disease study conducted between 1994 and 2001. It had a population of 76 million in 2001, with 27% urban (20.8 million people), and showed a 1:3 ratio of urban to rural disease burden in terms of DALYs lost (Mahapatra, 2001). The burden of disease rates was 19% higher in rural than in urban areas, as measured by DALYs lost per 1,000 population (Figure 1-4).

The Burden of Disease and Injury in New Zealand, 1996

Age and ethnicity are key characteristics of a population that require a disaggregation of the burden of

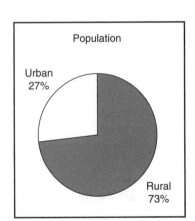

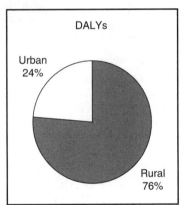

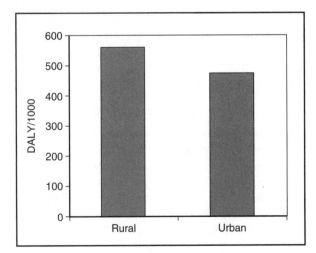

Figure 1-4 Burden of Disease in Andhra Pradesh, 2001, by Region. Based on Mahapatra, P. (2001). "Estimating National Burden of Disease: The Burden of Disease in Andhra Pradesh 1990s." Hyberdad: Institute of Health Systems. Accessed August 17, 2004, from http://www.insnet.org.in/BurdenOfDisease/APBurdenofDiseaseStudy.htm.

Note: Total DALYs lost in Andhra Pradesh = 5 million.

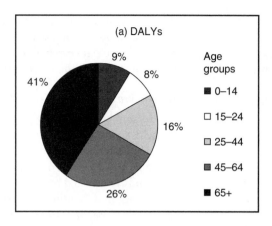

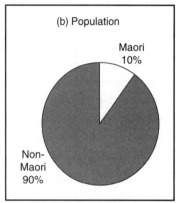
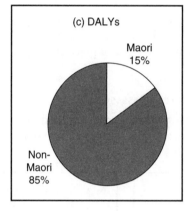

Note: Total DALYs lost in New Zealand for 1996 = 500,000.

Figure 1-5 Burden of Disease in New Zealand, 1996, by Age (a) and Ethnicity (b and c). Based on data from New Zealand Ministry of Health. (2001). "Burden of Disease and Injury in New Zealand." Accessed on August 17, 2004, from http://www.moh.govt.nz/moh.nsf/.

disease. The national burden of disease study of New Zealand (population in 1996, 3.6 million) provides a clear example of how the DALYs lost in 1996 were predominantly among the older age group (65+), though they represented about 12% of the population (New Zealand Ministry of Health, 2001). The identification of 15% of the burden in the indigenous Maori population, compared with the 9.7% of the population they constitute, was an important finding (Figure 1-5).

The Burden of Disease in Chile, 1993

A disaggregated burden analysis by gender can also be seen in the work done in Chile in 1993, where at that time 49.6% of the population was male. The study found that 56% of the DALYs lost were among males (Figure 1-6). The distribution of the burden by major disease groups (see Figure 1-6) showed the dominance of chronic conditions in the burden (Concha, 1993).

The Burden of Disease Estimates for South Africa, 2000

HIV/AIDS is ravaging Africa, and thus the impact of HIV/AIDS on the burden of disease in African countries can be significant. In South Africa, 30% of the 15 million DALYs lost in 2000 could be attributed to HIV/AIDS (Figure 1-7) (Burden of Disease Research Unit, 2003); for a population of 45 million, this means 0.33 DALYs per capita. Such data are important for national decision making.

The Burden of Disease and Injury in Australia, 1996

The distribution of disease burden by socioeconomic variables is important for poverty and equity analysis. The national burden of disease analysis in Australia for 1996 presented results based on socioeconomic status (defined by the social and economic characteristics of the living area), disaggregated by gender, for both mortality (YLL) and disability (YLD) (Figure 1-8) (Mathers, Vos, & Stevenson, 1999). These show the high disability losses for

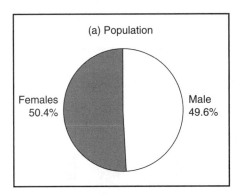

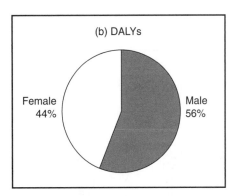

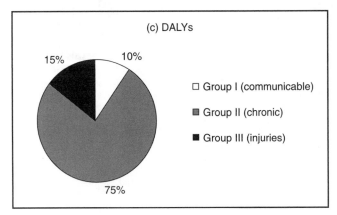

Note: Total DALYs lost in Chile for 1993 = 2 million.

Figure 1-6 Burden of Disease in Chile, 1993, by Gender (a and b) and Disease Groups (c). Based on data from Concha, M. (1993). "Burden of Disease in Chile." Accessed on August 17, 2004, from http://www.globalforumhealth.org/Non_compliant_pages/forum3/forum3doc823.htm.

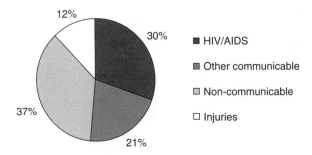

Note: Total DALYs lost in South Africa for 2000 = 15 million.

Figure 1-7 Burden of Disease in South Africa, 2000, by Disease Groups. Based on data from Burden of Disease Research Unit. (2003). "Initial Burden of Disease Estimates for South Africa, 2000." South Africa: South African Medical Research Council. Accessed on August 17, 2004, from http://www.mrc.ac.za/bod/bod.htm.

women and the poor. Such explorations of intranational distributions of disease burden are useful in studying the disproportionate impact of ill health on the poor and women.

The Burden of Disease and National Income

WHO has categorized member states by income levels into high-, middle-, and low-income nations. The population of the world in 2000 was slightly more than 5 billion people, with 85% in the low- and middle-income nations (Figure 1-9). As may be expected, more than 90% of the global burden is found in the low- and middle-income nations reflecting the double challenge faced by the majority of people in the world: They are poor and they are unhealthy. This relationship between ill-health and poverty has long been recognized as complex and has been the object of much research and inquiry.

The Burden of Disease by Disease Groups

Another way to disaggregate data is to explore the disease burden based on disease groups: group I (communicable, infectious, maternal, and perinatal), group II (noncommunicable, chronic), and group III (injuries and violence). There is great variation in the portions allocated to these groups; for example, group I may be responsible for 12% to 70% of the burden.

Males   Females

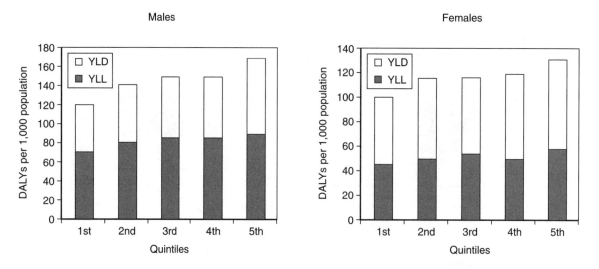

Note: The first quintile corresponds to the highest socioeconomic group, and the fifth quintile to the lowest. Each quintile contains approximately 20% of the total Australian population. Total DALYs lost in Australia for 1996 = 2.5 million.

Figure 1-8 Burden of disease in Australia, 1996, by Socioeconomic Status and Gender. Based on data from Mathers, C., Vos, T. & Stevenson, C. (1999). "The Burden of Disease and Injury in Australia." Australian Institute of Health and Welfare. Accessed on August 17, 2004, from http://www.aihw.gov.au/.

Population   Disease Burden

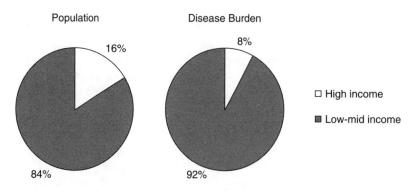

Note: Total global disease burden for 2000 = 1.46 billion DALYs.

Figure 1-9 Global Burden of Disease, 2000, by Income Level of Countries. Based on data from World Health Organization. (2000). "The World Health Report 2000." Geneva, Switzerland.

When the countries are stratified by GNP per capita as a measure of development, an important trend can be seen (Table 1-4). As income rises, the proportion of the burden attributable to group I decreases, while that of group II increases. The effect is progressive, although countries such as Turkmenistan (middle income) still retain a high group I burden. This is consistent with the theory of epidemiologic transition predicting a change in disease profile with economic development.

Intentional and unintentional injuries are responsible for 4% to 40% of the disease burden. Injuries contribute significantly to premature death and disability in low- and middle-income countries. The primary causes within this category also tend to change with development, although causes such as road traffic crashes are ubiquitous.

Global Assessments of Disease Burden

Information regarding health and disease for all countries of the world can be collated to provide a picture of global health status. In addition, global health assessments may be done as a separate activity, and such data can then be disaggregated into regional information. Global assessments serve to highlight major challenges facing the world community, and trends

Table 1-4	Distribution of Disease Burden Within Countries		
Disease Burden in Disease Categories (of 100%)			
Country	Group I	Group II	Group III
Low-income nations			
(GNP per capita of $635 or less)[a]			
Andhra Pradesh	54	30	16
Guinea	70	23	7
Lower medium-income nations			
(GNP per capita > $635 ≤ $2,555)			
Colombia	22	39	39
Jamaica	16	60	24
Turkmenistan	51	45	4
Uzbekistan	46	40	14
Upper medium-income nations			
(> $2,555 ≤ $7,911)			
Mauritius	16	74	10
Mexico	32	48	20
Uruguay	12	73	15

Note: Disease classification system—Group I: communicable, infectious, maternal, and perinatal; group II: noncommunicable and chronic; group III: injuries and accidents.

[a]GNP per capita from the World Bank (1993).

in such assessments indicate progress, if any, in improving the health of people worldwide. Such information is critical to the work of organizations such as WHO and UNICEF in their efforts to combat ill health and disease worldwide.

This section highlights results of global exercises for assessment of the disease burden, recent evaluations, and projections for the future.

The Global Burden of Disease

The Global Burden of Disease 2000 study presented estimates for mortality, disability, and DALYs by cause for regions of the world. Demographic estimates of deaths in 2000 by age and sex form the basis of this work, in addition to assessment of disability for evaluation of the disease burden using DALYs. The results were based on a variety of sources, including vital registrations systems, special studies, surveys, and expert opinion.

Mortality. Globally, in 2000, ischemic heart disease, cerebrovascular disease, and respiratory infections were the top three causes of death, while 10 causes accounted for 54% of deaths worldwide. One death in 10 was from injuries, with road traffic accidents included in the top 10 causes of deaths. The low- and middle-income world accounted for 98% of all deaths in children, 83% of deaths in persons aged 15

to 59 years, and 59% of deaths in persons aged 70+ years. Of all deaths in the low- and middle-income world, 28% were in children. Thus, an inordinate proportion of the mortality burden at the beginning of this decade is in low- and middle-income countries, even at adult and older ages.

Table 1-5 shows the differences in the 10 leading causes of deaths for 2000 for the high-income and the low- and middle-income world. The presence of perinatal conditions, tuberculosis, HIV/AIDS, and malaria in the low- and middle-income world is indicative of the high impact of these conditions on premature mortality. These conditions are absent from the top 10 causes in the high-income world, reflecting the success in combating these infectious conditions. It is important to note that noncommunicable diseases such as ischemic heart disease were already prominent causes of premature death in the low- and middle-income world in 2000.

Disability. The Global Burden of Disease 2000 study also evaluated the contribution of conditions to disability in the world. Leading causes of disability in 2000 worldwide are shown in Table 1-6. Neuropsychiatric and behavioral conditions dominate the causes of disability, represented by 4 of the top 10 conditions. However, a diverse spectrum of conditions, such as hearing loss, congenital anomalies, and osteoarthritis, also appears on the list. This has been a unique contribution of the Global Burden of Disease work—placing nonfatal health outcomes in the center of international health policy in recent years. The important, and yet often ignored, impact of these conditions is obvious once disability is counted in estimates of disease burden.

Disease Burden. Based on the estimation of deaths and disability presented previously, the global disease burden for 2000 was estimated using DALYs. Leading causes of the global burden of 2000 (Table 1-7) indicate the impact of those conditions affecting the low- and middle-income world. The top 10 list is a mixture of the unfinished agenda of communicable and perinatal conditions, noncommunicable diseases, and road traffic injuries. This situation highlights the challenge facing the global health community as it continues fighting the infectious diseases, improving the response to chronic conditions, and preparing to meet the increasing impact of injuries, all at the same time.

Age and Disease Distributions. Figure 1-10 presents the distribution of the global burden in 2000 by disease groups and demonstrates the growing relative impact of chronic diseases (group II) over infectious diseases (group I). Comparable figures for loss of healthy life in sub-Saharan Africa, the Middle Eastern crescent, Latin America, and the Caribbean

Table 1-5	Leading Causes of Deaths in High-Income and Low- and Middle-Income Countries, 2000		
High-Income Countries		**Low- and Middle-Income Countries**	
Rank	Cause	Rank	Cause
1	Ischemic heart disease	1	Ischemic heart disease
2	Cerebrovascular disease	2	Cerebrovascular disease
3	Trachea, bronchus, lung cancers	3	Lower respiratory infections
4	Lower respiratory infections	4	HIV/AIDS
5	Chronic obstructive pulmonary diseases	5	Perinatal conditions
6	Colon and rectum cancers	6	Chronic obstructive pulmonary diseases
7	Diabetes mellitus	7	Diarrheal diseases
8	Stomach cancer	8	Tuberculosis
9	Breast cancer	9	Road traffic accidents
10	Alzheimer and other dementias	10	Malaria

Based on data from Murray, C. J., Lopez, A. D., Mathers, C. D., et al. (2001). "The Global Burden of Disease 2000 Project: Aims, Methods and Data Sources." Geneva, Switzerland: World Health Organization.

Table 1-6	Leading Causes of Disability Losses Globally, 2000
Rank	Cause
1	Unipolar major depression
2	Hearing loss, adult onset
3	Alcohol use disorders
4	Osteoarthritis
5	Schizophrenia
6	Perinatal conditions
7	Bipolar disorders
8	Chronic obstructive pulmonary disease
9	Congenital anomalies
10	Asthma

Note: Disability losses are defined by years of life lived with disability—YLDs.

Based on data from Murray, C. J., Lopez, A. D., Mathers, C. D., et al. (2001). "The Global Burden of Disease 2000 Project: Aims, Methods and Data Sources." Geneva, Switzerland. World Health Organization.

Table 1-7	Leading Causes of Global Burden of Disease, 2000
Rank	Cause
1	Lower respiratory conditions
2	Perinatal conditions
3	HIV/AIDS
4	Unipolar major depression
5	Diarrheal diseases
6	Ischemic heart disease
7	Cerebrovascular diseases
8	Road traffic accidents
9	Malaria
10	Tuberculosis

Based on data from Murray, C. J., Lopez, A. D., Mathers, C. D., et al. (2001). "The Global Burden of Disease 2000 Project: Aims, Methods and Data Sources." Geneva, Switzerland. World Health Organization.

are presented in Figure 1-11. It is important to note that communicable diseases still represent a considerable portion of the disease burden in 2000, especially in sub-Saharan Africa due to HIV/AIDS.

The analyses indicate that subregions within middle- and low-income countries are at different stages of the epidemiologic transition. The influx of chronic diseases has added another layer of problems, while the burden of communicable diseases has not yet been eradicated. This double burden is a major challenge for the health systems in these nations. In addition, the scarcity of resources in many of these countries makes the situation even more critical, and it becomes imperative to define interventions that are cost-effective and able to reduce the burden.

Other Ways Burden Can Be Measured

Mortality and morbidity alone have been used for decades for international comparisons of disease burden. Child mortality under the age of 5 years is considered a sensitive indicator of the overall health of nations, especially women and children. UNICEF publishes an annual *State of the World's Children* report that includes a ranking of nations based on this indicator (Table 1-8). Gross national income (GNI) per

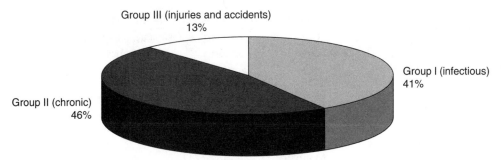

Figure 1-10 Global Burden of Disease 2000 by Disease Groups. Based on data from Murray, C. J., Lopez, A. D., Mathers, C. D., et al. (2001). "The Global Burden of Disease 2000 Project: Aims, Methods and Data Sources." Geneva, Switzerland. World Health Organization.

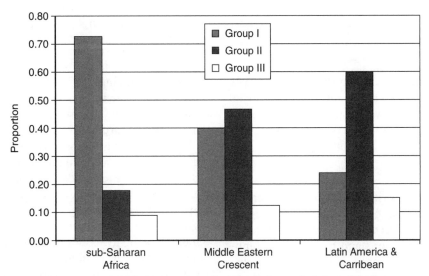

Figure 1-11 Proportion of Disease Burden by Disease Groups in Selected Regions, 2000. Based on data from Murray, C. J., Lopez, A. D., Mathers, C. D., et al. (2001). "The Global Burden of Disease 2000 Project: Aims, Methods and Data Sources." Geneva, Switzerland. World Health Organization.

capita is an indicator of national wealth, and the relationship between these variables usually follows an expected sequence in which the country with the lowest GNI per capita has the worst indicators of health. However, as Table 1-8 indicates, countries that have relatively higher per capita income can have poor indicators of health service accessibility (e.g., coverage of tetanus toxoid vaccination for pregnant women) and health impact (e.g., prevalence of anemia in pregnant women). For example, Bhutan has a per capita GNI that is higher than Mongolia, but it ranks lower in child mortality and life expectancy. These examples demonstrate that the relationship between health and poverty is complex and needs in-depth investigation. To improve the health of nations, the disparities within societies that are impediments to the empowerment of the poor and needy, especially women and children, need to be addressed as well as absolute poverty.

In 1999 UNICEF reported a new risk index for children in countries worldwide. This proposed index was developed with the intent of measuring children's welfare in a new manner. This national index measures countries on a scale of 0 to 100 and is based on the following factors: mortality rate of children under 5, percentage of children who are moderately or severely underweight, access to primary schooling, risks from armed conflict, and risks from HIV/AIDS. The high-income nations—United States, Australia, New Zealand, and Japan— are in the lowest risk index, whereas the poorest nations of Angola, Sierra Leone, and Afghanistan are in the highest risk category. As a continent, Africa is in the highest risk category. This index does not consider other factors that impinge on child welfare, such as child labor, sexual exploitation, and lack of family support. However, the collation of traditional indicators of child and

Table 1-8	Health Status Indicators and National Income for Selected Developing Nations				
Country	Ranking by Child Mortality (<5 years)	Life Expectation (years)	Stunted Children <5 years (%)	Coverage of Tetanus Vaccination Among Pregnant Women (%)	GNI per Capita (U.S. dollars)
Niger	2	46	40	36	170
Sierra Leone	1	34	34	60	140
Angola	3	40	45	62	660
Afghanistan	4	43	52	34	250
Mongolia	64	64	25	—	440
Pakistan	44	61	37	56	410
Bhutan	50	63	40	70	590
Nicaragua	82	69	20	95	370
Peru	86	70	25	57	2,050
Guatemala	74	67	46	38	1,750

Source: United Nations Children's Fund, *The State of the World's Children 2004* (New York: UNICEF, 2004). Reprinted with permission.

national health (such as child mortality) with issues of access (to primary education) and emerging threats (HIV) makes for an innovative approach to measuring the suffering linked to poverty and bringing it to the attention of the global community.

Future Projections

Future projections of disease burden have been attempted, with the intent of providing some basis for health planning. This is a challenging task that requires further data manipulations and the use of assumptions. These assumptions must predict changes in disease prevalence and incidence over time, the effect of interventions, and other factors. As a result, all projections are estimates with substantial variations that are highly dependent on the data used to derive them.

The GBD study for 1990 attempted to project the global burden in the future to the year 2020. These estimates were based on projected changes in the expectation of life, age structure of the global community, disease profiles based on current states, and other relevant parameters (Murray & Lopez, 1996a). In addition, the projections were guided by forecasts for income per capita, human capital, and smoking intensity. The results of this exercise reveal the leading causes of projected global burden of disease for 2020, as shown in Table 1-9. The domination of chronic diseases is obvious, although respiratory conditions still appear to be important. Injuries from road traffic crashes are projected to become the third leading cause of the global disease burden. It is interesting to note that the mortality and disability consequences of war make it the eighth leading cause of projected global disease burden. In addition, the lower ranking of HIV in the list reflects the assumption that interventions for this condition will suc-

ceed in reducing the burden in the intervening decades. This may or may not hold true, and other assumptions may be used to project a different scenario for the future.

The growing importance of noncommunicable diseases may be a global phenomenon, and their impact on low- and middle-income countries and regions needs to be assessed. Table 1-9 also shows the projected leading causes of the disease burden in the low- and middle-income world for 2020. Here again, four of the top five conditions are chronic diseases and injuries. However, unlike the list for the world, the persistent burden of respiratory infections and diarrheal diseases is evident. The situation in the low- and middle-income world is one in which the triple burden of persistent communicable diseases, prevalent noncommunicable conditions, and increasing injuries will call for an appropriate response.

Burden of Risk Factors

An analysis of risk factors that underlie many important disease conditions can be useful for assisting policy decisions concerning health promotion and disease reduction interventions. Smoking, alcohol, hypertension, and malnutrition are risk factors for a variety of health outcomes, and there are specific interventions that may help reduce their prevalence. Risk factors include an array of human behaviors, nutritional deficiencies and excesses, substance abuse, and certain characteristics such as hypertension. Some may be both an outcome and a risk factor (e.g., hypertension), whereas others are difficult to measure (e.g., violence), and yet others lead to many outcomes (e.g., smoking and alcohol use). The linkage between an identified risk factor and the set of associated health outcomes

Table 1-9	Projected Leading Causes of Disease Burden in 2020		
Global		**Developing Regions Only**	
Rank	Cause	Rank	Cause
1	Ischemic heart disease	1	Unipolar major depression
2	Unipolar major depression	2	Road traffic accidents
3	Road traffic accidents	3	Ischemic heart disease
4	Cerebrovascular disease	4	Chronic pulmonary obstructive diseases
5	Chronic pulmonary obstructive diseases	5	Cerebrovascular disease
6	Lower respiratory infections	6	Tuberculosis
7	Tuberculosis	7	Lower respiratory infections
8	War	8	War
9	Diarrheal diseases	9	Diarrheal diseases
10	HIV	10	HIV

Source: C. J. L. Murray and A. D. Lopez (Eds.), *The Global Burden of Disease and Injury 1990* (Geneva, Switzerland: World Health Organization, 1996).

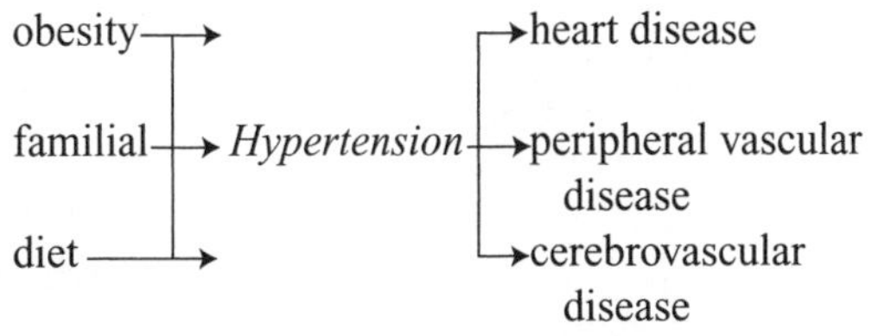

Figure 1-12 Linkages of risk factors with health outcomes.

may be difficult to directly quantify, and the portion of specific diseases attributable to any one factor may be difficult to estimate. Relationships such as those shown in Figure 1-12 need careful assessment to determine the burden from heart disease that can be attributed to hypertension in relation to other interacting causal factors. The best way to determine the portion of disease that may be attributed to hypertension is through a randomized trial and careful assessment of disease outcomes over time: Results from such studies have shown a reduction of death and disability from not only cardiac disease but also cerebrovascular and renal diseases.

Because the purpose of risk factor analysis is to assist in decisions concerning the allocation of resources, the link between the risk factor and the potential intervention to reduce the risk should be clear. The effectiveness of interventions against risk factors ultimately should be judged by their ability to reduce the healthy life lost attributed to the diseases that the risk factor affects. For the evaluation of an interven-

tion that reduces hypertension, the HeaLY losses from the entire range of diseases that hypertension influences are required.

The Burden of Selected Major Risk Factors

As reviewed in this chapter, a substantial body of work has focused on the quantification of trends in mortality and, more recently, burden of disease.[1] However, reliable and comparable analyses of risks to health, key for preventing disease and injury, have not been quantified as well. Most analyses of the relation of risk factors to specific diseases have been done in the context of individual risk factors, in limited settings, and with wide variations in the criteria for risk assessment. This has made comparisons of risk factors on a population health level difficult. As a result, the Comparative Risk Assessment (CRA) project of the Global Burden of Disease 2000 study attempted a systematic evaluation of the contributions of selected risk factors to global and regional burden using a specific model for analysis (Murray et al., 2001).

The model used in CRA for causal attribution of health outcomes was based on counterfactual analysis (Ezzati et al., 2002). Under this analysis, the contribution of one or a group of risk factors to disease or mortality is estimated by comparing the current or

---

[1]This section is based on a paper by Ezzati et al. (2002).

future disease burden with the levels that would be expected under an alternative hypothetical scenario (referred to as the counterfactual). In this case, the CRA project's estimates of burden of disease and injuries due to risks were based on a counterfactual exposure distribution that would result in the lowest population risk. This involves an evaluation of the effect a risk factor has on the disease or mortality by setting the risk factor to its minimum while keeping all other factors constant. This method has the advantage of showing the potential gains by risk reduction from all levels of suboptimal exposure in a consistent way across risk factors (Ezzati et al., 2002).

Twenty-five risk factors were selected by the CRA project based on how likely they were to be among the leading causes of death and disease, the likelihood of causality, the availability of data, and whether or not they were modifiable. For each risk factor, an expert working group did a comprehensive review of published work and other sources to obtain the data on prevalence of risk factor exposure and hazard size.

The results of this analysis show the contribution of the 20 leading global risk factors for the world and for three broad combinations of regions: demographically and economically developed, lower-mortality developing, and high-mortality developing (Figure 1-13). Undernutrition was the single leading global cause of health loss, with 140 million DALYs lost; 9.5% of this was from underweight, 2.4% from iron deficiency, 1.8% from vitamin A deficiency, and 1.9% from zinc deficiency. Although the prevalence of underweight has decreased as a global average, it has increased in sub-Saharan Africa, where its effects are disproportionately large due to simultaneous exposure to other childhood disease risk factors. At the same time, risk factors for noncommunicable diseases—high blood pressure, high cholesterol, and high body mass index (BMI)—are also widely prevalent and causing substantial losses to healthy life. The lower-mortality developing regions (40% of the global population) suffer from risk factors affecting both developed and high-mortality developing regions.

An important finding of this analysis is the key role of nutrition in health worldwide. Approximately 15% of the global disease burden can be attributed to the joint effects of childhood and maternal underweight or micronutrient deficiencies. In addition, almost as much can be attributed to risk factors that have substantial dietary determinants—high blood pressure, high cholesterol, high BMI, and low fruit and vegetable intake.

Some risk factors may have little impact on the total global burden of disease, but they may be very important locally within certain populations and regions. For example, iodine deficiency still affects important parts of the developing world, resulting in substantial disability in those populations. The approach used in CRA was new and innovative, but has not yet been widely used at the national level. With further experience and additional refinements, studies concerned with interventions directed toward risk factors will play an increasing role in improving the health of populations.

Conclusion

The health of populations is the fundamental concern of international public health. The first step in the pursuit of population health improvement is the measurement of health and disease. Measurement is required to establish the magnitude of disease problems, define causal factors, explore potential solutions, and determine the impact of interventions. Measuring the impact of diseases on populations in terms of mortality and morbidity and their consequences is essential for planning effective ways to reduce the burden of illness and for setting priorities.

The burden of disease in populations has been gauged in many ways: Examples include measures of mortality such as infant mortality rates; demographic measures such as expectation of life at birth; and measures of morbidity such as days away from work. However, for purposes of comparison among populations and for assisting in health planning and resource allocation, a common denominator combining these factors is needed. Composite summary measures of population health based on the amount of healthy life lost from disability and from death have been developed to serve that purpose. Composite indicators (such as HeaLYs and DALYs) use duration of time (years, weeks, days) to measure the loss of healthy life from disease and the gain from interventions. These are coming to be important tools for assisting health-related decision making, but to avoid misuse, it is critical for those using them to understand the underlying assumptions and limitations and also to meet the rather formidable data requirements. These summary measures also could be used to examine the burden of disease among subpopulations according to socioeconomic, cultural, and especially vulnerable groups and to ensure that health-related decisions consider equity as well as cost-effective criteria.

Trends in disease burden provide important clues to the success of ongoing health programs and the need for development of new interventions. At the

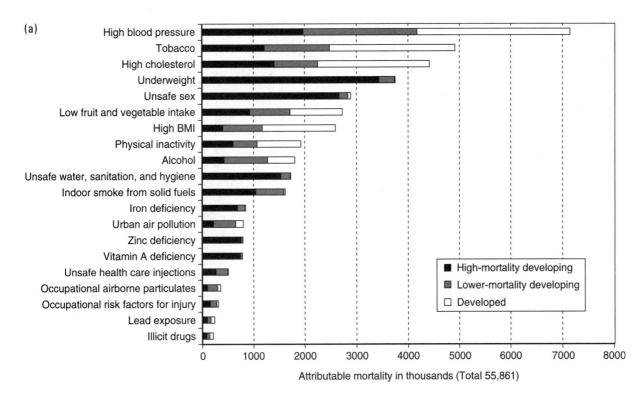

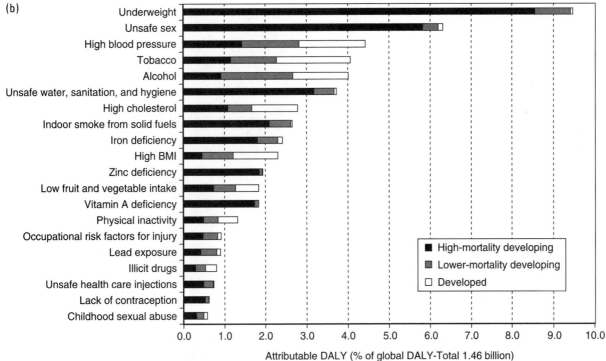

Figure 1-13 Mortality (a) and Burden of Disease (b) Due to Leading Global Risk Factors. Based on data from Ezzati, M., Lopez, A., Vander Hoorn, S., Rodgers, A., Murray, C. J. L., & the Comparative Risk Assessment Collaborative Group (2002). "Selected Major Risk Factors and Global Regional Burden of Disease." *Lancet, 360* (9343), 1347–1360.

same time, they reflect non-health factors that are important to the production or maintenance of health in populations. Intercountry and interregional comparisons allow for measuring progress among nations and can highlight inequalities in health status and examine these in relation to social, economic, educational, and other factors as well.

Health systems across the world are greatly affected by changes in disease profiles and population dynamics. These systems must develop the capacity to respond to such changes effectively within the resources of each nation. Decisions must be based on evidence about the patterns of diseases, their risk factors, and the effectiveness of alternative interventions. Timely collection and analysis of appropriate, high-quality data to support such evidence are prerequisites for improving equitable global health development.

● ● ● DISCUSSION QUESTIONS

1. What is the primary purpose of a health system in a country? How can data help achieve this purpose?
2. What are the essential elements of health information, and what types of data are required to assess ill health?
3. What are the relative strengths and weaknesses of composite indicators compared with more traditional indicators of disease burden?
4. In your country, what would be the most appropriate set of indicators to assess the impact of diseases on the population? Why?

● ● ● References

Anand, S., & Ranaan-Eliya, R. (1996). *Disability adjusted life years: A critical review* (Working Paper No. 95-06). Boston: Harvard Center for Population and Development Studies.

Barendregt, J. J., Bonneux, L., & Van Der Maas, P. J. (1996). DALYs: The age weights on balance. *Bulletin of the World Health Organization, 74,* 439–443.

Barker, C., & Green, A. (1996). Opening the debate on DALYs. *Health Policy and Planning, 11*(2), 179–183.

Barnum, H. (1987). Evaluating healthy days of life gained from health projects. *Social Science and Medicine, 24,* 833–841.

Blumstein, J. (1997). The Oregon experiment: The role of cost-benefit analysis in the allocation of Medicaid funds. *Social Science and Medicine, 45,* 545–554.

Bobadilla, J. L. (1998). *Searching for essential health services in low and middle income countries.* Washington, DC: Inter American Development Bank.

Burden of Disease Research Unit. (2003). *Initial burden of disease estimates for South Africa, 2000.* South Africa: South African Medical Research Council. Retrieved August 17, 2004, from http://www.mrc.ac.za/bod/ bod.htm.

Busschbach, J. J. V., Hesing, D. J., & de Charro, F. T. (1993). The utility of health at different stages of life: A qualitative approach. *Social Science and Medicine, 37*(2), 153–158.

Coale, A. J., & Demeney, P. (1983). *Regional model life tables and stable populations.* New York: Academic Press.

Coale, A. J., & Guo, G. (1989). Revised regional model life tables at very low levels of mortality. *Population Index, 55,* 613–643.

Concha, M. (1993). *Burden of disease in Chile.* Retrieved August 17, 2004, from http://www.globalforumhealth.org/Non_compliant_pages/forum3/forum3doc823.htm.

Crooper, M., & Kopits, E. (2003). *Traffic fatalities and economic growth* (World Bank Policy Research Working Paper 3035). Washington, DC: World Bank.

Eddy, D. (1991). Oregon's methods: Did cost-effectiveness analysis fail? *Journal of the American Medical Association, 266,* 2135–2141.

Evans, J. R., Hall, K. L., & Warford, J. (1981). Health care in the developing world: Problems of scarcity and choice. *New England Journal of Medicine, 305,* 1117–1127.

Ezzati, M., Lopez, A., Vander Hoorn, S., Rodgers, A., Murray, C. J. L., & the Comparative Risk Assessment Collaborative Group. (2002). Selected major risk factors and global and regional burden of disease. *Lancet, 360*(9343), 1347–1360.

Feachem, R. G. A., & Kjellstrom, T. (Eds.). (1992). *The health of adults in the developing world.* New York: Oxford University Press.

Ghana Health Assessment Team. (1981). A quantitative method for assessing the health impact of different diseases in less developed countries. *International Journal of Epidemiology, 10,* 73–80.

Gold, M. R., Siegel, J. E., Russel, L. B., & Weinstein, M. C. (Eds.). (1996). *Cost-effectiveness in health and medicine.* New York: Oxford University Press.

Gudex, C., & Kind, P. (1988). *The QALY toolkit.* York, England: Centre for Health Economics, University of York.

Hill, K. (2001). Demographic techniques: Indirect estimation. In *International encyclopedia of social and behavioral sciences.* Oxford, England: Elsevier Science.

Hyder, A., & Morrow, R. (1999). Steady state assumptions in DALYs: Effect on estimates of HIV impact. *Journal of Epidemiology and Community Health, 53,* 43–45.

Hyder, A. A., & Morrow, R. H. (2000). Applying burden of disease methods in developing countries: A case study from Pakistan. *American Journal of Public Health, 90*(8), 1235–1247.

Hyder, A. A., Rotllant, G., & Morrow, R. H. (1998). Measuring the burden of disease: Healthy life years. *American Journal of Public Health, 88,* 196–202.

Joint United Nations Programme on HIV/AIDS. (2003). *Global summary of the HIV and AIDS epidemic in 2003.* Retrieved October 13, 2004, from http://www.unaids. org/en/resources/ epidemiology/epicorejuly2004.asp.

Kaplan, R. M. (1990). The general health policy model: An integrated approach. In B. Spilker (Ed.), *Quality of life assessment in clinical trials.* New York: Raven Press.

King, M. (1990). Health is a sustainable state. *Lancet, 336,* 664-667.

Last, J. M. (Ed.). (2000). *A dictionary of epidemiology* (4th ed.). New York: Oxford University Press.

Lopez, A., Ahmad, O., Guillot, M., Inoue, M., Fergusson, B., Salomon, J., Murray, C. J. L., & Hill, K. (2002). *World mortality in 2000: Life tables for 191 countries.* Geneva, Switzerland: World Health Organization.

Mahapatra, P. (2001). *Estimating national burden of disease: The burden of disease in Andhra Pradesh, 1990s.* Hyderabad, India: Institute of Health Systems. Retrieved August 17, 2004, from http://www.ihsnet.org.in/ BurdenOfDisease/APBurdenofDiseaseStudy.htm.

Mathers, C., Vos., T., Lopez, A., Salomon, J., Lozano, R., & Ezzati, M. (Eds.). (2001). *National burden of disease studies: A practical guide* (Edition 2.0). Geneva, Switzerland: World Health Organization.

Mathers, C., Vos, T., & Stevenson, C. (1999). *The burden of disease and injury in Australia.* Canberra, Australia: Australian Institute of Health and Welfare. Retrieved August 17, 2004, from http://www.aihw.gov.au/.

Morrow, R. H. (1984). The application of a quantitative approach to the assessment of the relative importance of vector and soil transmitted diseases in Ghana. *Social Science and Medicine, 19,* 1039–1049.

Morrow, R. H., & Bryant, J. H. (1995). Health policy approaches to measuring and valuing human life: Conceptual and ethical issues. *American Journal of Public Health, 85,* 1356–1360.

Mosley, H. W., Jamison, D. T., Bobadilla, J. L., & Meashem, A. (Eds.). (1993). *Disease control priorities in the developing world.* New York: Oxford University Press.

Murray, C. J. L., & Chen, L. C. (1992). Understanding morbidity change. *Population and Development Review, 18*(3), 481–503.

Murray, C. J. L., & Lopez, A. D. (1994a). *Global comparative assessments in the health sector.* Geneva, Switzerland: World Health Organization.

Murray, C. J. L., & Lopez, A. D. (1994b). Quantifying disability: Data, methods and results. *Bulletin of the World Health Organization, 72,* 481–494.

Murray, C. J. L., & Lopez, A. D. (Eds.). (1996a). *The global burden of disease 1990.* Geneva, Switzerland: World Health Organization.

Murray, C. J. L., & Lopez, A. D. (Eds.). (1996b). *Global health statistics 1990.* Geneva, Switzerland: World Health Organization.

Murray, C. J. L., & Lopez, A. D. (1999). On the comparable quantification of health risks: Lessons from the Global Burden of Disease study. *Epidemiology, 10,* 594–605.

Murray, C. J. L., Lopez, A. D., Mathers, C. D., et al. (2001). *The Global Burden of Disease 2000 project: Aims, methods and data sources.* Geneva, Switzerland: World Health Organization.

Murray, C. J. L., Salomon, J., Mathers, C., & Lopez, A. (2002). *Summary measures of population health: Concepts, ethics, measurement and applications.* Geneva, Switzerland: World Health Organization.

New Zealand Ministry of Health. (2001). *Burden of disease and injury in New Zealand.* Retrieved August 17, 2004, from http://www.moh.govt. nz/moh.nsf/.

Nord, E. (1992). Methods for quality adjustment of life years. *Social Science and Medicine, 34,* 559–569.

Nord, E. (1993). Unjustified use of the quality of well being scale in priority setting in Oregon. *Health Policy, 24,* 45–53.

Omran, A. (1971). The epidemiologic transition: A theory of the epidemiology of population change. *Milbank Memorial Fund Quarterly, 49,* 509–538.

Petiti, D. B. (1994). *Meta-analysis, decision analysis and cost-effectiveness analysis: Methods for quantitative synthesis in medicine.* New York: Oxford University Press.

Preston, S. H. (1976). *Mortality patterns in national populations.* New York: Academic Press.

Robine, J. M. (1994). Disability free life expectancy trends in France, 1981–1991: International comparisons. In C. Mathers et al. (Eds.), *Advances in health expectancies.* Canberra, Australia: Australian Institute of Health and Welfare.

Sullivan, D. F. (1971). A single index of mortality and morbidity. *HSMHA Health Reports, 86,* 347–354.

Torrence, G. W. (1986). Measurement of health state utilities for economic appraisal: A review. *Journal of Health Economics, 5,* 1–30.

UNAIDS. (2004). *AIDS epidemic update: 2004.* Retrieved July 13, 2005, from http://www.unaids.org/wad2004/report_pdf.html.

United Nations Children's Fund. (2004). *The state of the world's children 2004.* New York: UNICEF.

United Nations Population Division. (2002). *World population prospects: The 2002 revision population database.* Retrieved October 7, 2004, from http://esa.un.org/unpp.

Weinstein, M. C., Siegel, J. E., Gold, M. R., Kamlet, M. S., & Russell, L. B. (1996). Recommendations of the Panel on Cost-effectiveness in Health and Medicine. *Journal of the American Medical Association, 276,* 1253–1258.

World Bank. (1993). *World development report 1993: Investing in health.* New York: Oxford University Press.

World Health Organization. (1980). *International classification of impairments, disabilities and handicaps: A manual of classification relating to the consequences of disease.* Geneva, Switzerland.

World Health Organization. (1992). *International statistical classification of diseases and related health problems* (10th revision). Geneva, Switzerland.

World Health Organization. (2000). *The world health report 2000.* Geneva, Switzerland.

World Health Organization. (2001). *Macroeconomics and health: Investing in health for economic development. Report of the Commission on Macroeconomics and Health.* Geneva, Switzerland.

World Health Organization. (2002a). *The international classification of functioning, disability and health: Introduction.* Retrieved October 7, 2004, from http://www.who.int/ classification/ icf/intros/ICF-Eng-Intro.pdf.

World Health Organization. (2002b). *World report on violence and health.* Geneva, Switzerland.

World Health Organization. (2003). *The world health report 2003.* Geneva, Switzerland.

World Health Organization. (2004). *The world health report 2004.* Geneva, Switzerland.

Zeckhauser, R., & Shephard, D. (1976). Where now for saving lives? *Law and Contemporary Problems, 40,* 5–45.

CHAPTER

2

Culture, Behavior, and Health

SUSAN C. SCRIMSHAW

"If you wish to help a community improve its health, you must learn to think like the people of that community. Before asking a group of people to assume new health habits, it is wise to ascertain the existing habits, how these habits are linked to one another, what functions they perform, and what they mean to those who practice them" (Paul, 1955).

People around the world have beliefs and behaviors related to health and illness that stem from cultural forces and individual experiences and perceptions. A 16-country study of community perceptions of health, illness, and primary health care found that in all 42 communities studied, people used both the Western biomedical system and indigenous practices, including indigenous practitioners. Also, there were discrepancies between services the governmental agencies said existed in the community and what was really available. Due to positive experiences with alternative healing systems, and shortcomings in the Western biomedical system, people relied on both (Scrimshaw, 1992). Experience has shown that health programs that fail to recognize and work with indigenous beliefs and practices also fail to reach their goals. Similarly, research to plan and evaluate health programs must take cultural beliefs and behaviors into account if researchers expect to understand why programs are not working, and what to do about it.

This chapter draws on the social sciences, particularly anthropology, psychology, and sociology, to examine the cultural and behavioral parameters that are essential to understanding international health efforts. It begins with some key concepts from the field of anthropology and the subfield of medical anthropology. It continues with lists and brief descriptions of types of health belief systems and healers around the world. Next, some key theories of health behavior and behavioral and cultural change are described and discussed. Issues of health literacy and health communication are then addressed, along with health promotion strategies. Methodological issues are presented, followed by a case study of AIDS in Africa. The chapter concludes with a summary of how all these areas need to be considered in international health efforts.

Basic Concepts from Medical Anthropology

Health and illness are defined, labeled, evaluated, and acted on in the context of culture. In the 18th century, anthropologist Edmund Tylor defined culture as "that complex whole which includes knowledge, belief, art, morals, law, custom, and any other capabilities acquired by man as a member of society" (Tylor, 1871). Since those early days of anthropology, there have been literally hundreds of definitions of culture, but most have the following concepts in common (Institute of Medicine, 2002):

- Shared ideas, meanings, and values
- Socially learned, not genetically transmitted

Acknowledgments: I would like to thank Carolyn Cline for assistance in editing and preparing the bibliography, Pamela Ippoliti for editorial assistance, Susan Levy for providing key examples from the intervention literature, and Isabel Martinez and Janel Heinrich for assistance with the literature search, for helpful comments on the chapter, and, in particular, for preparing and revising the case study on AIDS. I am also grateful to Carole Chrvala for sharing notes on the various intervention theories.

- Patterns of behavior that are guided by these shared ideas, meanings, and values
- Often exists at an unconscious level
- Constantly being modified through "lived experiences"

The last of these concepts is a relatively new introduction. *Lived experiences* are defined as the experiences that people (and sometimes groups of people) go through as they live their lives. These experiences modify their culturally influenced beliefs and behaviors (Garro, 2000, 2001). This means culture is not static on either the group or individual level, because people are constantly changing. This concept helps allow for cultural change as people migrate to a new setting (community, region, or country), as people acquire additional education and experiences, and as conditions change around them (e.g., armed conflicts, economic changes in a country or region, political changes). This is a helpful viewpoint when looking at cultural change on both the individual and group levels.

Medical anthropologists observe different cultures and their perspectives on disease and illness by looking at the biological and the ecological aspects of disease, the cultural perspectives, and the ways in which cultures approach prevention and treatment.

To understand the cultural context of health, it is essential to work with several key concepts. First, the concepts of insider and outsider perspectives are useful for examining when we are seeing things from our point of view and when we are trying to understand someone else's view of things. The *insider perspective* (*emic* in anthropological terminology) shows the culture as viewed from within. It refers to the meaning that people attach to things from their cultural perspective. For example, some cultures view worms (*Ascaris*) in children as normal and believe they are caused by eating sweets. The *outsider perspective* (*etic* in anthropology) refers to the same thing as seen from the outside. Rather than meaning, it conveys a structural approach, or something as seen without understanding its meaning for a culture. It can also convey an outsider's meaning attached to the same phenomenon—for example, that ascariasis is contracted through ingesting eggs found in contaminated soil or in foods contaminated by contact with that soil. The eggs get into the soil through fecal wastes from infected individuals. The concepts of insider and outsider perspectives allow us to look at health, illness, and prevention and treatment systems from several perspectives, to analyze the differences between these perspectives, and to develop approaches that will work within a cultural context.

To continue the example, in Guatemalan villages where these beliefs prevailed, researchers learned that mothers believed that worms were normal and were not a problem unless they became agitated. In their view, worms live in a bag or sac in the stomach and are fine while so confined. Agitated worms get out and appear in the feces or may be coughed up. Mothers also believed that worms are more likely to become agitated during the rainy season because the thunder and lightning frightened them. From an outsider perspective, this makes sense: Sanitation is more likely to break down in the rainy season, so there is more chance of infection and more diarrheal disease, which will reveal the worms. The dilemma for the health workers was to get the mothers to accept deworming medication for their children, because most of the time worms were perceived as normal. If the health workers tried to tell the mothers that their beliefs were wrong, the mothers would reason that the health workers did not understand illness in a Guatemalan village and would reject their proposal. The compromise was to suggest that the children be dewormed just before the rainy season, in order to avoid the problem of agitated worms. It worked.[1]

The insider/outsider approach leads to another set of concepts. *Disease* is the outsider view, usually the Western biomedical definition. It refers to an undesirable deviation from a measurable norm. Deviations in temperature, white cell count, red cell count, bone density, and many others are seen as indicators of disease. *Illness,* on the other hand, means "not feeling well." Thus it is a subjective, insider view. This sets up some immediate dissonances between the two views. It is possible to have an undesirable deviation from a Western biomedical norm and to feel fine. Hypertension, early stages of cancer, HIV infection, and early stages of diabetes are all instances where people may feel well but have a disease. This means that health care providers must communicate the need for behaviors to address something that people may not realize is a problem.

It is also possible for someone to feel ill and for the Western biomedical system not to identify a disease. When this occurs, there is a tendency for Western-trained health care providers to say that nothing is wrong or that it is a psychosomatic problem. Although both of these can be the case, there are several other explanations for this occurrence. One possibility is that Western biomedical science has not yet figured out how to measure something.

---

[1] I am indebted to Elena Hurtado of Guatemala for this example.

Several recent examples of this include AIDS, generalized anxiety attacks, and chronic fatigue syndrome. All of these were labeled psychosomatic at one time and now have measurable deviations from a biological norm. Similarly, painful menstruation used to be labeled "subconscious rejection of femininity," but it is now associated with elevated prostaglandin levels and can be helped by a prostaglandin inhibitor.

Another possibility is something that anthropologists have called "culture-bound syndromes" (Hughes, 1990), but this might be better described as "culturally defined syndromes." Culturally defined syndromes are an insider way of describing and attributing a set of symptoms. They often refer to symptoms of a mental or psychological problem, but a physiological disease may exist, posing a challenge to the health practitioner. For example, Rubel and colleagues (1984) found that an illness called *susto,* or fright, in Mexico corresponded with symptoms of tuberculosis in adults. If people were told there was no such thing as *susto* and that they, in fact, had tuberculosis, they rejected the diagnosis and the treatment on the grounds that the doctors obviously knew nothing about *susto.* This was complicated by the fact that tuberculosis was viewed as serious and stigmatizing. The solution was to discuss the symptoms with people and mention that Western biomedicine had a treatment for those symptoms (Rubel et al., 1984). *Susto* may also be used to describe other sets of symptoms, for example, those of diarrheal disease in children (Scrimshaw & Hurtado, 1988).

With culturally defined syndromes, it is essential for an outsider to ask about the symptoms associated with the illness and to proceed with diagnosis and treatment on the basis of those symptoms. This is good practice in any event, because people often make a distinction between the cause of a disease or illness and its symptoms. Even if the perceived cause is inconsistent with the Western biomedical system, a disease can be diagnosed and treated based on the symptoms without challenging people's beliefs about the cause.

The term *Western biomedical system* is used throughout this chapter because a term such as *modern medicine* would deny the fact that there are other medical systems, such as Chinese and Ayurvedic medicine, that have modern forms. *Indigenous medical system* is used to refer to an insider (within the culture) system. Thus, the Western biomedical system is an indigenous medical system in some countries, but it still may exist side by side with other indigenous systems, even in the United States and western Europe. In most of the world, the Western biomedical system now coexists with, and often dominates, local or indigenous systems. Because of this, and because of class differences, physicians and policy makers in a country may not accept or even be aware of the extent to which indigenous systems exist and their importance. Also, many countries contain multiple cultures and languages. The cross-cultural principles discussed in this chapter may be just as important for working within a country as for working in multiple countries or cultures.

Another key concept from medical anthropology is that of ethnocentricism. *Ethnocentric* refers to seeing your own culture as best. This is a natural tendency, because the survival and perpetuation of a culture depend on teaching children to accept it and on its members feeling that it is a good thing. In the context of cross-cultural understanding, ethnocentricism poses a barrier if people approach a culture with the attitude that it is inferior. *Cultural relativism* in anthropology refers to the idea that each culture has developed its own ways of solving the problems of how to live together; how to obtain the essentials of life, such as food and shelter; how to explain phenomena; and so on. No one way is viewed as better or worse; they are just different. This works well for classic anthropology but is a challenge when international health is considered. What if a behavior is "wrong" from an epidemiologic perspective? How does one distinguish between dangerous behaviors (e.g., using an HIV-contaminated needle, swimming in a river with snails known to carry schistosomiasis, ingesting a powder with lead in it as part of a healing ritual) and behaviors that are merely different and therefore seem odd? For example, Bolivian peasants used very fine clay in a drink believed to be good for digestion and stomach ailments. Health workers succeeded in discouraging this practice in some communities because "eating dirt" seemed like a bad thing. The health workers then found themselves faced with increased caries and other symptoms of calcium deficiency. Upon analysis, the clay was found to be a key source of calcium for these communities. In addition, we use clay in Western biomedicine, but we color it pink or give it a mint flavor and put it in a bottle with a fancy label.

Thus, there is a delicate balance between being judgmental without good reason and introducing behavior change because there is real harm from existing behaviors. In general, it is best to leave harmless practices alone and focus on understanding and changing harmful behaviors. This is harder than it seems, because the concept of cultural relativism also applies to perceptions of quality of life. A culture in which people believe in reincarnation may approach death with equanimity and may not adopt drastic procedures that only briefly prolong life. In some cultures, loss of a body organ is viewed as impeding the ability to go to an afterlife or the next life, and such surgery may be refused. It is important in international public health for cultural outsiders to be cautious about statements about what is good for someone else.

The concept of holism is also useful in looking at health and disease cross-culturally. *Holism* is an approach used by anthropologists that looks at the broad context of whatever phenomenon is being studied. Holism involves staying alert for unexpected influences, because you never know what may have a bearing on the program you are trying to implement. For public health, this is crucial because there may be diverse factors influencing health and health behavior.

One classic example of this is the detective work that went into discovering the etiology of the New Guinea degenerative nerve disease kuru. Epidemiologists could not figure out how people contracted the disease, which appeared to have a long incubation period and to be more frequent in women and children than in men. Many hypotheses were advanced, including inheritance (genetic), infection (bacterial, parasitic), and psychosomatic origin. By the early 1960s the most accepted of the prevailing hypotheses was that it was genetically transmitted. Yet this did not explain the sex differences in infection rates seen in adults but not in children, nor how such a lethal gene could persist. Working with Gadjusek of the National Institutes of Health, cultural anthropologists Glasse and Lindenbaum used in-depth ethnographic interviews to establish that kuru was relatively new to that region of New Guinea, as was the practice of cannibalism. Women and children were more likely to engage in the ritual consumption of dead relatives as a way of paying tribute to them, which was culturally less acceptable for men. Also, this tissue was cooked, but women, who did the cooking, and children, who were around during cooking, were more likely to eat it when it was partially cooked and therefore still infectious. Lindenbaum and Glasse suggested the disease was transmitted by cannibalism. To confirm their hypothesis, Gadjusek's team inoculated chimpanzees with brain material from women who had died of kuru, and the animals developed the disease. The disease was found to be a slow virus, transmitted through the ingestion of brain tissue. Since then, the practice of cannibalism has declined and the disease has now virtually disappeared (Gadjusek, Gibbs, & Alpers, 1967; Lindenbaum, 1971).

In recent years, increasing attention has been focused on another area that intersects with culture in people's ability to understand and access health care. This is the concept of health literacy. *Health literacy* is defined as "the degree to which individuals have the capacity to obtain, process, and understand basic health information and services needed to make appropriate health decisions" (Ratzan & Parker, 2000). Health literacy has been most thoroughly explored in the United States and, until recently, was seen more as a literacy than a cultural issue. A 2004 Institute of Medicine report notes the importance of considering cultural issues, such as those discussed in this chapter, and of taking a more global look at the problem and needed interventions (Institute of Medicine, 2004).

It is particularly important to note that health literacy is as much the problem of the health care provider and health communication staff as it is of a patient or people in a community. If medical jargon is used, no amount of education short of medical or nursing school will help someone understand. Terms such as *oncology, nephrology,* and *gastroenterology* have meaning for the medical world, but not for patients. Health care providers outside the United States often have a better understanding of this than their U.S. counterparts.

Cultural Views of Health, Illness, and Healers

Cultures vary in their definitions of health and of illness. A condition that is endemic in a population may be seen as normal and may not be defined as illness. Ascariasis in young children has already been mentioned as a perceived normal condition in many populations. Similarly, malaria is seen as normal in some parts of Africa, because everyone has it or has had it. In Egypt, where schistosomiasis was common and affected the blood vessels around the bladder, blood in the urine was referred to as "male menstruation" and was seen as normal. These definitions may also vary by age and by gender. In most cultures, symptoms, such as fever, in children are seen as more serious than in adults. Men may deny symptoms more than women in some cultures, but women may do the same in others. Often, adult denial of symptoms is due to the need to continue working.

Sociologist Talcott Parsons (1948) first discussed the concept of the *sick role,* wherein an individual must "agree" to be considered ill and to take actions (or allow others to take actions) to define the state of his or her health, discover a remedy, and do what is necessary to become well. Individuals who adopt the sick role neglect their usual duties, may indulge in dependent behaviors, and seek treatment to get well. By adopting the sick role, they are viewed as having "permission" to be exempted from usual obligations, but they are also under an obligation to try to restore health. The process of seeking to remain healthy or to restore health will be discussed later.

Belief Systems

Table 2-1 depicts types of insider cultural explanations of disease causation. It is based on the literature and is an attempt to be as comprehensive as possible for cultures around the world. It is important to note that the table consists of generalizations about culture-specific health beliefs and behaviors and that generalizations cannot be assumed to apply to every individual from a given culture. We can learn about the hot/cold balance system of Latinos, Asians, and Middle Easterners, but the details of the system will vary from country to country, village to village, and individual to individual. When someone walks in the door of a clinic, you cannot know if he or she as an individual adheres to the beliefs described for his or her culture and what shape the individual's belief system takes. This makes the task both easier and harder.

It means a practitioner working with a Mexican population does not have to memorize which foods are hot and which are cold in Mexico, but the practitioner does need to know that the hot/cold belief system is important in Mexican culture and be able to be understanding and responsive when people bring up the topic.

The beliefs held by cultures around the world are classified into various categories, which are discussed in the following subsections. The categories are used for diagnosis and treatment and for explaining the etiology or origin of the illness. Often, multiple categories are used. For example, emotions may be seen as causing a "hot" illness.

Body Balances

In the category of body balances, the concept of hot and cold is one of the most pervasive around the world. It is particularly important in Asian, Latin American, and Mediterranean cultures. Hot and cold beliefs are part of what is referred to as *humoral medicine,* which is thought to have derived from Greek, Arabic, and East Indian pre-Christian traditions (Foster, 1953; Logan, 1972; Weller, 1983). This concept of opposites (such as hot and cold, wet and dry) also may have developed independently in other

Table 2-1	Types of Insider Culture Explanations of Disease Causation
Body Balances Temperature: Hot, cold Energy Blood: Loss of blood; properties of blood reflect imbalance; pollution from menstrual blood Dislocation: Fallen fontanel Organs: Swollen stomach; heart; uterus; liver; umbilicus; others Incompatibility of horoscopes **Emotional** Fright Sorrow Envy Stress **Weather** Winds Change of weather Seasonal disbalance **Vectors or Organisms** Worms Flies Parasites Germs	**Supernatural** Bewitching Demons Spirit possession Evil eye Offending God or gods Soul loss **Food** Properties: Hot, cold, heavy (rich), light Spoiled foods Dirty foods Sweets Raw foods Combining the "wrong" foods (incompatible foods) Mud **Sexual** Sex with forbidden person Overindulgence in sex **Heredity** **Old Age**

cultures (Rubel & Haas, 1990). For example, in the Chinese medical tradition, hot is referred to as *yin*, and cold as *yang* (Topley, 1976). In the hot and cold belief system, a healthy body is seen as in balance between the two. Illness may be brought on by violating the balance, such as washing the hair too soon after childbirth (cold may enter the body, which is still hot from the birth), eating hot/heavy foods at night, or breastfeeding while upset (the milk will be hot from the emotions and make the baby ill). It should be noted that *hot* does not always refer to temperature. Often foods such as beef and pork are classified as hot regardless of temperature, whereas fish may be seen as cold regardless of temperature. When illness has been diagnosed, the system is used to attempt to restore balance. Thus, in Central America some diarrheas in children are viewed as hot, and protein-rich "hot" foods such as meats are withheld, aggravating the malnutrition that may be present and may be exacerbated by the diarrheal disease (Scrimshaw & Hurtado, 1988). Extensive literature exists on the topic of hot and cold illness classifications and treatments for many of the world's cultures.

Energy balance is particularly important in Chinese medicine, where it is referred to as *chi*. When the balance is disturbed, there are internal problems of homeostasis. Foods (often following the hot/cold theories) and acupuncture are among the strategies used to restore balance (Topley, 1976).

Blood beliefs include the concept that blood is irreplaceable and that loss of blood, even small amounts, is a major risk. Adams (1955) describes a nutritional research project in a Guatemalan village where this belief inhibited the researcher's ability to obtain blood samples until the phlebotomists were instructed to draw as little blood as possible. Also, villagers were told that the blood would be examined to see if it was "sick" or "well" (another belief about blood) and they would be informed and given medicines if it were sick, which in fact did occur.

Menstrual blood is regarded as dangerous, especially to men, in many cultures, and elaborate precautions are taken to avoid contamination (Buckley & Gottlieb, 1988). As with the Guatemalan example, blood may have many properties that both diagnose and explain illness. Bad blood is seen as causing scabies in south India (Beals, 1976). Haitians have a particularly elaborate blood belief system, which includes concepts such as *mauvais sang* (literally, bad blood, which is when blood rises in the body and is dirty), *saisissement* (rapid heartbeat and cool blood, due to trauma), and *faiblesses* (too little blood). Blood may also be seen as opposites, such as clean/unclean,

sweet/normal, bitter/normal, high/normal, heavy/weak, clotted/thin, and quiet-turbulent (C. Scott, personal communication, 1976). It is easy to see how these concepts could be used in a current program to prevent HIV infection in a Haitian community, because the culture already has ways of describing problems with blood.

Dislocation of body parts may occur with organs, but also with a physical aspect, such as the fontanel, or "soft spot," in a baby's head where the bones do not come together in the first year or so to allow for growth. From the outsider perspective, a depression in this spot can be indicative of dehydration, often due to diarrheal disease; from the insider perspective, however, it is referred to as a cause of the disease (*caida de mollera*) in Mexico and Central America.

Many cultures associate illness with problems in specific organs. Good and Good (1981) talk about the importance of the heart for both Chinese and Iranian cultures. They discuss a case in which problems with cardiac medication were wrongly diagnosed for a Chinese woman who kept complaining about pain in her heart. In fact, she was referring to her grief over the loss of her son. The Hmong of Laos link many problems to the liver, referring to "ugly liver," "difficult liver," "broken liver," "short liver," "murmuring liver," and "rotten liver." These are said to refer to mental and emotional problems, and thus are idiomatic rather than literal (O'Connor, 1995).

Topley (1976) mentions incompatibility of horoscopes between mother and child as appearing in Chinese explanations for some children's illnesses.

Emotional

Illnesses of emotional origin are important in many cultures. Sorrow (as in the case of the Chinese woman mentioned earlier), envy, fright, and stress are seen as causing illnesses. In a Bolivian village in 1965, a young girl's smallpox infection was attributed to her sorrow over the death of her father.

Envy is believed to cause illness because people with envy could cast the evil eye on someone they envied, even unwittingly, or the envious person could become ill from the emotion (Reichel-Dolmatoff & Reichel-Dolmatoff, 1961). Fright, called *susto* in Latin America, has already been mentioned. In addition to the case of tuberculosis in adults discussed previously, it is a common explanation for illness in children. It is also mentioned for Chinese culture (Topley, 1976).

Weather

Everything from the change of seasons to unusual variations within seasons (too warm, too cold, too wet, too dry) can be blamed for causing illness. Winds, such as the Santa Ana in California or the Scirocco in the North African desert, are also implicated.

Vectors or Organisms

Vectors or organisms are blamed for illness in some cultures and represent a blend of Western biomedical and indigenous concepts. "Germs" is a catchall category, as is "parasites." Worms are seen as causing diarrhea, whereas flies are seen as causing illness and, sometimes, as carrying germs.

Supernatural

The supernatural is another frequently viewed source of illness, especially in Africa and Asia, but it is certainly not confined to those regions. In fact, the evil eye is a widespread concept, in which someone can deliberately or unwittingly bring on illness by looking at someone with envy, malice, or too hot a gaze. In cultures where most people have dark eyes, strangers with light eyes are seen as dangerous. In Latin America, a light-eyed person who admires a child can risk bringing evil eye to that child, but can counter it by touching the child. In other cultures, touching the child can be unlucky, so it is important to learn about local customs. Frequently, amulets and other protective devices, such as small eyes of glass, red hats, and a red string around the wrist, are worn to prevent the evil eye. These objects can be viewed as an opportunity to discuss preventive health measures, because they are an indication that people are thinking about prevention.

Bewitching is deliberate malice, either done by the individual who wishes someone ill (literally) or by a practitioner at someone else's request. Bewitching can be countered by another practitioner or by specific measures taken by an individual. In some regions of Africa, epidemics are blamed on "too many witches," and people disperse to get away from them, thus reducing the critical population density that had sustained the epidemic (Alland, 1970).

Belief in soul loss is widespread throughout the world. Soul loss can be caused by things such as fright, bewitching, the evil eye, and demons. It can occur in adults and children. Soul loss is serious and can lead to death. It must be treated through rituals to retrieve the soul. In Bolivia, a village priest complained that his attempt to visit a sick child was thwarted when the family would not allow him to enter the house. The family later reported that an indigenous healer was performing a curing ritual at the time, and the soul was flying around the house as they were trying to persuade it to reenter the child. Opening the door to the priest would have allowed the soul to escape. The child's symptoms were those of severe malnutrition.

Spirit possession is also a worldwide concept and is found frequently in African and Asian cultures. Writing about a village in South India, Beals (1976) mentions spirit possession in a daughter-in-law whose symptoms were refusing to work and speaking insultingly to her mother-in-law. He suggests that spirit possession is a "culturally sanctioned means of psychological release for oppressed daughters-in-law" (p. 188). Freed and Freed (1967) discuss similar cases in other parts of India. In Haiti, spirit possession is seen as a mark of favor by the spirits and is sought. One of the drawbacks, however, is that the possessing spirits object to the presence of foreign objects in the body, so some women do not want to use intrauterine devices.

Demons are viewed as causing illness in Chinese culture, whereas offending God or gods is a problem in others (Topley, 1976). In South India, epidemic diseases such as chickenpox and cholera (and, formerly, smallpox) are believed to be caused by disease goddesses. They bring the diseases to punish communities that become sinful (Beals, 1976). The concept of punishment from God is seen in a case study from Mexico, where onchocerciasis (river blindness), which is caused by a parasite transmitted by the bite of a fly that lives near streams, is often thought to be due to sins committed either by the victim or relatives of the victim. These transgressions against God are punished by God closing the victim's eyes (Gwaltney, 1970).

Food

Food can cause illness through its role in the hot and cold belief system, through spoiled foods, dirty foods, raw foods, and combining the wrong foods. Sweets are implicated as a cause of worms in children, and children who eat mud or dirt may get ill. Foods may also cause problems if eaten at the wrong time of day, such as "heavy" foods at night. There is an extensive literature on food beliefs and practices worldwide, which have important implications for public health practice.

Sexual

In Ecuador in the early 1970s, children's illnesses were sometime blamed on affairs between one of the child's parents and a *compadre* or *comadre*—one of the child's godparents (Scrimshaw, 1974). Such a relationship was viewed as incestuous and dangerous to the child. In India, sex is sometimes viewed as weakening to the man, so overindulgence is considered a cause of weakness. To return to the concept of blood beliefs, it is thought that 30 drops of blood are needed to make one drop of semen, thus weakening a man.

Heredity and Old Age

Heredity is sometimes blamed for illness, early death, or some types of death. Similarly, old age may be the simple explanation given for illness or death.

Illness in Various Forms

Table 2-2 illustrates the way in which some of these beliefs are used to explain a particular illness, diarrheal disease in Central America. It is typical of the way in which an illness may be seen as having different forms, or manifestations, with different etiologies. It is also typical of the way in which several different explanations may be used for one set of symptoms.

In this case, Table 2-2 and Figure 2-1, the diagram of treatments were key in expanding the orientation of the Central American diarrheal disease program. The program had intended to focus on the distribution of oral rehydration solutions (ORS) in the clinics, but the insider perception was that you usually only take a child to the clinic for the worst form of diarrhea, dysentery. Instead, the most common treatment consisted of fluids in the form of herbal teas or sodas with medicines added. Often, storekeepers and pharmacists were consulted. It made sense to provide the ORS at stores and pharmacies as well as at clinics, so that all diarrheas were more likely to be treated (Scrimshaw & Hurtado, 1988).

In a related situation, Kendall, Foote, and Martorell (1983) found that when the government of Honduras did not include indigenous or folk terminology for diarrheal disease in their mass media messages regarding oral rehydration, people did not use ORS for diarrheas attributed to indigenously defined causes.

Healers

Table 2-3 lists types of healers. This list includes types ranging from indigenous to Western biomedical. Pluralistic healers are those who mix the two traditions, although some Western biomedical healers and those from other medical systems may also mix traditions in their practices.

As with the types of explanations of disease, the types of healers listed here are found in different combinations in different cultures. There is always more than one type of healer available to a community, even if members have to travel to seek care. The 16-country study of health-seeking behavior described earlier found

that in all communities people used more than one healing tradition, and usually more than one type of healer (Scrimshaw, 1992). The processes of diagnosing illness and seeking a cure have been referred to as *patterns of resort* rather than the older term *hierarchy of resort* (Scrimshaw & Hurtado, 1987). This is because people may zigzag from one practitioner to another, crossing from type to type of healer and not always starting with the simplest and cheapest, but with the one they can best afford and who they feel will be most effective given the severity of the problem. Even middle- and upper-class individuals, who can afford Western biomedical care, may also use other types of practitioners and practices.

Indigenous practitioners are usually of the culture and follow traditional practices. Today they often mix elements of Western biomedicine and other traditional systems. In many instances, they are called to their profession through dreams, omens, or an illness, which usually can only be cured by their agreement to become a practitioner. Most learn through apprenticeship to other healers, but some are taught by dreams. Often they will take courses in Western practices in programs such as those developed to train "barefoot doctors" or community-based health promoters. In some instances, they must conceal their role as traditional healer from those running the training programs. The incorporation of some Western biomedical knowledge and skills often enhances a practitioner's prestige in the community.

Some indigenous practitioners charge for their services, but many do not, accepting gifts instead. In a few traditions (including some Chinese), practitioners are paid as long as family members are well, but they are not paid for illness treatment. The duty of the practitioner in those cases is to keep people well, which argues for the acceptability of prevention programs in those cultures.

For the most part, indigenous practitioners do "good," or healing. Some can do both good and ill (for example, shamans, sorcerers, and witches in many cultures). A few practice only evil or negative rituals (some shamans, sorcerers, and witches). Their work must then be countered by someone who does "good" magic. The power of belief is such that if individuals believe they have been bewitched, they may need a counteractive ritual, even if the Western biomedical system detects and treats a specific disease. In Guayaquil, Ecuador, one woman believed she had been *maleada* (cursed) by a woman who was jealous of her and that this was making her and her children ill. A *curandera* (curer) was brought in to do a *limpia* (ritual cleansing) of the house and family to remove the curse (Scrimshaw, 1974).

Table 2-2	Taxonomy of Diarrhea

CAUSE			SYMPTOMS All types have watery and frequent stools	TREATMENT
Mother's Milk	Physical activity	Hot		Not breastfeeding when hot
	Hot foods			Mother changes diet
	Pregnancy			Breastfeeding stops
	Anger	Emotional	Very dangerous	Home, drugstore, Injectionist, witch, spiritist
	Sadness			
	Fright			
Food		Bad food	Flatulence, feeling of fullness	Home, folk curer
		Excess		
		Does *not* eat *on* time		
	Hot	Quality		
	Cold			
Tooth Eruption			Tooth eruption	None
Fallen Fontanel, Fallen Stomach	Fallen stomach		Green with mucus	Folk curer
	Fallen fontanel		Sunken fontanel; vomiting; green in color	
Evil Eye			Fever	Folk curer
Stomach Worms			Worms	Drugstore, home, folk curer
Cold Enters Stomach	From feet		White in color	Folk curer
	From head			
Dysentery			Blood in stools, "urgency"; color is red or black	Home, drugstore, health post

Source: S. C. M. Scrimshaw and E. Hurtado, *Rapid Assessment Procedures for Nutrition and Primary Health Care: Anthropological Approaches to Improving Program Effectiveness (RAP)* (Los Angeles: UCLA Latin America Center, 1987), p. 26. Reprinted with permission of the Regents of the University of California.

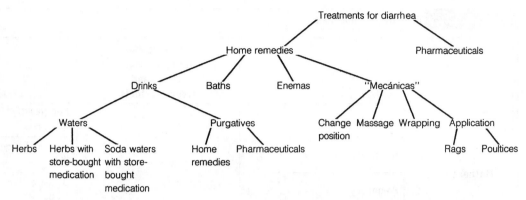

Figure 2-1 Taxonomy of Treatments for Diarrhea. *Source:* S. C. M. Scrimshaw and E. Hurtado, *Rapid Assessment Procedures for Nutrition and Primary Health Care: Anthropological Approaches to Improving Program Effectiveness (RAP)* (Los Angeles: UCLA Latin America Center, 1987), p. 26. Reprinted with permission of the Regents of the University of California.

Table 2-3	Types of Healers
Indigenous	**Western Biomedical**
Midwives	Pharmacists
Shamans	Nurse-midwives
Curers	Nurses
Spiritualists	Nurse practitioners
Witches	Physicians
Sorcerers	Dentists
Priests	Other health professionals
Diviners	
Herbalists	**Other Medical Systems**
Bonesetters	Chinese medical system
Massagers	Practitioners
	Chemists/herbalists
Pluralistic	Acupuncturists
Injectionists	Ayurvedic practitioners
Indigenous health workers	Taoist priests
Western-trained birth attendants	
Traditional chemists/ herbalists	
Storekeepers and vendors	

The importance of the power of belief is not confined to bewitching. One anthropologist working with a Haitian population discovered that a Haitian burn patient made no progress until she went to a *Houngan* (voodoo priest) on the patient's behalf and had the appropriate healing ritual conducted (J. Halifax-Groff, personal communication, 1976).

In some cultures some healers are seen as diagnosticians, while others do the treatment (Alland, 1970). Other healers may do both, but refer some kinds of illness to other practitioners. In Haiti, both midwives and voodoo priests refer some cases to the Western biomedical system. Healers who combine healing practices or who combine the ability to diagnose and to treat are viewed as more powerful than other types. Topley (1976) discusses this for Hong Kong and notes that Taoist priest healers are particularly respected. They are seen as both priest and doctor and "claim to combine the ethics of Confucianism, the hygiene and meditation of Taoism, and the prayers and self-cultivation of the Buddhist monk."

Pluralistic healers combine Western biomedical and indigenous practices. Injectionists will give an injection of antibiotics, vitamins, or other drugs purchased at pharmacies or stores. Sometimes these injections are suggested by the pharmacist or storekeeper; other times they are self-prescribed. Because antibiotics were so dramatic in curing infections when Western biomedicine was first introduced in many cultures, injections are seen as conveying greater healing than the same substance taken orally. Thus, many antibiotics now available orally and vitamins are injected. In today's environment this increases the risk of contracting HIV or hepatitis if sterile or new needles and syringes are not used.

Traditional chemists and herbalists, as well as storekeepers and vendors (many communities are too small to have a pharmacy), sell Western biomedical medications, including those that require a prescription in the United States and western Europe. Although prescriptions may be legally required in many countries, the laws are not rigorously enforced. This is also true for pharmacies, which are very important, sometimes the most important, sources of diagnosis and treatment in many communities around the world.

Western biomedical practitioners are an important source of care, but they may also be expensive or hard to access from remote areas. As mentioned earlier, if an individual believes that an illness is due to a cause explained by the indigenous system and a Western biomedical practitioner denies that cause, the individual may not return to that practitioner but seek help elsewhere.

As noted, there are other medical systems with long traditions, systematic ways of training practitioners, and well-established diagnostic and treatment procedures. Until recently Western biomedical practitioners totally rejected both these and indigenous systems, often failing to recognize how many practices and medicines in Western biomedicine were derived from other systems (e.g., quinine, digitalis, many anesthetics, aspirin, and estrogen). Elements of these systems that were derided in the past, such as acupuncture, have now found their way into Western biomedical practice and are being legitimized by Western research.

Theories of Health Behavior and Behavior Change

The fields of sociology, psychology, and anthropology have developed many theories to explain health beliefs and behaviors and behavior change. Some theories developed by sociologists and psychologists in the United States were developed first for U.S. populations and only later applied internationally. Others were developed with international and multicultural populations in mind from the beginning. Only a few of the many theories of health and illness beliefs and behavior are discussed here, but they are ones that have been quite influential in general or that are applicable for international work in particular.

Health Belief Model

The health belief model suggests that decision making about health behaviors is influenced by four basic premises—perceived susceptibility to the illness, perceived severity of the illness, perceived benefits of the prevention behavior, and perceived barriers to that behavior—as well as other variables, such as sociodemographic factors (Rosenstock, Strecher, & Becker, 1974). In general, people are seen as weighing perceived susceptibility (how likely they are to get the disease) and perceived severity (how serious the disease is) against their belief in the benefits and effectiveness of the prevention behavior they must undertake and the costs of that behavior in terms of barriers such as time, money, and aggravation. The

more serious the disease is believed to be, and the more effective the prevention, the more likely people are to incur the costs of engaging in the prevention behavior. This model has been extensively studied, critiqued, modified, and expanded to explain people's responses to symptoms and compliance with health care regimens for diagnosed illnesses. One concern has been that this model does not work as well for chronic problems or habitual behaviors because people learn to manage their behaviors or the health care system. Also, it has been accused of failing to take environmental and social forces into account, which in turn increases the potential for blaming the individual. The difficulty in quantifying the model for research and evaluation purposes is also a problem.

Work by Bandura led to the inclusion of self efficacy in the model. *Self-efficacy* has been defined as "the conviction that one can successfully execute the behavior required to produce the desired outcome" (Bandura, 1977, 1989). The concept of locus of control, or belief in the ability to control one's life, also has been used with this model. In one example, a comparison of migrant Yugoslavian and Swedish diabetic females revealed stronger locus of control in the Swedes and more passivity toward self-care in the Yugoslavs, who also had a lower self-efficacy that the authors attributed to the different political systems in the two countries—collectivism in Yugoslavia, individualism in Sweden (Hjelm, Nyberg, Isacsson, & Apelqvist, 1999).

The value of the four basic premises of the health belief model has held up well under scrutiny. Perceived barriers have the strongest predictive value of the four dimensions, followed by perceived susceptibility and perceived benefits. Perceived susceptibility is most frequently associated with compliance with health screening exams. Perceived severity of risk has been noted to have a weaker predictive value for protective health behaviors, while it is strongly associated with sick-role behaviors.

In *Medical Choice in a Mexican Village*, Young (1981) describes a health decision-making process very similar to that found in the health belief model. In choosing between home remedies, pharmacy or store, indigenous healer or doctor, the villagers weigh the perceived severity of the illness, the potential efficacy of the cure to be sought, the cost (money, time, and so on) of the cure, and their own resources to seek treatment and pay the cost as they make their decision. The simplest, least costly treatment is always the first choice, but the severity of illness and issues concerning efficacy may force a more costly option. Other studies of health-seeking behavior have found similar patterns throughout the world.

Theory of Reasoned Action

The theory of reasoned action was first proposed by Ajzen and Fishbein (1972) to predict an individual's intention to engage in a behavior in a specific time and place. The theory was intended to explain virtually all behaviors over which people have the ability to exert self-control. There are five basic constructs that precede the performance of a behavior. These are behavioral intent, attitudes, beliefs and evaluations of behavioral outcomes, subjective norms, and normative beliefs. Behavioral intent is seen as the immediate predictor of behavior. Factors that influence behavioral choices are mediated through this variable. In order to maximize the predictive ability of an intention to perform a specific behavior, the measurement of the intent must closely reflect the measurement of the behavior. Thus, measurement of the intention to begin to take oral contraceptives must include questions about the date a woman plans to visit a clinic and which clinic she plans to attend. The failure to address action, target, context, and time in the measurement of behavioral intention will undermine the predictive value of the model.

In a recent test of this theory in the prediction of intentions regarding condom use in a national sample of young people in England, measures of past behavior were the best predictors of intentions and attenuated the effects of attitude and subjective norms (Sutton, McVey, & Glanz, 1999).

Diffusion of Health Innovations Model

The diffusion of health innovations model proposes that communication is essential for social change, and that diffusion is the process by which an innovation is communicated through certain channels over time among members of a social system (Rogers, 1983; Rogers & Shoemaker, 1972). An *innovation* is an idea, practice, service, or other object that is perceived as new by an individual or group.

Ideally, the development of a diffusion strategy for a specific health behavior change goal will proceed through six stages:

1. Recognition of a problem or need

2. Performance of basic and applied research to address the specific problem

3. Development of strategies and materials that will put the innovative concept into a form that will meet the needs of the target population

4. Commercialization of the innovation, which will involve production, marketing, and distribution efforts

5. Diffusion and adoption of the innovation

6. Consequences associated with adoption of the innovation

According to classic diffusion theory, a population targeted by an intervention to promote acceptance of an innovation comprises six groups: innovators, early adopters, early majority, late majority, late adopters, and laggards. The rapidity and extent to which health innovations are adopted by a target population are mediated by a number of factors, including relative advantage, compatibility, complexity, communicability, observability, trialability, cost-efficiency, time, commitment, risk and uncertainty, reversibility, modifiability, and emergence. Relative advantage refers to the extent to which a health innovation is better (faster, cheaper, more beneficial) than an existing behavior or practice. Antibiotics were quickly accepted in most of the world because they were dramatically faster and more effective than traditional practices. Compatibility is the degree to which the innovation is congruent with the target population's existing set of practices and values. Polgar and Marshall (1976) point out that injectable contraceptives were acceptable in the village in India where Marshall worked because injections were viewed so positively due to the success of antibiotics. The degree to which an innovation is easy to incorporate into existing health regimens may also affect rates of diffusion. Iodized salt is an easier way to ensure people are receiving iodine than taking an iodine pill, because using salt is already a habit. Health innovations are also more likely to be adopted quickly and by larger numbers of individuals if the innovation itself can be easily communicated.

The concept of trialability involves the ease of trying out a new behavior. For example, it is easier to try a condom than to be fitted for a diaphragm. Observability refers to role models, such as village leaders volunteering to be the first in a vaccination campaign. A health innovation is also more likely to be adopted if it is seen as cost-efficient. A famous case study of water boiling in a Peruvian town demonstrated that the cost in time and energy of gathering wood and making a fire to boil the water far outweighed any perceived benefits, so water boiling was seldom adopted (Wellin, 1955). Successful health innovations are likely to be those that do not require expenditure of much additional time, energy, or other resources.

One of the overall messages regarding communication for the purposes of health education and promotion is that mass media and interpersonal communication channels should be used in conjunction (Rogers, 1973). Implementing both methods is of particular importance in developing countries, especially in rural communities. Rogers emphasizes that mass media deliver information to a large population to add knowledge, although interpersonal contacts are needed to persuade people to adopt new behaviors (thereby using the knowledge function, the persuasion function, and the innovation-decision process). According to Rogers's work and other work cited by him, "family planning diffusion is almost entirely via interpersonal channels" (1973, p. 263). He presented five examples in different countries, including India, Taiwan, and Hong Kong, in which interpersonal channels were the primary source for family planning information and were the motivating factors for seeking services.

The limitations to mass media in this area include the following:

- *Limited exposure:* In less developed countries, smaller audiences have access to mass media (radio is the most common mass media tool), and low literacy is also a barrier.

- *Message irrelevancy:* The content of mass media messages may be of no practical use for many rural and nonelite populations. Often instrumental information ("how to") is not included in the messages (e.g., information on where to receive services or on the positive and negative consequences of adopting a particular health behavior).

- *Low credibility:* For people to accept and believe the messages being diffused, trust needs to exist between the sender and receiver. Often radio and TV stations are a government monopoly and may be considered as government propaganda by the receivers.

The diffusion of innovations model focuses solely on the processes and determinants of adoption of a new behavior and does not help to understand or explain the maintenance of behavior change. Many health behaviors require permanent or long-term changes. Also, it is important to understand whether a new behavior is being conducted appropriately, consistently, or at all. One example is the story of condom use, which was demonstrated by unrolling the condom over a banana. Women who became pregnant while they reported using condoms had been faithfully putting them on bananas.

PRECEDE Model

The PRECEDE model of health promotion was first proposed by Green, Kreuter, Deeds, and Partridge in 1980. PRECEDE is an acronym for "predisposing, reinforcing, and enabling causes in educational diagnosis and evaluation." This model focuses on communities rather than individuals as the primary units of change. This approach incorporates specific recommendations

for evaluating the effectiveness of interventions and provides a highly focused target for the intervention.

The framework of the PRECEDE model outlines progression through seven phases. Phase 1, also known as social diagnosis, relies on assessment of the general problems of concern that have a negative impact on overall quality of life for members of the target population. Those populations might include patients, health care providers, family caregivers, lay health workers, or consumers of health care. During phase 1 there is an emphasis on identification of social problems encountered by the target population. This provides an important opportunity to involve the community. Community participation in and acceptance of programs greatly increase their likelihood of success.

Phase 2 focuses on epidemiologic diagnosis. Activities associated with phase 3 focus on the identification of nonbehavioral (and often nonmodifiable) causes and behavioral causes of the priority health problem. Phase 4 of the model is identified as educational diagnosis and consists of activities to identify predisposing, reinforcing, and enabling factors associated with the target health behavior. At phase 5 intervention planners must decide which of the factors are to be addressed by various aspects of the intervention. Phase 6 is administrative diagnosis and refers to the development and implementation of the intervention program. Viable intervention strategies suggested by Green and colleagues (1980) include group lectures, individual instruction, mass media messages, audiovisual aids, programmed learning, educational television, skill development workshops, simulations, role playing, educational games, peer group discussions, behavior modification, modeling, and community development. The seventh and final phase is focused on evaluation, which begins during each of the preceding six phases and ranges from simple process evaluation to impact and outcome evaluation.

Transtheoretical Model

Theories concerning the concept of stages of change have been evolving since the early 1950s. Currently the most widely accepted stage change model is the transtheoretical model of behavior change developed by Prochaska, DiClemente, and Norcross (1992). This model has four core constructs: (1) stages of change, (2) decisional balance, (3) self-efficacy, and (4) processes of change. Interventions relying on this model are expected to include all four constructs in the development of strategies to communicate, promote, and maintain behavior change.

The stages of change include several steps. The first is precontemplation, in which individuals have no intention to take action within the next 6 months. The contemplation stage refers to expressing an intention to take some action to change a negative health behavior or adopt a positive one within the next 6 months. The preparation stage refers to the intent to make a change within the next 30 days. The action stage is defined as the demonstration of an overt behavior change for an interval of less than six months. In the fifth stage, maintenance, a person will have sustained a change for at least 6 months.

Decisional balance is an assessment of the costs and benefits of changing, which will vary with the stage of change. Self-efficacy is divided into two concepts. The first is confidence that one can engage in the new behavior. Second, the temptation aspect of self-efficacy refers to factors that can tempt one to engage in unhealthy behaviors across different settings.

The fourth construct of the transtheoretical model deals with the process of change. This includes 10 factors that can affect the progression of individuals from the precontemplation to the maintenance stages.

Explanatory Models

Explanatory models were initially proposed by physician-anthropologist Kleinman (1980, 1986, 1988). They differ from some of the theories described earlier in this section in that they are designed for multicultural settings. They include models such as the meaning-centered approach to staff-patient negotiation described by Good and Good (1981). These models focus on individual interactions between physicians or other staff and patients, but the concepts, such as Kleinman's negotiation model, have proved useful for research and for behavioral interventions for larger populations. An explanatory model is seen as dynamic, and can change based on individual experiences with health, health information, or with the illness in question.

Table 2-4 adapts and summarizes concepts from Good and Good's description of the meaning-centered approach. The approach involves mutual interpretations across systems of meaning. The interpretive goal is understanding the patient's perspective. The underlying premise is that disorders vary profoundly in their psychodynamics, cultural influences in interpretation, behavioral expression, severity, and duration. As noted earlier, it is difficult to provide universal keys to culture and symptoms due to factors such as individual variation, groups assimilating or changing, and groups adding beliefs and behaviors from other cultures. For example, *espiritismo* (spiritism) was strongest in the Puerto Rican groups in the United

Table 2-4	Meaning-Centered Approach to Clinical Practice

Primary Principles

Groups vary in the specificity of their medical complaints.

Groups vary in their style of medical complaining.

Groups vary in the nature of their anxiety about the meaning of symptoms.

Groups vary in their focus on organ systems.

Groups vary in their response to therapeutic strategies.

Human illness is fundamentally sematic or meaningful (it may have a biological base, but is a human experience).

Corollary

Clinical practice is inherently interpretive.

Actions

Practitioners must

    Elicit patients' requests, questions, etc.

    Elicit and decode patients' semantic networks

    Distinguish disease and illness and develop plans for managing problems.

    Elicit explanatory models of patients and families, analyze conflict with biomedical models, and negotiate alternatives

Source: B. J. Good and M. J. D. Good, "The Meaning of Symptoms: A Cultural Hermeneutic Model for Clinical Practice," in I. Eisenberg and A. Kleinman, *The Relevance of Social Science for Medicine* (Dordrecht: Kluwer Academic Publishers, 1981). Adapted and reprinted with kind permission of Kluwer Academic Publishers.

States, but it has now been adopted by other cultures of Latin American origin as well. Instead of trying to provide formulas for understanding health and illness belief systems for different cultures, the focus is on the meaning of symptoms. The medical encounter is seen as involving the interpretation of symptoms and other relevant information. The suggestions in the "Actions" section of the table can be used both to explain insider/outsider views to health providers and to give them tools to work with individual patients or populations. (See Chapter 8 for further explanation of insider and outsider perspectives.)

Other Theories

A number of other theories can be useful in looking at culture and behavior. These include multiattribute utility theory, which predicts behavior directly from an individual's evaluation of the consequences or outcomes associated with both performing and not performing a given behavior. Some, such as social learning theory, have been criticized by anthropologists who argue against the notion that people are like a black box into which you can pour information and expect a specific behavior change.

Some Common Features of Successful Health Communication and Health Promotion Programs

When applied in practice, many of the principles discussed in this chapter help increase the success of health communication and health promotion programs. In particular, understanding and incorporating people's insider cultural values, beliefs, and behaviors; basing the program in the community with strong community participation; incorporating peer group education, including community-based outreach workers; and using multilevel intervention approaches have proved essential to program success.

For example, the Agita Sao Paulo Program provides a case study in using local culture to design both the content and delivery system for a program to use physical activity to promote health (Matsudo et al., 2003). Just the word *agita* (which means to move the body, to agitate in the sense of stirring, but also to change, is more culturally understood and internalized than a literal translation of *exercise*. In addition to careful work on culturally acceptable ways of delivering the message, the project provides multiple culturally valued ways to increase physical activity, and tailors these to the age, gender, and lifestyles of community members.

In a very different project, work in three townships in South Africa focused on identifying where AIDS prevention would be most effective from the culturally appropriate, insider perspective (Weir et al., 2003). Among other things, researchers learned that ideal prevention intervention sites varied depending on whether the central business district or the township was the location for initiating new sexual encounters. The type of sex (commercial vs. casual) as well as the availability of condoms varied with the site. The age of people engaging in risky behaviors and risk behaviors by gender also varied by site. Again, prevention programs needed to be tailored. In another AIDS prevention project, this time in Vietnam, paying attention to culture and religion was essential to program strategies (Rekart, 2002). In Belize, understanding adolescents and making sure the program met their needs in both culture- and age-appropriate ways was key (Martiniuk, O'Connor, & King, 2003).

Another example of focusing on understanding and changing cultural values in regard to unhealthy behaviors is found in the area of smoking cessation. Abdullah and Husten (2004) set forth a framework for public health intervention in this area that addresses multiple levels of society.

The need for the involvement of communities is also clearly demonstrated in the literature. Literally hundreds of references exist on this topic. A recent summary article outlines many of the broad principles in this approach. These include community analysis with community participation, action plans designed with community input, and community involvement in implementation. The latter can include community involvement in ongoing oversight and evaluation as well as the more usual modes of community outreach workers (e.g., see Thevos, Quick, & Yanduli, 2000), working through community organizations, and getting individuals involved (Bhuyan, 2004). A report from a recent project in Bolivia documents the success of involving community members in everything from mapping the villages to setting priorities for the program (Perry, Shanklin, & Schroeder, 2003).

Two projects in Chicago demonstrate the success of the community outreach worker approach. In one case, the project focuses on intravenous drug abusers, reducing their HIV/AIDS risk behaviors and helping them to initiate drug abuse treatment programs. This work simply could not be accomplished without community outreach workers, all of whom are former addicts who know how and when to reach current addicts. Also, the outreach workers are from the predominant cultural/ethnic group in each community (Ouellet, Huo, & Bailey, 2004). Similarly, the Chicago Project for Violence Prevention involves ex-gang members as outreach workers (Chicago Project for Violence Prevention, 2005). Both programs have been adopted internationally as well as in other cities in the United States. A similar focus on peer group education in Botswana led to increased knowledge and prevention behaviors among women at risk for HIV/AIDS infection (Norr et al., 2004).

Methodologies for Understanding Culture and Behavior

Many of the research methodologies developed in the United States did not translate easily, literally, or figuratively to international settings. Differences in linguistic nuances, in the meanings of words and concepts, and in what people would reveal to a stranger versus what they would reveal to someone from their community all complicated the application of the quantitative methodologies used by sociologists, psychologists, and epidemiologists. The realization of these problems came about gradually, through failed projects and missed interpretations, and particularly once AIDS appeared. As a disease whose only prevention is still behavioral, with many hidden or taboo behaviors involved, AIDS brought out the need for qualitative research and for research conducted by individuals from the cultures being studied. The field of international public health has now moved from an almost exclusively quantitative orientation to the recognition that we have a toolbox of methodologies. Some may be more valuable than others for some situations or questions; other times, a mix of several methodologies may offer the best approach. These methodologies derive from epidemiology, survey research, psychology, anthropology, marketing (including social marketing), and other fields. The biggest disagreement has been over the relative value of quantitative and qualitative methods.

The debate on the scientific value of qualitative versus quantitative research is well summarized by Pelto and Pelto (1978). They define science as the "accumulation of systematic and reliable knowledge about an aspect of the universe, carried out by empirical observation and interpreted in terms of the interrelating of concepts referable to empirical observations" (p. 22). The Peltos add that "if the 'personal factor' in anthropology makes it automatically unscientific, then much of medical science, psychology, geography, and significant parts of all disciplines (including chemistry and physics) are unscientific" (p. 23).

In fact, scientific research is not truly objective but is governed by the cultural framework and theoretical orientation of the researcher. One example is the past tendency of biomedical researchers in the United States to focus on adult men for many health problems that also occur in women (such as heart disease). The earlier example of kuru demonstrates the limitations of cultural bias.

The methodological concepts of validity and reliability provide a common foundation for the integration of quantitative and qualitative techniques. *Validity* refers to the accuracy of scientific measurement, "the degree to which scientific observations measure what they purport to measure" (Pelto & Pelto, 1978, p. 33). For example, in Spanish Harlem in New York City, the question "*¿Sabe como evitar los hijos?*" (Do you know how to avoid [having] children?) elicited responses on contraceptive methods and was used as the first in a series of questions on family planning. By not using family planning terminology at the outset, the study was able to avoid bi-

asing respondents (Scrimshaw & Pasquariella, 1970). The same phrase in Ecuador, however, produced reactions such as "I would never take out [abort] a child!" If the New York questionnaire had been applied in Ecuador without testing it through semistructured ethnographic interviews, the same words would have produced answers to what was in fact a different question (Scrimshaw, 1974). Qualitative methods often provide greater validity than quantitative methods because they rely on multiple data sources, including direct observation of behavior and multiple contacts with people over time. Thus they can be used to increase the validity of survey research.

Reliability refers to replicability: the extent to which scientific observations can be repeated and the same results obtained. In general, this is best accomplished through survey research or other quantitative means. Surveys can test hypotheses and examine questions generated through qualitative data. Qualitative methods may help us discover a behavior or how to ask questions about it, while quantitative data can tell us how extensive the behavior is in a population and what other variables are associated with it. Murray (1976) describes just such a discovery during qualitative research in a Haitian community, where the simple question "Are you pregnant?" had two meanings. Women could be pregnant with *gros ventre* (big belly) or could be pregnant and in *perdition*. Perdition meant a state in which a woman was pregnant, but the baby was "stuck" in utero and refused to grow. Perdition was attributed to causes such as cold, spirits, or ancestors. Women may be in perdition for years, and may be separated, divorced, or widowed, but the pregnancy is attributed to her partner when it commenced. Murray then included questions about perdition in a subsequent survey, which revealed that it was apparently a cultural way of making infertility or subfecundity socially acceptable, as many women in perdition fell into these categories.

Surveys are effective tools for collecting data from a large sample, particularly when the distribution of a variable in a population is needed (e.g., the percentage of women who obtain prenatal care) or when rarely occurring events (e.g., neonatal deaths) must be assessed. Surveys are also used to record people's answers to questions about their behavior, motivations, perception of an event, and similar topics. Although surveys are carefully designed to collect data in the most objective manner possible, they often suffer inaccuracies based on respondents' perceptions of their own behavior, their differing interpretations of the meaning of the question, or their desire to please the interviewer with their answers. Surveys also can have difficulty uncovering motives (i.e., why individuals behave as they do), and they are not apt to uncover behaviors that may be consciously or unconsciously concealed. In "Truths and Untruths in Village Haiti: An Experiment in Third World Survey Research," Chen and Murray (1976) describe some of these problems.

The traditional anthropological approach involves one person or a small team in a research site for at least a year. This is done in part to take into account the changes in people's lifestyles with the changes in seasons, activities, available food, and so on. Also, the anthropologist often needs time to learn a language or dialect and learn enough about the culture to provide a context for questions and observations. More recently a subset of anthropological tools (ethnographic interview, participant observation, conversation, and observation) plus the market researchers' tool of focus groups have been combined in a rapid anthropological assessment process known as Rapid Assessment Procedures (RAP) (Scrimshaw & Hurtado, 1987; Scrimshaw, et al., 1991, 1992).

The RAP evolved around the same time as Rapid Rural Appraisal was developed by rural sociologists (Chambers, 1992). Both methods made listening to community voices easier for program planners and health care providers and became a frequently used tool for program development and evaluation. RAPs have been developed for many topics, including AIDS, women's health, diarrheal disease, seizure disorders, water and health, and childhood obesity prevention. RAP has become a generic concept and has been modified for many uses. Modified titles include RARE and ERAP. Several versions of the RAP as adapted for different topics and related information can be found at www.uic.edu/sph/rap.

A final comment on methodology is that as the social sciences are increasingly combining methodologies and sharing each other's tools, it is also important to share theoretical approaches. Where methodology is concerned, this leads to using multilevel approaches to research, in which environment, biological factors, cognitive issues, societal and cultural context, and political and economic forces can all contribute to the analyses. This should take place at least to the extent that an examination is made of data one step above and one step below the phenomenon being explained (Rubenstein, Scrimshaw, & Morrissey, 2000).

An example of a logic framework using this approach can be found in the work of the Centers for Disease Control and Prevention (CDC) task force that has been developing the *Guide to Community Preventative Services,* which is a series of evidence-based recommendations for community public health practice based on a systematic and critical review of the evidence. Topics considered by the guide include major risk behaviors (tobacco use, alcohol abuse and misuse, other substance abuse, nutrition, physical activity, healthy sexual behavior), specific illnesses (e.g., cancer, diabetes), and one overarching topic, the sociocultural environment. Figure 2-2 contains the logic framework for this topic. The outcomes of community health (on the right) stem from factors in the physical environment, societal resources, and equity and social justice issues, shown on the left of the figure. The immediate outcomes are listed in the middle, and range from neighborhood living conditions to prevailing community norms to prevention and health care (Anderson et al., 2003a, 2003b). This approach greatly broadens the context for understanding and addressing the health of individuals and communities.

The CDC's guide can be accessed through the website www.thecommunityguide.org. The website and related publications listed there provide evidence-based guidelines for improving community health, many of which have global relevance.

Case Study: The Slim Disease— HIV/AIDS in sub-Saharan Africa

AIDS changed the way in which epidemiologic and behavioral research could be conducted and health interventions designed and carried out. This case study illustrates virtually all the topics covered in this chapter.[2]

Epidemiology

At the end of 2004, 39.4 (35.9–44.3) million adults and children were living with HIV/AIDS worldwide (UNAIDS, 2004). More than 60% of all HIV positive cases are in sub-Saharan Africa, where 17 million persons have died from AIDS and there are 23.4-28.4 million persons living with HIV. The virus is spreading throughout the African population at alarming rates. HIV prevalence among pregnant women has risen to between 15% and 30% in some provinces in South Africa alone (World Health Organization [WHO], 2004).

Unlike the West, where AIDS has been largely associated with gay men and injecting drug users, in Africa the most common transmission is through heterosexual sex. A husband often infects his wife as a result of his involvement with other partners. A

[2]This case study was developed by Isabel Martinez, MPH and updated by Janel Heinrich, MPH, MA.

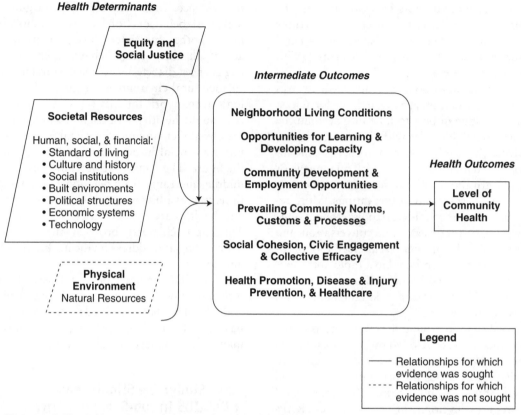

Figure 2-2 The *Guide to Community Preventive Service's* Social Environment and Health Model. *Source:* L. M. Anderson, S. C. Scrimshaw, M. T. Fullilove, et al., "The Community Guide's Model for Linking the Social Environment to Health," 2003, *American Journal of Preventive Medicine, 24*(3S), p. 13. Reprinted with permission.

pregnant, HIV-positive woman may transmit the virus to her fetus through the placenta or to her infant through breastfeeding. At the end of 2003, in sub-Saharan Africa, an estimated 1.9 million children are living with the virus as a result of mother-to-child transmission. Rural communities are not immune to HIV and AIDS, considering that the majority of the population lives in nonurban settings (Hunt, 1989; Salopek, 2000).

Generally, AIDS patients in Africa suffer from intestinal infections, skin disease, tuberculosis, herpes zoster, and meningitis. In the industrialized countries, AIDS is associated with Karposi's sarcoma (a skin cancer), meningitis, and pneumonia. So why does the same disease spread so differently from one region of the world to another? History, politics, economics, and cultural and social environments influence the course of a disease in a society. In the case of Africa, traditional family, social, and environmental structures were disrupted by European colonization, which imposed changes. Even after countries became independent from Europe, political, ecological, and economic struc-

tures remained disrupted and often unstable. Many of these factors contributed to an environment in which AIDS easily took hold (Akeroyd, 1997; Bond et al., 1997; Hunt, 1989). These factors and their association with the AIDS pandemic are described in the following sections. In addition to illustrating the relationship between cultural norms, prevention and health care access, and disease, the following discussion demonstrates the profound relationship between the general sociocultural, political, physical, and economic environment and health.

Risk of AIDS Associated with Migratory Labor

The integral family structure of the African culture has been broken up by the migratory labor system in eastern, central, and southern Africa. The migratory labor system is historically part of the regions' industrial development and colonization by European powers. These large industries, including mining, railroad work, plantation work, and primary production facilities such as oil refineries, absorbed massive labor from rural areas. Men typically left their homes and traveled outside their communities to work sites for long periods of time. This system has not only kept families apart, but has also increased the numbers of sex partners, thus giving rise to the prevalence of sexually transmitted infections (STIs) and later AIDS. In many African cultures, regular sex is believed essential to health. Men in the migratory labor system have sex with prostitutes close to their work sites, become infected, and eventually return home and infect their wives, whose babies may in turn become infected (Hunt, 1989; Salopek, 2000).

War

In 2001 there were 24 major armed conflicts globally, half of which occurred in Africa. A country at war faces the weakness of its political system, and the situation intensifies the impact of the AIDS epidemic. Several populations become more vulnerable to HIV/AIDS during wartime, including those affected by food emergencies and scarcity, displaced persons, and refugees. Women are especially at risk. They are six times more likely to contract HIV in refugee camps than populations outside. Women are victims of rape as a weapon of war by the enemy side. Armed forces and the commercial sex workers they interact with are also affected by the epidemic (Akeroyd, 1997; Carballo & Siem, 1996; Commission on Human Security, 2003; UNAIDS, 1999).

Gender Roles and Cultural Traditions

African women's struggle with the AIDS pandemic has been depicted often in the literature (Akeroyd, 1997; Carballo & Siem, 1996; Hunt, 1989; Messersmith, 1991; Salopek, 2000; UNAIDS, 1999a, 1999b). The risk to women from husbands or partners returning from work in other areas has already been discussed. Another risk factor—sex work or prostitution by women as a means of survival—is now almost a death sentence, considering the great risk of contracting HIV/AIDS. There are many reasons why some African women find the need to engage in sex work, though studies have linked the reasons to a political economy context. Sex in exchange for favors, material goods, or money is conducted at all socioeconomic levels, from female entrepreneurs in foreign trade having to use sexual ploys to ensure business to impoverished young women needing money to support themselves and their families. The women typically travel outside their community or country into urban areas and locations where tourists vacation. As mentioned earlier, prostitution also takes place in the surrounding communities near labor camps and vacation areas. Even if women in sex work are knowledgeable about preventing HIV infection through use of condoms, cost, availability, and the resistance of some men to using them raise barriers to their use and play a part in further transmission of the disease (Akeroyd, 1997; Messersmith, 1991).

Other cultural factors that place young women at greater risk for HIV infection include a superstition in some areas that having sex with a virgin will cure an HIV-infected man, and the practice of female circumcision. In both these circumstances, the risk of contracting HIV through sex or infected surgical instruments increases for adolescents (Akeroyd, 1997; Salopek, 2000).

These and additional cultural factors have contributed to the fact that for the first time in the history of the epidemic, more women than men are infected (Akeroyd, 1997; Hunt, 1989; Messersmith, 1991; Salopek, 2000). Across the region, there are 13 women living with HIV for every 10 men. For most countries of this region, women are being infected earlier than men, with the most pronounced difference in the 15 to 24 age group. For this population it has been estimated that for every 36 young women living with HIV there are 10 men. According to the UNAIDS *AIDs Epidemic Update* (2004a), in a study of women in Zimbabwe and South Africa, "66% reported having one lifetime partner, 79% had abstained from sex until at least their 17th birthday, and 79% said they used a condom. Yet 40% of the young women were HIV-positive."

Additional Cultural Beliefs

Secrecy regarding HIV/AIDS is common within regions of the sub-Saharan culture. Denying that AIDS is affecting one's community or that one is infected increases chances of transmitting the virus because preventive actions are not taken (Akeroyd, 1997; Salopek, 2000; UNAIDS & WHO, 1999; UNAIDS & Welcome Trust, 1999). Preventive actions go beyond preventing sexual transmission to concerns about transmission during treatment of ill individuals and during funeral practices.

In some parts of Africa, AIDS is referred to as the "slim disease" because of the wasting away that occurs as a result of the infection. Because of this belief, men prefer sex with plump women, believing that they are not infected. AIDS is called "whiteman's disease" in Gabon and "that other thing" in Zimbabwe. HIV and AIDS are a source of shame and denial in the culture. AIDS is also considered a punishment for overindulgence of the body. One *sangoma*, or faith healer, who has helped revive an ancient Zulu custom of virginity testing of young girls, supported her belief in reviving this custom, saying, "We have adopted too many

Western things without thinking, and we lost respect for our bodies. This has allowed things like AIDS to come torture us" (Akeroyd, 1997; Hunt, 1989; Salopek, 2000; UNAIDS & WHO, 1999).

Social and Economic Impacts

Two of the gravest social and economic consequences of the AIDS epidemic in sub-Saharan Africa are millions of orphaned children and a stifled economy for almost an entire continent. About half of HIV infections occur before the age of 25, and most of those afflicted die before 35. In Zimbabwe, for example, life expectancy was 52 years in 1990 but only 34 years in 2003 (UNAIDS, 2004a). This tragedy has left more than 12 million orphans in Africa—90% of the world's AIDS orphans. It is expected that by 2010, this number will rise to more than 18 million. Because this disease strikes people during their most productive years, the growth and development of Africa's economy is being threatened because infected people eventually become too weak to work, then die. This affliction has left many of Africa's traditionally prosperous industries, such as farming, mining, and oil, extremely vulnerable because of a lack of healthy workers and AIDS-related cost of workers' medical care. These social and economic crises may threaten political stability in many African countries and weaken the health of the population.

The AIDS epidemic in Africa will eventually have an impact on many parts of the world if the problem is not controlled. The increase of travel nationally and internationally has aided the spread of diseases. In addition, if the problems associated with the transmission of HIV/AIDS are not addressed, they will get worse, more threatening, and more expensive to control ("Africa Matters," 2000; Bartholet, 2000; Bond et al., 1997; Carballo & Siem, 1996; Hunt, 1989; Salopek, 2000; UNAIDS & WHO, 1999; UNAIDS, 2004b).

Barriers to Prevention or Treatment of HIV/AIDS

Many barriers to the prevention of HIV/AIDS exist in Africa. These include lack of financial resources and the allocation of funds to projects that might be less crucial than those related to health. For example, a foreign country funded a multimillion dollar hospital in Zambia, whereas the clinics in the rural areas where the majority of the population live are often not even stocked with aspirin. Treatment of HIV/AIDS with current Western therapies is so expensive that many countries cannot afford it, and negotiating with pharmaceutical companies for less expensive supplies has not always been successful (Bartholet, 2000; Salopek, 2000).

Changing people's health behaviors and addressing cultural beliefs have also been tough challenges in prevention. Promoting safe sex, the use of contraception, and abstention from some cultural rituals can be perceived as changing traditional gender roles for both men and women and can go against some religious values that are part of the core for some communities. The need to hide or look away from the problem of HIV/AIDS stems from the disgrace attached to the disease, which makes it difficult for people even to discuss it, much less be tested. The stigma of HIV/AIDS needs to be removed in order for prevention efforts to be accepted by the people ("Africa Matters," 2000; Akeroyd, 1997; Bartholet, 2000; Salopek, 2000; UNAIDS & WHO, 1999; King, 1999).

One project in Ghana used both the health belief model and social learning theory to examine the determinants of condom use to prevent HIV infection among youth. The authors of the study found that perceived barriers significantly interacted with perceived susceptibility and self-efficacy. Youth who perceived a high level of susceptibility to HIV infection and a low level of barriers to condom use were almost six times as likely to have used condoms at last intercourse. A high level of perceived self-efficacy and a low level of perceived barriers increased the likelihood of use three times (Adih & Alexander, 1999).

Prevention Efforts by Community and Governmental Agencies and NGOs

Uganda and Senegal have received much recognition for controlling the spread of HIV/AIDS. Both of these countries have reduced their infection rate through aggressive public education and condom promotion campaigns, expanded treatment programs for other sexually transmitted infections, and mobilization of nongovernmental organizations (NGOs). The current president of Uganda has worked to reduce the stigma for people with HIV/AIDS. Senegal reacted quickly to the threat of disease starting in the early 1990s. A survey of its citizens regarding sexual behavior, knowledge, and attitudes was conducted, followed by public education campaigns. Health officials believe the education efforts regarding AIDS have contributed to women choosing to remain virgins longer and to an increase in condom use among sex workers and men and women who have casual sex. A decrease of STIs in sex workers and pregnant women was also noted ("Africa Matters," 2000; UNAIDS & WHO, 1999; UNAIDS, 1999a).

The theory of self-efficacy has proved useful in addressing AIDS. For example, one study in South Africa found that knowledge of risk and its prevention was important, but not sufficient. The authors stress the need to improve personal autonomy in decision making about sexual behavior and condom use for both men and women through skills development programs that promote self-efficacy (Reddy, et al., 1999).

International health and development organizations have joined in the fight against AIDS in Africa. The United Nations and its specialized agencies have major programs assisting countries and communities in prevention efforts, including joining forces to accelerate the development of experimental vaccines. Academic institutions have also teamed up with local community and church organizations to create prevention projects and help organize the communities to reach more of the public. These efforts have assisted in empowering many volunteers, mostly women, to motivate others in their communities through education and increasing women's negotiation skills for safe sex or condom use (Msiza-Makhubu, 1997; UNAIDS & Wellcome Trust, 1999; World Health Organization, 1997).

There is also a growing movement of doctors in Africa working with traditional healers to do outreach and education on AIDS. As discussed earlier, traditional healers have better access to many populations. People seek their help because of tradition and lack of adequate health care (Associated Press, 2000; Green, 1994).

Antiretroviral Therapy

Globally, approximately, 3.1 million people died of HIV/AIDS or AIDS-related disease in 2004 (UNAIDS, 2004c).

Although there is no cure for HIV/AIDS at this time, the provision of antiretroviral (ARV) therapy will prolong and improve the quality of life for those suffering from this disease. In the past 10 years, various agencies, countries, and individuals have contributed resources (both human and financial) to improve HIV treatment and care options (services), namely in the form of antiretroviral drug therapy, in developing and transitional countries. Examples of donor agencies/organizations include the Global Fund to Fight AIDS, Tuberculosis, and Malaria, the U.S. President's Emergency Plan for AIDS Relief, the World Bank, the European Commission, the World Health Organization (WHO), and the Bill and Melinda Gates Foundation, to name a few. However, despite the increasing political attention paid to HIV/AIDS, and the increase in the level of financial resources available to fight this disease, the funds are not being applied in a fully effective, coordinated manner. In some instances, AIDS funding sits idle, blocked in govern-

ment bank accounts or stalled by rules of international funders (UNAIDS, 2004a; WHO, 2004).

The bureaucratic roadblocks to disseminating funds combined with the lack of knowledge about proper ARV therapy guidelines mean that more than 8,000 people are still dying daily from this easily preventable and treatable disease. Even though WHO estimates as of December 2004 were that 700,000 people had started receiving ARV therapy (up from 444,000 in July 2004) and this number represented a substantial increase compared with the 2001 estimates, coverage is still lowest in sub-Saharan Africa, where only 310,000 people were receiving treatment and 72% of the population's need for treatment are unmet. Furthermore, Nigeria and South Africa account for 41% of overall need for ARV therapy in the region. Access to antiretroviral treatment will ease the burden of those suffering from HIV/AIDS by improving their illness status (WHO, 2004; WHO et al., 2005).

The World Health Organization, through its 3 by 5 program, is one of the leaders in the effort to increase the provision of ARV therapy to people in developing and transitional countries. This program has the goal of providing 3 million people with access to antiretroviral treatment by the end of 2005. However, the 3 by 5 program is only the beginning, since the goal of 3 million represents only half of the estimated 6 million people who were living with HIV/AIDS in these countries at the end of 2003. Of the countries that have been identified as recipients of this program due to their limited resources and heavy prevalence of HIV/AIDS, sub-Saharan African has been identified as the region with the overall highest burden.

Goals of the 3 by 5 program include building capacity in these countries to disseminate information and assist with disease and treatment management. This includes increasing knowledge of ARV therapy programs within each country and improving (or building) tracking mechanisms to follow those who are receiving treatment. The 3 by 5 program uses the public health approach to train participant countries in national planning for antiretroviral therapy. This includes encouraging countries to develop and standardize ARV therapy treatment programs. This requires countries to select a single type of first-line treatment and a limited number of second-line ARV regimens and to refer those who cannot be treated in either format to specialists. In addition, it provides the ARV medicines at reduced prices. As a result, the cost of first-line treatment per person per year is now only US $150, a marked decrease compared with previous costs of US $300 or more (UNAIDS, 2004a, 2004b; WHO, 2004).

As with any international relief or assistance program, the WHO 3 by 5 program relies on long-term political support and funding. Because the most important outcome of this program is the provision of antiretroviral therapy, any reduction in, or loss of, support could have drastic results. Diminished support for ARV programs could lead to the interruption of treatment to HIV/AIDS patients. This has the potential to not only reverse the trend of improving quality of life and decreasing morbidity and mortality rates, but also to provide the HIV virus with the potential to become drug resistant. This has the potential of threatening individuals and society, because drug-resistant strains of the virus can spread and render entire treatment programs ineffective. In essence, the provision of HIV/AIDS treatment would be back at square one.

Other challenges include the shortage in Africa of health professionals, many of whom have left their countries for better opportunities in more developed, higher-income countries. In addition, a lack of health literacy is a huge challenge to effective antiretroviral treatment. In some African countries (and other developing countries), patients buy ARV medicines without medical advice and prescriptions, which leads to the potential of creating drug-resistant strains of the virus if the medicine is not taken properly. It also may mean that people desperate for treatment are taking medicines that may make them sicker or that are ineffective for their particular strain of HIV. (UNAIDS, 2004b).

The individual behaviors that place people at risk are part of larger root causes of the problem in Africa, including colonialism, big industry's design of mass labor migration, poverty, gender inequalities, and war. Ideal prevention and intervention strategies must address health behavior changes as well as economic and community barriers to the provision of social services and treatment options (Akeroyd, 1997; Bond et al., 1997; Tylor, 1871; King, 1999; UNAIDS & Wellcome Trust, 1996; WHO, 1997).

Conclusion

This has been a brief exploration of cultural and behavioral issues for international public health. Anthropology, sociology, and psychology have much greater depth in both method and theory than can be described in this chapter. There is a rich and extensive literature on health beliefs and behaviors, environmental and biological contexts, health systems, and programmatic successes and failures. It is essential to take these factors into account in considering international public health work. In addition, a program must consider structural factors, such as setting, hours, child care, and ambience, as well as factors of content, such as culturally acceptable services, which includes providers who treat patients with respect and understanding.

Research and preventive services regarding health beliefs and behaviors must accept and integrate concepts different from those of Western biomedicine, of middle- or upper-class health care providers, or of health care providers from an ethnic or cultural group that is different from their patients. This demands the ability inherent in some of the anthropological methods and approaches discussed earlier: the ability to get into someone's head and understand things from an insider perspective. There is nothing like the experience of spending time with people in their own homes or community and striving to reach that insider understanding.

● ● ● Discussion Questions

1. What prevention strategies would you develop for the prevention of AIDS if you were the minister of health of a sub-Saharan country? What would be your strategies if you were a community leader? Would these strategies differ? If yes, how? How would you address some of the cultural beliefs or traditions associated with HIV/AIDS mentioned in the case study?

2. If you were entering a community to introduce a health program, who would you talk to? What would you ask? Why?

3. What is the hot/cold illness belief system? Why is it important? How would you incorporate it into a maternal and child health program?

4. Many people believe that healers such as midwives and shamans are called to their profession by a greater spiritual power. What significance does this have for official health programs around the world? How should they address this belief?

5. If an indigenous practice seems peculiar to you, but does no apparent harm, what should you do?

6. How could you learn what people in a community really believe about health and illness?

● ● ● **References**

Abdullah, A., & Husten, C. (2004). Promotion of smoking cessation in developing countries: A framework for urgent public health interventions. *Thorax, 59,* 623–630.

Adams, R. N. (1955). A nutritional research program in Guatemala. In B. D. Paul (Ed.), *Health, culture, and community* (pp. 435–458). New York: Russell Sage Foundation.

Adih, W. K., & Alexander, C. S. (1999). Determinants of condom use to prevent HIV infection among youth in Ghana. *Journal of Adolescent Health, 24*(1), 63–72.

Africa matters: Interview with U.S. ambassador to the United Nations, Richard Holbrooke. (2000, January 17). *Newsweek.*

Ajzen, I., & Fishbein, M. (1972). Attitudes and normative beliefs as factors influencing behavioral intentions. *Journal of Personality and Social Psychology, 21*(1), 1–9.

Akeroyd, A. V. (1977). Sociocultural aspects of AIDS in Africa: Occupational and gender issues. In G. C. Bond, J. Kreniske, I. Susser, & J. Vincent (Eds.), *AIDS in Africa and the Caribbean.* Boulder, CO: Westview Press.

Alland, A. (1970). *Adaptation in cultural evolution: An approach to medical anthropology.* New York: Columbia University Press.

Anderson, L. M., Scrimshaw, M. T., & Fullilove, M. T., Fielding, J. E., and Task Force on Community Preventive Services. (2003a) The community guide's model for linking the social environment to health. *American Journal of Preventive Medicine, 24*(35), 12–20.

Anderson, L. M., Fielding, J. E., Fullilove, M. T., Scrimshaw, S. C., Carande-Kulis, V. G., & Task Force on Community Preventive Services. (2003b). Methods for conducting systematic reviews of the evidence of effectiveness and economic efficiency of interventions to promote healthy social environments. *American Journal of Preventive Medicine, 24*(53), 25–31.

Associated Press. (2000, February 8). Conference stresses uses for traditional healers in AIDS battle. Retrieved from http://www.intelihealth.com/IH/ihtIH/EMIHc000/333/333/268121/html.

Bandura, A. (1977). *Social learning theory.* Englewood Cliffs, NJ: Prentice Hall.

Bandura, A. (1989). Human agency in social cognitive theory. *American Psychologist, 44,* 1175–1184.

Bartholet, J. (2000, January 17). The plague years. *Newsweek.*

Beals, A. R. (1976). Strategies of resort to curers in south India. In C. Leslie (Ed.), *Asian medical systems: A comparative study* (pp. 184–200). Berkeley, CA: University of California Press.

Bhuyan, K. (2004). Health promotion through self-care and community participation: Elements of a proposed programme in the development countries. *BMC Public Health, 4,* 11. Retrieved from http://www.biomedcentral. com/1471-2458/4/11.

Bond, G. C., Kreniske, J., Susser, I., & Vincent, J. (1997). The anthropology of AIDS in Africa and the Caribbean. In G. C. Bond, J. Kreniske, I. Susser, & J. Vincent (Eds.), *AIDS in Africa and the Caribbean* (pp. 3–9). Boulder, CO: Westview Press.

Buckley, T., & Gottlieb, A. (Eds.). (1988). *Blood magic.* Berkeley, CA: University of California Press.

Carballo, M., & Siem, H. (1996). Migration, migration policy and AIDS. In M. Knipe & R. Rector (Eds.), *Crossing borders: Migration, ethnicity and AIDS* (pp. 31–48). London: Taylor and Francis.

Chambers, R. (1992). Rapid but relaxed and participatory rural appraisal: Towards applications in health and nutrition. In N. S. Scrimshaw & G. R. Gleason (Eds.), *Rapid assessment procedures: Qualitative methodologies for planning and evaluation of health related programmes* (pp. 295–305). Boston: International Nutrition Foundation for Developing Countries.

Chen, K.-H., & Murray, G. F. (1976). Truths and untruths in village Haiti: An experiment in third world survey research. In J. F. Marshall & S. Polgar (Eds.), *Culture, natality, and family planning* (pp. 241–262). Chapel Hill, NC: Carolina Population Center.

Chicago Project for Violence Prevention (CPVP) (2005). http://www.ceasefirechicago.org.

Commission on Human Security. (2003). People caught up in violent conflict. In *Human security now* (Chapter 2). New York: Commission on Human Security. Retrieved from http://www.humansecurity-chs.org/ finalreport/.

Community Outreach Intervention Projects (COIP). http://www.uic.edu/research_community_coip.htm.

Foster, G. M. (1953). Relationships between Spanish and Spanish-American folk medicine. *Journal of American Folklore, 66,* 201–217.

Freed, S. A., & Freed, R. S. (1967). Spirit possession as illness in a north Indian village. In J. Middleton (Ed.), *Magic, witchcraft, and curing* (pp. 295–320). Garden City, NY: Natural History Press.

Gadjusek, D. C., Gibbs, C. J., & Alpers, M. (1967). Transmission and passage of experimental 'kuru' to chimpanzees. *Science, 155,* 212–214.

Garro, L. (1996). Intracultural variation in causal accounts of diabetes: A comparison of three Canadian Anishinaabe (Okubway) communities. *Culture, Medicine and Psychiatry, 20,* 381–420.

Garro, L. (2000). Remembering what one knows and the construction of the past: A comparison of cultural consensus theory and cultural schema theory. *Ethos, 28,* 275–319.

Garro, L. (2001). Cultural, social and self processes in narrating trouble experiences. In C. Mattingly and U. Jensen (Eds.), *Narrative and Society* (pp. 165–196). Dordrecht, Holland: Reidel.

Good, B. J., & Good, M. J. D. (1981). The meaning of symptoms: A cultural hermeneutic model for clinical practice. In L. Eisenberg & A. Kleinman (Eds.), *The relevance of social science for medicine* (pp. 165–196). Dordrecht, Holland: Reidel.

Green, E. (1994). *AIDS and STDs in Africa: Bridging the gap between traditional healing and modern medicine.* Boulder, CO: Westview Press.

Green, L., Kreuter, M., Deeds, S., & Partridge, K. (1980). *Health education planning: A diagnostic approach.* Palo Alto, CA: Mayfield.

Gwaltney, J. L. (1970). *The thrice shy.* New York: Columbia University Press.

Hjelm, K., Nyberg, P., Isacsson, A., & Apelqvist, J. (1999). Beliefs about health and illness essential for self-care practice: A comparison of migrant Yugoslavian and Swedish diabetic females. *Journal of Advanced Nursing, 30*(5), 1147–1159.

Hughes, C. (1990). Ethnopsychiatry. In T. M. Johnson & C. E. Sargent (Eds.), *Medical anthropology: Contemporary theory and method.* New York: Praeger Publishers.

Hunt, C. W. (1989). Migration labor and sexually transmitted diseases: AIDS in Africa. *Journal of Health in Social Science Behavior, 30,* 353–373.

Institute of Medicine, Board on Neuroscience and Behavioral Health. (2002). *Speaking of health: Assessing health communication strategies for diverse populations.* Washington, DC: National Academies Press.

Institute of Medicine, Committee on Health Literacy. (2004). *Health literacy: A prescription to end confusion.* Washington, DC: National Academies Press.

Kendall, C., Foote, D., & Martorell, R. (1983). Anthropology, communications, and health: The mass media and health practices program in Honduras. *Human Organization, 42,* 353–360.

King, R. (1999). *Sexual behavior change for HIV: Where have theories taken us?* Geneva, Switzerland: UNAIDS.

Kleinman, A. (1980). *Patients and healers in the context of culture.* Berkeley, CA: University of California Press.

Kleinman, A. (1986). *Social origins of distress and disease.* New Haven, CT: Yale University Press.

Kleinman, A. (1988). *The illness narratives.* New York: Basic Books.

Lindenbaum, S. (1971). Sorcery and structure in Fore society. *Oceania, 41,* 277–287.

Logan, M. H. (1972). Humoral folk medicine: A potential aid in controlling pellagra in Mexico. *Ethnomedizin, 4,* 397–410.

Martiniuk, A., O'Connor, K., & King, W. (2003). A cluster randomized trial of a sex education programme in Belize, Central America. *International Journal of Epidemiology, 32*, 131–136.

Matsudo, S., Matsudo, V., Arugo, T., Andrade, D., Andrade, E., de Oliveira, L., & Braggion, G. (2003). The Agita São Paulo Program as a model for using physical activity to promote health. *Pan American Journal of Public Health, 14*(4), 265–272.

Messersmith, L. J. (1991). *The women of good times and Baba's place: The multi-dimensionality of the lives of commercial sex workers in Bamako, Mali.* Unpublished doctoral dissertation, University of California at Los Angeles.

Msiza-Makhubu, S. B. (1997). *Peer education and support for AIDS prevention among women in South Africa.* Unpublished doctoral dissertation, University of Illinois at Chicago.

Murray, G. F. (1976). *Women in perdition: Ritual fertility control in Haiti.* In J. F. Marshall & S. Polgar (Eds.), *Culture, natality, and family planning* (pp. 59–78). Chapel Hill, NC: Carolina Population Center.

Norr, K., Norr, J., McElmurray, B., Tlou, S., & Moeti, M. (2004). Impact of peer group education on HIV prevention among women in Botswana. *Health Care for Women International, 25*, 210–226.

O'Connor, B. (1995). *Healing traditions.* Philadelphia: University of Pennsylvania Press.

Ouellet, L. J., Huo, D., & Bailey, S. L. (2004). HIV risk practices among needle exchange users and non-users in Chicago. *Journal of Acquired Immune Deficiency Syndrome, 37*(1), 1187–1196.

Parsons, T. (1948). Illness and the role of the physician. In C. Kluckholm & H. Murray (Eds.), *Personality in nature, society, and culture.* New York: Alfred A. Knopf.

Paul, B. D. (Ed.). (1955). *Health, culture, and community.* New York: Russell Sage Foundation.

Pelto, P. J., & Pelto, G. H. (1978). *Anthropological research: The structure of inquiry.* New York: Cambridge University Press.

Perry, H., Shanklin, D., & Schroeder, D. (2003). Impact of a community-based comprehensive pri-

mary healthcare programme on infant and child mortality in Bolivia. *Journal of Health, Population, and Nutrition, 21*(4), 383–395.

Polgar, S., & Marshall, J. F. (1976). The search for culturally acceptable fertility regulating methods. In J. F. Marshall & S. Polgar (Eds.), *Culture, natality and family planning* (pp. 204–218). Chapel Hill, NC: Carolina Population Center.

Prochaska, J., DiClemente, C., & Norcross, J. (1992). In search of how people change: Applications to addictive behaviors. *American Psychologist, 47*, 1102–1104.

Ratzan, S. C., & Parker, R. M. (2000). Introduction. In C. R. Selden, M. Zorn, S. C. Ratzan, & R. M. Parker (Eds.), *Health literacy* (National Library of Medicine Publication No. CBM 2000-1). Bethesda, MD: National Institutes of Health.

Reddy, P., Meyer-Weitz, A., van den Borne, G., & Kok, G. (1999). STD-related knowledge, beliefs and attitudes of Xhosa-speaking patients attending STD primary health-care clinics in South Africa. *International Journal of Sexually Transmitted Diseases and AIDS, 10*(6), 392–400.

Reichel-Dolmatoff, G., & Reichel-Dolmatoff, A. (1961). *The people of Aritama.* London: Routledge and Kegan Paul.

Rekart, M. (2002). Sex in the city: Sexual behaviour, societal change, and STDs in Saigon. *Sexually Transmitted Infections, 78*(suppl I), i47–i54.

Rogers, E. M. (1973). *Communication strategies for family planning.* New York: Free Press.

Rogers, E. M. (1983). *Diffusion of innovations* (3rd ed.). New York: Free Press.

Rogers, E. M., & Shoemaker, F. F. (1972). *Communication of innovations* (2nd ed). New York: Free Press.

Rosenstock , I., Strecher, V., & Becker, M. (1974). Social learning theory and the health belief model. *Health Education Monograph, 2*, 328–386.

Rubel, A. J., & Haas, M. R. (1990). Ethnomedicine. In T. J. Johnson & C. D. Sargent

(Eds.), *Medical anthropology: Contemporary theory and method* (pp. 115–131). New York: Praeger.

Rubel, A. J., O'Nell, C. W., & Collado-Ardon, R. (1984). *Susto: A folk illness.* Berkeley, CA: University of California Press.

Rubenstein, R. A., Scrimshaw, S. C., & Morrissey, S. (2000). Classification and process in sociomedical understanding: Towards a multilevel view of sociomedical methodology. In G. L. Albrecht, R. Fitzpatrick, & S. C. Scrimshaw (Eds.), *The handbook of social studies in health and medicine* (pp. 36–49). London: Sage Publications.

Salopek, P. (2000, January 10). We die lying to ourselves. *Chicago Tribune.*

Scrimshaw, S. C. M. (1974). *Culture, environment, and family size: A study of urban in-migrants in Guayaquil, Ecuador.* Unpublished doctoral dissertation, Columbia University, New York.

Scrimshaw, S. C. M. (1992). Adaptation of anthropological methodologies to rapid assessment of nutrition and primary health care. In N. S. Scrimshaw & G. R. Gleason (Eds.), *Rapid assessment procedures: Qualitative methodologies for planning and evaluation of health related programmes* (pp. 25–49). Boston: International Nutrition Foundation for Developing Countries.

Scrimshaw, S. C. M., Carballo, M., Carael, M., Ramos, L., & Parker, R. G. (1992). *HIV/AIDS rapid assessment procedures: Rapid anthropological approaches for studying AIDS related beliefs, attitudes and behaviors.* Tokyo: United Nations University.

Scrimshaw, S. C. M., Carballo, M., Ramos, L., & Blair, B. A. (1991). The AIDS rapid anthropological assessment procedures: A tool for health education planning and evaluation. *Health Education Quarterly, 18*(1), 111–123.

Scrimshaw, S. C. M., & Hurtado, E. (1987). *Rapid assessment procedures for nutrition and primary health care: Anthropological approaches to improving program effectiveness (RAP).* Tokyo: United Nations University.

Scrimshaw, S. C. M., & Hurtado, E. (1988). Anthropological involvement in the Central American diarrheal disease control project. *Social Science and Medicine, 27*(1), 97–105.

Scrimshaw, S. C., & Pasquariella, B. G. (1970). Obstacles to sterilization in one community. *Family Planning Perspectives, 2*(4), 40–42.

Sutton, S., McVey, D., & Glanz, A. (1999). A comparative test of the theory of reasoned action and the theory of planned behavior in the prediction of condom use intentions in a national sample of English young people. *Health Psychology, 18*(1), 72–81.

Thevos, A., Quick, R., & Yanduli, V. (2000). Motivational interviewing enhances the adoption of water disinfection practices in Zambia. *Health Promotion International, 15*(3), 207–214.

Topley, M. (1976). Chinese traditional etiology and methods of cure in Hong Kong. In C. Leslie (Ed.), *Asian medical systems: A comparative study* (pp. 243–265). Berkeley, CA: University of California Press.

Tylor, E. B. (1871). *Primitive culture.* London: J. Murray.

UNAIDS. (1996b, May 6–8). HIV/AIDS in Africa: Socio-economic impact and response. Joint conference of African ministers of finance and ministers of economic development and planning. Addis-Abada, Ethiopia. Retrieved from http://www.unaids.org/publications/ graphics/addis/sld001.htm.

UNAIDS. (1999a). *Acting early to prevent AIDS: The case of Senegal.* Geneva, Switzerland: Author.

UNAIDS. (2004a). *AIDS epidemic update: 2004.* Geneva, Switzerland: Author. Retrieved from http://www.unaids.org/wad2004/EPIupdate2004_ html_en/epi04_00_en.htm.

UNAIDS. (2004b). *2004 report on the global HIV/AIDS epidemic: 4th global report.* Geneva, Switzerland: Author. Retrieved from http://www.unaids.org/bangkok2004/ GAR2004_html/GAR2004_00_en.htm.

UNAIDS. (2004c). *AIDS epidemic update: 2004.* Retrieved July 13, 2005, from http://www.unaids .org/wad2004/report_pdf.html.

UNAIDS & Wellcome Trust Centre for the Epidemiology of Infectious Disease. (1999). *Trends in HIV incidence and prevalence: Natural course of the epidemic or results of behavioural change?* Geneva, Switzerland: UNAIDS.

UNAIDS & World Health Organization. (1999). *AIDS epidemic update: December 1999.* Geneva, Switzerland: World Health Organization.

Weir, S. S., Pailman, C., Mahlalela, X., Coetzee, N., Meidany, F., & Boerma, J. T. (2003). From people to places: Focusing AIDS prevention efforts where it matters most. *AIDS, 17*(6), 895–903.

Weller, S. C. (1983). New data on intracultural variability: The hot-cold concept of medicine and illness. *Human Organization, 42,* 249–257.

Wellin, E. (1955). Water boiling in a Peruvian town. In B. D. Paul (Ed.), *Health, culture, and community* (pp. 71–103). New York: Russell Sage Foundation.

World Health Organization. (1997). *Women and HIV/AIDS prevention training manual.* Geneva, Switzerland: Author.

World Health Organization. (2004). *Investing in a comprehensive health sector response to HIV/AIDS: Scaling up treatment and accelerating prevention. WHO HIV/AIDS plan.* Geneva, Switzerland: Author. Retrieved from http://www .who.int/entity/3by5/en/ HIV_AIDSplan.pdf.

World Health Organization, UNAIDS, Global Fund, & U.S. Government. (2005). 700,000 people living with AIDS in developing countries now receiving treatment [Joint media release]. Retrieved from http://www.who.int/ mediacentre/news/ releases/2005/pr07/en.

Young, C. J. (1981). *Medical choice in a Mexican village.* New Brunswick, NJ: Rutgers University Press.

Reproductive Health

JANE MENKEN AND M. OMAR RAHMAN

Reproductive health in low- and middle-income countries has long been addressed primarily through family planning and maternal and child health programs and through programs to prevent and treat sexually transmitted infections (STIs) and their consequences. HIV/AIDS prevention and treatment is increasingly essential in addressing this area of international health.

Reproductive health is tied to policy concerns about population growth as well as health. In 1994, the United Nations (UN) sponsored the third decennial International Conference on Population and Development (ICPD) in Cairo. The previous two conferences had emphasized family planning and economic development, respectively, as the major focus of population policy—policy that was intended to reduce fertility and, thereby, population growth. The rationale for support of family planning programs included both the right of individuals to control their own fertility and the belief that reduced fertility would lead to reduced population growth, which would have benefits for individuals, nations, and the world. For the first time, in 1994, women's health advocates, many from nongovernmental organizations (NGOs), played a key role in the ICPD and brought to the fore issues of reproductive health that went beyond family planning. They called for a fundamental redefinition of population policy that focused on the status of women and gave "prominence to reproductive health and the empowerment of women while downplaying the demographic rationale for population policy" (McIntosh & Finkle, 1995, p. 223).

The 1994 ICPD adopted a Programme of Action that included the following as its definition of reproductive health:

> Reproductive health is a state of complete physical, mental and social well being, and not merely the absence of disease or infirmity, in all matters relating to the reproductive system and its processes. Reproductive health therefore implies that people are able to have a satisfying and safe sex life and that they have the capability to reproduce and the freedom to decide if, when, and how often to do so. Implicit in this last condition are the right of men and women to be informed and to have access to safe, effective, affordable and acceptable methods of family planning of their choice, as well as other methods of their choice for the regulation of fertility which are not against the law, and the right of access to appropriate health-care services that enable women to go safely through pregnancy and childbirth and provide couples with the best chance of having a healthy infant . . . It also includes sexual health, the purpose of which is the enhancement of life and personal relations, and not merely counseling and care related to reproduction and sexually transmitted diseases (United Nations, 1994).

This vision of reproductive health has, not unexpectedly, proved controversial and has not been achieved to the extent hoped for by its proponents (see, for example, "Population Control Measures," 1999; "Conference Adopts Plan," 1999). Nor have donors met the pledges made at the Cairo conference. The UN estimated in 2003 that the international donor community had contributed far less than the pledges for reproductive health made at Cairo. Of the $6.1 billion promised by 2005, just over $3 billion had been provided through 2003 (Population Reference Bureau, 2004; United Nations Commission on Population and Development, 2004).

A less controversial and more limited version of the vision for reproductive health guided the 1997 U.S. National Academy of Sciences report on reproductive health (Tsui, Wasserheit, & Haaga, 1997):

1. Every sex act should be free of coercion and infection.

2. Every pregnancy should be intended.

3. Every birth should be healthy for both mother and child.

Even so, no country, according to Tsui, Wasserheit, and Haaga (1997), had met these more limited goals by 1997, and the problems were greatest in the low- and middle-income countries.

In 2000, the United Nations Millennium Declaration was adopted as a commitment to "making the right to development a reality for everyone and to freeing the entire human race from want (United Nations General Assembly, 2000; United Nations Statistics Division, 2002). Eight Millennium Development Goals (MDGs) were established as part of the Roadmap toward the Implementation of the United Nations Millennium Declaration (United Nations General Assembly, 2001). Goal 5 is to improve maternal health with a specific target of reducing "by three quarters, between 1990 and 2015, the maternal mortality ratio." In mid-2005, the UN found little change in maternal mortality had occurred in sub-Saharan Africa and Southern Asia. Only in countries with moderate to low levels of maternal mortality in 1990 had there been significant improvement (United Nations Statistics Division, 2005a).

This chapter emphasizes both the older and the newer views of family planning and reproductive health. In the section on demographic trends, the focus is on population growth and change and the transitions under way around the world from situations of high fertility and high mortality to those of low fertility and low mortality. How people control their fertility and indices of the effects of various fertility determinants on overall fertility in a range of countries are then considered. The third section examines family planning programs and their role in the reduction of fertility and unintended pregnancy. The next two sections consider the role of fertility patterns in the health of children and women. The final section presents brief recommendations for future research and programs. Because Chapter 4 includes STIs and HIV/AIDS, these crucial aspects of reproductive health are only briefly mentioned here.

Demographic Trends and Fertility Determinants

History of Population Growth

To understand the context of the concerns about population and reproductive health in the world today, it is instructive to review the history of population growth and its associated impacts. Figure 3-1 shows the growth of world population and, in particular, the extraordinary changes of the past 200 years. World population reached 1 billion just after 1800. By the turn of the 20th century it had reached 1.6 billion, and before 1930 it had surpassed 2 billion. It had taken less than 125 years to add the second billion people, compared with the long sweep of history needed to reach the first billion. Population passed the 3 billion mark in 1960. Each additional billion has taken less time to add, so that, by mid-2000, population had reached 6 billion. Population had doubled between 1960 and 2000, adding 3 billion people in only 40 years (United Nations Population Division, 2005; Figure 3-1). The majority of this expansion has taken place in the low- and middle-income regions of Asia, Africa, Latin America, and Oceania (Figure 3-2), which accounted for 83% of the world's population in 2000, compared with 71% in 1950. The share of world population in these regions is expected to continue increasing, reaching 88% in the middle of the 21st century (United Nations Population Division, 2005).

The encouraging news is that the rate at which the world's population is growing has declined continuously since about 1960 (Figure 3-3), although the absolute *number* of people added in each decade has continued to increase. Only after 2000 was that number projected to decline. Population growth rates are declining in most of the low- and middle-income countries, but at an uneven pace, with some countries and regions experiencing much more rapid change than others. China is a particularly prominent example; its growth rate was 2.1% in 1960, increased to 2.6% in 1965, and steadily dropped to below 1% by 1995. The UN estimates that world population in the middle of the 21st century will be between 8 and 11 billion people. By that time, the growth rate will be well under 1% but will not yet have achieved the situation of no growth. Because of reduced fertility and increased life expectancy, the 2050 population will have more people over 60 than children under 15. As of 2005, 10% were over 60 and 28% under 15, but world population will continue to age, so that 22% are expected to be over 60 in 2050, while only 20% will be under 15 (United Nations Population Division, 2005).

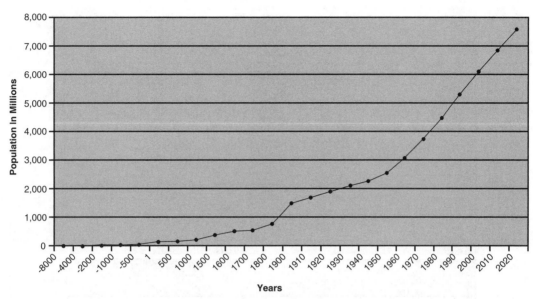

Figure 3-1 The Growth of Population and, in Particular, the Extraordinary Changes of the Past 200 Years. *Source:* Data for the years -8000 to 1900 from U.S. Census Bureau, Population Division, International Programs Center (http://www.census.gov/ipc/www/worldhis.html), and for the years 1910-2020 from United Nations Population Division, *World Population Prospects: The 2004 Revision Population Database* (http://esa.un.org/unpp/). Accessed June 22, 2005.

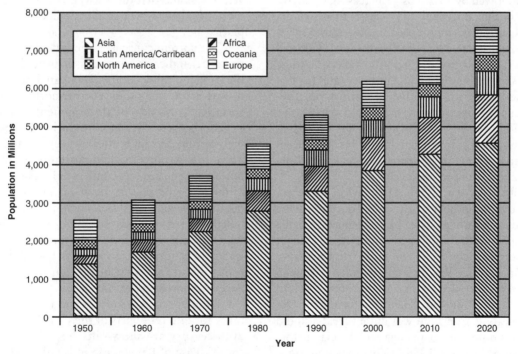

Figure 3-2 Population Size by Continent, 1950–2020. *Source:* Data from United Nations Population Division, *World Population Prospects: The 2004 Revision Population Database* (http://esa.un.org/unpp/). Accessed June 22, 2005.

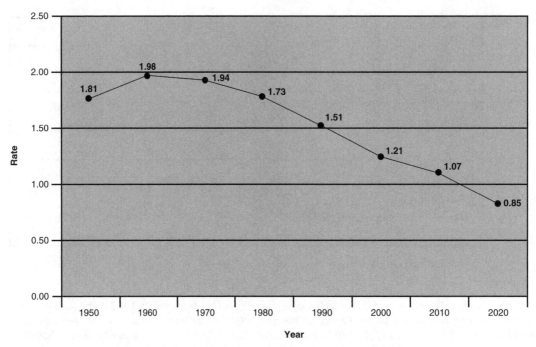

Figure 3-3 World Population Growth Rate: 1950–2020. *Source:* Data from United Nations Population Division, *World Population Prospects: The 2004 Revision Population Database* (http://esa.un.org/unpp/). Accessed June 22, 2005.

The Demographic Transition

What explains the historic experience of low initial growth followed by an explosive increase and, finally, a steady decline in growth? The classic theory of demographic transition proposed by Notestein (1953) and others postulated that all societies initially started off with high fertility and high mortality. At some point in societal development, mortality rates fell due to public health advances, while fertility rates remained high. This combination resulted in explosive population growth, with birth rates far exceeding death rates, until at some point birth rates also started to decline and a new equilibrium was reached at low fertility and low mortality levels.

Until fairly recently, the classic theory of demographic transition held sway, and all societies were supposed to go through it in a lock-step manner. In the early to mid-1970s, however, an international team of researchers participated in the Princeton University European Fertility Project and carefully examined historical fertility decline in Europe. They came to the somewhat surprising conclusion that the process of demographic transition was quite varied and did not always follow the path suggested by classic theory (Coale & Watkins, 1986). Under that scenario, a certain level of socioeconomic development was required for the initial mortality decline, which was followed, at some later point, by fertility decline.

Instead, the project found that mortality decline took place in different societies at different levels of development and that there was no magic threshold of mortality above which fertility decline would not take place.

The current consensus about demographic transition is that there is no specific sequence in which fertility and mortality decline. They can decline together, or one before the other. Furthermore, there are no specific thresholds of development required for either process to start. Finally, the interval between a high-fertility and high-mortality regime and a subsequent low-fertility and low-mortality regime is also not fixed and can vary considerably. The experience of the low- and middle-income countries has borne out this new consensus. Demographic transitions have taken place at different rates in different places and with different sequences; a common thread, however, is that the transition has often been considerably more rapid than those seen in the European or North American historical record.

Population growth rates and fertility and mortality for different parts of the world since the mid-20th century are shown in Table 3-1 and for the specific case of Bangladesh in Exhibit 3-1. Growth rates are given as percent change in population per year for the 5 years subsequent to the specified date. When a population stops changing in size, it be-

Table 3-1	Growth Rate, Total Fertility Rate, and Life Expectancy for Regions of the World, by Time Period					
Region	1950	1970	1990	2000	2010[a]	2020[a]
World						
Growth rate	1.81	1.94	1.51	1.21	1.07	0.85
TFR	5.02	4.49	3.04	2.65	2.46	2.31
Life expectancy	46.6	58.1	63.7	65.4	67.7	70.0
Less Developed Regions						
Growth rate	2.09	2.37	1.79	1.43	1.26	0.99
TFR	6.17	5.44	3.41	2.9	2.63	2.41
Life expectancy	41.1	54.8	61.5	63.4	65.9	68.4
More Developed Regions						
Growth rate	1.2	0.77	0.44	0.3	0.18	0.07
TFR	2.84	2.12	1.68	1.56	1.61	1.67
Life expectancy	66.1	71.4	74.0	75.6	77.0	78.8
Asia						
Growth rate	1.96	2.25	1.59	1.21	1.04	0.75
TFR	5.89	5.08	2.96	2.47	2.26	2.09
Life expectancy	41.4	56.4	64.0	67.3	70.2	72.5
Africa						
Growth rate	2.21	2.69	2.57	2.18	2.05	1.81
TFR	6.72	6.72	5.67	4.97	4.35	3.68
Life expectancy	38.4	46.7	50.8	49.1	51.8	55.9
Latin America & Caribbean						
Growth rate	2.56	2.46	1.72	1.42	1.15	0.87
TFR	5.89	5.05	3.03	2.55	2.26	2.06
Life expectancy	51.4	60.9	68.3	71.5	74.0	76.0
Oceania						
Growth rate	2.15	1.61	1.52	1.32	1.08	0.95
TFR	3.87	3.23	2.53	2.32	2.18	2.1
Life expectancy	60.4	65.8	71.5	74.0	76.2	77.9
Northern America						
Growth rate	1.71	0.97	1.08	0.97	0.84	0.68
TFR	3.47	2.01	1.99	1.99	1.93	1.83
Life expectancy	68.8	71.6	75.5	77.6	78.8	79.9
Europe						
Growth rate	0.99	0.59	0.18	−0.00	−0.13	−0.22
TFR	2.66	2.16	1.57	1.4	1.47	1.59
Life expectancy	65.6	71.0	72.6	73.7	75.0	77.0

Note: Growth rate (% per year), TFR, and life expectancy are for the subsequent 5-year period (e.g., 1950–1955). Life expectancy is for both sexes combined.

[a]Figures for 2010 and 2020 are from the medium-variant projection.

Source: Data from United Nations Population Division, *World Population Prospects: The 2004 Revision Population Database* (http://esa.un.org/unpp/). Accessed June 22, 2005.

comes stationary and its growth rate is zero. The *total fertility rate* (TFR) is the number of children women would bear, on average, if they lived to the end of the reproductive period under the childbearing pattern of a particular year (e.g., if they had, at age 15, the birth rate of 15-year-olds in 1970; at age 16, the birth rate of 16-year-olds in 1970; and so on).

Life expectancy at birth is the average number of years people would live if their entire lives were spent under the mortality conditions of a particular year (e.g., if they experienced the infant mortality of 1970, the death rate at age 1 of 1970, and so on). The numbers resulting from these examples would be the 1970 TFR and the 1970 life

| Exhibit 3-1 | Demographic Change in Bangladesh |

Bangladesh will be used as a case study throughout this chapter for a number of reasons. First it has experienced high population growth rates that were the result of continuing high fertility during a period when mortality was declining. At mid-century, life expectancy was under 40 years for both men and women and, in fact, was higher for males until the early 1990s. By that time, almost 20 years had been added to life expectancy, which was 56.36 years for both sexes. In 2004, life expectancy was around 62 for both sexes. Second, in the last quarter of the 20th century, the total fertility rate in Bangladesh dropped remarkably, from about 6.2 in 1970–1975 to 3.4 in the early 1990s. Fertility subsequently has plateaued at around 3 for the last decade. This situation may be described as a *stalled* fertility transition. As a consequence of the decline in mortality, the growth rate rose from 1.9% at mid-century to 2.3% for 1975–1980. The subsequent fertility decline caused the growth rate to decline to 2.0% for 1995–2000, and 1.9% for 2000–2004. Growth at this level, continued over many years, leads to a population doubling in size in only 43 to 46 years. And, finally, the Bangladesh fertility decline was accomplished in the context of a strong family planning program, which benefited from unusual systematic research efforts that were intended to improve the design of the program and delivery of services that were appropriate to the specific context of Bangladesh.

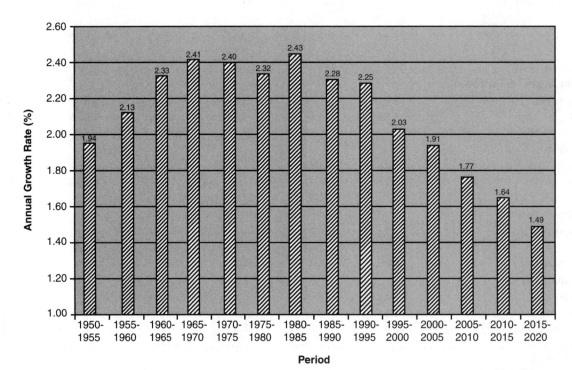

Period

Bangladesh Population Growth Rate (%)

Source: Data from United Nations Population Division, *World Population Prospects: The 2004 Revision Population Database* (http://esa.un.org/unpp/). Accessed June 22, 2005.

(continued)

Exhibit 3-1 | Continued

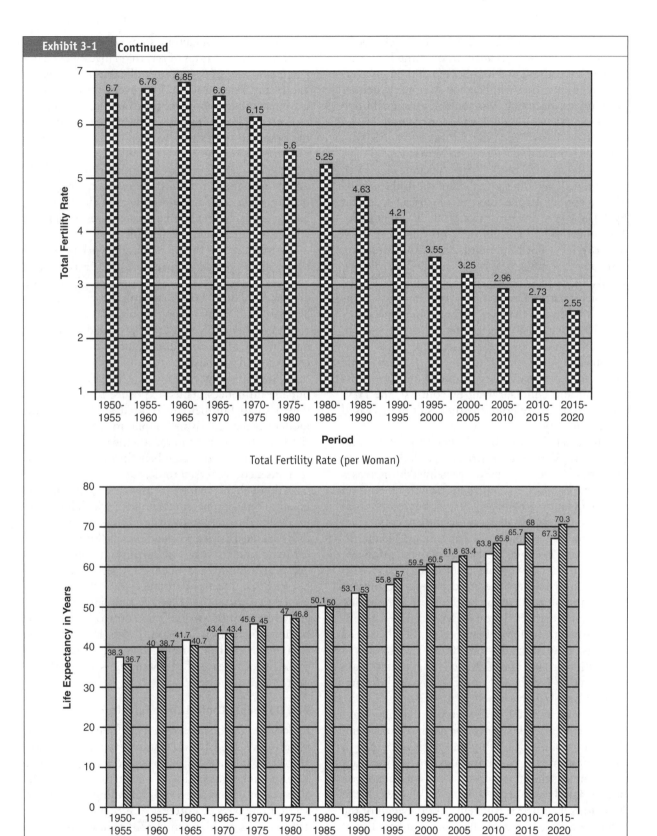

Total Fertility Rate (per Woman)

expectancy. A TFR of about 2.1 is usually referred to as *replacement-level fertility*. If, over the long run, women have about that number of children on average, the population will become stationary, neither growing nor declining. Women will be contributing to the next generation one child for themselves and one for their partner, and a bit more for girls who were born but did not survive to reproduce.

As shown in Table 3-1, life expectancy has risen continuously over the latter half of the 20th century. The exceptions are the countries of Africa hardest hit by AIDS, where disease is wiping out all earlier gains. Ten countries had an adult HIV prevalence of 10% or more in 2003: Swaziland, Botswana, Lesotho, Zimbabwe, South Africa, Namibia, Zambia, Malawi, Central African Republic, and Mozambique (United Nations Statistics Division, 2005b). The U.S. Census Bureau estimates that, on average, life expectancy in 2010 will be 30.5 years less in these countries than it would have been in the absence of AIDS (U.S. Census Bureau, 2002). Much of the increase in life expectancy in every country is due to improvements in infant and child survival; by contrast, the HIV-related declines are primarily the result of increased adult mortality.

Total fertility rate had declined by 1970 in all parts of the world except Africa. That decline was, in less industrialized regions, overwhelmed by increases in life expectancy, so that their growth rates—and their population growth—increased. But fertility continued to fall, and to do so sufficiently to counteract the continuing increased life expectancy. This fertility transition is serving to bring growth rates down in all low- and middle-income regions today. HIV/AIDS may be contributing to recent declines in fertility in the hardest hit parts of the world; there is mounting evidence that infected women have reduced fecundity (Gray et al., 1998; Lewis et al., 2004; United Nations Population Division, 2002). The changes in population growth rate, TFR, and life expectancy are illustrated in Exhibit 3-1, which provides information for Bangladesh from 1950 to 2020.

To understand the different types of fertility transitions that have taken place, we need to understand the determinants of fertility and fertility change in different contexts. There is an extensive literature that examines the impact of socioeconomic factors on desired family size (e.g., Bankole & Westoff, 1995; Bulatao & Lee, 1983; Rutstein, 1998). Much of the discussion is centered on the costs and benefits of children and the notion that couples desire additional children as long as the benefits are greater than the costs. These benefits and costs are, in turn, deter-mined by a range of factors, some of which are structural (e.g., wages, rates of return on investments, opportunity costs) and some attitudinal (e.g., changes in values and expectations). Improvements in the educational status of women, for example, are thought to decrease desired family size because they increase the potential wages that women can earn and thus raise the opportunity costs of childbearing and child rearing. Education may, in addition, lead to attitudinal change about trade-offs between quantity and quality when considering numbers of children (e.g., having fewer children so that greater investment in the education of each child is feasible).

Implicit in this theoretical framework is the idea that couples weigh a variety of alternatives, with childbearing being just one of the possible behavioral choices available. Other structural factors include changes such as increasing landlessness, which decreases the benefits of the labor provided by children and thereby tends to reduce family sizes. More recent research emphasizes attitudinal change. It posits that values and expectations can change as a result of outside influences. Thus, exposure to messages in which small families are treated as a marker for modernity may motivate couples to reduce their desired family sizes even in the absence of any changes in the structural costs and benefits of children. This remains a controversial topic.

Although this chapter focuses on low- and middle-income countries, in almost none of which has fertility declined to replacement level, it is worth noting that the industrialized world, especially Europe, is concerned about its very low fertility and population decline. For Europe as a whole, TFR declined below 1.9 before 1980 and has continued to decline. It is expected that the entire continent will have a negative growth rate for the period from 2000 to 2020 (United Nations Population Division, 2005). Understanding what maintains below-replacement fertility and what causes it to increase is an important issue for the industrialized countries.

How Do People Control Their Fertility?

In addition to considering *why* people control their fertility, we need to understand *how* people actually do so. It is useful first to consider the *proximate determinants* that lead to variation in fertility in the absence of deliberate family planning (Bongaarts, 1978; Bongaarts & Potter, 1983; Menken & Kuhn, 1996; Sheps & Menken, 1973). These proximate determinants can be divided into those that affect the *reproductive span* and those that influence the *intervals between successive births* within that span. As shown in Figure 3-4, the *effective reproductive span* exists within boundaries set by both the *biological* and the *social reproductive spans*. The former, the *biological reproductive span*, is the time during which a woman is capable of childbearing because she has the biological capacity to ovulate and to carry a pregnancy to a live birth. It is usually marked by menarche and menopause, but the first ovulation may occur well after menarche and last ovulation precedes menopause.

However, in no society do women devote their full biological span to reproduction. Were they to do so, according to Bongaarts (1978), women who survived to sterility would bear over 15 children on average. This figure is well beyond the maximum ever recorded for any population. Every society has social controls on the initiation and cessation of sexual activity. We will refer to entry into sexual activity as *marriage* and cessation as *marriage dissolution*. We use these terms as social markers rather than to represent legal ceremonies and arrangements of the state. Specifically, marriage dissolution can occur through breakup of the relationship or through widowhood. The *social reproductive span* is, therefore, the interval between initiation and cessation of sexual activity. The *effective reproductive span* is the overlap of the biological and the social spans. It begins with the later of menarche and marriage and ends with the earliest of sterility, death, and cessation of sexual activity. In many societies, this effective reproductive span is interrupted by time between successive unions or by temporary separation of spouses.

Within the effective reproductive span, the pace of childbearing is determined by the lengths of the successive intervals between births (B1, B2, etc., in Figure 3-4). We will first discuss *birth intervals* in the absence of deliberate family planning. The birth interval may be divided into several segments:

- The postpartum period after a birth until both *ovulation* and *sexual relations* resume
- The *time to conception*
- *Additional time* due to fetal loss through spontaneous abortion
- The *pregnancy leading to the next live birth*

Fertility in the Absence of Contraception and Induced Abortion

The postpartum period ends when both ovulation and intercourse have resumed. It is largely determined by the duration and intensity of breastfeeding and by postpartum taboos against intercourse by a nursing mother. Some populations, particularly in sub-Saharan Africa, have traditionally had taboos against intercourse that could increase the postpartum period beyond the resumption of ovulation, but these practices are rare outside this region and the observance is believed to be decreasing. Women who do not breastfeed usually menstruate for the first time about 2 months after the birth (Salber, Feinleib, & MacMahon, 1966), whereas frequent, intense breastfeeding can postpone the average time of ovulation to over 20 months (Wood et al., 1985). Breastfeeding not

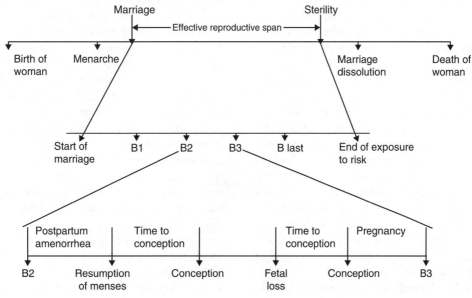

Figure 3-4 Reproductive Span and Birth Intervals.

only provides the child with nourishment but also, depending on the pattern of suckling, can postpone the return of ovulation for many months. Breastfeeding exerts this effect through a maternal response to suckling that suppresses the secretion of gonadotrophins. The classic studies of McNeilly (1996) and his coworkers have shown that "if the frequency of suckling is maintained above five times a day and the duration is maintained above 65 minutes a day, amenorrhea will often be the consequence." Others have found that night feeds are particularly important in maintaining amenorrhea (Jones, 1988). Women who fully breastfeed and are amenorrheic are highly unlikely to conceive in the first six months after a birth. A multinational study estimated that under 2% would do so (Labbok et al., 1997). In addition, demographic studies suggest that the duration of lactational amenorrhea increases with the age of the woman (Wood, 1994). The effects of breastfeeding patterns are so important that they are the major factor in explaining differences in fertility among populations in which no family planning was practiced.

The time to conception depends on the monthly probability of conception in the absence of birth control and can vary among populations, by age, and according to the frequency and pattern of intercourse. The monthly probability of conception, known as *fecundability*, is extremely difficult to measure, and available estimates differ in part because of the methods used to determine that a conception has occurred. If early fetal loss occurs before the woman is aware she is pregnant, then the estimates of conception are biased downward. According to Wood (1994), the best study of early fetal loss was by Wilcox and associates (1988), who followed a group of women aged 20 to 35 and collected blood and urine samples regularly. There were 198 pregnancies detected by assays of these samples; 43, or about 22%, were lost before the woman realized she was pregnant and before clinical diagnosis. Usually, however, fecundability has been measured by accepting a woman's report of her pregnancy. This measure of *apparent* fecundability has yielded values that range from about 0.10 to 0.30 for relatively young women (Menken, 1975; Wood, 1994). The waiting time to conception is, on average, the inverse of fecundability, so that this time is, for younger women, 3 to 10 months on average. In many cases, fecundability has been estimated from reported waiting times to conception using a variety of mathematical models (some of which are summarized by Wood, 1994).

Fecundability depends in part on a couple's frequency and pattern of intercourse, which determines the likelihood that coitus will occur during the woman's fertile period. Both those wishing to conceive a wanted child and those hoping to avoid pregnancy without the use of hormonal or barrier contraceptives depend on knowledge of the woman's cycle to time their sexual activity and thereby change their probability of conception. Whether ovulation is discerned by changes in cervical mucus or basal body temperature, conception is most likely when intercourse takes place shortly before ovulation (Colombo & Masarotto, 2000). Fecundability declines with the age of the woman, although there is increasing evidence that the decline does not take place until the late 30s, on average, if patterns of intercourse remain unchanged. Decline with age of the man is quite slow. Lactation has a fertility-reducing effect even after a woman has resumed menstruation and ovulation (Wood, 1994). Apparently, continued suckling beyond ovulation reduces fecundability through a response that interferes with the functioning of the corpus luteum. Although fertilization can occur, the corpus luteum may not produce sufficient progesterone for the pregnancy to continue (McNeilly, 1996). HIV also affects fertility by reducing conception rates beginning in the earliest asymptomatic stages of infection (Grey et al., 1998; Ross et al., 2004; United Nations Population Division 2002).

Spontaneous abortion occurs frequently; the rate, as already described, depends on how early the pregnancy is detected. From the time conceptions are *recognizable* by virtue of late menses, about 24% end in spontaneous abortion (French & Bierman, 1962). Even higher proportions of fertilized ovum do not lead to live births. Wilcox and associates (1988), in the study cited earlier in which urine specimens were collected so that early pregnancy could be detected, found that 31% of the pregnancies ended in fetal loss. Rates of spontaneous abortion increase with the age of the woman (Nybo Andersen et al., 2000; Wood, 1994) and, more slowly, of the man (Nybo Andersen et al., 2004; Slama et al., 2003). The time added to the birth interval by a recognized fetal loss is the sum of the time from pregnancy to the next ovulation (usually estimated to be just over 3 months on average, since the vast majority of spontaneous abortions occur very early in pregnancy) plus the time to the next conception. There is little evidence of much variation among populations in the rates of spontaneous abortion.

Gestation leading to a live birth does not vary much, usually lasting between 35 and 40 weeks, with little variation between population groups (Wood, 1994). There are two exceptions worth noting. If outstanding care is available, so that pregnancies that might otherwise have ended in fetal loss or stillbirth instead lead to a live birth, or if maternal risk of premature birth is increasing, gestation may be somewhat shorter on average. For the United States, the percent of livebirths reported as preterm (<37 weeks gestation) increased from 9.4% in 1981 to 12.1% in 2002, an increase of 29% (Martin et al., 2003)

A cross-cutting issue is that of infertility and sterility. Especially in parts of Africa, infertility and early sterility are affecting fertility. The effect may be through absolute sterility that causes the effective reproductive span to end early, or through decreased fecundability and/or increased risk of spontaneous abortion (Larsen, 1993, 2000). In most cases, however, the concern is with early sterility, much of which is believed to be due to sexually transmitted infections.

Thus, the main reasons that populations not practicing family planning vary in fertility are differences in the effective reproductive span and the duration of the postpartum amenorrheic period, with variation in time to conception and infertility playing a lesser role.

Deliberate Control of Fertility

People can deliberately reduce their fertility (1) by reducing the effective reproductive span through postponement of marriage or interrupted marriage or by sterilization that ends reproductive capacity early, (2) by using contraception (which increases the time to conception), and (3) by induced abortion (which increases the time added to the birth interval by pregnancies that do not lead to a live birth). Family planning programs can promote both the motivation to reduce fertility and the means to do so. Many governments encourage or enforce later marriage explicitly through changes in the legal age of marriage and implicitly through programs that foster female education. Family planning programs have traditionally focused on education regarding methods of fertility control, motivation to reduce the number of wanted children, and provision of family planning methods themselves. These methods include promotion of breastfeeding, both for the health of the infant and to prolong the postpartum period; contraception, intended to prolong the time to conception; and, except where there is opposition for religious reasons, abortion, which increases the time added to the birth interval.

Although specific family planning methods will be discussed in greater detail in the section on family planning programs, it seems appropriate to consider two important general issues here: Why is it that populations in which the desired number of children is low still have high proportions of unintended births? And why is reliance on abortion an inefficient approach to family planning?

Contraception, even when highly effective, may still not prevent all unintended pregnancies. A simple calculation makes this problem clear. Suppose a woman is using a highly effective method, one that reduces her probability of conceiving to about 1/1,000 per month. She begins using it at age 30 and wants no more children before she reaches menopause at age 45. We can calculate the probability that she has no pregnancy in each of 13 lunar months over the next 15 years, or 195 lunar months. The probability of succeeding (not getting pregnant) each month is .999. The probability of not getting pregnant in 195 months is $.999^{.195}$, which equals 0.38. In other words, she only has a 38% chance of avoiding pregnancy for 15 years. Among women like her, 62% will have at least one unintended pregnancy in that time period. For this reason, even women who are very serious users of contraception are at high risk of unintended pregnancy. Family planning program and health planners need to be aware of this high risk in developing their programs.

The second point concerns induced abortion. In a population that relies primarily on induced abortion to reduce fertility, if a woman becomes pregnant unintentionally, she may choose to have an abortion. About 3 months after the abortion, she again begins ovulating and is capable of conceiving. Suppose her time to conception averages 10 months. Then 13 months after the first abortion, she is again pregnant and must have another abortion if she is not to have an unwanted birth. And 13 months later, again an abortion, and so on. Preventing a birth for 15 years may require that many abortions. It is, therefore, not surprising that many women in eastern European countries that relied primarily on abortion for birth control reported numbers of abortions in the double digits. Women in the former Soviet Union, for example, are believed to have had six or more abortions on average over the course of their lifetime (David, 1992). Abortion, is, however, extremely effective as a backup to effective contraception. A woman who has an abortion and subsequently uses extremely effective contraception is unlikely to have more than one or two unintended pregnancies—but our previous analysis shows that she may have these one or two.

For these reasons, it is not surprising that sterilization, the one method that has a failure rate near zero, is widely selected by women and couples who want no additional children. In the United States in 2002, sterilization of the woman or of the man was the modal method selected when the woman is over 30 (Mosher et al., 2004). In low- and middle-income countries, 26% of married women relied on sterilization to prevent additional births (22% of wives and an additional 4% of their husbands had been sterilized) (Population Reference Bureau, 2002).

The Effect on Fertility of the Proximate Determinants

The Bongaarts's Indices

Bongaarts (1978) developed a set of indices to measure the effect on fertility of some of these proximate determinants. The derivation of these indices is not presented here. They are based on the assumption that there is some maximum potential fertility, *TF*, for women. This figure is usually estimated to be just over 15 children.

C_i *The index of postpartum infecundity* varies from 0 to 1. It represents the proportion of potential fertility, *TF*, remaining when the average postpartum period of the population of interest is taken into account. Therefore, $C_i = 1$ if the population does not breastfeed at all. The *fertility-reducing* effect of postpartum infecundity is $(1 - C_i)$.

C_A *The index of abortion* is the proportion of *TF, after postpartum infecundity is first taken into account*, remaining when the effect of induced abortion in reducing live births is taken into account. Spontaneous abortions are included in the original estimate of *TF*, since they are treated as a purely biological occurrence. Few countries have sufficient information available on abortion to make reasonable estimates of C_A, so it usually must be disregarded in application.

C_c *The index of contraception* is the proportion of *TF, after the effects of postpartum infecundity and induced abortion are taken into account*, remaining after contraceptive use is considered.

C_m *The index of marriage* is the proportion of *TF, after the first three factors are considered*, remaining when the particular marriage or sexual union pattern is taken into account.

Thus, in the Bongaarts decomposition of the total fertility rate,

$$TFR = TF \times C_i \times C_A \times C_c \times C_m$$

It should be noted that both C_c and C_m contain adjustments for infertility and/or sterility. In the first, the adjustment takes into account infertility and sterility and assumes no use of contraception by infertile and sterile couples. In the second, there is a weighting factor, in that nonmarriage has a greater effect on fertility reduction when the woman is young (e.g., the effect of nonmarriage is much greater for a 25-year-old than a 42-year-old).

Table 3-2 presents these indices, except for C_A, which is assumed to be 1 because of lack of data, for

a number of populations around 1970 and for several historical populations (Bongaarts & Potter, 1983). The major impact of breastfeeding can be seen through the values of the index C_i in countries that, at the period in question, used little contraception. All of the South and East Asian countries, as well as Kenya, have indices that do not exceed 0.67; thus, their potential fertility is reduced by at least a third by long postpartum periods. In fact, the long breastfeeding period practiced in Bangladesh and Indonesia reduced their fertility to only about half its potential. In Europe, the demographic transition to low levels of fertility was caused, to a great extent, by very late marriage and a relatively high degree of nonmarriage. The index of marriage is far lower, on average, for the industrialized countries around 1970 than for the low- and middle-income countries. But two historical populations shown had indices of marriage under 0.45, indicating that nonmarriage reduced their potential fertility by at least 55%. By 1970, fertility in all the industrialized countries shown was reduced by contraceptive use to no more than 30% of its potential level.

Thus, in industrialized countries, breastfeeding has little effect on fertility, but nonmarriage and use of contraception reduce the TFR to relatively low levels. In the 1970s, contraceptive use had little impact on fertility in the low- and middle-income countries included in this table; lower fertility was achieved in some of these countries through long-term breastfeeding (see Exhibit 3-2 for the example of Bangladesh). Populations that had very high TFRs achieved them through a combination of high indices of marriage and breastfeeding and little or no contraception.

Stover's Revision of Bongaarts's Indices

The indices of the effects of the proximate determinants on fertility have been revised a number of times by Bongaarts and others in order to take advantage of more detailed and reliable data and to substitute more realistic assumptions. Stover (1998), for example, dropped the original indices of marriage and contraceptive use and attempted to treat infertility and sterility more directly and to deal with sexual activity rather than the proxy of marriage or stable sexual union used in the earlier versions. He includes, instead, three new indices:

C_x *The index of sexual activity* depends on the reported proportion of women in the population who are sexually active. Its interpretation is, therefore, the proportion of potential fertility remaining after celibacy is taken into account.

Table 3-2	Estimates of Total Fertility Rate and the Bongaarts's Proximate Determinants Indices			
Region and Year	**Total Fertility Rate (TFR)**	**Index of Postpartum Infecundity (C_i)**	**Index of Marriage (C_m)**	**Index of Contraception (C_c)**
Low- and Middle-Income Countries				
Bangladesh, 1975	6.34	0.54	0.85	0.90
Colombia, 1976	4.57	0.84	0.58	0.61
Dominican Republic, 1975	5.85	0.61	0.60	1.0
Indonesia, 1976	4.69	0.58	0.71	0.75
Jordan, 1976	7.41	0.80	0.74	0.81
Kenya, 1976	8.02	0.67	0.77	1.0
Korea, 1970	3.97	0.66	0.58	0.68
Lebanon, 1976	4.77	0.78	0.58	0.69
Sri Lanka, 1975	3.53	0.61	0.51	0.74
Syria, 1973	7.00	0.73	0.73	0.86
Thailand, 1975	4.70	0.66	0.63	0.74
Industrialized Countries				
Denmark, 1970	1.78	0.93	0.55	0.23
France, 1972	2.21	0.93	0.52	0.30
Hungary, 1966	1.80	0.93	0.62	0.21
United Kingdom, 1967	2.38	0.93	0.61	0.27
United States, 1967	2.34	0.93	0.63	0.26
Historical Populations				
Bavarian villages, 1700–1850	4.45	0.85	0.37	0.91
Grafenhausen, 1700–1850	4.74	0.67	0.44	1.0
Hutterites	9.50	0.82	0.73	1.0
Quebec, 1700–1730	8.00	0.81	0.63	1.0

Note: Each index represents the proportion of potential fertility remaining after the particular factor is taken into account in the following order: postpartum infecundity, marriage, and contraceptive use.

Source: Adapted with permission of the Population Council, from John Bongaarts, "The Fertility-Inhibiting Effects of the Intermediate Fertility Variables," *Studies in Family Planning*, 13 (6/7), pp. 182–183.

Exhibit 3-2	Proximate Determinants of Fertility in Bangladesh

As shown in Table 3-2, fertility in Bangladesh was estimated to be over 6 in 1975. This high fertility was due to the combination of almost universal marriage for women of reproductive age ($C_m = 0.85$) and little fertility control within marriage ($C_c = 0.90$). Fertility could, however, have been much higher but for prolonged amenorrhea, which is related to the long breast-feeding period practiced in this country. Total fertility was just over half (0.54) of what it would have been if women had not breastfed at all. In fact, relative to the other countries with little contraceptive use and high proportions married, Bangladesh fertility was quite low.

Some early family planning programs specifically targeted women who had just delivered a baby. The rationale was that a woman would be more likely, at that point in her life, to be thinking about whether she wanted more children and, if she did, whether she would prefer to postpone the next birth. One of the lessons from the study of proximate determinants in Bangladesh and elsewhere is that contraceptive use in the postpartum period simply overlaps with a woman's natural immunity to conception and therefore fails to provide an additional protection against unintended pregnancy. This finding has been used by program designers in thinking about how best to use their scarce resources.

Recent estimates of the Bongaarts's proximate determinants of fertility for Bangladesh (TFR of 3 in 2004 versus TFR of 6 in 1974) indicate a significantly lower index of contraception (C_c of around 0.41 compared to 0.90), reflecting the rapid rise in contraceptive prevalence over the 30-year period to around 58%; a relatively unchanged index of marriage ($C_m = 0.80$ versus 0.85), reflecting the continuing high rates of marriage; and an increase in the index of postpartum infecundity from 0.54 to around 0.60, reflecting declining breastfeeding durations (Islam, 2003; Macro International, 2004).

C_f *The index of infecundity* reflects the effect on fertility of infecundity among sexually active women, and is simply $1 - f$, where f is the proportion reporting that they believe themselves infecund.

C_u *The index of contraceptive use* reflects actual contraceptive use by women who believe themselves to be fecund and who are not experiencing postpartum amenorrhea.

Thus, the fertility-reducing effect of the proximate determinants is given by

$$C_x \times C_i \times C_A \times C_f \times C_u$$

where, again, the index of abortion (C_A) can rarely be estimated.

These results show that the two main factors producing lower fertility in Latin America are relatively low participation in sexual activity and relatively high contraceptive use (Table 3-3). By contrast, in most countries of Africa, there is much higher participation in sexual activity and low use of contraception. Fertility would be even higher were it not for the effects of postpartum infecundity, which reduces fertility by at least 40% in the countries represented here. What is striking is the documentation of the rather large impact on

overall fertility (about 20%) in some countries due to infertility among sexually active women.

Family Planning Programs

A fundamental rationale for family planning programs is to reduce unintended fertility because of its negative health and welfare consequences and because control of fertility has been recognized as a human right of women and couples. Over the last 50 years, societal changes have occurred that include reduced infant mortality, increased urbanization, improved education for women, increased economic opportunities, and dissemination and adoption of modern ideas about small families. The response by couples in the low- and middle-income countries has been accelerated by changes in expectations about both the number and timing of births (Bongaarts, 1983; Freedman, 1987). In 1997, 155 countries had programs that subsidized the cost of family planning services (Gelbard, Haub, & Kent, 1999). However, in part due to the lack of available, accessible, and effective contraception, the gap between observed and desired fertility grew, leading in turn to an increase in unintended fertility (Bankole &

Table 3-3	Estimates of Total Fertility Rate (TFR) and Revised Bongaarts's Proximate Determinants Indices				
Region and Year	TFR	Index of Sexual Activity (C_x)	Index of Postpartum Infecundity (C_i)	Index of Infecundity (C_f)	Index of Contraceptive Use (C_u)
Africa					
Burkina Faso, 1993	6.9	0.66	0.49	0.88	0.94
Cameroon, 1991	5.8	0.69	0.57	0.81	0.84
Ghana, 1993	5.5	0.64	0.55	0.86	0.81
Madagascar, 1992	6.1	0.71	0.61	0.83	0.89
Namibia, 1992	5.4	0.59	0.59	0.86	0.70
Niger, 1992	7.4	0.86	0.58	0.78	1.0
Nigeria, 1990	6.0	0.73	0.53	0.80	0.93
Rwanda, 1992	6.2	0.60	0.56	0.85	0.86
Senegal, 1993	6.0	0.63	0.56	0.81	0.93
Zambia, 1992	6.5	0.69	0.60	0.86	0.90
Latin America and the Caribbean					
Brazil, 1991	3.7	0.59	0.83	0.88	0.39
Colombia, 1990	2.9	0.53	0.77	0.89	0.36
Dominican Republic, 1991	3.3	0.54	0.81	0.88	0.41
Paraguay, 1990	4.7	0.49	0.76	0.86	0.47
Peru, 1992	3.5	0.55	0.68	0.89	0.53

Source: Adapted with permission of the Population Council, from John Stover, "Revising the Proximate Determinants of Fertility Framework: What Have We Learned in the Past 20 Years?" 1998, *Studies in Family Planning, 29*(3), p. 263.

Westoff, 1995; Bulatao, 1998). In Bangladesh in 1996, 18% of women expressing a desire to control their fertility were not able to meet this need. By 2003, this figure had been reduced to 11% (Exhibit 3-3).

Unintended Fertility

A number of definitional issues underlie estimates of unintended fertility and its distribution. In general, data on unintended fertility come from representative population surveys in which women who are pregnant at the time of the survey or had at least one birth in the five years prior to the survey are asked whether each of those births (including the outcome of the current pregnancy) was *intended, mistimed* because it came too early but was still within the desired number of births, or *unwanted* in that no more children were desired. Unfortunately usage of these terms is not completely consistent; some authors include mistimed births as part of their estimates of unwanted births, while others count only those births that exceed the desired family size as unwanted (Brown & Eisenberg, 1995). The major weakness of this approach is that women may be reluctant to classify specific births as unwanted, leading to artificially low estimates of unwanted births.

Measurement of fertility intentions has been criticized because it relies exclusively on mothers' intentions and not the intentions of other family members, most importantly fathers, to gauge unintended fertility. It has been argued that the intentions of the mother, especially in many low- and middle-income countries, may not accurately reflect the desirability of a birth. Evidence suggests that intergenerational differences in family size

goals (i.e., preferences of grandparents versus parents) may be more pronounced than interspousal differences (Caldwell, 1986; Mason and Taj, 1987). Ultimately, the justification for relying on the stated preferences of the mother in determining desired family size and unintended or unwanted births stems from the fact that the mother is the person most responsible for the birth and child care (Tsui, Wasserheit, & Haaga, 1997).

Demographic and Health Surveys (DHS) have been fielded since 1984 in close to 70 low- and middle-income countries.[1] They are intended to provide comparable information on a variety of subjects related to health and fertility issues. DHS calculates, for each survey, both the TFR (the number of children a woman would bear were she to live her reproductive life under the fertility conditions just prior to the survey) and the unwanted TFR (the number of those children who would be unwanted) (Westoff, 2001). A birth is counted as unwanted only when the mother stated she wanted no more children at the time of the pregnancy. DHS fielded surveys in 1998-2003 in the 44 countries listed in Table 3-4. In nearly every country, TFR declined with education of the woman. On average, 20% of national total fertility was unwanted, with the percentage varying considerably by region. The lowest and the highest fertility regions (Central Asia and sub-Saharan Africa) had the lowest percentage unwanted (the mean percent of TFR unwanted was 6% for Central Asia and 15% for

---

[1]See www.measuredhs.com

Exhibit 3-3	Desired Family Size and Unmet Need for Contraception in Bangladesh

One rationale for family planning programs was that couples who wanted to have fewer children were unable to do so because they lacked either knowledge of the means of fertility control or access to those means, through lack of supplies or services. Even in the earliest surveys carried out in Bangladesh, a high proportion of married women reported they wanted no more children. In 1969, 44% reported they did not want to have another child. This proportion had risen only slightly by the early 1980s, but by 1993 nearly 58% reported wanting no more (Cleland et al., 1994). Remarkably, the proportion wanting to stop at two or three children had risen more than 20 percentage points in just 13 years. Over 80% of women with three or more children wanted no additional births.

In 1996, when asked their ideal number of children, women under 30 and women with 2 or fewer children reported 2.1 to 2.4 children as ideal, while those 30 to 49 or with 3 or more children responded with 2.4 to 3.0 on average. Yet before the inception of a well-run family planning program, among the barriers to achieving this low fertility were the economic costs of access to services, including the cost of transportation, and supplies; the social costs, such as travel by women whose mobility was traditionally constrained; the psychic costs of use in a society that offered little social or familial support for low fertility; and the health costs of side effects, whether subjective or objective, from contraceptive use.

These barriers have been overcome to the extent that in 2003, 58% of married women of reproductive age were current contraceptive users, compared with 44% in 1993; however, the need for contraception remains unmet for 11% of women at risk of pregnancy (Macro International, 2004).

sub-Saharan Africa). Some countries with high TFRs have low proportions unwanted (e.g., Niger). The highest percentages unwanted, a third or more, were in countries with TFRs between 3 and 5. Finally, in low-fertility countries where the TFR is below 4 births per woman, a substantial proportion of those births remain unwanted (Bongaarts, 1990, 1997a).

It is worth noting that this and earlier evidence suggests that increases in contraception prevalence rates do not necessarily cause a decline in the proportion of unwanted births and, in fact, may initially be associated with an increase in the proportion of unwanted births (Tsui, Wasserheit, & Haaga, 1997). This scenario can happen if desired fertility rates drop faster than the compensating rises in contraceptive prevalence rates and in the use of methods of fertility control so effective that unintended births rarely occur. Thus, when couples have very high fertility desires, it is difficult to exceed those desires, so nearly all children are wanted. As desired fertility falls, use and effective use of contraception or abortion may not increase quickly enough to avoid unwanted births. Finally, at low levels of fertility, women want so few children that there remain many years after the last wanted child during which an unwanted pregnancy and birth can, and frequently does, occur. The differences by education within a country can in part be explained by this phenomenon, in that more educated women within a society frequently are earlier adoptors of contraception and, because they desire few children, a higher proportion of their children may be unwanted.

With regard to mistimed births, DHS data from around 1990 suggest that roughly 20% of births in the low- and middle-income countries were mistimed (i.e., they come too early). There were no apparent regional differences in mistimed births and no clear association between contraceptive prevalence and the proportion of mistimed births. Thus, even in a region like sub-Saharan Africa, with low unwanted fertility, there was still considerable mistimed fertility. This finding suggests that there is a need for contraception to delay first births and control spacing of subsequent births even when there may be little demand for contraception to control the number of births (Bankole & Westoff, 1995; Rafailimanana & Westoff, 2001).

Consequences of Unintended Pregnancies and Births

Aside from helping individual couples fulfill their desires and expectations, why should we care about unintended pregnancies and births and, moreover, try to reduce them? A compelling public health reason is their negative consequences. Unintended pregnancies increase the lifetime risk of maternal mortality simply by increasing the number of pregnancies (Koenig et al., 1988). This topic is covered in greater detail in the next section. Unintended pregnancies can lead to unsafe abortion, poor infant health, and lower investment in the child.

Abortion

In many cases, unintended pregnancies are terminated by abortions, most of which are conducted illegally under unhygienic conditions and pose significant health risks to the mother. The legal status of abortion and, consequently, access to safe abortion services is highly variable. Roughly 25% of women live in countries where abortion is generally prohibited (Rahman, Katzive, & Henshaw, 1998). Women in low- and middle-income countries are much more likely to live under restrictive abortion laws than women in higher-income countries (Alan Guttmacher Institute, 1999a). Despite these differences in legal access, there is little difference in the likelihood of having an abortion. As a result, women in low- and middle-income countries (excluding China), are more likely to have illegal abortions. Their abortion mortality rate is many times higher than that for women in higher-income countries (330 deaths versus 0.2 to 1.2 deaths per 100,000 abortions) (Alan Guttmacher Institute, 1999b). Henshaw, Singh and Haas (1999) estimated that approximately 26 million legal and 20 million illegal abortions were performed worldwide in 1995, resulting in a worldwide abortion rate of 35 per 1,000 women aged 15 to 44. They report that eastern Europe had the highest abortion rate (90 per 1,000), and western Europe the lowest rate (11 per 1,000). Among countries where abortion is legal without restriction, the highest abortion rates in 1995 were reported for Vietnam (83 per 1,000), and the lowest for Belgium and the Netherlands (7 per 1,000).

Even where abortion is legal, access is very limited, there are poor systems of referral, and, very often, services are of poor quality. For example, despite the fact that manual vacuum extraction is much safer, the most frequently used method for abortion in most countries is dilatation and curettage, which has significant associated morbidity. The World Health Organization (WHO) estimated that there are about 20 million unsafe abortions (i.e., those not attended by a trained health professional) per year resulting in about 69,000 deaths in the low- and middle-income countries.

Table 3-4	Total Fertility Rate and Proportion Unwanted by Women's Education in Countries with DHS Surveys around 2000, by Region						
	No Education		Primary Education		Secondary or Higher Education		Total	
	TFR	Proportion Unwanted	TFR	Proportion Unwanted	TFR	Proportion Unwanted	TFR	Proportion Unwanted
sub-Saharan Africa								
Benin, 2001	6.3	0.17	4.9	0.18	3.6	0.25	5.6	0.18
Burkina Faso, 2003	6.3	0.13	4.5	0.13	2.5	0.08	5.9	0.14
Cameroon, 1998	6.1	0.03	5.0	0.14	3.6	0.17	4.8	0.10
Cote d'Ivoire, 1998/1999	6.1	0.11	4.7	0.17	2.3	0.17	5.2	0.13
Eritrea, 2002	5.5	0.07	4.2	0.07	3.1	0.06	4.8	0.08
Ethiopia, 2000	5.9	0.15	4.7	0.17	3.2	0.19	5.5	0.15
Gabon, 2000	5.1	0.16	5.3	0.17	3.5	0.17	4.2	0.17
Ghana, 2003	6.0	0.13	5.3	0.25	3.2	0.19	4.4	0.16
Guinea, 1999	5.9	0.08	4.8	0.10	3.5	0.20	5.5	0.09
Kenya, 2003	6.7	0.15	5.5	0.31	3.2	0.28	4.9	0.27
Madagascar, 2003/2004	6.5	0.11	5.7	0.12	3.4	0.12	5.2	0.12
Malawi, 2000	7.3	0.16	6.4	0.19	3.0	0.07	6.3	0.17
Mali, 2001	7.1	0.10	6.6	0.11	4.1	0.15	6.8	0.10
Mauritania, 2000/2001	4.8	0.06	4.7	0.15	3.2	0.16	4.5	0.09
Namibia, 2000	6.3	0.16	5.0	0.20	3.3	0.21	4.2	0.19
Niger, 1998	7.5	0.03	6.2	0.05	4.8	0.08	7.2	0.03
Nigeria, 2003	6.7	0.03	6.3	0.10	4.2	0.07	5.7	0.07
South Africa, 1998	4.5	0.27	3.7	0.24	2.5	0.20	2.9	0.21
Tanzania, 1999	6.5	0.14	5.2	0.13	3.5	0.06	5.6	0.14
Togo, 1998	6.3	0.16	4.6	0.22	2.7	0.22	5.2	0.19
Uganda, 2000/2001	7.8	0.19	7.3	0.23	3.9	0.18	6.9	0.23
Zambia, 2001/2002	7.4	0.11	6.5	0.15	3.9	0.23	5.9	0.17
Zimbabwe, 1999	5.2	0.12	4.5	0.16	3.3	0.12	4.0	0.15
North Africa/West Asia/Europe								
Armenia, 2000	–	–	0.7	0	1.7	0.12	1.7	0.12
Egypt, 2000	4.1	0.20	3.8	0.21	3.3	0.18	3.5	0.17
Jordan, 2002	3.6	0.50	3.7	0.30	3.6	0.28	3.7	0.30
Turkey, 1998	4.0	0.38	2.7	0.22	1.8	0.11	2.6	0.27
Central Asia								
Kazakhstan, 1999	0.9	–	–	–	2.1	0.10	2.0	0.05
Turkmenistan, 2000	3.7	0.22	2.0	0.10	2.9	0.07	2.9	0.07
South & Southeast Asia								
Bangladesh, 1999/2000	4.1	0.32	3.3	0.33	2.4	0.25	3.3	0.33
Cambodia, 2000	4.3	0.26	3.8	0.21	2.7	0.07	3.8	0.21
India, 1998/1999	–	–	–	–	–	–	2.8	0.25
Indonesia, 2002/2003	2.5	0.16	2.7	0.15	2.5	0.12	2.6	0.15
Nepal, 2001	4.8	0.38	3.2	0.38	2.2	0.23	4.1	0.39
Philippines, 2003	5.3	0.23	5.0	0.34	3.1	0.23	3.5	0.29
Vietnam, 2002	2.6	0.35	2.0	0.10	1.7	0.12	1.9	0.16
Latin America & Caribbean								
Bolivia, 2003	6.8	0.54	4.9	0.49	2.5	0.28	3.8	0.45
Colombia, 2000	4.0	0.50	3.6	0.36	2.2	0.23	2.6	0.31
Dominican Republic, 2002	4.5	0.33	3.6	0.25	2.5	0.12	3.0	0.23
Guatemala, 1998/1999	6.8	0.16	5.2	0.21	2.9	0.14	5.0	0.18
Haiti, 2000	6.1	0.41	5.3	0.36	2.7	0.30	4.7	0.40
Nicaragua, 2001	5.2	0.33	3.6	0.31	2.3	0.22	3.2	0.28
Peru, 2000	5.1	0.41	4.1	0.44	2.2	0.27	2.8	0.36

Note: – unavailable

Source: ORC Macro, 2005, MEASURE DHS STAT compiler, http://www.measuredhs.com. Accessed June 22, 2005.

Another abortion-related issue is the recent rise in the male to female sex ratio at birth in Southeast Asia. Data from a number of countries, including China and Korea, show that the sex ratio at birth is unusually high compared with the expected ratio of 1.06 male births to every female birth, and is steadily increasing. Rising sex ratios at birth suggest that selective abortion of female fetuses may be increasing (Arnold, Kishor, & Roy, 2002; Larsen, Chung, & Das Gupta, 1998; Westley, 1995). This practice is embedded in the context of strong societal preferences for male children and declining family size desires, which increase the incentives to have the desired family composition as well as the desired number of children. The recent availability of modern technology has provided the means to actualize these preferences. There are basically three different ways of determining the sex of a fetus: chorionic villus sampling, amniocentesis, and ultrasound. Ultrasound is the safest and cheapest method, but only works reliably around 5 to 6 months into the pregnancy (i.e., the end of the second trimester). It is widely available in rural areas in India, China, and other parts of East Asia. Despite strong legal sanctions against sex-selective abortion, the availability of relatively cheap ultrasound technology has promoted this practice, leading to deleterious consequences for women due to late-term, riskier abortions and possibly for children due to increasing sex imbalance.

Consequences for Infant Health

Information on the consequences of unintended births for infant health is available for the period before 1990. It shows these births were concentrated in demographically high-risk categories (Tables 3-5 to 3-7), that is, the proportion unintended was much higher in births to older mothers, higher-parity mothers, and following a short birth interval (Tsui, Wasserheit, & Haaga, 1997). Why these demographic characteristics are associated with high risks for infant health is discussed in greater detail in the next section. But unwanted births had higher mortality even when the pregnancy fits into otherwise demographically low-risk categories (mothers aged 24 to 29, and of parity 2 to 4).

Human Capital Investments

In addition to deleterious health consequences for the mother and the index child, unintended births have spillover and long-term cumulative effects by reducing human capital investments (i.e., allocation of resources for education and health) in the family as a whole. A

Table 3-5	Percentage Unintended of Most Recent Birth or Current Pregnancy by Mother's Age: Selected Countries		
	Mother's Age		
Country (Year)	<20	20–34	35+
Bolivia, 1993	41.5	53.9	74.0
Colombia, 1986	34.9	48.3	60.5
Egypt, 1988	13.9	41.3	75.0
Kenya, 1993	61.2	55.3	65.4
Nigeria, 1990	13.7	12.5	21.6
Philippines, 1993	37.6	46.4	58.2
Tanzania, 1991	22.7	26.1	31.7
Thailand, 1987	28.3	38.4	47.2

Source: Adapted with permission from A. O. Tsui, J. N. Wasserheit, and J. G. Haaga (Eds.), *Reproductive Health in Developing Countries: Expanding Dimensions, Building Solutions.* Copyright 1997 by the National Academy of Sciences, courtesy of the National Academies Press, Washington, D.C.

Table 3-6	Percentage Unintended of Most Recent Birth or Current Pregnancy by Birth Order: Selected Countries		
	Birth Order		
Country (Year)	1	2–4	5+
Bolivia, 1993	32.7	50.1	78.6
Colombia, 1986	25.0	50.7	68.8
Egypt, 1988	3.8	39.5	67.2
Kenya, 1993	52.1	52.1	66.2
Nigeria, 1990	11.2	9.9	22.7
Philippines, 1993	22.3	47.4	63.6
Tanzania, 1991	18.7	25.0	39.5
Thailand, 1987	20.7	36.3	64.4

Source: Adapted with permission from A. O. Tsui, J. N. Wasserheit, and J. G. Haaga (Eds.), *Reproductive Health in Developing Countries: Expanding Dimensions, Building Solutions.* Copyright 1997 by the National Academy of Sciences, courtesy of the National Academies Press, Washington, D.C.

number of studies in low- and middle-income countries have shown that older children, especially girls, suffer disproportionately in terms of lower educational attainment and health status as family size increases— the latter being a proxy for unwanted births (Bledsoe & Cohen, 1993; Desai, 1995; Frenzen & Hogan, 1982; Lloyd, 1994). Cross-sectional associations between large family sizes and lower health and educational attainments need to be interpreted cautiously due to the possibility that parents who choose to have large families may also choose to invest differently in different children (Knodel, Chamrathrithirong, & Debavalya, 1987). There is, however, some evidence, from a family planning quasi-experiment in which villages were as-

Table 3-7	Percentage Unintended of Recent Higher-Order Birth or Current Pregnancy by Interval from Previous Birth to Conception: Selected Countries	
	Interval from Previous Birth to Conception	
Country (Year)	**Birth Interval < 24 months**	**Birth Interval ≥ 24 months**
Bolivia, 1993	68.4	60.1
Colombia, 1986	67.6	49.2
Egypt, 1988	54.0	50.2
Kenya, 1993	67.2	56.1
Nigeria, 1990	21.1	13.0
Philippines, 1993	62.1	49.3
Tanzania, 1991	33.5	27.5
Thailand, 1987	53.4	36.5

Source: Adapted with permission from A. O. Tsui, J. N. Wasserheit, and J. G. Haaga (Eds.), *Reproductive Health in Developing Countries: Expanding Dimensions, Building Solutions.* Copyright 1997 by the National Academy of Sciences, courtesy of the National Academies Press, Washington, D.C.

signed different levels of family planning services, that part of the relationship between large family sizes and low human capital investments is causal (Foster & Roy, 1996).

Unmet Need for Contraception

A primary objective of family planning programs has been to reduce unintended births by addressing "the unmet need for contraception." This unmet need is conventionally estimated from representative population-based surveys of currently married women as the sum of the number of currently pregnant women who report that their pregnancy is unintended and the number of currently nonpregnant women who are not using contraception and would not like to have any more children, or, at least, none in the next 2 years (Bankole & Westoff, 1995). On the basis of this definition, unmet need for contraception (Table 3-8) is 15% or less for married women in countries with high contraceptive prevalence rates (55% or higher) and ranges up to 40% of women in countries with lower contraceptive prevalence rates.

The definition of unmet need for contraception described above has been criticized as an underestimate of actual need because it excludes both currently married women who are not pregnant and who are using inappropriate (because of health consequences or side effects) methods of contraception and sexually active women who are not currently married and who do not wish to become pregnant, at least in the next 2 years (Bongaarts, 1991; Dixon-Mueller & Germain, 1992; Pritchett, 1994a, 1994b). An additional criticism revolves around the issue of ineffective contraception. Large numbers of women currently use traditional methods, which have much higher failure rates than available modern contraceptives. Current estimates of unmet need do not include women who are using

traditional (i.e., ineffective) contraceptive methods. Recent estimates (Ross and Winfrey, 2002) consider unmarried as well as married women. They show that for all low- and middle-income countries, about 113.2 million women have an unmet need for contraception (105.2 million married and 8.4 million unmarried). This translates to 17% of married women having an unmet need compared to 3% of unmarried women, with women aged 15-24 accounting for one-third of the unmet need. Of this 17% total unmet need for contraception, 9% is attributed to the need to space births and 8.1% to the need to limit births. The total number of women whose needs are unmet results from the combination of upward pressure due to population growth and downward pressure due to the success of family planning programs, so that the proportion with unmet need is smaller (Ross & Winfrey, 2002). If the policy objective were defined as meeting the need for effective, modern contraceptives, estimates of unmet need would rise substantially (Ross & Winfrey, 2002).

Family planning programs have played an important role in reducing unmet need by making contraception physically accessible and financially affordable. Since the late 1950s, when the first national family planning programs in low- and middle-income countries began, there has been a significant increase in the prevalence of contraceptive use. This increase has played an important role in the significant reduction in fertility that has taken place especially over the last three decades in these regions, where the average number of births per couple has declined from over six to under three in the latter half of the 20th century. Program success in improving contraceptive prevalence rates has, however, been somewhat uneven. It has depended on a number of factors, including a receptive social and family environment that accepts fertility control as legitimate behavior, a favorable political and bureaucratic climate,

Table 3-8	Unmet Need for Contraception and Demand for Family Planning for Married Women in 55 Countries with DHS Survey in 1998–2000			
Country and Year	Unmet Need	Current Use of Contraception	Demand for Family Planning	Percentage of Total Demand Satisfied
sub-Saharan Africa				
Burkina Faso, 1998–1999	25.8	11.9	37.7	31.5
Cameroon, 1998	19.7	19.3	39.1	49.5
Ghana, 1998	23.0	22.0	45.0	48.8
Kenya, 1998	23.9	39.0	64.8	63.2
Malawi, 2000	29.7	30.6	60.3	50.8
Niger, 1998	16.6	8.2	24.9	33.0
Nigeria, 1999	17.5	15.3	32.8	46.7
South Africa, 1998	15.0	56.3	71.2	79.0
Uganda, 2000	34.6	22.8	57.3	39.7
Zimbabwe, 1999	12.9	53.6	68.2	81.0
North Africa				
Egypt, 2000	11.2	56.1	68.2	83.6
Asia				
Bangladesh, 1999/2000	15.3	53.8	70.8	78.3
Cambodia, 2000	32.6	23.8	56.4	42.2
India, 1998/1999	15.8	48.2	64.0	75.3
Indonesia, 1997	9.2	57.4	67.4	86.4
Philippines, 1998				
Latin America & Caribbean				
Bolivia, 1998	26.1	48.3	74.4	65.0
Colombia, 2000	6.2	76.9	86.3	92.8
Dominican Republic, 1999	11.8	69.5	82.6	85.7
Guatemala, 1998/1999	23.1	38.2	62.2	62.9
Haiti, 2000	39.8	28.1	67.8	41.4
Peru, 2000	10.2	68.9	82.5	87.6

Source: C. F. Westoff, *Unmet Need at the End of the Century* (Calverton, MD: ORC Macro, 2001). Accessed at http://www.measuredhs.com/pubs/pdftoc.cfm?ID=349. Accessed June 22, 2005.

a management structure that pays close attention to both quality and quantity of services, and reliable sources of funding. The programs that have succeeded have invested considerable resources in evaluation, research, and monitoring of services and have had the flexibility to adapt to local conditions (Bongaarts, 1997b; Bongaarts & Watkins, 1996; Bulatao, 1993, 1998; Freedman, 1987).

There has been a long-standing debate about the relative merits of so-called demand side versus supply side interventions to reduce unmet need in contraception (Bongaarts, 1997b; Pritchett, 1994a, 1994b). Demand-side proponents have argued that improvements in women's socioeconomic status are an essential and necessary prerequisite to the success of family planning programs. Thus, educated women with higher status are more likely to know about contraception and seek it out to actualize their latent fertility desires than are their less educated and lower-status peers. Supply-side proponents, on the other hand, are described as positing that family planning programs, when properly managed, can increase access to and availability of contraception even in the absence of changes in the socioeconomic status of women. Thus, programs can lead to increased contraceptive prevalence rates and initiation of fertility decline. The experience of many countries, however, shows that the onset of fertility decline[2] is not dependent on any particular threshold in socioeconomic factors such as levels of urbanization, female education, or infant mortality. Fertility decline appears to have started in a wide range of low- and middle-income countries at quite varied levels of socioeconomic status. Bangladesh

---

[2]The onset of fertility decline is usually dated from an initial decline of at least 0.7 points in total fertility over a five-year period, following Bulatao and Elwan (1985).

is frequently cited as the best example of improved contraceptive prevalence rates and dramatic fertility decline in the absence of socioeconomic improvements but in the presence of a well-run, focused family planning program (Cleland et al., 1994), although the absence of socioeconomic change has come under question (Caldwell et al., 1999; Menken, Khan & Williams, 1999). While there appears to be no magic threshold of socioeconomic development for initiation of fertility decline, the decline is faster in countries with greater levels of socioeconomic development (Bongaarts & Watkins, 1996).

The demand side versus supply side debate is basically a false dichotomy. Neither development nor family planning programs are necessary prerequisites, nor is either sufficient to induce fertility decline (Ross & Mauldin, 1996). They work in complementary fashions, with the time scale of their respective impacts being very different. Investments in improving women's status and educational attainment certainly have an important impact in reducing unmet need, but it is a long-term impact. On the other hand, family planning programs can increase access to contraception in the short run and thus enhance knowledge about use and availability and address many of the negative myths about particular methods of contraception. Appropriately crafted and focused media campaigns, implemented as part of family planning programs, can also help legitimize contraception as an acceptable and desirable form of behavior. Moreover, it is important to note that access to the means to limit fertility in and of itself helps improve the status of women. Family planning programs work synergistically with improvements in socioeconomic status and are most effective when there is an informed, educated, empowered client base (Freedman, 1987). In summary, Bongaarts (1997b) estimates that about 40% of the fertility decline in the last three decades of the 20th century in low- and middle-income countries (from a TFR of 6 to 3) can be attributed to family planning programs, and about 60% to changes in socioeconomic status, particularly for women.

The Challenges Facing Family Planning

Despite significant family planning program success in reducing the financial and logistic constraints to contraceptive access, unmet need for contraception remains high in many countries. Studies by Bongaarts and Bruce (1995) and Casterline and associates (1996) reported that the major barriers to use of contraception appeared to be lack of knowledge about contraception availability and use, concerns about the deleterious health consequences of contraception, and opposition from family and community to contraception use.

Given that physical access and financial constraints are not considered to be significant barriers to the use of contraception, the major challenges for family planning revolve around improving the quality of services, particularly in the areas of information exchange and method choice; integration with reproductive health services other than contraception; and last, but not least, financial sustainability.

Information Exchange

In upgrading the quality of family planning services, the major area of concern is information exchange between providers and clients. The fragmentary evidence that exists suggests that inadequate information is frequently provided about the proper use of contraceptives, alternatives in the event of nonoptimal use, contraceptive side effects, and the appropriateness of the chosen method for women who have particular health problems (Winikoff, Elias, & Beattie, 1994). For example, quite a few women who are using oral birth control pills do not know that they can make up for a missed day by taking two the next day. Similarly, not enough women know that birth control pills should not be used if a woman is a smoker or has a heart condition (Trottier et al., 1994). In general, far fewer than 50% of women have meaningful knowledge about contraceptive methods (Bongaarts & Bruce, 1995). This lack of specific knowledge often leads to exaggerated notions of the health risks of contraception (Casterline, Perez, & Biddlecom, 1996). It is worth reiterating that contraception is, by and large, very safe, especially when compared with the health risks deriving from an unplanned pregnancy. Ross and Frankenberg (1993) estimated that the mortality risk of an unplanned, unwanted pregnancy is 20 times the risk of any modern contraceptive method and 10 times the risk of a properly performed abortion. Although the last two decades have witnessed great success in social marketing, whereby most women are aware of the benefits of small families and the existence and availability of contraception, much more needs to be done to educate women about method choice and associated health risks and benefits.

Although concern about information exchange in family planning programs is long-standing, progress in addressing this problem is uneven. An issue that comes up repeatedly is whether there is a quality-quantity trade-off. Program managers voice a common complaint that they have their hands full just providing physical access to contraceptives. Many feel they do not have the luxury of providing extensive information about contraception because of the time-intensive nature of this type of activity.

It is important to recognize that there actually is little contradiction or trade-off between paying attention to quality issues and achieving quantity targets for numbers of users. The two are integrally linked in several ways. First, the key steps needed to improve quality—such as attention to logistics, adequate supervision, motivation of workers at every level, real feedback to managers and supervisors, and accountability for supplies and money—are exactly those steps needed to improve quantity. Second, family planning services are inseparable from information provision. In fact, provision of information is one of the key services that a family planning program can offer. Third, attention to quality will improve efficiency and will allow the addition of new users without new costs (Tsui, Wasserheit, & Haaga, 1997).

Contraceptive Use and Method Choice

Modern contraceptive methods are now so widely available in the low- and middle-income countries that about a third of all couples outside of China, and more than half of all couples in the industrialized countries in which the woman is of reproductive age were users by the early 1990s (Robey, Rutstein, & Morris, 1992). In 1993 the estimated number of contraceptive users in low- and middle-income countries was 436 million.

This number grew to 549 million in the year 2000, and is further expected to grow to 816 million during the next 25 years (Bongaarts & Johansson, 2002). This rapid growth is a result of population increases and a concomitant rise in contraceptive prevalence in low- and middle-income countries from 55% in 1993 to 60% in 2000 and a projected 67% in 2025 due to declines in desired fertility.

Table 3-9 shows the worldwide distribution of use according to method using the most recent data as of 2002. In addition to demonstrating the great variation in use, the data are remarkable in that they show that for much of the world, a high proportion of those couples using contraception are using sterilization—the one method that has almost zero risk of failure. Note that the average for low- to middle-income countries in Asia (64%) is heavily influenced by the very high rate of contraceptive prevalence in China (83%). Without China, the average for all low- and middle-income countries would drop from 55% to only 43% (Bongaarts & Johansson, 2002).

It is much harder to judge how much *choice* of method women in the low- and middle-income countries have, and how their array of choices has changed in recent years. With the exception of sub-Saharan Africa, where contraceptive prevalence rates are low, there has been significant progress in overall method availability in most countries between 1982 and 1994 (Ross & Mauldin, 1996). In all 22 countries (with the exception of Nigeria) where DHS surveys were conducted between 1990 and 1993, at least half of all

Table 3-9	Percentage Using Contraception, 2000: Married Couples[a] in Which the Woman Is of Reproductive Age, by Region					
	Sterilization					
Region	**Female**	**Male**	**Pill**	**IUD**	**Condom**	**Total**
World	21.0	4.0	7.0	15.0	5.0	61.0
Low- and middle-income regions						
Africa	2.0	0.1	7.0	5.0	1.0	26.0
Asia	25.0	4.0	5.0	18.0	4.0	64.0
Latin America and Caribbean	31.0	2.0	13.0	8.0	4.0	70.0
Oceania	12.0	9.0	21.0	2.0	9.0	59.0
Industrialized regions						
Japan	3.0	0.6	.8	1.5	43.0	56.0
Europe	4.0	2.0	16.0	15.0	10.0	67.0
Northern America	23.0	14.0	15.0	1.0	13.0	76.0
New Zealand	14.0	19.3	20.5	3.3	11.0	74.0

Note: The table is based on the most recent data available as of 2002; pertaining approximately to 2000.

[a]Including, where possible, those in consenual unions.

Source: Population Reference Bureau, *Family Planning Worldwide: 2002 Data Sheet.* Washington, DC: The Population Reference Bureau. Adapted with permission.

women had heard of at least one modern contraceptive method, and in 13 of these countries, more than 90% of women knew of at least one contraceptive method (Curtis & Neitzel, 1996).

Table 3-10 shows historical data on contraceptive method mix and alternative projections for the year 2015 (Bongaarts & Johansson, 2002). Although the two projection methodologies have varying estimates for specific methods, female sterilization will continue to remain the most popular method of choice, followed by IUDs and pills, in 2015. An issue of considerable concern is that despite evidence of a spreading HIV epidemic in low- and middle-income countries, condoms continue to have very low prevalences in these projections.

Largely due to a lack of funding and the long lead time required for new methods to gain acceptance, there has been relatively little innovation in contraceptive technology in the last 30 years, so that, in an era of increasing expectations for contraception, the menu of choices has not expanded greatly. As discussed earlier, given the AIDS pandemic, new contraceptive methods that are of high priority are vaginal microbicides that protect women from STIs in combination with spermicides that provide contraceptive protection (Bongaarts & Johansson, 2002; Harrison & Rosenfield, 1996; Tsui, Wasserheit, & Haaga, 1997).

In some situations, however, knowledge and use of existing technology have not been widely disseminated. One example is emergency contraception (the prevention of pregnancy through the use of contraceptive methods after unprotected sex), for which appropriate technologies (e.g., a combination of oral contraceptive pills, progestin-only pills, and the cop-per T IUD) have long been available but are not used by many women (e.g., victims of coercive sex) who could benefit from them (International Planned Parenthood Foundation, 1995; Trussell, Ellertson, & Stewart, 1996).

Political, Social, and Financial Constraints

Although high unmet need is in part a function of specific management deficiencies in family planning programs, it is important to recognize that broader political and societal constraints also play a role. Kenney (1993) has identified the policies in a variety of countries that retard access to safe contraception. They include health and safety regulations that restrict choice of methods or providers (e.g., the failure to approve oral contraceptives for use in Japan for over 9 years—a committee finally recommended their approval after the male impotence-relieving drug Viagra received endorsement within 6 months ["Insurance for Viagra," 1999]); taxes and barriers to trade that affect the importation of contraceptives; regulation of advertising (usually due to concerns about modesty and privacy); and restrictions on private-sector involvement in family planning. In addition, law and policies in many countries restrict or forbid access to abortion.

In any discussion of family planning programs and their performance, the issue of financial sustainability is key. Family planning expenditures in low- and middle-income countries as a whole are estimated to be slightly under US$10 billion annually, or roughly about $1 to $2 per person per year for the year 2000. In the last two decades, most of this expense has been paid for by national governments

Table 3-10	Estimates of Method Distribution in 1980 and 1993 and Alternative Projections for 2015, Low- and Middle-Income Countries			
	Past Estimates (%)		2015 Projections (%)	
Method	1980	1993	Futures Group	New Procedure
Female sterilization	24.0	39.0	26.0	37.0
Male sterilization	13.0	8.0	3.0	5.0
Pill	13.0	11.0	22.0	17.0
Injectables	0	4.0	6.0	5.0
IUD	32.0	26.0	18.0	20.0
Vaginal methods	0	0.3	0.6	0.4
Condom	5.0	4.0	10.0	9.0
Traditional methods	12.0	9.0	14.0	7.0
Total	100.0	100.0	100.0	100.0

Note: The figures for 1993 in Table 3-10 are proportions of total contraceptive use, whereas the analogous figures for 1993 in Table 3-9 are proportions of married women using contraceptives. Thus, in Table 3-9, 21% of married couples used female sterilization. Because the total number of married couples using contraceptive methods was 55%, this translates into 39% total contraceptive use (21/55)—the figure in Table 3-10.

Source: Adapted with permission of the Population Council, from John Bongaarts and Elof Johannsson, "Future Trends in Contraceptive Prevelance and Method Mix in the Developing World", *Studies in Family Planning, 33*(1), pp. 24–36.

(50%) and individual households (20%), with international donor assistance accounting for only about 30% of the total. If donor assistance for family planning were to keep pace with the historical record of 30%, it would have had to rise substantially from its 1994 level of US$1.37 billion to US$3.0 billion in the year 2000. However, there has been a decline rather than an increase in funding over the last few years. In particular, the share of funding provided by the United States, by far the largest historical donor for family planning programs, has fallen by about 30%. In the coming decades, rising demand for contraception and increasing budget constraints will require that programs either mobilize more public resources or increase the cost of family planning services to the individual so that more users can be accommodated (Bulatao, 1998).

The Broader Effects of Family Planning Programs

Even before the 1994 ICPD in Cairo, concerns were expressed, by women's groups and by policy makers, about the effects of family planning programs on the lives of individual women. Family planning programs have been criticized as exclusively concerned with reducing population growth. Studies in recent years have broadened research to include consideration of the effects of programs on the quality of life for women. In particular, the Women's Studies Project (1999) found that family planning programs provided benefits to women:

- Most women and men are convinced that practicing family planning and having smaller families provide health and economic benefits.
- Family planning offers freedom from fear of unplanned pregnancy and can improve sexual life, partner relations, and family well-being.
- Where jobs are available, family planning users are more likely than non-users to take advantage of work opportunities.
- Family planning helps women meet their practical needs and is necessary, but not sufficient, to help them meet their strategic needs (Women's Studies Project, 1999).

Exhibit 3-4 **The Bangladesh Family Planning Program**

Family planning in Bangladesh can be traced to the private Family Planning Association created in 1953, before Bangladesh achieved its independence from Pakistan. By 1960 Pakistan had begun public-sector programs, which Bangladesh continued after becoming a nation in 1971. The overall program has grown and changed over the years, but throughout there has been high-level political support and considerable funding from external donors. The program has emphasized provision of services, outreach activities at the village level, and mass communication through a variety of media.

As part of the early-1960s public-sector programs, family planning services were offered in government health clinics as part of regular health services. A system of using village aides to provide education was established but abandoned after only 18 months for a variety of reasons, including poor training of the aides, complaints that their services were directed only to family planning and not to other health problems, inadequate resources, and poor supervision. It was followed by renewed efforts run by a new Family Planning Board independent of the Ministry of Health.

Their efforts in the late 1960s met with little success, primarily because of poor-quality services provided by a program that had been instituted on a large scale with little pilot testing and poor organization. The program emphasized the IUD, which was met with resistance by many concerned about side effects and problems with its use. It did not help that the program was seen by many as having been imposed on Bangladesh, then East Pakistan, by a government whose political support was declining.

In the aftermath of the war for independence, although the health and social sectors of the government were particularly negatively affected, it was felt that family planning was urgently needed. A large and complex program was established. A separate Population Wing was created within the Ministry of Health and Population to run the program. Thus, health and family planning services were separated. At the local level, the primary health care staffs were predominantly male, in a society where, because there can be little interaction between women and men who are not members of their families, male workers cannot provide maternal and child health services except for immunizations. This staffing was a legacy of early programs to combat smallpox, tuberculosis, and malaria; it was ill-suited to the new focus. By contrast, local family planning workers were women, although their supervisors were men. They went directly to households and offered family planning counseling and free supplies. They spent some time on maternal and child health, although they were not well trained for this purpose.

Over the years, the program has continued to be revised and expanded. In all cases, the elements of strong political support, strong financial support, and extensive administrative support have remained.

Source: J. Cleland, J. F. Phillips, S. Amin, and G. M. Kamal, *The Determinants of Reproductive Change in Bangladesh* (Washington, DC: World Bank, 1994). Adapted with permission.

The Project also found costs to women, however:

- Contraceptive side effects—real or perceived—are a serious concern for many women, more so than providers realize.
- When partners or others are opposed, practicing family planning can increase women's vulnerability.
- When women have smaller families, they may lose the security of traditional roles and face new and sometimes difficult challenges, including the burden of multiple responsibilities at home and work (Women's Studies Project, 1999).

In addition, the Project found that the exclusion of men from most family planning programs affected the ability of women to take advantage of their services, because men play a dominant role in family planning decisions.

Most family planning programs have emphasized only the positive benefits of family planning; they are now being urged to pay attention to these broader considerations.

A Broader Definition of Family Planning and Reproductive Health Programs

As discussed earlier, the 1994 ICPD brought about an international reevaluation of the conceptualization of family planning programs. Such programs are now viewed as part of a larger rubric of more general reproductive health services and interventions, some of which are directly health related, while others are related indirectly. It is useful, however, to first consider conventional family planning programs.

Organization and Structure of Family Planning Programs

Although nearly all low- and middle-income countries have established infrastructure to deliver family planning services, their organization varies markedly. One exemplification, Bangladesh, is discussed in Exhibit 3-4. According to Tsui, Wasserheit, and Haaga (1997), successful performance is influenced by a focused commitment to achieving program objectives as well as by access to adequate resources. At the national level, strong leadership, clearly formulated policies, explicit goals and objectives, and a clear agenda for meeting those goals can all contribute to the success of programs. In some countries, political commitment is evidenced by placing the family planning

program under a national supervisory council or by establishing a separate ministry. Programs also need ways of assessing progress toward meeting their objectives. Indicators such as contraceptive prevalence, proportion of unwanted births, maternal morbidity and mortality, pregnancy complications and their management, and actual fertility levels all provide information that, over time, can permit program evaluation. Therefore, one element of successful programs is the definition of result measures to be used and establishment of mechanisms for collecting the needed information. Caution is in order, however. For example, goals that are defined in terms of targets, such as number of acceptors of particular methods in a given time, may lead workers to exert pressure on clients and reduce their options.

Family planning service programs have focused on a narrow set of goals—reducing unwanted fertility by providing access to the means of fertility control. Several models have been used for the design of programs. In the vertical model, family planning administration and service delivery are carried out by staff for whom this is their single function. In a second model, there is a separate family planning administration unit, but field staff at each level of the health care system can deliver a variety of linked services. In practice, the linkage between family planning and maternal and child health services has been the most common. Under the new, broader definition of reproductive health, other types of services are expected to be offered, so that the ways in which they are linked, both administratively and in provision of care, is also being addressed.

Whatever model is followed, the program design involves decisions on which services will be offered and at which level of the health care system. Tsui, Wasserheit, and Haaga (1997) illustrate the possibilities as follows:[2]

Level	Interventions for Prevention and Management of Unintended Pregnancies
Community	Information, education, and communication programs
	Community-based distribution
	Social marketing of condoms, oral pills

[2]*Source:* Adapted with permission from A. O. Tsui, J. N. Wasserheit, and J. G. Haaga (Eds.), *Reproductive Health in Developing Countries: Expanding Dimensions, Building Solutions.* Copyright 1997 by the National Academy of Sciences, courtesy of the National Academies Press, Washington, D.C.

Health post	Counseling/screening for contraception Counseling and referral for menstrual regulation or abortion Provision of injectable contraceptives IUD insertions Counseling and treatment of contraceptive side effects
Health center	Menstrual regulation/manual vacuum aspiration abortion Performing surgical contraception on set days Postabortion counseling and contraception Counseling and treatment of contraceptive side effects
District hospital	Surgical contraception Abortions through 20 weeks, where indicated Postabortion counseling and contraception

Their report concludes that the breadth and scope of the services to be delivered present a formidable challenge in design, execution, administration, and evaluation. Even if this challenge is met, a program can falter if inadequate resources are allocated to meet its needs for trained staff, equipment, and supplies. Additional demands will be placed on whatever system is in place if services related more generally to reproductive health are provided. Research on design and implementation can help improve family planning and reproductive health programs. Exhibits 3-5 and 3-6 illustrate the approach taken by Bangladesh in this regard.

Additional Reproductive Health Care Services

Some reproductive health services are closely linked to contraception; it is likely that, without much added expense, they can be integrated into conventional family planning programs relatively easily. These may include pregnancy tests, Pap smears, and screening for STIs. The latter has been carried out, in many cases, only in the context of separate programs to treat STIs. That type of intervention misses the general population of women who may not realize that they are infected or that they may pass their infection to their unborn or nursing children.

HIV/AIDS deserves special mention. The United Nations convened a conference in 1999 to assess progress since the 1994 ICPD. It concluded that the earlier conference had greatly underestimated the effects of HIV/AIDS on the populations of the low- and middle-income countries and called for specific programs and targets to reduce the spread of infection ("Conference Adopts Plan," 1999). Directly related to the family planning realm is their call for greater access to methods that can reduce or prevent transmission of the virus, such as female and male condoms. These and other approaches to preventing the spread of HIV/AIDS are discussed in Chapter 4.

Other desirable reproductive health interventions remain within the health realm but require significant changes in staffing and significantly more financial resources. These include emergency obstetrics, general women's health services, abortion services where they are not already available, infertility services, and greatly expanded testing and counseling for HIV/AIDS. Some infertility services are already provided within the context of programs to reduce sexually transmitted infections, since these are a major cause of infertility and premature sterility (Tsui, Wasserheit, & Haaga, 1997). All the others are generally lacking; however, without considerable expansion of the financial base for family planning and for the expanded reproductive health program, it is unlikely that these services can be provided in many of the low- and middle-income countries.

Reproductive Health Beyond Direct Health Care

Reproductive health interventions that go beyond the health care realm, while clearly valuable, are not linked in any obvious way to conventional family planning services. The Cairo agenda focused on improving the status of women. It called for interventions, such as income-generating activities for women and female education, that affect the overall status of women and for sex education for youth, both male and female, to increase responsible sexual behavior. The 1999 follow-up conference reiterated and intensified these calls ("Conference Adopts Plan," 1999).

Others have called for programs that decrease violence against women. Violence in women's intimate relationships can lead to death through homicide or through driving the woman to suicide. A less drastic outcome is loss of control by women over their sexuality and, therefore, their sexual health. A practice that is frequently interpreted as a kind of violence against women is female genital cutting, a practice that has been reported in over 40 low- and middle-income countries and has followed immigrants from these areas to industrialized countries (Tsui, Wasserheit, & Haaga, 1997). Although any type of genital cutting carries a risk of infection, the implications of genital cutting for long-term reproductive

Exhibit 3-5	Research to Improve the Family Planning Program in Bangladesh

How well does a family planning program work? Few experiments in applied research have been conducted to determine whether a particular design is effective in reaching the objectives of the program. The International Centre for Diarrhoeal Disease Research, Bangladesh (ICDDR, B) has carried out just these kinds of operations research experiments, which have served to improve the ways in which services are delivered within the Bangladesh family planning program.

An early effort, in 1975, was intended to test the hypothesis that there was latent demand for family planning. ICDDR, B maintains a field station in Matlab, approximately 40 km from the capital, Dhaka. A family planning program was introduced in roughly half of the area in which the center provided services, while people living in the remainder had access only to standard government or private services. Local women, mostly illiterate widows, were hired to visit households about every 90 days to offer oral contraception to women. Later, condoms were added to the offerings. The hypothesis was that couples wanted to reduce their fertility and would do so if only they were supplied with the means. Initial acceptance was good; prevalence of use rose in the early stage to almost 20% from its near-zero level prior to the program. But within less than 9 months, it had dropped, so that the program area prevalence was only 6 percentage points higher than in the comparison area. Lessons learned: This type of demand-oriented program was inadequate in a situation where women and couples had little social support for contraceptive use. Rather, a system that addressed the noneconomic costs of use—whether social, psychological, or based on health concerns—was essential. In addition, there were problems with a daily pill regimen, and condoms were not popular. Analysis of the experiment through interviews with people in the community also demonstrated the importance of the characteristics of the family planning worker. Women who had little status in the community and who were past the reproductive age themselves did not have sufficient credibility to help others withstand the social costs of use. Improving access was simply not enough.

A subsequent experiment begun in 1978 tested better follow-up for users; an expanded set of method choices; employment of better-educated, younger women; and new management strategies. These were undertaken to ensure that there were regular visits and that problems were addressed rapidly. A new dual leadership system was introduced in which there was both technical (paramedical) and administrative supervision. The interval between visits was reduced to 14 days. Within a year, nearly one-third of women in the study area were users, while there was little change in the comparison area. Increases in contraceptive use continued, so that by 1990 nearly 60% were users, compared with only about 25% in the comparison area. Clearly, taking advantage of latent demand for contraception required that the program address the social costs of contraceptive use. It also demonstrated the value of providing service in the home.

In 1983 a new experiment was begun outside of Matlab, to see if lessons learned there could be applied within the government family planning program and without major additional resources or changes in administration. This pilot project was carried out in two areas. Because of the success of this extension project, the government changed the national program to increase the number of female village workers, train them to provide injectable contraception within the home, and upgrade management to provide better support, both technical and supervisory, for local workers. In fact, one of the main lessons learned from these experiments was the need for careful supervision and support of workers. Another was the importance of designing a program for local cultural circumstances—in this case, providing basic services in the home. Since these experiments, other projects have tested variations of the extension project model to see how much it could be altered and still achieve the objectives of increased use of family planning and reduced fertility.

The extension project, later known as the Operations Research Project, has, since the International Conference on Population and Development, initiated studies of how the family planning program can be expanded to provide a wide array of reproductive and other health services under what is termed the Essential Services Package.

Source: J. Cleland, J. F. Phillips, S. Amin, and G. M. Kamal, *The Determinants of Reproductive Change in Bangladesh* (Washington, DC: World Bank, 1994). Adapted with permission.

health differ according to the severity of cutting, conditions of delivery, and sociodemographic factors. It is generally accepted that women who have undergone the most severe type of cutting, which includes removal of external genitalia and infibulation (stitching or narrowing of the vaginal opening), have an increased likelihood of delivery complications or obstetric morbidity (Slanger, Snow, & Okonofua, 2002). In some countries there is evidence that a growing proportion of these procedures are being carried out by medical personnel (Yoder, Abderrahim, & Zhuzhuni, 2004).

Can These Goals Be Achieved?

All parts of this new "beyond family planning" mandate are worthwhile. It is not clear, however, how this expansion, in the absence of clearly designated additional funds, will affect the ability of family planning programs to reach their objective of promoting safe contraception (Cleland et al., 1994; Finkle &

Exhibit 3-6	Strategies Used by the Bangladesh Family Planning and Reproductive Health Programs

According to Cleland and associates (1994), at least four sets of strategies have been implemented:

1. Strategies to improve the coverage and quality of services

- Clinics, located within 5 miles of most couples, now provide free contraception and treatment of side effects.
- Sterilization is offered without charge at all subdistrict hospitals and is carried out by well-trained personnel.
- Related health services for children and women are provided either in the home or in clinics.
- Community-based distribution of low-cost nonclinical contraceptives is provided through pharmacies and is well publicized through various media.

2. Strategies to improve awareness and motivation

- Mass media are used to provide extensive relevant information; family planning and reproductive health are openly discussed in public media.
- Focused programs (e.g., with religious leaders) are carried out to build awareness and consensus.

3. Strategies to foster village-based and household services

- Outreach involves female workers who deliver services in the home. These services are now provided by both the government and nongovernmental organizations.
- This strategy has been questioned by critics who say the time is past when women should be provided with services that encourage continued seclusion. They argue that the demand for family planning and reproductive health services is now so great that women will travel outside their homes to obtain these services and that this type of modernization is to be encouraged. In addition, the issue of the cost of maintaining a large cadre of home visitors is encouraging experimentation with less costly alternatives.

4. Strategies to foster community development and demand generation

- These strategies have not been carried out within the family planning program itself but are directed toward improving the status of women. They include micro-credit and other programs sponsored by local organizations, such as Grameen Bank and the Bangladesh Rural Advancement Committee, and government strategies to increase education of girls. In fact, education of women has increased substantially in recent years. In many parts of Bangladesh, nearly all children, male and female, are obtaining at least several years of primary schooling.

As a final note, the Bangladesh effort is characterized by the use of research to help determine the design of programs. Ongoing studies at ICDDR, B now the International Centre for Health and Population Research, include how the new Essential Services Package (which includes reproductive health, child survival, and curative care) can best be implemented within existing fixed service provision sites, how to meet the health needs of adolescents, strategies for improving prevention and management of reproductive tract and sexually transmitted infections, and strategies for providing essential obstetric care.

Source: J. Cleland, J. F. Phillips, S. Amin, and G. M. Kamal, *The Determinants of Reproductive Change in Bangladesh* (Washington, DC: World Bank, 1994). Adapted with permission.

Ness, 1985). In addition, there is concern that this expansion from family planning programs to reproductive health programs without additional funds will not only dilute what traditional family planning does reasonably well but will also fail to provide significant improvements in other areas. (Bulatao, 1998; Mukaire et al., 1997; Twahir, Maggwa, & Askew, 1996). See Exhibit 3-7 for a discussion of these issues in the context of Bangladesh.

In fact, the new agenda comes in an era when many industrialized countries are reducing their aid contributions. At Cairo, industrialized country donors pledged to provide $5.7 billion a year, but as of 1999, their contributions were only about $1.9 billion annually ("Population Control Measures,"

1999). Raising the political will and the funding for these new programs and for maintaining existing effective ones is perhaps the greatest challenge for reproductive health in the 21st century.

Impact of Reproductive Patterns on the Health of Children

Over the last several decades, an impressive body of evidence has accumulated suggesting that certain kinds of reproductive patterns are injurious to infant and child health (Table 3-11). The risk factors are usually discussed as if they were completely independent. There are, however, a number of problematic issues in

Exhibit 3-7	Challenges and Constraints with Regard to Family Planning and Fertility Reduction in Bangladesh

In the early 1990s, following the rapid decline in fertility from a TFR of 6.3 in 1975 to 3.4 in 1994, there was great optimism that fertility would continue to decline and that replacement-level fertility would be reached by 2005. However fertility in Bangladesh has plateaued at a TFR of around 3 children per woman for the last decade. This lack of change in fertility (which, by the way, is shared by its regional neighbor, India) has become a source of major concern and puzzlement. The initial dramatic fall in fertility took place in the context of relatively insignificant overt improvements in socioeconomic development, and was largely attributed to supply-side initiatives, that is, the impact of an intensive family planning program. In contrast, the last decade has witnessed quite significant improvements in socioeconomic development in Bangladesh, with rapid rise in educational enrollment for women and the rise of employment opportunities for women in the fast-growing garment sector in Bangladesh. Moreover, the family planning program has continued to enjoy high levels of funding and resources.

Various hypotheses have been put forth to explain this lack of progress in fertility. Advocates of conventional family planning programs suggest that this may be due to the change of focus in the mid-1990s, following the expansion of the family planning agenda to include broad-based reproductive health services; (see Exhibit 3-6) from household distribution of contraceptives by a vertical cadre of family planning workers to clinic-based family planning and reproductive health services provided by a unified integrated health and family planning service. They argue that this change has (1) reduced the motivation of the family planning workers, who now have an expanded set of health-related duties they are ill prepared to fulfill, and (2) made contraceptive provision just one of many activities, none of which has adequate resources committed to its fulfillment. Moreover, they question the optimism that family planning is so well established that women in rural Bangladesh no longer have social constraints regarding seeking family planning and reproductive health services outside the home.

Those who favor clinic-based services point out that contraceptive prevalence rates have continued to rise in Bangladesh over the last decade and that a change of method mix from predominantly oral contraceptives to more long-term methods with lower failure rates requires clinic-based initiatives. It is worth noting that due to the lack of progress in fertility, the government of Bangladesh has switched back from clinic-based services to household distribution.

Demand-side advocates, on the other hand, argue that the exclusive focus on fine-tuning family planning programs in order to bring about fertility reduction is misplaced. Their contention is that further reductions in fertility require broad-based initiatives to improve socioeconomic development (with a particular focus on improving women's status), which will help to reduce the benefits of additional children and increase their costs. They point to a continued desired fertility of 2.5 children per woman—still above replacement level, quite significant regional variations that can be correlated with differences in women's education and employment, and continued preference for sons.

The debate about demand- versus supply-side policy initiatives as the best approach to fertility reduction continues. Most researchers and policy makers feel that both kinds of initiatives are important. However, there is growing appreciation that the final stretch of fertility decline to replacement levels may well be a long, hard battle.

this approach to deleterious reproductive patterns. For example, many of the risk factors are integrally linked with one another, and their independent effects are difficult to disentangle. Thus, first births and young age of mothers are separately cited as risk factors, but young mothers usually are having their first birth. Similarly, children of high parity come from large families and are likely to have older mothers, yet all three are referred to individually.

Parity and Child Health

First births are known to be more dangerous for the child than subsequent births. But the excess risk relative to births of order 2 to 4 is limited to the first year of life (and particularly to the neonatal period, where the odds ratio for mortality is 1.7). There appears to be no survival disadvantage after the first birthday (Hobcraft, 1987; Hobcraft, McDonald, & Rutstein, 1985). Moreover, excess risk for firstborn children varies con-

siderably across countries. It is not clear whether it is due to inadequate physiologic adjustment of first-time mothers to pregnancy (leading to less intrauterine growth, shorter gestation, lower birth weight, a higher probability of birth trauma, higher risks of pregnancy-induced hypertension, higher prevalence of placental malaria in malaria-endemic areas, etc.) or due to the lack of experience of first-time mothers in care seeking and care taking. The latter is, of course, amenable to policy prescriptions that encourage first-time mothers to seek prenatal and postnatal care (Haaga, 1989; National Research Council, 1989).

Higher-order births may suffer due to poor maternal health as a result of cumulative exposure to previous pregnancies (Hobcraft, McDonald, & Rutstein, 1985; Pebley & Stupp, 1987). Mothers may suffer from inadequate recovery of their energy store after earlier pregnancies (maternal depletion hypothesis) and/or long-term cumulative effects of prior

Table 3-11	Mechanisms by Which Reproductive Patterns Affect Child Health
Reproductive Pattern	**Mechanism Through Which Child Health Is Affected**
Firstborn children	First-time mothers have a higher frequency of health problems during pregnancy and childbirth; parents have less experience with child care; poorer intrauterine growth
Higher-order children	Possible cumulative effect of earlier maternal reproductive injury ("maternal depletion" syndrome), leading to poorer intrauterine growth
Large families	Competition for limited resources, with some children, possibly disproportionately girls, losing out; possible spread of infection
Children born to very young mothers	Inadequate development of maternal reproductive system and incomplete maternal growth; young mothers less likely to know about and use prenatal and delivery care or provide good child care
Children born to older mothers	Greater risk of birth trauma; greater risk of genetic abnormalities
Short interbirth intervals	Inadequate maternal recovery time (maternal depletion); competition among similar-aged siblings for limited family resources; early termination of breast-feeding; low birth weight; increased exposure to infection from children of similar ages
Unwantedness	Conscious or unconscious neglect; child born into a stressful situation
Maternal death or illness (e.g., chronic infection such as AIDS)	Early termination of breastfeeding; no maternal care; disease may be passed to child
Contraceptive use	Hormonal contraception may interrupt breastfeeding

Source: Adapted with permission from *Contraception and Reproduction: Health Consequences for Women and Children in the Developing World.* Copyright 1989 by the National Academy of Sciences, courtesy of the National Academies Press, Washington, D.C.

delivery-related injuries. Thus, higher-order children (parity ≥ 5) may be at greater risk of poor intrauterine growth, greater trauma during birth, and, more generally, poorer health than lower-parity (2 to 4) children. Although these mechanisms are plausible, the empirical evidence is variable and suggests that there is little additional risk that can be attributed to higher-order births, once short birth intervals are taken into account (Gubhaju, 1986; Hobcraft, McDonald, & Rutstein, 1985; National Research Council, 1989).

In addition to physiologic deficiencies, higher-order children may suffer deleterious consequences of competition for limited family resources. Thus, they may get proportionately less food and less attention from their parents. This negative consequence of large families may not be limited only to higher-order births. If family resources are limited and there is no preference for specific children, all children may suffer as a result of large family sizes. There is, however, evidence that some children (particularly higher-order girls, and especially those with older sisters) suffer disproportionately from the impact of large family size in specific social settings (Muhuri & Menken, 1997).

Maternal Age

Hobcraft (1987) found that children born to teenaged mothers had significantly higher risks of dying than children born to mothers aged 25 to 34. This excess mortality risk was 1.2 for the neonatal period, 1.4 for the postneonatal period, 1.6 for toddlers, and 1.3 for children aged 2 to 5. There was, however, considerable variability among countries in excess mortality risk for children born to young mothers. Plausible explanations of both physiological and social causes have been offered for the health disadvantages of children born to young mothers. They may be disadvantaged because maternal reproductive systems are inadequately industrialized (Aitken & Walls, 1986) or because young mothers lack experience and knowledge about prenatal and postnatal care (Geronimus, 1987). Unfortunately, there is little solid empirical evidence from low- and middle-income countries. It has been difficult to study possible competition between fetal growth and maternal development as underlying the excessive mortality of children born to young mothers in the low- and middle-income countries. Due to lack of reliable data on gynecological age (i.e., age since menarche—a particularly important concern because of delayed age at menarche in low- and middle-income countries [Foster et al., 1986]) or chronological age below the age of 20, Haaga (1989) concluded that there was only weak evidence for this hypothesis. Studies that have addressed social causes (poor knowledge and use of prenatal care) have used socioeconomic status as a crude proxy for use of prenatal care services. In multivariate analyses, this measure fails to help explain the high risk of infants and children born to young mothers.

Children born to older mothers may suffer because of poorer maternal health due to age-related declines in physiologic function and a higher risk of genetic abnormalities (Hansen, 1986). However, there is little evidence to suggest that this is a major risk factor in low- and middle-income countries.

Short Birth Intervals

Short birth intervals, both prior and subsequent to the birth of a child, are probably the most consistent reproductive pattern identified as a risk factor for excess child mortality. Hobcraft (1987) reports that the excess mortality risk of children born less than 24 months after the preceding birth compared with those born 24 months or more after the preceding birth is 1.8 in the first year of life, 1.3 for toddlers (ages 1 to 2), and 1.3 for children aged 2 to 5. In terms of subsequent birth intervals, Hobcraft reports that on average, across 34 countries, children whose birth was followed by a subsequent birth within less than 24 months had 2.2 times the risk of dying of children for whom the subsequent birth interval was longer. As is the case for other demographic risk factors, there is considerable variation between countries in risks related to short birth intervals.

There are a number of plausible explanations for the relationship between short prior and subsequent birth intervals (<24 months) and a child's risk of poor health and increased mortality. First, due to maternal depletion resulting from inadequate recovery time from the nutritional burdens of breastfeeding and prior pregnancy (Merchant & Martorell, 1988), those born after a short birth interval may suffer poorer intrauterine growth, and possibly a higher risk of preterm birth. However, there is little empirical evidence to support this mechanism (Ferraz et al., 1988; National Research Council, 1989; Pebley & DaVanzo, 1988; Winikoff & Sullivan, 1987).

Second, children born before a short birth interval may suffer from premature cessation of breastfeeding, which has been shown to be an important correlate of child survival in low- and middle-income countries (Palloni & Millman, 1986), as the mother

shifts her attention to the recent arrival. However, studies that have controlled for the length of breastfeeding still show an association between short subsequent birth interval and high infant mortality (Pebley & Stupp, 1987). Thus, premature termination of breastfeeding does not entirely explain this effect.

Third, children born in close proximity to one another may suffer from competition for limited family resources of time and food. However, the evidence for this type of competition is unclear and sometimes contradictory (DaVanzo, Butz, & Habicht, 1983; Palloni, 1985).

Fourth, close birth spacing may increase the likelihood of transmission of infectious diseases such as diarrhea and measles, due to overcrowding and the presence of children of similar ages (Aaby et al., 1984). Finally, despite adequate controls for observable confounders in multivariate analyses, part of the relationship between short birth intervals (either preceding or following the index birth) and increased child mortality may be due to confounding from unobserved factors such as short gestational length or parental characteristics. Babies born before or after very short birth intervals are known to be at high risk for short gestational durations, which independently have been shown to increase child mortality dramatically (Miller, 1989; Pebley & Stupp, 1987).

In terms of unobserved parental characteristics, it is possible that women who are likely to have short birth intervals are inherently at higher risk for poorer child health outcomes than their peers who have longer birth intervals. This would lead to a spurious inference that short birth intervals are causally related to higher child mortality (Pebley & Stupp, 1987; Potter, 1988; Rosenzweig & Schultz, 1983).

Unwanted Pregnancy and Birth

As discussed previously, unwanted children have much higher risks of morbidity and mortality. They may suffer from both conscious and unconscious neglect due to lower allocations of food, parental time and attention, and access to health care. In countries with strong son preference (e.g., in South and Southeast Asia), there is significant evidence for higher mortality for female children relative to their male siblings (Das Gupta, 1987; D'Souza & Chen, 1980; Muhuri & Menken, 1997). Moreover, as discussed earlier, the recent rise in sex-selective abortion in China and Southeast Asia (which has led to a disproportionately high male to female sex ratio at birth) is evidence of the high risk of mortality for unwanted female fetuses (Larsen, Chung, & Das Gupta, 1998; Tsui, Wasserheit, & Haaga, 1997). The pattern of gender discrimination is complex and nuanced, however, and may vary by societal setting (Muhuri & Menken, 1997).

Maternal Health

Maternal morbidity and mortality can have profoundly negative effects on child health, leading to high rates of morbidity and mortality. Population-based studies in South and Southeast Asia suggest that over half of perinatal deaths (deaths in the first week of a child's life) are associated with poor maternal health and pregnancy and delivery-related complications (Fauveau et al., 1990; National Statistics Office [Philippines] & Macro International, 1994). These deleterious consequences may result from a combination of physiologic processes (e.g., cessation of breastfeeding following maternal morbidity and mortality; maternal fetal transmission of a variety of infectious agents, including HIV, toxoplasmosis, cytomegalovirus, rubella, hepatitis B virus, herpes simplex, syphilis, malaria, and tuberculosis) and emotional impacts and lower levels of caregiving (National Research Council, 1989; Overall, 1987; Turner, Miller, & Moses, 1989; Weinbreck et al., 1988). This is particularly a major concern in sub-Saharan Africa, where significant numbers of mothers are suffering from HIV and other sexually transmitted infections (National Research Council, 1989; Turner, Miller, & Moses, 1989; Weinbreck et al., 1988).

Methodological Concerns

The previously mentioned mechanisms by which specific reproductive patterns affect infant and child health are certainly plausible and suggestive. However, it is important to reiterate that the empirical evidence (in terms of the appropriateness of both data and statistical methods) supporting such mechanisms is variable and needs to be interpreted cautiously. Women have some control over their choices of reproductive patterns (i.e., whether to have children early or late, whether to have shorter or longer birth intervals, whether to have high-parity births). Therefore, unobservable factors that are associated with both reproductive patterns and child health may be operating, and reverse causality may be a problem. Thus, our estimates of the impact of specific reproductive patterns on the risk of poor infant and child health may be overstated.

For example, if women who choose to be young mothers are prone to behavior patterns that devalue prenatal and postnatal care, delaying childbirth for these women will not produce the salutary effects that our earlier discussion suggests. Similarly, there may be unobserved selection biases that operate so that a significant proportion of women who choose

to have births at older ages, higher-parity births, and closely spaced births are intrinsically in better health (most likely because of higher socioeconomic status). If that is the case, then reducing higher-parity births, increasing interbirth intervals, and reducing births to older women (>35) will not result in the degree of improvement that our current studies suggest.

With regard to reverse causality, one example is the often-cited relationship between the mortality of an index child and a short subsequent birth interval. The inference is that a child is at a higher risk of death if the next-younger sibling arrives after only a short interval—presumably because the pregnancy and the arrival of a newborn cause early cessation of breastfeeding for the older child and a shift of other maternal resources. However, it is quite possible that the subsequent birth interval is short because the index child died, or was ill and weaned earlier because of his or her existing health problems. Thus, the direction of causation is not from the short subsequent birth interval to the death of the preceding child but, instead, in the reverse direction—from the death of the preceding child to a short subsequent birth interval. Although in principle there are statistical methods to deal with this kind of potential bidirectionality (Rosenzweig & Schultz, 1983; Schultz, 1984), in practice relatively few published studies have employed such sophisticated methods of analysis. In summary, because of these methodological concerns, we should be careful not to overinterpret the evidence linking specific reproductive patterns and poor child health.

Summary of the Impact of Reproductive Patterns on Child Mortality

Despite these caveats about overinterpretation and overestimation, it is instructive to consider the impact of specific deleterious reproductive patterns on infant and child mortality. The National Research Council (1989) has simulated the impact of various reproductive patterns on child mortality rates using data from 18 low- and middle-income countries reported by Hobcraft (1987). The simulations in Table 3-12 refer to death rates that would be observed in individual families with particular reproductive patterns; they assume that the mortality risks associated with the specific reproductive pattern are causative. Table 3-12 shows that children of parity 2 and above are at much higher risk of mortality if they are born to teenaged mothers than if the mothers are aged 20 to 34. Moreover, both teenage and nonteenage mothers can significantly reduce the risks of child mortality by adopting better spacing patterns (i.e., birth intervals of 24 months or more). The best-case scenario for children of parity 2 and above occurs for

Table 3-12	Estimated Risk of Dying (Deaths per 1,000 Births) Prior to Their Second Birthday for Second and Higher-Order Births to Women with Different Reproductive Patterns		
Age of Mother	Better Spacing Pattern		Poor Spacing Pattern
Teenaged mothers	92		165
Mothers aged 20 to 34	67		120

Note: Better spacing pattern: Birth intervals both proceeding and subsequent to this birth were 24 months or more, and the older sibling survived. Poor spacing pattern: Birth intervals both preceding and subsequent to this birth were less than 24 months, and the older sibling survived.

Source: Data from the National Research Council, *Contraception and Reproduction: Health Consequences for Women and Children in the Developing World* (Washington, DC: National Academy Press, 1989); and J. N. Hobcraft, *Does Family Planning Save Lives?* Paper presented at the International Conference on Better Health for Women and Children Through Family Planning, Nairobi, October 5-9, 1987.

those born to mothers between the ages of 20 and 34, whose older sibling has survived, and whose birth interval is 24 months or more. Only 67 of 1,000 such children fail to reach their second birthday. This is less than half the mortality risk of their peers born to teenaged mothers, where their birth intervals are less than 24 months. In the latter situation, 165 of 1,000 such children die before age 2.

Other simulations show the deleterious consequences of increasing family size and birth intervals on the probability of a child surviving to his or her fifth birthday. The calculations were carried out under low, moderate, and high baseline child mortality rates (to take into account variation in overall mortality among populations). The baseline child mortality rates represent the probability of a child surviving to his or her fifth birthday for children who have the lowest risk profile (i.e., parity 2–3, preceding and subsequent birth intervals ≥ 24 months, and the older sibling survived). Thus, in a population with a baseline child mortality rate of 150/1,000, of 1,000 births of children who were parity 2 to 3, had long preceding and subsequent birth intervals (≥24 months), and whose older sibling survived, 150 would die before their fifth birthday. Mortality rates for specific combinations of parities below and above the baseline, of short and long intervals, and of survival of older sibling were estimated by Hobcraft (1987). He then simulated the average number of children per 1,000 births who would die before their fifth birthday. Here we discuss only those cases where the older sibling survived. In terms of family size, small families were much better off than large families. Regardless of the baseline mortality rates or the closeness of birth spacing, the greater the family size, the higher the child mortality rates. In all cases, four-child families experienced fewer than half the deaths per 1,000 births of nine-child families. Similarly, families with long spacing experienced half or less the mortality per 1,000 births of families with consistently short spacing. Clearly, the most beneficial scenario for children is that of well-spaced births and small overall family sizes.

Impact of Reproductive Patterns on the Health of Women

Pregnancy is one of the major health risks for women in the low- and middle-income countries. Nearly 530,000 women die worldwide each year due to pregnancy-related causes, and the vast majority (99%) of these deaths occur in the low- and middle-income countries (UNFPA, 2004). Although these numbers are alarming, it is important to recognize that there are 180 million pregnancies annually in the world, so that by and large reproduction is relatively safe for women. Maternal mortality risks are a fraction of infant mortality risks; for example, Bangladesh has both high infant mortality and very high maternal mortality risks, but the latter are roughly a tenth of the former. The maternal mortality ratio is about 380 deaths per 100,000 births, while the infant mortality rate (which has fallen considerably in the decade around 2000) is about 66 infant deaths per 1,000 births (Macro International, 2004; Tsui, Wasserheit, & Haaga, 1997).

Definitions

In any discussion of maternal mortality, a number of potentially confusing definitional issues arise. The first is the definition of a maternal death. A maternal death is usually defined as a death of a woman while pregnant or up to 42 days postdelivery from any cause (except accidents). There has been some discussion as to whether this definition is overly restrictive (i.e., leading to an undercount of maternal deaths) and should be expanded to include female deaths up to 90 days postdelivery. In reality, data from a number of well-conducted population-based studies using different postdelivery durations show that the majority of maternal deaths occur within 42 days postdelivery, and about 40% occur within 24 to 48 hours of delivery. Furthermore, extending the definition to up to 90 days would result in only a marginal increase (6%) in the number of deaths classified as related to maternal causes (Egypt Ministry of Health, 1994; Fauveau et al., 1988).

The second issue is the measure of maternal mortality risk that should be used in comparing and contrasting the situation in different populations both geographically and across time. Maternal mortality risks are conventionally described using three distinct measures. It is important to understand and to think of them separately, because they are conceptually distinct.

The first measure is the *maternal mortality ratio*, which is defined as the ratio of the number of maternal deaths to the number of pregnancies. It is an indicator of the risk of dying that a woman faces for each pregnancy she undergoes. Although conceptually the denominator for such a risk measure should include all pregnancies, operationally, because of the difficulty of counting miscarriages and induced abortions, the denominator used is live births.

The second measure is the *maternal mortality rate,* which is defined as the number of maternal deaths divided by the number of women of reproductive age (i.e., between ages 15 and 49). This is a composite measure that is the product of the maternal mortality ratio (deaths/births) and the birth rate in the reproductive age group (births/women between ages 15 and 49). The important point to note about the maternal mortality rate is that it can be changed by changing the frequency of pregnancies or births in the population without changing the risk of maternal death per pregnancy/birth. Although the maternal mortality ratio and the maternal mortality rate are conceptually distinct, they are often confused in the public health literature, with rates referring to ratios and vice versa. In this chapter, these two measures are carefully distinguished.

The third measure is the *lifetime risk of maternal mortality*. It is again a composite measure that takes into account not only the maternal mortality risk per pregnancy but also factors in the cumulative exposure to pregnancy that an individual woman experiences. The average cumulative exposure to pregnancy is usually taken to be the TFR for the population. It is an estimate of the number of births a woman in a particular society would have over her lifetime if she were to adhere to the current age-specific fertility rates in that population.

The lifetime maternal mortality risk for a woman in the low- and middle-income countries in 2000 was estimated to be 1/61 (Population Reference Bureau, 2005; UNFPA, 2004) This estimate can be interpreted as follows: a woman in the low- and middle-income countries who (1) has the same total number of pregnancies over her lifetime as the current fertility norm (estimated to be 3.7 pregnancies) and (2) experiences at each pregnancy the same independent risk of maternal death as the current maternal mortality ratio (440 maternal deaths per 100,000 births) would have 1 chance in 61 of dying from pregnancy-related causes. This lifetime risk captures both the risk of dying per pregnancy and the cumulative effect of exposure to multiple pregnancies.

Maternal Mortality Risks

A major constraint with respect to investigating the magnitude of maternal mortality risks and their determinants is the lack of available and reliable population-based data. Even in low- and middle-income countries, many of which have high maternal mortality rates and ratios, maternal deaths are relatively rare. For example, in sub-Saharan Africa and South Asia, where maternal mortality ratios of 800 maternal deaths per 100,000 live births have been reported, one would need very large sample sizes to get reasonable estimates of maternal mortality risks and their accompanying determinants. A sample of 10,000 births (a very large sample by any standards) would be expected to yield only 80 maternal deaths. In contrast, infant mortality rates in these settings are typically 15 times as large, and the same sample would yield 1,050 infant deaths. Relatively few large-scale population-based studies of maternal mortality have been conducted in low- and middle-income countries. They were carried out in Bangladesh (Alauddin, 1986; Chen et al.,1975; Khan, Jahan, & Begum, 1986; Fauveau et al., 1988; Koenig et al.,1988; Bangladesh Maternal Mortality Survey, 2004); Ethiopia (Kwast, Rochat, & Kildane-Mariam, 1986); Egypt (Egypt Ministry of Health, 1994; Fortney et al., 1985); and Jamaica (Walker et al., 1985). Estimates for other countries are derived from model-based assumptions and thus are not as precise.

There are huge disparities in maternal mortality among regions of the world. The disparity between the low- and middle-income countries and industrialized countries is much greater for maternal mortality (20 times higher risk of maternal death per pregnancy) than infant mortality (10 times higher risk of infant death per pregnancy). Lifetime risks of maternal mortality vary from 1/61 in the low- and middle-income countries to 1/2,800 in the industrialized countries (Table 3-13).

As is shown in Table 3-13, both the total number of pregnancies per woman and the individual risk of dying per pregnancy are much higher in the low- and middle-income countries than in the industrialized countries. But it is the risk of dying per pregnancy that accounts for the vast majority of the difference in lifetime risk of maternal mortality. Total fertility rates in the low- and middle-income countries are, on average, twice as high as in the industrialized countries (3.0 births per woman versus 1.6 births per woman). Maternal mortality ratios are 22 times as high (440 maternal deaths per 100,000 births in the low- and middle-income countries versus. 20 maternal deaths per 100,000 births in the industrialized countries). For most of the poor countries of the developing world (most of South Asia and Africa as opposed to the middle-income countries such as China, Egypt, Indonesia, Jordan, Mexico, Sri Lanka, and Tunisia), there has not been much change in the maternal mortality ratios between 1900 and 2000 (United Nations Statistics Division, 2005a).

Direct and Indirect Causes of Maternal Mortality and Morbidity

What does the mortality risk per pregnancy derive from? The causes of maternal mortality are conventionally divided into direct causes (those that occur only during pregnancy and the immediate postdelivery period) and indirect causes (those derived from conditions that precede, but are aggravated by pregnancy, such as anemia, diabetes, malaria, tuberculosis, cardiac disease, hepatitis, and, increasingly, AIDS).

In the low- and middle-income countries, direct causes account for 75% to 80% of maternal mortality and include, in approximate order of importance, hemorrhage, sepsis, hypertensive disorders of pregnancy (eclampsia), complications of unsafe abortion, and obstructed and/or prolonged labor (Fauveau et al., 1988; Maine & McGinn, 1999; World Health Organization, 1993c; World Health Organization & UNICEF, 1996). The vast majority of these maternal deaths can be attributed to just three causes: hemorrhage, sepsis, and eclampsia. Attribution of cause of

death is complicated by the fact that in most cases unsafe abortion and obstructed or prolonged labor eventually cause death via the proximate causes of hemorrhage and/or sepsis. There is variation in the order of importance of these causes in different studies from different parts of the world (Jamison et al., 1993), partly due to real differences in the availability and use of obstetric care and partly due to differences in the quality of reporting. Thus, in countries that have poor access to obstetric care facilities, the proportion of deaths attributed to hemorrhage, sepsis, and abortion is proportionately larger. Differential reporting, particularly reluctance to attribute maternal deaths to abortion in countries where it is illegal, also artifactually inflates the proportion of deaths attributed to hemorrhage and sepsis. For example, Jamison and associates (1993) estimated that, for the period 1980-85, 56% of maternal deaths in Indonesia were due to these two causes, 40% in Egypt, and 18% in the U.S.

The remaining 20% to 25% of maternal deaths can be attributed to illnesses aggravated by pregnancy (Jamison et al., 1993; World Health Organization, 1993b). Anemia hampers a woman's abilities to resist infection and to survive hemorrhage; it may increase the likelihood of her dying in childbirth by a factor of four (Chi, Agoestina, & Harbin, 1981). Hepatitis can cause hemorrhage or liver failure in pregnant women (Kwast & Stevens, 1987). Latent infections such as tuberculosis, malaria, or STIs can be activated or exacerbated during pregnancy and cause potentially severe complications for both mother and child (Jamison et al., 1993).

In keeping with the high rates of maternal mortality in the low- and middle-income countries, there are also high rates of maternal morbidity. There are estimated to be 30 to 50 morbidities (temporary and chronic) for every maternal death (Safe Motherhood

Table 3-13	TFR, Maternal Mortality Ratios, Lifetime Risks of Maternal Death, and Maternal Deaths by Region of the World in 2000			
	Total Fertility Rate	**Maternal Mortality Ratio**	**Maternal Deaths**	
Region	**(births per woman)**	**(deaths per 100,000 live births)**	**Lifetime Risk**	**Deaths per Year**
World Total	2.8	400	1 in 74	433,639
More Developed Countries	1.6	20	1 in 2,800	3,221
Less Developed Countries	3.0	440	1 in 61	424,098
Africa	5.1	830	1 in 20	223,000
Asia	2.6	330	1 in 94	202,340
Latin America and the Caribbean	2.6	190	1 in 160	17,625

Source: Population Reference Bureau, *Women of Our World: 2005 Data Sheet.* Washington, DC: The Population Reference Bureau. Accessed June 22, 2005 at (http://www.prb.org/Template.cfm?Section=PRB=/ContentManagement/ContentDisplay.cfm=12298). Adapted with permission.

Initiative, 2003). Approximately 30% to 40% of the approximately 180 million women who are pregnant annually in the world, or roughly 54 million women, report some kind of pregnancy-related morbidity annually (Koblinsky, Campbell, & Harlow, 1993; World Health Organization, 1993b). Of these, it is estimated that about 15 million a year develop relatively long-term disabilities deriving from complications from obstetric fistula or prolapse, uterine scarring, severe anemia, pelvic inflammatory disease, or reproductive tract infections, as well as infertility (Tsui, Wasserheit, & Haaga, 1997).

It is important to recognize that these figures are quite approximate, with significant variability from one country to another (Tsui, Wasserheit, & Haaga, 1997). For example, Guatemalan women report one in five pregnancies as being complicated (Bailey, Szaszdi, & Scheiber, 1994), women in West Java report one in three pregnancies being complicated (Alisjahbana et al., 1995), and two of three pregnancies in Ghana had some complications (De Graft-Johnson, 1994). This variability stems at least in part from differences in study design and data quality, as there have been relatively few population-based surveys. Moreover, much of the maternal morbidity data is based on self-reported symptoms, which have been shown to have relatively low reliability and validity (Stewart & Festin, 1995). There are a few data sets with reliable information from the United States and Canada (Koblinsky, Campbell, & Harlow, 1993; World Health Organization, 1994b) and from specific validation studies (Stewart & Festin, 1995). These data show that annually roughly 12% to 15% of women who are pregnant suffer life-threatening obstetric complications, that is, about 20 million women in the low- and middle-income countries (of the approximately 150 million women giving birth annually). In contrast to the evidence on acute pregnancy-related morbidity, little is known about the long-term chronic morbidity sequelae of pregnancy-related complications, which may significantly affect women's lives.

Specific Causes of Pregnancy-Related Morbidity and Mortality

This section focuses on some of the more prominent causes of pregnancy-related morbidity and mortality in the low- and middle-income countries.

Obstructed and Prolonged Labor

Obstructed and prolonged labor leads to about 40,000 maternal deaths annually, with high proportions of survivors suffering from obstetric fistulas and their newborn often suffering from long term sequelae of anoxia. Predictive risk factors are not particularly reliable (Fortney, 1995; Maine, 1991), and monitoring during labor using a partograph is the only effective way to detect such problems (World Health Organization, 1994a).

Obstetric Fistula and Genital Prolapse

It is important to focus attention on obstetric fistulas and genital prolapse because of their severe consequences. An obstetric fistula is a passage or channel from the vaginal wall to either the rectum (rectovaginal fistula) or the bladder (vesicovaginal fistula). It is usually a result of a tear in the vaginal wall during complicated labor. Risk factors for obstetric fistulas include the following: young mothers, stunted mothers, and mothers who have complicated labor and deliver in nonhospital settings with the help of traditional birth attendants (Lawson, 1992; Tahzib, 1983, 1985). Population-level estimates of obstetric fistulas are hard to come by, but fragmentary reports suggest that they are a significant cause of morbidity for pregnant women in low- and middle-income countries (Lawson, 1992; World Health Organization, 1991). The consequences of fistulas are quite severe, especially for young primiparas. The baby is often stillborn. The mother is incontinent of urine or feces or both. This condition is a source of enormous personal discomfort, exacerbated by social stigma. In many cases it leads to divorce and social ostracism— these women are often barred from food preparation or even participating in prayer because of lack of personal hygiene (Reed, Koblinsky, & Mosley, 2000).

Genital prolapse occurs when the vagina and uterus descend below their normal positions. It is usually a result of damage to supporting muscles and ligaments during childbirth and is most often associated with high parity. The condition is particularly uncomfortable for women who are squatting, which is the normal position for doing many chores in low- and middle-income countries. It can also lead to chronic backache, urinary problems, and pain during sexual intercourse. Subsequent pregnancies have a higher probability of fetal loss and further maternal morbidity.

Although good estimates of these conditions are hard to come by, some reliable population studies suggest very high prevalence rates in some countries— as many as one-third of all pregnant women (Omran & Standley, 1981; Younis et al., 1993). The Giza study (Younis et al., 1993), which clinically validated reported prolapse, found that a third of women suffered from genital prolapse; it also documented a relationship between genital prolapse and the risk of reproductive tract infections.

Anemia

Approximately 50% of pregnant women around the world are estimated to be anemic (i.e., have hemoglobin levels below 11g/dL). Dietary iron deficiency is the primary cause, followed by malaria, other parasitic diseases (schistosomiasis, hookworm), folate deficiency, AIDS, and sickle cell disease (Tsui, Wasserheit, & Haaga, 1997). In addition to its well-documented effects on pregnancy outcomes—prematurity, stillbirths, spontaneous abortions, and so forth (Levin et al., 1993)—anemia, even at fairly mild levels, has been implicated as directly contributing to maternal deaths (Harrison & Rossiter, 1985; United Nations, 1991). There is also some evidence that anemia predisposes women to higher risks of complications during pregnancy, including urinary tract infections, pyelonephritis, and preeclampsia (Kitay & Harbort, 1975). Anemia is also associated with reduced productivity and quality of life for women (Bothwell & Charllton, 1981).

The record of the impact of iron supplementation on reducing the prevalence of iron deficiency anemia is not encouraging (Sloan, Jordan, & Winikoff, 1992). Although a significant part of the failure to reduce anemia is due to the inadequate efforts to provide iron supplementation, it is important to acknowledge that even in situations where there have been properly conducted supplementation trials, these programs by and large appear not to be very effective in reducing baseline anemia levels (Sood et al., 1975). This may be due to the inadequacies of strategies that focus just on pregnant women. Long-term success in this effort probably involves the use of a multipronged strategy that includes iron supplementation schemes, efforts to raise household income, and efforts to reduce workload during pregnancy (Tsui, Wasserheit, & Haaga, 1997).

Pregnancy-Related Hypertension

Both eclampsia and preeclampsia are significant causes of maternal morbidity but appear to be difficult to predict and prevent, although routine prenatal blood pressure measurements and urinalysis for proteinuria in the first prenatal visit continue to be recommended (Rooney, 1992; Stone et al., 1994). Women with moderate hypertension and proteinuria require appropriate follow-up. Treatment options and their effectiveness vary, and no definitive conclusions or recommendations can be made. However, as a general rule, some combination of bed rest, antihypertensives, and anticonvulsants (especially magnesium sulfate for frank convulsions) provide some relief (Eclampsia Trial Collaborative Group, 1995; Rooney, 1992).

Consequences for Infants

Pregnancy- and delivery-related complications have important health consequences not only for mothers but also for infants, particularly in the perinatal period (i.e., the first 7 days of birth/delivery). For most low- and middle-income countries, perinatal mortality rates range from 40 to 60 deaths per 1,000 births, compared with 10 per 1,000 for the industrialized countries (note that this ratio includes still births in the denominator). As infant mortality rates drop, the proportion of infant deaths attributed to the perinatal period actually increases, since postneonatal deaths (those after the first 28 days of life and most sensitive to environmental contamination) are the first to drop. In general, perinatal deaths account for about 40% of infant deaths in most low- and middle-income countries, and an increasing percentage in industrialized countries.

Of the estimated 7.6 million perinatal deaths annually in low- and middle-income countries (World Health Organization, 1996), the vast majority are associated with maternal health problems during pregnancy and delivery (Fauveau et al., 1990). Women who have inadequate nutritional status (including short stature, poor prepregnancy weight, inadequate weight gain during pregnancy, and anemia) or infections during pregnancy are more likely to have low-birth-weight babies (World Health Organization, 1993b). The single most important risk factor for perinatal mortality is low birth weight, with babies below 2,500 grams having 20 to 30 times the mortality risk of fetuses of normal weight. In addition to increasing the risk of perinatal mortality, there is also a substantial burden of long-term disability (cerebral palsy, seizures, and severe learning disorders) for low-birth-weight babies who survive (Jamison et al., 1993; Tsui, Wasserheit, & Haaga, 1997).

High-Risk Pregnancies

For the sake of simplicity, the calculations of lifetime risk presented earlier assumed that the risk of maternal death per pregnancy is the same across women and across successive pregnancies within each woman. The reality is somewhat more complicated, with some types of pregnancies being riskier than others. These include pregnancies of first-time mothers, mothers with multiple previous pregnancies (five or more pregnancies), very young and older mothers, and women already in poor health, and pregnancies that are terminated by unsafe abortions (National Research

Council, 1989). Table 3-14 summarizes the hypothesized mechanisms by which different reproductive patterns affect maternal health.

First pregnancies have a higher risk of maternal mortality than subsequent pregnancies (up to five) both in the industrialized and the low- and middle-income countries. Population-based data from Bangladesh (Koenig et al., 1988), Ethiopia (Kwast, Rochat, & Kidane-Mariam, 1986), and Gambia (Greenwood et al., 1987) suggest that first pregnancies may be as much as three times riskier than later pregnancies.

The impact of young maternal age on maternal mortality is more difficult to evaluate because there are relatively few studies that have disaggregated the confounding effect of young maternal age and first pregnancy. Among those that have controlled confounding appropriately, the largest study to date looked at maternal mortality among 14,631 first births in rural Bangladesh (Koenig et al., 1988); it showed no age effect. However, other, smaller studies from the same area (Chen et al., 1975), Indonesia (Chi, Agoestina, & Harbin, 1981), and Jamaica (Walker et al., 1985) have shown a higher mortality risk for mothers below age 20 compared with mothers aged 20 to 24. A further problem that makes interpretation difficult is that maternal age below 20 is not disaggregated into single years of age; in fact, the highest risk may be for young teenaged mothers in the 15- to 17-year age group (Harrison & Rossiter, 1985).

The major causes of morbidity and mortality for young primigravidas include a high risk of pregnancy-induced hypertension (World Health Organization, 1988), a high frequency of obstructed labor due to the pelvis being too small for the child's head to pass (Aitken & Walls, 1986), and a high incidence of placental malaria (MacGregor, Wilson, & Billewicz, 1983).

A number of studies have shown that women with four or more pregnancies have about 1.5 to 3 times the risk of maternal death as women of parities 2 and 3. In general, within each parity, older women, particularly those over 35, have higher risks of maternal death (Koenig et al., 1988; Chi, Agoestina, & Harbin, 1981; Walker et al., 1985). A major cause of maternal morbidity and mortality for older multiparous women is the higher risk of malpresentation (in which the fetus lies in a position other than the usual head-first position, as in a breech or transverse lie presentation). Malpresentation of the fetus may occur due to the flacidity of the uterine wall from repeated stretching from successive pregnancies. It can lead to uterine rupture, hemorrhage associated with rupture, or infections resulting from unsuccessful attempts to deal with malpresentation. Another major cause of morbidity and mortality in older multiparous women is hemorrhage due to placental abnormalities such as placentia previa (where the placenta overlies the cervical opening of the uterus) and abruptia placenta (where the placenta separates prematurely

Table 3-14	Mechanisms by Which Reproductive Patterns Affect Maternal Health
Reproductive Pattern	**Mechanism Through Which Maternal Health Is Affected**
Number of pregnancies	Each pregnancy carries a risk of morbidity and mortality
High-risk pregnancies	
First-time mothers	Higher risk than pregnancies 2 through 4 for obstructed labor, pregnancy-induced hypertension, other obstetric complications due to initial adaptation to pregnancy
Higher-order pregnancies	Higher risk for hemorrhage and uterine rupture, due to cumulative toll of previous pregnancies and reproductive injuries
Pregnancy at very young maternal ages	Higher risk due to physiologically immature reproductive systems and reduced propensity for timely care seeking
Pregnancy at old maternal ages	Body in poorer condition for pregnancy and childbirth
Short interbirth intervals	Inadequate time to rebuild nutritional stores and regain energy levels
Unwanted pregnancies ending in unsafe abortions	Unsafe abortions increase exposure to injury, infection, hemorrhage, and death
Pregnancies for women already in poor health	Aggravated health condition

Source: Adapted with permission from *Contraception and Reproduction: Health Consequences for Women and Children in the Developing World.* Copyright 1989 by the National Academy of Sciences, courtesy of the National Academies Press, Washington, D.C.

from the uterus prior to delivery of the baby) (Faundes et al., 1974).

There has been much talk about the possibility of a maternal depletion syndrome, whereby multiple short birth intervals result in women not having enough time to recover their energy and nutritional levels, which in turn may lead to higher risks of maternal mortality (Jelliffe, 1976; Winikoff, 1983). However, no convincing evidence of this hypothesis has been presented (Koenig et al., 1988; National Research Council, 1989; Ronsman & Campbell, 1998). This could be due to the fact that intrinsically healthier women (in this case, women of higher socioeconomic status) may be more likely to have multiple short birth intervals, whereas less healthy women may take longer to have subsequent births (Duffy & Menken, 1998).

Pregnancy is more dangerous for women who are already in poor health; it increases the likelihood that a woman will die if she has certain preexisting conditions such as malaria, hepatitis, anemia, sickle cell disease, or rheumatic heart disease (Koblinsky, Campbell, & Harlow, 1995; Morrow et al., 1968; National Research Council, 1989; Tsui, Wasserheit, & Haaga, 1997; World Health Organization, 1993b).

Finally, unsafe abortions are a significant cause of maternal death in countries where abortion is not legal and regulated. Kwast, Rochat, and Kidane-Mariam (1986) report that the primary cause of maternal mortality in Addis Ababa, Ethiopia, especially among primigravid, unmarried women is complications from illegal abortions. In Bangladesh, Koenig and colleagues (1988) reported that 18% of all maternal deaths in the Matlab surveillance area were from abortion complications (see the earlier discussion of abortion and its health consequences for women).

Mechanisms to Reduce Maternal Morbidity and Mortality in Low- and Middle-Income Countries

The major emphasis in the last few decades in low- and middle-income countries in reducing maternal morbidity and mortality has been on decreasing the total number of pregnancies per woman. As documented earlier, the total number of pregnancies per woman has fallen quite sharply in many low- and middle-income countries; this drop has contributed significantly to the decrease in the lifetime risk of maternal mortality by reducing cumulative exposure. For example, assume a constant maternal mortality ratio of 650/100,000. In Bangladesh, if the TFR had remained at its 1975 level of over 7 instead of dropping to the 1998 level of 3.4, the lifetime risk of ma-

ternal mortality would have been 1/22 instead of 1/45. Now, of course, Bangladesh has a maternal mortality ratio of 380/100,000 and a TFR of 3.0 (Macro International, 2004). Both changes together have led to a decrease in the lifetime maternal mortality risk to 1/88.

In addition to the reduction in the TFR in low- and middle-income countries, there was been some progress over the 1960s and 1970s in reducing high parity births (Table 3-15), births to older women (Table 3-16), and births following short intervals (i.e., less than 24 months). By 2000, as fertility continued to decline in most of these countries, the proportion of births to older women increased again due to postponement of births (United Nations Population Division, 2005). Access to safe abortion has also increased (Tsui, Wasserheit, & Haaga, 1997). An often-overlooked benefit of fertility-reduction initiatives is their impact on reducing the frequency of unsafe abortions by providing access to effective contraception for those who want it (Bulatao, 1998; National Research Council, 1989).

Despite these positive efforts, there is a significant burden of maternal mortality that persists in low- and middle-income countries, despite the increase in the proportion of pregnancies that are in the demographically low-risk category (i.e., parity 2 to 4 among mothers aged 24 to 29 with birth intervals ≥ 24 months). There are two reasons. First, the absolute risk of maternal death is still very high in these settings, even for low-risk pregnancies. Second, some of the highest-risk pregnancies, such as first pregnancies, are unavoidable.

In this regard, it is worth considering the following scenario. Bangladesh (with its very high risks of maternal mortality per pregnancy) experiences no change in the mortality risk per pregnancy (now 380/100,000), but fertility declines to replacement levels (i.e., each woman had just 2.1 births over her lifetime). Under these conditions, the lifetime risk of maternal mortality would still be 1/125—almost 14 times as high as the lifetime maternal mortality risk (1/1,800) of a woman in the industrialized countries. Even this scenario may be overly optimistic. Our calculation does not allow for any heterogeneity in maternal mortality risks across pregnancies. If first pregnancies are intrinsically more dangerous or if healthier women were the ones who had more pregnancies, simply reducing the number of births would not achieve the reduction in maternal mortality just estimated. Finally, a number of studies have shown that older women with more surviving sons have significantly lower mortality than their peers with fewer

Table 3-15	Change in the Distribution of Birth Order over the Course of Fertility Decline and Percentage Decline in Total Fertility Rates for Selected Countries				
	Percentage of All Births of Order 1		Percentage of All Births of Order 5		
Country	1960s	1970s–1980	1960s	1970s–1980	Percentage Decline in TFR
Singapore	23	44	33	2	65
Hong Kong	25	43	23	4	64
Barbados	22	40	35	10	54
Mauritius	18	36	36	11	52
Costa Rica	18	32	45	17	50
Chile	25	41	31	9	49
Trinidad and Tobago	19	32	37	19	43
Puerto Rico	27	32	27	10	42
Panama	21	29	35	22	42
Malaysia	12	26	41	22	42
Fiji	23	35	36	13	41

Source: Adapted with permission from *Contraception and Reproduction: Health Consequences for Women and Children in the Developing World.* Copyright 1989 by the National Academy of Sciences, courtesy of the National Academies Press, Washington, D.C.

Table 3-16	Change in the Distribution of Births by Maternal Age in Selected Countries over the Course of Fertility Decline and Percentage Decline in Total Fertility Rates Between 1960 and 1980				
	Percentage of All Births to Women Under Age 20		Percentage of All Births to Women Aged 35 and Over		
Country	1960s	1970s–1980	1960s	1970s–1980	Percentage Decline in TFR
Singapore	8	4	14	5	65
Hong Kong	5	4	20	6	64
Barbados	21	25	15	6	54
Mauritius	13	14	15	7	52
Costa Rica	13	20	18	9	50
Chile	12	17	17	9	49
Trinidad and Tobago	17	19	11	8	43
Puerto Rico	18	18	11	7	42
Panama	18	20	11	9	42
Malaysia	11	7	14	13	42
Fiji	13	11	12	8	41

Source: Adapted with permission from *Contraception and Reproduction: Health Consequences for Women and Children in the Developing World.* Copyright 1989 by the National Academy of Sciences, courtesy of the National Academies Press, Washington, D.C.

sons (Rahman, 1998; Rahman, Menken, & Foster, 1992). This research suggests that although increased numbers of pregnancies may expose a woman to considerable risk of morbidity and mortality, women in certain social settings (where family support is crucial) are actually better off when they are older if they have had higher fertility. These considerations lead to the conclusion that, in order to reduce maternal deaths significantly in low- and middle-income countries, an emphasis on reducing overall fertility levels and the frequency of high-risk pregnancies is unlikely to be sufficient. The emphasis has to be on reducing the mortality risk for each and every pregnancy as well.

Obstetric Care

As pointed out earlier, the majority of maternal and perinatal mortality and morbidity stems from complications of the delivery process that are difficult to predict and avoid prenatally (Maine, 1991; National Statistics Office [Philippines] & Macro International, 1994; Thaddeus & Maine, 1994). Perhaps the most important benefit of prenatal care is in sensitizing the mother to the warning signs of obstetric emergencies and the need to seek appropriate obstetric care when they occur (Tsui, Wasserheit, & Haaga, 1997). It is instructive to review briefly what the basic acceptable package of obstetric care consists of. WHO uses the following criteria to assess the adequacy of obstetric care facilities (World Health Organization, 1995):

- The ability to carry out surgery such as caesarian section and removal of ectopic pregnancy, and the ability to treat infection, both orally and intravenously
- The ability to provide intravenous labor-inducing agents such as oxytocin
- The ability to provide anesthesia, ranging from mild sedation to epidural and full general anesthesia
- The facilities for the medical treatment of shock, sepsis, anemia, and hypertensive disorders of pregnancy
- The ability to provide blood transfusions
- The ability to provide manual procedures, including vacuum extractions
- The ability to monitor labor
- The ability to provide safe abortion services
- The ability to provide special care for neonates

The historical record in the United States and Europe (Hogberg, Wall, & Brostroin, 1986; Loudon, 1991) and the more recent experience of specific low- and middle-income countries such as Sri Lanka show that the implementation even of limited parts of the essential obstetric care package can result in major declines in maternal mortality. The maternal mortality ratio in Sri Lanka dropped dramatically from 555 per 100,000 births in the mid-1950s to 239 in the 1960s and to 95 in 1980 (World Health Organization, 1995). This was largely due to the expansion of health centers appropriately equipped for essential obstetric care and the increase in births attended by trained personnel.

For a variety of reasons (including cultural taboos, lack of social mobility, lack of economic resources, lack of logistic resources, and lack of information), women in low- and middle-income countries for the most part do not use appropriate obstetric care services, with the most vulnerable group in this regard being rural, less educated, and poorer women (Govindasamy et al., 1993). Only 37% of births in low- and middle-income countries take place in a health facility (World Health Organization, 1993a). The rest (some 55 to 60 million births) occur with the help of traditional birth attendants, family members, or no assistance at all. It is interesting to note that prenatal care services are used significantly more than obstetric care services. In 39 of 43 countries covered by DHS surveys between 1985 and 1994, prenatal care coverage was significantly higher than delivery care from a trained provider (doctor, nurse, or midwife) (Macro International, 1994). These results need to be viewed with some caution, because prenatal care is self-reported and may include very low and episodic use of appropriate services. There is considerable variation in the DHS countries in use of both prenatal and maternal care services. South Asia (with the exception of Sri Lanka) has particularly low uses of prenatal care and maternal care services.

The failure to use appropriate maternal care services can be viewed as resulting from a multipart process that includes (1) deficiencies in identifying life-threatening medical complications that would benefit from obstetric care services; (2) constraints that prevent the use of obstetric services even when appropriate conditions for such use are identified (these may include lack of financial resources, transportation difficulties, and other logistic problems); and finally (3) obstetric care facilities of such poor quality that they are ineffective in preventing obstetric complications and death, even when pregnant women come to such facilities (Thaddeus & Maine, 1994; Tsui, Wasserheit, & Haaga, 1997). Each of these problems is elaborated upon in the following subsections.

Identification of Serious Medical Complications That Will Benefit from Obstetric Care

It is important to reiterate that most women in low- and middle-income countries deliver at home, far away from even rudimentary obstetric care facilities, and are assisted for the most part by family members or traditional birth attendants. The ability to recognize a potentially life-threatening complication and its need for specialized obstetric care (such as obstructed or prolonged labor, incipient hemorrhage, or other fetal distress) depends on appropriate education and sensitization of both family members and traditional birth attendants, with the former being perhaps the more important constituency.

A number of cultural factors affect recognition that obstetric complications can benefit from specific kinds of medical care. When a woman is bleeding, the need for obstetric intervention by trained medical personnel is better recognized. Other complications are, however, generally not viewed as benefiting from specialized obstetric care. In some cultures, complications are seen as determined by fate, with little that can be done to alter the course of events. In Indonesia, for example, malposition of the fetus is seen as the domain of traditional birth attendants, who deal with it with soothing massage whereby pregnant women maintain the inner calm considered necessary for correcting the baby's position (Ambaretnani, Hessler-Radelet, & Carlin, 1993). As a result, referral to obstetric care services is often significantly delayed. There are other instances in which, due to concerns about privacy and modesty, the home is perceived as a more natural and fitting place for birth than any health care facility. For the Fulani and Hausa in Nigeria, pregnancy is seen as a shameful period with unpredictable outcome; thus, no preparations are made for referral for obstetric services (Public Opinion Polls, 1993; Tsui, Wasserheit, & Haaga, 1997).

It is clear from these examples that cultural sensitivities need to be taken into account when constructing appropriate educational messages that emphasize the identification of particularly serious obstetric risks and the need to refer them to health facilities with adequate obstetric care services. A purely technocratic approach, which focuses on modern systems of logic and evidence, may not be very effective in bringing about changes in behavior. Much attention has been focused on training birth attendants, given that they are present in the majority of births in low- and middle-income countries. However, the evidence suggests that focusing on just training birth attendants leads to mixed results in terms of increased referrals for appropriate conditions. In urban and periurban areas there appears to be no impact, whereas there is some improvement in rural areas with low prevalence rates of use of maternal care services (Alisjahbana et al., 1995; Bailey et al., 1991). The consensus from a number of sources suggests that husbands and possibly other family members (mothers-in-law, mothers, and sisters) are the key people who should be targeted, because they are the final decision makers with regard to whether the woman will go to a modern health care facility (Alisjahbana et al., 1995; Bailey, et al., 1991; Bower & Perez, 1993; Center for Health Research, Consultation and Education & MotherCare/John Snow, Inc., 1991; Howard-Grabman, Seoane, & Davenport, 1994).

Constraints Affecting Use of Obstetric Care Services Once Complications Are Identified

Several concerns affect the decision to use modern obstetric care services once a life-threatening complication is identified and the need for obstetric care is acknowledged. These include economic constraints (not being able to afford the costs of such care, including transportation costs), logistic constraints (taking time off to accompany the patient to often distant care facilities), and quality concerns (attitude and treatment of health care providers) (Sundari, 1992; Thaddeus & Maine, 1994).

It is important to recognize that the economic costs of care include not only the nominal costs charged by the health care facility for delivery-related services, but also transportation costs (which are not insubstantial in many rural settings), costs of medications, and costs of housing. In many cultures, family members need to accompany the patient, which adds to transportation and housing costs. In addition to these direct costs, there are opportunity costs or lost wages for the patient and particularly for family members who accompany the patient. There is relatively little population-based data to estimate all the various components of costs that are incurred for a maternal delivery in a health care facility, but some reports suggest that costs may in fact be a barrier to the use of obstetric services. For example, data from three countries in Africa (Nigeria, Ghana, and Sierra Leone) show that there were declines in deliveries in seven referral sites from 1983 to 1989, paralleling increases in costs to patients for drugs and services (Prevention of Maternal Mortality Network, 1995). The impact of user fees on the use of obstetric care for complicated cases (as opposed to normal deliveries) has been inadequately investigated. The existing evidence shows a mixed response to the imposition of user fees, with use of modern medical facilities for obstetric complications being reduced to different degrees in different countries (Ambaretnani, Hessler-Radelet, & Carlin, 1993; Prevention of Maternal Mortality Network, 1995).

Clearly, much more information needs to be collected to understand the changes in demand and use of obstetric care services with changes in costs of services. Special attention needs to be focused on getting data on the nonservice components of obstetric costs (travel costs, opportunity costs, etc.).

Aside from economic costs, transportation constraints are a major factor in the low use of maternal care services. In most low- and middle-income countries, advanced obstetric care (including surgical services with appropriate transfusion capabilities) is only available in a few health care facilities, often at a considerable distance from the patient. Transportation facilities are, for the most part, poorly developed and quite expensive. Thus, problems need to be anticipated in advance to allow enough time for the patient to reach the care facility. The degree to which lack of transportation is a major constraint to the use of modern obstetric services is not certain; the evidence is mixed. Data from rural Bangladesh suggest that relatively modest investments in transportation can have a significant impact on use of obstetric services, leading to reductions in maternal mortality (Fauveau et al., 1991; Maine et al., 1996). On the other hand, three different experiments that aimed at ensuring transport did not by themselves increase the use of obstetric services (Alisjahbana et al., 1995; Poedje et al., 1993; Prevention of Maternal Mortality Network, 1995).

Transportation concerns assume that the patient has to be brought to the care facility. A complementary approach is to bring the provider closer to the patient. There has been some limited success with posting certified midwives in health posts closer to the pregnant patient population, but such staffing may be difficult to sustain logistically and financially (Fauveau et al., 1991; Tsui, Wasserheit, & Haaga, 1997).

Finally, the perception of the welcoming nature of the referral site and its flexibility in accommodating accompanying family members are often ignored but particularly important constraints to seeking modern obstetric care. Often, referral sites are perceived as impersonal and unfriendly and are passed over in favor of care from traditional birth attendants (Bailey, Szaszdi, & Scheiber, 1994; Eades et al., 1993).

Quality of the Obstetric Care in the Care Facility

Relatively little systematic data on the quality of health care services in obstetric care facilities exists. The few studies that do exist suggest that the majority of obstetric care facilities in the low- and middle-income countries fall far short of minimal acceptable standards of care. Important indicators of quality include waiting time from admission to treatment, trends in numbers and rates of maternal and perinatal deaths, and trends in case fatality rates for all complications, including caesarians (O'Rourke, 1995; Prevention of Maternal Mortality Network, 1995).

Much of this problem can be traced to lack of adequate resources in terms of trained personnel, equipment, and bed capacity. For example, a UNICEF survey of three districts in India in 1993 found not only inadequate numbers of beds but also huge disparities in bed allocation between different levels of the health care system. The majority of beds were allocated to referral sites where a small minority of complicated births were managed. There were also major deficiencies in the availability of essential drugs and appropriately trained surgical and anesthesia professionals.

In addition to supply constraints, there are frequently major deficiencies in the management of services and in provider attitudes. Triaging is not done

systematically, and very sick patients are often left waiting for much longer than medically desirable, while others with less severe problems are treated before them. Obstetric care is often ad hoc, with no consistent set of case management algorithms being followed. Nursing is often seriously below standard, and basic levels of hygiene are not adhered to, leading to considerable postoperative morbidity and mortality.

In a nationally representative study of 718 maternal deaths in Egypt in 1992 (Egypt Ministry of Health, 1994), avoidable factors (i.e., those that could have been changed by either the health delivery system or the patient) were assessed by an expert panel. In about half the cases, the primary avoidable factor identified was poor management and diagnoses by health care professionals. For the rest, patient factors, particularly delay in seeking medical care (and/or compliance with medical recommendations) were implicated. It is interesting to note that the health professionals most cited for poor quality of care were not traditional birth attendants or general practitioners but, in fact, obstetricians with supposedly appropriate training. This sorry state of affairs is significantly related to the lack of consistent management guidelines for complicated obstetric cases.

Similar results have been reported from China (World Health Organization, 1994b), where a study of 1,173 maternal deaths in 1990 implicated deficiencies in the health care system as the highest contributor (48%), followed by individual and family delays in using health care and by transport problems. There appears to be a clear rural/urban divide, with rural areas having a much higher frequency of problems that are avoidable both from the point of view of the health care system and from the point of view of the patient.

Improvements in the quality of care require a number of simultaneous initiatives. Governments must appropriately fund health care referral facilities so that they have adequate supplies and equipment and are staffed by appropriate specialists. There must be a clear chain of referral whereby trained birth attendants refer complicated obstetric cases to higher-level facilities, where specialist care is available. Efforts must be made to follow consistent management protocols that are clearly articulated, and both birth attendants and specialists must be trained to adhere to them (Marshall & Buffington, 1991; Scheiber et al., 1995). There has to be a monitoring system that will provide regular audits of both process and outcome indicators, such as waiting times and case fatalities, and that will be used in a continuous process of review and upgrading (Egypt Ministry of Health, 1994).

If even some of these improvements in quality of care are made, they will not only improve outcomes for those women who reach the health facility but also will increase the demand for such services by pregnant women (Mantz & Okong, 1994; O'Rourke, 1995).

Conclusion

This chapter has outlined the need for reproductive health and family planning to help individual women and men and populations reduce fertility and maintain reproductive health. Population growth rates are declining in much of the world because people are reducing their fertility. The primary factors effecting this reduction are early termination of the reproductive period through sterilization, use of contraception to reduce conception rates, and induced abortion. Because of increased desire for smaller families, both unwanted fertility and unmet needs for family planning and reproductive health services exist in most of the low- and middle-income countries. To meet this challenge, improvements are needed in the quality of family planning services, especially in the areas of information exchange and method choice, integration of reproductive health services with contraceptive provision, and financial sustainability. Maternity care needs to be expanded so that the adverse sequelae of pregnancy and childbearing can be reduced. Preventive services need to be increased and targeted to those at greatest risk of adverse outcomes. These include education of both men and women regarding health and sexuality and regarding family planning and the prevention of STIs.

At the societal level, programs need to be supported to improve the status of women, whether through education or through changes in laws and culture to reduce violence. Although this may be unfamiliar territory to public health professionals, the consequences for the health of women and children make it essential that this broader perspective become part of health programs.

An overriding concern regarding continuing, let alone expanded, funding remains. Many industrialized countries have reduced their aid contributions; many low- and middle-income countries are undergoing financial and health crises. Part of the agenda for the future must be research to determine cost-effective and effective programs that will address the reproductive health needs of the 21st century.

● ● ● Discussion Questions

1. Using the proximate determinants framework (originally proposed by Bongaarts and subsequently revised by Stover), discuss the relative impacts of contraception, breastfeeding, abortion, sexual activity, and infecundity on total fertility rates in Latin America versus Africa. What are the policy implications of these findings?

2. Discuss fertility changes using the framework of wanted versus unwanted fertility and the forces that drive each of them. What are the policy approaches that stem from considering this kind of framework?

3. The 1994 Cairo ICPD substantially enlarged the scope of family planning to include a broader conception of women's health and development. Discuss the pros and cons of this expansion in the context of limited financial resources.

4. Discuss the impact of birth interval length, both prior and subsequent, on the health of children, taking into account methodological concerns about reverse causality. What are the implications for policy?

5. Consider the following statement: "Family planning has only a limited role to play in reducing the risk of maternal mortality." Discuss whether you agree with this statement and elaborate on the policy implications of your analysis.

6. "Specific health technological inputs are a necessary but not sufficient determinant of significant improvements in reproductive health." Using the example of changes in women's status, discuss the validity of this proposition.

● ● ● References

Aaby, P., Bukh, J., Lisse, I. M., & Smits, A. J. (1984). Overcrowding and intensive exposure as determinants of measles mortality. *American Journal of Epidemiology, 120*(1), 49–63.

Aitken, I. W., & Walls, B. (1986). Maternal height and cephalopelvic disproportion in Sierra Leone. *Tropical Doctor, 16*(3), 132–134.

Alan Guttmacher Institute (1999a). *Sharing Responsibility: Women, Society, and Abortion Worldwide*. New York: Alan Guttmacher Institute.

Alan Guttmacher Institute (1999b). *Facts in Brief: Induced Abortion Worldwide*. New York: Alan Guttmacher Institute.

Alauddin, M. (1986). Maternal mortality in rural Bangladesh: The Tangail district. *Studies in Family Planning, 17*(I), 13–21.

Alisjahbana, A. C., Williams, C., Dharmayanti, R., Hermawan, D., Kwast, B. E., & Koblinsky, M. (1995). An integrated village maternity service to improve referral patterns in a rural area in West Java. *International Journal of Gynecology and Obstetrics, 48*(Suppl.), s83–s94.

Ambaretnani, N. P., Hessler-Radelet, C., & Carlin, L. E. (1993). *Qualitative research for the social marketing component of the Perinatal Regionalization Project, Tanjungsari, Java* (MotherCare Working Paper No. 19, prepared for the U.S. Agency for International Development, Project No. 936-5966). Arlington, VA: John Snow, Inc.

Arnold, F., Kishor, S., & Roy, T.K. (2002). Sex-selective abortions in India. *Population and Development Review, 28*(4), 759–785.

Bailey, P. E., Dominik, R. C., Janowitz, B., & Aaujo, L. (1991). Obstetrica e mortalidade perinatal em uma area rural do nordeste Brasileiro. *Boletin de la Oficina Sanitaria Panamericana, 111*(4), 306–318.

Bailey, P. E., Szaszdi, J. A., & Scheiber, B. (1994). Analysis of the vital events reporting system of the Maternal and Neonatal Health Project: Quetzaltenango, Guatemala (MotherCare Working Paper No. 3, prepared for the U.S. Agency for International Development, Project No. DPE-5966-Z-00-8083-00). Arlington, VA: John Snow, Inc.

Bankole, A., & Westoff, C. F. (1995). *Childbearing attitudes and intentions* (DHS Comparative Studies No. 17). Calverton, MD: Macro International, Inc.

Bledsoe, C. H, & Cohen, B. (Eds.). (1993). *Social dynamics of adolescent fertility in sub-Saharan Africa*. Working Group on the Social Dynamics of Adolescent Fertility in Sub-Saharan Africa, Committee on Population, National Research Council. Washington, DC: National Academies Press.

Bongaarts, J. (1978). A framework for analyzing the proximate determinants of fertility. *Population and Development Review, 4*, 105–132.

Bongaarts, J. (1983). The proximate determinants of natural marital fertility. In R. A. Bulatao & R. D. Lee (Eds.), *Determinants of fertility in developing countries* (Vol. 1, pp. 103–108). New York: Academic Press.

Bongaarts, J. (1990). The measurement of unwanted fertility. *Population and Development Review, 16*(3), 487–506.

Bongaarts, J. (1991). Do reproductive intentions matter? *Demographic and Health Surveys World Conference, 1*, 223–248.

Bongaarts, J. (1997a). Trends in unwanted child-bearing in the developing world. *Studies in Family Planning, 28*(4), 267–277.

Bongaarts, J. (1997b). The role of family planning programs in contemporary fertility transitions. In G. W. Jones, R. M. Douglas, J. C. Caldwell, & R. M. D'Souza (Eds.), *The continuing demographic transition* (pp. 422–443). New York and Oxford: Oxford University Press.

Bongaarts, J., & Bruce, J. (1995). The causes of unmet need for contraception and the social context of services. *Studies in Family Planning, 26*(2), 57–76.

Bongaarts, J., & Johansson, E. (2002). Future trends in contraceptive prevalence and method mix in the developing world. *Studies in Family Planning, 33*(1), 24–36.

Bongaarts, J., & Potter, R. G., Jr. (1983). *Fertility, biology, and behavior: An analysis of the proximate determinants*. New York: Academic Press.

Bongaarts, J., & Watkins, S. C. (1996). Social interactions and contemporary fertility transitions. *Population and Development Review, 22*(4), 639–682.

Bothwell, T. H., & Charllton, R. (1981). Iron deficiency in women. Washington, DC: International Nutrition Anemia Consultative Group.

Bower, B., & Perez, A. (1993). *Final project report: Cochabamba Reproductive Health Project* (MotherCare Project No. 5966-C-00-3038-00). Arlington, VA: John Snow, Inc.

Brown, S. S., & Eisenberg, L. (Eds.). (1995). *The best intentions: Unintended pregnancy and the well-being of children and families*. Committee on Unintended Pregnancy, Institute of Medicine. Washington, DC: National Academies Press.

Bulatao, R. A. (1993). Effectiveness and evolution in family planning programs. In International Union for the Scientific Study of Population, *International Population Conference* (Vol. 1, pp. 189–200). Liege, Belgium: International Union for the Scientific Study of Population.

Bulatao, R. A. (1998). *The value of family planning programs in developing countries*. Santa Monica, CA: RAND Corporation.

Bulatao, R. A., & Lee, R. (1983). *Determinants of fertility in developing countries: Vol. I. Supply and demand for children*. New York: Academic Press.

Caldwell, J. C. (1986). Routes to low mortality in poor countries. *Population and Development Review, 12*(2), 171–200.

Caldwell, J. C., Barkat, H. B., Caldwell, B., Pieris, I., & Caldwell, P. (1999). The Bangladesh fertility decline: An interpretation. *Population and Development Review, 25*(1), 67–84.

Casterline, J., Perez, A. E., Biddlecom, A. E. (1996). *Factors underlying unmet need for family planning in the Philippines* (Research Division Working Paper No. 84). New York: Population Council.

Center for Health Research, Consultation and Education & MotherCare/John Snow, Inc. (1991). *Qualitative research on knowledge, attitudes, and practices related to women's reproductive health* (MotherCare Working Paper No. 9, prepared for the U.S. Agency for International Development, Project No. 936-5966). Arlington, VA: John Snow, Inc.

Chen, L. C., Gesche, M. C., Ahmed, S., Chowdhury, A. I., & Mosley, W. H. (1975). Maternal mortality in Bangladesh. *Studies in Family Planning, 5*(11), 334–341.

Cleland, J., Phillips, J. F., Amin, S., & Kamal, G. M. (1994). *The determinants of reproductive change in Bangladesh*. Washington, DC: The World Bank.

Coale, A. J., & Watkins, S. C. (1986). *The decline of fertility in Europe*. Princeton, NJ: Princeton University Press.

Colombo, B., & Masarotto, G. (2000). Daily fecundability: First results from a new data base. *Demographic Research*, 3(Article 5). Accessed June 22, 2005 at http//www.demographic-research.org/ Volumes/Vol3/5.

Conference adopts plan on limiting population. (1999, July 3). *New York Times*.

Curtis, S. L., & Neitzel, K. (1996). *Contraceptive knowledge, use, and sources* (DHS Comparative Studies No. 19). Columbia, MD: Institute for Resource Development.

Das Gupta, M. (1987). Selective discrimination against female children in rural Punjab. *Population and Development Review, 13*(1), 77–100.

DaVanzo, J., Butz, W. P., & Habicht, J. P. (1983). How biological and behavioral influences on mortality in Malaysia vary during the first year of life. *Population Studies, 37*(3), 381–402.

David, H. P. (1992). Abortion in Europe, 1920-91: A public health perspective. *Studies in Family Planning, 23*(1), 1–22.

De Graft-Johnson, J. (1994, May 5-7). *Maternal morbidity in Ghana*. Paper presented at the annual meeting of the Population Association of America, Miami, FL.

Desai, S. (1995). When are children from large families disadvantaged? Evidence from cross-national analyses. *Population Studies, 49*, 195–210.

Dixon-Mueller, R., & Germain, A. (1992). Stalking the elusive "unmet need" for family planning. *Studies in Family Planning, 23*(5), 330–335.

D'Souza, S., & Chen, L. C. (1980). Sex differentials in mortality in rural Bangladesh. *Population and Development Review, 6*(2), 257–270.

Duffy, L., & Menken, J. (1998). *Health, fertility, and socioeconomic status as predictors of survival and later health of women: A twenty-year prospective study in rural Bangladesh* (Working Paper WP-98-11). Boulder, CO: Population Program, Institute of Behavioral Science, University of Colorado.

Eades, C., Brace, C., Osei, L., & LaGuardia, K. (1993). Traditional birth attendants and maternal mortality in Ghana. *Social Science and Medicine, 36*(11), 1503–1507.

Eclampsia Trial Collaborative Group. (1995). Which anticonvulsant for women with eclampsia? Evidence from the Collaborative Eclampsia Trial. *Lancet, 345,* 1455–1463.

Egypt Ministry of Health. (1994). *National Maternal Mortality Study: Egypt, 1992-1993.* Alexandria, Egypt: Ministry of Health, Child Survival Project.

Faundes, A., Fanjul, B., Henriquez, G., Mora, G., & Tognola, C. (1974). Influencia de la edad y de la paridad sobre algunos parametros de morbilidad materna y sobre la morbimortalidad fetal. *Revista Chileña de Obstetrica y Ginecologia, 37*(1), 6–14.

Fauveau, V., Koenig, M., Chakraborty, J., & Chowdhury, A. (1988). Causes of maternal mortality in rural Bangladesh, 1976-1985. *Bulletin of the World Health Organization, 66*(5), 643–651.

Fauveau, V., Stewart, K., Khan, S. A., & Chakraborty, J. (1991). Effect on mortality of community-based maternity-care programme in rural Bangladesh. *Lancet, 338,* 1183–1186.

Fauveau, V., Wojtyniak, B., Mostafa, G., Sarder, A. M., & Chakraborty, J. (1990). Perinatal mortality in Matlab, Bangladesh: A community-based study. *International Journal of Epidemiology, 19,* 606–612.

Ferraz, E. M., Gray, R. H., Fleming, P. L., & Maria, T. M. (1988). Interpregnancy interval and low birthweight: Findings from a case-control study. *American Journal of Epidemiology, 128,* 1111–1116.

Finkle, J. L., & Ness, G. D. (1985). *Managing delivery systems: Identifying leverage points for improving family planning program performance.* Ann Arbor, MI: Department of Population Planning and International Health, University of Michigan.

Fortney, J. A. (1995). Antenatal risk screening and scoring: A new look. *International Journal of Gynecology and Obstetrics, 2*(Suppl.), s53–s58.

Fortney, J. A., Susanti, I., Gadalla, S., Saleh, S., Feldblum, P. J., & Potts, M. (1985, November 11-15). *Maternal mortality in Indonesia and Egypt.* Paper presented at the WHO Inter-regional Meeting on Prevention of Maternal Mortality, Geneva, Switzerland.

Foster, A., Menken, J., Chowdhury, A. K. M. A., & Trussell, J. (1986). Female reproductive development: A hazard model analysis. *Social Biology, 33*(3-4), 183–198.

Foster, A., & Roy, N. (1996). *The dynamics of education and fertility: Evidence from a family planning experiment.* Working paper, University of Pennsylvania, Department of Economics.

Freedman, R. (1987). The contribution of social science research to population policy and family planning effectiveness. *Studies in Family Planning, 18*(2), 57–82.

French, F. E., & Bierman, J. M. (1962). Probabilities of fetal mortality. *Public Health Report, 77,* 835–847.

Frenzen, P. D., & Hogan, D. P. (1982). The impact of class, education, and health care on infant mortality in a developing society: The case of rural Thailand. *Demography, 19,* 391–408.

Gelbard, A., Haub, C., & Kent, M. M. (1999). World population beyond six billion. *Population Bulletin, 54*(1), 1–40.

Geronimus, A. T. (1987). On teenage childbearing and neonatal mortality in the United States.

Population and Development Review, 13(2), 245–279.

Govindasamy, P., Stewart, K., Rutstein, S., Boerma, J., & Sommerfelt, A. (1993). *High-risk births and maternity care* (Demographic and Health Surveys Comparative Studies No. 8). Columbia, MD: Macro International, Inc.

Gray, R.H., Wawer, M.J., Serwadda, D., Sewankambo, N., Li, C., Wabwire-Mangen, F., Paxton, L., Kiwanuka, N., Kigozi, G., Konde-Lule, J., Quinn, T.C., Gaydos, C.A., McNairn, D. (1998). Population-based study of fertility in women with HIV-1 infection in Uganda. *Lancet, 351*(9096), 98–103.

Greenwood, A. M., Greenwood, B. M., Bradley, A. K., Williams, K., Shenton, F. C., Tulloch, S., Byass, P., & Oldfield, F. S. J. (1987). A prospective survey of the outcome of pregnancy in a rural area in the Gambia. *Bulletin of the World Health Organization, 65*(5), 635–643.

Gubhaju, B. (1986). Effect of birth spacing on infant and child mortality in rural Nepal. *Journal of Biosocial Science, 18*(4), 435–447.

Haaga, J. (1989). Mechanisms for the association of maternal age, parity, and birth spacing with infant health. In A. M. Parnell (Ed.), *Contraceptive use and controlled fertility: Health issues for women and children*. Washington, DC: National Academy Press.

Hansen, J. P. (1986). Older maternal age and pregnancy outcome: A review of the literature. *Obstetrical and Gynecological Survey, 41*, 726–742.

Harrison, K. A., & Rossiter, L. A. (1985). Child-bearing, health and social priorities: A survey of 22,774 consecutive hospital births in Zaria, Northern Nigeria. *British Journal of Obstetrics and Gynecology, 5*(Suppl.), 1–119.

Harrison, P. F., & Rosenfield, A. (Eds.). (1996). *Contraceptive research and development: Looking to the future*. Committee on Contraceptive Research and Development, Institute of Medicine. Washington, DC: National Academies Press.

Henshaw, S., K., Singh, S., & Haas, T. (1999). The incidence of abortion worldwide. *Family Planning Perspectives, 25*(Suppl.), S30–S38.

Hobcraft, J. N. (1987, October 5-9). *Does family planning save children's lives?* Paper presented at the International Conference on Better Health for Women and Children Through Family Planning, Nairobi.

Hobcraft, J. N., McDonald, J. W., & Rutstein, S. O. (1985). Demographic determinants of infant and child mortality: A comparative analysis. *Population Studies, 39*(3), 363–385.

Hogberg, U., Wall, S., & Brostroin, G. (1986). The impact of early medical technology on maternal mortality in late 19th century Sweden. *International Journal of Gynecology and Obstetrics, 24*, 251–261.

Howard-Grabman, L., Seoane, L. G., & Davenport, C. A. (1994). *The Warmi Project: A participatory approach to improve maternal and neonatal health. An implementor's manual*. Arlington, VA: MotherCare Project, John Snow, Inc.

Insurance for Viagra spurs coverage for birth control. (1999, June 30). *New York Times*.

International Planned Parenthood Foundation. (1995). *Consensus statement on emergency contraception*. London: International Planned Parenthood Federation.

Islam, A. M. (2003). *Plateauing of fertility level in Bangladesh: Exploring the reality*. Working paper, Centre for Policy Dialogue, Dhaka, Bangladesh.

Jamison, D. T., Mosley, W. H., Measham, A. R., & Bobadilla, J. L. (1993). *Disease control priorities in developing countries*. New York: Oxford University Press.

Jelliffe, D. B. (1976). Maternal nutrition and lactation. In CIBA Foundation Symposium, *Breastfeeding and the mother*. Amsterdam: Excerpta Medica.

Jones, R. E. (1988). A biobehavioral model for breastfeeding effects on return to menses postpartum in Javanese women. *Social Biology, 35*, 307–323.

Kenney, G. M. (1993). *Assessing legal and regulatory reform in family planning: Manual on legal and regulatory reform* (OPTIONS Projects Policy Paper No. 1). Washington, DC: The Futures Group.

Khan, A. R., Jahan, F. A., & Begum, S. F. (1986). Maternal mortality in rural Bangladesh: The Jamalpur district. *Studies in Family Planning, 17*(1), 7–12.

Kitay, D., & Harbort, R. (1975). Iron and folic acid deficiency in pregnancy. *Clinical Perinatology, 2,* 255–273.

Knodel, J., Chamrathrithirong, A., & Debavalya, N. (1987). Societal change and the demand for children. In *Thailand's reproductive revolution: Rapid fertility decline in a third world setting* (pp. 117–142). Madison: University of Wisconsin Press.

Koblinsky, M. A. (1995). Beyond maternal mortality—Magnitude, interrelationship, and consequences of women's health, pregnancy-related complications and nutritional status on pregnancy outcomes. *International Journal of Gynecology and Obstetrics, 48*(Suppl.), 21–32.

Koblinsky, M. A., Campbell, O., & Harlow, S. (1993). Mother and more: A broader perspective on women's health. In M. A. Koblinsky, J. Timyan, & J. Gay (Eds.), *The health of women: A global perspective.* Boulder CO: Westview Press.

Koenig, M. A., Phillips, J., Campbell, O., & D'Souza, S. (1988). Maternal mortality in Matlab, Bangladesh: 1976–1985. *Studies in Family Planning, 19*(2), 69–80.

Kwast, B. E., Rochat, R. W., & Kidane-Mariam, W. (1986). Maternal mortality in Addis Ababa, Ethiopia. *Studies in Family Planning, 17*(6), 288–301.

Kwast, B. E., & Stevens, J. A. (1987). Viral hepatitis as a major cause of maternal mortality in Addis Ababa, Ethiopia. *International Journal of Gynecology and Obstetrics, 25,* 99–106.

Labbok, M. H., Hight-Laukaran, V, Peterson, A. E., Fletcher, V., von Hertzen, H., & Van Look, P. F. (1997). Multicenter study of the Lactational Amenorrhea Method (LAM): I. Efficacy, duration, and implications for clinical application. *Contraception, 55*(6), 327–336.

Larsen, U. (1993). Levels, age patterns and trends of sterility in selected countries south of the Sahara. In International Union for the Scientific Study of Population, *International Population Conference,*

Montreal, Volume 1. Liege, Belgium: International Union for the Scientific Study of Population.

Larsen, U. (2000). Primary and secondary infertility in sub-Saharan Africa. *International Journal of Epidemiology, 29,* 285–291.

Larsen, U., Chung, W., & Das Gupta, M. (1998). Fertility and son preference in Korea. *Population Studies, 52*(3), 317–325.

Lawson, J. (1992). Vaginal fistulae. *Journal of the Royal Society of Medicine, 85,* 254–256.

Levin, H., Pollitt, E., Galloway, R., & McGuire, J. (1993). Micronutrient deficiency disorders. In D. Jamison, W. H. Mosley, A. Measham, & J. L. Bobadilla (Eds.), *Disease control priorities in developing countries.* New York: Oxford University Press.

Lewis, J. J. C., Ronsmans, C., Ezeh, A., & Gregson, S. (2004). The population impact of HIV on fertility in sub-Saharan Africa. *AIDS, 18*(Supplement 2), S35–S43.

Lloyd, C. (1994). Investing in the next generation: The implications of high fertility at the level of the family. In R. Cassen (Ed.), *Population and development: Old debates, new conclusions* (pp. 181–202). New Brunswick, NJ: Transaction Publishers.

Loudon, I. (1991). On maternal and infant mortality 1900–1960. *Social History of Medicine, 4*(1), 29–73.

MacGregor, I. A., Wilson, M. E., Billewicz, W. Z., (1983). Malaria infection of the placenta in the Gambia, West Africa: Its incidence and relationship to stillbirth, birthweight and placental weight. *Transactions of the Royal Society of Tropical Medicine and Hygiene, 77*(2), 232–244.

Macro International, Inc. (1994). Selected statistics from DHS. *Demographic and Health Surveys Newsletter,* no. 6, 2.

Macro International, Inc. (2004). *Bangladesh Demographic and Health Survey, 2001–2004* [Preliminary report]. Calverton, MD: National Institute of Population Research and Training, Bangladesh, Ministry of Health and Family Welfare; Mitra and Associates; and Macro International, Inc.

Maine, D. (1991). *Safe motherhood programs: Options and issues.* New York: Columbia University, Center for Population and Family Health, School of Public Health.

Maine, D., Akalin, M. Z., Chakraborty, J., de Francisco, A., & Strong, M. (1996). Why did maternal mortality decline in Matlab? *Studies in Family Planning, 27,* 179–187.

Maine, D., & McGinn, T. (1999). Maternal mortality and morbidity. Ch. 31. In M. Goldman and M. Hatch (Eds.), *Women and Health.* San Diego, California: Academic Press.

Mantz, M. L., & Okong, P. (1994). *Evaluation report: Uganda life saving skills program for midwives, October–November, 1994* (MotherCare Project No. 5966-C-00-3038-00, prepared for the U.S. Agency for International Development). Arlington, VA: John Snow, Inc.

Marshall, M. A., & Buffington, S. T. (1991). *Life-saving skills manual for midwives* (2nd ed.). Washington, DC: American College of Nurse-Midwives.

Martin, J.A., Hamilton, B.E., Sutton, P.D., Ventura, S.J., Menacker, F., & Munson, M.L. (2003). Births: Final Data for 2002. *National Vital Statistics Reports, 52*(10).

Mason, K. O., & Taj, A. M. (1987). Differences between women's and men's reproductive goals in developing countries. *Population and Development Review, 13*(4), 611–638.

McIntosh, C. A., & Finkle, J. L. (1995). The Cairo Conference on Population and Development: A new paradigm? *Population and Development Review, 21,* 223–260.

McNeilly, A. (1996). Breastfeeding and the suppression of fertility. *Food and Nutrition Bulletin, 17,* 340–345.

Menken, J. (1975). *Estimating fecundability.* Unpublished doctoral dissertation, Princeton University.

Menken, J., Khan, M. N., & Williams, J. (1999, March 27). *The role of female education in the Bangladesh fertility decline.* Paper presented at the annual meeting of the Population Association of America, New York.

Menken, J., & Kuhn, R. (1996). Demographic effects of breastfeeding: Fertility, mortality and population growth. *Food and Nutrition Bulletin, 17,* 349–361.

Merchant, K., & Martorell, R. (1988). Frequent reproductive cycling: Does it lead to nutritional depletion of mothers? *Progress in Food and Nutrition, 12,* 339–369.

Miller, J. E. (1989). Is the relationship between birth intervals and perinatal mortality spurious? Evidence from Hungary and Sweden. *Population Studies, 43*(3), 479–495.

Morrow, R. H., Jr., Smetana, H. F., Sai, F. T., & Edgcomb, J. H. (1968). Unusual features of viral hepatitis in Accra, Ghana. *Annals of Internal Medicine, 68*(6), 1250–1264.

Mosher, W. D., Martinez, G. M., Chandra, A., Abma, J. C., & Wilson, S. J. (2004). Use of contraception and use of family planning services in the United States: 1982-2002. *Advance Data from Vital and Health Statistics, Number 350.* Accessed June 22, 2005 at http://www.cdc.gov/nchs/data/ad/ad350.pdf.

Muhuri, P., & Menken, J. (1997). Adverse effects of next birth, gender, and family composition on child survival in rural Bangladesh. *Population Studies, 51,* 279–294.

Mukaire, J., Kalikwani, F., Maggwa, B. N., & Kisubi, W. (1997). *Integration of STI and HIV/AIDS services with MCH-FP services: A case study of the Busoga Diocese Family Life Education Program, Uganda.* Nairobi: Operations Research Technical Assistance, Africa Project II, Population Council.

National Research Council. (1989). *Contraception and reproduction: Health consequences for women and children in the developing world.* Committee on Population, Working Group on Healthy Consequences of Contraceptive Use and Controlled Fertility. Washington DC: National Academy Press.

National Statistics Office (Philippines) & Macro International, Inc. (1994). *Philippines National Safe Motherhood Survey, 1993.* Calverton MD:

National Statistics Office and Macro International, Inc.

Notestein, F. W. (1953). Economic problems of population change. In *Proceedings of the Eighth International Conference of Agricultural Economics* (pp. 13–31). London: Oxford University Press.

Nybo Andersen, A. M., Wohlfahrt, J., Christens, P., Olsen, J., & Melbye, M. (2000). Maternal age and fetal loss: Population based register linkage study. *British Medical Journal, 320*(7251), 1708–1712.

Nybo Andersen, A. M., Hansen, K. D., Andersen, P. K., & Davey Smith, G. (2004). Advanced paternal age and risk of fetal death: A cohort study. *American Journal of Epidemiology, 160*(12), 1214–1222.

Omran, A. R., & Standley, C. C. (Eds.). (1981). *Further studies on family formation patterns and health: An international collaborative study in Colombia, Egypt, Pakistan, and the Syrian Arab Republic.* Geneva, Switzerland: World Health Organization.

O'Rourke, K. (1995). The effect of hospital staff training on management of obstetrical patients referred by traditional birth attendants. *International Journal of Gynecology and Obstetrics, 48*(Suppl.), s95–s102.

Overall, J. C. (1987). Viral infections of the fetus and neonate. In R. D. Feigin & J. D. Cherry (Eds.), *Textbook of pediatric infectious diseases* (2nd ed., pp. 966–1007). Philadelphia: WB Saunders.

Palloni, A. (1985). Health conditions in Latin America and policies for mortality changes. In J. Vaillin & A. Lopez (Eds.), *Health policy, social policy, and mortality prospects. Proceedings of a seminar, Paris, February 28–March 4, 1983.* Liege: Ordina Editions.

Palloni, A., & Millman, S. (1986). Effects of interbirth intervals and breastfeeding on infant and early childhood mortality. *Population Studies, 40*(2), 215-236.

Pebley, A. R., & DaVanzo, J. (1988, April). Maternal depletion and child survival in Guatemala and Malaysia. Paper presented at the annual meet-ing of the Population Association of America, New Orleans, LA.

Pebley, A. R., & Stupp, P. W. (1987). Reproductive patterns and child mortality in Guatemala. *Demography, 24*(1), 43–60.

Poedje, R., Setjalilakusuma, L., Abadi, A., Soegianto, B., Rihadi, S., Djaeli, A., & Budiarto, W. (1993). *Final project report: East Java Safe Motherhood Study* (MotherCare Project No. 936-5966, prepared for the U.S. Agency for International Development). Arlington, VA: John Snow, Inc.

Population control measures to aid women are stumbling. (1999, April 10). *New York Times.*

Population Reference Bureau (2002). *Family Planning Worldwide 2002 Data Sheet.* Washington DC: Population Reference Bureau.

Population Reference Bureau (2004). *The unfinished agenda: Meeting the need for family planning in less developed countries.* PRB Policy Brief. Accessed June 22, 2005 at http://www.prb.org/Template.cfm?Section=PRB&template=/ContentManagement/ContentDisplay.cfm&ContentID=11948.

Population Reference Bureau (2005). *Women of our world: 2005 data sheet.* Washington DC: Population Reference Bureau. Accessed June 22, 2005 at (http://www.prb.org/Template.cfm?Section=PRB&template=/ContentManagement/ContentDisplay.cfm&ContentID=12298).

Potter, J. E. (1988). Does family planning reduce infant mortality? *Population and Development Review, 14*(1), 179–187.

Prevention of Maternal Mortality Network. (1995). Situational analyses of emergency obstetric care: Examples from eleven operations research projects in West Africa. *Social Science and Medicine, 40*(Suppl.), 657–667.

Pritchett, L. (1994a). Desired fertility and the impact of population policies. *Population and Development Review, 20*(1), 1–55.

Pritchett, L. (1994b). The impact of population policies: Reply. *Population and Development Review, 20*(3), 621–630.

Public Opinion Polls. (1993). *MotherCare Nigeria maternal healthcare project qualitative research* (MotherCare Working Paper No. 17B, prepared for the U.S. Agency for International Development, Project No. 936-5966). Arlington, VA: John Snow, Inc.

Rafailimanana, H. & Westoff C. F. (2001). *Gap between preferred and actual birth intervals in sub-Saharan Africa: Implications for fertility and child health.* Calverton, MD: ORC Macro. Accessed at http://www.measuredhs.com/pubs/pdf/AS2/AS2.pdf, June 22, 2005.

Rahman, A., Katzive, L., & Henshaw, S. K. (1998). A global review of laws on induced abortion, 1985–1997. *International Family Planning Perspectives, 24*(2), 56–64.

Rahman, O. (1998). Family matters. The impact of kin on elderly mortality in rural Bangladesh. *Population Studies, 53*(2), 227–235.

Rahman, O., Menken, J., & Foster, A. (1992). Older widow mortality in rural Bangladesh. *Social Science and Medicine, 34*(1), 89–96.

Reed, H. E., Koblinsky, M. A., & Mosley, W. H. (Eds.). (2000). *The consequences of maternal morbidity and maternal mortality.* Committee on Population, Commission on Behavioral and Social Sciences and Education, National Research Council. Washington, DC: National Academies Press.

Robey, B. K., Rutstein, S. O., & Morris, L. (1992). *The reproductive revolution: New survey findings* (Population Reports Series M, No. 11).

Ronsman, C., & Campbell O. (1998). Short birth intervals don't kill women: Evidence from Matlab, Bangladesh. *Studies in Family Planning, 29*(3), 282–290.

Rooney, C. (1992). *Antenatal care and maternal health: How effective is it? A review of the evidence* (WHO/MSM/92.4). Geneva, Switzerland: World Health Organization.

Rosenzweig, M. R., & Schultz, T. P. (1983). Estimating a household production function: Heterogeneity, the demand for health inputs, and their effects on birth weight. *Journal of Political Economy, 91*(5), 723–746.

Ross A., Van der Paal L., Lubega R., Mayanja B. N., Shafer L. A., Whitworth J. (2004). HIV-1 disease progression and fertility: The incidence of recognized pregnancy and pregnancy outcome in Uganda. *AIDS, 18*(5), 799–804.

Ross, J., & Frankenberg, E. (1993). *Findings from two decades of family planning research.* New York: Population Council.

Ross, J. A., & Mauldin, W. P. (1996). Family planning programs: Efforts and results, 1972–1994. *Studies in Family Planning, 27*(3), 137–147.

Ross, J. A., & Winfrey, W. L. (2002). Unmet need for contraception in the developing world and the former Soviet Union: An updated estimate. *International Family Planning Perspectives, 28*(3), 138–143.

Rutstein, S. O. (1998). *Change in the desired number of children: A cross-country cohort analysis of levels and correlates of change* (DHS Analytical Report No. 9). Calverton, MD: Macro International, Inc.

Safe Motherhood Initiative (2003). Accessed June 22, 2005 at http://www.safemotherhood.org.

Salber, E. J., Feinleib, M., & MacMahon, B. (1966). The duration of postpartum amenorrhea. *American Journal of Epidemiology, 82*, 347–358.

Scheiber, B. A., Mejia, M., Koritz, S., Gonsalez, C., & Kwast, B. (1995). *Medical audit of early neonatal deaths–INCAP: Quetzaltenango Maternal and Neonatal Health Project* (Technical Working Paper No. 1, prepared for the U.S. Agency for International Development, MotherCare Project 936-5966). Arlington, VA: John Snow, Inc.

Schultz, T. P. (1984). Studying the impact of household economic and community variables on child mortality. *Population and Development Review, 10*(Suppl.), 215–235.

Sheps, M. C., & Menken, J. (1973). *Mathematical models of conception and birth.* Chicago: University of Chicago Press.

Slama, R., Werwatz, A., Boutou, O., Ducot, B., Spira, A., & Hardle, W. (2003). Does male age affect the risk of spontaneous abortion? An approach using semiparametric regression. *American Journal of Epidemiology, 157*(9), 815–824.

Slanger, T. E., Snow, R. & Okonofua, F. E. (2002). The impact of female genital cutting on first delivery in southwest Nigeria. *Studies in Family Planning, 33*(2), 173–184.

Sloan, N. L., Jordan, E. A., & Winikoff, B. (1992). *Does iron supplementation make a difference?* (MotherCare Working Paper No. 15, prepared for the U.S. Agency for International Development, MotherCare Project No. 936-5966). Arlington, VA: John Snow, Inc.

Sood, S. K., Ramachandran, K., Mathur, M., Gupta, K., Ramalingaswamy, V., Swarnabai, C., Ponniah, J., Mathan, V. I., & Baker, S. J. (1975). WHO sponsored collaborative studies on nutritional anemia in India. Part I: The effects of supplemental oral iron administration to pregnant women. *Quarterly Journal of Medicine, 174,* 241–258.

Stewart, M. K., & Festin, M. (1995). Validation study of women's reporting and recall of major obstetric complications treated at the Philippine General Hospital. *International Journal of Gynecology and Obstetrics, 48*(Suppl.), s53–s66.

Stone, J. L., Lockwood, C. J., Berkowitz, G., Alvarez, M., Lapinski, R., & Berkowitz, R. (1994). Risk factors for severe preeclampsia. *Obstetrics and Gynecology, 83,* 357–361.

Stover, J. (1998). Revising the proximate determinants of fertility framework: What have we learned in the past 20 years? *Studies in Family Planning, 29*(3), 255–267.

Sundari, T. K. (1992). The untold story: How the health care systems in developing countries contribute to maternal mortality. *International Journal of Health Service, 22*(3), 513–528.

Tahzib, F. (1983). Epidemiological determinants of vesicovaginal fistulae. *British Journal of Obstetric Gynaecology, 90,* 387–391.

Tahzib, F. (1985). Vesicovaginal fistula in Nigerian children. *Lancet, 2*(8467), 1291–1293.

Thaddeus, S., & Maine, D. (1994). Too far to walk: Maternal mortality in context. *Social Science and Medicine, 38*(8), 1091–1110.

Trottier, D. A., Potter, L. S., Taylor, B., & Glover, L. H. (1994). User characteristics and oral contraceptive compliance in Egypt. *Studies in Family Planning, 25*(4), 284–292.

Trussell, J., Ellertson, C., & Stewart, F. (1996). The effectiveness of the Yuzpe regimen of emergency contraception. *Family Planning Perspectives, 28*(2), 58–87.

Tsui, A. O., Wasserheit, J. N., & Haaga, J. G. (Eds.). (1997). *Reproductive health in developing countries: Expanding dimensions, building solutions.* Panel on Reproductive Health, Committee on Population, Commission on Behavioral and Social Sciences and Education, National Research Council. Washington, DC: National Academies Press.

Turner, C. F., Miller, H. G., Moses, L. E. (Eds.). (1989). *AIDS, sexual behavior, and intravenous drug use.* Committee on AIDS Research and the Behavioral, Social, and Statistical Sciences. Commission on Behavioral and Social Sciences and Education, National Research Council. Washington, DC: National Academy Press.

Twahir, A., Maggwa, B. N., & Askew, I. (1996). *Integration of STI and HIV/AIDS services with MCH-FP services: A case study of the Mkomani Clinic Society in Mombasa, Kenya, Nairobi.* Operations Research Technical Assistance, Africa Project II, Population Council.

UNFPA (2004). *State of the world's population 2004: The Cairo Consensus at Ten: Population, reproductive health, and the global effort to end poverty.* Accessed June 22, 2005 at http://www.unfpa.org/swp/ swpmain.htm.

United Nations. (1991). *Controlling iron deficiency* (Nutrition State-of-the-Art Series, Nutrition Policy Discussion Paper No. 9). Geneva, Switzerland: United Nations.

United Nations. (1994). *Programme of action of the 1994 International Conference on Population and Development* (A/CONF.171/13). Reprinted in *Population and Development Review, 21*(1), 187–213 and 21(2), 437–461.

United Nations Commission on Population and Development (2004). *Flow of financial resources for assisting in the implementation of the*

Programme of Action of the International Conference on Population and Development: A 10-year review. Accessed June 22, 2005 at http://daccessdds.un.org/doc/UNDOC/GEN/N04/206/10/PDF/N0420610.pdf?OpenElement.

United Nations General Assembly (2000). *United Nations Millennium Declaration* (A/RES/55/2). Accessed June 22, 2005 at http://daccessdds.un.org/doc/UNDOC/GEN/N00/559/51/PDF/N0055951.pdf?OpenElement.

United Nations General Assembly (2001). *Road map towards the implementation of the United Nations Millennium Summit: Report of the Secretary-General* (A/56/326). Accessed June 22, 2005 at http://www.un.org/documents/ga/docs/56/a56326.pdf.

United Nations Population Division (2002). *HIV/AIDS and fertility in sub-Saharan Africa: A review of the research literature* (ESA/P/WP.174). Accessed June 22, 2005 at http://www.un.org/esa/population/publications/fertilitysection/HIVAIDSPaperFertSect.pdf.

United Nations Population Division (2005). World Population Prospects: The 2004 Revision Population Database. Accessed June 22, 2005 at http://esa.un.org/unpp/.

United Nations Statistics Division (2002). *Monitoring progress towards the achievement of the Millennium Development Goals* ST/ESA/STAT/MILLENNIUMINDICATORS DB/WWW). Accessed June 22, 2005 at http://millenniumindicators.un.org/unsd/mi/mi_highlights.asp.

United Nations Statistics Division (2005a). *Progress towards the Millennium Development Goals, 1990-2005.* Accessed June 22, 2005 at http://unstats.un.org/unsd/ mi/mi_coverfinal.htm.

United Nations Statistics Division (2005b). *Millennium Indicators Database.* Accessed June 22, 2005 at http://millenniumindicators.un.org/unsd/mi/mi_series_results.asp?rowId=729.

U.S. Census Bureau (2002). *Global Population Profile 2002: The Aids Pandemic in the 21st Century.* Accessed June 22, 2005 at http://www.census.gov/ipc/prod/wp02/wp-02006.pdf.

Walker, G. J., Ashley, D. E., McCaw, A., & Bernard, G. W. (1985). *Maternal mortality in Jamaica: A confidential enquiry into all maternal deaths in Jamaica, 1981–1983* (WHO FHE/PMM/85.9.10). WHO Inter-regional Meeting on Prevention of Maternal Mortality, Geneva, Switzerland.

Weinbreck, P. V., Loustaud, F., Denis, B., Vidal, M., Mounier, M., & DeLumley, L. (1988). Postnatal transmission of HIV infection. *Lancet, 1,* 482.

Westley, S. B. (1995). *Evidence mounts for sex-selective abortion in Asia* (Asia-Pacific Population and Policy No. 34). Honolulu: East-West Population Center.

Westoff, C.F. (2001). *Unmet need at the end of the century.* Calverton, MD: ORC Macro. Accessed June 22, 2005 at http://www.measuredhs.com/pubs/pdftoc.cfm?ID=349.

Wilcox, A. J., Weinberg, C. R., O'Connor, J. F., Baird, D. D., Schlatter, J. P., Canfield, R. E., Armstrong, E. G., & Nisula, B. C. (1988). Incidence of early loss of pregnancy. *New England Journal of Medicine, 319,* 189–194.

Winikoff, B. (1983). The effect of birthspacing on child and maternal health. *Studies in Family Planning, 18*(3), 128–143.

Winikoff, B., Elias, C., & Beattie, K. (1994). Special issues of IUD use in resource-poor settings. In C. W. Bardin & D. R. Mishell, Jr. (Eds.), *Proceedings of the Fourth International Conference on IUDs* (pp. 230–238). New York: Population Council.

Winikoff, B., & Sullivan, M. (1987). Assessing the role of family planning in reducing maternal mortality. *Studies in Family Planning, 18*(3), 128–143.

Women's Studies Project. (1999). *The impact of family planning on women's lives.* Research Triangle Park, NC: Family Health International.

Wood, J. W. (1994). *Dynamics of human reproduction: Biology, biometry, demography.* New York: Aldine de Gruyter.

Wood, J. W., Lai, D., Johnson, P. L., Campbell, K. L., & Maslar, I. A. (1985). Lactation and birth spacing in highland New Guinea. *Journal of Biosocial Science* (Suppl. 9), 157–173.

World Health Organization. (1988). Geographic variation in the incidence of hypertension in pregnancy. *American Journal of Obstetrics and Gynecology, 158*(1), 80–83.

World Health Organization. (1991). *Maternal mortality: A global factbook*. Geneva, Switzerland: World Health Organization.

World Health Organization. (1993a). *Coverage of maternity care: A tabulation of available information* (WHO/FHE/MSM/ 93.7). Geneva, Switzerland: World Health Organization.

World Health Organization. (1993b). *Making maternity care more accessible* (Press release No. 59). Geneva, Switzerland: World Health Organization.

World Health Organization. (1993c). *The global burden of disease*. Background paper prepared for the *World Development Report*. Geneva, Switzerland: World Health Organization.

World Health Organization. (1994a). *Maternal health and Safe Motherhood Programme: Research progress report 1987–1992* (WHO/FHE/MSM94.18). Geneva, Switzerland: World Health Organization.

World Health Organization. (1994b). *The mother-baby package: Implementing safe motherhood in countries* (Document FRH/MSM/94.11). Geneva, Switzerland: World Health Organization.

World Health Organization. (1995). Essential or emergency obstetric care. *Safe Motherhood Newsletter, 18*(2), 1–2.

World Health Organization. (1996). *Perinatal mortality* (Document FRH/MSM/96.7). Geneva, Switzerland: World Health Organization.

World Health Organization & UNICEF. (1996). *Revised estimates of maternal mortality: A new approach by WHO and UNICEF*. Geneva, Switzerland: World Health Organization.

Yoder, S., Abderrahim, N., & Zhuzhuni, A. (2004). *Female genital cutting in the demographic and health surveys: A critical and comparative analysis*. Calverton, MD: ORC Macro.

Younis, N., Khattab, H., Zurayk, H., el-Mouelhy, M., Fadle Amin, M., & Farag, A. M. (1993). A community study of gynecological and related morbidities in rural Egypt. *Studies in Family Planning, 24*(3), 175–186.

CHAPTER

4

Infectious Diseases

ARTHUR L. REINGOLD AND CHRISTINA R. PHARES

This chapter describes the epidemiological features of the infectious diseases of greatest public health significance in low- and middle-income countries and details available strategies to prevent and control them. Because these diseases cannot be covered in depth in a single chapter, the emphasis is on their unique epidemiological features and the relevant technological challenges, resource limitations and cultural barriers that have shaped current approaches to their prevention and control. Conceptually, these approaches include preventing exposure to the infectious agent; making otherwise susceptible individuals or populations immune to the infectious agent; treating infected individuals or populations to prevent illness and transmission of the agent to others; and improving the timeliness and appropriateness of care for symptomatic individuals so as to minimize morbidity and mortality and, in some instances, to reduce the likelihood of transmission to others. Examples of successful programs using one or more of these various conceptual approaches are discussed, as are the challenges and obstacles that confront low- and middle-income countries and their partners as they seek to reduce further the burden of disease caused by infectious agents.

Overview

Collectively, infectious diseases have undoubtedly been the single most important contributors to human morbidity and mortality throughout history. Over the past 150 years, the mortality attributable to them

has declined substantially in industrialized countries, and chronic diseases such as cardiovascular disease, cancer, stroke, chronic obstructive pulmonary disease, and diabetes mellitus have assumed prominence as the leading causes of death in these countries. Although there is uncertainty about the relative importance of various social, economic, environmental, and public health factors in this epidemiologic transition, most of these reductions in mortality attributable to infectious diseases clearly preceded any advances in clinical medicine and public health that plausibly could have had an impact on the infectious diseases of public health significance of the time (e.g., tuberculosis, rheumatic fever, scarlet fever, typhoid fever, and cholera). At present, only pneumonia, influenza, and human immunodeficiency virus (HIV)/ acquired immunodeficiency syndrome (AIDS) rank among the top 10 causes of mortality in the United States.

The global burden of disease and the epidemiologic transition are discussed in detail elsewhere in this book (see Chapter 1). Although current projections suggest that acute infectious diseases will decrease substantially in their absolute and relative importance as causes of death and disability in low- and middle-income countries in the decades to come, it is clear that today they remain of great public health significance. According to a World Health Organization (WHO) report (1999b), acute infectious diseases are, collectively, the leading cause of death among children and young adults, accounting for half of all deaths in low-income countries. In fact, in many countries the HIV/AIDS pandemic is reversing decades of progress

Acknowledgments: The authors acknowledge Colin Garrett for his assistance in the preparation of this chapter.

in reducing mortality due to acute infectious diseases, with a resulting decrease in life expectancy. Further, it is now well accepted that chronic infection contributes in important, if poorly understood, ways to the pathogenesis of a number of chronic diseases, including cervical cancer (in which human papilloma virus [HPV] plays a role), hepatic cancer and cirrhosis (in which hepatitis B virus [HBV] and probably hepatitis C virus [HCV] play a role), gastric cancer and peptic ulcer disease (in which *Helicobacter pylori* plays a role), and possibly cardiovascular disease (in which *Chlamydia pneumoniae* and perhaps other infectious agents may play a role). Hepatic cancer and cirrhosis due to HBV are the first vaccine-preventable chronic diseases, and if current attempts to develop a vaccine against HPV are successful, cervical cancer may also become vaccine preventable. Thus, for all the reasons just mentioned, infectious diseases and their prevention and control will remain of major public health importance for low- and middle-income countries for the foreseeable future.

Underlying virtually every infectious disease of public health importance in low- and middle-income countries is the significant role played by poverty and its associated problems. For example, both obvious and more subtle forms of malnutrition and micronutrient deficiencies are associated with an increased risk of severe morbidity and mortality from a wide range of infectious diseases. At the same time, lack of education, poor access to clean drinking water, inability to dispose properly of human waste, household crowding, and lack of access to medical care—all manifestations of poverty—also contribute substantially.

However, low- and middle-income countries and the people living in them cannot be lumped together into a single group insofar as their risk of various infectious diseases is concerned. There are important geographic differences in the incidence and public health significance of various infectious diseases, due to differences in climate, the distribution of insect vectors, and variations in other environmental, social, and cultural factors. In addition, all low- and middle-income countries are not equally resource poor—they vary enormously in the resources that are available to provide clinical services (e.g., oral rehydration therapy), mount public health programs (e.g., vaccination programs), and reduce environmental sources of infection (e.g., provide clean drinking water and adequate sanitation or control vector populations). Also, virtually all low- and middle-income countries include within them culturally, economically, and sometimes geographically diverse subpopulations with very different needs and resources, particularly with regard to infectious diseases. Given the diversity of the low- and middle-income countries and the infectious diseases that confront them, it will be possible in this chapter to discuss these diseases only selectively, using representative examples when appropriate.

Control of Infectious Diseases

The 20th century saw an ever-increasing number of programs to prevent morbidity and mortality from specific infectious diseases in low- and middle-income countries. Strategies that have been employed have included various combinations of vector control (e.g., for malaria, dengue, yellow fever, and onchocerciasis [river blindness]); vaccination (e.g., for smallpox, measles, polio, neonatal tetanus, diphtheria, pertussis, tetanus, hepatitis B, meningococcal meningitis, and yellow fever); mass chemotherapy (e.g., for hookworm, onchocerciasis, dracunculiasis [Guinea worm], and sexually transmitted infections [STIs]); improved sanitation and access to clean water (e.g., for diarrheal diseases); improved care seeking and caregiving (e.g., for diarrheal diseases, acute respiratory infections, and neonatal tetanus); and behavior change (e.g., for HIV and other STIs, diarrheal diseases, and dracunculiasis), among others. The successful eradication of smallpox in the late 1970s through a combination of enhanced case finding, containment, and vaccination gave considerable impetus to attempts to control other infectious diseases (Exhibit 4-1).

As the world health community has established goals for reducing morbidity and mortality from other infectious diseases, a variety of terms describing different levels of control have come into use. Organizations, such as WHO and its governing body, the World Health Assembly (WHA), have been careful to define their prevention goals vis-á-vis various diseases; these are set forth in appropriate sections of this chapter. A useful set of definitions of such terms was put forward at the Dahlem workshop on the Eradication of Infectious Diseases (Dowdle & Hopkins, 1998):

- *Control:* Reduction of disease incidence, prevalence, morbidity or mortality to a locally acceptable level as a result of deliberate efforts; continued intervention measures are required to maintain the reduction.

- *Elimination of disease:* Reduction to zero of the incidence of a specified disease in a defined geographic area as a result of deliberate efforts; continued intervention measures are required.

spread by oral-fecal route

| **Exhibit 4-1** | **Smallpox Eradication** |

Most individuals who work in the area of international health consider the eradication of smallpox to have been the single most important contribution of public health in the 20th century, and possibly the most significant accomplishment in the field of human health in recorded history. Although the ultimate eradication of smallpox through the use of vaccine was foreseen by Edward Jenner and President Thomas Jefferson at the beginning of the 19th century, it took more than 150 years for it to become a reality. Eradication of smallpox was possible because of several important features of the disease itself; technological advances in vaccine preparation and administration; development and application of a new approach to using the vaccine selectively rather than in mass campaigns; and a combination of international will and cooperation, strong leadership, and the focused effort of large numbers of health workers in multiple countries.

Features of smallpox that made it a candidate for eradication included its relatively inefficient transmission from person to person; the fact that individuals with smallpox were generally bedridden before the appearance of the rash, the stage in the illness when person-to-person transmission was most likely to occur; the facts that subclinical cases did not occur in unvaccinated individuals and that vaccinated individuals who developed mild smallpox did not efficiently transmit the virus; the lack of a carrier state; the presence of a single serotype of the virus; the marked seasonal fluctuation in cases; and the lack of a nonhuman reservoir for the virus in nature. Advances in vaccine development and delivery that were crucial to smallpox eradication included the development of a heat-stable, freeze-dried vaccine and of two improved methods of delivering the vaccine—a bifurcated needle that was inexpensive, easy to use, and economical in its use of a small volume of vaccine, and jet injector guns that allowed a team to vaccinate more than 1,000 persons per hour.

However, despite the availability of a heat-stable smallpox vaccine and the means of vaccinating large numbers of persons, mass vaccination campaigns intended to render entire populations immune to smallpox were unsuccessful in eradicating the disease, even in countries that achieved vaccine coverage in the range of 80% to 95%. Smallpox virus continued to circulate among the remaining unvaccinated individuals, who were extremely difficult to identify and vaccinate.

A delay in the arrival of sufficient vaccine to mount a mass campaign in Nigeria in 1966 led to the development of an alternative approach to preventing the spread of smallpox in an area: energetic case detection followed by isolation of all infected individuals and intense vaccination efforts focused on the area and population immediately surrounding a case. This approach, dubbed a *surveillance containment* strategy, proved to be remarkably successful in eradicating smallpox once imaginative and locally acceptable approaches to detecting all suspected cases, isolating individuals with smallpox, and vaccinating those around them were implemented. Surveillance containment ultimately replaced mass vaccination campaigns, and global efforts to complete eradication of smallpox relying on this approach gained momentum.

It has been estimated that in 1967 as many as 10 to 15 million cases of smallpox occurred in 33 countries with endemic smallpox and 14 other countries with imported cases of smallpox. These countries, with a total population of more than 1.2 billion persons, included many of the poorest countries in the world and those presenting the greatest logistical barriers to mounting an effective eradication program. As a result of the efforts of dedicated public health workers in these countries and a small cadre of public health professionals from unaffected countries, the last person with smallpox not caused by a laboratory accident had onset of a rash on October 26, 1977, in Somalia. On December 9, 1979, the World Health Organization's Global Commission for the Certification of Smallpox Eradication concluded that "smallpox eradication has been achieved throughout the world," a conclusion accepted by the World Health Assembly in May 1980.

- *Elimination of infection:* Reduction to zero of the incidence of infection caused by a specific agent in a defined geographic area as a result of deliberate efforts; continued measures to prevent reestablishment of transmission are required.

- *Eradication:* Permanent reduction to zero of the worldwide incidence of infection caused by a specific agent as a result of deliberate efforts; intervention measures are no longer needed.

- *Extinction:* The specific infectious agent no longer exists in nature or in the laboratory.[1]

In the near term, extinction is possible only for smallpox, although concerns about its use as an agent of bioterrorism have prevented the long-awaited destruction of the last known stocks of the virus. Eradication of other diseases, such as polio, measles, and dracunculiasis, is considered theoretically possible using existing control methods and is being actively pursued. However, for most of the infectious diseases responsible for the majority of morbidity and mortality in low- and middle-income countries at the turn of the 21st century, only their control is considered achievable in the foreseeable future (Table 4-1).

---

[1]*Source: The Eradication of Infectious Diseases: Report of the Dahlem Workshop on the Eradication of Infectious Diseases,* W. R. Dowdle and D. R. Hopkins, March 16–22, 1998. Copyright John Wiley & Sons Limited. Reproduced with permission.

Table 4-1	Levels of Control that Are Considered Achievable for Selected Infectious Diseases in the Foreseable Future Using Currently Available Methods			
Extinction	**Eradication**	**Elimination of Infection**	**Elimination of Disease**	**Control**
Smallpox	Polio	Onchocerciasis	Rabies	Neonatal teanus
	Measles		Trachoma	Malaria
	Dracunculiaisis			Cholera
	(Guineas worm)			Tuberculosis
				Schistosomiasis
				Diarrheal disease
				ARIs
				AIDS
				STIs
				Leprosy

Note: ARIs = acute respiratory infections; AIDS = acquired immunodeficiency syndrome; STIs = sexually transmitted infections.

Childhood Vaccine-Preventable Diseases: The Expanded Program on Immunization

Overview

Based on the success of the vaccination program mounted to control and then eradicate smallpox, WHO and various partner agencies launched the Expanded Program on Immunization (EPI, or PEV in French) in 1974. At that time it was estimated that fewer than 5% of infants and children in low- and middle-income countries were receiving relatively inexpensive and highly effective vaccines that had been licensed and available for a number of years. There were many obstacles to vaccinating them, including the lack of demand for vaccines on the part of the community; the small number of sources of vaccines of adequate quality; the lack of the infrastructure needed to purchase, store, and distribute vaccines, some of which were temperature sensitive; a deficiency in the number of trained personnel to administer vaccination programs; and insufficient funds to purchase vaccines and vaccination supplies and equipment. Further, most countries lacked health information and surveillance systems to assess the burden of disease caused by various vaccine-preventable diseases or to evaluate the impact of a vaccination program. Remarkable progress since 1974 in correcting these problems has led to the imminent eradication of polio; dramatic reductions in morbidity and mortality from measles and neonatal tetanus worldwide; and likely, but harder to demonstrate, reductions of a similar magnitude in morbidity and mortality from diphtheria and pertussis.

For the first 20 years or so of its existence, the EPI focused on diseases for which safe, effective, and inexpensive vaccines were available and could be given entirely during the first year of life. These included OPV (oral polio vaccine, a trivalent live vaccine against poliomyelitis), measles vaccine (a live vaccine), DPT (a three-component killed vaccine against diphtheria, pertussis, and tetanus), and BCG (bacillus Calmette-Guérin, a live vaccine against tuberculosis). Vaccination with tetanus toxoid (TT) was included for women of childbearing age to prevent neonatal tetanus in their newborn babies, even though the group being targeted for vaccination was not infants in the first year of life. Subsequently, it was recommended that vaccine against yellow fever be added in those countries where the disease is a threat. A vaccine against hepatitis B was then included after large quantities of relatively inexpensive vaccine became available. (See Table 4-2 for the current EPI schedule for infants.) Hepatitis B, yellow fever, and tuberculosis are discussed elsewhere in this chapter, so they will not be considered here.

Poliomyelitis

Etiologic Agent, Clinical Features, and Characteristics of the Currently Available Vaccines

Poliomyelitis (polio) is caused by any of the three known serotypes (1, 2, and 3) of poliovirus. Poliovirus is efficiently transmitted through the fecal-oral route. Ingestion of the virus leads to asymptomatic or mild, self-limited infection and shedding of the virus from the throat and gastrointestinal tract in the vast majority of those exposed. However, an estimated 1 in 100 to 1 in 850 infected persons develops symptomatic polio, with or without paralysis. Of those who develop paralysis, which primarily affects one or both legs, approximately 10% die acutely, 10% to 15% are left permanently unable to walk, and 10% to 15% are left lame (unable to walk normally). Treatment for polio is entirely supportive in nature. Before widespread vaccination,

Table 4-2	Current Recommended Schedule of Vaccination Under the Expanded Program on Immunization
Vaccine	**Age at Vaccination**
Bacillus Calmette-Guérin (BCG)	Birth
Oral polio vaccine (OPV)	Birth, 6, 10, and 14 weeks
Diptheria-pertussis-tetanus (DPT)	6, 10, and 14 weeks
Measles	9 months
Hepatitis B[a]	Scheme A: birth, 6, and 14 weeks
	Scheme B: 6, 10, and 14 weeks
Yellow fever[b]	9 months
Tetanus toxoid (TT)	Two doses for women of childbearing age

[a]Scheme A is recommended in countries where perinatal transmission of HBV is frequent (e.g., Southeast Asia), and scheme B is recommended in countries where perinatal transmission is less frequent (e.g., sub-Saharan Africa).

[b]In countries where yellow fever poses a risk.

polio was the leading cause of lameness in low- and middle-income countries, and many of its victims remain a visible sign of the ravages of the disease and will need assistance long after acute cases of polio have been eradicated.

Killed, injectable polio vaccine (IPV) and live, OPV became available in the 1950s and 1960s, respectively. Both are safe and highly effective, and each has been used successfully to eradicate disease caused by wild-type poliovirus in industrialized countries. Although there are extremely rare cases of polio caused by the vaccine strain of the virus when OPV is given, WHO and other supporters of the EPI have always considered OPV to be preferable to IPV for routine use in low- and middle-income countries. Reasons for preferring OPV have included its extremely low cost (approximately $0.02 per dose); its ease of administration; its ability to induce intestinal immunity that inhibits shedding of wild-type poliovirus; and its transmission to household and other close contacts through the fecal-oral route, providing repeated exposures to the vaccine and thus boosting immunity to polio in such contacts. However, for unclear reasons, the efficacy of OPV in low- and middle-income countries has consistently been found to be lower than that in industrialized countries (approximately 85% versus approximately 95% for the primary series) (Patriarca, Wright, & John, 1991).

Descriptive Epidemiologic Features and Risk Factors

Before the widespread use of polio vaccine, polio was endemic in virtually all low- and middle-income countries, and most children were asymptomatically infected during the first few years of life. Symptomatic acute polio was similarly seen primarily in infants and young children. Based on surveys of the preva-

lence of lameness in school-aged children, the annual incidence of symptomatic polio in low- and middle-income countries was estimated to be in the range of 20 to 40 per 100,000 total population (LaForce et al., 1980). As oral polio vaccine came into widespread use and vaccine coverage increased, endemic infections with wild-type poliovirus decreased. However, vaccine coverage levels in the range of 40% to 80%, combined with a vaccine efficacy of approximately 85%, led to an accumulation of susceptible individuals and subsequent outbreaks in many countries with "good" EPIs (Sutter et al., 1991). In the early 1980s, more than 50,000 cases of polio were being reported annually to WHO (Otten et al., 1992). By 1997 that number had been reduced by more than 90%.

Current Approaches to Prevention and Control

In 1988 the WHA set a goal of interrupting polio transmission worldwide by the year 2000 and certifying that polio had been eradicated by 2005. The polio eradication effort put into place at that time was based on a combination of ongoing routine immunization of infants, annual national immunization days, and house-to-house mop-up campaigns to vaccinate those missed by these other approaches (Hull et al., 1994). In addition, sensitive surveillance for and laboratory testing of specimens from individuals with acute flaccid paralysis were put into place to help identify cases of polio, thus allowing targeting of additional vaccination efforts and monitoring of the impact of the eradication program.

The last confirmed case of paralytic polio caused by wild-type poliovirus in the Western Hemisphere was detected in Peru in 1991, and three WHO regions (Americas, western Pacific, and European) had been certified as polio free by 2002 (Centers for Disease Control and Prevention [CDC], 2002). By

2003, the number of countries in the world where polio was endemic had decreased from 125 in 1988 to 6 (Afghanistan, Egypt, India, Niger, Nigeria, and Pakistan). However, major resurgences of polio were seen in selected states in India in 2002 and in northern Nigeria in 2003 and 2004, and the resurgence in Nigeria led to the reintroduction of wild-type polio into multiple neighboring countries and into other, more distant countries in North Africa and southern Africa. Intensive national and subnational supplemental immunization activities in and around the few remaining areas with endemic polio were being implemented in 2004, in hopes of eradicating wild-type polio by the end of 2004 or the middle of 2005 (Roberts, 2004), but these efforts may need to be continued into 2006 before eradication is achieved.

Measles

Etiologic Agent, Clinical Features, and Vaccine Characteristics

Measles is caused by measles virus. Although there is some genotypic variation, all measles virus strains are considered to be of a single type. Measles virus is spread via the respiratory route and is transmitted extremely efficiently. It is highly infectious, and in the absence of vaccine-induced immunity, virtually every child can be expected to develop measles if the virus is circulating in the community. Measles is characterized initially by fever, cough, runny nose, and malaise, making it indistinguishable from many other viral respiratory infections for the first several days, during which the child is highly infectious. A characteristic rash then appears. Although most cases are self-limited, complications commonly include pneumonia, diarrhea, and ear infections. Less common complications include encephalitis and blindness. Measles is not amenable to antibiotic therapy, but treatment with vitamin A reduces the case fatality ratio (Hussey & Klein, 1990).

Before widespread use of measles vaccine, measles was consistently one of the leading causes of death among children worldwide, accounting for an estimated 20% to 30% of such deaths (Walsh, 1983). Although the estimates of the case fatality ratio (CFR) for measles have varied from 1% to greater than 30%, depending in part on whether the studies were community or hospital based, it is clear that the most potent predictors of mortality among children with measles are young age and malnutrition, particularly vitamin A deficiency (Markowitz et al., 1989). Furthermore, measles frequently leaves a child weakened and at increased risk of illness and death from other causes for a year or more after the acute episode.

Measles vaccine consists of a live, attenuated strain of the measles virus. It is safe, inexpensive, and highly effective when given to a child after circulating measles antibody acquired from the mother has disappeared. Because maternal antibody tends to disappear somewhat later and exposure to measles virus is substantially less common in industrialized countries, measles vaccine is typically given at 15 months of age in such countries. In low- and middle-income countries, the intensity of exposure to measles and the poorly understood more rapid decline in maternal antibodies combine to put infants at much greater risk of acquiring measles at a young age, when complications and death are more likely. As a result, measles vaccine is typically given at 9 months of age in low- and middle-income countries.

Descriptive Epidemiologic Features and Risk Factors

In the absence of vaccination, every child in an area where measles virus is circulating would be expected to contract measles. In the early 1980s an estimated 3 million children died annually of measles and its sequelae. By the mid-1990s, with an estimated 80% of the world's children vaccinated against measles, the estimated annual number of deaths attributable to measles worldwide was 1 million. The age at which an unvaccinated child develops measles is a function of when maternal antibodies disappear (generally at 6 to 12 months of age) and the intensity of exposure to measles virus in the community. Thus, in crowded urban areas most unvaccinated children will develop measles between 6 months and 5 years of age, whereas in more sparsely populated, rural areas the age at acquisition of measles is older (Walsh, 1983). Family size, travel patterns, and types and locations of social interactions (e.g., marketplaces) also influence the local epidemiologic features of measles. HIV infection appears to increase the risk of acquiring measles in infancy, presumably by decreasing the level of circulating maternal antibody in the infant.

Current Approaches to Prevention and Control

Like smallpox, measles can, in theory, be completely eradicated because measles virus does not infect other species or live in the environment. However, because measles is more widespread and much more infectious than smallpox, and because there is substantial transmission of measles virus among infants below the age of routine vaccination, eradication of measles will be more difficult to achieve. Thus, rather than establish a goal of worldwide measles eradication, the WHA resolved in 1989 to reduce measles-related morbidity by 90% and measles-related mortality by

95% by the year 1995. As with polio, improved routine immunization of infants and periodic mass vaccination campaigns targeting infants and children from 9 months to 5 (or even up to 14) years of age have been undertaken as complementary strategies.

Based on substantial success in reducing the incidence of measles and even interrupting measles virus transmission over large geographic areas for substantial periods of time, the 1994 Pan American Sanitary Conference made elimination of measles from the Western Hemisphere a goal for the year 2000 (Pan America Health Organization, 1994). As a result of this concerted effort, indigenous measles virus circulation has not been observed in the region of the Americas since 2002, although continuing circulation of the virus elsewhere in the world means there is an ongoing threat of measles importations (de Quadros et al., 2004). Progress has also been made in reducing morbidity and mortality due to measles in Africa, where an estimated 58% of the world's 777,000 deaths due to measles occurred in 2000 (Stein et al., 2000). Through a combination of approaches, including supplemental immunization activities, improved surveillance, and improved case management, measles cases and deaths have been reduced in some African countries by 91% and 84%, respectively, compared with findings in the immediately preceding years (CDC, 2004). However, worldwide eradication of measles is unlikely in the immediate future.

Diphtheria

Etiologic Agent, Clinical Features, and Vaccine Characteristics

Diphtheria is caused by the bacterium *Corynebacterium diphtheriae*. It is spread primarily via the respiratory route, although in low- and middle-income countries the organism is a common cause of ulcerative skin lesions and can be transmitted from such lesions. Diphtheria is a disease of the upper respiratory tract, manifested by fever, sore throat, an inflamed pharynx (and possibly nose and larynx), and a grayish membrane covering the inflamed mucosa. With involvement of the larynx, the airways can be blocked and death can result. The disease is toxin mediated, and use of both antibiotics and diphtheria antitoxin (which is rarely, if ever, available in low- and middle-income countries) is beneficial in its treatment. The incidence of diphtheria and the morbidity and mortality attributable to it in low- and middle-income countries are largely unknown, but the disease is not believed to pose a major public health threat in such countries.

The diphtheria component of the DPT vaccine is composed of inactivated diphtheria toxin adsorbed to aluminum salts. Two or more doses of DPT result in protection against diphtheria in 90% to 100% of those vaccinated.

Descriptive Epidemiologic Features and Risk Factors

Although diphtheria is easier to diagnose than pertussis, it is likely that it is substantially underreported in many low- and middle-income countries. Thus, the estimated 15,000 to 50,000 cases of diphtheria reported to WHO annually in the mid-1990s almost certainly do not reflect the actual burden of disease (WHO, 1998c). Most cases of diphtheria occur in young children, primarily among those living in impoverished, crowded conditions. Lack of vaccination is undoubtedly the most important risk factor for developing or dying from diphtheria.

Current Approaches to Prevention and Control

The current approach to reducing morbidity and mortality from diphtheria is to improve levels of vaccine coverage achieved through ongoing infant immunization programs (i.e., the EPI) in various countries. Strategies for improving vaccine coverage include expanding the times when vaccinations are offered in clinics, reducing waiting times, and reducing the number of missed opportunities to vaccinate unvaccinated infants, among others. Because vaccination does not lead to elimination of carriage of C. *diphtheriae* from the nasopharynx, ongoing control of diphtheria will require achieving and maintaining high levels of vaccine coverage among the target population.

Pertussis

Etiologic Agent, Clinical Features, and Vaccine Characteristics

Pertussis (whooping cough) is caused by the bacterium *Bordetella pertussis*. Like measles, pertussis is spread via the respiratory route and is highly contagious, particularly within a household and in crowded institutional settings. In classic cases of pertussis, nonspecific respiratory tract symptoms are followed by severe and protracted bouts of coughing that typically end with an inspiratory whooping sound. These bouts of coughing can persist for many weeks and be quite debilitating, even when complications such as pneumonia and neurologic damage do not develop. Antibiotic treatment has little or no impact on the natural course of the disease once symptoms have begun, but probably shortens the time an individual is infectious.

Pertussis is believed to be the cause of substantial morbidity and mortality in the absence of high levels of coverage with pertussis vaccine, but it is difficult to assess what proportion of respiratory infections and related deaths is due to pertussis. In part, this difficulty arises from the fact that many infants with pertussis never have the characteristic whoop seen in older children. Similarly, there is growing evidence that in industrialized countries, and presumably in low- and middle-income countries as well, *B. pertussis* is the cause of many cough illnesses in young adults that are never recognized as pertussis. Finally, the laboratory diagnosis of pertussis has been plagued by the insensitivity, nonspecificity, technical difficulty, and cost of the various diagnostic tests, making research studies difficult and routine surveillance extremely inaccurate.

Pertussis vaccines have, until quite recently, consisted of killed whole bacteria adsorbed to aluminum salts to make them more immunogenic. In most instances, pertussis vaccine is given to infants and young children as a part of the DPT vaccine. When a full series of three doses is given, the efficacy of the pertussis component of DPT is in the range of 80%. Because whole-cell pertussis vaccine contains many bacterial products, it is the most reactogenic component of DPT and makes the vaccine the most reactogenic of those included in the EPI. Thus, pain and tenderness at the injection site, with or without fever, is common after a DPT injection. More serious but rare complications of whole-cell pertussis vaccine (e.g., encephalopathy) have been at the center of a protracted debate in many industrialized countries over its safety. Concern over these rare complications and attendant declines in vaccine acceptance led to the development and licensure of acellular pertussis vaccines that are far less reactogenic and equally efficacious, but also far more expensive than whole-cell pertussis vaccine. Because of this large difference in cost, the EPI continues to use whole-cell pertussis vaccine in virtually all low- and middle-income countries.

Descriptive Epidemiologic Features and Risk Factors

In the mid-1980s it was estimated that more than 600,000 children died of pertussis annually. The number of cases reported to WHO annually in the early 1980s was in the range of 1.5 to 2 million; by 1997, the number was less than 200,000 (WHO, 1998c). As noted earlier, any estimate of the burden of disease caused by pertussis is likely to underestimate the actual toll due to the difficulty of making the diagnosis. Limited studies suggest that most cases of pertussis in low- and middle-income countries occur in infancy

and early childhood and that the highest CFR is seen in infants. It is likely that poverty and the resultant crowding increase the risk of pertussis and that malnutrition increases the likelihood of dying among those who develop the disease, although lack of vaccination is undoubtedly the most important risk factor for developing or dying from pertussis at any age.

Current Approaches to Prevention and Control

As is the case for diphtheria, the current approach to reducing morbidity and mortality from pertussis is to improve levels of vaccine coverage through the EPI and strategies for improved vaccine coverage. Because vaccination does not lead to elimination of carriage of *B. pertussis,* ongoing control of pertussis will require high levels of vaccine coverage among the target population.

Tetanus

Etiologic Agent, Clinical Features, and Vaccine Characteristics

Tetanus is caused by the toxin produced by the anaerobic bacterium *Clostridium tetani*. It is commonly found in the gastrointestinal tract of many domesticated animals (e.g., cows, sheep, and goats). When deposited in the soil, *C. tetani* cells form spores that are highly resistant to heat and desiccation and remain viable for years or even decades. When these spores are introduced into a wound or other suitable environment, they sporulate and the bacterial cells reproduce, forming and releasing a highly potent neurotoxin as they grow. Symptoms produced by the neurotoxin include painful stiffening and spasms of the muscles, including those of the jaw (hence the name *lockjaw*), and, particularly in newborn infants, a resultant inability to suck or otherwise feed. Treatment of tetanus is largely supportive, even in the rare circumstance when tetanus antitoxin is available, and consists largely of giving muscle relaxants and fluids intravenously. However, even with supportive treatment, the CFR is very high, particularly in infants with neonatal tetanus, of whom 80% to 90% will die.

The vaccine against tetanus, either in a single preparation or in DPT, is a toxoid—an inactivated form of tetanus toxin, adsorbed to aluminum salts. Tetanus toxoid is extremely safe and produces few reactions. The three doses of DPT given to infants and the two doses of TT given to women of childbearing age or pregnant women through the EPI produce immunity in 90% to 100% of those vaccinated.

Descriptive Epidemiologic Features and Risk Factors

Whereas tetanus in adults is an avoidable and tragic illness, tetanus in newborn infants is a public health problem. Studies in the 1970s and 1980s showed that up to 60 newborn babies per 1,000 (6%) were developing neonatal tetanus in various low-income countries, primarily due to contamination of the umbilical stump, and that virtually all these babies died (Stanfield & Galazka, 1984). Deaths due to neonatal tetanus accounted for one-quarter to three-quarters of all neonatal deaths and up to one-quarter of infant mortality in these countries. In 1993 it was estimated that neonatal tetanus caused more than 500,000 deaths worldwide (WHO, 1994). Neonatal tetanus is more common in rural areas, particularly those where animal husbandry practices lead to substantial fecal contamination of the soil, and tends to be more common during the rainy season (Schofield, 1986). However, the key risk factors for neonatal tetanus clearly relate to where a delivery occurs, the level of training of the person assisting with the delivery, how the umbilical cord is cut, and the way the umbilical stump is treated. Because there is enormous diversity of cultural practices regarding how the cord is cut and what is placed on the umbilical stump (including mud, animal dung, clarified butter, and other nonsterile materials), the rate of and risk factors for neonatal tetanus vary substantially in different regions of the world (Stanfield & Galazka, 1984).

Current Approaches to Prevention and Control

Because the *C. tetani* spores that cause neonatal tetanus are ubiquitous in soil and can persist there indefinitely, the organism itself cannot be eradicated. Neonatal tetanus, however, can be controlled or eliminated as a public health problem (defined as fewer than 1 case per 1,000 live births in each health district) by ensuring that a high proportion of women giving birth have received two doses of TT or that the delivery and subsequent cord care practices minimize the chances that *C. tetani* spores will be introduced. Studies such as those conducted in Egypt (Figure 4-1) demonstrate clearly that immunization of women of reproductive age or of pregnant women has a dramatic impact on the risk of neonatal tetanus (Centers for Disease Control and Prevention, 1996). Other studies suggest that training and equipping birth attendants so they can perform a clean delivery (the "3 cleans"—delivery with clean hands, delivery on a clean surface, and use of clean instruments and dressings to cut and dress the umbilical cord) may be somewhat less effective at reducing the risk of neonatal tetanus but has a greater impact on the risk of neonatal mortality from all causes combined. These two approaches can and have been used

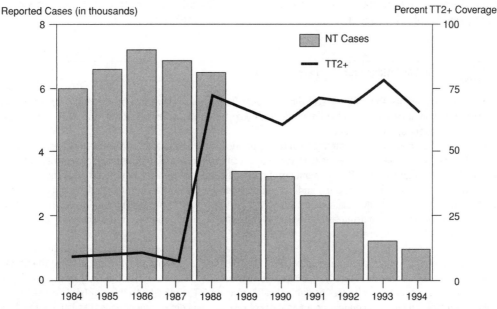

Figure 4-1 Number of Reported Cases of Neonatal Tetanus (NT) and Percentage of Pregnant Women Receiving at Least Two Doses of Tetanus Toxoid (TT2+), by Year, in Egypt, 1984–1994. *Source:* Centers for Disease Control and Prevention, "Progress Toward Elimination of Neonatal Tetanus: Egypt, 1988–1994," 1996, *Morbidity and Mortality Weekly Report, 45,* pp. 89–92. Reprinted with permission.

together. In recent years, the proportion of women giving birth in various geographic regions who have been adequately immunized with TT has increased substantially, but neonatal tetanus remains a problem in many low- and middle-income countries where many deliveries still occur at home.

Obstacles to Prevention and Control

Despite Herculean efforts on the part of WHO, UNICEF, and others, it has remained difficult to achieve and maintain high levels of vaccine coverage in many countries, particularly in rural areas of the low-income countries. For a number of years there was substantial controversy about the relative merits of vertical approaches to vaccinating children (i.e., mass campaigns) and horizontal approaches (i.e., improving access to and use of primary care services that provided routine immunizations). Although the debate over vertical versus horizontal programs continues in some health areas, it has largely been replaced with respect to vaccination of infants and children by a broad consensus that the two approaches can be complementary rather than conflicting. Thus, attempts to strengthen routine infant (and pregnant woman) immunization programs in low- and middle-income countries around the world have proceeded in parallel with mass campaigns intended to hasten the eradication of polio and measles.

Further reduction or elimination of the childhood vaccine-preventable diseases discussed in this section is contingent on the availability of sustained funding of and technical support for immunization programs, stimulation of increased demand for vaccination on the part of parents and communities, expanded access to immunization services, and effective surveillance for these diseases. At the same time, there is a need to continue to develop, test, and make available new and improved vaccines, to expand local production of existing vaccines in low- and middle-income countries, to ensure the potency and safety of the vaccines produced, and to ensure the availability and proper use of sterile injection equipment. The Global Alliance for Vaccines and Immunizations (GAVI) (Exhibit 4-2), together with the Bill and Melinda Gates Foundation and other partners, is working to ensure the earliest possible incorporation of other vaccines into the EPI.

Based on the model of smallpox eradication, one argument used to support the drive for worldwide polio eradication was that it would be possible to discontinue routine polio vaccination at some point after eradication was achieved. However, recent outbreaks of polio caused by circulating vaccine-derived polioviruses in Hispaniola, the Philippines, and Madagascar, together with the widespread presence of wild-type polio virus in numerous laboratories and vaccine production facilities around the world, have challenged previous notions about the need for ongoing polio vaccination after eradication (Fine, Oblapenko, and Sutter, 2004; Sutter, Cáceres, & Mas Lago, 2004).

| Exhibit 4-2 | The Global Alliance for Vaccines and Immunizations |

An estimated 2 million infants and children still die each year from diseases that can be prevented by currently available vaccines. Several million more infants and children die each year from tuberculosis, malaria, and AIDS, infectious diseases for which new vaccines are urgently needed.

Numerous obstacles, many of which are external to the public health and health care delivery systems, make it difficult to achieve and sustain high levels of coverage with existing vaccines in low- and middle-income countries. These obstacles include limited financial resources, insufficient numbers of trained health care workers, poor roads and other barriers to reaching remote parts of some countries, civil wars, and natural disasters. Other barriers retard the development, testing, licensure, and ultimate availability of new vaccines, including the cost of research and testing (and hence the eventual cost of new vaccines, particularly those requiring technological sophistication, such as conjugated vaccines) and liability concerns on the part of potential manufacturers.

Recognizing these problems and wishing to increase the speed with which current and new vaccines reach the world's children, a group of international agencies, including WHO, UNICEF, the World Bank, and others, launched the Global Alliance for Vaccines and Immunizations (GAVI) early in 2000. The mission of GAVI is "to fulfill the right of every child to be protected against vaccine-preventable diseases of public health concern." The initial activities of GAVI focused on establishing a children's vaccine fund and on conducting an analysis of research and development gaps that impede the development and distribution of vaccines. More recently, GAVI has begun working with multilateral and international agencies, vaccine manufacturers, foundations, and low- and middle-income countries to promote the rapid development of new vaccines and greater access to both current and new vaccines. For example, as of July 2003, an estimated 4.3 million children in poor countries had received *Haemophilus influenzae* b conjugate vaccine as a result of the efforts of GAVI and the Vaccine Fund.

The inexplicable and unfortunate increase in all-cause mortality seen in infants (primarily female infants) given experimental high-titer measles vaccine at a young age has clearly set back efforts to develop a more potent measles vaccine (Aaby et al., 1994). Therefore, for the foreseeable future, efforts to eliminate measles will, of necessity, have to make use of the currently available vaccine. Important unanswered questions, therefore, relate to how best to use the currently available vaccine and what vaccination strategies or combinations of strategies will be most effective in interrupting transmission of this highly infectious agent, particularly in Africa. Although there is a clear need to sustain high levels of routine immunization against measles at or about 9 months of age, the relative importance of various strategies for increasing population-level immunity, such as periodic mass campaigns and routinely giving a second dose of measles vaccine at some time after the first birthday, remains to be determined. It is, at best, uncertain whether a new vaccine that is immunogenic at a younger age (in the face of circulating maternal antibodies) and that is safe can be developed and tested, or whether it is even needed in order to eliminate measles.

Historically, rubella vaccine has not been included in the EPI package of vaccines, even though it has been available for 30 years. In recent years, however, there has been growing recognition that congenital rubella syndrome is a problem in low- and middle-income countries, where an estimated 110,000 cases occur annually (Cutts & Vynnycky, 1999). Although virtually all countries in the Americas now include rubella vaccine in the EPI package, consideration needs to be given to using it routinely in Africa and Asia as well (Banatvala & Brown, 2004).

Enteric Infections and Acute Respiratory Infections

Although it might seem odd to discuss enteric infections and acute respiratory infections (ARIs) together in one section, these seemingly disparate conditions have much in common. Each accounts for a substantial amount of childhood morbidity and mortality, as well as for a large proportion of outpatient visits and hospitalizations. Infants and young children almost uniformly experience multiple episodes of both types of illness, regardless of where they live. The identified risk factors for enteric infections and ARIs overlap substantially (e.g., poverty, crowding, lack of parental education, malnutrition, low birth weight, and lack of breastfeeding, and most of these are difficult to change

in the absence of major social change. Further, both enteric infections and ARIs are caused by a multitude of distinct microbial agents, for most of which no vaccine currently exists or is likely to be available in the near future. As a result, the overall approach to minimizing morbidity and mortality from both enteric infections and ARIs has been virtually identical—to accept the fact that such infections and illnesses will occur while attempting to ensure that prompt and appropriate care is sought and given.

Enteric Infections

Overview

Enteric infections encompass those viral, bacterial, and parasitic infections of the gastrointestinal tract that are, with the exception of typhoid fever, generally manifested as diarrhea, either alone or in combination with fever, vomiting, and abdominal pain. Although most episodes of diarrheal disease are mild and self-limited, the loss of fluids and salts accompanying severe diarrhea can be life threatening. Also, not all episodes of diarrheal disease are self-limited—various studies suggest that anywhere from 3% to 23% of diarrheal illnesses in infants and young children persist for longer than 2 weeks (Black, 1993). Both self-limited and persistent diarrhea can have a substantial negative impact on the growth of a child, through malabsorption of nutrients and reduced intake due to vomiting, loss of appetite, and undesirable changes in feeding practices in response to diarrheal illness. Thus, repeated episodes of diarrhea and persistent diarrhea often lead to malnutrition, which can, in turn, increase the likelihood of diarrhea persisting and producing a fatal outcome (El Samani, Willett, & Ware, 1988). It has been estimated that diarrheal disease has a more profound impact on the growth of children worldwide than any other infectious disease.

Cholera, while in a sense just one of many causes of watery diarrhea, is in many ways a disease unto itself. It can produce the most dramatic fluid losses of any enteric infection and, in the absence of appropriate replacement of fluid and salts, can cause death within 24 to 48 hours of onset. Cholera epidemics and pandemics can produce enormous numbers of cases and large numbers of deaths, resulting in profound social disruption. As a result, cholera has been accorded a special status by public health officials and agencies (see Introduction).

Many episodes of diarrheal disease in children in low- and middle-income countries are accompanied by bloody stools or frank dysentery (abdominal cramps; painful, strained defecation; and frequent stools containing blood and mucus), which is usually the result of an invasive infection that produces local tissue damage and inflammation in the intestinal mucosa. Although the fluid loss that accompanies such episodes is generally not profound, life-threatening local intestinal and systemic complications can result. Damage to the intestinal mucosa can also lead to substantial losses of protein, resulting in growth retardation. The clinical management of such episodes poses a number of distinctive challenges (see the section "Current Approaches to Prevention and Control").

On average, children under the age of 5 in low- and middle-income countries experience two to three episodes of diarrhea a year. The burden of disease attributable to diarrheal diseases worldwide is enormous. Despite the impressive accomplishments of diarrheal disease control programs, it is estimated that children under 5 years collectively experience more than 1 billion episodes of diarrhea annually, and diarrheal disease is estimated to cause approximately 3.3 million deaths each year (Bern et al., 1992). Thus, like ARIs, diarrheal disease accounts for roughly 25% of all deaths among those younger than 5 years of age (Black, Morris, & Bryce, 2003).

Typhoid fever, which results from an enteric infection and therefore shares many individual- and community-level risk factors with diarrheal disease, is not accompanied by diarrhea. Although it can be life threatening, typhoid fever has its most profound public health impact through its debilitating effects on school-aged children, causing substantial morbidity and absenteeism from school and work (Medina & Yrarrazaval, 1983).

Etiologic Agents

As noted earlier, diarrheal disease can be caused by a wide variety of viral, bacterial, and parasitic infections. In cases of endemic diarrheal disease, one or more etiologic agents can be identified in 70% to 80% of patients when state-of-the-art laboratory testing is performed. However, many of these agents can also be found in the stools of children who do not have diarrhea, and multiple infectious agents may be present in a child with diarrhea. Thus, the presence of a given causative agent in a stool sample may not mean that it is the cause of that episode of diarrhea.

These complications notwithstanding, the most important etiologic agents in young children in low- and middle-income countries are rotavirus, enterotoxigenic *Escherichia coli* (ETEC), shigella species, *Campylobacter jejuni,* and *Cryptosporidium parvum* (Parashar et al., 2003). Rotavirus is the single leading cause of nonbloody diarrhea in infants, whereas *Shigella* species appear to be the leading cause of

bloody diarrhea. Amebiasis (infection with *Entamoeba histolytica*), although frequently diagnosed, appears to be an extremely infrequent cause of bloody diarrhea in young children in low- and middle-income countries. *Vibrio cholerae* is the cause of a substantial fraction of cases of nonbloody diarrhea in endemic areas such as Bangladesh and India (Cholera Working Group, 1993; Nair et al., 1994); it is also the cause of large numbers of cases when epidemics of cholera occur in other regions, such as Africa and Latin America (Glass, Libel, & Brandling-Bennett, 1992; Goodgame & Greenough, 1975). Typhoid fever is caused by *Salmonella typhi.*

Descriptive Epidemiologic Features and Risk Factors

Children experience the highest risk of diarrheal illness between 6 and 11 months of age; risk declines steadily thereafter (Figure 4-2) (Bern et al., 1992). This age pattern is largely explained by the established risk factors for diarrheal disease and the likely sources of exposure to the causative agents. The risk of diarrheal disease in young infants is determined in large part by the feeding and hand-washing practices of the mother or other child care providers. Breastfeeding and lack of exposure to contaminated food, water, and other environmental sources are protective. As infants grow and become mobile, they begin to encounter numerous potential sources of infection with the agents of diarrheal disease, including contaminated water and weaning foods as well as human and animal waste that has not been disposed of properly. There is also evidence that uncontrolled fly populations can contribute to the risk of diarrheal illnesses, particularly those illnesses caused by etiologic agents requiring a small infectious dose (e.g., shigellosis).

As noted, diarrheal disease and malnutrition are intricately intertwined in infants and young children. Although it is not clear that malnutrition is associated with an increased incidence of diarrheal disease, there is strong evidence that malnutrition increases the likelihood that a child with diarrhea will die or develop persistent diarrhea, and that diarrhea in turn has a negative impact on nutritional status and growth.

Unlike diarrheal disease, typhoid fever has long been thought to be a problem primarily in school-aged children. However, infections with *S. typhi* clearly occur in infants and preschool-aged children, and *S. typhi* infections in this younger age group may be substantially underascertained (Sinha et al., 1999). It has been estimated that there are more than 20 million new cases of typhoid fever worldwide each year, with the highest rates seen in South

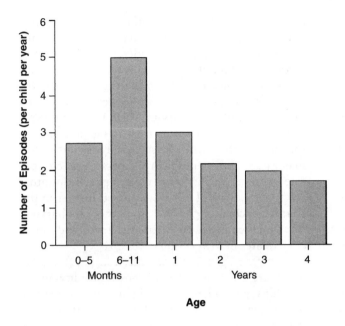

Figure 4-2 Estimated Median Diarrheal Morbidity for Under-Five-Year-Olds, Based on the Results from 18 Studies in Developing Countries. *Source:* C. Bern, J. Martines, I. de Zoysa, and R. I. Glass, "The Magnitude of the Global Problem of Diarrhoeal Disease: A Ten Year Update," 1992, *Bulletin of the World Health Organization, 70*(6), p. 707. Copyright 1992 by the World Health Organization. Reprinted with permission.

and Southeast Asia (Crump, Luby, & Mintz, 2004). *S. typhi* infection is primarily acquired from contaminated food and water.

Current Approaches to Prevention and Control

Unlike the case with ARIs (see later in this chapter), a number of approaches to the primary prevention of diarrheal illness have been studied and found to be successful at lowering the rate of diarrheal illness in the community. These include providing communities with a protected source of clean drinking water, making home treatment and safe storage of drinking water inexpensive and technologically feasible, improving sanitation through the provision of latrines, promoting hand washing and other personal hygiene habits, reducing the fly population in the community, promoting breastfeeding and proper weaning practices, and various combinations of these interventions (Huttly, Morris, & Pisani, 1997). Although these various approaches have been shown to be effective in well-funded research studies, the feasibility of fostering and sustaining such improvements across large areas and populations is directly linked to the availability of the financial resources and the political will to do so. In addition, such interventions can generally succeed only when the community is invested in making them work and when they are designed and introduced within a culturally acceptable framework (see Chapter 2).

In parallel with the testing of such primary prevention approaches to reduce the risk of diarrheal disease, there have been enormous efforts since the early

1980s to ensure that infants and children who develop diarrhea suffer a minimum of morbidity and mortality. These efforts have focused on prevention and early treatment of dehydration through proper case management in the home, maintenance of adequate nutritional intake to minimize the impact on growth, and appropriate treatment of infants and children who are brought to health facilities. Mothers and other caretakers of children are educated to use fluids available in the home to prevent dehydration, to use oral rehydration solutions (ORS) or cereal-based alternative solutions to prevent and treat dehydration, and to continue to breastfeed babies when they have diarrhea. ORS packets are now manufactured in many countries and widely distributed. At the same time, mothers and health care providers have been discouraged from using the wide range of largely ineffective, often expensive, and sometimes dangerous antimicrobial and antidiarrheal agents that are available. Care providers should reserve antimicrobial agents for the treatment of cholera and of dysentery suspected to be caused by shigellosis and to limit the use of intravenous fluids to those who are severely dehydrated. Although promoting and sustaining such changes in diverse countries and in the face of sometimes powerful cultural barriers requires a major effort, studies from Egypt and elsewhere suggest that morbidity and mortality from diarrheal disease have been reduced substantially by such efforts (El-Rafie et al., 1990).

Perhaps in part because of the emphasis given to primary prevention and proper case management for diarrheal disease, the role of vaccines in reducing morbidity and mortality from diarrhea has been quite limited until recently. Vaccines against cholera and typhoid that represent substantial improvements over older vaccines are now available, and a tetravalent rhesus-human reassortment vaccine against rotavirus was approved for use in the United States in 1999. However, that rotavirus vaccine was subsequently withdrawn in the United States because of what was perceived to be an unacceptably high rate of significant adverse reactions. Although a few countries in which typhoid fever is a major public health problem in school-aged children have begun to use typhoid vaccine in this age group, there is continued debate about the proper role for vaccines against enteric infections and under what circumstances they should be given routinely in low- and middle-income countries (Keusch & Cash, 1997). The withdrawal of the rhesus-human reassortment rotavirus vaccine in the United States has made its possible use in low- and middle-income countries politically and ethically contentious. However, clinical trials of human and bovine rotavirus vaccines are currently under way, and it is hoped that a safe and effective rotavirus vaccine will become available in the future (Glass et al., 2004).

Obstacles to Prevention and Control and Directions for Future Research

The greatest obstacle to reducing further the toll taken by diarrheal disease in low- and middle-income countries is the difficulty and expense of ensuring that everyone has regular access to clean, safe drinking water and adequate sanitation. Although WHO at one point envisioned reaching this goal by 1990, it is now clear that the obstacles to doing so are immense and extraordinarily complex. Substantial investments will be needed simply to improve antiquated and increasingly inadequate water treatment and sewage treatment facilities in the rapidly expanding urban centers of many low- and middle-income countries. The problems associated with ensuring a safe drinking water supply and adequate sanitation in rural areas, although different, are equally challenging to overcome.

Acute Respiratory Infections
Overview

Acute respiratory infections comprise infections of various parts of the respiratory tract, ranging from mild viral and bacterial infections of the upper respiratory tract (e.g., the common cold, viral and group A streptococcal pharyngitis, and middle ear infections) to life-threatening infections of the lower respiratory tract (e.g., bronchiolitis and pneumonia caused by a variety of bacterial and viral agents). Although upper respiratory tract infections globally cause substantial minor morbidity and economic loss through lost time at work, they rarely result in severe morbidity or in mortality. Interestingly, studies suggest that the incidence of upper respiratory tract infections, although varying with age and season, is remarkably similar in free-living populations throughout the world. Because they do not pose a major public health problem and because no effective interventions against them exist, upper respiratory tract infections will not be discussed further in this chapter, except for group A streptococcal pharyngitis, which can lead to rheumatic fever and is discussed later in this section.

Lower respiratory tract infections, on the other hand, are the cause of enormous morbidity and of mortality, particularly among infants and young children living in low- and middle-income settings, even when those settings are within generally industrialized countries. In low- and middle-income countries, particularly those with good childhood immunization and oral rehydration therapy programs, lower respiratory tract infections in general, and pneumonias in particular, are typically one of the leading causes of death among infants and children younger than 5 years (Graham, 1990). It is estimated that approximately 2.6 million children younger than 5 years die annually from pneumonia and other lower respiratory tract infections, most of them in low-income countries (Murray & Lopez, 1994). This estimate excludes deaths due to respiratory tract infections that are preventable with vaccines included in the EPI (e.g., measles and pertussis), discussed earlier. However, the accuracy of such estimates is limited because establishing a diagnosis of lower respiratory tract infection or pneumonia is difficult, particularly in settings where chest radiography is not available; many children die outside of hospitals; and other illnesses, such as malaria, make verbal autopsies (i.e., postmortem interviews of next-of-kin to determine the most likely cause of death) an unreliable means of establishing a definitive diagnosis. Although pneumonia and other lower respiratory tract infections also cause substantial morbidity and mortality in older children and adults, this section focuses on these infections in infants and young children. Pneumonia in adults is discussed briefly later, in the section on AIDS.

Etiologic Agent, Clinical Features, and Vaccine Characteristics

Lower respiratory tract infections can be caused by a variety of viral and bacterial agents, either singly or in combination. Numerous studies conducted in various countries around the world show similar results concerning the etiologic agents responsible for these infections in infants and young children. Excluding respiratory tract infections caused by agents included among the EPI vaccines, the most important viral causes of lower respiratory tract infections are influenza, parainfluenza, respiratory syncytial virus, and adenovirus (Avila et al., 1990). The most important bacterial causes of pneumonia, as determined by lung aspirate studies (in which a needle is passed through the chest wall into affected lung parenchyma, thus avoiding contamination of samples by flora in the upper airway), are *Streptococcus pneumoniae*, *Haemophilus influenzae*, and *Staphylococcus aureus* (Shann, 1986). However, many infants and young children have evidence of dual infections (e.g., a virus and a bacterium), and in as many as one-third of the cases, no etiologic agent can be found using state-of-the-art laboratory techniques.

Descriptive Epidemiologic Features and Risk Factors

Infants and young children living in low- and middle-income environments consistently have been found to experience high incidence rates of pneumonia (Selwyn, 1990). For example, in the Highlands of Papua New Guinea, cumulative incidence rates in the range of 250 to 300 per 1,000 infants per year have been observed, compared with a rate in the range of 10 per 1,000 infants per year among upper-middle-income children in the United States. At the same time, elevated incidence rates mirroring those in Papua New Guinea have been observed among Native American children living in poverty in the United States. Verbal autopsy studies suggest that 25% to 50% of deaths in children under 5 in low- and middle-income countries are due to pneumonia and other forms of lower respiratory tract infection (Sutrisna et al., 1993).

The single most important predictor of a child's risk of developing pneumonia or other lower respiratory tract infection is age. The cumulative incidence of lower respiratory tract infections is highest among young infants and drops rapidly with increasing age, reaching markedly lower levels by 2 or 3 years of age (Selwyn, 1990). Another important predictor of an increased risk of morbidity and mortality from lower respiratory tract infections is low birth weight. Other risk factors for either morbidity or mortality include exposure to indoor air pollution (from cooking, heating, and cigarette smoke), not breastfeeding, and malnutrition, including vitamin A deficiency, although these factors are closely intertwined with poverty and with each other, and their independent effects can be difficult to disentangle (Berman, 1991). HIV infection

is almost certainly another important risk factor, although its role in infants and young children has not been well studied.

Rheumatic fever following group A streptococcal pharyngitis occurs in a setting of poverty and household crowding. School-aged children are primarily affected acutely, but the damage done to heart valves is usually permanent, producing life-threatening disability. Population-based data concerning the incidence of acute rheumatic fever and the prevalence of rheumatic heart disease in low- and middle-income countries are infrequently available.

Current Approaches to Prevention and Control

In the 1980s WHO, together with various partners, began a multifaceted research program intended to develop an approach to reducing the substantial morbidity and mortality due to lower respiratory tract infections in infants and young children (WHO, 1981). This research program and the ARI control program that was subsequently developed were premised on the following observations:

- Upper respiratory tract infections, although frequent, are almost always benign and require only supportive care at home.

- Many lower respiratory tract infections in infants and young children are not preventable with existing vaccines.

- The major known risk factors for morbidity and mortality from lower respiratory tract infections (e.g., age, low birth weight, malnutrition, and indoor air pollution) are impossible or difficult to change.

- Most morbidity and mortality from lower respiratory tract infections occur in locales where access to medical care is limited and where there are few, if any, diagnostic facilities (i.e., the ability to perform chest x-rays, microbiologic cultures, and other tests).

Given these circumstances, it was decided that an ARI control program based on a triage performed by minimally trained village health workers according to readily observable clinical signs might be feasible, inexpensive, and effective at reducing at least mortality. As a result, a large body of multidisciplinary research relating to the various aspects of such a control program was commissioned and completed. Particularly important was research relating to which readily observable clinical manifestations (e.g., cough, fever, respiratory rate, and chest indrawing), singly or in combination, best distinguished infants or young children with various levels of severity of respiratory tract infection (initially classified as mild, moderate, and severe, but later as no pneumonia, pneumonia, and severe pneumonia).

Based on this research, intervention programs were developed. These were intended to train village health workers or their equivalents in how to assess and classify into one of these categories an infant or young child with signs of a respiratory tract infection. Based on their assessment, the village health workers were to recommend supportive care at home in cases of mild ARI (no pneumonia), provide an oral antimicrobial drug (either ampicillin or cotrimoxazole) and education about home care and follow-up in cases of moderate ARI (pneumonia), or refer the child immediately to the nearest hospital for assessment and inpatient care in cases of severe ARI (severe pneumonia). Well-designed intervention trials were carried out in a variety of countries to assess the efficacy of this approach in reducing mortality due to lower respiratory tract infections. As shown in a meta-analysis of these trials, they were almost all successful, reducing mortality due to lower respiratory tract infections and all-cause mortality in infants and in children aged 1 to 4 years (Sazawal & Black, 1992). It is important to note, however, that virtually all these trials assessed an intervention that included regular household visits by the village health workers in search of infants and children with signs of a respiratory tract infection.

Based on these favorable results, WHO promoted and supported the implementation of ARI control programs largely based on having village health workers (or their equivalent) assess infants and young children with suspected ARI, classify them by severity of illness, and treat or refer them. The impact of such programs on mortality, as distinct from the impact seen in the intervention trials, has not been adequately assessed. However, ARI control programs that do not include a proactive, outreach component that ensures early case detection (i.e., regular household visits) as was present in the intervention trials, and instead rely solely on maternal recognition of illness and appropriate, timely care seeking are not likely to have as large an impact. On the other hand, programs that include some form of regular household visits are likely to be difficult to sustain.

For a variety of reasons, the emphasis given to ARI control programs (and vertical disease-specific programs in general) by WHO and others has diminished in recent years, and attention has shifted to ensuring that any sick infant or child, regardless of his or her other signs and symptoms, receives appropriate evaluation and care. This approach, referred to as the Integrated Management of Childhood Illness, is described in Exhibit 4-3 (Gove, 1997; Lambrechts, Bryce, & Orinda, 1999; Perkins, Zucker et al., 1997; Weber et al., 1997). See also Table 4-3 (Gove, 1997).

Prevention of rheumatic fever depends on the recognition of streptococcal pharyngitis and treatment with an appropriate antimicrobial agent (e.g., penicillin or erythromycin). In populations with high rates of acute rheumatic fever, school-based and other programs to detect and treat streptococcal pharyngitis have been suggested (Bach et al., 1996).

Exhibit 4-3   Integrated Management of Childhood Illness

Throughout the 1970s and 1980s, concerted efforts were made to develop case management strategies for each of the infectious diseases that collectively accounted for the majority of morbidity and mortality among infants and young children in low- and middle-income countries—measles, malaria, diarrheal disease, and acute respiratory infections. Although each of these disease-specific case management strategies has been shown to be effective at reducing severe morbidity and mortality when properly implemented, it has been recognized that having multiple distinct disease-specific programs that all target the same health care providers can lead to overlap, inefficiency, and competition for the attention of an overworked health care worker. As a result, various programs within WHO and UNICEF have collaborated in the development of the Integrated Management of Childhood Illness (IMCI), which attempts to pull together into a single, more efficient program the approaches of the various disease-specific control programs (Gove, 1997).

The IMCI program includes both preventive strategies and case management approaches for the illnesses that collectively account for the majority of severe morbidity, mortality, and health care provider visits among infants and young children (see Table 4-3). The results of early field assessments of the IMCI algorithm in selected countries suggest that it can be an effective tool, although some modifications may be needed to maximize its usefulness (Lambrechts et al., 1999; Perkins, et al., 1997; Weber et al., 1997). A detailed evaluation of IMCI programs in five countries is currently under way (Bryce et al., 2004).

Table 4-3	Child Health Interventions Included in Integrated Management of Childhood Illness
Case Management Interventions	**Preventive Interventions**
Pneumonia	Immunization during sick child visits (to reduce missed opportunities)
Diarrhea	Nutrition counseling
Dehydration	Breastfeeding support (including the assessment and corrections of
Persistent diarrhea	breastfeeding technique
Dysentery	
Meningitis, sepsis	
Malaria	
Measles	
Malnutrition	
Anemia	
Ear infection	

Source: S. Gove, "Integrated Management of Childhood Illness by Outpatient Health Workers: Technical Basis and Overview," 1997, *Bulletin of World Health Organization, 75*(Suppl. 1), pp. 7-24. Copyright 1997 by the World Health Organization. Reprinted with permission.

Obstacles to Prevention and Control and Directions for Future Research

Primary prevention of lower respiratory tract infections remains a long-term goal, awaiting improvements in living conditions and socioeconomic status as well as the availability of affordable vaccines against the major etiologic agents that are effective when given in infancy. A safe, highly effective conjugate vaccine against *H. influenzae* type b has led to the virtual disappearance of invasive infections caused by this organism in the United States and other industrialized and middle-income countries, including a number of countries in Latin America. Once problems relating to the cost of adding this vaccine to the EPI have been dealt with, this vaccine will undoubtedly have a similar effect in other low- and middle-income countries. It is uncertain what proportion of morbidity and mortality related to lower respiratory tract infections in such countries will be prevented by this vaccine, because serotype b accounts for only a fraction of *H. influenzae* infections, but results from a study in Gambia suggest that conjugate *H. influenzae* b vaccine can prevent approximately 20% of radiologically confirmed pneumonias (Mulholland et al., 1997).

Conjugate pneumococcal vaccines including the most important serotypes of *S. pneumoniae* have been tested and have shown excellent efficacy and safety. A conjugate pneumococcal vaccine including those serotypes that collectively account for approximately 80% of invasive infections in infants in the United States was approved for use in that country in 2000 and has had a profound impact on the rate of invasive pneumococcal infections among infants; however, the current cost of the vaccine makes its use in low- and middle-income countries unaffordable. Also, certain pneumococcal serotypes that are more important causes of infection in low- and middle-income countries than in the United States are not included in the recently licensed vaccine. When pneumococcal vaccines that are specifically formulated for use in low- and middle-income countries are licensed, issues relating to how to finance their inclusion in the EPI will need to be addressed. When (indeed, if) vaccines against the various viruses that cause lower respiratory tract infections in infants and small children will become available is uncertain.

There are several barriers to reducing morbidity and mortality due to lower respiratory tract infections through means other than vaccination and the improvement of living conditions. The first set of barriers relates to how to ensure that the parents or guardians of a sick child will seek and have access to appropriate care in a timely fashion. A detailed discussion of care-seeking practices and obstacles to obtaining medical care is beyond the scope of this chapter, but the obstacles are multifaceted and difficult to overcome. There are also many challenges relating to ensuring that those ill infants and children who are brought to medical care facilities receive timely and appropriate care, including adequate assessment, treatment, and follow-up. Finally, there are concerns about the likelihood that increased use of currently effective and inexpensive antimicrobial agents, particularly use of inappropriate or inadequate regimens, may lead to the development of resistant strains of bacteria (particularly *S. pneumoniae*) that may then not respond to these inexpensive, oral treatment regimens.

Bacterial Meningitis

Overview

Meningitis is a nonspecific term that encompasses inflammation of the meninges (the membranous lining that covers the brain and spinal cord), which can be caused by a wide variety of infectious and noninfectious agents. Such inflammation, regardless of its cause, tends to produce a similar clinical picture: headache, stiff neck, fever, and variable other features. There is substantial overlap between the manifestations of meningitis, which is sometimes referred to as *spinal meningitis* or *cerebrospinal meningitis*, and those of many other infectious diseases. Although meningitis can be caused by a wide variety of viruses and other infectious agents (e.g., mycobacteria and parasites), meningitis caused by certain bacteria poses a substantial public health threat. Therefore, this section is confined to a discussion of bacterial meningitis, excluding tuberculous meningitis, which is discussed briefly in the section on tuberculosis.

From a public health perspective, it is important to subdivide bacterial meningitis into its endemic and epidemic forms. Endemic bacterial meningitis, while differing in a number of subtle ways with regard to its descriptive epidemiologic features and the distribution of etiologic agents in low- and middle-income countries versus industrialized countries, poses a similar set of challenges in these two different settings. The vastly different resources available in high- and low-income countries for prevention and control of endemic bacterial meningitis, although relatively less important only a few years ago, are now assuming greater importance as a result of the development and licensure of effective but expensive conjugate vaccines against the major etiologic agents causing endemic disease. Epidemic bacterial meningitis, for reasons that remain unexplained, has virtually ceased to be a public health problem in industrialized countries since World War II, although small clusters of cases or hyperendemic disease can still be a vexing problem. In a number of low- and middle-income countries, however, particularly those in the "meningitis belt" of sub-Saharan Africa, periodic epidemics of bacterial meningitis occur on a scale never documented in industrialized countries. These epidemics can be of such a magnitude and geographic scope as to be properly called public health disasters.

In industrialized countries, suspected bacterial meningitis is considered a medical emergency, requiring appropriate clinical specimens for diagnostic testing to be obtained and parenteral antimicrobial therapy in a hospital to be initiated immediately. Even under these ideal conditions, CFRs for bacterial meningitis range from 3% to 25%, depending primarily on the specific etiologic agent and the age of the patient. Further, many patients who survive the acute episode will be left with one or more serious sequelae, including deafness, blindness, mental retardation, and seizure disorders. Although the clinical outcomes of hospitalized cases of bacterial meningitis do not, in general, differ between low- and middle-income and industrialized countries, the resources available for treating such patients are obviously much more limited in low- and middle-income countries. Furthermore, it is evident that epidemics involving tens of thousands of such cases cannot be dealt with easily by countries with extremely constrained health budgets and facilities.

Endemic Meningitis

Etiologic Agents

Studies of the etiology of endemic bacterial meningitis in low- and middle-income countries have been hampered by the need for a reasonably well-equipped and staffed microbiology laboratory to conduct such studies. However, a number of hospital-based studies have been conducted in areas where or in time periods when epidemic meningitis has not been present. These studies are in general agreement that the leading causes of endemic bacterial meningitis in these settings are *S. pneumoniae, H. influenzae,* and *Neisseria meningitidis,* which also are responsible for most cases of bacterial meningitis in industrialized countries, although the introduction and use of conjugate vaccines against *H. influenzae* type b has led to the virtual disappearance of cases due to this organism in such countries. Other organisms that account for a reasonable proportion of cases in industrialized countries, such as group B streptococcus and *Listeria monocytogenes,* appear to be infrequent causes in low- and middle-income countries, although this apparent difference may be artifactual. At the same time, meningitis due to *Salmonella* species appears to be more common in low- and middle-income countries than in industrialized ones.

Descriptive Epidemiologic Features and Risk Factors

The overall cumulative incidence of endemic bacterial meningitis in low- and middle-income countries appears to be four or five times that in industrialized countries, although the available data are limited. It has been estimated that somewhere between 1 in 60 and 1 in 300 children die of bacterial meningitis before the age of 5 in nonepidemic areas (Greenwood, 1987). Endemic bacterial meningitis is primarily a problem in infants and young children, although age-specific incidence rates vary with the etiologic agent. Meningitis caused by *H. influenzae* occurs almost exclusively during the first 12 to 24 months of life. Although the highest rates of meningitis due to *S. pneumoniae* and endemic meningitis due to *N. meningitidis* occur in the first 12 to 24 months of life, cases also occur in older children and adults. Endemic bacterial meningitis probably occurs at approximately equal rates among males and females.

Because the three leading causes of endemic bacterial meningitis are all spread via respiratory droplets, poverty and the resulting crowding increase the risk of disease. Failure to breastfeed has been shown to be a risk factor in industrialized countries and probably increases the risk in low- and middle-income countries as well. Host factors also play an important role in determining the risk of endemic bacterial meningitis, most notably sickle cell disease and HIV infection. Sickle cell disease is associated with a markedly increased risk of infection with *S. pneumoniae*. Meningitis due to *S. pneumoniae*, like that caused by *Salmonella*, appears to occur at a substantially increased rate among HIV-infected children and adults. Malnutrition and anemia also have been suspected to be risk factors for bacterial meningitis.

Current Approaches to Prevention and Control

In most low- and middle-income countries, little or nothing is done to prevent endemic bacterial meningitis. Bacterial meningitis due to *H. influenzae* type b is now preventable with vaccines produced by conjugating the bacterial polysaccharide to one of several protein molecules. The widespread use of these vaccines has led to its virtual eradication in industrialized countries. However, because of their substantial cost, only a few middle-income countries (e.g., Brazil and Chile) have incorporated conjugate *H. influenzae* type b vaccine into their routine childhood immunization programs thus far. Recently, the GAVI has made substantial progress in making this vaccine more widely available in poor countries (see Exhibit 4-2). Although a portion of endemic meningitis caused by *N. meningitidis* could be prevented with existing purified polysaccharide vaccine against serogroup C and more recently developed vaccines against serogroup B, these vaccines are not in widespread use outside selected countries (e.g., Brazil and Cuba are routinely using a vaccine against serogroup B *N. meningitidis*). Endemic meningitis due to *S. pneumoniae* has not, until recently, been vaccine preventable in infants and young children, the highest-risk age

groups, but a conjugate *S. pneumoniae* vaccine formulated for use in the United States has recently been approved for use in infants there. Similar vaccines formulated for use in low- and middle-income countries are not yet available but are under development.

Chemoprophylaxis, the giving of a short course of an antimicrobial agent to individuals in close contact with someone with bacterial meningitis due to *N. meningitidis* or *H. influenzae* type b, has been used with some success in industrialized countries, but has not been widely advocated. It is virtually never used in low- and middle-income countries because of the small percentage of endemic cases that occur in close contacts of a known case, the cost and availability of the antimicrobial agents, the limited duration of the protection achieved, concerns about promoting the development of antimicrobial resistance, and logistical problems related to implementation.

Obstacles to Prevention and Control and Directions for Future Research

The primary obstacle to preventing endemic meningitis due to *H. influenzae* type b in low- and middle-income countries is the cost of the highly effective and safe conjugate vaccines now used in industrialized countries. If means of dramatically reducing the cost per dose of these vaccines and paying for them can be found, and high vaccine coverage can be achieved, endemic meningitis due to this organism can be virtually eliminated. If, as expected, the conjugate *S. pneumoniae* vaccines currently being developed for use in low- and middle-income countries prove successful in preventing pneumococcal meningitis (and other invasive infections caused by this organism), similar issues of how to make the vaccines affordable for use in such countries will arise. Prevention of endemic meningococcal meningitis must await the availability of serogroup B and C conjugate vaccines that are effective in infants, provide protection against multiple serotypes of serogroup B, and are affordable.

Epidemic Meningitis
Etiologic Agents

Epidemic bacterial meningitis is always caused by *N. meningitidis*. More specifically, serogroup A *N. meningitidis* causes most such epidemics, although epidemics due to serogroup C also have been well documented. Recently, explosive outbreaks caused by serogroup W-135 have complicated efforts to control or prevent epidemics of meningococcal meningitis using vaccines (Bertherat et al., 2002). Serogroup B *N. meningitidis*, one of the most important causes of endemic bacterial meningitis, has caused "epidemics" in a variety of industrialized and low- and middle-income countries, but these outbreaks are never of the scope and intensity of those caused by serogroup A, differing in overall attack rates by as much as two orders of magnitude (see the following section).

Descriptive Epidemiologic Features and Risk Factors

Epidemic bacterial meningitis, generally caused by serogroup A *N. meningitidis,* is one of the most interesting but least understood infectious disease problems in the world. Epidemics involving hundreds of thousands of cases and cumulative incidence rates of almost 2,000 per 100,000 total population have been observed in the "meningitis belt" of Africa (Figure 4-3) for more than 100 years (Moore, 1992). The epidemic there in the 1990s was one of the largest ever recorded and extended into parts of Africa not previously considered to be in the meningitis belt. In this region of Africa, epidemics in a given area last for 2 or 3 years and recur every 5 to 15 years. They occur only during the hot, dry season (January to April) and dissipate when the rains and cooler weather arrive, only to return the next dry season. The interepidemic period can vary from a few years to a decade or more, probably reflecting a combination of the time it takes to reaccumulate enough

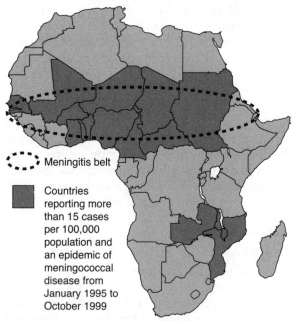

Figure 4-3 The Meningitis Belt of sub-Saharan Africa.
Source: WHO Report on Global Surveillance of Epidemic-Prone Infectious Diseases, Chapter 5, Meningococcal Disease, page 56. WHO/CDS/CSR/ISR/2000.1, World Health Organization, Department of Communicable Disease Surveillance and Response. Copyright 2000 by the World Health Organization. Reprinted with permission.

susceptible individuals to sustain an epidemic, the introduction of a new virulent strain of *N. meningitidis,* prior use of polysaccharide meningococcal vaccine in the population, and other poorly defined factors (Moore, 1992).

Epidemics of meningococcal meningitis also occur in Asia and Latin America. In western China and Nepal, the epidemics follow a pattern similar to that seen in Africa, except that they occur during a cold, dry season rather than a hot, dry season. In Latin America, Brazil has borne the brunt of such epidemics due to both serogroups A and C. Epidemics have also affected countries in the Middle East (e.g., Saudi Arabia) and the Pacific (e.g., New Zealand).

Current Approaches to Prevention and Control

Historically, efforts to reduce morbidity and mortality from epidemic meningococcal meningitis have been reactive in nature. Once an epidemic is detected, a vaccination campaign is implemented as rapidly as possible, along with making more available the antimicrobial agents and other materials needed to treat cases appropriately. This approach has been rightly criticized on the grounds that there are seemingly unavoidable delays in mounting such campaigns, during which time many cases (and resulting morbidity and mortality) occur. Such reactive vaccination campaigns are almost inevitably disruptive of other health programs, and the extent to which they actually reduce the size of the epidemic is often debated.

One approach to improving the control of such epidemics that has been suggested is to improve surveillance for bacterial meningitis in areas susceptible to epidemics (e.g., the meningitis belt of Africa), use a predetermined threshold rate of cases to declare an epidemic and mount a vaccination campaign, and have stockpiles of vaccine and other supplies and equipment in the immediate area (WHO, 1995). However, projections suggest that even these steps would result in the prevention of no more than 40% to 50% of the cases that would otherwise occur, and initial attempts to establish such early detection and response capabilities have demonstrated the limitations of this approach. Others have proposed routinely vaccinating all infants, children, and young adults in areas at risk of such epidemics with currently available meningococcal A polysaccharide vaccine (Robbins et al., 1997). However, the need to give three or more doses of this vaccine, and at least one of these at age 3 or 4 years in order to possibly achieve long-term protection, has raised concerns about the costs and feasibility of such an approach (Perkins et al., 1997). Furthermore, the recent large outbreak of meningococcal meningitis caused by serogroup

W-135 suggests that any meningococcal vaccine used routinely in this part of the world may need to contain at least three serogroups—A, C, and W-135.

Obstacles to Prevention and Control and Directions for Future Research

Pilot demonstration projects that attempt to incorporate the current meningococcal A purified polysaccharide vaccine into routine vaccination programs in countries in the meningitis belt of Africa are currently being discussed. However, the ultimate prevention of such epidemics may well have to await the availability of a multi-serogroup conjugate meningococcal vaccine that is immunogenic in infants, provides long-term protection when several doses are given within the first year of life, and is affordable. Such vaccines that appear promising are currently undergoing field trials in Africa, but it is unknown when they will become available or what they will cost (Jódar et al., 2002).

Mycobacterial Infections

Overview

Although many species of mycobacteria can infect people, only two of them cause sufficient human illness in low- and middle-income countries to warrant discussion here—*Mycobacteria tuberculosis,* the cause of tuberculosis, and *Mycobacteria leprae,* the cause of leprosy. Although *Mycobacteria bovis* (which is closely related to *M. tuberculosis*) can cause tuberculosis in humans, it accounts for a small percentage of cases, and these cases are generally not distinguishable from or in need of different treatment than cases caused by *M. tuberculosis.* Other than *M. leprae,* the various nontuberculous mycobacteria cause opportunistic infections that occur almost exclusively in immunocompromised individuals. Whereas these nontuberculous mycobacteria, particularly *Mycobacteria avium* complex, have caused substantial morbidity and mortality among AIDS patients in industrialized countries, they appear to be uncommon in AIDS patients in low- and middle-income countries.

Tuberculosis and infection with *M. tuberculosis* are, by every indicator available, among the most important public health problems in the world. It has been estimated that approximately one-third of the world's population (1.7 billion persons) is infected with *M. tuberculosis,* and that worldwide there were 8 to 9 million new cases of tuberculosis and almost 2 million deaths from tuberculosis in the year 2000 (Corbett et al., 2003). Among adults, tuberculosis is responsible for more deaths than any other single infectious agent. Because suppression of the body's immune system is the most important determinant of which individuals infected with *M. tuberculosis* will subsequently develop tuberculosis, the AIDS epidemic has had disastrous consequences for the control of tuberculosis, which was underfunded and inadequate in most low- and middle-income countries even before the arrival of AIDS. In recognition of the gravity of the problems posed by it, WHO declared tuberculosis to be a global emergency in 1993.

A disease that many believe to have been leprosy was described in the Old Testament of the Bible. Leprosy occupies a unique position among human diseases, in large part because of the disfigurement that it can produce and the belief in many cultures that it represents some form of divine punishment. Although leprosy was endemic to Europe during the 11th through 13th centuries, it had virtually disappeared from there by the 18th century, long before modern medicine arrived. There is speculation that it was the rise of tuberculosis and infection with *M. tuberculosis* that produced cross-immunity to *M. leprae* and led to the disappearance of leprosy from Europe. Some support for this theory comes from the observation that BCG, the vaccine intended to prevent tuberculosis, appears to be as or more effective in preventing leprosy. Whatever the cause of its virtual (but not complete) absence from industrialized countries, leprosy today is largely confined to a shrinking number of low- and middle-income countries.

Tuberculosis

Etiologic Agent, Clinical Features, and Vaccine Characteristics

Compared with other bacteria, mycobacteria are slow growing and have special nutritional needs. *M. tuberculosis* can be recovered from clinical specimens, particularly those from the respiratory tract, when appropriate artificial media and techniques are used, but the process takes many weeks and requires a laboratory with a modest level of sophistication and resources. Further, it can be difficult to obtain a specimen of respiratory tract secretions, particularly from a child. As a result, most cases of tuberculosis are diagnosed and treated based on examination of respiratory tract secretions under a microscope, radiologic findings on chest x-ray, or clinical grounds.

Descriptive Epidemiologic Features and Risk Factors

M. tuberculosis is spread via respiratory droplets produced when an individual with active pulmonary tuberculosis, particularly smear-positive tuberculosis (in which more organisms are present in the sputum), coughs or sneezes. Individuals in close contact with an untreated infected individual, particularly household contacts, are at highest risk of becoming infected. In low- and middle-income countries, the highest incidence rates of pulmonary tuberculosis are in men and women of reproductive age, meaning that there are often infants and young children in the same house-hold in close daily contact with individuals with active pulmonary tuberculosis. As a result, a high proportion of individuals will be exposed to and infected with *M. tuberculosis* before they reach adulthood.

Although a small proportion of infected infants and children will develop pulmonary or extrapulmonary tuberculosis soon after becoming infected, in most instances the immune system successfully walls off, but does not kill, all the *M. tuberculosis* organisms. As these infected children grow up, various factors, particularly HIV infection and malnutrition, can reduce the ability of the immune system to keep the organisms in check, and reactivation tuberculosis can occur. Before the AIDS epidemic, it was estimated that 5% of those infected as children developed tuberculosis soon after infection and another 5% developed tuberculosis at some point later in life. However, HIV infection is such a potent inhibitor of cell-mediated immunity (the part of the immune system that holds *M. tuberculosis* infection in check) that a high proportion of untreated dually infected individuals (i.e., infected with HIV and with *M. tuberculosis*) can be expected to develop tuberculosis unless they die of something else first or receive preventive therapy.

It was recently estimated that almost 2 million persons die from tuberculosis and that 8 million persons experience the onset of the disease each year, with the vast majority of these deaths and illnesses occurring in low-income countries. Although tuberculosis is a major public health problem in virtually every low-income country, the burden of disease attributable to tuberculosis varies by region and country, in part because of longstanding historical differences in the incidence of tuberculosis and the prevalence of infection with *M. tuberculosis,* in part because of local differences in the adequacy of the tuberculosis control program, and in part because of differences in the extent of the HIV/AIDS epidemic. Based on admittedly incomplete passive surveillance for reported cases of tuberculosis and on tuberculin skin test surveys, it appears that sub-Saharan Africa has the highest average annual risk of infection with *M. tuberculosis* and the highest crude incidence rate of cases of tuberculosis (Figure 4-4). However, the largest numbers of cases of tuberculosis are seen in the countries comprising the Southeast Asian

and the Western Pacific regions of WHO, which collectively account for almost two-thirds of the world's cases (Dolin, Raviglione, & Kochi, 1994). Because of the HIV/AIDS epidemic and unrelated demographic changes (e.g., population growth and increases in the numbers of individuals surviving to their 30s and 40s), it has been projected that the number of new cases of tuberculosis will increase in coming years in low- and middle-income countries in all the regions of the world.

Although tuberculosis occurs in individuals in all socioeconomic strata, it is quintessentially a disease of poverty. Through its effect on crowding, poverty increases the risk of airborne transmission of *M. tuberculosis*. At the same time, through its negative effect on nutritional status, poverty increases the likelihood that someone infected with *M. tuberculosis* will develop tuberculosis. HIV infection is also more prevalent among the poor, thus increasing the likelihood that an infected individual will develop tuberculosis. In addition, through its effect on access to curative medical care, poverty increases the likelihood that a patient with symptomatic pulmonary tuberculosis will remain untreated and hence infectious for a longer period of time.

Current Approaches to Prevention and Control

Tuberculosis control programs exist in virtually all low- and middle-income countries, although there is enormous variability in the resources at their disposal and their effectiveness. The current approach to controlling tuberculosis in low- and middle-income countries is based on a strategy of rapid detection of and provision of effective multidrug therapy to all infectious persons (i.e., patients with pulmonary tuberculosis, particularly smear-positive patients). Key components of a successful tuberculosis control program include a strong government commitment to the program; use of sputum smear microscopy to assess symptomatic patients who present at health care facilities; use of a standardized multidrug short-course regimen, with direct observation of drug ingestion for at least the first 2 months of treatment (directly observed treatment, short course [DOTS]); assurance of an uninterrupted supply of all essential antituberculosis drugs; and a standardized system of recording and reporting cases, treatment, and outcome. Whereas a survey conducted in 1996 showed that only 75 of the 180 responding countries had implemented such a program, and in only 39 of these countries was there nationwide implementation, by 2002 substantial progress had been made in widening coverage of DOTS (Figure 4-5). However, a WHA goal of detecting 70% of infectious cases and curing 85% of detected cases worldwide by December 2005 was in

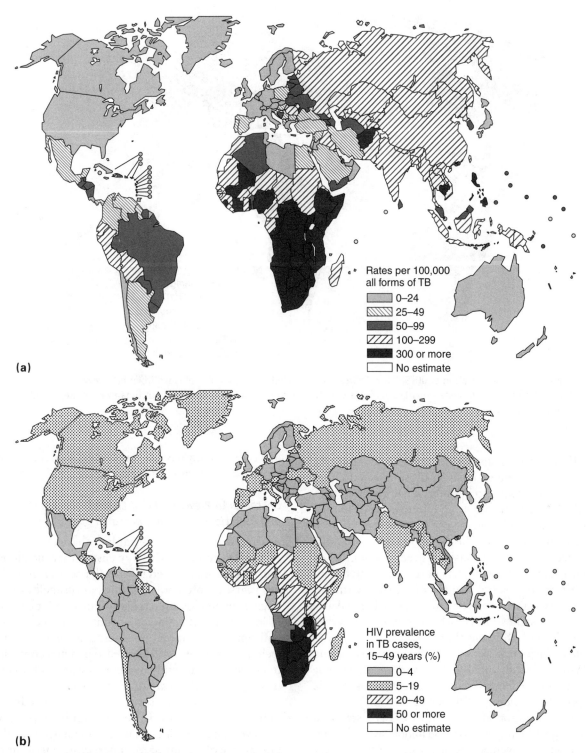

Figure 4-4 (a) Estimated Tuberculosis Incidence Rates, 2003; (b) Estimated HIV Prevalence in Tuberculosis Cases, 2003. *Source:* World Health Organization, 2003, 2004.

danger of not being met (Elzinga, Raviglione, & Maher 2004).

In the face of the limited resources available to ensure prompt diagnosis and treatment of infectious cases of tuberculosis among those who present spontaneously to health facilities, there has been an understandable reluctance to devote scarce resources to active searching for other cases in the households

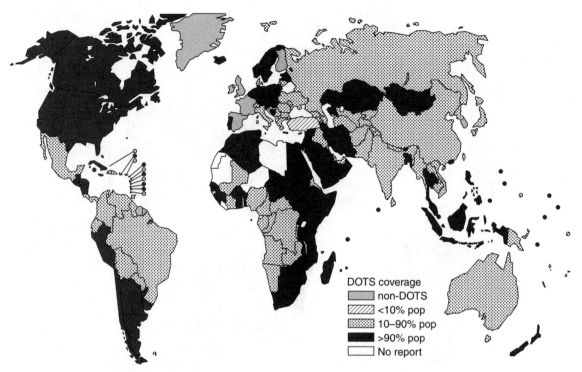

Figure 4-5 Implementation of DOTS, 2002. *Source:* Annex 5 World Maps, #3. Downloaded from: http:www.who.int/entity/tb/publications/global-report/2004/annex5.pdf. Copyright 2004 by the World Health Organization. Reprinted with permission.

of affected individuals or in the community. Similarly, prevention of tuberculosis in those infected either recently or longer ago in the past has not been considered a high priority or an effective use of limited resources. In addition, the use of a single drug, such as isoniazid, to reduce the likelihood of tuberculosis in infected individuals (as practiced in a number of industrialized countries) has raised the specter of inadvertent single-drug therapy of patients with unrecognized tuberculosis and an increased prevalence of drug-resistant strains of *M. tuberculosis*. However, clinical trials showing that preventive therapy is highly effective in preventing tuberculosis among HIV-infected individuals in low- and middle-income countries have focused renewed attention on the role of preventive therapy (Whalen et al., 1997).

Immunization at birth with BCG is a standard part of the EPI in every low- and middle-income country, and BCG coverage rates are high in virtually every such country. Infant immunization with BCG appears to be quite effective at reducing the risk of disseminated tuberculosis (e.g., tuberculous meningitis) in infants and children, but its efficacy against pulmonary tuberculosis in this age group is probably no better than 50% to 60%. Infant immunization with BCG probably has, at best, only a modest effect on the risk of developing pulmonary tuberculosis as an adult

and consequently has little or no impact on the spread of *M. tuberculosis* in the community.

Obstacles to Prevention and Control and Directions for Future Research

As noted earlier, demographic changes and the HIV/AIDS epidemic virtually ensure that the global burden of cases of tuberculosis will rise over the coming years. At present, the principal obstacles to reducing tuberculosis-related morbidity and mortality in low- and middle-income countries are economic and operational in nature. Increased financial and technical assistance will be needed in many countries to ensure that currently available strategies for controlling tuberculosis are fully implemented.

At the same time, further research is needed in multiple areas if control of tuberculosis is to be achieved and sustained. There is evidence that the prevalence of strains of *M. tuberculosis* resistant to one or more of the antimicrobial agents routinely used to treat tuberculosis is substantial and growing. This is occurring not only in those countries historically classified as resource poor, but also in Russia and some of the newly independent states of the former Soviet Union, where inadequate treatment of cases of tuberculosis has led to a rapid rise in drug-resistant strains.

Development of new drugs that are effective against *M. tuberculosis,* are affordable and safe, and can eradicate infection with a shorter duration of treatment is a high priority, but such drugs are unlikely to be available soon. Similarly, development of a vaccine against *M. tuberculosis* that can prevent pulmonary tuberculosis is a high priority, but is not currently within view. In the meantime, operational research into how to enhance case detection and ensure dispensing of and compliance with proper treatment, as well as how to prevent tuberculosis in high-risk individuals (e.g., those dually infected with *M. tuberculosis* and HIV) is urgently needed.

Leprosy
Etiologic Agent, Clinical Features, and Vaccine Characteristics

M. leprae cannot be grown on artificial media. In research laboratories, it can be isolated and propagated in the foot pad of a mouse or in armadillos, but these techniques have no relevance to diagnosing leprosy. The diagnosis of leprosy is made on clinical grounds, together with histopathologic examination of tissue biopsy material. *M. leprae* grows even more slowly than *M. tuberculosis.* The slow growth of both organisms is highly relevant to the control and prevention of tuberculosis and leprosy because of the consequent need to treat those who are infected for prolonged periods of time (months to years) and the resulting difficulty of ensuring compliance with antimicrobial therapy long after the individual feels well.

Descriptive Epidemiologic Features and Risk Factors

Although it is clear that prolonged, close contact (e.g., living in the same household) with someone with untreated leprosy, particularly someone with a high burden of organisms (i.e., multibacillary leprosy), is associated with a substantially increased risk of acquiring the disease, the routes of transmission are ill defined. It is assumed that transmission occurs primarily through skin-to-skin contact or exposure to respiratory tract (e.g., nasal) secretions. Environmental or animal reservoirs of *M. leprae* are thought to have little or no role in human infections. The exceedingly long incubation period for leprosy, which is believed to be years to decades, makes any study of transmission very difficult. Leprosy is primarily a disease of poverty, and even within a single relatively homogeneous community is disproportionately seen among the lowest-income members. Leprosy has often been described as being more common in rural than in urban populations and as having an association with proximity to water (e.g., lakes) or humidity, but clear differences in the prevalence of leprosy between neighboring communities are not well explained.

In the mid-1980s it was estimated that there were between 10 and 12 million persons with leprosy worldwide in endemic areas; the incidence of leprosy was 4 to 6 per 1,000, and the prevalence in affected countries often exceeded 10 per 1,000. However, control efforts had reduced the number of prevalent cases by more than 90% to an estimated 829,000 cases in 1998 (WHO, 1998a). In 2000, WHO reported there were 597,000 registered cases and 719,000 cases newly detected that year. Although leprosy previously existed throughout the world, and a handful of individuals living in industrialized countries such as the United States still develop leprosy each year (a few of whom have never traveled outside the United States), leprosy is now largely confined to a shrinking number of countries. In 2000, for example, more than 83% of the known cases in the world were in six countries, with one of those countries—India—accounting for approximately 64% of the cases. Other countries that continue to have substantial numbers of cases include Brazil, Burma, Madagascar, Nepal, and Mozambique, although other countries in Latin America, Africa, Asia, and the Middle East also have modest numbers (Britton & Lockwood, 2004; WHO Expert Committee on Leprosy, 1998).

Current Approaches to Prevention and Control

Early attempts to control leprosy were based on case finding and prolonged (i.e., multiyear) or lifetime treatment with dapsone, which had the advantages of being inexpensive and having few side effects. However, this approach failed to control leprosy, at least in part because *M. leprae* developed resistance to dapsone and it was difficult to ensure ongoing patient compliance with treatment over many years. In the early 1980s, multidrug treatment with two or three (depending on the stage of leprosy) effective antimicrobial agents was introduced and has produced the greater than 90% reduction in leprosy cases referred to earlier. WHO had set a goal of eliminating leprosy as a public health problem (i.e., achieving a prevalence of 1 case or fewer per 10,000) by the year 2000; that goal was reached in 107 of the 122 countries that had endemic leprosy in 1985.

Obstacles to Prevention and Control and Directions for Future Research

Because of its extremely long incubation period and the fact that infected individuals may transmit *M. leprae* for substantial periods of time prior to becoming symptomatic and being placed on multidrug therapy, it is likely that incident cases of leprosy will continue to occur in substantial numbers for years to come, even if the current leprosy elimination strategy substantially reduces transmission (Meima et al., 2004). The greatest threat to reducing further the prevalence and incidence of leprosy is complacency and consequent reduced funding for case detection and multidrug therapy, which is much more expensive than single-drug therapy with dapsone. The priority given to leprosy control and to leprosy-related research is likely to be reduced substantially as the prevalence of cases decreases.

The role, if any, for a vaccine in the immunotherapy or the prevention of leprosy remains uncertain. Numerous studies have suggested that BCG vaccine, given primarily to prevent various forms of disseminated tuberculosis in children, offers some protection. In fact, BCG may be more effective in preventing leprosy than in preventing tuberculosis, although the estimates of its efficacy in preventing leprosy span a very large range. Whether other candidate mycobacterial vaccines will offer even greater protection than BCG remains uncertain, as does their role, if any, in leprosy control.

Sexually Transmitted Infections and AIDS

Overview

Sexually transmitted infections (STIs) have historically been one of the most neglected areas of medicine and public health in low- and middle-income countries. Until the advent of the HIV/AIDS epidemic in the 1980s, remarkably little attention was paid to STIs in such countries, despite the fact that they collectively cause enormous morbidity, loss of productivity, and infertility, and result in substantial health care expenditures. The fact that HIV, the cause of AIDS and all its attendant morbidity and mortality, is transmitted sexually, together with the fact that the sexual transmission of HIV is facilitated by the presence of other STIs, has focused attention on and brought an infusion of resources into this long-neglected area. However, the myriad challenges confronting the treatment and control of STIs in low- and middle-income countries are multifaceted and complex. Among the most daunting are the difficulty of changing human sexual behavior; the frequency with which STIs are asymptomatic, particularly among women; the lack of simple, inexpensive diagnostic tests; and the lack of readily accessible, inexpensive, easy to administer, single-dose treatment regimens for most STIs.

Etiologic Agents

A variety of viruses and bacteria can be transmitted sexually (Table 4-4), including some (e.g., HBV) that are not traditionally grouped with other STIs. In this chapter, HBV is discussed with the other viruses that cause hepatitis. Many infectious agents that are transmitted sexually can also be transmitted via contaminated blood or injection equipment, and vertically from a mother to her newborn infant.

Of the infectious agents transmitted sexually, some initially cause ulcerative lesions, primarily on or near the genitalia (e.g., *Herpes simplex, Treponema pallidum,* and *Haemophilus ducreyii*); others initially cause urethral or vaginal discharge (e.g., *Neisseria gonorrhoea, Chlamydia trachomatis,* and *Trichomonas vaginalis*); and others cause only systemic manifestations (e.g., HIV). HPV, selected subtypes of which cause genital warts, plays an important role in the pathogenesis of cervical dysplasia and carcinoma, as well as in carcinoma of the penis, but most HPV infections are initially silent. Asymptomatic or minimally symptomatic infection with many of the sexually transmitted agents is common, greatly exacerbating the problem of interrupting transmission and reducing the prevalence and incidence of infection.

Many of the agents transmitted sexually not only produce acute symptoms referable to the lower genital tract, but also can produce other, often more serious manifestations. For example, untreated infections with *N. gonorrhoea* and *C. trachomatis* can ascend and produce pelvic inflammatory disease, tubal infertility, and ectopic pregnancy. Untreated primary syphilis in young adults can lead to life-threatening cardiac and neurologic complications due to tertiary syphilis years later, whereas congenital syphilis, the result of infection of a baby at the time of birth, produces profound systemic manifestations. As noted earlier, infection with HPV of selected subtypes is strongly associated with subsequent cervical dysplasia and cervical cancer. Finally, HIV causes profound damage to the host immune system and a virtually 100% CFR in the absence of treatment with antiretroviral drug regimens.

Descriptive Epidemiologic Features and Risk Factors

Data concerning the incidence of STIs in low- and middle-income countries are considered highly unreliable due to substantial underdiagnosis and underreporting. One estimate suggests that in 1999 there were 340 million new adult cases of curable STIs (e.g., gonorrhea, chlamydia, syphilis, and trichomoniasis) worldwide, the vast majority of which were in low- and

Table 4-4	Sexually Transmitted Infections of Importance in Low- and Middle-Income Countries		
Agent	**Disease**	**Vertical Transmission To Newborn Babies**	**Transmission via Blood Products**
Bacteria			
T. pallidum	Syphilis	Yes	Yes
N. gonorrhoea	Gonorrhea, pelvic inflammatory disease	Yes	Yes
C. trachomatis	Cervicitis, urethritis, lymphogranuloma venereum, pelvic inflammatory disease	Yes	No
H. ducreyii	Chancroid	No	No
Viruses			
Human immunodeficiency virus (HIV)	AIDS	Yes	Yes
H. simplex	Genital herpes	Yes	No
Human papilloma virus (HPV)	Genital warts, cervical dysplasia and cervical carcinoma	?	No
Hepatitis B virus[a]	Acute and chronic hepatitis, cirrhosis, and hepatocellular carcinoma	Yes	Yes
Other			
T. vaginalis	Vaginitis	No	No

[a]Discussed in the section on viral hepatitis.

middle-income countries (Figure 4-6). The number of noncurable STIs, including genital herpes, HPV, and HIV, is difficult to estimate. The passive surveillance for AIDS in place in most low- and middle-income countries is also not very sensitive or specific, making it necessary to estimate the number or incidence of AIDS cases. The most recent estimate is that in 2004 there were 36 to 44 million persons in the world living with HIV/AIDS, including 5 million people who became infected in 2004. While almost two-thirds of all people living with HIV in 2004 were in sub-Saharan Africa, the incidence of new infections is rising most rapidly in selected Asian countries (e.g., China, India, Vietnam, and Indonesia) and in eastern Europe (e.g., Estonia, Latvia, Ukraine, and the Russian Federation) (Figure 4-7; UNAIDS, 2004a). More than 20 million people have died of AIDS since the beginning of the epidemic through the end of 2001 (the last year for which estimates are available), and 14 million children have been orphaned (UNAIDS, 2004b). The vast majority of

deaths have been in low-income countries, particularly sub-Saharan Africa.

The prevalence of various STIs, particularly HIV, has been investigated in many low- and middle-income countries. The groups typically examined are those that can be studied easily and inexpensively, such as commercial sex workers, patients being treated for STIs or for tuberculosis, injection drug users, pregnant women or women giving birth, and blood donors. Prevalences of HIV infection as high as 70% to 85% have been seen among commercial sex workers, and prevalences in the range of 25% to 45% have been documented among pregnant women delivering at large urban hospitals in the worst-affected urban areas of sub-Saharan Africa (UNAIDS, 2002). Because an estimated 15% to 30% of untreated HIV-infected pregnant women will pass the virus to their newborn babies at or soon after delivery, large numbers of HIV-infected infants are also found wherever many women of reproductive age are infected. The result of widespread HIV infection among

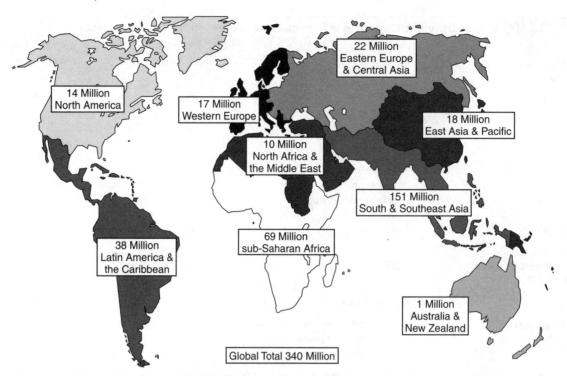

Figure 4-6 Estimated New Cases of Curable STIs Among Adults, 1999. *Source:* Global Prevalence and Incidence of Selected Curable Sexually Transmitted Infection: Overview and Estimates. World Health Organization, 2001, revised edition, November 2001. Reprinted with permission.

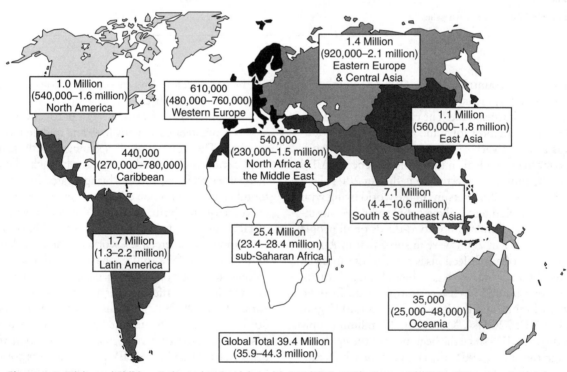

Figure 4-7 Adults and Children Estimated to Be Living with HIV/AIDS, 2004. *Source:* UNAIDS, *AIDS epidemic update: December 2004 and 2004 report on the global AIDS epidemic* (Geneva, Switzerland: UNAIDS/WHO, 2004a, b). Reprinted with permission.

men and women of reproductive age and among infants in the most severely affected countries has been a reversal of prior gains in life expectancy and prior reductions in infant and child mortality rates, an enormous increase in the numbers of orphaned children, and projected future declines in population size.

Given that the infectious agents under discussion are transmitted through sexual contact, it is not surprising that the highest incidences and prevalences of these infections are seen among men and women who are most sexually active, typically those 15 to 49 years of age, and that the most important risk factors for STIs—the number of sexual partners, the type of sexual partners, and whether barrier protection (e.g., a male condom) is used—are directly or indirectly related to the likelihood of exposure to one of the infectious agents. Thus, individuals with large numbers of sexual partners (e.g., commercial sex workers) who do not use barrier protection and those who have unprotected sex with such individuals are at highest risk. However, in societies in which it is considered acceptable for men to frequent commercial sex workers or have multiple sexual partners while women are expected to have a single partner, many monogamous women acquire STIs from their husbands. Other risk factors for STIs have been reported, such as lack of male circumcision, but are substantially less important than the number and type of sexual partners and the use or nonuse of barrier protection.

It is important to note the complex interplay between HIV infection and other STIs. There is strong evidence that infection with both ulcerative and nonulcerative STIs increases the likelihood of HIV being transmitted sexually between partners, either through the presence of disrupted mucosa or the presence in the genital tract of increased numbers of inflammatory cells and lymphocytes that can bind HIV.

Current Approaches to Prevention and Control

The current approach to the prevention and control of STIs, including HIV, focuses on improving the availability of and access to high-quality diagnostic and treatment services (especially in the case of HIV/AIDS), changing sexual practices through education and health promotion, increasing the availability and use of barrier methods that reduce transmission (e.g., male and female condoms), shortening the time between the onset of symptoms and the seeking of appropriate care, reducing the stigma attached to STIs, and improving surveillance. Not surprisingly, given the enormous cultural diversity that exists, approaches to delivery of risk-reduction messages (e.g., school-based programs, billboards, and radio), what groups to tar-

get (e.g., the entire population; individuals of reproductive age; school-aged children; high-risk groups such as commercial sex workers, migrant workers, truck drivers), and what messages to deliver (e.g., abstinence before marriage, monogamy, condom use) have varied greatly.

Because the laboratory facilities and trained staff needed to identify a specific etiologic agent in a given patient with a suspected STI are often lacking in many low- and middle-income countries, WHO has developed and promoted a syndromic approach to the management of STIs. This approach relies on classifying patients with a suspected STI into various groups depending on their symptoms and findings on physical examination (e.g., women with a vaginal discharge, men with urethral discharge and dysuria, and patients with genital ulcer) and then treating them with a regimen designed to cover the treatable etiologic agents that are likely to be responsible (e.g., *N. gonorrhoea* and *C. trachomatis* when a cervical or urethral discharge is present). Exhibit 4-4 provides an example of this approach.

Exhibit 4-4   Case Study of the Syndromic Management of Genital Ulcer

A study in Lesotho illustrates the promise and drawbacks of the syndromic approach (Htun et al., 1998). In an attempt to validate STI flowcharts for the management of genital ulcer, researchers found that syndromic protocols would have provided adequate treatment for at least 90% of their patient population, while the traditional, clinically directed protocol would have provided adequate treatment for only 62% of those same patients. On the other hand, syndromic protocols also would have led to the overtreatment of primary syphilis in about 60% of patients, while the clinically directed protocols would not have resulted in any such overtreatment.

A plurality of similar studies have shown that syndromic case management of STIs using flowcharts often leads to improved treatment in many patients as well as overtreatment in some patients. In general, to determine the appropriateness of implementing the syndromic approach in a given region, the costs of overtreatment (including the cost of the drugs themselves), the risk of promoting drug resistance, and the stigma of an STI diagnosis (which can lead to domestic violence against women) must be weighed against the benefits of improved treatment, including reductions in STI and HIV transmission, decreases in sequelae from untreated infections, and increased patient satisfaction. In view of the high prevalence of STIs in many low- and middle-income countries, this trade-off is often acceptable.

The finding that an intensive (and expensive) regimen of AZT (zidovudine) given to HIV-infected pregnant women in the United States substantially reduced vertical transmission of HIV to their newborn babies led to trials of simpler and cheaper AZT regimens in Thailand and the Ivory Coast. These trials showed that even these simpler regimens, which are given entirely by mouth and for a shorter period of time, are partially effective in reducing vertical transmission of HIV, and this regimen has been made more widely available in low- and middle-income countries (Shaffer et al., 1999; Wiktor et al., 1999). Similar trials using an even simpler dosing regimen and a less expensive drug, nevirapine, also have shown promising results (Jackson et al., 2003), although concerns about the possible promotion of antiretroviral drug resistance and reduced effectiveness of subsequent antiretroviral drug treatment in women treated with such regimens have arisen. Safe, effective, and inexpensive approaches to preventing vertical transmission during the postpartum interval also need to be developed, given the evidence that a substantial fraction of vertical transmission of HIV may occur via breastfeeding.

Previously, the prohibitive cost of antiretroviral drugs meant that the implementation of widescale treatment programs in low-income countries such as those of sub-Saharan Africa was unthinkable. As a result, fewer than 10% of people in low-income countries who needed antiretroviral treatment had access to it in 2003. In recent years, however, the introduction of generic competition in the global antiretroviral market has precipitated spectacular decreases in the cost of these drugs, making it conceivable to include antiretroviral treatment in the effort to control HIV-associated morbidity and early mortality for all affected groups. To this end, important developments include the WHO's 3 by 5 initiative (a plan to treat 3 million people with antiretroviral therapy by the year 2005); the establishment of the Global Fund to Fight HIV/AIDS, Tuberculosis, and Malaria; and the U.S. Emergency Plan for HIV/AIDS Relief, which seeks to treat 2 million people in selected low-income countries. Early reports from pilot programs to treat relatively large numbers of HIV-infected patients in low-income African settings suggest that expanded access to antiretroviral treatment is a feasible strategy, albeit enormously challenging (Katzenstein, Laga, & Moatti, 2003). Despite the challenges, the resources now being devoted to providing antiretroviral treatment in low-income countries have resulted in an estimated 700,000 HIV-infected persons having been begun on treatment by the end of 2004 (World Health Organization, 2004d; World Health Organization et al., 2005).

Obstacles to Prevention and Control and Directions for Future Research

There are enormous obstacles to changing the sexual behaviors of people, although there have been promising reductions in the frequency of high-risk sexual behaviors and the incidence of HIV infection in Thailand (Exhibit 4-5) (Celentano et al., 1996; Nelson et al., 1996; Rojanapithayakorn & Hanenberg, 1996) and Uganda (Kilian et al., 1999) in response to the AIDS epidemic. In many societies it is considered socially acceptable, even desirable, for men to visit commercial sex workers and have multiple sex partners. Many men do not want to use condoms, and a woman may risk physical abuse, rejection, or loss of financial support if she tries to insist that a condom be used by her husband, boyfriend, or customer. Women who learn they are infected with HIV also risk abandonment or abuse if they share this information. Thus, changing sexual behaviors requires the education of men as well as women, and reducing the incidence of STIs, including HIV, requires raising the status and improving the power of women in society. Similarly, economic and other practices that contribute to or promote risky sexual behaviors (e.g., forcing men to live apart from their wives in order to earn a living wage) need to be rethought.

Vaccines against STIs, particularly HIV, are desperately needed but have been difficult to develop. A vaccine against HPV is in the early stages of testing and appears promising, but it is likely to be a number of years until we know whether it is effective in preventing cervical dysplasia and cancer. The development of vaccines against HIV has been beset by many problems, and there is disagreement about what type of vaccine (inactivated whole virus, subunit, genetically engineered, live, attenuated, and so on) is likely to be safe and effective. Trials of a subunit HIV vaccine begun in the United States and Thailand in 1998-1999 showed that this vaccine was not effective in preventing acquisition of HIV infection (Cohen, 2003). Trials of other HIV vaccines are beginning in Thailand, Uganda, and elsewhere, but even under ideal circumstances, it is unlikely that an HIV vaccine can be available for widespread use for at least 5 to 10 years.

In the absence of vaccines against HIV and other STIs, other approaches to reducing morbidity and mortality beyond primary prevention of infection through behavior change are needed. For example, while

Exhibit 4-5	Case Study of a Successful Public Health Program: The Declining Spread of HIV Among Thai Military Conscripts

In the late 1980s heterosexual commercial sex was found to contribute significantly to the rapid spread of HIV in Thailand. Thai authorities responded swiftly to this observation and implemented public health programs that substantially increased the number of commercial sex acts protected by condoms, which in turn led to significant reductions in the rate of HIV infection among young men in Thailand. This case study tells the story of this public health success.

The first national serosurvey for HIV conducted in Thailand found that HIV was exceedingly prevalent among commercial sex workers. In June 1989, 44% of sex workers in the northern province of Chiang Mai were positive for HIV, a figure that would climb to 67% by June 1993 (Celentano et al., 1996). Commercial sex in Thailand is relatively common; for example, in the period from 1991 to 1993, more than 70% of Thai military conscripts were found to have engaged in at least one commercial sex act during their period of service. Because military conscripts are selected by a national lottery, these findings are applicable to the general population of young men in Thailand; thus, commercial sex was believed to be a common source of HIV infection.

To address this situation, Thai authorities implemented an HIV/AIDS prevention and control program that included the 100% Condom Campaign to promote condom use in commercial sex establishments. Under this campaign, free condoms were distributed to all sex establishments and the use of condoms was actively enforced by Thai authorities. The campaign was accompanied by mass advertising to promote condom use during commercial sex.

In the years following the initiation of the condom campaign, the use of condoms in sex establishments increased dramatically. National behavioral surveillance data revealed that the percentage of commercial sex acts in which condoms were used rose from approximately 14% in the years prior to 1989 to more than 90% by 1993 (Rojanapithayakorn & Hanenberg, 1996). Although the prevalence of HIV among sex workers has remained high, the prevalence among newly inducted military conscripts declined from greater than 10% in 1991 and 1993 to approximately 7% in 1995 (Nelson et al., 1996). Further, this decline occurred in the absence of a visible AIDS epidemic (Rojanapithayakorn & Hanenberg, 1996). Experts attribute these heartening findings, at least in part, to the swift implementation of the Thai HIV/AIDS prevention and control program, and especially to the success of the 100% Condom Campaign.

women in industrialized countries generally have access to regular screening for cervical dysplasia, which has been shown to be a highly effective tool for the secondary prevention of invasive cervical cancer, most women in low- and middle-income countries have not had access to such screening because of the cost and the need for moderately sophisticated laboratory support. Studies suggest that screening for cervical dysplasia using much simpler and less expensive technology may be possible in low- and middle-income countries (Cohen, 2003; University of Zimbabwe/JHPIEGO Cervical Cancer Project, 1999).

Universal access to antiretroviral therapy to treat HIV infection in low-income countries has become a top priority for international public health policy makers. However, the scientific community has just begun to grapple with the many medical, technical, and logistical difficulties associated with scaling up treatment programs in areas where public health infrastructure and resources are vanishingly scarce. Some of the major challenges will be to develop procedures for treating patients in the absence of laboratory-based monitoring for treatment failure and adverse events; to monitor and control emergent

drug resistance; and to develop creative ways to reach populations living in rural areas.

Viral Hepatitis

Overview

Hepatitis, which means inflammation of the liver, does not represent a single disease process, and can be caused on occasion by many viruses (as well as bacteria, protozoa, chemical agents, and some noninfectious diseases). However, there are at least five viruses that specifically infect the liver—hepatitis viruses A, B, C, D, and E. Each belongs to a different family and has unique clinical and epidemiologic features, necessitating diverse approaches to control and prevention.

Viral hepatitis is a major global public health problem. All five primary hepatitis viruses can cause acute disease. HBV, HCV, and hepatitis D virus (HDV) can also produce chronic infections. In many low- and middle-income countries, such persistent infections are the primary cause of serious liver disease, including chronic hepatitis, cirrhosis, and hepatocellular carcinoma, a common cancer that is almost always fatal. It is estimated that there are more than 350 million chronic carriers of HBV (WHO, 2001) and 170 million chronic carriers of HCV worldwide (WHO, 1997b).

Hepatitis A virus (HAV) and hepatitis E virus (HEV) cause acute self-limited disease; they do not cause chronic infection. Transmitted by the fecal-oral route, these viruses are endemic in many low- and middle-income countries with suboptimal environmental sanitation. HAV infections are typically asymptomatic when they occur in infants. In older children and adults, they generally produce a self-limited illness with few deaths. HEV infection results in more substantial morbidity and mortality, particularly when it occurs in pregnant women.

Etiologic Agents

The five primary hepatitis viruses (A, B, C, D, and E) account for almost all cases of viral hepatitis. Although other viruses (e.g., Epstein-Barr virus and cytomegalovirus) occasionally cause hepatitis, infections with these viruses do not principally involve the liver. Hepatitis G virus and GB virus C are isolates of the same virus (currently named HGV/GBV-C); this virus does not appear to cause liver disease (Bowden,

2001). The following discussion is limited to the five primary hepatitis viruses.

Descriptive Epidemiologic Features and Risk Factors

The prevalence of chronic HBV infection is moderate to high throughout low- and middle-income countries (Figure 4-8). For example, in sub-Saharan Africa, the Amazon Basin, and a number of countries in Asia, the prevalence of chronic HBV infection exceeds 8%, and the lifetime risk of infection is more than 60% (WHO, 2001). In these areas, most people who acquire HBV do so at the time of birth (through vertical transmission from an infected mother) or in infancy or childhood. Most such infections produce no acute symptoms. Unfortunately, the likelihood of chronic infection and risk of progression to chronic liver disease increases significantly as the age of acquisition decreases. The most common routes of transmission of HBV in low- and middle-income settings are perinatally, from mother to child, and horizontally, from one child to another. Transmission through the use of unsterilized needles for medical injections is also significant. Less frequent modes of transmission include sexual intercourse and needle sharing among injection drug users (the two principal modes of transmis-

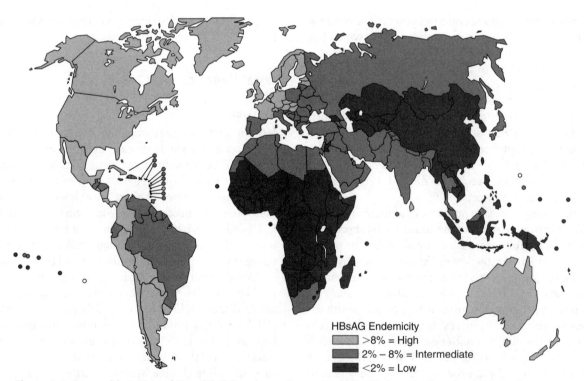

Figure 4-8 Geographic Pattern of Hepatitis B Prevalence. *Source:* World Health Organization, Department of Immunization, Vaccines and Biologicals, 2004, http://www.who.int/vaccines-surveillance/graphics/htmls/hepbprev.htm. Copyright 2004 by the World Health Organization. Reprinted with permission.

sion in industrialized countries). Additionally, practices such as tattooing, scarification, circumcision, body piercing, and acupuncture with unsterile instruments can spread HBV.

HDV is a defective virus, such that HDV infection can only be acquired in the presence of HBV infection. The distribution of HDV varies markedly by region but generally corresponds to the distribution of HBV, although there are some interesting exceptions to this pattern. For example, HDV infections are relatively rare in East and Southeast Asia, even though the prevalence of HBV is high in this area (Margolis, Alter, & Hadler, 1997). The primary mode of transmission of HDV is through percutaneous exposure to blood, as may occur through unsterile medical injections and the transfusion of unscreened blood. Perinatal and sexual transmission of HDV occur, but are less efficient than for HBV.

HCV virus is widespread throughout the world. Although HCV is not as infectious as HBV, HCV infection is much more likely to become chronic (as many as 80% of HCV-infected persons become chronically infected) (WHO, 1997a). In low- and middle-income countries, HCV prevalences in the general population range from 0% to greater than 10% (Figure 4-9) (WHO, 2002b). The principal modes of transmission of HCV in low- and middle-

income countries are believed to be the reuse of needles for medical injections and the transfusion of unscreened blood. Other percutaneous exposures to blood (needle sharing among drug users and traditional practices that involve piercing the skin) are important in some settings. There is evidence that HCV also can be spread perinatally and sexually, but this is probably uncommon.

HAV infection is endemic in most low- and middle-income countries. The primary mode of transmission of HAV is fecal-oral through person-to-person contact or the ingestion of contaminated food or water. In areas with poor environmental sanitation, HAV infection is virtually universal during the first few years of life. Infection in infancy and early childhood tends to be asymptomatic or mild and produces lifelong immunity. As sanitation improves, however, individuals are more likely to escape exposure to HAV in childhood. If they then are infected as teenagers or adults, the clinical manifestations tend to be more severe, albeit self-limited. Fatalities are uncommon.

HEV is also endemic in many low- and middle-income countries and causes substantial morbidity and mortality. HEV infection can be particularly deadly among pregnant women, with case fatality ratios approaching 30% for women who are infected with HEV during the last trimester (Jaiswal et al.,

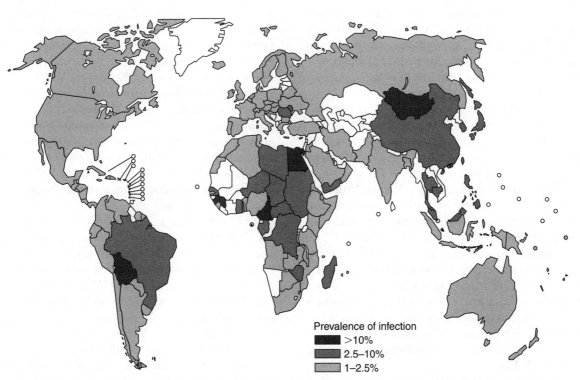

Prevalence of infection
- >10%
- 2.5–10%
- 1–2.5%

Figure 4-9 Prevalence of Hepatitis C Infection, 2002. *Source:* International Travel and Health, 2003, World Health Organization, Geneva. January, 2003, *Chapter 5, Infectious Diseases of Potential Risks for Travelers,* page 77. Copyright 2003 by the World Health Organization. Reprinted with permission.

2001; Khuroo et al., 1981). In endemic areas, HEV can produce cyclic outbreaks, as well as sporadic cases of hepatitis. HEV is acquired through the fecal-oral route, principally through ingestion of contaminated water. Person-to-person transmission of HEV can occur but is of lesser importance.

Current Approaches to Prevention and Control

A safe and effective vaccine for HBV has been available since 1982. In the early 1990s, the global advisory group of EPI and WHO recommended integrating the vaccine into the national immunization programs of all countries by 1997. One hundred fifty-one countries (79%) had achieved this goal as of May 2003 (WHO, 2003b). However, many low- and middle-income countries have not added HBV vaccine to their childhood immunization programs because of the associated costs, even though the vaccine is available at a cost of approximately 50 cents to 1 U.S. dollar per dose (WHO, 1999b). Although chronic HBV infection can be treated with interferon therapy or antiviral drugs such as lamivudine or adefovir, such costly options are not likely to contribute substantially to its control in low-income countries.

Vaccination against HBV infection is also effective against HDV coinfection. (As noted earlier, HDV infection requires the presence of HBV.) However, additional strategies are needed to prevent HDV superinfections among chronic carriers of HBV. Because there is no vaccine against HDV per se, the prevention of such superinfections depends on reducing percutaneous exposures to blood in medical and nonmedical settings among those who are chronically infected with HBV.

There is also no vaccine against HCV at this time. Treatment of chronic HCV infection with a combination of pegylated alpha interferon and ribavirin, the currently preferred therapy in high-income countries, is effective in approximately 40% to 80% of cases, depending on viral genotype (National Institutes of Health, 2002). However, such treatment is prohibitively expensive. Interrupting the transmission of HCV is currently the only feasible intervention. WHO recommends the following measures to prevent HCV infections: (1) screening blood and blood products worldwide, (2) effectively using universal precautions and barrier techniques, (3) destroying disposable needles and adequately sterilizing reusable injection materials, and (4) promoting public education about the risks of using unsterilized instruments to pierce the skin (WHO, 1997a).

The epidemiologic features of HAV infection vary by region and degree of sanitation, necessitating diverse approaches to control. An effective vaccine against HAV is available and may prove useful in controlling the periodic outbreaks among older children and adults that occur in areas of low endemicity. However, the current vaccine is licensed for use only in older children, not in infants. In most low- and middle-income countries, HAV infection is highly endemic and routinely acquired during infancy and early childhood, when it produces little morbidity or mortality. Consequently, the prevention of HAV infection in low- and middle-income countries is not a priority at this time, and the available vaccine is not licensed for use in the affected age group.

There is no vaccine against HEV, although this is an area of active research. Improved environmental sanitation, especially the provision of clean drinking water, remains the best strategy for prevention of HEV infections.

Obstacles to Prevention and Control and Directions for Future Research

Preventing HBV and HCV infections remains a major global public health goal. Universal coverage with the HBV vaccine reduces the incidence of HBV infection and serious liver disease and represents the best hope for reducing the acute and delayed morbidity and mortality caused by this virus. Unfortunately, the cost of supplying and distributing this relatively inexpensive vaccine in settings that have many competing needs remains a significant barrier to achieving universal immunization. Additionally, in areas where perinatal transmission of HBV is important, the vaccine should be given within 12 hours of birth (Margolis et al., 1997)—a difficult goal to achieve in most low- and middle-income settings. The costs and logistical problems associated with achieving high levels of coverage with routinely administered childhood vaccines are exacerbated as more and more vaccines (e.g., the *H. influenzae* type b vaccine) are added to the EPI. Depending on their cost, combined vaccines may help alleviate this difficulty in the future.

There are many obstacles to preventing HBV and HCV through means other than vaccination. The difficulty of ensuring safe medical injections and safe blood transfusions is a major barrier to reducing the bloodborne transmission of HBV and HCV; contaminated injections cause up to 21 million HBV infections and 2 million HCV infections per year, according to model-based estimates (Hauri, Armstrong, & Hutin, 2004). The prevention of HEV in the absence of a vaccine is no more tractable, because the problems of securing and sustaining a clean water supply are not easily overcome in low- and middle-income countries.

Malaria and Other Arthropod-Borne Diseases

Overview

Blood-sucking arthropods (including mosquitoes, flies, bugs, fleas, mites, and ticks) are efficient vectors for a host of pathogenic protozoa, bacteria, viruses, and worms that cause tremendous suffering and death around the world. Transmitted by mosquitoes, malaria is undoubtedly the most important parasitic disease in tropical regions of low- and middle-income countries. Malaria causes an estimated 700,000 to 2.7 million deaths each year, primarily (>75%) among African children (Breman, 2001). Mosquitoes also transmit dengue fever (an estimated 50 million cases per year) (WHO, 2002a), yellow fever, filariasis, and Japanese encephalitis, while various other arthropods spread trypanosomiasis, leishmaniasis, onchocerciasis (river blindness), and plague, to name but a few diseases. The public health importance of arthropod-borne diseases can scarcely be overstated—they contribute substantially to morbidity and mortality in affected countries and significantly encumber social, economic, and developmental progress.

Etiologic Agents and Clinical Features

As noted earlier , arthropod-borne diseases are caused by a wide variety of pathogens. However, this section is limited to a discussion of malaria, dengue fever, yellow fever, American trypanosomiasis, and African trypanosomiasis, although many of the prevention and control issues discussed in the context of these diseases are applicable to other arthropod-borne diseases. Onchocerciasis is discussed in the section on infectious causes of blindness.

Malaria is a febrile disease caused by five species of the parasitic *Plasmodium* protozoa: *P. malariae, P. falciparum, P. vivax, P. malariae,* and *P. ovale*. Dengue is caused by the four dengue viruses and occurs in two forms: dengue fever, which is self-limiting and rarely fatal; and dengue hemorrhagic fever/dengue shock syndrome, a more severe form of the disease that is associated with plasma leakage and bleeding and, occasionally, shock leading to death. Yellow fever is caused by a virus of the same name and is characterized by fever and, in severe cases, hemorrhage, jaundice, and liver and kidney involvement.

American trypanosomiasis (Chagas disease) is caused by the protozoan parasite *Trypanosoma cruzi*. Acute infections are usually mild, but about one-third of infected individuals develop more severe chronic manifestations after several years of asymptomatic infection, including digestive tract damage, neurologic involvement, and cardiac damage (most common) leading to heart failure. African trypanosomiasis (also known as sleeping sickness) is caused by two subspecies of the protozoan parasite *Trypanosoma brucei*, namely, *T.b. rhodesiense* and *T.b. gambiense*. Individuals infected with *T.b. rhodesiense* develop symptoms within weeks to months, whereas those infected with *T.b. gambiense* develop symptoms over a period of months to years. In both cases, the disease follows a course of central nervous system derangement, coma, and certain death if left untreated.

Descriptive Epidemiologic Features and Risk Factors

Although malaria is found in 100 countries around the world, more than 90% of cases occur in tropical Africa (WHO, 1997c). The parasite is transmitted between humans (who serve as the reservoir) by the female *Anopheles* mosquito. In endemic areas, where transmission is constant, individuals gradually develop immunity to severe disease. As a consequence, young children (who have not yet developed immunity) and pregnant women (who have depressed immune function) experience the highest rates of malaria morbidity and mortality. Susceptible individuals who enter endemic areas (e.g., migrant laborers, displaced persons, and travelers) are also at risk.

Approximately half the world's population lives in areas at risk for dengue virus infection, resulting in an estimated 50 million cases of dengue fever each year and 500,000 cases of dengue hemorrhagic fever, the more severe form of the disease (Figure 4-10) (WHO, 2002a). Major epidemics of dengue hemorrhagic fever to date have been largely limited to South and Southeast Asia and Latin America, whereas epidemics of dengue fever are more widespread. The geographic distribution of dengue fever and dengue hemorrhagic fever is growing rapidly.

There are four dengue virus serotypes. Infection with one serotype produces long-term immunity to that serotype, but limited cross-protection against the others. Evidence suggests that individuals who have preexisting antibody to a given dengue virus serotype from a previous infection have a higher risk of developing more severe disease upon reinfection with a different serotype than do individuals experiencing a primary infection. Viral virulence factors are also thought to influence the clinical outcome of infection. Dengue viruses have an urban or periurban transmission cycle (human-mosquito-human) in which the mosquitoes *Aedes aegypti* and *Ae. albopictus* are the principal vectors. Frequently, multiple dengue virus serotypes cocirculate in endemic urban cycles that periodically erupt in widespread epidemics (Gubler,

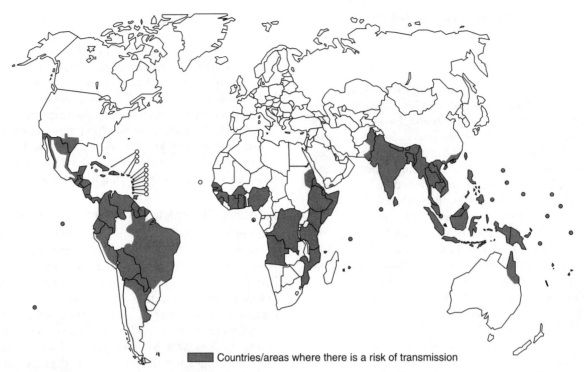

Countries/areas where there is a risk of transmission

Figure 4-10 World Distribution of Dengue Fever, 2003. *Source:* International Travel and Health, 2005, World Health Organization, Geneva. *Chapter 5, Infectious Diseases of Potential Risks for Travelers,* page 76. Copyright 2005 by the World Health Organization. Reprinted with permission.

1998). A rural transmission cycle also exists, but is less important from the public health perspective.

Yellow fever virus is endemic in 33 countries in sub-Saharan Africa and 9 countries in South America (WHO, 1998d). WHO estimates that 200,000 yellow fever cases occur annually, resulting in 30,000 deaths (WHO, 1998e). Yellow fever virus has an urban transmission cycle in which mosquitoes (typically *Ae. aegypti*) transmit yellow fever virus between humans. Large epidemics of yellow fever occur when the virus is acquired by the urban vector and introduced to susceptible populations. Yellow fever also has sylvatic and rural transmission cycles.

American trypanosomiasis occurs only in the Americas and is an important public health problem in Latin America, where it is estimated that 16 to 18 million persons are infected with *T. cruzi* (WHO, 2004a). Historically, *T. cruzi* has been (and continues to be) endemic in rural areas, where a variety of wild and domestic animals serve as reservoirs for the parasite. *T. cruzi* is transmitted to humans by triatomine bugs, which infest houses built with materials that shelter the bugs (e.g., thatched roofs or cracked mud walls). In recent decades, rural migration has introduced the disease to urban areas, where *T. cruzi* is spread via transfusions of infected blood. Congenital transmission also occurs. However, the

triatomine vector remains the most important source of infection.

African trypanosomiasis is found exclusively in sub-Saharan Africa, where the disease occurs in rural, endemic foci in 36 countries. An estimated 100,000 to 300,000 new cases occur annually, all of them fatal if left untreated (Pepin & Meda, 2001; WHO, 1998b). Although African trypanosomiasis was nearly eliminated by the early 1960s, the incidence of this disease has soared in recent decades, and devastating epidemics have occurred in the wake of civil disturbance, war, and population movements. The parasite that causes African trypanosomiasis, *T. brucei,* is transmitted to humans by the bite of the tsetse fly. Cattle and wild animals are the major reservoirs for *T.b. rhodesiense,* which is found in eastern Africa, whereas humans are the major reservoir for *T.b. gambiense,* which is found in western and central Africa.

Current Approaches to Prevention and Control

The historical context of the current malaria control strategy is instructive (Trigg & Kondrachine, 1998). To summarize, in the 1950s, malaria prevention programs focused on parasite eradication through the use of antimalarial drugs (e.g., chloroquine) to eliminate human infection and reduce the parasite reservoir, and residual insecticides (e.g., dichlorodiphenyltrichloroethane [DDT]) to interrupt malarial transmission via its mosquito vector. By the late 1960s, the incidence of malaria was greatly reduced in areas that implemented these programs, including Latin America and tropical Asia. These improvements proved unsustainable in part because of the rigidity of the eradication program, which was vertically structured and failed to consider regional differences in malaria epidemiology and public health infrastructure. Malaria resurged in the following decades (along with other mosquito-borne diseases, including dengue fever and yellow fever) as vector-control programs broke down. The goal of global malaria eradication was declared a failure and abandoned.

By the early 1990s, the international community identified malaria as a leading public health priority (again) and began to formulate new strategies for control. In 1998, the Roll Back Malaria (RBM) Partnership was established to coordinate an international effort to reduce the global burden of malaria—the first such campaign in more than three decades. The RBM strategy calls for the following:

1. Disease management through prompt (within 24 hours of the onset of symptoms) and affordable access to effective treatment, including artemisinin-based combination therapy.

2. Disease prevention through "personal and community protective measures," primarily increased access to insecticide-treated bed nets.

3. Targeted disease control and prevention for pregnant women. In areas of moderate or high endemicity, most adults have developed immunity to malaria. In these areas, infection during pregnancy is associated with severe maternal anemia and low-birth-weight babies (due to the presence of parasites in the placenta). In areas of low endemicity or epidemic transmission, where most women lack immunity, infection during pregnancy causes substantial maternal and neonatal mortality. Prevention efforts rely on the use of intermittent preventive treatment (at least two therapeutic doses of antimalarial drug administered to all pregnant women) and insecticide-treated bed nets.

4. Epidemic control through early detection and response.

The goal of the RBM Partnership is to halve the number of deaths due to malaria by 2010; however, despite renewed efforts, the burden of disease has remained high or increased in sub-Saharan Africa in recent years (WHO, 2003a). Adequate funding to implement key RBM strategies, particularly the provision of artemisinin-based combination therapy in areas where resistance has compromised the effectiveness of cheaper alternatives, has yet to materialize.

In summary, no antimalarial vaccines are currently available, although vaccine development is considered an achievable goal (Moorthy, Good, & Hill, 2004). Widescale chemoprophylaxis is not recommended because of drug resistance, cost, and sustainability. However, intermittent preventive treatment, in which individuals are presumptively treated with therapeutic doses of antimalarial drugs at specified intervals, for pregnant women, infants, and children is gaining acceptance. In addition, insecticide-treated bed nets have proved highly effective in reducing childhood mortality and morbidity from malaria (Lengeler, 2004) and are an important component of global control efforts.

There is no specific treatment for dengue fever or dengue hemorrhagic fever beyond attentive clinical management, and there are no vaccines currently available against dengue viruses, although a number of groups are working to develop them. Because of concerns that vaccine-induced antibody against fewer than all four serotypes could promote the development of dengue hemorrhagic fever, it is generally believed that only a vaccine that protects against all four serotypes can be safely developed, tested, and administered to populations at risk. Thus, the control and prevention of dengue fever currently depends on mosquito control, disease surveillance, and epidemic preparedness. A key component of *Aedes* control is source reduction through elimination of mosquito breeding sites.

Immunization is the most important prevention measure against yellow fever. The yellow fever vaccine, designated 17D, is safe, effective, and relatively inexpensive at 12 to 25 U.S. cents per dose (Vainio & Cutts, 1998). To prevent and control yellow fever in endemic areas, WHO recommends routine infant immunization against yellow fever (within the EPI), mass immunization campaigns (e.g., preventive catch-up campaigns), vigilant case and vector surveillance, reactive immunization to contain outbreaks, and careful management of the vaccine supply (WHO, 1998e).

No drugs are available for the treatment of chronic American trypanosomiasis, and the drugs used in the treatment of acute manifestations (benznidazole and nifurtimox) are expensive and toxic. Thus, the prevention and control of American trypanosomiasis is currently focused on interrupting vectorial transmission in addition to preventing transmission via the transfusion of units of infected blood. Vector-control efforts are centered on eradicating strictly domestic triatomine bugs and controlling domestic infestations of other (sylvatic) triatomine bugs, predominantly through indoor residual insecticide spraying in areas at high risk for American trypanosomiasis. The prevention of transfusion-related transmission is accomplished by screening all blood donors for *T. cruzi* antibodies and rejecting infected blood. The results of these efforts are encouraging—transmission has been interrupted in Uruguay, Chile, and most of Brazil; as a result, the incidence of *T. cruzi* infection among children has declined by 96% to 99% in these countries (WHO, 2004b). Similar results can be expected elsewhere once these strategies have been more widely deployed.

The current strategy for the control and prevention of African trypanosomiasis associated with *T.b. gambiense* involves active case-finding and early treatment, which reduces the human reservoir by curing the infection. Passive surveillance for *T.b. gambiense* is problematic because infected individuals are often infectious for months to years before developing symptoms that lead to (passive) detection. However, passive surveillance and epidemic preparedness are often adequate to control the transmission of *T.b. rhodesiense*, which quickly leads to symptoms of infection. The drugs used to treat African trypanosomiasis are highly unsatisfactory and excessively toxic. Melarsoprol, the first-line treatment for late-stage trypanosomiasis (i.e., central nervous system involvement) causes a reactive encephalopathy in 2% to 18% of patients, resulting in a considerable number of deaths (Pepin & Milord, 1994). The only other drug to treat late-stage disease, eflornithine, is expensive (US$700 per patient), difficult to administer, and ineffective against *T.b. rhodesiense,* and it produces undesirable side effects (albeit less severe than those associated with melarsoprol) (WHO, 1999a).

Obstacles to Prevention and Control and Directions for Future Research

Insecticide resistance presents a major challenge to prevention strategies based on vector control. Vectors for malaria, dengue, and yellow fever have all developed resistance to multiple insecticides, including the classic insecticides (e.g., DDT) and their replacements (e.g., organophosphates). Alternative insecticides have been developed but are often more costly and more toxic than the first-line agents. The dynamic ecology of vector-borne pathogens is an additional barrier to effective vector control. For example, changing land-use patterns, shifting weather patterns, urbanization, and population movements may result in new foci for

disease transmission. Finally, national and international travel and commerce represent continuing opportunities for reinfestation, necessitating continuous surveillance even in areas with good vector control.

Drug resistance is a serious problem for control strategies that rely on chemotherapy to treat disease and reduce the human reservoir. Nowhere is this problem more evident than in the management of malaria. Drugs that once provided cheap and effective means of antimalarial prophylaxis and therapy are now severely compromised in many parts of the world, necessitating the use of more expensive alternative drugs. The situation is most serious in parts of Southeast Asia, where multidrug resistance has been observed (Krogstad, 1996). Factors that promote drug resistance include mass chemoprophylaxis and treatment with suboptimal doses of drug. In addition, research and development for new drugs to treat diseases that are localized in low-income countries has long been neglected, and the continued manufacture of old drugs, especially those that have no other use, has come under threat on occasion.

Other barriers to the prevention and control of arthropod-borne diseases include the intermittent disruption of public health services as a consequence of civil disturbance or war and the ever-present problem of limited resources. Other problems include the difficulty of sustaining support for successful control measures (e.g., indoor insecticide spraying to control the vectorial spread of American trypanosomiasis) once the disease has been brought under control and thus is no longer a public health priority.

Future prospects for the improved prevention of arthropod-borne disease rest primarily on vaccine development. Current research is focused on developing candidate tetravalent dengue fever vaccines and antimalarial vaccines.

Helminthiases

Overview

It is estimated that more than one-third of the world's population is infected with parasitic helminths (Warren et al., 1993). The vast majority of infected individuals live in low- and middle-income countries where environmental sanitation is poor. Each parasite produces different manifestations according to the site, intensity, and length of infection. Host response also influences the clinical course of infection. In general, children experience the heaviest worm burden, and persistent infection throughout childhood is common in low- and middle-income settings. Heavy, prolonged infection produces adverse effects on growth and development and significantly increases childhood morbidity. In adults, helminthiases can produce acute and chronic morbidity, leading to impaired productivity, chronic disability, and reduced quality of life.

In terms of global prevalence, morbidity, and mortality, the most important helminthic infections are schistosomiasis (200 million cases) (WHO, 1993), ascariasis (1,450 million cases), trichuriasis (1,050 million cases), hookworm (1,300 million cases) (WHO, 2002c), onchocerciasis, and lymphatic filariasis. Although many of these infections are minimally symptomatic, the number of clinically significant cases is substantial. This section focuses on schistosomiasis and the most common intestinal helminthiases (ascariasis, trichuriasis, and hookworm). Dracunculiasis, a disease of considerable historical importance, is also considered.

Etiologic Agents and Clinical Features

Human schistosomiasis (also known as bilharziasis) is caused by a group of blood trematodes (flukes) known as schistosomes. The three main species that infect humans are *Schistosoma mansoni*, *Schistosoma japonicum*, and *Schistosoma haematobium*. Two other species, *Schistosoma mekongi* and *Schistosoma intercalatum*, also parasitize humans, but such infections are uncommon and will not be discussed further. Acute schistosomiasis (Katayama fever) is characterized by fever and chills, abdominal pain, diarrhea, and enlargement of the spleen or other organs. *S. japonicum* is most commonly associated with acute disease, although any type of schistosomiasis can cause these symptoms. Chronic disease is initiated by the deposition of schistosome eggs in the body, which induces inflammation and scarring. Chronic infection with *S. mansoni* or *S. japonicum* can lead to hepatosplenic and intestinal involvement, although most infected individuals are asymptomatic. Chronic infection with *S. haematobium* is associated with urinary tract disease, and a much higher proportion (50% to 70%) of infected individuals are symptomatic (WHO, 1993). *S. haematobium* infection is also associated with an increased risk for bladder cancer.

The most common intestinal helminthiases of humans are caused by *Ascaris lumbricoides*, *Trichuris trichiura* (whipworm), and two species of hookworm, *Ancylostoma duodenale* and *Necator americanus*. These parasites produce a diverse range of clinical symptoms, although light infections are generally asymptomatic. When worm burdens are heavy, *A. lumbricoides* infection is associated with malnutri-

tion and stunted growth. *A. lumbricoides* is also the largest of the intestinal helminths, measuring 15 to 35 centimeters in length; thus, single worms can cause obstruction and inflammation of the appendix, bile duct, or pancreatic duct, and a bolus of worms can cause intestinal obstruction leading to death. Trichuriasis is associated with abdominal pain, diarrhea, and general malaise when moderate worm loads are present, while nutritional deficiencies, anemia, and stunted growth can result from heavier worm loads. Hookworms attach to the intestinal mucosa, where they ingest 0.03 to 0.26 milliliters of blood per worm per day (Warren et al., 1993). The major clinical manifestations of hookworm infection are iron deficiency anemia and hypoalbuminemia resulting from chronic blood loss.

Dracunculiasis is caused by *Dracunculus medinensis* (Guinea worm), a long (60 to 90 centimeters), thin nematode. Symptoms of the disease are caused by the migration of the worm to the subcutaneous tissues and its eruption through the skin. Symptoms can include the formation of a blister or bleb at the site where the worm will emerge (usually the ankle or foot), hives, nausea, vomiting, diarrhea, and asthma. The blister ulcerates as the worm emerges, and local pain typically persists until the worm is expelled or extracted, which can take several weeks. Secondary infection of the worm track is common. Severe disability generally lasting 1 to 3 months occurs in most of those infected, and permanent disability occurs in 0.5% of infected individuals (Hunter, 1996). Even short-term disability can have a substantial economic impact, if the worm emerges during the months when important agricultural work is performed (Hopkins, 1984).

Descriptive Epidemiologic Features and Risk Factors

Schistosomiasis is the single most important helminthic disease and the second most important parasitic disease (after malaria) worldwide. An estimated 200 million persons in 74 countries and territories harbor this infection, yielding 20 million cases of severe disease and approximately 100 million symptomatic infections (WHO, 1993). *S. mansoni*, the most widespread of the schistosomes, is found in parts of Africa, the Middle East, the Caribbean, and South America; *S. haematobium* is restricted to Africa and the Middle East; and *S. japonicum* is currently found only in the Western Pacific countries. Overall, the vast majority of schistosome infections occur in sub-Saharan Africa.

The life cycle of the schistosome is quite complex, and a complete description is beyond the scope of this chapter, but a brief treatment is necessary. Adult worms live, mate, and deposit their eggs in the blood vessels lining the human intestines (*S. mansoni* and *S. japonicum*) or bladder (*S. haematobium*). These eggs migrate into the intestine or bladder and are passed out in the excreta. When deposited in fresh water, the eggs develop into immature parasites (miracidia) that infect fresh-water snails. The immature parasites then develop into infective larvae (cercariae). When released into the surrounding water, the larvae swim about, and those coming in contact with humans during this time penetrate through the skin and eventually reach the vascular system, completing the cycle. Thus, the maintenance of schistosomes in a given area requires the presence of the intermediate host, the contamination of water with egg-laden excreta, and the exposure of humans to contaminated water. Because schistosomes do not multiply in the human host, the intensity of infection is largely determined by the rate at which new worms are acquired. Studies have shown that the infection rate for schistosomes typically peaks during childhood and then declines with advancing age (Butterworth et al., 1996; Hagan, 1996). This finding is thought to reflect age-dependent changes in both water exposure and immunity to infection.

The public health impact of intestinal helminthiases on low- and middle-income countries is substantial. As noted earlier, *A. lumbricoides*, *T. trichiura*, and hookworm each infects about 1 billion individuals globally (WHO, 2002c). Although the morbidity and mortality associated with intestinal helminthiases is relatively low, the burden of illness and, to a lesser extent, death is considerable due to the extremely high prevalence of these infections (Bundy, 1990).

A. lumbricoides, *T. trichiura*, and hookworm share a relatively simple life cycle. The parasites mature and mate in the human intestines and produce eggs that are passed out in the feces. When deposited on moist soil, the eggs develop into the infective form of the parasite. (Because this part of the life cycle is spent in soil, these worms are collectively referred to as *geohelminths*.) Humans acquire the parasite when contaminated soil is ingested or, in the case of hookworm, when the infective larvae in the soil penetrate exposed skin. Thus, the maintenance of these helminths requires the deposition of feces in soil and the exposure of humans to that soil. For *A. lumbricoides* and *T. trichiura*, the peak intensity of infection typically occurs among young children, whereas for hookworm the peak occurs among adults (Bundy et al., 1992).

Dracunculiasis is contracted by drinking contaminated water. Parasitic larvae then migrate to the abdominal cavity, where they mature into adult worms over the course of a year. After copulation, the gravid female worm migrates through the body to the sub-cutaneous tissue and then secretes irritants that ulcerate the skin and expose the worm. When the affected body site is immersed in water, the worm expels clouds of larvae. The larvae are consumed by copepods (minute fresh-water crustaceans, also known as water fleas), which are in turn ingested by humans who drink contaminated water. Dracunculiasis occurs in individuals of all ages, but is less common in very young children, possibly because breastfeeding reduces water consumption (Hunter, 1996).

The global campaign to eradicate dracunculiasis was launched in the 1980s as a part of the United Nations International Drinking Water Supply and Sanitation Decade (1981–1990). Since then the incidence of dracunculiasis has declined from 4 million reported cases in 1981 (Hopkins, Ruiz-Tiben, & Ruebush, 1997) to just over 32,000 cases in 2003 (WHO, 2004c), and local eradication has occurred in many previously endemic countries. Endemic disease is now confined to just 12 African countries, and global eradication is considered an achievable goal (WHO, 2004c).

Current Approaches to Prevention and Control

The major strategies for the control of helminthic infections are chemotherapy, environmental sanitation and health education, and control or eradication of the intermediate host. No antihelminthic vaccines are currently available. For the control of schistosomiasis and geohelminths, WHO emphasizes first and foremost controlling morbidity by reducing the intensity of infection (the number of worms per person) rather than reducing the prevalence of infection (the number of persons with worms). The former is achieved in the short term through regular deworming, despite reinfection, whereas the latter requires improved environmental sanitation, intermediate-host control (in the case of schistosomiasis, for example), or both and is viewed as a long-term goal.

In most instances, WHO recommends targeted treatment in which all members of a risk group are presumptively dewormed at predefined intervals, as opposed to selective or universal treatment (Table 4-5). This approach is possible because safe, effective, and inexpensive oral treatments are available for the most common helminthiases. For schistosomiasis, praziquantel is the drug of choice. A single oral dose is well tolerated, relatively inexpensive (less than 7 U.S. cents), has an initial cure rate of 60% to 90%, and is effective against all species of *Schistosoma* (WHO, 1993). Albendazole and mebendazole, among other drugs, are commonly used to treat intestinal helminthiasis and

Table 4-5	World Health Organization–Recommended Treatment Strategies for Schistosome and Geohelminth Infections[a]	
Community Category	**Intervention in Schools (enrolled and nonenrolled children)**	**Health Services and Community-Based Intervention**
Geohelminth Infections		
High prevalence or high intensity	Targeted treatment of school-aged children, two to three times a year	Systematic treatment of preschool children and women of childbearing age in mother and child health programs
Moderate prevalence and low intensity	Targeted treatment of school-aged children, once a year	Systematic treatment of preschool children and women of childbearing age in mother and child health programs
Low prevalence and low intensity	Selective treatment	Selective treatment
Schistosome Infections		
High prevalence	Targeted treatment of school-aged children, once a year	Access to praziquantel for passive case treatment[b]; community-directed treatment for high-risk groups recommended
Moderate prevalence	Targeted treatment of school-aged children, once every two years	Access to praziquantel for passive case treatment[b]
Low prevalence	Targeted treatment of school-aged children twice during primary schooling (once on entry, again on leaving)	Access to praziquantel for passive case treatment[b]

[a]Treatment strategies should always be accompanied by efforts to improve water supply and sanitation.

[b]Can be done on presumptive grounds, according to diagnostic algorithms adapted to the endemic situation.

have moderate to very good activity against five of the most common species of worms (*A. lumbricoides, T. trichiura*, hookworms, *Strongyloides stercoralis*, and *Enterobius vermicularis*) (WHO, 1987). These drugs are also quite inexpensive, at less than 2 U.S. cents per tablet, and can be safely administered by nonmedical personnel.

Ultimately, most helminthiases are diseases of poor sanitation. Providing for the sanitary disposal of excreta prevents the contamination of soil and water and thus breaks the chain of transmission. However, environmental improvements must be made at the community level in order to be effective (Warren et al., 1993). Improvements in environmental sanitation are complemented by health education to promote healthy behaviors; for example, WHO has determined that schistosomiasis could be largely prevented by eliminating indiscriminate urination and defecation and increasing compliance with medical interventions (WHO, 1993).

Control of the intermediate host species for certain helminths, such as snail control for schistosomiasis, can also play an important role in preventing transmission. The primary strategies for snail control include application of molluscicidal agents and environmental management. Biological control strategies, such as the introduction of competitor snails, have not been successful and are not currently recommended (WHO, 1993). Control of the intermediate host also plays a crucial role in preventing the transmission of dracunculiasis. Much of the success of the eradication campaign has been achieved by teaching people to pour drinking water through a finely woven cloth to filter out the tiny crustaceans that carry the *Dracunculus* parasite. Chemical eradicants have also played a role.

Obstacles to Prevention and Control and Directions for Future Research

Major obstacles to the effective implementation of chemotherapy-based interventions are related to the logistical and financial difficulties of treating the large number of individuals in need. In addition, chemotherapy is not adequate to redress the conditions that led to the primary infection; thus, reinfection is likely to occur, necessitating repeated treatments and further cost. Widespread resistance to the antihelminthic agents in human infection has not yet emerged; however, resistance to benzimidazoles is often seen in veterinary practice, and there is some evidence to suggest rare instances of limited resistance to praziquantel (WHO, 2002c). These observations suggest that chemotherapeutic interventions should include provisions for detecting and, if necessary, managing drug resistance.

Adequate environmental sanitation is generally viewed as the only long-term solution to the control of intestinal helminthiases and schistosomiasis. However, providing safe drinking water and adequate disposal facilities in low- and middle-income areas has proved to be an extremely difficult, costly, and lengthy process. Current control efforts emphasize targeted chemotherapeutic interventions to relieve the immediate burden of disease while preserving universal sanitation as the long-term goal.

Zoonoses

Overview

Zoonoses are defined as diseases and infections naturally transmitted between vertebrate animals and humans. Zoonotic agents include a wide variety of bacteria, viruses, protozoa, and helminths, while their nonhuman hosts include wild animals and birds, food and draft animals, and domestic pets.

More than 200 different zoonoses are currently recognized (Hart, Trees, & Duerden, 1997). Zoonotic infections have a worldwide distribution and collectively produce significant morbidity and mortality. For example, indigenous rabies, which has a global distribution, causes more than 50,000 deaths per year (WHO, 2002d). *Yersinia pestis*, the bacterium that causes plague, remains enzoonotic in many parts of Africa, Asia, and South America, and in the southwestern United States. Although only 2,671 cases of human plague were reported to WHO in 2001 (WHO, 2003c), the control of human plague remains a public health priority because of its epidemic potential and relatively high CFR. In low- and middle-income settings, important zoonoses include rabies, plague, anthrax, leptospirosis, leishmaniasis, African trypanosomiasis, and a number of hemorrhagic fever viruses. Foodborne zoonoses, such as salmonellosis, campylobacteriosis, and certain *E. coli* infections, also contribute to the global burden of disease, while occupational zoonoses such as brucellosis, echinococcosis, and Q fever have regional significance. Finally, zoonotic infections are a rich source of emerging diseases such as severe acute respiratory syndrome (SARS), avian influenza in humans, Nipah virus encephalitis, variant Creutzfeldt-Jakob disease, and Ebola hemorrhagic fever, although the putative animal host for Ebola virus has yet to be identified.

Although zoonoses have a worldwide distribution, low- and middle-income countries bear a greater burden of disease than industrialized countries. This divergence reflects, in part, differences in opportunities for exposure to zoonotic pathogens. Residents of low- and middle-income countries typically experience more frequent and more intimate contact with animals, and often live in situations of suboptimal environmental sanitation (which promotes exposure to infective material such as contaminated animal excreta). In addition, many control measures that are readily available in industrialized countries (e.g., mass veterinary vaccination of domesticated animals) may not be available or affordable in low- and middle-income countries.

Zoonotic pathogens are transmitted to humans by five major routes:

1. *Inhalation:* transmission that occurs when infective materials are aerosolized and inhaled
2. *Ingestion:* transmission that occurs when humans consume contaminated meat, milk, or blood from infected animals or when foodstuffs (e.g., fruits and vegetables), drinking water, or hands are contaminated with infective materials, which are then ingested
3. *Nontraumatic contact:* transmission that typically occurs when pathogens enter through the skin (or mucosal surfaces or conjunctivae) as a result of direct or indirect contact with animal hides, hair, excreta, blood, or carcasses
4. *Traumatic contact:* transmission via animal bites or scratches
5. *Arthropod:* transmission by biting arthropods that feed on animals and humans

For some zoonoses, humans are an incidental, dead-end host. Human-to-human transmission of rabies or anthrax, for example, is extremely rare. For other zoonoses, humans may serve as a reservoir for infection, transmitting pathogens to other humans or even back to animals.

Zoonoses produce a wide variety of diseases with distinct clinical and epidemiologic characteristics, and are associated with many different animals occupying a number of ecologic niches, both urban and rural. Approaches to the control and prevention of zoonoses must necessarily reflect these differences.

General principles, however, often include good animal husbandry (including vaccination when appropriate), environmental sanitation, vector control, and the control or elimination of animal reservoirs (e.g., rats or other wild animals).

Rather than attempting to survey the entire range of zoonoses, this section is limited to a detailed discussion of rabies and leptospirosis, which are important zoonoses in many low- and middle-income countries.

Etiologic Agents and Clinical Features

Rabies is caused by the rabies virus, which is a *Lyssavirus* belonging to the Rhabdoviridae family. Typically transmitted by the bite of a rabid animal, human rabies is an acute, uniformly fatal encephalitic disease. Following inoculation, there is an asymptomatic incubation period typically lasting 1 to 3 months, although periods as short as a few days and as long as several years have been reported (Fishbein, 1991). (Postexposure prophylaxis must be initiated during this period in order to have an effect.) The prodromal period begins with the early signs of disease, which include nonspecific symptoms (e.g., fever and malaise) and abnormal sensations near the site of inoculation. This stage is followed by a 2- to 10-day period of acute neurologic dysfunction that manifests as furious rabies in about 80% of cases and paralytic (dumb) rabies in the remainder (Fishbein, 1991). Furious rabies is characterized by periods of extreme agitation and hyperactivity interspersed with periods of normalcy. Hydrophobia, aerophobia, combativeness, and hallucination may also occur. Features of paralytic rabies include paresthesia, weakness, and paralysis. The inevitable final stage of rabies (both furious and paralytic) is coma followed by death.

Leptospirosis is an acute febrile disease caused by pathogenic bacteria of the genus *Leptospira*. The clinical course of the disease is variable: The majority of infections result in subclinical or mild disease; however, 5% to 10% of those infected will develop more severe manifestations, including kidney failure and pulmonary hemorrhage (Levett, 2001). Ocular involvement may also occur. *Leptospira* is classified serologically into 200 serovars arranged in 24 serogroups; alternatively, the organism may be classified genotypically into genomospecies (Vinetz, 2001). The serologic classification scheme is more frequently used in epidemiologic studies. Certain serovars were once thought to be associated with more severe disease, but evidence in support of this hypothesis is lacking (Levett, 2001; Vinetz, 2001).

Descriptive Epidemiologic Features and Risk Factors

Rabies is a disease of animals; humans are incidentally infected and only rarely transmit the virus. Animal reservoirs include dogs, cats, and wild animals (notably foxes, skunks, wolves, coyotes, raccoons, mongooses, and bats). More than 99% of all human rabies cases are acquired from dogs, which are the major source of human infection in low- and middle-income countries (WHO, 2002d). In industrialized countries, where immunization of domestic animals is common, wild animals constitute the principal reservoir of infection and human rabies is extremely rare. Rabies virus is present in the saliva of infected animals and is typically transmitted to humans by the bite of a rabid animal. It may also be transmitted when intact mucous membranes are exposed to infective saliva. Not every exposure results in infection, but if infection occurs, it is fatal in the absence of postexposure prophylaxis.

Leptospirosis has a worldwide distribution, but its global incidence is difficult to assess. In general, the incidence and prevalence of infection are low in industrialized countries and higher in low- and middle-income countries (e.g., prevalences of infection ranging from 18% to 48% have been reported in some low- and middle-income communities) (Ellis, 1998). As with rabies, human infection with *Leptospira* is incidental, and humans do not contribute to the transmission of the bacteria. The main animal reservoirs for *Leptospira* serovars that cause human disease are rats, dogs, pigs, and cattle. Transmission of leptospires to humans typically occurs through contact with water contaminated with the urine of infected animals or through direct contact with infective animal urine. The bacteria infect humans by entering through broken skin, water-softened intact skin, mucosal surfaces, or conjunctivae. Human leptospirosis is traditionally considered an occupational disease among those whose professions involve contact with host animals (e.g., dairy farmers) or water (e.g., rice farmers). However, home and recreational exposures appear to be increasingly important, particularly in low- and middle-income settings. In addition, periodic flooding due to heavy rains can produce large epidemics of leptospirosis.

Current Approaches to Prevention and Control

The control of human rabies is achieved by the prevention of human exposure to the virus and the prevention of disease through postexposure prophylaxis when exposure does occur. Historically, rabies vaccines were not deemed suitable (i.e., sufficiently inexpensive, safe, and effective) for mass preexposure immunization of humans. However, WHO encourages research on the feasibility of incorporating rabies vaccination into the EPI for communities where rabies is a problem (WHO, 2002d).

The prevention of human exposure to rabies in low- and middle-income countries primarily depends on the control of dog rabies, which can be achieved through the widespread use of the parenteral dog rabies vaccine. The mass vaccination of owned dogs and the elimination of stray or feral dogs has proved successful in many countries. For example, in the United States, the incidence of human rabies cases was reduced from 0.03 per 100,000 per year in 1945 to less than 0.001 per 100,000 per year in the 1980s following the widespread control of dog rabies (Fishbein, 1991).

The prevention of human disease when exposure to rabies virus has occurred depends on good local wound care (e.g., flushing with soap and water) and postexposure prophylaxis, which entails passive immunization with immunoglobulin and active immunization with rabies vaccine. The complete postexposure regimen almost always prevents disease; however, the regimen must be delivered during the incubation period because neither immunization nor other treatments alter the fatal course of disease once symptoms develop. There are no diagnostic tests that detect rabies infection in humans prior to the onset of symptoms, and thus all suspected or possible infections must receive treatment.

The prevention of human leptospirosis depends on interrupting the transmission of leptospires to humans. Preventive measures include the vaccination of certain host animals (e.g., cattle) or the elimination of others (e.g., rats). Human vaccination has met with limited success and is not widely applied. Environmental control strategies aimed at reducing hazards such as stagnant bodies of water or the periodic flooding of residential areas, as well as educational campaigns aimed at decreasing unnecessary water exposures, may contribute to prevention efforts. Occupational improvements that curtail contact with host animals or contaminated water are also desirable. Antibiotic therapy with palliative care remains the treatment of choice, although evidence in support of antibiotic therapy is incomplete (Guidugli, Castro, & Atallah, 2000).

Obstacles to Prevention and Control and Directions for Future Research

The major obstacle to the improved control of rabies is the difficulty of achieving adequate vaccine coverage of dog populations in low- and middle-income countries. WHO estimates that 80% coverage is nec-

essary for effective control (WHO, 2002d). Ensuring the delivery of vaccine to stray and feral dogs (or eliminating these dogs altogether) is especially problematic. With sustained effort, WHO considers the global elimination of urban (dog) rabies to be an attainable goal.

The future control of leptospirosis is less promising. Animal vaccination may not be economically feasible for many farmers, and vaccines are not available or appropriate for every host species. The elimination of wildlife hosts (e.g., rats) is usually not feasible. Improvements in working and living conditions to reduce contact with animals and their excreta are desirable (for many reasons) but difficult to achieve in low- and middle-income settings. Until these difficulties are overcome, the control of leptospirosis must rely on health education to reduce risky behavior, veterinary education to promote good animal husbandry, and medical education to ensure the prompt diagnosis and treatment of leptospirosis.

Viral Hemorrhagic Fevers

Overview

The viruses that cause hemorrhagic fever (HF) belong to four different families (Table 4-6), and the illnesses they produce have distinct epidemiologic features. Despite their differences, these viruses produce a common clinical picture that is characterized by fever and hemorrhage, as the name suggests. Hemorrhagic manifestations can include petechiae, ecchymoses, bleeding gums, nosebleeds, vaginal bleeding, and bleeding from other mucosal surfaces, producing bloody urine, stool, and vomit. Complications can include cardiovascular and neurologic disturbances, shock, and death.

The spectrum of disease typically associated with each type of virus varies substantially. For example, Lassa virus infections result in inapparent or mild clinical symptoms in many people but cause severe life-threatening disease in others. Ebola virus and Marburg virus, on the other hand, appear to cause severe disease in virtually all those infected. The severity of the clinical illness that results from infection also varies according to differences in host response, viral virulence factors, and dose.

Infection with the HF viruses is, in general, relatively rare (Lassa virus is a notable exception). Although outbreaks are dramatic and lead to major responses on the part of public health and other officials, HF virus infections do not have the same public health impact in terms of morbidity and mortality as the infectious diseases that more commonly afflict the peoples of most low- and middle-income countries (WHO,

Table 4-6	Distribution and Modes of Transmission of Viral Hemorrhagic Fevers		
Family, Genus, and Virus	**Disease**	**Principal Means of Transmission**	**Principal Locations**
Flaviviridae			
Flavivirus			
Dengue	Dengue HF	Mosquito	Asia, Latin America
Yellow fever	Yellow fever	Mosquito	sub-Saharan Africa, South America
Kyasanur Forest disease	Kyasanur Forest disease	Tick	India
Omsk HF	Omsk HF	Tick, muskrat	Russia
Arenaviridae			
Arenavirus			
Lassa	Lassa fever	Rodent, person-to-person	West Africa
Junin	Argentine HF	Rodent	Argentina
Machupo	Bolivian HF	Rodent	Bolivia
Guanarito	Venezuelan HF	Rodent	Venezuela
Sabio	Brazilian HF	Unknown	Brazil
Bunyaviridae			
Phlebovirus			
Rift Valley fever	Rift Valley fever	Mosquito	Africa
Nairovirus			
Crimean-Congo HF	Crimean-Congo HF	Tick, person-to-person	Africa, Asia, Eastern Europe, Middle East
Hantavirus			
Hantaan, Seoul, and others	HF with renal syndrome	Rodent	Asia, Europe
Filoviridae			
Filovirus			
Marburg	Marburg HF	Person-to-person	Africa
Ebola	Ebola HF	Person-to-person	Africa

Note: HF = hemorrhagic fever.

1985). However, because most HF viruses are extremely virulent and capable of epidemic spread, developing strategies to control these viruses is a public health priority. In addition, some of the viruses, such as the South American HF viruses, pose regional public health hazards within their areas of endemicity.

All HF viruses are thought to be zoonotic. These viruses are proven or suspected to be transmitted from animals to humans by an arthropod vector (e.g., ticks or mosquitoes) or by direct or indirect contact with the animal reservoir (e.g., rodents) of the virus (see Table 4-6). In endemic areas, the temporal distribution of many viral HFs follows seasonal changes in the activity and density of the vector or animal reservoir, or seasonal changes in human activity. The age and sex distributions of infection and disease caused by some HF viruses reflect differences in exposure to the vector or reservoir, whereas other viruses affect persons of all ages and both sexes.

Several of the HFs have only recently been recognized and had their agents characterized. For example, the South American HFs, Ebola HF, and Marburg HF appear to have emerged in just the past 50 years, presumably as a result of increased human activity or settlement in areas where viruses circulate among their known or presumed zoonotic hosts. In some instances, such as with Argentine HF, the geographic range of the virus has expanded beyond its initial focus (and continues to spread) (Vainrub & Salas, 1994). The development of control and prevention strategies for newly emerging infections can pose special difficulties because investigators have not had time to conduct the research needed to formulate treatment modalities, vaccines, vector-control strategies, and other preventive measures

Etiologic Agents and Clinical Features

There are at least 14 different HF viruses (see Table 4-6). However, the public health significance of each virus differs substantially. The most prominent (in terms of annual incidence of disease) are Lassa virus, yellow fever virus, and dengue group viruses. The latter two are discussed in the section on arthropod-borne diseases. Ebola virus and Marburg virus are notable for their epidemic potential and extraordinarily high CFRs, whereas the South American HFs caused by Junin, Machupo, and Guanarito viruses have regional public health importance. Detailed discussion of the remaining HF viruses is beyond the scope of this work.

Descriptive Epidemiologic Features and Risk Factors

Ebola HF emerged in 1976 when concurrent epidemics occurred in the Democratic Republic of Congo (formerly Zaire) and Sudan. These outbreaks were caused by distinct subtypes of the virus and were characterized by high CFRs (88% in the Democratic Republic of Congo and 53% in Sudan). In total, 602 persons were infected and 431 died in the two outbreaks. Sudan experienced a second, smaller outbreak in 1979, and Gabon experienced three small outbreaks (each involving 60 or fewer cases) in the 1990s. A large outbreak occurred in Kikwit, the Democratic Republic of Congo, in 1995 and resulted in 315 cases and 244 deaths, for a CFR of 77%. The largest outbreak to date was in Uganda in 2000–2001, with 425 cases and 224 deaths (53%). Smaller outbreaks continued to recur in Gabon and the Republic of Congo from 2000 to 2003, resulting in a total of 302 cases and 254 deaths (84%).

The first recognized outbreak of Marburg HF occurred in Marburg, Germany, in 1967 among laboratory workers (and their contacts), who acquired the infection from monkeys imported from Uganda. Since then, a small number of cases have been reported in South Africa (1975) and Kenya (1980 and 1987), and more than 200 cases were identified in the Democratic Republic of Congo in the period from 1998 to 2000 (Bausch et al., 2003). The CFR of Marburg HF ranges from 26% to 83%.

Epidemics of Ebola HF have been sustained by person-to-person transmission through direct physical contact with infected persons or corpses (or with their bodily fluids or tissues) and the use of unsterile needles for medical injections. Person-to-person transmission is not very efficient, with secondary attack rates of 16% in household contacts (Dowell et al., 1999). Marburg virus is also transmitted by person-to-person contact. Fortunately, airborne transmission does not appear to be important for either virus. The ecologic niches of these viruses remain unknown, and zoonotic vectors and reservoirs have not been identified.

Lassa virus is widely distributed across West Africa, where it causes substantial morbidity and mortality. Although its precise incidence is unknown, it is estimated that as many as 100,000 to 300,000 new infections occur each year, with an overall CFR of about 1% to 2% (McCormick et al., 1987). Maternal death, fetal death, and permanent deafness are common complications (Cummins et al., 1990; Monson et al., 1987; Richmond & Baglole, 2003). Lassa virus is maintained in a rodent reservoir that is commonly found in the home. Virus is shed in rodent urine and droppings, and rodent-to-human transmission is believed to occur by aerosolization or ingestion of rodent excreta or by inoculation through broken skin. Rodent-to-human transmission may also occur when infected rodents are consumed as food (Ter Meulen et al., 1996). Person-to-person transmission occurs in community and hospital settings, and contributes substantially to epidemics of Lassa fever. This mode of transmission requires direct contact with infected persons. Person-to-person airborne transmission occurs rarely, if ever. Sexual transmission can occur; the importance of this mode of transmission is unknown.

Argentine HF, which is caused by Junin virus, was first described in 1955 in agricultural workers in the Argentine pampas. Several hundred cases of Argentine HF occur each year in large, primarily agricultural regions of the pampas. The region of endemicity is expanding, and is now nearly 10 times larger than its initial compass (Vainrub & Salas, 1994). Bolivian HF, which is caused by Machupo virus, was subsequently described in northeastern Bolivia, which is the only known endemic area. Outbreaks of Bolivian HF occurred in the 1960s and early 1970s, including large epidemics that affected hundreds of individuals. Although no cases were reported from 1976 to 1992, possibly due to effective host control, a small outbreak in 1994 and recent sporadic cases have marked its reemergence ("Reemergence of Bolivian Hemorrhagic Fever," 1994). Venezuelan HF, which is caused by Guanarito virus, was first recognized in 1989. During the period from September 1989 to January 1997, 165 cases were reported within the small region of central Venezuela where Guanarito virus is endemic (De Manzione et al., 1998). For infections caused by all three of these viruses, the case fatality ratio is in the range of 15% to 33% (De Manzione et al., 1998; Doyle, Bryan, & Peters, 1998).

Each of the three South American HF viruses is associated with a rodent reservoir that maintains the virus in the wild. As with Lassa fever, rodent-to-human transmission occurs by the aerosolization or ingestion of virus-laden rodent excreta or by inoculation through broken skin. The rodent that carries

Junin virus typically dwells in agricultural fields, whereas the rodent that carries Machupo virus readily enters the home. Rodent-control strategies must take such differences into account. Person-to-person transmission of Junin, Machupo, and Guanarito viruses is considered rare, and nosocomial outbreaks are uncommon.

Current Approaches to Prevention and Control

Field trials have demonstrated that a live, attenuated Junin virus vaccine is safe and provides effective protection against Argentine HF (Maiztegui et al., 1998) and may provide cross-protection against Bolivian HF as well. Vaccines are not available for Lassa fever, Ebola HF, or Marburg HF. In the absence of vaccines, reducing the morbidity and mortality caused by HF viruses depends on preventing primary transmission by limiting exposures to virus reservoirs and vectors and controlling secondary transmission (e.g., person-to-person transmission in the hospital, household, or community setting) through patient isolation and barrier nursing. In addition, the use of antiviral drugs or convalescent serum is effective in some instances.

Strategies to limit viral exposures are determined by the unique characteristics of the associated animal reservoir or vector and the distinct ways in which each of the viruses is transmitted. For example, the rodent that carries Machupo virus is frequently found in and around the home, and aggressive rodent eradication measures through trapping and poisoning appear to have been quite successful in controlling Bolivian HF (Kilgore et al., 1995). Conversely, the rodent reservoir of Junin virus lives in crop fields, where trapping and poisoning are difficult, necessitating the development of alternative rodent abatement strategies. Eradication (or even control) of the rodent reservoir of Lassa virus in West Africa is not considered feasible due to the density and wide distribution of the rodent that carries the virus. Preventing the primary transmission of Lassa virus has instead relied on educating at-risk communities about ways to reduce opportunities for exposure, such as never leaving food items uncovered and never consuming rodents as food. The development of control strategies for Ebola virus and Marburg virus awaits identification of the reservoir(s) and vector(s).

Historically, nosocomial and person-to-person transmission of Lassa fever, Ebola HF, and Marburg HF have contributed significantly to devastating outbreaks of these diseases. (The South American HF viruses are rarely transmitted by these routes.) Field experience indicates that epidemic control is readily achieved through simple barrier nursing techniques (e.g., wearing gloves, gowns, and masks; sterilizing equipment; and isolating patients), and epidemiologic studies support this conclusion. For example, serologic studies in Sierra Leone found that hospital personnel who used barrier techniques when caring for Lassa fever patients had no greater risk of infection than the local population (Helmick et al., 1986).

At present, few specific treatments are available for the viral HFs. Ribavirin (an antiviral drug) is effective in the treatment of Lassa fever (McCormick et al., 1986). Laboratory data suggest that ribavirin may also prove effective in treating South American HFs, although supporting clinical data are incomplete (Doyle, Bryan, & Peters, 1998). Ribavirin is unlikely to be beneficial in treating Ebola HF or Marburg HF. Convalescent serum is useful in the treatment of Argentine HF (WHO, 1985), but donors are not plentiful. Most people in low- and middle-income countries are not able to afford these therapies.

Obstacles to Prevention and Control and Directions for Future Research

The major obstacle to containing outbreaks of viral HFs (especially Ebola HF, Marburg HF, and Lassa fever) is inadequate disease surveillance, which results in delayed response and increased opportunity for epidemic spread. In many low- and middle-income countries, disease surveillance is impeded by the difficulty of making an early differential diagnosis in areas where illnesses with similar initial manifestations (e.g., malaria, influenza, typhoid fever, leptospirosis, meningococcemia, and hepatitis) are prevalent. The lack of ready access to diagnostic laboratories exacerbates this difficulty. In addition, because epidemics are unpredictable in time and place, surveillance efforts are difficult to maintain. Other obstacles to the control and prevention of viral HFs include the costliness of sustaining readiness for infection control measures (e.g., maintaining supplies for barrier nursing), lack of information about the vector(s) and reservoir(s) of Ebola and Marburg viruses, the difficulties of developing and maintaining vector- and rodent-control programs, and the limited availability of ribavirin (especially for the treatment of Lassa fever).

Infectious Causes of Blindness

Overview

Severely decreased visual acuity or complete blindness is profoundly disabling in any setting, but perhaps even more so in low- and middle-income countries. Among the known causes of blindness, two infectious agents play important etiologic roles in selected regions of the world: *C. trachomatis*, the cause of trachoma, and *Onchocerca volvulus*, the cause of onchocerciasis, also known as river blindness.

Trachoma

Etiologic Agents

C. trachomatis is a small bacterium that lives within selected types of human cells and is difficult to grow in the laboratory. Although *C. trachomatis* is also the cause of STIs, as discussed previously, different immunotypes of the bacterium cause trachoma and genital tract infections. Those that cause trachoma are spread person-to-person, most probably through eye and possibly nasal secretions on the hands. *C. trachomatis* is also spread mechanically by flies and probably by fomites such as washrags and handkerchiefs. Repeated episodes of infection in young (preschool) children lead to scarring of the eyelids, which in turn causes in-turned eyelashes that abrade the corneal surface, leading to subsequent corneal opacification and reduced visual acuity or blindness in adults.

Descriptive Epidemiologic Features and Risk Factors

Trachoma is the leading cause of preventable blindness in the world, accounting for an estimated 6 million or one-sixth of all cases (Mabey, Solomon, & Foster, 2003). In addition, roughly 150 million persons are infected with *C. trachomatis* and at risk of becoming blind. Trachoma is a disease of poverty that was described by the ancient Egyptians and previously was found throughout the world. Trachoma disappeared from Europe and virtually all of the United States long before antimicrobial agents became available in the 1930s and 1940s; improved standards of living and personal hygiene are credited with its disappearance. Trachoma is not a reportable condition, and what is known of its descriptive epidemiologic features comes from numerous surveys. Trachoma persists in hot, low- and middle-income countries, particularly in North Africa, the Middle East, sub-Saharan Africa, and drier regions of India and Southeast Asia. In hyperendemic areas, infection of the eye is virtually universal in children by their fifth birthday, but active disease is seen largely in older children. Repeated reinfection in children leads to the permanent damage to the eyes that results in subsequent blindness or visual impairment in adulthood. Although infection in childhood appears to be equally common in boys and girls, the blinding complications appear to be more common in women, perhaps because of repeated exposure to infected children.

Risk factors for trachoma in children largely relate to facial cleanliness, the presence of flies, and cultural practices that lead to an increased likelihood of person-to-person transmission of the etiologic agent, such as sharing washcloths and ways in which eye makeup is applied.

Current Approaches to Prevention and Control

Intervention studies have demonstrated that mass treatment with a variety of topical or oral antimicrobial agents and health educational programs that lead to improved facial cleanliness can substantially reduce the prevalence of trachoma in a community, as can fly control (Emerson et al., 2004). Reductions in trachoma in low- and middle-income countries in the absence of a specific control program have also been documented as access to water, access to health care, and hygiene have improved. The current approach to reducing trachoma-associated blindness in endemic areas is summarized in the acronym SAFE, which stands for (1) surgery to correct eyelid deformity, (2) antibiotics to treat acute eye infection and reduce sources of infection in the community, (3) facial cleanliness, and (4) environmental change that enhances availability of water and reduces the prevalence of flies. In 1997, WHO launched a new trachoma control program—Global Elimination of Trachoma by 2020 (GET 2020)—based on the SAFE approach.

Obstacles to Prevention and Directions for Future Research

Trachoma is likely to remain a persistent problem in endemic areas until rising socioeconomic conditions result in better access to water, improved personal hygiene and sanitation, reductions in the numbers of flies, and improved access to health care services. Although mass, community-wide treatment with antimicrobial agents can lead to reduced trachoma in such areas, these reductions have proven difficult to sustain unless such treatment is made a routine part of regularly available health services and is accompanied by improvements in hygiene. Although a vaccine against trachoma has been discussed for many years, it remains unclear whether an effective vaccine can or will ever be developed.

Onchocerciasis

O. volvulus is a filarial parasite that is spread through the bite of one of several species of Simulium black flies. During the bite of an infected female fly, larvae enter the body and ultimately develop into adult worms that form nodules, usually over bony prominences. Adult worms can survive inside these nodules for up to 15 years. The female adult worm produces microfilariae that migrate to the skin and the eye and are ingested by female flies when they bite an infected person, thus completing the cycle. In the skin, an inflammatory response to dead and dying microfilariae can lead to incapacitating itching and various types of degenerative, often unsightly, skin changes. In the eye, heavy and prolonged infection of the cornea with the microfilariae leads to opacification and reduced visual acuity or total blindness. The microfilariae can be detected by taking small snips of skin, immersing them in saline, and examining the saline microscopically.

Descriptive Epidemiologic Features and Risk Factors

Onchocerciasis is found only in a band of sub-Saharan African countries, parts of Central America, the northern part of South America, and the Arabian peninsula. It is estimated that almost 18 million persons worldwide are currently infected with the parasite and that more than 750,000 infected individuals are either blind or have severe visual impairment as a result, with the vast majority of these individuals living in Africa (especially Nigeria, Cameroon, Uganda, the Congo, and Ethiopia) (Greene, 1992). Within these affected regions, onchocerciasis occurs in foci, largely determined by distance from the black fly breeding sites. The intensity of infection (and hence the risk of visual impairment) increases with age, as the burden of adult female worms producing microfilariae increases, and tends to be greater in men than in women, perhaps reflecting work-related exposures to the flies.

Current Approaches to Prevention and Control

Approaches to the control of onchocerciasis and prevention of the blindness it causes have included vector control, mass treatment of infected individuals, and nodulectomy (removal of nodules to reduce the source and number of microfilariae that migrate to the eyes). Early attempts to control onchocerciasis targeted the Simulium flies that serve as vectors, the immature stages of which require running water (e.g., rivers and streams) for their development. Initially, DDT was the pesticide added to rivers that served as the breeding ground for the vector, but beginning in the 1970s other agents that target the larval stages of the fly (e.g., temephos) were used with great success, particularly in West Africa. These programs permitted resettlement of fertile areas that had been abandoned because of onchocerciasis, but the flies' development of resistance to temephos required switching to other larvacidal agents in some areas.

The control of onchocerciasis was revolutionized in the late 1980s with the introduction of ivermectin, a single dose of which eliminates microfilariae for a number of months. However, because ivermectin does not kill the adult worms, repeated treatment (e.g., every 6 to 12 months) of infected individuals over many years is needed to provide continued suppression of the number of microfilariae and to prevent visual damage. Treatment every 3 months may be even more effective at reducing both the number of female worms in nodules and symptoms (Gardon et al., 2002). Fortunately, in a noteworthy humanitarian gesture, the manufacturer of ivermectin has made a commitment to provide the drug free "for as long as necessary to as many as necessary." Given the availability of ivermectin, countries affected by onchocerciasis have developed control programs that identify endemic areas (typically by conducting nodule surveys) and then make the drug available in those areas (Pacqué et al., 1991). Various approaches to making the drug available have been used (e.g., passive health center–based programs and active community-based programs), and each has advantages and disadvantages.

Obstacles to Prevention and Directions for Future Research

Although it may be possible in some endemic areas to eradicate onchocerciasis through vector control or mass ivermectin treatment programs, in the most heavily affected parts of Africa complete eradication is not likely in the foreseeable future.

Emergence of New Infectious Disease Threats

The availability of a growing number of antimicrobial agents and vaccines in the 1950s through the 1970s simultaneously led to the burgeoning infectious disease prevention and control activities described in the preceding sections of this chapter and to a widely shared assumption that infectious disease threats to human (and animal) health would diminish over time. However, the unexpected emergence of new infectious diseases and the reemergence of previously controlled diseases that became apparent in the 1980s and 1990s made it clear that efforts to control existing infectious diseases needed to be accompanied by an improved global capacity for early detection and rapid response to newly emergent or reemergent infectious diseases. More recent concern about the possible intentional release of infectious agents in a deliberate effort to frighten, harm, or kill has given added impetus to efforts in this area.

The concept of emerging and reemerging infections, which began receiving prominent attention after the U.S. Institute of Medicine released a report entitled *Emerging Infections: Microbial Threats to Health in the United States* in 1992, encompasses several distinct phenomena that can produce unexpected and sometimes urgent infectious disease threats. Included under the rubric of emerging and reemerging infectious disease threats are diseases caused by microbial agents not previously known to cause illness in humans (e.g., SARS, Nipah virus encephalitis, and avian influenza in humans), the appearance in a new location of an infectious agent (e.g., the spread of West Nile virus to the United States), the appearance of a new epidemiologic pattern of disease caused by an infectious agent (e.g., epidemic meningococcal meningitis caused by serogroup W-135 *N. meningitidis*), the appearance or spread of new variants of an infectious agent (e.g., multidrug-resistant *M. tuberculosis*), and the resurgence of an infectious disease previously under good control (e.g., diphtheria in parts of the former Soviet Union).

The 1992 report by the Institute of Medicine, together with a follow-up report in 2003 (Smolinski, Hamburg, & Lederberg, 2003), outlined a number of factors that could promote the emergence or reemergence of infectious disease threats. In addition to microbial adaptation and change in response to selection pressures, numerous human and environmental factors can be involved in the emergence or reemergence of infectious diseases, including increased human susceptibility to infection; human demographic conditions and behaviors; international travel and commerce; economic development and land use; technologic change; climate and ecologic factors; breakdown of public health measures; war and famine; poverty and social inequality; lack of political will; and intent to harm. Individually and collectively, these factors can contribute to an increased likelihood that humans will come in contact with various infectious agents; a greater susceptibility to infection; enhanced and more rapid spread of infectious agents; and reduced capacity of communities to detect and respond effectively to infectious disease threats. Although the result can be dramatic outbreaks that command widespread public attention and political response (e.g., SARS and avian influenza), other equally serious infectious disease threats (e.g., multidrug-resistant tuberculosis) often go largely unnoticed by the general public and decision makers because they do not produce explosive epidemics.

The most dramatic example of an emerging infectious disease threat in recent years was the appearance of SARS. This life-threatening form of pneumonia appears to have originated in southern China in late 2002. Before the significance of these cases of pneumonia became apparent, the illness had spread to multiple other parts of Asia and eventually to Europe, North America, and elsewhere. By the middle of 2003, over 8,400 probable cases of SARS and over 800 SARS-related deaths had been reported from 30 countries, with China, Hong Kong, and Taiwan bearing the brunt of the epidemic. SARS is caused by a previously unknown member of the Coronaviridiae family that almost certainly originated in one or more animal reservoirs and that initially spread to humans with direct exposure to infected animals in southern China. However, the virus proved to be transmissible from person to person, particularly in the health care setting. Spread of the SARS-associated coronavirus was also documented on commercial airplanes, and the ease of modern travel from one part of the world to another clearly facilitated the rapid dissemination of the virus across the globe. In addition to the morbidity and mortality it caused, the SARS epidemic had an enormous economic impact; it has been estimated that the total cost of the epidemic to Asian economies alone was in the range of US$60 billion. In the absence of a vaccine, preventing further spread of the SARS epidemic required stringent isolation of patients, quarantine of exposed individuals, restrictions on travel, and various other measures that were highly disruptive of commerce, travel, and other aspects of life.

The few SARS cases that occurred in 2004 (largely due to laboratory accidents) were contained through stringent isolation and quarantine, preventing a recurrence of a broader epidemic. However, the experience with SARS in 2003 and the more recent experience with H5N1 influenza A (bird flu) in a number of Asian countries and monkey pox in the United States demonstrate that there is an ongoing threat of new infectious agents entering and causing disease in human populations, particularly from animal sources. Even as progress is made in eradicating or controlling historically important infectious diseases, there is a need for vigilance, preparedness, and a high level of international cooperation to detect and respond to new infectious disease threats that might emerge. WHO and others are currently working to improve global capacity in this area (see Exhibit 4-6).

Exhibit 4-6	Global Outbreak Alert and Response Network

Throughout the 1970s, 1980s, and 1990s, outbreaks of novel or high-impact infectious diseases (e.g., Ebola, cholera, and meningococcal meningitis) in poor- and middle-income countries often led to ad hoc responses by multiple national, international, academic, research, and private-sector organizations that were uncoordinated and sometimes duplicative or even competing in nature. Although the World Health Organization (WHO) was often looked to for leadership and technical assistance in such instances, it historically had very limited trained personnel and resources to devote to such efforts, as well as political and legal constraints that could limit its access.

In recognition of these problems, in 2000 WHO created the Global Outbreak Alert and Response Network (GOARN), which has its headquarters in Geneva. GOARN, which is intended to be an early warning system, receives a steady stream of daily reports concerning possible outbreaks from a global network of informants. GOARN also uses a newly developed software system to monitor news sources on the Internet. GOARN staff receive 10 to 20 leads a day, which they evaluate and, when appropriate, follow up. The network has proven extremely useful as SARS, avian influenza, and other outbreaks have appeared. However, increased staffing of GOARN and revisions to the International Health Regulations that would give WHO unimpeded access when important outbreaks occur are both needed to improve the functioning of this system.

Conclusion

The current status of infectious diseases in low- and middle-income countries reflects both the dramatic progress that has been made in controlling some diseases and the disappointing results to date in controlling others. The eradication of smallpox, the expected imminent eradication of polio, and impressive gains made against measles and neonatal tetanus all demonstrate what can be accomplished even in the lowest-income countries with an effective vaccine when concerted efforts are made to ensure that the vaccine reaches those in need. Similar progress in reducing morbidity from dracunculiasis and onchocerciasis demonstrates that, under the right conditions and with available resources, infectious diseases can be controlled through a combination of vector control and avoidance and treatment. At the same time, the reductions in the morbidity and mortality from

diarrheal diseases and acute respiratory infections that have been achieved are clear evidence that a combination of improved knowledge and access to reasonably inexpensive treatment modalities can also be highly effective.

Far less encouraging has been the progress made against malaria, dengue, tuberculosis, and AIDS, all of which continue to take a substantial toll. For diseases such as tuberculosis, much can be accomplished simply by improving diagnosis and treatment of cases using tried-and-true methods that have been available for many years. For diseases such as AIDS, behavior change and improved access to treatment of other STIs can reduce the risk of acquiring HIV infection, and expanded use of antiretroviral drugs can dramatically improve the lives of HIV-infected individuals and reduce vertical transmission of the virus, but development and widespread use of an effective vaccine is the only realistic long-term solution. For vector-borne diseases such as dengue and malaria, either new approaches to vector control or effective vaccines are urgently needed.

Progress to date in controlling the morbidity and mortality from infectious diseases in low- and middle-income countries demonstrates that much can be accomplished even in the absence of marked improvements in socioeconomic conditions. Ultimately, however, widespread improvements in education and socioeconomic conditions will be needed if such progress is to be maintained.

• • • Discussion Questions

1. What are the major different types of approaches that have been used to prevent morbidity and mortality from infectious diseases in low- and middle-income countries?

2. What are the major obstacles that have had and will have to be overcome in implementing various approaches to preventing morbidity and mortality from infectious diseases in low- and middle-income countries?

3. In the current year, what infectious diseases account for the most mortality in low-income countries? The most morbidity?

4. If you were working in the Ministry of Health of a low-income country and needed to set priorities concerning resource allocation, how could you go about determining the relative importance of various infectious diseases as causes of mortality in your country? The causes of morbidity/disability?

● ● ● References

Aaby, P., Samb, B., Simondon, F., Knudsen, K., Seck, A. M., Bennett, J., Markowitz, L., Rhodes, P., & Whittle, H. (1994). Sex-specific differences in mortality after high-titre measles immunization in rural Senegal. *Bulletin of the World Health Organization, 72,* 761–770.

Avila, M., Salomón, H., Carballal, G., Ebekian, B., Woyskovsky, N., Cerqueiro, M. C., & Weissenbacher, M. (1990). Role of viral pathogens in acute respiratory tract infections. *Reviews of Infectious Diseases, 12,* S974–S981.

Bach, J. F., Chalons, S., Forier, E., Elana, G., Jouanelle, J., Kayemba, S., Delbois, D., Mosser, A., Saint-Aime, C., & Berchel, C. (1996). 10–year educational programme aimed at rheumatic fever in two French Caribbean islands. *Lancet, 347,* 644–648.

Banatvala, J. E., & Brown, D. W. G. (2004). Rubella. *Lancet, 363,* 1127–1137.

Bausch, D. G., Borchert, M., Grein, T., Roth, C., Swanepoel, R., Libande, M. L., Talarmin, A., Bertherat, E., Muyembe-Tamfum, J. J., Tugume, B., Colebunders, R., Konde, K. M., Pirad, P., Olinda, L. L., Rodier, G. R., Campbell, P., Tomori, O., Ksiazek, T. G., & Rollin, P. E. (2003). Risk factors for Marburg hemorrhagic fever, Democratic Republic of the Congo. *Emerging Infectious Diseases, 9*(12), 1531–1537.

Berman, S. (1991). Epidemiology of acute respiratory infections in children of developing countries. *Reviews of Infectious Diseases, 13,* S454–S462.

Bern, C., Martines, J., de Zoysa, I., & Glass, R. I. (1992). The magnitude of the global problem of diarrhoeal disease: A ten-year update. *Bulletin of the World Health Organization, 70,* 705–714.

Bertherat, E., Yada, A., Djingarey, M. H., & Koumare, B. (2002). First major epidemic caused by *Neisseria meningitidis* serogroup W-135 in Africa. *Tropical Medicine, 62,* 301–304.

Black, R. E. (1993). Persistent diarrhea in children of developing countries. *Pediatric Infectious Disease Journal, 12,* 751–761.

Black, R. E., Morris, S. S., & Bryce, J. (2003). Where and why are 10 million children dying every year? *Lancet, 361,* 2226–2234.

Bowden, S. (2001). New hepatitis viruses: Contenders and pretenders. *Journal of Gastroenterology and Hepatology, 16*(2), 124–131.

Breman, J. G. (2001). The ears of the hippopotamus: Manifestations, determinants, and estimates of the malaria burden. *American Journal of Tropical Medicine and Hygiene, 64*(1–2 Suppl.), 1–11.

Britton, W. J., & Lockwood, D. N. (2004). Leprosy. *Lancet, 363,* 1209–1219.

Bryce, J., Victoria, C. G., Habicht, J.-P., & Black, R. E. (2004). The multi-country evaluation of the Integrated Management of Childhood Illness strategy: Lessons for the evaluation of public health interventions. *American Journal of Public Health, 94,* 406–415.

Bundy, D. A. (1990). New initiatives in the control of helminths. *Transactions of the Royal Society of Tropical Medicine and Hygiene, 84,* 467–468.

Bundy, D. A., Hall, A., Medley, G. F., & Savioli, L. (1992). Evaluating measures to control intestinal parasitic infections. *World Health Statistics Quarterly, 45,* 168–179.

Butterworth, A. E., Dunne, D. W., Fulford, A. J., Ouma, J. H., & Sturrock, R. F. (1996). Immunity and morbidity in *Schistosoma mansoni* infection: Quantitative aspects. *American Journal of Tropical Medicine and Hygiene, 55,* 109–115.

Celentano, D. D., Nelson, K. E., Suprasert, S., Eiumtrakul, S., Tulvatana, S., Kuntolbutra, S., Akarasewi, P., Matanasarawoot, A., Wright, N. H., Sirisopana, N., & Theetranont, C. (1996). Risk factors for HIV-1 seroconversion among young men in northern Thailand. *Journal of the American Medical Association, 275,* 122–127.

Centers for Disease Control and Prevention. (1996). Progress toward elimination of neonatal tetanus: Egypt, 1988–1994. *Morbidity and Mortality Weekly Report, 45,* 89–92.

Centers for Disease Control and Prevention. (1998). Progress toward poliomyelitis eradication: West Africa, 1997–September 1998. *Morbidity and Mortality Weekly Report, 45,* 89–92.

Centers for Disease Control and Prevention. (2002). Progress toward global eradication of poliomyelitis. *Morbidity and Mortality Weekly Report, 52,* 366–369.

Centers for Disease Control and Prevention. (2004). Measles mortality reduction—West Africa, 1996–2002. *Morbidity and Mortality Weekly Report, 53,* 28–30.

Cholera Working Group, International Centre for Diarrhoeal Diseases Research, Bangladesh. (1993). Large epidemic of cholera-like disease in Bangladesh caused by *Vibrio cholerae* O139 synonym Bengal. *Lancet, 342,* 387–390.

Cohen, J. (2003). AIDS vaccine still alive as booster after second failure in Thailand. *Science, 302,* 1309–1310.

Corbett, E. L., Watt, C. J., Walker, N., Williams, B. G., Raviglione, M. G., & Dye, C. (2003). The growing burden of tuberculosis: Global trends and interactions with the HIV epidemic. *Archives of Internal Medicine, 163,* 1009–1021.

Crump, J. A., Luby, S. P., & Mintz, E. D. (2004). The global burden of typhoid fever. *Bulletin of the World Health Organization, 82,* 346–353.

Cummins, D., McCormick, J. B., Bennett, D., Samba, J. A., Farrar, B., Machin, S. J., & Fisher-Hoch, S. P. (1990). Acute sensorineural deafness in Lassa fever. *Journal of the American Medical Association, 264,* 2093–2096.

Cutts, F. T., & Vynnycky, E. (1999). Modelling the incidence of congenital rubella syndrome in developing countries. *International Journal of Epidemiology, 28,* 1176–1184.

Dawson, C. (1999). Flies and the elimination of blinding trachoma. *Lancet, 353,* 1376–1377.

De Manzione, N., Salas, R. A., Paredes, H., Godoy, O., Rojas, L., Araoz, F., Fulhorst, C. F., Ksiazek, T. G., Mills, J. N., Ellis, B. A., Peters, C. J., & Tesh, R. B. (1998). Venezuelan hemorrhagic fever: Clinical and epidemiological studies of 165 cases. *Clinical Infectious Diseases, 26,* 308–313.

de Quadros, C. A., Izurieta, H., Venczel, L., & Carrasco, P. (2004). Measles eradication in the Americas: Progress to date. *Journal of Infectious Diseases, 189,* S227–S235.

Dolin, P. J., Raviglione, M. C., & Kochi, A. (1994). Global tuberculosis incidence and mortality during 1990–2000. *Bulletin of the World Health Organization, 72,* 213–220.

Dowdle, W. R., & Hopkins, D. R. (1998). *The eradication of infectious diseases: Report of the Dahlem Workshop on the Eradication of Infectious Diseases, Berlin, March 16–22, 1997.* Chichester, England: John Wiley & Sons.

Dowell, S. F., Mukunu, R., Ksiazek, T. G., Khan, A. S., Rollin, P. E., & Peters, C. J. (1999). Transmission of Ebola hemorrhagic fever: A study of risk factors in family members, Kikwit, Democratic Republic of the Congo, 1995. Commission de Lutte contre les Epidémies à Kikwit. *Journal of Infectious Diseases, 179,* S87–S91.

Doyle, T. J., Bryan, R. T., & Peters, C. J. (1998). Viral hemorrhagic fevers and hantavirus infections in the Americas. *Infectious Disease Clinics of North America, 12,* 95–110.

Ellis, W. A. (1998). Leptospirosis. In S. R. Palmer, E. J. L. Soulsby, & D. I. H. Simpson (Eds.), *Zoonoses: Biology, clinical practice, and public health control* (pp. 115–126). New York: Oxford University Press.

El-Rafie, M., Hassouna, W. A., Hirschhorn, N., Loza, S., Miller, P., Nagaty, A., Nasser, S., & Riyad, S. (1990). Effect of diarrhoeal disease control on infant and childhood mortality in Egypt: Report from the National Control of Diarrheal Diseases Project. *Lancet, 335,* 334–338.

El Samani, E. F., Willett, W. C., & Ware, J. H. (1998). Association of malnutrition and diarrhea in children aged under five years: A prospective follow-up study in a rural Sudanese community. *American Journal of Epidemiology, 128,* 93–105.

Elzinga, G., Raviglione, M. C., & Maher, D. (2004). Scale up: Meeting targets in global tuberculosis control. *Lancet, 363,* 814–819.

Emerson, P. M., Lindsay, S. W., Alexander, N., Bah, M., Dibba, S.-M., Faal, H. B., Lowe, K. O., McAdam, K. P., Ratcliffe, A. A., Walraven, G. E., & Bailey, R. L. (2004). Role of flies and provision of latrines in trachoma control: Cluster-randomized controlled trial. *Lancet, 363,* 1093–1098.

Fine, P. E. M., Oblapenko, G., & Sutter, R. W. (2004). Polio control after certification: Major issues outstanding. *Bulletin of the World Health Organization, 82,* 47–52.

Fishbein, D. B. (1991). Rabies in humans. In G. M. Baer (Ed.), *The natural history of rabies* (2nd ed., pp. 519–549). Boca Raton, FL: CRC Press.

Gardon, J., Boussinesq, M., Kamgno, J., Gardon-Wendel, N., Demanga-Ngangue, B., & Duke, O. L. (2002). Effects of standard and high doses of ivermectin on adult worms on *Onchocerca volvulus:* A randomized controlled trial. *Lancet, 360,* 203–210.

Gerbase, A. C., Rowley, J. T., & Mertens, T. E. (1998). Global epidemiology of sexually transmitted diseases. *Lancet, 351,* 2–4.

Glass, R. I., Bresee, J. S., Parashar, U. D., Jiang, B., & Gentsch, J. (2004). The future of rotavirus vaccines: A major setback leads to new opportunities. *Lancet, 363,* 1547–1550.

Glass, R. I., Libel, M., & Brandling-Bennett, A. D. (1992). Epidemic cholera in the Americas. *Science, 256,* 1524–1525.

Goodgame, R. W., & Greenough, W. B. (1975). Cholera in Africa: A message for the West. *Annals of Internal Medicine, 82,* 101–106.

Gove, S. (1997). Integrated management of childhood illness by outpatient health workers: Technical basis and overview. The WHO Working Group on Guidelines for Integrated Management of the Sick Child. *Bulletin of the World Health Organization, 75,* 7–24.

Graham, N. M. (1990). The epidemiology of acute respiratory infections in children and adults: A global perspective. *Epidemiologic Reviews, 12,* 149–178.

Greene, B. M. (1992). Modern medicine versus an ancient scourge: Progress toward control of onchocerciasis. *Journal of Infectious Diseases, 166,* 15–21.

Greenwood, B. M. (1987). The epidemiology of acute bacterial meningitis in tropical Africa. In J. D. Williams & J. Burnie (Eds.), *Bacterial meningitis* (pp. 61–91). London: Academic Press.

Gubler, D. J. (1998). Dengue and dengue hemorrhagic fever. *Clinical Microbiology Reviews, 11,* 480–496.

Guidugli, F., Castro, A. A., & Atallah, A. N. (2000). Antibiotics for treating leptospirosis. *Cochrane Database of Systematic Reviews, 2,* CD001306.

Hagan, P. (1996). Immunity and morbidity in infection due to *Schistosoma haematobium. American Journal of Tropical Medicine and Hygiene, 55,* 116–120.

Hart, C. A., Trees, A. J., & Duerden, B. I. (1997). Zoonoses. *Journal of Medical Microbiology, 46,* 4–6.

Hauri, A. M., Armstrong, G. L., & Hutin, Y. J. (2004). The global burden of disease attributable to contaminated injections given in health care settings. *International Journal of STD and AIDS, 15*(1), 7–16.

Helmick, C. G., Webb, P. A., Scribner, C. L., Krebs, J. W., & McCormick, J. B. (1986). No evidence for increased risk of Lassa fever infection in hospital staff. *Lancet, 2,* 1202–1205.

Hopkins, D. R. (1984). Eradication of dracunculiasis. In P. G. Bourne (Ed.), *Water and sanitation: Economic and sociological perspectives* (pp. 93–114). Orlando, FL: Academic Press.

Hopkins, D. R., Ruiz-Tiben, E., & Ruebush, T. K. (1997). Dracunculiasis eradication: Almost a reality. *American Journal of Tropical Medicine and Hygiene, 57,* 252–259.

Htun, Y., Morse, S. A., Dangor, Y., Fehler, G., Radebe, F., Trees, D. L., Beck-Sague, C. M., & Ballard, R. C. (1998). Comparison of clinically directed, disease specific, and syndromic protocols for the management of genital ulcer disease in Lesotho. *Sexually Transmitted Infections, 74,* S23–S28.

Hull, H. F., Ward, N. A., Hull, B. P., Milstien, J. B., & de Quadros, C. (1994). Paralytic poliomyelitis: Seasoned strategies, disappearing disease. *Lancet, 343,* 1331–1337.

Hunter, J. M. (1996). An introduction to Guinea worm on the eve of its departure: Dracunculiasis transmission, health effects, ecology and control. *Social Science and Medicine, 43,* 1399–1425.

Hussey, G. D., & Klein, M. (1990). A randomized, controlled trial of vitamin A in children with severe measles. *New England Journal of Medicine, 323,* 160–164.

Huttly, S. R., Morris, S. S., & Pisani, V. (1997). Prevention of diarrhoea in young children in developing countries. *Bulletin of the World Health Organization, 75,* 163–174.

Institute of Medicine. (1992). *Emerging infections: Microbial threats to health in the United States.* Washington, DC: National Academy Press.

Jackson, J. B., Musoke, P., Fleming, T., Guay, L. A., Bagenda, D., Allen, M., Nakabiito, C., Sherman, J., Bakaki, P., Owor, M., Ducar, C., Deseyve, M., Mwatha, A., Emel, L., Duefield, C., Mirochnick, M., Fowler, M. G., Mofenson, L., Miotti, P., Gigliotti, M., Bray, D., & Mmiro, F. (2003). Intrapartum and neonatal single-dose nevirapine compared with zidovudine for prevention of mother-to-child transmission of HIV-1 in Kampala, Uganda: 18-month follow-up of the HIVNET 012 randomised trial. *Lancet, 362*(9387), 859–868.

Jaiswal, S. P., Jain, A. K., Naik, G., Soni, N., & Chitnis, D. S. (2001). Viral hepatitis during pregnancy. *International Journal of Gynaecology and Obstetrics, 72*(2), 103–108.

Jódar, L., Feavers, I. M., Salisbury, D., & Granoff, D. M. (2002). Development of vaccines against meningococcal disease. *Lancet, 359,* 1499–1508.

Katzenstein, D., Laga, M., & Moatti, J. P. (Eds.). (2003). The evaluation of the HIV/AIDS drug access initiatives in Cote d'Ivoire, Senegal and Uganda: How access to antiretroviral treatment can become feasible in Africa. *AIDS, 17*(Suppl. 3), S1–S4.

Keusch, G. T., & Cash, R. A. (1997). A vaccine against rotavirus: When is too much too much? [Editorial]. *New England Journal of Medicine, 337,* 1228–1229.

Khuroo, M. S., Teli, M. R., Skidmore, S., Sofi, M. A., & Khuroo, M. I. (1981). Incidence and severity of viral hepatitis in pregnancy. *American Journal of Medicine, 70,* 252–255.

Kilgore, P. E., Peters, C. J., Mills, J. N., Rollin, P. E., Armstrong, L., Khan, A. S., & Ksiazek, T. G. (1995). Prospects for the control of Bolivian hemorrhagic fever [Editorial]. *Emerging Infectious Diseases, 1,* 97–100.

Kilian, A. H., Gregson, S., Ndyanabangi, B., Walusaga, K., Kipp, W., Sahlmuller, G., Garnett, G. P., AsiimweOkiror, G., Kabagambe, G., Weis, P., & von Sonnenburg, F. (1999). Reductions in risk behaviour provide the most consistent explanation for declining HIV-1 prevalence in Uganda. *AIDS, 13,* 391–398.

Krogstad, D. J. (1996). Malaria as a reemerging disease. *Epidemiologic Reviews, 18,* 77–89.

LaForce, F. M., Lichnevski, M. S., Keja, J., & Henderson, R. H. (1980). Clinical survey techniques to estimate prevalence and annual incidence of poliomyelitis in developing countries. *Bulletin of the World Health Organization, 58,* 609–620.

Lambrechts, T., Bryce, J., & Orinda V. (1999). Integrated management of childhood illness: A summary of first experiences. *Bulletin of the World Health Organization, 77,* 582–594.

Lengeler, C. (2004). Insecticide-treated bed nets and curtains for preventing malaria. *Cochrane Database of Systematic Reviews, 2,* CD000363.

Levett, P. N. (2001). Leptospirosis. *Clinical Microbiology Reviews, 14*(2), 296–326.

Mabey, D. C. W., Solomon, A. W., & Foster, A. (2003). Trachoma. *Lancet, 362,* 223–229.

Maiztegui, J. I., McKee, K. T., Jr., Barrera Oro, J. G., Harrison, L. H., Gibbs, P. H.,

Feuillade, M. R., Enria, D. A., Briggiler, A. M., Levis, S. C., Ambrosio, A. M., Halsey, N. A., & Peters, C. J. (1998). Protective efficacy of a live attenuated vaccine against Argentine hemorrhagic fever. AHF Study Group. *Journal of Infectious Diseases, 177,* 277–283.

Margolis, H. S., Alter, M. J., & Hadler, S. C. (1997). Viral hepatitis. In A. S. Evans & R. A. Kaslow (Eds.), *Viral infections of humans: Epidemiology and control* (4th ed., pp. 363–418). New York: Plenum Medical Books.

Markowitz, L. E., Nzilambi, N., Driskell, W. J., Sension, M. G., Rovira, E. Z., Nieburg, P., & Ryder, R. W. (1989). Vitamin A levels and mortality among hospitalized measles patients, Kinshasa, Zaire. *Journal of Tropical Pediatrics, 35,* 109–112.

McCormick, J. B., King, I. J., Webb, P. A., Scribner, C. L., Craven, R. B., Johnson, K. M., Elliott, L. H., & Belmont Williams, R. (1986). Lassa fever: Effective therapy with ribavirin. *New England Journal of Medicine, 314,* 20–26.

McCormick, J. B., Webb, P. A., Krebs, J. W., Johnson, K. M., & Smith, E. S. (1987). A prospective study of the epidemiology and ecology of Lassa fever. *Journal of Infectious Diseases, 155,* 437–444.

Medina, E., & Yrarrazaval, M. (1983). Typhoid fever in Chile: Epidemiological considerations. *Revista Medica de Chile, 111,* 609–615.

Meima, A., Smith, W. C. S., van Oortmarassen, G. J., Richardus, J. H., & Habbema, J. D. F. (2004). The future incidence of leprosy: A scenario analysis. *Bulletin of the World Health Organization, 82,* 373–380.

Monson, M. H., Cole, A. K., Frame, J. D., Serwint, J. R., Alexander, S., & Jahrling, P. B. (1987). Pediatric Lassa fever: A review of 33 Liberian cases. *American Journal of Tropical Medicine and Hygiene, 36,* 408–415.

Moore, P. S. (1992). Meningococcal meningitis in sub-Saharan Africa: A model for the epidemic process. *Clinical Infectious Diseases, 14,* 515–525.

Moorthy, V. S., Good, M. F., & Hill, A. V. (2004). Malaria vaccine developments. *Lancet, 363*(9403), 150–156.

Mulholland, K., Hilton, S., Adegbola, R., Usen, S., Oparaugo, A., Omosigho, C., Weber, M., Palmer, A., Schneider, G., Jobe, K., Lahai, G., & Jaffar, S. (1997). Randomised trial of *Haemophilus influenzae* type b tetanus protein conjugate for prevention of pneumonia and meningitis in Gambian infants. *Lancet, 349,* 1191–1197.

Murray, C. J. L., & Lopez, A. D. (1994). *Global comparative assessments in the health sector: Disease burden, expenditures, and intervention packages. Collected reprints from the Bulletin of the World Health Organization.* Geneva, Switzerland: World Health Organization.

Nair, G. B., Ramamurthy, T., Bhattacharya, S. K., Mukhopadhyay, A. K., Garg, S., Bhattacharya, M. K., Takeda, T., Shimada, T., Takeda, Y., & Deb, B. C. (1994). Spread of *Vibrio cholerae* O139 Bengal in India. *Journal of Infectious Diseases, 169,* 1029–1034.

National Institutes of Health. (2002). NIH consensus statement on management of hepatitis C: 2002. *NIH Consensus and State-of-the-Science Statements, 19*(3), 1–46.

Nelson, K. E., Celentano, D. D., Eiumtrakol, S., Hoover, D. R., Beyrer, C., Suprasert, S., Kuntolbutra, S., & Khamboonruang, C. (1996). Changes in sexual behavior and a decline in HIV infection among young men in Thailand. *New England Journal of Medicine, 335,* 297–303.

Otten, M. W., Jr., Deming, M. S., Jaiteh, K. O., Flagg, E. W., Forgie, I., Sanyang, Y., Sillah, B., Brogan, D., & Gowers, P. (1992). Epidemic poliomyelitis in the Gambia following the control of poliomyelitis as an endemic disease. I. Descriptive findings. *American Journal of Epidemiology, 135,* 381–392.

Pacqué, M., Muñoz, B., Greene, B. M., & Taylor, H. R. (1991). Community-based treatment of onchocerciasis with ivermectin: Safety, efficacy, and acceptability of yearly treatment. *Journal of Infectious Diseases, 163,* 381–385.

Pan America Health Organization. (1994, October). Measles elimination by the year 2000. *EPI Newsletter, 16,* 1–2.

Parashar, U. D., Hummelman, E. G., Bresee, J. S., Miller, M. A., & Glass, R. I. (2003). Global illness and deaths caused by rotavirus disease in children. *Emerging Infectious Diseases, 9,* 565–572.

Patriarca, P. A., Wright, P. F., & John, T. J. (1991). Factors affecting the immunogenicity of oral poliovirus vaccine in developing countries: Review. *Reviews of Infectious Diseases, 13,* 926–939.

Pepin, J., & Meda, H. A. (2001). The epidemiology and control of human African trypanosomiasis. *Advances in Parasitology, 49,* 71–132.

Pepin, J., & Milord, F. (1994). The treatment of human African trypanosomiasis. *Advances in Parasitology, 33,* 1–47.

Perkins, B. A., Broome, C. V., Rosenstein, N. E., Schuchat, A., & Reingold, A. L. (1997). Meningococcal vaccine in sub-Saharan Africa. [Letter]. *Lancet, 350,* 1708.

Perkins, B. A., Zucker, J. R., Otieno, J., Jafari, H. S., Paxton, L., Redd, S. C., Nahlen, B. L., Schwartz, B., Oloo, A. J., Olango, C., Gove, S., & Campbell, C. C. (1997). Evaluation of an algorithm for integrated management of childhood illness in an area of Kenya with high malaria transmission. *Bulletin of the World Health Organization, 75,* 33–42.

Re-emergence of Bolivian hemorrhagic fever. (1994). *Epidemiological Bulletin, 15,* 4–5.

Robbins, J. B., Towne, D. W., Gotschlich, E. C., & Schneerson, R. (1997). Love's labours lost: Failure to implement mass vaccination against group A meningococcal meningitis in sub-Saharan Africa. *Lancet, 350,* 880–882.

Roberts, L. (2004). Polio: The final assault? *Science, 303,* 1960–1971.

Rojanapithayakorn, W., & Hanenberg, R. (1996). The 100% Condom program in Thailand. *AIDS, 10,* 1–7.

Sazawal, S., & Black, R. E. (1992). Meta-analysis of intervention trials on case-management of pneumonia in community settings. *Lancet, 340,* 528–533.

Schofield, F. (1986). Selective primary health care: Strategies for control of disease in the developing world. XXII. Tetanus: A preventable problem. *Reviews of Infectious Diseases, 8,* 144–156.

Selwyn, B. J. (1990). The epidemiology of acute respiratory tract infection in young children: Comparison of findings from several developing countries. Coordinated Data Group of BOSTID Researchers. *Reviews of Infectious Diseases, 12,* S870–S888.

Shaffer, N., Chuachoowong, R., Mock, P. A., Bhadrakom, C., Siriwasin, W., Young, N. L., Chotpitayasunondh, T., Chearskul, S., Roongpisuthipong, A., Chinayon, P., Karon, J., Mastro, T. D., & Simonds, R. J. (1999). Short-course zidovudine for perinatal HIV-1 transmission in Bangkok, Thailand: A randomised controlled trial. *Lancet, 353,* 773–780.

Shann, F. (1986). Etiology of severe pneumonia in children in developing countries. *Pediatric Infectious Disease, 5,* 247–252.

Sinha, A., Sazawal, S., Kumar, R., Sood, S., Reddaiah, V. P., Singh, B., Rao, M., Naficy, A., Clemens, J. D., & Bhan, M. K. (1999). Typhoid fever in children aged less than 5 years. *Lancet, 354,* 734–737.

Smolinski, M. S., Hamburg, M. A., & Lederberg, J. (Eds.). (2003). *Microbial threats to health: Emergence, detection, and response.* Institute of Medicine. Washington, DC: National Academies Press.

Stanfield, J. P., & Galazka, A. (1984). Neonatal tetanus in the world today. *Bulletin of the World Health Organization, 62,* 647–669.

Stein, C., Birmingham, M., Kurian, M., Duclos, P., & Stebel, P. (2000). The global burden of measles in the year 2000—a model using country-specific indicators. *Journal of Infectious Diseases, 187,* S8–S14.

Sutrisna, B., Reingold, A., Kresno, S., Harrison, G., & Utomo, B. (1993). Care-seeking for fatal illnesses in young children in Indramayu, West Java, Indonesia. *Lancet, 342,* 787–789.

Sutter, R. W., Cáceres, V. M., & Mas Lago, P. (2004). The role of routine polio immunization in the post-certification era. *Bulletin of the World Health Organization, 82,* 31–39.

Sutter, R. W., Patriarca, P. A., Brogan, S., Malankar, P. G., Pallansch, M. A., Kew, O. M., Bass, A. G., Cochi, S. L., Alexander, J. P., Hall, D. B., Suleiman, A. J. M., Al-Ghassany, A. A. K., & El-Bualy, M. S. (1991). Outbreak of paralytic poliomyelitis in Oman: Evidence for widespread transmission among fully vaccinated children. *Lancet, 338,* 715–720.

Ter Meulen, J., Lukashevich, I., Sidibe, K., Inapogui, A., Marx, M., Dorlemann, A., Yansane, M. L., Koulemou, K., Chang-Claude, J., & Schmitz, H. (1996). Hunting of peridomestic rodents and consumption of their meat as possible risk factors for rodent-to-human transmission of Lassa virus in the Republic of Guinea. *American Journal of Tropical Medicine and Hygiene, 55,* 661–666.

Trigg, P. I., & Kondrachine, A. V. (1998). Commentary: Malaria control in the 1990s. *Bulletin of the World Health Organization, 76,* 11–16.

UNAIDS. (2002). *Report on the global HIV/AIDS epidemic 2002.* Geneva, Switzerland: UNAIDS/WHO.

UNAIDS. (2004a). *AIDS epidemic update: December 2004.* Geneva, Switzerland: UNAIDS/WHO.

UNAIDS. (2004b). *2004 report on the global AIDS epidemic.* Geneva, Switzerland: UNAIDS/WHO.

University of Zimbabwe/JHPIEGO Cervical Cancer Project. (1999). Visual inspection with acetic acid for cervical cancer screening: Test qualities in a primary-care setting. *Lancet, 353,* 869–873.

Vainio, J., & Cutts, F. (1998). *Yellow fever* (Document WHO/EPI/GEN/98.11). Geneva, Switzerland: World Health Organization.

Vainrub, B., & Salas, R. (1994). Latin American hemorrhagic fever. *Infectious Disease Clinics of North America, 8,* 47–59.

Vinetz, J. M. (2001). Leptospirosis. *Current Opinion in Infectious Diseases, 14*(5), 527–538.

Walsh, J. A. (1983). Selective primary health care: Strategies for control of disease in the developing world. IV. Measles. *Reviews of Infectious Diseases, 5,* 330–340.

Warren, K. S., Bundy, D. A., Anderson, R. M., Davis, A. R., Henderson, D. A., Jamison, D. T., Prescott, N., & Senft, A. (1993). Helminth infection. In D. T. Jamison, W. H. Mosley, A. R. Measham, & J. L. Bobadilla (Eds.), *Disease control priorities in developing countries* (pp. 131–160). New York: Oxford University Press.

Weber, M. W., Mulholland, E. K., Jaffar, S., Troedsson, H., Gove, S., & Greenwood, B. M. (1997). Evaluation of an algorithm for the integrated management of childhood illness in an area with seasonal malaria in the Gambia. *Bulletin of the World Health Organization, 75,* 25–32.

Whalen, C. C., Johnson, J. L., Okwera, A., Hom, D. L., Huebner, R., Mugyenyi, P., Mugerwa, R. D., & Ellner, J. J. (1997). A trial of three regimens to prevent tuberculosis in Ugandan adults infected with the human immunodeficiency virus. Uganda–Case Western Reserve University Research Collaboration. *New England Journal of Medicine, 337,* 801–808.

Wiktor, S. Z., Ekpini, E., Karon, J. M., Nkengasong, J., Maurice, C., Severin, S. T., Roels, T. H., Kouassi, M. K., Lackritz, E. M., Coulibaly, I., & Greenberg, A. E. (1999). Short-course oral zidovudine for prevention of mother-to-child transmission of HIV-1 in Abidjan, Côte d'Ivoire: A randomised trial. *Lancet, 353,* 781–785.

World Health Organization. (1981). Clinical management of acute respiratory infections in children: A WHO memorandum. *Bulletin of the World Health Organization, 59,* 707–716.

World Health Organization. (1985). *Viral haemorrhagic fevers: Report of a WHO Expert Committee* (WHO Technical Report No. 721). Geneva, Switzerland: World Health Organization.

World Health Organization. (1987). *Prevention and control of intestinal parasitic infections: Report of a WHO Expert Committee* (WHO Technical Report No. 749). Geneva, Switzerland: World Health Organization.

World Health Organization. (1991). *Management of patients with sexually transmitted diseases: Report of a WHO Study Group* (WHO Technical Report No. 810). Geneva, Switzerland: World Health Organization.

World Health Organization. (1993). *Control of schistosomiasis: The second report of the WHO Expert Committee* (WHO Technical Report No. 830). Geneva, Switzerland: World Health Organization.

World Health Organization. (1994). Expanded programme on immunization, Global Advisory Group. Part II. Achieving the major disease control goals. *Weekly Epidemiological Record, 69,* 29–31, 34–35.

World Health Organization. (1995). *Control of epidemic meningococcal disease: WHO practical guidelines.* Lyon, France: World Health Organization and Fondation Marcel Mérieux.

World Health Organization. (1997a). Hepatitis C. *Weekly Epidemiological Record, 72,* 65–69.

World Health Organization. (1997b). Hepatitis C: Global prevalence. *Weekly Epidemiological Record, 72,* 341–344.

World Health Organization. (1997c). World malaria situation in 1994. Part I. Population at risk. *Weekly Epidemiological Record, 72,* 269–274.

World Health Organization. (1998a). *Action programme for the elimination of leprosy: Status report 1998* (Document WHO/LEP/98.2). Geneva, Switzerland: World Health Organization.

World Health Organization. (1998b). *Control and surveillance of African trypanosomiasis* (WHO Technical Report No. 881). Geneva, Switzerland: World Health Organization.

World Health Organization. (1998c). *EPI information system: Global summary, September 1998* (Document WHO/EPI/GEN/98.10). Geneva, Switzerland: World Health Organization.

World Health Organization. (1998d). Yellow fever, 1996–1997. Part II. *Weekly Epidemiological Record, 73,* 370–372.

World Health Organization. (1998e). *Yellow fever technical consensus meeting* (Document WHO/EPI/GEN/98.08). Geneva, Switzerland: World Health Organization.

World Health Organization. (1999a). Orphan drug finds home [press release]. http://www.who.int/inf-pr-1999/en/pr99-74.html.

World Health Organization. (1999b). *Removing obstacles to healthy development* (Document WHO/CDS/99.1). Geneva, Switzerland: World Health Organization.

World Health Organization. (2001). *Introduction of hepatitis B vaccine into childhood immunization services* (Document WHO/V&B/01.31). Geneva, Switzerland: World Health Organization, Department of Vaccines and Biologicals.

World Health Organization. (2002a). Dengue prevention and control. *Weekly Epidemiological Record, 77*(6), 41–44.

World Health Organization. (2002b). Global distribution of hepatitis A, B, and C, 2001. *Weekly Epidemiological Record, 77*(6), 45–47.

World Health Organization. (2002c). *Prevention and control of schistosomiasis and soil-transmitted helminthiasis* (WHO Technical Report No. 912). Geneva, Switzerland: World Health Organization.

World Health Organization. (2002d). Rabies vaccines. *Weekly Epidemiological Record, 77*(14), 109–120.

World Health Organization. (2003a). *Africa malaria report 2003.* Geneva, Switzerland: World Health Organization/UNICEF.

World Health Organization. (2003b). Global progress towards universal childhood hepatitis B vaccination, 2003. *Weekly Epidemiological Record, 78*(42), 365–372.

World Health Organization. (2003c). Human plague in 2000 and 2001. *Weekly Epidemiological Record, 78*(16), 129–136.

World Health Organization. (2004a). *Chagas: Burdens and trends.* http://www.who.int/ctd/chagas/burdens.htm.

World Health Organization. (2004b). *Chagas: Recent epidemiological data*. http://www.who.int/ctd/chagas/epidemio.htm.

World Health Organization. (2004c). Dracunculiasis eradication. *Weekly Epidemiological Record, 79*(19), 181–192.

World Health Organization. (2004d). Investing in a comprehensive health sector response to HIV/AIDS: Scaling up treatment and accelerating prevention. *WHO HIV/AIDS plan*. Geneva, Switzerland: Author. Retrieved from

http://www.who.int/entity/3by5/en/HIV_AIDSplan.pdf.

World Health Organization Expert Committee on Leprosy. (1998). *Seventh report* (WHO Technical Report No. 874). Geneva, Switzerland: World Health Organization.

World Health Organization, UNAIDS, Global Fund, & U. S. Government. (2005). 700,000 people living with AIDS in developing countries now receiving treatment [Joint media release]. Retrieved from http://www.who.int/mediacentre/news/releases/2005/pro07/en.

5

Nutrition

KEITH P. WEST, JR., BENJAMIN CABALLERO, AND ROBERT E. BLACK

Nutritional concerns in low-income countries are diverse, ranging from deprivation, hunger, and consequent deficiencies that impair health, quality of life, and survival to a rising tide of obesity and ensuing risks of chronic disease in some regions. Undernutrition, reflected by high prevalences of wasting, stunting, and micronutrient deficiencies, is the predominant form of malnutrition throughout southern Asia and most of sub-Saharan Africa, while overweight status and obesity, often coexisting with stunting and micronutrient malnutrition, is an emerging concern in a number of regions, especially Latin America, northern Africa, the Middle East, and Central and East Asia.

Undernutrition has long been considered to represent both a consequence and cause of poor human health, development, and achievement throughout life (Administrative Committee on Coordination/Sub-Committee on Nutrition [ACC/ SCN], 2000; World Bank, 1993; World Health Organization [WHO], 2002). Although severe, wasting malnutrition, evident by classic clinical signs, can have profound effects on health and survival, it is becoming rare beyond areas of conflict and famine. More prevalent are less apparent, "hidden" forms of undernourishment with respect to energy, protein, and micronutrients that can adversely affect population distributions of child growth, development, and quality of life, impair resistance to infection, and decrease chances of survival. Groups at highest risk of undernutrition are the impoverished, who lack food security and the necessary resources to adequately feed and care for themselves. Within a population, groups at highest risk of undernutrition are those who, at certain stages in their lives, are exposed to its causes and most vulnerable to its consequences: the fetus, infants and

preschool-aged children, women of reproductive age, and older persons (Chilima & Ismail, 1998; Roubenoff, 2000), the last being the most rapidly growing demographic group in the world but who, at present, remain outside the reach of most nutrition policy initiatives.

Overnutrition largely affects groups or societies caught in a *nutrition transition:* a process marked by a shift in diet away from traditional staple diets toward more processed foods of higher energy (calorie) density from fat and refined sugars and decreased dietary fiber and roughage, coupled with lifestyle changes that lead to reductions in physical activity (ACC/SCN, 2000; Popkin, 1999). The nutrition transition parallels and is part of rapid economic, demographic, and health transitions under way in many previously underdeveloped societies. Although the rise from dietary deficit to one of relative adequacy in society has likely contributed to improved health and longevity across the globe (Popkin, 1999), excessive shifts toward overconsumption and inactivity along with other exposures of industrialization can increase the risk of degenerative, cardiovascular, and neoplastic (i.e., noncommunicable) diseases, which are rapidly becoming leading causes of adult morbidity and mortality throughout middle-income countries (James et al., 2004; WHO, 2002; World Bank, 1993).

The diversity and breadth of nutritional status in practically all countries, and the urgency to act to correct malnutrition, have been brought to the global development and political stages over the past 30 years in the form of several sequential and reinforcing international conferences directed toward improving food and nutritional conditions in the world and containing declarations of intent, strategic plans of action, follow-up planning sessions, and plans for monitoring member state compliance. Initial momentum provided by the World Food Conference in Rome in 1974, which issued a global call to abolish hunger and malnutrition (United Nations, 1982), stimulated the National Academy of Sciences in the United States to conduct the World Food and Nutrition Study in 1975 that concluded "in developing countries, effective nutrition interventions are likely to have more of an effect on human health than comparable investments in medical care" (National Research Council, 1977). These and other early convenings helped to develop the political will and evidence bases for global meetings that have served to coalesce global attention, commitment, and, gradually, action in recent years achieved through the World Summit for Children, International Conference on Nutrition, World Food Congress and Millenium Development Conference (Exhibit 5-1).

This chapter addresses nutritional problems of low-income countries that are motivating concern, research, and national and international response. These include the extent and causes of undernutrition, including its component protein-energy malnutrition, and deficiencies of multiple micronutrients (especially vitamin A, zinc, iron, and iodine) at vulnerable stages of life (especially in infants, children, during pregnancy and lactation, and at older ages); the basis for the food insecurity that envelopes malnutrition in most societies; interactions of nutrition and infection of public health consequence; roles of breastfeeding and complementary feeding in assuring healthy children; and seminal facets of the nutrition transition, including evidence of its origins in early life and adult manifestations of obesity and noncommunicable diseases. Throughout the chapter attention is drawn to approaches to prevention, where possible, taking into consideration the context of other health priorities, interventions, and development capacity.

Food Security

Food security exists when all people have reliable access to a sufficient amount of nutritious, safe, and culturally appropriate food. *Food insecurity*, then, refers to a state of chronic, deprived economic or physical access to food, either in quantity or quality, such that dietary intake fails to meet nutritional needs

---

Exhibit 5-1   The Art of Nutrition Policy Making and Advocacy Within the United Nations

Over the past 25 years, United Nations agencies have pressed the world to pay attention to the health and nutrition of children and women, motivated by recognized opportunities to improve health, survival, and quality of life, especially in disadvantaged societies. During the International Year of the Child of 1978, UNICEF rallied global attention concerning the neglect and nutritional plight of children, especially those in poor societies. A decade later, at the World Summit for Children, sponsored by UNICEF in New York in September 1989, 179 heads of state gathered to craft, sign, and commit to the principles and action plan of the Declaration on the Rights of the Child (UNICEF, 1991), which specified health and nutritional goals to achieve by the year 2000 that included a reduction in child mortality.

At the first-ever International Conference on Nutrition (ICN) held in Rome in 1992, and during the three years of national and regional preparations that preceded it, the Food and Agriculture Organization (FAO) and World Health Organization (WHO) seized the global momentum to secure ministerial commitments and signatures from 159 countries to a World Declaration and Plan of Action to develop goals for improving the nutritional health in their citizenry, especially vulnerable groups. Governments pledged to eliminate, before the year 2000, (1) famine and famine-related deaths, (2) starvation and nutritional deficiency diseases in communities affected by natural and human-made disasters, and (3) iodine and vitamin A deficiencies and to develop and implement national nutrition plans based on situational analyses within each country, using the ICN Plan of Action as a guide (Food and Agriculture Organization, 1992).

The World Food Summit, hosted by the FAO in Rome in 1996, seized momentum from the ICN and extended the timeline for governments to reduce, this time by 2015, the number of undernourished people in the world by half using 1990–1992 as the "baseline period" (World Food Summit, 1996), giving a sense of progress achieved toward a repackaged and longer-term goal.

This goal became the first of eight Millennium Development Goals (MDGs)—namely, to "halve the proportion of people who suffer from hunger by the year 2015"—that were adopted by world leaders at the United Nations Millennium Summit in September 2000 (United Nations, 2000). Subsequently, the World Bank and International Monetary Fund's Millennium Project—a network of policy makers, experts, and task forces—began meeting annually to manage and oversee strategies for achieving the MDGs (United Nations, 2004). Notwithstanding difficulties in definition and measurement, this advocacy process has led to many countries adopting and implementing elements of national nutrition policies that did not exist two decades ago.

and support the health of all individuals in a household or community. However, the concept extends to entire populations and to regions.

Food balance sheets maintained by the Food and Agriculture Organization (FAO) of the United Nations offer a composite view of the sufficiency and differences in regional availability that, when viewed over time, provide estimates of both status and trends (STAT) in gross levels of food security (FAOSTAT, n.d.). Estimates of kilocalories of energy and grams of protein per capita provide population growth–adjusted proxies for total food availability, while the latter also addresses a facet of nutritional quality of the food supply.

Table 5-1 indicates that, over a 10-year period from 1992 to 2002, world food production and availability increased approximately 5% on a per capita basis, with regional estimates ranging from no ap-

parent change in caloric availability in Central America to an 8% gain in North America. Protein availability increased by a similar percentage (6%) globally, with the largest relative gains seen in South America (+12%) and developing (or low-income) countries in general (+10%). However, regional disparities in calorie and protein availability that were evident in the early 1990s were virtually the same a decade later. For example, the per capita energy supply for sub-Saharan Africa remained just below 80% of the world average over the decade, at 2,346 kilcalories (kcal), or approximately 12% more than a full daily ration defined under disaster feeding conditions (WHO, 2000), while the European Union remained constant at 127% of the global average. Only in industrialized North America was there a substantial increase in food energy, from 129% to 134% of the world average, reflecting a per capita food energy

Table 5-1	Energy and Protein Supply on a Per Capita Per Day Basis, by Region of the World, Based on Food Balance Sheets of the Food and Agriculture Organization					
	Energy Supply (kcal)			Protein Supply (g)		
Region	1992	2002	Percent Change	1992	2002	Percent Change
World	2,708 (100)	2,804 (100)	+4	71 (100)	75 (100)	+6
Africa	2,346 (87)	2,425 (86)	+3	58 (82)	61 (81)	+5
sub-Saharan Africa	2,126 (78)	2,207 (79)	+4	51 (72)	54 (72)	+6
Asia	2,581 (95)	2,696 (96)	+4	65 (92)	70 (93)	+8
South America	2,703 (100)	2,851 (102)	+5	69 (97)	77 (103)	+12
North and Central America	3,260 (120)	3,449 (123)	+6	96 (135)	101 (135)	+5
North America, developed	3,492 (129)	3,756 (134)	+8	108 (152)	113 (150)	+5
Central America	2,935 (108)	2,941 (105)	0	77 (108)	83 (111)	+8
European Union	3,445 (127)	3,522 (127)	+2	104 (146)	108 (144)	+4
Developed countries	3,221 (119)	3,414 (122)	+6	98 (138)	100 (133)	+2
Developing countries	2,550 (94)	2,666 (95)	+5	63 (89)	69 (92)	+10

Note: Numbers in parentheses indicate percentages of the world per capita figures for 1992 and 2002, respectively.
Source: FAOSTAT data for 2004. http://faostat.fao.org/.

supply that is 70% greater than in sub-Saharan Africa. Thus, while overall, availability of food increased relative to population growth and improved in quality in most regions of the world, gross interregional inequities were unaltered. Although informative, food balance data remain crude indicators because the FAO regional divisions as defined for these estimates mask extensive within-region variation in food security as well as socioeconomic and other microlevel disparities in access.

At a more tangible level, causes of food insecurity can vary widely according to degree of urban/rural residence, socioeconomic exposures (e.g., prevailing food prices, adequacy of local food production, and trade and transport infrastructure) (Bouis, 1999), and level of disruption due to civil instability and conflict (Toole & Waldman, 1993; Yip & Sharp, 1993).

Although inequities of intrahousehold feeding can lead to poor nutrition of disfavored members (e.g., female children in some societies), as a public health problem undernutrition can usually be traced to chronic food insecurity at household, community, or larger aggregate levels of society.

Conceptual Models

Two conceptual models in common use help to visualize the continuum from food insecurity to undernutrition, the causal factors involved, and consequences. One, adapted from UNICEF (Figure 5-1), unites diverse basic (or root), underlying, and immediate causes of food insecurity and disease into a hierarchical causal path to undernutrition and its effects on health and disease (UNICEF, 1997). Implied in this model is the realization that there is no single cause of undernour-

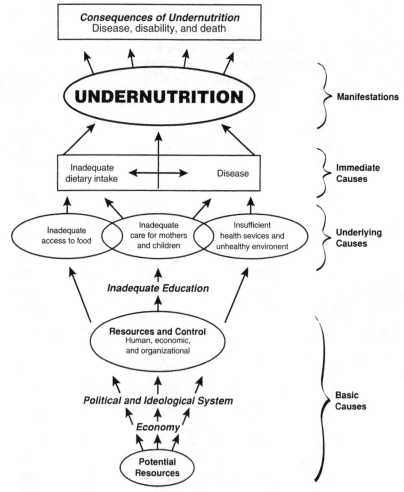

Figure 5-1 UNICEF Conceptual Model of the Causation of Undernutrition, Modified to Include Consequences. *Source:* UNICEF, *The State of the World's Children 1998* (New York: Oxford University Press, 1998), p. 24. Reprinted with permission.

ishment, but rather a set of contributing factors that vary in intensity, duration, specificity, and proximity to the undernourished individual. Another approach is to view the interacting forces as "component causes" that can unite in various ways to form a "completed" cause of undernutrition (Rothman & Greenland, 1998). Which are operating and how they interact determine the type and severity of malnutrition and the health or functional consequences, and offer insight into prevention.

For example, wasting malnutrition (defined later in this chapter) in a given set of children can result from being fed a diet chronically lacking sufficient energy and nutrient density, intensified by frequent episodes of diarrhea. Improving either of these conditions could prevent or lessen the severity of undernutrition. Both proximal conditions, however, arise from impoverished, food-insecure, and unhygienic conditions in the home or poor access to treatment, stemming from lack of family resources, due to poor education and unemployment, or of community resources (nonavailability of health care, poorly stocked food markets), providing modifiable underlying

causes that, if one or more were improved, could lower exposure to diarrhea or improve quality of diet. Underlying causes occur, in part, because of membership in particular social, cultural, or economic classes that have little influence on governance and control of resources. Typically, immediate and underlying causes operate through women, who as mothers serve as caretakers, allocators of food, and managers of resources in the household, suggesting that improving the status, education, and economic and political empowerment of women—addressing gender-related causes at nearly every level—could interrupt causal paths that lead to both child and maternal malnutrition (Haddad, 1999).

The second model illustrates a set of causes that affect individuals during different stages of the life cycle, and from generation to generation, within impoverished and chronically food-insecure families and communities (Figure 5-2). In this model, liveborn infants who may be growth retarded and developmentally delayed due to undernutrition face a sequence of nutritional, health, and developmental insults, compounded by deprived care and other resources, throughout

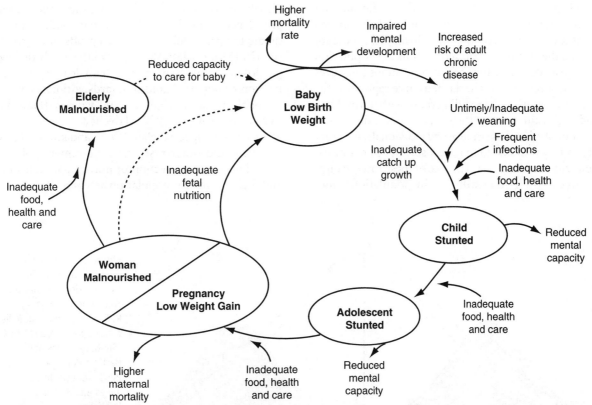

Figure 5-2 Conceptual Model of the Effects of Undernutrition Throughout the Life Cycle. *Source:* Administrative Committee on Coordination/Subcommittee on Nutrition, *Fourth Report on the World Nutrition Situation: Nutrition Throughout the Life Cycle* (Washington, DC: International Food Policy Research Institute, 2000). Reprinted with permission.

childhood, adolescence, and, for women, into the reproductive years (affecting offspring), as well as the vulnerable older years of life (ACC/SCN, 2000). It identifies times in the life cycle when malnutrition occurs, as well as potentially responsive causes and intermediate outcomes that could be altered by effective and timely intervention.

Population Spectrum of Nutritional Status

Although individuals usually must be exposed to poor diet, disease, and neglect over time to become malnourished, viewing the spectrum of nutritional status at a point in time (cross sectionally) provides the basis for quantifying the type, extent, and other aspects of malnutrition in the population. In this respect, the term *malnutrition* literally does not differentiate *undernutrition* from *overnutrition* (the former referring to deficiency states of energy, protein, or micronutrients, and the latter typically referring to states of excess energy stores), though its usage is most often linked with protein-energy malnutrition. Thus, in a single population three distributions can be envisioned with respect to nutritional status: those who are (1) normal, (2) undernourished or deficient, and (3) overnourished or obese, hypothetically illustrated in Figure 5-3. The overarching bell-shaped curve represents the status of all individuals in the population with respect to any number of continuous measures of nutritional status. The dashed curve represents the normally nourished, including those with normal low and high values, while the smaller curves depict undernourished and overnourished individuals. Intensity of shading is intended to reflect severity of malnutrition within each group. The size of these three groups relative to each other will vary by population under study (by region, socioeconomic status, age, gender, and other factors).

Neither malnourished group in Figure 5-3 can be perfectly identified, necessitating reliance on indicators of status, with cutoffs applied to define and estimate prevalence and, when combined with population data, numbers affected. It can be seen that drawing a cutoff line through either tail of the overall distribution to estimate proportions malnourished leads to classifying truly malnourished and truly normal individuals as being "malnourished" (true and false positives, respectively) and being "normal" (false and true negatives, respectively), revealing the challenges of nutritional assessment when the aim is to estimate prevalence, screen individuals for treatment or prevention, monitor shifts in proportions malnourished over time, or evaluate community program impact on malnutrition, since true distributions are rarely known.

Estimates of prevalence can be adjusted to remove the influence of misclassification and obtain the percentage of individuals lying outside a referent distribution (*standardized prevalence*) when indicator performance is known (i.e., sensitivity and specificity against a gold standard) and when the test and referent measurement values are assumed to be normally distributed (Figure 5-4). However, the standardized prevalence cannot be used to screen individuals or estimate the prevalence at specific cutoffs of degree of severity (Mora, 1989; WHO, 1995a). Clearly defined purposes for assessment that can lead to identification of potential gold standards, estimates of nutritional indicator reliability and validity (Habicht, Meyers, & Brownie, 1982; Habicht & Pelletier, 1990; Marks, Habicht, & Mueller, 1989), and knowledge of technical and other resource requirements ideally should inform the selection of nutritional indicators and their cutoffs for population assessment.

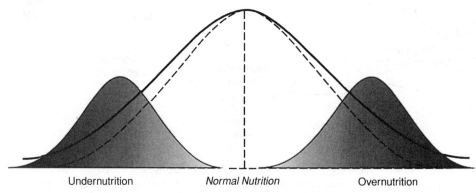

Undernutrition   *Normal Nutrition*   Overnutrition

Population Distribution

Figure 5-3 Spectrum of Nutritional Status in a Hypothetical Population. *Source*: M. H. Merson, R. E. Black, and A. J. Mills, *International Public Health* (Sudbury: Jones and Bartlett Publishers, Inc., 2001). Copyright 2001 by Jones and Bartlett Publishers, Inc. Reprinted with permission.

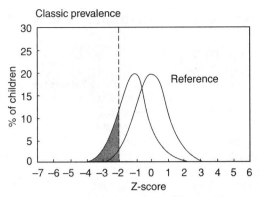
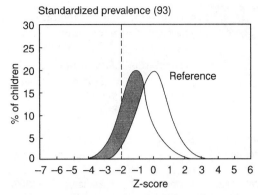

Figure 5-4 Classic and Standardized Approaches for Estimating Prevalence of Malnutrition, Illustrated with Undernutrition. *Source:* World Health Organization. (1995). *Physical status: The use and interpretation of anthropometry* (WHO Technical Report No. 854). Geneva: World Health Organization.

Undernutrition

Undernutrition inevitably represents a combination of deficiencies in energy, protein, and micronutrients, with manifestations that most often involve anthropometric deficit but may also include, depending on severity and duration, altered body composition (i.e., proportion of fat and lean mass), low tissue nutrient concentrations (e.g., plasma micronutrients), clinical signs (e.g., pedal edema), functional impairment (e.g., immune dysfunction), or other less specific indices of poor health (e.g., infection).

Protein-Energy Malnutrition

Acute or chronic protein-energy malnutrition (PEM) is usually considered the dominant cause of undernutrition. Universally, assessment of mild to moderate PEM in populations relies on comparative anthropometry, well-standardized procedures for measuring weight, length, or height, middle upper arm circumference (MUAC), and skinfolds at the tricipital and subscapular sites (Cameron, 1978; Gibson, 1990; Lohman, Roche, & Martorell, 1988). Composite indicators of weight, length, or height for age and weight for height, with cutoffs to define extremes of nutritional status, are derived from normative, gender-specific reference population data (Frisancho, 1981; WHO, 1995a), now maintained and freely available from WHO on the Web (www.who.int/nutgrowthdb). Anthropometric indicator cutoffs for estimating the prevalence of different aspects of undernutrition are conventionally based on standardized cutoffs (i.e., standard normal deviations, or Z-scores) below the median (Waterlow et al., 1977), which permit a child's status to be evaluated in the context of a reference distribution. Also in use at times are status values expressed as percentages of a referent median and, for relatively age-independent measures (e.g., MUAC from 1 to 5 years of age), absolute values (Table 5-2).

The weight of a child's age expressed as a standard normal deviation (Z-score) from the median weight of children of the same gender and month of age in the referent distribution (WHO, 1995a; WHO Global Database on Child Growth and Malnutrition, 2005), or weight for age, is the most commonly used indicator for assessing nutritional status and monitoring the growth of children (de Onis, Wijnhoven, & Onyango, 2004). Although low weight on its own does not differentiate between thinness (wasting) and stunting, both of which contribute to a low weight for age, underweight status, conventionally classified as Z-scores below −2, remains the dominant cause of disease burden (Ezzati et al., 2002). Child length (for those younger than 2 years) or height (for those older than 2 years), compared to the referent gender value for age, reveals the adequacy of linear growth (Hamill et al., 1979; WHO, 1995a). Stunting, discerned by a child's stature being 2 Z-scores below the median, reflects the growth consequences of chronic PEM (Waterlow et al., 1977). Because linear growth deceleration is a gradual process, stunting is often associated with other indicators of poverty and neglect (Martorell, Mendoza, & Castillo, 1988; Zeyre & McIntyre, 2003). Wasting, revealed by a child's weight being less than 2 Z-scores below the referent weight for the same height, identifies acute PEM (Waterlow et al., 1977), although in undernourished populations wasting can also persist in children for long periods of time. A MUAC measurement can detect a thin arm (e.g., less than 12.5 cm for a child 1 to 5 years

Table 5-2	Common Anthropometric Indicators with Cross-Sectional Cutoffs for Classifying Preschool Children by Severity of Undernutrition					
			Degree of Severity			
Indicator	**Interpretation**	**Classification System**	**Severe**	**Moderate to Severe**	**Mild or Worse**	**References**
Weight for age	Underweight	% Median	<60%	<75%	<90%	Gomez et al., 1956; Jelliffe, 1966
		Standardized	−3 Z	−2 Z	−1 Z	Hamill et al., 1979; Waterlow et al., 1977; WHO, 1995a
Height for age Length for age	Stunting	% Median	<85%	<90%	<95%	Jelliffe, 1966
		Standardized	−3 Z	−2 Z	−1 Z	Hamill et al., 1979; Waterlow et al., 1977; WHO, 1995a
Weight for height	Wasting	% Median	<70%	<80%	<90%	Jelliffe, 1966
		Standardized	−3 Z	−2 Z	−1 Z	Hamill et al., 1979; Waterlow et al., 1977; WHO, 1995a
MUAC	Wasting	Absolute	<11.5 cm	<12.5 cm	<13.5 cm	West et al., 1991

Notes: Cutoffs between classification systems are only approximately equal. The moderate to severe cutoff below −2 Z is conventionally used to define prevalence of underweight, stunting, and wasting. Comparisons are most suitable for children 12 to 59 months of age; below 12 months, care should be taken in interpreting populations against the current WHO reference (Victora et al., 1998; WHO, 1995a).

MUAC = middle upper arm circumference.

The NCHS (National Center for Health Statistics)/WHO reference anthropometric database for classifying, as well as ANTHRO software for analyzing, the status of local child populations using the standardized system can be accessed at http:/www.who.int/nutgrowthdb.

of age) and is an alternative indicator of wasting (Jelliffe, 1966; WHO, 1995a). When MUAC and a tricipital skinfold are both measured, upper arm muscle and fat areas can be calculated by standard formulas (Frisancho, 1981; Heymsfield et al., 1982), providing a relative measure of body composition that is in common use in population assessment (Hediger et al., 1998; Rivera et al., 1998; West, 1986).

While milder stages of PEM are often clinically inapparent (Figure 5-5, left child), severe PEM refers to two clinically distinct presentations, marasmus and kwashiorkor, and a mixed form, marasmic kwashiorkor. Marasmus, which typically occurs in infancy, is marked by severe wasting that is grossly clinically evident, accompanied by a weight for height usually below −3 Z-scores from loss of muscle and adipose; a resultant "baggy" appearance to the skin; moderate to severe stunting from a near cessation of linear growth; soft, sparse hair; absence of edema; alertness; and hunger (Reddy, 1991) (Figure 5-5, right child). *Kwashiorkor* is a Ghanain Ge tribal term for a condition that develops when the older child is displaced from the breast (Williams, 1933). As implied by the term, children 2 to 3 years of age are at highest risk of this condition. It is evident by edema (an essential feature), milder wasting, reddish hair changes, enlarged liver, frequent dermatosis (flaky-paint rash), and a state of misery and disinterest in food (Reddy, 1991). Children with either condition are at high risk for corneal xerophthalmia due to severe vitamin A deficiency (Sommer & West, 1996). Although both conditions are

considered to be caused by severe deficiencies in energy and protein, their distinct clinical and biochemical profiles (Torun & Chew, 1999) suggest this is an oversimplification, with differences in other nutrient deficiencies and oxidative stress offering potential explanations (Golden, 2002). Because of severe PEM's rare occurrence, outside of famine and other complex emergency conditions (Young et al., 2004), and high case fatality ratios (CFRs) when it does occur (Brown et al., 1981), population prevalence rates of severe PEM in most low-income countries are extremely low.

Extent of Undernutrition

The general magnitude of preschool child undernutrition can be gauged, nationally and by region, by indicators of prevalence of underweight, wasted, and stunted status, representing the global status around the year 1995 (Table 5-3) (de Onis & Blossner, 2000; de Onis et al., 2004a, 2004b). The largest percentages and numbers of undernourished children reside in South Central Asia (a UN subregion that includes India, Sri Lanka, Bangladesh, Nepal, Pakistan, Afghanistan, and Iran), where 45% of preschoolers are estimated to be underweight and stunted and 15% wasted. With 33% of the developing world's children, this region harbors 55%, 45%, and 55% of the global burden of underweight, stunted, and wasted children, respectively. Although high, regional redefinition masks still higher prevalence rates that continue to exist in South Asia (the Indian subcon-

Figure 5-5 Mild PEM (Clinically Normal Appearance) and Marasmus (Evident by Extreme Wasting of Limbs and Torso) in 1-Year-Old Bangladeshi Children. *Note:* The child on the left is a boy; the child on the right is a girl. *Source:* Photograph by K. P. West, Jr.

tinent), where surveyed prevalences of low weight for age exceed 50%, in contrast to rates of 4% to 18% in Central Asian member states in this region (WHO Global Database, 2005). Rates of underweight status among children in Southeast Asia (encompassing Indonesia, the Philippines, and the Indo-China peninsula) are presently about one-third lower than those observed in South Central Asia. In eastern Asia (predominantly China, with Japan and South Korea) and western Asia (most of the Middle East), childhood undernutrition is even lower, about one-third to one-half the burden reported among children in South Central Asia. Despite the continued burden of undernutrition, however, the prevalence of low weight for age among preschool Asian children is expected to decline considerably by the year 2015, based on trend analysis projections, to be nearly half of the levels observed in 1990 (de Onis et al., 2004a), signaling the potential for this massive region to

achieve the Millennium Development Goals target of reducing the prevalence of preschool child undernutrition during this period by 50%. Although all subregions appear poised to substantially contribute to the anticipated overall reduction, the greatest progress toward this goal is expected to be in eastern Asia, where the prevalence is projected to fall 84%, from 19% in 1990 to 3% in 2015 (de Onis et al., 2004a), a decline that raises concern about obesity becoming a public health problem in this subregion over the next two decades (Du et al., 2002).

In contrast to Asia, nutritional conditions have deteriorated over the past decade across most of sub-Saharan Africa, including eastern, middle, and western Africa plus the Sudan, where summaries in Table 5-3 show that approximately 27% of preschoolers are underweight, 34% to 44% are stunted, and 3% to 16% are wasted (de Onis & Blossner, 2000; de Onis et al., 2004b). While early childhood wasting rates generally remain lower across Africa than in South Asia, the HIV/AIDS epidemic in Africa is expected to continue taking its nutritional toll on infected children and their families, with new generations of orphans and communities economically decimated by the disease (Anabwani & Navario, 2005). These effects, combined with the consequences of conflict (Salama et al., 2004), other governance and infrastructural problems, and survey trend data to date, indicate that nutritional status will either change little or continue to deteriorate through the year 2015, especially throughout eastern and sub-Saharan Africa (de Onis et al., 2004a).

The nature of undernutrition is quite different in Latin America and the Caribbean, where young children tend to be mildly underweight and moderately stunted, and tend to be more overweight for height than wasted (see Table 5-3) (addressed in a later section). The health consequences associated with undernutrition are considered next.

Undernutrition as a Risk Factor for Infection and Related Mortality

Undernutrition must be considered as a possible risk factor for infectious morbidity and associated case fatality among children in low-income countries. Because gestational age and size for gestational age are possibly correlated with nutritional status during early childhood, it is appropriate to consider these as part of a continuum of possible risk. Nevertheless, studies have generally examined separately the risk related to status at birth in the neonatal or infant period and the risk related to nutritional status throughout childhood, at least up to age 5 years.

| Table 5-3 | Regional Prevalence and Numbers of Underweight, Stunted, Wasted, and Overweight Preschool-Aged Children |

UN Region[a]	Underweight		Stunted		Wasted		Overweight	
	%	No. ($\times 10^6$)	%	No. ($\times 10^6$)	%	No. ($\times 10^6$)	%	No. ($\times 10^6$)
Africa	**23.9**	**27.8**	**36.1**	**41.9**	**9.6**	**11.1**	**3.9**	**4.5**
Eastern	27.9	10.9	44.4	17.3	7.0	2.7	NA	—
Middle	26.9	4.2	40.0	6.3	8.6	1.4	NA	—
Northern	10.9	2.3	24.4	5.1	7.2	1.5	8.1	1.6
Southern	13.9	0.8	25.0	1.4	2.9	0.2	6.5	0.4
Western	27.5	9.6	33.8	11.8	15.6	5.3	2.6	0.9
Asia	**31.5**	**116.3**	**35.4**	**130.8**	**10.4**	**37.9**	**2.9**	**10.6**
Eastern	13.2	14.5	21.5	23.5	3.4	3.7	4.3	4.7
South Central	45.2	80.9	45.2	81.0	15.4	27.3	2.1	3.7
Southeastern	31.2	18.1	36.8	21.0	10.4	5.8	2.4	1.3
Western	12.1	2.8	21.7	5.0	5.1	1.1	NA	—
Latin America and the Caribbean	**7.3**	**4.0**	**15.9**	**8.8**	**2.9**	**1.6**	**4.4**	**2.4**
Caribbean	7.8	0.3	9.6	0.4	NA	—	NA	—
Central America	10.7	1.7	23.0	3.7	4.9	0.8	3.5	5.6
South America	5.7	2.0	13.3	4.7	1.8	0.6	4.9	1.7
Developing countries	**27.3**	**148.2**	**33.5**	**181.5**	**9.4**	**50.6**	**3.3**	**17.6**
Developed countries[b]	**1.4**	**1.0**	**2.8**	**2.0**	**0.7**	**0.5**	**4.5**	**3.9**

Notes: Prevalence is the percentage below −2 standard normal deviations (SND) from the WHO/NCHS reference (median) value of weight for age (underweight), height for age (stunted), and weight for height (wasted), and above 2 SND from the reference value of weight for height (overweight), from national surveys, averaged for the year 1995, of children younger than 6 years in 139 countries (de Onis et al., 2004a, 2004b), except for estimates of the prevalence of overweight, which are based on national surveys from 79 countries (de Onis & Blossner, 2000).

NA = not available

[a]Member states within each region can be retrieved at http://esa.un.org/unup/index.asp?panel=5.

[b]Developed country prevalence estimates for wasting and overweight are based on a national survey of children aged 2 to 59 months in the United States as of 1994 (NCHS/CDC, 1994), which were applied against the developed country population estimates.

Low Birth Weight

Low birth weight is usually defined as a weight at birth less than 2,500 grams (approximately 5 lb, 14 oz). The incidence of low-weight births varies inversely with level of economic development (ACC/SCN, 1992), as does the proportion of these births that is due to fetal malnutrition (i.e., intrauterine growth retardation) versus preterm delivery of less than 37 weeks' gestation (de Onis, Blossner, & Villar, 1998). Intrauterine growth retardation is usually defined as a birth that is more than 2 standard deviations (SDs) below the median weight expected for that gestational age (or, alternatively but not equivalently, below the 10th percentile). The rate of low-birth-weight deliveries in low- and middle-income countries ranges from approximately 10% in most countries in Latin America to 30% to 50% in South Asian countries (de Onis, Blossner, & Villar, 1998). In settings with a high incidence of low birth weight, two-thirds or more of these low-weight births are due to intrauterine growth retardation. In settings with a low inci-

dence of low birth weight, most are due to preterm delivery.

To examine the role of nutritional risk factors for morbidity and mortality, it is important to evaluate births that have intrauterine growth retardation. Unfortunately, many of the studies provide information only on low-birth-weight births rather than distinguishing these by the cause of the low weight. Low-birth-weight babies have the largest increase in risk during the neonatal period, and they continue to have additional risk in the postneonatal period of infancy. In high-income countries, birth weights of 3,500 to 4,500 grams (7 lb, 11 oz to 9 lb, 14 oz) are associated with the lowest risk of neonatal mortality. The relative risk of neonatal mortality increases with birth weights below 2,500 grams and increases even more for very low-birth-weight babies of less than 1,500 grams (3 lb, 3 oz) (Ashworth, 1998).

In low-income countries, the data are more limited due to the difficulty of obtaining accurate birth-weight measurements for deliveries that are predominantly in the home. In most low-income-country populations, at least 20% to 40% of births are classified as low birth weight, which appears to be predominantly due to intrauterine growth retardation. In these settings, the neonatal mortality rates range to 50 deaths per 1,000 live births and increase with decreasing birth weight. In two studies that were able to cross-classify births by nutritional status for gestational age (to determine if the birth had intrauterine growth retardation) and gestational age, the results varied substantially. In Brazil, babies with intrauterine growth retardation had a fivefold increase in the risk of death (Barros et al., 1987), whereas in Bangladesh the risk was only slightly increased (El-Arifeen, 1997). During the postneonatal period, low-weight births continued to have higher mortality than babies born with a higher weight. Again, the data are limited, but in Brazil babies born with intrauterine growth retardation had a fourfold increase in postneonatal mortality, and such births in Bangladesh had about a 50% increase in postneonatal deaths (Barros et al., 1987; El-Arifeen, 1997).

Because of the importance of diarrhea and pneumonia as causes of death in children in low-income countries, a few studies have evaluated whether low birth weight confers additional risk for deaths from these two causes. In three studies in low-income countries, the increased risk of diarrheal deaths during infancy was 2.5 to 2.8-fold for low-birth-weight babies (Ashworth & Feachem, 1985). Likewise, the risks of death from acute lower respiratory infections were increased, but with more variability, with a relative risk ranging from 1.6 to 8.0 (Victora et al., 1999).

As might be expected from these studies of infant mortality, low birth weight has also been shown to be a risk factor for diarrheal and respiratory morbidity (Ashworth & Feachem, 1985; Victora et al., 1999). Studies in Papua New Guinea (Bukenya, Barnes, & Nwokolo, 1991), Thailand (Ittiravivongs et al., 1991), and Brazil (Victora et al., 1990) found a relative risk, adjusted for other possible determinants of illness, ranging from 1.6 to 3.9 for acute diarrhea. Studies in China (Chen, Yu, & Li, 1988), Argentina (Cerqueiro et al., 1990), and Brazil (Victora et al., 1989; Victora et al., 1990) found a relative risk ranging from 1.4 to 2.2 for acute lower respiratory infection or pneumonia hospitalization.

The consequences of low birth weight, however, may extend into adulthood. It has been hypothesized that nutritional insult during fetal life, reflected by intrauterine growth retardation, may lead to increased risk of coronary heart disease (Barker et al., 1989), hypertension (Barker et al., 1990), and diabetes (Hales et al., 1991). Although studies to date have been un-

able to explain such associations by confounding socioeconomic and dietary influences (Leon, 1998), the hypothesis remains controversial (Joseph & Kramer, 1996). In the Gambia, however, the risk of all-cause mortality in a cohort of individuals more than 14.5 years of age, followed from birth, was fourfold greater among individuals born during the preharvest "hungry" than in the postharvest season. Death beyond 25 years of age was 10 times more likely among individuals born during the hungry season (Moore et al., 1999). Most known causes of death were reportedly infectious-related causes. The etiological importance of maternal undernutrition in hungry-season low-birth-weight incidence has been confirmed by low maternal weight gain and birth weight (Prentice et al., 1983) and the responsiveness of birth weight and neonatal survival to maternal supplementation with food (providing approximately 1,000 kcal per day) in this season (Ceesay et al., 1997). Both seasonal birth cohorts were comparable in nutritional status in their second year of life, however, suggesting a latent effect of gestational insult on subsequent health and survival. It has been hypothesized that intrauterine or early postnatal undernutrition may leave an "imprint" on an individual (e.g., through defects of thymic and other lymphoid tissues at critical developmental periods) that could in later life impair host resistance to infection (Moore et al., 1999; Prentice, 1998) or otherwise predispose individuals to disease (Barker et al., 1989; Leon, 1998).

Childhood Undernutrition

This section focuses on the risk of infectious disease and related mortality in early childhood as a function of anthropometric status, since risk from micronutrient deficiency is considered separately in the chapter. It is clear that severe malnutrition carries a risk of death, but it is the potentially causal interaction of undernutrition with common infectious diseases in low-income countries that is of far greater importance. It has long been postulated that there is a synergy between undernutrition and infectious diseases, in which the combination of these conditions results in much greater mortality than either independently (Scrimshaw, Taylor, & Gordon, 1967). This appears to be because infectious diseases are more severe in undernourished children and carry a higher case fatality rate, although an increased incidence of infectious diseases may also play some role.

A review of the observational studies of anthropometric status as a risk factor for child mortality in low-income countries demonstrated that each level of worsening weight for age below the international median is associated with increased mortality (Figure 5-6a) (Pelletier, Frongillo, & Habicht, 1993). Similar increases in mortality risk have been observed with decrements in MUAC, adjusted (Sommer & Loewenstein, 1975) or unadjusted (Briend & Zimicki, 1986; Briend, Wojtyniak, & Rowland, 1987; West et al., 1991) for height, across all preschool ages, including early infancy once arm size is adjusted for age (De Vaquera et al., 1983; West et al., 1991). Stunting early in life (younger than 3 years), adjusted for wasting, carries a disproportionate risk of mortality (Katz et al., 1989; Smedman et al., 1987).

It is important to note that even mild undernutrition puts a child at increased risk of mortality. Because the greatest number of undernourished children have mild to moderate rather than severe malnutrition, most of the excess risk of death is attributable to the less severe forms of undernutrition. Also important is the observation that with worsening levels of weight for age, the mortality rate increases logarithmically (Figure 5-6b). Across studies, children were estimated to experience an approximately 7% compound increase in risk of dying for every percent decrease in weight for age below the referent median (Pelletier et al., 1993), suggesting the absence of an often-posited threshold phenomenon (Pelletier, 1994). The effect is consistent, however, with the postulated synergistic interaction between nutrition and infection, because nearly all the deaths are due to infectious diseases. It was estimated that 53% of all childhood deaths could be explained by the potentiating effects of undernutrition on infectious morbidity (Caulfield et al., 2004).

Thus, reductions in mortality may be achieved either through improving nutritional status or by reducing the incidence or case fatality from infectious diseases; however, improvements in both at the same time would be expected to have a synergistic benefit. In addition, improving nutritional well-being to reduce these excess deaths will require approaches that correct underlying inequities in impoverished communities through broad-based programs that improve food security and diets (or nutrient intakes through fortification), since poor screening specificity (that correctly excludes large numbers of children unlikely to die) in a mildly to moderately malnourished population could overwhelm targeted nutrition programs.

Diarrheal diseases and pneumonia are the two most important causes of death in children under 5 years of age in low-income countries. These two conditions have a higher case fatality rate in undernourished children compared with those who are well nourished. For example, malnourished children who

were discharged from a hospital after treatment for diarrheal illness in Bangladesh had a 14-fold greater risk of dying comparing with better-nourished controls (Roy, Chowdhury, & Rahaman, 1983). In a community-based study in rural India, severely malnourished children had a 24-fold higher diarrheal case fatality rate compared with better-nourished children (Bhandari, Bhan, & Sazawal, 1992), and in Mexico, undernourished children had an 8-fold greater risk of death with severe diarrhea (Tome et al., 1996). Studies in the Philippines (Tupasi et al., 1990), Papua New Guinea (Shann, Barker, & Poore, 1989), Bangladesh (Rahman et al., 1990), and Argentina (Weissenbacher et al., 1990) of acute lower respiratory infection and pneumonia found a 2- to 3-fold increase in case fatality rate in undernourished versus better-nourished children.

Prospective studies to evaluate the role of undernutrition, assessed by anthropometry, in predisposing children to cause-specific mortality have found a progressively increased risk with worsening nutritional status. In a meta-analysis of 10 longitudinal studies, there were significantly increased risks for diarrhea and pneumonia mortality associated with a Z-score below -1 for weight for age (Table 5-4). It was estimated from this relationship that 61% of diarrhea mortality and 52% of pneumonia mortality could be attributed to undernutrition (Fishman et al., 2004)

It has long been observed that measles has been associated with undernutrition in children in low-income countries. This association and the apparent higher case fatality rate for measles in malnourished children led many to conclude that there was again a synergistic relationship. A recent meta-analysis of longitudinal studies found that there is a significant relationship between weight for age and measles mortality. This analysis estimated that 45% of measles mortality could be attributed to undernutrition (Fishman et al., 2004). The observation in several African settings that vitamin A supplementation during acute measles can substantially reduce the severity and case fatality of measles (Barclay, Foster, & Sommer, 1987; Coutsoudis et al., 1992; Hussey & Klein, 1990) also speaks for the importance of nutritional risk factors in affecting survival from measles.

The role of undernutrition in predisposing children to malaria is controversial. Early observations from the 19th century reported that malaria was more frequent in those with inadequate diets or with undernutrition (Garnham, 1954). However, studies in the latter part of the 20th century appeared to show that malnutrition could actually be protective for

(a)

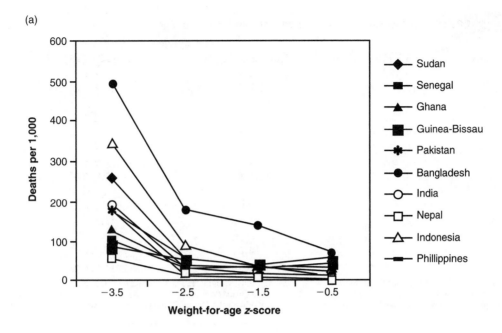

(b)

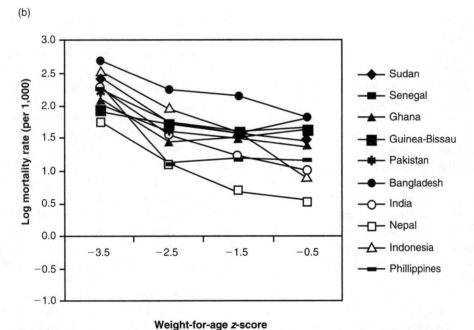

Figure 5-6 Association Between Weight for Age (Z-Score) and Risk of All-Cause Mortality Among Children 6 to 59 Months of Age at Baseline, Followed for Periods of 6 to 24 Months, in Longitudinal Population Studies in 10 Countries. (a) Deaths Per 1,000 Per Year. (b) Logarithm of Deaths per 1,000 Children Per Year. *Source:* S. M. Fishman, L.E. Caulfield, M. de Onis, M. Blossner, A. A. Hyder, L. Mullany, & R. E. Black. (2004). Childhood and maternal under-nutrition. In: M. Ezzati, A. D. Lopez, A. Rodgers, C. J. L. Murray. (Eds). Comparative Quantification of Health Risks: Global and Regional Burden of Disease Attributable to Selected Major Risk Factors (pp. 39–162). Geneva: World Health Organization.

Table 5-4	Relative Risk of Mortality Associated with Low Weight for Age			
	Weight for Age			
Cause of Death	≤ −3 Z (95% CI)	−2 to −3 Z (95% CI)	−1 to -2 Z (95% CI)	≥−1 Z
Diarrhea	12.5 (7.2, 21.7)	5.4 (3.7, 7.8)	2.3 (1.9, 2.8)	1.0
Pneumonia	8.1 (4.4, 15.0)	4.0 (2.7, 6.1)	2.0 (1.6, 2.5)	1.0
Malaria	9.5 (3.2, 27.7)	4.5 (2.2, 9.2)	2.1 (1.5, 3.0)	1.0
Measles	5.2 (2.3, 11.9)	3.0 (1.7, 5.2)	1.7 (1.3, 2.3)	1.0
All causes	8.7 (5.6, 13.7)	4.2 (3.1, 5.7)	2.1 (1.8, 2.4)	1.0

Source: S. Fishman, L. E. Caulfield, M. de Ois, M. Blössner, A. A. Hyder, L. Mullany, and R. E. Black, "Childhood and Maternal Underweight," in M. Ezzati, A. D. Lopez, A. Rodgers, & C. J. L. Murray (Eds.), *Comparative Quantification of Health Risks: Global and Regional Burden of Disease Attributable to Selected Major Risk Factors* (Geneva, Switzerland: World Health Organization, pp. 39–162). Reprinted with permission.

malaria. This was based on observational studies (Hendrickse et al., 1971) or on interventions such as the refeeding of famine victims (Murray et al., 1975) in which an exacerbation of malaria appeared to occur. Animal studies seemed to support the suppressive effects of a poor diet on malaria, leading to the belief that undernourished children are less susceptible to infection with and the consequences of malaria.

More recent studies, however, indicate strongly that the relationship between nutritional status and malaria is complex and that undernutrition serves as a risk factor for increased malaria mortality and morbidity. A recent meta-analysis of longitudinal studies found a significant relationship between weight for age and malaria mortality, resulting in an estimate of 57% of malaria mortality being attributable to undernutrition (Caulfield, Richard, & Black, 2004; Fishman et al., 2004). Additional studies indicate that specific micronutrients, such as vitamin A, zinc, iron, and others, affect the risk of infection and severity of illness with malaria as well (Caulfield, Richard, & Black, 2004). Although it is now believed that undernutrition is a risk factor for malaria, it is also a consistent observation that refeeding a malaria-infected, starved host can reactivate the low-grade infection, making it more severe. One implication is that antimalarial measures should be included during nutritional rehabilitation of famine victims who are likely to have malaria infection.

Nutritional status has been assessed widely as a risk factor for the severity and incidence of diarrheal diseases. As might be expected with the reported higher case fatality rate in undernourished children, there is an association with disease severity. One measure of this is the duration of the illness. In studies in several countries, the duration of diarrhea in mild to moderately malnourished children was shown to be up to 3-fold longer than for better-nourished children (Black, Brown, & Becker, 1984b). Undernutrition is also an important risk factor for the occurrence of persistent diarrhea (Baqui et al., 1993). This relationship has also been demonstrated for specific types of diarrhea, such as episodes due to *Shigella* species and enterotoxigenic *Escherichia coli,* where the illness duration in Bangladeshi children was 2.5-fold longer in undernourished children (Black, Brown, & Becker, 1984b). Poorer nutritional status has also been documented to be associated with increased rate of stool output in children, leading to an increased risk of dehydration (Black et al., 1984). These mechanisms likely explain the increased risk for hospitalization and length of hospital stay due to diarrhea in undernourished children (Man et al., 1998; Victora et al., 1990).

The effect of undernutrition on diarrheal incidence has been more variable in different settings. Some studies show no increased risk of overall incidence, whereas others have found a 30% to 70% increased risk of incident diarrhea in undernourished children (Black et al., 1984; Checkley et al., 2002; Guerrant et al., 1992; El Samani, Willett, & Ware, 1986). A meta-analysis has estimated that underweight status (≤2 Z-scores weight for age) has an increased relative risk of diarrhea of 1.23 (95% confidence interval [CI]:1.12, 1.35) (Fishman et al.,

2004). Some enteropathogens causing diarrhea, such as *Cryptosporidium parvum*, may be particularly selected as a cause of infection in undernourished children (Checkley et al., 1998).

The role of undernutrition as a risk factor for severity or incidence of acute lower respiratory infections or pneumonia has also received extensive study. Evidence would support an association between undernutrition and severity of respiratory infection, with such associations being found in both hospital-based and community-based studies. Undernutrition has been found to increase the likelihood that a child will have bacteremia, pleural effusion, and other complications (Johnson, Aderele, & Gbadero, 1992). Studies in the Philippines, Costa Rica (James, 1972), and Brazil (Fonseca et al., 1996; Victora et al., 1989) found a modestly increased incidence of acute lower respiratory infections in undernourished children, but studies in Papua New Guinea (Smith et al., 1991), Uruguay (Selwyn, 1990), and Guatemala (Cruz et al., 1990) did not find any relationship. A meta-analysis found that underweight status (≤2 Z-scores weight for age) has an increased relative risk of pneumonia of 1.86 (95% CI: 1.06, 3.28) (Fishman et al., 2004). One study in the Gambia found that the development of pneumococcal infection was associated with a history of poor weight gain prior to the illness compared with other children in the community (O'Dempsey et al., 1996). It appears that undernutrition is associated with increased severity and complications of illness, as well as case fatality, and with an increased incidence of pneumonia.

Contributions of Infection to Undernutrition

Infections in childhood have long been recognized to influence physical growth and rates of malnutrition among children in low- and middle-income countries. After initial observation of the relationship, more recent work has assessed the size of this effect and moderating influences. This has been done largely in prospective community-based studies, which use intensive surveillance to assess episodes of illness and growth performance. These studies examined the most frequent childhood infectious diseases, especially diarrhea and respiratory diseases. Some have assessed the effects of measles, malaria, and other infections, such as those of the skin. It is clear from the studies to date that infectious morbidity, particularly diarrheal disease, has an important effect on weight gain. A similar effect on linear growth was generally observed in these studies.

The negative effect of diarrhea on weight and often height gain of children during and after an episode of acute diarrhea has been documented in diverse low-income-country settings. Nevertheless, the magnitude of the effect on growth faltering has varied widely in these studies (Black, Brown, & Becker, 1983). Some studies, such as those in Guatemala (Martorell et al., 1975), Mexico (Condon-Paoloni et al., 1977), and Bangladesh (Black, Brown, & Becker, 1984a), have reported that 10% to 24% of the growth faltering could be explained statistically by the prevalence of diarrhea, whereas studies in other countries, such as Uganda (Cole & Parkin, 1977), the Gambia (Rowland, Cole, & Whitehead, 1977), and Sudan (Zumrawi, Dimond, & Waterlow, 1987) have reported that diarrhea could explain as much as 40% to 80% of observed faltering. In nearly all instances, these percentages of growth faltering explained by diarrhea were higher than those explained by other infectious diseases, again demonstrating the quantitative importance of the relationship between diarrhea and growth faltering. Infectious diseases generally result in poorer weight gain or weight loss, which may be due to loss of appetite (Brown et al., 1985) or increased metabolism. With diarrhea there may also be intentional withholding of food, as well as malabsorption of ingested food in the damaged intestine (Behrens et al., 1987; Lunn, Northrop-Clewes, & Downes, 1991). Variation in these factors may explain some of the differences in the magnitude of effect in various low-income-country settings, but it is necessary also to consider factors such as the etiology of diarrhea, the age pattern of infection, feeding pattern and dietary intake, treatment practices, and the length of the convalescent period.

Few studies have examined the differential effect of diarrhea due to specific etiologic agents on growth. In Bangladesh, enterotoxigenic *E. coli* and *Shigella* species had the strongest effects on growth, whereas rotavirus and other enteropathogens, in part due to their lower prevalence, did not have a significant effect (Black, Brown, & Becker, 1984a). The seasonal pattern of particular enteropathogens causing diarrhea may explain part of the seasonality in growth seen in some low-income-country settings. In regard to clinical syndromes, it has been noted that dysentery (bloody diarrhea) and persistent diarrhea (defined by the World Health Organization as an episode lasting more than 14 days) have particularly important adverse effects on the growth of children (Black, 1993). As one might expect, the magnitude of the weight deficit is inversely related to the duration of the diarrheal episode. Persistent diarrheal episodes usually occur in children who also have, in general, a higher burden of diarrhea, so that both the persistent episodes and the high prevalence of diarrhea adversely affect growth.

Asymptomatic as well as symptomatic infections can have an adverse effect on growth. Infection with *C. parvum,* with or without illness, in Peruvian children was associated with a reduction in weight gain, controlling for other variables (Checkley et al., 1998). Even though the effect size was lower with asymptomatic infections than with symptomatic ones, asymptomatic infections had a greater overall impact on growth than symptomatic infections because of the former's higher prevalence. Children after illness have the potential to grow more rapidly than they were growing previously; this is known as catch-up growth. Children with a *C. parvum* infection in the first 6 months of life did not have catch-up growth, showing that there was a long-lasting adverse effect on linear growth, whereas children with infections at an older age did have some catch-up growth.

The feeding practices of a child at the time of illness can modify the effect of diarrhea on growth. Infants who are exclusively or predominantly breastfeeding experience fewer adverse effects of diarrhea (Launer, Habicht, & Kardjati, 1990). This may be because breastfeeding ameliorates the severity of the illness or because breastfeeding generally seems to be continued without reduction in most circumstances during illness (Brown et al., 1985; Hoyle, Yunus, & Hen, 1980), whereas other foods may be reduced due to medical or cultural practices or to anorexia caused by the illness. Children in the first 6 months of life who are exclusively or predominantly breastfed may have less severe consequences of diarrhea or other infectious diseases (Khin-Maung-U et al., 1985; Launer, Habicht, & Kardjati, 1990; Rowland, Rowland, & Cole, 1988). On the other hand, if very young children become ill with diarrhea there may be long-term height deficits, effects that may be greater than for diarrhea at an older age (Checkley et al., 2003).

There is also a modifying effect of diet on the relationship between diarrhea and growth (Brown et al., 1988). Diarrhea has a lesser effect among children whose usual dietary intake is greater or of better quality, or among children who receive food supplements, compared with children with poorer diets or those not receiving food supplements in the same setting (Lutter et al., 1989).

Appropriate treatment of diarrheal illnesses may reduce the adverse effects of diarrhea on growth. The replacement of fluid and electrolytes with oral rehydration therapy may restore appetite and improve bowel function. Also, continued feeding during the illness has been demonstrated in clinical trials to result in improved weight gain in comparison with partial withholding of food during the acute phase (Brown et al., 1988). Although antibiotics are not necessary for most cases of acute diarrhea, appropriate antibiotic treatment of dysentery would be expected to shorten the illness and, therefore, the period of adverse effects on growth.

Catch-up growth seems possible without specific supplementary feeding programs, due to the child's increased consumption of available food; however, some diarrheal disease control programs recommend additional feeding in the convalescent period after illness. Unfortunately, the opportunity for catch-up growth may be limited by the duration of the healthy period between illnesses. Studies in Bangladesh (Black, Brown, & Becker, 1983) and Zimbabwe (Moy et al., 1994) have shown that it requires about 2 weeks following diarrhea for children to recover to their pre-illness weight and about 4 weeks to grow to the weight expected if these children had continued the rate of growth that they had prior to the illness. Another illness occurring during this month long convalescent period may result in insufficient time for catch-up growth to occur and could add additional nutritional insult. The net effect in the long term is a reduction in both ponderal and linear growth.

Acute respiratory infections, predominantly upper respiratory infections, have a high prevalence worldwide. Children in low-income countries, while having a similar prevalence of upper respiratory infections as children in more industrialized countries, have a substantially higher rate of acute lower respiratory infections or pneumonia (Graham, 1990). Most of the studies of the effect of acute respiratory infections on growth have included both upper and lower respiratory infections and have generally not found an effect of the illnesses on growth. In a Gambian study, children under 2 years of age with acute lower respiratory infections diagnosed by a pediatrician had a loss of 14.7 grams of weight per day of illness, slightly but not significantly greater than the reduction observed with diarrheal diseases (Rowland, Rowland, & Cole, 1988). However, the prevalence of diarrhea was much higher than that of acute lower respiratory infections, so that diarrheal diseases explained one-half and respiratory infections only one-quarter of the observed weight deficit. Other studies in the Philippines (Adair et al., 1993), Papua New Guinea (Smith et al., 1991), Guatemala (Cruz et al., 1990), and Brazil (Victora et al., 1990) have also indicated that acute lower respiratory infections adversely affect growth.

Acute respiratory illnesses have been shown to be associated with a 10% to 20% reduction in food intake, possibly due to a reduction in the child's appetite (Brown et al., 1985; Mata et al., 1977). As with other illnesses, catabolism may also play a role. Further studies are required to assess the magnitude of the adverse effects of acute lower respiratory infections on growth and to document if there are modifying factors, as there appear to be with diarrheal diseases.

A few studies have attempted to document whether malaria has an adverse effect on growth in children in low-income countries. In the Gambia, malaria prevalence adversely affected weight gain but not linear growth (Rowland, Cole, & Whitehead, 1977). Subsequent studies in Uganda (Cole & Parkin, 1977) and the Gambia (Rowland, Rowland, & Cole, 1988) were not able to demonstrate an effect of malaria on the growth of children.

Although it has been believed for many years that measles causes a reduction in growth, this has been difficult to document on a population basis. This is in part because of the low incidence of measles found in prospective studies, which in some cases was due to the administration of measles vaccine in the study cohort. Older studies suggest that children with measles lose weight or have reduced growth velocity (Reddy, 1991), but measles has been best recognized as an illness that precipitates severe clinical forms of malnutrition. In children with previous undernutrition, measles can precipitate kwashiorkor or marasmus (DeMaeyer & Adiels-Tegman, 1985) as well as xerophthalmia (Sommer, 1982). Measles can also predispose to subsequent diarrhea and pneumonia, which will have additional adverse effects on nutritional status.

Intestinal helminthic infections, especially with *Acaris lumbricoides,* in children in low- and middle-income countries have been associated with poor growth (Rousham & Mascie-Taylor, 1994). In such populations, periodic deworming of children using a mass treatment approach has been demonstrated to improve growth (Adams et al., 1994; Stoltzfus et al., 1998; Willett, Kilama, & Kihamia, 1979). Because children are reinfected rapidly after treatment, such approaches should be routine and combined with environmental sanitation and hygiene education.

Micronutrient Deficiencies

Essential micronutrients comprise vitamins and minerals that are required by the body in minute amounts from the diet to support tissue growth, development, function, maintenance, and repair. Micronutrient deficiency, frequently accompanied by degrees of PEM,

progressively impairs normal physiologic processes with increasing severity, duration, and mix of dietary deficits, depending on concurrent health conditions and timing or stage of life. Historically, the severity of micronutrient deficiency has been interpreted to parallel its progression in clinical signs (e.g., mild eye signs of xerophthalmia equals mild vitamin A deficiency), with little attention given to subacute deficiency, similar to historic neglect of the extent and consequences of mild weight deficit in children (Pelletier, Frongillo, & Habicht, 1993). However, improved methods to assess biochemical and functional aspects of deficiency in populations, greater cognizance that clinical signs reflect moderate to severe nutrient depletion (tip of the iceberg), and revelations about the morbidity and mortality risks associated with more prevalent subacute stages of deficiency have prompted efforts to assess and prevent the full spectrum of micronutrient deficiencies and their impact on health.

Estimates of the extent of micronutrient undernutrition vary widely, from 20% of the world's population—or more than 1 billion persons—being deficient in one or more essential micronutrients (Trowbridge et al., 1993) to more than 2 billion being iron deficient alone (UNICEF, 1997). Despite the imprecision of global estimates, dietary deficit or imbalance in essential micronutrients represents an enormous problem of "hidden hunger" (Ramalingaswami, 1995), with global health consequences, especially in the low-income countries (Howson, Kennedy, & Horwitz, 1998; McGuire & Galloway, 1994; Trowbridge et al., 1993). Among the multiple micronutrient deficiencies affecting health, four have gained widespread attention for their relevance to child and maternal health, development, and survival: vitamin A, iron, iodine, and zinc. These are each discussed in the following sections.

Vitamin A Deficiency

Vitamin A deficiency is the leading cause of preventable pediatric blindness and a major determinant of childhood morbidity and mortality in low-income countries (Rice, West, & Black, 2004; Sommer & West, 1996). A current, likely conservative, estimate based on extrapolation from population biochemical and clinical survey data is that there are 127 million vitamin A–deficient preschool-aged children living in lower-income countries, with deficiency defined as plasma retinol concentrations below 0.70 μmol/L (20 μg/dL). Roughly 4.4 million, or 3% of those deficient, have ocular manifestations of xerophthalmia (West, 2002). These estimates are far lower than the

WHO estimates of up to 250 million deficient children a decade ago (WHO, 1993), which appears largely to be attributed to combined effects of an earlier calculating error related to "country weights" and actual reductions that have occurred following intensive prevention program activity over the past several years (Goodman et al., 2000). Notwithstanding, combined prevalence data for both xerophthalmia and hyporetinolemia show that vitamin A deficiency remains a major public health problem across southern Asia, South Central Asia, and sub-Saharan Africa and, at a less severe level, in the western Pacific, Central and South America, and in the Carribean region (Figure 5-7). Although the annual incidence of potentially blinding corneal xerophthalmia is suspected to be lower than the half-million new cases initially estimated based on prospective population data from Indonesia two decades ago (Sommer et al., 1981), there are no recent reliable cohort data on which to change this estimate.

Data are emerging, however, to reveal the extent of vitamin A deficiency in older age and life-stage groups. For example, based on a limited number of reports, approximately 23% of children 5 to 15 years

of age in Southeast Asia (or 83 million) have recently been estimated to have a plasma retinol concentration below the conventional cutoff of 0.70 μmol/L, among whom 11% (2.6% overall) have mild xerophthalmia (Singh & West, 2004). Corneal xerophthalmia appears to be virtually absent at this age. Limited reports suggest that the magnitude of adolescent deficiency in sub-Saharan Africa is at least as great as in Southeast Asia. Surveys in undernourished populations of South Asia, rural Africa, and in Latin America typically report 10% to 20% of women experiencing night blindness during pregnancy (Christian et al., 1998a; Kamal, Ahsan, & Salam, 1998; Katz et al., 1995; Pradhan et al., 1997; West, 2002), a condition attributed largely to vitamin A deficiency (Christian et al., 1998b; Dixit, 1966; Mandal, Nanda, & Bose, 1969). Based on the numbers and fertility of women of childbearing age (Parikh & Shane, 1998) and the likely regional prevalence of maternal night blindness, at least 6 million pregnant women develop night blindness each year (West, 2002). Experience to date suggests that the number of pregnant women with marginal vitamin A status (based on serum retinol <30 μg/dL or poor dark adaptation) can be expected to be two to three

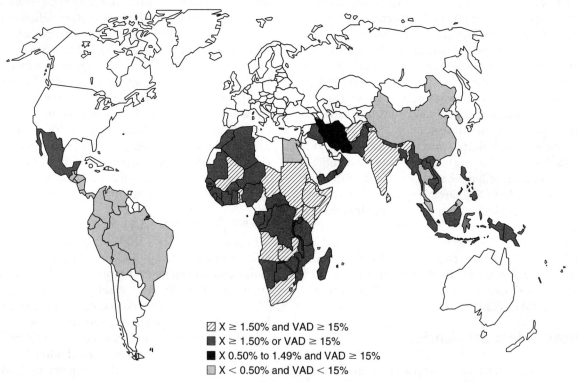

Figure 5-7 Countries Categorized by Degree of the Joint Distribution of Xerophthalmia (X) and Vitamin A Deficiency (VAD) Among Preschool Children. *Note:* Blank color denotes lack of data. *Source:* K. P. West, Jr. (2002). Extent of vitamin A deficiency among preschool children and women of reproductive age. *Journal of Nutrition*, 132, 2857S–2866S, American Society for Nutritional Sciences.

times the prevalence of night blindness (Christian et al., 1998b).

Function, Requirements, and Assessment

Vitamin A is an essential nutrient that participates in the visual cycle and, at the genomic level, in regulating cell proliferation and differentiation (Blomhoff, 1994). Normally, rod and cone photoreceptor cells in the retina of the eye produce photosensitive pigments that respond to light, triggering neural impulses along the optic nerve to the brain that result in vision. Rhodopsin ("visual purple") is the vitamin A–dependent photosensitive pigment that accumulates in rod cells, enabling vision under conditions of low illumination (scotopic vision) (Wald, 1955). Vitamin A deficiency leads to decreased availability of retinaldeyhde (retinal) and decreased production of rhodopsin, raising the minimum threshold of light required to see in the dark. This impairment of rod function leads to night blindness, a condition that is recognized by affected individuals (Sommer & West, 1996).

Other, more pervasive functions of vitamin A draw on its role in gene regulation, especially evident in rapidly dividing, bipotential cells. Within the nucleus, vitamin A metabolic intermediates (retinoic acids) interact with receptor proteins that, in turn, influence transcription by activating or inhibiting nearby target genes (Kastner, Chambon, & Leid, 1994), thereby directing protein synthesis and cell differentiation and proliferation. Adequate vitamin A nutriture, therefore, helps to maintain, for example, the function and integrity of mucus-secreting, epithelial, immunologic, and osteogenic cells in the body. Deficiency of vitamin A can change the types of cells produced, causing keratinizing metaplasia of epithelial surfaces, evident by xerotic (drying) changes on ocular surfaces that lead to xerophthalmia (Sommer, 1995). These cellular changes may disrupt the barrier function of epithelial surfaces. Further, vitamin A deficiency can alter the expression and function of immune effector cells and their ability to clear pathogens (Ross, 1996). These pathophysiologic processes can lead to impaired host resistance to infection (Stephensen, 2001).

Vitamin A status is commonly assessed by clinical, biochemical, and functional indicators. Assessment and staging of xerophthalmic eye signs, following a widely accepted WHO classification system (Table 5-5) (Sommer, 1995), provide standardized criteria for evaluating the extent of moderate to severe deficiency, screening individuals for treatment, and, because xerophthalmia occurs in clusters (Katz, Zeger, & Tielsch, 1988; Katz et al., 1993), identifying communities at risk. Biochemical and functional indicators, in the absence of clinical signs, are best applied toward estimating levels of deficiency in groups of individuals.

Table 5-5	WHO Classification and Minimum Prevalence Criteria for Xerophthalmia and Vitamin A Deficiency as a Public Health Program		
Definition (Code)	**Minimum Prevalence (%)**		**Highest-Risk Groups**
Night blindness (XN)			
Children 2–5 years of age	1.0		Entire age group
Women during recent pregnancy	5.0		Women with previous episode of XN
Conjunctival xerosis (X1A)	—		
Bitot's spots (X1B)	0.5		
Corneal xerosis (X2)			
Corneal ulceration keratomalacia (X3)	0.01		Children 1–3 years
Xerophthalmic corneal scar (XS)	0.05		Cumulative >1 year
Serum retinol <0.70 mol L	15.0		
Abnormal CIC/RDR/MRDR	20.0[a]		

Notes: CIC = conjunctival impression cytology; RDR = relative dose response; MRDR = modified RDR.

[a]Provisional cutoffs above which community interventions may be warranted.

Source: A. Sommer and F. R. Davidson, "Assessment and Control of Vitamin A Deficiency: The Annecy Accords," 2002, *Journal of Nutrition, 132,* pp. 2845S–2850S. Reprinted with permission.

Serum (plasma) retinol is the most commonly measured biochemical indicator of vitamin A status. Although homeostatically controlled within a broad range of nutritional adequacy, plasma retinol concentration falls progressively with liver and total body vitamin A depletion (Olson, 1992; Underwood, 1990). Serum retinol eluted from a filter paper blood spot has shown promise as a practical and inexpensive field approach to population assessment (Craft et al., 2000). Serum retinol response tests following receipt of a standard, small oral dose of vitamin A are based on retinol kinetics (relative dose response [RDR] and modified RDR) that allow the relative liver adequacy of vitamin A to be estimated (Flores et al., 1984; Loerch, Underwood, & Lewis, 1979; Tanumihardjo et al., 1990).

Other functional, preclinical measures for evaluating community vitamin A status include breast milk retinol concentration (Stoltzfus & Underwood, 1995), conjunctival impression cytology (Natadisastra et al., 1988; Stoltzfus, Miller, et al., 1993; Wittpenn, Tseng, & Sommer, 1986), and dark adaptometry (Congdon & West, 2002). Cutoffs established by WHO and the International Vitamin A Consultative Group (IVACG), and other provisional cutoffs for evaluating community risk by various means, are listed in Table 5-6 (Congdon & West, 2002; Sommer & Davidson, 2002; WHO, 1996a).

The Recommended Dietary Allowance (RDA) for vitamin A, expressed as retinol activity equivalents, is 300 to 600 μg per day for children up to 13 years of age, and 700 to 900 μg per day thereafter for both sexes, including during pregnancy (Table 5-7). The RDA increases substantially (to 1,300 μg per day) during lactation (Institute of Medicine, 2001).

Health Consequences

Consequences of vitamin A deficiency that are of public health importance in low-income countries relate to increased risks of xerophthalmia and its blinding sequelae, infectious morbidity and mortality, and, to some extent, poor growth.

Xerophthalmia. Active stages of xerophthalmia due to vitamin A deficiency include night blindness; conjunctival xerosis (dryness), usually with Bitot's spots; corneal xerosis; ulceration; and necrosis (keratomalacia, or softening of the cornea). Corneal lesions may heal to form a scar (leukoma), become phthisic (shrunken globe), or form a staphyloma (bulging eye) (Sommer, 1995). Noncorneal xerophthalmia indicates mild eye disease but moderate to severe deficiency, revealed by a low serum retinol concentration and increased risks of morbidity and mortality (Sommer & West, 1996). Corneal involvement is a medical emergency because it is potentially blinding and is associated with a case fatality rate of 5% to 25% (Sommer, 1982). WHO has classified the stages of xerophthalmia and provided prevalence estimates as minimum criteria for defining vitamin A deficiency as a public health problem (see Table 5-5). The vitamin A treatment schedule for xerophthalmia is well standardized (see Table 5-6) (Sommer, 1995; WHO/UNICEF/IVACG, 1997).

Morbidity and Mortality. A dose-responsive, strong, and consistent association has been shown to exist between clinical vitamin A deficiency, represented by mild xerophthalmic eye signs, and short-term risk of child mortality (Sommer et al., 1983; Sommer & West, 1996). The causality of this association has been borne out by eight community intervention trials, enrolling more than 165,000 children, conducted in

Table 5-6	Vitamin A Treatment and Prevention Schedules			
			Prevention	
Age	**Treatment at Diagnosis[a] (Dosage)**	**Dosage**	**Frequency**
<6 months				
Shortly after birth	50,000 IU	50,000 IU	Once or split doses[b]
Postneonatally	50,000 IU	50,000 IU	6, 10, and 14 weeks of age
6–12 months	100,000 IU	100,000 IU	Every 4–6 months
≥1 year	200,000 IU	200,000 IU	Every 4–6 months
Women	200,000 IU[c]	400,000 IU	≤6 weeks after delivery

[a]Treat all cases of xerophthalmia and measles with the same age-specific dosage the next day and again 1 to 4 weeks later.

[b]Unofficial recommendation for non-HIV areas, based on recent trials from Indonesia and India that show potential to reduce infant mortality.

[c]For women of reproductive age, give 200,000 IU only for corneal xerophthalmia; for milder eye signs (night blindness or Bitot's spots), give women 5,000 to 10,000 IU per day or up to 25,000 IU per week for 4 weeks or more.

Source: A. Sommer and F. R. Davidson, "Assessment and Control of Vitamin A Deficiency: The Annecy Accords," 2002, *Journal of Nutrition, 132,* pp. 2845S–2850S. Reprinted with permission.

Table 5-7	Recommended Dietary Allowances (RDA) for Selected Micronutrients				
			Zinc (mg/d)		
	Vitamin A (μg/d)[a]	Iron (mg/d)	Condition 1[b]	Condition 2[c]	Iodine (μg/d)
Infants					
0–6 mo	400	11	4	5	110
7–11 mo	500	11	4	5	130
Children					
1–3 yr	300	7	3	3	90
4–8 yr	400	10	4	5	90
Boys					
9–13 yr	600	8	6	9	120
14–18 yr	900	11	10	14	150
Girls					
9–13 yr	600	8	6	9	120
14–18 yr	700	15	9	11	150
Men					
19–70 yr	900	8	13	19	150
Women					
19–70 yr	700	18[d]	8	9	150
Pregnant	770	27	10	13	220
Lactating	1300	9	9	10	290

Notes: RDA values are adapted from Institute of Medicine (2001) for all nutrients except zinc, for which modified estimates judged to be more appropriate for dietary conditions in lower-income countries have been obtained from the International Zinc Nutrition Consultative Group (IZiNCG) (Hotz & Brown, 2004)

[a]Expressed as Retinol Activity Equivalents that allow for a dietary carotenoid to vitamin A conversion ratio of 12:1 for beta-carotene and 24:1 for other provitamin A carotenoids.

[b]Under usual conditions of a mixed or refined vegetarian diet.

[c]Under usual conditions of an unrefined cereal-based diet.

[d]Value for perimenopausal women; RDA decreases to 8 mg/d above 50 years of age.

South and Southeast Asia and Africa over the past 20 years (Figure 5-8). Overviews indicate that their findings are compatible with reductions of 23% to 34% in preschool child mortality following vitamin A prophylaxis by direct supplementation or routine consumption of vitamin A–fortified food (Beaton et al., 1993; Bishai et al., 2005; Fawzi et al., 1993; Glasziou & Mackerras, 1993; Tonascia, 1993).

Embedded in this impact on all-cause death are likely to be strong effects of vitamin A supplementation in reducing the severity and case fatality of measles, as seen in both community-based (Rahmathullah et al., 1990; West et al., 1991) and hospital-based clinical trials (Barclay, Foster, & Sommer, 1987; Coutsoudis et al., 1992; Ellison, 1932; Hussey & Klein, 1990), diarrhea and dysentery (Arthur et al., 1992; Banajeh, 2003), and *Plasmodium falciparum* malaria (Shankar, Genton, Semba, et al., 1999). Although vitamin A programs have made substantial progress, currently an estimated 650,000 preschool children die each year from infections such as measles, malaria, diarrhea, and

other infections that could be averted by preventing underlying vitamin A deficiency, down from a midrange estimate of 1.9 miillion deaths more than a decade ago (Humphrey & West, 1992), plausibly attributed to, in large measure, vastly increased global vitamin A program activity in recent years (Exhibit 5-2).

Newborn supplementation with 50,000 IU (International Unit) within days following birth represents a new potential child survival approach. Two randomized trials in southern Asia to date—one in Indonesia (Humphrey et al., 1998) and the other in southern India (Rahmathullah et al., 2003)—have reported reductions of more than 20% in mortality of infants following large-dose vitamin A receipt. The latter site represents an area of South Asia where early infantile keratomalacia is routinely reported (Rahmathullah & Chanravathi, 1997). Plausible mechanisms include delayed pneumococcal colonization of the respiratory tract (Coles et al., 2001), a leading cause of pneumonia and death among young infants, among other potential mechanisms of host

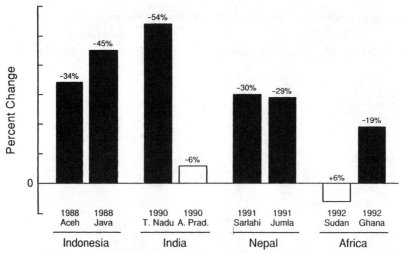

Figure 5-8 Summary of Percent Change in Mortality of Children Receiving Vitamin A Versus No Vitamin A (Controls) in Eight Field Intervention Trials. *Notes:* Ages of children range from approximately 6 months to 72 months. Black bars represent statistically significant reductions; white bars represent nonsignificant change. Total N (across trials) >165,000 children. Meta-analyses show overall reductions in mortality with vitamin A of 23% to 34%. *Source:* A. Sommer and K. P. West, Jr., *Vitamin Deficiency: Health, Survival, and Vision* (New York: Oxford University Press, 1996), Figure 2.5, p. 30. Used by permission of Oxford University Press, Inc.

Exhibit 5-2   **The Vitamin A Campaign Trail**

Field research has shown that vitamin A supplementation can reduce preschool child mortality by 25% to 35% and can virtually eliminate nutritional blindness in many low- and middle-income countries (Sommer & West, 1996). In recent years, high-potency vitamin A delivery has been redesigned as a semiannual national campaign, with widely advocated, highly organized distribution days set 6 months apart. On two days each year, government, communities, and local, national, and international agencies focus on distributing a US$0.02 vitamin A capsule (VAC) to children. Integration of VAC distribution into the WHO Expanded Program on Immunization or National Immunization Days (NIDs) during the late 1990s and first years of this decade (WHO, 1998) provided an ideal opportunity for delivery and for raising community awareness and demand for this service.

Since 2002, as the NID program has undergone its planned phase-out, demand and program momentum have motivated governments and service agencies to set up new semiannual mechanisms through which to sustain VAC distribution, such as Operation Timbang, a national child-weighing day program in the Philippines (Klemm et al., 1997), National Vitamin A Week in Bangladesh (where VACs have been distributed since 1973) (Helen Keller International, 1998), and various forms of National Child Health or Vitamin A Days or Weeks in several countries throughout Africa, southern Asia, and Latin America. VAC delivery has frequently been combined with other services, such as immunizations, deworming, oral rehydration solution distribution, and health education, to create a semiannual community-based health event (Mora et al., 2004). In mountainous Nepal, a model national program was launched in 1993 that, supported by USAID and UNICEF, was organized around community mobilization from its outset. As of the year 2004, all 75 districts of the country achieved semiannual coverage of approximately 90% among more than 2.5 million children through the efforts of approximately 25,000 local female community health volunteers. Recent program evaluations, combining coverage estimates with data from periodic Demographic Health Surveys, reflect a reduction in child mortality that is consistent with those observed by two previous randomized trials in the country (Shrestha et al., 2004). Knowledge that vitamin A saves lives, coupled with a reinvigorated campaign approach to VAC delivery, has led vitamin A delivery to be considered an essential component of child survival strategies.

resistance to infection. A recent trial in Zimbabwe, however, failed to find any survival benefit of either newborn or postpartum maternal vitamin A supplementation in adequately vitamin A–nourished mothers and infants (Malaba et al., 2005), suggesting regional differences, possibly reflecting nutritional and health differences, between South Asian and sub-Saharan African population responses to vitamin A.

Finally, maternal vitamin A deficiency may be a cause of pregnancy-related morbidity and mortality, at least in high-mortality, undernourished settings in southern Asia. A recent trial in the southern plains of Nepal reported maternal night blindness to be associated with increased risks of infectious and reproductive morbidity, general malnutrition (Christian et al., 1998b), and prolonged mortality for up to 2 years following the pregnancy and accompanying episode of maternal night blindness (Christian et al., 2000). Further, routine, low-dose vitamin A or beta-carotene supplementation of women reduced mortality related to pregnancy by more than 40% in this undernourished, high-mortality-risk population (West et al., 1999). Plausible causal pathways that vitamin A or beta-carotene could affect include infections, obstetric hemorrhage, hypertensive illness, and anemia (Faisal & Pittrof, 2000). Although no overall reductions were observed in fetal or early infant death (Katz et al., 2000), infant mortality was approximately 25% lower among children of night-blind women if the mothers had routinely received vitamin A (Christian et al, 2001).

Poor Growth. Vitamin A is required for mammalian growth. The discovery of vitamin A early in the 20th century was prompted by observations that young animals deprived of an ether-soluble fraction in egg yolk and milk ("fat-soluble factor A") failed to gain weight and eventually died (McCollum & Davis, 1915). Preschool-aged children, who wax and wane in vitamin A nutriture, decelerate in linear growth as they enter a mildly xerophthalmic state, only to recover height growth more slowly relative to weight as apparent vitamin A intake improves (Tarwotjo et al., 1992). Thus, different rates of recovery by aspect of growth might explain, in part, a rather consistent association between mild xerophthalmia and stunting (Khatry et al., 1995; Mele et al., 1991; Sommer & West, 1996). However, growth responses to population-based vitamin A supplementation have been mixed, with many studies finding no effect (Fawzi et al., 1997; Kirkwood et al., 1996; Lie et al., 1993; Rahmathullah et al., 1991; Ramakrishnan, Latham, & Abel, 1995). Others have reported improved weight without height gain (Bahl

et al., 1997; West et al., 1988), height without weight gain (Humphrey et al., 1998; Muhilal et al., 1988), or acceleration in both aspects in high risk subgroups (Donnen et al., 1998; Hadi et al., 2000; West et al., 1997). Presence of infection may also blunt a potential growth response (Hadi et al., 1999), which could explain observed seasonal differences in growth response to vitamin A (Hadi, Dibley, & West, 2004). On balance, it appears that some aspect of growth may improve with vitamin A supplementation of children for whom, or during seasons when, vitamin A deficiency is moderate to severe and is growth limiting among competing nutrition and disease factors.

Prevention

Prevention of vitamin A deficiency should be guided by epidemiologic insight. For example, mild xerophthalmia has been observed to cluster by region (Cohen et al., 1987), community (Katz, Zeger, & Tielsch, 1988; Mele et al., 1991; Sommer, 1982), and household, where siblings of cases have been reported to be 7 to 13 times more likely also to have or develop xerophthalmia (Katz et al., 1993) and twice as likely to die (Khatry et al., 1995) than children living in homes with no history of xerophthalmia. Recently, this clustering of deficiency was extended intergenerationally in Cambodia, whereby a mother or her preschool child was 4 to 9 times more likely to have xerophthalmia if the other was a case (Semba et al., 2004). Vitamin A deficiency often exhibits seasonality (Sinha & Bang, 1973). Knowledge of spatial, temporal, and generational patterns of clustering can help target high-risk groups and seasons for programs.

Three broad strategies exist to prevent vitamin A deficiency: direct supplementation with high-potency vitamin A, food fortification, and a wide range of dietary approaches to increase vitamin A intake. In addition, measures taken to prevent and control infection, which depletes vitamin A stores through increased use and excretion in the body (Campos, Flores, & Underwood, 1987; Mitra, Alvarez, & Stephensen, 1998), may conserve vitamin A in the body and, therefore, may be viewed as an indirect way to prevent vitamin A deficiency.

High-potency vitamin A supplementation is the most common, direct strategy to increase vitamin A intake and status. Typically, a large oral dose of vitamin A (see Table 5-6) is delivered either as a gelatinous capsule or in oily syrup to preschool children on a periodic basis, providing a theoretically sufficient supply of the nutrient for a 4- to 6-month period (Bloem et al., 1995). Improvement in serum retinol concentration can be variable, ranging from a few weeks to a few months, although prophylactic efficacy against xerophthalmia and child mortality can last for 6 to 12 months (Banajeh, 2003; Sommer & West, 1996). Vitamin A can be delivered as a community-based intervention (Bloem et al., 1995) or through clinic-based treatment and prevention programs (West & Sommer, 1987). UNICEF supports national vitamin A delivery programs through distribution of 400 to 800 million supplements to low- and middle-income countries each year (see Exhibit 5-2) (N. Dalmiya, personal communication). Current, revised recommendations are to provide a 400,000 IU oral dose of vitamin A to women within 6 weeks postpartum as a means to improve maternal and, via breastfeeding, infant stores (see Table 5-6). Although effective in improving the short-term vitamin A status of women and their breastfed infants, other sustained dietary or supplementary approaches are probably also required to sustain adequate maternal and infant vitamin A status (Rice et al., 1999; Stoltzfus, Hakimi et al., 1993).

Fortification is increasingly assuming importance as a means to improve routine intake of vitamin A. Many food vehicles can be technically fortified with vitamin A in that the nutrient can be added in efficacious amounts without affecting organoleptic qualities, under ambient conditions of production and consumer use. Successful commercial food items should, ideally, be produced or processed centrally in a limited number of units (to maintain quality control), have wide market penetration in high-risk areas, be consumed by target groups within a relatively narrow band of intake (to set effective and safe nutrient levels), and be produced and packaged to maintain adequate shelf life at low cost, while maintaining standards set by government regulatory bodies.

A few products that have been fortified with vitamin A have been shown to be effective in improving and maintaining adequate vitamin A status in high-risk populations. Most successful has been the fortification of sugar in Guatemala and elsewhere in Central and South America, where population vitamin A status has been effectively improved over the past 2.5 decades (Arroyave, Mejia, & Aguilar, 1981; Dary, 1994; Krause, Delisle, & Solomons, 1998). Monosodium glutamate fortification with vitamin A was shown to improve status and reduce child mortality in Southeast Asia (Muhilal et al., 1988; Solon et al., 1979; Sommer & West, 1996), but organoleptic changes hindered its further use (Solon et al., 1985). Other successfully tested products include nonrefrigerated margarine (Solon et al., 1996) and centrally processed wheat flour (Solon et al., 2000) in the Philippines, and a va-

riety of long-standing food aid commodities such as dried skim milk powder, vegetable oil, and cereal grain flours.

Improved intake of vitamin A through other food-based means inevitably leads to a diversified diet and increased intakes of many micronutrients (Combs et al., 1996). Highly bioavailable, preformed vitamin A is found in liver, fish liver oil, cheese, milk, and other full-fat dairy products. Such foods, however, typically constitue 10% to 15% of all food sources of vitamin A in low income settings. Provitamin A carotenoids (e.g., beta-carotene) derived from deeply colored yellow and orange fruits and vegetables and dark green leaves historically have been viewed to contribute more than 85% of food-based vitamin A in the developing world (FAO, 1988). Although apparently effective in preventing moderate to severe vitamin A deficiency (Sommer & West, 1996), the efficiency of bioconversion of plant-based carotenoids to retinol has been deemed to be at least half that previously calculated (i.e., from a beta-carotene to retinol conversion ratio by weight of 6:1 to 12:1) (Institute of Medicine, 2001), particularly from dark green leaves (West, Eilander, & van Lieshout, 2002). The new dietary conversion data suggest that poor, undernourished societies may not be able to optimize their vitamin A status subsisting on a strictly vegetarian diet (De Pee, Bloem, Gorstein, et al., 1998; De Pee et al., 1995; De Pee et al., 1999).

Children with xerophthalmia tend to be breastfed less frequently, weaned from the breast at an earlier age, and given foods high in vitamin A content less often than clinically normal children (Mahalanabis, 1991; Mele et al., 1991; Sommer & West, 1996; Tarwotjo, Sommer, & Soegiharto, 1982; West et al., 1986). Thus, infant and child feeding approaches should encourage continued breastfeeding into the third year of life, while nutritious complementary foods such as egg, ripe mango and papaya, cooked carrot, and dark green leaves are introduced at appropriate times (De Pee, Bloem, Satoto, et al.,1998; Kuhnlein, 1992; Seshadri,1996; Tarwotjo, Sommer, & Soegiharto, 1982). Who children eat their meals with may also affect the quality of their diet. In Nepal, young children sharing a meal plate with other children and adults were more likely to eat a nutritious variety of foods at mealtime than children eating alone, particularly if the person with whom a plate was shared was an adult female (Shankar et al., 1998). Social marketing programs have been effective in increasing household purchases and intakes of vitamin A food sources such as dark green leaves (Smitasiri, Attig, & Dhanamitta, 1992) and egg (De Pee, Bloem, Satoto, et al., 1998). Home gardening, where commonly practiced, provides an excellent means to increase the variety of provitamin A carotenoid-rich foods (Talukder et al., 1993). Although effects of homestead gardening on vitamin A status remain inconclusive, other food security, nutritional, and economic benefits can accrue from such programs (Marsh, 1998).

Iron Deficiency and Anemia

Iron is essential in the body for oxygen transport and cellular respiration, functions that are especially critical in red cells, brain, and muscle (Beard, 2001). Iron deficiency is considered the most common micronutrient deficiency in the world, with anemia, characterized by abnormally low blood hemoglobin concentration, being its major clinical manifestation. Although anemia is not specific to iron deficiency, the two conditions are inseparable in most malnourished populations, making anemia the most frequently reported clinical index of iron deficiency in the low-income countries (Yip, 1994).

An estimated 1.3 to more than 2 billion women, children, and men in the world are anemic (DeMaeyer & Adiels-Tegman, 1985; Stoltzfus, Mullany, & Black, 2004; WHO, 1992a). Approximately half of the global burden of anemia appears to be due solely to iron de-

ficiency. On the other hand, depletion of body iron stores (with or without impaired red cell production) is likely to be twice as prevalent as anemia (Cook, Finch, & Smith, 1976; Yip, 1994), leading to roughly similar global estimates of the prevalence of anemia (from all causes) and iron deficiency. The term *nutritional anemia* includes the anemic burden due to deficiency in iron plus other vitamins, particularly folate, vitamin B_{12} (Fishman, Christian, & West, 2000), and vitamin A (Sommer & West, 1996), and trace elements that participate in erythropoiesis (WHO, 1992a). Major nonnutritional causes of red cell mass loss or destruction and consequent anemia are hookworm (Albonico et al., 1998; Brooker et al., 1999; Hopkins et al., 1997; Stoltzfus et al., 1997; Stoltzfus et al., 1998) and malarial (Beales, 1997) infections, respectively, both of which occur in large areas of low-income countries. HIV/AIDS has also emerged as an important cause of anemia in sub-Saharan Africa (Vetter et al., 1996).

Pregnant women, infants, and young children are at highest risk of iron deficiency anemia. According to population surveys conducted from 1970 through the late 1980s, nearly half of women of reproductive age in low-income countries are anemic (Table 5-8) based on conventional hemoglobin (Hb) concentration cutoffs (Table 5-9) (Stoltzfus, 2003). On average, an even

Table 5-8	Prevalence of Anemia by Life Stage and Geographic Region of the World		
	Women (15–44 yr)	**Men (15–49 yr)**	**Children (0–4 yr)**
Africa	41%	28%	60%
Latin America	23%	11%	46%
Eastern Mediterranean	44%	17%	63%
Southeast Asia[a]	49%	32%	49%
Southeast Asia[b]	60%	36%	66%
North America	8%	5%	7%

Note: Several countries are excluded within each region due to lack of population anemia prevalence data.

[a]Indonesia, Sri Lanka, and Thailand

[b]Bangladesh, Bhutan, Democratic People's Republic of Korea, India, Maldives, Myanmar, and Nepal.

Source: R. J. Stoltzfus, "Iron Deficiency: Global Prevalence and Consequences," 2003, *Food and Nutrition Bulletin, 24*, pp. S99–S103. Reprinted with permission.

Table 5-9	Hemoglobin and Hematocrit Cutoffs Used to Define Anemia		
	Hemoglobin Cutoff (g/L)		**Hematocrit Cutoff (%)**
Target Group	**Any**	**Moderate to Severe[a]**	**Any**
Children 0–5 years	<110	<90	<33
Children 6–14 years	<120	<100	<36
Nonpregnant women	<120	<100	<36
Pregnant women	<110	<90	<33
Men	<130	<110	<39

[a]Suggested cutoffs are motivated by discussions in Stoltzfus (1997) and Yip (1994), indicating a cutoff for moderate anemia at approximately 20 g/L below that for mild anemia, and findings from the U.S. National Collaborative Perinatal Project (Garn et al., 1981).

higher percentage of preschool-aged children are anemic due to iron deficiency, affecting an estimated 750 million worldwide (UNICEF, n.d.). Southeast Asia shoulders the greatest burden of anemia, and presumably iron deficiency, where approximately two-thirds of women and young children have anemia. Data from Central Asia suggest that Central Asia bears a comparable risk, with 40% to 60% of women of reproductive age reported to be anemic (Sharmanov, 1998). Moderate to severe maternal anemia, defined at Hb cutoffs ranging from below 90 or below 100 g/L, can be expected to affect far fewer women, but the use of such cutoffs may differentiate, with greater clarity, populations lying along an anemia health risk continuum (Stoltzfus, 1997). Severe anemia (Hb cutoffs ranging from <50 to <70 g/L) generally occurs in less than 5% of women in high-risk populations (Sharmanov, 1998; Stoltzfus, 1997). The World Health Organization is presently updating its database from surveys conducted after 1991; however, most later survey data examined to date suggest little change over the past 15 years (Mason et al., 2001), permitting previous aggregate data to be used and adjusted to estimate burdens of iron deficiency anemia and its health consequences in populations (Stoltzfus, Mullany, & Black, 2004).

Function, Requirements, and Assessment

In the body, iron is found in metabolically active "functional" and "storage" pools, accounting for approximately 75% and 25% of total body iron, respectively (Lynch, 1999). Approximately 80% of functional iron complexes with Hb during erythropoiesis, where it plays a central-role in oxygen transport to cells. Ten percent of this metabolic iron pool is incorporated into intracellular myoglobin, where oxygen is stored for use during muscle respiration and contraction. In addition, iron serves as a cofactor in 200 or more heme and nonheme enzymes involved in cellular respiration, division, neurotransmission, immunity, and growth (Beard, 2001; Dallman, 1986; Ryan, 1997; Viteri, 1998). These ubiquitous functions highlight the importance of adequate iron nutriture in achieving health benchmarks as diverse as physical performance, a normal pregnancy outcome, and full motor and cognitive potential (Ryan, 1997; Viteri, 1998).

Metabolic and functional pathways of iron in the body provide the basis for indicators used to assess iron status, and thus are important to understand. Total body iron balance is largely regulated at the point of absorption. Approximately 12% to 25% of dietary heme iron (e.g., from red meat) is taken up by the small intestinal mucosa (Bothwell & Charlton, 1981), versus a much smaller fraction, typically less than 5%, of dietary nonheme iron from cereal-based diets. Absorption depends on the iron status and requirements of the host, the food matrix, and the presence of dietary factors that inhibit or enhance absorption (Bothwell et al., 1982). Newly absorbed iron as well as endogenous iron released from normal degradation of senescent red blood cells is transported to tissues by plasma transferrin. Although virtually all cells require iron, approximately 80% of transferrin-bound iron is delivered to bone marrow for red cell production, mediated by expression of a specific transferrin receptor that reflects tissue iron need (Skikne, Flowers, & Cook, 1990). Normally, up to 30% of body iron is stored in association with the intracellular protein ferritin, from which iron can be released into circulation to maintain homeostasis, or as hemosiderin, which is a less available, longer-term intracellular storage form of tissue iron (Dallman, 1986). During prolonged dietary deficit, iron is released from intracellular ferritin into circulation via transferrin to support hematopoiesis, thus decreasing iron stores. As iron depletion progresses, transferrin carries and delivers a diminishing supply of iron to the marrow and other tissues. This stage of iron deficiency without anemia is reflected by increased transferrin receptor expression on cell surfaces, a low level of transferrin being saturated with iron, and increased amounts of circulating erythrocyte protoporphyrin, a protein that accumulates in red blood cells lacking iron (Skikne, Flowers, & Cook, 1990). Finally, iron deficiency anemia develops as Hb concentration falls, red cells become smaller in size (microcytic) and more pale in color (hypochromic), and mean corpuscular volume decreases (Ryan, 1997).

Several indicators track these changes in iron status, only a few of which are commonly used and are discussed here. Assessment of Hb or hematocrit (Hct) concentrations, evaluating their distributions against conventional cutoffs by age, life stage, and gender (Table 5-9), is the standard approach for diagnosing and estimating the prevalence of anemia. Field assessment of Hb has advanced greatly through use of the HemoCue, a battery-operated portable photometer (Anglholm, Sweden) (Burger & Pierre-Louis, 2003; Yip, 1994). In populations where iron deficiency is known to be the single major cause of anemia, comparing the distribution of Hb values against a referent distribution free of iron deficiency can reveal the total burden of anemia that should be amenable to iron intervention (Yip, 1994; Yip, Johnson, & Dallman, 1984). Estimating the prevalence of moderate to severe anemia, with its greater health risk (Dallman, 1986) and responsiveness to intervention, may improve the interpretation of population anemia burden over the use of cutoffs that define mild anemia or worse status (Stoltzfus, 1997). Assessing Hb response to supplementation provides another, more accurate but complex approach to estimating the extent of iron deficiency anemia (Yip, 1994).

Although ferritin is an intracellular iron storage protein, it also appears in circulation, giving rise to its use as an indicator of tissue iron stores (Cook et al., 1974), with each 1 μg/L concentration of plasma ferritin reflecting approximately 8 to 10 mg of tissue iron. Concentrations below 12 μg/L are conventionally taken to represent a state of body iron depletion (Bothwell & Charlton, 1981), although plasma ferritin may be elevated in response to acute infection or chronic inflammation (Walter et al., 1997). Measurement of soluble transferrin receptor in plasma has been shown to provide a dependable estimate of tissue iron need (Cook, Baynes, & Skikne, 1994) under conditions of chronic disease or inflammation (Ferguson et al., 1992), undernutrition (Kuvibidila et al., 1996), and pregnancy (Akesson et al., 1998) but remains little used in low-income countries. Another common measure of iron status is percent transferrin saturation, which reflects the adequacy of iron delivery to tissues (Bothwell & Charlton, 1981). The conceptual spectrum of deficiency, with illustrated cutoffs for serologic indicators

commonly used in low-income countries, is depicted in Figure 5-9 (Bothwell & Charlton, 1981).

Simple diagnostic tools available to assess anemia in primary care settings include the clinical diagnosis of pallor (palmar, tarsal conjunctival, and nail bed), which can diagnose severe anemia (Hb <50 to <70 g/L or Hct <15%) with approximately 10% to 50% sensitivity and 90% to 100% specificity (Kalter et al., 1997; Luby et al., 1995; Stoltzfus et al., 1999; Zucker et al., 1997). A simple color scale has shown promise as a tool for field use in diagnosing low hemoglobin from a fresh blood spot (Lewis, Stott, & Wynn, 1998; Stott & Lewis, 1995). Inexpensive instruments for detecting anemia in primary care settings have also been tested (Robinett, Taylor, & Stephens, 1996).

The RDA for iron has been established based on complex considerations of requirements at various life stages in healthy populations, the proportion of heme to nonheme dietary iron, and other factors. A bioavailability of 18% is presumed for most estimates, recognizing that one-half to one-third of this percentage of ingested iron is likely to be typically bioavailable from grain-based diets lacking meat, as found in most low-income countries. With this caveat in mind, an RDA has been set at 8 mg per day for men of all ages and for postmenopausal women. Premenopausal intake should be 18 mg per day, intended to replace menstrual losses. The RDA throughout pregnancy is 27 mg per day, based on third-trimester needs that are intended to permit iron

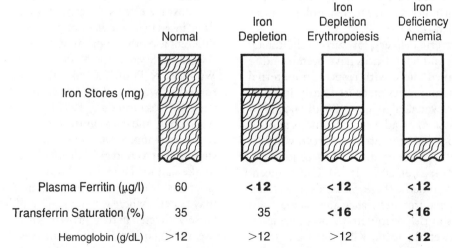

Figure 5-9 Relationship Between Depletion in Body Iron Stores and Change in Selected Indicators of Iron and Anemia Status. *Note:* Bold values represent deficient status. *Source:* T. H. Bothwell, & R. W. Charlton. (1981). *Iron Deficiency in Women.* Report from the International Nutritional Anemia Consultative Group (INACG). Washington, DC: The Nutrition Foundation.

stores to build during early gestation (Institute of Medicine, 2001).

Health Consequences

The highest-risk groups in terms of both probability of becoming anemic from iron deficiency and of suffering its consequences are women of reproductive age, especially during pregnancy; infants older than 6 months of age; and young children.

Pregnancy-Related Vital Outcomes. Women are at high risk of anemia due to periodic menstrual blood loss and increased requirements during pregnancy due to expanded red blood cell mass and accretion of iron in fetal tissue and placenta. Thus, gestational iron deficiency anemia is likely to be harmful to the mother, as suggested by evidence from several observational studies over the past 40 years linking moderate anemia (Hb 40–80 g/L) to a 1.35-fold higher risk of maternal mortality (95% CI: 0.92–2.00) and severe anemia (<47 g/L) to a 3.51-fold higher risk (95% CI: 2.05–6.00) of maternal death compared with nonanemic gravida (Brabin, Hakimi, & Pelletier, 2001). Although no experimental trials exist to demonstrate that iron supplementation reduces maternal mortality, plausible causes associated with moderate to severe anemia include puerperal cardiac failure or hemorrhage (Allen, 1997). A more formal, recent meta-analysis suggests there is a continuous risk reduction in maternal mortality risk, reflected by a protective odds ratio of 0.75 (95% CI: 0.62–0.89), with each 10 g/L increase in blood Hb concentration (Stoltzfus, Mullany, & Black, 2004). However, data revealing the incidence and severity of maternal morbidity relative to hematologic status are lacking (Allen, 1997).

Risks of preterm delivery, low birth weight, fetal malformations, and fetal deaths have been found to follow a U-shaped curve with respect to maternal hemoglobin (hematocrit) measured early in pregnancy, with an elevated Hb (e.g., >130 g/L) posing as much or more risk of an adverse outcome as a lower (<90 g/L) hemoglobin concentration (Dreyfuss, 1998; Scholl et al., 1992; Steer et al., 1995; Yip, Johnson, & Dallman, 1984; Zhou et al., 1998). Causal mechanisms that may underlie these risks are not well understood. Maternal iron deficiency anemia may also place newborns at risk of low iron stores during infancy (Hokama et al., 1996; Kilbride et al., 1999; Preziosi et al., 1997). Recently, iron supplementation during pregnancy was found to improve newborn length, Apgar score, and survival (Preziosi et al., 1997; Christian, 1998) and lead to larger infant iron stores (plasma ferritin concentrations) at 3 months of age.

In Nepal, a randomized, multiple-arm antenatal micronutrient supplementation trial observed that daily iron (60 mg) and folic acid (400 µg) intake reduced the risk of low birth weight (<2,500 g) by 16% (Christian, Khatry, et al., 2003)—a change, however, that appeared to confer no apparent advantage to infant survival through 3 months of age (Christian, West, et al., 2003), leaving unclear the benefits of maternal iron supplementation to infant survival.

Growth. Late infancy and early childhood is a high-risk period for becoming iron deficient and anemic because of the high iron levels required to support rapid growth coupled with poor dietary intake of bioavailable iron (Gibson, Ferguson, & Lehrfeld, 1998; Ryan, 1997). Iron deficiency anemia has been associated with stunted growth (Chwang, Soemantri, & Pollitt, 1988), and in some trials iron supplementation (e.g., at approximately 2–3 mg per kilogram body weight per day) has improved both ponderal and linear growth of initially anemic and iron-deficient children (Angeles et al., 1993; Aukett et al., 1986; Chwang, Soemantri, & Pollitt, 1988; Lawless et al., 1994). Yet in other trials, including studies done in populations where iron deficiency anemia prevails, daily iron had no effect on child growth (Rahman et al., 1999; Rosado et al., 1997), and in one study supplemental iron mildly suppressed weight gain (Idjradinata, Watkins, & Pollitt, 1994). Recent trials in Sweden and Honduras (Dewey et al., 2002) observed bone growth deceleration and possible increased frequencies of diarrhea with daily iron supplementation in nonanemic breastfed infants, whereas anemic infants may have experienced less diarrhea.

Positive effects on growth of school-aged children in Kenya (Lawless et al., 1994), qualitatively different growth responses within similar populations (Chwang, Soemantri, & Pollitt, 1988; Idjradinata, Watkins, & Pollitt, 1994), and lack of effects observed in wasted (Rahman et al., 1999) and nonwasted (Rosado et al., 1997) populations, coupled with small and nonsignificant effect sizes obtained from meta-analyses (Ramakrishnan et al., 2004), all suggest that a child growth effect from increased iron intake cannot be expected. Of more concern is the emerging evidence of an interaction: Anemic children may benefit, whereas nonanemic children may be adversely affected in their growth with iron supplement use, raising questions about the need for targeted interventions in the future.

Development. Persistent deficits in learning, psychomotor, behavioral interactions, and educational achievement have been observed more often in anemic infants and young children than in children with normal hematologic status (Aukett et al., 1986; Lozoff et al., 1998; Pollitt et al., 1995), but such abnormalities may also result from malnutrition, other health problems (Heywood et al., 1989), and inadequate stimulation at home (Lozoff et al., 1998). Perhaps not surprisingly, some trials have reported improved behavioral (Oski et al., 1983), developmental (Aukett et al., 1986), and learning-achievement scores with daily iron supplementation of children (Bruner et al., 1996; Soemantri, Pollitt, & Kim, 1985), whereas other trials have failed to reverse early psychomotor deficits with iron (Lozoff, Wolf, & Jimenez, 1996; Walter, 1989). Still, the potential for infantile and early childhood iron deficiency to compromise child development provides strong impetus to advance both iron deficiency prevention programs and research agendas.

Prevention

Programs should seek first to prevent iron deficiency anemia among pregnant and postpartum women and infants 6 to 24 months of age (Stoltzfus & Dreyfuss, 1998). Ideally, women entering their reproductive years (Viteri, 1998) and preschool children provide additional potentially anemic groups to target (Stoltzfus & Dreyfuss, 1998). Effective planning should establish proportions of the anemic burden attributable to iron deficiency, malaria, hookworm, or other causes (Yip, 1997). For example, anthelminthic prophylaxis may prove highly effective where hookworm and trichuris are endemic (Albonico et al., 1998; Brooker et al., 1999; Christian, Khatry, & West, 2004; Hopkins et al., 1997; Stoltzfus et al., 1998). Malarial prophylaxis programs may also re-

duce the risk of anemia (Beales, 1997; Huddle, Gibson, & Cullinan, 1999). Iron deficiency is the underlying cause of anemia, however, in most populations, which can be directly addressed through iron supplementation, food fortification, or other dietary measures.

Iron Supplementation. Guidelines have been developed in accordance with WHO recommendations for the use of iron and folic acid supplements to prevent and treat iron deficiency anemia (Table 5-10) (Stoltzfus & Dreyfuss, 1998). Daily iron supplementation can effectively raise blood Hb and plasma ferritin levels among pregnant women. Inclusion of folic acid can guard against megaloblastic anemia, neural tube abnormalities if women are supplemented periconceptionally (MRC Vitamin Study Research Group, 1991), and other consequences of folate deficiency that may affect malnourished populations (Fishman, Christian, & West, 2000). A long-standing debate over whether prophylactic iron may be contraindicated where malaria is endemic (Menendez et al., 1997; Murray et al., 1975; Oppenheimer, 2001) has been refueled by the findings of two randomized trials: one in Zanzibar, reporting that preschool child iron supplementation in a *P. falciparum* malaria endemic area may increase risk of hospitalization and mortality in nonanemic children (Sazawal, 2004), and one in a nonmalarious area of Nepal, where no such effect was observed (J. Tielsch, et al., personal communication, 2005). To date, though, low-cost systems for routine and high-compliance delivery of oral iron to infants and young children in typical low-income-country settings remain to be implemented.

Table 5-10	Guidelines for Supplementing Pregnant Women and Infants with Iron			
	Daily Dosage			
Prevalence of Anemia	**Iron (mg)**	**Folic Acid (μg)**	**Condition**	**Duration**
Pregnant Women				
<40%	60	400	In pregnancy	6 months[a]
≥40%	60	400	In pregnancy	6 months[a]
			Postpartum	3 months
Infants				
<40%[b]	12.5[c]	50	Birth weight ≥ 2,500 g	6–12 months
			Birth weight < 2,500 g	2–24 months
≥40%[b]	12.5[c]	50	Birth weight ≥ 2,500 g	6–24 months
			Birth weight < 2,500 g	2–24 months

[a]If 6-month duration cannot be achieved in pregnancy, continue supplement to 6 months postpartum or increase dose to 120 mg iron per day.

[b]If prevalence in infants is not known, assume the same prevalence as observed in pregnant women in the same population.

[c]Iron dosage is based on 2 mg iron per kg body weight per day.

Source: R. J. Stoltzfus and M. L. Dreyfuss, M. L., *Guidelines for the Use of Iron Supplements to Prevent and Treat Iron Deficiency Anemia* (Washington, DC: ILSI Press, 1998). Reprinted with permission. Rates are based on cutoffs proposed by Stoltzfus and Dreyfuss (1998).

Fortification. Iron fortification has been successfully carried out in a number of foodstuffs, such as fish sauces, curry powder, sugar, salt, dairy products, and infant formulas (Stoltzfus & Dreyfuss, 1998), though few large-scale iron fortification programs exist in low- and middle-income countries (Yip, 1997). Several food-grade forms of iron are available for use, depending on the type of food vehicle, methods of preparation, storage, and other factors. For example, ferrous sulfate can be used in liquids but may discolor dry foods or make fatty foods rancid (International Nutritional Anemia Consultative Group, 1997). Iron EDTA (ethylenediaminetetraacetic acid) has been shown to permit efficient absorption of nonheme iron in the presence of dietary inhibitors of absorption (Lynch et al., 1993). As with supplementation, two primary target groups exist for fortification—infants and young children, and women—for whom different food vehicles may need to be considered.

Powdered milk, frequently given to children in low-income, aid-recipient families, was fortified with both iron and vitamin C and shown to improve iron status of young children in Chile (Yip, 1997). "Sprinkles," single-meal sachets of lipid-encapsulated ferrous fumarate in powdered form, which can be sprinkled onto porridge, offer a promising "home fortification" approach to increasing iron intake in infants (Zlotkin et al., 2001). First proposed in 1996, iron-fortified sprinkles have been shown in seven randomized trials conducted in four low-income countries to be equivalent to iron sulfate drops in curing infantile anemia (Zlotkin et al., 2005). Presently, assistance is being offered to transfer the sprinkles production capabilities to several low-income-country governments. Several Caribbean, South American, and South Asian countries have begun to fortify wheat flour with iron (Yip, 1997). Yet, to date, one large, community-based wheat fortification trial in Sri Lanka, using either electrolytic or reduced iron, failed to improve Hb status in children of either preschool or school ages, or in nonpregnant women (Nestel et al., 2004). Alternatively, trials in Morocco have demonstrated significant improvements in a range of iron status indicators in school-aged children consuming salt fortified with either iron plus iodine (Zimmermann et al., 2003; Zimmermann, Wegmueller, et al., 2004a) or iron, iodine, and vitamin A (Zimmermann, Wegmueller, et al., 2004b). Adverse effects, as seen with iron supplements, have not been reported from fortification trials.

Dietary Approach. Typically, the iron density of diets in low-income regions ranges from 4.5 to 7.5 mg per 1,000 kilocalories (ACC/SCN, 1992), largely consisting of nonheme iron from grains, nuts, vegetables, and fruits, from which iron is poorly absorbed (Bothwell et al., 1982; Lynch, 1997). Phytates in foods, tannins and polyphenols in tea, calcium in dairy products and green leaves, and animal protein from whole milk, cheeses, and egg whites further inhibit the absorption of nonheme iron (Hallberg, et al., 1991; Lynch, 1997; Ryan, 1997). Concurrent intakes of ascorbic acid (e.g., from citrus) or meat, poultry, and fish (Bothwell et al.,1982; Monsen et al., 1978) can enhance nonheme absorption in a dose-response manner. However, dietary programs to prevent anemia in low-income countries have been few and have achieved little success (Yip, 1997).

Iodine Deficiency

Iodine is an essential component of thyroid hormones that control cellular metabolism and neuromuscular tissue growth and development. Deficiency in iodine and consequent thyroid hormone production during critical periods of organogenesis can thus damage the brain and nervous tissue, causing irreversible mental retardation and other developmental abnormalities. The spectrum of mild through severe health consequences causally linked to iodine deficiency at different stages of life (Table 5-11) are collectively known as iodine deficiency disorders, or IDD (Delange, 1994). Although these effects vary in their specificity with respect to deficiency of iodine, the term has propelled greater understanding of the multiple health and societal consequences of this nutrient deficiency. Informative treatises exist on the histories of goiter and cretinism, the two most notable clinical syndromes of iodine deficiency (Hetzel, 1989).

As an element in the Earth's crust, iodine can be either sufficient or in varying stages of depletion in areas of the world. Thus, the iodine adequacy of all flora and fauna, and therefore food, in a general locale is dependent on the adequacy of the nutrient in soil (Houston, 1999). Major mountainous regions of the world, such as the Himalayas, Andes, and Alps, are severely depleted in soil iodine, resulting from erosion due to glacier activity, rain, and deforestation (Dunn & van der Haar, 1990). However, plains regions of central Africa, Asia, and Europe, as well as major riverine and deltaic areas affected by frequent flooding, such as Gangetic South Asia and the valleys of the Yellow, Rhine, and Amazon rivers, also lack iodine (Dunn & van der Haar, 1990) (Figure 5-10). In some areas of Central Africa, such as Zaire, where environmental iodine and intake are marginal to low, iodine deficiency is augmented by routine consumption

Table 5-11	Spectrum of Iodine Deficiency Disorders
Fetus	
Abortion	
Stillbirth	
Congenital anomalies	
Increased perinatal mortality	
Increased infant mortality	
Endemic cretinism	
Deaf mutism	
Neonate	
Neonatal goiter	
Neonatal hypothyroidism	
Increased susceptibility to nuclear radiation[a]	
Child and Adolescent	
Goiter	
Juvenile hypothyroidism	
Impaired mental function	
Retarded physical development	
Increased susceptibility to nuclear radiation[a]	
Adult	
Goiter with its complications	
Hypothyroidism	
Impaired mental function	
Iodine-induced hyperthyroidism	
Increased susceptibility to nuclear radiation	

[a]Due to increased uptake of radioactive iodine by the thyroid gland.

Source: F. Delange, "The Disorders Induced by Iodine Deficiency," 1994, *Thyroid, 4,* pp. 107–128. Reprinted with permission.

of goitrogenic substances, such as linamarin, a cyanide-containing compound found in the root of cassava (Delange et al., 1982). Thiocyanates, which result from detoxification of linamarin in the liver, decrease iodine uptake by the thyroid gland and suppress circulating thyroid hormone, leading to secondary iodine deficiency.

As of the early 1990s, an estimated 1.6 billion persons, or nearly 30% of the world's population, were thought to be at risk of iodine deficiency (WHO, 1993), based on documented occurrence of goiter (prevalence >5%) and the sizes of populations living in iodine-depleted regions of the world (Houston, 1999). Revised estimates of the extent of iodine deficiency obtained from WHO's global database for the 192 member states of the United Nations suggest that nearly 2 billion people, or approximately 35% of the world's population living in 53 countries, have an insufficient intake of iodine based on urinary iodine status, and 16% of the world's populations are affected by goiter (de Benoist et al., 2004) (Table 5-12).

Estimates of the numbers affected by cretinism (approximately 11 million worldwide) have not changed in recent years. Perhaps of greatest concern is the likelihood that more than 43 million persons in 118 affected countries throughout the world have some degree of mental impairment resulting from iodine deficiency (WHO, 1994).

Function

Iodine, ingested as iodide or iodate, is an essential constituent of thyroid hormones. Once in circulation, nearly all body iodide is actively trapped by follicle cells of the thyroid gland, where it is oxidized to iodine and bound to tyrosine amino acids, catalyzed by an iron-containing peroxidase, to form the thyroid hormones T_3 (triiodothyronine) and T_4 (tetraiodothyronine, or thyroxine) (Houston, 1999; Tortora & Grabowski, 1996). T_3 and T_4 are stored in the thyroid gland in association with the glycoprotein thyroglobulin.

Following stimulation from the hypothalamus, thyroid-stimulating hormone (TSH) is released from the anterior pituitary gland, which induces thyroid hormone release into circulation bound to circulatory carrier proteins (Houston, 1999). As T_3 and T_4 levels rise, the hypothalamic–anterior pituitary–thyroid axis maintains homeostasis by reducing thyroid hormone release. Within target cells, thyroid hormones regulate oxygen use, basic metabolic rate, protein synthesis, and thermogenesis; this is accomplished largely by influencing gene transcription (Stein, 1994). During gestation, both maternal as well as fetally derived T_3 and T_4 contribute to the regulatory thyroxine pool that, acting in concert with other hormones (e.g., growth hormone, insulin), directs fetal tissue function, growth, and development. In particular, thyroid hormones influence the development of the brain and other neural tissue, giving rise to their, and iodine's, key role in regulating fetal and infant growth, physical and mental function, and development (Tortora & Grabowski, 1996). Paradoxically, excess build-up of iodine in the thyroid gland can suppress the release of T_3 and T_4, leading to concern about risks of toxicity associated with rapid correction of iodine deficiency in some endemic areas (Corvilain et al., 1998; Dunn, Semigran, & Delange, 1998; Stanbury et al., 1998), similar to risks observed in areas of chronically high iodine intake (Konno et al., 1994).

Health Consequences

Among the disorders caused by lack of iodine, fetal and neonatal hypothyroidism due to maternal iodine depletion is by far the most serious, with widespread

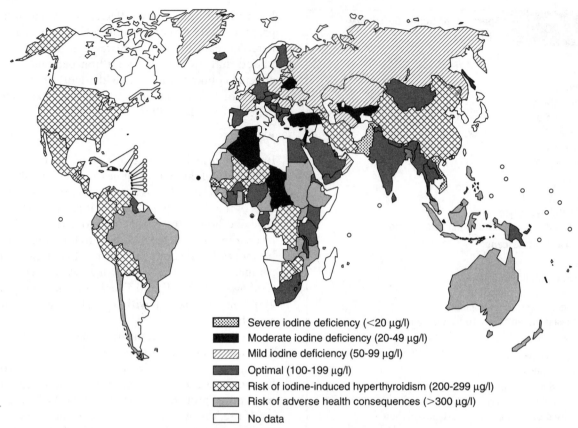

Severe iodine deficiency (<20 µg/l)
Moderate iodine deficiency (20-49 µg/l)
Mild iodine deficiency (50-99 µg/l)
Optimal (100-199 µg/l)
Risk of iodine-induced hyperthyroidism (200-299 µg/l)
Risk of adverse health consequences (>300 µg/l)
No data

Figure 5-10 Prevalence of Worldwide Iodine Deficiency Disorders Based on Assessment of the Total Goiter Rate in School-Aged Children. *Source:* B. De Benoist, M. Andersson, I. Egli, B. Takkouche, & H. Allen (Eds). (2004). *Iodine status worldwide.* WHO global database on iodine deficiency. Geneva: World Health Organization.

Table 5-12	Iodine Deficiency by United Nations Region							
	Countries				**Population**[b]			
	Surveyed[c]		**Deficient**[d]		**Insufficient Intake**[e]		**Goiter Rate**	
UN Region[a]	No.	%	No.	%	No. (millions)	%	No. (millions)	%
Africa	38	72	16	42	324.2	43.0	202.1	26.8
Asia	34	72	17	50	1239.3	35.6	504.8	14.5
Europe	30	73	16	53	330.8	52.7	102.3	16.3
Latin America and the Caribbean	19	58	2	11	47.4	10.0	22.3	4.7
Northern America	1	50	0	0	27.6	9.5	—	—
Oceania	4	25	3	75	19.2	64.5	3.84	12.9
Total	126	67	54	42	1988.5	35.2	835.3	15.8

[a]United Nations designated regions, with 192 member states distributed as follows: Africa (53), Asia (47), Europe (41), Latin America & Caribbean (33), Northern America (2), and Oceania (16).

[b]Population across all ages.

[c]Number (%) of countries within each region with national or subnational urinary iodine (UI) surveys for school-aged children (6–12 yr).

[d]Number (%) of surveyed countries considered to have at least mild iodine deficiency based on the median UI levels in school-aged children being less than 100 µg/L.

[e]Estimates extrapolated to general population based on surveyed UI levels (<100 µg/L) and total goiter rates in school-aged children (de Benoist et al., 2004).

consequences. This disorder permanently alters the structure and function of the brain and other nervous tissue during critical stages of development, giving rise to permanent neurologic and developmental abnormalities (Hetzel, 1994; Stein, 1994). Postnatal iodine deficiency perpetuates thyroid failure that, depending on its duration and severity, can lead to continued hypothyroidism, growth retardation, sexual immaturity, and impaired cognition and motor development (Halpern, 1994).

Severe iodine deficiency can result in spontaneous abortion, stillbirth, and congenital abnormalities among surviving offspring (Pharoah, Buttfield, & Hetzel, 1971). Cretinism (Figure 5-11), representing the most severe clinical spectrum of IDD, is usually manifest by severe mental and growth retardation, paraplegia, rigidity, deaf-mutism, and facial disturbances (Hetzel, 1994). The type and severity of brain

Figure 5-11 Cretinism. *Source:* Photograph copyright John Dunn.

and other neurologic and musculoskeletal deficits appear to arise from the timing, duration, and severity of insult. For example, the central nervous system defects associated with cretinism can be linked to severe gestational iodine deficiency in the second trimester of pregnancy (DeLong et al., 1994; Halpern, 1994), a period when the cerebral cortex, basal ganglia, and cochlea undergo rapid growth and development. Severe fetal hypothyroidism thus gives rise to the neurologic cretin. Severe growth retardation, sexual delay, and musculoskeletal deformity, with continued neurologic damage, can be attributed largely to severe postnatal iodine deficiency, giving rise to the myxedemetous cretin (Boyages, 1994).

Mild, biochemical, or noncretinous hypothyroidism due to iodine deficiency is a major public health concern due to its frequency in infancy and early childhood. Decreased infant survival may be a little-suspected consequence of mild neonatal hypothyroidism (Cobra et al., 1997). More fully appreciated is the observation that children living in iodine-deficient communities, usually exhibiting one or more indications of iodine deficiency, exhibit a lower intelligence quotient and perform more poorly in cognition, motor function, and school achievement tests than peers with normal status growing up under iodine-sufficient surroundings (Bleichrodt & Born, 1994; Huda et al., 1999). Historically, the strength of evidence for a unique contribution of mild iodine deficiency to impaired cognition, has been tempered by lack of control in studies for community differences in nutritional, health, education, and socioeconomic factors that can also influence child stimulation and achievement. Some of these concerns for confounders, however, are being addressed. An observational study of young, mildly hypothyroid and euthyroid Bangladeshi school children, matched on school, grade, and local area and controlled for numerous potential confounders related to child health and household status, still observed deficient performance of hypothyroid children in terms of abilities to spell and read (Huda et al., 1999). Recognition and quantification of this subclinical base of the IDD iceberg have been key motivating factors for invigorated efforts to prevent iodine deficiency (Hetzel, 1989).

Goiter is an enlarged thyroid gland and is the most commonly observed clinical manifestation of iodine deficiency. Chronic deficiency of iodine lowers thyroid hormone output, which, in turn, leads to increased TSH release from the anterior pituitary to stimulate increased T_3 and thyroxine production. Failure results in compensatory growth of the thyroid gland (Kavishe, 1999). Goiter size can range from barely palpable with the neck extended to grotesquely visible from a distance. An enlarged thyroid due to iodine deficiency poses little known health risk. However, hyperthyroidism reflecting a state of thyrotoxicosis may serve as an indicator of cardiac risk in some elderly groups who respond abnormally to iodine prophylaxis (Corvilain et al., 1998; Dunn, Semigran, & Delange, 1998; Stanbury et al., 1998).

Assessment

Iodine status can be assessed through clinical and biochemical means. Indicators with suggested cutoffs, target populations for assessment, and criteria related to severity of iodine deficiency as a public health problem have been published by WHO and the International Council for Control of Iodine Deficiency (WHO, 1994) (Table 5-13).

Virtually all goiter occurring in iodine-deficient areas can be attributed to iodine deficiency; thus, goiter prevalence can serve as a useful population indicator of risk. Reliable thyroid examination by palpation requires well-trained observers (Peterson et al., 2000). In 1960 the WHO established a five-stage goiter classification system (Perez, Scrimshaw, & Munoz, 1960) that served as the basis for evaluating the public health significance of iodine deficiency over the subsequent three decades (WHO, 1993). The minimum clinical cutoff for estimating the total goiter rate (TGR) was a palpable glandular mass with each lobe being at least as large as the distal phalanx of the subject's thumb. A TGR of more than 10% was set as the minimum public health criterion for iodine deficiency (Perez, Scrimshaw, & Munoz, 1960). In 1994 the WHO simplified the scheme to two clinical grades,

defining goiter as a palpable mass of any size with the neck in a normal position, and lowered the minimum TGR of public health significance to greater than 5% (WHO, 1994). Although motivated to improve diagnostic reliability, the reverse may have occurred by changing the minimum cutoff to a milder, less discernible stage of thyroid enlargement (Peterson et al., 2000).

Thyroid volume is more reliably and accurately assessed by ultrasonography than by palpation, providing a clear method of choice where resources permit (Pardede et al., 1998; Tajtakova et al., 1990). In recent years, normative standards have been developed for evaluating ultrasound-derived thyroid volume distributions in adults (Delange et al., 1997) and in school-aged children for screening and population assessment (Zimmermann, Hess, et al., 2004). Thus, the TGR remains an important population indicator of iodine deficiency risk; however, given the slowness and variability of goiter to respond to increased iodine intake (for example, from more than 6 months to 4 years) (Elnagar et al., 1995; Hintze et al., 1988), other indicators of iodine status should be employed for surveillance and program evaluation (Zimmermann, 2004) .

Urinary iodine (UI) concentration serves as the conventional biochemical measure of current iodine intake and status of a population. Fasting morning samples of urine can be used to assess the iodine status of a community (Thomson et al., 1997; WHO, 1994), although high day-to-day variability requires 24-hour urine collection on more than one day for reliable individual assessment (Rasmussen, Ovesen, & Christiansen, 1999; Thomson et al., 1997). UI is preferably reported as μg/L (WHO, 1994), although

Table 5-13	WHO Minimum Criteria for Iodine Deficiency as a Public Health Problem				
				Severity of IDD	
				Mild	**Severe**
Indicator	**Cutoff**	**Target Population**		**Percent Affected**	
Goiter	Grade >0	Schoolchildren		5–19	≥30
Thyroid volume[a]	>97th percentile	Schoolchildren		5–19	≥30
TSH[b]	>5 μm/L	Neonates		3–19	≥40
	Unit			**Median Concentration**	
Urinary iodine	μg/L	Schoolchildren		50–99	<20
Thyroglobulin	ng/mL	Children and adults		10–19	≥40

[a] Assessed by ultrasonography.

[b] Whole blood thyroid stimulating hormone.

Source: World Health Organization, Indicators for Assessing Iodine Deficiency Disorders and Their Control Through Salt Iodization, WHO/NUT/94.6 (Geneva, Switzerland: World Health Organization, 1994). Adapted with permission.

creatinine-adjusted concentrations are frequently used and, at least in otherwise normally nourished populations, the two measures can be equated (1 μg/L equals approximately 1 μg/g) (Dunn & van der Haar, 1990). A median value of more than 100 μg/L urine is considered to be reflective of a normal (average) iodine intake (i.e., >150 μg per day) and adequate status in the community (Dunn & van der Haar, 1990). Notably, median urinary iodine concentrations correlate negatively with the prevalence of goiter across communities (Bar-Andziak et al., 1993; Caron et al., 1997; Delange et al., 1997; Kimiagar et al., 1990; Pardede et al., 1998; Rasmussen, Ovesen, & Christiansen, 1999) and correlate positively with iodine intake (e.g., r = 0.3 to 0.6) (Bar-Andziak et al., 1993; Brussard et al., 1997; Kim et al., 1998), serving to affirm population-based assessments of risk based on this measure.

Additional iodine status indicators include serum, whole blood, or whole blood spot TSH and serum thyroglobulin concentration. TSH measurement is recommended for screening neonates for hypothyroidism, which also can indicate population iodine status (Delange, 1998; Dunn, 1996; Lixin et al., 1995). Neonatal TSH tends to be negatively correlated (e.g., r = −0.5) with maternal urinary iodine, thus reflecting the status of the maternofetal dyad (Lixin et al., 1995). Thyroglobulin concentration reflects increased turnover of thyroid cells due to hypertrophy and hyperplasia. Both indicators rise with increasingly severe iodine deficiency (decreasing median iodine intakes and UI excretion levels) (WHO, 1994).

Prevention

Unlike other micronutrient deficiencies that might be corrected by diversifying the local diet, iodine deficiency correction in an endemic area is largely dependent on consuming foods grown in iodine-sufficient soil or fortified with iodine (iodization). Pilot projects in China have successfully demonstrated the beneficial impact of iodinating irrigation water used for crop production on the iodine status of humans and animal herds.

An average dietary iodine intake of approximately 150 μg per day is recommended for adults to maintain adequate iodine status (Delange, 1993; Institute of Medicine, 2001). A usual intake of 50 μg per day is considered a minimum requirement, below which thyroid enlargement can be expected (Delange, 1993). U.S. RDAs during infancy through age 3 years, which range from 40 μg to 70 μg per day, are premised on an adequate maternal iodine intake and breast milk iodine concentration. The question-

able applicability of these assumptions in iodine-deficient regions of the world has motivated some experts to suggest raising the recommendation to 90 μg per day for these young ages (Delange, 1993).

Universal salt iodization (USI) remains the longest-standing, most adapted, and most cost-effective approach to preventing iodine deficiency and its disorders throughout the world. Begun in the United States and selected European countries in the 1920s, USI programs are now under way in at least 82 of the 118 countries where risk of IDD is a public health concern (Underwood, 1994). Salt iodization technology is straightforward, typically involving the dry mixing or spraying of potassium iodate or iodide with food-grade salt (Mannar & Dunn, 1995). Levels of iodization vary across and within countries, after considering salt consumption patterns, the iodine gap in the diet, ambient exposures, packaging, transport, and other conditions. Often the iodine concentration will range from 10 ppm to 80 ppm of elemental iodine (Mannar & Dunn, 1995). In recent years, several trials have demonstrated an ability of salt fortified with iodine plus iron (Zimmermann et al., 2003; Zimmermann, Wegmueller, et al., 2004a) and iodine, iron, and vitamin A (Zimmermann, Wegmueller, et al., 2004b) to improve the status of all three nutrients in school-aged children, opening up possibilities for salt to serve as a vehicle for preventing multiple micronutrient deficiencies.

In addition to the expected efficacy of the intended dosage, the success of salt iodization rests on numerous other political, legislative, management, and marketing and salt use factors that must be synchronous to be effective (Exhibit 5-3). Failure in these other program elements has led to disappointingly small changes in iodine status in many settings, even after decades of salt iodization (Langer et al., 1994; Lindberg, Andersson, & Lamberg, 1989; Metges et al., 1996; Syrenicz et al., 1993). Still, USI remains a viable goal in most countries in need of iodine deficiency control.

Where salt iodization is not practical, other means must be found to deliver adequate iodine to high-risk groups (Solomons, 1998). Annual or biannual supplementation with iodized oil improves iodine status (Peterson et al., 2000) and has been shown to markedly lower risk of maternal hypothyroidism, cretinism, and fetal/infant mortality (Pharoah, Butterfield, & Hetzel, 1971). An annual dose of 200 mg of iodine has been shown to optimize iodine status while minimizing risk of toxicity in adults (Peterson et al., 2000). Under consideration is the possibility of delivering a single, oral dose of iodized

---

Exhibit 5-3 | **Salt Iodization: Ensuring Quality, Maintaining Impact**

Salt remains a common dietary item for people of all ages, cultures, and geographic and socioeconomic bounds. Industrialized countries have had iodized salt to prevent iodine deficiency for several decades; however, the full impact of salt iodization has yet to be achieved in most low- and middle-income countries. Iodizing salt is straightforward, but many factors impede progress. Key steps for cost-effective salt iodization were laid out in a 1996 quality assurance workshop for producers, policy makers, scientists, and programmers (Quality Assurance Workshop, 1997). These included the following.

Producers

- Upgrade raw salt production through quality control and training
- Batch process salt and iodate by a mechanized, noncorrosive blender or mixer, with manual backup for power outage; or for continuous processing, use a screw/auger mixer during or after adding iodate dosing pumps and spray methods for uniform iodization
- Package bulk salt in lined or laminated bags of less than 50 kg, using semiautomated filling, sealing, and stitching procedures
- Label bulk bags with "Use No Hooks," "Iodized Salt," producer's name/address, and bag weight
- Retail salt in smaller (<1 kg), heat-sealed bags
- Support government efforts to monitor and achieve iodized salt standards
- Monitor with salt test kits
- Self-police through producer associations

Governments

- Pass and review as needed enabling salt iodization legislation (setting ranges versus absolute concentrations for iodine content) that includes packaging, labeling, transport, and marketing policies
- Hold stakeholder meetings to provide updates on IDD control and discuss new technology
- Develop methods for small producers to meet standards
- Create national database of producers to ensure training
- Strictly monitor and provide incentives for compliance, focusing on low-coverage areas
- Modernize test laboratories
- Accelerate consumer demand for small (<1 kg) retail packages
- Enforce policies related to national standards
- Monitor IDD impact

Agencies

- Develop and distribute information for producers
- Help improve government-industry-international exchange
- Monitor and provide information on the potassium iodate market
- Help increase consumer demand for small packages of salt
- Assist in capacity building and quality assurance agenda

---

oil to young infants at the time of oral polio vaccine, possibly through the WHO Expanded Program on Immunization. In one randomized trial, neutralizing antibody responses to oral polio vaccine were unaffected by iodized oil intake (Taffs et al., 1999), while infant mortality was reduced (Cobra et al., 1997).

Irrespective of the choice of iodine intervention, sound programming principles must be followed, which include involving key stakeholders (from government to the private sector) in planning, educating the targeted public (especially important with voluntary salt iodization), implementing proper monitor-

ing, and taking adequate steps to solve problems and ensure sustainability (Dunn, 1996).

Zinc Deficiency

Zinc is essential for many metabolic functions, growth, and survival in mammals, poultry, and some plants; thus, zinc deficiency has many serious consequences (Hambidge & Krebs, 1999; Keen & Gershwin, 1990; Solomons, 1999). Yet to date zinc deficiency has been one of the least visible micronutrient deficiencies. Evidence of some of the clinical abnormalities due to human zinc deficiency became clear in the 1960s

(Prasad, 1985), but its prevalence was difficult to ascertain due to absence of adequate, nationally representative data on zinc status (ACC/SCN, 2000). This uncertainty, attributed to a lack of reliable indicators or lack of consensus regarding their use and interpretation (Black, 1997), coupled with limited experience to date in prevention programs (Gibson & Ferguson, 1998b) may have been factors that led to the near exclusion of zinc on the global micronutrient agenda until very recently (*Ending Hidden Hunger,* 1992; McGuire & Galloway, 1994; Trowbridge et al., 1993). Extensive evidence accumulated in the last decade, primarily from randomized trials of zinc supplementation in children and pregnant women in low-income countries, has now conclusively demonstrated the importance of zinc deficiency in these settings in regard to growth, risk of infectious disease morbidity and mortality, and other outcomes.

This evidence, coupled with new estimates indicating that zinc deficiency is highly prevalent in low- and middle-income countries (Hotz & Brown, 2004), has resulted in a better appreciation of the magnitude of the problem. The WHO now estimates that the global burden of disease attributable to zinc deficiency is comparable to that due to deficiency of vitamin A or iron (Ezzati et al., 2002). These calculations indicate that zinc deficiency results in 789,000 deaths and 28 million disability-adjusted life years (DALYs), or about 2% of global DALYs annually (Caulfield & Black, 2004). With this new recognition of the magnitude of the problem has come more attention to the development of programs to prevent or rectify the deficiency.

Function, Requirements and Assessment

Zinc is found in all cells, serving as a constituent of more than 200 enzymes and numerous transcription proteins (as a "zinc finger") that regulate nucleic acid synthesis; metabolism of protein, lipid, and carbohydrate; and cell differentiation (Cousins & Hempe, 1990; Stipanuk, 2000). These functions confer on zinc important roles in organogenesis, tissue growth, functional development, and immunity (Shankar & Prasad, 1998; Stipanuk, 2000). Such broad involvement in metabolism virtually assures zinc an important role in maintaining health.

Zinc is absorbed by both passive diffusion across a concentration gradient and by energy-dependent processes when intake is low (Stipanuk, 2000). Specific transporter proteins may facilitate absorption (McMahon & Cousins, 1998). In mixed diets, the efficiency of zinc absorption can vary widely, from practically nil to 40%, with the lowest absorption associated with high grain and plant consumption and the highest with breast milk and meat. Absorption tends to be higher in zinc deficiency (Solomons, 1999). Uptake into tissues appears to be regulated, although the mechanisms are poorly understood. About 85% of total body zinc resides in skeletal muscle, calcified bone, and marrow, mostly bound to the storage protein metallothionein. This leaves only a small exchangeable body pool that can respond to short-term variation in zinc intake. Less than 1% of body zinc is in circulation (Cousins & Hempe, 1990). There are no large body reserves of zinc in the conventional sense, but bone may serve as a passive reserve, with zinc being made available during normal turnover.

RDAs for zinc in healthy individuals have been available from WHO and were updated with new values by the Institute of Medicine in the United States (Institute of Medicine, 2001) that have been considered by many to be low for grain-based, low-meat diets, leading to a more recent revision by the International Zinc Nutrition Consultative Group (Hotz & Brown, 2004), which are presented in Table 5-7. For children these range from 3 to 14 mg per day depending on age, weight, sex, and the bioavailability of dietary zinc. For adults the recommended intakes range from 8 to 15 mg per day depending on sex and physiologic state (e.g., pregnancy or lactation). Because zinc is lost during diarrhea and may be consumed more rapidly during infections, the need for dietary zinc may be increased at such times.

Zinc status may be assessed by a combination of clinical, biochemical, test-response, and dietary methods (Gibson, 1990; Gibson & Huddle, 1998). Clinical signs of moderate to severe zinc deficiency, including marked growth retardation, dermatitis and other skin changes, poor appetite, and mental lethargy, are either rare or lack sufficient specificity to be useful for population assessment. Diagnosis of more prevalent mild zinc deficiency usually rests on determining serum or plasma zinc concentration. Although unreliable for individual assessment, the distribution of serum zinc concentrations or the responsiveness of the lower end of the distribution to intervention can identify groups at risk (Hotz & Brown, 2004). Serum zinc concentration varies by time of day, largely related to food ingestion, and can be lowered by infection because of cytokine-mediated shifts into the liver. Extensive recent work has resulted in suggested lower cutoffs for the assessment of serum zinc concentration depending on time of day, fasting state, age, sex, and pregnancy (Table 5-14) (Hotz & Brown, 2004). Hair zinc concentration may be used as a static indicator to identify groups of individuals likely to be zinc deficient, with

1.68 μmol/g suggested as a cutoff (Gibson & Huddle, 1998). In comparison with serum zinc, hair zinc measurement has the advantages that concentrations are more stable, reflecting longer-term status, and that collection of hair is easier than collection of blood. The disadvantages are that there are limited reference data and the possibility that zinc deficiency may stunt hair growth, resulting in normal hair zinc concentrations. Stable isotope dilution methods may be used to assess total body zinc stores, though the cost and complexity of this approach limits its use to evaluating small numbers of individuals and validating other indicators (Hambidge & Krebs, 1995; Hambidge, Krebs, & Miller, 1998).

Dietary assessment can provide valuable insight with respect to the bioavailable dietary zinc from local food resulting from concurrent estimation of zinc and phytate content, but alone it cannot reflect the status of an individual or population (Gibson & Ferguson, 1998a). Extensive guidelines on conducting and interpreting dietary surveys to assess the adequacy of dietary zinc intake have been published (Hotz & Brown, 2004).

Other possible measures of zinc deficiency in a population are the functional responses to zinc supplementation, such as improved growth and reduced infections, which will be considered in the next subsection. Because of the association of zinc deficiency with growth stunting (low height for age), as well as dietary inadequacy, the International Zinc Nutrition Consultative Group has used a composite index composed of the percentage of preschool children who are stunted and the percentage of individuals at risk of inadequate zinc intake (from national food balance sheets) to classify countries by their risk of zinc deficiency (Figure 5-12) (Hotz & Brown, 2004).

Health Consequences

As predicted by Prasad (1991), the past decade has witnessed an explosion of research to elucidate zinc's role in health. Preschool children who exhibit a low serum zinc level are more likely to develop diarrhea and experience more severe episodes of diarrhea or acute respiratory infection than children with adequate zinc status (Bahl et al., 1998). The causality of this association has been examined by quantifying the impact of zinc supplementation on the incidence, duration, and severity of acute and persistent diarrhea or dysentery (Faruque et al., 1999; Penny et al., 1999; Rosado et al., 1997; Roy et al., 1999; Ruel et al., 1997; Sazawal et al., 1995, 1996; Sazawal, Black et al., 1997; Sazawal, Jalla et al., 1997; Sazawal et al., 1998; Zinc Investigators' Collaborative Group, 1999), acute respiratory infections (Roy et al.,1999; Ruel et al., 1997; Sazawal et al., 1998), malaria (Shankar & Prasad, 1998), immune competence (Sazawal, Jalla et al., 1997; Shankar & Prasad, 1998), and growth (Brown, Peerson, & Allen, 1998; Rosado et al., 1997) in young children. The number, specificity, and timeliness of the trials, coupled with an urgent need to grasp the health implications of adequate zinc nutriture for policy and program purposes, have stimulated overview analyses to better discern the health benefits of improved zinc nutriture, especially for high-risk populations.

Diarrhea. Evidence for a role of zinc in reducing the incidence, severity, and duration of diarrhea is remarkably consistent. Data from seven clinical trials evaluating the efficacy of continuous, daily zinc supplementation of preschool children were pooled for analysis (Zinc Investigators' Collaborative Group, 1999). Eligible trials provided 5 to 20 mg of zinc (as sulfate, gluconate, or methionate) for periods of 12 to 54 weeks to preschoolers. The benefit of zinc supplementation was consistent with average reductions of 18% in the incidence (odds ratio [OR] = 0.82; 95% CI: 0.72–0.93) (Figure 5-13a) and 25% (OR = 0.75; 95% CI: 0.63–0.88) in the prevalence (days ill per 100 person-days) (Figure 5-13b) of diarrhea. The apparent greater impact on prevalence can be expected because prevalence includes episodic duration, which was also reduced by zinc supplementation

Table 5-14	Suggested Lower Thresholds for Mean Serum Zinc Concentrations (μg/dL) to Classify Populations at Risk of Zinc Deficiency		
		Age Group	
		≥10 years	
Time of Day of Blood Sample	**<10 years**	**Nonpregnant Females**	**Males**
Morning, fasting	Unknown	70 (10.7)	74 (11.3)
Morning, other	65 (9.9)	66 (10.1)	70 (10.7)
Afternoon/evening	57 (8.7)	59 (9.0)	61 (9.3)
Note: 1 μmol/L = 6.54 μg/dL.			

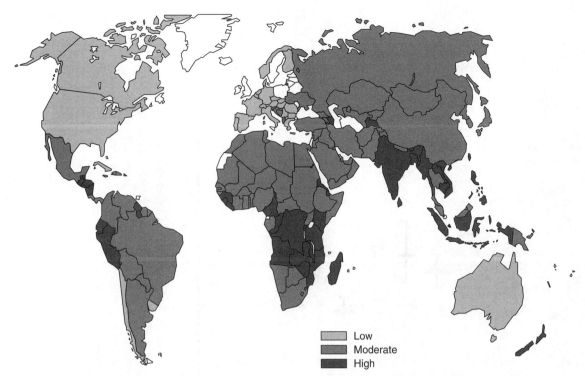

Low
Moderate
High

Figure 5-12 National Risk of Zinc Deficiency Based on Combined Data on Prevalence of Child Growth Stunting and Percentage at Risk of Inadequate Zinc Intake. *Source:* C. Hotz and K. H. Brown (Eds.), International Zinc Nutrition Consultative Group (IZiNCG) Technical Document No. 1: Assessment of the Risk of Zinc Deficiency in Populations and Options for Its Control [Special issue], 2004, *Food and Nutrition Bulletin, 25*(Suppl. 2). Reprinted with permission.

(Faruque et al., 1999; Hambidge, Krebs, & Miller, 1998; Roy et al., 1997; Ruel et al., 1997). Zinc therapy also reduced the frequency of prolonged diarrhea (Black, 1998). Zinc supplementation has been found to be safe in HIV-positive individuals and to reduce the incidence of diarrhea in children in South Africa (Moss et al., unpublished manuscript, 2005; Siberry, Ruff, & Black, 2002).

Zinc has also been successfully used in therapy of acute and persistent diarrhea. In a meta-analysis of five randomized, controlled trials in acute diarrhea, the summary estimate of the effect of zinc supplements was a 16% reduction in episode duration (Zinc Investigators' Collaborative Group, 1999). Also in this systematic review of five trials of zinc supplements in persistent diarrhea (enrollment duration of 14 days or more), the summary estimate was a 29% reduction in duration. Many subsequent trials have confirmed the findings that zinc supplements as adjunctive therapy with oral rehydration reduce the duration and severity of the episode (Bahl et al., 2001, Baqui et al., 2002). Of additional interest is that zinc supplements given for 2 weeks during and following diarrhea have been shown to reduce the incidence of

diarrhea in the subsequent 2 to 3 months (Zinc Investigators' Collaborative Group, 1999).

Respiratory Infection. A number of studies have evaluated the effects of zinc on acute lower respiratory infection. Four zinc supplementation trials that examined this question were analyzed together (Ninh et al., 1996; Penny et al., 1999; Sazawal et al., 1998; Zinc Investigators' Collaborative Group, 1999). These studies revealed an average reduction of 41% in the incidence of pneumonia among zinc-supplemented versus control children (OR = 0.59; 95% CI: 0.41–0.83). A subsequent trial confirmed this benefit (Bhandari et al., 2002).

Zinc has also been shown to have benefit as an adjunctive therapy along with antibiotics for pneumonia. Trials in Bangladesh and India found that children with severe pneumonia who received zinc had a shorter duration of illness and a lower rate of failure of initial antibiotic therapy (Brooks et al., 2004; Mahalanabis et al., 2004).

Malaria. Experimental zinc deficiency impairs host defenses against malarial infection (Shankar & Prasad, 1998). *Plasmodium falciparum* parasitemia has also been negatively associated with measures of

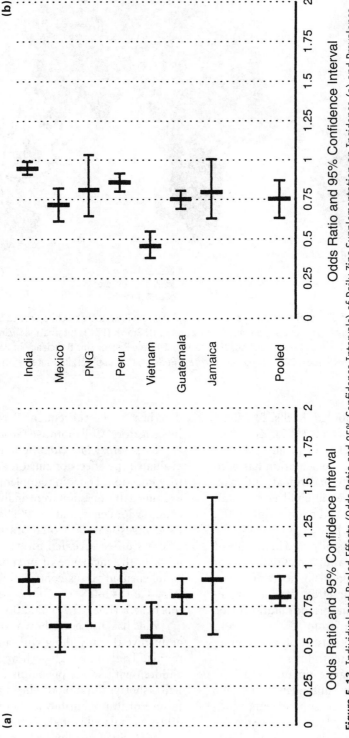

Figure 5-13 Individual and Pooled Effects (Odds Ratio and 95% Confidence Intervals) of Daily Zinc Supplementation on Incidence (a) and Prevalence (b) of Early Childhood Diarrhea in Seven Randomized, Double-Masked, Continuous Supplementation Trials. *Source:* Zinc Investigators' Collaborative Group, "Prevention of Diarrhea and Pneumonia by Zinc Supplementation in Children in Developing Countries: Pooled Analysis of Randomized Controlled Trials," 1999, *Journal of Pediatrics, 135,* p. 693. Copyright 1999 by Mosby, Inc. Reprinted with permission.

zinc status or intake in Africa (Gibson & Huddle, 1998) and Southeast Asia (Gibson et al., 1991). The public health impact of this association has been tested in four randomized, double-masked field trials. The largest was conducted among 274 children aged 6 to 60 months in Papua New Guinea. Children who received 10 mg of zinc, 6 days per week for 10 months, experienced a 38% reduction (95% CI: 3% to 60%) in *P. falciparum* malaria episodes (fever plus parasitemia greater than 9,200 per μL) and a 69% reduction in episodes with heavy parasitemia (>100,000 μL) (Shankar, Genton, Tamja et al., 1999). Similar reductions in malarial illness have been reported from the Gambia (30%, not statistically significant) (Bates et al., 1993) and from another trial among nursery school children in Uganda, where zinc supplementation throughout the school year was associated with a 25% reduction in weekly illness event rates (*p* < 0.05), more than 80% of which were classified as malaria attacks (Kikafunda et al., 1998). On the other hand, a trial in Burkina Faso did not find an effect of zinc supplementation on the incidence of malaria, possibly because the community-based design led to early treatment and illness definitions that may not have reflected clinically important malaria (Müller et al., 2001). In addition, zinc has not been shown to be efficacious in treatment of *P. falciparum* malaria (Zinc Against Plasmodium Study Group, 2002).

With mounting evidence that adequate zinc nutriture can reduce the incidence and intensity of infections, it is plausible that child mortality could be reduced by preventing even mild zinc deficiency through supplementation or dietary enhancement, including fortification. Two trials provide evidence that zinc supplementation resulted in a large reduction in child mortality. One trial in full-term small-for-gestational-age Indian infants, who received daily zinc supplements from 1 to 9 months of age, found a reduction by two-thirds in deaths compared with infants receiving a control supplement without zinc (Sazawal et al., 2001). In a large trial in Bangladesh, preschool children who received a zinc supplement along with oral rehydration therapy for diarrhea had 50% fewer deaths than children receiving oral rehydration alone (Baqui et al., 2002).

Poor Growth. A 2002 overview clarified the extent and type of growth response that may occur when prepubescent children are given zinc on a daily basis: 33 controlled trials were included in a meta-analysis that examined the effect of dosing children under 12 years with a range of 1 to 20 mg zinc daily for periods of 8 weeks to 15 months (mean approximately 7 months) (Brown et al., 2002). Differences in ponderal and linear growth were expressed as an "effect size" ([mean change in treatment group − mean change in control group] / pooled standard deviation of the difference between groups), weighted by sample size, expressed as a standard deviation. The analysis revealed modest but statistically significant increases in weight (0.31 SD, *p* < 0.001) and height (0.35 SD, *p* < 0.0001), with larger effects seen for weight in children with lower weight for age, and for height/length in more stunted study children (Brown et al., 2002). Zinc supplementation has, in some settings, also increased tricipital skinfold size (Kikafunda et al., 1998), middle upper arm circumference (Cavan et al., 1993; Kikafunda et al., 1998), and lean body mass, supporting a role for zinc in maintaining body composition.

Reproductive Health. Zinc is required for normal maternal health, fetal growth, and development and parturition (Caulfield et al., 1998). Experimental zinc deficiency leads to poor pregnancy outcomes (Apgar, 1985; Bunce et al., 1994), but evidence linking human maternal zinc deficiency to intrauterine growth retardation, prematurity, low birth weight, and complications at delivery is conflicting (Tamura et al., 2000). Several trials have reported modest increases (approximately 0.5 wk) in length of gestation (Caulfield et al., 1998; Cherry et al., 1989; Garg, Singhla, & Arshad, 1993; Goldenberg et al., 1995; Kynast & Saling, 1986; Ross, Nel, & Naeye, 1985) and improved birth weight (Garg, Singhla, & Arshad, 1993; Goldenberg et al., 1995) following maternal zinc supplementation, whereas others carried out in low-income countries have failed to find any effect on newborn size (Caulfield et al., 1999; Fawzi et al., 2005; Osendarp et al., 2000; Ross, Nel, & Naeye, 1985). A meeting to review the consequences of maternal zinc deficiency concluded that the evidence is conflicting on its relationship with labor or delivery complications, gestational age at birth, birth weight, and fetal development (Osendarp et al., 2003). However, more subtle relationships may exist, such as improved fetal neurobehavioral development following maternal zinc supplementation (Merialdi et al., 1998).

Zinc also plays a known role in mammalian cell differentiation and turnover, ontogeny of mammalian systems, and thymic and other lymphoid tissue development and function (Cousins & Hempe, 1990), which, for example, could predispose individuals deprived of essential zinc in utero to permanent impairment in immunity and host resistance (Beach, Gershwin, & Hurley, 1982). Evidence from trials of zinc supplementation in pregnancy supports a beneficial effect on neonatal and infant infectious disease morbidity (Osendarp et al., 2001).

Prevention

The ubiquitous role of zinc in nature and its potential to affect many facets of health make zinc deficiency one of the most compelling of all micronutrient deficiencies to address. Yet little has been done to prevent zinc deficiency to date. Prevention strategies could employ dietary, fortification, supplementary, and agricultural approaches. Excellent sources of bioavailable zinc include red meat, liver and other organ meats, poultry, shellfish, eggs, and milk. These foods often contribute less than 10% of dietary zinc among low-income populations (Gibson & Ferguson, 1998b). The adequacy of dietary zinc depends on both its quantity and bioavailability, the latter being a function of the presence of compounds in foods that inhibit absorption of zinc. These compounds include phytates, found abundantly in whole-grain cereals and legumes; dietary fiber; oxalates; polyphenols; and other binding compounds (Oberleas & Harland, 1981; Solomons, 1999). A dietary phytate-to-zinc molar ratio of more than 15 (Gibson, 1990), common in many traditional diets in low- and middle-income countries (Ferguson et al., 1993), has been associated with low zinc status (WHO, 1996b). Phytates may be reduced in some whole grains (e.g., wheat, rice, and sorghum) by milling, which can remove the phytate-rich aleurone layer, or by methods that induce enzymatic (phytase) hydrolysis of phytic acid, thereby disabling its ability to complex with zinc in the gut (Lonnerdal et al., 1989). These latter methods include soaking of cereals or legumes, germination, and fermentation of cereals and related products (Gibson et al., 1998), methods that are easily applied in rural areas. Plant breeding strategies may provide new generations of staple crops in the future that increase zinc and decrease phytic acid content, while enhancing yield (Gibson & Ferguson, 1998b; Graham, Ascher, & Hynes, 1992; Ruel & Bouis, 1998).

Fortification, either with zinc alone or, more likely, with zinc plus other micronutrients, offers promise as processed staple grains and other food commodities increasingly penetrate the low-income markets. Micronutrient premixes containing zinc have been proposed as complementary and special transitional foods for children in refugee settings (Gibson & Ferguson, 1998b) based on the estimated needs of infants and young children (Brown, Dewey, & Allen, 1998). Direct supplementation offers the most immediate approach for improving the zinc status of mothers and children, most probably in combination with other micronutrients.

The extensive evidence that zinc supplements started during a diarrheal episode reduce the severity of that episode and the incidence of subsequent episodes has led to a joint recommendation from WHO and UNICEF that zinc be used to treat all episodes of watery diarrhea and dysentery (WHO/UNICEF, 2004). Implementation of this recommendation is beginning in many countries.

Diet and Undernutrition

From the foregoing sections, it should be apparent that young children, in particular, are vulnerable to protein, energy, and micronutrient deficiencies. Diet in childhood should be adequate to meet all normal energy and nutrient requirements to support tissue growth, maintenance and function, and physical activity. Health and developmental consequences can occur when diet continually fails to meet these nutritional demands. Family and the mealtime conditions under which food is eaten often reflect broader issues of child care and nurturing in the home that can influence child development.

Most childhood undernutrition results directly from a diet that is chronically inadequate in quantity—conventionally taken to mean low in energy and protein—and quality, more broadly reflecting poor biological value of protein (e.g., low amino acid score), low or imbalanced micronutrient density, or low bioavailability due to high "antinutrient" content (e.g., phytate, fiber, oxalates). Poor quality may also refer to nonhygienic aspects of the food consumed, which could lead to food contamination and increased disease risk. Often the diet of the undernourished encompasses most of these features to varying degrees. Nutrient supplements are generally not viewed as part of the diet. Fortified food, though still rare in the diets of most low-income people, is increasingly being viewed as contributing to dietary quality. Dietary needs and the major ways these are met in infancy and early childhood are the focus of this section.

The Continuum from Breastfeeding to Complementary Feeding

Ideally, the infant-to-child feeding continuum should be viewed as a process, involving first breastfeeding and then transitional feeding, that results in adequate nourishment of children to support normal growth, health, and development from birth through the early childhood years. The process of establishing exclusive breastfeeding, followed by phasing in complementary feeding and eventually transitioning to family foods, is illustrated in Figure 5-14 and provided as a series of steps and principles in Exhibit 5-4. The con-

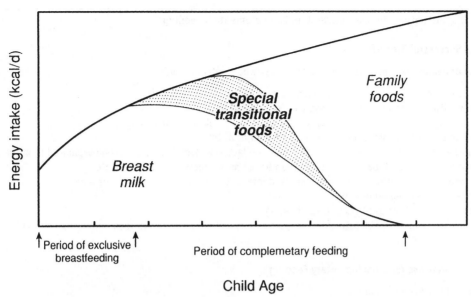

Figure 5-14 Illustration of the Sequential Phases of Early Childhood Feeding. *Source:* K. H. Brown, K. Dewey, and L. Allen, *Complementary Feeding of Young Children in Developing Countries: A Review of Current Scientific Knowledge,* WHO/NUT/98 (Geneva, Switzerland: World Health Organization, 1998). Reprinted with permission.

cept is advanced by clear definitions of feeding states that have emerged in recent years. Thus, exclusive (or full) and almost exclusive breastfeeding are differentiated due to the potential pathogen exposure and risk of infection that accompanies the latter (Labbok & Krasovec, 1990). Partially breastfed infants are usefully subdivided according to their consumption of nonhuman milk, solid foods, and frequency of breastfeeding or percentage of total daily energy consumed from breast milk (Piwoz et al., 1996). Complementary feeding begins with the onset of partial breastfeeding. Complementary foods, or "special transitional foods," are "any nutrient containing foods or liquids other than breast milk given to young children during the period of complementary feeding" (Brown, Dewey, & Allen, 1998). Their purpose is to adequately nourish infants as they transition to the family diet, while trying to minimize breast milk displacement. It has been suggested that the term *weaning food* be avoided because it may convey the wrong goal of displacing breast milk with another, even if nutritious, food (Brown, Dewey, & Allen, 1998). Finally, the complementary feeding period passes when an infant is fully weaned from the breast, although infrequent (token) breastfeeding may persist prior to complete cessation, with likely little nutritional or growth benefit (Labbok & Krasovec, 1990; Piwoz et al., 1996). By that age, often 3 to 4 years, a child has passed through the period of highest risk for growth faltering, serious infectious illness, and mortality. Dietary progression to a full household diet is likely to follow patterns established during complementary feeding.

An empirical example of the feeding continuum can be derived from data on breastfeeding prevalence among nearly 21,000 children participating in the Botswana Nutritional Surveillance System (Figure 5-15) (Michaelson, 1988). The pattern is typical of many rural areas of Africa and other low-income regions, whereby initial, (almost) exclusive breastfeeding rapidly gives way to partial breastfeeding by 6 months of age, and gradual weaning by 3 years of age.

The slopes of the transition curves depend on cultural and socioeconomic norms, and especially maternal, caregiver, and family preferences related to breastfeeding initiation; frequency and duration; the availability of hygienic (Rowland, Barrell, & Whitehead, 1978), affordable, and nutritious complementary foods; emerging changes in women's roles in communities; and other lifestyle, socioeconomic, food security, and disease factors (Begin, Frongillo, & Delisle, 1999; Galler et al., 1998; Underwood & Hofvander, 1982). For example, HIV-positive mothers in sub-Saharan Africa are likely to be increasingly advised to abruptly wean an infant after 6 months

Exhibit 5-4	Promoting Successful Breast and Complementary Feeding

Ten Steps to Successful Breastfeeding

Every facility providing maternity services and care for newborn infants should:

1. Have a written policy that is routinely communicated to all health care staff
2. Train all health care staff in skills necessary to implement this policy
3. Inform all pregnant women about the benefits and management of breastfeeding
4. Help mothers initiate breastfeeding within a half-hour of birth
5. Show mothers how to breastfeed, and how to maintain lactation even if they should be separated from their infants
6. Give newborn infants no food or drink other than breast milk, unless medically indicated
7. Practice rooming-in, that is, allowing mothers and infants to remain together 24 hours a day
8. Encourage breastfeeding on demand
9. Give no artificial teats or pacifiers to breastfeeding infants
10. Foster the establishment of breastfeeding support groups and refer mothers to them on discharge from the hospital or clinic

WHO Recommendations for Complementary Feeding

- Give breast milk alone for 6 months.
- Give complementary foods from 6 months onward.
- If a child aged 4 through 6 months is not gaining weight adequately despite appropriate breastfeeding or receives frequent breastfeeds but appears hungry soon after, give complementary foods.
- When starting complementary foods, continue breastfeeding as often and as long as before.
- Give complementary foods that are rich in energy and nutrients, clean and safe, easy to prepare from family foods, and locally available and affordable.
- Give complementary foods three times daily to breastfed babies aged 6 to 7 months, increasing to five times daily by 12 months.
- Start with a few teaspoons and gradually increase the amount and variety.
- Actively encourage a child to eat.
- Make sure all utensils are clean.
- Spoon-feed foods from a cup or bowl.
- If foods are not refrigerated, feed them within 2 hours of preparation.
- During and after illness, breastfeed more frequently than usual and give extra meals.
- After illness, encourage a child to eat as much as possible at each meal, until the lost weight is regained.
- Keep a chart of the child's weight.

Source: E. G. Piwoz, S. L. Huffman, and V. J. Quinn, "Promotion and Advocacy for Improved Complementary Feeding: Can We Apply the Lessons Learned from Breastfeeding?" 2003, *Food and Nutrition Bulletin,* 24, pp. 29–44. Reprinted with permission.

(e.g., within a month's time) in accordance with the WHO/UNAIDS/UNICEF recommendations for breast milk replacement feeding options beyond 6 months of age being promoted as a strategy to reduce risk of viral transmission through breast milk (Table 5-15) (Papathakis & Rollins, 2004). Abrupt weaning would, in the Botswana example, virtually eliminate the extended period of partial breastfeeding (area under upper curve) in Figure 5-15, collapsing the period of transition from being breastfed only to not breastfed or fully weaned.

Reflecting regional variation in other determinants, women in South and Southeast Asia tend to extend the period of partial breastfeeding for a longer duration, indicated by prevalence rates of any breastfeeding of 50% to 80% during the third year of life (Brown, Black, & Becker, 1982; Grummer-Strawn, 1996; Huffman et al., 1980; Khatry et al., 1995), whereas the period of transition to family food tends to be shorter in Latin America (Grummer-Strawn, 1996) and China (Taren & Chen, 1993).

Breastfeeding

It is now recommended that exclusive breastfeeding be practiced for the first 6 months of life (WHO/UNICEF, 2001), based on a consensus that breastfeeding can provide adequate energy, nutrients, and fluid, protect against infection, and permit normal growth for in-

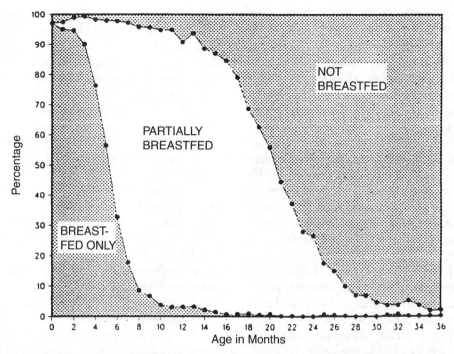

Figure 5-15 Actual Distributions of Preschool Children in Botswana by Breastfeeding Status. *Note: Partially breastfed* implies a period of complementary feeding, and *not breastfed* is interpreted to denote a period of transition to family foods. *Source:* K. F. Michaelsen (1988). Value of prolonged breastfeeding (letter). *Lancet* 2, pp. 788–789. Reprinted with permission from Elsevier.

Table 5-15	WHO/UNAIDS/UNICEF Feeding Options for Infants of HIV-Infected Mothers

Breast Milk

1. Exclusive breastfeeding by the mother for first 6 months and continuing until age 2 years, or as long as mother chooses
2. Exclusive breastfeeding by the mother with early cessation, with rapid weaning to replacement milk as early as feasible
3. Breast milk expression with heat treatment; expressed milk fed via cup
4. Wet nursing by an HIV-uninfected mother

Replacement Milks

1. Commercial infant formula, prepared according to manufacturer's directions
2. Fresh full-cream milk, with added water, sugar, and micronutrients; boiled before use
3. Evaporated full-cream milk or powdered full-cream milk, with added water, sugar, and micronutrients

Note: All feeding options recommend introduction of complementary foods at 6 months of age.

Source: P. C. Papathakis and N. C. Rollins, "Are WHO/UNAIDS/UNICEF-Recommended Replacement Milks for Infants of HIV-Infected Mothers Appropriate in the South African Context?" 2004, *Bulletin of the World Health Organization, 82,* pp. 164–171. Reprinted with permission.

fants through this early period of life. Early nutrient- and energy-dense colostrum is important in this process. During the first 6 months of life, average breast milk intakes for populations of infants have been noted to range between 700 and 800 mL per day in both low-income and industrialized countries (Brown, Dewey, & Allen, 1998; Dewey & Brown,

2003), an amount that is adequate to meet average nutritional needs. This is reflected in the growth of exclusively breastfed infants, reared in both industrialized countries (Dewey, Heinig, & Nommsen-Rivers, 1995) and in families of high socioeconomic standing in low-income countries (Pathak, Shah, & Tataria, 1993), following or exceeding the WHO/NCHS median weight-for-age curve through the first 3 months of life (Victora et al., 1998; WHO Working Group on Infant Growth, 1994).

Although the 6-month exclusive breastfeeding recommendation safely applies to populations of infants, it is important to recognize that individual needs, due to malnutrition, disease, or other factors, inevitably lead to individual adjustment (Black & Victora, 2002). Lower milk production (for example, 400 to 600 mL/d), as has been observed in some malnourished groups of women (Jelliffe & Jelliffe, 1978), might suggest a need to introduce complementary foods at an age that is closer to 4 than 6 months. The degree to which frequent exposure to infection, as often occurs among young infants in poor societies, changes energy and nutrient requirements and the consequent ability of exclusive breastfeeding to meet increased nutritional needs are inadequately known (Brown, Dewey, & Allen, 1998; Butte, 1996). In some studies, infection has been noted to have relatively little effect on breast milk intake during early infancy (Brown et al., 1985; Brown et al., 1990). Interaction with infection, however, could partly explain the frequent occurrence of growth failure among almost exclusively breastfed infants during the first 3 to 6 months of life in poorly nourished groups (Rivera & Ruel, 1997).

Beyond energy and nutrients, breast milk contains a repertoire of antimicrobial and anti-inflammatory factors, hormones, digestive enzymes, transport molecules, and growth modulators that appear to confer substantial protection from infection and other harmful agents (Prentice, 1996). These factors, along with the nutritional qualities of human milk, provide biological plausibility for observed reductions in persistent or severe diarrheal morbidity (Victora et al., 1992), including episodes of cholera and shigellosis (Clemens et al., 1986; Clemens et al., 1990), among breastfed versus nonbreastfed infants and young children. Lower risk of sick child visits and reported episodes of diarrhea, ear infection, and respiratory infection have also been associated with early breastfeeding in industrialized countries (Raisler, Alexander, & O'Campo, 1999).

Breastfeeding markedly improves an infant's chances of surviving the first 2 to 3 months of life, an age at which a pooled analysis from observational studies in three countries revealed a 75% to 80% lower risk of death among breastfed infants relative to nonbreastfed infants. A stronger protective effect was observed against diarrhea-related fatality (85% reduction) than acute respiratory infection–related fatality (58% reduction) at that age (WHO Collaborative Study Team, 2000). These findings are supported by the findings of a multipronged breastfeeding education trial in India that led to approximately 17-fold higher odds of sustained exclusive breastfeeding to 6 months of age and, among intervened communities, a 30% lower prevalence of diarrhea at 3 months of age (Bhandari et al., 2003). Continued breastfeeding into midinfancy (4 to 8 months) and into the second year of life has been associated with approximately 50% and 33% reductions in risk of death, respectively (WHO Collaborative Study Team, 2000).

The survival effect of any breastfeeding appears to disproportionately benefit at least two groups at high risk: severely malnourished children (Briend, Wojtyniak, & Rowland, 1988), among whom breastfeeding has been associated with a strong protection into the third year of life (Briend & Bari, 1989), and children from low-income households (e.g., homes with high maternal illiteracy and poor sanitation). The likely benefits to survival among low-income children are fully consistent with observations linking extended, partial breastfeeding to protection against consequences of moderate to severe micronutrient deficiencies, such as xerophthalmia (Mahalanabis, 1991; West et al., 1986). Better educated women, on the other hand, while less likely to breastfeed, are also more likely to use promotive and curative health services (Becker et al., 1993) and ensure a more nutritious diet that can lead to improved child survival (Bairagi, 1980; Bouis & Novenario-Reese, 1997).

One paradoxical, largely cross-sectional observation in recent years has been that breastfed children in late infancy through the third year of life are generally, though not always (Taren & Chen, 1993), lower in weight and shorter in height than their weaned peers of the same age (Brakohiapa et al., 1988; Castillo et al., 1996; Caulfield, Bentley, & Ahmed, 1996; Grummer-Strawn, 1996; Victora et al., 1984). The finding has persisted despite repeated attempts to adjust for multiple possible confounding factors. It has been difficult, however, to develop plausible explanations for how breastfeeding could depress physical growth while improving survival and reducing risks of micronutrient deficiencies, given the lack of evidence that breastfeeding specifically increases the risk of infection or reduces appetite and, thus, nutrient delivery to the infant. The association is more likely to be explained by factors related to (1) cross-sectional study designs that cannot reveal the temporal dimension of the breastfeeding–nutritional status relationship; (2) residual confounding, despite adjustment for multiple factors as measured that may influence both the mother's decision to breastfeed and the nutritional health of children; and (3) reverse causality, which could lead mothers to continue breastfeeding their children because they are malnourished (Caulfield, Bentley, & Ahmed, 1996).

Relevant to understanding this phenomenon, a prospective study in Kenya assessed the growth of 264 partially breastfed children between approximately 14 to 20 months of age by their longitudinal breastfeeding and weaning habits over a 6-month period. Children who continued to breastfeed for the entire follow-up period gained more in height (+0.6 cm) and weight (+230 g) than children who breastfed for a medium duration (50% to 99% of the 6-month follow-up) and 3.4 cm and 370 g more in weight and height, respectively, than children whose breastfeeding duration was shortest (<50% of the follow-up period) (Onyango, Esrey, & Kramer, 1999). These findings agree with two other longitudinal studies of breastfeeding and growth (Adair et al., 1993; Marquis et al., 1997), reinforcing the need for prospective studies that collect sufficient data on breastfeeding, diet, morbidity, care, and other factors to clarify this issue, short of an (unlikely) randomized trial.

Among the few negative effects of breastfeeding, that of greatest public health importance is the potential for breast milk to carry HIV and thus serve as a vehicle for vertical transmission of the virus from mother to infant (Dunn et al., 1992; Kreiss, 1997). It is estimated that breastfeeding may account for 5% to 15% of all postnatal HIV infection among infants (Leroy et al., 1998). HIV infection is associated with marked changes in maternal wasting and micronutrient status, which could affect the pathogenesis and transmission of disease (Mostad et al., 1997; Semba & Tang, 1999) and infant survival (Fawzi et al., 1998). Viral load and mastitis may interact to increase risk of vertical transmission to breastfed infants (Semba et al., 1999). For these reasons, it is hoped that the new WHO/UNAIDS/UNICEF guidelines on breastfeeding and use of replacement milks (see Table 5-15) will help health care providers advise HIV-positive mothers to adopt feeding options that can reduce viral exposure to infants. However, effective translation of these recommendations into practice requires a thorough understanding of breastfeeding and infant feeding practices in HIV-affected cultures (de Paoli, Manongi, & Klep, 2004; Poggensee et al., 2004).

Promotion and adoption of appropriate breastfeeding practices is considered one of the most cost-effective interventions within the low-income world for increasing DALYs, a quantitative index of burden of disease (Horton et al., 1996; Murray & Lopez, 1997; Sanghvi & Murray, 1997; World Bank, 1993)

(Figure 5-16). The most widely adopted and cost-effective program to date has been the global Baby Friendly Hospital Initiative developed and promoted by WHO and UNICEF (Sanghvi & Murray, 1997). However, the effectiveness of targeting a range of health care providers and services with interventions to promote exclusive breastfeeding has also begun to be tested. For example, a breastfeeding education program implemented in India through Anganwadi workers, traditional birth attendants, and other local service providers, and evaluated in the context of a randomized trial, increased the odds of exclusive breastfeeding to 6 months of age by approximately 17-fold and, among intervened communities, lowered by 30% the prevalence of diarrhea at 3 months of age (Bhandari et al., 2003).

Complementary Feeding

Although considerable agreement exists about the value of exclusive breastfeeding through 6 months of age and the basic sequences of early childhood feeding, opinions vary about the specific types of foods infants can tolerate, their order of introduction, the frequency and mode of feeding, preparation, and the degree to which variation in these facets of child feeding affects the health, growth, and development of children (Dewey & Brown, 2003). Most evidence relates to the effects of diverse feeding interventions on growth and development.

Impact on Growth

Growth is expected to improve when undernourished children are fed more food, although the evidence for such impact varies. Randomized complementary feeding trials were carried out among Honduran infants between 4 and 6 months of age who had been normal (Cohen et al., 1994) and small (Dewey et al., 1999) for gestational age at birth. No growth differences through 12 months of age could be attributed to infant receipt of a nutritious menu of complementary foods during the 3-month period compared with exclusively breastfed control infants. In both studies, by 6 months of age early complementary feeding had displaced breast milk intake slightly, despite maintaining a normal frequency of breastfeeds. In only one of four randomized feeding trials conducted in Senegal, the Congo, Bolivia, and New Caledonia did intake of a standardized, fortified instant gruel, providing approximately 200 kcal daily to 4- to 7-month old infants, have any impact on growth. In Senegal, where malnutrition was highest, linear growth improved by approximately 0.5 cm among supplemented over nonsupplemented infants

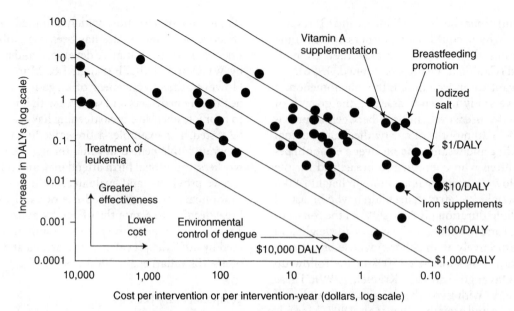

Figure 5-16 Comparison of the Cost-Effectiveness of Several Nutrition Interventions (Labeled as Vitamin A Supplementation, Breastfeeding Promotion, and Iodized Salt) in Relation to Other Public Health and Treatment Programs in Terms of Disability-Adjusted Life Years (DALYs) Gained. *Notes:* DALYs (Horton et al., 1996), are a summary measure of "life years lost due to premature mortality and years lived with disability adjusted for severity" (Murray & Lopez, 1997). Calculated DALYs gained due to vitamin A did not consider impact on child mortality (World Bank, 1993), leading to an underestimate of effectiveness. *Source:* T. G. Sanghvi and J. Murray, *Improving Health Through Nutrition: The Nutrition Minimum Package* (Arlington, VA: Basic Support for Institutionalizing Child Survival [BASICS] Project, for the U.S. Agency for International Development, 1997), p. 6. Reprinted with permission.

(Simondon et al., 1996). These results generally agree with observational studies indicating that the growth of exclusively breastfed infants either parallels or exceeds that of partially or fully weaned infants through the first 6 months of life (Brown, Dewey, & Allen, 1998). An exception lies in a well-described trial in Colombia during which mothers were randomized in the third trimester of pregnancy to receive a family food package each week, including a skim-milk and vegetable protein mixture for their infants starting at 3 months of age (providing 670 kcal and 23 g of protein daily). Supplemented infants exhibited a 0.6 cm and 162 g increase in length and weight, respectively, over controls by 6 months of age (Lutter et al., 1990; Mora et al., 1981), although breastfeeding patterns were not reported and the effect may have been partly influenced by improved maternal intake during pregnancy and lactation.

A well-known study by the Instituto Nutricional de Central America y Panama (INCAP), conducted from 1969 to 1977, showed that infants fed a high-protein, multinutrient supplement (*atole*) daily for 3 years increased linear growth by 2.5 cm over children given a low-calorie supplement (*fresca*). Most of the im-

provement occurred in late infancy, and the effect was permanent, persisting into adolescence (Ruel et al., 1995). In Ghana, the efficacy of Weanimix, a cereal-legume transitional food (containing maize, soybean, and ground nut) developed by UNICEF, was tested by itself and when fortified with added vitamins and minerals, and against two other mixes using fish powder and koko, a fermented maize porridge. Six-month-old infants randomized to consume one of four mixtures daily were comparable in growth and morbidity over the 6-month period of intervention, although fortification improved iron and vitamn A status, based on changes in plasma ferritin and retinol concentrations (Lartey et al., 1999). In the Colombian study described earlier, continued supplementation with the protein-calorie gruel further increased weight (+110 g) and length (+0.45 cm) between 9 and 12 months of age, with smaller increments observed through 36 months of age (Lutter et al., 1990). In Jamaica, children 9 to 24 months of age given a weekly take-home milk formula (providing approximately 100 kcal per day above usual home intakes) showed improved weight, length, and head circumferential growth over controls during an initial 6-month period, but not thereafter (Walker et al., 1991). In Indonesia, infants 6 to 20 months of age given a 400-kcal/d dietary supplement for 3 months accelerated weight but not height gain, perhaps reflecting an insufficient time to affect linear growth (Husaini et al., 1991).

The effectiveness of feeding activites in improving child growth or reducing protein-energy malnutrition in large programs may be difficult to discern. This is illustrated by a recent evaluation of a massive ($60 million) integrated nutrition program in Bangladesh that included growth monitoring, promotion, and screening with daily take-home food packets (containing 300 kcal and 8 g protein) given to parents of severely malnourished children (<60% weight for age), or half this amount for growth-faltering children. A postprogram comparison with matched, nonproject villages revealed no evidence of program impact in reducing prevalences of moderately or severely low weight or height for age in children 6 to 23 months of age (Hossain, Duffield, & Taylor, 2005). Rather, other factors such as socioeconomic status, maternal education, and maternal nutritional status were more strongly associated with childhood nutritional status. These outcomes, coupled with varied micronutrient supplement effects noted earlier, suggest that the growth impact of feeding undernourished children can be expected to depend on many local dietary, disease, socioeconomic, and seasonal factors, but in any event, may be disappointingly small. Paradoxically, enhanced complementary feeding that is not, or perhaps no longer (Kain, Vio, & Albala, 1998), indicated by a population's nutritional status might in some cultures promote obesity by stimulating adequately nourished children to gain too much weight (Uauy, Albala, & Kain, 2001).

Development Effects

Nutritious, complementary feeding early in life may improve childhood developmental indices. In the INCAP study, *atole* recipients later in childhood were found to register higher scores on aptitude and cognitive tests than children given *fresco* (Pollitt et al., 1995). Four years after completion of the Jamaican trial described earlier, previously supplemented children showed a modest increase in perceptual-motor scores over those not supplemented. However, children who had been stunted and had smaller head circumferences at the trial's outset had significantly lower intelligence scores, irrespective of supplement receipt (Grantham-McGregor et al., 1997), possibly indicating early cognitive impairment that has been observed in children born with intrauterine growth retardation (Villar et al., 1984). Mental and psy-

chomotor test scores also improved over the 3-month period during which Indonesian infants had been given the energy- and protein-dense supplement (Husaini et al., 1991). Observed effects of zinc (Bentley et al., 1997; Black, 1998), iron (Aukett et al., 1986; Bruner et al., 1996; Oski et al., 1983; Soemantri, Pollitt, & Kim, 1985), and iodine (Bleichrodt & Born, 1994; Huda et al., 1999) supplementation on early childhood cognition and development suggest that a usual dietary intake of foods rich in such micronutrients could perhaps provide a greater benefit, representing an urgent area for additional research.

Malnutrition Among Older Persons

A largely unrecognized group at high risk of undernutrition has been the rapidly growing segment of older persons (>60 years), particularly those living in impoverished settings where deteriorating health, strength, and capability are further stressed by the need to continue economically supporting themselves. Aging in such populations is often accompanied by decreased access to resources that are essential to maintain a minimum standard of quality of life, including adequate food, health and dental care, social and welfare services, and family support. As life expectancy continues to rise (Roubenoff, 2000; World Bank, 1993), so too is the number of older persons, expected to exceed 1.2 billion by the year 2025, two-thirds of whom will live in the low- and middle-income countries (ACC/SCN, 2000).

Undernutrition, due to coexisting primary deficiency and a condition secondary to chronic disease, is likely to be widely prevalent among older urban and rural people in low- and middle-income countries. For example, limited survey data obtained from peri-urban slums of Mumbai, India (ACC/SCN, 2000), and rural villages of Malawi (Chilima & Ismail, 1998) suggest that 25% to 35% of free-living older persons in low-income populations may be in a chronic state of acute undernourishment, reflected by a low body mass index (<18.5 kg of weight per m^2 of height).

An interaction between undernutrition and chronic disease likely exists among older persons in many low- and middle-income countries, sharing basic causes in poverty and its determinants. Specific age-related disorders that may be exacerbated by chronic intercurrent malnutrition and disease and that are likely to be of considerable public health importance include sarcopenia (loss of muscle mass and strength), with consequent muscle weakness, impaired mobility, and body function (Kehayias et al., 1997; Roubenoff, 2000); osteoporosis, with resultant bone fractures (Wark, 1999); and various dementias of potential nutritional origin (Riggs et al., 1996; Rosenberg & Miller, 1992; Tucker, 2000). Sarcopenia is a universal consequence of aging, the etiology of which is complex (Roubenoff, 2000); however, inadequate energy and protein intakes can lead to sustained negative nitrogen balance that, over time, can be an important factor in accelerated muscle loss (Kamel, 2003). Osteoporosis (loss of bone mass) may be attributable in part to chronic calcium (and vitamin D) insufficiency (Peacock, 1998), a low intake of which is likely to be common among women (Islam et al, 2003). Evidence is slowly accumulating to suggest that undernutrition among older persons is an immense and growing problem in low- and middle-income countries, providing impetus to define accurately the population-based extent and severity of nutritional deficiencies and potentially related disabilities and diseases in this age group, understand causes, and identify resources to enable healthy aging among poor populations, for whom programs are virtually nonexistent at present.

The Nutrition Transition

The changes in the demographic, social, and economic conditions of many low- and intermediate-income developing countries are modifying rapidly the pattern of noncommunicable chronic diseases, particularly in countries with emerging market economies. The contributions of diet and lifestyle to these changes have been clearly established, and the framework in which they operate in the developing world has been studied under the name of the *nutrition transition* (Caballero & Popkin, 2002; Popkin, 1994). The concept of transition was first applied to the field of epidemiology about 35 years ago (see also Chapter 6) (Omran, 1971) to describe the changes in demographic and disease patterns in populations. The nutrition transition refers specifically to population shifts in dietary patterns considered to increase risks of obesity and chronic disease, including type 2 diabetes, hypertension, cardiovascular disease, and cancer (Adair, 2002; Popkin, 1998), driven by three major ecologic factors: demographic changes in populations, urbanization, and changes in dietary trends as a result of shifts in food production and marketing. Advances in transportation and communications are also important contributors by facilitating penetration of markets with highly processed, energy-dense foods

and a rapid dissemination of information that can influence trends in lifestyle and food preferences across the globe. Regions of the world where the nutrition transition has accelerated in recent decades include Latin America (Monteiro, Conde, & Popkin, 2002; Uauy, Albala, & Kain, 2001), northern Africa (Mokhtar et al., 2001), and China (Du et al., 2002).

Demographic Trends

A key factor sustaining the nutrition transition is the demographic transition, that is, the slowing in population growth with an associated decline in mortality. The overall decline in population growth reflects a reduction in the younger population combined with a continuing increase in the older population (Zlotnik, 2002). These trends result in an increasing proportion of people in the age range where chronic diseases are more prevalent (see also Chapter 1).

Urbanization

Urban residence continues to increase throughout the world. It is predicted that by the year 2025, the majority of the world's population, including those living in low-income countries, will reside in urban areas (Zlotnik, 2002). This phenomenon is another key element of the nutrition transition, since urban dwelling has several activity, lifestyle, and dietary characteristics that affect dietary intake and energy balance. In the urban environment, some of the most energy-demanding survival activities of rural life, such as securing water and firewood, are minimal or nonexistent. Urban employment, often comprising sedentary office or service jobs, typically requires less energy than rural agricultural work and labor. These types of jobs are increasingly available in urban centers of lower-middle-income countries, for example, as a result of globalization and technological advances that are permitting industrialized countries to outsource service jobs (e.g., computer operators, data processing clerks, archivists) to a cheaper labor force. Further, mechanized transport and centralized public services also reduce energy spent on displacement to and from work. Dietary energy availability and consumption also tend to be higher in the urban than rural environment, and may provide higher amounts of calories derived from saturated fat and refined sugars (Popkin, 1999). Under these conditions, without deliberate effort to increase energy expenditure through recreational physical activity and change of diet, excess dietary energy intake and reduced physical activity can result in excess weight gain and obesity.

Dietary Trends

FAO projections anticipate a continued rise in total dietary energy availability, as seen in Table 5-1, and in the contribution of vegetable oils to daily energy intake. Modest increases in meat availability are also projected, reflected in part by the continued rise in protein availability (see Table 5-1). Projections also predict a decline in cereal production over the next 30 years (FAO, 2002). These gross changes in per capita energy availability, especially from increasingly cheap vegetable oils, in conjunction with an accelerated pace of urbanization and emergence of market economies, broadly influence the availability of foods in regional markets, which contributes to the rapid pace of dietary change in many low- to middle-income, transitioning countries—for example, in China, where per capita daily caloric availability has increased by 1,000 kcal over the past 20 years (WHO/FAO, 2003). Global production of soy, palm, and rapeseed oils rose to over 70 million metric tons by 1996, while animal fat remained essentially unchanged (Popkin & Gordon-Larsen, 2004; Smil, 2002). Cultural perceptions, advertisement, and the search for convenience have also increased consumption of prepared ("fast") foods, including prepackaged foods that may have a higher content of refined sugars (Drewnowski & Popkin, 1997; USDA Economic Research Service, 2001).

Notwithstanding the global, epidemiologic characteristics of this transitional phenomenon, especially in lower-income sectors of lower-middle-income countries (Blakely et al., 2005; Monteiro et al., 2004), obesity as a consequence of developmental and urban transition is not a fait accompli. In South Korea, for example, which has undergone a transition over the past 30 years, there has been an increase in the prevalence of adult overweight status, but not obesity, attributed to retained dietary elements of high cereal grain (rice) and vegetable intakes in the population (Popkin, Horton, & Kim, 2001).

The Dual Burden of Countries in Transition

Early on in the study of the nutrition transition, experts had assumed that the emergence of obesity and noncommunicable diseases in the developing world would be most evident in those countries at more advanced stages of economic development. Furthermore, within a country, the prevalence of obesity would be higher at higher socioeconomic levels. In sum, there would be a positive correlation between income (per capita gross national product) and obesity prevalence (Sobal & Stunkard, 1989). A recent analysis, however, suggests that the relationship between income and obesity risk is more complex (Monteiro et al., 2004), with obesity prevalence shifting toward the poor. This phenomenon is illustrated by relative risks of obesity among women by quartile of education within a series of studies across 37 developing countries (Figure 5-17). Indeed, low-income countries (those with a gross national product [GNP] of less than $800 per year) generally have a low overall prevalence of obesity, since food scarcity and relatively high levels of physical activity may prevent accumulation of surplus energy in the form of body fat. In these countries, the poorer the socioeconomic status, the lesser the risk of obesity and greater the risk of undernutrition (see Figure 5-17). A similar but weaker dose-response trend is apparent in lower-middle-income countries, where upper socioeconomic strata tend to show a higher risk of obesity. However, in upper-middle-income countries (those with a GNP of approximately $2,000 per year), the opposite occurs: Risk of obesity is highest among women in the poorer sectors of society, whose years of schooling are below the national median, and risk is lowest in the upper quartiles of education.

Paradoxically, it is increasingly common among the poor of transitional countries to find obesity and undernutrition coexisting within the same household (Doak et al., 2000; Garrett & Ruel, 2003), with some experts estimating that in some eastern Asian and western Pacific countries as many as 60% of the households have at least one overweight and one underweight member, frequently an obese mother with an underweight or stunted child (Popkin, Horton, & Kim, 2001). This phenomenon has been termed the *dual burden* of populations in nutrition transition (Doak et al., 2005). Data from China are consistent with the notion that the move from very low to intermediate income may in fact have a negative effect on the diet of the urban poor (Du et al., 2004).

Early Origins of Chronic Diseases and the Nutrition Transition

The observations of Barker and others on the impact of fetal growth and birth weight on the prevalence of diabetes and cardiovascular disease in adult life prompted much inquiry into the effects of early nutritional factors on adult disease (Barker, 2004; Cheung et al., 2000; Eriksson et al., 1999; Forsen et al., 2000). The so-called Barker hypothesis, or fetal origins hypothesis, proposes that undernutrition at different phases of intrauterine and postnatal growth results in an increased risk for certain noncommunicable chronic diseases in adulthood. The mechanism is hypothesized to be related to irreversible structural or functional differentiation ("programming") of systems that are

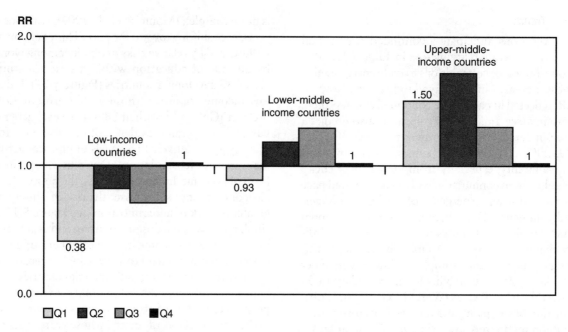

Figure 5-17 Relative Risk (RR) of Obesity Among Women by Quartiles (Q) of Years of Schooling in 37 Low-Income Countries, 1992–2002. *Source:* C. A. Monteiro, W. L. Conde, and B. M. Popkin, "Trends in Under- and Overnutrition in Brazil," in B. Caballero & B. M. Popkin (Eds.), *The Nutrition Transition: Diet and Disease in the Developing World,* Food Science and Technology International Series (London: Academic Press, 2002), pp. 224–140. Reprinted with permission.

critical for maintenance of energy balance and vascular tone, among others. For example, a restriction in energy availability to the fetus may trigger differentiation of systems in a way that would maximize energy conservation and glucose uptake. This irreversible adaptative response would become a maladaptation when this individual is exposed, as an adult, to an abundant supply of dietary energy, and would favor the development of obesity or type 2 diabetes (Eriksson et al., 1999; Forsen et al., 2000).

Mechanistic studies have focused on the effects of transitions in growth velocity during childhood (i.e., slow to fast or vice versa) on the programming of metabolic systems related to body fat accumulation and distribution, insulin sensitivity, and vascular tone (Martorell, Stein, & Schroeder, 2001; Schroeder, Martorell, & Flores, 1999; Susser & Stein, 1994). Other than physiological transitions, like the adiposity rebound that occurs around 5 years of age (Rolland-Cachera et al., 1984), these rapid changes in growth velocity are typical of children recovering from a period of undernutrition, a response called catch-up growth (Adair, 2002; McMillen, Adam, & Muhlhausler, 2005). The limited availability of birth weight and longitudinal growth records in developing countries, and lack of longitudinal follow-up of

individuals participating in nutrition trials in utero or as infants, has made it difficult to fully evaluate the Barker hypothesis, although new evidence is emerging from well-designed studies in the Philippines (Adair, Kuzawa, & Borja, 2001), India (Yajnik et al., 2003), and other countries. The implications of these phenomena for developing countries are obvious. Because of the high prevalence of impaired fetal and postnatal growth, developing countries could have large proportions of their populations at increased risk for noncommunicable diseases in adulthood.

In summary, diet-related chronic diseases are increasing at a fast pace in the developing world, particularly in middle-income countries. The major factors fueling this increase are population trends that are increasing the number of individuals reaching older adult age; urbanization, with its associated changes in diet patterns and lifestyle and changes in food availability, price, and choices leading to increases in total and fat-derived energy intake; and an increasingly sedentary lifestyle in some sectors, with consequent reduction in daily energy expenditure. These factors have already resulted in dramatic shifts in the disease burden of the urban poor, who in many middle-income countries are now bearing the dual costs of undernutrition plus obesity. The WHO and other agencies have formulated global action strategies to address the health effects of the nutrition transition (WHO/FAO, 2003; WHO/NPH, 2002), and it is hoped that these measures will eventually be incorporated into the national health policies of the most affected countries.

● ● ● Discussion Questions

1. The same population may be affected by multiple micronutrient deficiencies, although different life stages and socioeconomic or geographic groups may be more vulnerable to individual nutrient deficiencies. Discuss ways in which prevention strategies for single-micronutrient deficiencies might be combined, integrated, or coordinated to achieve cost-effective control.

2. A lower-middle-income country may be afflicted with both high rates of childhood undernutrition and a rising epidemic of obesity among its lower socioeconomic groups while undergoing a nutrition transition. Discuss the challenges this situation poses for the government in developing food and nutrition policies as well as national dietary guidelines for healthy eating.

3. The Ministry of Health of a lower-income country has decided to institute a national nutrition surveillance system to monitor the country's most pressing child and maternal nutrition problems. Discuss the kinds of nutritional problems, target groups, approaches to assessment, options for routine contact in the community, and types of agencies to organize into a surveillance system that need to be considered.

• • • **References**

Adair, L. S. (2002). Early nutrition conditions and later risk of disease. In B. Caballero & B. M. Popkin (Eds.), *The nutrition transition: Diet and disease in the developing world* (pp. 129–145). London: Academic Press.

Adair, L. S., Kuzawa, C. W., & Borja, J. (2001). Maternal energy stores and diet composition during pregnancy program adolescent blood pressure. *Circulation, 104,* 1034–1039.

Adair, L., Popkin, B. M., Van Derslice, J., Akin, J., Guilkey, D., Black, R., Briscoe, J., & Flieger, W. (1993). Growth dynamics during the first two years of life: A prospective study in the Philippines. *European Journal of Clinical Nutrition, 47,* 42–51.

Adams, E. J., Stephenson, L. S., Latham, M. C., & Kinoti, S. N. (1994). Physical activity and growth of Kenyan school children with hookworm: *Trichuris trichiura* and *Ascaris lumbricoides* infections are improved after treatment with albendazole. *Journal of Nutrition, 124,* 1199–1206.

Administrative Committee on Coordination/Sub-Committee on Nutrition (ACC/SCN). (1992, October). *Second report on the world nutrition situation: Vol. I. Global and regional results.* Geneva, Switzerland: World Health Organization.

Administrative Committee on Coordination/Sub-Committee on Nutrition (ACC/SCN). (2000). *Fourth report on the world nutrition situation: Nutrition throughout the life cycle.* Washington, DC: International Food Policy Research Institute.

Akesson, A., Bjellerup, P., Berglund, M., Bremme, K., & Vahter, M. (1998). Serum transferrin receptor: A specific marker of iron deficiency in pregnancy. *American Journal of Clinical Nutrition, 68,* 1241–1246.

Albonico, M., Stoltzfus, R. J., Savioli, L., Tielsch, J. M., Chwaya, H. M., Ercole, E., & Cancrini, G. (1998). Epidemiological evidence for a differential effect of hookworm species, *Ancylostoma duodenale* or *Necator americanus,* on iron status of children. *International Journal of Epidemiology, 27,* 530–537.

Allen, L. H. (1997). Pregnancy and iron deficiency: Unresolved issues. *Nutrition Reviews, 55,* 91–101.

Anabwani, G., & Navario, P. (2005). Nutrition and HIV/AIDS in sub-Saharan Africa: An overview. *Nutrition, 21,* 96–99.

Angeles, I. T., Schultink, W. J., Matulessi, P., Gross, R., & Sastroamidjojo, S. (1993). Decreased rate of stunting among anemic Indonesian preschool children through iron supplementation. *American Journal of Clinical Nutrition, 58,* 339–342.

Apgar, J. (1985). Zinc and reproduction. *Annual Review of Nutrition, 5,* 43–68.

Arroyave, G., Mejia, L. A., & Aguilar, J. R. (1981). The effect of vitamin A fortification of sugar on the serum vitamin A levels of preschool Guatemalan children: A longitudinal evaluation. *American Journal of Clinical Nutrition, 34,* 41–49.

Arthur, P., Kirkwood, B., Ross, D., Morris, S., Gyapong, J., Tomkins, A., & Addy, H. (1992). Impact of vitamin A supplementation on childhood morbidity in northern Ghana. *Lancet, 339,* 361–362.

Ashworth, A. (1998). Effects of intrauterine growth retardation on mortality and morbidity in infants and young children. *European Journal of Clinical Nutrition, 52,* S34–S42.

Ashworth, A., & Feachem, R. G. (1985). Interventions for the control of diarrhoeal diseases among young children: Prevention of low birthweight. *Bulletin of the World Health Organization, 63,* 165–184.

Aukett, M. A., Parks, Y. A., Scott, P. H., & Wharton, B. A. (1986). Treatment with iron increases weight gain and psychomotor development. *Archives of Diseases in Childhood, 61,* 849–857.

Bahl, R., Bhan, M. K., Bhatnagar, S., Black, R. E., Brooks, A., Cuevas, L. E., Dutta, P., Frischer, R., Ghosh, S., Malhotra, S., Penny, M., Roy, S. K., Sachdev, H. P. S., Sack, D. A., Sazawal, S., Strand, T., Fontaine, O., Patwari, A. K., Raina, N., & Khanum, S. (2001). Effect of zinc supplementation on clinical course of acute diarrhea. Report of a meeting, New Delhi, 7–8 May 2001. *Journal of Health Population and Nutrition, 19,* 338–346.

Bahl, R., Bhandari, N., Hambidge, K. M., & Bhan, M. K. (1998). Plasma zinc as a predictor of diarrheal and respiratory morbidity in children in an urban slum setting. *American Journal of Clinical Nutrition, 68,* 414S–417S.

Bahl, R., Bhandari, N., Taneja, S., & Bhan, M. K. (1997). The impact of vitamin A supplementation on physical growth of children is dependent on season. *European Journal of Clinical Nutrition, 51,* 26–29.

Bairagi, R. (1980). Is income the only constraint on child nutrition in rural Bangladesh? *Bulletin of the World Health Organization, 58,* 767–772.

Banajeh, S. M. (2003). Is 12-monthly vitamin A supplementation of preschool children effective? An observational study of mortality rates for severe dehydrating diarrhea in Yemen. *South African Journal of Clinical Nutrition, 16,* 137–142.

Baqui, A. H., Black, R. E., El Arifee, S., Yunus, M., Chakraborty, J., Ahmed, S., & Vaughan, J. P. (2002). Effect of zinc supplementation started during diarrhea on morbidity and mortality in Bangladeshi children: Community randomized trial. *British Medical Journal, 325,* 1059–1065.

Baqui, A. H., Sack, R. B., Black, R. E., Chowdhury, H. R., Yunus, M., & Siddique, A. K. (1993). Cell-mediated immune deficiency and malnutrition are independent risk factors for persistent diarrhea in Bangladeshi children. *American Journal of Clinical Nutrition, 58,* 543–548.

Bar-Andziak, E., Lazecki, D., Radwanowska, N., & Nauman, J. (1993). Iodine intake and goiter incidence among schoolchildren living in Warsaw region (Warsaw and Ciechanow Voivodships–Warsaw Coordinating Center). *Edokrynologia Polska, 44,* 288–295.

Barclay, A. J. G., Foster, A., & Sommer, A. (1987). Vitamin A supplements and mortality related to measles: A randomised clinical trial. *British Medical Journal, 294,* 294–296.

Barker, D. J. P. (2004). The developmental origins of adult disease. *Journal of the American College of Nutrition, 23,* 588S–595S.

Barker, D. J. P., Bull, A. R., Osmond, C., & Simmonds, S. J. (1990). Fetal and placental size and risk of hypertension in adult life. *British Medical Journal, 301,* 259–262.

Barker, D. J. P., Osmond, C., Winter, P. D., Margetts, B., & Simmonds, S. J. (1989). Weight in infancy and death from ischaemic heart disease. *Lancet, 2,* 577–580.

Barros, F. C., Victora, C. G., Vaughan, J. P., Teixeira, A. M. B., & Ashworth, A. (1987). Infant mortality in southern Brazil: A population based study of causes of death. *Archives of Diseases in Childhood, 62,* 487–490.

Bates, C. J., Evans, P. H., Dardenne, M., Prentice, A., Lunn, P. G., Northrop-Clewes, C. A., Hoares, S., Cole, T. J., Horan, S. J., Longman, S. C., Stirling, D., & Aggett, P. J. (1993). A trial of zinc supplementation in young rural Gambian children. *Journal of Nutrition, 69,* 243–255.

Beach, R. S., Gershwin, M. E., & Hurley, L. S. (1982). Gestational zinc deprivation in mice: Persistence of immunodeficiency for three generations. *Science, 218,* 469–471.

Beales, P. F. (1997). Anaemia in malaria control: A practical approach. *Annals of Tropical Medicine and Parasitology, 91,* 713–718.

Beard, J. L. (2001). Iron biology in immune function, muscle metabolism and neuronal functioning. *Journal of Nutrition, 131,* 568S–580S.

Beaton, G. H., Martorell, R., Aronson, K. J., Edmonston, B., McCabe, G., Ross, A. C., & Harvey, B. (1993). *Effectiveness of vitamin A supplementation in the control of young child morbidity and mortality in developing countries* (ACC/SCN State of the Art Series Nutrition Policy Discussion Paper No. 13). Geneva, Switzerland: Administrative Committee on Coordination/ Subcommittee on Nutrition.

Becker, S., Peters, D. H., Gray, R. H., Gultiano, C., & Black, R. E. (1993). The determinants of use of maternal and child health services in Metro Cebu, the Philippines. *Health Transition Reviews, 3,* 77–89.

Begin, F., Frongillo, E. A., & Delisle, H. (1999). Caregiver behaviors and resources influence child height-for-age in rural Chad. *Journal of Nutrition, 129,* 680–686.

Behrens, R. H., Lunn, P. G., Northrop, C. A., Hanlon, P. W., & Neale, G. (1987). Factors affecting the integrity of the intestinal mucosa of Gambian children. *American Journal of Clinical Nutrition, 45,* 1433–1441.

Bentley, M. E., Caulfield, L. E., Ram, M., Santizo, M. C., Hurtado, E., Rivera, J. A., Ruel, M. T., & Brown, K. H. (1997). Zinc supplementation affects the activity patterns of rural Guatemalan infants. *Journal of Nutrition, 127,* 1333–1338.

Bhandari, N., Bahl, R., Mazumdar, S., Martines, J., Black, R. E., Bhan, M. K., & the other members of the Infant Feeding Study Group. (2003). Effect of community-based promotion of exclusive breast-feeding on diarrhoeal illness and growth: A cluster randomised controlled trial. *Lancet, 361,* 1418–1423.

Bhandari, N., Bahl, R., Taneja, S., Strand, T., Molbak, K., Ulvik, R. J., Sommerfelt, H., & Bhan, M. K. (2002). Effect of routine zinc supplementation on pneumonia in children aged 6 months to 3 years: Randomized controlled trial in an urban slum. *British Medical Journal, 324,* 1358–1361.

Bhandari, N., Bhan, M. K., & Sazawal, S. (1992). Mortality associated with acute watery diarrhea, dysentery, and persistent diarrhea in rural north India. *Acta Paediatrica Supplement, 381,* 3–6.

Bishai, D., Kumar, K. C. S., Waters, H., Koenig, M., Katz, J., Khatry, S. K., & West, K. P., Jr. (2005). The impact of vitamin A supplementation on mortality inequalities among children in Nepal. *Health Policy and Planning, 20,* 60–66.

Black, M. M. (1998). Zinc deficiency and child development. *American Journal of Clinical Nutrition, 68,* 464S–469S.

Black, R. E. (1993). Persistent diarrhea in children of developing countries. *Pediatric Infectious Diseases Journal, 12,* 751–761.

Black, R. E. (1997). *Zinc for child health: Child Health Research Project special report.* Johns Hopkins University, Baltimore, MD.

Black, R. E. (1998). Therapeutic and preventive effects of zinc on serious childhood infectious diseases in developing countries. *American Journal of Clinical Nutrition, 68,* 476S–479S.

Black, R. E., Brown, K. H., & Becker, S. (1983). Influence of acute diarrhea on the growth parameters of children. In J. A. Bellanti (Ed.), *Acute diarrhea: Its nutritional consequences* (pp. 75–84). New York: Vevey-Raven Press.

Black, R. E., Brown, K. H., & Becker, S. (1984a). Effects of diarrhea associated with specific enteropathogens on the growth of children in rural Bangladesh. *Pediatrics, 73,* 799–805.

Black, R. E., Brown, K. H., & Becker, S. (1984b). Malnutrition is a determining factor in diarrheal duration, but not incidence, among young children in a longitudinal study in rural Bangladesh. *American Journal of Clinical Nutrition, 39,* 87–94.

Black, R. E., Merson, M. H., Eusof, A., Huq, I., & Pollard, R. (1984). Nutritional status, body size, and severity of diarrhoea associated with rotavirus or enterotoxigenic *Escherichia coli. Journal of Tropical Medical Hygiene, 87,* 83–89.

Black, R. E., & Victora, C. G. (2002). Optimal duration of exclusive breast feeding in low income countries. Six months as recommended by WHO applies to populations, not necessarily to individuals. *British Medical Journal, 325,* 1252–1253.

Blakely, T., Hales, S., Kieft, C., Wilson, N., & Woodward, A. (2005). The global distribution of risk factors by poverty level. *Bulletin of the World Health Organization, 83,* 118–126.

Bleichrodt, N., & Born, M. P. (1994). A meta-analysis of research on iodine and its relationship to cognitive development. In J. B. Stanbury (Ed.), *The damaged brain of iodine deficiency* (pp. 195–200). New York: Cognizant Communication Corporation.

Bloem, M. W., Hye, A., Wijnroks, M., Ralte, A., West, K. P., Jr., & Sommer, A. (1995). The role of universal distribution of vitamin A capsules in combating vitamin A deficiency in Bangladesh. *American Journal of Epidemiology, 142,* 843–855.

Blomhoff, R. (1994). Introduction: Overview of vitamin A metabolism and function. In R. Blomhoff (Ed.), *Vitamin A in health and disease* (pp. 1–35). New York: Marcel Dekker.

Bothwell, T. H., & Charlton, R. W. (1981). *Iron deficiency in women.* Report for the International Nutritional Anemia Consultative Group (INACG). Washington, DC: Nutrition Foundation.

Bothwell, T. H., Hallberg, L., Clydesdale, F. M., Van Campen, D., Cook, J. D., Wolf, W. J., & Dallman, T. R. (1982, June). *The effects of cereals and legumes on iron bioavailability.* Report for the International Nutritional Anemia Consultative Group (INACG). Washington, DC: Nutrition Foundation.

Bouis, H., & Hunt, J. (1999). Linking food and nutrition security: Past lessons and future opportunities. In J. Hunt & M. G. Quibria (Eds.), *Investing in child nutrition in Asia* (pp. 168–213). Manila: Asia Development Bank.

Bouis, H., & Novenario-Reese, M. J. G. (1997). *The determinants of demand for micronutrients: An analysis of rural households in Bangladesh* (FCND Discussion Paper No. 32). Washington, DC: International Food Policy Research Institute.

Boyages, S. C. (1994). The damaged brain of iodine deficiency: Evidence for a continuum of effect on the population at risk. In J. B. Stanbury (Ed.), *The damaged brain of iodine deficiency* (pp. 251–257). New York: Cognizant Communication Corporation.

Brabin, B. J., Hakimi, M., & Pelletier, D. (2001). An analysis of anemia and pregnancy-related maternal mortality. *Journal of Nutrition, 131,* 604S–615S.

Brakohiapa, L. A., Bille, A., Wuansah, E., Kishi, K., Yartey, J., Harrison, E., Armar, M. A., & Yamamoto, S. (1988). Does prolonged breastfeeding adversely affect a child's nutritional status? *Lancet, 2,* 416.

Briend, A., & Bari, A. (1989). Breastfeeding improves survival, but not nutritional status, of 12- to 35-months-old children in rural Bangladesh. *European Journal of Clinical Nutrition, 43,* 603–608.

Briend, A., Wojtyniak, B., & Rowland, M. G. M. (1987). Arm circumference and other factors in children at high risk of death in rural Bangladesh. *Lancet, 2,* 725.

Briend, A., Wojtyniak, B., & Rowland, M. G. M. (1988). Breast feeding, nutritional state, and child survival in rural Bangladesh. *British Medical Journal, 296,* 879.

Briend, A., & Zimicki, S. (1986). Validation of arm circumference as an indicator of risk of death in one- to four-year-old children. *Nutrition Research, 6,* 249–261.

Brooker, S., Peshu, N., Warn, P. A., Mosobo, M., Guyatt, H. L., Marsh, K., & Snow, R.W. (1999). The epidemiology of hookworm infection and its contribution to anaemia among pre-school children on the Kenyan Coast. *Transactions of the Royal Society for Tropical Medical Hygiene, 93,* 240–246.

Brooks, W. A., Yunus, M., Santosham, M., Wahed, M. A., Nahar, K., Yeasmin, S., & Black, R. E. (2004). Zinc for severe pneumonia in very young children: Double-blind placebo-controlled trial. *Lancet, 363,* 1683–1688.

Brown, K. H., Black, R. E., & Becker, S. (1982). Seasonal changes in nutritional status and the prevalence of malnutrition in a longitudinal study of young children in rural Bangladesh. *American Journal of Clinical Nutrition, 36,* 303–313.

Brown, K. H., Black, R. E., Robertson, A. D., & Becker, S. (1985). Effects of season and illness on the dietary intake of weanlings during longitudinal studies in rural Bangladesh. *American Journal of Clinical Nutrition, 41,* 343–355.

Brown, K. H., Dewey, K., & Allen, L. (1998). *Complementary feeding of young children in developing countries: A review of current scientific knowledge* (WHO/NUT/98). Geneva, Switzerland: World Health Organization.

Brown, K. H., Gastanaduy, A. S., Saavedra, J. M., Lembcke, J., Rivas, D., Robertson, A. D., Yolken, R., & Sack, R. B. (1988). Effect of continued oral feeding on clinical and nutritional outcomes of acute diarrhea in children. *Journal of Pediatrics, 112,* 191–200.

Brown, K. H., Gilman, R. H., Gaffar, A., Alamgir, S. M., Strife, J. L., Kapikian, A. Z., & Sack, R. B. (1981). Infections associated with severe protein-calorie malnutrition in hospitalized infants and children. *Nutrition Research, 1,* 33–46.

Brown, K. H., Peerson, J. M., & Allen, L. H. (1998). Effect of zinc supplementation on children's growth: A meta-analysis of intervention trials. *Bibliotheca Nutritio et Dieta, 54,* 76–83.

Brown, K. H., Peerson, J. M., Rivera, J., & Allen, L. H. (2002). Effect of supplemental zinc on the growth and serum zinc concentration of prepubertal children: A meta-analysis of randomized controlled trials. *American Journal of Clinical Nutrition, 75,* 1062–1071.

Brown, K. H., Stallings, R. Y., Creed de Kanashiro, H., Lopez de Romana, G., & Black, R. E. (1990). Effects of common illnesses on infants' energy intakes from breastmilk and other foods during longitudinal community-based studies in Huascar (Lima), Peru. *American Journal of Clinical Nutrition, 52,* 1005–1013.

Bruner, A. B., Joffe, A., Duggan, A. K., Casella, J. F., & Brandt, J. (1996). Randomised study of cognitive effects of iron supplementation in non-anaemic iron-deficient adolescent girls. *Lancet, 348,* 992–996.

Brussard, J. H., Brants, H. A. M., Hulshof, K. F. A. M., Kistemaker, C., & Lowik, M. R. H. (1997). Iodine intake and urinary excretion among adults in the Netherlands. *European Journal of Clinical Nutrition, 51,* S59–S62.

Bukenya, G. B., Barnes, T., & Nwokolo, N. (1991). Low birthweight and acute childhood diarrhoea: Evidence of their association in an urban settlement of Papua New Guinea. *Annals of Tropical Paediatrics, 11,* 357–362.

Bunce, G. E., Lytton, F., Gunesekera, B., Vessal, M., & Kim, C. (1994). Molecular basis for abnormal parturition in zinc deficiency in rats. In L. Allen, J. King, & B. Lonnerdal (Eds.), *Nutrient regulation during pregnancy, lactation, and infant growth.* New York: Plenum Press.

Burger, S., & Pierre-Louis, J. (2003). *A procedure to estimate the accuracy and reliabiity of HemoCue*^TM *measurements of survey workers.*

Washington, DC: International Life Sciences Institute.

Butte, N. F. (1996). Energy requirements of infants. *European Journal of Clinical Nutrition, 50,* S24–S36.

Caballero, B., & Popkin, B. M. (2002). *The nutrition transition: Diet and disease in the developing world.* Food Science and Technology, International Series. London: Academic Press.

Cameron, N. (1978). The methods of auxological anthropometry. In F. Falkner & J. M. Tanner (Eds.), *Human growth: A comprehensive treatise. Vol. 3. Methodology, ecological, genetic, and nutritional effects on growth* (2nd ed., pp. 3–46). New York: Plenum Press.

Campos, F. A., Flores, H., & Underwood, B. A. (1987). Effect of an infection on vitamin A status of children as measured by the relative dose response (RDR). *American Journal of Clinical Nutrition, 46,* 91–94.

Caron, P., Hoff, M., Bazzi, S., Dufor, A., Faure, G., Ghandour, I., Lauzu, P., Lucas, Y., Maraval, D., Mignot, F., Ressigeac, P., Vertongen, F., & Grange, V. (1997). Urinary iodine excretion during normal pregnancy in healthy women living in the southwest of France: Correlation with maternal thyroid parameters. *Thyroid, 7,* 749–754.

Castillo, C., Atalah, E., Riumallo, J., & Castro, R. (1996). Breast-feeding and the nutritional status of nursing children in Chile. *Bulletin of the Pan American Health Organization, 30,* 125–132.

Caulfield, L. E., Bentley, M. E., & Ahmed, S. (1996). Is prolonged breastfeeding associated with malnutrition? Evidence from nineteen demographic and health surveys. *International Journal of Epidemiology, 25,* 693–703.

Caulfield, L., & Black, R. E. (2004). Zinc deficiency. In M. Ezzati, A. D. Lopez, A. Rodgers, & C. J. L. Murray (Eds.), *Comparative quantification of health risks: Global and regional burden of disease attributable to selected major risk factors* (pp. 257–280). Geneva, Switzerland: World Health Organization.

Caulfield, L. E., de Onis, M., Blossner, M., & Black, R. E. (2004). Undernutrition as an underlying cause of child deaths associated with diarrhea, pneumonia, malaria, and measles. *American Journal of Clinical Nutrition, 80,* 193–198.

Caulfield, L. E., Richard, S. A., & Black, R. E. (2004). Undernutrition as an underlying cause of malaria morbidity and mortality in children less than five years old. *American Journal of Tropical Medicine, 71*(Suppl. 2), 55–63.

Caulfield, L. E., Zavaleta, N., Figueroa, A., & Leon, Z. (1999). Maternal zinc supplementation does not affect size at birth or pregnancy duration in Peru. *Journal of Nutrition, 129,*1563–1568.

Caulfield, L. E., Zavaleta, N., Shankar, A., & Merialdi, M. (1998). Potential contribution of maternal zinc supplementation during pregnancy for maternal and child survival. *American Journal of Clinical Nutrition, 68,* S499–S508.

Cavan, K. R., Gibson, R. S., Grazioso, C. F., Isalgue, A. M., Ruz, M., & Solomons, N. W. (1993). Growth and body composition of periurban Guatemalan children in relation to zinc status: A longitudinal zinc intervention trial. *American Journal of Clinical Nutrition, 57,* 344–352.

Ceesay, S. M., Prentice, A. M., Cole, T. J., Ford, F., Weaver, L. T., Poskitt, E. M. E., & Whitehead, R. G. (1997). Effects on birthweight and perinatal mortality of maternal dietary supplements in rural Gambia: 5-year randomised controlled trial. *British Medical Journal, 315,* 786–790.

Cerqueiro, M. C., Murtagh, P., Halac, A., Avila, M., & Weissenbacher, M. (1990). Epidemiologic risk factors for children with acute lower respiratory tract infection in Buenos Aires, Argentina: A matched case-control study. *Reviews of Infectious Diseases, 12,* S1021–1028.

Checkley, W., Epstein, L. D., Gilman, R. H., Black, R. E., Cabrera, L., & Sterling, C. R. (1998). Effects of *Cryptosporidium parvum* infection in Peruvian children: Growth faltering and subsequent catch-up growth. *American Journal of Epidemiology, 148,* 497–506.

Checkley, W., Epstein, L. D., Gilman, R. H., Cabrera, L., & Black, R. E. (2003). Effects of acute diarrhea on linear growth in Peruvian children. *American Journal of Epidemiology, 157,* 166–175.

Checkley, W., Gilman, R. H., Black, R. E., Lescano, A. G., Cabrera, L., Taylor, D. N., & Moulton, L. H. (2002). Effects of nutritional status on diarrhea in Peruvian children. *Journal of Pediatrics, 140,* 210–218.

Chen, Y., Yu, S., & Li, W. (1988). Artificial feeding and hospitalization in the first 18 months of life. *Pediatrics, 81,* 58–62.

Cherry, F. F., Sandstead, H. H., Rojas, P., Johnson, L. K., Batson, H. K., & Wang, X. B. (1989). Adolescent pregnancy: Associations among body weight, zinc nutriture, and pregnancy outcome. *American Journal of Clinical Nutrition, 50,* 945–954.

Cheung, Y. B., Low, L., Osmond, C., Barker, D., & Karlberg, J. (2000). Fetal growth and early postnatal growth are related to blood pressure in adults. *Hypertension, 36,* 795–800.

Chilima, D. M., & Ismail, S. J. (1998). Anthropometric characteristics of older people in rural Malawi. *European Journal of Clinical Nutrition, 52,* 643–649.

Christian, P. (1998). Antenatal iron supplementation as a child survival strategy [Letter]. *American Journal of Clinical Nutrition, 68,* 403–404.

Christian, P., Khatry, S. K., Katz, J., Pradhan, E. K., LeClerq, S. C., Shrestha, S. R., Adhikari, R. K., Sommer, A., & West, K. P., Jr. (2003). Effects of alternative maternal micronutrient supplements on low birth weight in rural Nepal: Double blind randomised community trial. *British Medical Journal, 326,* 571–576.

Christian, P., Khatry, S. K., & West, K. P., Jr. (2004). Antenatal anthelmintic treatment, birthweight, and infant survival in rural Nepal. *Lancet, 364,* 981–983.

Christian, P., West, K. P., Jr., Khatry, S. K., Katz, J., LeClerq, S., Pradhan, E. K., & Shrestha, S. R. (1998a). Vitamin A or β-carotene supplementation reduces but does not eliminate maternal night blindness in Nepal. *Journal of Nutrition, 128,* 1458–1463.

Christian, P., West, K. P., Jr., Khatry, S. K., Katz, J., Shrestha, S. R., Pradhan, E. K., LeClerq, S. C., & Pokhrel, R. P. (1998b). Night blindness of pregnancy in rural Nepal: Nutritional and health risks. *International Journal of Epidemiology, 27,* 231–237.

Christian, P., West, K. P., Jr., Khatry, S. K., Kimbrough-Pradhan, E., LeClerq, S. C., Katz, J., Shrestha, S. R., Dali, S. M., & Sommer, A. (2000). Night blindness during pregnancy and subsequent mortality among women in Nepal: Effects of vitamin A and β-carotene supplementation. *American Journal of Epidemiology, 152,* 542–547.

Christian, P., West, K. P., Jr., Khatry, S. K., LeClerq, S. C., Kimbrough-Pradhan, E., Katz, J., & Shrestha, S. R. (2001). Maternal night blindness increases risk of mortality in the first 6 months of life among infants in Nepal. *Journal of Nutrition, 131,* 1510–1512.

Christian, P., West, K. P., Jr., Khatry, S. K., LeClerq, S. C., Pradhan, E. K., Katz, J., Shrestha, S. R., & Sommer, A. (2003). Effects of maternal micronutrient supplementation on fetal loss and infant mortality: A cluster-randomized trial in Nepal. *American Journal of Clinical Nutrition, 78,* 1194–1202.

Chwang, L., Soemantri, A. G., & Pollitt, E. (1988). Iron supplementation and physical growth of rural Indonesian children. *American Journal of Clinical Nutrition, 47,* 496–501.

Clemens, J. D., Sack, D. A., Harris, J. R., Khan, M. R., Chakraborty, J., Chowdhury, S., Rao, M. R., van Loon, F. P., Stanton, B. F., & Yunus, M. (1990). Breastfeeding and the risk of severe cholera in rural Bangladeshi children. *American Journal of Epidemiology, 131,* 400–411.

Clemens, J. D., Stanton, B., Stoll, B., Shadid, N. S., Banu, H., & Chowdhury, A. K. (1986). Breast-feeding as a determinant of severity in shigellosis: Evidence for protection throughout the first three years of life in Bangladeshi children. *American Journal of Epidemiology, 123,* 710–720.

Cobra, C., Muhilal, Rusmil, K., Rustama, D., Djatnika, Suwardi, S. S., Permaesih, D., Muherdiyantiningsih, Martuti, S., & Semba, R. D. (1997). Infant survival is improved by oral iodine supplementation. *Journal of Nutrition, 127,* 574–578.

Cohen, N., Rahman, H., Mitra, M., Sprague, J., Islam, S., Leemhuis de Regt, E., & Jalil, M. A. (1987). Impact of massive doses of vitamin A on nutritional blindness in Bangladesh. *American Journal of Clinical Nutrition, 45,* 970–976.

Cohen, R. J., Brown, K. H., Canahuati, J., Rivera, L. L., & Dewey, K. G. (1994). Effects of age of introduction of complementary foods on infant breast milk intake, total energy intake, and growth: A randomised intervention study in Honduras. *Lancet, 344,* 288–293.

Cole, T. J., & Parkin, J. M. (1977). Infection and its effect on the growth of young children: A comparison of the Gambia and Uganda. *Transactions of the Royal Society for Tropical Medicine and Hygiene, 71,* 196–198.

Coles, C. L., Rahmathullah, L., Kanungo, R., Thulasiraj, R. D., Katz, J., Santhosham, M., & Tielsch, J. M. (2001). Vitamin A supplementation at birth delays pneumococcal colonization in South Indian infants. *Journal of Nutrition, 131,* 255–261.

Combs, G. F., Jr., Welch, R. M., Duxbury, J. M., Uphoff, N. T., & Nesheim, M. C. (1996). *Food-based approaches to preventing micronutrient malnutrition: An international research agenda.* Ithaca, NY: Cornell International Institute for Food, Agriculture, and Development.

Condon-Paoloni, D., Joaquin, C., Johnston, F. E., deLicardi, E. R., & Scholl, T. O. (1977). Morbidity and growth of infants and young children in a rural Mexican village. *American Journal of Public Health, 67,* 651–656.

Congdon, N. G., & West, K. P., Jr. (2002). Physiologic indicators of vitamin A status. *Journal of Nutrition, 132,* 2889S–2894S.

Cook, J. D., Baynes, R. D., & Skikne, B. S. (1994). The physiological significance of circulating transferrin receptors. In L. Allen, J. King, & B. Lonnerdal (Eds.), *Nutrient regulation during pregnancy, lactation, and infant growth.* New York: Plenum Press.

Cook, J. D., Finch, C. A., & Smith, N. J. (1976). Evaluation of the iron status of a population. *Blood, 48,* 449–455.

Cook, J. D., Lipschitz, D. A., Miles, L. E. M., & Finch, C. A. (1974). Serum ferritin as a measure of iron stores in normal subjects. *American Journal of Clinical Nutrition, 27,* 681.

Corvilain, B., Van Sande, J., Dumont, J. E., Bourdoux, P., & Ermans, A. M. (1998). Autonomy in endemic goiter. *Thyroid, 8,* 107–113.

Cousins, R. J., & Hempe, J. M. (1990). Zinc. In M. L. Brown (Ed.), *Present knowledge in nutrition* (6th ed., pp. 251–260). Washington, DC: ILSI Press.

Coutsoudis, A., Kiepiela, P., Coovadia, H. M., & Broughton, M. (1992). Vitamin A supplementation enhances specific IgG antibody levels and total lymphocyte numbers while improving morbidity in measles. *Pediatric Infectious Diseases Journal, 11,* 203–209.

Craft, N. E., Haitema, T., Brindle, L. K., Yamini, S., Humphrey, J. H., & West, K. P., Jr. (2000). Retinol analysis in dried blood spots by HPLC. *Journal of Nutrition, 130,* 882–885.

Cruz, J. R., Pareja, G., de Fernandez, A., Peralta, F., Caceres, P., & Cano, F. (1990). Epidemiology of acute respiratory tract infections among Guatemalan ambulatory preschool children. *Reviews of Infectious Diseases, 12,* S1029–S1034.

Dallman, P. R. (1986). Biochemical basis for the manifestation of iron deficiency. *Annual Review of Nutrition, 6,* 13–40.

Dary, O. (1994). Avances en el proceso de fortificacion de azucar con vitamina A en Centro America. *Boletin de la Oficina Sanitaria Pan Americana, 117,* 529–536.

de Benoist, B., Andersson, M., Egli, I., Takkouche, B., & Allen, H. (Eds). (2004). *Iodine status worldwide. WHO global database on iodine deficiency.* Geneva, Switzerland: World Health Organization.

Delange, F. (1993). Requirements of iodine in humans. In F. Delange (Ed.), *Iodine deficiency in Europe.* New York: Plenum Press.

Delange, F. (1994). The disorders induced by iodine deficiency. *Thyroid, 4,* 107–128.

Delange, F. (1998). Screening for congenital hypothyroidism used as an indicator of the degree of iodine deficiency and of its control. *Thyroid, 8,* 1185–1192.

Delange, F., Benker, G., Caron, P., Eber, O., Ott, W., Peter, F., Podoba, J., Simescu, M., Szybinsky, Z., Vertongen, F., Vitti, P., Wiersinga, W., & Zamrazil, V. (1997). Thyroid volume and urinary iodine in European school children: Standardization of values for assessment of iodine deficiency. *European Journal of Endocrinology, 136,* 180–187.

Delange, F., Thilly, C., Bourdoux, P., Hennart, P., Courtois, P., & Ermans, A. M. (1982). Influence of dietary goitrogens during pregnancy in humans on thyroid function of the newborn. In F. Delange, F. B. Iteke, & A. M. Ermans (Eds.), *Nutritional factors involved in goitrogenic action of cassava* (pp. 40–50). Ottawa: International Developmental Research Centre Publications.

DeLong, R., Tai, M., Xue-Yi, C., Xin-Min, J., Zhi-Hong, D., Rakeman, M. A., Ming-Li, Z., & Heinz, R. (1994). The neuromotor deficit in endemic cretinism. In J. B. Stanbury (Ed.), *The damaged brain of iodine deficiency* (pp. 9–13). New York: Cognizant Communication Corporation.

DeMaeyer, E. M., & Adiels-Tegman, M. (1985). The prevalence of anemia in the world. *World Health Statistics Quarterly, 38,* 302–316.

de Onis, M., & Blossner, M. (2000). Prevalence and trends of overweight among preschool children in developing countries. *American Journal of Clinical Nutrition, 72,* 1032–1039.

de Onis, M., Blossner, M., Borghi, E., Frongillo, E. A., & Morris, R. (2004a) Estimates of global prevalence of childhood underweight in 1990 and 2015. *Journal of the American Medical Association, 291,* 2600–2606.

de Onis, M., Blossner, M., Borghi, E., Morris, R., & Frongillo, E. A. (2004b). Methodology for estimating regional and global trends of child malnutrition. *International Journal of Epidemiology, 33,* 1260–1270.

de Onis, M., Blossner, M., & Villar, J. (1998). Levels and patterns of intrauterine growth retardation in developing countries. *European Journal of Clinical Nutrition, 52,* S5–S15.

de Onis, M., Wijnhoven, T. M. A., & Onyango, A. W. (2004). Worldwide practices in child growth monitoring. *Journal of Pediatrics, 144,* 461–465.

de Paoli, M. M., Manongi, R., & Klepp, K. (2004). Are infant feeding options that are recommended for mothers with HIV acceptable, feasible, affordable, sustainable and safe? Pregnant women's perspectives. *Public Health Nutrition, 7,* 611–619.

De Pee, S., Bloem, M. W., Gorstein, J., Sari, M., Satoto, Yip, R., Shrimpton, R., & Muhilal. (1998). Reappraisal of the role of vegetables in the vitamin A status of mothers in Central Java, Indonesia. *American Journal of Clinical Nutrition, 68,* 1068–1074.

De Pee, S., Bloem, M. W., Satoto, Yip, R., Sukaton, A., Tjiong, R., Shrimpton, R., Muhilal, & Kodyat, B. (1998). Impact of a social marketing campaign promoting dark-green leafy vegetables and eggs in Central Java, Indonesia. *International Journal of Vitamin and Nutrition Research, 68,* 389–398.

De Pee, S., Bloem, M. W., Tjiong, R., Martini, E., Satoto, Gorstein, J., Shrimpton, R., & Muhilal. (1999). Who has a high vitamin A intake from plant foods, but a low serum retinol concentration? Data from women in Indonesia. *European Journal of Clinical Nutrition, 53,* 288–297.

De Pee, S., West, C. E., Muhilal, Karyadi, D., & Hautvast, J. G. A. J. (1995). Lack of improvement in vitamin A status with increased consumption of dark-green leafy vegetables. *Lancet, 346,* 75–81.

De Vaquera, M. V., Townsend, J. W., Arroyo, J. J., & Lechtig, A. (1983). The relationship between arm circumference at birth and early mortality. *Journal of Tropical Pediatrics, 29,* 167–174.

Dewey, K. G., & Brown, K. H. (2003). Update on technical issues concerning complementary feeding of young children in developing countries and implications for intervention programs. *Food and Nutrition Bulletin, 24,* 5–28.

Dewey, K. G., Cohen, R. J., Brown, K. H., & Rivera, L. L. (1999). Age of introduction of complementary foods and growth of term, low-birth-weight, breast-fed infants: A randomized intervention study in Honduras. *American Journal of Clinical Nutrition, 69,* 679–686.

Dewey, K. G., Domellof, M., Cohen, R. J., Rivera, L. L., Hernell, O., & Lonnerdal, B. (2002). Iron supplementation affects growth and morbidity of breast-fed infants: Results of a randomized trial in Sweden and Honduras. *Journal of Nutrition, 132,* 3249–3255.

Dewey, K. G., Heinig, M. J., & Nommsen-Rivers, L. A. (1995). Differences in morbidity between breast-fed and formula-fed infants. *Journal of Pediatrics, 126,* 696–702.

Dixit, D. T. (1966). Night blindness in third trimester of pregnancy. *Indian Journal of Medical Research, 54,* 791–795.

Doak, C. M., Adair, L. S., Bentley, M., Monteiro, C., & Popkin, B. M. (2005). The dual burden household and the nutrition transition paradox. *International Journal of Obesity and Related Metabolic Disorders, 29,* 129–136.

Doak, C. M., Adair, L. S., Monteiro, C., & Popkin, B. M. (2000). Overweight and underweight coexist within households in Brazil, China and Russia. *Journal of Nutrition, 130,* 2965–2971.

Donnen, P., Brasseur, D., Dramaix, M., Vertongen, F., Zihindula, M., Muhamiriza, M., & Hennart, P. (1998). Vitamin A supplementation but not deworming improves growth of malnourished preschool children in eastern Zaire. *Journal of Nutrition, 128,* 1320–1327.

Drewnowski, A., & Popkin, B. M. (1997). The nutrition transition: New trends in the global diet. *Nutrition Reviews, 55,* 31–43.

Dreyfuss, M. L. (1998). *Anemia and iron deficiency during pregnancy: Etiologies and effects on birth outcomes in Nepal.* Unpublished thesis, Johns Hopkins University, Baltimore, MD.

Du, S., Lu, B., Zhai, F., & Popkin, B. M. (2002). The nutrition transition in China: A new stage of the Chinese diet. In B. Caballero & B. M. Popkin (Eds.), *The nutrition transition: Diet and disease in the developing world* (Vol. 11, pp. 205–221). London: Academic Press.

Du, S., Mroz, T. A., Zhai, F., & Popkin, B. M. (2004). Rapid income growth adversely affects diet quality in China–particularly for the poor! *Social Science and Medicine, 59,* 1505–1515.

Dunn, D. T., Newell, M. L., Ades, A. E., & Peckham, C. S. (1992). Risk of human immuno-deficiency virus type 1 transmission through breast-feeding. *Lancet, 340,* 585–588.

Dunn, J. T. (1996). Seven deadly sins in confronting endemic iodine deficiency, and how to avoid them. *Journal of Clinical Endocrinological Metabolism, 81,* 1332–1335.

Dunn, J. T., Semigran, M. J., & Delange, F. (1998). The prevention and management of iodine-induced hyperthyroidism and its cardiac features. *Thyroid, 8,* 101–106.

Dunn, J. T., & van der Haar, F. (1990). *A practical guide to the correction of iodine deficiency.* The Netherlands: International Council for Control of Iodine Deficiency Disorders.

El-Arifeen, S. (1997). Birthweight, intrauterine growth retardation and prematurity: A prospective study of infant growth and survival in the slums of Dhaka, Bangladesh. Unpublished doctoral dissertation, Johns Hopkins School of Public Health, Baltimore, MD.

Ellison, J. B. (1932). Intensive vitamin therapy in measles. *British Medical Journal, 2,* 708–711.

Elnagar, B., Eltom, M., Karlsson, F. A., Ermans, A. M., Gebre-Medhin, M., & Bourdoux, P. P. (1995). The effects of different doses of oral iodized oil on goiter size, urinary iodine, and thyroid-related hormones. *Journal of Clinical Endocrinological Metabolism, 80,* 891–897.

El Samani, F. Z., Willett, W. C., & Ware, J. H. (1986). Predictors of simple diarrhoea disease surveillance in a rural Ghanaian pre-school child population. *Transactions of the Royal Society for Tropical Medicine and Hygiene, 80,* 208–213.

Ending hidden hunger: Proceedings of a policy conference on micronutrient malnutrition, Montreal, Quebec, Canada, 10–12 October 1991. (1992). Atlanta, GA: Task Force on Child Survival and Development.

Eriksson, J. G., Forsen, T., Tuomilehto, J., Reunanen, A., Osmond, C., & Barker, D. (1999). Size at birth, growth in childhood and future risk of type 2 diabetes. *Diabetes, 48,* A72.

Ezzati, M., Lopez, A. D., Rodgers, A., Vander Hoorn, S., Murray, C. J. L., & the Comparative Risk Assessment Collaborating Group. (2002). Selected major risk factors and global and regional burden of disease. *Lancet, 360,* 1347–1360.

Faisel, H., & Pittrof, R. (2000). Vitamin A and causes of maternal mortality: Association and biological plausibility. *Public Health Nutrition, 3,* 321–327.

FAOSTAT. (n.d.). FAO statistical databases. http://faostat.fao.org.

Faruque, A. S. G., Mahalanabis, D., Haque, S. S., Fuchs, G. J., & Habte, D. (1999). Double-blind, randomized, controlled trial of zinc or vitamin A supplementation in young children with acute diarrhoea. *Acta Paediatrica, 88,* 154–160.

Fawzi, W. W., Chalmers, T. C., Herrera, G., & Mosteller, F. (1993). Vitamin A supplementation and child mortality: A meta-analysis. *Journal of the American Medical Association, 269,* 898–903.

Fawzi, W. W., Herrera, G., Willett, W. C., Nestle, P., El Amin, A., & Mohamed, K. A. (1997). The effect of vitamin A supplementation on the growth of preschool children in the Sudan. *American Journal of Public Health, 87,* 1359–1362.

Fawzi, W. W., Msamanga, G. I., Spiegelman, D., Urassa, E. J. N., McGrath, N., Mwakagile, D., Antelman, G., Mbise, R., Herrera, G., Kapiga, S., Willett, W. C., & Hunter, D. J., for the Tanzania Vitamin and HIV Infection Trial Team. (1998). Randomised trial of effects of vitamin supplements on pregnancy outcomes and T cell counts in HIV-1-infected women in Tanzania. *Lancet, 351,* 1477–1482.

Fawzi, W. W., Villamor, E., Msamanga, G. E., Antelman, G., Aboud, S., Urassa, W., & Hunter, D. (2005). Trial of zinc supplements in relation to pregnancy outcomes, hematologic indicators, and T cell counts among HIV-1-infected women in Tanzania. *American Journal of Clinical Nutrition, 81,* 161–167.

Ferguson, B. J., Skikne, B. S., Simpson, K. M., Baynes, R. D., & Cook, J. D. (1992). Serum transferrin receptor distinguishes the anemia of chronic disease from iron deficiency anemia. *Journal of Laboratory Clinical Medicine, 19,* 385–390.

Ferguson, E. L., Gibson, R. S., Opare-Obisaw, C., Ounpuu, S., Thompson, L. U., & Lehrfeld, J. (1993). The zinc nutriture of preschool children living in two African countries. *Journal of Nutrition, 123,* 1487–1496.

Fishman, S., Caulfield, L. E., de Ois, M., Blossner, M., Hyder, A. A., Mullany, L., & Black, R. E. (2004). Childhood and maternal underweight. In M. Ezzati, A. D. Lopez, A. Rodgers, & C. J. L. Murray (Eds.), *Comparative quantification of health risks: Global and regional burden of disease attributable to selected major risk factors* (pp. 39–162). Geneva, Switzerland: World Health Organization.

Fishman, S. M., Christian, P., & West, K. P., Jr. (2000). The role of vitamins in the prevention and control of anaemia. *Public Health and Nutrition, 3,* 125–150.

Flores, H., Campos, F., Araujo, C. R. C., & Underwood, B. A. (1984). Assessment of marginal vitamin A deficiency in Brazilian children using the relative dose response procedure. *American Journal of Clinical Nutrition, 40,* 1281–1289.

Fonseca, W., Kirkwood, B. R., Victora, C. G., Fuchs, S. R., Flores, J. A., & Misago, C. (1996). Risk factors for childhood pneumonia among the urban poor in Fortaleza, Brazil: A case-control study. *Bulletin of the World Health Organization, 74,* 199–208.

Food and Agriculture Organization of the United Nations. (1988). *Requirements of vitamin A, iron, folate, and vitamin B12: Report of a joint FAO/WHO expert committee.* Rome: Food and Agriculture Organization.

Food and Agriculture Organization of the United Nations. (2002). *World agriculture: Towards 2015/2030.* Rome: Food and Agriculture Organization of the United Nations.

Food and Agriculture Organization of the United Nations & World Health Organization. (1992). *World declaration and plan of action for nutrition.* Rome: International Conference on Nutrition.

Forsen, T., Eriksson, J., Tuomilehto, J., Reunanen, A., Osmond, C., & Barker, D. (2000). The fetal and childhood growth of persons who develop type 2 diabetes. *Annals of Internal Medicine, 133,* 176–182.

Frisancho, A. R. (1981). The norms of upper limb fat and muscle areas for assessment of nutritional status. *American Journal of Clinical Nutrition, 34,* 2540–2545.

Galler, J. R., Ramsey, F. C., Harrison, R. H., Brooks, R., & Weiskopf-Bock, S. (1998). Infant feeding practices in Barbados predict later growth. *Journal of Nutrition, 128,* 1328–1335.

Garg, H. K., Singhla, K. C., & Arshad, Z. (1993). A study of the effect of oral zinc supplementation during pregnancy on pregnancy outcome. *Indian Journal of Physiology and Pharmacology, 37,* 276–284.

Garn, S. M., Ridella, S. A., Petzold, A. S., & Falkner, F. (1981). Maternal hematologic levels and pregnancy outcomes. *Seminars in Perinatology, 5,* 155–162.

Garnham, P. C. C. (1954). Malaria in the African child. *East African Medical Journal, 31,* 155–159.

Garrett, J. L., & Ruel, M. T. (2003). *Stunted child-overweight mother pairs: An emerging policy concern?* (FCSD Discussion Paper No. 148). Washington, DC: International Food Policy Research Institute.

Gibson, R. S. (1990). *Principles of nutritional assessment.* New York: Oxford University Press.

Gibson, R. S., & Ferguson, E. L. (1998a). Assessment of dietary zinc in a population. *American Journal of Clinical Nutrition, 68,* 430S–434S.

Gibson, R. S., & Ferguson, E. L. (1998b). Nutrition intervention strategies to combat zinc deficiency in developing countries. *Nutrition Research Reviews, 11,* 115–131.

Gibson, R. S., Ferguson, E. L., & Lehrfeld, J. (1998). Complementary foods for infant feeding in developing countries: Their nutrient adequacy and improvement. *European Journal of Clinical Nutrition, 52,* 764–770.

Gibson, R. S., Heywood, A., Yaman, C., Sohlstrom, A., Thompson, L. U., & Heywood, P. (1991). Growth in children from the Wosera sub-district, Papua New Guinea, in relation to energy and protein intakes and zinc status. *American Journal of Clinical Nutrition, 53,* 782–789.

Gibson, R. S., & Huddle, J. M. (1998). Suboptimal zinc status in pregnant Malawian women: Its association with low intakes of poorly available zinc, frequent reproductive cycling, and malaria. *American Journal of Clinical Nutrition, 67,* 702–709.

Gibson, R. S., Yeudall, F., Drost, N., Mtitimuni, B., Cullinan, T. (1998). Dietary interventions to prevent zinc deficiency. *American Journal of Clinical Nutrition, 68,* 484S–487S.

Glasziou, P. P., & Mackerras, D. E. M. (1993). Vitamin A supplementation in infectious diseases: A meta-analysis. *British Medical Journal, 306,* 366–370.

Golden, M. H. N. (2002). The development of concepts of malnutrition. *Journal of Nutrition, 132,* 2117S–2122S.

Goldenberg, R. L., Tamura, T., Neggers, Y., Copper, R. L., Johnston, K. E., DuBard, M. B., & Hauth, J. C. (1995). The effect of zinc supplementation on pregnancy outcome. *Journal of the American Medical Association, 274,* 463–468.

Gomez, F., Ramos-Galvan, R., Frenk, R., Cravioto, J. M., Chavez, R., & Vasquez, J. (1956). Mortality in second and third degree malnutrition. *Journal of Tropical Pediatrics, 2,* 77–85.

Goodman, T., Dalmiya, N., de Benoist, B., & Schultink, W. (2000). Polio as a platform: Using national immunization days to deliver vitamin A supplements. *Bulletin of the World Health Organization, 78,* 305–314.

Graham, N. M. H. (1990). The epidemiology of acute respiratory infections in children and adults:

A global perspective. *Epidemiologic Reviews, 12,* 149–178.

Graham, R. D., Ascher, J. S., & Hynes, S. C. (1992). Selecting zinc-efficient cereal genotypes for soils of low zinc status. *Plant and Soil, 146,* 241–250.

Grantham-McGregor, S. M., Walker, S. P., Chang, S. M., & Powell, C. A. (1997). Effects of early childhood supplementation with and without stimulation on later development in stunted Jamaican children. *American Journal of Clinical Nutrition, 66,* 247–253.

Grummer-Strawn, L. M. (1996). The effect of changes in population characteristics on breastfeeding trends in fifteen developing countries. *International Journal of Epidemiology, 25,* 94–102.

Guerrant, R. I., Schorling, J. B., McAuliffe, J. F., & de Souza, M. A. (1992). Diarrhea as a cause and an effect of malnutrition: Diarrhea prevents catch-up growth and malnutrition increases diarrhea frequency and duration. *American Journal of Tropical Medicine and Hygiene, 47,* 28–35.

Habicht, J. P., Meyers, L. D., & Brownie, C. (1982). Indicators for identifying and counting the improperly nourished. *American Journal of Clinical Nutrition, 35,* 1241–1254.

Habicht, J. P., & Pelletier, D. L. (1990). The importance of context in choosing nutritional indicators. *Journal of Nutrition, 120,* 1519–1524.

Haddad, L. (1999). Women's status: Levels, determinants, consequences for malnutrition, interventions, and policy. In J. Hunt & M. G. Quibria (Eds.), *Investing in child nutrition in Asia* (pp. 96–131). Manila: Asian Development Bank.

Hadi, H., Dibley, M. J., & West, K. P., Jr. (2004). Complex interactions with infection and diet may explain seasonal growth responses to vitamin A in preschool aged Indonesian children. *European Journal of Clinical Nutrition, 58,* 990–999.

Hadi, H., Stoltzfus, R. J., Dibley, M. J., Moulton, L. H., West, K. P., Jr., Kjolhede, C. L., & Sadjimin, T. (2000). Vitamin A supplementation selectively improves the linear growth of Indonesian preschool children: Results from a randomized controlled trial. *American Journal of Clinical Nutrition, 71,* 507–513.

Hadi, H., Stoltzfus, R. J., Moulton, L. H., Dibley, M. J., & West, K. P., Jr. (1999). Respiratory infections reduce the growth response to vitamin A supplementation in a randomized controlled trial. *International Journal of Epidemiology, 28,* 874–881.

Hales, C. N., Barker, D. J. P., Clark, P. M. S., Cox, L. J., Fall, C., Osmond, C., & Winter, P. D. (1991). Fetal and infant growth and impaired glucose tolerance at age 64. *British Medical Journal, 303,* 1019–1022.

Hallberg, L., Brune, M., Erlandsson, M., Sandberg, A. S., & Rossander-Hulten, L. (1991). Calcium: Effects of different amounts on nonheme- and heme-iron absorption in humans. *American Journal of Clinical Nutrition, 53,* 112–119.

Halpern, J. P. (1994). The neuromotor deficit in endemic cretinism and its implications for the pathogenesis of the disorder. In J. B. Stanbury (Ed.), *The damaged brain of iodine deficiency* (pp. 15–24). New York: Cognizant Communication Corporation.

Hambidge, K. M., & Krebs, N. F. (1995). Assessment of zinc status in man. *Indian Journal of Pediatrics, 62,* 169–180.

Hambidge, K. M., & Krebs, N. F. (1999). Zinc, diarrhea, and pneumonia. *Journal of Pediatrics, 135,* 661–664.

Hambidge, K. M., Krebs, N. F., & Miller, L. (1998). Evaluation of zinc metabolism with use of stable-isotope techniques: Implications for the assessment of zinc status. *American Journal of Clinical Nutrition, 68,* 410S–413S.

Hamill, P. V. V., Drizid, T. A., Johnson, C. L., Reed, R. B., Roche, A. F., & Moore, W. M. (1979). Physical growth: National Center for Health statistics percentiles. *American Journal of Clinical Nutrition, 32,* 607–629.

Hediger, M. L., Overpeck, M. D., Kuczmarski, R. J., McGlynn, A., Maurer, K. R., & Davis, W. W. (1998). Muscularity and fatness of infants and young children born small- or large-for-gestational-age. *Pediatrics, 102,* 60–67.

Helen Keller International. (1998). *Current status of preschool vitamin A capsule supplementation program in rural Bangladesh.* Bangladesh: Helen Keller International.

Hendrickse, R. G., Hasan, A. H., Olumide, L. O., & Akinkunmi, A. (1971). Malaria in early childhood: An investigation of five hundred seriously ill children in whom a "clinical" diagnosis of malaria was made on admission to the children's emergency room at University College Hospital, Ibadan. *Annals of Tropical Medicine and Parasitology, 65,* 1–20.

Hetzel, B. S. (1989). *The story of iodine deficiency: An international challenge in nutrition.* Oxford and Delhi: Oxford University Press.

Hetzel, B. S. (1994). Historical development of the concepts of the brain-thyroid relationships. In J. B. Stanbury (Ed.), *The damaged brain of iodine deficiency* (pp. 1–7). New York: Cognizant Communication Corporation.

Heymsfield, S. B., McManus, C., Stevens, V., & Smith, J. (1982). Muscle mass: Reliable indicator of protein-energy malnutrition severity and outcome. *American Journal of Clinical Nutrition, 35,* 1192–1199.

Heywood, A., Oppenheimer, S., Heywood, P., & Jolley, D. (1989). Behavioral effects of iron supplementation in infants in Madang, Papua New Guinea. *American Journal of Clinical Nutrition, 50,* 630–640.

Hintze, G., Emrich, D., Richter, K., Thal, H., Wasielewski, T., & Kobberling, J. (1988). Effect of voluntary intake of iodinated salt on prevalence of goitre in children. *Acta Endocrinologica (Copenhagen), 117,* 333–338.

Hokama, T., Takenaka, S., Hirayama, K., Yara, A., Yoshida, K., Itokazu, K., Kinjho, R., & Yabu, E. (1996). Iron status of newborns born to iron deficiency anaemic mothers. *Journal of Tropical Pediatrics, 42,* 75–77.

Hopkins, R. M., Gracey, M. S., Hobbs, R. P., Spargo, R. M., Yates, M., & Thompson, R. C. A. (1997). The prevalence of hookworm infection, iron deficiency, and anaemia in an Aboriginal community in north-west Australia. *Medical Journal of Australia, 166,* 241–244.

Horton, S., Sanghvi, T., Phillips, M., Fieldler, J., Perez-Escamilla, R., Lutter, C., Rivera, A., & Segall-Correa, A. M. (1996). Breastfeeding promotion and priority setting. *Health Policy and Planning, 11,* 156–168.

Hossain, S. M. M., Duffield, A., & Taylor A. (2005). An evaluation of the impact of a US$60 million nutrition programme in Bangladesh. *Health Policy and Planning, 20,* 35–40.

Hotz, C., & Brown, K. H. (Eds.). (2004). International Zinc Nutrition Consultative Group (IZiNCG) Technical Document No. 1: Assessment of the risk of zinc deficiency in populations and options for its control [Special issue]. *Food and Nutrition Bulletin, 25*(Suppl. 2), S94–S203.

Houston, R. (1999). *The Nepal national vitamin A program: Elements of success.* Kathmandu, Nepal: Nepali Technical Assistance Group and John Snow, Inc., for the Ministry of Health, U.S. Agency for International Development, and UNICEF.

Howson, C. P., Kennedy, E. T., & Horwitz, A. (1998). *Prevention of micronutrient deficiencies: Tools for policymakers and public health workers.* Washington, DC: National Academy Press.

Hoyle, B., Yunus, M., & Hen, L. C. (1980). Breastfeeding and food intake among children with acute diarrheal disease. *American Journal of Clinical Nutrition, 33,* 2365–2371.

Huda, S. N., Grantham-McGregor, S. M., Rahman, K. M., & Tomkins, A. (1999). Biochemical hypothyroidism secondary to iodine deficiency is associated with poor school achievement and cognition in Bangladeshi children. *Journal of Nutrition, 129,* 980–987.

Huddle, J. M., Gibson, R. S., & Cullinan, T. R. (1999). The impact of malarial infection and diet on the anaemia status of rural pregnant Malawian women. *European Journal of Clinical Nutrition, 53,* 792–801.

Huffman, S. L., Chowdhury, A. K. M., Chakraborty, J., & Simpson, N. K. (1980). Breast-

feeding patterns in rural Bangladesh. *American Journal of Clinical Nutrition, 33,* 144–154.

Humphrey, J. H., Agoestina, T., Juliana, A., Septiana, S., Widjaja, H., Cerreto, M. C., Wu, L. S. F., Ichord, R. N., Katz, J., & West, K. P., Jr. (1998). Neonatal vitamin A supplementation: Effect on development and growth at 3 years of age. *American Journal of Clinical Nutrition, 68,* 109–117.

Humphrey, J. H., West, K. P., Jr. (1992). Vitamin A deficiency and attributable mortality among under-5-year-olds. *Bulletin of the World Health Organization, 70,* 225–232.

Husaini, M. A., Karyadi, L., Husaini, Y. K., Sandjaja, B., Karyadi, D., & Pollitt, E. (1991). Developmental effects of short-term supplementary feeding in nutritionally at-risk Indonesian infants. *American Journal of Clinical Nutrition, 54,* 799–804.

Hussey, G. D., & Klein, M. (1990). A randomized, controlled trial of vitamin A in children with severe measles. *New England Journal of Medicine, 323,* 160–164.

Idjradinata, P., Watkins, W. E., & Pollitt, E. (1994). Adverse effect of iron supplementation on weight gain of iron replete young children. *Lancet, 343,* 1252–1254.

Institute of Medicine. (2001). *Dietary reference intakes for vitamin A, vitamin K, arsenic, boron, chromium, copper, iodine, iron, manganese, molybdenum, nickel, silicon, vanadium, and zinc.* Washington, DC: National Academies Press.

International Nutritional Anemia Consultative Group. (1997). *Iron EDTA for food fortification.* Washington, DC: Nutrition Foundation.

Islam, M. Z., Lamberg-Allardt, C., Karkkainen, M., & Ali, S. M. K. (2003). Dietary calcium intake in premenopausal Bangladeshi women: Do socioeconomic or physiological factors play a role? *European Journal of Clinical Nutrition, 57,* 674–680.

Ittiravivongs, A., Songchitratna, K. S., Ratthapalo, S., & Pattara-Arechachai, J. (1991). Effect of low birthweight on severe childhood diarrhea. *Southeast Asian Journal of Tropical Medicine and Public Health, 22,* 557–562.

James, J. W. (1972). Longitudinal study of the morbidity of diarrheal and respiratory infections in malnourished children. *American Journal of Clinical Nutrition, 25,* 690–694.

James, W. P. T., Jackson-Leach, R., Mhurchu, C. N., Kalamara, E., Shayeghi, M., Rigby, N. J., Nishida, C., & Rodgers A. (2004). Overweight and obesity (high body mass index). In M. Ezzati, A. D. Lopez, A. Rodgers, & C. J. L. Murray (Eds.), *Comparative quantification of health risks: Global and regional burden of disease attributable to selected major risk factors* (pp. 497–596). Geneva, Switzerland: World Health Organization.

Jelliffe, D. B. (1966). *The assessment of the nutritional status of the community* (WHO Monograph Series No. 53). Geneva, Switzerland: World Health Organization.

Jelliffe, D. B., & Jelliffe, E. F. P. (1978). The volume and composition of human milk in poorly nourished communities: A review. *American Journal of Clinical Nutrition, 31,* 492–515.

Johnson, W. B., Aderele, W. I., & Gbadero, D. A. (1992). Host factors and acute lower respiratory infections in pre-school children. *Journal of Tropical Pediatrics, 38,* 132–136.

Joseph, K. S., & Kramer, M. S. (1996). Review of the evidence on fetal and early childhood antecedents of adult chronic disease. *Epidemiology Reviews, 18,* 158–174.

Kain, J., Vio, F., & Albala, C. (1998). Childhood nutrition in Chile: From deficit to excess. *Nutrition Research, 18,* 1825–1837.

Kalter, H. D., Burnham, G., Kolstad, P. R., Hossain, M., Schillinger, J. A., Khan, N. Z., Saha, S., de Wit, V., Kenya-Mugisha, N., Schwartz, B., & Black, R. E. (1997). Evaluation of clinical signs to diagnose anaemia in Uganda and Bangladesh, in areas with and without malaria. *Bulletin of the World Health Organization, 75*(Suppl.), 103–111.

Kamal, M. K., Ahsan, R. I., & Salam, A. K. M. A. (1998). *Achieving the goals for children in Bangladesh.* Dhaka, Bangladesh: Bangladesh Bureau of Statistics/Ministry of Planning/ Government of the People's Republic of Bangladesh/UNICEF.

Kamel, H. K. (2003). Sarcopenia and aging. *Nutrition Reviews, 61,* 157–167.

Kastner, P., Chambon, P., & Leid, M. (1994). Role of nuclear retinoic acid receptors in the regulation of gene expression. In R. Blomhoff (Ed.), *Vitamin A in health and disease* (pp. 189–238). New York: Marcel Dekker.

Katz, J., Khatry, S. K., West, K. P., Jr., Humphrey, J. H., LeClerq, S. C., Pradhan, E. K., Pokhrel, R. P., & Sommer, A. (1995). Night blindness is prevalent during pregnancy and lactation in rural Nepal. *Journal of Nutrition, 125,* 2122–2127.

Katz, J., West, K. P., Jr., Khatry, S. K., Pradhan, E. K., LeClerq, S. C., Christian, P., Wu, L. S. F., Adhikari, R. K., Shrestha, S. R., & Sommer, A. (2000). Maternal low-dose vitamin A or beta-carotene supplementation has no effect on fetal loss and early infant mortality: A randomized cluster trial in Nepal. *American Journal of Clinical Nutrition, 71,* 1570–1576.

Katz, J., West, K. P., Jr., Tarwotjo, I., & Sommer, A. (1989). The importance of age in evaluating anthropometric indices for predicting mortality. *American Journal of Epidemiology, 130,* 1219–1226.

Katz, J., Zeger, S. L., & Tielsch, J. M. (1988). Village and household clustering of xerophthalmia and trachoma. *International Journal of Epidemiology, 17,* 865–869.

Katz, J., Zeger, S. L., West, K. P., Jr., Tielsch, J. M., & Sommer, A. (1993). Clustering of xerophthalmia within households and villages. *International Journal of Epidemiology, 22,* 709–715.

Kavishe, F. P. (1999). Iodine: Iodine deficiency disorders. In M. J. Sadler, J. J. Strain, & B. Caballero (Eds.), *Encyclopedia of human nutrition* (pp. 1146–1153). San Diego: Academic Press.

Keen, C. L., & Gershwin, M. E. (1990). Zinc deficiency and immune function. *Annual Review of Nutrition, 10,* 415–431.

Kehayias, J. J., Fiatarone, M. F., Zhuang, H., & Roubenoff, R. (1997). Total body potassium and body fat: Relevance to aging. *American Journal of Clinical Nutrition, 66,* 904–910.

Khatry, S. K., West, K. P., Jr., Katz, J., LeClerq, S. C., Pradhan, E. K., Wu, L. S., Thapa, M. D., & Pokhrel, R. P. (1995). Epidemiology of xerophthalmia in Nepal: A pattern of household poverty, childhood illness, and mortality. *Archives of Ophthalmology, 113,* 425–429.

Khin-Maung-U, Nyunt-Nyunt-Wai, Myo-Khin, Mu-Mu-Khin, Tin-U, & Thane-Toe. (1985). Effect on clinical outcome of breast feeding during acute diarrhoea. *British Medical Journal, 290,* 587–589.

Kikafunda, J. K., Walker, A. F., Allan, E. F., & Tumwine, J. K. (1998). Effect of zinc supplementation on growth and body composition of Ugandan preschool children: A randomized, controlled intervention trial. *American Journal of Clinical Nutrition, 68,* 1261–1266.

Kilbride, J., Baker, T. G., Parapia, L. A., Khoury, S. A., Shuqaidef, S. W., & Jerwood, D. (1999). Anaemia during pregnancy as a risk factor for iron-deficiency anaemia in infancy: A case-control study in Jordan. *International Journal of Epidemiology, 28,* 461–468.

Kim, J. Y., Moon, S. J., Kim, K. R., Sohn, C. Y., & Oh, J. J. (1998). Dietary iodine intake and urinary iodine excretion in normal Korean adults. *Yonsei Medical Journal, 39,* 355–362.

Kim, S., Moon, S., & Popkin, B. M. (2000). The nutrition transition in South Korea. *American Journal of Clinical Nutrition, 71,* 44–53.

Kimiagar, M., Azizi, F., Navai, L., Yassai, M., & Nafarabadi, T. (1990). Survey of iodine deficiency in a rural area near Tehran: Association of food intake and endemic goitre. *European Journal of Clinical Nutrition, 44,* 17–22.

Kirkwood, B. R., Ross, D. A., Arthur, P., Morris, S. S., Dollimore, N., Binka, F. N., Shier, R. P., Gyapong, J. O., Addy, H. A., & Smith, P. G. (1996). Effect of vitamin A supplementation on the growth of young children in northern Ghana. *American Journal of Clinical Nutrition, 63,* 773–781.

Klemm, R. D. W., Villate, E. E., Tuason-Lopez, C., Puertollano, E. P., Triunfante, J., del Rosario, A., & Dimaano, M. V. (1997). *Integrating vitamin A capsule supplementation into child weighing: A monitoring study on Philippine OPT Plus.* Manila,

Philippines: Helen Keller International and Nutrition Service, Department of Health.

Konno, N., Makita, H., Yuri, K., Iizuka, N., & Kawasaki, K. (1994). Association between dietary iodine intake and prevalence of subclinical hypothyroidism in the coastal regions of Japan. *Journal of Clinical Endocrinology and Metabolism, 78,* 393–397.

Krause, V. M., Delisle, H., & Solomons, N. W. (1998). Fortified foods contribute one half of recommended vitamin A intake in poor urban Guatemalan toddlers. *Journal of Nutrition, 128,* 860–864.

Kreiss, J. (1997). Breastfeeding and vertical transmission of HIV-1. *Acta Paediatrica, 421,* 113–117.

Kuhnlein, H. V. (1992). Food sources of vitamin A and provitamin A. *Food and Nutrition Bulletin, 14,* 3–5.

Kuvibidila, S., Warrier, R. P., Ode, D., & Yu, L. (1996). Serum transferrin receptor concentrations in women with mild malnutrition. *American Journal of Clinical Nutrition, 63,* 596–601.

Kynast, G., & Saling, E. (1986). Effect of oral zinc application during pregnancy. *Gynecology and Obstetrics Investigations, 21,* 117–123.

Labbok, M., & Krasovec, K. (1990). Toward consistency in breastfeeding definitions. *Studies in Family Planning, 21,* 226–230.

Langer, P., Tajtakova, M., Podoba, J., Jr., Kostalova, L., & Gutekunst, R. (1994). Thyroid volume and urinary iodine in school children and adolescents in Slovakia after 40 years of iodine prophylaxis. *Experimental Clinical Endocrinology, 102,* 394–398.

Lartey, A., Manu, A., Brown, K. H., Peerson, J. M., & Dewey, K. G. (1999). A randomized, community-based trial of the effects of improved, centrally processed complementary foods on growth and micronutrient status of Ghanaian infants from 6 to 12 months of age. *American Journal of Clinical Nutrition, 70,* 391–404.

Launer, L. J., Habicht, J. P., & Kardjati, S. (1990). Breast feeding protects infants in Indonesia against illness and weight loss due to illness. *American Journal of Epidemiology, 131,* 322–331.

Lawless, J. W., Latham, M. C., Stephenson, L. S., Kinoti, S. N., & Pertet, A. M. (1994). Iron supplementation improves appetite and growth in anemic Kenyan primary school children. *Journal of Nutrition, 124,* 645–654.

Lee, M.-J., Popkin, B. M., & Kim, S. (2002). The unique aspects of the nutrition transition in South Korea: The retention of healthful elements in their traditional diet. *Public Health Nutrition, 5,* 197–203.

Leon, D. A. (1998). Fetal growth and adult disease. *European Journal of Clinical Nutrition, 52,* S72–S82.

Leroy, V., Newell, M. L., Dabis F., Peckham, C., Van de Perre, P., Bulterys, M., Kind, C., Simmonds, R. J., Wiktor, S., & Msellati, P. (1998). International multicentre pooled analysis of late postnatal mother-to-child transmission of HIV-1. Ghent International Working Group on Mother-to-Child Transmission of HIV. *Lancet, 352,* 597–600.

Lewis, S. M., Stott, G. J., & Wynn, K. J. (1998). An inexpensive and reliable new haemoglobin colour scale for assessing anaemia. *Journal of Clinical Pathology, 51,* 21–24.

Lie, C., Ying, C., En-Lin, W., Brun, T., & Geissler, C. (1993). Impact of large-dose vitamin A supplementation on childhood diarrhoea, respiratory disease, and growth. *European Journal of Clinical Nutrition, 47,* 88–96.

Lindberg, O., Andersson, L. C., & Lamberg, B.-A. (1989). The impact of 25 years of iodine prophylaxis on the adult thyroid weight in Finland. *Journal of Endocrinology Investigations, 12,* 789–793.

Lixin, S., Zhongfu, S., Jiaxiu, Z., Qilin, M., Deming, K., Lifu, Y., & Ying, T. (1995). The measurement and application of TSH-IRMA levels among different age groups in areas with iodine deficiency disorders. *Chinese Medical Science Journal, 10,* 30–33.

Loerch, J. D., Underwood, B. A., & Lewis, K.C. (1979). Response of plasma levels of vitamin A to a dose of vitamin A as an indicator of hepatic vitamin A reserves in rats. *Journal of Nutrition, 109,* 778–786.

Lohman, T. G., Roche, A. F., & Martorell, R. (1988). *Anthropometric standardization reference manual.* Champaign, IL: Human Kinetics.

Lonnerdal, B., Sandberg, A. S., Sandstrom, B., & Kunz, C. (1989). Inhibitory effects of phytic acid and other inositol phosphates on zinc and calcium absorption in suckling rats. *Journal of Nutrition, 119,* 211–214.

Lozoff, B., Klein, N. K., Nelson, E. C., McClish, D. K., Manuel, M., & Chacon, M. E. (1998). Behavior of infants with iron-deficiency anemia. *Child Development, 69,* 24–36.

Lozoff, B., Wolf, A. W., & Jimenez, E. (1996). Iron-deficiency anemia and infant development: Effects of extended oral iron therapy. *Journal of Pediatrics, 129,* 382–399.

Luby, S. P., Kazembe, P. N., Redd, S. C., Ziba, C., Nwanyanwu, O. C., Hightower, A. W., Franco, C., Chitsulo, L., Wirima, J. J., & Olivar, M. A. (1995). Using clinical signs to diagnose anaemia in African children. *Bulletin of the World Health Organization, 73,* 477–482.

Lunn, P. G., Northrop-Clewes, C. A., & Downes, R. M. (1991). Intestinal permeability, mucosal injury, and growth faltering in Gambian infants. *Lancet, 338,* 907–910.

Lutter, C. K., Mora, J. O., Habicht, J. P., Rasmussen, K. M., Robson, D. S., & Herrera, M. G. (1990). Age-specific responsiveness of weight and length to nutritional supplementation. *American Journal of Clinical Nutrition, 51,* 359–364.

Lutter, C. K., Mora, J. O., Habicht, J. P., Rasmussen, K. M., Robson, D. S., Sellers, S. G., Super, C. M., & Herrera, M. G. (1989). Nutritional supplementation: Effects on child stunting because of diarrhea. *American Journal of Clinical Nutrition, 50,* 1–8.

Lynch, S. R. (1997). Interaction of iron with other nutrients. *Nutrition Reviews, 55,* 102–110.

Lynch, S. R. (1999). Iron: Physiology, dietary sources, and requirement. In M. J. Sadler, J. J. Strain, & B. Caballero (Eds.), *Encyclopedia of human nutrition* (pp. 1153–1159). San Diego: Academic Press.

Lynch, S. R., Hurrell, R. F., Bothwell, T. H., & MacPhail, A. P. (1993). *Iron EDTA for food fortification*. A report of the International Nutritional Anemia Consultative Group. Washington, DC: Nutrition Foundation.

Mahalanabis, D. (1991). Breast feeding and vitamin A deficiency among children attending a diarrhoea treatment centre in Bangladesh: A case-control study. *British Medical Journal, 303,* 493–496.

Mahalanabis, D., Lahiri, M., Paul, D., Gupta, S., Gupta, A., Wahed, M. A., & Khaled, M. (2004). Randomized, double-blind, placebo-controlled clinical trial of the efficacy of treatment with zinc or vitamin A in infants and young children with severe acute lower respiratory infection. *American Journal of Nutrition, 79,* 430–436.

Malaba, L. C., Iliff, P. J., Nathoo, K. J., Marinda, E., Moulton, L. H., Zijenah, L. S., Zvandasara, P., Ward, B. J., the ZVITAMBO Study Group, & Humphrey, J. H. (2005). Effect of postpartum maternal or neonatal vitamin A supplementation on infant mortality among infants born to HIV-negative mothers in Zimbabwe. *American Journal of Clinical Nutrition, 81,* 454–460.

Man, W. D., Weber, M., Palmer, A., Schneider, G., Wadda, R., Jaffar, S., Mulholland, E. D., & Greenwood, B. M. (1998). Nutritional status of children admitted to hospital with different diseases and its relationship to outcome in the Gambia, West Africa. *Tropical Medicine and International Health, 3,* 678–686.

Mandal, G. S., Nanda, K. N., & Bose, J. (1969). Night blindness in pregnancy. *Journal of Obstetrics and Gynecology of India, 19,* 453–458.

Mannar, M. G. V., & Dunn, J. T. (1995). *Salt iodization for the elimination of iodine deficiency*. Amsterdam, Netherlands: International Council for Control of Iodine Deficiency Disorders.

Marks, G. C., Habicht, J. P., & Mueller, W. H. (1989). Reliability, dependability, and precision of anthropometric measurements. The Second National Health and Nutrition Examination Survey 1976–1980. *American Journal of Epidemiology, 130,* 578–587.

Marquis, G. S., Habicht, J. P., Lanata, C. F., Black, R. E., & Rasmussen, K. M. (1997). Breast milk or animal-product foods improve growth of Peruvian toddlers consuming marginal diets. *American Journal of Clinical Nutrition, 66,* 1102–1109.

Marsh, R. (1998). Building on traditional gardening to improve household food security. *Food, Nutrition, and Agriculture, 22,* 4–14.

Martorell, R., Mendoza, F., & Castillo, R. (1988). Poverty and stature in children. In J. C. Waterlow (Ed.), *Linear growth retardation in less developed countries* (pp. 57–73). Nestle Nutrition Workshop Series, Vol. 14. New York: Vevey-Raven Press.

Martorell, R., Stein, A. D., & Schroeder, D. G. (2001). Early nutrition and later adiposity. *Journal of Nutrition, 131,* 874S–880S.

Martorell, R., Yarbrough, C., Lechtig, A., Habicht, J. P., & Klein, R. E. (1975). Diarrheal diseases and growth retardation in preschool Guatemalan children. *American Journal of Physical Anthropology, 43,* 341–346.

Mason, J. B., Lotfi, M., Dalmiya, N., Sethuraman, K., & Deitchler, M. (2001). *The micronutrient report. Current progress and trends in the control of vitamin A, iodine, and iron deficiencies*. Ottawa: The Micronutrient Initiative.

Mata, L. J., Cromal, R. A., Urrutia, J. J., & Garcia, B. (1977). Effect of infection of food intake and the nutritional state: Perspectives as viewed from the village. *American Journal of Clinical Nutrition, 30,* 1215–1227.

McCollum, E. V., & Davis, M. (1915). The essential factors in the diet during growth. *Journal of Biological Chemistry, 23,* 231–254.

McGuire, J., & Galloway, R. (1994). *Enriching lives: Overcoming vitamin and mineral malnutrition in developing countries*. Washington, DC: World Bank.

McMahon, R. J., & Cousins, R. J. (1998). Mammalian zinc transporters. *Journal of Nutrition, 128,* 667–670.

McMillen, I. C., Adam, C. L., & Muhlhausler, B. S. (2005). Early origins of obesity: Programming the appetite regulatory system. *Journal of Physiology, 565,* 9–17.

Mele, L., West, K. P., Jr., Kusdiono, Pandji, A., Nendrawati, H., Tilden, R. L., Tarwotjo, I., & ACEH Study Group. (1991). Nutritional and household risk factors for xerophthalmia in Aceh, Indonesia: A case-control study. *American Journal of Clinical Nutrition, 53,* 1460–1465.

Menendez, C., Kahigwa, E., Hirt, R., Vounatsou, P., Aponte, J. J., Font, F., Acosta, C. J., Schellenberg, D. M., Galindo, C. M., Kimario, J., Urassa, H., Brabin, B., Smith, T. A., Kitua, A. Y., Tanner, M., & Alonso, P. L. (1997). Randomised placebo-controlled trial of iron supplementation and malaria chemoprophylaxis for prevention of severe anaemia and malaria in Tanzanian infants. *Lancet, 350,* 844–850.

Merialdi, M., Caulfield, L. E., Zavaleta, N., Figueroa, A., & DiPietro, J. A. (1998). Adding zinc to prenatal iron and folate tablets improves fetal neurobehavioral development. *American Journal of Obstetrics and Gynecology, 180,* 483–490.

Metges, C. C., Greil, W., Gartner, R., Rafferzeder, M., Linseisen, J., Woerl, A., & Wolfram, G. (1996). Influence of knowledge on iodine content in foodstuffs and prophylactic usage of iodized salt on urinary iodine excretion and thyroid volume of adults in southern Germany. *Zeitschrift Ernahrungswiss, 35,* 6–12.

Michaelsen, K. F. (1988). Value of prolonged breastfeeding [Letter]. *Lancet, 2,* 788–789.

Mitra, A. K., Alvarez, J. O., & Stephensen, C. B. (1998). Increased urinary retinol loss in children with severe infections. *Lancet, 351,* 1033–1034.

Mokhtar, N., Elati, J., Chabir, R., Bour, A., Elkari, K., Schlossman, N. P., Caballero, B., & Aguenaou, H. (2001). Diet culture and obesity in northern Africa. *Journal of Nutrition, 131,* 887S–892S.

Monsen, E. R., Hallberg, L., Layrisse, M., Hegsted, D. M., Cook, J. D., Mertz, W., & Finch, C. A. (1978). Estimation of available dietary iron. *American Journal of Clinical Nutrition, 31,* 134–141.

Monteiro, C. A., Conde, W. L., & Popkin, B. M. (2002). Trends in under- and overnutrition in Brazil. In B. Caballero & B. M. Popkin (Eds.), *The nutrition transition: Diet and disease in the developing world* (pp. 224–140). Food Science and

Technology International Series. London: Academic Press.

Monteiro, C. A., Moura, E. C., Conde, W. L., & Popkin, B. M. (2004). Socioeconomic status and obesity in adult populations of developing countries: A review. *Bulletin of the World Health Organization, 82,* 940–946.

Moore, S. E., Cole, T. J., Collinson, A. C., Poskitt, E. M. E., McGregor, I. A., & Prentice, A. M. (1999). Prenatal or early postnatal events predict infectious deaths in young adulthood in rural Africa. *International Journal of Epidemiology, 28,* 1088–1095.

Mora, J. O. (1989). A new method for estimating a standardized prevalence of child malnutrition from anthropometric indicators. *Bulletin of the World Health Organization, 67,* 133–142.

Mora, J., Bonilla, J., Navas, G. E., & Largaespada, A. (2004). *Vitamin A deficiency is virtually under control in Nicaragua.* Paper presented at the twenty-second IVACG meeting, Lima, Peru.

Mora, J. O., Herrera, M. G., Suescun, J., de Navarro, L., & Wagner, M. (1981). The effects of nutritional supplementation on physical growth of children at risk of malnutrition. *American Journal of Clinical Nutrition, 34,* 1885–1892.

Mostad, S. B., Overbaugh, J., DeVange, D. M., Welch, M. J., Chohan, B., Mandaliya, K., Nyange, P., Martin, J. L., Jr., Ndinya-Achola, J., Bwayo, J. J., & Kreiss, J. K. (1997). Hormonal contraception, vitamin A deficiency, and other risk factors for shedding of HIV-1 infected cells from the cervix and vagina. *Lancet, 350,* 922–927.

Moy, R. J. D., Marshall, T. F. de C., Choto, R. G. A. B., McNeish, A. S., & Booth, I. W. (1994). Diarrhoea and growth faltering in rural Zimbabwe. *European Journal of Clinical Nutrition, 48,* 810–821.

MRC Vitamin Study Research Group. (1991). Prevention of neural tube defects: Results of the Medical Research Council vitamin study. *Lancet, 338,* 131–137.

Muhilal, Permeisih, D., Idjradinata, Y. R., Muherdiyantiningsih, & Karyadi, D. (1988).

Vitamin A-fortified monosodium glutamate and health, growth, and survival of children: A controlled field trial. *American Journal of Clinical Nutrition, 48,* 1271–1276.

Müller, O., Becher, H., van Zweeden, A. B., Ye, Y., Diallo, D. A., Konate, A. T., Gbangou, A., Kouyate, B., & Garenne, M. (2001). Effect of zinc supplementation on malaria and other causes of morbidity in west African children: Randomized double blind placebo controlled trial. *British Medical Journal, 322,* 1567–1571.

Murray, C. J. L., & Lopez, A. D. (1997). Global mortality, disability, and the contribution of risk factors: Global burden of disease study. *Lancet, 349,* 1436–1442.

Murray, M. J., Murray, N. J., Murray, A. B., & Murray, M. B. (1975). Refeeding-malaria and hyperferraemia. *Lancet, 1,* 653–654.

Natadisastra, G., Wittpenn, J. R., Muhilal, West, K. P., Jr., Mele, L., & Sommer, A. (1988). Impression cytology: A practical index of vitamin A status. *American Journal of Clinical Nutrition, 48,* 695–701.

National Research Council. (1977). *World food and nutrition study: The potential contributions of research.* Washington, DC: National Academy of Sciences.

Nestel, P., Nalubola, R., Sivakaneshan, R., Wickramasinghe, A. R., Atukorala, S., Wickramanayake, T., & the Flour Fortification Trial Team. (2004). The use of iron-fortified wheat flour to reduce anemia among the estate population in Sri Lanka. *International Journal of Vitamin and Nutrition Research, 74,* 35–51.

Ninh, N. X., Thissen, J. P., Collette, L., Gerard, G. G., Khoi, H. H., & Ketelslegers, J. M. (1996). Zinc supplementation increases growth and circulating insulin-like growth factor I (IGF-I) in growth-retarded Vietnamese children. *American Journal of Clinical Nutrition, 63,* 514–519.

Oberleas, D., & Harland, B. F. (1981). Phytate content of foods: Effect on dietary zinc bioavailability. *Journal of the American Dietetic Association, 79,* 433–436.

O'Dempsey, T. J., McArdle, R. F., Lloyd-Evans, N., Baldeh, I., Lawrence, B. E., Secka, O., & Greenwood, B. (1996). Pneumococcal disease among children in a rural area of west Africa. *Pediatric Infectious Disease Journal, 15,* 431–437.

Olson, J. A. (1992). Measurement of vitamin A status. *Netherlands Journal of Nutrition, 53,* 163–167.

Omran, A. R. (1971). The epidemiologic transition: A theory of the epidemiology of population change. *Milbank Memorial Fund Quarterly, 49,* 509–538.

Onyango, A. W., Esrey, S. A., & Kramer, M. S. (1999). Continued breastfeeding and child growth in the second year of life: A prospective cohort study in western Kenya. *Lancet, 354,* 2041–2045.

Oppenheimer, S. J. (2001). Iron and its relation to immunity and infectious disease. *Journal of Nutrition, 131,* 616S–635S.

Osendarp, S. J. M., van Raaij, J. M. A., Arifeen, S. E., Wahed, M. A., Baqui, A. H., & Fuchs, G. J. (2000). A randomized, placebo-controlled trial of the effect of zinc supplementation during pregnancy on pregnancy outcome in Bangladeshi urban poor. *American Journal of Clinical Nutrition, 71,* 114–119.

Osendarp, S. J. M., van Raaij, J. M. A., Darmstadt, G. L., Baqui, A. H., Hautvast, J. G. A., & Fuchs, G. J. (2001). Zinc supplementation during pregnancy and effects on growth and morbidity in low birthweight infants: A randomized placebo controlled trial. *Lancet, 357,* 1080–1085.

Osendarp, S. J. M., West, C. E., & Black, R. E., on behalf of the Maternal Zinc Supplementation Study Group. (2003). The need for maternal zinc supplementation in developing countries: An unresolved issue. *Journal of Nutrition, 133,* 817S–827S.

Oski, F. A., Honig, A. S., Helu, B., & Howanitz, P. (1983). Effect of iron therapy on behavior performance in nonanemic, iron-deficient infants. *Pediatrics, 71,* 877–880.

Papathakis, P. C., & Rollins, N. C. (2004). Are WHO/UNAIDS/UNICEF-recommended replacement milks for infants of HIV-infected mothers appropriate in the South African context? *Bulletin of the World Health Organization, 82,* 164–171.

Pardede, L. V. H., Hardjowasito, W., Gross, R., Dillion, D. H. S., Totoprajogo, O. S., Yosoprawoto, M., Waskito, L., & Untoro, J. (1998). Urinary iodine excretion is the most appropriate outcome indicator for iodine deficiency at field conditions at district level. *Journal of Nutrition, 128,* 1122–1126.

Parikh, L., & Shane, B. (1998). *Women of our world.* Washington, DC: Population Reference Bureau.

Pathak, A., Shah, N., & Tataria, A. (1993). Growth of exclusively breastfed infants. *Indian Pediatrics, 30,* 1291–1300.

Peacock, M. (1998). Effects of calcium and vitamin D insufficiency on the skeleton. *Osteoporosis International, 8,* S45–S51.

Pelletier, D. L. (1994). The potentiating effects of malnutrition on child mortality: Epidemiologic evidence and policy implications. *Nutrition Reviews, 52,* 409–415.

Pelletier, D. L., Frongillo, E. D., & Habicht, J. P. (1993). Epidemiologic evidence for a potentiating effect of malnutrition on child mortality. *American Journal of Public Health, 83,* 1130–1133.

Penny, M. E., Peerson, J. M., Marin, M., Duran, A., Lanata, C. F., Lonnerdal, B., Black, R. E., & Brown, K. H. (1999). Randomized, community-based trial of the effect of zinc supplementation, with and without other micronutrients, in the duration of persistent childhood diarrhea in Lima, Peru. *Journal of Pediatrics, 135,* 208–217.

Perez, C., Scrimshaw, S., & Munoz, A. (1960). Technique of endemic goitre surveys. In *Endemic goitre* (pp. 360–383). Geneva, Switzerland: World Health Organization.

Peterson, S., Sanga, A., Eklof, H., Bunga, B., Taube, A., Gebre-Medhin, M., & Rosling, H. (2000). Classification of thyroid size by palpation and ultrasonography in field surveys. *Lancet, 355,* 106–110.

Pharoah, P. O. D., Buttfield, I. H., & Hetzel, B. S. (1971). Neurological damage to the fetus resulting from severe iodine deficiency during pregnancy. *Lancet, 1,* 308–310.

Piwoz, E. G., Creed de Kanashiro, H., Lopez de Romana, G., Black, R. E., & Brown, K. H. (1996). Feeding practices and growth among low-income Peruvian infants: A comparison of internationally recommended definitions. *International Journal of Epidemiology, 25,* 103–114.

Piwoz, E. G., Huffman, S. L., & Quinn, V. J. (2003). Promotion and advocacy for improved complementary feeding: Can we apply the lessons learned from breastfeeding? *Food and Nutrition Bulletin, 24,* 29–44.

Poggensee, G., Schulze, K., Moneta, I., Mbezi, P., Baryomunsi, C., & Harms, G. (2004). Infant feeding practices in western Tanzania and Uganda: Implications for infant feeding recommendations for HIV-infected mothers. *Tropical Medicine and International Health, 9,* 477–485.

Pollitt, E., Gorman, K. S., Engle, P. L., Rivera, J. A., & Martorell, R. (1995). Nutrition in early life and the fulfillment of intellectual potential. *Journal of Nutrition, 125,* 1111S–11118S.

Popkin, B. M. (1994). The nutrition transition in low-income countries: An emerging crisis. *Nutrition Reviews, 52,* 285–298.

Popkin, B. M. (1998). The nutrition transition and its health implications in lower-income countries. *Public Health and Nutrition, 1,* 5–21.

Popkin, B. M. (1999). Urbanization, lifestyle changes, and the nutrition transition. *World Development, 27,* 1905–1915.

Popkin, B. M., & Doak, C. M. (1998). The obesity epidemic is a worldwide phenomenon. *Nutrition Reviews, 56,* 106–114.

Popkin, B. M, & Gordon-Larsen, P. (2004). The nutrition transition: Worldwide obesity dynamics and their determinants. *International Journal of Obesity and Related Metabolic Disorders, 28,* S2–S9.

Popkin, B. M., Horton, S. H., & Kim, S. (2001). The nutrition transition and prevention of diet-related diseases in Asia and the Pacific. *Food and Nutrition Bulletin, 22,* 3–57.

Pradhan, A., Aryal, R. H., Regmi, G., Ban, B., & Govindasamy, P. (1997). *Nepal Family Health Survey 1996.* Kathmandu, Nepal, and Calverton, MD: Ministry of Health (Nepal), New ERA, and Macro International.

Prasad, A. S. (1985). Clinical manifestations of zinc deficiency. *Annual Review of Nutrition, 5,* 341–363.

Prasad, A. S. (1991). Discovery of human zinc deficiency and studies in an experimental human model. *American Journal of Clinical Nutrition, 53,* 403–412.

Prentice, A. M. (1996). Constituents of human milk. *Food and Nutrition Bulletin, 17,* 305–312.

Prentice, A. M. (1998). Early nutritional programming of human immunity. In *Annual report, 1998* (pp. 53–64). Laussanne: Nestle Foundation for the Study of Problems of Nutrition in the World.

Prentice, A. M., Whitehead, R. G., Watkinson, M., Lamb, W. H., & Cole, T. J. (1983). Prenatal dietary supplementation of African women and birthweight. *Lancet, 1,* 489–492.

Preziosi, P., Prual, A., Galan, P., Daouda, H., Boureima, H., & Hereberg, S. (1997). Effect of iron supplementation on the iron status of pregnant women: Consequences for newborns. *American Journal of Clinical Nutrition, 66,* 1178–1182.

Quality Assurance Workshop for Salt Iodized Programs. (1997). Program Against Micronutrient Malnutrition, Opportunities for Micronutrient Interventions, and John Snow, Inc.

Rahman, M. M., Akramuzzaman, S. M., Mitra, A. K., Fuchs, G. J., & Mahalanabis, D. (1999). Long-term supplementation with iron does not enhance growth in malnourished Bangladeshi children. *Journal of Nutrition, 129,* 1319–1322.

Rahman, M. M., Huq, F., Sack, D. A., Butler, T., Azad, A. K., Alam, A., Nahar, N., & Islam, M. (1990). Acute lower respiratory infections in hospitalized patients with diarrhea in Dhaka, Bangladesh. *Reviews of Infectious Diseases, 12,* S899–S906.

Rahmathullah, L., & Chandravathi, T. S. (1997). Aetiology of severe vitamin A deficiency in chil-

dren. *Natational Medical Journal of India, 10,* 62–65.

Rahmathullah, L., Tielsch, J. M., Thulasiraj, R. D., Katz, J., Coles, C., Devi, S., John, R., Prakesh, K., Sadanand, A. V., Edwin, E., & Kamaraj, C. (2003). Impact of supplementing newborn infants with vitamin A on early infant mortality: Community based randomized trial in southern India. *British Medical Journal, 327,* 254–259.

Rahmathullah, L., Underwood, B. A., Thulasiraj, R. D., & Milton, R. C. (1991). Diarrhea, respiratory infections, and growth are not affected by a weekly low-dose vitamin A supplement: A masked, controlled field trial in children in southern India. *American Journal of Clinical Nutrition, 54,* 568–577.

Rahmathullah, L., Underwood, B. A., Thulasiraj, R. D., Milton, R. C., Ramaswamy, K., Rahmathullah, R., & Babu, G. (1990). Reducing mortality among children in southern India receiving a small weekly dose of vitamin A. *New England Journal of Medicine, 323,* 929–935.

Raisler, J., Alexander, C., & O'Campo, P. (1999). Breastfeeding and infant illness: A dose-response relationship. *American Journal of Public Health, 89,* 25–30.

Ramakrishnan, U., Aburto, N., McCabe, G., & Martorell, R. (2004). Multimicronutrient interventions but not vitamin A or iron interventions alone improve child growth: Results of 3 meta-analyses. *Journal of Nutrition, 134,* 2592–2602.

Ramakrishnan, U., Latham, M. C., & Abel, R. (1995). Vitamin A supplementation does not improve growth of preschool children: A randomized, double-blind field trial in South India. *Journal of Nutrition, 125,* 202–211.

Ramalingaswami, V. (1995). New global perspectives on overcoming malnutrition. *American Journal of Clinical Nutrition, 61,* 259–263.

Rasmussen, L. B., Ovesen, L., & Christiansen, E. (1999). Day-to-day and within-day variation in urinary iodine excretion. *European Journal of Clinical Nutrition, 53,* 401–407.

Reddy, V. (1991). Protein-energy malnutrition. In P. Stanfield, M. Brueton, M. Chan, M. Parkin, &

T. Waterston (Eds.), *Diseases of children in the subtropics and tropics* (4th ed., pp. 335–357). London: Hodder & Stoughton.

Rice, A. L., Stoltzfus, R. J., de Francisco, A., Chakraborty, J., Kjolhede, C. L., & Wahed, M. A. (1999). Maternal vitamin A or β-carotene supplementation in lactating Bangladeshi women benefits mothers and infants but does not prevent subclinical deficiency. *Journal of Nutrition, 129,* 356–365.

Rice, A. L., West, K. P., Jr., & Black, R. E. (2004). Vitamin A deficiency. In M. Ezzati, A. D. Lopez, A. Rodgers, & C. J. L. Murray (Eds.), *Comparative quantification of health risks: Global and regional burden of disease attributable to selected major risk factors* (pp. 211–256). Geneva, Switzerland: World Health Organization.

Riggs, K. M., Spiro, A. L. I., Tucker, K., & Rush, D. (1996). Relations of vitamin B12, vitamin B6, folate, and homocysteine to cognitive performance in the Normative Aging Study. *American Journal of Clinical Nutrition, 63,* 306–314.

Rivera, J., & Ruel, M. T. (1997). Growth retardation starts in the first three months of life among rural Guatemalan children. *European Journal of Clinical Nutrition, 1,* 92–96.

Rivera, J. A., Ruel, M. T., Santizo, M. C., Lönnerdal, B., & Brown, K. H. (1998). Zinc supplementation improves the growth of stunted rural Guatemalan infants. *Journal of Nutrition, 128,* 556–562.

Robinett, D., Taylor, H., & Stephens, C. (1996). *Anemia detection in health services: Guidelines for program managers* (2nd ed.). Seattle: Program for Appropriate Technology in Health.

Rolland-Cachera, M.-F., Deheeger, M., Bellisle, F., Guilloud-Bataille, M., & Patois, F. (1984). Adiposity rebound in children: A simple indicator for predicting obesity. *American Journal of Clinical Nutrition, 39,* 129–135.

Rosado, J. L., Lopez, P., Munoz, E., Martinez, H., & Allen, L.H. (1997). Zinc supplementation reduced morbidity, but neither zinc nor iron supplementation affected growth or body composition of Mexican preschoolers. *American Journal of Clinical Nutrition, 65,* 13–19.

Rosenberg, I. H., & Miller, J. W. (1992). Nutritional factors in physical and cognitive functions of elderly people. *American Journal of Clinical Nutrition, 55,* 1237S–1243S.

Ross, A. C. (1996). The relationship between immunocompetence and vitamin A status. In A. Sommer & K. P. West, Jr. (Eds.), *Vitamin A deficiency: Health, survival, and vision* (pp. 251–273). New York: Oxford University Press.

Ross, S. M., Nel, E., & Naeye, R. (1985). Differing effects of low- and high-bulk maternal dietary supplements during pregnancy. *Early Human Development, 10,* 295–302.

Rothman, K. J., & Greenland, S. (1998). Causation and causal inference. In K. J. Rothman & S. Greenland (Eds.), *Modern epidemiology* (2nd ed., pp. 7–28). Philadelphia: Lippincott-Raven.

Roubenoff, R. (2000). Sarcopenia and its implications for the elderly. *European Journal of Clinical Nutrition, 54,* S40–S47.

Rousham, E. K., & Mascie-Taylor, C. G. (1994). An 18-month study of the effect of periodic anthelminthic treatment on the growth and nutritional status of pre-school children in Bangladesh. *Annals of Human Biology, 21,* 315–324.

Rowland, M. G. M., Barrell, R. A. E., & Whitehead, R. G. (1978). Bacterial contamination in traditional Gambian weaning foods. *Lancet, 1,* 136–138.

Rowland, M. G. M., Cole, T. J., & Whitehead, R. G. (1977). A quantitative study into the role of infection in determining nutritional status in Gambian village children. *British Journal of Nutrition, 37,* 441–450.

Rowland, M. G. M., Rowland, S. G. J. G., & Cole, T. J. (1988). Impact of infection on the growth of children from 0 to 2 years in an urban West African community. *American Journal of Clinical Nutrition, 47,* 134–138.

Roy, S. K., Chowdhury, A. K., & Rahaman, M. M. (1983). Excess mortality among children discharged from hospital after treatment for diarrhoea in rural Bangladesh. *British Medical Journal, 287,* 1097–1099.

Roy, S. K., Tomkins, A. M., Akramuzzaman, S. M., Behrens, R. H., Haider, R., Mahalanabis, D., & Fuchs, G. (1997). Randomised controlled trial of zinc supplementation in malnourished Bangladeshi children with acute diarrhoea. *Archives of Diseases in Childhood, 77,* 196–200.

Roy, S. K., Tomkins, A. M., Haider, R., Behrens, R. H., Akramuzzaman, S. M., Mahalanabis, D., & Fuchs, G. J. (1999). Impact of zinc supplementation on subsequent growth and morbidity in Bangladeshi children with acute diarrhoea. *European Journal of Clinical Nutrition, 53,* 529–534.

Ruel, M. T., & Bouis, H. E. (1998). Plant breeding: A long-term strategy for the control of zinc deficiency in vulnerable populations. *American Journal of Clinical Nutrition, 68,* 488S–494S.

Ruel, M. T., Rivera, J., Habicht, J. P., & Martorell, R. (1995). Differential response to early nutrition supplementation: Long-term effects on height at adolescence. *International Journal of Epidemiology, 24,* 404–412.

Ruel, M. T., Rivera, J. A., Santizo, M.-C., Lonnerdal, B., & Brown, K. H. (1997). Impact of zinc supplementation on morbidity from diarrhea and respiratory infections among rural Guatemalan children. *Pediatrics, 99,* 808–813.

Ryan, A. S. (1997). Iron-deficiency anemia in infant development: Implications for growth, cognitive development, resistance to infection, and iron supplementation. *Yearbook of Physical Anthropology, 40,* 25–62.

Salama, P., Spiegel, P., Talley, L., & Waldman, R. (2004). Lessons learned from complex emergencies over the past decade. *Lancet, 364,* 1801–1813.

Sanghvi, T. G. (1995). *Improving the cost-effectiveness of breastfeeding promotion in maternity services. Summary of the USAID/LAC HNS Study in Latin America (1992–1995).* Arlington, VA: U.S. Agency for International Development.

Sanghvi, T., & Murray, J. (1997). *Improving child health through nutrition: The Nutrition Minimum Package.* Arlington, VA: Basic Support for Institutionalizing Child Survival (BASICS) Project, for the U.S. Agency for International Development.

Sazawal, S. (2004). *Effect of iron-folate supplementation on hospitalization and mortality in a high malaria transmission setting.* Paper presented at the INACG Symposium on Iron Deficiency in Early Life: Challenges and Progress, Lima, Peru.

Sazawal, S., Black, R. E., Bhan, M. K., Bhandari, N., Sinha, A., & Jalla, S. (1995). Zinc supplementation in young children with acute diarrhea in India. *New England Journal of Medicine, 333,* 839–844.

Sazawal, S., Black, R. E., Bhan, M. K., Jalla, S., Bhandari, N., Sinha, A., & Majumdar, S. (1996). Zinc supplementation reduces the incidence of persistent diarrhea and dysentery among low socioeconomic children in India. *Journal of Nutrition, 126,* 443–450.

Sazawal, S., Black, R. E., Bhan, M. K., Jalla, S., Sinha, A., & Bhandari, N. (1997). Efficacy of zinc supplementation in reducing the incidence and prevalence of acute diarrhea: A community-based, double-blind, controlled trial. *American Journal of Clinical Nutrition, 66,* 413–418.

Sazawal, S., Black, R. E., Jalla, S., Mazumdar, S., Sinha, A., & Bhan, M. K. (1998). Zinc supplementation reduces the incidence of acute lower respiratory infections in infants and preschool children: A double-blind controlled trial. *Pediatrics, 102,* 1–5.

Sazawal, S., Black, R. E., Menon, V. P., Dhingra, P., Caulfield, L. E., Dhingra, U., & Bagati, A. (2001). Zinc supplementation in infants born small for gestational age reduces mortality: A prospective randomized controlled trial. *Pediatrics, 108,* 1280–1286.

Sazawal, S., Jalla, S., Mazumder, S., Sinha, A., Black, R. E., & Bhan, M. K. (1997). Effect of zinc supplementation on cell-mediated immunity and lymphocyte subsets in preschool children. *Indian Pediatrics, 34,* 589.

Scholl, T. O., Hediger, M. L., Fischer, R. L., & Shearer, J. W. (1992). Anemia vs iron deficiency: Increased risk of preterm delivery in a prospective study. *American Journal of Clinical Nutrition, 55,* 985–988.

Schroeder, D. G., Martorell, R., & Flores, R. (1999). Infant and child growth and fatness and fat distribution in Guatemalan adults. *American Journal of Epidemiology, 149,* 177–185.

Scrimshaw, N. S., Taylor, C. E., & Gordon, J. E. (1967). *Interactions of nutrition and infection* (WHO Monograph Series). Geneva, Switzerland: World Health Organization.

Selwyn, B. J. (1990). The epidemiology of acute respiratory tract infection in young children: Comparison of findings from several developing countries. *Reviews of Infectious Diseases, 12,* S870–888.

Semba, R. D., de Pee, S., Panagides, D., Poly, O., & Bloem, M. W. (2004). Risk factors for xerophthalmia among mothers and their children and for mother-child pairs with xerophthalmia in Cambodia. *Archives of Ophthalmology, 122,* 517–523.

Semba, R. D., Kumwenda, N., Hoover, D. R., Taha, T. E., Quinn, T. C., Mtimavalye, L., Biggar, R. J., Broadhead, R., Miotti, P. G., Sokoll, L. J., van der Hoeven, L., & Chiphangwi, J. D. (1999). Human immunodeficiency virus load in breast milk, mastitis, and mother-to-child transmission of human immunodeficiency virus type 1. *Journal of Infectious Diseases, 180,* 93–98.

Semba, R. D., & Tang, A. M. (1999). Micronutrients and the pathogenesis of human immunodeficiency virus infection. *British Journal of Nutrition, 81,* 181–189.

Seshadri, S. (Ed.). (1996). *Use of carotene-rich foods to combat vitamin A deficiency in India: A multicentric study* (Scientific Report No. 12). New Delhi: Nutrition Foundation of India.

Shankar, A. H., Genton, B., Semba, R. D., Baisor, M., Paino, J., Tamja, S., Adiguma, T., Wu, L., Rare, L., Tielsch, J. M., Alpers, M. P., & West, K. P., Jr. (1999). Effect of vitamin A supplementation on morbidity due to *Plasmodium falciparum* in young children in Papua New Guinea: A randomised trial. *Lancet, 354,* 203–209.

Shankar, A. H., Genton, B., Tamja, S., Arnold, S., Wu, L., Baisor, M., Paino, J., Tielsch, J. M., West, K. P., Jr., & Alpers, M. A. (1999). Zinc supplementation can reduce malaria-related morbidity in preschool children. *American Journal of Tropical Medicine and Hygiene, 57,* A434.

Shankar, A. V., Gittelsohn, J., West, K. P., Jr., Stallings, R., Gnywali, T., & Faruque, F. (1998). Eating from a shared plate affects food consumption in vitamin A-deficient Nepali children. *Journal of Nutrition, 128,* 1127–1133.

Shankar, A. H., & Prasad, A. S. (1998). Zinc and immune function: The biological basis of altered resistance to infection. *American Journal of Clinical Nutrition, 68,* 447S–463S.

Shann, F., Barker, J., & Poore, P. (1989). Clinical signs that predict death in children with severe pneumonia. *Pediatric Infectious Disease Journal, 8,* 852–855.

Sharmanov, A. (1998). Anaemia in Central Asia: Demographic and health survey experience. *Food and Nutrition Bulletin, 19,* 307–317.

Shrestha, R., Pandey, P., Whalley, A., Pandey, S., Mathema, P., Quinley, J., & Dharampal, R. (2004). *Scaling-up child health services: A decade's experience of the Nepal National Vitamin A Program (NVAP).* Paper presented at the twenty-second IVACG Meeting, Lima, Peru.

Siberry, G. K., Ruff, A. J., & Black, R. (2002). Zinc and human immunodeficiency virus infection. *Nutrition Research, 22,* 527–538.

Simondon, K. B., Gartner, A., Berger, J., Cornu, A., Massamba, J. P., San Miguel, J. L., Ly, C., Missotte, I., Simondon, F., Traissac, P., Delpeuch, F., & Maire, B. (1996). Effect of early, short-term supplementation on weight and linear growth of 4–7-month-old infants in developing countries: A four-country randomized trial. *American Journal of Clinical Nutrition, 64,* 537–545.

Singh, V., & West, K. P., Jr. (2004). Vitamin A deficiency and xerophthalmia among school-aged children in southeastern Asia. *European Journal of Clinical Nutrition, 58,* 1342–1349.

Sinha, D. P., & Bang, F. B. (1973). Seasonal variation in signs of vitamin-A deficiency in rural West Bengal children. *Lancet, 2,* 228–231.

Skikne, B. S., Flowers, C. H., & Cook, J. D. (1990). Serum transferrin receptor: A quantitative measure of tissue iron deficiency. *Blood, 75,* 1870–1876.

Smedman, L., Sterky, G., Mellander, L., & Wall, S. (1987). Anthropometry and subsequent mortality in groups of children aged 6–59 months in Guinea-Bissau. *American Journal of Clinical Nutrition, 46,* 369–373.

Smil, V. (2002). Food production. In B. Caballero & B. M. Popkin (Eds.), *The nutrition transition: Diet and disease in the developing world* (pp. 25–50). London: Academic Press.

Smitasiri, S., Attig, G. A., & Dhanamitta, S. (1992). Participatory action for nutrition education: Social marketing vitamin A-rich foods in Thailand. *Ecology of Food and Nutrition, 28,* 199–210.

Smith, J. C., Makdani, D., Hegar, A., Rao, D., & Douglass, L. W. (1999). Vitamin A and zinc supplementation of preschool children. *Journal of the American College of Nutrition, 18,* 213–222.

Smith, T. A., Lehman, D., Coakley, C., Spooner, V., & Alpers, M. P. (1991). Relationships between growth and acute lower-respiratory infections in children <5 years in a highland population of Papua New Guinea. *American Journal of Clinical Nutrition, 53,* 963–970.

Sobal, J., & Stunkard, A. J. (1989). Socioeconomic status and obesity: A review of the literature. *Psychological Bulletin, 105,* 260–275.

Soemantri, A. G., Pollitt, E., & Kim, I. (1985). Iron deficiency anemia and educational achievement. *American Journal of Clinical Nutrition, 42,* 1221–1228.

Soewarta, K., & Bloem, M. W. (1999). The role of high-dose vitamin A capsules in preventing a relapse of vitamin A deficiency due to Indonesia's current crisis. *Helen Keller International Indonesia Crisis Bulletin, 1,* 1–4.

Solomons, N. W. (1998). There needs to be more than one way to skin the iodine deficiency disorders cat: Novel insights from the field in Zimbabwe. *American Journal of Clinical Nutrition, 67,* 1104–1105.

Solomons, N. W. (1999). Malnutrition: Secondary malnutrition. In M. J. Sadler, J. J. Strain, & B. Caballero (Eds.), *Encyclopedia of human nutrition* (pp. 1254–1259). San Diego, CA: Academic Press.

Solon, F. S., Fernandez, T. L., Latham, M. C., & Popkin, B. M. (1979). An evaluation of strategies to control vitamin A deficiency in the Philippines. *American Journal of Clinical Nutrition, 32,* 1445–1453.

Solon, F. S., Klemm, R. D. W., Sanchez, L., Darnton-Hill, I., Craft, N. E., Christian, P., & West, K. P., Jr. (2000). Efficacy of a vitamin A-fortified wheat-flour bun on the vitamin A status of Filipino school children. *American Journal of Clinical Nutrition, 72,* 738–744.

Solon, F. S., Latham, M. C., Guirriee, R., Florentino, R., Williamson, D. F., & Aguilar, J. (1985). Fortification of MSG with vitamin A: The Philippines experience. *Food Technology, 39,* 71–79.

Solon, F. S., Solon, M. S., Mehansho, H., West, K. P., Jr., Sarol, J., Perfecto, C., Nano, T., Sanchez, L., Isleta, M., Wasantwisut, E., & Sommer, A. (1996). Evaluation of the effect of vitamin A-fortified margarine on the vitamin A status of preschool Filipino children. *European Journal of Clinical Nutrition, 50,* 720–723.

Sommer, A. (1982). *Nutritional blindness: Xerophthalmia and keratomalacia.* New York: Oxford University Press.

Sommer, A. (1995). *Vitamin A deficiency and its consequences: A field guide to detection and control* (3rd ed.). Geneva, Switzerland: World Health Organization.

Sommer, A., & Davidson, F. R. (2002). Assessment and control of vitamin A deficiency: The Annecy Accords. *Journal of Nutrition, 132,* 2845S–2850S.

Sommer, A., Hussaini, G., Tarwotjo, I., & Susanto, D. (1983). Increased mortality in children with mild vitamin A deficiency. *Lancet, 2,* 585–588.

Sommer, A., & Loewenstein, M. S. (1975). Nutritional status and mortality: A prospective validation of the QUAC stick. *American Journal of Clinical Nutrition, 28,* 287–292.

Sommer, A., Tarwotjo, I., Hussaini, G., Susanto, D., & Soegiharto, T. (1981). Incidence, prevalence, and scale of blinding malnutrition. *Lancet, 1,* 1407–1408.

Sommer, A., & West, K. P., Jr. (1996). *Vitamin A deficiency: Health, survival, and vision.* New York: Oxford University Press.

Stanbury, J. B., Ermans, A. E., Bourdoux, P., Todd, C., Oken, E., Tonglet, R., Vidor, G., Braverman, L. E., & Medeiros Neto, G. (1998). Iodine-induced hyperthyroidism: Occurrence and epidemiology. *Thyroid, 8,* 83–100.

Steer, P., Alam, M. A., Wadsworth, J., & Welch, A. (1995). Relation between maternal haemoglobin concentration and birthweight in different ethnic groups. *British Medical Journal, 310,* 489–491.

Stein, S. A. (1994). Molecular and neuroanatomical substrates of motor and cerebral cortex abnormalities in fetal thyroid hormone disorders. In J. B. Stanbury (Ed.), *The damaged brain of iodine deficiency* (pp. 67–102). New York: Cognizant Communication Corporation.

Stephensen, C. B. (2001). Vitamin A, infection, and immune function. *Annual Review of Nutrition, 21,* 167–192.

Stipanuk, M. H. (2000). *Biochemical and physiological aspects of human nutrition.* Philadelphia: WB Saunders.

Stoltzfus, R. J. (1997). Rethinking anaemia surveillance. *Lancet, 349,* 1764–1766.

Stoltzfus, R. J. (2003). Iron deficiency: Global prevalence and consequences. *Food and Nutrition Bulletin, 24,* S99–S103.

Stoltzfus, R. J., Albonico, M., Chwaya, H. M., Tielsch, J. M., Schulze, K. J., & Savioli, L. (1998). Effects of the Zanzibar school-based deworming program on iron status of children. *American Journal of Clinical Nutrition, 68,* 179–186.

Stoltzfus, R. J., Chwaya, H. M., Tielsch, J. M., Schulze, K. J., Albonico, M., & Savioli, L. (1997). Epidemiology of iron deficiency anemia in Zanzibari school children. *American Journal of Clinical Nutrition, 65,* 153–159.

Stoltzfus, R. J., & Dreyfuss, M. L. (1998). *Guidelines for the use of iron supplements to prevent and treat iron deficiency anemia.* International Nutrition Anemia Consultative Group/World Health Organization/United Nations Children's Fund. Washington, DC: ILSI Press.

Stoltzfus, R. J., Edward-Raj, A., Dreyfuss, M. L., Albonico, M., Montresor, A., Thapa, M. D., West, K. P., Jr., Chwaya, H. M., Savioli, L., & Tielsch, J. (1999). Clinical pallor is useful to detect severe anemia in populations where anemia is prevalent and severe. *Journal of Nutrition, 129,* 1675–1681.

Stoltzfus, R. J., Hakimi, M., Miller, K. W., Rasmussen, K. M., Dawiesah, S., Habicht, J. P., & Dibley, M. J. (1993). High-dose vitamin A supplementation of breast feeding Indonesian mothers: Effects on the vitamin A status of mother and infant. *Journal of Nutrition, 123, 666–675.*

Stoltzfus, R. J., Miller, K. W., Hakimi, M., & Rasmussen, K. M. (1993). Conjunctival impression cytology as an indicator of vitamin A status in lactating Indonesian women. *American Journal of Clinical Nutrition, 58,* 167–173.

Stoltzfus, R. J., Mullany, L., & Black, R. E. (2004). Iron deficiency anaemia. In M. Ezzati, A. D. Lopez, A. Rodgers, & C. J. L. Murray (Eds.), *Comparative quantification of health risks: Global and regional burden of disease attributable to selected major risk factors* (pp. 163–209). Geneva, Switzerland: World Health Organization.

Stoltzfus, R. J., & Underwood, B. A. (1995). Breast-milk vitamin A as an indicator of the vitamin A status of women and infants. *Bulletin of the World Health Organization, 73,* 703–711.

Stott, G. J., & Lewis, S. M. (1995). A simple and reliable method for estimating haemoglobin. *Bulletin of the World Health Organization, 73,* 369–373.

Susser, M., & Stein, Z. (1994). Timing in prenatal nutrition: A reprise of the Dutch Famine Study. *Nutrition Reviews, 52,* 84–94.

Syrenicz, A., Napierala, K., Celibala, R., Majewska, U., Krzyzanowska, B., Gulinska, M., Gozdzik, J., Widecka, K., & Czekalski, S. (1993). Iodized salt consumption, urinary iodine concentration, and prevalence of goiter in children from four districts of northwestern Poland (Szczecin Coordinating Center). *Endokrynologia Polska, 44,* 343–350.

Taffs, R. E., Enterline, J. C., Rusmil, K., Muhilal, Suwardi, S. S., Rustama, D., Djatnika, Cobra, C., Semba, R. D., Cohen, N., & Asher, D. M. (1999). Oral iodine supplementation does not reduce neutralizing antibody responses to oral poliovirus vaccine. *Bulletin of the World Health Organization, 77,* 484–491.

Tajtakova, M., Hancinova, D., Langer, P., Tajtak, J., Foldes, O., Malinovsky, E., & Varga, J. (1990). Thyroid volume by ultrasound in boys and girls 6–16 years of age under marginal iodine deficiency as related to the age of puberty. *Klinisce Wochenschrift, 68,* 503–506.

Talukder, A., Islam, N., Klemm, R., & Bloem, M. (1993). *Home gardening in South Asia: The complete handbook.* Dhaka, Bangladesh: Helen Keller International.

Tamura, T., Goldenberg, R. L., Johnston, K. E., & Dubard, M. (2000). Maternal plasma zinc concentrations and pregnancy outcome. *American Journal of Clinical Nutrition, 71,* 109–113.

Tanumihardjo, S. A., Muhilal, Yuniar, Y., Permaeshi, D., Sulaiman, Z., Karyadi, D., & Olson, J. A. (1990). Vitamin A status in preschool-age Indonesian children as assessed by the modified relative-dose-response assay. *American Journal of Clinical Nutrition, 52,* 1068–1072.

Taren, D., & Chen, J. (1993). A positive association between extended breast-feeding and nutritional status in rural Hubei Province, People's Republic of China. *American Journal of Clinical Nutrition, 58,* 862–867.

Tarwotjo, I., Katz, J., West, K. P., Jr., Tielsch, J. M., & Sommer, A. (1992). Xerophthalmia and growth in preschool Indonesian children. *American Journal of Clinical Nutrition, 55,* 1142–1146.

Tarwotjo, I., Sommer, A., & Soegiharto, T. (1982). Dietary practices and xerophthalmia among Indonesian children. *American Journal of Clinical Nutrition, 35,* 574–581.

Thomson, C. D., Colls, A. J., Conaglen, J. V., Macormack, M., Stiles, M., & Mann, J. (1997). Iodine status of New Zealand residents as assessed by urinary iodide excretion and thyroid hormones. *British Journal of Nutrition, 78,* 891–912.

Thurnham, D. J., McCabe, G. P., Northrop-Clewes, C. A., & Nestel, P. (2003). Effects of subclinical infection on plasma retinol concentrations and assessment of prevalence of vitamin A deficiency: Meta-analysis. *Lancet, 362,* 2052–2058.

Tielsch, J. M., Stoltzfus, R. J., Khatry, S. K., Katz, J., LeClerq, S. C., Adhikari, R., Shrestha, S. R., Siegel, E., & Mullany, L. C. (2004). *Mortality risk is not affected by iron-folate supplementation among preschool children in Nepal.* Paper presented at the 2004 INACG Symposium, Iron Deficiency in Early Life: Challenges and Progress, Lima, Peru.

Tome, P., Reyes, H., Rodriguez, L., Guiscafre, H., & Gutierrez, G. (1996). Death caused by acute diarrhea in children: A study of prognostic factors. *Salud Publica de Mexico, 38,* 227–235.

Tonascia, J. A. (1993). Meta-analysis of published community trials: Impact of vitamin A on mortality. In Helen Keller International (Ed.), *Bellagio meeting on vitamin A deficiency and childhood mortality* (pp. 49–51). Proceedings of Public Health Significance of Vitamin A Deficiency and Its Control. New York: Helen Keller International.

Toole, M. J., & Waldman, R. J. (1993). Refugees and displaced persons. War, hunger, and public health. *Journal of the American Medical Association, 270,* 600–605.

Tortora, G. J., & Grabowski, S. R. (1996). The endocrine system. In G. J. Tortora & S. R. Grabowski (Eds.), *Principles of anatomy and physiology* (8th ed., pp. 501–550). New York: HarperCollins.

Torun, B., & Chew, F. (1999). Protein-energy malnutrition. In M. E. Shils, J. A. Olson, M. Shike, & A. C. Ross (Eds.), *Modern nutrition in health and disease* (pp. 963–988). Baltimore: Williams & Wilkins.

Trowbridge, F. L., Harris, S. S., Cook, J., Dunn, J. T., Florentino, R. F., Kodyat, B. A., Mannar, M. G. V., Reddy, V., Tontisirin, K., Underwood, B. A., & Yip, R. (1993). Coordinated strategies for controlling micronutrient malnutrition: A technical workshop. *Journal of Nutrition, 123,* 775–787.

Tucker, K. (2000). B vitamins, homocysteine, heart disease, and cognitive function. *SCN News, 19,* 30–33.

Tupasi, T. E., Mangubat, N. V., Sunico, M. E., Magdangal, D. M., Navarro, E. E., Leonor, Z. A., Lupisan, S., Medalla, F., & Lucero, M. G. (1990). Malnutrition and acute respiratory tract infections in Filipino children. *Review of Infectious Diseases, 12,* S1047–S1054.

Uauy, R., Albala, C., & Kain, J. (2001). Obesity trends in Latin America: Transiting from under- to overweight. *Journal of Nutrition, 131,* 893S–899S.

Underwood, B. A. (1990). Methods for assessment of vitamin A status. *Journal of Nutrition, 120,* 1459–1463.

Underwood, B. A. (1994). Current status of iodine deficiency disorders: A global perspective. *NU News on Health Care in Developing Countries, 8,* 4.

Underwood, B. A., & Hofvander, Y. (1982). Appropriate timing for complementary feeding of the breast-fed infant: A review. *Acta Paediatrica Scandinavica, 294*(Suppl.), 1–32.

UNICEF. (1991). *The state of the world's children 1991.* New York: Oxford University Press.

UNICEF. (1997). *The state of the world's children 1998.* New York: Oxford University Press.

UNICEF. (n.d.). Delivering essential micronutrients: Iron. http://www.unicef.org/nutrition/index_iron.html.

United Nations (1982, December 21). *Food problems* (A/RES/37/247). New York: United Nations.

United Nations. (2000, September 8). *United Nations Millennium Declaration* (A/RES/55/2). New York: United Nations.

United Nations. (2004, August 27). *Implementation of the United Nations Millennium Declaration* (A/59/282). New York: United Nations.

United Nations Population Division. (1988). *World urbanization prospects.* New York: United Nations.

United Nations Population Division. (2004). World population prospects: The 2004 revision population database. http://www.un.org/esa/population/unpop.htm/dataonline/definitionofregions.

USDA Economic Research Service. (2001). *Changing structure of global food consumption and trade.* Washington, DC: United States Department of Agriculture/ARS.

Vetter, K. M., Djomand, G., Zadi, F., Diaby, L., Brattegaard, K., Timite, M., Andoh, J., Adou, J. A., & DeCock, K. M. (1996). Clinical spectrum of human immunodeficiency virus disease in children in a west Africa city. Project RETRO-CI. *Pediatric Infectious Disease Journal, 15,* 438–442.

Victora, C. G., Barros, F. C., Kirkwood, B. R., & Vaughan, J. P. (1990). Pneumonia, diarrhea, and growth in the first 4 years of life: A longitudinal study of 5914 urban Brazilian children. *American Journal of Clinical Nutrition, 52,* 391–396.

Victora, C. G., Fuchs, S. C., Kirkwood, B. R., Lombardi, C., & Barros, F. C. (1992). Breast-feeding, nutritional status, and other prognostic factors for dehydration among young children with diarrhoea in Brazil. *Bulletin of the World Health Organization, 70,* 467–475.

Victora, C. G., Kirkwood, B. R., Ashworth, A., Black, R. E., Rogers, S., Sazawal, S., Campbell, H., & Gove, S. (1999). Potential interventions for the prevention of childhood pneumonia in developing countries: Improving nutrition. *American Journal of Clinical Nutrition, 70,* 309–320.

Victora, C. G., Morris, S. S., Barros, F. C., de Onis, M., & Yip, R. (1998). The NCHS reference and the growth of breast- and bottle-fed infants. *Journal of Nutrition, 128,* 1134–1138.

Victora, C. G., Smith, P. G., Barros, F. C., Vaughan, J. P., & Fuchs, S. C. (1989). Risk factors for deaths due to respiratory infections among Brazilian infants. *International Journal of Epidemiology, 18,* 918–925.

Victora, C. G., Vaughan, J. P., Martines, J. C., & Barcelos, L. B. (1984). Is prolonged breast-feeding associated with malnutrition? *American Journal of Clinical Nutrition, 39,* 307–314.

Villar, J., Smeriglio, V., Martorell, R., Brown, C. H., & Klein, R. E. (1984). Heterogeneous growth and mental development of intrauterine growth-retarded infants during the first 3 years of life. *Pediatrics, 74,* 783–791.

Viteri, F. E. (1998). A new concept in the control of iron deficiency: Community-based preventive supplementation of at-risk groups by the weekly intake of iron supplements. *Biomedical and Environmental Sciences, 11,* 46–60.

Wald, G. (1955). The photoreceptor process in vision. *American Journal of Ophthalmology, 40,* 18–41.

Walker, S. P., Powell, C. A., Grantham-McGregor, S. M., Himes, J. H., & Chang, S. M. (1991). Nutritional supplementation, psychosocial stimulation, and growth of stunted children: The Jamaican study. *American Journal of Clinical Nutrition, 54,* 642–648.

Walter, T. (1989). Infancy: Mental and motor development. *American Journal of Clinical Nutrition, 50,* 655–666.

Walter, T., Olivares, M., Pizarro, F., & Munoz, C. (1997). Iron, anemia, and infection. *Nutrition Reviews, 55,* 111–124.

Wark, J. D. (1999). Osteoporosis: A global perspective. *Bulletin of the World Health Organization, 77,* 424–426.

Waterlow, J. C., Buzina, R., Keller, W., Lane, J. M., Nichaman, M. Z., & Tanner, J. (1977). The presentation and use of height and weight data for comparing the nutritional status of groups of children under the age of 10 years. *Bulletin of the World Health Organization, 55,* 489–498.

Weissenbacher, M., Carballal, G., Avila, M., Salomon, H., Harisiadi, J., Catalano, M., Cerqueizo, M. C., & Murtagh, P. (1990). Hospital-based studies on acute respiratory tract infection in young children. *Review of Infectious Diseases, 12,* S889–S898.

West, C. E., Eilander, A., & van Lieshout, M. (2002). Consequences of revised estimates of carotenoid bioefficacy for dietary control of vitamin A deficiency in developing countries. *Journal of Nutrition, 132,* 2920S–2926S.

West, K. P., Jr. (1986). Peri-urban malnutrition in Bangladesh: Differential energy, protein, and growth status of children. *Ecology of Food and Nutrition, 19,* 99–112.

West, K. P., Jr. (2002). Extent of vitamin A deficiency among preschool children and women of reproductive age. *Journal of Nutrition, 132,* 2857S–2866S.

West, K. P., Jr. (2005). Famine. In M. Sadler, B. Caballero, & S. Strain (Eds.), *Encyclopedia of human nutrition.* London: Academic Press.

West, K. P., Jr., Chirambo, M., Katz, J., Sommer, A., & Malawi Survey Group. (1986). Breastfeeding, weaning patterns, and the risk of xerophthalmia in southern Malawi. *American Journal of Clinical Nutrition, 44,* 690–697.

West, K. P., Jr., Djunaedi, E., Pandji, A., Kusdiono, Tarwotjo, I., Sommer, A., & Aceh Study Group. (1988). Vitamin A supplementation and growth: A randomized community trial. *American Journal of Clinical Nutrition, 48,* 1257–1264.

West, K. P., Jr., Katz, J., Khatry, S. K., LeClerq, S. C., Pradhan, E. K., Shrestha, S. R., Connor, P. B., Dali, S. M., Christian, P., Pokhrel, R. P., Sommer, A., & the NNIPS-2 Study Group. (1999). Double blind, cluster randomised trial of low-dose supplementation with vitamin A or β-carotene on mortality related to pregnancy in Nepal. *British Medical Journal, 318,* 570–575.

West, K. P., Jr., LeClerq, S. C., Shrestha, S. R., Wu, L. S.-F., Pradhan, E. K., Khatry, S. K., Katz, J., Adhikari, R., & Sommer, A. (1997). Effects of vitamin A on growth of vitamin A-deficient children: Field studies in Nepal. *Journal of Nutrition, 127,* 1957–1965.

West, K. P., Jr., Pokhrel, R. P., Katz, J., LeClerq, S. C., Khatry, S. K., Shrestha, S. R., Pradhan, E. K., Tielsch, J. M., Pandey, M. R., & Sommer, A. (1991). Efficacy of vitamin A in reducing preschool child mortality in Nepal. *Lancet, 338,* 67–71.

West, K. P., Jr., & Sommer, A. (1987). *Delivery of oral doses of vitamin A to prevent vitamin A deficiency and nutritional blindness* (Nutrition Policy Discussion Paper No. 2). Rome: United Nations Administrative Committee on Coordination, Sub-Committee on Nutrition.

WHO Collaborative Study Team on the Role of Breastfeeding on the Prevention of Infant Mortality.

(2000). Effect of breastfeeding on infant and child mortality due to infectious diseases in less developed countries: A pooled analysis. *Lancet, 355,* 451–455.

WHO/FAO. (2003). *Diet, nutrition and the prevention of chronic diseases.* Geneva, Switzerland: World Health Organization.

WHO Global Database on Child Growth and Malnutrition. (n.d.). http://www.who.int/nutgrowthdb.

WHO/NPH. (2002). *Physical activity and health (PAH): Components of WHO strategic plan (2002–2003)* (WHO/NMH/NPH/PAH). Geneva, Switzerland: World Health Organization, Department of Prevention and Health Promotion.

WHO/UNICEF. (2001). *Global strategy for infant and young child feeding.* Geneva, Switzerland: World Health Organization.

WHO/UNICEF. (2004). *Clinical management of acute diarrhea.* Geneva, Switzerland: United Nations Children's Fund and the World Health Organization.

WHO/UNICEF/IVACG. (1997). *Vitamin A supplements: a guide to their use in the treatment and prevention of vitamin A deficiency and xerophthalmia* (2nd ed.). Geneva, Switzerland: World Health Organization.

WHO Working Group on Infant Growth. (1994). *An evaluation of infant growth.* Geneva, Switzerland: World Health Organization, Nutrition Unit.

Willett, W. C., Kilama, W. L., & Kihamia, C. M. (1979). Ascaris and growth rates: A randomized trial of treatment. *American Journal of Public Health, 69,* 987–991.

Williams, C. D. (1933). A nutritional disease of childhood associated with a maize diet. *Archives of Diseases in Childhood, 8,* 423–433.

Wittpenn, J. R, Tseng, S. C. G., & Sommer, A. (1986). Detection of early xerophthalmia by impression cytology. *Archives of Ophthalmology, 104,* 237–239.

World Bank. (1993). *World development report 1993: Investing in health.* New York: Oxford University Press.

World Food Summit, 13–17 November 1996, Rome, Italy. http://www.fao.org/wfs/index_en.htm.

World Health Organization. (1989). *Protecting, promoting, and supporting breast-feeding-the special role of maternity services.* Geneva, Switzerland: World Health Organization.

World Health Organization. (1992a). *Maternal health and safe motherhood programme. The prevalence of anaemia in women: A tabulation of available information* (2nd ed.) (WHO/MCH/MSM/92.2). Geneva, Switzerland: World Health Organization.

World Health Organization. (1992b). *Office of Information consensus statement: HIV and breast-feeding* (Press Release WHO/30). Geneva, Switzerland: World Health Organization.

World Health Organization. (1993). *Global prevalence of iodine deficiency disorders* (MDIS Working Paper No. 1). Geneva, Switzerland: Micronutrient Deficiency Information System/World Health Organization.

World Health Organization. (1994). *Indicators for assessing iodine deficiency disorders and their control through salt iodization* (WHO/NUT/94.6). Geneva, Switzerland: World Health Organization.

World Health Organization. (1995a). *Physical status: The use and interpretation of anthropometry* (WHO Technical Report No. 854). Geneva, Switzerland: World Health Organization.

World Health Organization. (1995b). *The global prevalence of vitamin A deficiency* (MDIS Working Paper No. 2; WHO/NUT/95.3). Geneva, Switzerland: World Health Organization.

World Health Organization. (1996a). *Indicators for assessing vitamin A deficiency and their application in monitoring and evaluating intervention programs* (WHO/ NUT/96.10). Geneva, Switzerland: World Health Organization.

World Health Organization. (1996b). *Trace elements in human health and nutrition.* Geneva, Switzerland: World Health Organization.

World Health Organization. (1998). *Integration of vitamin A supplementation with immunization: Policy and programme implications*. Report of a meeting 12–13 January, 1998, New York. Geneva, Switzerland: World Health Organization, Global Program for Vaccines and Immunization, Expanded Program on Immunization.

World Health Organization. (2000). *The management of nutrition in major emergencies*. Geneva, Switzerland: World Health Organization.

World Health Organization. (2002). *The world health report 2002: Reducing risks, promoting healthy life*. Geneva, Switzerland: World Health Organization.

Yadrick, M. K., Kenney, M. A., & Winterfeldt, E. A. (1989). Iron, copper, and zinc status: Response to supplementation with zinc or zinc and iron in adult females. *American Journal of Clinical Nutrition, 49*, 145–150.

Yajnik, C. S., Fall, C. H. D., Coyaji, K. J., Hirve, S. S., Rao, S., Barker, D. J. P., Joglekar, C., & Kellingray, S. (2003). Neonatal anthropometry: The thin-fat Indian baby. The Pune Maternal Nutrition Study. *International Journal of Obesity Related Metabolic Disorders, 27*, 173–180.

Yip, R. (1994). Iron deficiency: Contemporary scientific issues and international programmatic approaches. *Journal of Nutrition, 124*, 1479S–1490S.

Yip, R. (1997). The challenge of improving iron nutrition: Limitations and potentials of major intervention approaches. *European Journal of Clinical Nutrition, 51*, S16–S24.

Yip, R., Johnson, C., & Dallman, P. R. (1984). Age-related changes in laboratory values used in the diagnosis of anemia and iron deficiency. *American Journal of Clinical Nutrition, 39*, 427–436.

Yip, R., & Sharp, T. W. (1993). Acute malnutrition and high childhood mortality related to diarrhea. Lessons from the 1991 Kurdish refugee crisis. *Journal of the American Association, 270*, 587–590.

Young, H., Borrel, A., Holland, D., & Salama, P. (2004). Public nutrition in complex emergencies. *Lancet, 364*, 1899–1909.

Zeyre, E., & McIntyre, D. (2003). Inequities in under-five child malnutrition in South Africa. *International Journal for Equity in Health, 2*, 7–16.

Zhou, L.-M., Yang, W.-W., Hua, J.-Z., Deng, C.-Q., Tao, X., & Stoltzfus, R. J. (1998). Relation of hemoglobin measured at different times in pregnancy to preterm birth and low birthweight in Shanghai, China. *American Journal of Epidemiology, 148*, 998–1006.

Zimmermann, M. B. (2004). Assessing iodine status and monitoring progress of iodized salt programs. *Journal of Nutrition, 134*, 1673–1677.

Zimmermann, M. B., Hess, S. Y., Molinari, L., de Benoist, B., Delange, F., Braverman, L. E., Fujieda, K., Ito, Y., Jooste, P. L., Moosa, K., Pearce, E. N., Pretell, E. A., Shishiba Y. (2004). New reference values for thyroid volume by ultrasound in iodine-sufficient schoolchildren: A World Health Organization/Nutrition for Health and Development Iodine Deficiency Study Group report. *American Journal of Clinical Nutrition, 79*, 231–237.

Zimmermann, M. B., Wegmueller, R., Zeder, C., Chaouki, N., Rohner, F., Saissi, M., Torresani, T., Hurrell, R. F. (2004a). Dual fortification of salt with iodine and micronized ferric pyrophosphate: A randomized, double-blind, controlled trial. *American Journal of Clinical Nutrition, 80*, 952–959.

Zimmermann, M. B., Wegmueller, R., Zeder, C., Chaouki, N., Biebinger, R., Hurrell, R. F., & Windhab, E. (2004b). Triple fortification of salt with microcapsules of iodine, iron, and vitamin A. *American Journal of Clinical Nutrition, 80*, 1283–1290.

Zimmermann, M. B., Zeder, C., Chaouki, N., Saad, A., Torresani, T., & Hurrell, R. F. (2003). Dual fortification of salt with iodine and microencapsulated iron: A randomized, double-blind, controlled trial in Moroccan school children. *American Journal of Clinical Nutrition, 77*, 425–432.

Zinc Against Plasmodium Study Group. (2002). Effect of zinc on the treatment of *Plasmodium falciparum* malaria in children: A randomized controlled trial. *American Journal of Clinical Nutrition, 76*, 805–812.

Zinc Investigators' Collaborative Group. (1999). Prevention of diarrhea and pneumonia by zinc supplementation in children in developing countries: Pooled analysis of randomized controlled trials. *Journal of Pediatrics, 135,* 689–697.

Zinc Investigators' Collaborative Group. (2002). Therapeutic effects of oral zinc in acute and persistent diarrhea in children in developing countries: Pooled analysis of randomized controlled trials. *American Journal of Clinical Nutrition, 72,* 1516–1522.

Zlotkin, S. H., Arthur, P., Antwi, K. Y., & Yeung, G. (2001). Treatment of anemia with microencapsulated ferrous fumarate plus ascorbic acid supplied as "sprinkles" to complementary (weaning) foods. *American Journal of Clinical Nutrition, 74,* 791–795.

Zlotkin, S. H., Schauer, C., Christofides, A., Sharieff, W., Tondeur, M. C., & Hyder, S. M. Z.

(2005). Micronutrient sprinkles to control childhood anaemia. *Public Library of Science Medicine, 2,* 24–28.

Zlotnik, H. (2002). Demographic trends. In B. Caballero & B. M. Popkin (Eds.), *The nutrition transition: Diet and disease in the developing world* (pp. 71–108). London: Academic Press.

Zucker, J. R., Perkins, B. A., Jafari, H., Otieno, J., Obonyo, C., & Campbell, C. C. (1997). Clinical signs for the recognition of children with moderate or severe anaemia in western Kenya. *Bulletin of the World Health Organization, 78*(Suppl.), 97–102.

Zumrawi, F. Y., Dimond, H., & Waterlow, J. C. (1987). Effects of infection on growth in Sudanese children. *Human Nutrition: Clinical Nutrition, 41,* 453–461.

6

Chronic Diseases and Risks

DEREK YACH, CORINNA HAWKES, JOANNE E. EPPING-JORDAN, AND KRISELA STEYN

Chronic diseases include a heterogeneous group of conditions that usually emerge in middle age after a long exposure to unhealthy consumption patterns. To a large extent, chronic diseases have common underlying characteristics: a few common risk factors that act independently and synergistically, a long latency between cumulative exposure to risk and disease outcomes, a high degree of preventability, a low cure rate necessitating decades of treatment, considerable comorbidity, and strong linkages to poverty and development. They are predominantly caused by non-infectious diseases.

The focus of this chapter is on leading chronic disease killers: cardiovascular diseases (mainly coronary heart disease and stroke), common cancers, chronic respiratory diseases (mainly chronic obstructive pulmonary disease and asthma) and diabetes. Other chronic diseases are covered elsewhere. Emphasis is given to unhealthy consumption and activity patterns—tobacco use, unhealthy diets, and physical inactivity—and the resulting intermediate risks, such as raised blood pressure, obesity, and abnormal glucose and lipid metabolism. The epidemiology, demography, current and future trends, and economic implications of these chronic diseases and their risks are briefly summarized. The policy responses and impediments to progress in addressing chronic diseases are briefly described.

Epidemiologic Trends

Disease Mortality and Burden

Worldwide, approximately 56 million deaths occurred in 2002, of which chronic diseases in adults accounted for 60% (see World Health Organizations's web site: http://www.who.int/topics/chronic_disease/en/)

(World Health Organization [WHO], 2003a). Cardiovascular diseases (CVD), especially coronary heart disease (CHD) and stroke, caused 16.7 million deaths; cancer, 7 million deaths; chronic respiratory disease, 5.2 million deaths; and diabetes, almost 1 million deaths (see Table 6-1 for the leading causes of death in 2000). Mental disorders are leading contributors to the burden of disease in many countries (WHO, 2001) and contribute significantly to the incidence and severity of many chronic diseases, including CVD and cancer. Three key risk factors—tobacco, the diet–physical activity complex, and alcohol—explain a significant proportion of the burden of chronic diseases.

Seventy-two percent of deaths from chronic diseases occur in low- and low-middle-income countries (WHO, 2003b) and, relative to higher-income nations, are more likely to occur among younger people (Leeder et al., 2004). Figure 6-1 shows a high prevalence of risk factors in high- and low-mortality developing countries,[1] and Figure 6-2 illustrates that chronic diseases rank as major causes of death in developing countries (WHO, 2003a). Age-specific death rates are higher in low- and low-middle-income countries relative to upper-middle and high-income countries (WHO, 2003b).

The shift toward a higher burden of chronic diseases in developing nations is well illustrated by China. By the late 1990s, 83% of rural deaths were

[1]To aid in cause of death and burden of disease analyses, the 192 member states of the World Health Organization have been divided into mortality strata. This classification was conducted using population statistics and estimates of mortality rates for 1999. Five mortality strata were defined in terms of quintiles of the distribution. Adult mortality was regressed and the regression line used to divide countries.

Table 6-1	Ten Leading Causes of Deaths in 2000, Globally and in Developing and Developed Countries				
World	**% of Total Deaths**	**Developed Countries**[a]	**% of Total Deaths**	**Developing Countries**	**% of Total Deaths**
1. Ischemic heart disease	12.4	1. Ischemic heart disease	22.6	1. Ischemic heart disease	9.1
2. Cerebrovascular disease	9.2	2. Cerebrovascular disease	13.7	2. Cerebrovascular disease	8.0
3. Lower respiratory infections	6.9	3. Trachea, bronchus, and lung cancers	4.5	3. Lower respiratory infections	7.7
4. HIV/AIDS	5.3	4. Lower respiratory infections	3.7	4. HIV/AIDS	6.9
5. Chronic obstructive pulmonary disease	4.5	5. Chronic obstructive pulmonary disease	3.1	5. Perinatal conditions	5.6
6. Perinatal conditions	4.4	6. Colon and rectum cancers	2.6	6. Chronic obstructive pulmonary disease	5.0
7. Diarrheal diseases	3.8	7. Stomach cancer	1.9	7. Diarrheal diseases	4.9
8. Tuberculosis	3.0	8. Self-inflicted injuries	1.9	8. Tuberculosis	3.7
9. Road traffic accidents	2.3	9. Diabetes	1.7	9. Malaria	2.6
10. Trachea, bronchus, and lung cancers	2.2	10. Breast cancer	1.6	10. Road traffic accidents	2.5

[a]Developed countries category includes European countries, former Soviet countries, Canada, the United States, Japan, Australia, and New Zealand.

Source: World Health Organization, *World Health Report, 2002* (Geneva, Switzerland: World Health Organization, 2002). Reprinted with permission.

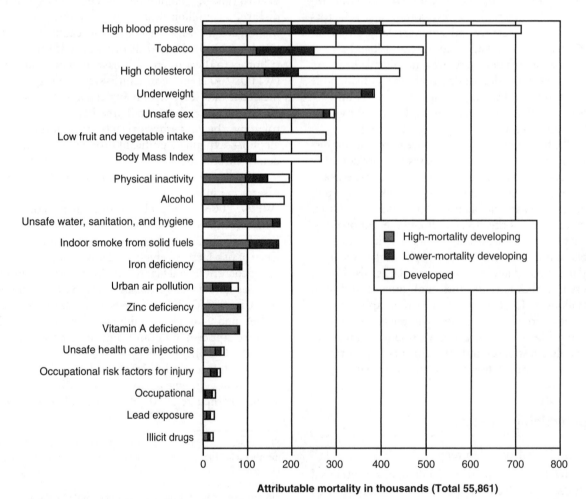

Figure 6-1 Mortality Attributable to 20 Leading Risk Factors, 2001. *Source:* World Health Organization, *World Health Report, 2002* (Geneva, Switzerland: World Health Organization, 2002). Reprinted with permission.

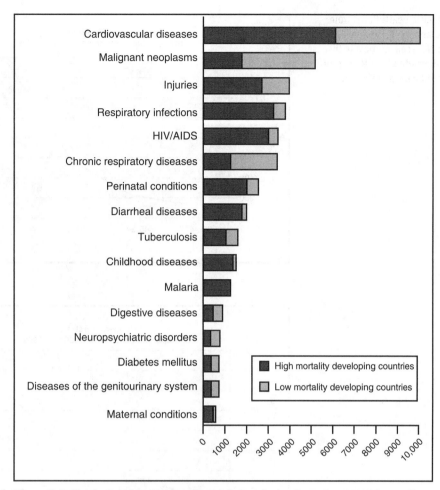

Figure 6-2 Sixteen Leading Causes of Death in Developing Countries, 2002. *Source:* Data from World Health Organization, *World Health Report, 2003* (Geneva, Switzerland: World Health Organization, 2003).

already caused by chronic diseases (Bumgarner, 2004). Age-specific death rates increased rapidly between 1986 and 1999 for CVD and cancers (Figure 6-3). It is predicted that deaths from diet-related chronic diseases will increase from 5 million in 1995 to 15.3 million in 2025. Although the percentage of deaths from chronic diseases tends to be lower in developing countries than in developed countries due to competing causes of death, absolute death rates can be higher, as illustrated by data in three areas of Tanzania (Figure 6-4) (Unwin et al., 2001).

The trend toward a higher burden of chronic diseases in developing countries has been termed the *epidemiologic transition*. Developed by Omran (1971), the theory conceptualizes three ages of disease epidemiologies: pestilence and famine, receding epidemics, and the current age of degenerative and human-made chronic diseases. Driving the transition to chronic diseases are three major sets of determinants: ecobiologic; socioeconomic, political, and cultural; and medical and public health interventions. Omran was correct in predicting a greater burden of chronic diseases. In Africa, for example, a substantial increase in the amount of chronic disease was first reported in the 1970s (Reis, 1978). In practice, however, chronic diseases have not smoothly displaced acute infectious diseases in developing countries. Rather, developing countries suffer from a polarized and protracted double burden of disease (Frenk et al., 1989). Developing countries now suffer double or triple burdens of disease. For example, in South Africa, infectious diseases account for 28% of years of life lost (YLLs), while chronic diseases account for 25% (Steyn et al., 2003). Figure 6-5

Figure 6-3 Age-Specific Death Rates from Cancer, China, 1986 and 1999. *Source:* J. R. Bumgarner, "China: Non-communicable Disease Issues and Options Revisited," 2004, *Oxford Vision 2020*. Reprinted with permission.

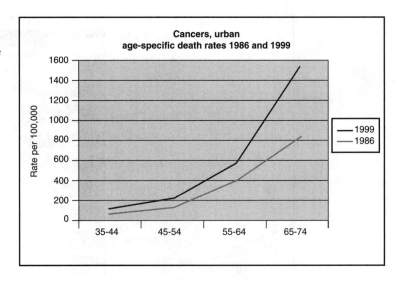

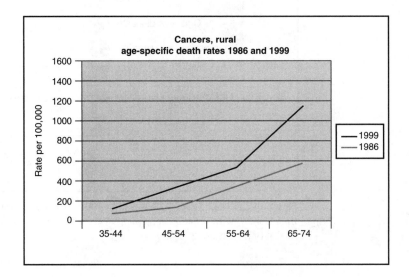

Common Chronic Conditions

The most common chronic conditions, their typical clinical features, and the diagnostic procedures required are presented in Table 6-2. The prevalence of these conditions varies significantly around the world. This is mainly determined by the extent to which populations have progressed along the process of the epidemiologic transition. All the conditions occur more frequently in middle-aged and older people and, with the exception of cancers, occur more frequently in urban than rural settings. Some chronic disease risk factors, such as hypertension and high blood lipid and

shows that in fact South Africa has a quadruple burden of HIV/AIDS, other infectious diseases, chronic diseases, and injuries (see also Chapter 1).

blood sugar levels, can be present without any signs or symptoms; therefore, their diagnoses depend either on regular screening by motivated health care providers or on the population asking for screening—usually after they have been prompted by health education initiatives targeting the whole population. Patients with strokes, heart attacks, and in diabetic coma present as medical emergencies requiring immediate hospitalization to ensure a high rate of survival.

Cardiovascular Diseases

Coronary heart disease and stroke are the two leading causes of death among both men and women in developing countries (as for developed countries) (WHO, 2003a) (see Figure 6-2). In absolute numbers, twice as many deaths from CVD occur in developing countries

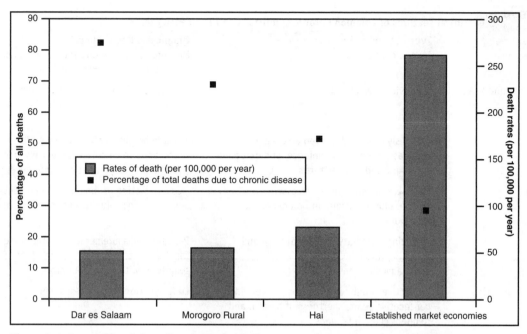

Figure 6-4 Rates of Death from Chronic Disease in Three Areas of Tanzania and Established Market Economies and Percentages of Total Deaths Due to Chronic Disease, Women 15–59 years. *Source:* N. C. Unwin et al., "Non-communicable Disease in Sub-Saharan Africa: Where Do They Feature in the Health Research Agenda?" 2001, *Bulletin of the World Health Organization, 79*(10), pp. 947–953. Reprinted with permission.

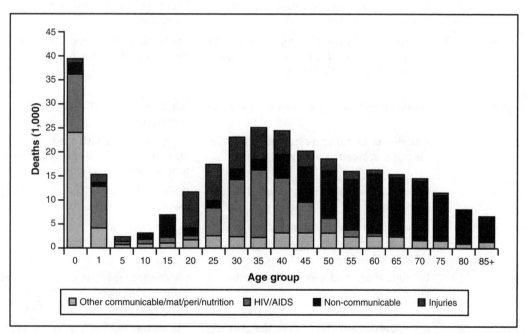

Figure 6-5 Male Deaths by Age, South Africa, 2000. *Source:* D. Bradshaw, P. Groenewald, R. Laubscher, N. Nannan, B. Nojilana, R. Norman, D. Pieterse, M. Schneider, D. Bourne, I. M. Timaeus, R. E. Dorrington, and L. Johnson, "Initial Burden of Disease Estimates for South Africa, 2000," 2003, *South African Medical Journal, 93*(9), pp. 682–688. Reprinted with permission.

Table 6-2	Clinical Features of Common Chronic Conditions and Their Risk Factors	
Conditions	**Typical Clinical Features**	**Diagnostic Requirements**
Hypertension	No obvious symptoms	Measure blood pressure following standardized procedures (e.g., WHO guidelines)
High blood lipid levels	No obvious symptoms	Measure total cholesterol, high-density lipoprotein cholesterol, and triglyceride levels in fasting blood samples
Obesity	Obviously overweight, often associated with tiredness, daytime somnolence, and excessive snoring; could have arthritis	Measure height (meters) and weight (kilograms) to calculate body mass index (weight/height^2); waist circumference
Diabetes	Malaise, excessive thirst, excessive urination, hunger, blurred vision, and proneness to infections	Measure fasting or random blood glucose levels and possibly glucose tolerance test
Asthma	Wheezing, difficulty with breathing, and coughing (bronchospasm) relieved by asthma medication	Peak flow measurements and other lung function tests, chest x-ray, and relief of symptoms with bronchodilators
Chronic bronchitis	Productive cough for 3 months per year in 2 consecutive years, shortness of breath, and frequent chest infections	Lung function tests; chest x-ray
Myocardial infarction (heart attack)	Sudden onset of severe crushing chest pain that could radiate down left arm, to neck or jaw, with associated sweating, faintness, shortness of breath, and nausea	Emergency—hospitalize; clinical examination, electrocardiograph, and blood tests for cardiac enzyme levels
Cerebrovascular disease (stroke)	Sudden weakness; loss of motor or sensory function, usually unilateral; inability to speak; vision disturbances or unconsciousness	Emergency—hospitalize; neurologic and full clinical examination; consider CAT scan and identify underlying causes
Angina	Central chest pain precipitated by exertion and relieved by resting	Electrocardiograph; pain relieved by angina medication
Transient ischemic attack	Same presentation as stroke, (e.g., weakness, loss of motor or sensory function, inability to speak, or vision disturbances), resolved within 24 hours	Neurologic and full clinical examination and identify underlying causes
Cancers in general	Unexplained loss of weight; malaise and tiredness	Full clinical examination and special investigations
Breast cancer	A painless lump in the breast or discharge from the nipple or breast deformity	Regular self-examination and by a doctor to identity lump early; mammogram; biopsy of lump for pathology diagnosis
Cervical cancer	Unexplained vaginal discharge or bleeding; pain on intercourse	Clinical examination; Pap smear; cytologic diagnosis
Lung cancer	Unexplained shortness of breath; chronic cough (could be blood stained); could have enlarged lymph nodes in neck	Clinical examination, sputum examination, chest x-ray, bronchoscopy, lung biopsy
Prostate cancer	Difficulty or pain with urination; frequent urination with dribbling	Clinical rectal examination, prostate specific antigen (PSA) blood test, biopsy, prostatectomy, and pathology diagnosis
Colon cancer	Ongoing abdominal pain or discomfort; change in bowel habits	Clinical examination, test for blood in the stool, barium enema and colonoscopy; surgery and pathology
Stomach cancer	Dyspepsia, ongoing upper abdominal pain or discomfort, nausea and vomiting	Clinical examination, barium meal, gastroscopy, surgery, and pathology

as in developed countries. CVD accounts for 2.8 million deaths a year in China and 2.5 million in India, dwarfing the combined totals of all deaths from infectious diseases in these countries (Beaglehole & Yach, 2003). In rural and urban Tanzania, stroke mortality rates are threefold higher than in the United Kingdom. Whereas CVD deaths have declined by 50% since the 1960s in the United States, the United Kingdom, and many other developed countries, they continue to increase rapidly in most developing countries (Leeder et al., 2004). Predictions for the next two decades include a near tripling of CHD and stroke mortality in Latin America, the Middle East, and even sub-Saharan Africa. Projected CHD mortality for all developing countries is anticipated to increase between 1990 and 2020 by 120% for women and 137% for men, compared with age-related increases of between 30% and 60% in developed countries (Leeder et al., 2004).

In developing countries, the age at which people die of CVD is significantly younger than in developed countries. CVD rates for 30- and 40-year-olds in many developing countries are now the same as for 40- and 50-year-olds in developed countries (WHO, 2003a). In India and South Africa, CVD death rates in working-age women are higher today than they were in U.S. women in the 1950s (Leeder et al., 2004). In Pakistan, the overall prevalence of coronary artery disease is 26.9% among men and 30.0% in women, which amounts to one in four middle-aged adults with prevalent coronary artery disease. The risk is uniformly higher in the young and in women (Nishtar, 2003). In rural Vietnam, CVD was found to account for around 20% of all deaths in 2000, with over 40% among people younger than 70 years (Minh, Byass, & Wall, 2003).

Diabetes

The global prevalence of diabetes among all age groups was estimated at 171 million (2.8% of the global population) in 2000, which is projected to increase to 366 million (6.5%) in 2030; 298 million of those affected will live in developing countries (Wild et al., 2004). The projected increase in developing countries will be 147%, compared with 54% for established market economies (Table 6-3) (Wild et al., 2004). By 2030, most people with diabetes in developing countries will be between 45 and 64 years old. In developed countries, by contrast, most people with diabetes will be over 65 years old. These projections consider demographic changes and some aspects of urbanization, but not current increases in childhood and adult obesity in most urban settings, which will increase type 2 diabetes rates even more (Wild et al., 2004).

One example of rapid change and diabetes prevalence comes from the Pacific region. Diabetes was virtually nonexistent in populations indigenous to the Pacific who maintained a traditional lifestyle. However, in recent years, fueled by rapid change in diet and a reduction in physical activity, diabetes prevalence has soared (Foliaki & Pearce, 2003). A similar picture is emerging in many island states and even in some of the poorest countries of the world. For example, epidemiologic data indicate that diabetes prevalence in adults (35 years and over) in urban areas of Tanzania is at least 10% (Aspray et al., 2000). In China, a survey carried out in 2000–2001 showed that 5.2% of men aged 35 to 74 years (12.7 million) and 5.8% of women of the same age group (13.3 million) have diabetes (diagnosed and undiagnosed), far higher than previously reported (Gu et al., 2003).

Cancer

About 10 million people are diagnosed with cancer every year worldwide, and 7 million die of the disease. The International Agency for Research on Cancer (IARC) (see web site: http://www.iarc.fr/) estimates that cancer incidence increased 19% between 1990 and 2000 (Stewart & Kleihaus, 2003). The major causes of cancer are (1) tobacco use in both developed and developing countries, (2) chronic infections in devel-

Table 6-3	Projected Increase in Diabetes in Developing Countries		
Region	Estimated Number of People with Diabetes, 2000	Estimated Number of People with Diabetes, 2030	Percentage Change
India	31,705	79,441	151
China	20,757	42,321	104
Other Asia and Islands	22,238	58,109	148
sub-Saharan Africa	7,146	18,645	161
Latin America and the Caribbean	13,307	32,959	148
Middle Eastern crescent	20,051	52,794	163

Source: S. Wild, G. Roglic, A. Green, R. Sicree, and H. King, "Global Prevalence of Diabetes: Estimates for 2000 and Projections for 2003," 2004, *Diabetes Care, 27*, pp. 1047–1053. Reprinted with permission.

oping countries, and (3) a complex array of diet and physical activity factors (Figure 6-6). The prevalence of different types of cancers varies between developed and developing countries. Lung cancer, the most frequently occurring cancer worldwide and a type of cancer that is primarily due to tobacco use, accounts for 1.2 million deaths a year—12.3% of all cancer deaths. Cancers caused by tobacco are increasing in most developing countries and among women in almost all countries. In a few developed countries, tobacco-related cancer incidence has started to decline as men smoke less. In contrast, cancers caused by chronic infections and food contaminants and preparation methods have been in decline in developing countries for decades. There has been little change in the incidence of the two most common cancers in women: breast and cervix, over the last few decades. Survival rates remain very low for lung, liver, and stomach cancers, although they have increased for many other cancers in recent years, due mainly to early detection and increasingly effective treatments (Stewart & Kleihaus, 2003).

Figure 6-6 provides a summary of major differences in cancer incidence between developed and developing countries (Stewart & Kleihaus, 2003). It is estimated that the overall number of cancer cases will rise by 50% in the next 20 years, leading to a total of 15.3 million new patients with cancer per year—60% of whom will be living in developing countries (Ullrich et al., 2004).

Chronic Respiratory Diseases

Chronic respiratory diseases include two major groups of diseases: chronic obstructive pulmonary disease (COPD) and asthma. COPD accounts for 4.8% of all deaths worldwide (2.7 million a year), of which 50% of deaths occur in China and countries in the western Pacific, and a further 24% occur in India (WHO, 2003a). Major risk factors for COPD include tobacco, a range of occupational exposures, indoor air pollution from biomass fuel, and childhood exposure to respiratory infections (Ait-Khaled, Enarson, & Bousquet, 2001). These risk factors are substantially higher among people living in developing countries, and in poor communities in developed countries.

Comorbidity

Comorbidity refers to simultaneous occurrence in a person of two or more disorders. A notable form of comorbidity is between diabetes and CVD. Heart attacks, for example, are significantly higher in people with diabetes, as are deaths following a first heart attack (International Diabetes Federation, 2003). There are important comorbidities between mental disorders and other chronic diseases: People with chronic conditions have a greater probability of developing mental disorders such as depression (WHO, 2003c). The proportion of patients with depression who also have other common chronic diseases, such

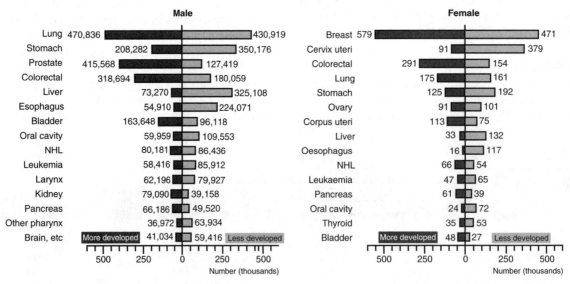

Figure 6-6 Comparison of the Most Common Cancers in More and Less Developed Countries in 2000. *Note:* NHL = non-Hodgkin's lymphoma. *Source:* International Agency for Research on Cancer, *World Cancer Report* (Lyon, France: IARC Press, 2003). Reprinted with permission.

as CVD, diabetes, and cancer, ranges from 22% to 33% (WHO, 2003c).

There are also interactive effects between certain infectious and noninfectious diseases. Several infectious agents cause cancer: Hepatitis B virus causes liver cancer; human papillomavirus (HPV) causes cervical cancer; *Helicobacter pylori* causes stomach cancer; HIV infection causes several cancers, including Kaposi's sarcoma and non-Hodgkin's lymphoma; and *Schistosoma haematobium* causes bladder cancer (Stewart & Kleihaus, 2003). All these cancers are common in the least-developed countries, where resources for treatment are extremely inadequate. Vaccines to prevent these infections and effective drugs to treat them could greatly reduce the cancer burden in these countries.

Finally, there are interactions between risk factors and death rates from other diseases. Tobacco increases the death rate from tuberculosis (TB)—a classic disease of poverty—in those already infected. In India, smokers are 4.5 times more likely to die of TB than nonsmokers (Gajalakshmi et al., 2003). An estimated 80% of TB patients smoke. As a result, tobacco is probably the major cause of death in treated TB patients (Yach & Raviglione, 2004).

Risk Factors

Major Risk Factors

Over the last 50 years, epidemiologic studies have provided evidence of which risk factors cause chronic diseases. This chapter focuses mainly on three: tobacco, diet, and physical activity. These major risk factors explain the incidence of most chronic diseases. Many are common to several chronic diseases, and most are modifiable. The strength of the evidence and the quality of studies have been strongest for tobacco. Since the first Surgeon General's report on smoking in 1964 (U.S. Department of Health, Education, and Welfare, 1964) the criteria for deciding whether tobacco causes a disease have been refined, the evidence of the impact of tobacco on specific causes has strengthened, and the number of diseases and conditions listed as being causally related to tobacco has lengthened. The recent 50-year follow-up of doctors quantifies the long-term impact of tobacco in a unique way (Figure 6-7) and shows that risks of smoking remain substantial well into the eighth decade of life and, conversely, that quitting confers life-extending benefits at advanced ages (Doll et al., 2004). In the Surgeon General's report of 2004 (U.S. Department of Health and Human services

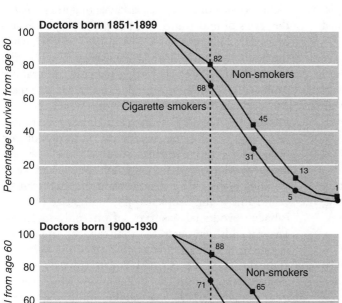

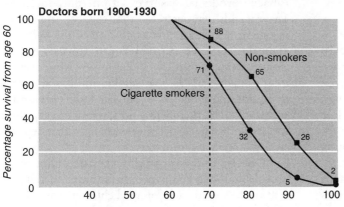

Figure 6-7 Survival from Age 60 for Continuing Cigarette Smokers and Lifelong Nonsmokers Among UK Male Doctors Born 1851–1899 (Median 1889) and 1900–1930 (Median 1915), with Percentages Alive at Each Decade of Age. *Source:* R. Doll, R. Peto, J. Boreham, and I. Sunderland, "Mortality in Relation to Smoking: 50 Years' Observations of Male British Doctors," 2004, *British Medical Journal, 328*, p. 1519. Reprinted with permission from the BMJ Publishing Group.

Table 6-4	Diseases and Other Adverse Health Effects for Which Smoking Is Identified as a Cause in the 2004 Surgeon General's Report
Cancers	Bladder, cervix,[a] esophagus, kidney,[a] larynx, acute myeloid leukemia,[a] lung, oral cancer, pancreas,[a] stomach
Cardiovascular diseases	Abdominal aortic aneurysm,[a] atherosclerosis, cerebrovascular disease, coronary heart disease
Respiratory diseases	Chronic obstructive pulmonary disease, pneumonia,[a] respiratory effects in utero, respiratory effects on children and adolescents
Reproductive effects	Fetal deaths and stillbirths, infertility (in women), low birth weight, pregnancy complications
Other effects	Cataract,[a] diminished health status,[a] hip fractures, low bone density, periodontitis,[a] peptic ulcer disease

[a]Added as being "causally associated with smoking" in 2004.

Source: U.S. Department of Health and Human Services, *The Health Consequences of Smoking: A Report of the Surgeon General* (Atlanta, GA: Centers for Disease Control and Prevention, 2004). Reprinted with permission.

[US DHHS], 2004), several diseases were added to previous lists (see Table 6-4 for the full list of causally associated diseases).

In contrast, there have not been as many major reviews of the impact of specific dietary factors and physical activity on specific outcomes. One of the most recent international reviews on the topic is summarized in Table 6-5. The causal criteria differ from those used for tobacco, and there have been substantially fewer cohort studies of long duration in the areas of diet and nutrition compared with tobacco. Taken together, the causal studies on tobacco, diet, and physical activity indicate that several major diseases are closely and negatively associated with just these three risk factors.

The reports just described have been used with the latest information on prevalence of risks and levels of disease and deaths to determine global impacts of major risks, which are summarized in WHO's 2002 *World Health Report*. In the poorest group of developing countries (high mortality in Figure 6-1), 4 chronic disease risk factors—tobacco, high blood pressure, indoor air pollution, and high cholesterol—are among the 10 leading risk factors contributing to the burden of disease (WHO, 2003a). In contrast, in low-mortality developing countries, 7 chronic disease risk factors—alcohol, blood pressure, tobacco, overweight, cholesterol, low fruit and vegetable intake, and indoor air pollution—are among the 10 leading risk factors contributing to the overall burden of diseases. In developed countries, 7 chronic disease risk factors—tobacco, high blood pressure, alcohol, increased cholesterol, increased body mass index, low fruit and vegetable intake, and physical inactivity—are among the 10 leading risk factors contributing to the overall burden of disease.

It is clear from the global analyses that tobacco and high blood pressure are major universal threats to health. Diet-related risks dominate in all parts of the world, albeit with varying contributions coming from underconsumption and overconsumption in different parts of the world. A lack of fruit and vegetables is evident in most countries and has implications not just for chronic noncommunicable disease but also for infectious diseases.

Risk Factor Trends

Trends in risk factors for chronic diseases in developing countries are not encouraging. The number of cigarettes smoked has more than doubled since 1960 (Mackay & Eriksen, 2002). There have been positive dietary trends over the past decades that are reducing the levels of undernutrition, but the supply of fat increased by 28% between 1977 and 1997 to 1999, while the Food and Agriculture Organization (FAO) of the United Nations predicts further increases in total per capita consumption of vegetable oils, sugar, and meat and declines in cereal consumption (WHO, 2003d). Importantly, children are increasingly exposed to risk factors, portending a massive increase in chronic disease occurrence in future decades. Alcohol abuse is becoming more widespread among youth. Age of uptake of smoking is showing a trend toward the early teenage years, and young people exhibit high usage of other tobacco products. A survey of one million 13- to 15-year-olds demonstrated that tobacco use occurs in one in five children in almost all of the over 100 countries surveyed (Global Youth Tobacco Survey Collaborating Group, 2003) (Table 6-6). Moreover, almost as many girls as boys smoke, and in some areas more girls smoke than boys. This can be linked with advertising and marketing practices, which target girls as well as women by associating smoking with independence, glamour, and romance.

Obesity and overweight are becoming more prevalent among young people (Table 6-7). Ten percent of the world's school-aged children are now estimated to be carrying excess body fat (Lobstein,

Table 6-5	Selective Summary of the Evidence for Obesity, Type 2 Diabetes, Cardiovascular Disease (CVD), Cancer, Dental Disease, and Osteoporosis					
	Obesity	**Type 2 Diabetes**	**CVD**	**Cancer**	**Dental Disease**	**Osteoporosis**
Energy and Fats (High Intake)						
Energy-dense foods	C+					
Saturated fats		P+	C+			
Transfatty acids			C+			
Dietary cholesterol			P+			
Fish and fish oils			P−			
Carbohydrate (High Intake)						
Dietary fiber	C−	P−	P−			
Free sugars					C+	
Vitamins						
Vitamin D					C−	C−
Minerals						
High sodium			C+			
Local fluoride					C−	
Fruits and Vegetables	C−	P−	C−	P−		
Beverages, Nonalcoholic						
Sugar-sweetened soft drinks	P+				P+	
Beverages, Alcoholic						
High alcohol intake			C+	C+		C+
Low to moderate intake			C−			
Weight and Physical Activity						
Overweight and obesity		C+	C+	C+		
Voluntary weight loss		C−				
Regular physical activity	C−	C−	C−	C−		C−
Physical inactivity	C+	C+				
Other Factors						
Exclusive breastfeeding	P+					
Environmental Factors						
Heavy marketing of energy-dense foods and fast-food outlets	P+					

C+ = convincing increasing risk; C− = convincing decreasing risk; P+ = probable increasing risk; P− = probably decreasing risk.

Source: World Health Organization, *Diet, Nutrition, and the Prevention of Chronic Diseases,* Technical Report No. 916 (Geneva, Switzerland: World Health Organization, 2003). Reprinted with permission.

Bauer, & Uauy, 2004). Of these overweight children, one-quarter are obese. Though the prevalence of overweight is dramatically higher in economically developed regions, it is rising significantly in most parts of the world. The International Obesity Taskforce attributes rising levels of overweight and obesity to a range of factors, including greater availability and marketing of energy-dense foods and a fall in opportunities for physical activity (see web site: http://www.iotf.org/).

The examples of China and South Africa illustrate the accumulation of risk factors in both adults and children. In 2003, there were 320 million smokers in China over the age of 15, compared with 250 million in 1986. If current smoking patterns remain unchanged, it is predicted that 100 million men now under age 30 will die of smoking-related diseases (Zhang & Baiqiang, 2003). Dietary intake in China has changed significantly over the past decades: The percentage of energy obtained from fat for 20- to 25-year-old adults rose from 19.3% in 1989 to 27.3% in 1997 (Du et al., 2002). In the same time period, the overall prevalence of obesity among children aged 2 to 6 years increased from 4.2% to 6.4% (1.5% to 12.6% in cities) (Luo & Hu, 2002). In Beijing, 18.2% of local primary and middle school students suffer from obesity, far higher than the 10.6% recorded in 1991 (Chinese Center for Disease Control and Prevention, 2004).

Table 6-6	Percentage of Students Aged 13 to 15 Who Currently Smoke Cigarettes		
	Boys	**Girls**	**Boys/Girls Ratio**
Overall (Median)	**15.0**	**6.6**	**1.9:1.0**
Africa	10.4	4.6	2.2:1.0
Burkina Faso	28.6	9.6	3.0:1.0
South Africa	21.0	10.6	2.0:1.0
The Americas	**16.6**	**12.2**	**1.2:1.0**
Columbia	31.0	33.4	0.9:1.0
United States	17.7	17.8	1.0:1.0
Eastern Mediterranean	**22.8**	**5.3**	**4.3:1.0**
Jordan	22.0	9.9	2.2:1.0
Europe	33.9	29.0	1.2:1.0
Bulgaria	26.0	39.4	0.7:1.0
Czech Republic	34.0	35.1	1.0:1.0
Southeast Asia	**13.5**	**3.2**	**4.2:1.0**
Indonesia	38.9	4.7	8.3:1.0
Myanmar	19.0	3.2	5.9:1.0
Western Pacific	**11.0**	**6.4**	**1.7:1.0**
Palau	20.0	23.3	0.9:1.0

Source: Global Youth Tobacco Survey Collaborating Group, "Differences in Worldwide Tobacco Use by Gender: Findings from the Global Youth Tobacco Survey," 2003, *Journal of School Health, 73,* pp. 207–215. Reprinted with permission.

Table 6-7	Prevalence of Overweight and Obesity Among School-Aged Children in Global Regions		
	Obesity (%)	**Overweight (%)**	**Obesity and Overweight (%)**
Worldwide	2.7	7.6	10.3
Americas	8.2	23.6	31.8
Europe	4.6	15	19.6
Near/Middle East	6.2	9.7	15.9
Asia Pacific	1	4.1	5.1
sub-Saharan Africa	0.2	1.1	1.3

Source: T. Lobstein, L. Baur, and R. Uauy, "Obesity of Children and Young People: A Crisis in Public Health," 2004, *Obesity Reviews, 5*(Suppl. 1), pp. 4–85. Reprinted with permission.

In South Africa, the results of the 1999 National Food Consumption Survey of 1- to 8-year-olds showed that 19.3% of children were stunted (height for age less than or equal to −2 standard deviations of National Center for Health Statistics 50th percentile) and that the prevalence of overweight and obesity (body mass index [BMI] greater than or equal to 25) was 17.2%, with levels of overweight being significantly higher in children from urban areas and those living in homes with refrigerators, stoves, and television sets (Steyn et al., 2004). In adults, a strong gender difference is evident with respect to underweight and overweight. Data from the nationally representative South African Demographic and Health Survey of 1998 showed that 12.9% of men and 4.8% of women aged 15 to 65 were underweight (BMI less than 18.5). In contrast, 25.4% of men and 68.5% of women were overweight or obese (Bourne, Lambert, & Steyn, 2002). Not surprisingly, there are reports of

increased type 2 diabetes and high levels of hypertension in the country.

Not discussed in depth are the importance of intermediate risk factors such as hypertension and hypercholesterolemia. Exhibit 6-1 describes major trends and the importance of these risks in the poorest region of the world, Africa.

Accumulation of Risks over the Life Course

The current burden of chronic diseases reflects cumulative risks over lifetimes. Figure 6-8 indicates that the future global burden of chronic disease will be determined by current population exposures to the major chronic disease risk factors.

The major risks for cancer, CVD, and diabetes accumulate from early in fetal life. Early-life risk factors—such as suboptimal diets, early termination of breastfeeding, exposure to tobacco and alcohol, exposure to indoor air pollution from biomass fuels,

| Exhibit 6-1 | Hypercholesterolemia and Hypertension in Africa |

After many decades of scientific debate and data published from large community-based trials in the 1970s and 1980s, high total blood cholesterol levels were proven to be an independent major risk factor for atherosclerosis-related chronic diseases such as coronary heart disease and cerebrovascular diseases (strokes). Total blood cholesterol levels vary considerably between populations with different dietary patterns. Most people of Africa still following traditional diets have far lower blood cholesterol levels than those found in people of Europe or the United States, or in people of India who migrated and adopted typical Western lifestyles. These differences among people with different lifestyles are present from a young age. In Johannesburg and Soweto, Steyn and associates (2000) found that the mean total cholesterol level in African and colored 5-year-old children was 3.9 mmol/L, compared with 4.1 mmol/L for Indian and 4.4 mmol/L for white children. These group differences in total cholesterol profiles tend to continue into adolescence and adulthood. Several African studies have shown that total cholesterol levels usually differ between urban and rural settings, reflecting the effects of urbanization on increasing total cholesterol levels (Knuiman et al.,1980; Seftel et al.,1993; Swai et al.,1993).

It is estimated that between 10 and 20 million people in sub-Saharan Africa alone have hypertension and, further, that adequate hypertension treatment could prevent about 250,000 deaths in this region (Cappuccio et al., 2000). However, hypertension is universally underdiagnosed or inadequately treated, or both, with the result that extensive end-organ damage and premature death is often seen. Furthermore, hypertension is frequently coexistent with other noncommunicable disease risk factors, such as diabetes.

Early surveys in sub-Saharan African countries showed that the lowest prevalence of hypertension occurred in the poorest countries, but as affluence increased, the prevalence increased. They also found that hypertension was more common in urban than rural settings in the region (Nissinen et al., 1988). The elegant Kenyan Luo migration study of Poulter and colleagues (1990) was the first to show that migration of people living in traditional rural villages on the northern shores of Lake Victoria to the urban settings of Nairobi, was associated with an increase in blood pressure. The urban migrants had higher body weights, pulse rates, and urinary sodium/potassium ratios than those who remained in the rural areas. This suggests a marked change in the diet of the new arrivals in Nairobi, with a higher salt and calorie intake along with a reduced potassium intake due to consuming fewer fruit and vegetables.

A high intake of sodium is common in sub-Saharan Africa, as it is used to preserve food or to make food tastier. For example, Cappuccio and associates (2000) described the diet in Ghana as consisting mostly of unprocessed food and highly salted fish and meat. Substantial amounts of salt are added to food while cooking, and monosodium glutamate–based flavoring cubes or salts are widely used to give food taste. In addition to a high salt intake, people in sub-Saharan Africa frequently eat little fruit and vegetable, resulting in low potassium intakes.

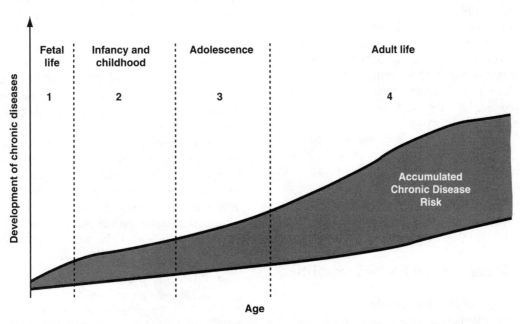

Figure 6-8 A Life Course Approach to Chronic Disease Prevention. *Source:* I. Aboderin, A. Kalache, Y. Ben-Shlomo, J. W. Lynch, C. D. Yajnik, D. Kuh, and D. Yach, *Life Course Perspectives in Coronary Heart Disease, Stroke and Diabetes: Key Issues and Implications for Policy and Research* (Geneva, Switzerland: World Health Organization, 2001). Reprinted with permission.

and repeated respiratory infections—are important for the development of chronic diseases in adulthood. Recent research derived from birth cohort studies has documented how and when these life-course influences happen (Aboderin et al., 2001; Batty & Leon, 2002). The risk of developing CVD or diabetes is influenced by biological and social factors at all stages of the life course, from fetal life to adulthood. Some life-course influences are disease specific, whereas others are cohort specific. Known risk factors remain the most firmly established link to many major chronic diseases. For example, 80% to 90% of patients who develop clinically significant CHD and more than 95% of patients who have experienced a fatal CHD event had at least one of the major cardiac risk factors—smoking, diabetes, hypertension, and hypercholesterolemia (Canto & Iskandrian, 2003). The link between infant nutrition and chronic disease has been the subject of much research and debate. The most recent studies indicate that early postnatal nutrition permanently affects the major components of the metabolic syndrome that affect propensity to CVD (Singhal & Lucas, 2004) and that influences in fetal life and early childhood are related to systolic blood pressure (Levitt et al., 1999).

COPD and lung function in adults are also the result of cumulative exposures that start early in life. South African studies have shown that what were assumed to be racial or genetic differences in lung size are probably due to early childhood respiratory infections occurring in crowded homes where biomass fuel is used, combined with tobacco use and adverse occupational exposures (Goldin et al., 1996). More recent analyses of the determinants of chronic bronchitis based on a population survey of 5,671 men and 8,155 women in South Africa estimated the following population-attributable fractions in men: 25% for tobacco use, 14% for occupational exposure, and 10% for past TB. In women, these fractions were 14% for use of smoky domestic fuel, 10% for past TB, and 11% for tobacco use (Ehrlich et al., 2004). This study demonstrates how multiple assaults on the lung—including an infectious agent, fuel use, exposure at work, and tobacco use—are important in chronic lung disease. All these factors have been shown to be also related to poverty.

Economic Impacts and Health Inequalities

Economic Costs of Selected Chronic Diseases and Risks

Chronic diseases have a significant impact on national economies by disabling and killing the working-age population (Leeder et al., 2004). This results in high direct costs (health care, treatment) and indirect costs (number of productive years lost, social security and pension costs). Owing to the relatively high rates of chronic disease among people with potential to contribute to economic productivity, the economic impact of chronic diseases resulting from lost productivity is likely to be particularly significant in developing countries.

Evidence is already emerging that the growing burden of chronic disease in developing countries is having a significant impact on health care costs and lost productivity. For example, Popkin and associates (2001) estimated that in 1995, diet-related chronic diseases (cancer, coronary heart disease, stroke, hypertension, and diabetes) accounted for 22.6% of health care costs (primarily state costs) in China, while the estimated cost of lost productivity was 0.5% of gross domestic product (GDP). In India in the same year, diet-related chronic diseases accounted for 13.9% of health care costs (primarily individual expenditures) and 0.7% of GDP in lost productivity. It should be noted that these estimates of lost productivity are underestimates because they are based on mortality and do not consider the lost productivity resulting from morbidity.

Estimates have also been made for specific diseases and risk factors.

Cardiovascular Disease

CVD is known to have significant economic costs in the developed world. In the United States, CVD accounts for approximately 61% of all health care spending (US DHHS, 2001). In the United Kingdom, the total cost of coronary heart disease in 1999 was £7.06 billion, comprising £1.73 million costs to the U.K. health care system, £2.42 million in informal care, and £2.91 million in friction period–adjusted productivity loss (24.1% due to mortality and 75.9% to morbidity) (Liu et al., 2002).[2]

The potential economic costs of CVD are potentially even higher in emerging economies owing to the burden of CVD mortality and morbidity among the workforce that occurs at a relatively young age. Leeder and associates (2004) have provided compelling information on the macroeconomic costs of CVD in Brazil, China, India, Russia, and South Africa and have estimated the following.

- *Productive years of life lost (PPYLL, years lost in the age range 35–64):* In the five countries, PPYLL are predicted to be 33.7 million by

---

[2]The friction period is the period of an employee's absence from work before the employer replaces him or her with another worker.

2030, an increase from 20.5 million in 2000. Compared with 2000, the number of PPYLL to cardiovascular disease will increase in 2030 by 64% in Brazil, 57% in China, and 95% in India. This compares with 20% in the United States and 30% in Portugal.

- *Payroll losses:* In India, payroll losses in a single year (2000) from CVD were estimated at US$198 million (not including health care costs).

- *Social security costs arising from disability:* Based on the conservative assumption that disability from CVD lasts on average 3 years, in India the wage losses due to disability disrupting gainful employment is calculated at $30 million over 3 years. In South Africa, it is estimated that the disabled workforce cost R 453 million (US$64 million) in public disability payments in 2000, predicted to rise to R 3.9 billion (US$550 million) in 2040.

- *Direct health care costs:* In South Africa, direct health systems costs from CVD totaled between US$230 million and US$300 million in 1991 (US$310–470 million at more current values); data from a region of Brazil indicate that patients admitted for circulatory disease account for 10.5% of hospital days but 20% of costs. In China, hospital costs at-

tributable to cardiovascular conditions totaled over US$9.6 billion in 1998 (20% of all costs).

Diabetes

There have been numerous estimates of the health care costs of diabetes. The direct health care costs of diabetes, including the treatment of complications, range from 2.5% to 15% of national annual health care budgets, depending on diabetes prevalence and the level of treatment available (WHO, 2003b). For example:

- In Latin America and the Caribbean, the direct health care costs of diabetes were estimated at US$10.7 billion in 2000 (Barceló et al., 2003). Indirect costs were over five times higher than the direct costs, estimated at US$54.9 billion, making a total cost for the region of US$65.2 billion (Figure 6-9).

- In the United States, the direct costs of diabetes over all age groups were estimated at US$91.8 billion in 2002 (American Diabetes Association [ADA], 2003), an increase from US$44 billion in 1997 (ADA, 1998).

- Studies in India estimate that, for a low-income Indian family with an adult with diabetes, as much as 25% of family income can be devoted to diabetes care (Shobana et al., 2000).

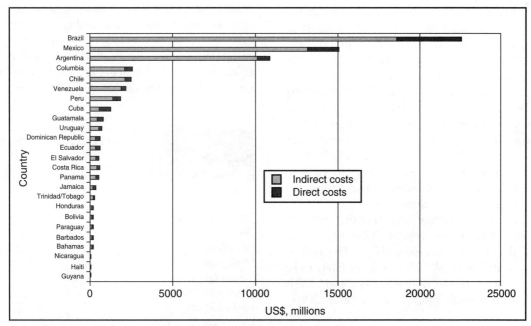

Figure 6-9 Estimated Total Indirect and Direct Costs Attributed to Diabetes in Latin America and the Caribbean, 2000. *Source:* A. Barceló, C. Aedo, S. Rajpathak, and S. Robles, "The Cost of Diabetes in Latin America and the Caribbean," 2003, *Bulletin of the World Health Organization, 81*(1), pp. 19–27. Reprinted with permission.

- In WHO's Western Pacific region, a recent analysis of health care expenditure has shown that 16% of hospital expenditure was due to people with diabetes (WHO, 2002a). In the Republic of the Marshall Islands, this figure was 25%. Twenty percent of offshore expenditure on health by Fiji—instances where facilities for care were not available in Fiji, so patients had to travel elsewhere—was on diabetes-related complications.

- Many estimates have been made on the costs of diabetes in Sweden. Most recently, direct and indirect costs per person were estimated at approximately US$8,500 per year, taking into account comorbidity (Norlund et al., 2001). Twenty-eight percent of the costs were for health care, 41% for lost productivity, and 31% for the municipality and for relatives.

- There are little data from African or Middle Eastern countries, but studies from the early 1990s again suggest costs are high. In Tunisia, an estimate from the early 1990s placed the total annual costs of medication and outpatient care for people with diabetes at 2.6 times that for people without diabetes (US$179 versus US$68) (Chale et al., 1992).

The International Diabetes Federation has estimated the annual direct health care costs of diabetes worldwide and expressed them in international dollars. (International dollars are a common currency unit that takes account of the relative purchasing power of various currencies.) For people in the 20 to 79 age bracket, costs are at least 153 million international dollars, and may be as much as 286 billion international dollars or more. It is predicted that if diabetes continues to climb, total direct health care expenditure will be between 213 billion and 396 billion international dollars. This means that the proportion of the world health care budget being spent in 2025 on diabetes care will be between 7% and 13%, with high-prevalence countries spending up to 40% of their budget. Estimates of indirect costs are just as high—or even higher—as direct costs.

Recent studies show that the cost of treating CVD is the largest identifiable proportion (26.4%) of the overall diabetes health care expenditure. This reflects two factors: Patients with CVD are more likely to be hospitalized and consume more medicines, and CVD is prevalent in people with diabetes (Simpson et al., 2003).

Asthma

The medical costs for asthma are considerable. For example, they constitute 1.3% of Singapore's total health care cost (i.e., US$33.93 million per year), and 1.4% of direct health care costs, or 2.1 million EUR, in Estonia, where medication expenses are 53% of the total (Chew, Goh, & Lee, 1999; Kiivet, 2001) .

Risk Factors

Tobacco has many negative economic impacts. The most authoritative review of the economic impact of tobacco by the World Bank provided estimates from developing and developed countries of annual health care costs (Table 6-8). The substantial economic impact of tobacco in developing countries led major development agencies, including the European Commission, to conclude that tobacco was truly a poverty-related issue requiring urgent attention. More recently this was restated by the United Nations Economic and Social Council (Economic and Social Council, 2004).

National health care spending attributable to obesity has been estimated to range from 2% and 6% for high-income countries (Finkelstein, Fiebelkorn, & Wang, 2003, 2004; Kuchler & Ballenger, 2002; Thompson & Wolf, 2001). These estimates deal only with direct health care spending rather than decreased productivity and other indirect measures. The data referred to earlier in relation to the costs of diet-related chronic diseases in China and India include the impact of obesity (Popkin et al., 2001).

Macroeconomic Impacts

Indirect productivity losses incurred because of chronic diseases have the potential to affect the global macroeconomy. Evidence is strengthening to show that premature death and disability from chronic diseases affect national emerging economies by dampening the engine of productivity and reducing economic growth (Leeder et al., 2004). This hypothesis can also be extended to the global level, because

Table 6-8	Health Care Costs Attributable to Tobacco
Country	**Costs (US$)**
Australia	$6 billion
Canada	$1.6 billion
China	$3.5 billion
Germany	$14.7 billion
New Zealand	$84 million
Philippines	$600 million
South Africa	$1 billion
United Kingdom	$2.25 billion
United States	$76 billion

Note: Costs are for 2002 or latest available estimates.

Source: J. Mackay and M. Eriksen, *The Tobacco Atlas* (Geneva, Switzerland: World Health Organization, 2002). Reprinted with permission.

workers in emerging markets are not only generating growth in their home economies but in developed nations are well. In fact, arguments are emerging that the potential returns for developed country investors from emerging markets could be higher than the OECD (Organization for Economic Cooperation and Development) countries over the long term, especially in the light of low expected returns in mature markets (Clark & Hebb, 2002; Heller, 2003; Kimmis et al., 2002). If chronic diseases do diminish productivity as predicted, then investor returns in developing countries will in turn be affected, with impacts on growth in OECD countries.

Both transnational corporations (TNCs) and pension funds face risks. Where TNCs are direct employers with health insurance liabilities, the lesson of HIV/AIDS is that chronic conditions can place heavy financial burdens on the company, especially when treatment is expensive. United States–based TNCs already face huge health care costs at home. A recent study estimated health and productivity expenses incurred by six large employers in the United States at US\$3,524 per eligible employee in 1999 (Goetzel et al., 2003). Although "short-termism" is still endemic in pension fund investments, recent trends show a growing interest in more long-term value investing, and some companies with direct investments overseas are themselves arguing the need to incorporate longer-term upfront investments into their business practice in developing countries in order to sustain profitability over the long term (Clark & Hebb, 2002).

Impact on Health Inequalities

Emergence of Inequalities

As put by Gunnar Myrdal, the Nobel Prize winner for economics in the 1950s, people are sick because they are poor, and become poorer because they are sick (Myrdal, 1952). This downward spiral occurs with chronic diseases. Increased cumulative exposure to risk factors over the life course, combined with social and economic inequalities, leads to the levels of inequalities seen in later adult life (see Figure 6-8).

Chronic diseases impose a significant burden on low-income populations. In developed countries, the relationships among poverty and cardiovascular disease, cancer, diabetes, and their associated risk factors are well described. It is also established that chronic diseases explain health inequalities by social class, ethnicity, and gender (Aboderin et al., 2001; Batty & Leon, 2002; Brands & Yach, 2001; Kogevinas et al., 1997; Mackenbach et al., 2000; Marmot et al., 1978; Wong et al., 2002).

Chronic diseases are not common among the very poorest people in developing countries, but neither do they affect only the affluent. As risks accumulate over the life course and over generations, this will become more evident. In developed countries, risk factor exposure (tobacco, alcohol, poor diet and physical activity) is directly associated with poverty, social class, and level of education. These risks have accumulated into higher rates of chronic diseases among poorer populations. The same applies in Europe's poorest countries. In developing countries, the poorest populations already exhibit the highest risks for tobacco and alcohol use (Jha & Chaloupka, 2000), but the relationship with intermediate risk factors and diseases is complex and varies between countries, as discussed in the following.

- *India:* Currently, rates of hypertension, cholesterol, diabetes, and cardiovascular disease increase directly with socioeconomic status (Singh et al., 1999; Vikram et al., 2003). Yet, high rates of hypertension and LDL cholesterol are now being measured in urban slums (Misra et al., 2001), and tobacco consumption is higher among the most poorly educated. Death rates from TB—a disease associated with poverty—are four times higher among people who smoke relative to nonsmokers (Gajalakshmi et al., 2003). Poorer people also suffer from relatively higher rates of complications from diabetes, owing to exposure to multiple risk factors (Ramachandran et al., 2002).

- *Brazil:* In urban Brazil, an inverse relationship between socioeconomic status and smoking and alcohol consumption in men and women was measured in the 1980s (Duncan et al., 1993). Also identified were inverse links between socioeconomic status and hypertension in men, and between sedentary lifestyle and obesity in women.

- *Jamaica:* Obesity increases with income level strongly in men and weakly in women (owing to high levels of obesity among the poorest women) (Mendez et al., 2004). The relationship between income, diabetes, and hypertension, however, is nonlinear. In women, there is a U-shaped curve for diabetes and hypertension, and the highest rates of diabetes are found in the poorest women. Obesity and diabetes are strongly related, especially among poor women. The lack of a strong income gradient in hypertension or diabetes—despite a strong relationship between income and obesity—might be partly attributable to greater adverse effects of obesity among the poor.

- *China*: In China, there is a U-shaped relationship between socioeconomic status and hypertension in women. This result in part reflects the fact that poorer women tend to have lower body mass indices and to smoke less but do less physical activity, and vice versa for the wealthiest group (Bell, Adair, & Popkin, 2004).

Owing to the long and often variable lag times between exposure to risk factors and disease onset, exposure to chronic disease risks in developing countries has yet to fully develop into a direct relationship among poverty, intermediate risk factors, and chronic disease. Over time, accumulation of risk among poorer groups will increase as availability and marketing of products increases with economic development. There are concerns that over the long term, this will lead to a pronounced association between chronic diseases and poverty.

Data on obesity illustrate that the risk factor gradient will increasingly tilt toward poorer groups as economies develop. Until the late 1980s, socioeconomic status and obesity tended to be inversely related in developed populations and directly related in developing populations (Sobal & Stunkard, 1989). In other words, in developing economies, obesity was associated with more affluent groups. But more recent work from Brazil indicates that over time, female obesity shifts toward lower-income groups in economically more developed regions and urban areas. Although low socioeconomic status still confers protection from obesity in low-income nations, when national GNP reaches a value of about US$2,500 per capita, obesity rates become directly associated with low socioeconomic status (Monteiro et al., 2004; Peña & Bacallao, 2000).

A recent study comparing the relationship between social class and consumption patterns in the United States and China illustrates this point (Kim, Symons, & Popkin, 2004). Using a composite lifestyle index (LI) that included data on diet, smoking, alcohol, and physical activity, the authors showed that there was an inverse relationship between socioeconomic status and the LI in the United States, but a direct relationship in China. China is on the ascending limb, and the U.S. population would be on the descending limb. This phenomenon suggests that policy makers in low- and middle-income countries should not wait for a social class gradient to appear in the occurrence of chronic disease (or risk factors) before implementing strong preventive and health-promoting policies.

Determinants of Major Chronic Diseases

Demographic Change

Aging

The aging of populations, due mainly to a decline in fertility rates and a higher proportion of children living into adulthood, is an important underlying determinant of chronic disease epidemics (Beaglehole & Yach, 2003). Although demographic change has been well described in respect of developed countries, the pace and impact of aging in developing countries is only starting to be appreciated. Recent UN projections suggest that the population share of those over 60 years of age will rise from the range of 5% to 6% to that of 14% to 15% in Algeria, Egypt, Iran, South Africa, and Tunisia. Developed countries are already under pressure to address the pensions and social insurance demands of aging populations; developing countries will soon have to do so, albeit from a starting base of substantially fewer resources (Heller, 2003).

Aging need not be a risk factor per se for increased morbidity caused by chronic diseases. Fries first postulated in 1980 that if health promotion and disease prevention programs were successful, it would be possible to have continued increases in longevity without a concomitant increase in morbidity and disability. In his model of "compression of morbidity," Fries (1980) theorized that the means are available to modify and improve the quality of aging. The model proposes that sufficient postponement can mean the avoidance of chronic symptoms until the natural lifespan has run its course—in which case chronic disease is effectively prevented. As the rates of premature death decline, the survival curve becomes increasingly rectangular. Evidence is emerging that has been the case in the United States for the last decade (Fries, 2003). During this time, mortality rates have dropped by 1% per year and disability rates by 2% a year, suggesting that compression of morbidity with longevity is possible. Increases in life expectancy past the age of 65 have been, and are expected to remain, modest.

The decline in disability in people over the age of 65 has been much more dramatic and continues at a relatively rapid rate. The avoidance of health risks, such as smoking, lack of exercise, and obesity, has been shown to be a major factor in the postponement of disability, leading to the conclusion that health enhancement interventions for the elderly and the implementation of disability postponement measures into health care systems as part of broad health policy initiatives are the best means to facilitate the further compression of morbidity (Fries, 2003). The expected cumulative health expenditures in healthier elderly persons, despite their greater longevity, were similar to those for less healthy persons (Lubitz et al., 2003). These relatively recent findings suggest that risk factor prevention and health promotion will save lives and money.

Urbanization

From just 16 cities in the world having over a million people at the beginning of the 20th century, there are now around 400, about three-quarters of which are in developing countries (Cohen, 2004). Further dramatic expansion of giant metropolises in the developing world is predicted (Heller, 2003), and long-term projections show that globally, urban populations will soon exceed rural populations.

Urbanization can stimulate chronic disease prevention efforts by improving access to a wider variety of foods, to health systems for early diagnosis and effective treatment, and to knowledge and information about healthy living. At the same time, urban areas are magnets for the flow of goods, investment, technology, and marketing, which subsequently attract flows of people from rural areas. Urbanization thus does not cause chronic diseases per se, but rather creates conditions in which a mass of people are exposed to products, technologies, marketing, and a different working and social environment. Urban populations develop high levels of branded cigarette consumption following exposure to advertising (Yach, Mathews, & Buch, 1990). Diets in urban areas tend to be higher in fat, animal products, and processed foods (Popkin, 1999). Urbanization also distances people from the point of food production, with implications for dietary intake (WHO, 2003d). When people move to urban areas, they adopt less physically demanding types of employment, such as manufacturing and services (Popkin & Doak, 1998), and unplanned urban sprawl may not be conducive to pedestrian activity.

Evidence from South Africa in the 1960s suggests urbanization is associated with the development of diabetes (Seftel & Schultz, 1961), while more recent data point to an association with an earlier incidence of stroke (Vorster, 2002). In Thailand, city dwellers have higher blood pressure, BMIs, and cholesterol levels (InterASIA Collaborative Group, 2003).

Economic Development

The world economy is now more integrated than ever before, with increased trade, investment, and communications flowing between countries. Changes could be even more dramatic over the next 50 years as Brazil, China, India, and Russia become much larger economic forces (Wilson & Purushothaman, 2003).

With economic growth comes the potential for better health: Average life expectancy has increased in the past 30 years as average incomes have risen. Yet growth also brings with it economic, cultural, and social shifts. Among these shifts are the spread of risk factors for chronic diseases. This spread is not inevitable, but probable if unchecked, and will lead to a deterioration of chronic disease profiles.

This process can be conceptualized by a chronic disease consumption curve, based on both empirical data and well-founded assumptions (Figure 6-10). Empirical data show increasing levels of tobacco use and obesity with economic development (Popkin & Doak, 1998; Yach, 1990); lag times between uptake of risk factors and onset of disease; and declines in mortality and morbidity from chronic disease in the OECD countries (Leeder et al., 2004). Data on tobacco use and obesity apply more widely to other risks associated with consumption behavior, while declining mortality from chronic diseases is associated with very high levels of social and economic development. Thus, in the absence of policy actions, consumption of tobacco, alcohol, and foods high in fat, salt, and sugar grows with GNP, followed by associated increases in chronic diseases decades later (curve 1). This contrasts with infectious diseases, which in general decline with economic growth (McKeown, 1988). Chronic disease risk rates do not begin to fall until high levels of wealth and literacy are reached, whereupon governments are more likely to respond to public health concerns and use a broad range of policy instruments to influence consumption trends.

Globalization

Globalization is part of the process of global economic development. Important processes in globalization—trade, foreign investment, marketing, and the spread of technologies—have implications for the spread and alleviation of chronic diseases. These flows drive, and are driven by, the process of globalization and the development of global production systems. Flows of tobacco are always negative; flows concerning food, alcohol, and goods and services related to physical activity can be both positive and negative. A detailed discussion of the relationship between globalization and chronic diseases is contained in Chapter 15.

Policy Responses to the Growing Burden of Chronic Diseases

There are many impediments to addressing chronic diseases, not least owing to the myths perpetuated regarding the burden of chronic diseases and the most

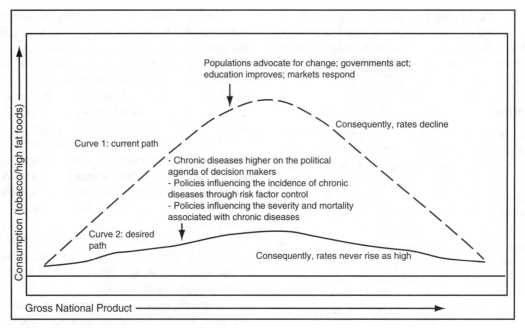

Figure 6-10 Chronic Disease Consumption Curve.

appropriate way to control them (Table 6-9). As already shown by the evidence presented here, these myths are false but create a policy-making environment in which it is easy to justify neglect.

Key stakeholders have met the growing burden of chronic diseases with a patchwork of responses. Overall, there is a lack of policy coherence between different stakeholders, exacerbated by the absence of adequate global governance of chronic diseases (Yach et al., 2004). Table 6-10 summarizes the range of policy responses to chronic diseases.

Governments

At a national level, many ministries of health do recognize chronic disease prevention and control as a significant health priority, but this has not translated into comprehensive policy development or fiscal and human resources (Alwan, Maclean, & Mandil, 2001). Based on a review of government policies and actions in 185 countries (Alwan, Maclean, & Mandil, 2001), the following conclusions emerged:

- The capacity of health systems to prevent and treat chronic diseases is generally low.

- Few countries have developed comprehensive national plans to address chronic diseases.

- Needed legislative and fiscal policies to support health promotion and prevention are not in place.

- Most governments do not provide a budget line for chronic disease control.

- Few countries have essential medicines for chronic disease management readily available in their primary care settings.

World Health Organization

The World Health Organization (WHO) has responsibility for addressing the global burden of chronic diseases. Many WHO functions and goals are directly related to chronic disease control, including "strengthen health services," "control endemic and other diseases," and "propose conventions, agreements and regulations" (Article 2). WHO member states first requested action on chronic diseases at the Ninth World Health Assembly in 1956, with a resolution from India requesting the Director General to establish an expert committee on CVD and hypertension (WHO, 1956). Member states from both developed and developing countries have demanded action since then, including the global strategy on the prevention and control of noncommunicable diseases in 2000; the landmark resolution on the Framework Convention on Tobacco Control (FCTC) in 2003; and a resolution and strategy on diet, physical activity, and health in 2004.

However, with the important exception of tobacco control, financial resources for chronic disease control across WHO remain small when compared with other major contributors to the global burden of

Table 6-9	Eight Myths of Chronic Disease Burden and Control

1. We can wait until infectious diseases are controlled.

False! As development progresses, chronic diseases do not smoothly displace acute diseases. Many countries have a double burden of disease; thus we must deal with both and develop the health system accordingly. Further, some infectious diseases, such as HIV/AIDS, are chronic in nature.

2. Economic growth will improve all health conditions.

False! Economic development can improve health in developing countries. Yet, economic growth can also exacerbate chronic diseases.

3. Chronic diseases are diseases of affluence.

False! Chronic diseases are not solely diseases of affluence in developed and most developing countries. Low socio-economic status leads to cumulative exposure to risk factors, greater comorbidity, and decreased access to quality health care.

4. Chronic diseases are diseases of the elderly.

False! Chronic diseases in developing countries are no longer just diseases of the elderly. Chronic diseases in developing countries affect a much higher proportion of people during their prime working years, compared to developed countries.

5. Chronic diseases result from freely adopted risks.

False! Chronic diseases cannot be blamed solely on the failure of individual responsibility, because the cultural and environmental context in any society or community inevitably affects personal choices. Thus governments, industry, and others also play a role.

6. The benefits of chronic disease control accrue only to individuals.

False! Chronic disease control fosters positive social development and benefits societies economically, and therefore benefits the public as a whole. Like acute disease control, chronic disease control is an appropriate public investment.

7. Acute, infectious disease models are applicable to chronic diseases.

False! Interventions for acute diseases are relatively simple, whereas chronic diseases require a planned, proactive approach to health care, and the active participation of patients, families, and communities.

8. Treating individuals in the health sector is the only appropriate chronic disease strategy.

False! The medical community has focused on using traditional approaches to screen high-risk individuals with a high probability of contracting chronic diseases. Yet, prevention requires a multisectoral commitment in addition to more comprehensive health service interventions for clinical prevention.

disease. In 2002, WHO allocated 3.5% of its total budget (US$43.6 million) to noncommunicable diseases, of which almost equal shares were allocated to country and regional activities (US$22.7 million) and to global and interregional activities (US$21.5 million) (C. M. Michaud, unpublished data, October 2003).

Donor Agencies

Health has not traditionally been a priority area for many donors, and chronic diseases in developing countries have received substantially less attention than other health issues. Although official development assistance for health has increased in the past 5 years, this has been almost entirely absorbed by HIV/AIDS in sub-Saharan Africa (C. M. Michaud, unpublished data, October 2003). Bilateral aid agencies rarely prioritize chronic disease or related risk factors. Official overseas development aid (ODA) to the health sector in 2002 reached $2.9 billion, of which 0.1% was allocated to chronic diseases (in-

cluding mental disorders) (C. M. Michaud, unpublished data, October 2003). The true figure may be higher because about 30% of ODA to health goes to basic health services, of which a proportion would benefit chronic disease control.

United Nations Agencies

UN health and development reports play a major role in setting priorities for global health. Persistent problems that hinder development, such as infant and maternal mortality, malnutrition, and HIV/AIDS, have appropriately received priority in the poorest countries. Despite their impact in low- and middle-income countries, chronic diseases are not recognized as a health and development issue. Millennium Development Goal 6 is "Combat HIV/AIDS, malaria and other diseases" (United Nations Development Program [UNDP], 2001). Though "other diseases" theoretically includes chronic diseases, in practice they are ignored when resources are allocated to health and when countries report on how

Table 6-10	Summary of Key Players' Policy Responses to the Global Burden of Chronic Diseases	
Key Players	**Policy Responses**	
	Positive	**Neutral or Negative**
Heads of state	• G8: Recognition that "health is the key to prosperity" and "poor health drives poverty" • G77: Recent support for the FCTC	• G8: Mobilization of resources for Global Fund in 2001 but no commitment to chronic diseases • G77: No concerted effort on chronic diseases; critical of the draft global strategy on diet, physical activity, and health
Health ministries	• High recognition of problem of chronic diseases	• Inadequate capacity and budget for chronic disease prevention and control in most countries
World Health Organization	• 46 chronic disease resolutions since 1956 • Noncommunicable disease cluster established in 1998 and capacity later developed in regions	• Commitment not followed by funding or high-level advocacy
International donors	• Modest support for tobacco control • Increased health support by donors mostly directed toward HIV/AIDS	• Minimal support for chronic diseases
World Bank and regional development banks	• World Bank recognizes impact of risk factors on poor and is developing a Policy Note on chronic diseases • Policies on chronic diseases and risks emerging in some regional development banks	• Not yet reflected by coherent policy response, investment, or inclusion in poverty reduction strategies • Regional development banks' health sector strategies concentrate on communicable diseases, and funding is minimal or nonexistent
UN initiatives related to health and development	• World Summit of Sustainable Development's Plan of Implementation includes chronic diseases • WHO Commission on Macroeconomics and Health now giving greater consideration to chronic disease threat • International Labor Organization (ILO) SOLVE program addresses chronic disease risks in the workplace	• Millennium Development Goals exclude chronic diseases • United Nations Population Fund does not include chronic diseases or risk factors in strategy on population and development • UNICEF's goal-setting program excludes reference to risk factors for chronic diseases among children • ILO report to the World Commission on the social dimension of globalization and the MNE Declaration do not refer to chronic diseases
International NGOs	• High potential for national capacity building and wide geographic reach • GLOBALink and Framework Convention Alliance supporting FCTC was effective	• Integrated support by NGOs for chronic diseases is insufficiently mobilized
Agricultural and trade sectors	• Links made between tobacco production and health • Increasing research into relationships between agriculture, trade, and chronic diseases	• Linkages between agriculture, trade, and chronic disease insufficiently recognized • Research is receiving insufficient support
Business and investment community	• Some companies developing new business models for chronic disease prevention • Investment community warning of risks associated with chronic diseases	• Companies are largely restricted to corporate social responsibility initiatives, which rarely refer to chronic diseases • Powerful commercial interests have attempted to thwart chronic disease prevention initiatives
Academic health centers, research institutions, and journals	• Active research and development programs between developing and developed countries and research groups • International committees recognize chronic disease research is necessary • Recent editions suggest major journal editors are giving more attention to chronic disease in developing countries	• U.S. academic health centers and international schools of public health have not adequately incorporated chronic diseases into teaching or research • Funding for research is not proportionally allocated • Tiny proportion of developing country researchers publish papers on chronic diseases

they are addressing MDG goals (UNDP, 2001). The UN Population Fund (UNFPA) does not mention chronic illnesses in its strategy on population and development (UNFPA, 1995); and the recent goal-setting program of the UN Children's Fund (UNICEF), A World Fit for Children, excludes risk factors for chronic conditions for children from the 25 action points proposed to "promote healthy lives," despite strong global evidence that tobacco use and obesity are ubiquitous risks among children in developing countries (UN General Assembly, 2002). The Plan of Action of the World Summit on Sustainable Development (WSSD) does, however, state that it will "develop or strengthen, where applicable, preventive, promotive and curative programs to address noncommunicable diseases and conditions . . . and associated risk factors, including alcohol, tobacco, unhealthy diets and lack of physical activity" (WSSD, 2002).

The World Bank has been active in health for decades and is aware of the need to address chronic diseases. It was instrumental in defining the economic basis for action against tobacco (World Bank, 1999). However, of the US$4.25 billion allocated to loans for health between 1997 and 2002, only 2.5% was explicitly for chronic disease control programs.

Nongovernmental Organizations

Nongovernmental organizations (NGOs) have a wide geographic spread and the ability to build capacity. Nationally, NGOs are reported to play a variety of roles in chronic disease control, but their precise roles and effectiveness are not well known (Alwan, Maclean, & Mandil, 2001). There is only limited advocacy at the global level for a chronic disease prevention and control agenda. The most effective advocates for prevention have focused on specific diseases or risks. Internationally, NGOs proved critical in the development of the WHO FCTC. Yet overall, there has been no concerted effort to promote and develop a comprehensive prevention and management approach to chronic diseases by NGOs. NGOs concerned with diet and nutrition in developed countries have not built capacity in developing countries. International consumer group input is inadequate. Initiatives such as "sustainable development" and "corporate social responsibility" have not been applied to chronic diseases.

Private Sector

Sustained engagement by the private sector has been insufficient, although new business models are emerging as investors warn of risks (Table 6-11) and enlightened companies recognize that profitability and public health can coexist. Over recent years, tobacco companies such as Philip Morris and BAT have developed corporate social responsibility (CSR) initiatives aimed at persuading the public that their products are less dangerous. Their efforts are not supported by public health authorities. CSR criteria have to date focused on environmental factors, labor standards, and human rights and not on health considerations. If health were to be considered a key factor when deciding on whether a CSR program was really responsible, tobacco companies would be immediately excluded.

Several food companies have issued guidelines on marketing to children (Hawkes, 2004a). The impact of the guidelines has not been formally evaluated, and it appears that structures have not been put in place to monitor their effects on diet. Self-regulatory guidelines on marketing adopted by alcohol companies have proved useful in some ways, but tend to fall short of their claims (Babor et al., 2003).

Certain TNCs and associated lobbyists have actively tried to thwart action by national governments and WHO in addressing risk factors. The tobacco industry has asserted that the WHO should not focus on the "lifestyle issues" of affluent Western countries. It has also attempted to redirect WHO policies on tobacco, alleging that the WHO is misspending its budget "at the expense of more urgent public health needs, particularly in developing countries, such as prevention of malaria and other communicable diseases" (WHO, 2000). Lobbyists for tobacco, sugar, and some other food interests have worked hard to keep attention away from the need to address consumption patterns that drive chronic diseases (Brownell & Hagen, 2004).

There are currently few private-public partnerships addressing chronic disease prevention. One new such initiative is the Oxford Health Alliance that brings together academics, nongovernmental organizations, international health groups and the private sector (see web site: http://www.oxha.org/). Novo Nordisk has played an initiating role with Oxford and Yale Universities in this endeavor. New community based research projects to determine how best to prevent chronic diseases in 20 developing and developed countries are being supported through the Alliance, which regularly convenes major players involved in chronic disease prevention in order to find practical means of increasing advocacy and funding. The focus is on reducing tobacco use, improving diets and levels of physical activity in order to make an impact on cardiovascular disease, certain cancers, diabetes and chronic respiratory diseases.

Academic and Research Community

The academic response to chronic disease prevention and control in developing countries has been mixed. Few developing country–oriented courses on

Table 6-11	Equity and Market Research into the Future of the Tobacco and Food Industry

- Moody's Investors Service, 2003: "FDA regulation is a real possibility and would transform the industry. Easing the introduction of reduced-risk products would be an advantage to Philip Morris" (Razaire et al., 2005).
- Swiss Reinsurance Company, 2004: "The increasing prevalence of obesity has financial implications for consumers of life insurance products and society as a whole. . . As consumers' Body Mass Index goes up, so too will their premiums" (Swiss Reinsurance Company, 2004).
- JP Morgan, 2003: The food industry should "review its marketing practices and transform itself" (Langlois, Adam, & Powell, 2003, p. 1).
- UBS Warburg, 2002: "There are risks associated with obesity that have not yet been factored into share prices" (Streets et al., 2002, p. 1).
- Datamonitor, 2002: "[Food] manufacturers have a great opportunity for product leadership and category reinvention" (Datamonitor, 2002).
- JP Morgan, 2004: "R&D is making safer cigarettes a reality" (JP Morgan, 2004).

chronic disease epidemiology and control exist anywhere in the world, and few developing country research institutes support research into chronic disease risks and prevention programs. Notably, there is a paucity of research conducted on chronic diseases by researchers in developing countries (Figure 6-11). This can be explained by the levels of investment in health research for chronic disease prevention and control. About $10 billion was spent on CVD disease research, and a further $1.6 billion on diabetes research globally in 2000–2001. Of that, about 75% was spent in the United States, Japan, United Kingdom, France, and Italy. Further, somewhere over 95% is spent on new drug development—very little is spent on community-based prevention research. There are few significant funders of chronic disease research in developing countries. One such funder, the Fogarty International Center of the National Institutes of Health (NIH), supports tobacco control research in developing countries (see web site: http://www.fic.nih.gov).

Against this backdrop, it is not surprising that authors from the United States and United Kingdom dominated research output in all chronic disease and

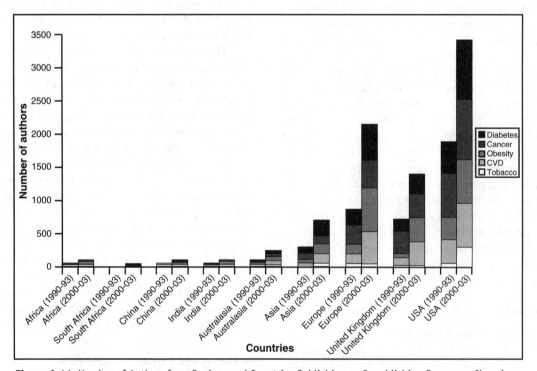

Figure 6-11 Number of Authors from Regions and Countries Publishing or Copublishing Papers on Chronic Diseases or Their Major Risk Factors in 1990–1993 and 2000–2003.

risk categories, accounting for 80% of research on tobacco and cancer, 75% on diabetes and cardiovascular disease, and 60% on obesity (see Figure 6-11). India and China produced less than 3.5% in all categories, despite being home to 40% of the world's population and a large share of the chronic disease burden. Articles about tobacco with authors from Africa, China, Europe, India, and the United Kingdom declined as a percentage of total papers, though increased by over 20% for authors from the United States.

Preventing and Managing Chronic Diseases: What Needs to Be Done

For progress in chronic disease control, the following is required: solid evidence of what should be done; acknowledgment by key players of roles and responsibilities; and recognition of the actions that are required at local, national, and international levels.

Several approaches as to what should be done have been proposed, usually summarized as involving either the promotion of healthy lifestyles for the whole population or the early diagnosis and cost-effective management of risk factors and disease. In reality, it is useful to split this distinction further because it has implications for who should take responsibility for actions. Thus, three sets of actions are necessary: All are required.

1. Health promotion aimed at shifting the entire distribution of risks in populations through intersectoral actions

2. Prevention programs aimed at reducing the prevalence of specific major risks, especially tobacco use and unhealthy diets

3. Health service programs to identify and reduce risk for patients with risk behavior and/or preclinical signs of chronic diseases, and programs to prevent the onset of complications in those with disease

These three interrelated actions are described in the following subsections.

Systems That Promote Health

Over the years, the phrase *health systems* has been used to refer to all forms of treatments for diseases, some aspects of rehabilitation, and a few aspects of primary prevention or health promotion. Health departments of countries manage health care systems and receive "health" budgets to do so. This narrow perspective leads to public confusion and a lack of clarity about who is really responsible for broader aspects of health promotion.

For chronic diseases such as HIV/AIDS, TB, cancer, diabetes, and cardiovascular disease, there is a long lag between exposure to risks for disease and the occurrence of clinical disease. Acting on risks will reduce incidence, and effective treatment will prevent serious complications and death. About half of the decline in CVD mortality in the United States over the last two decades is ascribed to better treatment, half to better prevention of risks. For a few cancers, treatment has led to dramatic increases in survival. However, this has not been the case with two major tobacco-related cancers: lung and larynx.

Advocacy groups for patients' rights to treatment have successfully changed drug pricing policies and improved access to diagnosis and treatment for a range of diseases, such as HIV/AIDS, breast cancer, and epilepsy. In contrast, the voices calling for prevention and health promotion are relatively mute. The political pressure for greater investments in prevention and health promotion has until recently been lacking. Stronger systems are needed to promote health and prevent risk, and better health care systems are needed to address failures of prevention and conditions for which causes (and also successful interventions) remain unknown (McGinnis, Williams-Russo, & Knickman, 2002).

How Is a System for Health Promotion Broader Than a Health Care System?

The goals of a system concerned with health promotion would be broader and focused more on determinants and underlying causes of ill health and on ways of promoting health, compared with health care systems. Health care systems usually focus on providing treatment within a system that emphasizes quality of care, cost-effectiveness, and equity in access to lifelong care. Within government, many sectors play a role in promoting health or causing disease. A system for health promotion would recognize this and ensure that all policies were evaluated in relation to their impact on health and not just from a narrow sectoral perspective. Health care systems are funded mainly from health department budgets, some form of social insurance, and through private out-of-pocket expenditure. In contrast, a system for health promotion could tap into funding within many sectoral departments—from agriculture and sports to education and welfare. Health care system debates at a national level tend to focus on whether programs should be vertical or horizontal, and how to achieve cost-containment and equity goals. Debates within government on systems for health promotion would address complex and profound issues involving trade-offs between development priorities and between allocations that would benefit current as opposed to future generations. Policy impact evaluations would be required to ensure that decisions are made in a transparent manner.

The principle of policy impact assessments has for years been accepted in relation to the environment or in relation to long-term impacts on budgets but has been neglected from a health perspective. The result has been profoundly negative for health promotion. For example:

- Urban design decisions rarely consider the impact on physical activity and consequently on obesity, diabetes, and CVD.

- Agricultural policies are not developed from a health perspective but primarily for short-term commercial and political reasons. Thus, there are subsidies for products harmful to health, such as tobacco; subsidies that protect developed countries' farmers at the cost of developing countries' economies; and few incentives for farmers to grow more fruit and vegetables.

- Trade policies often place protection of patents ahead of public health concerns—particularly those of the poorest countries and communities.

- Decisions related to foreign direct investment (FDI) are usually neutral with regard to the impact of new investments on health outcomes. It is often assumed that FDI will bring new jobs and economic growth and thus is always good for societies. Contrary evidence suggests that certain types of FDI promote rapid acquisition of unhealthy consumption patterns for products such as tobacco, foods with a high fat, sugar, and salt content, and alcohol (Table 6-12).

Systems for health promotion would be governed at the national level by the cabinet as a whole and not just by the ministry or department of health. In a few countries, ministries of health are often mandated to lead on all issues related to health. This usually occurs when there is a strong and dynamic minister.

The report by Derek Wanless in the United Kingdom entitled *Securing Good Health for the Whole Population* (see web site: http://www.hm_treasury.gov.uk/consultations_and_legislation/wanless/consult_wanless04_final.cfm) provides detailed guidance to sectoral ministries on how they could contribute to improving health overall, and especially how they could reduce inequalities in health (Wanless, 2004). What makes Wanless's work so important is that it was commissioned and coordinated by the UK Treasury, albeit by drawing heavily on public health expertise. The report must rank as one of the most important contributions to public health anywhere, and certainly has implications for how one can take a step-by-step approach to building true systems for health promotion. Unlike so many other report a cited by Wanless over the last few decades, this one is likely to be backed by government finance and, where required, legislation and taxation; it is already strongly supported by a newly activated public health community.

Table 6-12	Foreign Direct Investment: Foreign Assets and Employment of Tobacco, Alcohol, Food, and Retail Companies in the World's Largest 100 Transnational Corporations, 2001			
Sector	**Corporation**	**Home Economy**	**Foreign Assets (Rank) US$ billion**	**Foreign Employment**
Food and Beverage	Hutinson Whampoa Limited	Hong Kong	40.9 (17)	53,478
	Nestle SA	Switzerland	33.1 (21)	223,000
	Unilever	UK/Netherlands	30.5 (25)	204,000
	Diageo	UK	19.7 (47)	60,000
	Procter & Gamble	USA	17.3 (58)	43,381
	Coca-Cola Company	USA	17.1 (59)	26,000
	McDonalds	USA	12.8 (79)	251,000
	Danone Group SA	France	11.4 (86)	88,000
Retail	Carrefour SA	France	29.3 (29)	235,894
(food and drink)	Wal-Mart Stores	USA	26.3 (24)	303,000
	Royal Ahold NV	Netherlands	19.9 (44)	183,851
Alcohol	Diageo	UK	19.7 (47)	60,000
Tobacco	Phillip Morris	USA	19.3 (49)	39,000
	BAT	UK	10.4 (92)	59,000

Note: Eleven automobile and 10 pharmaceutical companies are also among the top 100 transnational corporations.

Source: United Nations Conference on Trade and Development, *World Investment Report 2003* (Geneva and New York: UNCTAD, 2003). Reprinted with permission.

What Types of Conflicts Occur?

Progress in much of infectious disease control is achievable with additional funding for surveillance, effective treatment, and new drugs and vaccines where existing ones are ineffective or are not available; it also requires general improvements in housing and related infrastructure (water, sanitation, and energy). All of these investments are now regarded as noncontentious. Even the tough issues of improving access to drugs in poor countries are being addressed nationally and internationally within the context of the Doha trade round. Conflicts that do remain are subsiding, and the move is now to seek funds for effective action.

In contrast, progress in promoting health often involves WHO and public health agencies urging individuals to stop smoking; eat less fat, sugar, and salt; do more physical activity; and eat more fruits, vegetables, nuts, and grains. They do so knowing that individual responsibility without supportive government and multisectoral action does not lead to sustained change. Further, unless "healthy choices are made," in the words of the Ottawa Charter, "the easy choices," such as unhealthy consumption patterns, will persist, especially among the poor, where they often become entrenched as the easiest and most affordable choices.

Table 6-13 summarizes a number of policy issues that require resolution at a level of government outside of the health department. The table lists some traditional opponents to healthy public policies, along with possible supporters of change. Tobacco and diet/physical activity are major contributors to the burden of disease in developed and developing countries.

Because of their disproportionate impact, special emphasis is given to the nature of conflicts and trade-offs that have occurred in these areas. The call to stop smoking has unified a variety of opposition groups—the tobacco industry itself, the hospitality and entertainment industries, farmers, advertising companies, and often the media. All are told a simple message: If people smoke less, they will all lose jobs. It has taken decades of policy work by economists,

public health advocates, and practitioners to correct myths propagated by the tobacco industry surrogates. Examples of such myths include the following:

- Restaurants and pubs will go bankrupt if smoke-free policies are introduced. The opposite is the truth.

- Finance departments will lose revenue from smuggling and reduced tax receipts if excise taxes increase. Actually, smuggling may have a small impact on revenue, but the solution is not to condone crime but rather to strengthen customs and excise controls.

- Farmers in countries such as Zimbabwe and Malawi will be unemployed in a few years as consumption declines. Unfortunately, from a public health perspective, consumption does not fall at a rate faster than 5% per year, and usually rates of 2% have been regarded as impressive if maintained for years. At those rates, and in the face of continued population growth, the demand for leaf tobacco will remain high for many decades. The immediate threat to African tobacco farmers comes more from the introduction of mechanization locally and subsidies in developed countries than from less smoking.

The public health statement "Consume sugar sparingly," which seems like common sense to most people, evokes strong responses from a wide range of special interests. During the development of the WHO Global Strategy on Diet, Physical Activity and Health, the full range of possible arguments against this simple message about sugar emerged (A. Waxman, 2004; H. Waxman, 2004). Soda manufacturers have led the global efforts to deny that sugar causes obesity or dental caries, or that specific levels of sugars are desirable. Sugarcane farmers in developing countries are concerned that if new WHO/FAO guidelines on sugar consumption were applied globally, they would lose their jobs. The economic stakes are much more

Table 6-13	Supporters and Opponents of Selected Policy Issues		
Major Risk Factor	**Policy Issue**	**Supporters**	**Opponents**
Tobacco	Excise tax	Finance, World Bank	Tobacco industry
	Advertising bans	N/A	Advertisers, media, libertarians
	Smoke-free areas	Restaurants	Hospitality and restaurant sector
	Agricultural subsidies	Enlightened countries	Farmers, rural voters
	Advertising to children	N/A	Advertisers, multinational food companies, media
Diet, nutrition	Commodity changes, sugar	Fruit, vegetables	Sugar farmers, producers, lobbyists
	Promotion to children	Sports, gyms	Sports, toys, fast food

N/A = not applicable.

substantive for sugar as opposed to tobacco; the size of the lobbying community is far greater and the evidence base on the economics of sugar use is not as well described as it is for tobacco.

For several years, efforts were made to be prepared for critique of any efforts to control tobacco use. These included engaging with the Food and Agriculture Organization, the World Bank, the IMF, UNICEF, and other UN partners and jointly agreeing that the key policy goal in relation to tobacco was demand reduction. Supply-related issues would need to be addressed but should not block action on making public health gains. In the process, new research by the World Bank showed that tobacco control was sound economic and health policy, and the FAO showed that farmers' short-term fears were exaggerated. Within the UN family, policy coherence was achieved. This was later reflected in increased policy coherence within governments. Similar work is yet to emerge with respect to many food policy issues. They are inherently more complex, involve a wider array of players, and will need to address the reality that there may be some losers over the long term, but that these are likely to be more than offset by winners, particularly in the fruit, vegetable, and nuts sectors. As with tobacco, and opposite to what lobbyists maintain, there will only be very modest impacts on the demand for sugar over the next few decades even if the WHO recommendations were fully implemented (LMC International, 2004).

Specific Prevention Programs to Address Tobacco, Diet, and Physical Activity

Tobacco

Since the first major reports of harm in the early 1960s, there has been an evolution in the development of policies to tackle tobacco. This evolution has unfolded in different ways in different geographic regions. By the early 1970s, the content of a comprehensive package of interventions to address tobacco had been accepted as the way forward and had been incorporated into national law in several Nordic countries, as well as in Singapore, Australia, and New Zealand. A very similar package was adopted three decades later as the basis for action—the WHO FCTC (see later in this chapter) (see WHO FCTC's web site: http://www.who.int/tobacco/framework/en). None of the early-adopter countries was home to multinational tobacco companies. All had a strong history of open and critically transparent parliamentary processes that gave emphasis to health.

In the United States, tobacco company efforts ensured that few attempts by the federal government succeeded and that tobacco control was based on a strong educational component. Innovation was left to the states and, increasingly, to local cities and towns. In California, for example, the freedom that came with statehood stimulated local initiatives that were well funded and politically supported. Sensing the threat posed by the increasing evidence that interventions were effective in reducing smoking, the tobacco industry hired large numbers of consultants, including economists, journalists, advertisers, physicians, and philosophers, to dispute this evidence. This led to the strange situation whereby tobacco control experts could discover what really made a difference simply by studying where opposition was strongest. Thus, taxes, advertisement bans, smoke-free policies, and litigation, which the industry argued would "not work," should be emphasized. In contrast, industry-favored policies such as education at schools, voluntary agreements on advertising, and accommodation between smokers and nonsmokers are largely ineffective. In many cases, the industry actively commissioned research that was either methodologically flawed or simply fraudulent to give weight to its arguments.

The same approaches, although in some cases at lower levels of intensity, were adopted by major tobacco companies based in Japan, Germany, and the United Kingdom.

Paradoxically, some of the earliest countries to act against tobacco introduced effective policies even though the evidence from research was not yet available. Randomized control studies of advertising bans or tax increases were not possible. Rather, professional judgment and common sense played a key role. Decades later, developing countries introducing these same measures are being challenged by tobacco companies that dispute their now well-established effectiveness.

The accumulation of experience from many countries means that it is now much clearer what works and what does not. It confirms the wisdom of the early adopters: Be comprehensive; keep the debate alive, interesting, and provocative in the media; incrementally tighten laws as public support and demand for action increases; move to make smoking an unacceptable and antisocial behavior; and globalize action to counter the global reach and strategies of tobacco companies—particularly their marketing and investment practices. International consensus of what constitutes the key elements of a comprehensive approach to tobacco control is now enshrined in the text of the FCTC, which by August 2004 had been adopted by 192 countries, signed by 170, and ratified by 29.

Table 6-14	Potential Relevance of FCTC Provisions to Diet and Physical Activity	
Measure	**FCTC Tobacco Provision**	**Application to Diet and Physical activity**
Pricing and taxes	Increase price by raising excise taxes and imposing prohibitions or restrictions on sales/imports of tax- and duty-free tobacco products	Use price measures to make fruit and vegetables more affordable; conduct research to consider whether taxing certain foods will promote healthier eating
Exposure to environmental tobacco smoke	Measures aimed at protecting the public from exposure to environmental tobacco smoke	Not applicable
Packaging and labeling requirements	Provisions address the size of health warnings and labeling, especially with respect to misleading language (Article 11)	Health warnings and disclosure of nutritional information: adherence to Codex nutrition labeling guidelines and science-based criteria for health claims
Product content	Guidelines for testing, measuring, and regulating the contents and emissions of tobacco products (Article 9)	Regulation of harmful ingredients; labeling that discloses significant ingredients; food safety regulations
Education campaigns	Promotion of public awareness of health risks of tobacco use/exposure to tobacco smoke, and of the benefits of cessation of tobacco use and of tobacco-free lifestyles	Educational campaigns in schools, workplaces, primary health care settings, and other sites reaching the general public; information and skill building to encourage optimal nutrition and physical activity
Restrictions on advertising, sponsorship, and promotion	Restrictions (preferably a complete ban) on advertising, sponsorship, and promotion of tobacco products	Restrictions on advertising, sponsorship, and promotion of some food products to children; discouragement of sedentary behavior and unhealthy lifestyles
Clinical interventions	Cessation programs; diagnosis and treatment of tobacco dependence	Clinical interventions based on collaborative goal setting, skill building, self-monitoring, personalized feedback, planned follow-up, and links to community resources

Source: D. Yach, C. Hawkes, J. E. Epping-Jordan, and S. Galbraith, "The World Health Organization's Framework Convention on Tobacco Control: Implications for the Global Epidemics of Food-Related Deaths and Disease," 2003, *Journal of Public Health Policy,* 24(2–3), pp. 274–290. Reprinted with permission.

Diet

With the enormous contemporary focus on obesity, it is easy to ignore the profound changes that have occurred with respect to many other aspects of healthy diets. Salt levels in processed foods have declined in many countries, often stimulated by government regulations; consumption of saturated fat has been reduced in many developed countries as a result of education, better product choices provided by companies, and media coverage (but this took three decades); and the need for all people to eat more fruits and vegetables is now accepted widely even though consumption remains way below suggested levels. The combined impact of these dietary changes has led to a striking reduction in the incidence of CVD in industrialized countries, with the impact especially apparent in the former communist countries of east-

ern Europe, now members of the European Union, where change proceeded rapidly after 1990.

Yet at the same time as the progress just described has occurred, some aspects of diet have worsened. More sugar is consumed by children in many countries, and physical activity levels have collapsed. In developing countries, a more rapid nutrition transition is under way than ever occurred in developed countries, with "bads" increasingly displacing "goods."

Governments worldwide are now struggling to develop effective approaches to obesity. The recently adopted WHO Global Strategy on Diet, Physical Activity and Health proposes a range of key elements of a comprehensive approach. However, this issue is only now reaching the policy agenda, and, compared with tobacco, the level of active intervention and support by many governments has been low.

Table 6-14 considers which key elements of the FCTC have implications for diet and physical activity. A few points are worth noting:

- Increasing prices through excise tax works well for tobacco control but remains technically doubtful as a means of influencing food choices. Currently, taxes on soft drinks are used to raise revenue for health promotion. Measures to make fruit and vegetables more affordable may be a better alternative.

- Several recent studies suggest that fear works in tobacco control communications to adults and children. But this seems to have limited use in influencing food choices or in promoting physical activity.

- Few of the interventions for tobacco or diet/physical activity have been explicitly designed or evaluated in terms of their impact on reducing risks among the poorest communities and their impact on minorities. Evidence suggests that most tobacco control measures have mainly benefited the most educated and the wealthiest in countries. This issue requires serious research and policy attention because chronic diseases already contribute to inequalities in survival by social class and area.

Have Risk Factor—Specific Policies Made a Difference?

The impact of policies on tobacco use, and on the health consequences that follow, has been well documented. In many developed countries, male smoking rates reached 50% to 60% by the early 1960s—now they are around 20% to 30%, and in some places, such as California, have fallen to 11%. Cardiovascular disease, lung cancer, and other tobacco-related diseases have declined in these countries—in some cases, the declines have been rapid and substantial. There is growing evidence that the intense public and media debates over several decades have themselves played a powerful role in changing behaviors.

There has been much less progress among women. In some developed countries, their smoking rates are still increasing—and along with them CVD and, after a further lag period, lung cancer rates. Among adults, the greatest declines have been in higher social classes, with very modest progress evident among manual workers, marginalized groups, and people with the lowest levels of education. Smoking prevalence among children in many developed countries remains high. In many countries, girls are more likely to smoke than boys, portending

future reversals of the traditional female advantage in life expectancy.

Several developing countries and countries in transition have also made real progress, but in only a few, such as Poland, has this so far translated into fewer deaths. A World Bank review of strategies and successes in tobacco control in Brazil, South Africa, Thailand, Poland, Bangladesh, and Canada showed that a range of policies and regulations had contributed to reduced smoking prevalence (de Beyer & Brigden, 2003).

For many developing countries, the fundamental challenge is different from that in developed countries: how to stop an increase in smoking against a backdrop of historically relatively low rates (especially among women and children). In developed countries, the goal has primarily been to reduce already high rates among men, while in countries in transition it is also important to prevent the rise in female smoking. The different policy approaches called for when the goal is to stop an increase compared to when it is to reduce already high rates have never been carefully distinguished. Taxes, advertising bans, and early introduction of smoke-free policies may well be most effective and cost-effective in settings where education levels are low, where health services, including cessation, are underdeveloped, and where the unchecked impact of the tobacco industry is greatest.

Achievements in relation to diet have been less clear-cut. Although increased consumption of micronutrients, especially from fresh fruit and vegetables, and reductions in consumption of saturated fat have led to declines in stroke and CVD, the growth of obesity has fueled an epidemic of type 2 diabetes. As time passes, this can be expected to reverse the earlier gains, this time driven not by saturated fat but by excessive calories, carbohydrates, hypertension, and diabetes itself.

The Limitations of Studies on Cost-Effectiveness for Chronic Disease Prevention

Many interventions for chronic disease prevention and health promotion have been tried and tested, notably by the Cochrane Collaboration process. As summarized in Table 6-15, Cochrane reviews of several interventions are now available (Riemsma et al., 2002), and a global task force has identified additional priority areas for future research (Doyle et al., 2005). As identified in the lessons learned from the tobacco experience (Exhibit 6-2), success in health promotion and chronic disease prevention depends on having a comprehensive set of interventions that taken together make it possible for healthy choices to be the easy choices. Several

Table 6-15	Cochrane Reviews of Effective Interventions in Chronic Disease Risk Factors		
Risk Factor Area	**Examples of Published Cochrane Reviews**	**Cochrane Reviews in Progress (Published Protocol or Registered Title)**	**Examples of Interventions Needing Review**
Tobacco	• Community interventions for preventing smoking in young people • Impact of tobacco advertising and promotion on increasing adolescent smoking behaviors • Workplace interventions for smoking cessation	• Stage-based interventions for smoking cessation • Mass media interventions for smoking cessation in adults (registered title only)	• Interventions targeted by gender to decrease tobacco initiation • Interventions utilizing marketing strategies to promote healthy behaviors in young people, focusing on tobacco
Obesity	• Advice on low-fat diets for obesity • Interventions for preventing childhood obesity	• Exercise for obesity	
Diet	• Reduced or modified dietary fat for preventing cardiovascular disease	• Interventions for promoting the initiation of breastfeeding	• Interventions utilizing marketing strategies to promote healthy behaviors in young people, focusing on food[a] • Interventions for healthier food choices[a] (e.g., sales promotion strategies of supermarkets to increase healthier food purchase and/or pricing policies to increase healthy food choices)
Physical activity	• Exercise for preventing and treating osteoporosis in postmenopausal women • Exercise to improve self-esteem in children and young people	• Interventions for promoting physical activity • Interventions implemented through sporting organizations for increasing participation in sport (registered title only) • School-based physical activity programs for promoting physical activity and fitness in children and adolescents aged 6 to 18 (registered title only)	• Physical exercise to improve mental health outcomes for adults[a] • Interventions to minimize the impact of urban sprawl on physical activity[a] • Interventions to increase the supply of sidewalks and walking trails for the public • Healthy cities project to reduce cardiovascular risk factors[a] (could apply to all risk factors)

[a] Identified as priority topics for review by the Cochrane Collaboration process.

Source: R. P. Riemsma, J. Pattenden, C. Bridle, A. J. Sowden, L. Mather, I. S. Watt, and A. Walker, "A systematic review of the Effectivenss of Interventions Based on a Stages-of-Change Approach to Promote Individual Behaviour Change," 2002, *Health Technology Assessment,* 6(24), pp. 1–231. Reprinted with permission.

studies carried out in school, workplace, or health care settings have demonstrated short-term effects in relatively small groups of people—effects that are rarely replicated across large populations. Further, the types of interventions with the greatest probability of influencing the behavior of populations—namely, those involving regulatory actions, changes in fiscal policy, or intersectoral actions—do not lend themselves to randomized control studies of the type usually reported in Cochrane reviews.

More complex approaches are needed to evaluate such interventions. One recent initiative by WHO researchers provides an example of what could be done more broadly. A comprehensive review that applies to all countries, at all levels of development, used methods that could be applied to the full range of chronic diseases and risks (Murray et al., 2003). The study used the output of systematic reviews as a basis for developing evidence on effectiveness and costs of interventions to lower population-wide measures of systolic blood pressure and cholesterol. The results showed that nonpersonal health interventions, including government action to stimulate a reduction in the salt content of processed foods, are cost-effective ways to limit CVD. Combination treatment is also cost-effective for people whose risk of a CVD event over the next 10 years is above 35%. Together, personal and nonpersonal health interventions (excluding those related to tobacco) could lower the global incidence of CVD events by as much as 50% (Murray et al., 2003).

Management of Chronic Diseases by Health Care Systems

Health Care Quality and Access

Universally, health care systems are not organized to provide effective and efficient prevention and care for chronic diseases. Countries often struggle with the complexity of insufficient resources combined with inadequate access to necessary drugs and technologies. Chemotherapeutic agents most effective against the 10 leading cancers are not available in many developing countries, where they are often subject to high import duties (IARC, 2003). Inhaled beclomethasone is often not available or affordable in developing countries, placing patients with COPD and asthma at considerable risk for premature death (Ait-Khaled, Enarson, & Bousquet, 2001).

Opportunities for secondary prevention are being missed. The WHO PREMISE study of secondary prevention of CHD and cerebrovascular disease showed that knowledge and treatment of these dis-

---

Exhibit 6-2	Twelve Lessons from the Experience of Tobacco That May Be Applicable to Policy Development Relating to Diet and Nutrition

1. *Address the issue of individual responsibility versus collective/environmental action early and often.* This issue pervades debates on the role of government versus the individual. Both sides of the issue need to be addressed, with emphasis being given to the Ottawa Charter statement that "healthy choices need to be the easy choices."

2. *Evidence of harm is necessary but not sufficient to motivate policy change.* There is a need for some essential epidemiologic gaps to be closed in relation to diet and outcomes in developing countries, but there is already sufficient knowledge to act now, rather than using the call for research as a means of delaying action.

3. *Decisions to act need not wait for evidence of the effectiveness of interventions.* Initial tobacco control interventions were not evidence based but represented sound judgment at the time. We know now what has worked for tobacco and can adapt some elements immediately. For others, we should introduce interventions in such a way that they can be critically evaluated in terms of effectiveness and adjustments can be made over time.

4. *The real and perceived needs and concerns of developing countries need to be addressed even if they involve going beyond the initial scope of the risk being addressed.* For tobacco control, this meant addressing all forms of tobacco use, not just cigarettes, and considering the concerns of tobacco farmers and providing convincing evidence that their livelihoods were not under threat in the mid-term. For the diet/nutrition area, this will be more complex and require that close interaction be sought between those working to address hunger, micronutrient deficiencies, and undernutrition in general and those working to develop policies for overweight and chronic disease prevention. The goal should be to promote the optimal diet for all. It also requires that the complex agricultural issues related to subsidies and decisions about what gets cultivated receive greater attention.

5. *The more comprehensive the package of measures considered, the greater the impact.* Most approaches currently discussed in relation to diet and physical activity tend to emphasize very narrow approaches: more exercise at schools or more education at work, for example. Few take a broad perspective. Within a comprehensive package, those working in tobacco and diet/physical activity need to understand where governments have constraints and help them to address them. For example, some countries have a constitutional impediment to a complete ban on tobacco advertisement.

6. *Broad-based vertical and horizontal coalitions, well networked, are key.* Vertical coalitions include all those in health—from the local health department to the regional and national authority and to WHO. What is increasingly clear is that the wide array of players outside the traditional boundaries of health need to be engaged and to lead on certain aspects of the problem. But health still needs to provide overall direction and leadership. This has been achieved for the FCTC process within the UN, among NGOs, and to a limited extent across departments inside many governments. It remains to be done for diet and physical activity.

(continued)

Exhibit 6-2	Continued

7. *Media-savvy individual and institutional leadership matters.* Say no more!

8. *Change in support for tobacco control took decades of dedicated effort by all.* The global breakthrough came with the then director general of WHO, Dr. Brundtland, being willing to tackle an unpopular topic by speaking out often to heads of state, major donors, and those in the industry about tobacco use being a real global concern. But progress had been happening well before, in developing the basis for having content that would work in the FCTC, and in having a network of advocates and NGOs ready to rally in support.

9. *Modest, well-spent funds can have a massive impact, but without clear goals they may not be sustainable.* For both tobacco and diet, there are no agreed targets or internationally accepted indicators of progress. Some countries have set targets for tobacco control but then did not provide resources for their attainment.

10. *Complacency that past actions will serve well in the future may retard future progress.* Despite all the progress in tobacco control, the bottom line remains that global consumption continues to increase, albeit slowly; few countries have achieved sustained declines of more than 2% prevalence per year for a decade (Canada has come close, and South Africa has reported a 65% decline per year for 8 years). Such slow rates of decline must mean that we need to reconsider our policies and interventions and consider what is needed to reach an 8% to 10% decline per year and then to maintain levels well below 10% in all subgroups. It might be that stronger emphasis on smoke-free policies combined more tightly with access to cessation programs and increased prices could together achieve such levels of decline. New approaches, including the use of plain packaging, need to be considered as well. For diet, and especially obesity, investment in large-scale community-based research is needed to yield the first signs of progress.

11. *Rules of engagement with the tobacco and food industries need to be different and continually under review.* Until now, the public health community has not officially met with the tobacco industry—exceptions being the CDC and WHO as part of their on-the-record interactions in relation to product regulation. As time passes, there will be a need to meet with tobacco industry scientists to review their progress on potentially reduced-risk products and to consider what criteria should be used to judge their claims of reduced harm. A new set of rules for engagement is required to extract possible areas of progress. At this stage, interaction in relation to youth smoking, marketing, taxes, and smoke-free public places does seem warranted. With respect to the food industry, the issue is more complex, and at this stage an agreed sets of rules for engagement should be developed that could include guidance on how to find common solutions to issues related to marketing to children, product content and safety, joint action to promote physical activity and healthy eating, and support for priority research.

12. *Risk factor envy is harmful.* As the media shift to focus on obesity, funders are shifting too. There is a real danger that one major health problem will be displaced by another. There is an urgent need to build synergies between those active in tobacco and others addressing diet and physical activity, as well as diseases associated with them. A grand coalition of the willing could do more good for public health by pushing for sustained policy and financial change together than by competing against each other.

eases is underutilized for patients in low- and middle-income countries. Most patients were aware of the preventive effects of lifestyle factors, such as quitting smoking, eating a healthier diet, and performing physical activity, but did not necessarily follow these recommendations. Many patients were not receiving preventive medication such as aspirin. Measurement of cardiovascular risk factors, such as blood sugar and blood cholesterol levels and blood pressure, was not sufficiently regular. Inadequate resources and facilities of health care systems in low- and middle-income countries are largely responsible for the insufficiencies of secondary prevention (WHO PREMISE).

Quality gaps extend beyond medication availability, however. In the Caribbean, for example, a medical record review of over 1,600 patients attending health care clinics for diabetes indicated that over a 12-month period, fewer than one-third had received dietary advice and only 5% had received exercise advice (Gulliford et al., 1996). Similar findings have been reported in South Africa (Beattie et al., 1998) and India (Raheja et al., 2001).

Another complicating factor in health care access and quality is the double burden of noncommunicable and communicable diseases. Many developing countries are struggling to manage infant mortality and malnutrition alongside infectious and noncommunicable chronic diseases.

Underlying Drivers of the Problem

Most health care systems have not kept pace with the decline in acute health problems and the increase in chronic disease and are still trying to manage chronic problems using acute care mentality, methods, and systems. Because current health care systems developed in response to acute problems and the urgent needs of patients, they are designed to address pressing concerns. Health care interactions are characterized by one-to-one visits with health care workers whose purpose is to diagnose and treat a patient's pressing complaint. Testing, diagnosing, relieving symptoms, and expecting cure are characteristic of this kind of health care, and these functions fit the needs of patients experiencing acute and episodic health problems.

There are obvious problems with the application of this typical visit format to chronic conditions. One problem is the discrete nature of the interactions, which belies the importance of promoting planned and proactive care. Clearly, chronic conditions are not a series of disconnected complaints. Yet frequently, people with chronic disease are treated as if this were the case. This approach is wasteful and inefficient given that complications and the eventual outcomes of poorly managed chronic conditions follow a known and predictable course. Chronic diseases require health care that is proactive and organized around the concepts of planned care and prevention.

A second major problem is that health care workers frequently fail to recognize the importance of empowering patients to become active participants in their ongoing care. There is substantial evidence from more than 400 published articles that interventions designed to promote patients' roles in the prevention and management of chronic diseases are associated with improved outcomes. What patients do for themselves on a daily basis—engage in regular physical activity, eat properly, avoid tobacco use, sleep regularly, adhere to treatment plans—influences their health far more than biomedical interventions alone. There is also ample scientific evidence demonstrating that successful health care interventions *do* exist for changing patients' health behavior and increasing their adherence to treatments. However, these interventions, which could prevent many chronic diseases and improve their management once they occur, are frequently missing from current systems of care.

Characteristics of Effective Systems of Care for Chronic Diseases

Health care for patients with chronic conditions requires a fundamental change in perspective from the familiar acute care model. The magnitude of the challenge is eased somewhat by the fact that chronic conditions share many common features. Whereas biomedical management depends on the unique features of the specific disease, the general components of care organization and delivery for patients with chronic conditions are essentially the same. These components include a well-defined care plan, patient self-management, scheduled follow-up appointments, monitoring of outcome and adherence, and stepwise treatment protocols. Collectively, these approaches represent a significant shift in health care practices (Table 6-16). The differences between typical current and desired future approaches are described in the following subsections.

Patient Centered. Patient-centered care recognizes the patient as a person; fully informs patients about the risks and benefits of treatment options; tailors decision making in response to individual patients' values, needs, and expressed preferences; shares power and responsibility among patients and providers; and develops patients' abilities to participate in their care. Across its multiple meanings, research shows that patient-centered care is crucial for obtaining good outcomes for chronic conditions.

Several experiences within developing countries demonstrate the utility of patient-centered care across diverse cultures and resource contexts. WHO's Integrated Management of Adult Illness (IMAI) general principles of chronic care, for example, are focused on equipping first-level health care workers to provide patient-centered health care. Specifically, the guidelines and related training materials prepare health care workers to solicit patients' concerns and preferences, work in collaboration with patients to decide specific goals and treatment plans, and support patients in their daily efforts regarding prevention, medication adherence, and self-management.

Early results indicate that this approach is understandable and usable by first-level health workers. Physicians, nurses, and lay providers have been trained in Burkina Faso, Burundi, Ethiopia, Sudan, and Uganda. In Shanghai, China, a community-based chronic disease

Table 6-16	Elements of Effective Care for Chronic Conditions
Typical Current Approach	**Desired Future Approach**
Disease centered	Patient centered
Specialty care/ hospital based	Primary health care based
Individual patients: focus of concern	Population needs: focus of concern
Reactive, symptom driven	Proactive, planned
Treatment focused	Prevention focused

self-management program has been shown to improve health status and reduce hospitalizations among patients with hypertension, heart disease, chronic lung disease, arthritis, stroke, and diabetes. Participants learn to take responsibility for the day-to-day management of their disease(s) and the physical and emotional problems caused by their disease(s). The program is led by lay people with chronic conditions, who follow a detailed leader's manual throughout the program (Fu et al., 2003).

Primary Health Care Based. In developing countries, patients with chronic conditions present and need to be managed mainly at the primary health care level. This represents a shift from health care systems that are driven by tertiary care, specialty settings. Oman has successfully made the shift to a decentralized primary health care system, in which health programs and activities are coordinated with the regional health services via referrals and linkages (WHO, 2002e). Similarly, the health policy of the Islamic Republic of Iran is based on primary health care, with particular emphasis on the expansion of health networks and programs in rural areas.

Population Based. Health care for chronic conditions is most effective when policies, plans, and practices prioritize the health of a defined population rather than the single unit of a patient seeking care. A population focus implies that health care systems assess and monitor the health of communities, emphasize prevention and promote healthy behavior, assure universal access to appropriate and cost-effective services, and contribute to the evidence base for effective treatments and systems of care.

Cuba's family doctor program is an application of population-based care. Each family doctor is responsible for the general health of the entire population in a small, defined area. They are expected to provide preventive, maternal, and curative services to children and adults, and to monitor all patients with chronic conditions. They live in the communities that they serve, often sharing the same apartment block as their patients. In addition to medical consultations, Cuba's family doctors play an active role in promoting health among the communities they serve. They provide informal advice and counseling to community members, and they run regular prevention and self-management groups concerning a range of issues. They are also expected to set a positive example for their patients in the conduct of their day-to-day lives (Warman, 2001).

Proactive. Proactive care anticipates patients' needs rather than relying on a patient-initiated, often acute care–focused interaction. In rural South Africa,

a proactive noncommunicable disease management program for hypertension, diabetes, asthma, and epilepsy was established within primary health care. The program emphasized planned care: Clinic-held treatment cards and registries were introduced, and diagnostic and management protocols were followed, which included regular, planned follow-up with a clinic nurse. Using this proactive care approach, nurses were able to achieve good disease control among most of the patient population: 68% of patients with hypertension, 82% of those with diabetes, and 84% of those with asthma (Coleman, Gill, & Wilkinson, 1998).

A Model of Care: Innovative Care for Chronic Conditions

A model based on these approaches has been developed by the World Health Organization. The Innovative Care for Chronic Conditions (ICCC) framework provides a road map for decision makers who want to improve their health system's capacity to manage chronic conditions (WHO, 2002b) (Figure 6-12). This framework is composed of fundamental components within the levels of patient interactions, organization of health care, community, and policy. These components are described as building blocks that can be used to help decision makers progressively create or redesign a health care system to expand its capacity to manage long-term health problems. Although the framework does not prescribe specific changes, which must be tailored to unique needs and resources, it highlights the need for comprehensive system design or change in the requirements for effective care.

Comprehensive Care Applied to Clinical Prevention

The preponderance of the evidence suggests that effective health care strategies for reducing risk do exist, but tend to be weakly implemented (Coffield et al., 2001). Many professional competencies for delivering effective clinical prevention are outside the scope and culture of clinical medicine, so health care professionals frequently have little or no training in the skills required to improve care (Glasgow, Orleans, & Wagner, 2001).

Many opportunities for better integration of the treatment of chronic diseases and the prevention of risk factor behaviors remain largely untapped. For example, stronger support for smoking cessation among TB patients would save lives in the long term, and smoking cessation among patients with CHD is the single most effective intervention for reducing mortality in patients with CHD who smoke. With a

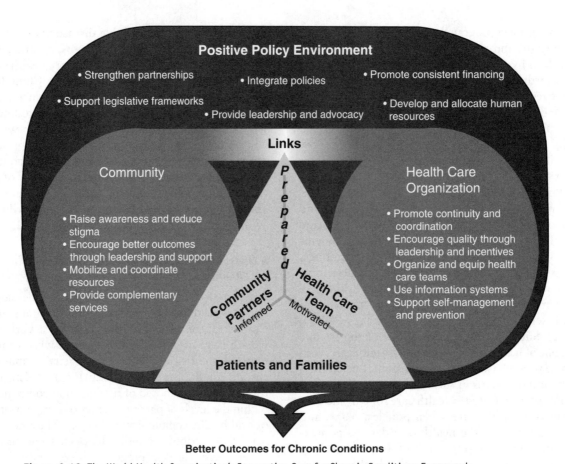

Figure 6-12 The World Health Organization's Innovative Care for Chronic Conditions Framework.

36% reduction in the relative risk of mortality among CHD patients who quit, smoking is at least as important as other secondary prevention measures such as statins (a 29% reduction), aspirin (15%), beta-blockers (23%), or ACE inhibitors (23%) (Critchley & Capewell, 2003). Smoking cessation is also a priority for people with mental disorders. In one of the major studies on comorbidity between tobacco use and depression, researchers found that people with mental disorders are almost twice as likely to smoke as other persons. Further, they found that people with a mental disorder had consumed about 44.3% of all cigarettes smoked by a nationally representative sample in the previous days (Lasser et al., 2000).

Another challenge is that effective clinical prevention services must extend beyond the mere provision of information to patients. The era of exhortation by health care professionals to "eat better" or "drop some weight" is long passed: Modern, evidence-based interventions emphasize shared decision making and collaborative goal setting among providers and pa-

tients (Serdula, Khan, & Dietz, 2003). The clearer and more personalized the goal, the better (Estabrooks, Glasgow, & Dzewaltowski, 2003). Skill building to overcome barriers, self-monitoring, personalized feedback, and systematic links to community resources such as peer support groups are other important elements for success (Steptoe et al., 2003). Many health care settings deliver these kinds of interventions in group formats, which enhances the efficiency of health care professionals and provides the added element of social support (Noel & Pugh, 2002).

Comprehensive Care Applied to Adherence

The ICCC framework recognizes the importance of treatment adherence as a primary determinant of the effectiveness of treatment. Good adherence confers both health and economic benefits. Adherence has been associated with improved blood pressure control (Luscher, 1985) and lessened complications of hypertension (Morisky et al., 1983; Psaty et al., 1990). Despite the clear importance of treatment adherence, a number of rigorous reviews have found that in developed countries, adherence among patients with chronic diseases averages only 50%; it is even lower in developing countries. In Gambia, China, and the United States, only 27%, 43%, and 51%, respectively, of patients adhere to their medication regimen for high blood pressure. Similar patterns have been reported for other conditions, such as depression (40% to 70%), asthma (43% for acute treatments and 28% for maintenance), and HIV/AIDS (37% to 83%) (WHO, 2003e).

Adherence is a complex behavioral process that is influenced by five interacting dimensions: social and economic factors, health care system factors, condition-related factors, therapy-related factors, and patient-related factors. Each dimension plays an important role in determining adherence rates (WHO, 2003e). All dimensions should be considered when designing interventions to improve outcomes. The most effective interventions have been shown to be multilevel, targeting more than one factor with more than one intervention (Dickinson, Wilkie, & Harris, 1999).

Contemporary perspectives have pointed out the importance of conceptualizing adherence as the active, voluntary involvement of the patient in the management of his or her disease, including a mutually agreed-upon course of treatment and sharing of responsibility between the patient and health care providers (Flood & Chiang, 2001). In this regard, adherence is an active, responsible, and flexible process of self-management, in which the person strives to achieve good health by working in close collaboration with health care staff instead of simply following rigidly prescribed rules.

Summary of Effective Health Care

Reviews of interventions to improve health care for chronic conditions have demonstrated the importance of using multifaceted approaches as opposed to magic-bullet or single-lever interventions (Grimshaw et al., 2001; Renders et al., 2002; Wagner et al., 2001). Models of integrated, coordinated care, such as the ICCC framework, capture this complexity in an organized way.

Several key concepts have emerged from the evidence. First, it is necessary to work across multiple levels in a coordinated fashion to effect meaningful change in health care for chronic diseases. Second, organized systems of care, not just individual health care workers, are essential in producing positive outcomes for chronic disease. Third, it is crucial to work across the disease continuum in a comprehensive way. Comprehensive care for chronic conditions must span from clinical prevention to treatment, rehabilitation, and palliation.

The Role of National Governments

Primary prevention and health promotion requires a careful balance between individual, family, and community responsibility; government regulations and policies; and multisectoral actions by government, industry, and civil society (Yach, 2005).

A key role for government is to embrace strategies that reduce exposure to risk factors and attempt to influence individual behavior (Leeder et al., 2004). There are a range of scales at which the government can operate to influence the degree of risk exposure, conceptualized by the WHO as a stepwise approach to chronic disease control (Table 6-17). Examples include population-based cross-sectoral interventions, fiscal policies, and regulations on the information provided to consumers. There are a few documented examples of how effective such approaches can be when governments provide leadership over a sustained period of time. Some are described in the following subsections.

Comprehensive Community-Based Programs of Prevention and Health Promotion

Finland provides one such example of success that is applicable to developed and developing countries. Health promotion efforts in Finland began in 1972 in the province of North Karelia, where rates of heart disease were double that of the rest of the country, at a time when Finland was not the wealthy country it is now. Taking a population-wide approach, the North Karelia project encouraged change across sectors: diversification of agriculture away from meat and dairy; encouragement of individual lifestyle shifts to better diets, more exercise, and less smoking; and training of medical professionals to increase monitoring of blood pressure. The program was expanded to the rest of Finland in 1977. Although cholesterol-lowering drugs may also have played a role, in the past 30 years deaths from heart disease and deaths from lung cancer in North Karelia have fallen by around 70% each. Male life expectancy has increased, as has per capita vegetable consumption. Under the auspices of WHO, pilot projects based on North Karelia have been developed in regions of China and in Chile, Iran, and Oman.

Governments have been successful in introducing some elements of the comprehensive approach as well. Raising the tobacco excise tax can reduce consumption effectively, increase government revenue, and reduce the burden of disease (de Beyer & Brigden, 2003; Guindon, Tobin, & Yach, 2002). A precedent has been set by Thailand, which has identified health promotion as a priority area to reduce the incidence of chronic

Table 6-17	Stepwise Policy and Program Targets for National Prevention and Control of Chronic Diseases		
	Population Approaches		
Resource Level	National Level	Community Level	Individual High-Risk Approaches
Step 1: Core	WHO Framework Convention on Tobacco Control (FCTC) is ratified in every country. Tobacco control legislation consistent with the elements of the FCTC is enacted and enforced. A national nutrition and physical activity policy consistent with the global strategy is developed and endorsed at the cabinet level, including laws. Health impact assessment of public policy is carried out; priority areas: transport, urban planning, taxation, trade, and agriculture	Local infrastructure plans include the provisions and maintenance of accessible and safe sites for physical activity (such as parks and pedestrian-only areas). Health-promoting community projects include participatory actions to cope with the environmental factors that predispose to risk of chronic diseases: inactivity, unhealthy diet, and tobacco and alcohol use. Active health promotion programs focusing on chronic diseases are implemented in different settings—villages, schools, and workplaces—and explicitly aim to reach poor communities.	Context-specific guidelines for chronic disease prevention and control have been adopted and are used at all health care levels. A sustainable, accessible, and affordable supply of appropriate medication is assured for priority chronic diseases. A system exists for the consistent, high-quality application of clinical guidelines and for the clinical audit of services offered. A proactive follow-up system for patients with diabetes and hypertension is in operation.
Step 2: Expanded	Tobacco legislation provides for incremental increases in tax on tobacco, and a proportion of the revenue is earmarked for health promotion. Food standards legislation is enacted and enforced, including nutrition labeling. Sustained, well-designed, national programs (counteradvertising) are in place to promote nonsmoking lifestyles, fruits and vegetables, and physical activity. Country standards are established that regulate marketing of unhealthy food to children.	Sustained, well-designed programs are in place to promote tobacco-free lifestyles (e.g., smoke-free public places, smoke-free sports), healthy diets (e.g., low-cost, low-fat foods, fresh fruit and vegetables); and physical activity (e.g., "movement") in different domains (occupational and leisure).	Systems are in place for selective and targeted prevention aimed at high-risk populations, based on absolute levels of risk. Publicly financed quit-line for smokers; weight control line.
Step 3: Optimal	Policies shown to work for chronic disease prevention and control are implemented Policy coherence is achieved between agricultural systems and chronic diseases. Country standards are established that regulate marketing of unhealthy food to children.	Recreational and fitness centers are available for community use.	Opportunistic screening, case finding, and management programs are implemented. Self-management groups are fostered for tobacco cessation and overweight reduction. Appropriate diagnostic and therapeutic interventions are implemented.

Source: World Health Organization, *World Health Report, 2003* (Geneva, Switzerland: World Health Organization, 2003). Adapted with permission.

disease (WHO Thailand, 2000). The Thai government set up the Thai Health Promotion Foundation (ThaiHealth) in April 2001, sustained by a dedicated 2% surcharge tax on alcohol and tobacco products. Although inevitably prone to shifts in the tax regime, the funding provides a relatively sustainable source of revenue.

The power of advocacy supported by government and executed by NGOs is demonstrated by the work of Heartfile in Pakistan (Nishtar, 2003). Created to focus on CVD prevention and health promotion, Heartfile's tactics for targeting cardiovascular disease have been wide-ranging. Community intervention programs have been composed of print and electronic media campaigns and other public health promotion campaigns carried out in various aspects of the community, such as restaurants. Other activities have been directed at the reorientation of health services, research, and advocacy to highlight CVD in the government agenda. Heartfile has been successful in establishing strong and effective links at regional, national, and international levels, paving the way for private-sector-based initiatives, collaboration with health service providers, and more effective dissemination of information in the future. In more countries—and globally—strong and broad alliances of major health professional organizations, consumer groups, enlightened businesses and industries, and academic institutions are needed to better prioritize prevention strategies against chronic disease in developing countries.

Specific regulations can control the information environment regarding risk factors. Reducing the marketing of tobacco products is known to reduce consumption (World Bank, 1999). By providing information to consumers, warnings and labels can also affect consumption. Warnings on cigarette packages have been shown to be effective, while for food, evidence from middle- and high-income countries indicates that consumers use nutrition labels to make food choices (Hawkes, 2004b).

Reorient Health Services to Address Chronic Disease

Many lives are lost prematurely because of inadequate treatment and long-term management of chronic diseases, even though simple and inexpensive approaches exist. Even in wealthy countries, the potential of these interventions is not fully utilized. The situation in both poorer countries and poor communities within rich countries is even less satisfactory. In most countries, effective means of preventing, treating, and providing palliative care for cancer exist, but are not implemented. There are many opportunities for coordinated risk reduction, care, and long-term management of chronic disease. For example, smoking cessation is a priority for all patients who smoke; dietary and physical activity information and skill building should be provided to most patients in virtually all health care settings. Few efforts have been made to explicitly target poor communities with such interventions.

Considerable progress has been made in improving access to, and reducing the price of, antiretroviral agents for HIV/AIDS, drugs to treat TB, and several vaccines. Similar progress has yet to be made for essential drugs that are required to improve survival for treatable cancers, diabetes, and CVD. A patient with heart disease in a poor nation has the same right to effective drug treatment as a patient with malaria, tuberculosis, or HIV/AIDS. Nongovernmental organizations have yet to advocate as effectively for better access to chronic disease treatment as they have for selected infectious diseases, despite the huge savings in lives and suffering that would result.

Continued strengthening of certain aspects of infectious disease control, particularly related to chronic infectious diseases such as TB and HIV/AIDS, will benefit the control of CVD, diabetes, and cancer. The same transformation of health care systems is required to address prevention and long-term disease management for both infectious and noninfectious chronic diseases. For sub-Saharan African countries, there is an opportunity to ensure that the new platforms for health service delivery that are being built to expand access to treatment for HIV/AIDS also address noninfectious chronic diseases. The marginal increased investments required would in all likelihood yield substantial gains for public health among poor communities who already suffer from CVD, diabetes, and cancer.

Promote Broader Societal Changes

Many aspects of chronic disease prevention require legislative, financial, and engineering approaches. These aspects, often not under the control of health departments, can complement educational programs. Educational programs have a limited impact, especially among the poor and illiterate. Implementation of the following measures can bring about a disproportionately large positive impact for poor populations: infrastructural changes that promote public transport and physical activity, laws that ban tobacco advertising and smoking in public places, tax policies that raise excise taxes on tobacco, and agricultural policies that provide schools and poor communities with easy, government-funded access to fruits, vegetables, and other food staples.

Acting Globally to Achieve Sustained National Benefits

In an era of globalization, national governments need to act together to address several global threats to health and to maximize the potential benefits that accrue through globalization. Some of these actions that relate specifically to chronic diseases are described here. Further details are contained in Chapter 15.

Redirecting Investment

The tremendous financial inflows into chronic disease risk factors in developing nations have the potential to be reoriented to investments that assist in the prevention of chronic diseases, rather than propel them. Flows of certain goods, technology, marketing, and FDI into weakly regulated markets is undermining healthy public policy. These investments could be shifted from financing associated with promoting behaviors that lead to chronic diseases to products, marketing, and services aligned with public health goals. This is essentially a process of making markets work for chronic disease prevention. For example, businesses could make core business investments that are positive for health, encouraged by conditionalities placed on investment in risk-creating products. It is in government and company self-interest to channel financial resources to reduce chronic diseases. Equity research is already showing it is in the tobacco and food industry's interest to invest in healthier products and more responsible marketing (see Table 6-11).

Implementing Global Norms and Standards

Global norms and standards have an important role to play in the prevention of chronic diseases. Many developing countries lack the basic human resources to develop and implement laws and regulations, as well as the tax policies that are so important to many aspects of chronic disease control. For them, international support is often the spur to national action, and global norms provide the umbrella of legitimacy that they need to develop and implement national laws. There is also an increasing need to establish global norms in a wide range of spheres that affect transnational influences on chronic diseases—from marketing and trade to human resource flows. Such norms can balance the otherwise unrestrained influences of powerful actors and can assist countries that have limited national public health and regulatory ability. To do so, public health capacities in trade and political science must be strengthened so as to (1) effectively participate in the World Trade Organization, where health issues are in-creasingly considered, and (2) develop stronger norms that could be used as the basis for resolving trade disputes concerning products associated with adverse health impacts.

The FCTC is one example of a global norm that can protect developing countries from industry pressures as they introduce effective tobacco control. The FCTC is the first time WHO used its treaty-making right to advance public health goals. The FCTC was adopted by all the countries in the world (all 192 WHO member states) in May 2003. The pioneering convention aims to protect health and save the lives of billions in present and future generations through tobacco advertising bans, larger health warning labels on tobacco products, measures to protect against secondhand smoke, tobacco tax and price increases, and efforts to eliminate illicit trade (see Table 6-14). Other norms that are important for noncommunicable disease control include the International Code of Marketing of Breast-milk Substitutes and the Codex Alimentarius Commission (with its likely increased focus on food labeling and health claims).

Treaties are probably not the solution to the complex issues related to nutrition transition or physical inactivity. At the global level, combinations of multistakeholder and intergovernmental codes are better options to pursue, especially in relation to restricting the marketing of alcohol and foods to young children. Such approaches are already being used in many ways in many developing countries to improve labor conditions, environmental quality, and protection of human rights. These approaches are cheaper and quicker to implement than traditional legislative approaches, but require strong independent oversight to ensure they have the desired impact.

Globalization of Civil Society

NGOs have a set of potentially critical abilities: to unite both developed and developing country interests in the face of common threats over a wide geographic range, to build national capacity, to channel individual concern into productive societal change, and to place on the ground "connectors" who can implement policy and technical advice provided by national and international authorities. Another characteristic of NGOs is that their advocacy activities calling for government action can somewhat offset the argument that a government is a "nanny state" if it institutes regulations designed to facilitate pro-health choices (Leeder et al., 2004). A global network of all different categories of NGOs, all committed to chronic disease prevention and control, could lobby governments and WHO and would be a useful force for global and national advocacy, enhance national capacity, and have a wide geographic reach.

Several elements of such a network already exist. The International Union Against Cancer (UICC) hosts Globalink, an Internet-based network of over 4,000 tobacco advocates and policy makers who together have moved the FCTC process ahead, and influenced many national and local initiatives in tobacco control by combining forces across the world. ProCOR, an e-mail and Internet-based service for chronic disease researchers and policy makers in developing countries, provides practical and essential educational material to people involved in policy and program development (Lown, 2004).

● ● ● **Discussion Questions**

1. Given current trends, what are likely to be the major causes of death and disability in low- and middle-income countries in the 2020s?

2. What policies and actions taken over the next decade at national and international levels could influence these trends?

3. What are the major impediments to introducing these policies and actions?

4. Outline major gaps in knowledge and research that hamper progress in chronic disease control in developing countries.

5. Describe how globalization could be positively harnessed for chronic disease prevention. In doing so, consider how multinational companies could play a more effective role in health promotion.

• • • References

Aboderin, I., Kalache, A., Ben-Shlomo, Y., Lynch, J. W., Yajnik, C. D., Kuh, D., & Yach, D. (2001). *Life course perspectives on coronary heart disease, stroke and diabetes: Key issues and implications for policy and research*. Geneva, Switzerland: World Health Organization.

Ait-Khaled, N., Enarson, D., & Bousquet, J. (2001). Chronic respiratory diseases in developing countries: The burden and strategies for prevention and management. *Bulletin of the World Health Organization, 79*(10), 971–979.

Alwan, A., Maclean, D., & Mandil, A. (2001). *Assessment of national capacity for noncommunicable disease prevention and control*. Geneva, Switzerland: World Health Organization.

American Diabetes Association. (1998). Economic consequences of diabetes mellitus in the U.S. in 1997. *Diabetes Care, 21*, 296–309.

American Diabetes Association. (2003). Economic consequences of diabetes mellitus in the U.S. in 2002. *Diabetes Care, 26*, 917–932.

Aspray, T. J., Mugusi, F., Rashid, S., Whiting, D., Edwards, R., Alberti, K. G., & Unwin, N. C. (2000). Essential Non-Communicable Disease Health Intervention Project. Rural and urban differences in diabetes prevalence in Tanzania: The role of obesity, physical inactivity and urban living. *Transactions of the Royal Society of Tropical Medicine and Hygiene, 94*(6), 637–644.

Babor, T., Caetano, R., Casswell, S., Edwards, G., Giesbrecht, N., Graham, K., Grube, J., Grunewald, P., Hill, L., Holder, H., Homel, R., Osterberg, E., Rehm, J., Room, R., & Rossow, I. (2003). *Alcohol: No ordinary commodity*. Oxford, England: Oxford University Press.

Barceló, A., Aedo, C., Rajpathak, S., & Robles, S. (2003). The cost of diabetes in Latin America and the Caribbean. *Bulletin of the World Health Organization, 81*(1), 19–27.

Batty, G. D., & Leon, D. A. (2002). Socio-economic position and coronary heart disease risk factors in children and young people. *European Journal of Public Health, 12*, 263–272.

Beaglehole, R., & Yach, D. (2003). Globalisation and the prevention and control of noncommunicable disease: The neglected chronic diseases of adults. *Lancet, 362*, 903–908.

Beattie, A., Kalk, W. J., Price, M., Rispel, L., Broomberg, J., & Cabral, J. (1998). The management of diabetes at primary level in South Africa: The results of a facility-based assessment. *Journal of the Royal Society of Health, 118*(6), 338–345.

Bell, A. C., Adair, A. S., & Popkin, B. M. (2004). Understanding the role of mediating risk factors and proxy effects in the association between socio-economic status and untreated hypertension. *Social Science and Medicine, 59*, 275–283.

Bourne, L. T., Lambert, E. V., & Steyn, K. (2002). Where does the black population of South Africa stand on nutrition transition? *Public Health Nutrition, 5*(1A), 157–162.

Bradshaw, D., Groenewald, P., Laubscher, R., Nannan, N., Nojilana, B., Norman, R., Pieterse, D., Schneider, M., Bourne, D., Timaeus, I. M., Dorrington, R. E., & Johnson, L. (2003). Initial burden of disease estimates for South Africa, 2000. *South African Medical Journal, 93*(9), 682–688.

Brands, A., & Yach, D. (2001). *Noncommunicable diseases and gender*. Geneva, Switzerland: World Health Organization.

Brownell, K. D., & Hagen, K. B. (2004). *Food fight: The inside story of the food industry. America's obesity crisis, and what we can do about it*. Chicago: Contemporary Books.

Bumgarner, J. R. (2004). China: Non-communicable disease issues and options revisited. *Oxford Vision 2020*.

Canto, J. G., & Iskandrian, A. E. (2003). Major risk factors for cardiovascular disease. Debunking the "only 50%" myth. *Journal of the American Medical Association, 290*, 947–949.

Cappuccio, F. P., Plange-Rhule, J., Phillips, R. O., & Eastwood, J. B. (2000). Prevention of hypertension and stroke in Africa. *Lancet, 356*, 677–678.

Chale, S. S., Swai, A. B., Mujinja, P. G., & McLarty, D. G. (1992). Must diabetes be a fatal disease in Africa? Study of costs of treatment. *British Medical Journal, 304,* 1215–1218.

Chew, F. T., Goh, D. Y., & Lee, B. W. (1999). The economic cost of asthma in Singapore. *Australian and New Zealand Journal of Medicine, 29*(2), 228–233.

Chinese Center for Disease Control and Prevention, cited in Xinhua News Agency. (2004, January 24). Unhealthy lifestyles cause disease among one third of Beijing residents.

Clark, G. L., & Hebb, T. (2002). *Understanding pension fund corporate engagement in a global arena.* Paper prepared for the seminar Understanding Pension Fund Corporate Engagement in a Global Arena, November 24–26, Oxford University, England.

Coffield, A. B., Maciosek, M. V., McGinnis, J. M., Harris, J. R., Caldwell, M. B., Teutsch, S. M., Atkins, D., Richland, J. H., & Haddix, A. (2001). Priorities among recommended clinical preventive services. *American Journal of Preventive Medicine, 21*(1), 1–9.

Cohen, B. (2004). Urban growth in developing countries: A review of current trends and a caution regarding existing forecasts. *World Development, 32*(1), 23–51.

Coleman, R., Gill, G., & Wilkinson, D. (1998). Noncommunicable disease management in resource-poor settings: A primary care model from rural South Africa. *Bulletin of the World Health Organization, 76*(6), 633–640.

Critchley, J., & Capewell, S. (2003). Mortality risk reduction associated with smoking cessation in patients with coronary heart diseases: A systematic review. *Journal of the American Medical Association, 290,* 86–97.

Datamonitor. (2002). *Childhood obesity 2002: How obesity is shaping the U.S. food and beverage markets.* New York, Datamonitor.

de Beyer, J., & Brigden, L. W. (2003). *Tobacco control policy: Strategies, successes and setbacks.* Washington, DC: World Bank/Research for International Tobacco Control.

de Onis, M., Blossner, M., Borghi, E., Frangillo, E. A., & Morris, R. (2004). Estimates of global prevalence of childhood underweight in 1995 and 2015. *Journal of the American Medical Association, 291*(21), 2600–2606.

Dickinson, D., Wilkie, P., & Harris, M. (1999). Taking medicines: Concordance is not compliance. *British Medical Journal, 319*(7212), 787.

Doll, R., Peto, R., Boreham, J., & Sunderland, I. (2004). Mortality in relation to smoking: 50 years' observations of male British doctors. *British Medical Journal, 328,* 1519–1528.

Doyle, J., Waters, E., Yach, D., McQueen, D., De Francisco, A., Stewart, T., Reddy, P., Gulmezoglu, A. M., Galea, G., & Portela, A. (2005). Global priority setting for Cochrane systematic reviews of health promotion and public health research. *Journal of Epidemiology and Community Health, 59,* 193–197.

Du, S., Lu, B., Zhai, F., & Popkin, B. M. (2002). A new stage of the nutrition transition in China. *Public Health Nutrition, 5*(1A), 169–174.

Duncan, B. D., Schmidt, M. I., Achutti, A. C., Polanczyk, C. A., Benia, L. R., & Maia, A. A. (1993). Socioeconomic distribution of noncommunicable disease risk factors in urban Brazil: The case of Pôrto Alegre. *Bulletin of the Pan American Health Organization, 27*(4), 337–349.

Economic and Social Council. (2004). *Ad hoc interagency task force on tobacco control: Report of the Secretary-General* (E/2004/55). New York: United Nations.

Ehrlich, R. I., White, N., Norman, R., Laubscher, R., Steyn, K., Lombard, C., & Bradshaw, D. (2004). Predictors of chronic bronchitis in South African adults. *International Journal of Tuberculosis and Lung Disease, 8*(3), 369–376.

Estabrooks, P. A., Glasgow, R. E., & Dzewaltowski, D. A. (2003). Physical activity promotion through primary care. *Journal of the American Medical Association, 289*(22), 2913.

Finkelstein, E. A., Fiebelkorn, I. C., & Wang, G. (2003). National medical spending attributable to overweight and obesity: How much, and who's paying? *Health Affairs*, W3-219–W3-226.

Finkelstein, E. A., Fiebelkorn, I. C., & Wang, G. (2004). State-level estimates of annual medical expenditures attributable to obesity. *Obesity Research*, 12(1), 18–24.

Flood, R. G., & Chiang, V. W. (2001). Rate and prediction of infection in children with diabetic ketoacidosis. *American Journal of Emergency Medicine 19*, 270–273.

Foliaki, S., & Pearce, N. (2003). Prevention and control of diabetes in Pacific people. *British Medical Journal, 327*, 437–439.

Frenk, J., Bobdilla, J. L., Sepulveda, J., & Cervantes, L. M. (1989). Health transition in middle income countries: New challenges for health care. *Health Policy and Planning, 4*(1), 29–39.

Fries, J. F. (1980). Ageing, natural death, and the compression of morbidity. *New England Journal of Medicine, 303*, 130–135.

Fries, J. F. (2003). Measuring and monitoring success in compressing morbidity. *Annals of Internal Medicine, 139*, 455–459.

Fu, D., Fu, H., McGowan, P., Shen, Y., Zhu, L., Yang, H., Mao, J., Zhu, S., Ding, Y., & Wei, Z. (2003). Implementation and quantitative evaluation of chronic disease self-management programme in Shanghai, China: Randomized controlled trial. *Bulletin of the World Health Organization, 81*(3), 174–182.

Gajalakshmi, V., Peto, R., Kanaka, T. S., & Jha, P. (2003). Smoking and mortality from tuberculosis and other diseases in India. *Lancet, 362*, 507–515.

Glasgow, R. E., Goldstein, M. G., Ockene, J. K., & Pronk, N. P. (2004). Translating what we have learned into practice: Principles and hypotheses for addressing multiple behaviors in primary care. *American Journal of Preventive Medicine, 27* (2 Suppl.), 88–101.

Glasgow, R. E., Orleans, C. T., & Wagner, E. H. (2001). Does the chronic care model serve also as a template for improving prevention? *Milbank Quarterly, 79*(4), 579–612.

Global Youth Tobacco Survey Collaborating Group. (2003). Differences in worldwide tobacco use by gender: Findings from the Global Youth Tobacco Survey. *Journal of School Health, 73*, 207–215.

Goetzel, R. Z., Hawkins, K., Ozminkowski, R. J., & Wang, S. (2003). The health and productivity cost burden of the "top 10" physical and mental health conditions affecting six large US employers in 1999. *Journal of Occupational and Environmental Medicine, 45*, 5–14.

Goldin, J. G., Louw, S. J. & Joubert, G. Spirometry of healthy adult South African men. Part I. Interrelationship between socio-environmental factors and 'race' as determinant of spirometry. *South African Medical Journal, 86*(7), 820–826.

Grimshaw, J. M., Shirran, L., Thomas, R., Mowatt, G., Fraser, C., Bero, L., Grilli R., Harvey, E., Oxman, A., & O'Brien, M. A. (2001). Changing provider behavior: An overview of systematic reviews of interventions. *Medical Care, 39*, 112–145.

Gu, D., Reynolds, K., Duan, X., Xin, X., et al. (2003). Prevalence of diabetes and impaired fasting glucose in the Chinese adult population: International Collaborative Study of Cardiovascular Disease in Asia (InterASIA). *Diabetologia, 46*(9), 1190–1198.

Guindon, G. E., Tobin, S., & Yach, D. (2002). Trends and affordability of cigarette prices: Ample room for tax increases and related health gains. *Tobacco Control, 11*, 35–43.

Gulliford, M. C., Alert, C. V., Mahabir, D., Ariyanayagam-Baksh, S. M., Fraser, H. S., & Picou, D. I. (1996). Diabetes care in middle-income countries: A Caribbean case study. *Diabetic Medicine, 13*(6), 574–581.

Hawkes, C. (2004a). *Marketing food to children: The global regulatory environment*. Geneva, Switzerland: World Health Organization.

Hawkes, C. (2004b). *Nutrition labels and health claims: The global regulatory environment*. Geneva, Switzerland: World Health Organization.

Heller, P. S. (2003). *Who will pay? Coping with aging societies, climate change, and other long-term fiscal challenges.* Washington, DC: International Monetary Fund.

InterASIA Collaborative Group. (2003). Cardiovascular risk factors levels in urban and rural Thailand: The International Collaborative Study of Cardiovascular Diseases in Asia (InterASIA). *European Journal of Cardiovascular Prevention and Rehabilitation, 10*(4), 249–257.

International Agency for Research on Cancer. (2003). *World cancer report.* Lyon, France: IARC Press.

International Diabetes Federation. (2003). *Diabetes atlas* (2nd ed.). Brussels: International Diabetes Federation.

Jha, P., & Chaloupka, F. J. (Eds.). (2000). *Tobacco control in developing countries.* New York: Oxford University Press.

JP Morgan. (2004, July 26). *The path to a safer cigarette. Global equity research.* New York: JP Morgan.

Kiivet, R. A., Kaur, I., Lang, A., Aaviksoo, A., & Nirk, L. (2001). Costs of asthma treatment in Estonia. *European Journal of Public Health, 11*(1), 89–92.

Kim, S., Symons, M., & Popkin, B. M. (2004). Contrasting socioeconomic profiles related to healthier lifestyles in China and the United States. *American Journal of Epidemiology, 159*(2), 184–191.

Kimmis, J., Gottchalk, R., Armendariz, E., & Griffith-Jones, S. (2002). *Making the case for UK pension fund investment in developing country assets.* Unpublished manuscript, Institute for Development Studies, University of Sussex, Brighton, England.

Knuiman, J. T., Hermus, R. J. J., & Hautvast, J. G. A. J. (1980). Serum total and high-density lipoprotein (HDL) cholesterol concentrations in rural and urban boys from 16 countries. *Atherosclerosis, 36,* 529–537.

Kogevinas, M., Pearce, N., Susser, M., & Boffetta, P. (Eds.). (1997). *Social inequalities and cancer* (IARC Scientific Publications No. 138). Lyon, France: IARC.

Kuchler, F., & Ballenger, N. (2002). Societal costs of obesity: How can we assess when federal interventions will pay? *Food Review, 25*(3), 33–37.

Langlois, A., Adam, V., & Powell, A. (2003). *Food manufacturing. Obesity: The big issue.* London: JP Morgan European Equity Research.

Lasser, K., Boyd, J. W., Woolhandler, S., Himmelstein, D. U., McCormick, D., & Bor, D. H. (2000). Smoking and mental health: A population-based prevalence study. *Journal of the American Medical Association, 284,* 2606–2610.

Leeder, S., Raymond, S., Greenberg, H., Liu, H., & Esson, K. (2004). *A race against time: The challenge of cardiovascular disease in developing economies.* New York: Columbia University.

Levitt, N. S., Steyn, K., de Wet, T., Morrell, C., Edwards, R., Ellison, G. T. H., & Cameron, N. (1999). An inverse relationship between blood pressure and birth weight among 5 year old children from Soweto, South Africa. *Journal of Epidemiology and Community Health, 53,* 264–268.

Liu, J. L. Y., Maniadakis, N., Gray, A., & Rayner, M. (2002). The economic burden of coronary heart disease in the UK. *Heart, 88,* 597–603.

LMC International. (2004, May). *Implications of the WHO/FAO expert consultative report on the sugar market.* Unpublished manuscript, LMC International, London.

Lobstein, T., Baur, L., & Uauy, R. (2004). Obesity in children and young people: A crisis in public health. *Obesity Reviews, 5*(Suppl. 1), 4–85.

Lown, B. (2004, June 16). *A cardiologist's perspective on the crisis and challenges of biotechnology.* Plenary address to the fifth International Heart Health Conference, Milan, Italy.

Lubitz, J., Cai, L., Kamarow, E., & Lentzner, H. (2003). Health, life expectancy, and health care spending among the elderly. *New England Journal of Medicine, 349*(11), 1048–1055.

Luo, J., & Hu, F. B. (2002). Time trends of obesity in pre-school children in China from 1989 to 1997. *International Journal of Obesity, 26*(4), 553–558.

Luscher, T. F., Vetter, H., Sigenthaler, W., & Vetter, W. (1985). Compliance in hypertension: Facts and concepts. *Journal of Hypertension, 3,* 3–9.

Mackay, J., & Eriksen, M. (2002). *The tobacco atlas.* Geneva, Switzerland: World Health Organization.

Mackenbach, J. P., Cavelaars, A. E. J. M., Kunst, A. E., et al. (2000). Socio-economic inequalities in cardiovascular disease mortality. An international study. *European Heart Journal, 21,* 1141–1151.

Marmot, M. G., Adelstein, A. M., Robinson, N., & Rose, G. A. (1978). Changing social-class distribution of heart disease. *British Medical Journal, 2*(6145), 1109–1112.

McGinnis, J. M., Williams-Russo, P., & Knickman, J. R. (2002). The case for more active policy attention to health promotion. *Health Affairs, 21*(2), 78–93.

McKeown, T. (1988). *The origins of human disease.* Oxford, England: Basil Blackwell.

Mendez, M. A, Cooper, R. S., Luke, A., Wilks, R., Bennett, F., & Forrester, T. (2004). Higher income is more strongly associated with obesity than with obesity-related metabolic disorders in Jamaican adults. *International Journal of Obesity, 28*(4), 543–550.

Minh, H. V., Byass, P., & Wall, S. (2003). Mortality from cardiovascular diseases in Bavi District, Vietnam. *Scandinavian Journal of Public Health, S62,* 26–31.

Misra, A., Pandey, R. M., Devi, J. R., Sharma, R., Vikram, N. K., & Khanna, N. (2001). High prevalence of diabetes, obesity and dyslipidaemia in urban slum populations in northern India. *International Journal of Obesity, 25,* 1–8.

Monteiro, C. A., Conde, W. L., Lu, B., & Popkin, B. M. (2004, June 22). Obesity and health inequities in the developing world [Advance online version]. *International Journal of Obesity,* 1–6.

Morisky, D. E., Levine, D. M., Green, L. W., Shapiro, S., Russell, R. P., & Smith, C. R. (1983). Five year blood pressure control and mortality following health education for hypertensive patients. *American Journal of Public Health, 73,* 153–162.

Murray, J. L., Lauer, J. A., Hutaberry, R. C. W., Niessen, L., Tamijuma, N., Rodgen, A., Lawes, C. M. M., & Evans, D. B. (2003). Effectiveness and costs of interventions to lower systolic blood pressure and cholesterol: A global and regional analysis on reduction of cardiovascular disease rate. *Lancet, 361,* 717–725.

Myrdal, G. (1952). *Economic aspects of health.* Address to the World Health Assembly, World Health Organization, Geneva, Switzerland.

Nchinda, T. C. (2002). Research capacity strengthening in the South. *Social Science and Medicine, 54,* 1699–1711.

Nishtar, S. (2003). Cardiovascular disease prevention in low resource settings: Lessons from the Heartfile experience in Pakistan. *Ethnicity and Disease, 13*(2 Suppl. 2), 138–147.

Nissinen, A., Bothig, S., Granroth, H., & Lopez, A. D. (1988). Hypertension in developing countries. *World Health Statistics Quarterly, 41,* 141–154.

Noel, P. H., & Pugh, J. A. (2002). Management of overweight and obese adults. *British Medical Journal, 325*(7367), 757–761.

Norlund, A., Apelqvist, J., Bitzen, P. O., Nyberg, P., & Schersten, B. (2001). Cost of illness of adult diabetes mellitus underestimated if comorbidity is not considered. *Journal of Internal Medicine, 250,* 57–65.

Omran, A. R. (1971). The epidemiologic transition. A theory of the epidemiology of population change. *Milbank Memorial Fund Quarterly, 49,* 509–538.

Peña, M., & Bacallao, J. (2000). Obesity among the poor: An emerging problem in Latin America and the Caribbean. In M. Peña & J. Bacallao (Eds.), *Obesity and poverty: A new public health challenge* (Scientific Publication No. 576). Washington, DC: Pan American Health Organization.

Popkin, B. M. (1999). Urbanization, lifestyle changes and the nutrition transition. *World Development, 27*(11), 1905–1916.

Popkin, B. M., & Doak, C. M. (1998). The obesity epidemic is a worldwide phenomenon. *Nutrition Reviews, 56*(4), 106–114.

Popkin, B. M., Horton, S., Kim, S., Mahal, A., & Shuigao, J. (2001). Trends in diet, nutritional status and diet-related noncommunicable diseases in China and India: The economic costs of nutrition transition. *Nutrition Reviews, 59,* 379–390.

Poulter, N., Khaw, K. T., Hopwood, B. E., Mugambi, M., Peart, W. S., Rose, G., & Sever, P. S. (1990). The Kenyan Luo migration study: Observations on the initation of a rise in blood pressure. *British Medical Journal, 300,* 967–972.

Poulter, N., Khaw, K. T., Hopwood, B. E., Mugambi, M., Peart, W. S., & Sever, P. S. (1985). Determinants of blood pressure changes due to urbanization: A longitudinal study. *Journal of Hypertension, 3*(Suppl.), S375–377.

Psaty, B. M., Koepsell, T. D., Wagner, E. H., Lo Gerfo, J. P., & Inui, T. S. (1990). The relative risk of incident coronary heart diseases associated with recently stopping the use of β-blockers. *Journal of the American Medical Association, 73,* 1653–1657.

Raheja, B. S., Kapur, A., Bhoraskar, A., Sathe, S. R., Jorgensen, L. N., Moorthi, S. R., Pendsey, S., & Sahay, B. K. (2001). DiabCare Asia—India Study: Diabetes care in India—current status. *Journal of the Association of Physicians of India, 49,* 717–722.

Ramachandran, A., Snehalatha, C., Vijay, V., & King, H. (2002). Impact of poverty on the prevalence of diabetes and its complications in urban southern India. *Diabetic Medicine, 19,* 130–135.

Razaire, C. (2003). *Industry outlook: Tobacco.* New York: Moody's Investor Service.

Reis, C. S. (1978). Demographic and epidemiological transition in Africa. *Tropical Doctor, 8,* 229–233.

Renders, C. M., Valk, G. D., Griffin, S. M., Wagner, E. H., Eijk, J. T., & Assendelft, W. J. (2002). Interventions to improve the management of diabetes in primary care, outpatient and community settings: A systematic review. *Diabetes Care, 24,* 1821–1833.

Riemsma, R. P., Pattenden, J., Bridle, C., Sowden, A. J., Mather, L., Watt, I. S., & Walker, A. (2002). A systematic review of the effectiveness of interventions based on a stages-of-change approach to promote individual behaviour change. *Health Technology Assessment, 6*(24), 1–231.

Seftel, H., Asvat, M. S., Joffe, B. I., Raal, F. J., Panz, V. R., Vermaak, W. J. H., Loock, M. E., Rajput, M. C., Omar, M. A. K., Jeenah, M. S., Steyn, K., & Becker, P. J. (1993). Selected risk factors for coronary heart disease in male scholars from the major South African population groups. *South African Medical Journal, 83,* 891–897.

Seftel, H. C., & Schultz, E. (1961). Diabetes mellitus in the urbanised Johannesburg African. *South African Medical Journal, 35,* 66–70.

Serdula, M. K., Khan, L. K., & Dietz, W. H. (2003). Weight loss counseling revisited. *Journal of the American Medical Association, 289*(14), 1747–1750.

Shobana, R., Rama Rao, P., Lavanya, A., Williams, R., Vijay, V., & Ramachandran, A. (2000). Expenditure on health care incurred by diabetic subjects in a developing country—a study from southern India. *Diabetes Research and Clinical Practice, 48,* 37–42.

Simpson, S., Corabian, P., Jacobs, P., & Johnson, J. A. (2003). The cost of major comorbidity in people with diabetes mellitus. *Canadian Medical Association Journal, 168,* 1661–1667.

Singh, R. B., Beegom, R., Mehta, A. S., Niaz, M. A., et al. (1999). Social class, coronary risk factors and undernutrition, a double burden of diseases, in women during transition, in five Indian cities. *International Journal of Cardiology, 69*(2), 139–147.

Singhal, A., & Lucas, A. (2004). Early origins of cardiovascular disease: Is there a unifying hypothesis? *Lancet, 363,* 1642–1645.

Sobal, J., & Stunkard, A. J. (1989). Socioeconomic status and obesity: A review of the literature. *Psychological Bulletin, 105*(2), 260–275.

Steptoe, A., Perkins-Porras, L., McKay, C., Rink, E., Hilton, S., & Cappuccio, F. P. (2003). Behavioural counselling to increase consumption of fruit and vegetables in low income adults: Randomised trial. *British Medical Journal, 326*(7394), 855.

Stewart, B. W., & Kleihaus, P. (Eds.). (2003). *World cancer report*. Lyon, France: IARC Press.

Steyn, K., Bradshaw, D., Norman, R., & Laubscher, R. (2003). *Determinants and treatment of hypertension in South Africa/Determinants of hypertension and its treatment in South Africa during 1998: The first Demographic and Health Survey* [Draft]. Tygerburg, South Africa: South Africa Medical Research Council.

Steyn, K., de Wet, T., Richter, L., Cameron, N., Levitt, N. S., & Morrell, C. (2000). Cardiovascular disease risk factors in five-year-old urban South African children—the Birth to Ten study. *South African Medical Journal, 90*(7), 719–726.

Steyn, N. P., Labadarios, D., Nel, J., & Lombard, C. (2005). Secondary data analysis of the National Food Consumption Survey in South Africa: Prevalence of stunting and overweight. *Nutrition, 21*(1), 4–13.

Streets, J., Levy, C., Erskine, A., & Hudson, J. (2002). *Absolute risk of obesity*. London: UBS Warburg Global Equity Research.

Swai, A. B., McLarty, D. G., Kitange, H. M., Kilima, P. M., Tatalla, S., Keen, N., Chuwa, L. M., & Alberti, K. G. (1993). Low prevalence of risk factors for coronary heart disease in rural Tanzania. *International Journal of Epidemiology, 22*(4), 651–659.

Swiss Reinsurance Company. (2004). *Too big to ignore: The impact of obesity on mortality trends*. Zurich: Swiss Reinsurance Company.

Thompson, D., & Wolf, A. M. (2001). The medical-care cost burden of obesity. *Obesity Reviews, 2*, 189–197.

Ullrich, A., Sepulveda, C., Waxman, A., Costa e Silva, V. L., Beaglehole, R., Bettcher, D., & Vestal, G. (2004). Cancer prevention in the political arena: The WHO perspective. *Annals of Oncology, 15*(Suppl. 4), 249–256.

United Nations Conference on Trade and Development (UNCTAD). (2003). *World investment report 2003*. Geneva and New York: UNCTAD.

United Nations Development Program (UNDP). (2001). *Implementing the Millennium Declaration*.

New York: UNDP. Available at http://www.undp.org/mdg/goal6.pdf.

UNFPA. (1995). State of the World's Population 1996. Changing places: Population, development, and the urban future. Annual report.

United Nations General Assembly. (2002, October 11). *A world fit for children* (S-27/2). New York: United Nations.

Unwin, N. C., Setel, P., Rashid, S., Mugusi, F., Mbanya, J. C., Kitange, H., Hayes, L., Edwards, R., Aspray, T., & Alberti, K. G. (2001). Non-communicable diseases in sub-Saharan Africa: Where do they feature in the health research agenda? *Bulletin of the World Health Organization, 79*(10), 947–953.

US Department of Health, Education and Welfare. (1964). *Smoking and health: Report of the Advisory Committee to the Surgeon General of the Public Health Service* (PHS Publication No. 1103). Washington, DC: US Department of Health, Education and Welfare.

US Department of Health and Human Services. (2001). *The Surgeon General's call to action to prevent and decrease overweight and obesity*. Rockville, MD: US Department of Health and Human Services.

US Department of Health and Human Services. (2004). *The health consequences of smoking: A report of the Surgeon General*. Atlanta, GA: Centers for Disease Control and Prevention.

Vikram, V. M., Pandey, R. M., Misra, A., Sharma, R., Devi, J. R., & Khanna, N. (2003). Non-obese (body mass index < 25 kg/m^2) Asian Indians with normal waist circumference have high cardiovascular risk. *Nutrition, 19*(6), 503–509.

Vorster, H. H. (2002). The emergence of cardiovascular disease during urbanisation of Africans. *Public Health Nutrition, 5*(1A), 239–243.

Wagner, E. H., Glasgow, R. E., Davis, C., Bonomie, A. E., Provost, L., McCulloch, D., Carver, P., & Sixta, C. (2001). Quality improvement in chronic illness care: A collaborative approach. *Joint Commission Journal on Quality Improvement, 27*, 63–80.

Walkenhorst, P. (2001). The geography of foreign direct investment in Poland's food industry. *Journal of Agricultural Economics, 52*(3), 71–86.

Wanless, D. (2004). *Securing good health for the whole population: Final report.* London: Her Majesty's Treasury.

Warman, A. (2001). Living the revolution: Cuban health workers. *Journal of Clinical Nursing, 10*(3), 311–319.

Waxman, A. (2004). The WHO Global Strategy on Diet, Physical Activity and Health: The controversy on sugar. *Development, 47*(2), 75–83.

Waxman, H. A. (2004). Politics of international health in the Bush administration. *Development, 47*(2), 24–30.

WHO PREMISE (Phase I) Study Group. *Gaps in secondary prevention of myocardial infarction and stroke: World Health Organization study on Prevention of Recurrences of Myocardial Infarction and Stroke (WHO PREMISE) in low and middle income countries.* WHO bulletin. Publication pending.

Wild, S., Roglic, G., Green, A., Sicree, R., & King, H. (2004). Global prevalence of diabetes: Estimates for 2000 and projections for 2030. *Diabetes Care, 27,* 1047–1053.

Wilson, D., & Purushothaman, R. (2003). *Dreaming with BRICS: The path to 2050.* New York: Goldman Sachs.

Winocour, P. H. (2002). Effective diabetes care: A need for realistic targets. *British Medical Journal, 324*(7353), 1577–1580.

Wong, M. D., Shapiro, M. F., Boscardin, W. J., & Ettner, S. L. (2002). Contribution of major diseases to disparities in mortality. *New England Journal of Medicine, 347*(20), 1585–1592.

World Bank. (1999). *Curbing the epidemic: Governments and the economics of tobacco control.* Washington, DC: World Bank.

World Health Organization. (1956). *Cardiovascular diseases and hypertension* (WHA9.31 21). Geneva, Switzerland: World Health Organization.

World Health Organization. (2000). *Tobacco company strategies to undermine tobacco control activities at the World Health Organization: Report of the Committee of Experts on Tobacco Industry Documents.* Geneva, Switzerland: World Health Organization.

World Health Organization. (2001). *World health report, 2001.* Geneva, Switzerland: World Health Organization.

World Health Organization. (2002a). *The cost of diabetes* (WHO Fact Sheet 236). Geneva, Switzerland: World Health Organization.

World Health Organization. (2002b). *Innovative care for chronic conditions: Building blocks for action.* Geneva, Switzerland: World Health Organization.

World Health Organization. (2002c). *Active ageing: A policy framework.* Geneva, Switzerland: World Health Organization.

World Health Organization. (2002d). *World health report, 2002.* Geneva, Switzerland: World Health Organization.

World Health Organization. (2002e). *WHO report on the consultative meeting on primary health care policy review in the Eastern Mediterranean Region, Muscat, Oman, 28–30 January 2002.* Cairo, Egypt: World Health Organization.

World Health Organization. (2003a). *World health report, 2003.* Geneva, Switzerland: World Health Organization.

World Health Organization. (2003b). *Global burden of disease estimates. GBD 2002 estimates: Estimates by income level.* http://www3.who.int/whosis/menu.cfm?path=evidence,burden,burden_estimates&language=english.

World Health Organization. (2003c). *Investing in mental health.* Geneva, Switzerland: World Health Organization.

World Health Organization. (2003d). *Diet, nutrition and the prevention of chronic diseases* (Technical Report No. 916). Geneva, Switzerland: World Health Organization.

World Health Organization. (2003e). *Adherence to long-term therapies: Evidence for action.* Geneva, Switzerland: World Health Organization.

World Summit on Sustainable Development. (2002). *Plan of implementation.* http://www.johannesburgsummit.org/html/documents/summit_docs/2309_planfinal.htm.

Yach, D. (1990). Tobacco-induced diseases in South Africa. *International Journal of Epidemiology, 19*(4), 1122–1123.

Yach, D. (2005). Chronic disorders: Cardiovascular disease, cancer, and diabetes. In B. S. Levy & V. W. Sidel (Eds.), *Social injustice and public health.* Oxford, England: Oxford University Press.

Yach, D., Hawkes, C., Epping-Jordan, J. E., & Galbraith, S. (2003). The World Health Organization's Framework Convention on Tobacco Control: Implications for the global epidemics of food-related deaths and disease. *Journal of Public Health Policy, 24*(2–3), 274–290.

Yach, D., Hawkes, C., Gould, C. L., & Hofman, K. J. (2004). The global burden of chronic diseases: Overcoming impediments to prevention and control. *Journal of the American Medical Association, 291*(21), 2616–2622.

Yach, D., Mathews, C., & Buch, E. (1990). Urbanisation and health: Methodological difficulties in undertaking epidemiological research in developing countries. *Social Science and Medicine, 31*(4), 507–514.

Yach, D., & Raviglione, M. (2004). TB and tobacco. *Evidence-Based Health Care, 8,* 28.

Zhang, H., & Baiqiang, C. (2003). The impact of tobacco on lung health in China. *Respirology, 8,* 17–21

Unintentional Injuries and Violence

ROBYN NORTON, ADNAN A. HYDER, AND GOPALAKRISHNA GURURAJ

Injuries are no "accident." Recognition that a scientific approach to the prevention and control of injuries can and must be implemented, as with other health conditions, has significantly raised the profile of injuries on the public health agenda. Twenty years ago the topic hardly received mention in the curricula of most schools of public health, whereas today it has become an integral part of a well-balanced training in public health, not only in most high-income countries but also in increasing numbers of low- and middle-income countries.

Injuries have traditionally been defined as physical damage to a person caused by an acute transfer of energy (mechanical, thermal, electrical, chemical, or radiation energy) or by the sudden absence of heat or oxygen. However, it is now recognized that this definition is too narrow and should be broadened to include impacts that result in psychological harm, maldevelopment, or deprivation (WHO Global Consultation on Violence and Health, 1996).

Injuries can be categorized in various ways, but commonly they have been categorized in terms of whether or not the injury was planned or intended. Unintentional injuries comprise that subset of injuries for which there is no evidence of predetermined intent and includes injuries sustained as a result of road traffic crashes, poisonings, falls, burns, and drowning, as well as occupational injuries and sports injuries.

Violence or intentional injuries are those injuries for which there is evidence that the injury was planned or intended. However, more recently this definition has been refined to recognize that this category includes injuries where there may have been an intention to use force or to use violence but not necessarily an intention to injure (Krug et al., 2002). Violence can be categorized, depending on the characteristics of those who commit the violent act, into self-directed violence (violence a person inflicts upon himself or herself), interpersonal violence (violence inflicted by another individual or a small group of individuals), and collective violence (violence inflicted by larger groups, such as states, organized political groups, religious groups, militia groups, and terrorist organizations). Self-directed violence covers a broad spectrum, including completed suicides, attempted suicides, suicidal ideation, and suicidal behaviors, as well as self-abuse. Interpersonal violence includes family and intimate partner violence as well as community violence, while collective violence can be subdivided into social, political, and economic violence.

Evidence to show intent may not always be available, and as a consequence such injuries are generally classified as being of undetermined intent, although for legal or social reasons they may well be classified as unintentional injuries.

This chapter considers both unintentional injuries and violence and, in particular, examines issues relating to a number of cause-specific injuries. The latter include those injuries that are routinely analyzed and published by the World Health Organization (WHO) and which individually constitute the greatest injury burden in terms of mortality and disability-adjusted life years (DALYs). These include road traffic injuries, poisonings, falls, burns, and drowning, as well as self-directed violence, interpersonal violence (including youth violence, child abuse and neglect, violence by intimate partners, abuse of the elderly, and sexual violence), and collective violence (including war-related injuries).

The first section of the chapter provides an overview of the global burden of injuries. This section includes discussion about data sources and the challenges associated with obtaining accurate injury data, especially in low- and middle-income countries.

The next section of the chapter outlines known and potential causes or risk factors for unintentional injuries and violence. Discussion is included on the extent to which knowledge about risk factors in one setting can be applied to other settings, and especially the extent to which knowledge about risk factors can be transferred from high-income country settings to low- and middle-income country settings.

Current evidence about effective interventions to prevent and control injuries is then outlined. Again, the extent to which evidence of effectiveness in high-income countries can be extrapolated to middle- and low-income countries is considered, and particular attention is given to the relevance of operational research in identifying how best evidence about effective interventions in high-income countries can be implemented in low- and middle-income settings.

The last section of the chapter considers the opportunities and challenges that exist in moving the injury prevention agenda forward. Issues that are considered include the continued need for advocacy for injury prevention, the importance of research, the significance of a trained workforce, and the role of national and international organizations.

The Global Burden of Injuries

Data Sources

Data on injuries and violence may be obtained from two types of sources—within the health sector and outside the health sector. Data sources within the health sector include both those that are usual sources for information about other health conditions, such as health information systems, vital registration systems, and hospital discharge data, and those that are more specific to injuries and violence, such as ambulance data and trauma registries. Sources outside the health sector cover a wide spectrum, depending on the type and nature of injuries. Common non-health-sector data sources are police data, transport sector data, legal records, and insurance company claims. Innovative data sources for injuries have also been used, such as newspapers and consumer reports. This diversity of data sources makes the field of injuries and violence unique and challenging—unique, in terms of the intersectoral nature of the information, and challenging because the biases and nature of the data from each source need to be understood.

Comprehensive global data on all injuries and violence are only available from the work of WHO (see website http://who.int/violence_injury_prevention), including data from the Global Burden of Disease study. Attempts to compile and make available consistent and internationally comparable data have been made by WHO, and such information is updated regularly. WHO data have limitations, though, in that data on burns include only fire burns (and not scalds), and data on drowning do not include drowning due to floods. However, the aggregation of all injuries into one unified system of information makes WHO data most useful for public health purposes. For specific types of injury, alternative data sources are available, although they frequently provide slightly different estimates to those provided by WHO. For example, the International Road and Traffic Accident Database (see web site: http://www.bast.de/htdocs/fachthemen/irtad), the World Bank (see web site: http://www.worldbank.org), and Transport Research Laboratory (United Kingdom) (see web site: http://www.trl.co.uk/) provide estimates of deaths from road traffic injuries—estimates that are somewhat lower than those provided by WHO.

It is important to note that the quantity and quality of data for different health outcomes from injuries vary. Generally more and better quality data are available for deaths from injuries than for morbidity and disability. Data on the types and severity of nonfatal health outcomes are important and yet challenging to obtain, especially from the developing world. Data on nonfatal health outcomes have primarily been derived from high-income countries, although in the past decade significant information on injuries has emerged from low- and middle-income countries. In general, though, the state of routine health information in the developing world has been fragile, especially in regions such as sub-Saharan Africa and South Asia, and thus it is not surprising that there has been little tradition of developing specific information sources for injuries. Population-based studies from low- and middle-income countries, though, frequently suggest that the injury burden is higher than reported in national official statistics, indicating that injuries are significantly underreported in these reports.

Estimates of Injury Mortality and Disability

Most of the data presented in the following subsections have been derived from WHO reports for the years 1998 to 2002. It is to be noted that WHO still uses the word *accident* in its data for road traffic injuries. Additionally, specific studies or sources have been quoted to highlight recent information from the developing world.

Over 5.1 million deaths occurred from all injuries worldwide in 2001, of which nearly 4.7 million were in low- and middle-income countries (WHO, 2002). Nearly 25% of these deaths were caused by road traffic injuries, with self-inflicted injuries and violence constituting a further 17% and 11% of deaths, respectively (Figure 7-1). Notably, about 18% of deaths were classified as "other" unintentional injury deaths. Not surprisingly, injury death rates were highest for road traffic injuries, followed by "other" unintentional injuries, self-inflicted injuries, and violence (Figure 7-2). Somewhat similar patterns were observed for nonfatal health outcomes (using DALY rates) (Figure 7-3), although the rates were highest for all "other" unintentional injuries, no doubt reflecting challenges in coding the specific causes of nonfatal unintentional injuries.

Unintentional Injuries

Road traffic injuries alone killed almost 1.2 million people in 1998, qualifying these types of injuries as the tenth leading cause of death worldwide (WHO, 1999). Road traffic injuries accounted for 2.2% of global mortality, resulting in a heavy death toll for people in all age categories. According to the Global Burden of Disease study, death and disability from road traffic injuries are projected to rise substantially in future years to become the third leading cause of DALYs lost worldwide by 2020 (Murray & Lopez, 1996).

Globally, 1.0 million of those killed during 1998 were from low- or middle-income countries, and 142,000 were from high-income countries, corresponding to 20.7 and 15.6 deaths per 100,000 population, respectively. The absolute number of fatalities and the mortality rate resulting from road traffic injuries vary considerably across countries. An estimated 40,000 people are killed annually in the member states of the European Union, with an accompanying economic cost of 160 billion Euros (ICF Consulting & Imperial College Centre for Transport Studies, 2003).

Although all age groups are affected by fatalities resulting from road traffic injuries, young adults, particularly males, are most at risk of loss of life. Children are also affected by road traffic injuries. Of people killed in 1998, 844,700 were aged 45 years or younger (WHO, 1999). Since this age group corresponds to the most economically productive segment of the population, road traffic injuries have serious implications for national economies.

The WHO estimates that there were over 3 million cases of acute, severe poisoning and a greater number of mild to moderate cases, resulting in an estimated 349,000 deaths in 2001. These deaths demonstrated a 2:1 male to female ratio, and over 90% of these occurred in low- and middle-income countries.

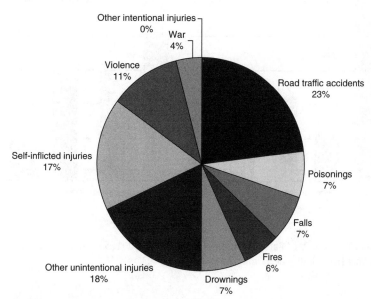

Figure 7-1 Distribution of Global Deaths from Injuries, 2001. *Source:* Based on Global Burden of Disease data from the World Health Organization, 2001.

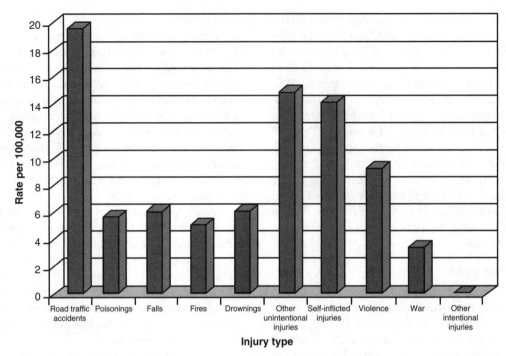

Figure 7-2 Global Injury Death Rates per 100,000 Population, 2001. *Source:* Based on Global Burden of Disease data from the World Health Organization, 2001.

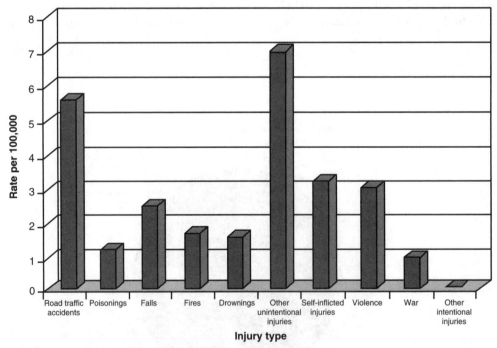

Figure 7-3 Global Injury DALY Rates per 100,000 Population, 2001. *Source:* Based on Global Burden of Disease data from the World Health Organization, 2001.

Nonfatal unintentional poisonings resulted in a loss of over 7.5 million DALYs globally.

Falls caused more than 387,000 deaths worldwide in 2001, with nearly 310,000 in low- and middle-income countries, and a 2:1 male to female ratio. These numbers translate to a mortality rate of 6 per 100,000 globally and more than 15 million DALYs lost per year (loss of 2 DALYs per 1,000 population), signifying the important contribution of morbidity and disability in falls.

WHO only registers data for burns as a result of fires and not scalds (water burns)—an important limitation. Over 300,000 deaths were caused by fires in 2001, resulting in more than 10 million DALYs lost. Unlike other injuries, more females than males died from fires (male to female ratio of 0.6:1.0).

Drowning is the process of experiencing respiratory impairment from submersion or immersion in liquid. Drowning outcomes are classified as death, morbidity, and no morbidity. Agreed terminology is essential to describe the problem and to allow effective comparisons of drowning trends. Thus, the definition of drowning just given, which was adopted by the 2002 World Congress on Drowning, should be widely used (WHO, 2003). Eight percent of all injury deaths in 2000 were from unintentional drowning, and 97% of these occurred in low- and middle-income countries. In 2000 an estimated 409,272 people drowned, making it the second leading cause of unintentional injury death globally after road traffic injuries. One-third of drowning cases occur in the Western Pacific region, though the African region has the highest drowning fatality rate (Table 7-1). Overall, the male rate of drowning is more than twice that for females. The rate of drowning in the African region is more than four times, and the Western Pacific region more than twice, that of the Americas—the region with the lowest rate. It is important to note that these data include only accidental drowning and sub-mersion and exclude drowning due to floods (cataclysms), boating, and water transport.

Drowning has been studied in a few developing countries, especially in the 1980s and early 1990s. South Africa reported drowning as the second leading cause of injury mortality for children younger than 15 years (Kibel, Joubert, & Bradshaw, 1990) and demonstrated an increasing trend in drowning deaths for all ethnic groups in the 1980s (Cywes et al., 1990; Kibel, Bradshaw, & Joubert, 1990). A review of more than 300 pediatric deaths (0–14 years) in the United Arab Emirates revealed that drowning was the second leading cause of death for both genders (Bener, 1998). Drowning is also the second leading cause of death for the 10- to 19-year age group in Taiwan, while it remains the number one cause for males aged 10 to 14 years (Lu, Lee, & Chou, 1998). Table 7-2 shows selected indices of the burden of drowning in two low- and middle-income countries—China and India—the most populous developing nations of the world (WHO, 2003). Both have high drowning mortality rates and together contribute 43% of the world drowning deaths and 41% of the total DALYs attributed to drowning globally.

Violence (Intentional Injuries)

Self-inflicted injuries caused the deaths of over 850,000 people globally in 2001, resulting in more than 20 million DALYs lost. These injuries include suicides, attempted suicide, self-destructive behaviors, and self-mutilation. Data on self-directed injuries are challenging to obtain, but case studies from several parts of the world indicate that they are being increasingly documented globally (see Exhibit 7-1).

Interpersonal violence disproportionately affects low- and middle-income countries. An estimated 90% of all interpersonal violence–related deaths occurred in these countries in 2000. The estimated rate of violent death in low- and middle-income countries was 32.1

Table 7-1	Global Drowning Deaths by Gender in Each WHO Region, 2000						
Region	**World**	**AFR**	**AMR**	**EMR**	**EUR**	**SEAR**	**WPR**
Males	281,717	67,654	20,181	20,712	30,322	55,258	87,600
Females	127,554	23,311	4,408	6,904	7,196	36,520	49,216
Total	409,271	90,965	24,589	27,616	37,518	91,778	136,816
M:F ratio	2.2:1	2.9:1	4.6:1	3:1	4.2:1	1.5:1	1.8:1
Percent	100	22	6	7	9	22	33
Rate[a]	6.8	14.2	3	5.7	4.3	6	8.1

Note: AFR = African region of WHO; AMR = American region; EMR = Eastern Mediterranean region; EUR = European region; SEAR = South East Asian region; WPR = Western Pacific region.

[a] Rate per 100,000 people.

Source: World Health Organization, *Facts About Injuries: Drowning* (Geneva, Switzerland: World Health Organization, 2003). Reprinted with permission.

Table 7-2	Drowning in China and India, 2000	
Marker	China	India
Drowning deaths	129,000	86,000
Mortality rate[a]	10.2	8.5
Percentage of global unintentional drowning mortality	26	17
Rank, leading cause of unintentional death[b]	3	4
DALYs[c]	3,567,000	2,445,000
Percentage of total DALYs	24	17

[a]All rates per 100,000 people.

[b]Ranked 1–6 of leading cause of disability due to unintentional injury.

[c]DALY: disability-adjusted life year.

Source: World Health Organization, *Facts About Injuries: Drowning* (Geneva, Switzerland: World Health Organization, 2003). Reprinted with permission.

per 100,000 people in 2000, compared with 14.4 per 100,000 in high-income countries (Krug et al., 2002). Estimates of different types of interpersonal violence have been developed by WHO as well.

Youth violence is defined as violence committed by or against individuals between the ages of 10 and 29 years. In 2000, an estimated 199,000 youth homicides were committed globally—9.2 per 100,000 individuals. This rate varied from 0.9 per 100,000 in high-income countries to 17.6 in Africa and 36.4 in Latin America. Based on studies of nonfatal violence, it has been further estimated that for every youth homicide there are 20 to 40 victims of nonfatal youth violence receiving hospital treatment (Krug et al., 2002).

The extent of child abuse and neglect is difficult to gauge because much, if not most, of it is unreported. The 2002 *World Report on Violence and Health* estimates that the rates of homicide of children under 5 years of age were 2.2 per 100,000 for boys and 1.8 per 100,000 for girls in high-income countries. In low- and middle-income countries, the corresponding rates were 6.1 and 5.1 per 100,000 for boys and girls, respectively. In Africa, the rates were 17.9 per 100,000 for boys and 12.7 per 100,000 for girls (Krug et al., 2002).

According to the WHO, intimate partner violence is defined as "any behavior within an intimate relationship that causes physical, psychological or sexual harm to those in the relationship." Such behaviors include "acts of physical aggression—such as slapping, hitting, kicking and beating; psychological abuse—such as intimidation, constant belittlement and humiliation; forced intercourse and other forms of sexual coercion; and various controlling behaviors—such as isolating a person from their family and friends, monitoring their movements, and restricting their access to information or assistance"

Exhibit 7-1	Suicides in South Asia: Case Study from Pakistan

There are no official data on suicide from Pakistan, a conservative South Asian Islamic country with traditionally low suicide rates. As a result, national rates on suicide are neither known nor reported to the World Health Organization (WHO). However, there is accumulating anecdotal evidence that suicide rates have been gradually increasing in Pakistan over the last few years. In addition, both suicide and attempted suicide are understudied and underresearched subjects in Pakistan.

A general lack of trained mental health researchers in the country is partly to blame. Furthermore, a lack of interest by available researchers may be related to the generally held belief that suicide and attempted suicide are rare events in Muslim countries and therefore unworthy of scientific study. Other reasons may be the difficulty in gaining access to such data, because there are many legal, social, and cultural issues related to suicide and attempted suicide. Both suicide and attempted suicide are illegal acts, socially and religiously condemned, making research in this area difficult.

Recent work explores police data in Sindh—one of the four provinces of Pakistan—and provides a unique picture of trends of suicide over 15 years (1985–1999). During this period there were 2,568 reported suicides (71% men, 39% women; ratio 1.8:1.00). The lowest number was 90 in 1987; the highest was 360 in 1999. Poisoning by organophosphates was the most common method, followed by hanging. These data, although limited in scope and from only one data source, provide evidence of an increase in suicide rates in Pakistan. There is urgent need for further research on suicide in Pakistan. Interventions for suicide prevention in the country can then be planned.

Selected References

Khan, M., & Hyder, A. A. (2004). *Suicides in the Developing World—Case Study from Pakistan.* Karachi, Pakistan: Aga Khan University.

Khan, M., & Prince, M. (2003). Beyond rates: The tragedy of suicide in Pakistan. *Tropical Doctor, 33,* 67–69.

Source: World Health Organization. (2000). *Preventing suicide: A resource for primary health care workers.* (WHO/MNH/MBD/00.4). Geneva, Switzerland, World Health Organization.

(Krug et al., 2002). The true extent of intimate partner violence is unknown. Surveys suggest a wide range of prevalence estimates, but the results are difficult to compare given cultural differences and social taboos in responding to questions. In Paraguay and the Philippines, 10% of women surveyed reported being assaulted by an intimate partner, compared with 22% in the United States, 29% in Canada, and 34% in Egypt (Krug et al., 2002). Other studies have shown that 3.0% or less of women in Australia, the United States, and Canada had been assaulted by a partner in the previous 12 months, compared with 27% of ever-partnered women in León, Nicaragua, 38% of currently married women in South Korea, and 53% of currently married women in the West Bank and Gaza (Krug et al., 2002).

Abuse of the elderly is a category of violence that incorporates physical, sexual, emotional, and psychological acts or neglect directed toward older people. It is an important type of violence, especially because it is predicted that the global population of those over 65 years of age will soon reach over a billion (Krug et al., 2002). Over 80% of these older people will be in low- and middle-income countries where they will compose over 12% of the population. Such abuse occurs in both the home and institutional settings and is very difficult to measure; there is a lack of global statistics on this issue. Surveys in the developed world indicate a prevalence of 4% to 6% (Krug et al., 2002).

Sexual violence includes rape (by an intimate partner or stranger), attempted rape, gang rape, and other forms of forced sexual acts in any setting (e.g., home, work). Surveys indicate that between 0.3% and 8% of women (over 16 years) report experiencing sexual violence within the past 5 years, while up to 27% report experiencing sexual violence from an intimate partner in the past year (Krug et al., 2002).

War is an important form of collective violence and was estimated by WHO to cause more than 200,000 deaths worldwide in 2001. There is a 9:1 male to female ratio of deaths under this category. It is important to note that this is an estimate of deaths caused directly by war and does not include deaths caused indirectly by war, such as those as a result of a disrupted health system or those that occur after the end of war.

Estimates of the Economic and Social Costs of Injury

Loss of life and health is only one dimension of why injuries are an important public health problem. Other important dimensions include their social and economic toll on individuals, families, and societies. The death of loved ones, lifelong disabilities resulting in unemployment, and the staggering costs of medical care are some of the effects of injuries that need to be described. In addition, factors such as lost productivity, insurance, replacement income activities, and family consequences are important. Unfortunately, such information is not readily available and is uncommon from large parts of the world; as a consequence, our knowledge of the economic and social impacts of injuries is limited.

The following paragraphs, although not presenting a comprehensive review of the economic and social costs of all injuries, provide examples of the breadth and, importantly, the limitations of what has been documented for road traffic injuries and interpersonal violence.

Despite the global significance of road traffic injuries in terms of mortality and disability, the economic and social consequences of such injuries have only recently been documented. Work undertaken by TRL (Transport Research Laboratory) Ltd., based on road crash costs from 21 developed and developing countries, found that the average annual cost of road crashes was about 1% of GNP in developing countries, 1.5% in countries in economic transition, and 2% in highly motorized countries. As a result, it suggests that the annual burden of the economic costs of road traffic injuries globally is about US$518 billion, with the annual costs of road traffic injuries in low- and middle-income countries being about US$65 billion, exceeding the total annual amount received by these countries in development assistance (Jacobs, Aeron-Thomas, & Astrop, 2000).

More recently published work has attempted to document and compare the impact of road traffic injuries on low-income households in Bangladesh and India (Aeron-Thomas et al., 2004). In both countries, males who provided the majority of the household income were the most common victims of road traffic fatalities, and consequences included reduced household income and reduced food consumption for the victim's family. Although poor households did not report higher rates of fatal and nonfatal road traffic injuries than nonpoor households, the poor were found to spend a much greater proportion of their income on medical and funeral costs than the nonpoor.

Interpersonal violence is expensive. Estimates of the cost of violence in the United States reach 3.3% of the gross domestic product (GDP). In England and Wales, the total costs from violence—including homicide, wounding, and sexual assault—amount to an estimated $40.2 billion annually. Interpersonal violence disproportionately affects low- and middle-income countries. The economic effects are also likely to be more severe in poorer countries. However, as a recent report shows, there is a scarcity of studies of the economic effects of this violence in low- and middle-income countries (Waters et al., 2004). Estimates from low- and middle-income countries indicate that the overall costs of violence are substantial, ranging up to 25% of annual GDP (Table 7-3).

Comparisons with high-income countries are complicated by the fact that economic losses related to productivity tend to be undervalued in lower-income countries since these losses are typically based on foregone wages and income. For example, a single homicide is calculated to cost, on average, $15,319 in South Africa, $602,000 in Australia, $829,000 in New Zealand, and more than $2 million in the United States (all monetary values have been converted to 2001 U.S. dollars to enable comparisons and to adjust for inflation and varying exchange rates).

Many of the studies detailing the costs of specific types of violence are from the United States (Waters et al., 2004). Child abuse results in $94 billion in annual costs to the U.S. economy (1% of GDP). Direct medical treatment costs per abused child have been calculated by different studies to range from $13,781 to $42,518 per child. Intimate partner violence costs the U.S. economy $12.6 billion on an annual basis (0.1% of GDP), compared with 1.6% of GDP in Nicaragua and 2.0% of GDP in Chile. Gun violence, which includes suicides, has alone been calculated at $155 billion annually in the United States, with lifetime medical treatment costs per victim ranging from $37,000 to $42,000.

Table 7-3	The Costs of Social Violence in Latin America
Country	% 1997 GDP Lost Due to Social Violence
Brazil	10.5
Colombia	24.7
El Salvador	24.9
Mexico	12.3
Peru	5.1
Venezuela	11.8

Note: The definition of violence for this table includes collective violence.

Source: M. Buvinic, A. R. Morrison, and M. Shifter. "Violence in Latin America and the Caribbean: A Framework for Action," in Andrew R. Morison and Maria Loreto Biehl (Eds.), *Too Close to Home: Domestic Violence in the Americas* (New York: Inter-American Development Bank, 1999). Reprinted with permission.

Evidence abounds that the public sector—and thus society in general—picks up much of the tab for interpersonal violence. Several studies in the United States show that from 56% to 80% of the costs of care of gun and stabbing injuries are either directly paid by public financing or are not paid at all, in which case they are absorbed by government and society in the form of uncompensated care financing and overall higher payment rates. In low- and middle-income countries, it is also probable that society absorbs much of the costs of violence, through direct public expenditures and negative effects on investment and economic growth.

Studies documenting the economic effects of interpersonal violence have used a broad range of categories of costs. Those estimating indirect costs—including the opportunity cost of time, lost productivity, and reduced quality of life—provide higher cost estimates than studies that limit the costs of violence to direct costs alone. Other key methodological issues include the economic values assigned to human life, lost productive time, and psychological distress. The rate at which future costs and benefits are discounted, in accounting terms, also varies across studies.

Risk Factors for Unintentional Injuries and Violence

As with most diseases, the causes of unintentional injuries and violence are considered to be multifactorial. The traditional epidemiologic paradigm of host (including biological and behavioral), vector, and environmental factors that in combination contribute to the incidence of disease has been readily adapted and applied in determining the causes of unintentional injury. This paradigm has been extended, though, to consider each factor in relation to the timing of the injury occurrence—that is, factors operating prior to, during, and after the injury that might be associated with both the incidence and the severity of the injury (Haddon, 1968). In determining the causes of violence, especially interpersonal violence, a somewhat different model (described as an ecological model) has more commonly been utilized, which focuses on the interplay between individual, relationship, community, and societal factors (Krug et al., 2002).

In the past two decades, the evidence base identifying risk factors for unintentional injuries and violence has increased dramatically as the numbers of injury researchers and research institutions have increased. The application of public health research methods, commonly used in identifying risk factors for other causes of death and disability, to the problems of unintentional injuries and violence has undoubtedly contributed to the growth in this knowledge. For example, case control and cohort studies now likely contribute as much to the evidence base in the injury field as they do for other leading causes of death and disability, such as cancer and heart disease.

Most of this research, though, has been undertaken in high-income countries, in large part given the preponderance of injury researchers and research institutions in these countries. Nevertheless, the evidence base identifying risk factors for unintentional injuries in low- and middle-income countries is growing with the increasing recognition that certain types of injuries are unique to these countries and that although some risk factors may be common across a wide range of settings (e.g., alcohol use), other risk factors are unique to the environments in which they occur (e.g., the significance of water wells in increasing the risks of drowning in low-income countries).

This section outlines known and potential risk factors for the leading cause-specific injuries, highlighting specifically the extent to which knowledge has been obtained exclusively in high-income countries, the extent to which this knowledge might be transferred to middle- and low-income countries, and the areas where the evidence base is still minimal.

Risk Factors for Road Traffic Injuries

Not surprisingly, given the significant burden of road traffic injuries, much is known about risk factors for such injuries, as outlined in detail in the recently published *World Report on Road Traffic Injury Prevention* (Peden et al., 2004). The report describes road traffic injury risk in terms of four functions: factors affecting exposure to risk, factors influencing crash involvement, factors influencing crash injury severity, and factors influencing severity of postcrash injuries.

Factors Influencing Exposure to Risk

Increasing motorization is, without doubt, one of the main factors contributing to the increase in road traffic injuries worldwide and especially in low- and middle-income countries. Motorization rates rise with income (Kopits & Cropper, 2003), and in a growing number of low- and middle-income countries where economies are experiencing growth there has been a corresponding increase in the numbers of motor vehicles (Ghaffar et al., 1999).

Unfortunately, in some low- and middle-income countries, traffic growth has been led by an increase in less safe forms of travel—namely, motorized two-

wheeled vehicles—resulting in concurrent increases in related injuries (Zhang et al., 2004). This growth in motorized two-wheel vehicles is not, however, unique to low- and middle-income countries as high-income countries try to find solutions to the problems of growing traffic congestion. In London, England, for example, due to the introduction of policies that encourage the use of such vehicles, deaths and injuries among users of motorized two-wheelers are increasing (Peden et al., 2004).

Projected demographic changes in high-income countries over the next 20 to 30 years are likely to result in greater numbers of people over the age of 65 years being exposed to traffic risk, and, given their greater physical vulnerability, greater numbers sustaining injury. By comparison, in low- and middle-income countries, increasing economic growth is fueling both the aspirations of younger people to drive motor vehicles and the need to travel greater distances to work. As a consequence, in many low- and middle-income countries, this vulnerable road user group will continue to be the predominant group involved in road crashes.

Transport, land use, and road network planning have been shown to be important in determining exposure to injury risk. Whereas many of the technical aspects of planning, highway design, traffic engineering, and traffic management have been the hallmarks of transport systems in high-income countries, such planning systems are frequently absent in low- and middle-income countries. However, the necessity for such planning is probably even greater in low- and middle-income countries than high-income countries, given the extremely diverse and multiple modes of both motorized and nonmotorized traffic seen in these countries (Tiwari, 2000).

Factors Influencing Crash Involvement

The overwhelming influence of speed and alcohol consumption on the risk of crash involvement has been shown, primarily in studies undertaken in high-income countries, but also in an increasing number of studies undertaken in low- and middle-income countries. A number of other host-related factors, as outlined here, have also been postulated as increasing the risk of crash involvement, although evidence to support their involvement is still limited and mostly restricted to studies undertaken in high-income countries.

There is very good evidence from high-income countries to show a strong relationship between increasing vehicle speeds and increasing risk of crash, both for motor vehicle occupants and for vulnerable road users, particularly pedestrians (European Road

Safety Action Program, 2003). This relationship is likely to be true for low- and middle-income countries, and indeed data obtained from routinely collected police reports in a number of low- and middle-income countries show that speed is listed as the leading causal factor in road traffic crashes (Afukaar, Antwi, & Ofosu-Amah, 2003; Odero, Khayesi, & Heda, 2003; Wang et al., 2003), accounting for up to 50% of all crashes.

The observation, in studies of victims and perpetrators, that alcohol is associated with an increased risk of road crashes has been confirmed in several case control studies conducted in high-income countries (Peden et al., 2004), as well as in studies conducted in low- and middle-income countries, where alcohol has been shown to be present in between 33% and 69% of fatally injured drivers and in between 8% and 29% of drivers involved in crashes who were not fatally injured (Odero & Zwi, 1995). Alcohol consumption by pedestrians has also been shown to increase their risk of injuries. In high-income countries and in at least some low- and middle-income countries, the prevalence of alcohol among fatally injured pedestrians has been shown to be greater than 50% (Peden et al., 1996).

Other factors that have been shown to increase the risks of road crashes in high-income countries include fatigue, use of hand-held mobile telephones, and inadequate visibility of vulnerable road users (Peden et al., 2004), all of which are equally likely to increase risks in low- and middle-income countries. Indeed, a recent case control study from China showed a twofold increased risk of car crash associated with driver chronic sleepiness (Liu et al., 2003), while surveys of commercial and public road transport in a number of African countries have shown that drivers often work unduly long hours and go to work when exhausted (Mock, Amegashi, & Darteh, 1999; Nafukho & Khayesi, 2002). Studies in Malaysia have clearly shown that motorcyclists who use daytime running lights have a crash risk about 10% to 29% lower than those that do not (Radin Umar, Mackay, & Hills, 1996).

Clearly, road-related and vehicle-related risk factors may increase the risk of crash involvement. Specific factors related to road planning that have been suggested as risk factors for crashes include traffic passing through residential areas, conflicts between pedestrians and vehicles near schools located on busy roads, lack of segregation of pedestrians and high-speed traffic, lack of median barriers to prevent dangerous overtaking on single-carriage roads, and lack of barriers to prevent pedestrian access to high-

speed roads. However, studies that have examined the risks associated with each of these factors are lacking (Ross et al., 1991). Data from both large in-depth studies conducted in high-income countries and from a number of African countries suggest that although vehicle-related risk factors do contribute to crash involvement, their contribution may account for less than 5% of crashes (Odero, Garner, & Zwi, 1997; Van Schoor, van Niekerk, & Grobbelaar, 2001).

Factors Influencing Injury Severity

In-vehicle crash protection is undoubtedly a factor relating to crash injury severity. Although significant improvements have been made to private vehicles in the past decade, there is evidence to show that many of these improvements are still not present in vehicles in low- and middle-income countries (Odero, Garner, & Zwi, 1997). However, the issue of crash protection that reduces injury severity to vulnerable road users is probably of greater relevance, especially in low- and middle-income countries, where vulnerable road users are predominant. In few countries, however, whether high or low income, are there requirements to protect vulnerable road users by means of crash-worthy designs for the front of cars or buses (Mohan, 2002).

A significant risk factor for increased injury severity in users of motorized two-wheeled vehicles is non-use or inappropriate use of motorcycle helmets (Kulanthayan et al., 2000; Liu et al., 2004). Even where there are mandatory helmet wearing laws, nonuse of helmets, use of nonstandard helmets, and improperly secured helmets are not uncommon, especially in many low- and middle-income countries (Conrad et al., 1996; Kulanthayan et al., 2000). Similarly, a risk factor for increased injury severity in bicyclists is nonuse of helmets, again despite evidence of their efficacy (Attewell, Glase, & McFadden, 2001). Similarly, while failure to use seat belts is still a significant risk factor associated with injury severity in vehicle occupants in high-income countries, in many low- and middle-income countries, no requirements for seat belts to be fitted or used are in place (Peden et al., 2004).

Studies in high-income countries suggest that roadside hazards, such as trees, poles, and road signs, may contribute to between 18% and 42% of road crash fatalities (Kloeden et al., 1998), although the extent to which this is also true in low- and middle-income countries has not been determined.

Factors Influencing Severity of Postcrash Injuries

Both the availability and quality of prehospital and in-hospital care are major influences on the severity of the injuries sustained postcrash. Comparisons between high-income countries and low- and middle-income countries show clear differences in the proportions of injured individuals who die before reaching a hospital, in large part reflecting the limited access to prehospital medical services in low- and middle-income countries. (Mock et al., 1998). Factors that determine survival and outcome are early availability of care, time interval between injury and reaching a definitive hospital, referral based on triage, and availability of physical and human resources.

Risk Factors for Poisonings

The global literature on unintentional poisonings includes significant information on occupation-related poisonings, especially pesticide poisonings, and a growing body of information on environmental poisoning, especially lead poisoning. The particular focus of this section, however, is on risk factors for other unintentional poisonings, insofar as the other two issues are covered in Chapter 9 under the topic of environmental health.

The literature in this area almost exclusively considers risk factors for poisonings in young children. In high-income countries, product accessibility, in terms of both safe packaging and storage, has long been recognized as the key risk factor (Shannon, 2000); as a consequence, a number of highly effective interventions to address this risk factor have been introduced. There is a relative paucity of controlled studies that have sought to identify other potential risk factors for childhood poisoning in high-income countries.

By comparison, several case control studies have been conducted in a number of low- and middle-income countries and show evidence of the importance of a number of sociodemographic risk factors, including young age of parents, residential mobility, and limited adult supervision of children (Azizi, Zulkifli, & Kasim, 1993; Soori, 2001). The studies also suggest that previous poisoning may be a risk factor (Soori, 2001). Importantly in low- and middle-income countries, storage issues also appear to be risk factors for poisoning, including the numbers of used storage containers in the residence; the use of nonstandard containers for storage, for example, Coca-Cola bottles for the storage of kerosene; and the storage of poisons at ground level (Azizi, Zulkifli, & Kasim, 1993; Chatsantiprapa, Chokkanapitak, & Pinpradit, 2001; Soori, 2001).

Risk Factors for Fall-Related Injuries

Older people are at particularly high risk of fall-related injuries compared with other age groups, in large part related to their greater susceptibility to sus-taining an injury following a fall, both as a result of reduced protective responses that minimize the impact of a fall and of their greater bone fragility. Consequently, it might be expected that risk factors for falling and risk factors for sustaining an injury following a fall differ somewhat between older and younger people. As a result, these risk factors are discussed separately.

Fall-Related Injuries in Older People

Risk factors for fall-related injuries in older people are generally considered in terms of risk factors for falling, risk factors associated with the severity of the impact following the fall, and risks factors associated with low levels of bone mineral density, insofar as almost all fall-related injuries in older people involve broken bones. An extensive body of literature examining risk factors for hip fractures in older people exists, including large multicountry studies, such as the European-based EPIDOS study. These analytical studies have generally shown that risk factors for fall-related injuries, and especially hip fractures, are consistent across most countries, whether they are high- or low-income countries. These risk factors include low bone density; poor nutritional status and low body mass index (BMI); low calcium intake; comorbid conditions, such as hypertension and diabetes; poor performance in activities of daily living (ADLs and instrumental ADLs); low levels of engagement in physical activity; poor cognitive function; poor perceived health status; poor vision; environmental factors affecting balance or gait; family history of hip fracture; and alcohol consumption (Boonyaratavej et al., 2001; Clark et al., 1998; Cummings et al., 1995; Dargent-Molina et al., 1996).

Some studies, though, have identified other factors that have not previously been identified and may be more relevant in the context of low- and middle-income countries. For example, studies in Thailand have suggested that factors associated with poor socioeconomic status may be risk factors, for example, lack of electricity in the house and living in Thai-style houses or huts (Jitapunkul, Yuktananandana, & Parkpian, 1998).

Fall-Related Injuries in Younger People

The identification of risk factors for falls in younger people, especially in high-income countries, has predominantly emerged from descriptive studies that have sought to identify factors associated with falls from heights. These descriptive studies have recognized the importance of falls from balconies and apartment windows (Istre et al., 2003), falls associated with beds/bunks (Macgregor, 2000) and nursery equipment (including baby walkers), and falls from playground equipment (Dedoukou et al., 2004). Similarly, from the relatively few studies reporting falls in younger children in low- and middle-income countries, the emphasis appears to be on identifying the nature of falls from heights, including falls from rooftops and falls from trees (Adesunkanmi, Oseni, & Badru, 1999; Bangdiwala & Anzola-Perez, 1990; Kozik et al., 1999; Raja, Vohra, & Ahmed, 2001).

Risk Factors for Burn-Related Injuries

Despite the focus of the WHO data on burn-related injuries sustained as a result of fires, in a number of countries scalds from hot water may be equal or more important causes of burn-related injuries than fires (Chan et al., 2002; Delgado et al., 2002; Forjuoh, Guyer, & Smith, 1995; Rossi et al., 1998; Torova & Sinha 1996).

Overall, women are at greater risk of fire-related burn injuries compared with men. However, data from population-based and medical center surveys comprising all types of burns patients suggest that in some settings males may be at greater risk of burns than females (Chan et al., 2002; Zhu, Yang, & Meng, 1998). In many studies, burn-related injuries account for a much higher proportion of injuries in young children compared with other age groups (Jie & Ren, 1992; Liu et al., 1998).

In high-income countries, much of our knowledge about risk factors for fire-related injuries has come from cross-sectional studies and only a few case control studies. From these studies a number of consistent risk factors have been identified. Nonmodifiable risk factors include both young and older age, male gender, nonwhite race, low income, disability, and late night/early morning occurrence (Warda, Tenenbein, & Moffatt, 1999a). Modifiable risk factors include place of residence, type of residence (such as mobile homes and homes without a smoke detector or telephone), smoking, and alcohol use (Warda, Tenebein, & Moffatt, 1999a). By comparison, few controlled studies have examined risk factors for hot water burns, and most discussion in the literature focuses on the lack of temperature controls for hot water systems or taps (Jaye, Simpson, & Langley, 2001).

Case control studies aimed at identifying risk factors for burn-related injuries have been undertaken in South America, Africa, and Asia; all focus on the identification of risk factors in children. A case control study conducted in Peru (Delgado et al., 2002) identified a range of sociodemographic factors that were associated with increased risk of injury, including lack of water supply, low income, and crowding. The presence of a living room and better maternal education were identified as protective factors. A comparable focus and identification of sociodemographic risk factors was also observed in a study in Brazil (Werneck & Reichenheim, 1997). Children who lived in crowded households, who were not the firstborn, had a pregnant mother, had a mother recently dismissed from a job, or who had recently moved their residence were found to be at increased risk. In contrast, history of previous injury had a significant protective effect among males who lived in good environmental conditions.

A case control study conducted in Ghana focused less on sociodemographic factors than on other potential risk factors, including environmental factors (Forjuoh et al., 1995). The presence of a preexisting impairment in a child was the strongest risk factor in this population, with other significant risk factors including sibling death from a burn, history of burn in a sibling, and storage of a flammable substance in the home. Maternal education had a protective effect against childhood burns, although this effect was not strong.

In a case control study conducted in Bangladesh (Daisy et al., 2001), highly significant associations were found between burns and lack of alertness to burns among parents, clothing of human-made fabrics, and cooking equipment in the kitchen within reach of children. There was a significant association between burns and illiteracy of parents, housing located in slums and congested areas, presence of preexisting impairment in children, presence of a history of burns among siblings, and low economic status of the parents.

Risk Factors for Drowning

In high-income countries, the majority of drowning incidents are associated with recreation or leisure activities, including swimming pools (Brenner, 2003), whereas in most low- and middle-income countries they are associated with everyday activities near bodies of water, including rivers, water wells, or buckets (Celis, 1997; Hyder et al., 2003; Kobusingye, Guwatudde, & Lett, 2001).

Men constitute a higher proportion of drowning incidents than women, and children aged 1 to 4 years and young people appear to be at greatest risk, with drowning accounting for a high proportion of injury-related deaths in these age groups (Celis, 1997; Davis & Smith, 1985; Kibel et al., 1990; Kibel, Joubert, & Bradshaw, 1990; Kozik et al., 1999; Tan, Li, & Bu, 1998; Wyndham, 1984; Zhang et al., 2003). Some surveys also suggest that older people may be at particularly high risk (Tan, Li, & Bu, 1998). Descriptive surveys show that in low- and middle-income countries, those living in rural areas are at greater risk than those living in urban areas (Kobusingye, Guwatudde, & Lett, 2001), suggesting a greater exposure to unprotected rural water surfaces.

In a number of studies, mostly descriptive, both in high-income countries and low- and middle-income countries, there is consistent evidence that the majority of adult drowning incidents appear to be associated with positive blood alcohol tests (Carlini-Cotrim & da Matta Chasin, 2000; Celis, 1997; Davis & Smith, 1985; Driscoll, Harrison, & Steenkamp, 2004). In descriptive studies also, a significant proportion of drowning incidents in young children appear to be associated with lapses in parental supervision (Brenner, 2003).

Case control studies of drowning in young children in low- and middle-income countries have identified both sociodemographic risk factors and risk factors associated with proximity to bodies of water. In a study in Bangladesh (Ahmed, Rahman, & van Ginneken, 1999), the risk of drowning was shown to increase with the age of the mother and much more sharply with the number of living children in the family. In a case control study conducted in Mexico (Celis, 1997), the risk of drowning associated with having a water well at home was almost seven times that of children in homes without a water well.

Risk Factors for Self-Directed Violence (see also Chapter 8)

The *World Report on Violence and Health* provides a comprehensive overview of known risk factors for suicidal behavior based on the findings of an extensive body of research, primarily in high-income countries, that has examined the role of psychiatric, biological, social, and environmental factors as well as factors related to an individual's life history (Krug et al., 2002).

Case control studies using psychological autopsies (information gathered after death from relatives, health care professionals, and medical records) have played an important role in identifying psychiatric risk factors for suicide, as have longitudinal studies. Depression is perhaps the leading psychiatric condition associated with an increased risk of suicidal behaviors, and because it is relatively common, it is not surprising that a large proportion of all suicides are believed to be related to this condition. Other conditions associated with increased risk include schizophrenia, anxiety disorders of conduct and personality, impulsivity, and a sense of hopelessness. Alcohol and

drug abuse also play significant roles, although the close relationship between the latter and depression makes it difficult to determine the independent contributions of these conditions. Without doubt another important risk factor is previous suicidal attempt, with some studies suggesting that the risk could be as high as 20 to 30 times the risk seen in the general population.

Among the biological and medical markers that have been identified as risk factors, family history of suicide is one of the strongest markers, suggesting the possibility of a genetic predisposition, which has been supported by twin studies. Other evidence in support of a biological basis for suicide comes from studies of neurobiological processes, particularly those that have examined serotonin levels in psychiatric patients, suggesting that altered serotonin levels may, in part, be linked to greater risks of suicide. Suicide may also be the consequence of severe and painful illness, although the extent to which any such relationship is independent of psychiatric illness cannot yet be determined.

Certain negative life events may be precipitating factors for suicide for some individuals, including personal loss (whether through divorce, separation, or death), interpersonal conflict (including bullying), a broken or disturbed relationship, and legal or work-related problems. In particular, studies have shown a higher risk of suicide attempts among victims of violence between intimate partners due to unresolved conflicts, as well as in individuals with a history of physical or sexual abuse in childhood. Although in many countries marriage and children do appear to be protective factors, those who marry early may not be equally protected. Studies undertaken in Pakistan and China suggest that married women, especially older married women, may not necessarily be protected (Khan & Reza, 1998; Yip, 1998). In contrast, individuals who are socially isolated appear to be at increased risk, including homosexual adolescents and the elderly.

Social and environmental factors that are believed to increase the risk of suicidal behavior include the availability of the means of suicide; a person's place of residence, employment, or immigration status; affiliation to a religion; and economic conditions. Numerous studies, undertaken in a wide range of both high-income countries and low- and middle-income countries, provide clear evidence that not only the ready availability of means but also the lethality of the available methods influences the incidence of both suicide attempts and completions. Likewise, studies conducted in both high-income countries and low- and middle-income countries show that rural residence is an important risk factor for suicide, possibly related to issues of social isolation and increased accessibility to means. Both the economic prosperity of a community and personal economic circumstances appear to be related to risk of suicide, as observed in various studies in both high-income countries and low- and middle-income countries. Although some exceptions exist, there does appear to be a consistent relationship between greater religious involvement and lower risk of suicide.

Risk Factors for Interpersonal Violence

The *World Report on Violence and Health* also comprehensively reviews risk factors for youth violence, child abuse and neglect by parents and other caregivers, violence by intimate partners, abuse of the elderly, and sexual violence (Krug et al., 2002). The quantity and nature of the research on risk factors differs across these different categories, as does the extent to which the research has focused on risk factors associated with perpetrators and risk factors associated with victims.

Although certain risk factors are specific to the different types of self-directed violence and to perpetrators or victims, a number of common risk factors have been observed across at least three of these different categories and to some extent in both high-income and low- and middle-income countries (Rosenberg et al., in press). In terms of individual risk factors, these include being male and young, being an abuser of alcohol and other drugs, and being a victim of child abuse or neglect. Family risk factors include low socioeconomic status of the household, marital discord, and parental conflict involving the use of violence. Community risk factors include low social capital in the community, high crime levels in the community of residence, low access to or inadequate medical care, and situational factors. Lastly, societal risk factors include rapid social change (leading to the breakdown of traditional value and social support networks), economic inequality, poverty, weak economic safety nets, poor rule of law and high corruption, a culture of violence, gender inequalities, high firearm availability, and punitive responses to perpetrators and conflict/postconflict.

Individual risk factors that have additionally been linked to the perpetrators of youth violence include hyperactivity, impulsiveness, poor behavioral control and attention problems, and high levels of daring or risk-taking behavior. Low intelligence and low levels of achievement have likewise been found to be associated with youth violence. In terms of relationship risk factors, poor monitoring and supervision of children by parents and the use of harsh physical punishment to discipline children have been shown to be strong predictors of violence during adolescence and adulthood. Children growing up in single-parent households have also been shown to be at increased risk, as have those having delinquent friends, including friends who use drugs.

Although there has been only limited research identifying risk factors for child abuse and neglect, a range of factors, not previously highlighted, may be important. Girls rather than boys tend to be the victims of most forms of child abuse and neglect, and there is some suggestion that premature infants, twins, and handicapped children may be particularly vulnerable. Although women are often more likely than men to be the perpetrators, men are more likely to inflict serious injuries, including sexual abuse. Parents who abuse their children tend to have low self-esteem, poor control of their impulses, and mental health problems and to display antisocial behavior. They also may have unrealistic expectations about child development. Stress and social isolation of parents may be linked to increased risk of abuse, and, as with youth violence, children living in single-parent homes appear to be at increased risk.

Research identifying individual and community risk factors for partner violence has been undertaken primarily in North America, and many of the risk factors described previously as common risk factors for most forms of interpersonal violence are relevant risk factors for perpetrators of partner abuse as well. Additionally, depression and personality disorders have been suggested as individual risk factors, and weak community sanctions against domestic violence have been linked with a greater incidence of such violence (Exhibit 7-2).

Risk factor research on elder abuse is still very much in its infancy. Although various risk factors have been hypothesized, evidence to support many of these hypotheses, such as the significance of caregiver stress, is not convincing. One of the most consistent findings, though, is the important role of social isolation. Additionally, although there is little empirical evidence, cultural norms relating to ageism and sexism are thought to play an important role.

The identification of risk factors for sexual violence has focused both on risk factors for victimization and risk factors for perpetration, with victims predominantly female and perpetrators predominantly male. In addition to being married or cohabitating with a partner, the identified risk factors for victimization include being young, consuming alco-

| Exhibit 7-2 | Intimate Partner Violence Among Refugee Populations |

The rates of intimate partner violence seem to be particularly high in vulnerable situations such as refugee camps. It has been suggested that the difficulties and stresses of poverty, in combination with their vulnerabilities and insecurities, lead men to use violence in order to reclaim their sense of power and control. In Ngara, Tanzania, relief workers concur that gender-based violence is prevalent among the Burundian refugee population, while in a study at an Ethiopian camp, women reported that violence had increased since being in the camp. In the Ngara camp, 95% of the reported cases of sexual and gender-based violence were related to domestic violence.

The prevalence of domestic violence in refugee camps varies internationally; however, the presence of this type of violence is widely recognized. According to a survey of Somali and Sudanese refugee women in the Kakuma camp in Kenya, 12% of the women reported that someone in their home had hit them in the past month. There have also been numerous reports of domestic violence in Burmese refugee camps in Thailand. Thirty percent of Palestinian women refugees surveyed in Lebanon reported being abused by their husbands at least once.

Despite recent repatriation efforts, Afghans still make up one of the largest refugee populations in the world. Unfortunately, the status of women in refugee camps in Pakistan is not significantly better than in Afghanistan. The culture and norms that accept domestic violence continue and, perhaps, are amplified in refugee camp settings. According to one survey by the International Rescue Committee of 200 women in refugee camps near Peshawar, Pakistan, 79% of the women reported having been beaten by their husbands. A study in a district in the Northwest Frontier province of Pakistan by Save the Children in 1997 found that there was a "potentially" high rate of domestic violence through their discussions with refugees. Some of the men and women justified domestic violence by stating that a man had the right to discipline his wife if she misbehaved or disobeyed. The report also revealed that it was believed by some that younger brides were more likely to suffer abuse.

Data like these are few and limited in scope. In most refugee camps, there is no effective reporting system, and there is still uncertainty about how to respond to such reports from victims. In refugee settings, women often do not know where to turn if they need help and are unfamiliar with the host country's laws regarding domestic violence. Often the police do not report or investigate these cases because it is considered a "private matter".

In a culture in which domestic violence is prevalent, women's personal and interpersonal methods for dealing with violence on a day-to-day basis may be critical to helping women lead productive lives. A better understanding of these methods may serve as a catalyst for the development of innovative approaches to the problem of domestic violence in the refugee setting.

Selected References

Jewkes, R. (2002). Intimate partner violence: Causes and prevention. *Lancet, 359*, 1423–1429.

United Nations Office for the Coordination of Humanitarian Affairs. Burundi-Tanzania: Focus on sexual violence among Burundi refugees. *Integrated Regional Information Network*. http://www.reliefweb.int.

McGinn, T. (2000). Reproductive health of war-affected populations: What do we know? *International Family Planning Perspectives, 26*(4), 174–180.

hol and other drugs, previous victimization, having many sexual partners, involvement in sex work, becoming more educated and economically empowered, and poverty. By comparison, identified risk factors for perpetration, in addition to the common risk factors identified previously, include personal attitudes and beliefs supportive of sexual violence, impulsive and antisocial tendencies, preference for impersonal sex, and hostility toward women. Peer and family risk factors associated with increased risk of perpetration include association with delinquent peers and a family environment that is strongly patriarchal, emotionally unsupportive, and values family honor above the health and safety of a victim. Community and societal systems that both tolerate sexual assault and have weak community sanctions

against perpetrators, combined with views that enforce male superiority and sexual entitlement, have also been shown to be associated with increased levels of sexual violence.

Risk Factors for Collective Violence

As outlined in greater detail in the *World Report on Violence and Health*, the Carnegie Commission on Preventing Deadly Conflict (1997) has identified a range of factors that either alone or in combination may precipitate the risk of political violence. In brief, the Commission has suggested that political and economic factors (including lack of democratic processes, unequal access to power, unequal distribution of and access to resources, and control over both key natural resources and drug production or trading), societal and community factors (including inequalities between groups, fueling of group fanaticism, and readily available weapons), and demographic factors (particularly rapid demographic change) likely play important roles.

Finally, recent research has found an absence of positive protective factors, such as coping abilities, critical thinking, social support systems, communication, attachment and bonding, among persons completing or attempting suicide (Gururaj et al., 2004).

Interventions to Prevent Unintentional Injuries and Violence

Interventions to prevent unintentional injuries have traditionally been considered in terms of the three E's—education, enforcement, and engineering—and also within the framework of the Haddon matrix, that is, in terms of preventing the occurrence of the injury event, minimizing the severity of injury at the time of the injury event, and minimizing the severity of injury following the injury event. By comparison, interventions aimed at reducing violence have focused on individual, relationship, community, and societal approaches, mirroring the ecological model outlined in the previous section. Passive interventions rather than active interventions—that is, those that require little behavior change by an individual—have traditionally been espoused as those likely to have the greatest success in reducing injuries.

Although randomized controlled trials, whether they involve individuals or communities, provide the gold standard by which the effectiveness of injury interventions might best be assessed, such trials are still relatively uncommon in the injury field. Studies comparing the incidence of injury before and after the implementation of an intervention, sometimes with reference to a control population in which the intervention has not been introduced, more commonly provide the only evidence of effectiveness. In some areas, the findings from observational studies, such as case control studies, provide the best available evidence. However, randomized controlled trials are clearly not needed for all interventions because their benefits are obvious, whereas for other interventions, particularly those that may have modest but important benefits, rigorous evaluation methods are required.

Evidence of effectiveness of interventions in low- and middle-income countries, as distinct from their effectiveness in high-income countries, is also relatively uncommon. Although the proven efficacy of some interventions (e.g., using motorcyle helmets) in high-income countries does not require replication in low-income countries, strategies that may be effective in increasing the rates of helmet wearing in high-income countries may not necessarily be appropriate in low- and middle-income countries, and thus specific evidence of their effectiveness is required. Tailoring interventions found effective in high-income countries to low- and middle-income countries with rigorous evaluation is thus increasingly being endorsed (Peden et al., 2004).

Interventions to Prevent Road Traffic Injuries

Safer roads, safer vehicles, and safer people has been the motto traditionally employed by many working to reduce road traffic injuries. More recently this motto has been augmented by the recognition that managing exposure to the risk of a road traffic injury through appropriate transport and land use policies may also play an important role in reducing such injuries (Peden et al., 2004).

Managing exposure to risk involves strategies aimed at reducing motor vehicle traffic, encouraging the use of safer modes of traffic, and minimizing exposure to high-risk scenarios. Reductions in motor vehicle traffic, are possible through efficient fuel taxes; land use; safety impact assessments of transport and land use plans; the provision of shorter, safer routes; and trip reduction measures, including greater emphasis on the development and use of public transport systems. Minimizing exposure to high-risk scenarios includes strategies such as restricting access to different parts of the road network, giving priority in the road network to higher-occupancy vehicles or to pedestrians and slow-moving transport, restricting speed and engine performance of motorized two-wheelers, separating different traffic modes, increasing the legal age for motorized two-wheelers, and instituting graduated driver licensing systems. Evidence from Malaysia shows that increasing the legal age of motorcyclists from 16 to 18 years has been beneficial (Norghani et al., 1998), but evidence of effectiveness for many of the other strategies is not yet available from low- and middle-income countries.

Safer Roads

Intervention strategies focusing on safer roads should incorporate safety awareness in planning road networks, incorporate safety features into road design, and take remedial action at high-risk crash sites. Many of these strategies, though not examined in rigorously controlled studies, have been adapted and adopted over many years in high-income countries and form the basis of best-practice guidelines and manuals that are now being used in low- and middle-income countries (Ross et al., 1991).

Traffic-calming measures are among the strategies recommended with respect to incorporating safety features into road design. A systematic review of studies conducted in high-income countries shows that reductions in pedestrian injuries are likely following the conversion of intersections with traffic signals or stop signs to roundabouts (Retting, Ferguson, & McCartt, 2003). Another review also suggests there is potential for traffic-calming measures to reduce road traffic injuries, although evidence from randomized controlled trials is not yet available (Bunn et al., 2003). Most recently, a before-and-after study conducted in Ghana showed that speed bumps were effective in reducing traffic injuries and especially pedestrian injuries (Afukaar, Antwi, & Ofosu-Amah, 2003).

The introduction of speed cameras has been shown to be highly cost-effective in reducing road traffic injuries in high income countries. A U.K. study showed that the use of speed cameras resulted in a 35% reduction in fatalities and serious injuries and a 14% reduction in injury crashes (Department for Transport, 2003), and an overall summary of research findings has suggested that automated speed enforcement reduces speeds by about 7%—reducing average speeds by several kilometers per hour and virtually eliminating speeding where installed (ICF Consulting, Ltd., and Imperial College Centre for Transport Studies, 2003).

Other safety features that might be incorporated in road design include provision for slow-moving traffic and for vulnerable road users, lanes for overtaking, median barriers, street lighting, advisory speed limits, and systematic removal of roadside hazards such as trees or utility poles (Peden et al., 2004).

Safer Vehicles

Strategies focusing on safer vehicles that have been suggested as likely to decrease the incidence of road traffic injuries include improving the visibility of vehicles, designing crash-protective vehicles, and further developing intelligent vehicles. However, in low- and middle-income countries, strategies that simply ensure regular maintenance of older vehicles may be effective, although evidence to support the latter is limited. Specifically, it has been suggested that vehicle regulation/licensing and inspection has the potential to be cost-effective in low- and middle-income countries (Peden et al., 2004).

Meta-analyses of the effects of automatic daytime running lights on cars have consistently showed that they reduce road crashes, including reductions in

pedestrian and cycle crashes (Elvik & Vaa, 2004; Koornstra, Bijleveld, & Hagenzieker, 1997). Similar positive effects of daytime running lights on motorcycles have also been shown, including before-and-after studies undertaken in both Singapore and Malaysia (Radin Umar, Mackay, & Hills, 1996; Yuan, 2000). The installation and maintenance of seat belts in cars, including child restraint systems, is probably the most well known and most effective vehicle design strategy. Although the fitting of seat belts is covered by technical standards worldwide and in most countries is mandatory, anecdotal evidence suggests that vehicles in many low- and middle-income countries lack functioning seat belts (Forjuoh, 2003). Among the intelligent vehicle devices that might prove useful in low- and middle-income countries are speed limiters and alcohol ignition interlock devices.

Safer People

An increasing focus of effective intervention strategies aimed at improving road user behavior is on the introduction and enforcement of relevant legislation rather than educational efforts. The focus of these legislative intervention strategies includes speeding, alcohol impairment, fatigue, seat belt and child restraint use, and motorcycle and bicycle helmet use. Recent research from Brazil, involving a before-and-after design, has shown, for example, that generic increases in fines and driver license withdrawal had an immediate impact on reduction of road traffic injury deaths and injuries (Poli de Figueiredo et al., 2001).

A large body of research, although little of it was conducted in low- and middle-income countries, shows that the setting and enforcement of speed limits leads to reductions of up to 34% in road traffic injuries (Peden et al., 2004). Similarly, there is a large body of research that shows that the setting and enforcement of legal blood alcohol limits, minimum drinking-age laws, and alcohol checkpoints lead to important reductions in road traffic injuries, of varying magnitude (Peden et al., 2004). Legislation and enforcement of hours of driving for commercial vehicles and drivers have been suggested as potentially effective interventions, but little research is available to support this suggestion.

The introduction of mandatory seat belt laws and mandatory child restraint laws has been shown to have a major impact in reducing occupant deaths and injuries (reductions of up to 25%). Such laws, however, have not been introduced into all low- and middle-income countries and are clearly likely to show benefits when introduced. Systematic reviews have shown the greater effectiveness of enforcement strategies that allow enforcement officers to specifically stop and check seat belt use (primary enforcement) compared with strategies that only allow seat belt use to be checked when other enforcement strategies are the focus (secondary prevention) (Dinh-Zarr et al., 2001; Rivara et al., 1999), and many studies have shown that enforcement needs to be selective, highly visible and well publicized, and conducted over a sufficiently long period and repeated several times a year (Jonah, Dawson, & Smith, 1982; Jonah & Grant, 1985; Solomon, Ulmer, & Preusser, 2002).

Both bicycle and motorcycle helmets have been shown to have a significant impact in reducing head injuries among riders (reductions of up to 85%) (Thompson, Rivara, & Thompson, 1989). Although education may be effective in increasing helmet use, legislation and enforcement of legislation are likely to have a greater impact, as has been shown in countries such as Malaysia (see Exhibit 7-3) and Thailand (Ichikawa, Chadbunchachai, & Marui, 2003; Supramaniam, van Belle, & Sung, 1984).

Interventions to Prevent Poisonings

The prevention of unintentional poisonings includes consideration of both occupational and nonoccupational poisonings, including household poisonings. The former has been extensively considered and includes the promotion, legislation, and enforcement of nonchemical methods of pest control and the promotion of the safe use of pesticides when nonchemical methods are not feasible. Interventions such as these largely fall within the domain of those working in occupational and environmental health and are not considered further in this chapter.

Suggested interventions to reduce exposure to nonoccupational poisonings include better storage of poisons, both in terms of the storage position and in terms of the nature of the storage vessels (Nixon et al., 2004). With respect to the former, the suggested interventions include storing poisons outside the home, and at levels beyond the reach of children (above head height). With respect to the nature of the storage containers, it has been suggested that efforts need to be directed toward reducing the use of secondhand household containers (for example, Coca-Cola bottles), including the introduction and enforcement of legislation to prohibit sales of poisons in such containers (Nhachi & Kasilo, 1994).

Although these interventions clearly have merit, evidence to show that they are effective is lacking. However, the efficacy of child-resistant containers in preventing access to poisons has been shown, and data from a controlled before-and-after study undertaken in South Africa has shown that the free distribution of child-resistant containers appears to be a highly effective means of preventing poisoning in children (Krug et al., 1994).

Other interventions that have been suggested, but not rigorously examined, include the use of warning labels on poison packaging, appropriate first aid education, and the introduction of poison control centers to monitor the incidence of poisonings and

---

| Exhibit 7-3 | Motorcycle Safety Programs in Malaysia |

Motorcycles represent half (51%) of the total vehicles registered in Malaysia (an upper-middle-income economy) and account for 49% of all reported crash cases and 68% of all road injuries and deaths in 1997. Motorcycle-related injuries led to 60% of all road fatalities, while head injuries accounted for 49% of all motorcycle fatalities in 1997 (Royal Malaysian Police, 1998). Given that helmet laws have been in place since 1971, these data raise issues regarding the improper use of helmets. A study conducted by Kulanthayan and colleagues (2000) showed that only 54% of motorcyclists in Malaysia used helmets properly. Twenty-one percent used them improperly, and 24% did not wear helmets. In regression analysis, statistically significant contributors ($p < 0.05$) to improper helmet usage were age, gender, race, formal education level, prior accident experiences, and type of license held.

Following the creation of the Malaysian Motorcycle Safety Program in September of 1997, a study conducted by Umar and Law (1999) looked at the effects of safety interventions on changes in road use behavior, and the effects of campaigns promoting these interventions on motorcycle crashes and casualties. The intervention led to a statistically significant ($p < 0.05$) reduction of 32% in motorcycle casualties.

The utilization of helmets by motorcycle drivers and their passengers has also been studied in other East Asian countries. For example, as a result of the enactment of a helmet law in Thailand, the number of injured motorcyclists declined by 2,414 cases (34%). Only 5% used a helmet before the law was passed, increasing to 23% in the period following the act (Ichikawa, Chadbunchachi, & Marui, 2003). In regard to helmet effectiveness, a study conducted in Indonesia showed a head injuries rate of 32% in helmet users and 52% in non-helmet users. The relative risk of injury among non-helmet users was calculated at 1.7 (Conrad et al., 1996).

provide appropriate preventive advice (Nixon et al., 2004).

Interventions to Prevent Fall-Related Injuries

Fall-Related Injuries in Older People

The range of interventions that have been shown to be effective in preventing falls in older people in high-income countries includes muscle strengthening and balance retraining, individually prescribed at home by a trained health professional; tai chi group exercise; home hazard assessment and modification that is professionally prescribed for older people with a history of falling; and multidisciplinary, multifactorial health and environmental risk factor screening and intervention programs, both for unselected community-dwelling older people and for high-risk older people, such as those with a history of falling or other known risk factors (Chang et al., 2004; Gillespie et al., 2003). Although reduction in psychotropic medication has been shown to be efficacious, questions remain about the effectiveness of this strategy in practice (Campbell et al., 1999). Most recently, meta-analyses suggest that supplementation with vitamin D may also reduce falls (Bischoff-Ferrari et al., 2004).

Hip protectors were initially shown to be a promising intervention to reduce the impact of a fall for older people. However, a growing number of studies are now questioning the effectiveness of these devices, given the relatively poor compliance rates that are achieved in real-life settings (Parker, Gillespie, & Gillespie, 2003). Effective strategies to maximize bone strength include calcium and vitamin D supplementation, the use of bisphosphonates, and the use of hormone replacement therapy (Brown et al., 2002).

Fall-Related Injuries in Younger People

Other than general recommendations about increased supervision of children, for which there is little evidence of effectiveness, two areas show promise as avenues for the prevention of falls in children, both targeting falls from heights in children in high-income countries.

The Children Can't Fly program has been shown to reduce falls from windows in low-income areas in the United States. The program has four major components: (1) reporting of falls by hospital emergency rooms and police precincts, followed up by counseling, referral, and data collection by public health nurses; (2) a media campaign to inform the public and elevate their awareness of the hazards; (3) community education for prevention through door-to-door hazard identification, counseling by outreach workers, and community organization efforts with schools, tenant groups, clinics, churches, health care providers, and so on; and (4) provision of free, easily installed window guards to families with young children living in high-risk areas (Spiegel & Lindaman, 1977). Extrapolation of this program to countries where, for example, children play on rooftops might provide comparable benefits.

A second major focus in high-income countries has been in the area of minimizing falls from playground equipment, with the focus being on both height reductions and, more important, appropriate ground surfacing (Laforest et al., 2001). To date, however, evidence to support the effectiveness of related interventions is lacking.

Interventions to Prevent Burn-Related Injuries

There is limited evidence for the effectiveness of interventions to prevent fire-related injuries. Studies in high-income countries have examined targeted smoke detector giveaway programs, community- and school-based educational campaigns, and community-based burn prevention measures (Warda, Tenenbein, & Moffatt, 1999b). However, the most rigorous of these studies, a randomized, controlled trial of a smoke detector giveaway program in inner London, was unable to show evidence of effectiveness on the incidence of fires and fire-related injuries (DiGuiseppi et al., 2002). A more recent study, though, suggests that installation programs, rather than giveaway programs, may be effective in increasing the use of these alarms (Harvey et al., 2004).

Interventions that have been proposed but not yet shown to be effective involve, in large part, efforts to reduce exposure to fires and flames. These include separating cooking areas from living areas (including efforts to reduce the use of indoor fires for cooking), ensuring cooking surfaces are at appropriate heights, reducing the storage of flammable substances in households, and greater supervision of younger children (Forjuoh, in press).

The introduction, monitoring, and enforcement of standards and codes for and the wearing of fire-safety garments have also been proposed. Such standards and codes must, however, be based on data from studies that examine the flammability of materials in circumstances that most closely mimic real-life circumstances (Bawa Bhalla, Kale, & Mohan, 2000).

Evidence for the effectiveness of interventions to prevent water-related burn injuries is minimal, but promising. In an increasing number of high-income countries, much effort has been directed toward measures that not only educate communities about the dangers of high tap water temperatures but also legis-late and enforce efforts to regulate the temperature of water flowing from household taps (Macarthur, 2003). However, in low-income countries, scalds due to hot water are more likely to be associated with cooking and boiling of water, rather than water from taps.

Many of the same interventions proposed in re-lation to the separation of the cooking areas from living and play areas have been proposed for water-related burn injuries, as well as suggestions that cook-ing vessels holding water might be better designed to minimize the chances of spillage.

Finally, interventions directed at increasing aware-ness of burn prevention (whether they be fire or wa-ter related) have been proposed, in large part as a result of the success of safe-community interventions involving a multitude of strategies (Ytterstad & Sogaard, 1995). Similarly, relevant to both types of burn injuries is the issue of immediate first aid re-sponses and the importance of education to ensure that the most appropriate first aid strategies are applied (Ghosh & Bharat, 2000; Sunder & Bharat, 1998).

Interventions to Prevent Drowning

Evidence for the effectiveness of interventions to pre-vent drowning, whether in high- or low-income coun-tries, is almost nonexistent. The only available data providing some evidence of effectiveness come from case control studies undertaken in high-income coun-tries, suggesting that fencing of domestic swimming pools reduces the risks of drowning (Thompson & Rivara, 2000). Although the observational nature of these studies still leaves open the possibility that the apparent effectiveness of fencing may be explained by uncontrolled confounding, there would be few who would not agree that at least some protection must be afforded by limiting exposure to water. Extrapolation of these findings to a low-income setting would sug-gest that measures to limit exposure to bodies of wa-ter close to dwellings might be effective in reducing drowning. Examples that have been proposed include covering wells with grills, fencing close-by lakes or riverbanks, and building flood control embankments.

The effectiveness of learn-to-swim programs, while a common component of prevention programs in high-income countries, has not been examined in rigorously controlled studies. However, few would argue that teaching both children and adults to swim does not have the potential to reduce drowning both in high-income countries and low- and middle-income countries.

Education regarding the burden and risk factors for drowning, including, in particular, the risks posed by prior consumption of alcohol, has also been pos-tulated as a potential intervention strategy (Celis, 1991). Increased supervision of children around bod-ies of water and the provision of lifesavers at popular swimming areas have been proposed as other measures that might reduce drowning (Hyder et al., 2003).

Interventions to prevent water-related transport drowning include equipping boats with flotation de-vices, ensuring that boats and flotation devices are well maintained, passing legislation and enforcing reg-ulations relating to the maximum numbers of indi-viduals who might be carried on boats, and providing of fully trained and responsive coast guard services (World Health Organization, 2003). However, as with the preventive measures designed to prevent non-transport-related drowning, evidence that any of these interventions is effective is unavailable.

Interventions to Prevent Self-Directed Violence (see also Chapter 8, Exhibit 8.4)

Although many interventions to prevent self-directed violence have been available for some time, there is very limited evidence to show the effectiveness of these interventions in terms of reductions in suicidal behavior (Krug et al., 2002). Individual approaches to prevention include both treatment approaches and behavioral approaches, with the former focusing on identifying and managing mental disorders that have been shown to be associated with increased risk of self-directed violence (primarily with pharmacother-apy). Behavioral therapy approaches focus particu-larly on identifying situations and issues that may place individuals at high risk and considering ways in which individuals can be better equipped to address these situations. Relationship approaches to preven-tion focus on enhancing social relationships so as to reduce repeated suicidal behaviors.

Community-based prevention efforts include en-couraging attendance at suicide prevention centers and self-help groups and school-based interventions that in-volve training of school staff, community members, and health care providers to identify those at risk and refer them to treatment. By comparison, societal ap-proaches include both restricting access to means and managing media reports of suicides. The former ap-proach has included reducing access to sedatives, pes-ticides, carbon monoxide in domestic gas and in car exhausts, and the possession of handguns in the home.

Interventions to Prevent Interpersonal Violence

Interventions to prevent interpersonal violence have been categorized not only in terms of the various phases encompassed in the ecological model but also in terms of the developmental phases spanning from the infant and toddler years (ages <3) through childhood (3–11 years) and adolescence (12–19 years) to adulthood (>19 years). The *World Report* outlines in some detail, for the various types of interpersonal violence, a range of both effective and ineffective interventions that can be considered in this way (Krug et al., 2002).

Individual interventions that have been shown to be effective in reducing youth violence, primarily in high-income countries, include social development programs that improve competency and social skills with peers, commonly introduced in school settings. Relationship approaches attempt to influence the type of relations that young people have with others with whom they regularly interact. Home visitation programs in infancy, training in parenting during early childhood, and mentoring programs during adolescence have all been shown to be effective interventions. Although a range of community and societal interventions strategies have also been proposed, to date, evidence of their effectiveness is lacking.

Although the effectiveness of home visitations in preventing child abuse and neglect has been well documented, few other interventions in this field have been evaluated. Very few of the proposed interventions focus on primary prevention, and most focus on the management of victims or perpetrators of violence. Proposed intervention strategies include family support approaches (including home visitations), health service approaches that include screening by health professionals and the training of health professionals, and therapeutic approaches comprising services for victims, services for children who witness violence, and services for adults abused as children. Legal and related interventions that have been recommended and implemented include mandatory and voluntary reporting schemes, child protection services, child fatality review teams, various arrest and prosecution policies, and court-mandated treatment for offenders. Community-based intervention strategies include school-based programs, prevention and educational campaigns, and interventions to change community attitudes and behavior, while societal approaches include the introduction of national policies and programs and international treaties.

In the arena of violence by intimate partners, very few interventions have been rigorously evaluated. Interventions that have been implemented include support for victims, including the provision of safe houses or shelters and the introduction of legal remedies and judicial reforms that include the criminalization of abuse, laws and policies relating to the arrest of perpetrators, alternative sanctions such as protection orders, and, in a few countries, especially in Latin America, the introduction of all-women police stations. Treatment programs for perpetrators have been introduced in some countries, although evidence to support the effectiveness of such programs is very mixed. A range of health service interventions for victims have been implemented, focusing in large part on increasing the identification of victims in emergency departments or through primary care services. Community-based initiatives that been introduced include outreach work, co-coordinated community interventions, prevention campaigns, and school programs.

Very few evaluated interventions exist in the area of elder abuse, with none involving a comparison group. Interventions that have and continue to be considered include both national-level responses, such as establishing national bodies to address the issue, and local-level responses. The latter include the provision of appropriate social services and health care, legal actions, and educational and public awareness campaigns.

As with most of the other areas of interpersonal violence just discussed, the number of interventions addressing sexual violence is limited and few have been well evaluated. Similarly, few of these interventions have been implemented or evaluated in low- and middle-income countries. Individual intervention approaches include services that provide psychological care and support for victims, programs for perpetrators, and life-skills and other educational programs. Health care responses include the provision of medico-legal services, training for health care professionals, prophylaxis programs for HIV infection, and centers providing comprehensive care to victims of sexual assault. Community-based efforts include prevention campaigns, community activism by men, and school-based programs. Legal and policy responses to sexual violence include approaches to the reporting and handling of cases of sexual violence, legal reform, and international treaties. Finally, a range of actions to prevent other forms of sexual violence have been proposed relating to sexual trafficking, female genital mutilation, child marriage, and rape during armed conflicts, although evidence to support the effectiveness of any of these interventions is lacking.

Interventions to Prevent Collective Violence

The prevention of collective violence lies in reducing the potential for violent conflicts and in providing appropriate responses to violent conflicts when they occur. Not surprisingly, scientific evidence about the effectiveness of interventions is lacking (Krug et al., 2002). However, policies that facilitate reductions in poverty, that make decision making more accountable, and that reduce inequalities between groups, as well as policies that reduce access to biological, chemical, nuclear, and other weapons, have been recommended. When planning responses to violent conflicts, recommended approaches include assessing at an early stage who is most vulnerable and what their needs are, coordinating of activities between various players, and working toward global, national, and local capabilities so as to deliver effective health services during the various stages of an emergency (Krug et al., 2002).

The Role of Health Services in Preventing Death and Disability from Unintentional Injuries and Violence

Although the focus of this section has been on identifying strategies to prevent the occurrence of injuries, it is important to recognize that access to health services has a major role to play in preventing death and disability from injuries. Differential access to health and medical services has been identified in other fields of health as having an important bearing on long-term outcomes, and the importance of such services is increasingly being recognized in the injury field (Razzak & Kellermann, 2002).

For example, although prehospital transport systems exist in major cities in low- and middle-income countries, in rural areas the prehospital care that is delivered to trauma victims in the field is minimal or nonexistent. The lack of quality emergency medical services care and timely transport to the hospital translates into higher rates of death for patients. For example, one study reported up to 58% prehospital mortality for intentional injuries in Pakistan (Chotani, Razzack, & Luby, 2002).

In a recent review of trauma outcomes, mortality was 65% in resource-poor settings, compared with 55% and 35% in moderate- and good-resource settings, respectively (Mock et al., 1998). Significant improvements, with reductions in mortality, have been reported as a result of improvements in trauma care (Mock, Quansah et al., 2004). WHO has recently suggested that even in less-resourced environments, injury mortality and disability can be reduced by reorganizing systems, upgrading the skills of health staff, and ensuring minimum physical and human resources (Mock, Lormand et al., 2004).

The availability and quality of nonacute services, especially rehabilitation services, are also relevant to the long-term outcomes of injured individuals. Although a detailed review of the significance of such services is beyond the scope of this chapter, there is increasing recognition of the importance of an integrated response to injury prevention that includes primary prevention as well as secondary and tertiary prevention.

Economic Analyses of Interventions to Prevent Unintentional Injuries and Violence

There is a dearth of literature on economic evaluations of interventions for injuries, in large part reflecting the infancy of the field and the limited but growing evidence base identifying effective preventive strategies. However, even for interventions that are routinely used in high-income countries, the evidence for their cost-effectiveness is not easily or widely available. The situation is more critical in low- and middle-income countries, where evaluations for these interventions are generally not available.

Exemplifying this paucity, but the potential importance of such data, are the findings of two recent reviews that have documented available economic analysis on interventions for road traffic injuries (Hyder et al., 2004; Waters, Hyder, & Phillips, 2004). These reviews, almost entirely undertaken using data from high-income countries, suggest that interventions such as mandatory helmet laws, laws requiring that motor vehicles be inspected, the installation of automatic daytime running lights, and seat belt laws are likely to provide widespread benefits with high benefit to cost ratios, even in low- and middle-income countries.

Similarly, although there are relatively few published economic evaluations of interventions targeting interpersonal violence, the available studies suggest that behavioral, legal, and regulatory interventions cost less money than they save, in some cases by several orders of magnitude (Waters et al., 2004). For example, the 1994 Violence Against Women Act in the United States has resulted in an estimated net benefit of $16.4 billion, including $14.8 billion in averted victims' costs. A separate analysis shows that providing shelters for victims of domestic violence would result in a benefit to cost ratio of between 6.8 and 18.4. Similarly, the costs of a program to prevent child abuse through counseling equal 5% of the costs of child abuse itself. Implementation of a gun registration law in Canada costs $70 million, in comparison with a total annual cost of $5.6 billion for firearm-related injuries in that country. Interventions that target juvenile offenders—including aggression replacement training and foster care treatment—have been shown to result in economic benefits that are more than 30 times greater than the corresponding costs.

Moving Forward the Injury Prevention Agenda: Opportunities and Challenges

In the past 20 years, our knowledge about the burden of injuries, risk factors for injuries, and effective interventions has increased exponentially. In many high-income countries, the benefits of this increased knowledge have resulted in significant declines in injury mortality rates. However, for many low- and middle-income countries, increases in injury mortality and morbidity are predicted over the next 20 years, both as a result of changing sociodemographic patterns and as these countries increasingly address the burdens of communicable disease and maternal and child ill health. Consequently, there is an imperative to move ahead with an injury prevention agenda, while recognizing that many of the challenges faced by low- and middle-income countries will be different from those that have been faced in the previous 20 years.

Advocacy for Injury Prevention

It remains critical that the global health community understand the health, economic, and social effects of unintentional injuries and violence. It is equally important that the health sector recognize that there are clearly defined risk factors for these injuries and, even more important, that there are effective interventions that can prevent these injuries and reduce the burden of death and disability from this preventable cause of ill health. However, despite the recent efforts by WHO and many injury professionals throughout the world, there is still only limited recognition by many governments and the wider community that injuries are no accident and that we can work to prevent the predicted global increases in injury mortality and disability. As a result, it is clear that targeted and evidence-based advocacy is essential at local, national, and international levels.

The key messages to be transmitted in advocacy efforts include the fact that injuries and violence cause considerable death and disability, are predictable events with clearly identified causes, and can be effectively prevented. Moreover, there is a great need, especially in low- and middle- income countries, to initiate national dialogues regarding key injury issues and to stimulate an intersectoral approach to address them. The *World Report on Road Traffic Injuries Prevention*, for example, proposes such an approach to national stakeholders and stresses the need for national ownership and local action (Peden et al., 2004).

Research and Development Needs

To date, global investments for injury research and interventions, compared with other health areas, do not match the burden of disease. For example, road traffic injuries have been identified as a highly neglected area for investments compared with the burden of disease they represent, measured in dollars per DALY (approximately US$0.40/DALY), especially when considered in relation to other major health problems (Ad Hoc Committee on Health Research Relating to Future Intervention Options, 1996). It is not surprising, therefore, that national analyses of safety investments have demonstrated very low investment rates in low-income countries such as Pakistan and Uganda—approximately US$0.07 per capita in Pakistan (Bishai et al., 2003). Consequently, although there is much that we already know about the burden, causes, and effective interventions for injury, significant gains in our understanding of these factors could be made if equitable resources were directed to the injury field.

Since 90% of the world's population lives in low- and middle-income countries, and the burden of injuries is predicted to increase in these countries, it is imperative that future research and development activities focus especially on the needs of these countries. Although it would be inappropriate to outline a detailed agenda for future research and development that is relevant to all countries, a generic framework that encompasses the type of research that is required can be recommended, as described in the following paragraphs.

Epidemiologic research in describing the existing burden, causes, and distribution of unintentional injuries and violence is still needed in low- and middle-income countries. Assessing the loss of health and life from unintentional injuries and violence, who they affect, how, and under what specific circumstances is thus a continuing research agenda for low- and middle-income countries. Problems of underreporting and other biases in available data need to be addressed as well.

It is critical to not only identify the determinants of unintentional injuries and violence but also to address them. The lack of intervention research in low- and middle-income countries is a huge gap in health research globally. Scientific trials of injury interventions have largely not been conducted in low- and middle-income countries, and there is a great need to modify, adapt, and test existing as well as new interventions in these specific settings. Although clearly some might argue that such research should be a priority in most low- and middle-income countries, unless the basic underpinning research on the burden and determinants of unintentional injuries and violence has been undertaken, the political and financial support for such research will not be forthcoming.

The lack of empirical information on the cost-effectiveness of injury interventions, not only in high-income countries but also in low- and middle-income countries, is a major policy issue, especially because there is the potential for interventions used in high-income countries to be transferred to low- and middle-income countries without regard to their appropriateness or relevance. Perhaps equally important is the concern that without such research, highly cost-effective interventions will not be implemented at all. Policy-oriented research that identifies the barriers to implementation is thus an essential component of moving forward an injury prevention agenda.

The Significance of a Trained Workforce

Research and programs in the field of unintentional injuries and violence require trained individuals with specific skills and tools. Injury and violence prevention is a science with conceptual frameworks, epidemiologic approaches, intervention testing methods, and analysis techniques. There are well-developed training programs in high-income countries that produce a workforce that can take the injury and violence prevention agenda forward. However, there is a general lack of such trained human resources in the developing world; as a consequence, capacity development for human resources must necessarily focus on developing capacity in low-and middle-income countries.

Issues of both quantity and quality arise in the production of a trained workforce. Clearly, there needs to be a critical mass of trained injury and violence prevention professionals in a country to understand, develop, and implement interventions. On the other hand, this field is multisectoral, and so a wide diversity of skills is needed for prevention. Epidemiology, statistics, health information systems, health policy, economics, sociology, and law are only some of the fields that have a role in reducing the burden of disease from injuries and violence. In this context, the role of the public health sector is both to assume leadership in developing and organizing a response to injuries and violence and to facilitate the inputs by other fields and disciplines. As a result, management and leadership skills also become important for a well-trained workforce in injury and violence prevention.

The Role of National and International Organizations

Finally, the role of international organizations (such as WHO or the World Bank) and national agencies (such as ministries of health or medical research councils) needs to be emphasized in moving ahead the injury prevention agenda.

The role of international organizations can be summarized as follows.

- *Strategic:* in terms of first internally recognizing the toll on societies of injuries and violence, and then convincing governments externally to appreciate the same (as has been done in the case of road traffic injuries by the joint World Bank/WHO report)
- *Facilitation:* in terms of providing technical assistance, appropriate advice, and relevant tools for national policies and action
- *Resource mobilization:* in terms of demonstrating true commitment to supporting the implementation of effective interventions in countries and promoting research in the field

The role of national organizations will encompass elements of the functions just mentioned but also include the following.

- *Advocacy:* in terms of accepting ownership of the problem and promoting engagement with other national institutions
- *Implementation:* in terms of policy development and ensuring programs on the ground in countries for addressing injuries and violence
- *Evaluation:* in terms of a continuous process of assessing interventions and programs, in addition to supporting nationally relevant research

The international movements currently under way for violence prevention and road traffic injuries prevention as promulgated through the two *World Reports* are examples of how joint global and national partnerships are needed for making change.

Conclusions

Unintentional injuries and violence present a major global health problem, which will increase in magnitude unless systematic, scientifically based approaches to prevention are implemented. Although the public health community has only relatively recently recognized the significance of the global injury epidemic, much new knowledge has been generated in a very short time, as illustrated in the current chapter. However, much of this new knowledge has focused on the burden of injury in high-income countries, and thus the challenge for the future must be to extend our knowledge to the growing injury burden faced by low- and middle-income countries.

The international public health community has an important role to play in addressing this challenge, through facilitating the description of the problem, the development of solutions, the implementation of programs, and the analysis of effects. Moreover, the public health community can also play a leadership role in galvanizing a multisectoral response to injuries, advocating for investments at national and international levels, and catalyzing the sharing of experiences around the world. The large and often devastating health impact of injuries and violence on humans makes it imperative that the international public health community not only take an interest but be proactive in addressing the burden of disease from injuries and violence at local, national, and international levels.

By way of example, the role of the public health sector in drowning prevention has been described clearly by WHO as follows:

- to describe the magnitude of the problem by collecting data on drowning deaths and morbidity
- to identify vulnerable populations and address their needs
- to undertake research to identify risk factors, protective factors, and exposure measures
- to identify the economic impact of drowning, in order to provide a basis for cost-benefit analysis for safety improvements

- to promote, facilitate, and catalyze the implementation of drowning prevention measures and policies
- to monitor and evaluate interventions
- to advocate for more attention to drowning prevention
- to strengthen emergency response services

The extension of this paradigm to all cause-specific unintentional injuries and violence should thus be advocated and implemented.

In summary, injuries are no accident, but are highly predictable and preventable events. The international public health community has already played an important role in taking this message forward—the challenge is to continue to do so, to prevent the predicted epidemics of unintentional injuries and violence in low- and middle-income countries.

● ● ● **Discussion Questions**

1. Why should public health programs in low- and middle-income countries address injuries and violence?

2. The lack of good global and regional statistics on injuries and violence is apparent. How can this situation be improved? Who should improve it?

3. Choose a specific type of injury. What steps can be taken to reduce the burden of this injury in low- and middle-income countries?

4. Suppose you were funding research on injuries and violence. Describe five topics or studies that would be your priority for research in low- and middle-income countries.

• • • References

Adesunkanmi, A. R., Oseni, S. A., & Badru, O. S. (1999). Severity and outcome of falls in children. *West African Journal of Medicine, 18*(4), 281–285.

Ad Hoc Committee on Health Research Relating to Future Intervention Options. (1996). *Investing in health research and development* (Document TDK/Gen/96.1). Geneva, Switzerland: World Health Organization.

Aeron-Thomas, A., Jacobs, G. D., Sexton, B., Gururaj, G., & Rahmann, F. (2004). *The involvement and impact of road crashes on the poor: Bangladesh and India case studies* (Published Project Report No. PRP 010). Crowthorne, United Kingdom: Transport Research Laboratory.

Afukaar, F. K. (2003). Speed control in low- and middle-income countries: Issues, challenges and opportunities in reducing road traffic injuries. *Injury Control and Safety Promotion, 10*(1–2), 77–81.

Afukaar, F. K., Pantwi, P., & Ofosu-Amah, S. (2003). Pattern of road traffic injuries in Ghana: Implications for control. *Injury Control and Safety Promotion, 10*(1–2), 69–76.

Ahmed, M. K., Rahman, M., & van Ginneken, J. (1999). Epidemiology of child deaths due to drowning in Matlab, Bangladesh. *International Journal of Epidemiology, 28*(2), 306–311.

Attewell, R. G., Glase, K., & McFadden, M. (2001). Bicycle helmet efficacy: A meta-analysis. *Accident Analysis and Prevention, 33*(3), 345–352.

Azizi, B. H., Zulkifli, H. I., & Kasim, M. S. (1993). Risk factors for accidental poisoning in urban Malaysian children. *Annals of Tropical Paediatrics, 13*(2), 183–188.

Bangdiwala, S. I., & Anzola-Perez, E. (1990). The incidence of injuries in young people: II. Log-linear multivariable models for risk factors in a collaborative study in Brazil, Chile, Cuba and Venezuela. *International Journal of Epidemiology, 19*(1), 125–132.

Bawa Bhalla, S., Kale, S. R., & Mohan, D. (2000). Burn properties of fabrics and garments worn in India. *Accident Analysis and Prevention, 32*(3), 407–420.

Bener, A., Al-Salman, K. M., & Pugh, R. N. H. (1998). Injury mortality and morbidity among children in the United Arab Emirates. *European Journal of Epidemiology, 14*, 175–178.

Bischoff-Ferrari, H. A., Dawson-Hughes, B., Willett, W. C., Staehelin, H. B., Bazemore, M. G., Zee, R. Y., & Wong, J. B. (2004). Effect of vitamin D on falls: A meta-analysis. *Journal of the American Medical Association, 291*(16), 1999–2006.

Bishai, D., Hyder, A. A., Ghaffar, A., Morrow, R. H., & Kobusingye, O. (2003). Rates of public investment for road safety in developing countries: Case studies of Uganda and Pakistan. *Health Policy and Planning, 18*(2), 232–235.

Boonyaratavej, N., Suriyawongpaisal, P., Takkinsatien, A., Wanvarie, S., Rajatanavin, R., & Apiyasawat, P. (2001). Physical activity and risk factors for hip fractures in Thai women. *Osteoporosis International, 12*(3), 244–248.

Brenner, R. A. (2003). Prevention of drowning in infants, children and adolescents. *Pediatrics, 112*(2), 440–445.

Brown, J. P., Josse, R. G., Scientific Advisory Council of the Osteoporosis Society of Canada. (2002). 2002 clinical practice guidelines for the diagnosis and management of osteoporosis in Canada. *Canadian Medical Association Journal, 167*(10 Suppl.), S1–S34.

Bunn, F., Collier, T., Frost, C., Ker, K., Roberts, I., & Wentz, R. (2003). Traffic calming for the prevention of road traffic injuries: Systematic review and meta-analysis. *Injury Prevention, 9*(3), 200–204.

Buvinic, M., Morrison, A. R., & Shifter, M. (1999). Violence in Latin America and the Caribbean: A framework for action. In Andrew R. Morison and Maria Loreto Biehl (Eds.), *Too close to home: Domestic violence in the Americas.* New York: Inter-American Development Bank.

Campbell, A. J., Robertson, M. C., Gardner, M. M., Norton, R. N., & Buchner, D.M. (1999). Psychotropic medication withdrawal and a home-based exercise program to prevent falls: A randomized controlled trial. *Journal of the American Geriatrics Society, 47*(7), 850–853.

Carlini-Cotrim, B., & da Matta Chasin, A. A. (2000). Blood alcohol content and death from fatal injury: A study in metropolitan area of Sao Paulo, Brazil. *Journal of Psychoactive Drugs, 32*(3), 269–275.

Carnegie Commission on Preventing Deadly Conflict. (1997). *Preventing deadly conflict: Final report.* New York: Carnegie Corporation.

Celis, A. (1991). Drowning in Jalisco: 1983–1989. *Saluda Publica Mexico, 33*(6), 585–589.

Celis, A. (1997). Home drowning among preschool age Mexican children. *Injury Prevention, 3*(4), 252–256.

Chan, K. Y., Hairol, O., Imtiaz, H., Zailani, M., Kumar, S., Somasundaram, S., & Nasir-Zahari, M. (2002). A review of burns patients admitted to the burns unit of Hospital Universiti Kebangsaan Malaysia. *Medical Journal of Malaysia, 57*(4), 418–425.

Chang, J. T., Morton, S. C., Rubenstein, L. Z., Mojica, W. A., Maglione, M., Suttorp, M. J., Roth, E. A., & Shekelle, P. G. (2004). Interventions for the prevention of falls in older adults: Systematic review and meta-analysis of randomised clinical trials. *British Medical Journal, 328*(7441), 653–654.

Chatsantiprapa, K., Chokkanapitak, J., & Pinpradit, N. (2001). Host and environment factors for exposure to poisons: A case control study of preschool children in Thailand. *Injury Prevention, 7*(3), 214–217.

Chotani, H. A., Razzak, J. A., & Luby, S. P. (2002). Patterns of violence in Karachi. *Injury Prevention, 8*(1), 57–59.

Clark, P., de la Pena, F., Gomez Garcia, F., Orozco, J. A., & Tugwell, P. (1998). Risk factors for osteoporotic hip fractures in Mexicans. *Archives of Medical Research, 29*(3), 253–257.

Conrad, P., Bradshaw, Y. S., Lamsudin, R., Kasniyah, N., & Costello, C. (1996). Helmets, injuries, and cultural definitions: Motorcycle injury in urban Indonesia. *Accident Analysis and Prevention, 28*(2), 193–200.

Cummings, S. R., Nevitt, M. C., Browner, W. S., Stone, K., Fox, K. M., Ensrud, K. E., Cauley, J., Black, D., & Vogt, T. M. (1995). Risk factors for hip fracture in white women. *New England Journal of Medicine, 332*(12), 767–773.

Cywes, S., Kibel, S. M., Bass, D. H., Rode, H., Millar, A. J. W., & De Wet, J. (1990). Paediatric trauma care. *South African Medical Journal, 78,* 413–418.

Daisy, S., Mostaque, A. K., Bari, T. S., Kahn, A. R., Karim, S., & Quamruzzaman, Q. (2001). Socioeconomic and cultural influence in the causation of burns in the urban children of Bangladesh. *Journal of Burn Care and Rehabilitation, 22*(4), 269–273.

Dargent-Molina, P., Favier, F., Grandjean, H., Baudoin, C., Schott, A. M., Hausherr, E., Meunier, P. J., & Breart, G. (1996). Fall-related factors and risk of hip fracture: The EPIDOS prospective study. *Lancet, 348*(9021), 145–149.

Davis, S., & Smith, L. S. (1985). The epidemiology of drowning in Cape Town 1980–1983. *South African Medical Journal, 68*(10), 739–742.

Dedoukou, X., Spyridopoulos, T., Kedikoglou, S., Alexe, D. M., Dessypris, N., & Petridou, E. (2004). Incidence and risk factors of fall injuries among infants: A study in Greece. *Archives of Pediatric and Adolescent Medicine, 158*(10), 1002–1006.

Delgado, J., Ramirez-Cardich, M. E., Gilman, R. H., Lavarello, R., Dahodwala, N., Bazan, A., Rodriguez, V., Cama, R. I., Tovar, M., & Lescano, A. (2002). Risk factors for burns in children: Crowding, poverty, and poor maternal education. *Injury Prevention, 8*(1), 38–41.

Department for Transport. (2003). *A cost recovery system for speed and red light cameras: Two-year pilot evaluation.* London: Department for Transport, Road Safety Division.

DiGuiseppi, C., Roberts, I., Wade, A., Sculpher, M., Edwards, P., Godward, C., Pan, H., & Slater, S. (2002). Incidence of fires and related injuries after giving out free smoke alarms: Cluster randomized controlled trial. *British Medical Journal, 325*(7371), 995.

Dinh-Zarr, T. B., Sleet, D. A., Shults, R. A., Zaza, S., Elder, R. W., Nichols, J. L., Thompson, R. S., Sosin, D. M., Task Force on Community Preventive

Services. (2001). Reviews of evidence regarding interventions to increase the use of safety belts. *American Journal of Preventive Medicine, 21* (4 Suppl.), 48–65.

Driscoll, T. R., Harrison, J. A., & and Steenkamp, M. (2004). Review of the role of alcohol in drowning associated with recreational aquatic activity. *Injury Prevention, 10*(2), 107–113.

Elvik, R., & Vaa, T. (2004). *Handbook of road safety measures.* Amsterdam: Elsevier.

European Road Safety Action Program. (2003). *Halving the number of road accident victims in the European Union by 2010: A shared responsibility.* Brussels: European Commission. http://europa .eu.int./comm/transport/road/roadsafety/rsap/ index_en.htm.

Forjuoh, S. N. (2003). Traffic-related injury prevention interventions for low income countries. *Injury Control and Safety Promotion, 10*(1–2), 109–118.

Forjuoh, S. N. (in press). *Preventing burns in low and middle-income countries.* Disease Control Priorities Project Working Paper.

Forjuoh, S. N., Guyer, B., & Smith, G. S. (1995). Childhood burns in Ghana: Epidemiological characteristics and home-based treatment. *Burns, 21*(1), 24–28.

Forjuoh, S. N., Guyer, B., Strobino, D. M., Keyl, P. M., Diener-West, M., & Smith, G. S. (1995). Risk factors for childhood burns: A case-control study of Ghanaian children. *Journal of Epidemiology and Community Health, 49*(2), 189–193.

Ghaffar, A., Hyder, A. A., Mastoor, M. I., & Shaikh, I. (1999). Injuries in Pakistan: Directions for future health policy. *Health Policy and Planning, 14*(1), 11–17.

Ghosh, A., & Bharat, R. (2000). Domestic burns prevention and first aid awareness in and around Jamshedpur, India: Strategies and impact. *Burns, 26*(7), 605–608.

Gillespie, L. D., Gillespie, W. J., Robertson, M. C., Lamb, S. E., Cumming, R. G., & Rowe, B. H. (2003). Interventions for preventing falls in elderly people. *Cochrane Database of Systematic Reviews,* no. 4, CD000340.

Gururaj, G., Isaac, M. K., Subbakrishna, D. K., & Ranjani, R. (2004). Risk factors for completed suicides: A case-control study from Bangalore, India. *Injury Control and Safety Promotion, 11*(3), 183–191.

Haddon, W., Jr. (1968). The changing approach to the epidemiology, prevention, and amelioration of trauma: The transition to approaches etiologically rather than descriptively based. *American Journal of Public Health and the Nation's Health, 58*(8), 1431–1438.

Harvey, P. A., Aitken, M., Ryan, G. W., Demeter, L. A, Givens, J., Sundararaman, R., & Goulette, S. (2004). Strategies to increase smoke alarm use in high-risk households. *Journal of Community Health, 29*(5), 375–385.

Hyder, A. A., Arifeen, S., Begum, N., Fishman, S., Wali, S., & Baqui, A. H. (2003). Death from drowning: Defining a new challenge for child survival in Bangladesh. *Injury Control and Safety Promotion, 10*(4), 205–210.

Hyder, A. A., Waters, H., Philipps, T., & Rehwinkel, J. (2004). *Exploring the economics of motorcycle helmet laws: Implications for low and middle-income countries.* Baltimore: Johns Hopkins University.

ICF Consulting, Ltd., & Imperial College Centre for Transport Studies. (2003). *Cost-benefit analysis of road safety improvements: Final report.* London: ICF Consulting, Ltd.

Ichikawa, M., Chadbunchachai, W., & Marui, E. (2003). Effect of the helmet act for motorcyclists in Thailand. *Accident Analysis and Prevention, 35*(2), 183–189.

Istre, G. R., McCoy, M. A., Stowe, M., Davies, K., Zane, D., Anderson, R. J., et al. (2003). Childhood injuries due to falls from apartment balconies and windows. *Injury Prevention, 9*(4), 349–352.

Jacobs, G., Aaron-Thomas A., Astrop A. (2000) *Estimating global road fatalities.* (TRL Report 445). Crowthorne, United Kingdom: Transport Research Laboratory.

Jaye, C., Simpson, J. C., & Langley, J. D. (2001). Barriers to safe hot tap water: Results from a national study of New Zealand plumbers. *Injury Prevention, 7,* 302–306.

Jie, X., & Ren, C. B. (1992). Burn injuries in the Dong Bei area of China: A study of 12,606 cases. *Burns, 18*(3), 228–232.

Jitapunkul, S., Yuktananandana, P., & Parkpian, V. (2001). Risk factors of hip fracture among Thai female patients. *Journal of the Medical Association of Thailand, 84*(11), 1576–1581.

Jonah, B. A., Dawson, N. E., & Smith, G. A. (1982). Effects of a selective traffic enforcement program on seat belt usage. *Journal of Applied Psychology, 67,* 89–96.

Jonah, B. A., & Grant, B. A. (1985). Long-term effectiveness of selective traffic enforcement programs for increasing seat belt usage. *Journal of Applied Psychology, 70*(2), 257–263.

Khan, M. M., & Reza, H. (1998). Gender differences in non-fatal suicidal behavior in Pakistan: Significance of sociocultural factors. *Suicide and Life-Threatening Behavior, 28,* 62–68.

Kibel, S. M., Joubert, G., & Bradshaw, D. (1990). Injury-related mortality in South African children, 1981–1985. *South African Medical Journal, 78*(7), 398–403.

Kibel, S. M., Nagel, F. O., Myers, J., & Cywes, S. (1990). Childhood near-drowning-A 12-year retrospective review. *South African Medical Journal, 78*(7), 418–421.

Kloeden, C. N., McLean, A. J., Baldock, M. R. J., & Cockington, A. J. T. (1998). *Severe and fatal car crashes due to roadside hazards: A report to the Motor Accident Commission.* Adelaide, Australia: National Health and Medical Research Council Road Accident Research Unit, University of Adelaide.

Kobusingye, O., Guwatudde, D., & Lett, R. (2001). Injury patterns in rural and urban Uganda. *Injury Prevention, 7*(1), 46–50.

Koornstra, M., Bijleveld, F., & Hagenzieker, M. (1997). *The safety effects of daytime running lights* (Report R-97-36). Leidschendam, The Netherlands: Institute for Road Safety Research.

Kopits, E., & Cropper, M. (2003). *Traffic fatalities and economic growth* (Policy Research Working Paper 3035). Washington, DC: World Bank.

Kozik, C. A., Suntayakorn, S., Vaughn, D. W., Suntayakorn, C., Snitbhan, R., & Innis, B. L. (1999). Causes of death and unintentional injury among schoolchildren in Thailand. *Southeast Asian Journal of Tropical Medicine and Public Health, 30*(1), 129–135.

Krug, A., Ellis, J. B., Hay, I. T., Mokgabudi, N. F., & Robertson, J. (1994). The impact of child-resistant containers on the incidence of paraffin (kerosene) ingestion in children. *South African Medical Journal, 84*(11), 730–734.

Krug, E. G., Dahlberg, K. L., Mercy, J. A., Zwi, A. B., & Lozano, R. (Eds.). (2002). *World report on violence and health.* Geneva, Switzerland: World Health Organization.

Kulanthayan, S., Umar, R. S., Hariza, H. A., Nasir, M. T., & Harwant, S. (2000). Compliance of proper safety helmet usage in motorcyclists. *Medical Journal of Malaysia, 55*(1), 40–44.

Laforest, S., Robitaille, Y., Lesage, D., & Dorval, D. (2001). Surface characteristics, equipment height, and the occurrence and severity of playground injuries. *Injury Prevention, 7*(1), 35–40.

Liu, B., Ivers, R., Norton, R., Blows, S., & Lo, S. K. (2004). Helmets for preventing injury in motorcycle riders. *Cochrane Database of Systematic Reviews,* no. 4, CD004333.

Liu, E. H., Khatri, B., Shakya, Y. M., & Richard, B. M. (1998). A 3 year prospective audit of burns patients treated at the Western Regional Hospital of Nepal. *Burns, 24*(2), 129–133.

Liu, G. F., Han, S., Liang, D. H., Wang, F. Z., Shi, X. Z., Yu, J., Wu, Z. L. (2003). Driver sleepiness and risk of car crashes in Shenyang, a Chinese northeastern city: Population-based case-control study. *Biomedical and Environmental Sciences, 16*(3), 219–226.

Lu, T. H., Lee, M. C., & Chou, M. C. (1998). Trends in injury mortality among adolescents in Taiwan, 1965–94. *Injury Prevention, 4,* 111–115.

Macarthur, C. (2003). Evaluation of Safe Kids Week 2001: Prevention of scald and burn injuries in young children. *Injury Prevention, 9*(2), 112–116.

Macgregor, D. M. (2000). Injuries associated with falls from beds. *Injury Prevention, 6*(4), 291–292.

Mock, C., Amegashi, J., & Darteh, K. (1999). Role of commercial drivers in motor vehicle related injuries in Ghana. *Injury Prevention, 5*(4), 268–271.

Mock, C. J., Jurkovich, G. J., nii-Amon-Kotei, D., Arreola-Risa, C., & Maier, R. V. (1998). Trauma mortality patterns in three nations at different economic levels: Implications for global trauma system development. *Journal of Trauma, 44*(5), 804–812.

Mock, C., Lormand, J. P., Joshipura, M., Goosen, J., & Peden, M. (2004). *Guidelines for essential trauma care.* Geneva, Switzerland: World Health Organization.

Mock, C., Quansah, R., Krishnan, R., Arreola-Risa, C., & Rivara, F. (2004). Strengthening the prevention and care of injuries worldwide. *Lancet, 363*(9427), 2172–2179.

Mohan, D. (2002). Road safety in less-motorized environments: Future concerns. *International Journal of Epidemiology, 31*(3), 527–532.

Murray, C., & Lopez, A. (1996). *Global burden of disease and injuries.* Cambridge, MA: Harvard University Press.

Nafukho, F. M., & Khayesi, M. (2002). Livelihood, conditions of work, regulation, and road safety in the small-scale public transport sector: A case of the matatu mode of transport in Kenya. In X. Godard & I. Fatonzoun (Eds.), *Urban mobility for all. Proceedings of the Tenth International CODATU Conference, Lome, Togo, 12–15 November 2002* (pp. 241–245). Lisse, The Netherlands: AA Balkema Publishers.

Nhachi, C. F., & Kasilo, O. M. (1994). Household chemicals poisoning admissions in Zimbabwe's main urban centres. *Human and Experimental Toxicology, 13*(2), 69–72.

Nixon, J., Spinks, A., Turner, C., & McClure, R. (2004). Community based programs to prevent poisoning in children 0–15 years. *Injury Prevention, 10*(1), 43–46.

Norghani, M., Zainuddin, A., Radin Umar, R. S., & Hussain, H. (1998). *Use of exposure control methods to tackle motorcycle accidents in Malaysia* (Research Report 3/98). Serdang, Malaysia: Road Safety Research Center, University Putra Malaysia.

Odero, W., Garner, P., & Zwi, A. B. (1997). Road traffic injuries in developing countries: A comprehensive review of epidemiological studies. *Tropical Medicine and International Health, 2*(5), 445–460.

Odero, W., Khayesi, M., & Heda, P. M. (2003). Road traffic injuries in Kenya: Magnitude, causes and status of intervention. *Injury Control and Safety Promotion, 10*(1–2), 53–61.

Odero, W. O., & Zwi, A. B. (1995). Alcohol-related traffic injuries and fatalities in low- and middle-income countries: A critical review of literature. In C. N. Kloeden & A. J. McLean (Eds.), *Proceedings of the 13th International Conference on Alcohol, Drugs, and Traffic Safety, Adelaide, 13–18 August 1995* (pp. 713–720). Adelaide, Australia: Road Accident Research Unit.

Parker, M. J., Gillespie, L. D., & Gillespie, W. J. (2003). Hip protectors for preventing hip fractures in the elderly. *Cochrane Database of Systematic Reviews,* no. 3, CD001255.

Peden, M., Knottenbelt, D., Van der Spuy, J., Oodit, R., Scholtz, M. J., & Stokol, J. M. (1996). Injured pedestrians in Cape Town: The role of alcohol. *South African Medical Journal, 86*(9), 1103–1105.

Peden, M., Scurfield, R., Sleet, D., Mohan, D., Hyder, A. A., Jarawan, E., & Matherc, C. (Eds). (2004). *World report on road traffic injury prevention.* Geneva, Switzerland: World Health Organization.

Poli de Figueiredo, L. F., Rasslan, S., Bruscagin, V., Cruz, R., & Rocha e Silva, M. (2001). Increases in fines and driver licence withdrawal have effectively reduced immediate deaths from trauma on Brazilian roads: First-year report on the new traffic code. *Injury, 32*(2), 91–94.

Radin Umar, R. S., Mackay, G. M., & Hills, B. L. (1996). Modelling of conspicuity-related motorcycle accidents in Seremban and Shah Alam, Malaysia. *Accident Analysis and Prevention, 28*(3), 325–332.

Raja, I. A., Vohra, A. H., & Ahmed, M. (2001). Neurotrauma in Pakistan. *World Journal of Surgery, 25*(9), 1230–1237.

Razzak, J. A., & Kellermann, A. L. (2002). Emergency medical care in developing countries: Is it worthwhile? *Bulletin of the World Health Organization, 80*(11), 900–905.

Retting, R. A., Ferguson, S. A., & McCartt, A. T. (2003). A review of evidence-based traffic engineering measures designed to reduce pedestrian-motor vehicle crashes. *American Journal of Public Health, 93*(9), 1456–1463.

Rivara, F. P., Thompson, D. C., Beahler, C., & MacKenzie, E. J. (1999). Systematic reviews of strategies to prevent motor vehicle injuries. *American Journal of Preventive Medicine, 16*(1 Suppl.), 1–5.

Rosenberg, M., Butchart, A., Mercy, J., Narasimhan, V., & Waters, H. (in press). Violence. In D. Jamieson et al. (Eds.), *Disease control priorities in developing countries* (2nd ed). New York: Oxford University Press.

Ross, A., Baguley, C., Hills, V., McDonald, M., & Silcock, D. (1991). *Towards safer roads in developing countries. A guide for planners and engineers.* Crowthorne, United Kingdom: Transport Research Laboratory.

Rossi, L. A., Braga, E. C., Barruffini, R. C., & Carvalho, E. C. (1998). Childhood burn injuries: Circumstances of occurrences and their prevention in Ribeirao Preto, Brazil. *Burns, 24*(5), 416–419.

Royal Malaysian Police. (1998). *Statistical report road accidents Malaysia-1997.* Kuala Lumpur: PNMB Publishers.

Shannon, M. (2000). Ingestion of toxic substances by children. *New England Journal of Medicine, 342*(3), 186–191.

Solomon, M. G., Ulmer, R. G., & Preusser, D. F. (2002). *Evaluation of click it or ticket model programs* (DOT HS-809-498). Washington, DC: National Highway Traffic Safety Administration.

Soori, H. (2001). Developmental risk factors for unintentional childhood poisoning. *Saudi Medical Journal, 22*(3), 227–230.

Spiegel, C. N., & Lindaman, F. C. (1977). Children Can't Fly: A program to prevent childhood morbidity and mortality from window falls. *American Journal of Public Health, 67*(12), 1143–1147.

Sunder, S., & Bharat, R. (1998). Industrial burns in Jamshedpur, India: Epidemiology, prevention, and first aid. *Burns, 24*(5), 444–447.

Supramaniam, V., van Belle, G., & Sung, J. (1984). Fatal motorcycle accidents and helmet laws in peninsular Malaysia. *Accident Analysis and Prevention, 16*(3), 157–162.

Tan, Z., Li, X., & Bu, Q. (1998). Epidemiological study on drowning in Wujin, Jiangsu, 1997. *Zhonghua Liu Xing Bing Xue Za Zhi, 19*(4), 208–210.

Thompson, D. C., & Rivara, F. P. (2000). Pool fencing for preventing drowning in children. *Cochrane Database of Systematic Reviews*, no. 2, CD001047.

Thompson, R. S., Rivara, F. P., & Thompson, D. C. (1989). A case-control study of the effectiveness of bicycle safety helmets. *New England Journal of Medicine, 320*(21), 1361–1367.

Tiwari, G. (2000). Traffic flow and safety: Need for new models for heterogeneous traffic. In D. Mohan & G. Tiwari (Eds.), *Injury prevention and control* (pp. 71–88). London: Taylor and Francis.

Torova, F., & Sinha, S. N. (1996). Burns admissions to Port Moresby General Hospital 1978–1984. *Papua and New Guinea Medical Journal, 39*(2), 111–116.

Umar, R. S., & Law, T. H. (1999). *Preliminary evaluation of the targeted motorcycle safety program in Malaysia* (Road Safety Research Center Research Report). Malaysia: Motorcycle Safety Program, Ministry of Transport.

Van Schoor, O., van Niekerk, J., & Grobbelaar, B. (2001). Mechanical failures as a contributing cause to motor vehicle accidents: South Africa. *Accident Analysis and Prevention, 33*(6), 713–721.

Wang, S., Chi, G. B., Jing, C. X., Dong, X. M., Wu, C. P., & Li, L. P. (2003). Trends in road traffic crashes and associated injury and fatality in the

People's Republic of China, 1951–1999. *Injury Control and Safety Promotion, 10*(1–2): 83–87.

Warda, L., Tenenbein, M., & Moffatt, M. E. K. (1999a). House fire injury prevention update. Part I. A review of risk factors for fatal and non-fatal house fire injury. *Injury Prevention, 5*(3), 145–150.

Warda, L., Tenenbein, M., & Moffatt, M. E. K. (1999b). House fire injury prevention update. Part II. A review of the effectiveness of preventive interventions. *Injury Prevention, 5*(3), 217–225.

Waters, H. R., Hyder, A. A., & Phillips, T. L. (2004). Economic evaluation of interventions for reducing road traffic injuries—A review of literature with applications to low- and middle-income countries. *Asia Pacific Journal of Public Health, 16*(1), 23–31.

Waters, H., Hyder, A., Rajkotia, Y., Basu, S., Rehwinkel, J. A., & Butchart, A. (2004). *The economic dimensions of interpersonal violence.* Geneva, Switzerland: World Health Organization.

Werneck, G. L., & Reichenheim, M. E. (1997). Paediatric burns and associated risk factors in Rio de Janeiro, Brazil. *Burns, 23*(6), 478–483.

WHO Global Consultation on Violence and Health. (1996). *Violence: A public health priority* (WHO/EHA/SPI.POA.2). Geneva, Switzerland: World Health Organization.

World Health Organization. (1999). *Injury: A leading cause of the global burden of disease.* Geneva, Switzerland: World Health Organization.

World Health Organization. (2002). *The world health report 2002: Reducing risks, promoting healthy life.* Geneva, Switzerland: World Health Organization.

World Health Organization. (2003). *Facts about injuries: Drowning.* Geneva, Switzerland: World Health Organization.

Wyndham, C. H. (1984). Leading causes of death among children under 5 years of age in the various population groups of the RSA in 1970. *South African Medical Journal, 66*(19), 717–718.

Yip, P. S. F. (1998). Age, sex, marital status and suicide: An empirical study of East and West. *Psychological Reports, 82,* 311–322.

Ytterstad, B., & Sogaard, A. J. (1995). The Harstad injury prevention study: Prevention of burns in small children by a community-based intervention. *Burns, 21*(4), 259–266.

Yuan, W. (2000). The effectiveness of the 'Ride Bright' legislation for motorcycles in Singapore. *Accident Analysis and Prevention, 32*(4), 559–563.

Zhang, J., Norton, R., Tang, K. C., Lo, S. K., Jiaton, Z., & Wenkui, G. (2004). Motorcycle ownership and injury in China. *Injury Control and Safety Promotion, 11*(3), 159–163.

Zhang, P. B., Chen, R. H., Deng, J. Y., Xu, B. R., & Hu, Y. F. (2003). Evaluation on intervening efficacy of health education on accidental suffocation and drowning of children aged 0–4 in countryside. *Zhonghua Er Ke Za Zhi, 41*(7), 497–500.

Zhu, Z. X., Yang, H., & Meng, F. Z. (1988). The epidemiology of childhood burns in Jiamusi, China. *Burns, Including Thermal Injury, 14*(5), 394–396.

Mental Health

VIKRAM PATEL, ALAN J. FLISHER, AND ALEX COHEN

Mental disorders have been increasingly recognized as a major contributor to the burden of global ill health and disability, especially since the publication of the *World Development Report, 1993* (World Bank, 1993). This report showed, to the surprise even of most public health experts, that the burden attributable to mental disorders was also significant in low- and middle-income countries, in spite of the coexisting burden of infectious and other noncommunicable diseases. This double burden is, in part, the result of the epidemiologic and demographic transition evident in most countries, and leads to unique challenges in securing a place for mental health in public health policy in low- and middle-income countries. Globally, there is increasing recognition that mental health and well-being are essential components of a healthy society. This recognition is evidenced by the continuing importance given to mental health in international public health documents, culminating most notably in the *World Health Report* of 2001, which was devoted to mental health (World Health Organization [WHO], 2001b).

Despite this recognition, the fact remains that the vast majority of people affected by mental disorders go without appropriate care or any care whatsoever, that the human rights of persons in mental hospitals are routinely compromised, that resources for the promotion of mental health or the primary or secondary prevention of mental disorder are extremely limited, and that national or regional mental health policies are either absent or poorly implemented. There has been little research on models of sustainable mental health care delivery. There are limited opportunities for training in mental health research or policy development. The existing evidence base of the burden and risk factors for mental disorders has spurred the development of new mental health programs in low- and middle-income countries. However, the stigma associated with mental illness, the shortage of human skills, and competing public health concerns are some of the major reasons that potentially impede the implementation of such programs.

This chapter considers the current evidence base on international public mental health. A useful starting point for the discussion is to chart the historical development of public mental health. Next, the chapter considers the concepts and classification of mental disorders, noting in particular the influence of cultural factors in the development of psychiatric classifications, as well as the universal nature of symptoms and major syndromes of mental disorders. Then, it considers the global burden of mental disorders, focusing on the prevalence and incidence of these disorders, and the social and economic impact of mental disorders. Next, it considers the evidence base on the etiology of mental disorders, a crucial link to our consideration of potential preventive strategies. Here, the discussion highlights the multifactorial nature of most mental disorders, demonstrating that both biologic and socioeconomic risk factors best explain the etiology and course of mental disorders. The chapter then briefly reviews the evidence for the primary, secondary, and tertiary prevention of major groups of disorders and follows this with a discussion of mental health at the extremes of the life cycle (namely, childhood and adolescence, and old age). Finally, it discusses each of the ten recommendations of the 2001 *World Health Report* and considers examples of how the goals of public mental health can be achieved.

Historical Development of Public Mental Health

It is possible to find the origins of public mental health in the early Islamic world of North Africa, Spain, and the Middle East. Following the belief that insane people were loved by God, asylums were established, first in Baghdad in the 8th century, and later in Cairo, Damascus, and Fez (Mora, 1980). One might also point to Flanders and the establishment, between the 12th and 15th centuries, of mental hospitals in Ghent, Bruges, and Antwerp, as well as the famous Colony of Gheel (Pierloot, 1975). Or, one can see the origins of public mental health in how a 13th century priory house in London was transformed into Bethlem Hospital, which later became infamous for the brutality shown to its inmates and whose nickname—Bedlam—came to signify any asylum or person who was mad (Andrews et al., 1997).

However one sees these early developments, it is probably fair to mark the beginning of modern public mental health to the shift in beliefs about the nature of mental illness that took place in the late 18th century. Before this time, madness was associated with a loss of rationality, which meant that mentally ill individuals were considered as less than human and, in an effort to restore them to reason, were treated as brutes (Scull, 1989). "Moral treatment," which was developed simultaneously and independently in France (Pinel, 1977) and England (Digby, 1985), rejected the notion that mentally ill people lacked reason and believed, instead, that tolerance and confinement in a well-ordered and pleasant environment could restore a person to mental health (Grob, 1994).

In Europe and North America during the first half of the 19th century, this new perspective brought about a powerful movement to abolish the abuses of the past and to establish a public system of mental institutions that would offer beneficent care and the prospect of recovery to mentally ill persons (Scull, 1989). However, as soon as the public asylums were opened, they were filled beyond capacity and, throughout the second half of the 19th century, the notion of small curative institutions was forgotten under the dual pressures of increasing demands for services and a reluctance on the part of governments to allocate more and more funds for the care of mentally ill indigents (Grob, 1994; Scull, 1989). In addition, as conditions in the asylums grew worse, many physicians began to question their usefulness (Scull, MacKenzie, & Hervey, 1996). Thus, by the late 19th century, public mental health efforts were inextrica-

bly associated with the wretched, overcrowded conditions in the mental asylums.

Beginning in the 1950s, then continuing through the 1960s and 1970s, there were efforts in North America and western Europe to remove long-term patients from psychiatric facilities and place them in community-based treatment and care. The impetus of this so-called *deinstitutionalization* movement came from a convergence of several forces. First, with the successes in treating soldiers traumatized by their experiences in World War II, psychiatrists became optimistic about their ability to effectively treat other mental disorders outside of hospital settings (Grob, 1994). Second, there was a growing awareness that the abusive conditions found in most state psychiatric hospitals, and the negative effects of long-term institutionalization, were at least as harmful as chronic mental disorder itself. Third, fiscal conservatives were concerned with the enormous expense of caring for patients in large institutions. Finally, the discovery in 1954 of chlorpromazine, the first effective antipsychotic medication, offered people with chronic mental disorders the prospect of living in community rather than hospital settings (Greenblatt, 1992). All together, these forces brought about a dramatic shift in admission and discharge practices in psychiatric hospitals. In the United States, the dramatic effects of these changes can be seen in the following data: In 1955, 559,000 patients were living in state and county psychiatric hospitals, whereas only 138,000 were living in such facilities 25 years later (Goldman, 1983).

There is consensus that the deinstitutionalization movement in the United States has not achieved its aims. The odd alliance of fiscal conservatives and civil rights advocates that gave rise to the movement brought about the discharge of tens of thousands of patients from psychiatric hospitals with little planning and without sufficient comprehensive community mental health centers and support services (e.g., housing and rehabilitation programs). Thus, neglect in the community took the place of abuse in the asylum. In fact, deinstitutionalization is a misnomer for what took place, at least in the United States. *Dehospitalization* is a more accurate term. Great numbers of patients were discharged from hospitals only to be accommodated in other institutional settings—prisons and jails, nursing homes, and adult residences—that often replicated the worst aspects of the old asylums (Jencks, 1994; Levy, 2002). Other countries—Australia, for example—have better managed the process of deinstitutionalization (Whiteford, Buckingham, & Manderscheid, 2002). In brief,

Australia (the state of Victoria in particular) closed many of its psychiatric hospitals and, in their place, developed a wide range of community services and acute psychiatric units in general hospitals. With these efforts, clinical opportunities for providing care in the community have increased, and the civil rights of patients have been expanded. Thus, Australia has managed to avoid most of the worst experiences of de-institutionalization in the United States.

Community-Based Mental Health Services

The community mental health movement was both an impetus for and a product of deinstitutionalization. Although the belief in the ability to treat people with mental disorders outside of hospital settings was established sometime prior to the discovery of effective antipsychotic medications, the development and evolution of community-based services came about with the realization that treatment and care involved more than dispensing medication: A range of social and rehabilitation services were necessary. Thus, although the definition of community care may have once simply meant care outside hospitals, it now encompasses professional services in community settings and social reintegration and support services (i.e., housing, employment, medical care, and welfare) (Tansella & Thornicroft, 2001). Community-based mental health represents an ideology as much as a set of psychiatric practices (Mechanic, 2001). Indeed, the ideology has come to signify a set of principles that shape the planning and delivery of services: openness and honesty, respect, fair and equitable allocation of care and treatment, responsiveness to the changing needs of clients, and openness to learning and change (Tansella & Thornicroft, 2001). In addition, proponents of community-based care recognize that the parties involved in mental health services (e.g., government funding agencies, mental health professionals, the users of mental health services and their families, and researchers) may hold conflicting values and interests, and that managing disparate views is a major challenge to providing effective services where they are most needed (Szmukler & Thornicroft, 2001). For example, professionals may offer efficacious medications, but patients may consider the side effects of those medications, or the need for housing and income, as far more critical to their well-being than the reduction of symptoms.

Colonial Psychiatry

During the 19th and early 20th centuries, European colonial governments established large psychiatric institutions throughout Asia and Africa. These institutions have often been depicted as being a form of social control of indigenous populations (Goddard, 1992; Jackson, 1999; Schmidt, 1967; Swartz, 1999). Although it may be true that the majority of colonial asylum administrators were racist and that indigenous people suffering from mental illness did not receive the best available care, it is also true that asylums in the colonies merely reflected their counterparts in Europe. Thus, asylums in the colonies were run according to much the same precepts as asylums in Europe.

After the end of European rule, the old asylums were the only mental health facilities that remained in the former colonies. In a terrible irony, the end of colonialism came about just prior to the move toward community-based care in many of the wealthy countries of the West, leaving the former colonies saddled with outmoded hospital-based systems of care and lacking the resources to carry out reforms. Given this situation, which has not changed substantially in the past 50 years, it would be easy to recommend deinstitutionalization. But that would be naïve. For example, India has only about 40 public mental hospitals (with a total bed capacity of approximately 20,000) to serve a population of more than one billion people. This is clearly inadequate. What is needed is not deinstitutionalization (although establishing community facilities would make it possible to discharge many chronic patients) but improvements in the hospitals to strengthen respect for human rights (Exhibit 8-1) and *more* hospital facilities to handle patients in crisis.

The Present

Since the early 1990s, the field of international mental health has been transformed from a subdiscipline that attracted only a handful of anthropologists, psychiatrists, and psychologists into a major focus of international public health. As noted earlier, the *World Development Report 1993* demonstrated the huge burden of disease that was imposed by neuropsychiatric disorders in wealthy countries and low- and middle-income countries alike. Two years later, the publication of *World Mental Health* (Desjarlais et al., 1995) highlighted the mental health crisis in low-income countries. The following year, WHO established Nations for Mental Health, a program that supported demonstration projects for underserved populations in more than a dozen low-income countries around the world. In 1998, the World Bank—the largest external funder of health projects in the world—created a position within its Health, Nutrition

Exhibit 8-1	Human Rights and Mental Illness

The past two decades have seen increased attention to the human rights of people suffering from mental disorders (WHO, 2001b). The United Nations General Assembly Resolution *The Protection of Persons with Mental Illness and the Improvement of Mental Health Care* (United Nations, 1991), the Declaration of Caracas (WHO, 2001b), and the Declarations of Hawaii and Madrid (Helmchen & Okasha, 2000) set forth principles that establish basic rights for persons suffering from mental illnesses, among them the right to the best available mental health care, protection from exploitation and discrimination, the right to be treated in the least restrictive environment possible, and the right of confidentiality. In view of past abuses in psychiatry (Birley, 2000; Bloch, 1997), these documents have served to raise awareness about the need to be vigilant on behalf of persons with mental disorders. With these guidelines in place, it is unfortunate that many countries do not have relevant policies, programs, or legislation that protect the human rights of persons with mental disorders. Abuses in psychiatric facilities in low- and middle-income countries are not uncommon (Alem, 2000; Levav & Gonzalez Uzcategui, 2000; National Human Rights Commission, 1999).

and Population Sector for a specialist to stimulate and review proposals for mental health projects.

Without doubt, the year 2001 was a high point for international mental health. It was the focus of the WHO *World Health Report* (WHO, 2001b) and of a report by the Institute of Medicine (Institute of Medicine, 2001) in the United States. In addition, WHO initiated the Atlas Project (http://www.cvdinfobase.ca/mh-atlas/), whose goal is to collect and disseminate information about mental health resources in countries throughout the world. Finally, the Fogarty International Center of the U.S. National Institutes of Health established the International Clinical, Operational, and Health Services Research and Training Award, whose major focus is on research and training in the fields of mental health and substance abuse.

Despite these advances, the future prospects for continued development in international mental health are not clear. The growing HIV/AIDS pandemic and renewed concerns about tuberculosis, malaria, and other infectious diseases are attracting the great bulk of attention and resources from international health and donor agencies. Although infectious diseases may bring about significant mental health problems, which, in turn, may lead to nonadherence to medication regimens, it is an open question whether mental health will be seen as a priority.

Concepts and Classification

The classification of diseases leads, in theory, to more accurate diagnoses and more effective treatments. Valid and reliable systems of classification make it possible to determine accurate prevalence and incidence rates and, therefore, should guide decisions about the development of services. However, the classification of mental disorders presents a particular challenge. Many authors have noted that psychiatric diagnoses do not "carve nature at the joint" and that the boundaries between different conditions may not be distinct (Blacker & Tsuang, 1992; Kendler & Gardner, 1998; Tsuang, Stone, & Faraone, 2000). Problems with classification increase when one moves from the world of academic research, clinical samples, and controlled trials to mental disorders as they occur in the community, where comorbidity is the rule rather than the exception (Kessler et al., 1994). These problems are compounded by cultural variations in the expression of mental distress (Kleinman, 1988). Most of these difficulties have been recognized for more than 100 years. Following a visit to Java, the German psychiatrist Emil Kraepelin (2000/1904) wrote, "Reliable comparison is, of course, only possible if we are able to draw clear distinctions between identifiable illnesses, as well as between clinical states" and went on to note that although it was possible to recognize schizophrenia and bipolar disorder among the Javanese, "comparison between the native and the European populations is made more difficult . . . by the fact that the clinical symptomatology, while broadly in agreement with that seen [in Europe], presents certain very noteworthy differences in individual instances."

A key characteristic that differentiates the process of classification of mental disorders from other health problems is that, for most mental disorders, there are no specific and replicable pathophysiological changes that can be reliably identified in a clinical setting. Virtually all the diagnostic categories used in psychiatry are essentially those of "illnesses" as compared with "diseases." This distinction implies that classification is based on the nature of symptoms and syndromes, rather than their etiology (as, for example, in the case of infectious diseases) or their pathology (as, for example, in the case of vascular disease). The classification of mental disorders is thus influenced by cultural factors, such as the language of emotional distress, and the ways in which these are conceptualized by a particular culture. In the absence of demonstrable disease processes, a variety of explanations are likely to arise that are heavily influenced by other belief systems, notably religious beliefs. Historically, a number of different classifications of mental disorders have coexisted in different cultures, each with its own taxonomy and causal models for various disorders. This section considers the history behind the emergence of the current, phenomenologically oriented diagnostic system, largely based on descriptions of mental disorders in the United States and Britain. We also describe the role and relevance of alternative worldviews in understanding mental disorders.

The Evolution of Culturally Sensitive Biomedical Classifications

Historically, cross-cultural studies in psychiatric epidemiology have suffered several problems. First, case identification techniques varied from site to site, and methods were not standardized. These inconsistencies led to a movement to standardize the process of psychiatric measurement and diagnosis. This process of standardization was driven by psychiatric classification systems originating in Euro-American societies. Standardized interviews that mimicked clinical psychiatric evaluations were developed and became the criteria for determining "caseness" in epidemiologic investigations (World Bank, 1993). After standardizing the interview schedules in Euro-American cultures, the interviews were subsequently used in other cultures. Most of these subsequent cross-cultural psychiatric investigations relied on implicit, largely untested assumptions: (1) the universality of mental illnesses, implying that regardless of cultural variations, disorders as described in Euro-American classifications occur everywhere; (2) invariance, implying that the core features of psychiatric syndromes are invariant; and (3) validity, implying that although refinement is possible, the diagnostic categories of current classifications are valid clinical constructs (Beiser, Cargo, & Woodbury, 1994). This approach, termed the *etic* or universalist approach, became the most popular method for epidemiologic investigations of mental illness across cultures. The etic approach offered the perspective that because mental illness was similar throughout the world, psychiatric

taxonomies, their measuring instruments, and models of health care were also globally applicable.

Many researchers have cautioned that there was a risk of confounding culturally distinctive behavior with psychopathology on the basis of superficial similarities of behavior patterns or phenomena in different cultures (Kleinman, 1988). It was argued that classification of psychiatric disorders largely reflected American and European concepts of psychopathology based on implicit cultural concepts of normality and deviance. Critics accused the etic approach of contributing to a worldview that "privileges biology over culture" (Eisenbruch, 1991) and of ignoring the cultural and social contexts of psychiatric disorders. In contrast, the *emic* approach argued that the culture-bound aspects of biomedicine, such as its emphasis on medical disease entities, limited its universal applicability. More specifically, this approach argued that culture played such an influential role in the presentation of psychiatric disorders that it was wrong to presume a priori that Euro-American psychiatric categories were appropriate throughout the world (Littlewood, 1990). The emic approach proposed to evaluate phenomena from within a culture and its context, aiming to understand its significance and relationship with other intracultural elements. The emic approach has also drawn its share of criticism, the most fundamental one being that it is unable to provide data that can be compared across cultures. These studies are usually small in scale and are unable to resolve questions of long-term courses and treatment outcomes. The emic approach has been criticized for not suggesting plausible alternatives, such as a set of principles that would help ensure cultural sensitivity, or models upon which to fashion culturally sensitive nosologies (Beiser, Cargo, & Woodbury, 1994).

Thus, both the etic and emic approaches in cross-cultural psychiatry have strengths and weaknesses. It is widely accepted that the integration of their methodological strengths is essential for the development of the "new cross-cultural psychiatry" or a culturally sensitive psychiatry (Kleinman, 1988; Littlewood, 1990). Value must be given to both folk beliefs about mental illness as well as to the biomedical system of psychiatry. It is important to investigate patients' explanatory models, that is, how patients understand their problems, their nature, origins, consequences, and remedies, because these can radically assist patient-doctor negotiations over appropriate treatment (Kleinman, 1988). Similarly, researchers should examine the psychiatric symptoms of persons who are considered to be mentally ill by the local population and to determine the relationship of the diagnostic system used by local health care providers with psychiatric diagnostic categories. In essence, the central aim of the "new" cross-cultural psychiatry would be to describe mental illness in different cultures using methods that are sensitive and valid for the local culture and resulting in data that are comparable across cultures. In order to tackle this difficult task, psychiatric research needs to blend both ethnographic and epidemiologic methods, emphasizing the unique contribution of both approaches to the understanding of mental illness across cultures.

There are two main biomedical systems of psychiatric classification: the *International Classification of Diseases* (ICD) of the World Health Organization, and the *Diagnostic and Statistical Manual* (DSM) of the American Psychiatric Association. Diagnostic criteria of syndromes can and do change over time, as is well demonstrated by the regular revisions of international psychiatric classifications, which are considerably influenced by attitudinal, political, and historical factors. Both major classifications of mental disorders have attempted to improve their cross-cultural and international validity.

The tenth revision of the ICD (ICD-10) was developed with the explicit purpose of being an international standard. Thus, efforts were made to ensure that the drafters of the ICD-10 were drawn from as many countries as was feasible. The classification itself was field-tested in 39 countries from all continents, though the largest number of centers were in European or developed countries, and by over 700 clinicians. In these field trials, two or more clinicians rated a consecutive group of new patients presenting to the service and made an ICD-10 diagnosis according to the manual; the inter-rater reliability coefficient for each disorder was then calculated. The vast majority of ICD-10 conditions had reasonable reliability (Sartorius et al., 1993). In addition to reliability, the cultural validity of diagnostic categories has also been attempted by classifications, for example, by including guidelines for clinicians to make a "cultural formulation" of a person's mental health problem (Exhibit 8-2).

Alternative Worldviews of Mental Illness

Indigenous classifications, by and large, are based on spiritual, supernatural, or humoral etiological theories (Murdock, Wilson, & Frederick, 1980) that are not tenable in the practice of biomedicine. Broadly, there is a general classification of illness into two categories, "normal" and "abnormal." The former are perceived as being caused by physical agents

---

Exhibit 8-2	**Cultural Formulation in the DSM-IV**

This formulation implies the clinician provides a narrative summary on the following.

- The cultural identity of the individual (e.g., language abilities, cultural preference group, degree of involvement with other cultures in community)

- Cultural explanations of the illness (similar to the explanatory models, described earlier and including prominent idioms of distress, causal models, and treatment preferences)

- Cultural factors related to the psychosocial environment and functioning (culturally relevant interpretations of social stressors, available social support, and disability)

- Cultural elements of the relationship between the individual and the clinician (identify differences and similarities in cultural and social status that might influence diagnosis and treatment)

- Overall cultural assessment: a conclusion formulating how these cultural considerations influence diagnosis and treatment decisions

---

(such as infections and climatic changes) and considered to be treated effectively by either biomedical or traditional treatments, whereas the latter are perceived to be caused by spiritual or supernatural causes, and are thus brought principally to traditional healers. A further classification of "unnatural" causes is a model in which illness is brought about by supernatural forces or other human beings, or caused by the behavior of an individual or his family. The classifications used are typically flexible and patient dependent; thus, even though phenomenology may be used by a healer to understand the nature of the illness, an etiological model is almost always provided since it gives the illness experience meaning for the patient.

There is evidence that with the influence of urbanization and other changes in society, views about illness are also changing. Thus, biomedical diagnostic systems are increasingly being used in low- and middle-income countries, and multiple illness models are held simultaneously. It is therefore not uncommon in many low- and middle-income countries for a person with a mental illness to consult both traditional/religious and biomedical health care providers. Most commonly, the explanatory models of mental illness equate them with psychotic or severe mental disorders. For these disorders, there is a striking similarity in the behavioral symptoms across cultures, with some behaviors, such as incoherent speech, talking to oneself, disrobing, wandering, and aggression, being particularly common (Patel, 1995). However, there is much less emphasis on cognitive features, such as delusions, which are central to the diagnosis in the biomedical model. Disorders resembling depression and anxiety, though often not perceived to be mental disorders, are still recognized by local people and traditional healers as being sources of illness, suffering, and misfortune.

Although the ICD-10 is an international system and does include a section on culture-specific disorder (Exhibit 8-3) it was not at least initially intended

to supplant local classificatory systems. However, most countries have gradually shed their national classification schemes; of the few that remain, there have been attempts to make them conform to the ICD as closely as possible. China is, possibly, the only low- and middle-income country that has its own, separate classification of mental disorders. The first Chinese Classification of Mental Disorders (CCMD) appeared in 1979; since then, it has undergone several revisions. Its third and most recent version has been heavily influenced by the ICD-10 and DSM-IV systems but still retains certain local features. The main differences between the ICD-10 and the CCMD-3 are summarized by Lee (2001). Notable among these are the retention of the term *neurosis* and the retention of some specific categories of neurotic disorder, such as neurasthenia. Personality disorder is less often diagnosed in Chinese populations, possibly because deviant behavior is dealt with by the penal system. Thus, two categories of personality disorder—borderline personality disorder and avoidant personality disorder—are excluded from the Chinese scheme. The Chinese task force excluded borderline personality disorder from the CCMD-3 because it felt that impulsivity and emotional instability were character traits that should not be medicalized. The CCMD also includes its own section of culture-related mental disorders, such as *qigong*-induced mental disorder. *Qigong* is a trance-based form of a traditional Chinese healing system. The disorder is similar to a dissociative state, with identity disturbance, irritability, hallucinations, and aggressive and bizarre behaviors. These are often acute, brief episodes and are linked to excessive practice of *qigong* meditation by physically or psychologically ill subjects.

Exhibit 8-3	Culture-Bound Syndromes

The ICD-10 defines culture-specific disorders as sharing two cardinal characteristics:

1. They are not easily accommodated by the categories in established and internationally used psychiatric classifications.

2. They were first described in, and subsequently closely or exclusively associated with, a particular population or cultural area.

Examples of culture-bound categories include the following: *amok*, the *dhat* syndrome, and *koro* in Asian cultures; *latah* in indigenous cultures of Scandinavia, the Americas, and Asia; *susto* in Latin America; *windigo* among the indigenous peoples of North America; and *taijin kyofusho* in Japan. None of the culture-specific syndromes resembles severe mental disorders; all occur in the context of severe stress and are phenomenologically closest to the neurotic and dissociative disorders and neurotic disorders. Many conditions bear considerable similarity with one another and with a multitude of other conditions described in diverse cultures.

Susto and *nervios* are folk idioms of distress; Arctic hysteria and *windigo* are culturally stereotyped reactions to extreme environmental conditions; *koro* and *dhat* are related to a cultural concern regarding fertility and procreation; *latah* and *amok* are related to a cultural emphasis on learned dissociation; and *brain fag* is an example of a syndrome related to acculturative stress on adolescents (the pressure of academic performance in some cultures). A culture-bound syndrome should not in itself constitute a complete psychiatric diagnosis. Just as a diagnosis of anxiety disorder can signify anything from a hidden malignancy to a marital problem, so too all patients must be fully investigated to clarify any underlying pathology.

The Burden of Mental Disorders

Prevalence of Mental Disorders
Common Mental Disorders

Common mental disorders (CMDs) include depressive and anxiety disorders. Among community samples, rates of CMDs generally range from about 10% to 20%, but have been found to be as high as 46% and 66% in samples of women from two rural communities in Pakistan. In India, rates are relatively low (<15%), while in South Africa they average about 25%. Not surprisingly, prevalence rates among attendees of primary health care facilities are somewhat higher, tending to range between 15% and 30%, but rates of 45% or more are not uncommon and have been found in samples from Chile, India, Jordan, and Nicaragua (Cohen, 2001). Despite inconsistencies in diagnostic criteria and sampling methods, research clearly demonstrates large variations in prevalence rates from one sociocultural environment to another, as well as the large global burden of disease that is imposed by CMDs.

Recent advances in the development of valid and reliable diagnostic interviews, the initiation of multiple cross-national surveys of mental disorders, and continued research in clinical epidemiology have all improved the ability of psychiatric epidemiologists to determine prevalence rates of mental disorders in a variety of settings (Kessler, 2000). Currently, the best example of these advances is found in the work of the World Mental Health Survey Consortium (WHO World Mental Health Survey Consortium, 2004), which has conducted a survey of the prevalence, severity, and treatment of nonpsychotic mental disorders (anxiety, mood, impulse control, and substance abuse disorders) among more than 60,000 persons in six less developed and eight developed countries. Overall 12-month prevalence rates ranged from a low of 4.3% in Shanghai to a high of 26.4% in the United States. Anxiety and mood disorders were the most common, followed by substance abuse and impulse disorders. Looking at the results by country, the United States and Colombia had relatively high rates for all types, while the Netherlands and Ukraine displayed high rates for most. In contrast, prevalence rates were comparatively low in Italy, and were low for all types in Nigeria and Shanghai.

A major improvement of the World Mental Health Survey over much previous research was that it included precise measures of the levels of severity and impairment that are associated with mental disorders. In general, mild forms of disorders are more prevalent than either moderate or serious forms, and the proportion of mild disorders did not fall below 33% anywhere. In some countries the proportion of mild disorders approached or even exceeded the proportion of moderate and serious disorders combined. For example, the ratio of mild to moderate/serious cases was a little more than 4 to 1 in Nigeria, whereas it was about 1 to 1 in six countries of Europe. Not surprisingly, level of severity was associated with level of impairment in all countries: Persons with serious disorders reported 30 or more days in the past year of being incapable of normal functioning, whereas persons with moderate and mild disorders reported far fewer days out of role as a result of mental health problems.

The World Mental Health Survey also gathered information about treatment for mental disorders and found an association between the level of severity and the likelihood of being in treatment: Persons with serious disorders were the most likely to have been in treatment, no matter where they lived. However, it must be noted that the proportion of people with serious disorders who received treatment never exceeded 65% in any of the countries, and was as low as about 15% in Lebanon. At the same time, the survey data show that persons with either mild disorders or no disorder make up about half of all respondents who reported being in treatment during the previous year. Together, these results indicate that many serious cases are not receiving treatment and that available resources do not always go toward the treatment of those persons most in need of care. The results of the World Mental Health Survey are consistent with previous research (e.g., Ustun & Sartorius, 1995), although a question remains about the validity of the findings regarding the large variation in cross-national prevalence rates. As acknowledged by the investigators, the instruments used in the survey were developed in studies conducted primarily in wealthy Western countries, and their use in different settings may not be valid. Nevertheless, the survey is a major advance in psychiatric epidemiology. Even if the national prevalence rates are not all accurate, the information about, for example, rates of treatment will inform health policy development.

Severe Mental Disorders

The investigation of the cross-cultural epidemiology of severe mental disorders, notably schizophrenia, was initiated with Kraepelin's visit to Java in 1904 (Kraepelin, 2000/1904). Over the next 100 years, numerous researchers have produced extensive evidence on the topic (Kulhara & Chakrabarti, 2001). However, in all that time, only one project—the WHO Determinants of Outcome of Severe Mental Disorders—conducted epidemiologic investigations into the incidence of schizophrenia in different countries (Jablensky et al., 1992). This research found that the incidence of schizophrenia ranged from 7 to 14 per 100,000 among populations at risk (15–44 years). The extent of this variation was not statistically significant, and experts in the field have concluded that, in general, the incidence of schizophrenia is similar in different populations.

To test this assumption, researchers at the University of Queensland conducted a meta-analysis of 158 studies and determined that the median value of the rates was 15.2 per 100,000, with a range of 7.7 to 43.0 per 100,000 (McGrath et al., 2004). From the evidence, the investigators concluded that there *are* significant differences in incidence rates across populations. Furthermore, the meta-analysis determined that rates were higher among men than among women, higher in urban areas, and higher in migrant groups. Further research is required to determine the reasons for the variation.

Virtually no data exist on the prevalence and course of bipolar disorders, another type of severe mental disorder, in low- and middle-income countries.

Substance Abuse Disorders

The burden of substance abuse disorders varies considerably according to the substance being abused, across countries, within countries, and between various groups in a given population. If we exclude tobacco dependence (arguably the most common substance to be abused), alcohol abuse is the commonest substance abuse disorder in most countries. Point prevalence of alcohol use disorders (harmful use and dependence) in adults has been estimated to be around 1.7% globally, according to the Global Burden of Disease (GBD) 2000 analysis. The rates are 2.8% for men and 0.5% for women. The prevalence of alcohol use disorders varies widely across different regions of the world, ranging from very low levels in some Middle Eastern countries to over 5% in North America and parts of eastern Europe. Alcohol abuse contributes to an enormous burden of ill health through its contribution to injuries, accidents, liver disease, neuropsychiatric disease, and other medical complications. Alcohol use is rising rapidly in some of the developing regions of the world (WHO, 2001b), which is likely to escalate alcohol-related problems.

Besides tobacco and alcohol, a large number of other substances, generally grouped under the broad category of drugs, are also abused. These include illicit drugs such as heroin, cocaine, and cannabis. The period prevalence of drug abuse and dependence ranges from 0.4% to 4%, but the type of drugs used varies greatly from region to region. Global Burden of Disease 2000 analysis suggests that the point prevalence of heroin and cocaine use disorders is 0.25%. Substance abuse is strongly associated with the risk for other mental health problems, notably suicide.

Epilepsy

Epilepsy has been included in this chapter because, in many countries, persons with epilepsy are cared for in mental health care settings. The prevalence of epilepsy is about 4 to 8 per 1,000 in industrialized countries and three to five times higher in developing countries (Desjarlais et al., 1995). There are about 50 million people worldwide with epilepsy, 80% of whom live in developing countries. The aggregate burden due to epilepsy is about 0.5% of the total disease burden, according to the GBD 2000. There are frequently serious adverse psychological and social consequences of epilepsy, partly because of the stigma that is associated with this disorder (WHO, 2001b).

Mental Retardation

Mental retardation is defined as subnormal intelligence (intelligence quotient [IQ] more than two standard deviations below the population mean), accompanied by limitations in related skills areas. Depending on IQ, mental handicap can be classified as mild (IQ from 50–55 to approximately 70), moderate (IQ from 35–40 to 50–55), severe (IQ from 20–25 to 35–40), and profound (IQ less than 20 or 25) (American Psychiatric Association, 1994). In the developed world, approximately 3% of the population have an IQ of less than 70, and only 4 in a thousand have an IQ of less than 50—that is, have moderate, severe, or profound mental handicap (Molteno & Westaway, 2001). Comprehensive prevalence rates are not available for any countries in the developing world. However, some studies have provided prevalence estimates for severe mental handicap that suggest that the rates are higher in developing countries (Institute of Medicine, 2001).

The Impact of Mental Disorders

Disability-adjusted life years (DALYs) are a measure that combines the impact of morbidity and mortality into a single statistic and makes it possible to compare the burden of disease imposed by a variety of health conditions (Murray & Lopez, 1996). Previously, rates of mortality dominated assessments of public health priorities. Therefore, mental disorders, which are mainly associated with disability, were not considered important. The use of DALYs changed this by demonstrating, as of 2000, that 12.3% of the global burden of disease was the result of mental disorders. Three conditions—unipolar depressive disorders, alcohol use disorders, and self-inflicted injuries (which are often associated with mental illness)—were among the 20 leading causes of the global burden of disease. Among persons aged 15 to 44 years, a particularly productive age group, six of the leading causes were mental disorders, and the burden of depression (8.6%) was second only to that of HIV/AIDS (13%) (Table 8-1). Even in those countries that continue to experience high rates of morbidity and mortality—due to infectious diseases, as well as maternal, perinatal, and nutritional conditions—mental disorders constituted 8% of the total burden of disease (WHO, 2001b).

The direct and indirect economic costs of mental disorders are substantial. Rice, Kelman, and Miller (1992) estimated that the total amounted to $103.7 billion in 1985 in the United States. Of this, direct costs (e.g., professional services, medication, and hospitalization) were $42.5 billion, or 11.5% of spending for all illnesses. Indirect costs due to disability (e.g., lost and reduced work productivity) amounted to $47.4 billion. Indirect costs due to lost productivity as the result of premature death amounted to $9.3 billion.

Other researchers have attempted to estimate the costs of specific classes of mental disorders. For example, studies in the United States have found that in 1990 the cost of anxiety disorders and depression totaled $42.3 billion (Greenberg et al., 1999) and $43.7 billion (Greenberg et al., 1993), respectively. We do not have comparable data for schizophrenia, but Knapp (2000) suggests that the costs are very high, especially if one considers that the hidden costs (e.g., unemployment and lost productivity) are substantial and fall not only on persons who suffer from schizophrenia but also on "their families and other caregivers and [on] the wider society."

Alcohol disorders impose a great economic burden on society. One estimate has put the yearly economic cost of alcohol abuse in the United States at $148 billion, including $19 billion for health care expenditures. In Canada, the economic costs of alcohol, tobacco, and illicit drugs in 1992 amounted to $18.4 billon (Canadian dollars), representing 2.7% of the gross domestic product. Alcohol alone was responsible for $7.52 billion (Canadian dollars) in costs. Studies in other countries have estimated the cost of alcohol-related problems to be around 1% of the gross domestic product (WHO, 2001b). There are few comparable studies of the costs of mental disorders in low- and middle-income countries (Shah, 1999); these have typically found a considerable economic impact of severe mental disorders such as schizophrenia on household finances (Westermeyer, 1984).

A substantial burden is attributable to mental retardation. For the individual and family, this may include attending to activities of daily living and self-care. Also, it is difficult for people with a mental handicap to secure remunerative employment, so there may be a financial burden. For the education system, there is the challenge of providing appropriate educational services, which can range from segregated specialized residential and day schools, to special classes in regular schools, to mainstreaming or inclusive education. In the developing world, there are frequently no services for children with mental handicap, which implies that such children do not receive the benefits of any education whatsoever. For the health system, there is the burden attributed to associated disabilities, such as cerebral palsy (present in 20% of people with mental handicap), sensory deficits (present in 10%), epilepsy (present in 30%), and comorbid mental disorders (Molteno & Westaway, 2001). It is difficult to estimate the proportion of people with mental handicap who suffer from a comorbid mental disorder because of diagnostic uncertainties. However, it is estimated that rates are generally two to three times

Table 8-1	Leading Causes of Disability-Adjusted Life Years in 15- to 44-Year-Olds, by Sex, Estimates for 2000				
Both Sexes, Ages 15–44	**% Total**	**Males, 15–44 Years**	**% Total**	**Females, 15–44 Years**	**% Total**
HIV/AIDS	13.0	HIV/AIDS	12.1	HIV/AIDS	13.9
Unipolar depressive disorders	8.6	Road traffic accidents	7.7	*Unipolar depressive disorders*	10.6
Road traffic accidents	4.9	*Unipolar depressive disorders*	6.7	Tuberculosis	3.2
Tuberculosis	3.9	*Alcohol use disorders*	5.1	Iron deficiency anemia	3.2
Alcohol use disorders	3.0	Tuberculosis	4.5	*Schizophrenia*	2.8
Self-inflicted injuries	2.7	Violence	3.7	Obstructed labor	2.7
Iron deficiency anemia	2.6	*Self-inflicted injuries*	3.0	*Bipolar affective disorder*	2.5
Schizophrenia	2.6	*Schizophrenia*	2.5	Abortion	2.5
Bipolar affective disorder	2.5	*Bipolar affective disorder*	2.4	*Self-inflicted injuries*	2.4
Violence	2.3	Iron-deficiency anemia	2.1	Maternal sepsis	2.1

Note: Disorders in italics are mental disorders.

Source: World Health Organization, *Mental Health: New Understanding, New Hope* (Geneva, Switzerland: World Health Organization, 2001). Reprinted with permission.

greater in people with mental handicap compared with the general population.

There is abundant evidence that mental health is closely linked with virtually all global public health priorities. Substance abuse disorders are associated with increased risk for sexually transmitted infections, particularly HIV/AIDS, through the use of unsafe injections by intravenous drug users and unsafe sexual behavior among substance abusers in general. Depression increases the risk of myocardial infarction and worsens its prognosis. Mental disorders are major risk factors for road traffic accidents, a subject that was the focus of the *World Health Report* in 2004. Depression in mothers has been shown to be strongly associated with depression and childhood failure to thrive in South Asia, a region where failure to thrive affects more than one in three children (Patel et al., 2004). Violence, especially domestic violence, is a global health priority. Alcohol abuse and personality disorder frequently precede violence. If we were to incorporate these broader outcomes, the overall impact of mental disorders would be inestimable.

Etiology

Biological Factors

It is difficult to overstate the influence of biological and physical factors such as genes, infections, physical trauma, nutrition, hormones, and toxins on the development of mental disorders (WHO, 2001b). This section focuses only on genes and infections, because they are attracting considerable research attention that will have substantial clinical and public health implications.

Genes

Until the 1950s, the dominant notions about the etiology of mental disorders were environmental in nature. For example, schizophrenia was attributed to abnormal parenting, and obsessive compulsive disorder to anal aggression. However, beginning in the 1960s, a more balanced view began to take root (Plomin, Owen, & McGuffin, 1994). Consensus developed that both environmental and genetic influences contribute to the development of mental disorder. The question changed from *which* was relevant for a specific disorder to *how much* each contributed (Anastasi, 1958). However, this question, too, was based on an incorrect assumption, namely, that the environmental and genetic factors exert their

influences in an additive and independent manner. There is now a recognition that they exert their influences in an interactive manner. Contemporary scientists are attempting to answer the question of *how* they interact.

What is the explanation for such a rapid change in the consensus about the genetic contribution to the etiology of mental disorder? One important factor was a compelling set of results from adoption studies, which allow conclusions about the reasons for the well-known fact that schizophrenia runs in families (Slater & Cowie, 1971). For example, Heston (1966) reported that the rate of schizophrenia was 11% in adopted-away children of mothers with schizophrenia, compared with 0% in control adoptees. Twin studies confirmed the results of adoption studies by demonstrating that the concordance rates of schizophrenia (and many other mental disorders) are higher in monozygotic twins than dizygotic twins. In one study, for example, the rate for the former was 58% and for the latter 6% (for twins of the opposite sex) (Shields & Slater, 1975).

The incontrovertible nature of these findings should not distract from the fact that the risk of the common forms of mental illness is genetically complex (WHO, 2001b). After causative genes were discovered for cystic fibrosis and Huntington's disorder, it was assumed that it was a matter of time before evidence would emerge that psychiatric disorders such as schizophrenia could also be attributed to a single gene. However, it is now clear that the common forms of mental disorder are caused by multiple genes. The inheritance patterns are not clear-cut. The manner in which the genes manifest themselves in the anatomy, physiology, biochemistry, and psychology of the individual (phenotype) is heterogeneous. Nevertheless, it is clear that genetic vulnerabilities are implicated in the etiology of disorders such as schizophrenia, mood disorders (particularly bipolar affective disorder), anxiety disorders, Tourette's disorder, and attention deficit hyperactivity disorder (Kaliski, 2001).

Ironically, genetic research has provided evidence of the role of environmental influences on development. Genetic research has proved that most psychiatric disorders show as much environmental as genetic influence. Furthermore, many measures that are commonly assumed to reflect environmental influences are themselves influenced by genetic factors. Examples of such variables include parenting, childhood accidents, television viewing, classroom environments, peer groups, social support, work environments, life events, divorce, exposure to drugs, and education (Plomin, Owen & McGuffin, 1994).

Thus, the interaction between genes and environment assumes a higher level of complexity.

Infection

It has been known for over a century that infectious agents can cause mental disorders (U.S. Department of Health and Human Services, 1999). For example, cerebral infection with *Treponema pallidum* causes tertiary syphilis, which is manifest by neurologic deterioration, psychosis, paralysis, and death. Tertiary syphilis is close to elimination, at least in the developed world, where there is widespread access to antibiotics. A second example is cerebral infection by the human immunodeficiency virus (HIV), which can cause depression, psychosis, dementia, and delirium. The rates of these disorders are high in HIV-positive people; for example, the rates of dementia range from 15% to 44% (Grant et al., 1987, McArthur et al., 1993), and the rate of delirium is in excess of 65% in those with advanced disease (Breitbart et al., 1996; Work Group on HIV/AIDS, 2000). This has increased the burden of mental disorders, especially in sub-Saharan Africa, which accounts for 10% of the world's population but 75% of AIDS deaths (World Bank, 2000). Other examples of mental disorders caused by infectious agents include encephalitis, meningitis, Lyme disease, and a form of obsessive compulsive disorder (pediatric autoimmune neuropsychiatric disorders associated with streptococcal infection [PANDAS]).

Socioeconomic Determinants

This section considers four major social determinants of mental disorders, namely, poverty, gender, conflict, and the marginalization experienced by indigenous communities across the world.

Poverty

There is now substantial evidence that demonstrates the relationship between poverty and socioeconomic inequalities and both common and severe mental disorders. In the United Kingdom, for example, there is good evidence showing an association between low standards of living and the prevalence of depression (Weich & Lewis, 1998). Evidence is also beginning to accumulate demonstrating a similar association between economic disadvantage and the presence of depression in developing countries. A recent review of 11 community-based epidemiologic studies—from six countries—in Latin America (Brazil, Chile), Africa (Lesotho, Zimbabwe), and Asia (Pakistan, Indonesia)—found that 10 studies showed a statistically significant

relationship between prevalence of common mental disorder and indicators of low socioeconomic status. The most consistent relationship was between low education and mental disorder. Significant associations were evident for most associations of other socioeconomic indicators, such as being in debt, and common mental disorders (Patel & Kleinman, 2003). Studies in developed countries have shown that mortality and morbidity rates are more affected by relative, rather than absolute, living standards. A survey in the United States, for example, showed an independent association between low income and living in income-unequal states with depression in women (Kahn et al., 2000).

The association between inequality and poor mental health may be mediated by both individual psychological factors, such as low self-esteem and frustration, and a breakdown in structural factors in the community, such as less social cohesion and poorer infrastructure. The lack of social support and the breakdown of kinship structures are probably the key stressors for the millions of migrant laborers to the urban centers of Asia, Africa, and South America, as well as the millions of dependents who are left behind in rural areas and whose only hope of survival is the remittances relatives send from distant cities. In developed countries, increased mobility of labor has reduced family ties and also led to the decline of the extended family.

The social consequences of low education are obvious, especially in developing countries that are facing a growing lack of security for employees as economies are reformed. Lack of secondary education may represent a diminished opportunity for persons who are depressed, especially women, to access resources to improve their situation (Patel et al., 1999). People living in conditions of poverty are at greater risk for physical health problems, and there is abundant evidence demonstrating the high degree of comorbidity between physical and mental illnesses.

Gender

The female excess for depression has been demonstrated in most community-based studies in all regions of the world (Patel et al., 1999). The social gradient in health is heavily gendered, and women are disproportionately affected by the burden of poverty, which, in turn, may influence their vulnerability for depression. Women are far more likely to be victims of violence in their homes; women who experience physical violence by an intimate partner are significantly more likely to suffer depression, abuse drugs, or attempt suicide. Women who were sexually abused as children are significantly more likely to suffer depression in adulthood, and sexual and other forms of violence in youth are associated with depression in adolescence (Astbury, 2001).

A study from Ghana investigating women's perceptions of their health found that the most important health concern was "thinking too much"; the explanations given were attributed to heavy workloads, financial insecurity, and the burden of caring for children, duties that were heavily gendered in their distribution (Avotri & Walters, 1999). Examples of the cultural context of some of these gendered stressors are illustrated by several studies. Research on depression in women in low-income townships of Harare, Zimbabwe, reported that nearly 18% of the women had a current episode of depression, compared with only 9% of their counterparts in Camberwell, a deprived inner-London district thought to have a relatively high rate of depression (Broadhead & Abas, 1998). More women in Harare had experienced a severe life event (54%) in the preceding 12 months than had women in Camberwell (31%). A notable finding in Harare was the high proportion of events involving humiliation and entrapment that were related to marital crises, such as being deserted by husbands and left to care for several children, premature death, illness in family members, and severe financial difficulties occurring in the absence of an adequate welfare safety net. Studies in South Asia have shown that marital violence and the culturally determined value placed on boys (as compared with girls) adversely influence maternal mental health. Three cohort studies from India and Pakistan have demonstrated the greater risk for postnatal depression in mothers who have a girl child, especially if the desired sex was a boy or if the mother already had living girl children (Patel et al., 2004).

The male excess for alcohol abuse has been demonstrated in every community study from every region of the world, although the disparities are greatest in developing countries. The wide sex differences in alcohol abuse in Latin American countries and the Caribbean have been attributed to a number of gender factors (Pyne, Claeson, & Correia, 2002). Women, for example, face strict social scrutiny about many behaviors, drinking among them. Men's consumption of alcohol takes place in the public realm, whereas women's more often occurs in private. Drinking among men has social meanings, such as maintaining friendships, while refusing a drink can imply lack of trust and denial of mutual respect. At the other extreme, intoxication of men is more socially acceptable than that of women; indeed, women often tolerate their male partners' intoxication as being a "natural"

condition of manhood. Drinking and drunkenness are more often perceived to be consistent with gendered notions of masculinity; thus, men who conform closely to cultural norms are more likely to drink. Drinking may also be a coping strategy when men are faced with serious life difficulties, such as unemployment, and are unable to live up to the traditional expectations. Finally, in many cultures, but perhaps most well recognized in Latin American cultures, *machismo* (i.e., the importance of male sexuality) plays a role in shaping alcohol consumption. Thus, young men may consume excess alcohol with the deliberate intent of getting drunk because excessive drinking "celebrates male courage, sexual prowess, maturity and the ability to take risks, including sexual risks." (Pyne, Claeson & Correia, 2002)

The evidence that gender plays a role in eating disorders stems from two observations: the enormous sex difference (females outnumbering men), and the fact that cultures that have been relatively immune to the media-driven creation of the ideal body image for women have very low rates of these disorders. Recently, a study from Fiji has demonstrated that the introduction of television in a media-naïve non-Westernized population is associated with a rise in attitudes favoring thinner body image and self-induced vomiting in girls (Becker et al., 2002), adding credence to the theory that the emphasis on women's thinness by the media and fashion industries is now leading to a rise in disordered eating in societies that, through the forces of globalization, are being increasingly influenced by Western imagery and values.

Conflict and Refugees

According to the UNHCR there were an estimated 9.2 million refugees and 7.6 million internally displaced and stateless persons as of the end of 2004 (UNHCR, 2005). Many of these refugees will have experienced enormous trauma in the form of violence, crime, or other humiliations, physical injury, economic dispossession, and disruption of family and community structures. Thus, the rates of mental disorder among these people would be expected to be at least as high and probably higher than for migrants in general. A recent study of over 3,000 respondents from post-conflict communities in Algeria, Cambodia, Ethiopia, and Palestine found that post-traumatic stress disorder, a psychiatric disorder that is considered a specific response to trauma, was the most likely disorder in individuals exposed to violence associated with armed conflict (de Jong et al., 2003). In addition to exposure to trauma, a number of other factors may predispose refugees and immigrants to mental disorders, such as marginalization and minority status, socioeconomic disadvantage, poor physical health, the loss of social support systems, and cultural alienation in the new society. For illegal immigrants, there is also the constant fear of being found out and repatriated; therefore, access to possible sources of help is severely limited.

It is relevant to note that the universal application of trauma-related mental disorders, in particular post-traumatic stress disorder, has been criticized because it is itself based on culturally influenced notions of how a person is supposed to react to trauma. Thus, in narrating the experience of Cambodian refugees, Eisenbruch (1991) described patients who are "possessed by spirits, troubled by visitations of ghosts from the homeland . . . and feel he or she is being punished for having survived." The cultural construction of symptoms is also an important determinant of help-seeking behavior; thus, Buddhist monks might work as "allies to the clinician in clarifying the diagnosis of cultural bereavement" in Cambodia. Although there is consensus that trauma does negatively affect a person's mental health, the question of whether this negative impact should be conceptualized in psychiatric terms (with the concomitant implications of diagnosis and treatment) or in social and cultural terms remains unresolved. (See also Chapter 10).

Indigenous Communities

It is estimated that there are between 220 and 300 million indigenous persons living in 5,000 to 6,000 distinct groups in more than 70 countries. They exhibit a wide diversity of lifestyles, cultures, social organization, histories, and political realities. Nevertheless, they share certain historical and political realities, including being subject to violence and genocide, depopulation from infectious diseases such as smallpox and measles, dislocation from traditional lands, extreme poverty due to the destruction of their subsistence economies, and state-organized attempts to repress and eradicate their cultures. Given this history, it is not surprising that the indigenous peoples of the world now experience relatively high rates of depression, alcoholism, and suicide, as well as high rates of infectious diseases and relatively short life expectancies (Cohen, 1999).

The case of the indigenous communities of Australia serves to illustrate the confluence of these historical, political, social, and economic forces for understanding why the rates of mental disorders are higher among indigenous peoples. The indigenous peoples of Australia had a diversity of cultures dating back at least 40,000 years before the arrival of European settlers just over 200 years ago. The societies had a rich cultural belief system that attributed spiritual importance to land. Social relationships were governed by codes of behavior, and local taxonomies of illness guided the treatment of health problems. The brutal history of colonization, which ultimately led to the destruction and devastation of hundreds of indigenous nations, each with a distinct language and lineage, was marked by a number of severe social adversities. Notable among these were exposure to new diseases, removal from traditional lands, enslavement on white farms, imprisonment without trials, denial of basic political rights, brutal violation of human rights, sexual abuse of women, and perhaps most tragic of all, the "stolen generations," that is, the children who were forcibly removed from their parents and fostered by white families in an effort to "breed out" the native population. The consequences of this history are reflected in socioeconomic, psychosocial, and health indicators of all kinds, including high rates of unemployment, low levels of income, and poor educational status; age-specific mortality rates two to seven times higher than, and life expectancies more than 15 years shorter than, those of the general population; and high levels of alcoholism and suicide (Cohen, 1999). It is impossible to interpret the poor mental health without considering the social and historical contexts of the systematic abuse of aboriginal communities. *Ways Forward*, the national inquiry into indigenous mental health conducted in the early 1990s, prioritized holistic conceptions of emotional and social well-being. From these developments greater emphasis has been given to providing access to culturally appropriate services within mainstream health care settings. Today, even as efforts are made for a national reconciliation between indigenous and new Australians, the considerable gap between these two communities in their social and health indicators is a reminder of the distance that still needs to be covered.

Interventions

Only a small proportion of people suffering from mental disorders receive effective interventions. This is particularly the case in low- and middle-income countries, where mental health services are scarce. There are few low-income countries that have more than one psychiatrist per 10,000 people, and in many countries the bulk of the resources available for mental health services are devoted to large psychiatric hospitals (WHO, 2001b). In these contexts, people with serious psychiatric disorders and who cause public disturbance tend to receive the few available resources. Selected approaches to extending services beyond this core group are presented in the last section of this chapter.

Some important barriers prevent people from accessing even the limited services that exist. These include demographic factors (e.g., race/ethnicity or gender), attitudes (e.g., fear of being stigmatized, thinking that no one can help, and a belief in solving problems independently), cost (even for those with insurance, mental health coverage is frequently inferior to that for other medical conditions), and organizational factors (e.g., fragmentation of services and lack of availability) (Sussman, Robin, & Earls, 1987). These organizational factors are frequently more pertinent for people who are members of racial or ethnic minorities or who are poor (U.S. Department of Health and Human Services, 1999). The fact that effective treatments exist for the majority of mental disorders amplifies the urgency of addressing the barriers that prevent people from receiving interventions from which they would benefit.

Finally, it has been recognized for some time that there is an "efficacy-effectiveness gap." This refers to the phenomenon that pharmacological and psychotherapeutic treatments have a greater benefit in clinical trial settings as opposed to everyday practice. Some key differences between these settings account for the differences in response to treatment. For example, in everyday practice, patients are more heterogeneous and ethnically diverse, have one or more comorbid disorders, are less compliant, are less likely to be seen in specialty settings, and are less likely to have their progress carefully and objectively monitored (Dixon, Lehman, & Levine, 1995). Almost all efficacy studies involving psychiatric treatments have been conducted in the developed world. As great as the differences are between the clinical trial setting and the real-world setting in developed countries, those differences are still greater in low- and middle-income countries, where evidence from clinical trials may have little relevance because resource scarcity and lack of training profoundly shape clinical practices. Thus, it is particularly crucial to conduct effectiveness studies in low- and middle-income countries (Institute of Medicine, 2001). The section on clinical and public health interventions provides examples of interventions for disorders that represent substantial public health challenges in low- and middle-income countries and for which effective interventions are available.

Principles of Intervention

Interventions for mental health problems can be classified into three major activities: prevention, treatment, and maintenance (Institute of Medicine, 2001; WHO, 2001b).

Prevention involves interrupting the development of disorder by altering factors that affect the development of mental health problems. These factors can be divided into risk and protective factors. The former refers to factors that make it more likely that an individual will develop mental health difficulties, whereas the latter refers to factors that mediate and reduce the effects of risk exposure. Risk and protective factors can exist in the biologic, psychologic, and social domains (Table 8-2). Preventive interventions can be indicated (where the target is high-risk individuals who are showing evidence of early disorder), selective (where the target is high-risk groups), or universal (where the target is the entire population). There is overlap between mental health prevention and promotion, which is most evident with universal preventive interventions. Thus, an activity such as providing increased opportunities for more optimal use of leisure time could be construed as both a universal preventive intervention and as a mental health promoting activity. Other examples of interventions that straddle prevention and promotion include raising public awareness about mental disorders with a view to reducing stigma and school-based health programs that aim to reduce substance use (Flisher, Brown, & Mukoma, 2002).

Treatment for mental disorders has progressed enormously in recent years, to the point that effective treatments are available for the majority of mental disorders. Treatments may involve pharmacotherapy or psychotherapy, or both. Examples of the former include neuroleptics (for schizophrenia), antidepressants, stimulants (for attention deficit hyperactivity disorder), mood stabilizers such as lithium (for bipolar affective disorder), and anxiolytics (for anxiety disorders). Considerable progress has been made in the development of newer psychotropic agents, for example, neuroleptics and antidepressants. In general, these newer agents may not be more effective than their older counterparts, but they have fewer side effects. However, they are generally more expensive, which means that people in low- and middle-income countries are unlikely to enjoy the benefits of recent psychopharmacological advances.

Psychotherapy refers to planned and structured interventions aimed at influencing behavior, mood, and emotional patterns of reaction to different stimuli through verbal and nonverbal psychological means

(WHO, 2001b). There are a range of models of psychotherapy—for example, psychoanalysis, cognitive behavior therapy, and interpersonal psychotherapy. Each model can be applied in a range of individual, family, or group settings. Although there is increasing evidence of the effectiveness of many psychotherapies, we are still at an early stage in our understanding of the mechanisms through which this effectiveness is achieved. For many disorders, the optimum approach is to provide a combination of pharmacotherapy and psychotherapy.

Maintenance has two main aspects: preventing relapse or recurrence and providing rehabilitation. The former generally involves a combination of pharmacotherapy and psychotherapy as outlined earlier. The latter aims to facilitate optimal functioning. It involves improving both individual skills and capacities and the environment in which the person lives. This can be achieved by improving social competence, reducing discrimination and stigma, providing family support, providing social support (including basic needs related to housing, employment, social networks, and leisure), and facilitating consumer empowerment (WHO, 1995).

Specific Mental Disorders

Depression

Depression is a common mental disorder characterized by symptoms of low mood and loss of interest in daily activities. Most persons also experience a range of somatic symptoms (such as tiredness) and so-called biologic symptoms (such as sleep and appetite disturbances). In severe cases, psychotic and suicidal symptoms (Exhibit 8-4) may be experienced.

Prevention. The epidemiology of depression strongly indicates that treatment alone is unlikely to reduce its prevalence. Even in rich countries such as the United States, only about 20% of individuals with major depression actually receive mental health treatment. Most individuals with major depression do visit their primary care providers; unfortunately, major depression is recognized in only a third to a half of cases. Once recognized, not all those afflicted obtain treatment, and of those who do, many are inadequately treated. Even when treated, relapse rates are as high as 50% after one episode and 90% after 3 years (Cooper et al., 2002). These figures strongly suggest the need to prevent the first episode.

Community approaches to prevention of depression can focus on several levels: At the individual level, one can strengthen mood management skills, self-efficacy, and self-esteem; at the system level, one can focus on social support networks and increased employment. Such interventions aim to prevent the development of depressive symptoms to the point at which they become severe enough to cross the threshold into a major depressive episode. Interventions in the workplace tend to focus on stress and stress management approaches, with a secondary aim of reducing possible psychiatric symptomatology such as depression and anxiety. Some interventions target all or part of an organization. For example, the Caregiver Support Program for human service workers (cited in Jané-Llopis, Muñoz, & Patel, in press) has demonstrated that improving individual skills and changing organizational processes reduced depressive symptomatology. Effective workplace policies—from worker health and safety laws to employee assistance programs for alcohol, drug, and mental health problems—are also likely to have an impact on depressive symptomatology.

Indicated prevention has focused on those suffering from chronic medical conditions or from associated depressive symptomatology. Postpartum depression prevention in the forms of support provision and antenatal education has been attempted in several trials. In spite of the lack of evidence of the effectiveness of antenatal programs in preventing postpartum depression, they have led to other positive health outcomes related to children and mothers, such as mother-infant engagement (Cooper et al., 2002). Selective prevention strategies that have proved effective for adults focus on stressful life events that have a direct or indirect relation with depression and depressive symptoms. For example, a focus on providing support to unemployed persons has led to reductions in depressive symptoms. A number of randomized trials have also attempted to test whether the incidence of major depressive episodes can be reduced (Muñoz et al., 2002). In sum, although there is evidence that it is possible to reduce the onset of major depressive episodes in adolescents using indicated interventions, preventive interventions for adults have not yet yielded significant reduction in the incidence of major depressive episodes. Notably, there are no published studies on the effectiveness of preventive strategies for depression in developing countries.

Treatment and Maintenance. A large body of evidence from randomized controlled trials demonstrates the efficacy of both drug and psychosocial treatments for depression (Paykel & Priest, 1992). These studies showed the following. First, antidepressants were moderately superior to placebo, and this effect was most clearly evident in the short term. Thus, depressed persons were more likely to recover

Table 8-2	Selected Risk and Protective Factors for Mental Health	
Domain	**Risk Factors**	**Protective Factors**
Biological	Exposure to toxins (e.g., tobacco and alcohol) during pregnancy	Age-appropriate physical development
	Genetic tendency to psychiatric disorder	Good physical health
	Head trauma	Services provided at mother-baby clinics
	HIV infection and other physical illnesses	
Psychological	Maladaptive personality traits	Ability to learn from experiences
	Effects of emotional and sexual abuse and neglect	Good self-esteem
	Difficult temperament	High level of problem-solving ability
		Social skills
Social		
Family	Divorce	Family attachment
	Family conflict	Opportunities for positive involvement in family
	Poor family discipline	Rewards for involvement in family
	Poor family management	
	No family	
School or work place	Failure to perform at the expected level	Opportunities for involvement in school or occupational activities
	Low degree of commitment to school or workplace	
	Inadequate/inappropriate educational provision or training opportunities	
Community	Community disorganization	Connectedness to community
	Effects of discrimination	Opportunities for constructive use of leisure
	Exposure to violence	Positive cultural experiences
	Social conflict and migration	Positive role models
	Poverty	Rewards for community involvement
	Transitions (e.g., urbanization)	

Source: World Health Organization, *Child and Adolescent Mental Health* (Geneva, Switzerland: World Health Organization, in press). Reprinted with permission.

quickly if receiving antidepressants. Second, efficacy is similar between the older tricyclic antidepressants and newer drugs, including the selective serotonin reuptake inhibitors. The newer drugs have milder side effect profiles than the tricyclic antidepressants and are therefore more likely to be tolerated at therapeutic doses. Third, of the psychosocial treatments with demonstrated efficacy, the most widely accepted are cognitive-behavioral approaches. Alone or in combination, drug and psychosocial treatments speed recovery from acute episodes. Maintenance treatment with drugs decreases relapse risk. There is some evidence that a course of psychotherapy may also delay relapses.

A number of randomized controlled trials studying the efficacy and cost-effectiveness of the treatment of depression in low- and middle-income countries have been recently published (Patel, Araya, & Bolton, 2004). Each study provided evidence for the efficacy of depression interventions that are locally feasible and cost-effective among the poorest people in that setting. The associated improvement in function suggests benefits beyond mental health and beyond the individual who was treated, since improved function should benefit both family and community and enable the person to cope better with his or her social and economic difficulties. The studies demonstrate that some interventions found to be effective in developed countries were also found to be effective at these study sites, whereas others were not, perhaps due to local factors such as low adherence and lack of acceptability of specific treatments. Both elements suggest that it is worth trying interventions found to be effective in other cultures, but that their effectiveness needs to be tested when applied to new populations. In Chile, the trial evidence has been integrated into a nationwide program of integrating depression management into primary care settings.

Schizophrenia

Schizophrenia is a severe mental disorder that lasts for at least 6 months and includes at least 1 month of active symptoms such as delusions (false beliefs), hallucinations (disembodied voices or visions), disorganized speech, grossly disorganized or catatonic behavior, and negative symptoms (apathy and lack of drive). Onset is typically in late adolescence or early adulthood. The course is variable, with about 10% continuing to experience substantial impairment in their daily functioning (WHO, 2001b). However, about two-thirds achieve recovery or significant improvement (Harding, Zubin, & Strauss, 1987; Hopper, 1991).

Prevention. At present, there are no risk factors for schizophrenia that are sufficiently sensitive and specific to serve as a screening test for schizophrenia. Even if such a test were to be developed, there are no interventions that would stop the development of schizophrenia (Institute of Medicine, 2001). There is, however, a randomized controlled trial that provides grounds for hope. McGorry and associates (2002) compared two groups of people at risk for progression to a first episode of psychosis. One group received needs-based supportive psychotherapy plus a specific preventive intervention comprising a low dose of antipsychotic medication (risperidone), while the other group received only needs-based supportive psychotherapy. The results suggest that it might be

---

Exhibit 8-4	Suicide

Suicide is a major public mental health problem. In most countries where data are available, suicide ranks among the three leading causes of death in the age range from 15 to 44 years. Approximately 1 million people die from suicide annually. The magnitude of the challenge is magnified when one considers that for every completed suicide there are at least 20 attempted suicides (WHO, n.d.). There is no clear indication of an increase or decrease in global suicide rates over the past decades (WHO, 2001b). There are, however, important differences between and within countries and regions. For example, rates are low in South and Central America; intermediate in North America, India, and a few countries in western Europe; and high in most of Australasia and Europe (WHO, n.d.). It is not the case that suicide is a major challenge in industrialized countries only; for example, Sri Lanka and China have among the highest rates in the world (Desjarlais et al., 1995). The reasons for these differences remain obscure. Likewise, the associations between suicide and social factors such as unemployment, exposure to war, and poverty are inconsistent.

Suicidal behavior does not constitute a syndrome or series of syndromes, nor does it occur randomly. A heuristic *suicide pathway* can assist in the management of suicidal people and the prevention of suicidal behavior (Flisher, 1999). Step 1 consists of factors that generally predispose to suicidal behavior. These include demographic factors (male and female gender for completed and attempted suicide, respectively; increasing age); biologic factors (family history of psychopathology); psychopathology (especially alcohol use and depression); social context (high community base suicide rates, not adhering to a religion in which suicide is proscribed); and a family or personal history of attempted suicide. In addition, certain cultures are characterized by specific patterns that may predispose to suicide—for example, dowry dispute in India. Step 2 involves a precipitating event, which converts a predisposition toward suicidal behavior to actual behavior. Such events can include stressful life events, altered states of mind (fear, intoxication), a suicide cluster in one's social network, reports of suicide in the media, or spring season. Step 3 refers to the opportunity that needs to be present to make a suicide attempt, such as a method of suicide and privacy. Step 4 is the actual suicidal behavior.

Strategies to prevent suicide should aim to intervene in this pathway. For example, in step 1, one can aim to identify and provide mental heath services for those at risk, such as people suffering from alcohol dependence or depression. In step 2, one can increase access to crisis intervention services or provide life skills training to assist people in responding to stressful life events in an adaptive manner without resorting to suicide; implement postvention, in which one intervenes with members of a social network in which there is a suicide cluster; and work with the media to discourage glamorizing suicide. In step 3, one can reduce opportunities by limiting access to firearms, pesticides, or fatal household gas. In step 4, one can increase access to and improve the quality of emergency medical care following suicide attempts.

possible to delay or prevent progression to a first episode of psychosis.

Treatment. It is important to commence treatment as soon as possible after the disorder becomes apparent. The mainstay of treatment is neuroleptic medication, which is indicated over extended periods of time for almost all patients with schizophrenia. There are two families of neuroleptic medications, the conventional and the atypical neuroleptics. Both have equivalent effectiveness, although the latter are preferable in terms of adverse effects, acceptability, and treatment adherence (Institute of Medicine, 2001; Wahlbeck, Cheine, & Essali, 2000). Whether the atypical neuroleptics are more cost-effective has not been established (even in developed countries), although the conventional neuroleptics are clearly less expensive. Given that most people with schizophrenia in the developing world do not receive any treatment at all, it may make sense to promote the use of the less expensive conventional neuroleptic drugs, at least until inexpensive generic versions of the atypical neuroleptics are available (Institute of Medicine, 2001).

Maintenance. Medication remains crucial in the maintenance phase. Family interventions have also been shown to be effective in reducing relapse in patients with schizophrenia, both in the developed world and in low- and middle-income countries (Xiong et al., 1994). Major components of such family interventions include a collaborative relationship with the family in a no-fault atmosphere, education about schizophrenia, strategies for coping with the illness, communication training, problem-solving training, and crisis intervention (Asarnow, Tompson, & McGrath, 2004). Other psychological interventions that have been shown to be effective in the treatment of schizophrenia include cognitive behavioral psychotherapy and reality-oriented therapy (Pilling et al., 2002).

The generic principles of rehabilitation that were introduced in the section on principles of intervention earlier in this chapter are all particularly applicable to schizophrenia. In addition, intensive case management is frequently necessary because people suffering from schizophrenia frequently need an array of clinical, rehabilitative, and social services (Asarnow, Tompson, & McGrath, 2004). Assertive community treatment (ACT) is one form of intensive case management, which emphasizes coordination, integration, and continuity of services (Lehman & Steinwachs, 1998). Randomized clinical trials have demonstrated the superiority of case management, in general, and ACT, in particular, for a range of outcomes, including relapse risk (Asarnow,

Tompson, & McGrath, 2004). Although there is much less evidence for community interventions in low- and middle-income countries, a recent study has reported the efficacy of community-based rehabilitation in improving clinical and disability outcomes in persons with chronic schizophrenia from a rural setting in India (Chatterjee et al., 2003) (see Exhibit 8-7, later in this chapter).

Substance Abuse

Substance abuse disorders cover a wide range of psychotropic substances, including tobacco (not covered in this chapter), alcohol, and drugs such as heroin and cocaine.

Prevention. Effective interventions, strategies, and policies to prevent and reduce substance use disorders can be categorized as regulatory, community based (including education), and health service based. The evidence base is largely restricted to high-income countries, although it is expanding in low- and middle-income countries. Prohibition has been attempted for alcohol products and is currently in place in some countries, and is in place for classes of substances such as opioids, cannabinoids, and cocaine in most countries. Although prohibition can dramatically reduce substance use disorders in the short term, the costs in terms of civil disobedience and crime are enormous, so much so, that, in general, prohibition is not regarded as an acceptable policy option, with the exception of specific circumstances, such as drinking alcohol and driving (Anderson, Biglan, & Holder, in press).

Regulatory interventions include taxation, restrictions on availability, and total bans on all forms of direct and indirect advertising. Increases in alcohol taxes reduce both the prevalence and consumption of alcohol products. For young people, laws that raise the minimum legal drinking age reduce alcohol sales and problems among young drinkers. Reductions in the hours and days of sale, numbers of alcohol outlets, and restrictions on access to alcohol are all associated with reductions in both alcohol use and alcohol-related problems. There is limited evidence regarding the impact of prohibition or regulatory interventions on illicit drug use. Surveys of drug users tend to show rising or constant patterns of use in many countries, and falls in others, though strong regulatory interventions are evident in most.

Research paints a fairly dismal picture of the results of efforts to limit the supply of illicit drugs. Community mobilization and education have been used to prevent substance abuse in many countries (Exhibit 8-5). A crucial setting for prevention is in schools, where the goal of most alcohol education

| Exhibit 8-5 | Community Mobilization and Substance Abuse in Developing Countries |

Two examples from developing countries demonstrate the impact of community interventions. In India, a community-based approach to combating alcoholism included education and awareness building, action against drunken men, advocacy to limit the sale and distribution of alcohol in bars and shops, and mass oaths for abstinence. The program was implemented through a community movement led by young people and women and the *Darumukti Sangathana* (Liberation from Liquor) village groups. The program has led to a marked reduction in the number of alcohol outlets in the area, and a 60% reduction in alcohol consumption (Bang & Bang, 1991).

An unblinded, matched, community-based trial in Yunnan, China, involved multiple sectors and leaders in the community and emphasized community participation and action, education in schools, literacy improvement, and employment opportunities. The program led to a significant reduction in the incidence of drug abuse (Wu et al., 2002).

programs is to change the adolescent's drinking beliefs, attitudes, and drinking behaviors, or to modify factors such as general social skills and self-esteem that are assumed to underlie adolescent drinking. Scientific evaluations of school-based interventions have generally produced small effects that are short-lived unless accompanied by ongoing booster sessions.

Treatment and Maintenance. The management of substance abuse begins with motivating the person to acknowledge dependence and to agree on a management plan. A management plan will involve either a cessation of substance use or a minimization of the risk of continued use. In the former, cessation can be either sudden or gradual. Withdrawal syndromes must be managed with psychological support and drug treatments, if indicated. In the latter, harm minimization may take the form of switching from harmful patterns of substance use, for example, injecting street heroin, to oral methadone maintenance. The most recent and comprehensive meta-analysis comparing brief interventions (defined as those providing no more than four intervention sessions) to control conditions found significant effect sizes in changes in alcohol consumption at 6 to 12 months' follow-up (Moyer et al., 2002).

The more challenging next phase is to prevent relapse to the original levels of abuse. A variety of psychological interventions, from brief counseling for use by general practitioners to more elaborate interventions based on cognitive-behavior therapy, group therapy, therapeutic communities, and motivational interviewing, have been shown to increase the cessation rates and the duration of time that individuals are able to remain sober or drug free. Relapse rates in alcohol-dependent patients may be reduced by the agents which reduce craving for alcohol such as naltrexone, ondansetron and acamprosate. Relapse rates in opiod-dependent patients may be reduced by methadone and buprenorphine.

Epilepsy

Epilepsy is characterized by two or more unprovoked seizures that are caused by outbursts of excessive electrical activity in the brain. The manifestations of epilepsy depend on whether the entire brain or only part is affected. However, loss of consciousness and spasmodic body movements are frequently present.

Prevention. Preventive efforts are directed to reducing the risk factors for epilepsy. The following strategies are recommended for the prevention of epilepsy (Institute of Medicine, 2001; WHO, 1998):

- *Prenatal care:* Immunization of pregnant women, improvement of mothers' nutritional status, detection of high-risk pregnancies, and control of infectious diseases in pregnancy

- *Safe delivery:* Avoidance of labor and delivery complications, labor surveillance, and detection and early treatment of neonatal hypoxia

- *Fever control in children:* Avoidance of febrile illnesses in children, control of high temperatures in children, and neurologic consultation if a child presents with recurrent febrile seizures

- *Reduction of the causes of brain injury:* Enforcement of traffic regulations and speed limits; punishment for drunken driving; compulsory use of seat belts, children's safety seats, and helmets; safety precautions for stairs and windows; and avoidance of toxins such as alcohol in pregnancy, lead, and pesticides

- *Control of infectious and parasitic diseases:* Extension of immunization programs, environmental control of parasitic diseases, and detection and treatment of vectors

- *Genetic counseling:* Accurate information and counseling for potential parents who have epilepsy

Sustained intersectoral collaboration with a view to implementing these measures will have substantial favorable effects on the incidence of epilepsy.

Treatment. Almost all people with epilepsy should receive pharmacological treatment, with which the vast majority would remain seizure free. The drug of choice in low- and middle-income countries is phenobarbitol, which is inexpensive, effective, and has an acceptable side effect profile (Mani et al., 2001). Surgery may be a cost-effective intervention for intractable epilepsy in low-income countries, since the expenses of life-long pharmacological treatment are avoided and the costs of the surgery may be relatively less than in industrialized countries (Wieser & Silfvenius, 2000). The gap between the number of people needing treatment and those receiving it is on the order of 90% in many low- and middle-income countries (Shorvon & Farmer, 1988). There are two main reasons for the gap: delays in help seeking due to ignorance, fear, illiteracy, and cultural attitudes toward treatment (e.g., attributing epilepsy to possession), and reduced availability of drugs due to poor production facilities and inability of individuals or health systems to pay for treatment (Desjarlais et al., 1995).

Maintenance. In the case of epilepsy, there is an overlap between maintenance and treatment since the goal of even the initial treatment is to prevent recurrence. However, rehabilitation is an aspect of maintenance that is particularly important because stigma has such a pervasive influence on the economic, social, and marital opportunities of people with epilepsy. Important aspects of rehabilitation include public education, providing a reliable supply of medication, counseling the family, demonstrating that patients can resume or assume a role in the community, and providing or enhancing social support through social networks and constructive leisure time utilization (Desjarlais et al., 1995). All of these interventions can be expected to reduce the extent of stigma.

Mental Retardation

Mental handicap is defined as subnormal intelligence (IQ more than two standard deviations below the population mean), accompanied by limitations in related skills areas.

Prevention. Prevention aims mainly to reduce or eliminate the influence of biologic risk factors. For example, genetic risk can be reduced by improving contraception services to women over the age of 35 years, which will reduce the number of children with Down syndrome, an important cause of mental hand-

icap. There is a higher rate of mental handicap and other genetic conditions for the offspring of consanguineous marriages, which are common in many parts of the world. Educational campaigns and genetic counseling may contribute to reducing the incidence of mental handicap that is attributable to consanguineous marriages. Screening programs for conditions that are known to be associated with mental handicap (e.g., hypothyroidism, phenylketonuria, and syphilis) are a cost-effective prevention strategy in both the developed and developing world.

Four micronutrient deficiencies are associated with mental handicap: iodine, vitamin A, iron, and folic acid. Cost-effective interventions that contribute to increased intake of these micronutrients and hence reduce the prevalence of mental handicap include education about dietary sources of these nutrients and strategies for ensuring adequate intake; fortification of the food supply (e.g., salt or milk); supplementation to ensure adequate intake by vulnerable individuals; and control of infectious or parasitic diseases that cause a reduction in the levels of these nutrients. Other interventions that aim to reduce the impact of risk factors include the prevention and treatment of infections that cause mental handicap, such as congenital rubella, malaria, bacterial meningitis, measles, and HIV infection; reducing environmental levels of toxins such as lead; improving prenatal care and perinatal services; preventing trauma; and appropriate management of patients who have been exposed to trauma (Institute of Medicine, 2001).

Treatment. Because there are no treatments for the mental handicap per se, the focus of treatment is on comorbid conditions such as mental disorder. The first challenge is to make the correct diagnosis, as symptoms of comorbid psychiatric disorders may be falsely attributed to the mental handicap. For example, the excitement and increased levels of sexual activity that constitute aspects of a manic episode may be attributed to the disinhibition associated with mental handicap. The challenge is compounded by the inability of many people with mental disorder to provide the kind of history that facilitates diagnosis. The treatment may involve improving living circumstances, such as allowing personal choices to be implemented and enhancing competence; behavior management, such as encouraging positive behavior; and medication (Molteno & Westaway, 2001).

Maintenance. In the context of mental handicap, maintenance refers to rehabilitation. The most appropriate setting for rehabilitation is the community, as opposed to hospitals or institutions. The aim is the social integration of people with mental handicap, with a view to decreasing isolation and stigma. The emphasis is moving from restoration of function in individuals to changing public attitudes and environmental barriers that reduce participation in society (Institute of Medicine, 2001). However, community facilities such as group homes, protected workshops, and activity centers are key requirements for the successful implementation of a community-based approach to rehabilitation. One aspect of the normalization of people with mental handicap is the recognition of their rights to engage in fulfilling sexual relationships (Molteno & Westaway, 2001).

Mental Illness Across the Life Span

Earlier, this chapter discussed interventions for mental disorders that occur primarily in adults. Here it considers the public health implications of mental disorders at the two extremes of the life span.

Childhood and Adolescence

Mental disorders are common in childhood and adolescence. Examples include mood disorders (e.g., depression), anxiety disorders (e.g., post-traumatic stress disorder), and others (e.g., attention deficit hyperactivity disorder and conduct disorder). Overall, prevalence rates on the order of 10–20% for such disorders have been documented in community-based studies in several national and cultural contexts (Bird, 1996; Verhulst, 1995; WHO, 2001b).

The points that were made earlier about the causes of mental disorder also apply to children and adolescents. However, the importance of social context is even more pronounced. Also, mental disorders in childhood and adolescence need to be considered in relation to development. Thus, the extent and nature of the influence of the social context (e.g., family relationships, peer and neighborhood factors, and the larger sociocultural context) depend on the developmental stage of the child or adolescent. The impact of the primary caregiver and peers on mental health, for example, is likely to be particularly important during infancy and adolescence, respectively. Interventions that fail to take into account these developmental specificities are unlikely to achieve their maximal impact. Another implication of a developmental approach is that symptoms have different implications depending on when they are present: Temper tantrums in a 2-year-old generally have less pathological significance than in an adolescent. This accounts for the finding that prevalence rates of psychopathology vary substantially depending on the extent to which functional impairment is necessary for diagnosis (Shaffer et al., 1996). Finally, the developmental approach implies that service delivery can be planned on the basis that specific mental disorders generally present at specific times during the course of child and adolescent development—for example, attachment disorders present in the first few years of life, while schizophrenia generally presents in adolescence.

The treatment approaches mentioned previously are in general also applicable to children and adolescents, although the evidence base for both psychosocial and pharmacological interventions is less extensive than for adults. There is disagreement as to whether child and adolescent mental health services should constitute a discrete area of health care (which can make it more likely that the necessary funding will be forthcoming) or should be integrated into pediatric or general psychiatric services (which can increase access in contexts where limited child and adolescent mental health personnel are available).

The Elderly

By 1990, a majority (58%) of the world's population aged 60 years and over were already living in developing countries. By 2020 this proportion will have risen to 67%. For older people, mental health problems are an important cause of morbidity and premature mortality. Among the neuropsychiatric conditions, dementia and major depression were the leading contributors, accounting for one-quarter and one-sixth, respectively, of all DALYs in this category. As dementia research has evolved in developed countries, early differences in age-specific prevalence turned out to be largely explained by methodological effects. The EURODEM concerted action, which identified recent studies that had used comparable methods, showed no important variation in dementia prevalence (Hofman et al., 1991). A number of studies in low- and middle-income countries have reported strikingly low prevalence rates of dementia (Hendrie et al., 1995). There seems to be a general trend for age-adjusted prevalence estimates from low- and middle-income countries to be lower than those for developed countries. Confirmation and elaboration of this fascinating discrepancy will require more studies in more settings, using appropriately harmonized dementia diagnostic procedures.

Mental disorders in the elderly are neither well understood nor acknowledged either by the community or the medical profession in low- and middle-income countries. Ethnographic studies have shown that symptoms of depression and dementia are attributed to tension, family conflict, and lack of family affection rather than a biomedical psychiatric problem (Patel & Prince, 2001). In many countries, there are no social welfare systems for the aged, a situation compounded by the gradual breakdown of the traditional extended family that has formed the bulwark for the care of the disabled and chronically ill. There is good evidence from developed countries regarding the effectiveness of interventions focusing on supporting carers and improving the behavioral and cognitive symptoms of persons with dementia. There is a need to evaluate the effectiveness of such interventions in low-resource settings.

Public Mental Health: Priorities for Developing Countries

The 2001 *World Health Report* (WHO, 2001b) set out 10 key recommendations for public mental health in low- and middle-income countries (Table 8-3). This chapter concludes by considering the evidence for each of these recommendations and suggesting future strategies and directions.

Provide Treatment in Primary Care

More than 30 years of epidemiologic studies suggests that between 15% and 30% of attendees in primary care settings in low-income countries suffer from some mental disorder, predominantly depression and anxiety (Cohen, 2001). This, in combination with an acute shortage of mental health professionals, points to the need for providing mental health treatment in primary care settings. Over the past 30 years, this notion has been a mantra of international psychiatry

Table 8-3	Public Mental Health Priorities
1. Provide treatment in primary care	
2. Make psychotropics medications available	
3. Give care in the community	
4. Educate the public	
5. Involve communities, families, and consumers	
6. Establish national policies and legislation	
7. Develop human resources	
8. Link with other sectors	
9. Monitor community health	
10. Support more research	

Source: World Health Organization, *Mental Health: New Understanding, New Hope* (Geneva, Switzerland: World Health Organization, 2001). Reprinted with permission.

(WHO, 1975, 2001b), even though we have little evidence of its effective implementation (Cohen, 2001).

That the integration of mental health services into primary care is believed to be an easily achieved panacea (Jenkins & Strathdee, 2000) is puzzling in light of research from North America and Europe that has repeatedly demonstrated that it is not a straightforward task and instead requires multifaceted strategies that include training, patient education, follow-up, and ongoing supervision by mental health professionals (Katon et al., 1996; Lin, 1999). Furthermore, discussions of this policy frequently do not consider the nature of primary care itself. Health workers' lack of knowledge about mental disorders, in combination with the demands of treating physical disorders, and within the context of scarce resources, usually means that mental health issues are pushed to the bottom of priority lists. Finally, discussions usually assume that "primary care" represents a single model, rather than acknowledging the existence of vast differences in the organization and resources of health systems across South America, Africa, and Asia (Patel & Cohen, 2003). Although attention is usually focused on public health systems, private medical practitioners (both traditional healers and biomedical physicians) constitute a large and growing proportion of the health system. Thus, it is necessary to consider these diverse sectors and challenges if we are to develop coherent policies that improve mental health services in primary care.

Although recent trials have begun to provide the evidence necessary for establishing effective mental health services in primary care in low- and middle-income countries (Araya et al., 2003; Bolton et al., 2003; Patel et al., 2003), large-scale implementation of these interventions will be difficult because of resource shortages, and many organizational barriers remain. The barriers include markedly different priorities in public health (e.g., HIV/AIDS in some countries), varying levels of risk factors (e.g., violence), the heterogeneous nature of primary health care systems, and the extent to which a variety of health resources are available. There is no question that the provision of effective mental health services in primary care is essential if we are serious about addressing the global burden of disease imposed by mental disorders. Nevertheless, it is dangerous to plunge ahead with untested assumptions and ignore the inherent difficulties of this task (Abas et al., 2003; Acland, 2002; Petersen, 2000). To meet the challenge, it will be necessary to consider the clinical issues involved in the treatment of mental disorders, the structural barriers that make such treatment a low priority,

Exhibit 8-6	Do Talking Treatments Work in Low-Income Countries?

Interpersonal psychotherapy is a form of psychological treatment that has been extensively used, and evaluated, for the treatment of depression in developed countries. However, the applicability and effectiveness of such "talking treatments" in non-Western settings have not been studied.

A team of investigators from the United States and Uganda adapted this intervention for use in a rural setting in Uganda that had high rates of HIV infection and other communicable diseases. They chose a group setting for delivering the intervention since this would enable reaching out to more patients and would be more cost-effective in a low-resource setting. The intervention was tested in a cluster randomized controlled trial in which 30 villages were randomized. Men received the intervention in half the villages, and women in the other half. Depression was diagnosed using locally validated questionnaires. The intervention consisted of weekly group therapy sessions lasting about 90 minutes each, over 16 weeks.

Whereas about 90% of subjects in both arms (intervention and control) met criteria for a major depressive disorder at recruitment, only 6.5% of subjects in the intervention villages were depressed at the end of the trial, as compared with over half the subjects in the control villages ($p < .001$). This trial demonstrated not only the effectiveness of a relatively cheap and safe treatment for depression in a rural setting of a poor country but also the feasibility of complex trials for mental disorders in low-resource settings (Bolton et al., 2003).

and sociocultural factors, such as stigma and discrimination, that make the implementation of change so difficult.

Make Psychotropic Medications Available

Despite the evidence for the efficacy and, in some instances, the cost-effectiveness of drug treatments for a range of mental disorders, there is very limited access to these in most low- and middle-income countries.

In many low- and middle-income countries, most persons will not have access to a reliable supply of psychotropic drugs. Table 8-4 shows the availability of various psychotropic drugs in different regions of the world. These figures, however, hide the considerable variations between and within countries in each region and between social classes. Thus, in many low- and middle-income countries, the urban middle class may be able to access the newest psychotropic drugs, whereas the majority of the urban poor and rural populations have access to only the old psychotropics, or no psychotropics at all. Another problem is irrational drug use—polypharmacy, in particular. This leads to the paradoxical situation wherein the majority of the population does not have access to even basic drugs, while many of those who do, often receive inappropriate treatments (Patel & Andrade, 2003).

A key priority is to ensure the reliable and affordable access to a basic list of essential drugs for psychiatric disorders. As important as a reliable supply of affordable medication is the need to ensure that those who are authorized to prescribe these drugs are fully aware of their indications and adverse effects. In countries in which there is minimal mental health personnel, this may mean providing basic training on diagnosis and treatment to general

health workers. In other countries, where there are more mental health personnel, the emphasis may lie in ensuring a reliable supply of drugs and on continuing education of psychiatrists on the need for rational drug use. Equally important, there is a need to recognize that drugs must be provided in the context of a multimodal approach to care. Finally, if, as we hope, radically new treatments are patented for mental disorders, advocacy will be required to ensure that the cost of these treatments do not limit their availability to poorer populations.

Give Care in the Community

Deinstitutionalization of mentally ill persons through the closure of mental hospitals and the development of community care programs is arguably one of the most impressive public mental health achievements of the latter half of the last century. As noted earlier, these changes have led to vast improvements in the quality of care and, importantly, in the rights of patients. However, these sweeping changes have not been as visible in developing countries. Indeed, institutional care still remains the norm even in countries with relatively numerous mental health human resources, such as Brazil and India. Thus, mental hospital beds account for a large proportion of psychiatric beds in most low- and middle-income countries (instead of general hospital psychiatric units in developed countries), and community programs are either symbolic demonstration projects or small-scale programs run in the nongovernmental sector.

The managed closure of mental hospitals must be accompanied by a carefully planned strategy to ensure that mentally ill persons do not simply end up living on the streets. Half-way and rehabilitation homes may

Table 8-4	Percentage of Drug Availability per Region (Among Countries Responding)					
	Africa	**America**	**Eastern Mediterranean**	**Europe**	**Southeast Asia**	**Western Pacific**
Carbamazepine	77.8	100.0	84.2	100.0	88.9	96.3
Valproate	48.9	67.9	73.7	87.0	77.8	63.0
Amitriptylline	71.1	93.3	84.2	100.0	88.9	96.3
Chlorpromazine	97.8	93.3	89.5	84.8	90.0	96.3
Diazepam	97.7	100.0	94.7	95.7	100.0	100.0
Fluphenazine	60.0	64.3	68.4	84.8	80.0	63.0
Haloperidol	84.4	100.0	84.2	97.8	66.7	96.3
Lithium	36.4	83.3	52.6	95.6	55.6	70.4
Biperiden	33.3	50.0	42.1	80.0	11.1	22.1

Source: World Health Organization, *Atlas: Country Profiles of Mental Health Resources* (Geneva, Switzerland: World Health Organization, 2001). Reprinted with permission.

be needed for some persons who are severely disabled by their mental illness and who do not have adequate social support networks. For others, community care, linked with support from a mental health professional when available, must be the goal for mental health systems in all countries. That community care can be implemented using locally available resources, and that it can improve clinical outcomes, is evident from the description of a number of models in low- and middle-income countries. One such example is the Ashagram model in rural India (Exhibit 8-7).

Educate the Public

There is low awareness regarding mental illness and the importance of mental health in most countries, but most markedly in low- and middle-income countries.

Raising awareness about mental illness may help improve understanding about the risks to mental health, and methods of coping with these risks, and thus promote mental health in the community. One such awareness program, delivered through schools, was assessed in a controlled trial in Rawalpindi, Pakistan. The intervention was delivered in two secondary schools, and the outcome measurement was based on a self-report questionnaire about various aspects of mental health and illness. The experimental group showed significantly better improvement in scores as compared with the control group (Rahman et al., 1998). More impressive was the finding that parents, friends, and even neighbors of the students in the experimental group showed significant improvements as compared with the control group. This trial has shown that delivering education regarding mental

Exhibit 8-7	Community Care for Severe Mental Disorders in Low-Resource Settings

A community mental health program for severe mental disorders in a rural setting in India was initiated in partnership with Ashagram ("village of hope"), a nongovernmental organization (NGO) working toward the rehabilitation of people affected by leprosy. The NGO was located in Barwani, one of the poorest districts in India. Mental health care was routinely provided through an outpatient clinic, which required patients to travel to the hospital to be assessed and to receive treatment.

A community-based rehabilitation (CBR) model was devised for patients with chronic schizophrenia, based on a three-tiered service delivery system. CBR is a model of community care based on the active participation of the disabled and their families in rehabilitation that takes specific cognizance of prevailing social, economic, and cultural issues. At the top was outpatient care. The second tier was composed of mental health workers drawn from the local community. After a 60-day training program, they worked with patients, families, and the local community in providing services. Each of these mental health workers serviced five to six contiguous villages and carried a total case load of 25 to 30 patients, including some of the study subjects. The third tier consisted of family members and other key persons in the community who formed the local village health groups (*samitis*). These groups were a forum for the members to plan relevant rehabilitation measures and reduce social exclusion. All patients were started on antipsychotic medication.

The evaluation of the CBR program showed that, among compliant subjects, the CBR model is more effective than standard outpatient treatment on a range of clinical and functional outcomes (Chatterjee et al., 2003). Since the lack of professional resources is the reality in low-income countries, the CBR method offers a model that involves active local community participation and low levels of technical expertise to deliver services.

health and illness to secondary school students is effective in raising awareness in the wider community and may thus help raise mental health literacy and promote mental health at large.

Nongovernmental organizations in many developing countries are now playing a key role in raising awareness about mental health and pioneering a range of community programs targeted to different population groups to promote mental health and prevent mental illnesses. A recent book has documented 17 such programs being implemented in India (Patel & Thara, 2003). Public education and awareness campaigns on mental health are essential, feasible, and effective. The main goal is to reduce barriers to treatment and care by increasing awareness of mental disorders and their treatability. The care choices available and their benefits should be widely disseminated so that responses from the general population, professionals, media, policy makers, and politicians reflect the best available knowledge. Well-planned public awareness and education campaigns can reduce stigma and discrimination, increase the use of mental health services, and bring mental and physical health care closer to each other (WHO, 2001b).

Involve Communities, Families, and Consumers

Involving diverse sectors is a key aspect of public mental health in all settings, and arguably even more so in developing countries where the formal mental health care system is inadequately developed. This chapter has presented a number of examples of intersectoral, community action, for example, the programs to prevent alcohol and drug abuse and the community-based rehabilitation model for schizophrenia. This section highlights one specific sector that has made an important contribution to mental health care and reforms in developed countries and is only recently achieving recognition in low- and middle-income countries: consumer- and family-led movements.

The World Fellowship for Schizophrenia and Allied Disorders and Alzheimer's Disease International are NGOs that have their origins in developed countries, where strong consumer movements led by families of persons with schizophrenia and Alzheimer's disease led to their establishment. In the past decade, both NGOs have had a growing presence in low- and middle-income countries. Similarly, Befriender International, a voluntary group that provides support to persons who are suicidal, has spread to a number of developing countries. Local NGOs led by families of persons affected by mental illness are also mushrooming in developing countries (Patel & Thara, 2003). There are fewer examples of community move-

ments that are led by persons who are themselves suffering from mental disorders. Perhaps the best example is Alcoholics Anonymous, which is widely represented internationally and is one of the most well-described examples of an effective community-based strategy for the prevention of any mental disorder.

All of these NGOs share many characteristics. All have a strong community orientation, with an explicit space for families and users of services to express their views and set the agenda for action. Advocacy to policy makers, the media, and other sectors in the health system is a core activity. Documentation and dissemination of relevant facts and research, and lobbying policy makers for changes in the law are vital instruments for improving mental health care. Prominent examples of the success of these advocacy efforts are the inclusion of mental disabilities in the disability legislation of some countries. Many groups also provide services, usually in the form of support groups or networking for affected families; the larger groups even support research activities and medical care.

Establish National Policies and Legislation

A mental health policy presents the values, principles, and objectives for improving the mental health of people and reducing the burden of mental disorders in a population. It should define a vision for the future and help to establish a model for action. A policy should be distinguished from a plan, which is a strategy for implementing actions to achieve the objectives of a policy. In some countries, mental health policies are restricted to psychiatric services. However, a broader scope is preferable, one in which mental health services in general are addressed. These can include primary care and specialized care, and all three aspects of intervention mentioned earlier (prevention, treatment, and maintenance) (WHO, 2003b). Policies need to address the coordination between mental health services themselves and also between mental health services and other services such as housing, education, and employment. Other key aspects that policies should address include the financial arrangements for the private and public sectors, expenditure prioritization, and individual and organizational capacity development (WHO, 2001b). Finally, there needs to be continuous evaluation of mental health outcomes to ensure that the policy remains appropriate to contemporary circumstances and information.

A country's capacity to deliver appropriate mental health services to its population is seriously hampered by the absence of a mental health policy. It is thus a cause for concern that only 60% of countries have mental health policies. Developing countries are less likely to have policies; for example, only 48% of countries in Africa and the western Pacific have policies (WHO, 2001a). Partly in response to this, the World Health Organization has developed the Mental Health Policy and Service Guidance Package. The package consists of a series of interrelated user-friendly modules designed to assist with policy development and service planning. One module provides a series of steps that can be taken to develop mental health policies: Assess the population's needs; gather evidence for effective policy; consult and negotiate; exchange with other countries; set out the vision, values, principles, and objectives of the policy; determine areas for action; identify the roles and responsibilities of different sectors; and conduct pilot studies (WHO, 2003b).

Legislation is essential to complement and reinforce mental health policy. It provides the legal framework for issues such as human rights; community integration of the mentally ill; links with other sectors; access to care, rehabilitation, and aftercare; enhancing the quality of care; the prevention of mental disorders; and the promotion of mental health (WHO, 2003a). Worldwide, only 75% of countries have any mental health legislation (WHO, 2001a). However, in contrast with mental health policies, it is not the case that developing countries are less likely to have legislation. In Africa, for example, 71% of countries have mental health legislation. A module in the World Health Organization's Mental Health Policy and Service Guidance Package addresses mental health legislation and human rights (WHO, 2003a). The module presents a step-by-step approach to each of the following phases of the legislative process: preliminary activities, the drafting process, adoption of legislation, and implementation.

Develop Human Resources

The implementation of mental health policies and plans is dependent on the quantity and quality of the personnel who will implement the three aspects of interventions mentioned earlier: prevention, treatment, and maintenance. There are vast differences between regions of the world in terms of the availability of mental health professionals (Table 8-5). In almost all countries, there is a gap between the supply of personnel and the demand for their services. The deleterious consequences of the low numbers of mental health professionals are magnified when one considers that the distribution of mental health professionals is frequently uneven between countries in each region and within countries (with the number of

mental health workers per 100,000 being considerably higher in metropolitan areas, for example) (WHO, 2005). Also, the available personnel are not used appropriately, and many staff are demoralized and demotivated (WHO, 2005).

The development of human resources should thus constitute a key component of an effort to improve the public mental health. The World Health Organization (2005) suggests that several steps can be taken to address this need: Countries need to develop policies for increasing human resources in mental health; they need a systematic method of calculating how many mental health staff are required and what skill mix is optimal; they need to develop appropriate management strategies for leadership, motivation, and deployment of scarce personnel; training of mental health staff needs to be reviewed and improved, in keeping with the mental health needs of the population; and, once professionals are qualified, continuing education, training, and supervision needs to be developed for the provision of the best care.

Mental health programs require a cadre of well-trained mental heath specialists, for example, psychiatrists, psychologists, mental health occupational therapists, and psychiatric nurses (Desjarlais et al., 1995). They are responsible for functions such as the management of patients with complex conditions, supervision and training of other specialists and generic health workers, research, planning, management, and consultation-liaison. It is clearly vital that specialists are abreast of modern international developments that are relevant for the functions they perform. However, the application of such developments should be informed by local research and experience. Training efforts for specialists should occur in parallel with training for generic health workers such as doctors and nurses, who provide the majority of care in developing countries.

Link with Other Sectors

Many of the social determinants of mental health cut across a range of sectors, such as labor and employment, commerce and economics, education, housing, other social welfare services, and the criminal justice system. Mental health input is thus necessary in many departments to ensure that policies improve the mental health of the population and do not have the opposite effect. For example, mental health input in the criminal justice system can prevent the inappropriate imprisonment of people with mental disorders, make treatment for mental disorders available in prisons, and reduce the mental health sequelae of imprisonment for prisoners and their families (WHO, 2001b).

Table 8-5	Median Number of Mental Health Professionals per 100,000 Population in each WHO Region and in the World			
WHO Region and the World	Psychiatrists	Psychiatric Nurses	Psychologists Working in Mental Health	Social Workers Working in Mental Health
Africa	0.05	0.20	0.05	0.04
Americas	1.60	2.70	2.80	1.90
Eastern Mediterranean	0.95	0.50	0.20	0.40
Europe	9.00	27.50	3.00	2.35
Southeast Asia	0.21	0.16	0.02	0.05
Western Pacific	0.28	1.10	0.03	0.13
World	1.00	2.00	0.40	0.30

Source: World Health Organization, *Atlas: Country Profiles of Mental Health Resources* (Geneva, Switzerland: World Health Organization, 2001). Reprinted with permission.

There are several other important reasons for linking with other sectors, including promoting political will for the implementation of policies and legislation that are optimal for the public mental health; exploiting the potential to meet mental health needs in a number of settings (e.g., the school, workplace, and community); increasing buy-in from other sectors; educating people as to the potential contribution of their sector to the public mental health; increasing the comprehensiveness and holism with which an issue is regarded; encouraging a continuum of care; enabling a range of different approaches to be brought to bear in addressing an issue; and increasing efficiency and cost-effectiveness through reducing duplication and enhancing synergy between sectors. It is important to keep these reasons in mind when engaging with other sectors so that steps can be taken to ensure that the full benefits of such linkages are realized.

One sector that is particularly important in developing countries is the traditional health sector. In many developing countries, the majority of people seek care from traditional healers before seeing allopathic healers. The report of the Alma-Ata International Conference on Primary Health Care concluded:

> Traditional medical practitioners and birth attendants are found in most societies. They are often part of a local community, culture and tradition, and continue to have high social standing in many places, exerting considerable influence on local health practices. It is therefore well worthwhile exploring the possibilities of engaging them in primary health care and of training them accordingly. (WHO, 1978)

There are several ways in which they can be engaged. They can operate side by side with allopathic mental health services, perhaps even operating from the same premises; they can be trained to recognize mental dis-orders and refer people suffering them to allopathic services; and they can be recruited and trained to function as allopathic mental health workers.

Whatever arrangements are made at an organizational level, individual mental health service providers should attempt to establish whether their patients are being subjected to any traditional interventions that are harmful. If they are, they should receive education and counseling that aim to reduce exposure to such negative interventions. Mental health service providers should also attempt to ascertain whether their patients are taking traditional medicines. This is important because such medicines may produce dangerous side effects, especially if there is interaction with allopathic medicines. Conversely, traditional practices that are helpful can be incorporated into allopathic care (Institute of Medicine, 2001).

Monitor Community Health

A major lacunae in community health surveillance and monitoring is the lack of mental health indicators. A number of new initiatives are being planned that aim to integrate mental health as part of routine demographic and health surveillance. For example, the follow-up of the 1999 National Family Health Survey in India included a short screening questionnaire to measure common mental disorders. A new mental health group has been formed by the International Network of field sites with continuous Demographic Evaluation of Populations and Their Health (INDEPTH Network), linking 36 field sites from 18 low-income countries in Africa, Asia, and South America; this offers a timely opportunity to implement community monitoring of mental health simultaneously with the monitoring of other demographic and health indicators in developing countries. New, short, and relatively simple screening measures for common mental (e.g., the K6 questionnaire) and alcohol use (e.g., the AUDIT questionnaire) disorders are a more accurate way of monitoring community mental health because of low recognition rates for these disorders among health workers.

The WHO is attempting to bridge this information gap, at least in part, through the development of a set of indicators to monitor mental health systems and services at the country level (S. Saxena, personal communication). The implementation of these indicators could lead to substantial gains in the current status of mental health information. Countries would be able to monitor progress in the implementation of their reform policies, provision of community services and activities, and involvement of the communities, consumers' and families' associations, and other governmental sectors in mental health promotion, prevention, care, and rehabilitation. Countries would thus reach a clearer and more comprehensive picture of the main mental health issues and be able to assess improvement over time. Furthermore, at the country level, indicators may prompt governments and health systems managers to build a data infrastructure, implement information systems, and foster the use of surveys of mental disorders.

Support More Research

Research is essential to generate the necessary evidence for guiding an appropriate response by policy makers and practitioners to the large unmet needs of care for mental illnesses, particularly in developing countries. The need for psychiatric research to reflect the diverse realities of health systems and cultural factors is crucial if research is to inform local health policy and practice. As with most areas of health, the contribution of developing countries to mental health research is very low. Surveys of high-impact journals typically show that less than 10% of published research originates from developing countries, and the vast majority of journals published in developing countries are nonindexed, limiting their impact (Patel & Sumathipala, 2001). A major factor that is impeding the use of more appropriate interventions or a greater prominence to mental illness in policy is the lack of evidence about treatments and the tendency for research to be focused on psychiatrists and psychiatric contexts. Arguably, if there was evidence that treatments were efficacious and cost-effective and that they were clearly linked to other community health problems, then they would be more widely adopted by health workers and health policy makers. It is clearly time, then, to move from surveys demonstrating prevalence to research. Future psychiatric research in developing countries needs to be more action-oriented, in the form of actual intervention trials or studies with the explicit goal of influencing the integration of mental health care in existing community health services and public health priorities. The research must be sensitive to local needs and involve active participation from potential users of the findings. In selecting settings for intervention research, a variety of health systems should be considered to ensure that findings can be generalized to many regions of the world.

Perhaps the most important strategy to support mental health research in developing countries is to raise skills and capacity for research in diverse regions of the world. There are some existing resources for mental health research in developing countries. These include collaborative relationships between institutions, international networks for research, a growing number of donors willing to fund mental health research, and a variety of training programs for research. However, since there is still a large gap between what is available and what is needed, it is necessary to strengthen existing resources and develop new ones. The ultimate goals for sustainable research in developing countries include creating a network of researchers, research centers, and forums for information exchange; making a career in research an attractive option for mental health and public health professionals in developing countries; ensuring that research findings are taken seriously by practitioners and policy makers; and securing sufficient funding, commensurate with the global burden of mental disorders and, in particular, sufficient to enable research in developing countries.

• • • Discussion Questions

1. It is difficult to place mental health high on the public health agenda of low-income countries that face an enormous burden of communicable diseases. What evidence-based arguments can you make to challenge the notion that mental health is a luxury item on the health agenda of such countries?

2. The classification of mental disorders is mainly derived from the description of these disorders in developed countries. Some argue that this fact limits the application of psychiatric knowledge and evidence to non-Western cultures. How valid are these concerns? In what ways have the Western bias been addressed in the classification of mental disorders in international public health?

3. A major obstacle to implementing public mental health programs in low-resource

settings is the lack of human resources. What alternatives can be considered to overcome this limitation? For example, what is the role of nonspecialist health and nonhealth resources for mental health care?

4. Diseases that disproportionately affect the poor are typically prioritized by governments and donors. Many people believe that disorders such as depression and alcohol abuse are problems of the middle class and affluent, and thus they do not deserve allocation of scarce resources. What is the evidence linking poverty with mental disorders? How might poverty interact with mental health?

5. A range of factors, biological and social, have been identified in the etiology of mental disorders. Describe the different factors associated with the causes of both common and severe mental disorders. How does an understanding of etiology inform the development of treatment and prevention?

● ● ● **References**

Abas, M., Mbengeranwa, O. L., Chagwedera, I. V., Maramba, P., & Broadhead, J. (2003). Primary care services for depression in Harare, Zimbabwe. *Harvard Review of Psychiatry, 11*(3), 157–165.

Acland, S. (2002). Mental health services in primary care: The case of Nepal. In A. Cohen, A. Kleinman, & B. Saraceno (Eds.), *The world mental health casebook: Social and mental health programs in low-income countries* (pp. 121–152). New York: Kluwer Academic/Plenum Press.

Alem, A. (2000). Human rights and psychiatric care in Africa with particular reference to the Ethiopian situation. *Acta Psychiatrica Scandinavica Supplementum, 399,* 93–96.

American Psychiatric Association. (1994). *Diagnostic and statistical manual of mental disorders, 4th edition.* Washington, DC: American Psychiatric Association.

Anastasi, A. (1958). Heredity, environment and the question 'How'? *Psychological Review, 65,* 197–208.

Anderson, P., Biglan, A., & Holder, H. (in press). Reducing the onset of substance use disorders. In C. Hosman, C. Jané-Llopis, & S. Saxena (Eds.), *Prevention of mental disorders: An overview on evidence-based strategies and programs.* Oxford, England: Oxford University Press.

Andrews, J., Briggs, A., Porter, R., Tucker, P., & Waddington, K. (1997). *The history of Bethlem.* London: Routledge.

Araya, R., Rojas, G., Fritsch, R., Gaete, J., Rojas, M., Simon, G., & Peters, T. J. (2003). Treating depression in primary care in low-income women in Santiago, Chile: A randomised controlled trial. *Lancet, 361*(9362), 995–1000.

Asarnow, J. R., Tompson, M. C., & McGrath, E. P. (2004). Annotation: Childhood-onset schizophrenia: Clinical and treatment issues. *Journal of Child Psychology and Psychiatry and Allied Disciplines, 45,* 180–194.

Astbury, J. (2001). Gender disparities in mental health. In *Mental health: A call for action by World Health Ministers* (pp. 73–92). Geneva, Switzerland: World Health Organization.

Avotri, J. Y., & Walters, V. (1999). "You just look at our work and see if you have any freedom on earth": Ghanaian women's accounts of their work and health. *Social Science and Medicine, 48,* 1123–1133.

Bang, A., & Bang, R. (1991). Community participation in research and action against alcoholism. *World Health Forum, 12,* 104–109.

Becker, A. E., Burwell, R. A., Gilman, S. E., Herzog, D. B., & Hamburg, P. (2002). Disordered eating behaviors and attitudes follow prolonged exposure to television among ethnic Fijian adolescent girls. *British Journal of Psychiatry, 180,* 509–514.

Beiser, M., Cargo, M., & Woodbury, M. (1994). A comparison of psychiatric disorder in different cultures: Depressive typologies in South-East Asian refugees and resident Canadians. *International Journal of Methods in Psychiatric Research, 4,* 157–172.

Bird, H. (1996). Epidemiology of childhood disorders in a cross-cultural context. *Journal of Child Psychology and Psychiatry and Allied Disciplines, 37,* 35–49.

Birley, J. L. (2000). Political abuse of psychiatry. *Acta Psychiatrica Scandinavica Supplementum, 399,* 13–15.

Blacker, D., & Tsuang, M. T. (1992). Contested boundaries of bipolar disorder and the limits of categorical diagnosis in psychiatry. *American Journal of Psychiatry, 149*(11), 1473–1483.

Bloch, S. (1997). Psychiatry: An impossible profession? *Australian and New Zealand Journal of Psychiatry, 31,* 172–183.

Bolton, P., Bass, J., Neugebauer, R., Verdeli, H., Clougherty, K. F., Wickramaratne, P. J., Speelman, L., Ndogoni, L., & Weissman, M. M. (2003). Group interpersonal psychotherapy for depression in rural Uganda. *Journal of the American Medical Association, 289,* 3117–3124.

Breitbart, W., Marotta, R., Platt, M. M., Weisman, H., Derevenco, M., Grau, C., Corbera, K., Raymond, S., Lund, S., & Jacobson, P. (1996). A double-blind trial of haloperidol, chlorpromazine, and lorazepam in the treatment of delirium in hospitalized AIDS patients. *American Journal of Psychiatry, 153,* 231–237.

Broadhead, J. C., & Abas, M. A. (1998). Life events, difficulties and depression among women in an urban setting in Zimbabwe. *Psychological Medicine, 28*(1), 29–38.

Chatterjee, S., Patel, V., Chatterjee, A., & Weiss, H. (2003). Evaluation of a community-based rehabilitation model for chronic schizophrenia in rural India. *British Journal of Psychiatry, 182,* 57–62.

Cohen, A. (1999). *The mental health of indigenous people: An international overview.* Geneva, Switzerland: World Health Organization.

Cohen, A. (2001). *The effectiveness of mental health services in primary care: The view from the developing world.* Geneva, Switzerland: World Health Organization.

Cooper, P., Landman, M., Tomlinson, M., Molteno, C., Swartz, L., & Murray, L. (2002). The impact of a mother-infant intervention in an indigent peri-urban South African context: A pilot study. *British Journal of Psychiatry, 180,* 76–81.

de Jong, J. T. V. M., Komproe, I. H., & Ommeren, M. V. (2003). Common mental disorders in post-conflict settings. *Lancet, 361,* 2128–2130.

Desjarlais, R., Eisenberg, L., Good, B., & Kleinman, A. (1995). *World mental health: Problems and priorities in low-income countries.* New York: Oxford University Press.

Digby, A. (1985). Moral treatment at the Retreat, 1796–1846. In W. F. Bynum, R. Porter, & M. Shepherd (Eds.), *The anatomy of madness: Essays in the history of psychiatry* (Vol. II, pp. 52–72). London: Tavistock Publications.

Dixon, L. B., Lehman, A. F., & Levine, J. (1995). Conventional antipsychotic medications for schizophrenia. *Schizophrenia Bulletin, 21,* 567–577.

Eisenbruch, M. (1991). From post-traumatic stress disorder to cultural bereavement: Diagnosis of Southeast Asian refugees. *Social Science and Medicine, 33,* 673–680.

Flisher, A. J. (1999). The management of suicidal behaviour in adolescents. *Specialist Medicine, 21,* 418–423.

Flisher, A. J., Brown, A., & Mukoma, W. (2002). Intervening through school systems. In W. R. Miller & C. M. Weisner (Eds.), *Changing substance abuse through health and social systems* (pp. 171–182). New York: Kluwer Academic/Plenum Press.

Goddard, M. (1992). Bedlam in paradise: A critical history of psychiatry in Papua New Guinea. *Journal of Pacific History, 27,* 55–72.

Goldman, H. H. (1983). The demography of deinstitutionalization. *New Directions for Mental Health Services, 17,* 31–40.

Grant, I., Atkinson, J. H., Hesselink, J. R., Kennedy, C. J., Richman, D. D., Spector, S. A., & McCutchan, J. A. (1987). Evidence for early central nervous system involvement in the acquired immunodeficiency syndrome (AIDS) and other human immunodeficiency virus (HIV) infections. Studies with neuropsychologic testing and magnetic resonance imaging. *Annals of Internal Medicine, 107*(6), 828–836.

Greenberg, P. E., Sisitsky, T., Kessler, R. C., Finkelstein, S. N., Berndt, E. R., Davidson, J. R., Ballenger, J. C., & Fyer, A. J. (1999). The economic burden of anxiety disorders in the 1990s. *Journal of Clinical Psychiatry, 60*(7), 427–435.

Greenberg, P. E., Stiglin, L. E., Finkelstein, S. N., & Berndt, E. R. (1993). The economic burden of depression in 1990. *Journal of Clinical Psychiatry, 54,* 405–418.

Greenblatt, M. (1992). Deinstitutionalization and reinstitutionalization of the mentally ill. In M. J. Robertson & M. Greenblatt (Eds.), *Homelessness: A national perspective* (pp. 47–56). New York: Plenum Press.

Grob, G. N. (1994). *The mad among us: A history of the care of America's mentally ill.* New York: Free Press.

Harding, C. M., Zubin, J., & Strauss, J. S. (1987). Chronicity in schizophrenia: Fact, partial fact, or artifact? *Hospital and Community Psychiatry, 38,* 477–486.

Helmchen, H., & Okasha, A. (2000). From the Hawaii Declaration to the Declaration of Madrid. *Acta Psychiatrica Scandinavica Supplementum, 399,* 20–23.

Hendrie, H., Osuntokun, B., Hall, K., Ogunniyi, A., Hui, S., Unverzagt, F., Gureje, O., Rodenberg, C., Baiyewu, O., & Musick, B. (1995). Prevalence of Alzheimer's disease and dementias in two communities: Nigerian Africans and African Americans. *American Journal of Psychiatry, 152,* 1485–1492.

Heston, L. L. (1966). Psychiatric disorders in foster-home reared children of schizophrenic mothers. *British Journal of Psychiatry, 112,* 819–825.

Hofman, A., Rocca, W. A., Brayne, C., Breteler, M. M., Clarke M., Cooper, B., Copeland, J. R., Dartigues, J. F., da Silva Droux, A., Hagnell, O., et al. (1991). The prevalence of dementia in Europe: A collaborative study of 1980–1990 findings. *International Journal of Epidemiology, 20,* 736–748.

Hopper, K. (1991). Some old questions for the new cross-cultural psychiatry. *Medical Anthropology Quarterly, 5,* 299–330.

Institute of Medicine. (2001). *Neurological, psychiatric, and developmental disorders: Meeting the challenge in the developing world.* Washington, DC: National Academy Press.

Jablensky, A., Sartorius, N., Ernberg, G., Anker, M., Korten, A., Cooper, J. E., Day, R., & Bertelsen, A. (1992). *Schizophrenia: Manifestations, incidence, and course in different cultures. A World Health Organization ten-country study.* Psychological Medicine Monograph Supplement 20. Cambridge, England: Cambridge University Press.

Jackson, L. A. (1999). The place of psychiatry in colonial and early postcolonial Zimbabwe. *International Journal of Mental Health, 28*(2), 38–71.

Jané-Llopis, E., Muñoz, R. F., & Patel, V. (in press). Prevention of depression and depressive symptomatology. In C. Hosman, E. Jané-Llopis, & S. Saxena (Eds.), *Prevention of mental disorders: An overview on evidence-based strategies and programs.* Oxford, England: Oxford University Press.

Jencks, C. (1994). *The homeless.* Cambridge, MA: Harvard University Press.

Jenkins, R., & Strathdee, G. (2000). The integration of mental health care with primary care. *International Journal of Law and Psychiatry, 23,* 277–291.

Kahn, R. S., Wise, P. H., Kennedy, B. P., & Kawachi, I. (2000). State income inequality, household income, and maternal mental and physical health: Cross-sectional national survey. *British Medical Journal, 321,* 1311–1315.

Kaliski, S. (2001). The prevalence and aetiology of psychiatric disorders. In B. Robertson, C. Allwood, & C. Gagiano (Eds.), *Textbook of psychiatry for Southern Africa* (pp. 14–34). Cape Town, South Africa: Oxford University Press.

Katon, W., Robinson, P., Von Korff, M., Lin, E., & Bush, T. (1996). A multifaceted intervention to improve treatment of depression in primary care. *Archives of General Psychiatry, 53,* 924–932.

Kendler, K. S., & Gardner, C. O., Jr. (1998). Boundaries of major depression: An evaluation of DSM-IV criteria. *American Journal of Psychiatry, 155,* 172–177.

Kessler, R. C. (2000). Psychiatric epidemiology: Selected recent advances and future directions. *Bulletin of the World Health Organization, 78*(4), 464–474.

Kessler, R. C., McGonagle, K. A., Zhao, S., Nelson, C. B., Hughes, M., Eshlerman, S., Wittchen, H.-U., & Kendler, K. S. (1994). Lifetime and 12-month prevalence of DSM-III-R psychiatric disorders in the United States. *Archives of General Psychiatry, 51,* 8–19.

Kleinman, A. (1988). *Rethinking psychiatry: Cultural category to personal experience.* New York: Free Press.

Knapp, M. (2000). Schizophrenia costs and treatment cost-effectiveness. *Acta Psychiatrica Scandinavica, 102*(Suppl. 407), 15–18.

Kraepelin, E. (2000/1904). Comparative psychiatry. In R. Littlewood & S. Dein (Eds.), *Cultural psychiatry and medical anthropology: An introduction and reader* (pp. 38–42). London: Athlone Press.

Kulhara, P., & Chakrabarti, S. (2001). Culture and schizophrenia and other psychotic disorders. *Psychiatric Clinics of North America, 24,* 449–464.

Lee, S. (2001). From diversity to unity: The classification of mental disorders in 21st-century China. *Psychiatric Clinics of North America, 24,* 421–431.

Lehman, A. F., & Steinwachs, D. M. (1998). Translating research into practice: The Schizophrenia Patient Outcomes Research Team (PORT) treatment recommendations. *Schizophrenia Bulletin, 24,* 1–10.

Levav, I., & Gonzalez Uzcategui, R. (2000). Rights of persons with mental illness in Central America. *Acta Psychiatrica Scandinavica Supplementum, 399,* 83–86.

Levy, C. J. (2002, April 28). Ingredients of a failing system: A lack of state money, a group without a voice. *New York Times.*

Lin, E. H. B. (1999). Improving management of depression by primary care physicians. In M. Tansella & T. Graham (Eds.), *Common mental disorders in primary care: Essays in honour of Professor Sir David Goldberg* (pp. 116–128). London: Routledge.

Littlewood, R. (1990). From categories to contexts: A decade of the "New Cross-Cultural Psychiatry." *British Journal of Psychiatry, 156,* 308–327.

Mani, K. S., Rangan, G., Srinivas, H. V., Srindharan, V. S., & Subbakrishna, D. K. (2001). Epilepsy control with phenobarbital or phenytoin in rural south India: The Yelandur study. *Lancet, 357*(9265), 1316–1320.

McArthur, J. C., Hoover, D. R., Bacellar, H., Miller, E. N., Cohen, B. A., Becker, J. T., Graham, N. M., McArthur, J. H., Selnes, O. A., Jacobson, L. P., et al. (1993). Dementia in AIDS patients: Incidence and risk factors. Multicenter AIDS Cohort Study. *Neurology, 43*(11), 2245–2252.

McGorry, P. D., Yung, A. R., Phillips, L. J., Yuen, H. P., Francey, S., Cosgrave, E. M., Germano, D., Bravin, J., McDonald, T., Blair, A., Adlard, S., & Jackson, H. (2002). Randomized controlled trial of interventions designed to reduce the risk of progression to first-episode psychosis in a clinical sample with subthreshold symptoms. *Archives of General Psychiatry, 59*(10), 921–928.

McGrath, J., Saha, S., Welham, J., El Saadi, O., MacCauley, C., & Chant, D. (2004). A systematic review of the incidence of schizophrenia: The distribution of rates and the influence of sex, urbanicity, migrant status and methodology. *BMC Medicine, 2*(13).

Mechanic, D. (2001). The scientific foundations of community psychiatry. In G. Thornicroft & G. Szmukler (Eds.), *Textbook of community psychiatry* (pp. 41–52). Oxford, England: Oxford University Press.

Molteno, C., & Westaway, J. (2001). Mental handicap. In B. Robertson, C. Allwood, & C. Gagiano (Eds.), *Textbook of psychiatry for Southern Africa* (pp. 345–357). Cape Town, South Africa: Oxford University Press.

Mora, G. (1980). Historical and theoretical trends in psychiatry. In H. I. Kaplan, A. M. Freedman, & B. J. Sadock (Eds.), *Comprehensive textbook of psychiatry* (3rd ed., pp. 4–98). Baltimore: Williams and Wilkins.

Moyer, A., Finney, J. W., Swearingen, C. E., & Vergun, P. (2002). Brief interventions for alcohol problems: A meta-analytic review of controlled investigations in treatment-seeking and non-treatment-seeking populations. *Addiction, 97,* 279–292.

Muñoz, R. F., Le, H. N., Clarke, G., & Jaycox, L. (2002). Preventing the onset of major depression. In I. H. Gotlib & C. L. Hammen (Eds.), *Handbook of depression* (pp. 343–359). New York: Guilford.

Murdock, G. P., Wilson, S. F., & Frederick, V. (1980). World distribution of theories of illness. *Transcultural Psychiatry Research Review, 17,* 37–64.

Murray, C. J. L., & Lopez, A. D. (1996). *The global burden of disease: A comprehensive assessment of mortality and disability from diseases, injuries, and risk factors in 1990 and projected to 2020.* Cambridge, MA: Harvard School of Public Health.

National Human Rights Commission. (1999). *Quality assurance in mental health.* New Delhi, India: National Human Rights Commission of India.

Patel, V. (1995). Explanatory models of mental illness in sub-Saharan Africa. *Social Science and Medicine, 40,* 1291–1298.

Patel, V., & Andrade, C. (2003). Pharmacological treatment of severe psychiatric disorders in the developing world: Lessons from India. *CNS Drugs, 17,* 1071–1080.

Patel, V., Araya, R., & Bolton, P. (2004). Treating depression in developing countries. *Tropical Medicine and International Health, 9,* 539.

Patel, V., Araya, R., de Lima, M., Ludermir, A., & Todd, C. (1999). Women, poverty and common mental disorders in four restructuring societies. *Social Science andFe for South Africa: Pipedream or possibility? Social Science and Medicine, 51,* 321–334.

Patel, V., Chisholm, D., Rabe-Hesketh, S., Dias-Saxena, F., Andrew, G., & Mann, A. (2003). Efficacy and cost-effectiveness of drug and psychological treatments for common mental disorders in general health care in Goa, India: A randomised, controlled trial. *Lancet, 361,* 33-39.

Patel, V., & Cohen, A. (2003). Mental health services in primary care in 'developing' countries. *World Psychiatry, 2*(3), 163-164.

Patel, V., & Kleinman, A. (2003). Poverty and common mental disorders in developing countries. *Bulletin of the World Health Organization, 81,* 609-615.

Patel, V., & Prince, M. (2001). Ageing and mental health in a developing country: Who cares? qualitative studies from Goa, India. *Psychological Medicine, 31,* 29-38.

Patel, V., Rahman, A., Jacob, K. S., & Hughes, M. (2004). Effect of maternal mental health on infant growth in low income countries: New evidence from South Asia. *BMJ, 328*(7443), 820-823.

Patel, V., & Sumathipala, A. (2001). International representation in psychiatric literature: Survey of six leading journals. *British Journal of Psychiatry, 178,* 406-409.

Patel, V., & Thara, R. (2003). *Meeting mental health needs in developing countries.* New Delhi: Sage (India).

Paykel, E. S., & Priest, R. (1992). Recognition and management of depression in general practice: Consensus statement. *British Medical Journal, 305,* 1198-1202.

Petersen, I. (2000). Comprehensive integrated primary mental health care for South Africa: Pipedream or possibility? *Social Science & Medicine, 51,* 321-334.

Pierloot, R. A. (1975). Belgium. In J. G. Howells (Ed.), *World history of psychiatry* (pp. 136–149). New York: Brunner/Mazel.

Pilling, S., Bebbington, P., Kuipers, E., Garety, P., Geddes, J., Martindale, B., Orbach, G., & Morgan, C. (2002). Psychological treatments in schizophrenia: II. Meta-analyses of randomized controlled trials of social skills training and cognitive remediation. *Psychological Medicine, 32*(5), 783–791.

Pinel, P. (1977). A treatise on insanity. In J. C. Shershow (Ed.), *Delicate branch: The vision of moral psychiatry* (pp. 1–38). Oceanside, NY: Dabor Science Publications.

Plomin, R., Owen, M. J., & McGuffin, P. (1994). The genetic basis of complex human behaviors. *Science, 264*(5166), 1733–1739.

Pyne, H. H., Claeson, M., & Correia, M. (2002). *Gender dimensions of alcohol consumption and alcohol-related problems in Latin America and the Caribbean.* Washington, DC: World Bank.

Rahman, A., Mubbashar, M. H., Gater, R., & Goldberg, D. (1998). Randomised trial of impact of school mental-health programme in rural Rawalpindi, Pakistan. *Lancet, 352,* 1022–1025.

Rice, D. P., Kelman, S., & Miller, L. S. (1992). The economic burden of mental illness. *Hospital and Community Psychiatry, 43* (12), 1227–1232.

Sartorius, N., Kaelber, C. T., Cooper, J. E., Roper, M. T., Rae, D. S., Gulbinat, W., Ustun, T. B., & Regier, D. A. (1993). Progress toward achieving a common language in psychiatry. *Archives of General Psychiatry, 50,* 115–124.

Schmidt, K. E. (1967). Mental health services in a developing country in South-East Asia (Sarawak). In H. C. Freeman & J. Farndale (Eds.), *New aspects of the mental health services.* Oxford, England: Pergamon Press.

Scull, A. (1989). *Social order/mental disorder: Anglo-American psychiatry in historical perspective.* Berkeley: University of California Press.

Scull, A. T., MacKenzie, C., & Hervey, N. (1996). *Masters of Bedlam: The transformation of the mad-doctoring trade.* Princeton, NJ: Princeton University Press.

Shaffer, M. D., Fisher, P., Dulcan, M. K., Davies, M., Piacentini, J., Schwab-Stone, M. E., Lahey, B. B., Bourdon, K., Jensen, P. S., Bird, H. R., Canino, G., & Regier, D. A. (1996). The NIMH Diagnostic Interview Schedule for Children Version 2.3 (DISC-2.3): Description, acceptability, prevalence rates, and performance in the MECA study. *Journal of the American Academy of Child and Adolescent Psychiatry, 35,* 865–875.

Shah, A., & Jenkins, R. (2000). Mental health economic studies from developing countries reviewed in the context of those from developed countries. *Acta Psychiatrica Scandinavica, 101,* 87–103.

Shields, J., & Slater, E. (1975). Genetic aspects of schizophrenia. *British Journal of Psychiatry, Special 9,* 32–40.

Shorvon, S. D., & Farmer, P. J. (1988). Epilepsy in developing countries: A review of epidemiological, sociocultural, and treatment aspects. *Epilepsia, 29*(Suppl. 1), S36–S54.

Slater, E., & Cowie, V. (1971). *The genetics of mental disorder.* London: Oxford University Press.

Sussman, L. K., Robins, L. N., & Earls, F. (1987). Treatment-seeking for depression by black and white Americans. *Social Science and Medicine, 24,* 187–196.

Swartz, S. (1999). "Work of mercy and necessity": British rule and psychiatric practice in the Cape Colony, 1891–1910. *International Journal of Mental Health, 28*(2), 72–90.

Szmukler, G., & Thornicroft, G. (2001). What is community psychiatry? In G. Thornicroft & G. Szmukler (Eds.), *Textbook of community psychiatry* (pp. 1–12). Oxford, England: Oxford University Press.

Tansella, M., & Thornicroft, G. (2001). The principles underlying community care. In G. Thornicroft & G. Szmukler (Eds.), *Textbook of community psychiatry* (pp. 155–165). Oxford, England: Oxford University Press.

Tsuang, M. T., Stone, W. S., & Faraone, S. V. (2000). Toward reformulating the diagnosis of schizophrenia. *American Journal of Psychiatry, 157,* 1041–1050.

UNHCR. (2005). *2004 global refugee trends: Overview of refugee populations, new arrivals, durable solutions, asylum-seekers, stateless and other persons of concern to UNHCR.* Retrieved July 7, 2005 from http://www.unhcr.ch/cgibin/fexis/vtx/event/opendoc.pdf?tbl=STATISTICS&id=42b 283744.

United Nations. (1991). *The protection of persons with mental illness and the improvement of mental health care* (A/RES/46/119). New York: United Nations.

U.S. Department of Health and Human Services. (1999). *Mental health: A report of the Surgeon General.* Rockville, MD: Center for Mental Health Services, National Institutes of Health.

Ustun, T. B., & Sartorius, N. (1995). *Mental illness in general health care: An international study.* Chichester, England: John Wiley & Sons.

Verhulst, F. C. (1995). A review of community studies. In F. C. Verhulst & H. M. Koot (Eds.), *The epidemiology of child and adolescent psychopathology.* Oxford, England: Oxford University Press.

Wahlbeck, K., Cheine, M., & Essali, M. A. (2000). Clozapine versus typical neuroleptic medication for schizophrenia. *Cochrane Database of Systematic Reviews* (2), CD000059.

Weich, S., & Lewis, G. (1998). Poverty, unemployment and the common mental disorders: A population based cohort study. *British Medical Journal, 317,* 115–119.

Westermeyer, J. (1984). Economic losses associated with chronic mental disorder in a developing country. *British Journal of Psychiatry,* 144, 475–481.

Whiteford, H., Buckingham, B., & Manderscheid, R. (2002). Australia's National Mental Health Strategy. *British Journal of Psychiatry, 180,* 210–215.

WHO World Mental Health Survey Consortium. (2004). Prevalence, severity, and unmet need for treatment of mental disorders in the World Health Organization World Mental Health Surveys. *Journal of the American Medical Association, 291,* 2581–2590.

Wieser, H. G., & Silfvenius, H. (2000). Overview: Epilepsy surgery in developing countries. *Epilepsia, 41*(Suppl. 4), S3–S9.

Work Group on HIV/AIDS. (2000). Practice guideline for the treatment of patients with HIV/AIDS. *American Journal of Psychiatry, 157*(Suppl. 11), 1–62.

World Bank. (1993). *World development report 1993: Investing in health.* New York: Oxford University Press.

World Bank. (2000). *Intensifying action against HIV/AIDS: Responding to the development crisis.* Washington, DC: World Bank.

World Health Organization. (1975). *Organization of mental health services in the developing countries.* Geneva, Switzerland: World Health Organization.

World Health Organization. (1978). *Primary health care: Report of the international conference.* Geneva, Switzerland: World Health Organization.

World Health Organization. (1995). *Psychosocial rehabilitation: A consensus statement.* Geneva, Switzerland: World Health Organization.

World Health Organization. (1998). *Primary prevention of mental, neurological and psychosocial disorders.* Geneva, Switzerland: World Health Organization.

World Health Organization. (2001a). *Atlas: Country profiles of mental health resources.* Geneva, Switzerland: World Health Organization.

World Health Organization. (2001b). *Mental health: New understanding, new hope.* Geneva, Switzerland: World Health Organization.

World Health Organization. (2003a). *Mental health legislation and human rights.* Geneva, Switzerland: World Health Organization.

World Health Organization. (2003b). *Mental health policy, plans and programmes.* Geneva, Switzerland: World Health Organization.

World Health Organization. (2005). *Child and adolescent mental health.* Geneva, Switzerland: World Health Organization.

World Health Organization. (2005). *Human resources and training in mental health.* Geneva, Switzerland: World Health Organization.

World Health Organization. (n.d.). *Suicide prevention: Live your life.* http://www.who.int/mental_health/management/en/SUPRE_flyer1.pdf.

Wu, Z., Detels, R., Zhang, J., Li, V., & Li, J. (2002). Community base trial to prevent drug use amongst youth in Yunnan, China. *American Journal of Public Health, 92,* 1952–1957.

Xiong, W., Phillips, M. R., Hu, X., Wang, R., Dai, Q., Kleinman, J., & Kleinman, A. (1994). Family-based intervention for schizophrenic patients in China: A randomised controlled trial. *British Journal of Psychiatry, 165,* 239–247.

Environmental Health

ANTHONY J. McMICHAEL, TORD KJELLSTROM, AND KIRK R. SMITH

This chapter first explores the definition of "environment" and its ways of affecting human health. In doing so, it takes note of several key disciplinary perspectives, the international spectrum of environmental health issues, and the ongoing emergence of larger-scale environmental problems. The main conceptual and methodological issues that relate to environmental health research and public health action are discussed. Subsequently, using a five-way subdivision of "environment" classified by scale and setting, the profiles of environmental health hazards are discussed within the domestic setting, the workplace, the community, and on regional and global scales. Illustrative case studies are presented.

The final section considers the issues and prospects that bear on the future of environmental health research and policy. What priorities apply in a politically and economically unequal world? What are the environmental hazards of globalization, in its several guises? How can environmental health hazards be addressed via a more integrated, "ecological" understanding of how the complex interplay between human populations and the natural "environment" affects population health?

Definition and Scope of Environment

The word "environment" is broad and elastic in scope. In this chapter, "environment" refers to external physical, chemical, and microbiological exposures and processes that impinge upon individuals and groups and are beyond the immediate control of individuals. This definition excludes exposures that occur largely because of individual choice, such as active cigarette smoking and personal dietary habits. It also excludes

risk factors that arise within the sociocultural environment, such as violent crime and community stress (see Chapter 7). Further, environmental conditions associated with risk of physical injury (such as traffic, workplace, and home) will only be discussed briefly (for further details, see Chapter 7).

The "environment" can be categorized several ways, including in relation to environmental media (air, water, soil, and food), economic sector (transport, land use, and energy generation), physical scale (local, regional, global), setting (household, workplace, and urban environment), and disease outcomes (cancers, congenital anomalies, and others). A classification that comprises five categories is used here, defined jointly by physical scale and by setting. The five categories are as follows:

1. household
2. workplace
3. community
4. regional
5. global

A sixth category, that of cross scale, should also be included. This recognizes that the scale at which an environmental health impact eventually occurs may not be the scale at which the exposure was initiated.

Consider the hierarchy of environmental health consequences of energy use. The environmental impacts of energy production and use contribute significantly to the total human impact on the "environment" at each of the six above-mentioned levels. That is, the extraction, harvesting, processing, distribution, and use of fuels and other energy sources have major environmental impacts at all scales, from individual households to the globe itself. Combustion occurs locally, causing local air pollution, indoors and outdoors, but it also contributes to regional acid rain and, globally, to the accumulation of carbon dioxide as a heat-trapping greenhouse gas in the lower atmosphere.

In defining environment, there are two other points to note. First, some environmental exposures arise because of natural variation, whereas others are due to human interventions. Natural exposures arise from seasonal, latitudinal, or altitudinal gradients in solar irradiation, extremes of hot and cold weather, the occurrence of physical disasters, and local micronutrient deficiencies in soil. The usual environmental concern, however, is with exposure to human-made hazards. In industrialized countries, attention has focused in recent years on the many chemical contaminants entering the air, water, soil, and food and on physical hazards such as ionizing radiation, urban noise, and road trauma. In low- and middle-income countries, the major environmental concerns are with the microbiological quality of drinking water and food, the physical safety of housing and work, indoor air pollution, and road hazards. Those hazards are kept under control in industrialized countries through major investments in good-quality housing and community infrastructure (drinking water supply, sewerage, solid waste collection, and others).

Second, there are two qualitatively different dimensions of environment that are relevant to human health risks. There is the familiar local physicochemical and microbiological environment as the vehicle for various specific hazards able to cause injury, toxicity, nutritional deficiency, or infection. Less familiar are the hazards that arise from today's emerging disruptions to the biosphere's ecological and geophysical system—that is, the life-support systems that stabilize, replenish, recycle, cleanse, and produce, thereby providing climatic stability, food yields, clean freshwater, nutrient cycling, and sustained biodiversity (see also the section "Environment: Encompassing Both Hazard and Habitat," later in this chapter).

Scale and Distribution of Environmental Risks to Health

The relative importance of environmental exposures as a cause of human disease and premature death remains contentious. The question is difficult, because knowledge about disease etiology is incomplete and because the statistic is a moving target because of the usual latency period between environmental change and nonacute health outcomes. Many of today's chronic diseases are the result of past exposures that have either changed (such as urban air pollution) or essentially ceased.

The complex bidirectional relationships among environmental conditions, socioeconomic circumstances, demographic change, and human health present a further difficulty in estimating the environmental contribution to disease burden (Shahi et al., 1997). For example, the combination of population pressure and poverty among rural populations in low- and middle-income countries often leads to land degradation, deforestation, flooding, further impoverishment, and increased risks to health from infectious disease, food shortages, and nutritional deficiencies. The plight of sub-Saharan Africa, with its persistent poverty, environmental stresses, and marginalization in the global economy, illustrates well these complex relationships. Many of the erstwhile gains in sub-Saharan Africa's health, education, and living standards have been reversed in the past two decades: A majority of people live in absolute poverty, with more than 50% still lacking safe drinking water, and 70% lacking proper sanitation, and the spread of desertification and deforestation is affecting some regions (Logie & Benatar, 1997). According to the World Health Organization (WHO) (1999), infant mortality rates in sub-Saharan African countries are 55% higher than in other low- and middle-income countries, and average life expectancy is about a decade less.

In general, there is a tendency for environmental health risks to shift during the economic development process, first from household to community and then to regional and global scales, as part of the "environmental risk transition" (Smith, 1997; Smith & Ezzati, 2005). Environmental risks in low- and middle-income societies are dominated by poor food, water, and air quality at the household level from inadequate sanitation, contaminated water, and low-quality fuels (WHO, 1997). Some of the activities that help solve these problems act to transfer problems to the community level in the form of urban air pollution, hazardous waste, and chemical pollution. In the industrialized societies, where most community and household problems have come under considerable control, problems have been shifted to the global scale, for example, through greenhouse gas emissions.

As discussed in Chapter 1, the shift in diseases during the epidemiologic transition—although its details vary substantially in different places and times—has been one of the most important features of economic development. Before there can be a shift in age-specific disease patterns, however, there needs to be a shift in the within-population pattern of risks that lead to disease. Another important characteristic that shifts is temporal scale. Many important infectious diseases, such as diarrhea, malaria, and measles, for example, have relatively short latency periods (hours to weeks) between exposure to risk factors and development of disease. Cancer and other chronic noninfectious diseases, however, often entail time delays of several decades. Global processes such as anthropogenic climate change may involve even longer time periods. Thus, the risk transition tends to involve a shift in temporal characteristics, which has important implications for research and social policy.

Depending on definitions, assumptions, and choice of reference populations, estimates of the environmental contribution to the total avoidable global burden of disease span a wide range. In the first systematic use of a standardized metric—the disability-adjusted life year (DALY) (Murray & Lopez, 1996), which combines morbidity and mortality data in a manner suitable for international comparisons—the World Bank (1993) attributed about 50% of all global DALYs to diseases associated with environmental (including microbiological) exposures in the household and an additional 30% to diseases associated with the community environment. However, only a small proportion of these DALYs were deemed amenable to feasible preventive interventions (World Bank, 1993). A reassessment conducted for the fifth anniversary of the Rio Earth Summit (WHO, 1997) estimated that about 25% of global DALYs were caused by environmental hazards, including the workplace environment. Smith, Corvalan, and Kjellstrom (1999), in a more comprehensive analysis, estimated that 25% to 33% of the global burden of disease and premature death is attributable to direct environmental risk factors.

The first truly integrated comparative risk assessment of the global and regional burden of disease due to major risk factors was organized by WHO and summarized in its *World Health Report 2002* (WHO, 2002). For the first time, risks from major environmental hazards were evaluated on a common basis not only among themselves, but also for comparison with such nonenvironmental hazards as smoking, unsafe sex, malnutrition, high blood pressure, and so on. The environmental hazards included unsafe water, sanitation, and hygiene; urban air pollution; indoor smoke from solid fuels; lead exposure; climate change; and five types of occupational risks. The results are likely to be underestimates, because a rather conser-

vative definition of acceptable evidence of cause-effect relationships was used in order to provide consistency across risk factors. This is particularly so for occupational risks in poor countries, where much work occurs in informal sectors that were not addressed by this risk assessment.

As shown in Table 9-1, in the poorest developing countries with high mortality, unsafe water and indoor smoke are ranked as numbers three and five among the leading risk factors for burden of disease, while in low-mortality (middle income) developing countries they ranked twelfth and tenth. In contrast, they are not among the top 15 in developed countries (Smith & Ezzati, 2005). Note the relative importance of occupational risks at every level of development.

As shown in Figure 9-1, the largest environmental health burdens occur in low- and middle-income countries with significant household-level risks, which also tend to affect young children in particular. Indeed, as a percentage of total burden as well as in absolute terms (e.g., DALYs per capita), environmental risks are most important in the poorest populations. Globally, the "environment" is least important in both absolute and percentage terms as a factor in ill-health in rich countries, where behavorial risks (smoking, diet, physical activity, etc.) tend to dominate. Also, as shown in the figure, although household environmental risks tend to decline with development, community-level environmental risks, such as urban air pollution, tend first to rise with development and then to fall at later stages. Although the burden due to global level risks (climate change) is highest in poor countries, the imposition of these risks is primarily due to greenhouse-gases emitting activities in rich countries. This phenomenon is called the "environmental risk transition."

It should be noted here that global statistical data sources are becoming increasingly ambitious and sophisticated. Global and national time trend analyses for certain environmental health hazards are becoming more feasible than in the past. This has been facilitated by the inclusion of several health- and environment-related indicators for the monitoring of progress toward the United Nations Millennium Development Goal (United Nations Development Program [UNDP], 2004), agreed to in 2000 by all member states. These indicators include the proportions of population with sustainable access to an improved water source; with access to improved sanitation; using solid fuels; and with access to secure residential tenure (an indicator of slum-dwelling patterns).

Table 9-1	**Ranking of Health Burden Due to Environmental Risk Factors in 2000 by Development Status** (Percent of total disability-adjusted lost life years due to each risk factor)						
High-Mortality (Poor) Developing Countries (population = 2.3 billion)	**% of Burden**	**Rank**	**Low-Mortality (Middle-Income) Developing Countries (pop. = 2.4 billion)**	**% of Burden**	**Rank**	**Developed Countries (pop. = 1.4 billion)**	**% of Burden**	**Rank**
Underweight	14.7	1	Alcohol	6.3	1	Tobacco	12.2	1
Unsafe sex	10.0	2	Blood pressure	5.0	2	Blood pressure	10.9	2
Unsafe water, sanitation, and hygiene	5.5	3	Tobacco	4.0	3	Alcohol	9.2	3
Lack of vaccination for child cluster diseases	5.3	4	**Road traffic**	3.3	4	Cholesterol	7.6	4
Indoor smoke from solid fuels	3.6	5	Underweight	3.1	5	Overweight	7.4	5
Zinc deficiency	3.2	6	Overweight	2.7	6	Low fruit and vegetable intake	3.9	6
Iron deficiency	3.1	7	**Occupation**	2.4	7	Physical inactivity	3.3	7
Vitamin A deficiency	3.0	8	Cholesterol	2.1	8	**Road traffic**	1.9	8
Blood pressure	2.4	9	Low fruit and vegetable intake	1.9	9	Illicit drugs	1.8	9
Tobacco	2.0	10	**Indoor smoke**	1.9	10	**Occupation**	1.5	10
Occupational risks	1.1	14	**Unsafe water**	1.8	12	**Lead exposure**	0.65	13
Lead exposure	0.70	19	**Lead exposure**	1.4	14	**Urban air**	0.55	15
Climate change	0.61	20	**Urban air**	0.99	17	**Unsafe water**	0.39	16
Urban air pollution	0.32	23	**Climate change**	0.07	24	**Indoor smoke**	0.26	19
Road traffic accidents	0.31	24				**Climate change**	0.01	23

Environmental risks are shown in bold type.

Source: Smith & Ezzati, 2005. Source of data: WHO, 2002 and WHO's GBD Database for 2000.

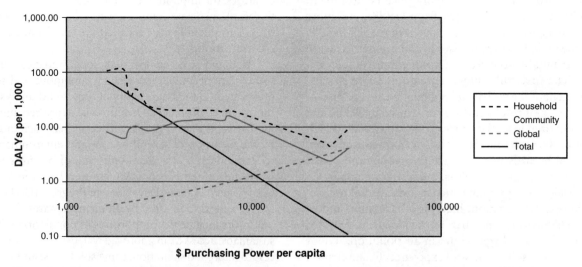

Figure 9-1 Environmental Risk Transition for Household, Community, and Imposed Global Environmental Risks in 2000. Note that household risks decline with rising income, imposed global risks rise, and community risks first rise and then fall. *Source:* Adapted from Smith and Ezzati, 2005, using WHO data.

Environment: Encompassing Both Hazard and Habitat

Most analyses of environmental health effects focus on specific, direct-acting hazards within a localized setting. Exposure is assessed either at the individual or group level, health outcomes are assessed, and dose-response relationships are estimated, usually by fitting statistical models. Where data are sparse, model fitting may be guided by theoretical considerations. Once dose-response relationships have been satisfactorily estimated, and if the causal interpretation is convincing, then the results can be used to guide environmental policy. However, exposures have often been higher in workplaces than in the ambient environment, and many of the published dose-response relationships are based on occupational epidemiologic studies.

During recent decades this mode of environmental and occupational health research, culminating in formal risk assessment (Samet, Schnatter, & Gibb, 1998), has prevailed in industrialized countries. Ambient and workplace environmental exposure standards have thereby been set for several hundred specific environmental exposure agents. There are currently more than 80,000 human-made chemical substances in commercial use worldwide, and 4,000 of these are in widespread use. Further, thousands of naturally occurring chemicals are in general use, including many in low- and middle-income countries. Evidently there are insufficient epidemiologic and toxicologic data to evaluate the potential health effects of most of these chemicals (Moochhala, Shahi, & Cote, 1997).

Meanwhile, a larger scale of environmental hazard to human health began to emerge in the final decades of the 20th century. With increased emissions of greenhouse gases and various ozone-destroying gases, the basic composition of the world's lower and middle atmospheres is, for the first time, being altered by human actions. The world's great geochemical cycles of sulfur and nitrogen are also being perturbed by human actions. Meanwhile, human-induced environmental changes are causing worldwide depletion of soil fertility, aquifers, ocean fisheries, and—perhaps most serious—biologic diversity. These human-induced changes are beginning to weaken the world's life-supporting systems and change the conditions of the biosphere—our habitat. Various serious consequences for human health must be expected, such as changes in the pattern of infectious diseases and in regional agricultural and aquatic yields and in the impacts of economic hardship or demographic displacement.

Therefore, the scope of the environmental health framework must be extended to include the impairment of our habitat. Meanwhile, hazard-oriented environmental health research must also be maintained. As the environmental impact grows larger, so do the dimensions of the research, risk management, and policy development tasks.

Environmental Health Research, Risk Assessment, and Monitoring

Research Scope and Strategies

Environmental health research seeks to elucidate causal relations between environmental exposures and impaired states of health, prioritize and develop appropriate interventions to reduce risks to health, and evaluate the effectiveness of such interventions. Epidemiology is the basic quantitative science of environmental health research. In essence, epidemiologic research describes and explains variations and temporal changes in the pattern of illness and disease between and within populations. Most environmental epidemiology is observational (that is, nonexperimental), which introduces some important issues in research design and data interpretation (Morgenstern & Thomas, 1993). However, where health benefit is anticipated from exposure-reducing interventions, experimental studies may be carried out.

Historically, epidemiology has played a crucial and largely self-sufficient role in identifying the environmental health hazards posed by relatively high levels of exposure—such as to severe air pollution (e.g., the "London Fog" of 1952), to heavy metals in water and food, and to solar ultraviolet radiation (UVR). Those studies were mostly done in industrialized countries, where research expertise existed and where technical and information resources were available. Increasingly, studies of physicochemical environmental exposures are being done in low- and middle-income countries, as well as in the former territories of the Soviet Union, where extensive environmental pollution and degradation often occurred. Meanwhile, many of the environmental health questions now being addressed in industrialized countries refer to more subtle exposures, such as electromagnetic fields as a putative cancer risk and chemical exposures that act cumulatively over decades on fertility and reproduction (especially via endocrine-disrupting chemicals) and on the functioning of the central nervous system and the immune system.

Many environmental exposures occur at levels that are low by comparison with occupational exposures and personal habits, such as cigarette smoking. For example, in terms of the inhalation of fine particulates and various noxious gases, living in a heavily air-polluted city entails exposures equivalent to smoking no more than several cigarettes per day. Yet most of the convincing epidemiologic studies of cigarette smoking and disease have depended on comparing persons smoking 10-plus cigarettes per day with nonsmokers. This typically lesser level of ambient environmental exposure renders difficult the task of detecting modest increments in risk. Yet the importance of such environmental exposures is threefold: (1) They typically impinge on many persons, perhaps whole populations, thereby causing a large aggregate health impact (an economic-political criterion); (2) they are encountered on an essentially involuntary, and often unequal, basis (an ethical criterion); and (3) they are often amenable to control at the source (a practical criterion).

The epidemiologist faces two other recurrent difficulties. First, these real-world exposures are likely to be accompanied (that is, confounded) by various other exposures or risk factors—some of which may be unknown to the investigator, or indeed to science. Second, the exposure-effect relationships often entail long-term, chronic, and sometimes subtle causal processes.

Because of these complexities, environmental health research must often be tackled in a multidisciplinary fashion in order to attain a sufficiently broad basis of evidence for causal inference. For example, causal inferences about the effect of low-level environmental lead exposure on the cognitive development of young children has required the integrated consideration of the results of epidemiologic studies, animal experimental research, and neuropathological and molecular toxicological studies.

Extra leverage may be gained via interdisciplinary research in which the techniques of several disciplines are combined within one (usually epidemiologic) study. For example, the development of molecular biology over the past several decades has yielded many new techniques for measuring internal exposure, especially in relation to carcinogenesis. Molecular biological markers may also elucidate the biological mechanism, thus strengthening the basis for causal inference. Further, these epidemiology-based research approaches, focusing on cause-effect relationships and underlying biological mechanisms, should be complemented by technical/engineering, behavioral, and policy research in order to develop feasible interventions. In the environmental health arena, the contribution of these nonhealth disciplines may be crucial for developing effective health protection.

Causation and Other Methodological Issues

Etiologic studies examine associations between exposure and health outcome, assess the causal nature of the association, and, where possible, estimate the quantitative variation in risk as a function of variation in exposure. Epidemiologic research, predominantly nonexperimental, seeks research settings and study designs that can maximize the signal-to-noise ratio, since studies of disease etiology in free-living populations, with heterogeneous exposures and circumstances, usually entail substantial background noise. The quality of the measurement of exposure and of health status is often much less than in controlled clinical trials or laboratory-based studies. There may be many potential confounding variables (such as sex, age, and smoking habit)—that is, factors that are statistically associated with the exposure variable of interest and that are also predictive of the health outcome—that must be controlled for by study design or analysis. The sample of persons studied may not be a random sample of the source population with respect to the relationship that the sample either actually displays (selection bias) or apparently displays (classification bias) between exposure and outcome.

Once a sufficient number of studies have been done, in diverse settings and with adequate attention to minimizing the sources of random error (a property of a stochastic universe), systematic error (procedural bias), and logical error (confounding), then causation can be assessed. Over recent decades epidemiologists have developed a set of criteria specifically suited to their predominantly nonexperimental, bias-prone, confounding-rich research, with particular emphasis upon the temporality of the relationship, its strength, the presence of a plausible dose-response relationship, the consistency of findings in diverse studies, and coherence with other disciplinary findings and biomedical theory (Beaglehole, Bonita, & Kjellstrom, 2002).

Etiologic research in environmental epidemiology entails several distinctive methodological issues, including the following:

- Choice of the appropriate level of comparison (population, local community, or individual). Many environmental exposures (such as ambient air pollution or fluoride levels in drinking water) impinge on whole communities, with minimal exposure difference between individuals.

- Definition of *exposure* and choice of the mode of exposure assessment.
- Choice of the relevant reference exposure (the theoretical minimum exposure level that a society could achieve).
- Dealing with multiple coexistent, potentially interacting environmental exposures.

These and other issues are discussed in the following sections.

Study Design Options

The same basic set of study designs used in general epidemiology are also used in environmental epidemiology. The studies can be descriptive, analytic, or experimental (Beaglehole, Bonita, & Kjellstrom, 2002).

Descriptive Studies: Trends and Correlations

In descriptive studies, the pattern of variation in a population's or community's environmental exposure or health status or both is described, usually in relation to time, place, or category of person (e.g., age, sex, ethnicity). If the data are appropriate, the relationship between exposure factors and health status may be described. Such studies aid in identifying research priorities and in guiding the design of etiologic studies. For example, a study may show that the exposure levels are not high enough to warrant more detailed epidemiologic study. The time trend of exposure may influence how further studies are designed. Seasonal variations can be an important indicator of effects of exposures to environmental hazards that vary with season. The spatial distribution of exposure may indicate how to define subgroups with different exposure levels within the population.

With adequate data and sufficient variation in exposure, it is possible to examine the statistical correlation, over time or space (or both), between the descriptive population-level measure of exposure and health. Usually, such studies cannot yield definite conclusions about etiology—most often because there is inadequate information on confounding factors or because an association observed at the population level does not necessarily exist at the individual level (the so-called ecologic fallacy). Note, however, that the latter problem is much less important for exposures that impinge relatively homogeneously throughout a specified population. Thus, one can reasonably compare the acute respiratory symptom prevalence rates between Beijing and Singapore in the knowledge that all Beijing dwellers are exposed to high levels of ambient air pollution while all Singaporeans are not. Such a correlation analysis would be much improved by increasing the number of observation units (populations), maximizing the variation in exposure between them, and adjusting for important confounders (e.g., age distribution and cigarette smoking prevalence).

For microecological studies that examine exposure-related variations in health status between small, usually contiguous, groups of people or households, small-area study designs are used. A substantial body of theory has evolved recently for this type of study, and various statistical techniques for smoothing the data and adjusting for autocorrelation between adjoining spatial (and temporal) units have been developed. These designs are useful for examining relationships such as the variation in respiratory disease rates in relation to residential distance from major highways, or the variation in congenital anomaly rates in relation to residential distance from high-temperature incinerators. Whether working at the small, medium, or large spatial scale, there are increasingly sophisticated techniques for spatial analysis.

Time-series studies have a special role in environmental epidemiology. Some environmental exposures vary on a short-term basis, especially levels of urban air pollution and weather conditions. There are intrinsically interesting questions about the acute health impact of fluctuations in air pollution or temperature, such as whether asthma attacks increase on high-pollution days or whether daily death rates increase on days of extreme temperature. The statistical analytic techniques for time-series analyses have been acquired variously from econometrics and engineering research. They include sophisticated adjustments for lower-frequency (e.g., seasonal) cyclical variations, background secular trends, and autocorrelation. Time-series studies benefit from the fact that ongoing characteristics of the study population, such as age distribution, socioeconomic profile, and smoking habits, remain essentially constant over time. Further, since the comparison is made entirely within the chosen population, there can be no problem of interpopulation confounding.

Analytic Studies

Analytic studies examine formal statistical associations between an exposure variable and a health outcome variable at the level of the individual or small homogeneous exposure group (Beaglehole, Bonita, & Kjellstrom, 2002). Are individuals with higher exposure to indoor air pollution more likely to develop respiratory disease than those with low exposure? Are individuals who develop diarrheal disease in a coastal city more likely to have been swimming in contaminated seawater recently than individuals without such disease? The studies can be designed to start from exposures (cohort studies, such as the indoor air pollution example described earlier) or from the health effect (case control studies, such as the diarrheal disease example described earlier).

The study of the relationship of early-life environmental lead exposure to child cognitive-intellectual development began with various types of cross-sectional studies in the 1970s. However, it was not possible to establish from those studies the temporal relationship between occurrence of exposure and occurrence of intellectual or behavioral deficit. Cohort studies were required, in which infants and children were followed from birth, with systematic documentation of their early-life lead exposure history and cognitive-intellectual development. The largest of these, carried out in and around the lead smelting town of Port Pirie, South Australia (Tong et al., 1998), provided the type of data (Figure 9-2) necessary to resolve this important public health issue and to estimate the magnitude of the risk (see also Exhibit 9-1).

An important issue in environmental epidemiology studies is how to deal with the problem of confounding by factors that are statistically associated with the exposure variable and, also, are independently predictive of the health outcome. If, in the previously described cohort study example, those people with high indoor air pollution exposure also smoke more on average than people with low exposure, then smoking habits would confound the assessment of the relationship between indoor air pollution and respiratory disease. The higher rates of disease in the more polluted households may actually be due to the greater amount of smoking. Similarly, in the above-mentioned case control study, if the people with diarrheal disease (cases) are more likely to have eaten contaminated shellfish than people without diarrhea (controls), then shellfish consumption would confound the assessment of the relationship between diarrhea and having swum in contaminated seawater. The issue of confounding is pervasive in epidemiologic research, reflecting the nonrandom distribution of risk factors in real-world populations. It is usually more amenable to control in analytic individual-level studies than in population-level correlation analyses.

Experimental Studies

Experimental studies (or intervention studies) begin with sets of reasonably similar populations or groups, which can then be allocated, preferably randomly, to "intervention" or "control" categories. The statistical analysis compares outcome rates in the two or more groups (the intervention may be applied at more than one level). The clinical randomized controlled trial (RCT) is the model for this type of design.

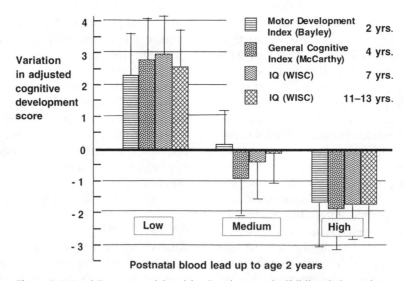

Figure 9-2 Lead Exposure and Cognitive Development in Childhood. One point approximates to a 1% change. Low, medium, and high lead exposure categories have mean blood lead concentrations of 12.5, 18.5, and 25.9 μg/dL, respectively. *Source:* S. Tong et al., "Lifetime Exposure to Environmental Lead and Children's Intelligence at 11–13 Years: The Pt. Pirie Cohort Study," 1996, *British Medical Journal, 312,* pp. 1569–1570. Adapted with permission.

Exhibit 9-1	Environmental Lead Exposure and Childhood Cognitive Development

Lead is the most abundant heavy metal. It may have been the first metal smelted, dating from 7000 to 6500 B.C. The ancient civilizations of Phoenicia, Egypt, Greece, Rome, China, and India used lead for vessels, roofs, water ducts, utensils, ornaments, and weights. There was a great resurgence in its use during the Industrial Revolution. The subsequent development of the automobile hugely increased lead usage, in lead-acid batteries and as an anti-knock additive in gasoline. The lead content of Greenland ice layers shows a strong rise over the past thousand years, reaching 100 times the natural background level in the mid-1990s. The natural background (preindustrial) blood lead concentration of humans is estimated to be much lower than the lowest reported levels in contemporary humans living in remote regions.

Lead has adverse effects on various organ systems, most importantly the gastrointestinal tract, central nervous system, kidneys, and blood (hemoglobin synthesis). High levels of exposure (with blood lead concentrations of 50 to 100μg/dL) typically occur in the workplace, including lead smelting, battery recycling, lead soldering, and various lead-based craft activities. Such exposures occurred often 50 to 150 years ago in today's developed countries, during earlier stages of industrialization, and they remain widespread in many of today's less developed countries.

Over the past two decades, epidemiologic evidence has accrued indicating that low-level environmental lead exposure in early childhood causes a deficit in neurocognitive development (Tong et al., 1998; see also Figure 9-2). Evidence from animal experimental studies and neuropathologic analyses corroborates this causal interpretation. Meta-analyses estimate that a doubling in blood lead concentration from 10 to 20 μg/dL—a range of lead exposure typically found between high and low tertiles in poorly controlled urban environment—is associated with a deficit in intelligence quotient of 1 to 3 points, that is, 1% to 3% of the expected average IQ score of 100 (Pocock, Smith, & Baghurst, 1994). Indeed, subtle effects on IQ result from blood lead levels as low as 5 μg/dL. A loss of IQ points will have greater impact in children with an IQ score just above 69 (mild mental retardation is defined as an IQ score of 50 to 69) than in those with a higher IQ.

Many high-income countries, including the United States and Australia, have recently set new, lower standards on environmental lead levels, to protect young children. However, childhood lead poisoning is an increasing problem in many low- or middle-income countries. For example, the lead content of gasoline sold in Africa is the highest in the world and is associated with high lead concentrations in the atmosphere, dust, and soils. Many other exposures to lead in Africa result from industrial, cottage industry, and domestic sources. Survey research has shown that over 90% of the children in Cape Province, South Africa, had blood lead levels over 10 μg/dL (Nriagu, Blankson, & Ocran, 1996). In Dhaka, Bangladesh, the airborne lead concentration is one of the highest in the world, and the mean blood lead concentration in 93 randomly chosen rickshaw pullers was 53 μg/dL—five times higher than the acceptable limit in high-income countries. A recent study in six Indian cities found that more than 50% of children had blood lead concentrations higher than 10 μg/dL, and more than 12% of the children tested had concentrations higher than 20 μg/dL. In China, where industrialization and motor vehicle usage are rapidly increasing, childhood exposure to lead is becoming a significant public health issue.

There are difficulties in including cognitive and intellectual impairment in the risk assessment equation for evaluating and controlling environmental lead as a public health hazard. This particular functional health deficit—a subtle neurologic impairment that will be most marked on the social and psychological development of children who already have a low IQ score—does not readily translate into the standard currency of deficit due to disease, disability, or death (the disability-adjusted life year, DALY). Hence, the burden of disease caused by relatively low but widespread exposures to lead can be readily underestimated by policy makers. Although overt lead-induced toxicity is apparent in individuals experiencing high levels of exposure, the full public health impact of widespread exposure to a range of environmental lead levels requires evaluation of more subtle health, behavioral, and developmental effects (Moore, 2003).

In developing a policy on environmental lead, and taking the evidence of cognitive impairment into account, two further questions arise. First, does the neurodevelopmental deficit persist over time? The currently available epidemiologic evidence suggests that the deficit persists through late childhood and early adulthood. Second, because few data are available in the very low exposure range, it remains uncertain if there is an exposure level below which no neurotoxicologic effect occurs. Overall, there is a strong case for public health measures to prevent exposure in early childhood. Because lead exposure tends to be ubiquitous within a population, a modest health impact upon each individual would yield a substantial aggregate impact for the total population. Assessments of population-attributable burden are given in Ostro (1994) and Schwartz (1994). Phasing out leaded gasoline is the most effective way to reduce population exposure to lead. However, a number of countries are still endangering their populations by allowing use of leaded gasoline (Moore, 2003; World Resources Institute, 1998).

Some types of environmental epidemiologic questions can be addressed experimentally at the individual level—for example, testing whether the installation of household humidifiers reduces the prevalence of respiratory symptoms, or whether the provision of masks to reduce workplace exposure to fumes reduces headaches. However, comparisons are more usually made at the supraindividual level—for example, testing the effectiveness of the broadcasting of safety promotion advertisements on television. A well-known historical example from the 1940s was the experimental addition of fluoride to the drinking water of four towns in North America, but not in four other similar towns, thereby allowing subsequent comparison of dental decay prevalence in children. For ethical reasons, experimental studies cannot be carried out with exposures that might be harmful to those who are exposed, although it may be ethical to test experimentally the short-term, reversible effect of annoyance factors (such as the acute effect of loud noise on blood pressure or of odors on mood).

A less rigorous approach to testing an environmental intervention is to carry out a before-and-after approach within a single group or population. However, it is often difficult to be sure that nothing else of relevance changed between the timing of the two periods.

Exposure and Dose: Assessment and Definitions

Paracelsus, the 16th-century German physician/alchemist who is often credited with being the founder of environmental health and toxicology, wrote: "Poison is in everything, and nothing is without poison. The dosage makes it either poison or remedy" (Deishmann & Henschler, 1986). This statement lies at the heart of environmental health science, as illustrated in the environmental pathway shown in Figure 9-3.

Although some idea of the health effects of an environmental contaminant can be obtained by measuring the quantity of toxin at the source or in emissions or as environmental concentrations, these can be misleading measures because they do not directly indicate how much actually reaches the population. There is a huge amount of toxic mercury in the oceans, for example, but little reaches people in normal circumstances. Volcanoes emit vast amounts of toxic gases, but fortunately few persons are usually nearby to breathe them. Far more precise for predict-

ing health effects would be measurements of dose itself, that is, the amount of toxins that has actually reached the vulnerable parts of the body. Unfortunately, it is difficult to measure dose directly for most toxins, either because it involves sophisticated, expensive, and invasive procedures (such as extracting and analyzing blood or tissue samples) or, for many toxins, because it is beyond our current scientific abilities. In addition, in a sense it is too late because once the toxin has entered the critical body organs the options for mitigation are limited.

Scientific and policy attention has therefore increasingly focused on the intermediate part of the environmental pathway—exposure (see Figure 9-3), which lies directly at the interface of the "environment" and the body. *Exposure* is the amount of toxin actually encountered by humans in the course of their activities. More explicitly, it is the amount of material or energy in the air, water, food, and soil that reaches the body's protective barriers of the respiratory and digestive systems, skin, eyes, and ears (Figure 9-4). Exposure differs from dose in that it does not encompass any of the body's internal mechanisms for absorption, transformation, excretion, and storage of the toxin. Exposure differs from concentrations by incorporating not only measures of the levels of the pollutant in the "environment" but also who experiences them and for how long. Thus, exposure integrates information about where the pollution is and also where the people are.

Total Exposure Assessment

Another important concept is that of total exposure assessment (TEA). To understand the full impact of a pollutant, it is necessary to examine all the ways it might reach people and not just rely on measurements made in the most convenient places. This is especially important for pollutants that can reach people through several different routes. For example, airborne lead pollution, arising mainly from vehicles, can spread through the "environment" to reach vul-

Figure 9-3 Environmental Pathway. *Source:* K. R. Smith, *Biofuels, Air Pollution, and Health: A Global Review* (New York: Plenum Publishing, 1987). Reprinted with permission.

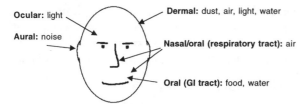

Ocular: light

Aural: noise

Dermal: dust, air, light, water

Nasal/oral (respiratory tract): air

Oral (GI tract): food, water

Figure 9-4 Routes of Exposure.

nerable groups, particularly children, not only through the air but also through water, soil, and food. Even though the original emissions are only to air, confining attention only to the air route would greatly underestimate the actual total exposure (see also Exhibit 9-1). It is total exposure, of course, that determines the risk to health.

The idea of TEA also applies to pollutants that only contaminate one medium. Consider, for example, the woman with the daily pattern of activities shown in Figure 9-5. What would be her health risk due to exposure to particulate air pollution? She lives in an urban slum of a low-income country where outdoor air pollution levels are fairly high. Her total exposure, however, is higher still because she spends considerable time in locations where particulate concentrations are higher than the outdoor levels. During the working day, she works as a sweeper on busy streets, where particulate levels are higher than the average outdoor level because of proximity to traffic. In the morning and evening, she experiences even higher levels as household cook because her family can only afford poor-quality cooking fuels that produce much air pollution, such as briquettes made from coal dust.

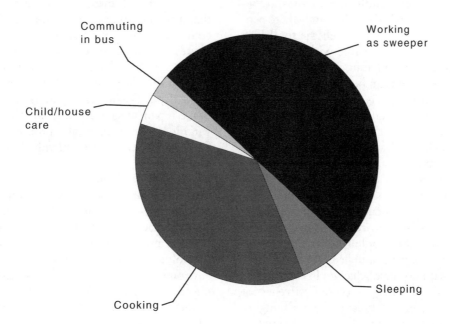

Activity	Hours/Day	Particulate Concentration ($\mu g/m^3$)	Daily Exposure Equivalent ($\mu g/m^3$)	Proportion of Total Exposure
Sleeping	7	100	29.2	0.07
Cooking	3	1,200	150.0	0.36
Child/house care	3	120	15.0	0.04
Commuting in bus	1	300	12.5	0.03
Working as sweeper	10	500	208.3	0.50
Total	24	mean = 415	415	1

Figure 9-5 Total Particulate Exposure for a Woman in an Urban Slum.

In the evening, she is exposed to the environmental tobacco smoke (ETS) from her husband's cigarettes. Her total exposure over the day is best estimated by the daily sum of the pollutant concentration in each major microenvironment where she spends time, weighted by the fraction of time she spends in it.

The TEA approach can cause profound changes in the ranking of pollution sources. Consider, again, the category of persons represented by the woman in Figure 9-5. Although power plants and factories produce by far the most emissions and thus affect outdoor concentrations most, they do not produce the most exposure for those persons. Poorly maintained cars and motorbikes add significantly to outdoor concentrations of air pollution, but they have an even greater impact on actual exposure because they release their pollution in places where people spend time. Household stoves add little to the outdoor air pollution, but they profoundly affect exposure because their pollution is released when and where people are present. Finally, even though the total ETS emissions are negligible compared with those from outdoor sources, their contribution to the personal exposure of nonsmokers can be considerable.

The importance of TEA is thus severalfold. It can change the relative importance of sources of pollution, and it can uncover important new sources of personal risk, such as ETS, that may not appreciably affect environmental concentrations. It also reveals a new dimension of potential control measures. For example, chimneys for household stoves that would not change emissions at all—and might even increase outdoor concentrations—can lower exposures substantially by separating the people from the pollution. Laws to reduce smoking in public places can lower ETS exposure with no actual changes in total smoking emissions. In some cases, the cost-effectiveness of such exposure-control measures can be much higher than exposure reduction through generalized control of outdoor sources. Although ideally all pollution sources should be controlled, in reality there is always a limit to the resources available. Choosing the most cost-effective control measures first will ensure that the most public health protection is achieved with whatever resources are available.

The central task in most environmental epidemiologic studies is to estimate the quantitative link between ill health and a particular environmental exposure. Risks can be estimated in relation to a number of possible exposure indices that refer to ambient environmental exposure (e.g., average level of air pollution within district), microecological exposures (e.g., neighborhood quality of housing),

personal-behavioral characteristics (e.g., time spent exposed to indoor air), or actual measurement of TEA. The choice of which to use depends on the accuracy needed and, as always, the resources available.

Biological Markers of Dose

Although not available for all situations, many types of biological markers (dose indices) are possible, such as heavy metals in hair, nails, and blood; metabolites in urine; chlorinated organic chemicals in adipose tissue; radionuclides in bone; and antibody titers in relation to infectious agents. The advent of increasingly specific and sensitive laboratory assays has greatly expanded the possibilities of measuring dose. Such assays include modem fluorometric methods, atomic absorption spectroscopy, high-performance chromatography, immunosorbent assays, and the use of various molecular biological markers.

For all such measures, it must be remembered that a biological assay estimates the integrated outcome of a sequence of physiological and metabolic processes. Since individuals vary, for constitutional reasons, in such things as the efficiency of intestinal absorption, the profile of hepatic metabolic pathways, deposition in peripheral tissues, excretion, and tissue repair mechanisms, whatever interindividual variation exists in external exposure will be randomly amplified by these interindividual biological differences.

The field of molecular epidemiology became prominent during the 1990s as an approach to studying the cause—especially the environmental cause—of cancer (McMichael, 1994). This same field has also become important in modem infectious disease epidemiology, particularly for the determination of environmental sources and transmission pathways for infections such as Legionnaires' disease, tuberculosis, influenza, cholera, and food-poisoning organisms. Molecular assays make use of the variation in structure of macromolecules, particularly DNA. One example in which DNA measurement has assisted the conventional epidemiologic study of causation has been in studies of dietary aflatoxin as a cause of liver cancer (McMichael, 1994). Aflatoxin is a biotoxin produced by the *Aspergillus flavus* mold in stored foods in warm, humid environments. Because it was not previously possible to determine directly an individual's level of aflatoxin intake, epidemiologists were limited to demonstrating ecological correlations, in eastern Africa and within China, between average aflatoxin concentrations in local diets and rates of liver cancer mortality. However, it is now possible to measure the concentration of excised, excreted, aflatoxin-DNA adducts in urine and to use this as a measure of recent individual exposure. This particular measure was used successfully in a cohort study of 18,000 Chinese men in Shanghai who were followed for liver cancer incidence. The study revealed a positive association, at the individual level, between initial adduct level and cancer occurrence.

Exposure Assessment at Individual and Population Levels

In studies of the health effects of ETS, for example, it has been common to classify exposures according to whether an adult has a smoking spouse or a child has a smoking parent. Clearly, someone living with a smoker is more likely to experience greater ETS levels than someone who does not, but this does not guarantee that this is so in every case. A child with no smoking parent, for example, may have four smoking grandparents who visit every day. Another child may have smoking parents who are careful to refrain from smoking anywhere near their child. In these cases, classification of these children by the smoking status of their parents would lead to exposure misclassification and a consequent attenuated estimate of the true effect. The risk of such exposure misclassification can be reduced by careful questionnaire design and by exposure-verification techniques, such as checking a sample of the children's urine for specific metabolites of nicotine.

The population-level classification of exposure, of whole subpopulations classified according to ecological indicators such as location within a city, is often inexpensive and convenient. However, it can yield exposure misclassification if not done carefully. It is common, for example, to conduct air pollution epidemiology by dividing urban populations into exposure classes according to the measurements made at the nearest outdoor air pollution monitoring station or even to use one or a few monitors to represent the exposure of an entire city for comparison with other cities. If the prevalence of local exposure sources (dirty household fuels, heavily trafficked roads, and others) differs in different parts of the city or in different cities, much exposure misclassification could result. Indeed, this problem is one of the main reasons why time-series studies have become more popular in recent decades (see also "Descriptive Studies," earlier in this chapter).

Health Outcome Assessment

Many studies of the health impacts of air pollution have examined associations with mortality. Yet the underlying pyramid of nonfatal health effects is very broad based; there is much to learn about the impacts of air pollution on hospitalizations, primary care consultations, existence of chronic conditions, impaired lung function (which requires testing of individuals), and self-assessed symptoms.

There is a natural tendency for researchers and data-collection agencies to prefer "hard" endpoints that are well defined clinically and amenable to clear-cut counting or measurement. Yet community surveys or consultations often indicate that the main perceived health impacts of environmental factors have to do with social, behavioral, and psychological disruptions, such as the mental stress of noisy environments, headaches or nausea from unpleasant odors, or underexercised, overweight children who are constrained by traffic and lack of neighborhood facilities.

Having decided on the category of health outcome, a formal case definition must be made. For those outcomes with preexisting population-based case registration—for example, cancers and congenital anomalies—case definition is relatively simple. However, when working anew from medical records, questionnaires, or test results, clear and stringent criteria must be specified.

Comparison of health status between populations usually necessitates adjustments for differences in basic demographic characteristics such as age distribution, sex ratio, ethnic composition, and socioeconomic profile.

Are preclinical changes useful as health outcomes? In principle, such "outcomes" would enable earlier answers to be obtained to urgent questions, including in relation to newly introduced exposures. For example, is there any form of early evidence available to access whether there has been a change in skin cancer risk due to increased ultraviolet irradiation caused by stratospheric ozone depletion? If, for example, UVR-specific mutations in skin could be identified and assayed, that would accelerate the answering of that question.

Data Analysis and Interpretation

In correlation studies, the data are assembled at a group or population level, and associations are based on comparing average exposure levels and the rates or levels of health outcomes in the different groups. Depending on the data sources, the health outcomes can be expressed as prevalence rates (e.g., health survey data on blood pressure) or incidence rates (e.g., rmortality data or cancer registration data). The comparison may involve just two groups at different exposure levels or a series of groups for which a

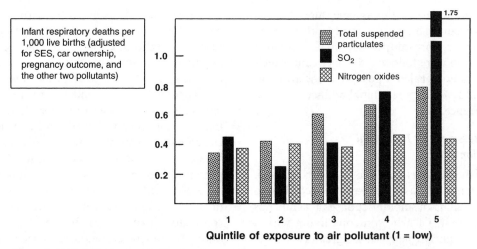

Figure 9-6 Air Pollution and Infant Respiratory Disease Mortality in Eastern Europe. *Source:* Data from M. Bobak and D. Leon, "Air Pollution and Infant Mortality in the Czech Republic 1968–1988," 1992, *Lancet, 340,* pp. 1010–1014.

dose-response relationship can be analyzed (e.g., see Figure 9-6; Bobak & Leon, 1992).

In correlation studies dependent on the use of pre-existing aggregated data, the lack of data on potential confounding factors may weaken the analysis. In analytic or experimental studies, the observed association between exposure and health outcome is generally thought to be more valid because of the readier control of confounding, the observable conjunction of exposure and health outcome at the individual level, and knowledge of the temporal relationship between those two variables. Nevertheless, if information about a potential confounding factor has not been recorded in the study, or if the data have been collected or classified in biased fashion, the interpretation of the results may still be misleading.

The presentation of the results is important for effective risk communication. The statistical analysis may have shown that the mortality rate within a community for a particular disease has gone up by a factor of 1.3, with a 95% confidence interval of 1.1 to 1.6. What does this relative risk of 1.3 really mean? If the disease in question is rare, the 1.3-fold increase of the absolute risk may represent a few cases per million exposed people per year. If, on the other hand, the disease is quite common, a relative risk of 1.3 may imply a major public health impact. Risk estimates can also be presented in the form of the number of exposure-attributable cases per year or as the number of cases that would occur in a longer time period (e.g., a lifetime) within a community; these are sometimes called public health impact estimates. These measures are the most intuitively understandable to the lay person (e.g.,

27 persons dying each year due to the environmental exposure, against a background expectation of 90 deaths), and they may assist decision makers more than would the more abstract epidemiologic measures of health effects. Ideally, for risk communication purposes, all three ways of expressing health risk associated with an exposure situation should be used.

Thus, it is important to consider whether the results of a study are of public health significance, in addition to being statistically significant. The analysis and presentation of the results can highlight the public health significance of that particular problem by a combination of risk estimates, as mentioned earlier, comparing the absolute risk estimates and public health impact estimates to the corresponding estimates for other health problems. This will provide an impression of the importance of the health effects identified. A problem in such comparisons is that it is difficult to measure the total health impact of an environmental exposure in a way that combines impacts on mortality and morbidity. In recent years various approaches have been proposed, such as the loss of quality-adjusted life years (QALYs), of health expectancy (an extension of the concept of life expectancy, the latter being confined to mortality data), or of DALYs. The DALY combines years of life lost from premature death and years lived with nonfatal conditions (assigned a disability weighting) (Murray & Lopez, 1996). The DALY was designed for comparative risk assessment and for economic impact analysis, and therefore it incorporates discount rates for the future value of healthy life. This measure has been promoted by the World Bank (1993) and WHO

(2002) as a tool for priority setting in health sector investments (see Chapter 1).

These different ways of expressing the health risk of an environmental exposure may lead to different interpretations of the results of environmental epidemiology studies. No standardized approach is available yet. Note, however, that in the first published ranking of the different determinants of global burden of disease (Murray & Lopez, 1996), occupational health hazards and outdoor air pollutants were included in the top 10. In the more recent analysis (WHO, 2002), several environmental health hazards were included, and poor water and sanitation as well as indoor air pollution from solid fuel burning were ranked among the top 10 global burden of disease risks (see Table 9-1).

Environmental Health Indicators and Monitoring

Environmental health issues are increasingly recognized as being part of a broader development-environment-health perspective. To achieve a lasting, sustainable impact leading to improved public health, the intervention must address underlying processes that create the exposure in the first place. In epidemiologic studies, the more direct the associations under study, the less likely are confounding and other complexities to cloud the interpretation. However, for effective decision making, the relationships between underlying factors and health outcomes may be more important than acquiring detailed information about the exposure-effect relationships. The dramatic contamination of the human food chain by dioxins in animal feeds in Belgium in 1999 raised upstream questions about the monitoring and regulation of feed production and about the social and economic pressures that heighten the risk of such episodes occurring.

Most industrialized countries have established a range of environmental performance indicators based on this approach. The most widely used scheme is that developed by the Organization of Economic Cooperation and Development (1993): the pressure-state-response (PSR) model. To analyze human health risks of environmental conditions, an expanded framework that better represents the cause-and-effect relationships between human activities, environmental change, and human health has been developed (Corvalan, Briggs, & Kjellstrom, 1996; Kjellstrom & Corvalan, 1995). According to this framework, driving forces lead to pressures; those pressures then affect the environmental quality (state), resulting in exposures (to humans) and then effects (in humans). The response to this cycle has

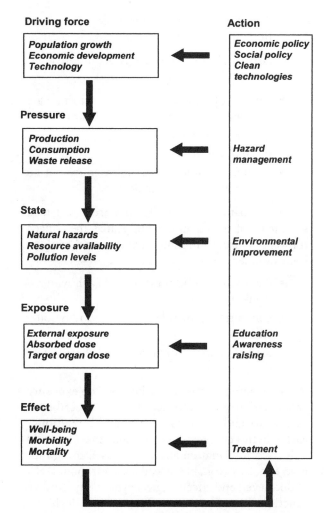

Figure 9-7 The DPSEEA Framework to Define Environmental Health Indicators. *Source:* T. Kjellstrom, and C. Corvalan, "Framework for the Development of Environmental Health Indicators," 1995, *World Health Statistics Quarterly, 48,* pp. 144–154; and C. Corvalan, D. Briggs, and T. Kjellstrom, "Development of Environmental Health Indicators," in D. Briggs, C. Corvalan, & M. Nurminen (Eds.), *Linkage Methods for Environment and Health Analysis,* Document WHO/EHG/95.26 (Geneva, Switzerland: World Health Organization). Adapted with permission.

been labeled *actions* to highlight an active role of society rather than a passive response. The framework was termed the DPSEEA model (Figure 9-7).

Driving force indicators are likely to be qualitative and are often expressed as yes/no answers. For example:

- Is there a policy to redirect all storm water to treatment plants?
- Are sedimentation dams in operation upstream in potentially cadmium-contaminated rivers?

- Are safety regulations for nuclear power stations adhered to?

Pressure indicators are usually quantitative. For example:

- amount of sewage-contaminated storm water entering a beach or river after heavy rain
- amount of cadmium transported via river water to paddy fields
- amount of radionuclides released from a nuclear power station accident

The most common indicators are direct measurements of the environmental state—the concentration of a hazard in some environmental medium. For example:

- enterococci concentration in beach water or drinking water
- concentration of cadmium in rice paddy soil or rice
- level of radioactive strontium in lichens or reindeer meat

Exposure indicators may be based on exposures calculated from state indicators, as described in "Exposure and Dose: Assessment and Definitions," earlier in this chapter. Biological indices add individual-based information and can be used to monitor both exposure (e.g., blood lead concentration, DNA-adduct level) and effects (e.g., enzyme assays for liver function, blood pressure). The marked decline in breast milk concentrations of dichlorodiphenyltrichloroethane (DDT) around the world is illustrated

in Figure 9-8 (Smith, 1999). The most commonly used materials are blood and urine, although hair, nails, saliva, exhaled air, breast milk, and biopsy (or autopsy) materials from internal organs are also used in special circumstances.

Ideally, an indicator of health effects should identify early effects that precede irreversible health damage. Examples include free erythrocyte protoporphyrin measurements in the blood of lead-exposed people and temporary threshold shift in hearing acuity after noise exposure. The next level of indicator includes early pathological change that may be reversible. An example is early tubular proteinuria after cadmium exposure (WHO, 1992). In some situations clinical symptoms or disease can be used in the monitoring, particularly after interventions to reduce environmental exposures. It would also be appropriate to use such indicators when there is disagreement about the actual existence of an environmental health problem. For particulate air pollution and other common air pollutants, for example, mortality monitoring may be useful, because the pathogenesis underlying increased mortality at relatively low levels of PM10 (particulate matter of less than 10 microns diameter) and carbon monoxide remains uncertain.

Assessment of Environmental Health Impacts and Risks

Introduction to Risk Assessment

Risk assessment is conventionally viewed as a five-point sequence. This begins with the research-based identification of an environmental hazard. Subsequent

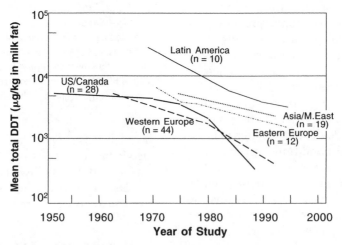

Figure 9-8 Worldwide Trends in DDT Levels in Human Breast Milk.
Note: n = number of studies. *Source:* D. Smith, "Worldwide Trends in DDT Levels in Human Breast Milk," 1999, *International Journal of Epidemiology, 28,* pp. 179–188. Copyright 1999 by Oxford University Press, Inc. Reprinted by permission of Oxford University Press, Inc.

| Exhibit 9-2 | Risk Assessments Can Provide Additional Information for Decision Making but Are Not Substitutes for Decision Making |

Consider that a proposal has been made to build a large new power plant near your community. Everyone agrees on the need for more power and that there are only two viable alternatives available: coal and nuclear (the actual case in many parts of the world). These are found to cost about the same. A full probabilistic risk assessment is done to compare the health implications of the two plants. The results are shown in the following illustration:

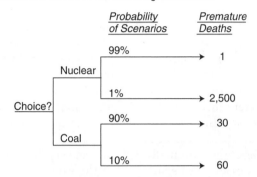

The coal plant, although of the best design, will still produce impacts because of air pollution and coal mining accidents. There is relatively little uncertainty about these factors—the PRA finds that there is a 90% chance that 30 persons will die prematurely because of the operation of the plant over its lifetime. Because there might be a large accident at the coal mine or a fire at the coal plant during meteorological conditions that lead to severe local air pollution, there is a 10% likelihood of killing 60 persons.

The nuclear plant, on the other hand, is given a 99% chance of doing very little damage (i.e., shortening only one person's life from the small amount of radiation released routinely). Unlike the coal plant, however, there is a small chance (here set at 1%) of a terrible accident in which 2,500 persons die from the radiation released. Which plant is safer? Which would you rather live alongside? There are at least three ways to answer, none necessarily right or wrong, but all dependent on the set of values of the people making the decision:

- *Maxi-min* (maximize the chance of the minimum consequence): Since 99% of the time little damage is done and more may be learned in the future on how to reduce the chance of accidents, choose nuclear.

- *Mini-max* (minimize the chance of the maximum consequence): Since a nuclear accident would be a tragedy (cause international headlines, go down in history, destroy the community, and so on), coal should be used so as not to have any chance of such an event.

- *Expected value* (calculate the odds): Since the expected value of deaths from the coal plant is 33 ($0.9 \times 30 + 0.1 \times 60$) and for nuclear, 26 ($0.99 \times 1 + 0.01 + 2500$), choose coal.

Although the particular numbers used here are fictional and real probabilistic risk assessments for such facilities are much more complicated (involving hundreds of branches on the risk trees shown in the figure), the overall results are often similar. Nuclear plants generally have a lower expected value of damage but carry a small probability of terrible events (much less than 1%). Coal plants produce more damage on average but do not impose anxiety about large negative events (although growing concerns about possible climate change from release of carbon dioxide from coal plants may change this perception). The fact that groups of perfectly rational people may choose different decision rules does not mean than any group is right in an absolute sense, only that they start with different values. Indeed, although there are many other factors to consider, the big difference in public acceptance of nuclear power between, say, France and Sweden, can be partially accounted for by such different values.

studies then estimate, first, the exposure- or dose-response relationship between the hazard and the specified health outcome, and, second, the distribution of exposure (doses) within the population of interest. From these two sets of information the overall risk to the population is then characterized, and risk management strategies are formulated. Although there is now some agreement about how to calculate risks, there is no completely objective way to compare alternatives with different patterns of risk. This is illustrated in Exhibit 9-2, which presents a choice between two ways of producing electric power with different patterns of risk and explains how reasonable consumers with different views of risk could rationally choose one over the other. This difference in risk perception is why people buy life insurance (risk aversion) and why insurance companies sell it (profits based on expected-value calculations).

Many other considerations would be included in a full assessment of alternative power plants. These include various outcomes of social importance other than those directly related to health. Thus the example illustrates that a decision about how much of what kind of risk to take demands substantial scientific input but is to a considerable extent a social and political choice.

Probabilistic Risk Assessment

Since nuclear power plant operation is a relatively new enterprise, few accident statistics are available, particularly for large accidents in modern plants. How, then, can overall risk be determined? For this purpose, a technique called *probabilistic risk assessment* (PRA) is applied to understand the potential for adverse consequences. Developed originally by NASA for assessing the risks of manned space flight, the technique basically breaks down the extremely complicated systems of large-scale technologies for which there are no overall accident information into subsystems. These subsystems may need to be further broken down into even smaller components until a level is reached for which failure data are available. Then, the failure data for each subsystem are combined to predict the performance of the total system.

There is no information that would enable one to predict directly how a new type of nuclear plant will operate over time. However, it is made up of thousands of components for which information is available. There will be information, for example, about how often pumps of a certain size, switches of a certain voltage, or warning gauges of a particular brand will fail under various conditions. Even if a new type of component is introduced, its failure rate can be experimentally determined without putting anyone at risk, unlike testing the entire power plant.

Such PRAs, of necessity, are extremely complex and difficult for even specialists to evaluate. In particular, it is hard to tell whether all possible accident scenarios have been taken into account and whether there might be unforeseen events, such as human sabotage, that could circumvent many subsystems at once. It also assumes that the context in which each component was originally tested is not materially different in critical respects (e.g., temperature or vibration) from the working context of the assembled plant.

Where an assessment reveals a potential or actual exposure to a chemical for which there is no human exposure history, a similar dilemma results. It would be dangerous and unethical, not to mention time-consuming, to deliberately expose enough people to

the chemical to discover its true risk. Various techniques have been developed to estimate the risks of human exposures in this situation. The most common is to expose laboratory animals, usually rats and mice, to high enough doses of the chemical to observe effects within their relatively short life spans. When effects, such as tumors or reproductive failure, are observed, then there is legitimate concern that such effects might also be seen in humans. To quantify that risk, however, requires extrapolating from high doses in animals to (usually) low doses in humans. This involves using a mathematical model that, ideally, is based on knowledge of metabolism, tumor induction, and other often poorly understood biological processes. Frequently, though, alternate animal models that are equally plausible biologically predict very different human risks for the same dose of the same chemical. (Had the antinausea drug thalidomide been tested in rats, not rabbits, the tragedy of limbless babies would probably have been averted.) It is necessary, therefore, to establish standard conventions for which model will be used in which circumstances so that consistent risk estimates are made. At present, many of the model choices depend more on scientific intuition than actual demonstrated knowledge. Finding more reliable and scientifically valid ways of doing such assessments is a very active research arena.

It might seem best to establish the convention of always using the most conservative model, that is, the model that predicts the largest risk. This would seem to fit the classic public health dictum that, in cases of uncertainty, it is better to err on the side of caution than to underestimate potential risk. Indeed, for this reason, such a conservative approach is used in formulating official policy by some regulatory agencies. Unfortunately, and perhaps counterintuitively, if this approach is taken for each chemical independently, it can lead to the opposite effect, that is, exposing the public to unnecessary risks. This is because the degree of conservatism (or the size of the safety factor) for specific chemicals can be quite different, depending on how well their observed animal or human impact actually compares with the predictions of the mathematical model employed. Thus, society might end up spending much to control one chemical based on a risk assessment that uses a conservative safety factor of 1,000 because it appears to be more dangerous than another that is in reality more dangerous, but whose estimated risk is based on a safety factor only 10 times its true value. Since it is rarely necessary to protect the population from only one hazard at a time, it is preferable to make judgments based on the best estimate of the actual risks rather than incorporating large, but varying, safety factors. In the real world of limited resources and time to deal with many possible hazards, an overly cautionary approach might be described as "too safe is unsafe."

Measures of Ill Health for Risk Assessment Purposes

As discussed in Chapter 6, various measures of ill health have been proposed to take into account, separately or in combination, the degree of prematurity of death and the time lived with nonfatal disease. There are several choices to be made in such calculations—for example, whether to use different life expectancies for men and women or for different regions, how to weigh the severity of different kinds of disease, and whether to discount the value of lost life years in the future (as is the practice in economics). Whatever choices are made, it seems clear that measures of lost healthy life years, due both to death and disease, are useful as a primary indicator of ill health. Indeed, even more than money, time is a universal asset among humans in all societies. Unlike money, time is also something shared approximately equally—or it would be if all people were not differentially burdened by risk factors such as malnutrition, vaccinations, medical care, and environmental pollution. Thus, the extent to which someone is denied a full healthy life span is arguably the best measure of the value lost, not only in practical terms but also in philosophical terms.

Such measures of forfeited healthy person-time, such as the DALY used by WHO for burden of disease estimates, are coming into increasing use. However, to date few current epidemiologic studies or risk assessment methods have directly applied them. More specifically, better estimates are needed of how much of the global burden of disease is due to environmental factors.

As the environmental risk transition progresses, and as the time between creation of a risk factor and its expression as disease tends to lengthen, the need for risk assessment increases (Smith, 1997). For evaluating measures to control diarrhea, it is reasonable to monitor diarrhea rates, for the diarrhea of today is due largely to environmental exposures within a few preceding days. For controlling environmental carcinogens or greenhouse gases with their decades-long latency periods, however, waiting until ill effects start to occur would be far too late. It is thus necessary to conduct risk assessments as best we can to predict well in advance, so that appropriate measures can be taken in time. As a result, these actions—sometimes difficult and expensive actions—will have to be taken without confirmation that they will really be needed. Indeed, in some cases, confirmation may not even be attained in retrospect. However, society will usually gain collateral public health, social, and often economic benefits from expending resources to reduce longer-term risks.

Assessing Risk: Compared with What?

Risk assessments, done in isolation, can be misleading. The following two examples are illustrative. Determining the risk imposed by an activity requires, explicitly or implicitly, choosing an appropriate baseline. In discussing the health effects of smoking, the appropriate baseline is arguably zero. It is possible for people to quit or not take up smoking. For air pollution, however, the choice is not as clear. There are natural sources of many pollutants, and human sources that are so difficult and expensive to control that a zero baseline is not feasible for many. What level is then appropriate? The national standard or the WHO guideline value? The level of the cleanest city? It is necessary to choose something in order to calculate the risk of the incremental pollution above the baseline.

Most human endeavors that are subject to risk assessment (technologies, industries, chemicals, regulations, and others) actually result in a mix of risk lowering and risk raising. A new factory in a low-income country, for example, might impose pollution on the public and accident risk on the workers, but it may provide jobs, housing, training, security, and other benefits that could lead to substantial improvements in health. Just because these effects are less direct than the accident risk does not mean they are small. Indeed, the overall impact of industrialization must be risk lowering—otherwise, it would be the industrialized countries that would be unhealthy rather than the low- and middle-income countries without industry. Such risk lowering also occurs in industrialized countries as well. Consider, for example, a pesticide residue on vegetables. Looked at in isolation, it may appear unacceptably risky. Looked at in terms of the overall impact on food cost and intake for low-income people, occupational risks to farm workers, and other factors, however, it may actually lower the overall risk compared with alternatives. This is not to say that all polluting activities will lower risks, but that all technologies should be judged on both their risk lowering and their risk raising. There are also often important equity and justice issues relating to who experiences the raised and who the lowered risk. However, our current risk assessment methods are not well developed for determining risk lowering, and this potentially biases the results.

In both these cases, to be fair and done well, assessment needs to be grounded, that is, the assessor should explicitly answer the question "Compared with what?" and inform the reader why this particular comparison has been chosen. An example might be a risk assessment of the small cancer risk created by chlorinating drinking water (from the chemicals produced by the reaction of chlorine and organic compounds in the water). In a place where the microbiological risks in drinking water remain high, the small incremental cancer risk may be well worth the trade-off.

Some Special Considerations in Environmental Health Research

Several other considerations have recently assumed increasing importance in environmental health research and practice. There is a greater emphasis on seeking upstream (social, economic, political, etc.) explanations of environmental health hazards, particularly because downstream (end-of-pipe) solutions are often ineffective (see also the discussion of the assessment of drivers, pressures, and environmental state changes in the earlier section, "Environmental Health Indicators and Monitoring"). Meanwhile, advances in biomedical science have yielded a better understanding of how various body systems function as complex, dynamic, adaptive systems and of how their integrity might be affected, subclinically, by diverse environmental exposures. Finally, the understanding of the determinants of population and individual vulnerability to environmental stresses is improving.

Specific Observable Toxicity Versus Subclinical Organ System Effects

Most toxicological and environmental epidemiologic studies aim to characterize effects and risks associated with specific exposure agents. When such exposures yield specific avoidable disease outcomes (e.g., bronchitis or bladder cancer), then this approach makes good sense. However, the functioning of certain organ systems can be cumulatively affected by multiple and continuing repeated exposures over time, resulting in immune system suppression, endocrine disruption, or cognitive impairment.

Both the immune system and the endocrine system entail complex interactive networks of organs, cells, and chemical messengers. It is not surprising that many exogenous organic chemicals can cause metabolic disturbance of these systems. Those are not so much toxic as pharmacologic effects. A growing body of evidence implicates pesticide exposures in suppression of the human immune system (Repetto & Belagi, 1996). This is also the case for other environ-mental exposures, such as air pollution and ultraviolet radiation. There is suggestive, but inconclusive, evidence of an environmentally induced decline in human sperm count in industrialized countries over the past half century, although the constituent data sets are neither representative nor standardized. Supportive evidence comes from observations of impaired fertility and reproduction in other mammals, birds, and fishes due to endocrine-disrupting chemicals released by human societies (Colborn, Vom Saal, & Soto, 1993).

Determinants of Population Vulnerability

In general, low- and middle-income populations are the most vulnerable to the health impacts of environmental degradation and change. They are typically more exposed, in terms of residential and occupational location, and have fewer resources for taking protective or adaptive action. The various social, cultural, and political influences on population vulnerability to environmental change include poverty, environmentally destructive growth, political rigidity, dependency, and isolation (Woodward, Hales, & Weinstein, 1998). Changes in the age structure of populations also affect vulnerability. As average life expectancies increase, populations become more vulnerable to many environmental stressors because of the increasing proportion of elderly persons.

More than 460 extra deaths were attributed to the effects of an extreme heat wave in Chicago in July 1995. The rate of heat-related death was much greater in blacks than in whites, and in persons bedridden or otherwise confined to poorly ventilated inner-city housing. In the correspondingly severe 1995 heat wave in England and Wales, a 10% excess of deaths occurred in all age groups. In greater London, where daytime temperatures were higher and there was lesser cooling overnight, mortality increased by around 15%. The excess mortality risks were generally greater in socioeconomically deprived groups. Similar patterns probably apply in low- and middle-income countries, although little such research has yet been done.

The impact of regional changes in food and water availability will be greatest in potentially vulnerable regions where population growth is pronounced and food insecurity exists. Interactions between local environmental degradation and larger-scale environmental changes are likely to be important in determining the net impacts on human health. For example, local deforestation due to population pressure may directly alter the distribution of vector-borne diseases and the likelihood of flooding, both of which are also liable to increase because of global climate change.

Determinants of Individual Susceptibility to Effects of Environmental Exposures

Constitutional characteristics frequently influence an individual's susceptibility to environmental exposures. Ready examples include skin pigmentation modulating the risk of solar-induced skin cancer, and age modulating the efficiency of intestinal absorption of lead. Many physiological and biochemical functions of the human body—such as kidney function, liver function, eyesight, and hearing—decline with age after early adulthood. Individual variations in metabolic phenotype, substantially determined by genotype, are also important. There are many enzyme pathways known to be involved in the activation or deactivation of potentially carcinogenic or other toxic chemicals, such as the various oxidizing enzymes of the mitochondrial P450 system, the acetylation pathway (yielding phenotypically "fast" and "slow" acetylators), the glutathione transferase pathway, and the alpha-antitrypsin pathway. There has been a steady accrual of epidemiologic evidence that these polymorphisms modify the disease-inducing impact of an external environmental exposure; that is, a gene-environment interaction is observable at the individual level.

This raises important opportunities for higher-resolution research. When study subjects are stratified on a metabolic polymorphic characteristic relevant to the external exposure, then the effect within the susceptible subgroup will become more evident than when the effect is diluted (averaged) across the susceptible and nonsusceptible subgroups.

This, of course, also creates new possibilities for future environmental risk management. The possibility of genetic screening in the occupational setting raises some particular dilemmas in terms of ethics, social priorities, and public health strategies. Are we going to refocus on assessing individual susceptibility and give less emphasis to reducing the occupational or ambient environmental exposure that is the external trigger for the increase in risk?

Household Exposures

Because the house is where much human activity takes place, the potential for damaging exposures in households is high if pollutants are present. Unfortunately, two of the most fundamental and mundane human household activities—defecation and cooking—produce significant volumes of health-damaging waste products. When human waste is not removed completely from the household "environment" and iso-lated from drinking water supplies, it leads to outbreaks of diarrhea and other waterborne diseases. When the smoke from cooking fires fueled with wood, coal, and other low-quality fuels is released into households, it leads to respiratory diseases and other health impacts. Indeed, together these two environmental health impacts account for the largest environmental burden of ill health globally and probably account for a larger burden than any other major risk factor, environmental or not, except malnutrition.

Sanitation and Clean Drinking Water

Ever since hunter-gatherers turned to cultivation and settled living, sanitation has been a public health problem for human societies. Further, as urban populations increase in size, the pressure on local sources of fresh drinking water increases. Today, these two perennial difficulties remain widespread health hazards in the world, particularly in low- and middle-income countries in semiarid regions. Approximately 40% of the world's population does not have ready access to clean, safe drinking water, and approximately 60% does not have satisfactory facilities for the safe disposal of human excreta.

Water shortage amplifies the risk of many "water-washed" infectious diseases, such as *Chlamydia* and scabies. Water shortage in combination with local fecal contamination increases the likelihood of transmission of waterborne diarrheal diseases, cholera, campylobacteriosis, and other infections. Every year, several million children die from diarrheal diseases contracted from infectious agents in drinking water and on food (see Chapter 4).

Solid Household Fuels

The oldest of human energy technologies, the home cooking fire using wood or other biomass, remains the most prevalent fuel-using technology in the world today. Indeed, in more than 100 countries, household fuel demand makes up more than half of the total energy demand.

A useful framework for examining the trends and impacts of household fuel use is the "energy ladder." It ranks household fuels along a spectrum running from the simple biomass fuels (dung, crop residues, and wood) through the fossil fuels (kerosene and gas) to the most modern form, electricity. In moving up the ladder, the fuel and stove combinations that represent the higher rungs increase the desirable characteristics of cleanliness, efficiency, storability, and controllability. On the other hand, capital cost and dependence on centralized fuel cycles also tend to increase with upward movement. Although there are local exceptions, history has generally shown that when alternatives are affordable and available, populations tend to naturally move up the ladder to higher-quality fuel and stove combinations. Although all of humanity had its start a quarter of a million years ago at what was then the top of the energy ladder, wood, only about half has moved to higher-quality rungs. The remaining half is either still using wood or has been forced down the ladder by local wood shortages to crop residues, animal dung, or, in some severe situations, to the poorest-quality fuels, such as shrubs and grass.

Throughout history, shortage of local wood supplies led some populations to move to coal for household use in places where it was easily available. This occurred in the early 1800s in the United Kingdom, for example, although it is relatively uncommon there today. In the past 150 years, such transitions occurred in eastern Europe and China, where household coal use still persists in millions of households (Figure 9-9). In the framework of the energy ladder, coal represents an upward movement in terms of efficiency and storability. Because of these characteristics and its higher energy densities, coal can be shipped economically over longer distances than wood and, can efficiently supply urban markets: In this regard, it is like other household fossil fuels. Unlike kerosene and gas, however, coal often represents a decrease in cleanliness as compared with wood.

The two characteristics of fuels that most affect their pollutant emissions when burned are physical form and contaminant content. Generally, it is difficult to premix solid fuels sufficiently with air to ensure good combustion in simple small-scale devices such as household stoves. Consequently, even though most biomass fuels contain few noxious contaminants, they are usually burned incompletely in household stoves and produce a wide range of health-damaging pollutants (HDPs). Table 9-2 lists some of the many hundred HDPs emitted as products of incomplete combustion from a range of household stoves in India. Even though biomass fuels would produce little other than carbon dioxide and water when combusted completely, in practice as much as one-fifth of the fuel carbon is diverted to products of incomplete combustion, many of which are important HDPs. Coal, on the other hand, is not only difficult to bum completely because of being solid, but it also often contains significant intrinsic contaminants. Most prominent among such emissions from coal, as shown in Table 9-2 are sulfur oxides. Coal in many areas also contains arsenic, fluorine, lead, mercury, or other toxic elements that lead to serious HDPs.

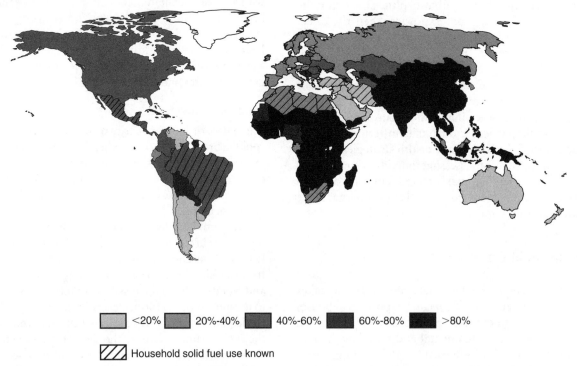

<table>
<tr><td><20%</td><td>20%-40%</td><td>40%-60%</td><td>60%-80%</td><td>>80%</td></tr>
</table>

Household solid fuel use known

Figure 9-9 National Household Solid Fuel Use, 2000. *Source:* K. R. Smith, S. Mehta, and M. Maeusezahl-Feuz, "Indoor Smoke from Household Solid Fuels," in M. Ezzati, A. D. Rodgers, A. D. Lopez, and C. J. L. Murray (Eds.), *Comparative Quantification of Health Risks: Global and Regional Burden of Disease Due to Selected Major Risk Factors,* Vol. 2 (Geneva, Switzerland: World Health Organization, 2004). Reprinted with permission.

Table 9-2	Pollutants in Solid Fuel (Biomass and Coal) Smoke from Household Stoves in Poor Countries

- Small particles, carbon monoxide, nitrogen dioxide
- Formaldehyde, acrolein, benzene, 1,3-butadiene, toluene, styrene, and many other toxic volatile organic chemicals
- Polyaromatic hydrocarbons, such as benzo(alpha)pyrene
- Coal produces all the above, plus may emit sulfur dioxide and toxic elements, such as arsenic, lead, mercury, and fluorine
- In simple stoves, biomass and coal burning produce significant non-CO_2 greenhouse pollutants, such as methane and black carbon

Source: K. R. Smith, *Biofuels, Air Pollution, and Health: A Global Review* (New York: Plenum Publishing, 1987). Reprinted with permission.

Petroleum-based liquid and gaseous fuels, such as kerosene and liquid petroleum gas, can also contain sulfur and other contaminants, but in much smaller amounts than in many coals. Further, their physical forms allow much better premixing with air in simple devices, thus assuring substantially higher combustion efficiencies and lower HDP emissions. In addition, kerosene and gas stoves tend to be much more energy efficient. Hence, the HDP emissions per meal from these fuels are at least an order of magnitude less than those from solid fuels.

Unfortunately, not only do solid-fuel stoves produce substantial HDPs, but a large fraction also lack chimneys for removing the emissions. Consequently, indoor HDP concentrations can reach very high levels for various important HDPs, including fine particulates and carbon monoxide. Fine particulate levels often reach 20 to 40 times the WHO guideline levels set to protect health. Even in households with chimneys, heavily polluting solid-fuel stoves can produce significant local outdoor pollution. This is particularly true in dense urban slums, where such neighborhood pollution can greatly exceed the urban average levels.

Pollution from household stoves is released in every household every day. This is the setting for high pollution exposures: significant amounts of pollution frequently released in poorly ventilated spaces at the times when people are present. Moreover, because they are usually responsible for cooking, women and their accompanying youngest children generally are the most exposed. Thus, although the total amount of HDP pollution released from stoves worldwide is not high compared with that from large-scale use of fossil fuels, the total human exposures to a number of important pollutants are actually much larger than those created by outdoor pollution. As a result, the health effects can be expected to be higher as well.

Despite the sizes of the exposed populations and the HDP exposures involved, there has been relatively little scientific investigation of the health effects of indoor air pollution in low- and middle-income countries compared with studies of outdoor air pollution

in urban populations (McMichael & Smith, 1999). Nevertheless, enough has been done to enable estimates of the magnitude of their impact, at least for women and young children, who receive the highest exposures. The impacts of the high concentrations experienced by a larger number of people with generally lower overall health status exceed those for outdoor air pollution (Exhibit 9-3).

Housing Quality

General housing quality involves such factors as ventilation, drainage, crowding, dustiness, materials that resist pests, and insulation from sun, wind, and cold. All these factors have a significant influence on health. Indeed, much of the improvement in health that occurred in western Europe and North America during the latter part of the 19th and early part of the 20th centuries is attributable to improved housing—although it is difficult to separate the relative benefits of improved housing from those due to concurrent changes in nutrition and personal hygiene behavior. Studies in some communities in low- and middle-income countries, however, indicate that health gains require improvements in a mix of factors, including general housing quality, rather than in just one factor at a time.

Good-quality housing for low- and middle-income communities can protect health in various ways. It provides shelter from cold, hot, or wet weather conditions. Incremental improvements of traditional designs that are basically adapted to the local conditions would be the most cost-effective means of improving shelter. A factor of importance is the structural integrity of the housing in the face of typhoons, floods, or earthquakes. The location of the house is also of importance. The houses of many persons injured or killed in floods are in low-lying areas prone to flooding.

The risk of physical injuries is another important aspect of housing quality. Children and elderly need to be protected from falls. Animals, machinery, vehicles, and cooking stoves and non-CO_2 greenhouse gases, such as methane heaters, need to be separated from areas to which small children have access.

Exhibit 9-3	Health Impacts of Indoor Air Pollution in Low- and Middle-Income Countries

Three main categories of health effects from indoor air pollution are thought to occur, based on studies in solid-fuel households and corroborated by studies of active and passive smoking and outdoor air pollution:

- infectious respiratory diseases, such as acute respiratory infections and, perhaps, tuberculosis
- chronic respiratory diseases, such as chronic bronchitis and lung cancer
- adverse pregnancy outcomes, such as stillbirth and low birth weight in infants born to women exposed during pregnancy

In addition, there is some evidence that air pollution from the household use of solid fuel increases the risks of blindness, asthma, and heart disease.

The best available estimates of the range of potential health effects within the low- and middle-income country setting come from the comparative risk assessment done by the World Health Organization, summarized in the *World Health Report 2002* and in Ezzati and associates (2002). This large multi-institution effort compared the burden of death and disease from more than two dozen major risk factors globally by age, sex, and region. To facilitate comparison, the studies were done under rules of "consensual discipline" in which, as much as possible, common criteria for acceptance of evidence were adopted. Under these rules, only the evidence for acute lower respiratory infections in young children and chronic obstructive pulmonary disease and lung cancer in women was deemed sufficiently robust for these conditions to be included as outcomes of indoor air pollution (Smith, Mehta, & Maeusezahl-Feuz, 2004).

The result was an estimate of 1.6 million premature deaths annually, about 1 million in young children. This makes up about 2.6% of the total global burden of disease and is thus larger than the contribution from all tuberculosis and is more than half that from all cancer. In mortality, it is substantially greater than the toll from malaria. The impacts occur largely in poor countries of South Asia (one-third), sub-Saharan Africa (one-third), and China (one-sixth). See Table 9-1 for a comparison of the impact of indoor air pollution compared with other risk factors, environmental and otherwise.

Although it is tempting to promote technical fixes for household environmental health problems in low- and middle-income countries, alone they are often of only limited success, although in the case of China some 180 million improved stoves have been introduced (Sinton et al., 2004). Provision of improved biomass-burning cooking stoves with chimneys often fails to reduce indoor air pollution because of poor maintenance and lack of consideration of local cooking practices. Promoting the use of cleaner fuels is difficult among populations that have little disposable income but have free access to local biomass resources. In general, reducing the risks related to such activities as cooking, defecation, and hygiene requires both technical and behavioral changes. Finding effective ways to achieve this is an important research task.

Source: Data from K. R. Smith, *National Burden of Disease from Indoor Air Pollution in India* (Mumbai: Indira Gandhi Institute of Development Research, 1998).

Another factor of importance in tropical countries is the avoidance of breeding sites for insect vectors of disease. Good drainage around the home and elimination of any sites where water can stagnate and mosquitoes can breed are of great importance to prevent malaria and dengue fever. In parts of Latin America, the prevention of Chagas disease (South American sleeping sickness) and the elimination of its vector, the triatomine bug, depend on the use of solid ceiling and wall materials without cracks.

The Workplace Environment

The workplace "environment" is generally more dangerous to health than the ambient external environment. Machinery, chemicals, dusts, ergonomic hazards, and the fact that much work is carried out with the body at its peak performance all contribute to the overall level of risk. Nevertheless, many of the same specific hazards occur in the workplace and the general environment, and hence there are many similarities in how their effects can be monitored and managed (Yassi & Kjellstrom, 1998).

There are various textbooks on occupational health and occupational medicine describing the many workplace hazards to health (e.g., Levy & Wegman, 2000; Rosenstock & Cullen, 1994; Stellman, 1998). The issues in low- and middle-income countries have been highlighted by Kjellstrom (1994), and a detailed treatise is given by Herzstein and colleagues (1998). The following text summarizes several key areas.

Important phenomena in the workplace "environment" of low- and middle-income countries are the specific problems occurring at the time of rapid industrialization. Agricultural societies are transformed, often without the infrastructure for environmental and workplace health protection that was built up in industrialized countries over decades of industrial development. Sometimes the new industries replace existing cottage industries, and conditions may improve.

In other cases industries with outmoded, dangerous technology are moved from developed countries, creating new hazards in the receiving country. The phrase *"export of hazards"* has been used to describe this problem (LaDou & Jeyaratnam, 1994).

Agriculture

Agriculture is the most common occupation in rural areas of low- and middle-income countries, where most of the world's population lives. Most workers are engaged in subsistence agriculture, in which the boundaries between work and other aspects of daily life are fluid. Workplace hazards in this type of situation include the generally poor and unhealthy living environments, with unsafe drinking water, poor sanitation, and inadequate shelter.

Further, there are specific hazards, such as injury hazards from tools used in tilling the soil, vector-borne diseases related to walking in water or mud, hazardous heat exposure under extreme conditions, bites from insects and animals, and falls or drowning from working on hillsides or riversides. The health risks are further increased because subsistence farm work involves the whole family, including children and the elderly. Epidemiologic evidence of these types of health risks is scanty.

As the planting and harvesting processes become more advanced and farmers develop cash crop production, new hazards emerge. The tools involved become more mechanized, which creates new types of injury risks, particularly because the use of these tools is unfamiliar to many of the workers. Pesticides are introduced, often without full equipment and training (WHO, 1990). It has been estimated that each year at least 1 million cases of unintentional pesticide poisoning occur among agricultural workers in low- and middle-income countries (WHO, 1990). In addition, there may be as many as 2 million suicide attempts annually, using pesticides, in these countries.

Agricultural work hazards are not only related to planting and harvesting food crops. An important activity is the collection of fuel wood for cooking and heating. Wood and agricultural waste is often collected in local forests by women (Sims, 1994). An analysis of time use for these activities, along with water collection and cooking, in four low-income countries showed that women spent 9 to 12 hours per day doing this, whereas men spent 5 to 8 hours. Firewood collection may be combined with harvesting of wood for local use in construction and small-scale cottage industry manufacturing. A number of health hazards are associated with the basic conditions of the forest, including insect bites, stings from poisonous plants, cuts, falls, and drowning. In countries with tropical heat and humidity, great physiological strain is placed on the body, whereas the cold is a potential hazard in temperate countries. In countries with a high sunshine level, UVR can be another health hazard, increasing the risk of skin cancer and cataracts (WHO, 1994). All forestry work is hard physical labor, with a risk of ergonomic damage, such as painful backs and joints as well as fatigue, which increases the risk of injuries from falls, falling trees, or equipment (Poschen, 1998). Women carrying heavy loads of firewood are common in areas with subsistence forestry (Sims, 1994). Further, the living conditions of forestry workers are often poor, and workers may spend long periods in simple huts in the forest with limited protection against the weather and poor sanitary facilities.

Urbanization leads to the development of a commercial market for firewood and larger-scale production of firewood from logs or from smaller waste material left over after the logs have been harvested. Energy forestry then becomes more mechanized, and workers are exposed to additional hazards associated with commercial forestry (Poschen, 1998). Motorized hand tools (e.g., the chain saw) become more commonly used, which leads to high injury risk, as well as noise-induced hearing loss and "white finger disease" caused by vibration of the hands. In addition, fertilizer and pesticides become a part of the production system, with the potential for pesticide poisoning among sprayers. As the development of forestry progresses, more of the logging becomes mechanized with large machinery, reducing the direct contact between worker and materials. Workers in highly mechanized forestry have only 15% of the injury risk of highly skilled forestry workers using chain saws (Poschen, 1998). However, firewood production continues to require manual handling and may therefore remain a hazardous operation.

Mining and Extraction

Mining is inherently dangerous to the mine workers, and most countries, including low- and middle-income countries, have recognized this by developing specific legislation and systems to protect mine workers (Stellman, 1998). There are two major types of mining, with somewhat different patterns of health hazards: underground mining and open-cast mining. Ergonomic hazards and physical (accident-inducing) hazards occur in both, but underground work includes the added hazards of being crushed by falling rock, poisoned by gas or dust build-up, or affected by heat or radiation. Each type of mine entails specific hazards associated with the rock from which the ore is excavated. Most types of rock contain high levels of silica, leading to high levels of silica dust in the air of a mine and the risk of silicosis in workers. Certain types of rock (particularly uranium ore) contain radioactive compounds that emanate as the gas radon, which increases the risk of lung cancer. Other types of rock contain metals that are inherently poisonous (e.g., lead and cadmium) and that in certain conditions can cause dangerous exposures.

According to the United Nations' *Demographic Yearbooks*, miners constitute a large occupational group in the international statistics. They represent up to 2% of the economically active population in some countries. Although 1% of the global work force is engaged in mining, it contributes 8% of the global fatal occupational accidents—about 15,000 per year. A detailed review of occupational health and safety issues in mining is available in Armstrong and Menon (1998).

Mining is thus a particularly dangerous occupation. Table 9-3 (Kjellstrom, Koplan, & Rothenberg, 1992) highlights the high overall occupational mortality rates in low- and middle-income countries, where reported rates are around 10 times higher than in industrialized countries, despite considerable underreporting.

In low- and middle-income countries, coal mining employs millions of people. Coal is a major global energy source, contributing 24% of total energy consumption (WHO, 1997). It was the primary source between 1900 and 1960, but subsequently has been overtaken by oil. Coal can be produced through surface mining (open cast) or underground mining. Both operations are inherently dangerous to the health of the workers.

Underground coal miners are exposed to the hazards of excavating and transporting materials underground. This includes injuries from falling rocks and falls into mine shafts, as well as injuries from machinery used in the mine. There are no reliable global data on injuries of this type from low- and middle-income countries (Jennings, 1998), but in industrialized countries miners have some of the highest rates of compensation for injuries. In addition, much of the excavation involves drilling into silica-based rock, creating high levels of silica dust inside the mine. Pneumoconiosis silicosis is therefore a common health effect in coal miners (Jennings, 1998). In addition, it has been shown that coal miners with silicosis have an increased risk of lung cancer.

Other health hazards specific for underground coal mining include the coal dust, which can cause "coal worker's pneumoconiosis," or anthracosis, often combined with silicosis. The coal dust is explosive, and explosions in underground coal mines are an ever-present danger for coal miners. Fires in coal mines are not uncommon, and once started may be almost impossible to extinguish. Apart from the danger of burns, the production of smoke and toxic fumes creates great health risks for the miners. Even without fires, the coal material produces toxic gases when it is disturbed: carbon monoxide, carbon dioxide, and methane. Carbon monoxide binds to hemoglobin in the blood, blocking oxygen transport and causing chemical suffocation. It is a colorless and odorless gas and therefore gives no warning before the symptoms of drowsiness, dizziness, headache, and unconsciousness occur. Carbon dioxide displaces oxygen in the underground air and can cause suffocation.

Table 9-3	Occupational Death Rates in selected Countries and Relative Rates for Miners and Construction Workers		
Country	Crude Death Rate, All Occupations (Deaths per 1,000 workers per year, 1980s)	Ratio of Crude Death Rate in Mining Relative to Rate in All Occupations	Ratio of Crude Death Rate in Construction Relative to Rate in All Occupations
Guatemala	0.54	3	2
South Korea	0.33	13	1
Zimbabwe	0.28	4	1.5
Hong Kong	0.075	23	12
United States	0.060	5	3
Sweden	0.036	6	2
Japan	0.020	19	4
United Kingdom	0.017	10	6

Source: R. Feachem, T. Kjellstrom, C. J. L. Murray, M. Over, & M. A. Phillips (Eds.), *The Health of Adults in the Developing World* (Oxford, England: Oxford University Press, 1992). Copyright 1992 by International Bank for Reconstruction and Development/The World Bank. Reprinted by permission of Oxford University Press, Inc.

Another health hazard is exhaust fumes from the diesel engines used in machinery or transport vehicles underground. These contain very fine particles, nitrogen oxides, and carbon monoxide, all of which can create serious health problems. Underground mining may also expose the workers to extreme heat stress due to high temperature or humidity. The climatic conditions underground need to be assessed when scheduling work shifts and breaks.

Surface coal mining avoids the hazards of working underground but still involves risk from machinery, falls, and falling rocks. In addition, coal mining is very energy-intensive work, similar to forestry, and heat, humidity, and other weather factors can affect the worker's health. The machinery used is noisy, and hearing loss is a common effect in miners. Another health hazard is the often squalid conditions under which many coal workers in low- and middle-income countries live, creating particular risks for the diseases of poverty.

A special type of mining is the extraction of oil and gas to supply the energy needs of industrializing societies. Oil and gas exploration, drilling, extraction, processing, and transportation involve a number of the hazards mentioned previously: heavy workload, ergonomic hazards, injury risk, noise, vibration, and chemical exposures (Kraus, 1998). This type of work is often carried out in isolated geographic areas with inclement weather conditions. Long-distance commuting may also be involved, causing fatigue, stress, and traffic accident risks. The ergonomic hazards lead to risk of back pain and joint pain. Injuries include burns and those caused by explosions. Skin damage from exposure to the oil itself and from chemicals used in the drilling processes creates a need for well-designed protective clothing. In addition, many oil and gas installations have used asbestos for heat-insulating cladding of pipes and equipment. This creates the hazard of inhalation of asbestos dust in the installation and repair of such equipment, which increases the risk of lung cancer, asbestosis, and mesothelioma (WHO, 1998).

Much exploration and drilling for oil and gas now occur offshore. This involves underwater diving work, which is inherently dangerous. In addition, the weather-related exposures can be extreme, particularly because the work often requires continuous operations around the clock (Kraus, 1998).

Construction

Construction work is another dangerous occupation with potential exposures to a variety of hazards (Weeks, 1998). This includes injuries from falls and falling objects, and injuries from machinery or related to excavation or underground work. Because much construction work is carried out in the open, weather conditions create hazards of heat, cold, UVR, and dust storms. Construction work involves heavy lifting of materials and activities in awkward body positions, leading to ergonomic hazards. Injuries, strains, and sprains are common. Many injuries are severe, leading to the high ratio of construction workers in the occupational mortality statistics (see Table 9-3).

Construction work also involves exposures to noise, chemicals, and biological hazards. Much of the machinery used is noisy, and this problem has increased with the increasing mechanization of the industry. Demolition is a common aspect of construction work, and demolition activities are inherently noisy. Noise-induced hearing loss is therefore common among construction workers. Another aspect of the noisy "environment" is the increased safety problems caused by the masking of warning calls or other alarms.

Chemical and dust exposures are related to the composition of the building materials. Asbestos, which has been used as insulation and as a component of asbestos-cement pipes and sheets, has been a prime example of a hazardous material. Asbestosis (a form of pneumoconiosis), lung cancer, and mesothelioma (another fatal cancer) have been found in many construction workers (WHO, 1998). Mesothelioma is one of the most prominent occupational diseases in most countries where records are kept, but underreporting of asbestos-related lung cancer is common. It has been estimated that in high-income countries as many as 20,000 cases of lung cancer and 10,000 cases of mesothelioma occur each year due to asbestos exposures in workplaces that occurred 20 to 40 years ago (Tossavainen, 2000). The use of asbestos has been reduced in most industrialized countries and banned in some, but asbestos-cement building products are still widely used in low- and middle-income countries because these materials have attractive technical qualities. Alternatives to asbestos exist for almost every use, and their cost is often similar to asbestos.

It is clear that the use of asbestos in low- and middle-income countries is still widespread (Kazan-Allen, 2003; Tossavainen, 2004). The epidemic of serious health effects takes decades to develop, so preventive actions need to be taken at an early stage. Some developing countries have instituted bans, which would be the most effective prevention. The epidemic is still on the ascendancy in a number of high-income countries, even though virtual bans were instituted in the 1980s—for example, in New Zealand, where the full epidemic of asbestos cancer over 40 years may kill at least 2,000 to 3,000 workers (Kjellstrom, 2004).

Other chemical and dust exposures include cement dust among bricklayers and concrete workers (Weeks, 1998). This dust causes dermatitis. Sandblasting or rock drilling creates silica dust in the air, which can lead to silicosis in the exposed workers. Construction work often involves welding, which adds further health hazards, such as inhalation of welding fumes that leads to bronchitis. Paint fumes often contain organic solvents that may cause neurologic disorders. The hazards of dusts and fumes are increased inside confined spaces, where these concentrations can reach extremely high levels.

Because of climate conditions, work in the construction industry is often seasonal, and contract workers therefore rely on other work during parts of each year. The intermittent character of the work creates problems in maintaining efficient prevention programs to protect workers against these hazards (Weeks, 1998). This is particularly so in low- and middle-income countries. Subcontracting or informal employment relations often reduce the responsibility taken by the main employer or contractor on a construction site. The responsibility for health and safety is dispersed among many individuals, so the protection against hazards may become insufficient. In construction work it is therefore important that contracts include the necessary safety provisions and that there are systems in place for monitoring and enforcing these provisions.

Manufacturing

Manufacturing workplaces can involve any of a textbook list of occupational hazards, some of which were mentioned in previous sections. A recent review of the various hazards is included in the *Encyclopaedia of Occupational Health and Safety*, published by the International Labor Organization (Stellman, 1998). Manufacturing involves ergonomic injury hazards from improper work positions, heavy lifts, and dangerous machinery; physical hazards, such as noise, heat, poor lighting, and, occasionally, radiation; and chemical exposures of many kinds. However, as in the history of today's industrialized countries, the major chemical exposure problems in low- and middle-income countries include lead, cadmium, chromium, mercury, other metals, organic solvents, and welding fumes. Increasingly, the most hazardous industries and processes are exported from industrialized to low- and middle-income countries (LaDou & Jeyaratnam, 1994), without the technological improvements that have reduced workers' exposures in the industrialized countries. In addition, stress and other psychosocial hazards of long work hours and shiftwork are common in an industry that has large investments in machinery, from which economic benefit only accrues when it is in operation.

Of the various manufacturing industries, some with particular health risks are worth highlighting. In electrical appliance manufacturing (Stellman, 1998), a major problem is lead-acid battery manufacture, which produces batteries for vehicles. Because such batteries are too heavy to transport over long distances, local production is usually established at an early stage of the "motor car society." The operation of these factories typically involves many workers who receive unacceptably high lead exposures. The usual approach is to monitor workers' blood lead levels; if the levels exceed the national standard, the worker is excused for a few weeks. Indeed, this type of risk management is enshrined in occupational health law in many countries. This approach displaces the exposure problem to the individual rather than analyzing the workplace "environment" as a whole. Cadmium is another toxic metal of increased importance because it is used in rechargeable batteries in modern electronic equipment such as mobile phones. The manufacturing of cadmium batteries involves even more risks than lead battery production. Vigilant exposure monitoring and effective protection are essential to avoid chronic poisoning in the form of kidney and lung diseases (Friberg et al., 1986).

Another manufacturing industry common in industrializing countries is metal processing and metal working. Smelting and refining of any metal provides a major potential for occupational exposures to many types of hazards, and a particular risk of exposure to toxic metal dusts, sulfur dioxide, and other fumes. Because these industries are often of very large scale, even small concentrations of toxic compounds in the processes can yield substantial emissions into the workplace and the surrounding environment. The experience from lead smelters in many countries is similar: high lead exposures for workers and contamination of the local environment. Often the workers and their families live in the vicinity of the industry, and high lead exposures in children from dust emissions are found. These exposure situations have been studied in detail in the United States and Australia, and epidemiologic research there has produced some of the most valuable quantitative data on the health risks of lead in children and workers (see also Exhibit 9-1).

Service Occupations

Many service industries involve important occupational hazards. The services reviewed by the International Labor Organization include those with specialized and sometimes severe hazards, such as emergency and security services (e.g., fire fighting and law enforcement), public and government services (e.g., garbage collection and hazardous waste disposal), and health care services (Stellman, 1998). The review also includes those likely to have less severe hazards, such as retail trades, banking, administrative services, telecommunications, restaurants, education, and entertainment.

Fire fighting involves exposure to carbon monoxide and toxic fumes, as well as the heat from the fire itself. Injuries from falling debris, falls, or working in awkward positions are also of concern. Protection of workers depends on protective equipment, which in low- and middle-income countries may be in short supply. Law enforcement is another high-risk occupation, which involves hostile contacts with other persons who may be armed.

Garbage collection exposes workers to risks of cuts and other injuries from the garbage itself, as well as heavy lifts. A particular risk group in low- and middle-income countries is the people who scavenge on garbage dumps for recyclable materials from which to glean a meager existence. Sometimes these scavengers actually live on the garbage dump, with the associated risks of infectious disease, bites from rats and dogs, and other dangers. Hazardous wastes are not always separated and therefore add to the risks of the garbage collectors and scavengers. In areas where hazardous wastes are separated, the storage and handling of these requires sophisticated protective equipment, detailed information about the hazards, and efficient management systems. These are often missing even in industrialized countries.

Health care workers face other hazards, such as infections from patients, transmission of HIV or hepatitis from needle pricks, and allergies to drugs given patients or to cleaning and disinfection chemicals. However, the most common problem is ergonomic hazards from lifting or moving patients, leading to back injuries. This creates great problems for nurses and nurse aides, and in many cases curtails their careers.

One special hazard for people in service trades that involve continuous work at computer keyboards is the development of repetitive strain injury, or as it is also called, occupational overuse syndrome. The repetitive keyboard finger work, or the repetitive fine movement of the computer mouse, creates a wear-and-tear reaction in tendons and muscles that can lead to chronic pain. As with the situation for bad backs, these painful conditions are not always accompanied by measurable anatomical or pathological changes, which has caused substantial arguments among medical practitioners as to the genuineness of the disease. However, as many peo-

ple using modern computers attest, the short-term pain after intensive use of a keyboard or a mouse is real. The ergonomic design of a computer work station and the provision of regular work breaks are essential for preventing this occupational hazard. The height of the keyboard should be adjusted to the individual user. These conditions may be difficult to achieve in low- and middle-income countries.

Other Occupations

Among the other occupational exposure situations of particular importance, especially in low- and middle-income countries, are cottage industries of various types. At an early stage of industrialization, small-scale operations based on family members may be the mainstay of certain industries. This may be in the form of work contracted out from a larger enterprise, or it may arise directly in relation to the local market. The production of handicrafts, clothing, and consumer items for local households may be the starting point. However, more hazardous activities, such as recycling car batteries, may also develop initially as a cottage industry. This may entail extreme exposures to toxic chemicals, with little or no protection either for the workers or other family members. Ergonomic hazards, injuries, noise damage, and all other occupational hazards are likely to be a greater danger in these cottage industries than in more organized enterprises.

Community-Level Exposures

The community level is the level at which much environmental epidemiologic research has concentrated, particularly in relation to ambient air pollution, industrial emissions, the problems associated with urban transport systems, contamination of local drinking water and local food supplies, and waste management. Difficult methodological choices often confront researchers at this level, particularly whether to attempt to measure exposures and make comparisons at the individual, small-group (microecological) or community level.

Outdoor Air Quality

Urban air pollution has, in recent decades, become recognized as a worldwide public health problem (World Resources Institute, 1998). In the industrialized countries, the earlier industrial and household air pollution from coal burning has been replaced by pollutants from motorized transport that form photochemical smog, including ozone (a strong irritant that affects eyes, upper airways, and lungs) in summer and a heavy haze of particulates and nitrogen oxides in winter. Although many industrialized cities do not yet meet annual standards for every pollutant, conditions are generally much better than in the past. Nevertheless, air pollution has become a renewed concern in various industrialized cities where it was believed that the historic problems had been solved. The experience of severe air pollution incidents around the mid 20th century, most famously in London in 1952 (the "London Smog" incident) when the daily mortality was doubled during a 2-week period, finally led to a political agreement to act against air pollution. During that episode, the daily peaks were several thousand $\mu g/m^3$ for each of the pollutants. Those earlier problems were caused mainly by the industrial and household burning of coal without efficient emission controls, leading especially to high breathing zone concentrations during temperature inversions. During the subsequent decades, the annual average and daily peak levels of particulate matter and sulfur dioxide were decreased tenfold or more in most cities of industrialized countries.

In low- and middle-income countries, urban air pollution has recently attained alarming levels in many cities. In New Delhi, Beijing, and several other Indian and Chinese cities, for example, the annual average concentrations of particulates have been 5 to 10 times greater than the WHO air quality guideline (Exhibit 9-4). In China, the main source of pollution is combustion of coal. Industrial, neighborhood, and household sources all contribute, how-ever, and emissions from automobiles are increasing sharply (Florig, 1997). The estimated morbidity and mortality in Chinese cities due to air pollution is now increasing markedly (see Exhibit 9-4). Meanwhile, in many of the cities of central and eastern Europe, the mix of industrial emissions and car exhausts has caused increases in air pollution. In eastern Germany and in southern Poland in the late 1980s, winter concentrations of sulfur dioxide from coal burning were even higher than those in London during the infamous 1952 smog episode.

Studies relating ambient air pollution levels to health risks were, until the 1970s, largely confined to examining the health impacts of particular extreme episodes of very high outdoor air pollution levels. Subsequent studies, based on daily mortality time series, have elucidated the role of respirable particulates, ozone, and nitrogen oxides in acute mortality (Schwartz, 1994). The advantages and attractions of daily time-series statistical analysis have been discussed in the section "Study Design Options" earlier in this chapter. However, this acute component of mortality due to daily fluctuations in air pollution levels needs to be carefully distinguished from the long-term effect of chronic exposure at an elevated level (McMichael et al., 1998). Long-term follow-up studies to of populations exposed to different levels of air pollution, especially particulates, indicate that the higher the levels of exposure, the greater the mortality risk. A 16-year follow-up of 500,000 people in

---

Exhibit 9-4   Urban Air Pollution and Health in India and China

The two largest countries in the world, India and China, share an unfortunate characteristic: They rely on dirty coal for large fractions of their commercial energy. In addition, being low income, they have not been able to devote significant resources to either cleaning the coal before it is burned or capturing the emissions in the smokestacks before they are released into the environment. Furthermore, they have many relatively small coal-burning sources, including small factories, commercial activities such as restaurants, and, in China, boilers for heating buildings and cookstoves, from which the pollution is difficult to control. The result is high air pollution levels in many cities in both countries.

Data show, for example, that the average annual outdoor concentration of PM10 (airborne particulate matter of diameter less than 10 microns) in large Indian cities is about 190 $\mu g/m^3$ This is six to eight times the levels in U.S. and European cities. Mean PM10 levels in large Chinese cities are similar, perhaps 180 $\mu g/m^3$, but, unlike India, China's coal also contains significant amounts of sulfur; thus, sulfur dioxide levels are sometimes markedly elevated, although progress is being made to reduce them (International Scientific Oversight Committee, 2004).

Although fossil fuels dominate energy use in the urban sectors of all countries, small-scale combustion of biomass in households and small enterprises still contributes substantial pollution in many cities in India. For example, small particles from biomass combustion make up 10% to 29% of the particles in Delhi and 17% to 32% in Kolkata, depending on the season (Chowdhury, Zheng, & Russel, 2004).

Although estimations in this context are difficult, it appears that the resulting burden of disease in each country is high. The WHO Comparative Risk Study (see Table 9-1) found about 300,000 premature deaths per year in China and 110,000 in India from urban outdoor air pollution (Cohen et al., 2004). However, in addition to other uncertainties, such calculations depend on what baseline is assumed, that is, how low pollution levels could realistically become. Given natural background environmental factors, a level of zero is simply not feasible.

the United States was used to link urban air pollution exposures to mortality with appropriate control of founding factors (Pope et al., 2002). An increased mortality in cardiopulmonary diseases was found, and the strongest relation to air pollution (particulate matter of less than 2.5 μm diameter) was found for lung cancer. The effects of long-term exposure can also be studied with small-scale spatial analysis within cities, taking confounding factors into account. In one such study (Scoggins et al., 2004), a significant increase in mortality attributable to local air pollution was found in a city with relatively low air pollution levels (Auckland, New Zealand).

Asthma, which has been increasing in industrialized countries for three decades, has a still unresolved relationship to external air pollution. Although some studies indicate a contributory role of air pollution as a trigger, if not as the initiator, in this marked rise in asthma rates, other studies are less conclusive. The apparent increasing susceptibility of successive modern generations of children to asthma may well derive from changes in human ecology that have altered early-life immunological experience, such as reduced exposure to common childhood infections (due to smaller family sizes) or allergenic household exposures (e.g., house-dust mites or fungal spores), or modern vaccination regimes.

Epidemiologists have developed a diverse and increasingly sophisticated set of methods for assessing the health impacts of air pollution. Nevertheless, the issue remains bedeviled by difficulties in exposure assessment, the uncertain differentiation of acute and chronic effects, the need to sort out independent and interactive effects between air pollutants that are often highly correlated, and the fact that the profile of air pollution keeps evolving as human activity patterns change. Although there are many uncertainties, there is general agreement that significant health effects occur at pollutant concentrations that used to be considered benign. In the case of small particulates, which can penetrate deeply into the respiratory system, there is no evidence of a threshold exposure below which no effect occurs. This absence of a safe lever complicates the development of guidelines and standards. Recently, WHO decided instead to publish a table of exposure-response relationship functions (WHO, 2002). Policy makers are thus forced to decide what level of health risk is acceptable in order to determine an appropriate exposure standard.

Traffic and Transport

As cities grow in size, urban transport systems expand and evolve. In particular, private car ownership and travel have increased spectacularly over the past half-century, creating new opportunities and freedoms—and new social and public health problems (Fletcher & McMichael, 1997). Currently, there seems to be no agreed vision of an urban future that is not dominated by privately owned vehicles.

Transportation is one of the key polluters in the process of economic development, urbanization, and industrialization. In traditional subsistence agricultural societies, the community's basic needs could be met within a relatively localized distance. Increases in population size and density mean that specialized resources for the community, such as firewood, must be acquired from increasingly distant sources, which creates transportation needs. Modern economic development has accelerated this process by further specialization of economic tasks and dependence on resources from distant areas. Energy sources, such as coal, have had to be transported from afar to sustain local cottage industries; this was also the case with food items to sustain people in places where little could be grown or gathered for much of the year.

Initially, transportation by waterways was favored, requiring no investment in tracks for vehicles. During the 20th century, railways and roadways dominated. Motor cars and trucks with internal combustion engines have subsequently had a significant impact on the "environment" and health. Combustion of petroleum fuel produces various toxic emissions: particulate matter (dust), carbon monoxide, nitrogen oxides, hydrocarbon remnants from the oil, and a variety of complex hydrocarbons. The health effects of these pollutants range from minor respiratory symptoms to asthma attacks, lung cancer, and death from heart or lung disease. In addition, some of these pollutants react with oxygen in strong sunlight to form ozone.

Today, the automobile has become the dominant source of air pollution in many cities (World Resources Institute, 1998). Current technical solutions to this problem include making car engines more energy efficient and using pollution control devices, such as catalytic converters. The obvious, more radical solution is to reduce dependence on car traffic by encouraging people to walk and to travel by trains, buses, or bicycles. Such measures, carried out as part of a clean air implementation plan, can significantly reduce automotive air pollution, as shown in certain towns in the United States and Germany (WHO, 1997). However, in cities in low- and middle-income countries, the problems have grown even faster. Whereas in Europe a local transport infrastructure based on railways, trams, and buses was already in place when the car boom emerged in the 1960s, low- and middle-income countries often have negligible transport infrastructure. Hence, with increasing affluence and urbanization, the automobile is seen as the best solution for individual families. Cities such as Mexico City have, consequently, experienced a rapidly deteriorating air pollution situation (WHO, 1997). However, the recent experience of Mexico City also provides a case study of an effective reduction of car-generated air pollution (Exhibit 9-5).

Since the first oil crisis in the 1970s, the average fuel efficiency of the world's automobiles has increased substantially, largely through major improvements in North America up to the mid-1990s that brought efficiencies nearly to European levels. Emissions of air pollutants have also been greatly reduced, partly through combustion modifications and partly through extensive application of end-of-pipe controls, in the form of catalytic converters. It is clear, however, that if the number of automobiles in low- and middle-income countries continues to grow as it has in recent years, unacceptable air pollution levels will persist for many decades even with the best current auto technology. Fortunately, several near-commercial technologies promise much better efficiency and lower emissions. Electric cars will probably have increasing, but still specialized, applications. However, because of weight, capacity, cost, and lifetime limitations of batteries, they show no sign of being able to serve the main market. Hybrid cars, which are now becoming available, combine the best features of both fuel and electric drive systems and can significantly increase efficiency and lower emissions without the changes in fuel delivery systems required by all-electric vehicles. Even more promising, although not yet commercially available, are cars powered by fuel cells. These can be extremely efficient and produce only tiny amounts of pollution when powered by clean fuels such as methane or hydrogen. Both hybrid and, particularly, fuel-cell cars would also reduce the emission of carbon dioxide, the main anthropogenic greenhouse gas contributing to climate change (see "Climate Change," later in this chapter).

The motor car–based transport system poses several other health risks. Most obvious, internationally, is the great and increasing burden of disease due to car crash injuries (Murray & Lopez, 1996). Much of the additional future health impact will occur in the currently low- and middle-income countries. Road fatality rates per thousand vehicles are around 30 times higher in Africa than in Norway, the United Kingdom, and the United States, for example. These differences highlight the injury risks at an early stage of motorization when roads are still undeveloped, pedestrians and drivers are not adjusted to one another, drivers have poor driving skills, and the vehicles are not prop-

erly maintained (see Chapter 7). The dramatic public health impact of traffic crash injuries, shown in Table 9-1, has great influence on the health services through the intensive and acute treatments that are required; in this manner, road traffic injuries threaten services for other health problems (WHO, 2004).

Car traffic also creates a major noise hazard. This greatly impairs quality of life for millions of people living close to busy roads, especially in countries with tropical climates where windows of dwellings are seldom closed. Traffic noise disturbs sleep and impairs communication (of particular importance in schools). The proliferation of roads and highways can disrupt social interactions within communities. Unless town planning attends to the needs of pedestrians, cars and roadways tend to dominate the built-up landscape. In Britain the proportion of primary school children walking to school has fallen over the past two decades from a clear majority to a shrinking minority, as traffic has become more intense and walking along roads less safe. Another problem with the trend toward more private motor vehicle use for daily transport needs is the reduction in daily natural exercise that follows. This has been labeled an "obesogenic environment" and is contributing to the global epidemic of obesity and associated disease problems (Kjellstrom et al., 2003).

Road building and the resultant large land area covered in tar-seal constitute yet another form of environmental hazard by greatly increasing the storm water runoff during heavy rains. Storm water drains are needed, which inevitably will be contaminated by road dust and other surface contaminants. Often the storm water drains are connected to the community sewerage system, creating sewage overflow during rains.

Industry and Manufacturing

Industrialization brings many benefits in the form of income and jobs, but, unless regulated in some fashion, can lead to significant occupational and public health hazards. The public hazards may be in the form of releases of toxic or potentially toxic material—as in the notorious cases in postwar Japan (Exhibit 9-6). Some industrial facilities carry the risk of large-scale accidental releases of toxic materials. The biggest such release in world history occurred in Bhopal, India, where an explosion at a pesticide manufacturing plant resulted in some 3,000 deaths caused by the chemical methyl-isocyanate and significant health impairment in many tens of thousands. The impact of this accident at the facility was exacerbated by the lack of urban zoning controls, with hundreds of households having been built directly adjacent to the plant. There was also inadequate planning for alert-

Exhibit 9-5	Automobile Air Pollution in Mexico City: Thinking Things Through

Mexico City has often been cited as having some of the worst urban air pollution conditions in the world, although, from a health perspective, the large Asian coal-burning cities probably create higher risk for their residents. The pollution in Mexico City has been so intense because a large industrializing population lives within a bowl-shaped valley that experiences frequent meteorological conditions that limit circulation of clean air from outside. (Indeed, having nearly 20 million persons living in such an arrangement has been termed a serious "topological error.") The rapidly growing number of automobiles in the city is a major cause not only of the pollution, but also of serious traffic congestion, with consequent negative impacts on economic and social interactions.

In the late 1980s it was proposed to reduce vehicle pollution in the city by imposing the "Day without a car" (*hoy no circula*) program, in which all cars would be prohibited from driving one weekday every week, the day depending on the last digit on each car's license plate. The reasoning was that pollution emissions and congestion would thus be reduced approximately 20% by forcing people to carpool or use public transit more often.

For the first few weeks, data showed that there seemed to be a drop in pollution and congestion. The response of the population over the longer term, however, was different than anticipated. Many thousands of persons purchased second cars with a different license plate number so that they could still drive every day. Of course, once they had a second car, they tended to drive more than they would have with just one. In addition, many of these second cars were older used cars, which tend to have higher emissions levels. Thus, one unintended result of the regulation was to draw older, more polluting cars into Mexico City from other parts of the country.

When proposing new pollution regulations, it is important to consider the full ramifications. This is particularly so when dealing with pollution caused by behavior at the individual level, such as use of private vehicles. Economists and other social scientists need to be involved from the start, and household surveys and pretesting are needed to gauge impacts before full implementation is attempted.

To address this issue, a new scheme was implemented in 1996 by the local authorities. Cars were assigned to three broad categories according to age, pollution control technology, and emission levels:

- 1993 and newer cars, which all have a three-way catalytic converter, can obtain a verification sticker with a number 0 if they emit less than 100 parts per million (ppm) of total hydrocarbons (HC) and less than 1% of carbon monoxide (CO). This sticker means that they have "zero" restrictions and can be driven every day.

- Cars without a three-way catalyst but with an electronic fuel injection system can obtain a sticker number 1 if they emit less than 200 ppm of HC and less than 2% of CO, the city standards. These must comply with the "day without a car" (DWC) constraint.

- If these vehicles exceed the city standard but comply with the more lenient federal standard, they receive a number 2 sticker and must comply with the DWC as well as with additional restrictions during high pollution episodes. Cars without catalysts and without electronic fuel injection systems can only obtain a sticker number 2 if they pass the federal limits.

The differential treatment of cars according to such criteria is probably the best approach. One reason is that it gives the opportunity to combine this measure with other policy instruments. For instance, the triggering point (ambient ozone levels) for the application of the episode alert can be lowered over time without changing stickers. In 2000 a car with a sticker number 1 is prohibited 52 days a year, and a car with a sticker number 2 might be prohibited 60 to 70 times. In the future the number of days of prohibition of the more-polluting 2 cars could be increased considerably by lowering the triggering point, thus putting increasing pressure on people to move to more modem and less-polluting cars.

Such an approach recognizes the now well-demonstrated fact that most car pollution comes from a small fraction of the cars. Pollution regulations that focus on the few heavy polluters can be more effective and less economically and administratively burdensome than those that apply to all cars.

ing and evacuating the public once the accident had occurred.

Waste Management

Few issues in environmental health have generated such attention and controversy as the management of hazardous wastes, whether chemical or radioactive. This has come about through a strong sense of public outrage about numerous publicized cases in which hazardous materials have been dumped indiscriminately or clandestinely, thus leaving expensive and dirty waste sites for others to handle. Both industry and governments have been responsible for creating such sites, which, in industrialized countries, have become very expensive to clean up. Indeed, the USEPA spends 20-25% of its entire

| Exhibit 9-6 | Minamata and Itai-Itai Disease: Classic Environmental Health Disasters |

Environmental health disasters have been important triggers for national and international action to prevent environmental pollution. The best-known such disaster may be Minamata disease, which struck the small coastal town of Minamata, Japan, in 1956 (WHO, 1990). Hundreds of people were seriously affected by methylmercury poisoning, and many victims died. This type of poisoning affects the nervous system, with symptoms ranging from slight numbness of the fingers to loss of the ability to talk and walk. The source of the methylmercury was a chemical production factory that used mercury as a catalyst in one of its processes. Surplus mercury was discharged via spill water into a nearby bay, and this mercury accumulated in bottom sediments. Microbes in the sediments converted the mercury to methylmercury, which eventually entered the food chain of fish and caused very high methylmercury levels in the local fish. Minamata had a substantial population of small family fisheries, and these families were the most affected.

The outbreak of disease developed over several months, and it was initially thought that a new type of infectious disease affecting the nervous system was occurring. It took months of detailed epidemiologic research to conclude that the cause of the disease was associated with the consumption of fish. Further toxicologic and epidemiologic research over many years eventually identified the specific chemical involved. A second outbreak of similar methylmercury poisoning, in Niigata, Japan, intensified the search for a definite cause. In 1968 the Japanese government committee responsible for elucidating the cause finally incriminated methylmercury—12 years after the disease was first reported.

A similar story can be told about Itai-Itai disease, a form of chronic cadmium poisoning that developed in farmers in Toyama, Japan, at about the same time as the first outbreak of Minamata disease (Friberg et al., 1986; WHO, 1992). Painstaking research identified that the consumption of cadmium-contaminated rice and drinking water was the cause. The cadmium, from a mining area and a lead/zinc ore concentration plant, had reached the affected community via a river that they used to irrigate their rice fields. The farming families in the contaminated area had small subsistence farms, providing for all their family needs. Thus, if a family's farm was contaminated, the family members ended up with very high daily cadmium intake. Cadmium is a cumulative poison that eventually damages the kidneys, indirectly leading to bone deformities and fractures because of severe osteomalacia and osteoporosis.

At the time when these two disease outbreaks occurred, Japan was a low-income country trying to recover from the disastrous economic effects of World War II. The living conditions were not dissimilar to those in today's low-income countries undergoing rapid industrialization. Rural populations consumed mainly locally produced food. Health care services were basic, and the environmental pollution situation was not closely monitored or managed. Local industry discharged waste into air, rivers, or sea without much pollution control equipment. A country with similar conditions to erstwhile Japan is China, with lead, zinc, and copper mining; rice farming; and high local food content in the diet. Indeed, cadmium-polluted areas have been found in China (Cai et al., 1995), and environmental epidemiologic studies have discovered exposures and effects similar to the polluted areas of Japan.

budget to clean up chemically contaminated industrial sites, amounting to many tens of billions of dollars over the decades, with additional costs for industry itself. The cost of cleaning up the chemical and radioactive contamination left as remnants of a half-century of cold war nuclear weapons development and manufacture add significantly to this cost.

Perhaps surprisingly, in spite of the large public concern in industrialized nations, as evidenced by the resources devoted to cleanup, the actual health impact of hazardous waste is not significant in most areas. Although there are egregious examples of highly contaminated sites that impose notable risks on local communities, as a societal health issue hazardous waste lies far behind more mundane forms of air and water pollution. One exception, however, is hazardous waste from the military activities (including weapons manufacture) of the former Soviet Union; this waste is at such a scale that it significantly affects the health of tens of thousands of persons today.

There also seem to be cases in China of widespread contamination of aquifers by chromium and other wastes, for example. Even in these countries, however, environmental health risks are dominated by more traditional water and air pollutants and by occupational hazards. In the United States, for example, it has been estimated that the current approach to hazardous waste cleanup costs an average of about $12 billion per cancer case averted, a huge expense when there is so much health improvement that could be achieved at much lower cost (Viscusi et al., 1999).

It is interesting to speculate why hazardous wastes attract so much more attention than the actual health risk warrants. It is partly due to what has been called the outrage factor—that is, the understandable violation felt because of the inexcusably negligent and sometimes criminal behavior of industries and governments in the past. It is also due to a natural human tendency to treat "waste" with a high degree of suspicion. In reality, however, people show relatively little apparent concern for exposure to the same chemicals at much higher levels while using household and agricultural chemicals, vehicle fuel, and other toxic solvents. From the perspective of the human body, there are no differences in the ill effect of, for example, benzene molecules from one source or another. Finally, and more important, by its high attention to waste, society may be expressing a type of concern not well captured by formal health risk analyses, that is, that the incremental health gains and other benefits of the activities that produce the waste are no longer worth the incremental risks, even if those risks are relatively small.

Globally, the less exotic forms of waste generated by household garbage, mine tailings, and vegetation cuttings undoubtedly cause the most pervasive health damage year in and year out. Uncollected garbage breeds disease-carrying pests of many sorts, including rats and flies. Leached toxic materials and floods from unmanaged mine tailing ponds create health hazards as well. The spontaneous and purposeful burning of garbage, coal mine tailings, and vegetation cuttings is a major source of health-damaging air pollution worldwide, although largely controlled in industrialized countries. As discussed in the following section, garbage collection is also a significant source of occupational hazards in low- and middle-income cities.

The related problem of the export of hazardous wastes, from the more to the less industrialized countries, is addressed in "The Export of Hazard," later in this chapter.

Microbiological Contamination of Water and Food

Diarrheal disease from contaminated water and food remains one of the world's great public health problems, as discussed earlier. Although the hazard is in a sense generated at the household level, failure to initiate community controls can lead to large-scale outbreaks.

An important example is cholera, which spread worldwide during the 1990s. The seventh, and largest ever, cholera pandemic is now causing cases throughout Asia, the Middle East, Europe (occasionally), Africa (where the disease has become endemic for the first time), and Latin America, where it spread widely during the 1990s, causing more than 1 million cases and 10,000 deaths. Meanwhile, an apparently new epidemic of cholera was detected in the early 1990s, appearing first in southern India and caused by a new strain (number 0139) of *Vibrio cholerae*. The spread of cholera has been greatly enhanced by the increasing number of slum dwellers in low- and middle-income countries, the speed and distance of modern

tourism, and an apparent increase in extreme weather events, such as the massive EI Niño–associated floods in Kenya in 1997 that caused epidemics of cholera in two regions of the country.

In the villages and slums of low- and middle-income countries, poor household water quality and sanitation often lead to food contamination. The widespread and unregulated commercial street-food sector in cities offers additional opportunities for exposure. Food contamination remains a concern even in industrialized countries where food is supplied to most of the population via long agriculture, processing, and distribution chains.

The reported rates of food poisoning have increased in industrialized countries during the past two decades—and almost doubled in the United Kingdom during the 1990s. The spread of the potentially lethal toxin-producing *Escherichia coli* in North America and Europe in the mid-1990s appears to have accompanied beef imported from infected cattle in Argentina. As long-distance trade expands, as commercial supply lines lengthen in large cities, and as people more frequently opt for convenience or fast foods, the opportunities for food-borne illness increase.

The intensification of meat production is another hot spot for infectious disease problems, as recently evidenced by these three examples: mad cow disease in Britain and its human counterpart (a variant of Creutzfeldt-Jakob disease); the outbreak of a new strain of influenza in chickens in Hong Kong in 1997; and the surprise appearance in 1999 of the newly named (and often fatal) Nipah virus in intensively produced Malaysian pigs and in several hundred human contacts, many of whom died (Weiss & McMichael, 2004).

Chemical Contamination of Water and Food

The sources of chemical contamination are: (1) industrial wastes and emissions and household and agricultural chemicals (Exhibit 9-7); (2) chemicals that form during the storage and handling of food, such as the biotoxin aflatoxin; and (3) natural chemical contaminants.

Several major contamination episodes have occurred in Europe. In 1981 the toxic Spanish oil episode occurred, in which edible vegetable oil was adulterated with industrial oil, causing several hundred deaths and several thousand severe illnesses. In 1985 batches of Austrian and Italian wine were found adulterated with alcohol-containing antifreeze, a toxic compound. In both those episodes, the hazardous substances were added surreptitiously, for commercial

---

Exhibit 9-7   Learning from Bitter Experience: The Banning of Methylmercury Fungicides

The infamous methylmercury poisoning catastrophe in Minamata, Japan, in 1956 highlighted the severe public health problems that could occur after environmental pollution with organic chemicals (WHO, 1990). The same chemical was used in the 1950s and 1960s as a fungicide to prevent fungal growth, which impairs crop-seed viability and causes mold damage in paper pulp. The use in the paper industry caused increased concentrations of mercury in the factories' wastewater and thus methylmercury contamination of fish. In the late 1960s, Swedish ornithologists had identified both this and the use of fungicide-treated seeds as a potential cause of infertility in wild birds. A major environmental pollution debate followed, and eventually these fungicides were banned, not only in Sweden but in most countries with functioning regulatory systems.

In 1971 Iraq received a large consignment of fungicide-treated wheat seeds from USAID. They arrived when much of rural Iraq was suffering from severe drought, and farming families had little food. The seeds for planting had been dyed red to indicate that they should not be eaten, but the farmers soon found out that washing the seeds in water eliminated the dye. Unfortunately, the fungicide stayed in the seeds. The farmers then used the seeds to make bread, and about 2 months later a major epidemic of serious neurologic diseases began. Eventually 500 people died and about 5,000 were hospitalized.

This was the largest known epidemic of this type. Previously some smaller outbreaks had occurred in Africa from the same seed fungicide. After the disastrous Iraq epidemic a new level of awareness arose about such problems, and the use of this fungicide was subsequently banned in most countries. This is an example of successful chemical safety management, based on the scare caused by a major epidemic of toxicity.

---

gain, by persons ignorant of (or indifferent to) the potential risks to public health. In 1999 in Belgium, dioxin-contaminated fats entered the animal feed manufacturing process, leading to the contamination of pigs, poultry, and dairy cattle on 1,500 Belgian farms and to thousands of tons of contaminated food products. The potential for the rapid globalization of such environmental problems in the modern free-trading world became quickly apparent (McMichael, 1999): Countries in the Middle East, the Americas, and Southeast and eastern Asia quickly declared a ban on Belgian food imports.

Similar problems can affect the quality of drinking water. The widespread problem with arsenic in local drinking water supplies in various communities around the world, particularly in Bangladesh and West Bengal, India, is illustrative (Exhibit 9-8).

Urbanization

A spectacular shift of human populations into the world's cities is occurring. The urbanized proportion of the world's population has grown from around 5% to 50% in the past two centuries and is still rising. This urban migration reflects, variously, the advent of industrialization, the contraction of rural employment, the flight from food insecurity and other forms of insecurity, and the search for jobs, amenities, or a stimulating environment.

The urban "environment" confers various benefits upon human health and well-being. There is better access to education and health, financial, and social services. The urban "environment" is rich with new opportunities. Yet big cities are often impersonal and sometimes menacing. Noise, traffic congestion, and residential crowding are stress-inducing. The air quality is poor in many cities around the world.

The mortality impact of heat waves is typically greatest in urban centers, where temperatures tend to be higher than in the leafier suburbs and the surrounding countryside, and the relief of night-time cooling is lessened. This "heat island" effect is due to the large heat-retaining structures and treeless asphalt expanses of inner cities and the physical obstruction of cooling breezes. Each population has a middle temperature range to which it is well adapted physiologically, behaviorally, and technically. As temperatures become colder, daily death rates gradually increase. As temperatures rise above that middle comfort zone, daily deaths increase—and they often do so rather abruptly once a threshold temperature is exceeded. This threshold is much more evident in some populations than in others. In China there is a clear threshold at 34°C (93°F) in Shanghai, but no evident threshold in warmer and more humid Guangzhou. Little is known about the health impacts of extremes of heat and cold in low- and middle-income urban populations.

Urban populations play a dominant role in the mounting pressures that today jeopardize the sustainability of current human ecology. Cities have increasingly large "ecologic footprints" (Rees, 1996). There are undoubted ecological benefits of urbanism, including economies of scale, shared use of resources, and opportunities for reuse and recycling. Equally, though, urban populations depend on the natural resources of ecosystems that, in aggregate, are vastly

Exhibit 9-8	Arsenic in Groundwater

The concentration of various elements, such as fluorine and arsenic, varies naturally in groundwater supplies around the world. In countries such as Taiwan and Argentina, the high levels of arsenic in the drinking water have been recognized as a health hazard since the mid-1900s, causing keratoses, hyperpigmentation, and skin cancer. High levels also exist in Chile, inner Mongolia, parts of the United States, Hungary, Thailand, and China. More recently the exposure has assumed epic proportions in Bangladesh and neighboring West Bengal, India, where several million persons in recent decades have been drinking arsenic-contaminated water obtained via tubewells, and where the number already manifesting toxic effects, especially skin lesions, is probably in the hundreds of thousands (Khan et al., 1997).

The prolonged consumption of arsenic causes a succession of toxic effects, typically appearing 5 to 10 years after first exposure. There is some evidence that these are greatest in low-income rural villagers with malnutrition, but this may be co-incidental rather than causal. Early manifestations include keratosis and skin pigmentation, followed by dysfunction of kidneys and liver, and, perhaps, peripheral neuropathy. With continued exposure, the arsenicosis progresses to liver failure and may cause gangrene and cancer. It is well established that arsenic in drinking water increases severalfold the incidence of cancers of the bladder, skin, lung, and kidney (Smith et al., 1998); indeed, arsenic appears to be the most widespread cancer hazard in drinking water in the world. In Chile, for example, 5% to 10% of all deaths over age 30 have been attributed to arsenic-induced cancers (Smith et al., 1998). A cross-sectional study in Bangladesh has compared the prevalence of diabetes mellitus in persons living in areas with high water arsenic levels and areas without arsenic contamination of drinking water (Rahman et al., 1998). Diabetes prevalence was clearly higher in the exposed population. However, there were no historical time-trend data on water arsenic concentration for either population.

West Bengal shares with Bangladesh a subterranean geologic continuity with arsenic-rich sediments. Much of the drinking water comes from the several hundred thousand tubewells sunk over the past two decades to provide villagers with safe drinking water, thus avoiding the hazard of fecally contaminated surface water. The problem was first identified in Bangladesh in 1993. It is thought that the aeration of the deep sediment by the many bore holes leads to oxidation of the natural arsenopyrite and mobilization of arsenic into water. Many of the tubewells yield water with arsenic concentrations 10 to 50 times higher than the WHO guideline (0.01 mg/L). In the village of Samta (population 4,800), in the Jessore district on the Bangladesh and West Bengal boundary, approximately 90% of the 265 tubewells had arsenic concentrations above 0.05 mg/L, and 10% exceeded 0.5 mg/L (Biswas et al., 1998).

Mitigation of the problem can be complex and costly. Various chemical treatments of the water remove arsenic by absorption onto activated salts and elements, reverse osmosis, ion exchange, or oxidation. Cheaper physical methods involve sand filtration and clarification. The simplest physical solution, where possible, is to drill the tubewells deeper, in conjunction with rapid field testing able to identify contamination above 0.05 mg/L. This is being done in parts of Bangladesh and West Bengal. Meanwhile, tubewells with very high contamination should be identified and, as soon as an acceptable alternative is found, closed. The practical solution includes restricting the use of arsenic-contaminated water to washing only and to avoid using it for cooking or drinking.

---

larger in area than the city itself. The highly urbanized Netherlands consumes resources from a total surface area approximately 20 times larger than itself. The estimated consumption of resources—wood, paper, fibers, and food (including seafood)—by 29 cities of the Baltic Sea region, and the absorption of their wastes, depends on a total area 200 times greater than the combined area of the 29 cities (Folke, Larsson, & Sweitzer, 1996). The scale of these externalities of urbanism is growing, and includes massive contributions to global greenhouse gas accumulation, stratospheric ozone depletion, land degradation, and coastal zone destruction. The urbanized developed world, with one-fifth of the world population, currently contributes three-quarters of all greenhouse gas emissions (Intergovernmental Panel on Climate Change, 2001).

Regional Exposures: Transboundary Problems

As the scale of human economic activity has increased, environmental problems have increasingly spilled over beyond local community boundaries. Regional watersheds become contaminated from multiple sources; radioactive wastes and emissions spread regionally; land-use practices affect infectious disease patterns; and the industrial emissions of sulfur and nitrogen oxides acidify the regional atmosphere. Via these larger-scale pathways, environmental changes can adversely affect human health.

Atmospheric Dispersion of Contaminants

Following the surge of industrial growth in developed countries in the third quarter of the 20th century, the transboundary problem of acid deposition (commonly referred to as *acid rain*) became increasingly problematic. It featured prominently at the 1972 UN Conference on the Human Environment in Stockholm. By that time, eastern Canada was experiencing problems from acidic emissions traveling northeast from the United States, and Scandinavia was exposed to emissions from the United Kingdom and highly industrialized areas of West and East Germany. More recently, the strong increase in China's industrial production has subjected Japan to acid deposition from that source. Acid levels are rising in other parts of Asia as energy use grows.

The hazards to human health are neither extreme nor direct. However, the acidification of waterways and soils has demonstrably increased the mobilization of various elements—particularly heavy metals and aluminum—enabling them to enter the drinking water and the food chain. Human exposures to these elements have thus increased in several regions.

Another type of regional air pollution was the release of radionuclides from the Chernobyl nuclear power plant in the 1986 disaster (WHO, 1996). Much of this radioactive material was deposited within a 125-mile radius of the plant, but significant radionuclide contamination also resulted from dispersal by winds to areas several thousand miles away. About 4 million persons in the most contaminated adjoining areas were significantly exposed, via the food chain, or were otherwise affected by restrictions on the use of their land for farming. A great increase in the incidence of child thyroid cancer was found in the most polluted areas during the decade after the disaster. Further afield, such as in northern Finland, Sweden, and Norway, health protection measures had major economic impacts. Reindeer farming is the major economic enterprise in these areas, and thousands of reindeer had to be slaughtered and discarded because of high radiation levels in their meat.

The impact of regional climatic variations on human well-being and health has created great recent research interest. There is new understanding about the regional pattern of storms, floods, cyclones, and droughts in response to these quasi-periodic cycles. Indeed, advance warning of interannual variations in rainfall and drought conditions (with their implications for regional food production and outbreaks of certain infectious diseases) is now becoming possible. An interesting example of a regional impact occurred in the United States, where the El Niño event of the early 1990s was associated, initially, with drought conditions in the Southwest (in the "four corners" region where Arizona, Colorado, Utah, and New Mexico meet). This led to a drop in vegetation and in animal populations, including the natural predators of the deer mouse. When heavy rains occurred in 1993, with resultant profuse growth of piñon nuts, there was an uncontrolled proliferation in the deer mouse population. These rodents harbor a virus, transmissible to humans via dried excreta, that causes hantavirus pulmonary disease—first described at that time (Duchin et al., 1994). This disease has subsequently spread to many contiguous states and to western Canada and much of South America.

The El Niño event of 1997–1998 created unusually strong drought conditions in Southeast Asia, which exacerbated the size and duration of forest fires originally lit to clear land. The result, in addition to extensive damage to the forests, was regional air pollution in the form of wood smoke plumes that extended over thousands of miles and could easily be seen by satellites. The forest fires actually raised outdoor particulate levels to several times the acceptable upper limit in a number of large cities in the region for a period of days to weeks, apparently with significant accompanying adverse health effects. Although larger than in previous years, the same phenomenon has been occurring for decades in the region, and is likely to be repeated often unless land-use practices are modified.

Land Use and Water Engineering

Regional tensions over freshwater supplies are increasing in many locations as population pressures increase and an increasing proportion of agricultural production comes to depend on irrigation (Gleick, 1998). Water is essential for domestic hygiene, communal sanitation, and economic vitality. The problems in the West Bengal region, where freshwater availability is declining as the hydrologic cycle is perturbed by human interventions and where surface water is widely fecally contaminated, are described in Exhibit 9-8.

During the third quarter of the 20th century it became clear that large-scale human interventions in the natural environment—dams, irrigation schemes, land reclamation, road construction, and population resettlement program—often affected infectious disease patterns. In particular, the composition of vector species generally changes following alterations in environmental conditions. Such large-scale developments in the eastern Mediterranean, Africa, South America, and Asia have been consistently associated with increases in vector-borne diseases, especially schistosomiasis and filariasis. In the Sudan in the 1970s, for example, schistosomiasis appeared soon after the start of the Gezira scheme, a large irrigated cotton project; the prevalence of malaria also increased markedly in this region (Fenwick, Cheesmond, & Amin, 1981; Gruenbaum, 1983). In Africa the building of large dams in the Sudan, Egypt (the Aswan High Dam), Ghana, and Senegal caused the prevalence of schistosomiasis in the surrounding populace to increase from very low levels to more than 90% (WHO, 1997).

An example of a disastrous land-use decision, with major regional environmental health consequences, is the fate of the Aral Sea in Central Asia. This inland sea is dependent on the inflow of water from two major rivers. Until about 1960 the sea level was constant, and large populations in the countries surrounding the Aral Sea sustained their economies through fishing and agriculture. In the 1950s large-scale cotton farming was developed along the two major rivers based on irrigation water diverted from those rivers. This farming used large amounts of pesticides, which contaminated the water and the soil. Signs of environmental damage began emerging in the 1960s. The level of the Aral Sea sank, the irrigated farm soils became salinated, and soil erosion by wind became an increasing problem. Since then the Aral Sea has continued to shrink, the fishing industry has collapsed, and agriculture has been increasingly impaired. Adverse health impacts in the regional population of 30 million persons have been reported—although not yet satisfactorily confirmed—apparently in association with direct toxic pesticide exposures and with the socioeconomic decline caused by the environmental disaster.

Deforestation has had variable effects on malaria mosquito vectors. In some parts of Southeast Asia, deforestation has enabled malaria-transmitting *Anopheles punctulatus* species to become established. In contrast, several *Anopheles* species, including *Anopheles dirus* in Thailand and *Anopheles darlingi* in South America, have disappeared following deforestation that removed the flora and fauna upon which they depended for feeding. Forest clearance in South America during recent decades to extend agricultural land has mobilized various viral hemorrhagic fevers that previously circulated quietly in wild animal hosts. For example, the Junin virus, which causes Argentine hemorrhagic fever, naturally infects wild rodents. However, extensive conversion of grassland to maize cultivation in recent decades stimulated a proliferation of the reservoir rodent species, thus exposing human farmworkers to this "new" virus. In the past 35 years, the land area carrying this new human disease has expanded sevenfold, now causing several hundred

infected cases annually on average, up to one-third of whom die (WHO, 1997).

Because changes in land-use patterns are typically accompanied by changes in population density, population mobility, pesticide usage, and regional climate, it is difficult to assign specific causal explanations. Indeed, many of the health outcomes result from interactions between these various change processes.

Global Environmental Change and Population Health

A major consequence of the increasing scale of the human enterprise is the potentially important health impact of global environmental changes. Humankind is now disrupting some of the biosphere's life-support systems—the natural processes of stabilization, production, cleansing, and recycling that our predecessors were able to take for granted in a less human-dominated world (Daily, 1997; McMichael, 1993). We no longer live in such a world. The composition of both the lower and middle atmospheres is changing. There is a net loss of productive soils on all continents, most ocean fisheries have been overfished, aquifers on which irrigated agriculture depends have been depleted, and whole species and many local populations are being extinguished unprecedentedly fast. These large-scale environmental changes pose long-term, and unfamiliar, risks to human population health.

Climate Change

The United Nations' Intergovernmental Panel on Climate Change (IPCC) stated that "the balance of evidence suggests a discernible human influence on global climate" (2001). Further, trends in greenhouse gas emissions will, in, the IPCC's estimation, cause an increase in average world temperature of approximately 1 to 3°C over the coming century. Rainfall patterns will also change, and so too, probably, will the variability of weather patterns. All these changes would vary considerably by region (Exhibit 9-9). The health effects of climate change would encompass direct and indirect, and immediate and delayed effects (McMichael et al., 2003). Although some health outcomes in some populations would be beneficial—some tropical regions may become too hot for mosquitoes, for example, and winter cold snaps would become milder in temperate-zone countries where death rates typically peak in wintertime—most of the anticipated health effects would be adverse (IPCC, 2001; McMichael et al., 2003).

Exhibit 9-9	Modeling the Future Impacts of Climate Change on Malaria Transmissibility

Mosquitoes, the vector organisms for malaria, are very sensitive to temperature and humidity. Further, patterns of rainfall, river flow, and surface water affect their opportunity to breed. Scientists therefore anticipate that a change in world climatic conditions during the 21st century will affect the pattern of potential transmission of malaria. Temperature and humidity affect the growth, biting rate, reproductive cycle, and longevity of the mosquito. Mosquitoes are most comfortable in the temperature range from 20 to 30°C and at around 60% humidity. The malarial parasite, a single-celled sexually reproducing plasmodium, is also affected by temperature during the extrinsic phase of its complex life cycle when forming sporozoites within the mosquito. The two major species of plasmodia have minimum temperature requirements: For *Plasmodium vivax* a minimum of 16°C is required, whereas for the potentially fatal *Plasmodium falciparum* a temperature of approximately 18°C is required. Within the above-mentioned comfort range, the higher the temperature the more rapid the incubation—and hence the sooner the opportunity for transmission to another mosquito-bitten human.

From studies done during the 1980s and 1990s it is clear that malaria outbreaks are closely related to inter-annual climatic variations in many countries. In Venezuela, for example, the incidence of malaria consistently surged upward throughout the 20th century in the year following an El Niño event. This is most probably due to the combination of above-average rainfall in the post-Niño year and the drop in acquired immunity in the population because of the low malaria incidence during the dry El Niño year. Studies in India, Pakistan, and Sri Lanka all display similarly strong associations with El Niño events and the associated monsoonal changes. A correspondingly strong correlation with interannual variations in temperature and rainfall has been reported for outbreaks of dengue fever (a mosquito-borne infectious disease) in Pacific island populations (Hales et al., 1999).

The science of forecasting climatic fluctuations 3 to 6 months in advance is steadily improving. Indeed, there is considerable economic incentive to improve the forecasting of El Niño and La Nina events, as these have global repercussions on regional agricultural yields. With sufficient advance warning, farmers can switch to more appropriate crops. The equivalent approach will soon be possible for the forecasting of malaria outbreaks, enabling public health interventions (e.g., activated population-based surveillance, surface water control, insecticide-impregnated bed nets, and antimalarial prophylaxis).

Longer-term global and local forecasting are being facilitated as information accrues about the way malaria has responded to the generalized warming that has occurred since the 1970s. Forecasts on this decadal scale are relevant for inclusion in the estimation of aggregate burden of adverse health impacts that could accrue if climate change were to occur as predicted. Mathematical models are required for this type of long-range forecasting of changes in the potential transmission of malaria. Such a model integrates, for units of time (typically months) and units of surface area (e.g., 100 square kilometers), the estimated future climatic conditions (as a function of continuing excess emissions of greenhouse gases) and characteristics of the mosquito and parasite "system" and of the human population (size, age distribution, prior immunity).

Because other determinants of malaria occurrence will also inevitably change over coming decades (e.g., vaccine efficacy, human demography, land-use patterns, or parasite resistance to drugs), the modeling of climate change impacts typically only indicates changes in potential transmission (see Figure 9-10). Nevertheless this is an important consideration in the formulation of long-term priorities and policies. In the future, more comprehensive modeling will be able to take these other covariables into account.

Direct health effects would include changes in mortality and morbidity from an altered pattern of exposure to thermal extremes; the respiratory health consequences of increased exposures to photochemical pollutants and aeroallergens; and the physical hazards of the increased occurrence of storms, floods, or droughts, in at least some regions. Intensified rainfall, with flooding, can overwhelm urban wastewater and sewer systems, leading to contamination of drinking water supplies. This is most likely in large crowded cities where infrastructure is old or inadequate, as illustrated by an outbreak of typhoid in Tajikistan in 1994 when the city wastewater system flooded during unusual torrential rains.

Indirect health effects are likely to have a greater aggregate impact over time. They would include alterations in the range and activity of vector-borne infectious diseases (e.g., malaria, dengue fever, and leishmaniasis). These diseases are spread by vectors (e.g., mosquitoes) that are very sensitive to climatic conditions (Figure 9-10), as is the parasite's development while incubating in the vector. Scenario-based mathematical modeling has suggested that the geographic zone and seasonality of potential transmission of malaria or dengue fever will increase in many parts of the world (IPCC, 2001; McMichael et al., 2003). In temperate Europe and North America, climate-sensitive, vector-borne infections include tick-borne encephalitis and Lyme disease. Other indirect effects would include altered transmission of person-to-person infections (especially summertime food- and waterborne pathogens). Of great potential impor-

Change in Seasonality

- ▇ 3 to 5 months
- ▇ 1 to 2 months
- ▇ −2 to −1 months
- ▢ −5 to −3 months

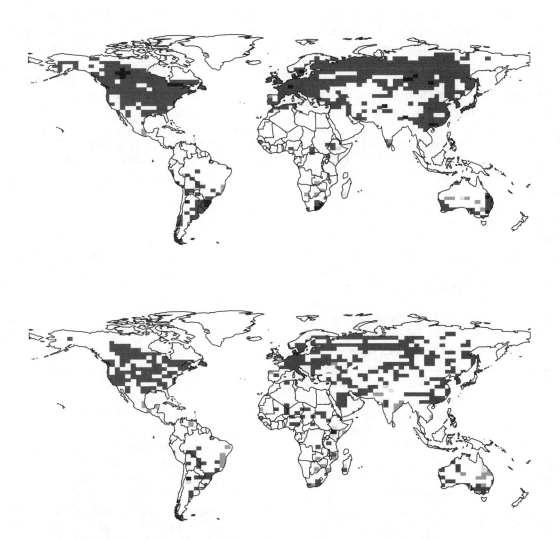

Figure 9-10 Future Changes in Seasonality of Potential Transmission of Malaria, 2080s versus Present. (A) Change in number of transmissions per year under a future scenario of unconstrained emissions of carbon dioxide. (B) Change in number of months of potential transmission per year, under a future scenario of constrained emissions of carbon dioxide (such that atmospheric concentration stabilizes at 550 parts per million). *Source:* P. Martens et al., "Climate Change and Future Populations at Risk of Malaria," 1999, *Global Environmental Change, 9,* pp. S89–S107. Adapted with permission of Elsevier Science.

tance to population health would be the adverse nutritional consequences of the likely regional declines in agricultural productivity, estimated at around 10% to 20% by the latter half of the 21st century in many already food-insecure populations in low-latitude regions. Finally, there would be inevitable adverse physical and psychological health consequences resulting from population displacement and economic disruption due to rising sea levels (e.g., small island states, coastal Bangladesh, and the Nile Delta), agroecosystem decline, and freshwater shortages.

Stratospheric Ozone Depletion

Stratospheric ozone depletion is essentially a separate phenomenon from greenhouse gas accumulation in the troposphere. Ozone depletion is causing an increase in ultraviolet irradiation at Earth's surface. This increase in ultraviolet exposure is expected to peak sometime within the next two decades and then decline slowly over several decades, in response to the phasing out of the major ozone-destroying industrial and agricultural chemicals. For the first half of this century, increases are expected in the severity of sunburn and in the incidence of skin cancers in fair-skinned populations and of various disorders of the eye (especially cataracts). Some UVR-induced suppression of immune functioning may also result, thus increasing susceptibility to infectious diseases and perhaps reducing vaccination efficacy (United Nations Environment Program, 1998; WHO, 1994).

Persistence of the ozone losses of the 1979–1992 period for several decades would cause the annual incidence of basal cell carcinoma (the dominant skin cancer type) to increase by an estimated 1% to 2% at low latitude (5°), 14% at 55° to 65° in the northern hemisphere (e.g., the United Kingdom), and 25% at that latitude in the south (Madronich & de Gruijl, 1993). The estimated percentage increases in incidence of squamous cell carcinoma would be twice as great. More sophisticated mathematical modeling indicates that nonmelanoma skin cancer rates would rise to a peak excess incidence of approximately 10% in the United States and Europe around the middle of the 21st century (Slaper et al., 1996).

A potentially more important, although much more indirect, health detriment could arise from ultraviolet-induced impairment of photosynthesis on land (terrestrial plants) and at sea (phytoplankton). Although such an effect could reduce the world's food production, few quantitative data are yet available.

Biodiversity: Losses and Invasions

Through humankind's spectacular reproductive and technological success, the natural habitats of many other species have been occupied, damaged, or eliminated. Biologists estimated that this fastest mass extinction might cause around one-third of all species alive in the 1800s to be gone before the end of the 21st century (Pimm et al., 1995). "A more recent analysis agrees with this rate of extinctions (UNEP, 2004) and states that a major reason for current extinctions is habitat loss due to human activities." The loss of var-

ious key species would weaken whole ecosystems, with consequences that would often be adverse to human interests, such as disturbing the ecology of vector-borne infections and food-producing systems that depend on pollinators and the predation of pests, and impairing the cleansing of water and the circulation of nutrients that normally pass through ecosystems. A rich repertoire of genetic and phenotypic material would also be lost. To maintain the hybrid vigor and environmental resilience of food species, a diversity of wild species needs to be preserved as a source of genetic additives. Similarly, a high proportion of modern medicinal drugs in Western medicine has natural origins, and many defy synthesis in the laboratory. Scientists test thousands of novel natural chemicals each year, seeking new drugs to treat HIV, malaria, drug-resistant tuberculosis, and cancers.

The other side of this coin is the accelerating spread of invasive species, as long-distance trade, tourism, and migration increase in intensity. Several examples with public health consequences are given in the section "Environmental Hazards Resulting from Forms of Globalization," later in this chapter. There are many others. For example, the vast proliferation of water hyacinth (a decorative plant from Brazil) in Lake Victoria, eastern Africa, has extended the breeding grounds for the water snail that transmits schistosomiasis. The planting of *Lantana camerata* as a garden border shrub in Uganda, and its subsequent dispersed spread, has increased the habitat for the tsetse fly that transmits the trypanosome that causes African sleeping sickness.

Land Degradation, Food, and Malnutrition

The increase in land degradation has implications for food supplies and therefore for nutrition, child development, and health. During the 1980s the combination of erosion, desiccation, and nutrient exhaustion, plus irrigation-induced water-logging and salinization, rendered unproductive one-fifteenth of the world's 1.5 billion hectares of readily arable farmland (World Resources Institute, 1998). The Green Revolution, which fed much of the expanding human population during the 1960s to the 1980s, depended on laboratory-bred, high-yield cereal grains, fertilizers, groundwater, and arable soils. In retrospect, those productivity gains appear to have come substantially from using up exhaustible ecological capital—especially topsoil and groundwater. As greater food yields to feed ever-more people are pursued, almost one-tenth of the world's population is malnourished in ways that impair health. Meanwhile, at sea, many of the world's great fisheries are now on the brink of being overexploited. The Food and Agriculture Organization (FAO) of the

United Nations estimates that the sustainable fish-catch limit has been neared—around 100 million tonnes per year (FAO, 2002).

Persistent Organic Pollutants

Various chemical pollutants, particularly the many chlorinated organic chemicals such as the polychlorinated biphenyls (PCBs), are persistent and have become globally pervasive. They are referred to as persistent organic pollutants (Watson, Dixon, & Hamburg, 1998). The semivolatile members of this class of chemicals undergo a type of serial distillation process in the atmosphere as they pass from low to high latitudes, ultimately impinging at higher concentrations in the circumpolar regions. Some of these chemicals are likely to affect neurologic, immune, and reproductive systems in humans, who feed at the top of the increasingly contaminated food chain. Weakening of ecosystems may also occur, with various additive environmental health effects in human populations (Colborn, Vom Saal, & Soto, 1993).

Pathways to the Future in an Unequal World

Sometimes low- and middle-income countries are criticized for not imposing stricter environmental and occupational standards. Too often, there are indeed situations where minimal efforts could achieve great reductions in health risks. In addition, given the likely increase in public willingness to pay for stricter standards as development continues, the early imposition of reasonable standards can often be quite cost-effective using standard economic criteria. On the other hand, most large low- and middle-income countries today have standards that are much stricter than those in the industrialized countries at the corresponding level of development. Indeed, although there are cases of the export of environmental hazard and the degradation of local environments by exploitative and destructive commercial practice (see "The Export of Hazard," later in this chapter), the overall impact of globalization may be a net export of environmental health. That is, through education, political and public pressures, technology transfer, trade agreements, and other initiatives, low- and middle-income countries have, on average, better environmental quality than would otherwise be the case.

Setting Standards: Too Safe Can Be Unsafe

Setting and enforcing environmental standards for protection of the public and workers is a difficult exercise, even in industrialized countries with substantial resources. In low- and middle-income countries, which face a number of critical needs with few resources, the process is even more troublesome. Although official rhetoric about setting standards often states that the only concern is protection of health, in reality there are always economic and other trade-offs involved. It is too expensive and there are too many other demands on resources to bring every pollutant under the maximum control quickly. Politically, however, it is often difficult for governments in low- and middle-income nations to set standards that are significantly less stringent than those in industrialized countries. As a result, sometimes standards are unrealistically strict and cannot be met. This leads to graft, cynicism, apathy, and, too often, to exposures and ill health above what could be achieved by more realistic approaches.

One way out of this dilemma is to emphasize environmental health protection and standard setting as dynamic and evolutionary processes rather than static one-time-forever efforts. In this way a country might set 20-year goals for its standards that are as strict as any in the world, while establishing interim objectives that become progressively more strict. Thus, pollutants and industries that pose the most risk can be emphasized first, while control over other pollutants and industries (of the kind that now attract attention in industrialized countries) can be postponed to a later period. No hazard is ignored, but merely put into a rational order of priority. Industrial interests are likely to be more willing to accept stricter standards under such a scheme because they tend to have shorter-term financial goals, facilitated by clarity of the regulatory environment, whereas they are unsettled by longer-term uncertainty. A recurring problem, however, is attaining sufficient stability within governments to implement such a long-term approach.

The Export of Hazard

In recent years there has been concern about the potential export of environmental hazard that may be occurring as part of the globalization of the world economy (LaDou, 1992). Since environmental and occupational standards and enforcement tend to be less strict in low- and middle-income countries, polluting activities may tend to migrate to those countries, thereby imposing excess risk on workers and public. Studies of international industrial trends, however, have identified few cases where differences in environmental and occupational standards have been the critical determinants of such shifts, compared with labor costs, tax regimes, and other business factors. Indeed, locally owned industries tend to have higher emissions and occupational hazards than do facilities owned by multinational corporations, which often feel considerable pressure to maintain higher standards. Besides, the mere fact of a difference in standards does not necessarily mean that an injustice exists. As noted earlier, nations at different stages of development may quite rationally choose different trade-offs between standards, job creation, and infrastructure development. The most outrageous examples of injustice arise where decisions about such trade-offs are made by a small oligarchy without considering the needs and wishes of the population as a whole. In these cases, perhaps the only way to protect the interests of those in the low- and middle-income countries would be to establish international norms.

Flagrant examples of the problems created by the exporting of hazard exist along borders between industrialized and low- and middle-income countries. On the Mexican side of the long U.S.-Mexican border, for example, there are many highly polluting industries with poor occupational safety and health conditions relative to standards on the U.S. side of the border. Because of the proximity, both the pollution and health problems tend to cross the border, frustrating attempts by U.S. border communities to maintain acceptable conditions. Attempts to impose U.S. standards on Mexican facilities, however, understandably create friction. There have been some encouraging successes in joint efforts by neighboring Mexican-U.S. communities to address these issues jointly in a way that takes into account the need for jobs and for clean working and living conditions on both sides.

The political and moral dilemmas are manifest. Today's industrialized world followed a path to development and wealth that put economic gains ahead of human welfare and environmental conservation for most of the 19th century. Today's low- and middle-income countries are dissuaded, if not formally barred, from following the equivalent pathway because (1) their populations have access to more information and hence have higher expectations; (2) the industrialized world has a moral obligation to assist via the transfer of knowledge, wealth, and technology; (3) it is now clear that the integrity of the biosphere at large is jeopardized by the prospect of huge populations in these countries accruing wealth via environmentally damaging behaviors; and (4) there is pressure from public opinion in industrialized countries to achieve higher standards.

Environmental Hazards Resulting from Forms of Globalization

A dominant trend in the global economic "environment" over the past 50 years has been the rapid growth in international trade in goods, services, and human resources. The globalizing processes of the past quarter century have transformed patterns of connectedness around the world and have created new power relations among countries, international and national governance, and the public and private sectors (see Chapter 15).

In traditional agrarian-based societies that produce, consume, and trade on a local basis and with relatively low-impact technologies, the impacts on the "environment" are predominantly local. Few such societies remain today, in the face of strong and pervasive economic, technologic, and cultural influences. The industrialization of the past century and the more recent globalizing processes have altered the scale of contact between societies, intensified environmental impacts, and extended the public health impacts of one society on another. In the name of economic development and free markets, low- and middle-income countries have come under pressure to grant unrestricted access to their resources, work forces, and consumer markets. This process has been associated with increasing poverty in many parts of the world, widening inequalities between and within countries, expanding pressures to reduce the power of the state, and subordinating national programs of social welfare and environmental protection to the agenda of economic growth.

Following the international debt crisis of the early 1980s, many struggling low- and middle-income countries were obliged to accept the economic stringencies of the World Bank's structural adjustment program. This entailed a reduction in spending on health throughout the 1980s and into the 1990s. There is evidence that these policies adversely affected the public health capacity of those countries, with some serious health implications (Hoogvelt, 1997). This included, in many countries, a diminished capacity to respond to the resurgence of TB, maintain environmental controls on vector-borne infectious diseases, and provide basic primary family health care. In its current form, the world's globalizing economy operates to the general disadvantage of low- and middle-income countries. The exacerbation of land degradation, rural unemployment, food shortages, and urban crowding all contribute to health deficits for the rural dispossessed, the underfed, and the slum dweller.

Many features of today's globalizing world contribute to the spread of infectious diseases (Weiss and McMichael, 2004; Wilson, 1995). Human mobility has escalated dramatically, in volume and speed, between and within countries. Long-distance trade facilitates the geographic redistribution of pests and pathogens—well illustrated in recent years by the HIV pandemic, the worldwide dispersal of rat-borne hantaviruses, and the rapid dissemination of a new epidemic strain of bacterial meningitis along routes of travel and trade. Likewise, there has been shipborne introduction of the Asian tiger mosquito, *Aedes albopictus*—a vector for yellow fever and dengue—into South America, North America, and Africa (Morse, 1995) and of the cholera bacterium into South American coastal waters (Colwell, 1996). In an analysis of cholera outbreaks since 1817, Lee and Dodgson (2000) argue that the current, seventh, pandemic is clearly different from earlier ones, reflecting the unprecedented scale of social and environmental change in the world over recent years, the exacerbation of urban poverty, and the rapidity and intensity of intercontinental contacts.

An aspect of globalization that may have negative effects on "environment" and health is the harmonization of trade-related rules and legislation via the World Trade Organization (WTO). Particular attention has been paid to nontariff trade barriers, which comprise any national regulation or legislation that hinders trade and is not a financial levy on the trade itself. For instance, if country A legislates that the maximum level of mercury in fish sold in that country should be 0.5 mg/kg, another country B cannot sell fish with a higher mercury level to country A. If in country B, fish with levels up to 1 mg/kg can be freely sold, then country B can claim that the fish-mercury regulation of country A is a nontariff trade barrier. However, country A may have made a health risk assessment based on the local fish consumption patterns and decided that 0.5 mg/kg is the maximum acceptable. How should this be resolved? Current WTO practice means that only internationally agreed health guidelines can be implemented in this situation, and, if no such guidelines exist, country A is not allowed to have a stricter environmental health rule than country B unless country A can convince the WTO disputes committee that the trade restrictioin is implemented for good reasons.

Similar situations develop with the banning of hazardous products such as asbestos. If, for example, there is no international health guideline banning the use of asbestos, then any country taking a unilateral decision to ban asbestos use would risk trade sanctions from other countries wanting to export asbestos. If the trend in international environmental and occupational health guidelines went toward stricter prevention, this harmonization via trade rules could be good for health and the "environment". However, the intense lobbying from commercial groups and countries that would benefit from lax rules makes it likely that the opposite will happen. Compromises toward less protection will be made (LaDou, 1992).

Population Health: Index of Social and Environmental Sustainability

Current models of government reflect the compartmentalization of knowledge and policy that grew out of the classic development of scientific disciplines in the 19th century. In order to deal with a multifaceted world, our predecessors defined sectors of knowledge, policy, and social action: environment, industry, agriculture, transport, health, social welfare, and education. Subsequently, however, one of the great lessons to emerge from 20th-century science, with its origins in the realm of physics (the 1920s debate about quantum mechanics and uncertainty), is that the complexities of the real world require us to think in more integrative ways, across disciplines and topics, elevating holism (or ecological thinking) above mechanistic, reductionist thinking.

It is within that type of integrative framework that population health can be understood as part of the total social experience, a manifestation of how well the social and natural environments are being managed. Population health should therefore be a primary criterion for all social policy making, particularly in relation to achieving the "sustainability transition." Health is therefore not just a type of sideshow in the policy arena. Rather, it is affected by the social, environmental, and (in the longer term) the ecological consequences of policies in all sectors. Population health should therefore be an integrating index of social policy across all sectors.

Conclusion

The perceived importance of environmental exposures as health hazards—at local, regional, and global levels—has increased steadily over the past several decades. Currently, scientists estimate that from one-quarter to one-third of the global burden of disease and premature death is attributable to ambient (including domestic) environmental risk factors.

In the developed world during much of the past four decades, the generally greater ease of measurement of specific exposures relating to individual lifestyle (eating, smoking, and sexual behaviors) and the workplace, compared with the more diffuse lower-concentration exposures in the external environment, resulted in the latter topic area attracting less attention and having lower credibility. More recently, improvements in exposure assessment, the harnessing of time-series analyses, the advent of spatial analytic techniques, the recognized legitimacy of population-level analyses, and the extra leverage afforded by molecular biological indices of exposure, susceptibility, and biological damage have all helped reveal the range and extent of ambient environmental risks to health.

Meanwhile, in developing countries, the age-old scourges of diarrheal disease, acute respiratory infections, TB, and vector-borne infections have remained the dominant health problems. The ascendancy of specific health system interventions for those problems—sanitation, domestic hygiene, vaccination, pesticides, and drug treatment—has led to their wider ecological dimensions being somewhat overlooked. Many problems of environmental contamination have their origins in poverty; deficient regulation of mining, industry, and agriculture; and mismanagement of surface and ground water supplies. Domestic exposure to indoor air pollution reflects division of labor (women are mostly exposed), low-grade technology, and the biomass fuels of poverty. Infectious diseases are often spread by environmental encroachments—land clearing, water damming, irrigation, and expanded trade.

The environmental health agenda is becoming ever broader. Today the burden of human numbers and aggregate consumption and waste generation is beginning to overload various of the planet's great natural systems. The resultant global environmental changes, signifying that the biosphere's human population carrying capacity is being exceeded, pose yet further risks to human health. Therefore, even as environmental health scientists strive to improve their research methods for characterizing the health risks associated with local physical, chemical, and microbiological hazards, they must also extend their ideas and methods to encompass larger-scale environmental hazards and the health consequences of disrupted ecosystems. Policy makers, in many sectors, must understand the tendency of human-wrought changes in the social, built, and natural environments to affect health—if not immediately, then in the longer term, and sometimes via pathways with which we yet have little familiarity.

● ● ● Discussion Questions

1. What should be the scope of the term "environment"?

2. What methodological problems are particularly characteristic of environmental epidemiology?

3. How can the differences be explained in the profile of environmental health problems between industrialized and low- and middle-income countries? Are the differences a function of history, demography, wealth, knowledge, or something else?

4. What are the characteristics of particular environmental health problems that render them more, or less, tractable to amelioration or elimination?

5. As the scale of human impact on the global "environment" increases, people become more concerned about the consequences of disruption of our "habitat." What does this signify?

• • • **References**

Armstrong, J., & Menon, R. (1998). Mining and quarrying. In J. M. Stellman (Ed.), *Encyclopaedia of occupational health and safety* (4th ed., Vol. III). Geneva, Switzerland: International Labor Office.

Beaglehole, R., Bonita, R., & Kjellstrom, T. (2002). *Basic epidemiology* (Updated edition). Geneva, Switzerland: World Health Organization.

Biswas, B. K., Dhar, R. K., Samanta, G., Mandal, B. K., Chakraborti, D., Faruk, I., Islam, K. S., Chodhury, M. M., Islam, A., & Roy, S. (1998). Detailed study report of Samta, one of the arsenic-affected villages of Jessore District, Bangladesh. *Current Science, 74*, 134–145.

Bobak, M., & Leon, D. A. (1992). Air pollution and infant mortality in the Czech Republic, 1986–1988. *Lancet, 340*, 1010–1014.

Cai, S., Yue, L., Shang, Q., & Nordberg, G. (1995). Cadmium exposure among residents in an area contaminated by irrigation water in China. *Bulletin of the World Health Organization, 73*, 359–367.

Chowdhury, Z., Zheng, M., & Russel, A. (2004). *Source apportionment and characterization of ambient fine particles in Delhi, Mumbai, Kolkata, and Chandigarh.* Washington, DC: World Bank.

Cohen, A. J., Anderson, H. R., Ostro, B., Pandey, K. D., Krzyzanowski, M., Kuenzli, N., Gutschmidt, K., Pope, C. A., Romieu, I., Samet, J. M., & Smith, K. R. (2004). Mortality impacts of urban air pollution. In M. Ezzati, A. D. Rodgers, A. D. Lopez, & C. J. L. Murray (Eds.), *Comparative quantification of health risks: Global and regional burden of disease due to selected major risk factors* (Vol. 2). Geneva, Switzerland: World Health Organization.

Colborn, T., Vom Saal, F., & Soto, A. (1993). Developmental effects of endocrine-disrupting chemicals in wildlife and humans. *Environmental Health Perspectives, 101*, 378–384.

Colwell, R. (1996). Global climate and infectious disease: The cholera paradigm. *Science, 274*, 2025–2031.

Corvalan, C., Briggs, D., & Kjellstrom, T. (1996). Development of environmental health indicators. In D. Briggs, C. Corvalan, & M. Nurminen (Eds.), *Linkage methods for environment and health analysis* (Document WHO/EHG/95.26). Geneva, Switzerland: World Health Organization.

Daily, G. C. (Ed.). (1997). *Nature's services.* Washington, DC: Island Press.

Deishmann, W., & Henschler, D. (1986). What is there that is not poison? A study of the *Third Defense* by Paracelsus. *Archives of Toxicology, 58*(4), 207–213.

Duchin, J. S., Koster, F. T., Peters, C. J., Simpson, G. L., Tempest, B., Zaki, S. R., Ksiazek, T. G., Rollin, P. E., Nichol, S., & Umland, E. T. (1994). Hantavirus pulmonary syndrome: A clinical description of 17 patients with a newly recognized disease. *New England Journal of Medicine, 330*, 949–955.

Ezzati, M., Lopez, A. D., Rodgers, A., Vander Hoorn, S., Murray, C. J. L., et al. (2002). Selected major risk factors and global and regional burden of disease. *Lancet, 360*, 1347–1360.

Ezzati, M., Vander Hoorn, A., Rodgers, A., Lopez, A. D., Mathers, C. D., & Murray, C. J .L. (2003). Estimates of global and regional potential health gains from reducing multiple major risk factors. *Lancet, 362*, 271–280.

Fenwick, A., Cheesmond, A. K., & Amin, M. A. (1981). The role of field irrigation canals in the transmission of *Schistosoma mansoni* in the Gezira Scheme, Sudan. *Bulletin of the World Health Organization, 59*, 777–786.

Fletcher, T., & McMichael, A. J. (1997). *Health at the crossroads: Transport policy and urban health.* Chichester, England: John Wiley & Sons.

Florig, K. (1997). China's air pollution risks. *Environmental Science and Technology, 31*, 276–279.

Folke, C., Larsson, J., & Sweitzer, J. (1996). Renewable resource appropriation. In R. Costanza & O. Segura (Eds.), *Getting down to Earth.* Washington, DC: Island Press.

Food and Agriculture Organization. (2002). *State of world fisheries and aquaculture.* Rome, Italy: Food and Agriculture Organization.

Friberg, L., Elinder, C.-G., Kjellstrom, T., & Nordberg, G. F. (Eds.). (1986). *Cadmium and health* (Vol. 2). Boca Raton, FL: CRC Press.

Gleick, P. H. (1998). *The world's water: The biennial report on freshwater resources 1998–1999*. Washington, DC: Island Press.

Gruenbaum, E. (1983). Struggling with the mosquito: Malaria policy and agricultural development in Sudan. *Medical Anthropology, 7,* 51–62.

Hales, S., Weinstein, P., Souares, P., & Woodward, A. (1999). El Niño and the dynamics of vector-borne disease transmission. *Environmental Health Perspectives, 107,* 99–102.

Herzstein, J. A., Bunn, W. B., Fleming, L. E., Harrington, J. M., Jeyaratnam, J., & Gardner, I. R. (1998). *International occupational and environmental medicine*. St. Louis, MO: Mosby.

Hoogvelt, A. (1997). *Globalisation and the post-colonial world*. London: Macmillan.

Intergovernmental Panel on Climate Change. (2001). *Third assessment report: Climate change 2001* (Vols. I–III). New York: Cambridge University Press.

International Scientific Oversight Committee. (2004). *Health effects of outdoor air pollution in developing countries of Asia: A literature review* (Special Report 15). Boston: Health Effects Institute. http://www.healtheffects.org/Pubs/SpecialReport15.pdf.

Jennings, N. S. (1998). Mining: An overview. In J. M. Stellman (Ed.), *Encyclopaedia of occupational health and safety* (4th ed., Vol. III, pp. 74.2–74.4). Geneva, Switzerland: International Labor Office.

Kazan-Allen, L. (2003). The asbestos war. *International Journal of Occupational and Environmental Health, 9,* 173–193.

Khan, A. W., Ahmad, A., Sayed, M. H. S. U., Hadi, A., Khan, M. H., Jalil, M. A., Ahmed, R., & Faruquee, M. H. (1997). Arsenic contamination in ground water and its effect on human health with particular reference to Bangladesh. *Journal of Preventive and Social Medicine, 16,* 65–73.

Kjellstrom, T. (1994). Issues in the developing world. In L. Rosenstock & M. Cullen (Eds.), *Textbook of clinical occupational and environmental medicine* (pp. 25–31). Philadelphia: W.B. Saunders.

Kjellstrom, T. (2004). The epidemic of asbestos-related diseases in New Zealand. *International Journal of Occupational and Environmental Health, 10,* 212–219.

Kjellstrom, T., & Corvalan, C. (1995). Framework for the development of environmental health indicators. *World Health Statistics Quarterly, 48,* 144–154.

Kjellstrom, T., Koplan, J. P., & Rothenberg, R. B. (1992). Current and future determinants of adult ill health. In R. G. A. Feachem, T. Kjellstrom, C. J. L. Murray, M. Over, & M. A. Phillips (Eds.), *The health of adults in the developing world*. Oxford, England: Oxford University Press.

Kjellstrom, T., van Kerkhoff, L., Bammer, G., & McMichael, T. (2003). Comparative assessment of transport risks—how it can contribute to health impact assessment of transport policies. *Bulletin of the World Health Organization, 81,* 451–458.

Kraus, R. S. (1998). Oil exploration and drilling. In J. M. Stellman (Ed.), *Encyclopaedia of occupational health and safety* (4th ed., Vol. III). Geneva, Switzerland: International Labor Office.

LaDou, J. (1992). The export of industrial hazards to developing countries. In J. Jeyaratnam (Ed.), *Occupational health in developing countries* (pp. 340–360). Oxford, England: Oxford University Press.

LaDou, J., & Jeyaratnam, J. (1994). Transfer of hazardous industries: Issues and solutions. In J. Jeyaratnam & K. S. Chia (Eds.), *Occupational health in national development*. River Edge, NJ: World Scientific Publications.

Lee, K., & Dodgson, R. (2000). Globalisation and cholera: Implications for global governance. *Global Governance, 6,* 213–236.

Levy, B. S., & Wegman, D. H. (Eds.). (2000). *Occupational health: Recognizing and preventing work-related disease and injury* (4th ed.). Philadelphia: Lippincott, Williams and Wilkins.

Logie, D. E., & Benatar, S. R. (1997). Africa in the 21st century: Can despair be turned to hope? *British Medical Journal, 315,* 1444–1446.

Madronich, S., & de Gruijl, F. R. (1993). Skin cancer and UV radiation. *Nature, 366,* 23–25.

McMichael, A. J. (1993). *Planetary overload: Global environmental change and the health of the human species.* Cambridge, England: Cambridge University Press.

McMichael, A .J. (1994). "Molecular epidemiology": New pathway or new traveling companion? *American Journal of Epidemiology, 140,* 1–11.

McMichael, A. J. (1999). Dioxins in the Belgian food chain: Chickens and eggs. *Journal of Epidemiology and Community Health, 53,* 742–743.

McMichael, A. J., Anderson, H. R., Brunekreef, B., & Cohen, A. (1998). Inappropriate use of daily mortality analyses for estimating the longer-term mortality effects of air pollution. *International Journal of Epidemiology, 27,* 450–453.

McMichael, A. J., Campbell-Lendrum, D., Ebi, K., Githeko, A., Scheraga, J., & Woodward, A. (Eds.). (2003). *Climate change and human health: Risks and responses.* Geneva, Switzerland: World Health Organization.

McMichael, A. J., & Smith, K. R. (1999). Air pollution and health: Seeking a global perspective [Editorial]. *Epidemiology, 10,* 1–4.

Moochhala, S. M., Shahi, G. S., & Cote, I. L. (1997). The role of epidemiology, controlled clinical studies, and toxicology in defining environmental risks. In G. S. Shahi, B. S. Levy, A. Binger, T. Kjellstrom, & R. Lawrence (Eds.), *International perspective on environment, development and health: Toward a sustainable world* (pp. 341–352). New York: Springer.

Moore, C. F. (2003). *Silent scourge: Children, pollution and why scientists disagree.* Oxford, England: Oxford University Press.

Morgenstern, H., & Thomas, D. (1993). Principals of study design in environmental epidemiology. *Environmental Health Perspectives Supplement, 101,* 23–38.

Morse, S. S. (1995). Factors in the emergence of infectious diseases. *Emerging Infectious Diseases, 1,* 7–15.

Murray, C. J. L., & Lopez, A. D. (1996). *The global burden of disease: A comprehensive assessment of mortality and disability from diseases, injuries, and risk factors in 1990 and projected to 2020.* Cambridge, MA: Harvard University Press.

Nriagu, J. O., Blankson, M. L., & Ocran, K. (1996). Childhood lead poisoning in Africa: A growing public health problem. *Science of Total Environment, 181,* 93–100.

Organization of Economic Cooperation and Development. (1993). *OECD core set of indicators for environmental performance reviews* (Environmental Monograph No. 83). Paris: Organization of Economic Cooperation and Development.

Ostro, B. (1994). *Estimating the health effects of air pollutants* (Policy Research Working Paper No. 1301). Washington, DC: World Bank.

Pimentel, D., Tort, M., D'Anna, L., Krawic, A., Berger, J., Rossman, J., Mugo, F., Doon, N., Shriberg, M., Howard, E., Lee, S., & Talbot, J. (1998). Ecology of increasing disease. *Bioscience, 48,* 817–826.

Pimm, S. L., Russell, G. J., Gittleman, J. L., & Brooks, T. M. (1995). The future of biodiversity. *Science, 269,* 347–354.

Pocock, S. J., Smith, M., & Baghurst, P. (1994). Environmental lead and children's intelligence: A systematic review of the epidemiological evidence. *British Medical Journal, 309,* 1189–1197.

Pope C. A., III, Burnett, R. T., Thun, M. J., Calle, E. E., Krewski, D., Ito, K., & Thurston, G. D. (2002). Lung cancer, cardiopulmonary mortality, and long-term exposure to fine particulate air pollution. *Journal of the American Medical Association, 287,* 1132–1141.

Poschen, P. (1998). General profile (forestry). In J. M. Stellman (Ed.), *Encyclopaedia of occupational health and safety* (4th ed., Vol. III, pp. 68.2–68.6). Geneva, Switzerland: International Labor Office.

Rahman, M., Tondel, M. J., Ahmad, S. A., & Axelson, O. (1998). Diabetes mellitus associated with arsenic exposure in Bangladesh. *American Journal of Epidemiology, 148,* 198–203.

Rees, W. (1996). Revisiting carrying capacity: Area-based indicators of sustainability. *Population and Environment, 17,* 195–215.

Repetto, R., & Belagi, S. S. (Eds.). (1996). *Pesticides and the immune system: The public health risks.* Washington, DC: World Resources Institute.

Rosenstock, L., & Cullen, M. (1994). *Textbook of clinical occupational and environmental medicine.* Philadelphia: W.B. Saunders.

Samet, J. M., Schnatter, R., & Gibb, H. (1998). Invited commentary: Epidemiology and risk assessment. *American Journal of Epidemiology, 148,* 929–936.

Schwartz, J. (1994). Low level lead exposure and children's IQ: A meta-analysis and search for a threshold. *Environmental Research, 65,* 42–45.

Scoggins, A., Kjellstrom, T., Fisher, G. W., Connor, J., & Gimson, N. R. (2004). Spatial analysis of annual air pollution exposure and mortality. *The Science of the Total Environment, 321,* 71–85.

Shahi, G. S., Levy, B. S., Binger, A., Kjellstrom, T., & Lawrence, R. (Eds.). (1997). *International perspective on environment, development and health: Toward a sustainable world.* New York: Springer.

Sims, J. (1994). *Women, health and environment: An anthology* (Document WHO/EHG/94.11). Geneva, Switzerland: World Health Organization.

Sinton, J., Smith, K. R., Peabody, J. W., Liu, Y., Zhang, X., Edwards, R., & Gan, Q. (2004). An assessment of programs to promote improved household stoves in China. *Energy for Sustainable Development, 8*(3), 33–52.

Slaper, H., Velders, G. J. M., Daniel, J. S., de Gruijl, F. R., & van der Leun, J. C. (1996). Estimates of ozone depletion and skin cancer incidence to examine the Vienna Convention achievements. *Nature, 384,* 256–258.

Smith, A. H., Goycoleam, M., Haque, R., & Biggs, M. L. (1998). Marked increase in bladder and lung cancer mortality in a region of northern Chile due to arsenic in drinking water. *American Journal of Epidemiology, 147,* 660–669.

Smith, D. (1999). Worldwide trends in DDT levels in human milk. *International Journal of Epidemiology, 28,* 179–188.

Smith, K. R. (1997). Development, health, and the environmental risk transition. In G. Shahi, B. S. Levy, & A. Binger (Eds.), *International perspectives in environment, development, and health* (pp. 51–62). New York: Springer.

Smith, K. R., Corvalan, C., & Kjellstrom, T. (1999). How much global ill-health is attributable to environmental factors? *Epidemiology, 10,* 573–584.

Smith, K. R., & Ezzati, M. (2005). How environmental health risks change with development: The environmental risk and epidemiologic transitions revisited. *Annual Review of Energy and Resources, 30* (in press).

Smith, K. R., Mehta, S., & Maeusezahl-Feuz, M. (2004). Indoor smoke from household solid fuels. In M. Ezzati, A. D. Rodgers, A. D. Lopez, & C. J. L. Murray (Eds.), *Comparative quantification of health risks: Global and regional burden of disease due to selected major risk factors* (Vol. 2, pp. 1437–1495). Geneva, Switzerland: World Health Organization.

Stellman, J. M. (Ed.). (1998). *Encyclopaedia of occupational health and safety* (4th ed.). Geneva, Switzerland: International Labor Organization.

Tong, S., Baghurst, P. A., Sawyer, M. G., Burns, J., & McMichael, A. J. (1998). Declining blood lead levels and cognitive function during childhood—the Port Pirie Cohort Study. *Journal of the American Medical Association, 280,* 1915–1919.

Tossavainen, A. (2000). International expert meeting on new advances in the radiology and screening of asbestos-related diseases. Consensus report. *Scandinavian Journal of Work, Environment and Health, 26,* 449–454.

Tossavainen, A. (2004). Global use of asbestos and the incidence of mesothelioma. *International Journal of Occupational and Environmental Health, 10,* 22–25.

United Nations. (Annual). *United Nations demographic yearbook*. New York: United Nations.

United Nations Development Program. (2004). *Human development report 2004*. New York: United Nations Development Program.

United Nations Environment Program. (1998). *Environmental effects of ozone depletion*. Nairobi: United Nations Environment Program.

UNEP. (2004) *GEO: Global Environmental Outlook 3*. Nairobi: United Nations Environment Program.

U.S. Congress, Subcommittee on Finance and Hazardous Materials. (1998, February). *Status of the Superfund program*. Washington, DC: Government Printing Office.

Viscusi, W. K., & Hamilton, J. T. (1999). Are risk regulators rational? Evidence from hazardous waste cleanup decisions. *American Economic Review, 89*(4), 1010–1027.

Watson, R. T., Dixon, J. A., & Hamburg, S. P. (Eds.). (1998). *Protecting our planet, securing our future: Linkages among global environmental issues and human needs*. Nairobi: UNEP/ USNASA/World Bank.

Weeks, J. L. (1998). Health and safety hazards in the construction industry. In J. M. Stellman (Ed.), *Encyclopaedia of occupational health and safety* (4th ed., Vol. III, pp. 93.2–93.8). Geneva, Switzerland: International Labor Office.

Weiss, R., & McMichael, A. J. (2004). Social and environmental risk factors in the emergence of infectious diseases. *Nature Medicine, 10*, S70–S76.

Wilson, M. E. (1995). Infectious diseases: An ecologic perspective. *British Medical Journal, 311*, 1681–1684.

Woodward, A., Hales, S., & Weinstein, P. (1998). Climate change and human health in the Asia Pacific region: Who will be the most vulnerable? *Climate Research, 11*, 31–38.

World Bank. (1993). *World development report 1993. Investing in health*. Washington, DC: World Bank.

World Health Organization. (1990). *Public health impact of the use of pesticides in agriculture*. Geneva, Switzerland: World Health Organization.

World Health Organization. (1992). *Cadmium* (Environmental Health Criteria No. 134). Geneva, Switzerland: World Health Organization.

World Health Organization. (1994). *Ultraviolet radiation* (Environmental Health Criteria No. 160). Geneva, Switzerland: World Health Organization.

World Health Organization. (1996). *Health effects of the Chernobyl accident* (Document WHO/EHG/96.X). Geneva, Switzerland: World Health Organization.

World Health Organization. (1997). *Health and environment in sustainable development* (Document WHO/EHG/97.8). Geneva, Switzerland: World Health Organization.

World Health Organization. (1998). *Chrysotile asbestos* (Environmental Health Criteria No. 190). Geneva, Switzerland: World Health Organization.

World Health Organization. (1999). *World health report 1999. Making a difference*. Geneva, Switzerland: World Health Organization.

World Health Organization. (2000). *Air quality guidelines for Europe* (2nd ed.). Geneva, Switzerland: World Health Organization.

World Health Organization. (2002). *World health report 2002. Reducing risks, promoting healthy life*. Geneva, Switzerland: World Health Organization.

World Health Organization. (2004). *World report on road traffic injury prevention*. Geneva, Switzerland: World Health Organization.

World Resources Institute. (1998). *World resources 1998–99*. Oxford, England: Oxford University Press.

Yassi, A., & Kjellstrom, T. (1998). Environmental health hazards. In J. M. Stellman (Ed.), *Encyclopaedia of occupational health and safety* (4th ed., Vol. II, pp. 53.1–53.33). Geneva, Switzerland: International Labor Office.

Complex Emergencies

MICHAEL J. TOOLE, RONALD J. WALDMAN, AND ANTHONY ZWI

This chapter focuses on public health emergencies that arise from complex political crises. Terminology changes frequently, and different definitions emphasize different aspects of a concept. The term *complex humanitarian emergencies* came into popular use following the Kurdish refugee exodus in 1991. It was defined by the Centers for Disease Control and Prevention (CDC) as "a situation affecting large civilian populations which usually involves a combination of factors including war or civil strife, food shortages, and population displacement, resulting in significant excess mortality" (Burkholder & Toole, 1995). Goodhand and Hulme (1999) defined *complex political emergencies* as conflicts that combine a number of features: They often occur within but also across state boundaries; they have political antecedents, often relating to competition for power and resources; they are protracted in duration; they are embedded in and are expressions of existing social, political, economic, and cultural structures and cleavages; and they are often characterized by predatory social formations. This latter definition clearly locates the causes and effects in the political sphere, a point echoed by numerous other writers, which has considerable implications for those working in these settings with a primarily public health agenda. In the new millennium these terms have merged into *complex emergencies*, the term that we use in this chapter to maintain simplicity and consistency.

The chapter grapples with current understanding of complex emergencies (CEs) and their political causes and considers their impact on populations and health systems.[1] It highlights current knowledge in humanitarian assistance and indicates that effective technical interventions are possible to help alleviate suffering and limit adverse effects on the health of populations. We draw attention to current efforts by the humanitarian community to improve the effectiveness, efficiency, and equity of humanitarian responses, and consider how the pattern of early responses may influence the longer-term survival of populations and systems and the nature of any post-conflict society established. We are acutely aware, however, that the solutions to CEs are political and not humanitarian, and that it is in the political sphere that both upstream and downstream responses to complex emergencies must receive priority.

Although the impact of natural disasters is not the subject of this chapter, we have made one important exception: the destructive tsunami that originated off the coast of Indonesia on December 26, 2004. We include this catastrophic event because it had many elements of a complex emergency. It caused more than 230,000 deaths and injuries in eight countries and displaced more than 1.5 million people from their homes (United Nations Office for the Coordination of Humanitarian Affairs, 2005). Two of the areas

---

[1]The emphasis in this chapter is on complex political emergencies and not on more traditional forms of interstate conflict and war. Furthermore, although we comment on other forms of intrastate conflict and repression, such as torture and disappearance, these forms of violence are not the focus of this chapter. Where possible, however, we have briefly highlighted these issues either through the presentation of an exhibit or through reference to the literature.

Acknowledgments: The authors wish to acknowledge the advice provided on food and nutrition by Professor Michael Golden.

most severely affected (Aceh province of Indonesia and northeast Sri Lanka) have experienced several decades of armed conflict. More than 127,000 Burmese refugees were living in the five Thai provinces affected by the tsunami: At least 1,000 perished, and a further 1,000 were still missing in late January 2005 (United States Committee for Refugees, 2005). The massive displacement and disruption to food and water supplies, shelter, and sanitation created conditions similar to those experienced by refugees and internally displaced persons (IDPs) fleeing armed conflict. No natural disaster in the past 50 years has led to such life-threatening conditions.

In the period from the end of World War II to the end of the Cold War, most conflicts took place in the developing regions of the world, primarily in Africa, the Middle East, Asia, and Latin America. The end of the Cold War, the break-up of the Soviet Union, and the pace and intensity of globalization led, in the 1990s, to major conflicts in Europe and the former Soviet Union, notably in Tajikistan, Chechnya, Georgia, Abkhazia, the former Yugoslavia, and Nagorno Karabakh. The number of armed conflicts globally reached a peak of 55 in 1992, with another peak of 37 conflicts in 1998–1999. Since then, there has been a steady decline, to a total of 21 during 2004 (Center for Defense Information, 2005). Recent peace agreements have been signed in Sudan, Angola, Liberia, Sierra Leone, Sri Lanka, and the Solomon Islands, ending, in some countries, decades of fighting (Figure 10-1).

Modern-day conflicts are increasingly internal rather than between states, and often have as a prime objective, alongside the quest for economic and political power, the undermining of the lives and livelihoods of civilian populations associated with opposing factions. Up to 90% of those affected in recent conflicts have been civilians, with all ages and both sexes affected. The distribution of impact and health outcomes will vary substantially, however, and will depend on the nature of the conflict and its history, its extent and form, and prior health and health systems status.

Many CEs have attracted considerable media attention and have caused people to seek to promote availability of at least a basic degree of humanitarian assistance, even if fundamental political solutions are not sought. However, other ongoing crises, despite causing massive loss of life, population displacement, and infrastructure destruction, are not necessarily explicitly recognized as CEs and as a result attract few resources and attention. These "hidden emergencies" nevertheless pose fundamental challenges to the health and well-being of affected populations. Ongoing conflicts in Burma, Colombia, western Sudan, Algeria, Nepal, Uganda, and the Democratic Republic of the Congo (DRC) seem to attract little attention and resources: Such discrepancies are likely to result from geopolitical concerns, media interest, and economic factors. The role of the media may be particularly powerful in annointing a country as a CE worthy of attention, such as the BBC did in Ethiopia in 1984 and

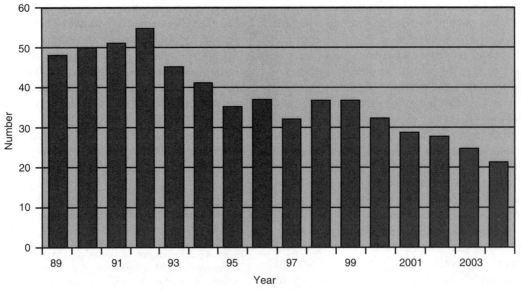

Figure 10-1 Armed Conflicts, 1989–2004. *Sources:* Data from P. Wallenstein and M. Sollenberg, "Armed Conflict 1989–1998," 1999, *Journal of Peace Research*, 36(5), pp. 593–606; and Centers for Defense Information, *Significant ongoing armed conflicts 2004*, 2005, http://www.cdi.org.

the *New York Times* in Somalia in 1993, which subsequently focused world attention and popular demands for action.

Some wars *are* still fought primarily between competing armies, such as the Iran/Iraq conflict from 1980 to 1988, in which an estimated 450,000 military personnel died (Sivard, 1996), the Gulf War of 1991, and the Eritrea/Ethiopia and India/Pakistan conflicts of 1999, but the vast majority now take place within states. However, in the aftermath of the September 2001 terrorist attacks on New York City and Washington, United States–led coalitions have used military force to change the regimes in Afghanistan and Iraq. These two conflicts represent a new trend in modern wars, with their huge disparities in military resources between the warring parties.

During the 60 years since the Holocaust, numerous episodes of massive human rights atrocities and genocide have been committed against particular groups: Pol Pot's killing fields in Cambodia, the Guatemalan government action against indigenous Mayan communities, and the genocide against Tutsis in Rwanda. Recent conflicts, such as that in West Darfur, Sudan, during 2004, highlight the nature of internal wars, including the use of repressive techniques to evict people from their homes and to undermine their sense of security and safety, accompanied by the targeted use of force to destroy social, political, and economic structures. A particularly insidious development is the targeting of violence toward individuals and groups on the basis of their ethnicity or religion. Such conflicts have been frequent enough that the term *ethnic cleansing* has entered the language. However, the reality has been that opportunistic politicians have often inflamed the perceived differences between groups, especially during times of economic and political uncertainty, resulting in open warfare.

In the same conflicts, we see evidence of other key features of modern-day CEs, such as

- the willingness of powerful segments of the international community to intervene in internal conflicts, and to do so in a way that minimizes their exposure to risk
- the changing nature of humanitarian assistance, which increasingly forms only one dimension to the management of conflicts, alongside political, economic, and military responses
- the changing role of the private sector, as well as the increasingly important role of local and global media

- trends in globalization that at the same time integrate peripheral areas within the global economy but contribute to their fragmentation as elites compete for access to the economic and political resources associated with integration in the global political economy

One consequence of the targeting of entire communities and their livelihoods has been the dramatic rise in numbers of forcibly displaced people. In 2004, there were an estimated 21.3 million IDPs and 11.5 million refugees (those seeking refuge across international borders), the vast majority fleeing conflict zones (United States Committee for Refugees, 2005). Those displaced within countries have less access to resources and services supported by the international community, may be at ongoing risk from violence perpetrated by the state and other powerful local actors, and have their needs more hidden than those displaced across borders.

Although refugee numbers are typically assessed in order to plan and provide relief, relatively little attention has been devoted to developing the most appropriate methods for establishing the precise composition of refugee and IDP populations, whether in terms of age, sex, religion, local geographic origin, or ethnicity. This imposes constraints given the differing needs and roles of groups within populations and may make it easier for the more complex issues of dealing with gender, equity, and ongoing intergroup rivalry to be overlooked. Particular groups, such as older adults, refugees not in camps, and IDPs, may neither be identified nor receive the required attention for their differing needs.

The changing pattern of conflict has been accompanied by significant changes in the delivery of humanitarian assistance. The number of agencies operating in these complex settings has increased dramatically; for example, there were over 240 nongovernmental organizations (NGOs) working in and around Rwanda in the aftermath of the genocide and over 100 agencies working with the Kosovar Albanians during 1999. Within one month after the 2004 Asian tsunami, more than 2,000 foreign medical personnel were working in the Indonesian province of Aceh. On the other hand, lower-profile CEs may be as severe and life-threatening to large populations, such as that in Sierra Leone in 1999, but attract much less media, intergovernmental, and humanitarian responses. New NGOs established in response to a specific conflict may be short-lived, inexperienced, and unable to cope with the challenges they face in providing services in complex political environments.

Ensuring one does more good than harm must underlie all interventions.

Every conflict has winners and losers; predators identify opportunities amidst the turmoil to further enrich themselves and entrench their political position. These players may therefore have an interest in perpetuating the conflict. Humanitarian aid itself may become a resource over which groups compete, and such assistance and resources may directly or indirectly stoke the conflict. In some distressing circumstances, humanitarian aid was used unwittingly to attract populations that were subsequently targeted by combatants, as in the DRC. Humanitarian workers have increasingly been directly targeted in latter-day conflicts, which has led to increased efforts to work closely with the military and security sector. Despite some benefits, such as improved logistics support, this trend may bring negative consequences and additional dangers and may threaten the neutrality and impartiality to which many agencies aspire.

NGOs are not a homogeneous community. Although some are highly professional and have given considerable thought to the development of humanitarian and technical policies and programs, there have been some negative consequences of the way in which humanitarian assistance has been provided. Recognition by the humanitarian community of these problems has led to a great deal of evaluation and introspection and measures to improve practice, including the development of codes of conduct for humanitarian agencies, the promotion of minimum standards for service provision, and debate regarding enhancing accountability to affected populations.

Promoting the derivation and uptake of good practice is particularly difficult in humanitarian agencies given rapid staff turnover, unwillingness to publicly acknowledge failures and limitations because of the possible funding consequences, and a culture of doing rather than reflecting. Interventions are often not evidence based, and, despite most agencies valuing the concept of coordination, few wish to be coordinated. The response to the Asian tsunami in 2004 once again witnessed an almost unseemly race to be "in charge" and to dominate the relief programs. Despite the overwhelming evidence that basic needs and public health interventions were the main priority among surviving communities, many donors insisted on sending highly visible field hospitals and surgical teams well after the need for such resources had passed. Poor-quality services have significant adverse consequences: increased morbidity, mortality, and disability; further spread of communicable diseases; community dissatisfaction and breakdown;

and psychosocial distress. Clear policy objectives for interventions are often lacking, and mechanisms for working with new players such as the military and the private sector remain inadequately developed. Despite recognition that the accountability of relief efforts to affected populations should be enhanced, mechanisms to assure this are in their infancy.

Ongoing humanitarian challenges include understanding how best to upgrade host population health services alongside efforts to improve those available to refugees, how to most humanely and efficiently provide good-quality services, and how to maintain the role of communities in structuring both the determination of priorities and the pattern of service provision. A key issue relates to how and whether to bolster and support resilient health and social systems and individual adaptations to conflict. Our level of knowledge regarding these responses, and the potential to further support them, is weak. A persistent challenge to humanitarian workers is to institutionalize a sensitive and inclusive evidence-based culture and to build sustainable mechanisms for crystallizing policy advice from the vast and valuable foundation of field experience.

Direct Public Health Impact of War

Measuring the impact and hidden costs of conflict is complex for a variety of reasons. These include methodological and theoretical shortcomings, inconsistencies in definitions and terms, restricted access to areas of conflict and sources of information, the rapid evolution of many emergencies, political manipulation of data, resource constraints, and the hidden or indirect nature of the impact. One of the consequences of the data limitations is difficulty in identifying more precisely which sections of the population are at greatest risk in order to develop more appropriate responses. Most poor countries lack reliable health information and vital registration systems, the absence of which increases the difficulties of determining the conflict-associated costs in terms of morbidity, mortality, and disability. Furthermore, CEs may seriously disrupt surveillance and information systems.

Lack of consistency in definitions used makes it difficult to compare within and across populations. Different agencies may define refugees and IDPs in different ways, case definitions for particular conditions vary, and techniques for estimating nutritional deficiencies, for example, may vary, among different agencies working with the same population. Data are at times incomplete because impartial observers who attempt to provide more accurate figures may not have access to witnesses or other reliable sources of information. On other occasions entire communities and detainees in camps may have been exterminated, leaving no witnesses.

During the last 10 years, there have been a number of expert meetings to develop more reliable methods of measuring both direct and indirect mortality resulting from CEs. Some of their proceedings have been published (Reed & Keeley, 2001). Cross-sectional retrospective mortality surveys have been increasingly employed to measure conflict-related mortality. In 2004 alone, large mortality surveys were conducted in three conflict zones: Iraq, the DRC, and the West Darfur region of Sudan. All surveys used cluster sampling methodology.

In Iraq, the survey compared preinvasion and postinvasion mortality (all ages) and found that the risk of death was 2.5-fold higher after the invasion when compared with the preinvasion period. Most of the 100,000 excess deaths were reported to be due to violence (Roberts et al., 2004). The DRC survey was the largest (n = 19,500 households) and the fourth such survey conducted in the country since 2001. The first three surveys found that an estimated 3.3 million people had died as a result of the armed conflict in the DRC, which commenced in 1998 (Roberts & Zantop, 2003). The fourth survey, conducted in 2004, found that the national crude mortality rate of 2 deaths per 1,000 per month was 67% higher than that reported before the war (Coghlan et al., 2004). In West Darfur, a survey was conducted among 215,000 internally displaced persons in four sites. The survey found that mortality prior to displacement ranged between 18 and 28 per 1,000 per month; violence caused between 68% and 93% of deaths, most of which occurred among adult men (Depoortere et al., 2004).

Although innovative techniques may be used to try to build up a picture of what transpired during a particular CE, what the needs were, and the nature of the response, the sources of data may be biased, as may the ways in which information has been collected. Despite this, innovative groups, often NGOs without a political agenda linked to any of the key players in the conflict, may be able to play a valuable role in documenting precisely what occurred and the nature of present needs. Médecins sans Frontières (MSF) has taken an innovative approach to documenting the impact of CEs through its *MSF Speaking Out* series, in which extracts from all relevant internal and external MSF documents are collated and annotated to form a compelling chronicle of a crisis (Binet, 2003).

Even where huge numbers of people are involved, agreement on the magnitude of impact varies. Estimates of the number of victims of the Rwandan genocide are still imprecise and vary from 500,000 to 1 million (best estimate: 800,000). Deaths during the 1991 Gulf War remain disputed; so too are likely to be the number of deaths experienced following the invasion of Iraq by the United States–led coalition in 2003. In Sudan, a nutrition and mortality assessment in 1993 acknowledged that reliable census data were not available for any of the four assessment sites, and that the size of the populations near airstrips where food was unloaded fluctuated according to the deliveries. Each party to the conflict has its own reasons for presenting data in a particular way; unless some more objective source is established, we will have to continue to be extremely cautious in the use of such figures. Moreover, the term *complex emergency* has sometimes been used incorrectly by some governments to describe what in essence has been genocide (e.g., Rwanda in 1994) in order to avoid their obligations under international law.

Particular affected populations may also be difficult to assess precisely, as in the case of war orphans or unaccompanied child refugees and IDPs. Unaccompanied children may account for 2% to 5% of the refugee population in camps, although this will clearly vary in different contexts. Massive population movements may occur over very short periods of time, such as the 1 million or more Hutu refugees who fled from Rwanda over a period of days. Even when the time scales are longer, considerable problems remain: For example, approximately 500,000 Liberian refugees fled to Guinea over a period of 5 years into an area that had a population of 1.2 million inhabitants (Van Damme, 1998). Such population flows present considerable challenges in terms of assessing health status, determining needs, and developing context-appropriate responses.

Political interests greatly affect which data are released, how and when this is done, and with what accompanying analyses. In the Kosovo conflict, NATO and the Yugoslav government tussled over a number of events in which civilian casualties occurred, with each side seeking to obtain maximum political and public relations benefits. Certain events, such as allegations of the use of systematic rape, only appeared at times when NATO was under pressure to justify its role and nature of engagement in the war.

Data on numbers of IDPs and refugees may be manipulated by states and organizations in an attempt to make a political point or to maximize access to resources. It has been alleged that some refugee camp administrators and refugees report fewer deaths than actually occur in order to maintain levels of international assistance. In Nepal, in an attempt to encourage reporting of deaths among Bhutanese refugees, free funeral shrouds were offered to relatives of the deceased together with assurances that the reporting would not result in decreases of rations.

Physical Impact

Political conflicts earlier this century were mostly waged between armies and trained combatants. The main direct results, in the form of deaths, morbidity, and disability, reflected the nature of the conflict, the level of technology and nature of weapons used, the prior preparation and protective clothing available to military personnel, and the quality of emergency medical care and evacuation facilities (Garfield & Neugat, 1991).

In the vast majority of latter-day conflicts, however, the entire population is often targeted, in part directly, but also with massive and sustained effort at reducing the viability and integrity of the affected community. In Mozambique, the antigovernment forces killed approximately 100,000 people in 1986 and 1987 alone, a massive proportion in a relatively small country (Cliff & Noormahomed, 1988). Injuries and disabilities may follow the use of firearms, but it is notable that technology levels need not be high to achieve terrible levels of destruction. The Rwandan genocide was largely committed with a combination of guns and machetes. Antipersonnel land mines are also responsible for significant population burdens, especially in a small number of heavily infested countries such as Angola, Cambodia, and Afghanistan.

The numbers of war disabled and their types of disability are not well known because only a few countries, such as Zimbabwe, El Salvador, and the Tigrayan region of Ethiopia, have attempted censuses of war-related disability. In Zimbabwe in 1981–1982, 13% of all disability was assessed as being war related, and in El Salvador in the mid-1990s, the census identified 12,041 war disabled, 82% of whom were combatants and the rest civilians. About one-third of the 300,000 soldiers returning from the front at the end of the war in Ethiopia had been injured or disabled. By 1984, well before the end of the war in 1991, over 40,000 people had lost one or more limbs in the conflict. During the bitter civil conflict in Sierra Leone between 1998 and 2002, an estimated 30,000 civilians, including children, had limbs hacked off by the rebels (Project Ploughshares, 2002).

Estimates of mine-related disabilities are sobering: 36,000 in Cambodia (1 in every 236 persons has lost

at least one limb), 20,000 in Angola, 8,000 in Mozambique, and 15,000 in Uganda. In the former Yugoslavia, over 3 million mines were laid; in late 1994, mine laying was occurring at a rate of 50,000 per week, with much of this unmarked and unmapped. The costs are both physical and social and affect all age groups. Between February 1991 and February 1992, approximately 75% of the land mine injuries treated worldwide were in children aged 5 to 15 years. Others affected may be aware of the dangers of mines but have to enter the mined areas in search of food or to continue their agricultural and pastoral activities. Many of the severely disabled will require permanent medical and social services and will strain the health resources of the country for many years. For years to come, the antipersonnel land mines and munitions will constitute a health hazard and contribute to thousands of deaths and severe disabilities, including many children.

Sexual Violence

Rape is increasingly recognized as a feature of internal wars but has been present in many different types of conflicts. In some conflicts, rape has been used systematically as an attempt to undermine opposing groups: This was noted in a very high-profile way in relation to the conflict in the former Yugoslavia, where Bosnian women were systematically abused (Stiglmayer, 1994), as well as in the Rwandan conflict. It has been argued that the more extensive development of women's organizations helped to ensure that these events were made more visible and that support for survivors was mobilized. It has also been suggested, however, that some forms of sexual abuse, such as male rape, for example, have as a result been poorly recognized, if at all. A study in Uganda found that despite widespread rape, few women spoke of their victimization (Bracken, Giller, & Kabaganda, 1992).

Rape, sexual violence, and exploitation may also be widespread in refugee camps, although the extent of their recognition is limited, and widely varying estimates of the numbers of victims have been reported. Violence against Somali women in refugee camps in northern Kenya attracted worldwide condemnation. Despite being relatively few in number, these incidents had a profound effect because they challenged the extent to which UN agencies, such as the Office of the United Nations High Commissioner for Refugees (UNHCR), were effective in assuring the protection of refugee populations against further abuse. In the former Yugoslavia, estimates of the number of rape survivors have ranged from 10,000 to 60,000 (Swiss & Giller, 1993) and have firmly placed the issue of systematic use of rape on the international agenda. Indirectly, such events have also highlighted the need for agencies working with conflict-affected populations to more widely consider their reproductive health needs (Palmer, Lush, & Zwi, 1999). However, sexual violence has continued to be a feature of recent conflicts. For example, an estimated 215,000 to 257,000 women were victims of sexual violence during the civil war in Sierra Leone (Project Ploughshares, 2002). Efforts to establish a permanent International Criminal Court, in which war crimes would be prosecuted, have clearly identified systematic use of rape in wartime as an issue to be addressed. Although sexual violence is most typically perpetrated by men against women, males and children of both sexes may be targeted and warrant attention, especially given the additional taboos and stigma associated with these circumstances.

In addition to long-lasting mental health disorders, rapes have resulted in the transmission of human immunodeficiency virus (HIV). Wars and political conflict present high-risk situations for the transmission of sexually transmitted infections (STIs), including HIV infection (Zwi & Cabral, 1991). War predisposes to STI and HIV transmission in various ways, such as the following:

- widespread population movement
- increased crowding
- separation of women from partners who normally provide a degree of protection
- abuses and sexual demands by military personnel and others in positions of power
- weakened social structures, thereby reducing inhibitions on aggressive behavior and violence against women

Aside from these additional exposures, access to barrier contraceptives, to treatment for STIs, to the prerequisites for maintaining personal hygiene, and to health promotion advice are all compromised in conflict situations.

Women who are on their own may find it more difficult to assure their safety and that of their children. They become targets of violence from three sides: the opposing army, the armed forces in the country to which they have fled, and finally sometimes from their own community (Palmer & Zwi, 1998). They may be forced to provide sex in exchange for food, shelter, or other necessities for self and family survival. The experience of Afghan refugees (Amnesty International, 1995) is illustrative: "In the camps in Pakistan, most of which are controlled by one or other of the warring Afghan factions, women have been attacked, particularly those who are unaccompanied by men. If they refuse sexual favours, they are often denied access to vital rations." In Somalia, fear of rape and shooting prevented women from leaving their homes.

Women's utilization of health care facilities may be severely reduced if males dominate service provision. Burmese Muslim women, many of whom had been raped, who fled to Bangladesh had difficulties in accessing health care due to the predominance of male providers, highlighting the importance of a gender-sensitive analysis of conflict (United Nations High Commissioner for Refugees [UNHCR], 1992). The issue of safety of women should be carefully considered when planning camp and other facilities: The placing of water, sewage removal facilities, and cooking fuels should be undertaken in such a way as to reduce risks of abuse and violence.

Human Rights

Article 25 of the Universal Declaration of Human Rights, proclaimed by resolution 217 A(III) of the United Nations General Assembly on 10 December 1948, states clearly that "[e]veryone has the right to a standard of living adequate for the health and well-being of himself and of his family, including food, clothing, housing and medical care." In times of war, this declaration and other laws, covenants, declarations, and treaties that constitute the body of human rights law are complemented by international humanitarian law. The latter is "a set of rules aimed at limiting violence and protecting the fundamental rights of the individual in times of armed conflict" (Perrin, 1996). These rules are intended to govern the conduct of war by banning the use of certain weapons and by minimizing the effects of armed conflicts, whether international or internal, on noncombatants. The protection of the rights of noncombatants in wartime is based primarily on the Geneva Conventions of 1949 and the two Additional Protocols of 1977. Yet, despite the existence of both of these bodies of international law, CEs are consistently associated with serious infringements of the dignity of individuals and, more specifically, with a major impact on the health status of affected individuals and populations.

General practices that can be considered to be clear violations of international humanitarian law include the intentional targeting of civilian noncombatants, medical personnel, and civilian health facilities. Protection is also conferred upon prisoners of war, wounded and ill combatants, and military medical installations. Violations by states and individuals occurred with great frequency during the second half of the 20th century. Some of the most prominent included the murder of civilians by the government of Guatemala during the 1980s (Yamauchi, 1993), the intentional destruction of health facilities by RENAMO forces seeking to bring down the government of Mozambique (Cliff & Noormahomed, 1988), and the genocidal activities perpetrated upon the Tutsi population of Rwanda in 1994. In the 1990s, the governments of Serbia and Croatia pursued ethnic cleansing policies (more accurately termed *ethnic repression*) against the populations of neighboring republics of the former Yugoslavia and, in the case of Serbia, the province of Kosovo. Arab militia in western Sudan, known as the *Janjaweed*, terrorized the Zaghawa, Masaalit, and Fur peoples between 2003 and 2005 with active support from the government of Sudan.

Violations of human rights law and international humanitarian law that target individuals can take many forms. Torture of civilians has been increasingly documented. More than 2,000 Bhutanese refugees in Nepal, about 2% of the total refugee population, reported having been tortured prior to their flight (Shrestha et al., 1998). Torture has also been reported as a frequently used weapon by China against Tibetans (Keller et al., 1997), and by Turkish authorities against dissenters to its regime (Iacopino et al., 1996). Sexual violence is also of increasing concern, as noted earlier in this chapter. UNHCR has noted the "widespread occurrence of sexual violence in violation of the fundamental right to personal security as recognized in international human rights and humanitarian law" (UNHCR, 1993).

The consequences of wartime human rights violations can be enduring. The physical and psychological consequences of bodily harm to individuals do not end with the cessation of hostilities. Most societies require years of reconstruction and redevelopment in order to restore viable and effective health systems to serve their surviving populations. One can only speculate as to how countries such as Cambodia, Angola, Sudan, Somalia, Rwanda, Liberia, Sierra Leone, the republics of the former Yugoslavia, and Timor L'Este will emerge from the gross abuses of human rights that occurred on their soil.

Although violations of human rights law and international humanitarian law are crimes, the legal systems for punishing the perpetrators and compensating the victims are grossly inadequate. To date, three international tribunals have been established to prosecute war criminals from the former Yu-

goslavia, Rwanda, and Sierra Leone. Although these courts help to move the punishment of war criminals from theory to practice, they have been very slow to act and very expensive to implement. The establishment of an International Criminal Court, a permanent standing body dedicated to the trial and punishment of individuals accused and convicted of violations of human rights law, is, at least conceptually, another step toward strengthening what has in many respects been a legal system without law enforcement capability.

Reporting and responding to reports of human rights violations pose major problems. Although wars and internal conflicts have been proximate causes of most humanitarian emergencies, few of the individuals and agencies who have been involved in providing relief to the individuals affected are trained in the recognition of human rights violations or know where and how to report them. Until more widespread attention is paid to these crimes against humanity, the victims will continue to suffer from preventable acute and chronic morbidity, and the perpetrators will go, for the most part, unpunished. It would be useful to treat human rights violations as a major cause of morbidity and mortality during wars and their aftermath and to establish the epidemiologic characteristics of their distribution (Spirer & Spirer, 1993).

Indirect Public Health Impact of Civil Conflict

This section focuses in detail on the impact on the health of populations that is not directly the consequence of violence. Although the chapter focuses on the public health consequences of armed conflict, there is a phased evolution of public health effects as a country or region moves from political disturbances, economic deterioration, and civil strife through armed conflict, population migration, food shortages, and the collapse of governance and physical infrastructure. Thus, this section attempts to frame the indirect consequences of civil conflict in the changing context of evolving humanitarian emergencies.

Food Scarcity

As political disturbances evolve in a country, there is generally a significant effect on national and local economies. In some cases, an economic crisis may initiate political turmoil where there have been underlying tensions between political factions, ethnic or religious groups, or disadvantaged geographic areas. Under such scenarios, especially in low-income countries, one of the first health effects is undernutrition in vulnerable groups, which is in turn caused by food scarcity (see Exhibit 10-1). Local farmers may not plant crops as extensively as usual, or may decrease the diversity of their crops due to the uncertainty created by the economic or political situation. The cost of seeds and fertilizer may increase and government agricultural extension services may be disrupted, resulting in lower yields. Distribution and marketing systems may be adversely affected. Devaluation of the local currency may drive down the price paid for agricultural produce, and the collapse of the local food processing industry may further diminish demand for agricultural products.

If full-scale armed conflict occurs, the fighting may damage irrigation systems, crops might be intentionally destroyed or looted by armed soldiers, distribution systems may collapse completely, and there may be widespread theft and looting of food stores. In countries that do not normally produce agricultural surpluses or that have large pastoral or nomadic communities, the impact of food deficits on the nutritional status of civilians may be severe, particularly in sub-Saharan Africa (see Exhibit 10-2). If adverse climatic factors intervene, as often happened in drought-prone countries such as Sudan, Somalia, Mozambique, and Ethiopia during the 1980s and 1990s, the outcome may be catastrophic famine.

Famine may be defined as high malnutrition and mortality rates resulting from inadequate availability of food. Lack of food availability may result from either insufficient production or inadequate or inequitable distribution.

In eastern Europe, when economic and political turmoil followed the collapse of the Soviet Union and its allies during the 1990s, currencies were devalued and the price of staple foods increased dramatically. Persons on fixed incomes, especially elderly pensioners and families with unemployed adults, found that their purchasing power decreased. This resulted in a large proportion of the population subsisting on inadequate diets. In industrialized countries affected by armed conflict, urban residents may be at higher risk than rural communities. For example, the 380,000 citizens of besieged Sarajevo in 1992 required approximately 270 metric tons (MT) of external food aid per day. However, in late 1992, an average of 216 MT of food was delivered daily, providing approximately 2,024 kilocalories per person per day, or 75% of the minimum average winter energy requirements (Toole, Galson, & Brady, 1993). In countries subject to sanctions or blockades, such as Armenia and Iraq during the 1990s, urban families are at particularly high risk of nutritional deficiencies.

When food aid programs are established, there may be inequitable distribution due to political factors, food stores may be damaged or destroyed, food may be stolen or diverted to military forces, and the distribution of food aid may be obstructed (Macrae & Zwi, 1994). The resulting food shortages may cause prolonged hunger and eventually drive families from their homes in search of relief. There have been many examples of food aid diversion, including

---

Exhibit 10-1	**Indonesia**

In Indonesia, the fourth most populous country in the world, an economic crisis occurred in 1997 at a time when dissatisfaction with the ruling oligarchy was high; within several months, widespread riots led to the resignation of the then president. Prior to the crisis, economic growth rates had been high, and food security was at its best level since independence. In 1997 and 1998, there was a dramatic flight of capital out of the country, an abrupt drop in foreign investment, widespread unemployment, and rising tensions within cities. The proportion of the population below the poverty line increased from 11% in 1996 to 14% in 1998, and unemployment increased from 4.7% to 20.3% within 1 year. By late 1999, there was secessionist violence in Aceh and Irian Jaya provinces, religious conflicts in the eastern provinces of Maluku and West Timor resulting in the loss of hundreds of lives, ethnic violence in West Kalimantan, and mass killings in Timor L'Este.

The nation faced near total collapse. Health budgets were halved, and existing health programs deteriorated in quality and coverage. Rice imports increased from 633,000 metric tons (MT) in 1994 to more than 3 million MT in 1998; with the greatly devalued currency, this led to the price of rice increasing threefold between 1997 and 1999. The price increases disproportionately affected the poor, who spent 25% of their incomes on rice, compared with only 5% among high-income households. Studies during 1998 showed decreases in the consumption of fish, eggs, and meat; increases in iron and vitamin A deficiency; increased prevalence of low body mass index (BMI) among women; and increased reported cases of severe wasting and nutritional edema among children.

Source: Data from M.J. Toole and A. Rodger, *The Impact of the Asian Financial Crisis on Health* (Canberra : Australian Agency for International Development, 2000).

Exhibit 10-2	West Darfur, Sudan

An armed conflict developed in Darfur, Sudan, in early 2003 with a major offensive by the progovernment *Janjaweed* militia against two rebel groups, the Sudan Liberation Army and the Justice and Equality Movement. The attacks led to the displacement of more than 1 million people within Darfur itself and more than 200,000 people into neighboring Chad. By late 2004, the security situation remained dire despite United Nations resolutions hinting at genocide and efforts by the African Union to halt the conflict. A World Food Programme food security assessment in October 2004 found that only 7% of IDPs were able to access sufficient food, compared with around 50% of nondisplaced residents. IDPs had lost 90% of their livestock and 80% of their grain stocks, and the area cultivated in 2004 was only 40% of that planted in 2003. Food prices were reported to be 60% above the normal level, and income had dropped by 80% and 70% for IDPs and residents, respectively.

Sources: E. Depoortere, F. Checchi, F. Broillet, S. Gerstl, A. Minetti, O. Gayraud, et al., "Violence and Mortality in West Darfur, Sudan (2003–2004): Epidemiological Evidence from Four Surveys," 2004 *Lancet*, 364, pp. 1315–1320; and United Nations Standing Committee on Nutrition, *Nutrition Information in Crisis Situations* (Report No. IV) Geneva, Switzerland: UN Standing Committee on Nutrition.

Mozambique and Ethiopia in the 1980s and Sudan and the former Yugoslavia in the 1990s and in the first years of the 21st century. Indeed, in latter-day CEs, targeting of relief assistance and the use of humanitarian aid as a resource that enables the warring parties to continue their violence is an ongoing challenge for humanitarian agencies.

Population Displacement

A common response by families and communities to civil conflict is to flee the violence. Individuals may flee because they fear persecution due to their particular political beliefs, ethnicity, or religion. In some societies, migration of part of the family to a safer area may be a traditional coping mechanism, with adult males staying behind to care for their land and animals. Some of these men may also be directly involved in the conflict. Mass migration and food shortages have been responsible for most deaths following civil conflicts in Africa and Asia.

Refugees are defined under several international conventions as persons who flee their country of origin through a well-founded fear of persecution for reasons of race, religion, social class, or political beliefs. The number of dependent refugees under the protection and care of the UNHCR steadily increased from approximately 6 million in 38 countries in 1980 to more than 17 million in 1992. By 2003, the number had declined to about 12 million due to a number of large repatriations of refugees to their homelands (United States Committee for Refugees, 2004). Table 10-1 notes major refugee populations as of December 2003.

Several of the world's largest ever mass migrations took place in the last decade of the 20th century. For example, in 1991, as many as 1 million Kurdish refugees fled Iraq for Iran or Turkey following the Gulf War. By early 1993, there were at least 1.5 million refugees or displaced persons within the republics of the former Yugoslavia. Between April and July 1994, an estimated 2 million Rwandan refugees fled into Tanzania, eastern Zaire, and Burundi, provoking the most serious refugee crisis in 20 years. In the final years of the 20th century and the first few years of the new millennium, major refugee flows occurred out of Kosovo, Timor L'Este, Sudan, Sierra Leone, and Côte d'Ivoire. Between March and June 1999, approximately 780,000 ethnic Albanians fled the Serbian province of Kosovo in one of the most dramatic examples of ethnic cleansing in the series of Balkan conflicts. This represented more than 50% of the Albanian population of the province prior to the war.

In June 1999, approximately 400,000 Kosovars spontaneously repatriated to their homes within 2 weeks of the end of the NATO bombing campaign. During the violence and destruction that followed the August 1999 referendum on independence in Timor L'Este, between 300,000 and 400,000 people were displaced (almost 50% of the population), of whom approximately 260,000 were forcibly moved into Indonesian-controlled West Timor.

In addition to those persons who meet the international definition of refugees, millions of people have fled their homes for the same reasons as refugees but remain internally displaced in their countries of origin. It has not proven easy to ascertain the number and location of the world's IDPs. This is due not only to definitional difficulties, but also to several institutional, political, and operational obstacles. Unlike the collection of refugee statistics, a task undertaken by UNHCR, no single UN agency has assumed responsibility for the collection of figures on internally displaced populations. The question of internal displacement is also a politically sensitive one. Governments are often unwilling to admit to the presence

Table 10-1	Origins of Ten Major Refugee Populations, December 2003	
Country of Origin	**Main Countries of Asylum**	**Estimated Number**
Palestinians	West Bank, Gaza, Jordan, Lebanon, other Middle Eastern countries	3,000,000
Afghanistan	Iran, Pakistan, India, western Europe	2,500,000
Sudan	Chad, Uganda, Ethiopia, Kenya, Central African Republic	351,300
Myanmar (Burma)	Thailand, Bangladesh, India	586,000
Democratic Republic of Congo (DRC)	Congo-Brazzaville, Angola, Burundi, Central African Republic, Rwanda, Tanzania, Zambia	440,000
Liberia	Guinea, Côte d'Ivoire, Ghana, Sierra Leone	384,000
Burundi	Tanzania, DRC, Rwanda, Zambia	355,000
Angola	DRC, Namibia, Zambia	323,000
Vietnam	China	307,000
Iraq	Iran, Syria, Saudi Arabia, Jordan	280,600

Source: United States Committee for Refugees, *World Refugee Survey, 2004* (Washington, DC: U.S. Committee for Refugees, 2004). Reprinted with permission.

of such populations on their territory, indicative as they are of the state's failure to protect its citizens. IDPs may themselves be reluctant to report to or register with the local authorities. Indeed, there is evidence to suggest that a large proportion of the world's IDPs live not in highly visible camps, but mingled with family members and friends, often in urban areas where they can enjoy a higher degree of anonymity.

Finally, there are some very obvious obstacles to the collection of data in areas affected by ongoing armed conflicts. In the combat zones of Liberia, Somalia, Sierra Leone, and Kosovo, for example, the international presence has been minimal or nonexistent, making it extremely difficult even to provide rough estimates of the number of people who have been displaced. Thus, in Sierra Leone, the statistics have been based on food aid beneficiary lists and probably reflect only a fraction of the displaced population. In other situations, such as Chechnya, IDPs are highly mobile, again making it very difficult to determine their exact numbers at any moment in time. Despite all of these difficulties, there was a broad international consensus that the global population of IDPs in 2003 stood somewhere in the region of 23 to 24 million (Figure 10-2): up to 13 million in Africa, 6 or 7 million in Asia and the Middle East, around 2 million in Europe (predominantly the former Yugoslavia and the Caucasus region), and up to 3 million in the Americas, almost all in Colombia (United States Committee for Refugees, 2004).

IDPs lack the international protection afforded by the international conventions and protocols on refugees. Nevertheless, the Geneva Conventions and certain articles of the United Nations Charter afford some protection to IDPs. During the 1990s, the United Nations took some extraordinary measures to protect these populations in southern Sudan, northern Iraq, the republics of the former Yugoslavia, Somalia, and Timor L'Este. There have been few such United Nations interventions since 2000.

Prior to 1990, most of the world's refugees had fled countries that ranked among the poorest in the world, such as Afghanistan, Cambodia, Mozambique, and Ethiopia. However, during the following decade, an increasing number of refugees originated in relatively more affluent countries, such as Kuwait, Iraq, the former Yugoslavia, Armenia, Georgia, and Azerbaijan. However, the reasons for the flight of refugees generally remain the same: war, civil strife, and persecution. Hunger, although sometimes a primary cause of population movements, is all too frequently only a contributing factor. For example, during 1992, although severe drought in southern Africa and the Horn of Africa affected food production in all countries in those regions, only in war-torn Mozambique and Somalia did millions of hungry inhabitants migrate in search of food.

The World Bank estimates that between 90 and 100 million people around the world have been forcibly displaced over the past decade as a result of large-scale development initiatives such as dam

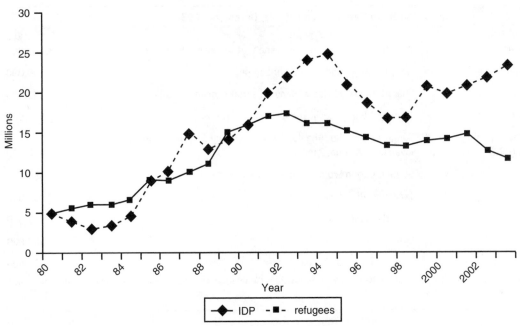

Figure 10-2 Comparison of Refugees and IDPs, 1986–2003. *Source:* Norwegian Refugee Council, *Internally Disabled Persons: A Global Survey* (London: Earthscan, 1997). Adapted with permission.

construction, urban development, and transportation programs. An unknown number have also been uprooted by lower-profile forestry, mining, game park, and land-use conversion projects. The scale of such displacement seems unlikely to diminish in the future, given the processes of economic development, urbanization, and population growth that are taking place in many low- and middle-income countries (United States Committee for Refugees, 1998).

The most common response to mass population movements, either across international boundaries or within countries, is to establish camps or settlements. In eastern Europe, many refugees and IDPs have been housed in hotels, resort camps, schools, and hostels, where environmental conditions have been relatively good. However, in low-income countries, most refugees and displaced persons have been placed in camps located in inappropriate border areas. Exceptions include Mozambican refugees in Malawi in the 1980s, Liberian refugees in Guinea in the early 1990s, and Kosovar Albanians in Macedonia and Albania in 1999. In all three situations at least 50% of refugees were housed in local villages. Conditions in camps have varied enormously; in general, camps with fewer than 20,000 residents have had more favorable environmental conditions than larger camps. Camps for Rwandan refugees in eastern Zaire in 1994 contained up to 300,000 persons; they were poorly planned and laid out, with inadequate sanitation and poor access to clean water. Relief

program managers found it difficult if not impossible to establish equitable systems of distribution of commodities, such as food and shelter materials, and there was a high frequency of violence and other crimes. By contrast, smaller refugee camps in Burundi were more easily managed and suffered fewer health consequences related to environmental conditions.

In addition to poor environmental conditions, crowded camps promote the spread of many communicable diseases, such as measles and acute respiratory infections. The overwhelming nature of these large camps also tends to promote a sense of loss of dignity and independence among mostly rural refugees and induces mental health disorders such as anxiety and depression.

Destruction of Public Utilities

Wars often involve the intentional or accidental destruction of public utilities, such as water and sewage systems, electricity sources and distribution grids, and fuel supplies. Although these disruptions mainly affect urban areas, local water supplies have also been destroyed in rural conflicts, such as in Somalia during the early 1990s. Land mines have also intentionally been laid close to public water outlets. During the long internal conflicts in Mozambique and Angola, large cities and towns were targeted by guerrilla forces, resulting in nonfunctioning public utilities for many years. During the last two decades of the 20th century, cities in Lebanon, Bosnia and Herzegovina,

Chechnya, Somalia, Sudan, Kuwait, Iraq, Serbia, and Kosovo were perhaps the most severely affected. In September 1999, Dili, the capital of newly independent Timor L'Este, was virtually destroyed in the ensuing violence.

Between 1992 and 1995, in Sarajevo, the capital, and other large cities in Bosnia and Herzegovina, municipal water supplies were destroyed by shelling; similar breakdowns in sewage systems and cross-contamination of piped water supplies led to widespread contamination of drinking water. These problems were compounded by the lack of electricity and diesel fuel needed to run generators. In the summer of 1993, residents of Sarajevo had on average only 5 liters of water per person per day, compared with the minimum of 15 to 20 liters recommended by the World Health Organization (WHO) and UNHCR. Although widespread epidemics of diarrheal disease were avoided, local health department data showed that the incidence of communicable diseases increased significantly after the beginning of the war. For example, between 1991 and 1993, the incidence of hepatitis A increased 6-fold in Sarajevo, 12-fold in Zenica, and 4-fold in Tuzla (CDC, 1993a). The incidence of dysentery caused by *Shigella* species increased 12-fold and 17-fold in Sarajevo and Zenica, respectively, during the same period.

Lack of electricity adversely affects urban health services, in particular, hospital and clinic curative services. During a conflict, hospital generators are often able to supply only operating rooms and emergency rooms, thus further promoting a concentration of services in the area of trauma management. Routine surgical procedures, inpatient medical care, and pediatric, obstetric and gynecological, and perinatal care services deteriorate. In addition, the cold chain required to maintain immunization programs is not sustainable.

Sanctions and blockades have a similar effect on public utilities, without any physical destruction. During the winter of 1992–1993, Armenian cities, such as the capital, Yerevan, were deprived of imported fuel, including petrol, coal, kerosene, and gas. Consequently, there was practically no electricity or cooking and heating fuels available to private homes while temperatures averaged well below zero. The cold increased the caloric requirements of individuals at a time when there were severe food shortages. Other health effects included increased rates of acute respiratory infections.

During the first Gulf War, allied bombing damaged Iraqi sewage treatment plants and water supplies, with available potable water declining to 1.5 million cubic meters per day. Shortages of chemicals to monitor water quality contributed to typhoid, cholera, and gastrointestinal diseases. Even in very poor settings, available local infrastructure may be specifically targeted. The Sudanese army deliberately destroyed hand water pumps in rebel areas, and the insurgency did likewise in government-held territory (Dodge, 1990). At the beginning of the 21st century, the Russian Army pounded Grozny, the capital city of Chechnya, with mortars and tanks in order to defeat the separatist movement based in the territory.

The Effects of Armed Conflict and Political Violence on Health Services

The model presented in Figure 10-3 offers a framework for describing the health service impact of conflict and CEs. The focus is on the health services within the countries affected by CEs; there are also related pressures and constraints on the health services of host countries to which refugees may flee.

Access to Services

The impact of conflict on health facilities and services depends on their prior availability, distribution, and utilization patterns. Where services were originally available, as in Iraq (prior to 1991) or the former Yugoslavia (prior to 1992), the conflict may cause rapid deterioration as a result of infrastructure and distribution systems damage, resource constraints, declining health personnel availability and morale, and reductions in access. The prewar Iraqi health system was extensive, accessible to 90% of the population, and reached 95% of the children requiring immunization (Lee & Haines, 1991). By the end of the Gulf War, many hospitals and clinics had been severely damaged or closed, those operating were overwhelmed with work, and damage to infrastructure, water supplies, electricity, and sewage disposal exacerbated problems in population health and health services activity.

Utilization is determined by geographic access (i.e., the services are not too far away), economic access (i.e., the services are affordable) and social access (i.e., there are no psychological or other barriers preventing use of services), all of which may be disrupted during CEs. Peripheral services may be directly targeted, as in Mozambique (Cliff & Noormahomed, 1988) or Nicaragua (Garfield & Williams, 1992) during the 1980s. Service access may be limited by fear of physical or sexual assault or by physical restrictions on access as a result of antipersonnel land mines, curfews, and, in some cases, the encirclement of areas. In Afghanistan, the Taliban imposed constraints on women accessing services that were previously

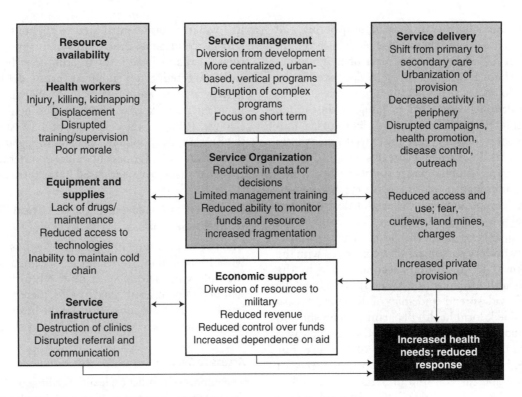

Figure 10-3 Impact of Conflict and Complex Emergencies on Health Services.

available to them. In other settings access may be restricted as a result of fear, insecurity, or lack of confidence in service providers. People injured in civil or political conflict may avoid using public services that carry a risk of security force surveillance. For example, in South Africa, the Philippines, and the occupied Palestinian territories, NGOs established alternative health services to allow those injured during uprisings against repressive regimes to seek care without fear of detection and detention.

Conflict may seriously disrupt links between services operating at different levels: Referrals will be disrupted by logistical and communication constraints, as well as physical and military barriers to access. Towns and cities may be besieged, with entry and exit controlled by militias, as in Beirut, Sarajevo, and Juba (Sudan). Health workers may move to urban areas to seek protection, other opportunities to make a living, or opportunities to provide health services privately with greater financial returns.

Health Services Adaptations

Health services may be affected in a variety of ways. For example, systems within conflict areas may shift away from primary and community-based care to secondary, hospital-based services. This is a reflection of the movement of health care providers to ur-

ban areas, increased efforts to respond to the most serious injuries and adverse health effects, and the greater difficulty of maintaining peripheral services. Even in situations where preventive care was identified as important, such as in the struggle for liberation in the Tigrayan province of Ethiopia, priority was given to dealing with the war wounded and maintaining the health of fighters (Barnabas & Zwi, 1997).

Emphasizing care and rehabilitation for war injuries indirectly de-emphasizes longer-term health development and community-based activities, including those focusing on disease control. Malaria control activities may be seriously compromised: Vector control, house spraying, environmental programs, information and education, training, and supervision may all be disrupted. Disease treatment may become nonstandardized, haphazard, incomplete, and uncoordinated, with considerable risk of the emergence of resistant organisms. These factors are especially important in relation to malaria, STIs, and tuberculosis control. Impaired surveillance and health information systems undermine the ability to detect unusual or exacerbated patterns of disease occurrence and to respond to them. Public health actions such as partner notification, screening, and community education efforts may be compromised. Activities may become increasingly limited to small areas or specific districts and populations, and service provision may be increasingly organized through vertical programs that allow control over activities to assess needs, deliver services, monitor performance, and track finances. The gap between better-funded vertical programs and the general health services may widen substantially, both during and in the aftermath of major conflicts.

Adaptation occurs, and other actors attempt to fill the gaps caused by retreating and contracting public sector services. Indigenous health care providers may become more important both in their role as healers more generally and as health care providers. The private health care sector expands, both through the provision of services by nonprofit NGOs and through the hemorrhage of public-sector workers into the private sector, whether officially or unofficially.

Infrastructure

Direct targeting of clinics, hospitals, and ambulances may be against international humanitarian law but has frequently been experienced in latter-day conflicts. In the siege of Vukovar in eastern Slavonia during the civil war in the former Yugoslavia, the hospital was seriously damaged and much of it destroyed. Related facilities, such as those necessary for water and sanitation, sewage removal, and electricity, have been directly targeted, the latter in Iraq and Serbia. In Nicaragua, the insurgency destroyed the main pharmaceutical storage facility of the country in Corinto, creating a severe shortage for months.

The destruction of nonhealth physical infrastructure such as roads, electrical plants, and communication systems has indirect health consequences. In Cape Town, South Africa, transport difficulties prevented health workers from attending work; experiences in the occupied Palestinian territories and other regions of active ongoing conflict have been similar. In some Iraqi hospitals, elevators did not work during energy blackouts, with the result that patients could not be moved to surgical theaters, and emergency interventions had to be delayed or take place in suboptimal conditions. The impact on health services of the electricity supply disruption instituted by NATO bombing in Serbia and Kosovo is unknown, as are the longer-term environmental and economic consequences.

Equipment and Supplies

Access to medicines and supplies is typically disrupted during conflicts. Drug shortages, especially where they were previously available, may lead to an increase in medically preventable causes of death, such as asthma, diabetes, and infectious diseases. Disruption to the Ugandan Essential Drugs Management Program, organized in the early 1980s, resulted in many rural dwellers who had gained access to modern medicines and vaccines being once more deprived of basic drugs. The quality of care available may suffer greatly. In Somalia, amputations performed without intravenous antibiotics led to higher rates of infection, and in the former Yugoslavia, operations were performed with inadequate anesthesia. Health care technologies, including x-rays and laboratories, are undermined through lack of maintenance, spare parts, skilled personnel, chemicals, and other supplies.

Additional problems may emerge as a result of the humanitarian response. Drug donations, if poorly coordinated and standardized, may lead to a large number of expired and inappropriate drugs being off–loaded in countries experiencing CEs. These may be unable to be used, but require to be safely and efficiently disposed of, placing an additional burden on the recipient country's pharmaceutical services. Another problem that typically arises results from the poor standardization of treatments, with different NGOs, host government, and other services all treating similar problems using different drugs, often with inappropriate treatment regimes, raising the risk of multiresistant organisms emerging.

Budgetary Impact

The conflict against the Ethiopian Derg led to increases in military expenditure from 11.2% of the government budget in 1974–1975 to 36.5% by 1990–1991 and to declines in the health budget from 6.1% in 1973–1974 to 3.5% in 1985–1986 and 3.2% in 1990–1991 (Kloos, 1992). The deterioration of the economy typically leads to reduced public expenditure as funds are shifted into supporting the war. In Uganda, the public health budget in 1986 was only 6.4% of what it had been in the early 1970s. In El Salvador the proportion of the national budget allocated to health during the civil war plummeted from 10% in 1980 to 6% in 1990, and the budget available to the ministry of health, as a percentage of the gross national product, declined from 2% to 0.9%. Prior to 1980, the health budget had been higher than the defense budget, but during the first year of the civil war more funds were allocated to the military than to health. At the peak of the conflict in 1986, even the official figures indicated that the military received about four times more than the health sector.

Human Resources

Injury, killing, kidnapping, and exodus of health workers are common during CEs. There is evidence of targeting health workers in many recent conflicts; this has been particularly well documented in Mozambique and Nicaragua. Even if not directly targeted, health workers may flee in search of safety and security. In Uganda, half the doctors and 80% of the pharmacists left the country between 1972 and 1985 (Dodge, 1990), and in Mozambique, only 80 of the 500 doctors present before independence remained after 1975 (Walt & Cliff, 1986). In Cambodia, Pol Pot's killing fields were directed at professional and educated people, among others, with brutal and long-lasting effects; there was some, as yet unconfirmed, evidence of professionals being similarly targeted in Kosovo. Administrative and planning capacity may be seriously undermined by the lack of data, lack of personnel, and lack of consensus-building opportunities through which policies can be negotiated, strategies developed, and planning undertaken. In the period leading up to the referendum on independence in Timor L'Este, there was an exodus of trained health personnel. The number of doctors in the province decreased from approximately 200 in 1998 to 69 in April 1999 (four months before the referendum) to only 20 in February 2000.

Community Involvement

In many latter-day conflicts and those of the Cold War period, which were described as "low intensity," community leaders and social structures were frequently targeted. Those who waged war against the Marxist Frelimo state in Mozambique attempted to reduce access to health care and educational services, which the state had prioritized as a symbol of its commitment to promoting more equitable development. A similar process took place in Nicaragua, where opposition forces targeted health and education services, a reflection of state commitment. Local systems of democracy and accountability are often seriously disrupted and involvement in community affairs discouraged; however, in some conflicts quite the reverse occurs, notably those in Mozambique, Vietnam, Eritrea, and Tigray.

Organizational or political responses to conflict may be positive, facilitating opportunities for health system and societal development. In the popular conflict against the Ethiopian Derg, community-based political movements in Eritrea and Tigray promoted community participation and control in decision making and facilitated the development of multisectoral health promotion strategies. The Tigrayan People's Liberation Front trained health workers and established mobile services and innovative community financing systems. Elected local governments, the *baitos*, were established, which played a significant role in mobilizing and distributing resources to ensure that

drugs and adequate services were available despite considerable constraints (Barnabas & Zwi, 1997).

Policy Formulation

Violent political conflict undermines the capacity to make decisions rationally and accountably. A key problem in conflict-affected settings is the wide range of actors operating and the confused lines of accountability. In typical health systems, peripheral-level services are accountable, usually within the health sector, to district or provincial health authorities, and these are, in turn, responsible to central health authorities. Conflict may lead to greater degrees of centralization of decision making, whereas the need is for increasingly decentralized decision making so as to ensure that peripheral services can respond appropriately to their local context.

The policy framework within which providers and purchasers of services operate may be compromised or nonexistent, leading to an inability to control and coordinate service provision. There may be a serious lack of data upon which to make important health policy decisions. Ongoing conflict may impede learning of lessons from experience, the build-up of institutional memory, and the stimulation of ongoing critical debate regarding health and social policies, both locally and in relation to current international debates. Locally available forums for debate, such as the media and professional organizations, may be controlled or less accessible. In the postconflict setting, a key challenge is to reestablish these forums for debate and to facilitate the exchange of ideas among the range of important stakeholders operating in the health environment.

New Actors

During internal conflicts, due to scarcity of resources and government difficulties in accessing populations under the control of insurgents, NGOs usually fill part of the vacuum left by the public sector. In recent conflict-related emergencies, various military forces have played a direct role in providing relief (e.g., northern Iraq, 1991), as have private companies contracted by government or UN agencies (e.g., Albania and Macedonia, 1999). The entry of these new players has further complicated the response to CEs. The role of NGOs is extremely important both during and in the aftermath of ongoing conflict. During conflicts, indigenous NGOs and church groups may be among the few service providers that continue to operate during the conflict, especially in rural areas and those more directly affected by violence. A key problem, however, is that these NGOs often provide a patchwork of services that are relatively independent of the state and do not necessarily fit in with other service provision approaches or priorities. They may communicate poorly with one another, adopt different approaches and standards of care and of health worker remuneration, and focus attention mostly at a very local level, with some impact on the equity of service availability across large regions.

Health-related peace-building initiatives may provide avenues for reconnecting people and social structures, lives, and livelihoods. Evidence for the extent and limitations of such approaches is slowly emerging but requires further critical analysis and debate. A key research challenge is to understand how health systems adapt and respond to conflict and to determine whether positive developments can be further reinforced and sustained. WHO assisted the Bosnian and Croatian health care systems to register and respond to the needs of disabled people during the war. These could be extended in the postwar period to ensure access to rehabilitation and social support services. Surgery services developed in response to antipersonnel land mine injuries should be extended to other forms of injury surveillance and treatment. Mechanisms to protect and maintain key elements of service provision and functioning, including information systems and supplies, are crucial to assuring ongoing system functioning. How best to promote this requires further exploration.

Specific Health Outcomes

Mortality

In this section, the impact of civil conflict and humanitarian emergencies on mortality rates will be confined to indirect causes, such as food scarcity, population displacement, destruction of health facilities and public utilities, and disruption of routine curative and preventive services. Mortality directly caused by the violence of war has been discussed earlier.

The most severe health consequences of conflict—population displacement, food scarcity, and siege situations—have occurred in the acute emergency phase, during the early stage of relief efforts, and have been characterized by extremely high mortality rates. Although the quality of the international community's disaster response efforts has steadily improved, death rates associated with forced migration have often remained high, as demonstrated by several emergencies during the 1990s. For example, the exodus of almost 1 million Rwandan refugees

into eastern Zaire in 1994 resulted in mortality rates that were more than 30 times the rates experienced prior to the conflict in Rwanda. A series of population surveys in the DRC between 2000 and 2004 found that approximately 3.8 million people had died as a result of the conflict in that country, which began in August 1998 (Coghlan et al., 2004). Death rates were highest in the eastern zones of the country, where the conflict had been most intense. Most of these excess deaths were due to easily preventable and treatable diseases; only 2% were caused by war-related injuries. In Darfur, Sudan, death rates among civilian populations as high as 9.5 per 10,000 per day were recorded (20 times higher than baseline mortality rates). In contrast to the DRC, between 68% and 93% of deaths in Darfur populations were due to violence (Depoortere et al., 2004).

Crude mortality rates (CMRs) have been estimated from burial site surveillance; administrative, hospital, and burial records; community-based reporting systems; and population surveys. The many problems in estimating mortality under emergency conditions have included the following:

- poorly representative or inaccurate population sample surveys
- failure of families to report all deaths for fear of losing food ration entitlements
- inaccurate estimates of affected populations for the purpose of calculating mortality rates
- lack of standard reporting procedures

In general, however, mortality rates have tended to be underestimated because deaths are usually underreported or undercounted, and population size is often exaggerated.

Early in an emergency, when mortality rates are elevated, the CMR is usually expressed as deaths per 10,000 population per day (CDC, 1992). The median annual CMR in developing countries is around 9 per 1,000, corresponding to a daily rate of approximately 0.25 per 10,000 (Reed & Keeley, 2001). A threshold of 1 per 10,000 per day has been used commonly to define an elevated CMR and to characterize a situation as an emergency (CDC, 1992). In one of the most severe refugee emergencies of the 1990s, the CMR among Rwandan refugees during the first month after their arrival in eastern Zaire was between 27 and 50 per 10,000 per day (Goma Epidemiology Group, 1995).

The most reliable estimates of mortality rates have come from well-defined and secure refugee camps where there is a reasonable level of camp organization and a designated agency has had responsibility for the collection of data (Table 10-2). The most difficult situations have been those where IDPs have been scattered over a wide area and where surveys could take place only in relatively secure zones (Table 10-3). These safe zones may have sometimes acted as magnets for the most severely affected elements of a population. For example, in 1998, a survey in Ajiep, southern Sudan, found that the CMR increased from 17.8 per 10,000 per day during the period June 3 to July 11 to 69.7 per 10,000 per day between July 12 and July 20 (Brown, Moren, & Paquet, 1999). The increase may have been due to an influx of displaced persons reaching Ajiep in a poor condition or by a decrease in the food available within the town. On the other hand, it is possible that the worst affected communities have been in areas that have been inaccessible by those performing the surveys. In either case, it has proved difficult to extrapolate the findings of surveys on mortality conducted in specific locations to broader populations in conflict-affected countries. Extensive differences in mortality

survey methods have been identified; for example, an evaluation of 23 field surveys performed in Somalia between 1991 and 1993 found wide variation in the target populations, sampling strategies, units of measurement, methods of rate calculation, and statistical analysis (Boss, Toole, & Yip, 1994).

Trends in death rates over time have varied from place to place. In refugee populations where the international response has been prompt and effective, such as was the case for Cambodians in eastern Thailand (1979) and Iraqis on the Turkish border (1991), death rates declined to baseline levels within 1 month. Among refugees in Somalia (1980) and Sudan (1985), death rates were still well above baseline rates 6 to 9 months after the influx of refugees occurred (Toole & Waldman, 1990). In the case of 170,000 Somali refugees in Ethiopia in 1988–1989, death rates actually increased significantly 6 months after the influx. This increase was associated with elevated malnutrition prevalence rates, inadequate food rations, and high incidence rates of certain communicable diseases. Although initial death rates among

Table 10-2	Estimated Daily Crude Mortality Rates (Deaths per 10,000 per Day) in Selected Refugee Populations, 1991–2004		
Period	**Country of Asylum**	**Country of Origin**	**Mean CMR for Period**
June 1991	Ethiopia	Somalia	2.3[a]
March–May 1991	Turkey	Iraq	4.7[b]
March–May 1991	Iran	Iraq	2.0[c]
March 1992	Kenya	Somalia	7.4[a]
March 1992	Nepal	Bhutan	3.0[d]
August 1992	Zimbabwe	Mozambique	3.5[e]
December 1993	Rwanda	Burundi	3.0[f]
August 1994	Tanzania	Rwanda	19.6–31.3[g]
May 1999	Albania	Yugoslavia (Kosovo)	0.5[h]
November 1999	Indonesia (Tuapukan camp, West Timor)	East Timor	2.1[i]
September 2004	Chad	Darfur, Sudan	1.3[j]

Note: CMR = crude mortality rate.

[a]Toole & Waldman (1993).

[b]Centers for Disease Control and Prevention (CDC) (1991b).

[c]Babille et al. (1994).

[d]Marfin et al. (1994).

[e]CDC (1993b).

[f]CDC (1994).

[g]UN Administrative Committee on Coordination, Sub-Committee on Nutrition (ACC/SCN) (1994a).

[h]UN ACC/SCN (1999).

[i]WHO Health Information Network for Advanced Planning (2000a).

[j]UN Standing Committee on Nutrition (2004d).

Table 10-3	Estimated Crude Mortality Rates (Deaths per 10,000 per Day), Internally Displaced Populations, 1991–2004	
Period	**Country (Region)**	**CMR for Period**
April 1991–March 1992	Somalia (Merca)	4.6[a]
April–November 1992	Somalia (Baidoa)	16.9[b]
April 1992–March 1993	Sudan (Ayod)	7.7[c]
April 1993	Bosnia and Herzegovina (Sarajevo)	1.0[d]
May 1995	Angola (Cafunfo)	8.3[e]
February 1996	Liberia (Bong)	5.5[f]
May 1998	Burundi (Cibitoke)	3.3[g]
June 3–July 20, 1998	Sudan (Ajiep)	26.0[h]
September 2001	Sierra Leone (Kono district)	1.4[i]
June 2002	Angola (Muacanhica, Muahimbo, Luena)	2.9–7.2[j]
February 2002	Sudan (Jonglei)	7.2[j]
April 2003	DRC (Katanga)	1.9[k]
April 2004	Sudan (Wade Saleh, Darfur)	3.6[l]

[a]Manoncourt et al. (1992).
[b]Moore et al. (1993).
[c]CDC (1993c).
[d]CDC (1993a).
[e]UN Administrative Committee on Coordination, Sub-Committee on Nutrition (ACC/SCN) (1995).
[f]UN ACC/SCN (1996).
[g]UN ACC/SCN (1998).
[h]Epicentre and MSF France, in UN ACC/SCN (1999).
[i]UN ACC/SCN (2002a).
[j]UN ACC/SCN (2002b).
[k]UN ACC/SCN (2003).
[l]UN Standing Committee on Nutrition (2004b).

Rwandan refugees in eastern Zaire were extremely high, they declined dramatically within 1 to 2 months (Figure 10-4). Surveys in Darfur, Sudan, in 2004 showed that mortality was higher in the predisplacement period and generally declined once people reached refugee or IDP camps (Depoortere et al., 2004).

Most deaths have occurred among children under 5 years of age; for example, 65% of deaths among Kurdish refugees on the Turkish border occurred in the 17% of the population younger than 5 years (Yip & Sharp, 1993). However, in some refugee situations, such as Goma during the first month after the refugee exodus, mortality rates were comparable in all age groups because the major cause of death was cholera, which is equally lethal at any age. Among IDPs in countries affected by severe famine, high adult mor-

tality has been reported. For example, in the Somali town of Baidoa, 59% of 15,105 deaths reported between August 1992 and February 1993 were among adults (Collins, 1993). In Ajiep, southern Sudan, the CMR among IDPs in August 1998 was equal to the under-5 mortality rate (Salama, 1999). In most reports from refugee camps, mortality rates have not been stratified by sex; however, the surveillance system for Burmese refugees in Bangladesh did estimate sex-specific death rates, demonstrating considerably higher death rates in females. Gendered analyses that take into account differences in the sociocultural position of women have been rare in emergency settings.

The major reported causes of death among refugees and displaced populations have been diarrheal diseases, measles, acute respiratory infections, and malaria, exacerbated by high rates of malnutri-

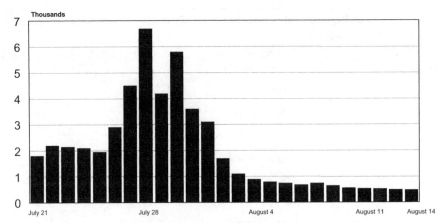

Figure 10-4 Number of Deaths per Day, July 21 to August 14, 1994, Rwandan Refugees, North Kivu Camps, Zaire. *Source:* Goma Epidemiology Group, "Public Health Impact of Rwandan Refugee Crisis: What Happened in Goma, Zaire, in July 1994?" 1995, *Lancet,* 345, pp. 339–344. Reproduced with permission.

tion. These diseases consistently account for between 60% and 95% of all reported causes of death in these populations. Measles epidemics caused high death rates among refugees during the 1980s. Epidemics of severe diarrheal disease have been increasingly common and contributed to high mortality. Cholera case fatality ratios (CFRs) in refugee camps have ranged between 3% and 30%, and dysentery CFRs have been as high as 10% among young children and the elderly.

In eastern European conflicts, a high proportion of mortality among civilians was caused by trauma associated with the violence. Nevertheless, there was also increased mortality in these conflicts due to the collapse of the public health system. Chronic conditions, such as cardiovascular diseases, cancer, and renal conditions, were inadequately treated because the health system was focused on the management of war-related injuries. Medical services in most parts of Bosnia and Herzegovina were overwhelmed by the demands of war casualties. The major hospital in Zenica reported that the proportion of all surgical cases associated with trauma steadily increased following the beginning of the war in April 1992, reaching 78% in November 1992. Preventive health services, including childhood immunization and antenatal care, ceased in many areas. Hospitals were systematic military targets in some areas, and in Sarajevo, 38 of the original 42 ambulances were destroyed (Toole, Galson, & Brady, 1993).

The collapse of health services in Bosnia and Herzegovina had significant public health effects. For example, perinatal mortality increased in Sarajevo from 16 deaths per 1,000 live births in 1991 to 27 per 1,000 during the first 4 months of 1993. The rate of

premature births increased from 5.3% to 12.9%, the stillbirth rate increased from 7.5 per 1000 to 12.3 per 1,000, and the average birth weight decreased from 3,700 g (8.2 lb) to 3,000 g (6.6 lb) during the same period (CDC, 1993a).

Recently, CEs have occurred without excess mortality being reported among displaced populations. For example, although mortality rates among Kosovar refugees in Albania and Macedonia remained below 1 per 10,000 per day, significant threats to the health of the affected populations were present. It is important to continue to monitor the changing epidemiology during the emergency phase and to be prepared to provide assistance targeted at those problems that are of highest priority.

Nutrition

Nutritional deficiencies are often the first public health effects of an evolving CE. Economic and political turmoil leads to food scarcity among vulnerable groups, as described earlier in this chapter. In many countries experiencing political and economic crises, certain ethnic groups are disadvantaged, as well as the unemployed and institutionalized individuals. In Africa and Asia, nomadic communities are often forced to sell their animals and other food reserves. Among refugees and IDPs, there are many factors that might lead to high rates of nutritional deficiency disorders, including prolonged food scarcity prior to and during displacement, delays in the provision of complete rations, problems with registration and estimation of the size of an affected population, and inequitable distribution systems.

In the emergency phase, acute energy depletion is a life-threatening condition and will lead to excess mortality. A critical factor is the synergy between malnutrition and infection; thus, malnutrition prevalence may be increased by high rates of infectious diseases, such as measles, diarrhea, dysentery, acute respiratory infections, malaria, and helminth infestation. Infections, on the other hand, lead to decreased appetite and increased metabolic rate, and exacerbate acute malnutrition. These factors may differentially affect certain demographic groups within the population. The most common vulnerable groups include children younger than 5 years of age, pregnant and lactating women, the elderly, unaccompanied children, the disabled, the chronically ill (e.g., tuberculosis patients), households lacking an adult male, and disadvantaged ethnic or religious groups. In the later stages of famine, there may be a high prevalence of acute malnutrition among adolescents and adults. In industrialized countries, the elderly are often most vulnerable, especially those living alone on fixed incomes.

Malnutrition

In estimating the prevalence of acute malnutrition in a population, the prevalence among children between 6 months and 5 years of age is usually used as a surrogate. This is because the relationship between weight and height in this age group is generally similar in all ethnic groups provided those children have access to adequate food. International reference tables may be used to define various degrees of acute malnutrition.

The prevalence of moderate to severe acute malnutrition in a random sample of children between 6 months and 5 years of age (or 110 cm in height) is generally a reliable indicator of this condition in a population. Since weight is more sensitive to sudden changes in food availability than height, nutritional assessments during emergencies focus on measuring weight for height. Moderate to severe acute malnutrition is defined as a weight-for-height measurement more than 2 standard deviations below the mean of the U.S. Centers for Disease Control and Prevention, National Center for Health Statistics, World Health Organization reference population (Z-score less than −2) (WHO, 1995). Severe acute malnutrition is defined as weight for height more than 3 standard deviations below the reference mean (Z-score less than −3). All children with edema are classified as having severe acute malnutrition. As a screening measurement, the middle upper arm circumference (MUAC) may also be used to assess acute malnutrition, although there is not complete agreement on which cutoff values should be used as indicators. Field studies indicate that a MUAC between 12.0 cm and 12.5 cm correlates with a weight-for-height Z-score of −2;

the lower figure (12.0 cm) is more appropriate in children younger than 2 years of age (WHO, 1995). Acute malnutrition without edema has been termed *wasting* or *marasmus,* and acute malnutrition with edema has been termed *kwashiorkor*; however, a combination of the two may occur in some children. Both are associated with anemia; however, this is often more severe in children (or adults) with kwashiorkor. The anemia may be exacerbated by local conditions, such as malaria and hookworm infection.

A meeting was convened in Nairobi in 2001 by the United Nations Sub-Committee on Nutrition to review the assessment of nutritional status in adults and adolescents. The meeting recommended that assessment of adult malnutrition should be considered under the following circumstances:

- if the crude mortality rate increases in relation to the under-five mortality rate

- if many adults are present at existing supplementary feeding centers

- where there are very high rates of under-five malnutrition in the absence of an epidemic outbreak

- if there is reasonable doubt that the child malnutrition rates do not reflect the nutritional status of the general population

- if the populations are entirely reliant on food aid and if data are required as an advocacy tool to leverage resources

The recommended indices that should be used are Cormic-adjusted body mass index (BMI) (population specific or Norgan correction) and MUAC. The Cormic index (sitting height to standing height ratio) may, to some extent, adjust for ethnic differences in body proportions; however, this technique has not been studied in adolescents (Woodruff & Duffield, 2000). Clinical criteria are recommended for screening adults and adolescents for severe malnutrition in order to determine the need for therapeutic feeding. In surveys of prepubertal adolescents, the extended weight-for-height chart developed by Action Contre la Faim (ACF) should be used. Moderate acute malnutrition is defined as a weight for height between 70% and 79% of the reference median (Z-scores are not used in this age group), and severe malnutrition as less than 70% of the median (Golden, 1999a).

Postpubertal adolescents and adults should be assessed using the BMI, which is the weight in kilograms divided by the height (in meters) squared (w/h^2). Genetic differences between ethnic groups are probably more significant among older age groups than among children younger than 5 years of age.

Therefore, the use of an international BMI reference poses considerable problems. For example, UNHCR and CDC conducted a nutrition survey of adolescents aged 10 to 19 years in four camps in Kenya housing Sudanese and Somali refugees. Comparing the BMI of the sampled adults to the WHO BMI-for-age reference population (which is based on Americans) and using the recommended cutoff, the prevalence of acute malnutrition was between 57% and 61%. However, morbidity and mortality data did not support these high estimates. The researchers strongly suggested that the WHO reference might not be appropriate for comparisons of all adolescents worldwide (Bhatia & Woodruff, 1999). Therefore, BMI for age is not currently recommended as a screening index (Golden, 1999a). MUAC for age is also a problematic screening tool in adolescents because there are no agreed-on cutoff points to define acute malnutrition.

MUAC is commonly used as a screening tool in adult populations. A MUAC of less than 23 cm in men and less than 22 cm in women has been proposed as indicating moderate malnutrition (corresponding to BMI values of less than 17). MUAC values of less than 20 cm in men and less than 19 cm in women were proposed as indicators of severe wasting, corresponding to BMIs below 13 (Ferro-Luzzi & James, 1996). Nevertheless, one reliable clinical sign of severe malnutrition commonly observed in adults is inability to stand.

In some settings, refugee children who were adequately nourished upon arrival in camps have developed acute malnutrition due either to inadequate food rations or to severe epidemics of diarrheal disease. In early 1991, the prevalence of acute malnutrition among Kurdish refugee children aged 12 to 23 months increased from less than 5% to 13% during a 2-month period following a severe outbreak of diarrheal disease (Yip & Sharp, 1993). Surprisingly, the malnutrition prevalence among children younger than 12 months was less than 4%; however, a survey revealed that the diarrhea-associated death rate in this age group was three times higher than the death rate among children 12 to 23 months of age. Thus, it is likely that many malnourished infants died, resulting in deceptively low malnutrition prevalence among the survivors.

North Korea experienced several years of severe food shortages between 1996 and 1999. In September 1998, UNICEF, the World Food Programme, and the European Community Humanitarian Office conducted a nutritional survey covering 61% of the counties and 71% of the country's population. The prevalence of wasting (low weight for height) was 15.6%, which was the highest in any country in East Asia that year. The prevalence was highest among children 12 to 35 months of age, and tended to be higher in boys than girls (European Union, UNICEF, & World Food Programme, 1998).

Prevalences of acute malnutrition among the internally displaced have tended to be extremely high. In southern Somalia during 1992, the prevalence of acute malnutrition among children younger than 5 years in displaced persons camps in Marka and Qorioley was 75%, compared with 43% among town residents (Manoncourt et al., 1992). Among the estimated 1 million IDPs in Darfur, Sudan, acute malnutrition prevalence ranged between 12.6% and 21.5% in March/April 2004, increasing to between 20.6% and 39% in May/June 2004. Following heightened international interest and assistance, rates of malnutrition generally decreased to a range of 10.7% to 23.6% by September 2004. (See Exhibit 10-3 for a discussion of malnutrition among Sudanese refugees.) The prevalence of acute malnutrition among children younger than 5 years of age in various displaced populations is presented in Table 10-4.

Micronutrient Deficiency Diseases

High incidence rates of several micronutrient deficiency diseases have been reported in many refugee camps, especially in Africa. Frequently, famine-affected and displaced populations have already experienced low levels of dietary vitamin A intake and, therefore, may have very low vitamin A reserves. Furthermore, the typical rations provided in large-scale relief operations lack vitamin A, putting these populations at high risk. In addition, those communicable diseases that are highly incident in refugee camps, such as measles and diarrhea, are known to rapidly deplete vitamin A stores. Consequently, young refugee and displaced children are at high risk of developing vitamin A deficiency. In 1990, more than 18,000 cases of pellagra, caused by food rations deficient in niacin, were reported among Mozambican refugees in Malawi (CDC, 1991a). Despite the increased awareness of micronutrient deficiencies among relief agencies, niacin was not a component of the general food ration for IDPs in Angola in 2000. A large outbreak of pellagra was documented, with attack rates among IDPs more than twice those of the nondisplaced population (Salama et al., 2001).

Numerous outbreaks of scurvy (vitamin C deficiency) were documented in refugee camps in Somalia, Ethiopia, and Sudan between 1982 and 1991. Cross-sectional surveys performed in 1986–1987 reported prevalence rates as high as 45% among females and

Exhibit 10-3	Sudanese Refugees in Chad, 2004

As a result of an armed conflict in Darfur, Sudan, that began in early 2003, around 100,000 refugees fled to Chad during 2003. Initially, they lived in makeshift camps and received very little international assistance. Early nutrition surveys indicated great variation between settlements; in November 2003, rates of acute malnutrition among children ranged from 7% to 27% (UN Standing Committee on Nutrition, 2004a). By May 2004, the camps were overcrowded, water and sanitation were inadequate, and an outbreak of the waterborne viral disease hepatitis E had occurred in some camps. In June, a joint agency survey found the overall acute malnutrition prevalence among children to be 35.6%, with 5.5% severely malnourished (UN Standing Committee on Nutrition, 2004c).

By the end of 2004, more than 200,000 Darfur refugees had fled to Chad. International media attention increasingly focused on both the conflict in Darfur and the plight of refugees and IDPs. International assistance increased, and by the end of 2004, most refugees were located in 11 camps run by UNHCR. Blanket supplementary feeding was introduced for all children under 5 and all pregnant and lactating women. According to food basket monitoring, the average energy content of the food ration reached 1,967 kilocalories per person per day by October 2004 (compared with an official ration of 2,063 kilocalories). A September survey in two camps found that the prevalence of acute malnutrition had dropped to 19.6%; although this represented an improvement, the rate remains very high by international standards (UN Standing Committee on Nutrition, 2004d).

36% among males; prevalence increased with age (Desenclos et al., 1989). The prevalence of scurvy was highly associated with the period of residence in camps, a reflection of the time exposed to rations lacking in vitamin C. Outbreaks of scurvy and beriberi were also reported among Bhutanese refugees in Nepal during 1993 (UN ACC/SCN, 1995). Iron deficiency anemia has been reported in many refugee populations, affecting particularly women of child-bearing age and young children. For example, a survey among IDPs in Darfur, Sudan, in 2004 found that 55% of children under 5 years were anemic, as well

Table 10-4	Prevalence of Acute Malnutrition Among Children Younger Than 5 Years in Internally Displaced and Conflict-Affected Populations, 1992–2004		
Date	**Country (Region)**	**Population Affected**	**Prevalence of (%) Acute Malnutrition**
1992	Southern Somalia	3,000,000	47–75[a]
1994	Sudan (Bahr el Ghazal)	345,000	36.1[b]
1994	Afghanistan (Sarashahi)	163,000	18.6[c]
1995	Angola (Cafunfo)	10,000	29.2[d]
1995	Liberia (Goba town, Margibi)	N/A	11.7[e]
1995	Sierra Leone (Bo)	250,000	19.8[d]
1996	Zaire (Masisi)	100,000	31.0[f]
1998	Burundi	N/A	14[g]
1999	West Timor, Indonesia	N/A	24[h]
2002	Sierra Leone (refugee camps)	50,000	6.6–22.2[i]
2003	Bay Region, Somalia	N/A	17.2[j]
2004	Darfur, Sudan	1,000,000	39[k]

Note: Acute malnutrition is defined either as weight for height 2 standard deviations below the reference mean or less than 80% of the reference median.

[a]Toole & Waldman (1993).

[b]Médecins sans Frontières (MSF) Belgium, in UN ACC/SCN (1994).

[c]MSF Holland, in UN ACC/SCN (1994).

[d]Action Contre la Faim (ACF), in UN ACC/SCN (1995).

[e]MSF Holland, in UN ACC/SCN (1995).

[f]MSF Holland, in UN ACC/SCN (1996).

[g]Concern International, in UN ACC/SCN (1998).

[h]World Health Organization, HINAP (2000a, 2000b).

[i]UN ACC/SCN (2003).

[j]UN Standing Committee on Nutrition (SCN) (2004a).

[k]UN SCN (2004c).

as 26.2% of women of reproductive age (UN Standing Committee on Nutrition [SCN], 2004d).

Impact of Communicable Diseases

In most CEs, the high rates of excess preventable mortality have been attributed primarily to communicable diseases. The specific causes of mortality, and their age and gender distribution, do not differ from those that prevail in nonemergency conditions. Accordingly, acute respiratory infections, diarrhea, measles, and malaria have been most frequently cited as proximate causes. Substandard conditions found in camps do not change the diseases that account for most of the morbidity and mortality in humanitarian emergency settings, but they do alter epidemiologic patterns in two important ways: The incidence, or attack, rates of commonly occurring and potentially fatal diseases are increased, and the case fatality ratios (CFRs) are higher than usual.

Measles

Measles has traditionally been among the most feared of communicable diseases in emergency settings. During the 1970s and 1980s, measles epidemics were common, and it was not unusual for measles to be the major cause of mortality in large, displaced populations. High incidence rates (particularly in populations with low levels of vaccination prior to displacement), high mortality rates, and unusually high CFRs are typical of measles outbreaks in emergencies. In an epidemic that occurred in the Wad Kowli refugee camp in eastern Sudan in 1985, the overall measles-specific mortality rate was 13 per 1,000 population per month, and the under-five mortality was 30 per 1,000 per month. CFRs in this outbreak reportedly reached an extraordinarily high level of 33%, probably due to a combination of underlying malnutrition, including widespread vitamin A deficiency, and inadequate medical services. Major outbreaks of measles have been uncommon in refugee camps since the late 1980s because of the high priority afforded to mass measles vaccination campaigns in the acute phase of humanitarian emergencies. However, major measles outbreaks, resulting in high mortality rates, were reported among IDPs in Ethiopia and the Democratic Republic of Congo during 2000 and 2001 because of delays in initiating vaccination campaigns (Salama et al., 2001).

In well-vaccinated populations, such as Bosnian and Kosovar refugees in the Balkans, Kurds in northern Iraq (1991), and Rwandans in Tanzania and eastern Zaire (1994), measles has been a less prominent public health problem. However, where unvaccinated populations reside in the midst of better protected ones, measles can still be an important problem. For example, indigenous populations living on the slopes of Mount Pinatubo, Philippines, who had not benefited from health services largely available to neighboring populations, were devastated by a measles epidemic that struck during their displacement following the eruption of the volcano in 1991.

Diarrhea

Unlike measles, which can be easily prevented, diarrheal diseases remain one of the top three causes of mortality in humanitarian emergencies. In Somalia (1979–1981), Ethiopia (1982), Sudan (1985), Malawi (1988), northern Iraq (1991), and Goma (1994), diarrheal diseases were responsible for between 25% and 85% of all mortality and accounted for a major share of all clinic visits as well (70% in northern Iraq). Although most often a condition of young children, cholera and dysentery, the major epidemic forms of diarrhea, affect people of all ages. Of all disease conditions, diarrhea is the most closely linked to poor sanitation, inadequate water quantity, and contaminated water.

Cholera epidemics have occurred frequently in emergency settings. Although deaths due to noncholera watery diarrhea have been far more numerous, cholera, in addition to being able to cause death rapidly from dehydration, incites fear and even panic in many populations. Its ability to affect other relief activities and to divert health personnel and supplies from other activities may even contribute to higher death tolls due to other diseases. Outbreaks of cholera have occurred in all parts of the world; large outbreaks were recorded in India (1971), Thailand (1979), Sudan (1985), Somalia (1985), Ethiopia (1984), Malawi (1988–1991), northern Iraq (1991), Goma (1994), and Rwanda (1996). Since 2000, there have been few outbreaks of cholera among refugees and IDPs; however, intermittent outbreaks occurred among the internally displaced in Burundi in 2004 and 2005.

In many of these settings, cholera was a recurrent problem, and in Malawi at least 20 separate outbreaks were recorded among Mozambican refugees during a 5-year period. Investigations of these outbreaks have documented numerous modes of transmission and risk factors, including contaminated water, shared water containers, inadequately heated leftover food, insufficient soap, and funeral gatherings for cholera victims. One of the most lethal cholera epidemics ever recorded occurred among refugees in Goma, Zaire, in 1994, when it was estimated that 45,000 people (about 9% of the total population) died in a 3-week period. The source of contamination is believed to have been Lake Kivu, the principal source of water on which the population depended. Epidemics due to *Shigella dysenteriae* type 1 have also been reported from a number of emergency settings and contributed to the high mortality in Goma.

Acute Respiratory Infection

Acute lower respiratory infection (ALRI), or pneumonia, has been an important cause of morbidity and mortality in emergency settings, and was recorded as one of the top three causes of mortality in Thailand (1979), Somalia (1980), Sudan (1985), and Honduras (1984–1987). Risk factors have included crowded conditions, inadequate shelter, vitamin A deficiency, and indoor air pollution, especially in societies that cook indoors (such as Nepal). ALRI is undoubtedly a major cause of morbidity and mortality in cold climates, such as northern Iraq, the Balkans, and the war-torn former Soviet republics. ALRI is the leading cause of death among children in low-income countries, but it has been less consistently reported and investigated than many other communicable diseases in emergency settings.

Malaria

In endemic areas, including Southeast Asia, the Indian subcontinent, and most of Africa, malaria is consistently among the leading causes of morbidity and mortality. It has been responsible for incidence rates as high as 1,034 per 1,000 per month (Thailand, 1984) and for as many as 30% of all deaths in displaced populations (Rwanda, 1994). It was the leading cause of mortality among Cambodian refugees in Thailand in 1978, Ethiopian refugees in Sudan in the mid-1980s, and Mozambican refugees in Malawi in the 1980s. It has been well established that populations that are displaced to areas of higher malaria endemicity than their place of origin have higher incidence rates and higher mortality. Following the collapse of health services during and following the conflict in East Timor, along with mass population displacement, the incidence of malaria increased significantly. In October 1999, approximately 30% of all morbidity was attributed to malaria, compared with 10% the previous year (WHO Health Information Network for Advanced Planning [HINAP], 2000a). The occurrence of epidemic malaria has also been more frequent in these circumstances. There is, however, little risk of displaced populations from areas of high malaria incidence causing increases in the diseases in areas to which they are displaced, because transmission is largely vector dependent.

Major risk factors for malaria in emergency settings include the lack of adequate housing, poor siting of refugee camps (especially when they are placed in marshy areas), overcrowding, proximity to livestock (which may be the primary targets of mosquito vectors), and a general lack of competently trained health personnel. Although it has not been clearly documented in emergencies, the association of malaria with low birth weight (especially in the offspring of first and second pregnancies) and with iron deficiency anemia may cause increases in incidence and CFR from a variety of causes, especially in children. High mortality was reported during severe epidemics of malaria in Burundi, Ethiopia, and Eritrea during the first few years of the 21st century. This was widely blamed on the continued use of antimalarial drugs that were no longer effective. In mid-2004, an international meeting of experts recommended that most countries with endemic malaria should change their first-line treatment regimen to artemesenin-based combination therapy. This recommendation was adopted by WHO.

Meningitis

Although not a consistent problem in emergencies, the threat of meningococcal (group A) meningitis is a formidable one. Overcrowding, especially during the drier seasons of the year, can be an important risk factor for this disease, which is transmitted via the respiratory route. In the Sakaeo camp in Thailand in 1980, a large outbreak of group A meningococcal meningitis had an attack rate of 130 per 100,000 population and an overall CFR of 28% (50% in children younger than 5 years). Other epidemics have occurred in Sudan (1989), Ethiopia (1993), Guinea (1993), and in Goma, where attack rates ranged from 94 to 137 per 100,000 population over a period of 2 months. Outbreaks of meningitis tend to be protracted, lasting from 1 to 2 months. Unless they are detected and controlled at an early stage, they can be directly responsible for high mortality; in addition, they can be resource intensive and detract attention from other high-priority health programs. In early 2005, an outbreak of the emerging W135 strain of meningococcus led to the vaccination of more than 150,000 Sudanese refugees in Chad.

Hepatitis E

Like meningitis, outbreaks of hepatitis E have not been frequent occurrences in emergencies but have had major consequences when they occurred. An enterically transmitted disease, usually linked to contaminated drinking water, especially when water quantity is compromised, hepatitis E is associated with a particularly high CFR in pregnant women. Clinical attack rates appear to be higher in adults, with children relatively spared. In Somalia in 1985, an outbreak of more than 2,000 cases was associated with an overall attack rate of 8% in adults. The overall CFR of 4% was more than quadrupled in pregnant women (17%). Outbreaks of similar magnitude occurred in Ethiopia (1989) and among Somali refugees in Liboi Camp, Kenya, in 1991. In the latter, the overall case fatality rate was 3.7%, but the CFR in pregnant women was 14%.

A severe epidemic occurred in 2004 among both IDPs in Darfur, Sudan, and refugees from Darfur in Chad. Starting in West Darfur in May, a total of 2,431 cases and 41 deaths (CFR 1.7%) of suspected hepatitis E was reported from health clinics in the Greater Darfur region. The most affected area was West Darfur state, with 66% of the total reported cases. A survey conducted in November 2004 found a CFR of 8.2% among pregnant women with hepatitis (Boccia, Klovstad, & Guthmann, 2004). Between June and September a total of 1,442 cases of suspected hepatitis E and 46 deaths (CFR 3.2%) were reported from two refugee camps and neighboring villages. Investigation of the epidemic was aided by the use of a newly licensed rapid diagnostic kit.

Tuberculosis

Tuberculosis (TB) is one of the most important communicable diseases to control in the postemergency phase. Its reemergence as a public health problem in many parts of the world is characterized by its close association with immune deficiency disorders, especially HIV/AIDS, and with the identification of multiple drug-resistant strains. TB can be quite common in some postemergency situations. It is highly prevalent during the emergency as well, but because of the difficulties in developing programs to control its transmission, diagnose the disease, and reliably treat it for adequate periods, other, more acute conditions are appropriately accorded priority. In Somalia, in 1985, more than one-quarter of all adult deaths were attributed to TB, which was the third leading cause of death overall. In Sudan in the mid-1980s and in Pakistan throughout the protracted displacement of Afghan refugees, TB also figured prominently.

Other Important Communicable Diseases

HIV/AIDS and other STIs are major problems among emergency-affected populations from areas where there is a high prevalence of these conditions. Until recently, there was a paucity of data on the prevalence of HIV in refugee populations. It has been postulated that refugees and other conflict-affected populations might be at greater risk of acquiring HIV because of sexual exploitation, the breakdown of traditional societies and values, and the disruption to STI treatment and condom promotion programs. Nevertheless, there is some evidence that conflict might actually inhibit the spread of HIV. When the 20-year conflict in Angola ended in 2002, the country had a significantly lower HIV prevalence (5% to 10% in Luanda and 1% to 3% in rural areas) than all other southern African countries (15% to 40%).

The population of Sierra Leone was thought to be highly vulnerable to HIV, especially given the widespread sexual violence during the civil conflict in the 1990s. Indeed, HIV prevalence among sex workers in the capital, Freetown, increased from 27% in 1995 to 71% in 1997 (a period of intense conflict); HIV prevalence among women in antenatal clinics increased from 4% to 7% in the same period; and 11% of Nigerian peacekeepers returning from Sierra Leone were HIV-positive, double the Nigerian prevalence at the time. However, in 2002, a rigorous study in Sierra Leone by the Centers for Disease Control and Prevention found much lower levels of HIV prevalence (1% to 4%) among the general population. The war made movement within the country and trade difficult and possibly insulated most of the population. Likewise, after 4 years of war and extensive documented sexual violence in Bosnia and Herzegovina, HIV prevalence remained below 0.01% in 2004.

Between 2001 and 2003, UNHCR surveys of pregnant women in 20 refugee camps in Kenya, Rwanda, Sudan, and Tanzania found *lower* HIV prevalence among refugees than in the surrounding population in three of the four countries (e.g., 5% versus 18% in Kenya), and in Sudan there was no significant difference. The report notes that most refugees moved from low- to high-prevalence countries, that most refugees lived in remote rural areas with restricted freedom of movement, and that NGOs had mounted HIV prevention programs targeted at easily accessible, "captive" populations.

Other communicable diseases that have occurred in emergency or postemergency settings have had a relatively minor impact. In the individual setting in which they occur, however, they command an important allocation of resources and may be important contributors to morbidity and mortality. Yellow fever, typhoid fever, relapsing fever, Japanese B encephalitis, dengue hemorrhagic fever, typhus, and leptospirosis are all real threats. Nevertheless, morbidity and mortality in

CEs has been shown time and again to be due to the same conditions that are responsible for the bulk of the disease burden in low-income countries in nonemergency settings. Important aspects concerning the control of these major communicable disease problems are presented later. Following the Asian tsunami in 2004, there was a significant outbreak of tetanus among wounded survivors of all ages in the Aceh province of Indonesia. Between 31 December 2004 and 25 January 2005, 91 cases of tetanus were hospitalized in Banda Aceh, Meulaboh, and Sigli (WHO, 2005). The outbreak reflected the low immunization coverage in Aceh, a likely outcome of decades of armed conflict.

Injuries

Injuries are widespread in all populations and are responsible for significant mortality, morbidity, and disability. Conflicts typically conjure up images of firearm-related morbidity and mortality, but other types of weapons, as high-tech as laser-guided missiles and chemical and biological warfare agents and as low-tech as machetes, can cause substantial morbidity and mortality. Injuries, aside from those that are directly war and conflict related, are typically neglected in preference for an emphasis on communicable diseases. This is unfortunate given the widespread occurrence of intentional (homicide, war, suicide) and unintentional (falls, traffic injuries, drowning, poisoning) injuries in many populations affected by conflict. Given exposure to firearms and other weapons, rapid and forced population movement, poor environmental conditions, and compromised safety and security, injuries of all sorts are bound to occur in these settings. In situations where injuries are shown to be major causes of morbidity and mortality, they should be addressed as vigorously as communicable diseases.

Most attention has been focused on land mine injuries, an area in which notable international successes have been achieved. The Ottawa process has led to the effective banning of the production and distribution of antipersonnel land mines, although a number of key countries, including the United States, have thus far refused to sign the relevant treaties. Evidence of the harmful effects of antipersonnel land mines and their concentration in the world's poorest countries, such as Angola, Ethiopia, Cambodia, and Afghanistan, has led to a dramatic increase in press and media interest and a related public policy response leading into the Ottawa process.

The spontaneous repatriation of refugees to Kosovo in mid-1999 was associated with a large number of land mine deaths and injuries. Aside from evidence of deaths and disability, the costs to the health

services of caring for and supporting disabled community members through the health services and, in the longer term, within the community are considerable. The opportunity costs are similarly important: Staff and equipment devoted to war surgery and specifically the treatment of injuries resulting from antipersonnel land mines could be devoted to other activities. Indeed, extending war surgery facilities introduced by organizations such as the International Committee of the Red Cross into resource-poor countries to facilitate the provision of a much wider range of treatment and rehabilitation services that would be available to those with any sort of injury is currently being promoted by WHO.

Aside from the direct health problems associated with antipersonnel land mines, they create a wide range of other problems—fear and insecurity, as well as limited access to areas affected by mines, which consequently become unavailable for agriculture and animal husbandry. Despite community knowledge of the sites of concentration of antipersonnel land mines, community members are often forced to enter these unsafe areas to collect firewood, water, or animals that have gone astray. The widespread availability of antipersonnel land mines has also led to their use for personal security, with community members in some cases using them to protect their homes at night or when they are away. In some situations, mines have been used to assist with tasks such as fishing, and children have been known to play with them. The long-term effects of land mines are serious: High levels of surgical skill and resources are required, and repeated refitting and modification of prostheses are necessary if disability is to be minimized.

Reproductive Health

Unfortunately, reproductive health services for refugees and displaced persons have often been considered to be secondary priorities; however, increased attention has been paid to reproductive health issues in the past 5 years. Although there is no doubt that the provision of food, water, sanitation facilities, and shelter is the highest priority during a complex humanitarian emergency, steps should be taken to ensure that other critical health needs of women, men, and adolescents are met as quickly as possible. Women are a particularly vulnerable subset of the population because the gender-based discrimination that is all too common in stable societies is frequently exacerbated in times of societal stress and meager resources. Uncontrolled violence and its aftermath are characterized by a number of specific features that negatively affect reproductive health. These include the breakdown of family networks and the consequent loss of protection and safety, as well as channels of information to adolescents and women of reproductive age.

Loss of revenue within the family can result in a restricted ability to make appropriate reproductive health choices, and may predispose women and adolescents to risk—for example, through engaging in commercial sex work. Increased sole responsibility, as manifested by an increase in the proportion of female-headed households, also changes the way women spend their time and money as they seek increased security and well-being for their families. Finally, as with all members of the affected population, women tend to pay more attention to securing health services for life-saving interventions than for nonemergency reproductive health services.

A minimum initial package of essential reproductive health services has been developed and is recommended by the major relevant international agencies. They are described later in this chapter. Interventions beyond this essential package require major investments of time and personnel that should not be diverted from the principal task of reducing excessive preventable mortality as rapidly as possible. In all cases, special care must be taken to ensure that women heads of household are being given equitable quantities of food and nonfood commodities for themselves and their families.

Mental Health

War and political violence have direct and indirect mental health consequences for victims, relatives, neighbors, and communities. The severity and type of mental health problems relate to the nature, intensity, and form of the violence, the relationship of the assessed person to others affected—self, family, and community members—the cause of the conflict, and the affected person's relationship to participation, victimization, or causation of the conflict. Anxiety, uncertainty, and fear about the future and about whether family members and homesteads remain alive and intact are a substantial cause of distress for affected individuals and communities. Among those who are forced to flee either as refugees or as internally displaced people, the lack of knowledge about relatives and property left behind causes stress and distress. Despite the ongoing challenges of maintaining lives and livelihoods, life as a refugee, especially in a camp situation, may be monotonous and conducive to stress, anxiety, and depression.

The extent of mental health trauma experienced during and in the aftermath of war and conflict is controversial, with some analysts identifying significant proportions of affected populations suffering from post-traumatic stress disorder, and others arguing that this term and the response to it medicalize an essentially social phenomenon. The former school calls for large-scale counseling and mental health support structures, whereas the latter, represented by Bracken, Giller, and Summerfield (1995), argue that reconstituting a sense of community and humanity and reestablishing livelihoods and community structures are far more important interventions than trauma centers and counseling. It is clear, and little disputed, that some individuals who experience particularly horrific experiences as victims of torture or gross human rights abuses during conflicts may well suffer from post-traumatic stress disorder. However, the debate centers on the extent to which this label can be applied to whole populations, rather than to the minority whose experiences have been particularly extreme. A key problem remains the difficulty of articulating the experiences suffered and of facilitating community- and individual-oriented systems of support. Women who had been raped during the civil war in Uganda benefited from opportunities to share their experiences with other women who had similarly been abused during wartime; in the absence of any health-related interventions, such experiences might well have remained bottled up and been cause for continuing distress. A key issue is to learn not only from those who succumb to the stresses placed upon them but also to understand and learn from the resilience of survivors. What mechanisms do they use to protect themselves and their mental health, and can others benefit from learning about such strategies?

Few national surveys of the mental health impact of conflicts are available, and even if such studies could be conducted, prior measurement of the distribution of mental health status within the population would be required to assess impact. A number of small and focused studies on particular subgroups of conflict-affected populations have been conducted, but their biomedical biases make them open to challenge. Little is known about the etiology of the symptoms of multiple trauma, the mental health consequences suffered by those who victimize, and the role of coping mechanisms. Anecdotal data indicate the serious mental strain, substance abuse, and high risk of suicide among some groups, such as South African policemen from the apartheid era and Vietnam veterans. The effects of personal experience of extreme violence, such as torture or rape, may be long lasting and may impede normal sexual and other social relationships.

Torture is a common practice in many conflicts, especially during the Cold War, when ideological factors were central to ongoing conflicts. The impact of torture has been extensively documented in Latin America and South Africa in particular. In so-called dirty wars of state-perpetrated internal repression, common in Latin America in the mid-1980s, torture was used systematically as a means of attempting to maintain societal structures through fear and intimidation. Mental health workers have identified *disintegration* as one of the consequences of torture and political repression: the destruction of the person as an autonomous subject with norms and values that inspired his or her political and social activities (Barudy, 1989).

The mental conditions of persons who move to other countries or are exiled vary according to specific circumstances. Although some political refugees and asylum seekers in industrialized nations have access to comprehensive health care, even these relatively more fortunate exiles are likely to experience severe cultural and language barriers when they attempt to access services. Uncertainty and guilt regarding relatives left behind, legal restrictions to employment, and ethnic discrimination are common causes of stress among exiles in advanced industrial nations.

A review of mental health studies and interventions in CEs in 2004 seemed to offer some consensus on the approach to this issue. A range of social and mental health strategies and principles seem to have broad support (Van Omeren et al., 2005).

Noncommunicable Diseases

Responding to the health needs of refugees and IDPs has traditionally emphasized the direct causes of ill health, such as firearms and other weaponry, as well as communicable diseases, which have been shown to pose a major problem in many CEs. In light of the aging of the population generally and of the changing geographic distribution of conflicts to include areas previously well served by health care, such as the former Yugoslavia, new problems are emerging.

Noncommunicable diseases are widespread in all populations of older adults worldwide. In those situations where medical care was at some stage available, the withdrawal or destruction of medical facilities and drug distribution mechanisms, and the withdrawal of health workers from areas of active conflict, all have an impact on the treatment and care available for noncommunicable diseases. Examples of reductions in the quality and availability of care for noncommunicable diseases come from Iraq in the aftermath of the Gulf War, from Sarajevo during its siege in the Yugoslav civil war, and from the Kosovar Albanians, especially those internally displaced people who lost access to services and care.

Conditions such as cardiovascular disease (including hypertension), diabetes, asthma, and cancer may deteriorate given the lack of access to medical care that typically occurs in conflict settings. Maintaining diagnostic and treatment services, drug supplies, and access to care is extremely difficult given destruction of infrastructure, targeting of health services, disruption of logistics and supply systems, and absolute resource constraints. In some conflicts, the imposition of sanctions may play some role in reducing access to technologies and drugs necessary for the diagnosis, treatment, and care of noncommunicable disorders.

Impact of Economic Sanctions and Embargoes

The imposition of economic sanctions has become a more common means of punishing nations and is increasingly considered as an alternative to war. The penalties and restrictions that constitute economic sanctions vary widely. Usually, trade in certain products, ranging from wheat and other agricultural products to high-technology instruments such as computers and to military equipment or items that can be used for military purposes, is limited or prohibited. At times, international travel, sporting events, and cultural exchanges can be curtailed. Assets held in foreign banks can be frozen. In each case, no matter what form the economic sanctions take, the goal of those imposing them is to achieve political objectives while avoiding the cost and destruction of war. Indeed, the popularity of economic sanctions parallels trends in military strategy: As governments appear to become increasingly hesitant to commit troops to fight foreign wars in which casualties may occur, they seek alternative ways of achieving political objectives. Sanctions tend to be used when diplomacy fails and when the costs and potential destruction that accompany military intervention are deemed to be excessive.

Sanctions can be imposed and administered by a single nation, a group of allied nations, or by the United Nations. The United States has used unilateral economic sanctions more than any other country and has been associated with imposing sanctions more than 100 times during the 20th century. More than one-third of those came during the 1990s. Also during that decade, the Security Council of the United Nations instituted multilateral economic sanctions against nine countries (Burundi, Haiti, Iraq, Liberia, Libya, Rwanda, Somalia, Sudan, and the former Yugoslavia) and against two nonstate parties (the Khmer Rouge in Cambodia, and the National Union for the Total Independence of Angola [UNITA]).

Although economic sanctions as an instrument of foreign policy are aimed at pressuring the targeted governments, experience has usually demonstrated that they are far from a benign weapon. They are rarely successful in achieving their desired political objectives, and they frequently take a very heavy toll on civilian populations. In fact, although the Geneva Conventions provide wartime protection to civilians by prohibiting the destruction of crops, livestock, sources of drinking water, and the like, few if any international standards protect civilians from the unintended consequences of broad economic sanctions imposed on their governments during peacetime. This is the case even when humanitarian exemptions are stipulated in the terms of the embargo. For example, although importation of measles vaccine intended for childhood vaccination programs in Haiti was allowed under the terms of the sanctions imposed upon that country in 1992, kerosene was not. As a result, refrigerators required to maintain the potency of the vaccine were unable to function and a large epidemic occurred.

Nowhere has the devastating effect of economic sanctions on a civilian population been better documented than in Iraq. It has been estimated that the sanctions imposed on that country were associated with the deaths of as many as 200,000 children younger than 5 years between 1991 and 1997 (Garfield, 1999). Dramatic increases in rates of malnutrition and preventable infectious diseases such as childhood diarrhea occurred. The prices of basic food items such as flour, rice, oil, meat, and milk soared out of proportion to wage increases as a result of trade restrictions. Distribution systems for food and other essential commodities were severely disrupted. In addition, by 1995, 4 years after the Gulf War, national water distribution was estimated to be only 50% of prewar levels and a UNICEF survey in that year found that 50% of the population had no access to potable water. Wastewater facilities and solid waste disposal systems were also destroyed during the war, and sanctions contributed to an inability to restore them. The lack of adequate quantities of food, water, and acceptable sanitation contributed to increased mortality in most segments of the population. The causes of mortality resembled those of a developing country more than those that occurred previously in a country with a relatively advanced health care system. Indeed, the number of deaths attributable to the imposition of economic sanctions following the 1991 war far exceeded those that occurred as a result of the war itself. Moreover, throughout it all, the government against which these severe sanctions were imposed remained in power.

Sanctions can be effective: They are felt to have played an important role in pressuring the pro-apartheid government of South Africa to relinquish power. For the most part, however, sanctions, in the form in which they have most frequently been applied, have not been able to produce their desired effect and have exacted an inappropriately severe toll on the most vulnerable elements of society, including children, women (especially pregnant women), and the elderly. In this sense, the imposition of economic sanctions has been a very blunt instrument of foreign policy. Critics have called for the development of "smart sanctions," that is, penalties on travel and on the assets of the wealthy and powerful elements of a targeted nation that will not have a destructive effect on social sectors, such as public health systems. Sanctions seem to be a good idea gone wrong: It is inappropriate to negatively affect the health status of a nation's civilian population when the objective is to bring about a change in its leadership.

Prevention and Mitigation of Complex Emergencies

The prevention of CEs is primarily the prevention of the conflicts that cause them; thus, the task is largely political. Since 1990, most CEs have had their roots in ethnic and religious conflicts within sovereign states. Since 2001, at least two major conflicts (Afghanistan and Iraq) had their origins in the need to protect the populations of western countries. The United Nations Charter has been ill equipped to intervene in issues deemed to be "internal" by member states. Chapters 6 and 7 of the Charter do allow the Security Council to authorize appropriate action, including the use of force, in situations that threaten international peace and security. During the Cold War, these provisions were rarely used because such action was likely to be vetoed by one of the five permanent members of the Security Council. However, Security Council resolutions supported intervention by the international community to protect civilians in conflicts in Somalia, Bosnia and Herzegovina, Haiti, Iraq, Angola, and East Timor during the 1990s. Since 2001, such international consensus has been rare. Armed interventions by the United States and its allies in Afghanistan and Iraq were not conducted under the auspices of the United Nations.

In general, however, the international community has had little success in resolving internal conflicts. Certain private organizations, such as the Carter Center in Atlanta, have attempted to facilitate the resolution of conflicts in Sudan, Haiti, Somalia, Afghanistan, the former Yugoslavia, and other countries. However, in these situations, the cessation of hostilities, if attained at all, has tended to be temporary. Sometimes, health campaigns have been used to seek a temporary halt to armed conflict, most commonly to implement child immunization programs. Such initiatives, for example, the Corridors of Tranquility and Health as a Bridge to Peace, have not addressed the root causes of the conflicts or led to permanent, peaceful resolution. A major victory for these efforts occurred in 2005 when the government of Sudan and the Sudan People's Liberation Front signed a peace agreement in Nairobi. Similar peace agreements have been signed since 2001 in Sri Lanka, Angola, Liberia, Sierra Leone, and the DRC (although the latter was fragile in 2005).

The United Nations has a poor record in conflict resolution. The internal conflict in Somalia was allowed to evolve over 5 years into the total disintegration of the nation state. Only when famine reached appalling levels in 1992 did the Security Council authorize extraordinary action to ensure the protection and care of the civilian population. Within 6 months of their arrival, UN troops became embroiled in the conflict itself, taking sides with or against certain armed factions. This led to heavy loss of life and the eventual withdrawal of the UN forces. In Bosnia and Herzegovina, between 1992 and 1995, the UN mobilized peacekeeping troops to safeguard the delivery of humanitarian supplies. However, these forces were not authorized to intervene to protect civilians from the violence intentionally directed at various ethnic groups; as a result, the international community's armed representatives were forced to silently witness gross abuses of human rights. This dilemma has been termed the *humanitarian trap*. One of the notable failures occurred when around 7,000 Muslim men in the so-called safe haven of Srebrenica in Bosnia were massacred by Bosnian Serbs despite the presence of UN peacekeeping forces in the area. When the genocide began in Rwanda in 1994, several Belgian peacekeepers already in the country with a UN contingent were killed by extreme Hutu nationalists. Instead of increasing the level of UN presence, the entire peacekeeping force was withdrawn, leaving civilians defenseless against these extremists. Eventually, more than half a million Rwandans were killed. It is likely that this string of UN failures led to NATO taking unilateral action in the form of a massive bombing campaign against Serbia to protect ethnic Albanians in 1999. Although appearing to be well intentioned, this action seemed to accelerate the pace of atrocities and ethnic cleansing instigated by the Serbs against the Kosovar Albanians.

The basis of protection of civilians in time of conflict is the Geneva Conventions of 1949 and the Additional Protocols of 1977. In addition, the 1951 Convention on the Prevention and Punishment of the Crime of Genocide was intended to protect civilians from the type of slaughters that occurred in Cambodia in the 1970s and Rwanda in 1994. General Assembly resolutions in 1971, 1985, and 1986 also elaborated on the protection of civilian populations. However, international human rights and humanitarian (armed conflict) laws are only as good as their enforcement. The UNCHR in Geneva is one of the primary official bodies that oversees this sometimes overwhelming task, relying on the documentation and testimony provided by accredited NGOs. Eleanor Roosevelt was instrumental in giving birth to the commission, along with the Frenchman Rene Cassin, who received the Nobel Peace Prize for authoring the Universal Declaration of Human Rights. Today, UNCHR passes influential resolutions on human rights abuses in member states and is the subject of intense lobbying by governments and NGOs. It is thanks to the efforts of a number of human rights advocacy groups that resolutions continue to be adopted by the commission condemning human rights violators. Such resolutions occasionally lead to action by the General Assembly and Security Council, which may dispatch peacekeeping forces to a troubled region (e.g., Central America in the 1980s and East Timor in 1999) to settle the conflicts giving rise to the violations in the first place. In 2004, a number of UN Security Council resolutions demanded that the government of Sudan remove its support for the genocidal militia in Darfur. Unusually, the African Union made strong statements on the affair and promised African peacekeeping troops. By the end of 2004, little progress in resolving the conflict had been achieved.

The United Nations Office for the Coordination of Humanitarian Affairs (OCHA), based in New York and Geneva, is the UN office responsible for coordinating efforts in early warning, prevention, mitigation, and response to disasters, including CEs. Its ReliefWeb project's purpose is to strengthen the capacity of the humanitarian relief community through the timely dissemination of reliable information on prevention, preparedness, and disaster response. Like many other similar projects, the information is available on the Internet (www.reliefweb.int).

Given the difficulty of preventing or resolving armed conflicts, what else can be done to prevent or mitigate the worst consequences of such conflicts on civilian populations? Although not yet tested, it may be possible during the early phase of national disintegration to focus development efforts on activities that strengthen the capacity of local organizations to implement life-saving programs. Accelerated training of health workers in emergency preparedness and response, support to local food production activities, and adaptation of health information systems to the priorities of an emergency assistance program may all help to minimize the eventual impact of the CE. Given the frequency of CEs in the past decade and the likelihood that they will continue to occur, donor governments should support pilot projects to examine what can and cannot be done to prepare for such emergencies.

Early Warning and Detection

Efforts to prevent and mitigate the impact of CEs on populations must rely on accurate and timely information to be effective. Given the enormous cost of military intervention (e.g., US$100 million a day in Kosovo in 1999) and major relief and rehabilitation programs, it is surprising that so little has been invested in early warning, emergency detection, preparedness, and mitigation projects. In the 1980s, the U.S. Agency for International Development (USAID) funded a Famine Early Warning System that focused on famine-prone countries, mainly in Africa. Most of the indicators routinely collected by the system related to agricultural and climatic conditions, economic conditions, nutritional indices, and population migrations. Although data on political factors were collected, there was no mechanism by which the world would respond if a certain threshold of instability or conflict was reached. The system did accurately predict a food shortage in southern Africa in 1992, but this was largely due to drought conditions rather than political instability.

In the late 1990s, there were a number of systems that collected, aggregated, and disseminated information on a number of indicators relevant to CEs. Most systems relied on information collected by other agencies, such as governments, UN agencies, and NGOs. ReliefWeb, a project of OCHA, has already been mentioned. The International Crisis Group has an active conflict monitoring system, which provides detailed reports on countries vulnerable to complex emergencies, including Indonesia, Burma, Algeria, and Burundi. A relatively new project is the Health Information Network for Advanced Planning (HINAP), which is based at WHO headquarters in Geneva. HINAP's major objective is to consolidate, sort, edit, organize, and redistribute background information and other existing sources of data to the right people, at the right time, in the right format.

The lack of preparedness for the mass exodus of hundreds of thousands of Kosovar refugees into neighboring countries in early 1999 by both UN agencies and NGOs seems surprising given the knowledge since 1989 that there was the potential for a major conflict in Kosovo province. This lack of preparedness was also evident in 1994 when more than 1 million Rwandan refugees crossed the border into eastern Zaire within 1 week.

Unlike natural disaster early warning systems and preparedness programs, monitoring and detecting CEs is fraught with political obstacles. The common adage that the first casualty in war is truth applies to attempts to collect accurate data on the health outcomes of war. The existence of armed conflicts is no secret; the political response is still inadequate. What would be valuable as CEs evolve would be a more accurate picture of which health interventions are going to be the highest priorities and most effective in preventing excess mortality and morbidity. In European wars, the most important public health priorities have been the direct effects of violence. Stopping the violence is a public health issue that can only be addressed by the world's leaders. In low-income countries, the priorities are most likely to be nutrition and communicable disease control. Thus, key indicators to monitor in early warning systems include food availability, nutritional status, immunization coverage, incidence of vaccine-preventable diseases, and antenatal program coverage.

In the late 1990s, as Indonesia went through economic and political turmoil, at least 20 different centers and institutes maintained information systems on economic and social indicators. However, very few were able to provide reliable information on health and nutrition outcomes. Systems of early warning, preparedness, and mitigation of the health effects of CEs are in their infancy. They should receive generous donor support if future humanitarian responses are to be based on science rather than instincts.

Responses to Complex Emergencies

Primary Prevention

Primary prevention is the basic strategy of public health, and epidemiology is one of its essential tools. In situations of armed conflict, however, epidemiology can be practiced safely and reliably in very few areas. Hence, the traditional documentation, monitoring, and evaluation elements of disease prevention may be ineffective in this situation. Because war and public health are essentially incompatible pursuits, the provision of adequate food, shelter, potable water, and sanitation as well as vaccination and other primary health care services has proved problematic in countries disrupted by war. Primary prevention in such circumstances, therefore, means stopping the violence. More effective diplomatic and political mechanisms need to be developed that might resolve conflicts early in their evolution prior to the stage when food shortages occur, health services collapse, populations migrate, and significant adverse public health outcomes emerge.

Secondary Prevention

Secondary prevention involves the early detection of evolving conflict-related food scarcity and population movements, preparedness for interventions that mitigate their public health impact, and the development of appropriate public health skills to enable relief workers to work effectively in emergency settings. Preparedness planning needs to take place both at a coordinated international level and at the level of countries where CEs might occur. Relief agencies need resources not only to respond to emergencies when they occur but also to implement early warning systems, maintain technical expertise, train personnel, build reserves of relief supplies, and develop their logistic capacity. At the country level, all health development programs should have an emergency preparedness component that should include the establishment of standard public health policies (e.g., rapid detection and management of epidemics, vaccination), treatment protocols, staff training, and the maintenance of reserves of essential drugs and vaccines for use in disasters.

Tertiary Prevention

Tertiary prevention involves prevention of excess mortality and morbidity once a disaster has occurred. The health problems that consistently cause most deaths and severe morbidity as well as those demographic groups most at risk have been identified. Most deaths in refugee and displaced populations are preventable using currently available and affordable technology. Relief programs, therefore, must channel all available resources toward addressing measles, diarrheal diseases, malnutrition, acute respiratory infections, and, in some cases, malaria, especially among women and young children. The challenge is to institutionalize this knowledge within the major relief organizations and to ensure that relief management and logistical systems provide the necessary resources to implement key interventions in a timely manner.

Initially, both refugees and displaced persons often find themselves in crowded, unsanitary camps in remote regions where the provision of basic needs is highly difficult. Prolonged exposure to the violence of war and the deprivations of long journeys by refugees cause severe physical and psychological stress. Upon arrival at their destination, refugees—most of whom tend to be women and childrenn—may suffer severe anxiety or depression, compounded by the loss of dignity associated with complete dependence on the generosity of others for their survival. If refugee camps are located near borders or close to areas of continuing armed conflict, the desire for security is an overriding concern. Therefore, the first priority of any relief operation is to ensure adequate protection; camps should be placed sufficiently distant from borders to reassure refugees that they are safe (Sphere Project, 2004).

To diminish the sense of helplessness and dependency, refugees should be given an active role in the planning and implementation of relief programs. Nevertheless, giving total control of the distribution of relief items to so-called refugee leaders may be dangerous. For example, leaders of the former, Hutu-controlled Rwandan government took control of the distribution system in Zairian refugee camps in July 1994, resulting in relief supplies being diverted to young male members of the former Rwandan Army. Even when their intentions are good, the priorities of communities may differ from those of international relief agencies. Whereas the latter may offer preferential treatment to children because mortality rates have been shown to be highest in younger age groups, a community may feel that the elderly, for example, deserve special care because they carry with them the traditions and customs of the culture. In general, the targeting of food and other supplies to communities and to vulnerable groups within those communities should be the subject of discussion between relief authorities and the communities (Jaspars & Shoham, 1999).

In the absence of conflict resolution, those communities that are totally dependent on external aid for their survival because they have either been displaced from their homes or are living under a state of siege must be provided the basic minimum resources necessary to maintain health and well-being. The provision of adequate food, clean water, shelter, sanitation, and warmth will prevent the most severe public health consequences of CEs. It would seem that the temporary location of refugees in small settlements or villages in the host country would have fewer adverse public health consequences than their placement in crowded, often unsanitary camps. Public health priorities include a rapid needs assessment, the establishment of a health information system, measles vaccination, the control of diarrheal and other communicable diseases, maternal and child health services, and nutritional rehabilitation. Critical to the success of the response is coordination of the many agencies involved in the relief effort.

Rapid Assessment

Displacement is the final, desperate act of a threatened population. Whenever possible, assessments of the public health needs of the population should be conducted prior to the act of migration or resettlement, whether it is within the country of origin or beyond its borders. Impending disasters, even the development of CEs, can frequently be predicted. Knowing the size of the population and its age and gender distribution, having baseline data concerning its health status and the level of health services available to it, and being aware of the characteristics of the place or places to which they are most likely to move can be of immense help in knowing what relief supplies will be needed and what kinds of health programs should be implemented. Needless to say, such predisplacement assessments have been rare.

Early assessments can be made by a variety of means. Technology-dependent methods such as satellite surveillance can provide information regarding crop growth, population densities, and even troop movements, although such technology is often unavailable to those agencies that need it the most. Reviews of existing documents and other information provided by a variety of United Nations agencies, bilateral governments, NGOs, and national authorities familiar with the situation can be helpful. On-the-ground economic evaluations, including a description of trends in market prices for food and essential commodities in foodbasket analyses, can be very helpful. More detailed information can frequently be obtained from visual inspection of the affected area, including mapping, key informant interviews, and observation of the affected population. For CEs, however, where political instability and increased violence are almost always compounding factors, more direct means of assessment prior to displacement are often impossible and the earliest assessment can only be conducted after the displaced have reached a relatively safe area of resettlement.

The purposes of early, rapid assessments are multiple. They can provide important information regarding the evolution of the emergency, identify groups and areas at greatest risk, evaluate the existing local response capacity, determine the magnitude of external resources required, and indicate which health programs will be required in the short and medium term. Every CE is characterized by a differ-

ent set of causes and consequences, and each should be assessed for its impact on the health of the population affected.

For CEs, early assessment should include both a description of the conflict and its sequelae, in terms of the affected areas and populations, and a characterization of the health consequences of displacement. In some cases, affected populations may not have migrated but rather may be trapped in a siegelike setting, such as in Sarajevo and Beirut. For the conflict, variables of particular significance include the duration of the conflict, the progress of negotiations (and the likelihood of an early return for the displaced), the patterns of violence, the size and location of inaccessible areas and populations, and the state of remaining available health services.

The highest priorities for early assessment are the availability and adequacy of drinking water, food, and shelter. Minimum standards described later in this chapter must be met. Regarding the health status of the population, perhaps the most important and most sensitive indicator is the mortality rate. Early documentation of mortality will establish an indispensable baseline and allow for the monitoring of trends that will attest to the overall effectiveness of the relief program. In an emergency, crude mortality rates are expressed as deaths per 10,000 per day. A CMR of greater than 1 has been used to define the existence of a public health emergency, and a CMR of greater than 2 indicates a critical situation. Of course, these thresholds are gross estimates. Whenever precrisis mortality rates are available, they should be taken into account. (Guha-Sapir & van Panhuis, 2004) Age- and gender-specific mortality should be assessed to identify population groups at the highest risk.

Rates of diseases commonly associated with high rates of preventable mortality should be assessed as early as possible. These include diarrheal illnesses, acute respiratory infections, and diseases with high epidemic potential, such as cholera, dysentery, measles, and meningitis. Where appropriate, the occurrence and risk of locally endemic diseases such as malaria and dengue should also be analyzed.

Complex emergencies are usually accompanied by food shortages that can lead to malnutrition. Assessment of protein-energy malnutrition among children should be undertaken as soon as possible. A variety of methods are available for doing so. Mass screening of all children is optimal, but an initial random sample of the population can establish the prevalence of malnutrition and indicate the need for targeted screening and feeding interventions. Vaccination coverage of children should also be assessed to determine the urgency of mounting vaccination campaigns, although in the absence of coverage data, measles vaccination should be considered a priority.

Rapid assessments require detailed planning and may fail because of the inadequacy of transport, maps, communications equipment, and fuel. In addition, attention needs to be given to the security situation in the affected area. An assessment is of limited value unless its results are communicated in a timely and effective manner to those who can act upon them. Presentation of the findings should be organized and clear, and the recommendations of the assessment team should indicate which actions are of highest priority, what a reasonable time frame for action would be, and what resources will be required. Without these, essential information required for the survival of large populations of displaced individuals may not be acted upon in time to prevent high levels of excess preventable mortality.

The potential usefulness of rapid assessment should not be underestimated. However, in the past there have often been *too many* assessments done by different agencies in an uncoordinated manner. It is essential that a designated lead agency coordinate rapid assessments, ensuring that sectoral assessments (e.g., water, medical services, food) are integrated and that the findings are used to inform program policies and planning. For example, in the post-tsunami relief effort of January 2005, the WHO organized teams from a number of UN and voluntary agencies, the Indonesian Ministry of Health, and the Indonesian military forces, and, using U.S. military assets for support, led a series of rapid assessments of stranded populations along the west coast of Aceh province on the island of Sumatra. These proved quite helpful in identifying remote populations and their needs and in targeting appropriate relief.

Health Information Systems

Epidemiologic surveillance is the ongoing and systematic collection, analysis, and interpretation of health data. This information is used for planning, implementing, and evaluating public health interventions and programs. Surveillance data are used both to determine the need for public health action and to assess the effectiveness of programs. In CEs, after the response to an initial rapid assessment has been instituted, the development and implementation of ongoing health information systems immediately becomes a high-priority activity. Although data on many of the subjects included in the rapid assessment will continue to be collected on a regular basis, routine health

information systems will allow for the monitoring of a significantly larger number of other potentially important health conditions and health programs.

Characteristics of Effective Health Information Systems

To be useful, surveillance systems must be relevant, especially in CEs, where time and resources are frequently in short supply. Data collection should be restricted to the most important of actual and potential public health problems. Equally important, data should only be collected if it will be useful in stimulating and guiding a response—if no intervention is feasible, there is little need to encumber the system with information on the problem.

The best health information systems are the simplest. In a number of CEs, difficulties have arisen in explaining the importance of the data to local staff responsible for its collection as well as to decision makers, who frequently do not appreciate the limitations of data of variable accuracy collected under the most difficult of circumstances. Case definitions must be clear, consistent, and suited to the local capacity to make accurate diagnoses. Where there are no microscopes, for example, malaria may have to be represented by "fever and chills." The data generated from simple systems must be represented for what it is worth and should not be overinterpreted. Nevertheless, good surveillance systems rely on laboratory confirmation of suspect or probable cases of diseases of public health importance. Efforts should be made to have available a basic public health laboratory, with appropriate supplies and technical expertise.

Representativeness is another essential element of health information systems that is related to the quality of the data. Careful interpretation of data collected from a surveillance system is required before extrapolations can be made to the general population. For example, in southern Sudan, nutrition and mortality assessments are hard to interpret because health information has been collected and reported from food distribution centers to which the displaced and most severely malnourished elements of the population were drawn. Mortality and malnutrition rates derived from these sites are not necessarily representative of the population of the region.

The organization and implementation of health information systems should be made the responsibility of one individual or agency that should also be responsible for ensuring widespread cooperation and coordination. It is important for the interpretation and response to the data that there be standardized case definitions, data collection methods, and conditions of reporting. This would avoid the problems described earlier in which different agencies used different data collection methods.

In emergencies, both reporting and the response to it must be timely. When the goal is to prevent excess mortality, undue delays between any two links of the surveillance chain, from the peripheral data-collection level to the more central, policy-making level and back to the periphery where action needs to be taken, can result in an unnecessary loss of life. Depending on the nature of the data, especially when an epidemic illness is deemed likely or is occurring, daily reporting of select information by telephone, text messaging, or messenger is not necessarily excessive. For other conditions, data are generally reported and analyzed on a weekly basis during the emergency period and monthly during the less acute phases of the crisis. Of course, data needs may change rapidly as an emergency evolves during a more steady state. For this reason, information systems must have a high degree of flexibility, and their response to new demands should be achieved with minimal disruption.

Methods

As long as they possess the qualities mentioned previously, surveillance systems may combine active and passive reporting mechanisms. Active reporting can include randomized population-based surveys aimed at gathering data on one or a selected few parameters, such as vaccination coverage or nutritional status. Alternatively, it can involve the hiring of personnel for the specific purpose of monitoring important health events that might occur outside the bounds of the health care system itself, such as hiring gravediggers to report on burials in order to determine mortality. Passive reporting generally refers to the routine collection and relaying of health statistics within the system itself, whether it is from community-based health posts, from primary care clinics, or from hospitals. Because access to the health care system may be limited and utilization may be low because of a variety of factors, such as fear or mistrust of the health care providers, unfamiliarity with the system, physical destruction of facilities, and other reasons that are frequently unrecognized by relief agencies, it is especially important that emergency health information systems be regularly evaluated for the characteristics described earlier.

Content of Health Information Systems in Complex Emergencies

Trends in crude mortality remain an important feature of surveillance throughout the emergency phase and beyond. In many cultures, death is a family and religious matter and deaths are not normally brought to the attention of the health care system. In fact, severely ill patients in hospitals are frequently taken home to die. For this reason, active surveillance is best for estimating mortality. Grave watchers, often those who dig the graves, can be hired on a 24-hour basis to report new burials and, if possible, to ascertain the age and gender of the deceased. In some cultures, the free distribution of burial shrouds or other materials used for burial or funerals can provide a useful incentive for reporting. At times, mortality can be determined by means of a population-based survey, but the data derived from these surveys are subject to different sorts of bias and are frequently dated. At times when large numbers of corpses are left unburied by families, as happened in Goma in 1994 because the ground was composed of volcanic rock that made it impossible to dig graves, or following extensive natural disasters such as the Indian Ocean tsunami of December 2004, where bodies were buried under rubble or swept away, it may be possible to ask those responsible for body collection and mass burial to keep count of the number of dead they see.

Health information systems should collect morbidity data on commonly occurring diseases and on diseases of epidemic potential. Diseases that have been prominent in all CEs include watery diarrhea, acute respiratory infections, malaria and other important endemic conditions, and malnutrition. Measles, meningitis, cholera, shigellosis (dysentery, or bloody diarrhea), and meningitis have all been responsible for major epidemics in emergency settings, and guidelines for the establishment of sensitive thresholds for the detection of each need to be followed where they already exist, or need to be developed. The detection of an epidemic should trigger an immediate and aggressive response.

In addition, at least two health programs—treatment of malnutrition and vaccination—need to be regularly monitored. Indicators of the numbers of patients in intensive or supplementary feeding programs need to be regularly tracked. Vaccination coverage rates also need to be estimated, and, when deemed appropriate, measles vaccination should be offered to all children aged 6 months to 15 years regardless of prior vaccination status as soon as resources permit. Routine vaccination with the six antigens of the WHO Expanded Program on Immunization should be established when feasible. Other vaccines may be offered after careful consideration by public health authorities of the epidemiology of diseases and the logistical implications.

Two areas that have been relatively neglected in CEs are those of reproductive health and psychosocial health. Ample evidence has accumulated to show that in emergencies, women of reproductive age, and especially pregnant women, need special attention, and their health conditions, including pregnancy, should be carefully monitored by surveillance mechanisms. Forced migration is itself a traumatic event and, when compounded by the ethnic strife and violence that frequently accompanies CEs, close attention should be paid not only to individuals who might be seriously affected by post-traumatic stress disorders but also to the reestablishment of community structures. Finally, when the emergency has subsided (e.g., when crude mortality rates drop below 1 per 10,000 per day), increased attention can be paid to dealing with more chronic or less fatal diseases, such as tuberculosis, STIs (including HIV), diabetes, hypertension, and elective surgical conditions.

The establishment of a useful health information system, with all of the characteristics described here, is an essential function of the health services. Without one, programs will be developed by guesswork and the effectiveness of program implementation will remain a matter for conjecture.

Shelter and Environment

As mentioned earlier, the placement of refugees and IDPs in small settlements or integration into local villages is preferable to the establishment of large camps. Health outcomes are probably better in these small settlements because environmental conditions are more favorable and there is less crowding. However, the provision of relief assistance to a large number of scattered settlements may pose a difficult management challenge and may provoke resentment in the surrounding communities. In Guinea in the early 1990s, food aid and other relief items were provided to communities for distribution to both Liberian refugees and local inhabitants. This system may have worked well because the refugees and locals were of the same ethnic origin and many were related. On the other hand, measles vaccination coverage of Mozambican refugees in Malawi who were absorbed into communities and were dependent on the national immunization program was considerably lower than that in refugee camps, where services were provided by the United Nations and international voluntary agencies.

When camps are unavoidable, three of the key determinants of location should be safety of residents, access to adequate quantities of clean water, and all-weather access by vehicles. In many instances, local politics determines the site, and the location is often less than desirable. For example, in 1988, the Ethiopian government placed Somali refugees in a large camp of 180,000 persons on a site that had no local supply of drinking water. The nearest source with an adequate quantity of water was situated in a town 100 km from the camp. For many years, water was delivered daily in convoys of trucks at enormous cost to the relief agencies. The Ethiopian government refused to move the refugees closer to town for fear of exacerbating political problems that it was experiencing with local ethnic Somalis. In 1981–1982, many camps for Ethiopian refugees in the central region of Somalia were flooded in the wet season, causing food trucks to be unable to reach them for weeks at a time.

Sites should be chosen with ease of water drainage in mind, though sometimes drainage systems have to be created at the time of camp construction. This is critical to ensure access by vehicles, limitation of disease vector breeding, and ease of access by refugees to services, such as health clinics and food distribution. When hundreds of thousands of refugees fled ethnic cleansing in Kosovo in 1999, spontaneous camps were established near the border of Macedonia, where up to 45,000 refugees were camped on a muddy, snowy field sheltered only by their vehicles and makeshift tents. An added hazard was a large quantity of land mines laid by Serb forces along the border; these mines killed several refugees. In Albania, tens of thousands of refugees brought their tractors with them and created a chaotic situation in which the delivery of services and the establishment of shelters were almost impossible. In Macedonia, Kosovar refugees were forcibly removed by bus from areas where the government did not want them located. Other inappropriate locations have included the swampy, malarious areas on the Thai border where Cambodian refugees were housed, the inhospitable mountainous area on the border between Iraq and Turkey to which the Kurdish population of Iraq fled in the wake of the 1991 Gulf War, and the volcanic, rocky ground in eastern Zaire where Rwandan refugee camps were placed, precluding both latrine construction and, as mentioned earlier, burial of the dead.

Ideally, the size of camps should be limited to 20,000 residents for reasons of security and ease of administration. Such camps should be further divided into sections of 5,000 persons for the purpose of service delivery. Shelter is an urgent priority. On average, the covered area provided per person should be 3.5 to 4.5 m^2 (Sphere Project, 2004). In warm, humid climates, shelters should have optimal ventilation and protection from direct sunlight. In cold climates, shelter material should provide adequate insulation combined with sufficient clothing, blankets, bedding, space heating, and caloric intake. Ideally, houses should be built using a traditional design and local materials. This may pose local environmental problems such as the destruction of trees, so building materials should be trucked in from areas remote from the camp. Waterproofing is essential and may be achieved with plastic sheeting or tarpaulins. Tents may provide temporary shelter; however, they deteriorate in rain and wind and should be replaced with local materials as soon as possible. To limit further environmental damage through deforestation, cooking fuel, such as charcoal, wood, oil, or kerosene, should be brought to the site from remote areas and fuel-efficient stoves provided or constructed. Camps may easily become fire hazards, and fire prevention should be an objective of proper camp design.

Water and Sanitation

When refugee camps are unavoidable, proximity to safe water sources needs to be recognized as the most important criterion for site selection. The Sphere Project minimum standard for water quantity is 15 liters of clean water per person per day for all domestic needs—cooking, drinking, and bathing. Other standards include at least one water point per 250 people and a maximum distance from shelter to the nearest water point of 500 meters. Ideally, both the quantity and quality of water provided to refugees and displaced persons should meet international standards; however, in many cases this is not possible. In general, ensuring access to adequate quantities of rel-

atively clean water is probably more effective in preventing diarrheal disease, especially bacterial dysentery, than providing small quantities of pure microbe-free water. Nevertheless, there have been some important exceptions to this rule (see Exhibit 10-4).

The usual options for supplying water to refugees and IDPs include surface water (lakes, rivers, streams, etc.), shallow wells, springs, bore wells, and trucked water from remote sources. Although surface water is often abundant, it needs to be treated, usually through a system of sedimentation and chlorination, and sometimes with filtration. A system of piped distribution and outlet taps needs to be developed to avoid crowding and drainage problems. Shallow wells and springs need to be protected and provided with a mechanism for drawing water, such as pumps. Deep-bore wells provide clean water at the source; however, it may take some time to bring in the necessary equipment.

In addition, measures to prevent postsource contamination need to be implemented, including treatment at the source (e.g., "bucket chlorination"). Sufficient collection and storage containers (at least three 20-liter containers per family), especially containers with narrow openings that prevent postcollection contamination, should be made available. A study in a Malawian refugee camp in 1993 demonstrated a significant reduction in fecal contamination of water stored in such buckets compared with standard buckets. In addition, the incidence of diarrhea among chil-

---

Exhibit 10-4	**Cholera in Goma, Zaire, Despite Large Quantities of Water Available**

Between July 14 and 17, 1994, large numbers of ethnic Hutus fled Rwanda and sought refuge in the North Kivu region of neighboring Zaire; initial estimates ranged as high as 1.2 million people. Many refugees entered through the town of Goma, at the northern end of a large body of deep water, Lake Kivu. Following the influx into Goma, many of the refugees were located near Lake Kivu, whose water flows very slowly, is carbonated by a volcanic bed, and is alkaline. These are favorable conditions for maintaining live *Vibrio cholerae*, which were endemic in the region. At the time there were no available means to purify and transport sufficient quantities of water to distribute to refugees. Although efforts were made by some agencies to chlorinate water in containers as refugees removed it from the lake, coverage was inadequate and most refugees consumed untreated water.

After 5 to 7 days, the refugees were moved to camps with no easy access to any water at all. Advisers to the relief program, especially the U.S. military, opted for a high-technology approach, namely, a large purification plant that was flown in after 1 week, and distribution of clean water to the camps by tankers. A few days after arrival, a diarrhea epidemic occurred among the population and was confirmed as being due to cholera. This epidemic had already peaked before July 29, when the relief operation was able to provide an average of only 1 liter of purified water per person per day. At least 58,000 cases of symptomatic cholera occurred in this population. Given the usual high ratio of asymptomatic to symptomatic infections (up to 10:1), it is likely that most refugees in the Goma area were infected with *V. cholerae*, and that few infections were prevented (Goma Epidemiology Group, 1995). In a subsequent evaluation of the epidemic, concerns regarding failure to adopt best treatment practices and poor coordination between agencies were highlighted.

Source: Data from Goma Epidemiology Group, "Public Health Impact of Rwandan Refugee Crisis: What Happened in Goma, Zaire, in July 1994?" 1995, *Lancet*, 345, pp. 339–344.

dren under 5 years of age in the households with the improved buckets was considerably lower than in control households (Roberts et al., 2001).

Adequate sanitation is an essential element of diarrheal disease prevention and a critical component of any relief program. While the eventual goal of sanitation programs should be the construction of one latrine per family, interim measures may include the designation of separate defecation areas and the temporary provision of neighborhood latrines. The Sphere Project minimum indicator of acceptable household-level sanitation is a maximum of 20 persons per latrine. Toilets should be segregated by sex and be no more than 50 meters from dwellings. To achieve maximal impact, these measures should be complemented by community hygiene education and regular distribution of at least 250 g of soap per person per month. Hygiene education has been shown to significantly increase the impact of sanitation programs. An analysis of data gathered in the Malawi study cited earlier demonstrated that the presence of soap in households significantly reduced the risk of diarrhea (Peterson et al., 1998). The objective of post-emergency sanitation measures should be to restore the predisaster levels of environmental services rather than attempting to improve on the original levels.

The provision of water and sanitation in emergency-affected populations in urban and rural areas of eastern Europe has posed different challenges. We have already discussed the problems caused by the destruction of public utilities in cities such as Beirut, Sarajevo, and Grozny. In general, the goal is to repair existing systems; however, interim measures may be required, such as rehabilitating old wells, providing generators to pump water from distant sources, such as rivers, and providing containers and security for residents to collect water at available sources.

Food Rations and Distribution

The quantity and quality of food rations is one of the most critical determinants of health outcomes in emergency-affected populations. During the early evolution of CEs, measures should be taken to increase access to food without forcing people to leave their homes. The establishment of "feeding camps" may act as a magnet for hungry families and lead to the spontaneous establishment of settlements and camps, with the subsequent health problems described earlier in this chapter. In addition, in conflict zones, warring parties may target areas where populations regularly congregate. Subsidized food shops; food-for-work or cash-for-work programs; emergency support for home food production, such as the distribution of fast-growing seed varieties and agricultural tools; and other measures may be effective prior to the onset of armed conflict.

Once armed conflict has commenced, either forcing people to flee their homes or be trapped in siege-like conditions, it is usually necessary to distribute food. General food rations should contain at least 2,100 kilocalories (kcal) of energy per person per day as well as the other nutrients listed in Table 10-5. Rations should take into consideration the demographic composition of the population, the specific needs of vulnerable groups, and access by the population to alternative sources of food and income. In cold climates, the minimum energy value of the ration should be adjusted upward. Pregnant women require

Table 10-5	Minimum Nutritional Requirements of Emergency-Affected Populations (for Planning Purposes During the Initial Stage of an Emergency)
Nutrient	**Mean Requirements (per person per day)**[a]
Energy	2,100 kcal
Protein	10%–12% total energy (52–63 g)
Fat	17% of total energy (40 g)
Vitamin A	1,666 IU
Thiamine	0.9 mg (or 0.4 mg per 1,000 kcal intake)
Riboflavin	1.4 mg (or 0.6 mg per 1,000 kcal intake)
Niacin	12.0 mg (or 6.6 mg per 1,000 kcal intake)
Vitamin C	28.0 mg
Vitamin D	3.2–3.8 micrograms calciferol
Iron	22 mg
Iodine	150 micrograms

[a]Based on standard age and sex distribution (World Food Programme/UNHCR, 1997)
Source: Sphere Project, *Humanitarian Charter and Minimum Standards in Disaster Response* (Geneva, Switzerland: The Sphere Project, 2004). Reprinted with permission.

on average an extra 285 kcal per day, and lactating women an extra 500 kcal. These extra requirements should be provided through distribution of rations within the household; however, this may need to be monitored, perhaps indirectly via the prevalence of low-birth-weight babies.

Food should be distributed regularly as dry items to family units, taking care that socially vulnerable groups, such as female-headed households, unaccompanied minors, and the elderly, receive their fair share (see Exhibit 10-5 for an exception). This requires an accurate registration system listing all residents in family groups. If a refugee or displaced population is organized in well-defined communities, food may be distributed to community leaders who then divide it further to the heads of households in quantities based on the number of family members. In other situations, food is distributed directly to heads of households, based on a ration card system. In low-income countries, food rations usually comprise a staple cereal, such as rice, wheat, or maize; a source of dense fat, such as vegetable oil; a source of protein, such as beans, lentils, groundnuts, or dried fish; and extra items such as salt, tea, and spices. Experience has shown that women are fairer than men in distributing each food item in the correct quantity. Standard serving containers based on a known weight or volume of food are essential for distribution centers. Guards are often necessary to maintain crowd control. Because of the indignity of being counted and the fact that many refugees are afraid to have their identities known and precise locations reported, attempts at registration for the distribution of humanitarian aid should be carried out with the security and cultural concerns of the population taken into careful consideration (Harrell-Bond, Voutira, & Leopold, 1992).

There is a widespread belief that currently available refugee rations, especially those distributed in non-European populations, are inadequate for nutrient requirements, which may be higher than the traditional recommended daily allowances. The best way to combat depletion of essential nutrients is to take active steps to increase the variety of the diet. This is not possible with relief foods that have to be capable of bulk storage and shipment—cereal, pulses, sugar, oil, and salt. For this reason, recipients of international aid should be encouraged to barter food items for local produce. Market facilities should be established, supported, and controlled by camp leaders. Seeds for leaf vegetables should be distributed as part of all relief activities, even in the acute phase. Every effort should be made to provide spices and herbs, used traditionally by the population, with all food baskets. There is no need for a special food basket for children or pregnant and lactating women—only a sufficiently varied diet for the whole family (Golden, 1999b).

In addition to food, adequate cooking fuel, utensils, and facilities to grind whole-grain cereals need to be provided to all families. Fuel-efficient stoves, often made of mud, may lead to more efficient use of scarce fuel. In children younger than 2 years, breastfeeding will provide considerable protection against communicable diseases, including diarrhea. Thus, attempts to introduce or distribute breast milk substitutes and infant feeding bottles should be strongly opposed in an emergency situation. The evidence that vitamin A deficiency is associated with increased childhood mortality and disabling blindness is now so convincing that supplements of vitamin A should be provided routinely to all refugee children under 5 years of age at first contact and every 3 to 6 months thereafter (Nieburg et al., 1988).

In eastern Europe, the same principles have been followed; however, the types of food have varied and have included cheese, meat, powdered orange juice, and fruit. In some industrialized countries experiencing economic and political instability, ration vouchers have been distributed to vulnerable persons, such as elderly pensioners, which can be redeemed for food at designated stores.

One of the main problems in Africa, and in some parts of Asia, has been providing refugees and IDPs with foods containing adequate quantities of micronutrients, especially niacin, riboflavin, thiamin, iron, and vitamin C. Epidemics of pellagra, scurvy, and beriberi have been common in African refugee camps. For many years, this was a blind spot in emergency food and nutrition planning; in recent years, although the problem has been acknowledged, solutions are still inadequate. In southern Africa, niacin has

Exhibit 10-5	Food Distribution in Somalia

During the civil conflict and famine in Somalia in 1992–1993, dry food rations distributed to families in Mogadishu were often stolen as families returned to their homes. Relief agencies were sometimes forced to establish feeding centers where cooked meals were served to people of all ages. This was an unusual exception from the general rule of providing dry food that families prepare at home, thus preserving some independence and dignity.

been added to maize flour during the milling process. However, vitamin C is water-soluble and very sensitive to heat, light, and bruising; thus, the transport, storage, and distribution of large quantities of foods such as citrus fruit have been problematic. One solution to this problem is to allow and encourage people to swap some of their ration items in local markets for vitamin C–containing foods, such as tomatoes, onions, potatoes, green chili peppers, and other fruits and vegetables. In addition, the provision of seeds to enable refugees to grow small amounts of vegetables in kitchen gardens is an effective measure. The provision of fortified blended cereals has also been proposed as a vehicle for ensuring adequate micronutrient intake. Studies in Ethiopia, Nepal, and Tanzania have shown that these cereals are generally acceptable; however, overcooking and consequent depletion of the vitamin C content may be a problem in some communities (Mears & Young, 1998). WHO has published a series of guidelines on the prevention of scurvy (WHO, 1999b), thiamine deficiency (WHO, 1999c), and pellagra (WHO, 2000a).

A food ration monitoring system is important to ensure that families are receiving fair and adequate quantities of food. On a food ration distribution day, monitoring teams can establish themselves at several points not far from the distribution center. They should be equipped with weighing scales and food composition tables. Families should be stopped randomly as they return to their homes and asked to participate. Each of the items in their ration should be weighed and converted to calories and other nutrients using the tables. The total weight of each food item (in grams) and the total nutrients provided should be divided by the number of family members and the number of days until the next distribution day. This will provide the average quantity per person per day and may be compared with the official ration and with standard tables of recommended daily allowances of nutrients.

Nutritional Rehabilitation

In general, the goal of an emergency feeding program is to provide adequate quantities of nutrients through the general household distribution of food rations. However, due to the many factors described earlier, there may be population subgroups who may either already be acutely malnourished or at high risk of becoming malnourished. These groups may require targeted feeding, or what is termed *selective feeding*. Figure 10-5 demonstrates the various kinds of selective feeding; however, these programs should be seen as additions to, not as substitutes for, the general feeding program. They need clear objectives and criteria

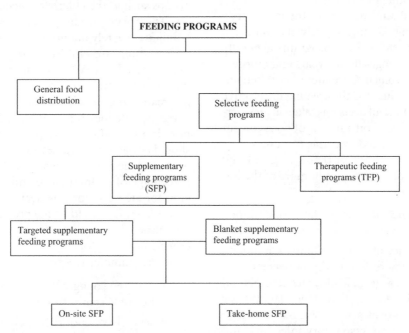

Figure 10-5 Overall Feeding Program Strategy. *Source:* United Nations High Commissioner for Refugees & World Food Programme, *Guidelines for Selective Feeding Programmes in Emergency Situations* (Geneva, Switzerland: UNHCR, 1999). Reprinted with permission.

for opening, admission, discharge, and closure that should be based on population-based anthropometry surveys and agreed-upon nutritional indices. In general, children are defined as acutely malnourished according to their weight-for-height index, although MUAC is also frequently used. Adolescents and adults may be defined according to their MUAC, BMI, or clinical signs. Selective feeding programs should be complemented by measures to improve the food ration distribution system, provide adequate clean water and sanitation, and control measles and other communicable diseases. They should be integrated into community health programs that offer other prevention and care services.

Supplementary feeding programs (SFPs) provide nutritious foods in addition to the general ration, with the aim of rehabilitating moderately malnourished individuals and decreasing the population prevalence of acute malnutrition. There are two kinds of SFPs: targeted and blanket. Each type may provide food supplements as on-site, precooked ("wet") or take-home ("dry") rations. Take-home rations are usually preferred because they require fewer resources, carry lower risks of cross-infection among recipients, and retain the family's primary responsibility for feeding. On-site feeding may be justified when the security situation is poor, the general ration is inadequate and thus food is likely to be shared within the household, or when cooking fuel is scarce.

A targeted SFP aims to prevent the moderately malnourished from becoming severely malnourished and to rehabilitate them. Such programs generally focus on children younger than 5 years and on pregnant and lactating women. Care should be taken not to apply strict guidelines for the opening of selective feeding programs. Like all decisions taken in an emergency, it should be based on a review of both current public health priorities and available resources.

Current guidelines suggest that a targeted SFP should be implemented when one or more of the following situations occur:

- The prevalence of acute malnutrition among children younger than 5 years is 10% to 14%.
- The prevalence of acute malnutrition among children is 5% to 9% in the presence of aggravating factors (e.g., inadequate general food ration, CMR greater than 1 per 10,000 per day, epidemics of measles or pertussis, and high incidence of acute respiratory infections and diarrheal diseases).

Criteria for admission should include the following:

- children under 5 years with a weight-for-height Z score between −3 and −2

- older children, adolescents, and adults who are moderately malnourished according to their MUAC, BMI, or clinical condition
- referrals of children graduating from therapeutic feeding programs
- selected pregnant women and nursing mothers

Blanket SFPs are meant to provide extra nutritious food to all members of groups at risk of malnutrition. They are started under the following conditions:

- general food distribution systems not yet in place
- problems in delivering and distributing the general ration
- prevalence of acute malnutrition equal to or greater than 15%
- prevalence of acute malnutrition of 10% to 14% in the presence of aggravating factors
- anticipated increase in acute malnutrition rates due to seasonally induced epidemics
- in the case of micronutrient deficiency disease outbreaks, to provide micronutrient-rich supplements to a target population

The primary recipients of blanket SFPs are all children younger than 5 years, pregnant women and nursing mothers (up to 6 months after delivery), and other groups such as the elderly or medically ill.

Therapeutic feeding programs (TFPs) aim to rehabilitate severely malnourished persons, the majority of whom are children with severe wasting or nutritional edema. A TFP should be initiated when the number of severely malnourished individuals cannot be treated adequately in other facilities. Although current guidelines for opening a TFP are based on population malnutrition prevalence, the decision should be based on an assessment of the public health needs and the resources available. In a large camp, the percentage of malnourished children may not be an appropriate basis for this decision. Perhaps a more practical guide would be the presence of, say, 50 potential beneficiaries in a settlement. The following criteria are used for admission (UNHCR & World Food Programme, 1999):

- children younger than 5 years with weight-for-height Z scores less than −3 or with edema
- severely malnourished children older than 5 years, adolescents, or adults assessed by other means
- low-birth-weight babies (less than 2,500 g)
- orphans younger than 1 year of age when traditional caring practices are inadequate

• mothers of children younger than 1 year with breastfeeding failure where relactation counseling has failed

Rehabilitation of severely malnourished individuals is a medical procedure demanding careful attention to detail; therefore, well-trained staff are essential. TFPs usually have two phases:

1. The intensive care phase includes 24-hour care with medical treatment to control infection and dehydration and correct electrolyte imbalance, and nutritional treatment. Very frequent feeds with therapeutic milk (F-75) are essential to prevent death from hypoglycemia and hypothermia. This phase usually lasts 1 week.

2. The rehabilitation phase provides at least six meals per day along with medical and psychological support, including for mothers of malnourished children. This phase usually lasts 5 weeks.

Details of the quantity and types of food recommended, discharge criteria, and reasons for stopping SFPs and TFPs are provided in two reference manuals (MSF, 1995; UNHCR & World Food Programme, 1999). In addition, detailed information on the management of severe malnutrition is provided in WHO manuals (WHO, 1999d; WHO, 2000b).

Health Services: Response to Complex Emergencies

Complex emergencies severely disrupt normal health care service activity (see Figure 10-3). In developing appropriate responses to this disruption, it is worth considering the impact on and response by at least three different sets of services:

• service provision in the country affected by the CE

• service provision in countries to which refugees have fled

• service provision by multilateral agencies and NGOs

Service Provision in Countries Directly Affected by Complex Emergencies

The main challenge in these settings is to seek to minimize the direct and indirect adverse impact of the conflict on the health services personnel and resources available. In many conflicts, as highlighted earlier, health services may be specifically targeted, as may health service providers. In such situations it may be extremely difficult to maintain services due to absent or fleeing health personnel, lack of drugs and equipment, disruption of referral systems, and destruction of physical infrastructure, including hospitals and clinics. Even if the official health system is destroyed, however, the health workers who previously worked within it may still be present within the community (unless they have themselves fled to safer areas) and may still be able to offer services and advice. The extent to which services can be maintained is in part dependent on earlier disaster preparedness activities, both in terms of training and of the prepositioning of drugs and other supplies in areas where logistic support was predicted to be vulnerable to disruption.

In some situations it has been possible to ensure that services likely to be disrupted have received prior stocks of drugs and equipment so as to maintain services despite the disruption of linkages to normal supply chains. Although this might be possible for certain forms of equipment and drugs, others, such as vaccination facilities (which are dependent upon maintaining an intact cold chain), and support activities, such as training and supervision, are invariably disrupted. Nevertheless, local-level responses are possible. In Afghanistan, despite the conflict in Kabul, the medical school was able to relocate to another city in order to continue its training activities. In relation to the availability of drugs for treatment, prior distribution of necessary drugs to responsible community members, such as community and other health workers, teachers, and in some cases patients with chronic conditions, may ensure their availability despite the population having to move suddenly. Patients with chronic conditions such as leprosy or TB could be issued with drug supplies for extended periods, assuming the drugs can be procured and distributed and that patients with these conditions will be able to adhere to the treatment regimes prescribed for them. The potential to distribute impregnated mosquito nets to populations on the move might be an option in areas of high malaria risk; some experience in this approach has been gained among the highly mobile Burmese refugees on the Thai border.

Service Provision in Countries to Which Refugees Have Fled

When refugees flee from their country and cross borders, their normal sources of health care are no longer available to them. Therefore, they may be dependent on what they can provide for themselves, which is often desperately little if they have been forced to flee suddenly, such as was the case with the Kosovar Albanians in 1999. Alternatively, they depend on what can be provided in the host country to which they have fled, either through existing host country services or through additional services mobilized through NGOs and other organizations. Host government services may rapidly become overwhelmed if large numbers of refugees suddenly move into an area and seek to use the local health system. In addition to their absolute numbers, the health condition of refugees may be poor, especially if their journey has been traumatic and unplanned or if their prior state of health was poor.

In most cases, at least in the short term, these local host-country services will not receive additional resources and will therefore have to cope as best they can with the additional service load. This may disadvantage local community members who ordinarily utilize such services, because the supply of drugs and usual access to health workers may be compromised. Communities will typically be willing to accept these hardships for a time, but if the situation becomes protracted and leads to a lasting decline in services, tension may develop between the host and refugee communities. Another point of friction occurs when refugees are offered access to host services at no cost, while local community members may be required to pay user charges, both informal and formal, to obtain care. Finally, different policies may be applied to refugee and local populations. For malaria treatment, for example, international organizations providing care to the emergency-affected population might opt for more effective drugs than those designated by existing national policies. Such was the case in Burundi in 2000–2001, where disagreements between MSF and the government of Burundi over malaria treatment policies took several months to resolve (MSF, 2001). Devoting attention to issues of equity and to ensuring that host and refugee communities gain similar access to services will be in the longer-term best interests of both groups.

A key challenge to the host community is to utilize opportunities presented by the influx of refugees, along with other organizations and resources, to ensure that their services are developed further and their capacity is strengthened. Unfortunately, this rarely happens, although increasing awareness of these problems has begun to highlight the need for more capacity-strengthening responses. When the Kosovar Albanians fled into Macedonia and Albania in 1999, for example, there were widespread calls for funds and other support to the health and welfare systems of these countries. This was in contrast with the lack of additional support provided to Tanzania, for example, in building a more appropriate system in response to the influx of Hutu refugees following the Rwandan genocide in 1994.

Even in circumstances where the international community, through UNHCR and a wide range of international NGOs, is providing services to the refugee community, an impact on local health services may be felt. This may result from the recruitment by these agencies of local health workers, depleting indigenous systems of their usually already inadequate human resources. Moreover, additional needs may be placed on other levels within the health system, such as referral, rehabilitation, and chronic disease services that the NGOs may be ill-prepared for or unwilling to address. Therefore, it is important to anticipate and provide support to the host health system to ensure that it is best able to respond to the increased needs without collapsing under the pressure of greater demands upon the services provided.

Service Provision by Multilateral Organizations and Nongovernmental Organizations

The key challenges for these organizations are, in the short term, to reduce excess loss of life and to reestablish an environment in which maintaining and promoting health is possible. Many of the subsequent sections deal with the nature of the health-related interventions that are necessary in these settings. A much debated issue is whether these interventions should focus solely on the immediate, short-term needs, or whether they should also have longer-term objectives. Many relief and humanitarian organizations see their primary role as saving lives that have been placed at risk as a result of extraordinary events. In such situations, doing whatever is necessary, with whatever resources are available, is deemed appropriate even if some of what is done cannot be replicated or sustained over the longer term.

In camp settings, health services should be organized to ensure that the major causes of morbidity and mortality are addressed through fixed facilities and outreach programs. An essential drug list and standardized treatment protocols are necessary elements of a curative program. It is not necessary to develop totally new guidelines in each refugee situation; several excellent manuals already exist, from which guidelines can be adapted to suit local conditions (WHO, 2003). Curative services should be decentralized in a camp system of community health workers, health posts, first-line outpatient clinics, and a small inpatient facility to treat severe emergency cases. Patients requiring surgery or prolonged hospitalization should be referred to a local district or provincial hospital that will require assistance with drugs and other medical supplies to cope with the extra patient load.

Organizations that typically espouse a development rather than relief-oriented approach have sought to place the issue of developmental relief onto the agenda, arguing that early attention to the difficult issues of efficiency, effectiveness, sustainability, equity, and local ownership will be beneficial in the longer term. If one adopted the latter approach, greater effort would be given to activities such as training, building local capacity, and keeping costs down, rather than seeing these as desirable, but not practical, goals given the acute needs faced in relation to saving lives.

An additional key concern facing the range of organizations offering services in response to humanitarian crises is the importance of coordination. Organizations need to work together very closely if they are to reinforce each other's actions, maximize the use of available resources, minimize duplication and overlap, and enhance effectiveness, equity, and efficiency. The Code of Conduct for Humanitarian Organizations highlights the need for effective coordination, usually under the aegis of a lead organization from the United Nations system, such as OCHA, UNHCR, or, in some cases (especially for the health sector), WHO or UNICEF.

Lastly, there has been considerable unease in recent years regarding the quality of much of the service provision by NGOs operating in CEs. A key problem is the lack of transparency and accountability of such services, and the fact that despite meaning well, some organizations may do more harm than good. Recent initiatives, such as the Sphere Project (see Exhibit 10-7, later in this chapter), seek to establish standard and minimum indicators of acceptable performance for organizations operating in these environments. Although no enforcement mechanisms, or even effective incentives, have been developed to ensure compliance with these suggested standards, many voluntary organizations have agreed to do what they can to comply. The increasing professionalization of the field of humanitarian assistance, briefly discussed toward the end of this chapter, similarly reflects these trends toward improved practice and accountability.

Refugee Health Workers

Community health workers (CHWs) were seen in many countries as the mainstay of primary health care promotion, although some critics have questioned their value to national primary health care programs (Walt, 1988). In refugee and displaced person settings, the selection and training of refugee health workers has been considered as one key mechanism by which health programs can work more closely with affected communities.

The principal advantages of refugee health workers may be related to their role as intermediaries between the affected community and the services provided by the humanitarian agencies, which are often led by expatriate staff. Refugee workers are more likely to understand the cultural, behavioral, and environmental influences on health status, to contribute to a growing potential for self-care and refugee-provided services within the community, to share the health service provision workload, to build capacity and skills that will potentially be available after repatriation, and to enhance the dignity of both the community and the health care providers themselves. CHWs who are relatively unskilled and trained within the community may be the mainstay of service provision. However, it is important to recognize that the presence of trained health workers within the affected community, whether these be midwives, nurses, doctors, or others, represents an extremely valuable resource whose role should be promoted in whatever services are developed with expatriate agency support.

The role of CHWs in refugee settings will depend on the public health needs, the availability of host country and NGO-provided services, the prior level of skill of the workers, and the extent and quality of training received. In many cases, refugee health workers have worked outside of health center settings and have performed a range of tasks, including the following:

- identifying sick and malnourished community members and assisting them in obtaining assistance
- collecting and reporting demographic data such as births and deaths
- providing first aid and basic primary care such as oral rehydration for children with diarrhea
- assisting in mass vaccination campaigns
- encouraging participation in health campaigns and disease control programs
- ensuring that the needs and perspectives of refugees are taken on board in the development of health programs

In many conflicts, notably those in Vietnam, Mozambique, Ethiopia, and Eritrea, liberation movements trained cadres of CHWs who played a valuable role in establishing core health care services. These initially focused on basic curative care, but eventually included preventive health and health promotion. In a number of these struggles, such health workers also played a role in community mobilization and in laying the foundations for primary care–oriented services.

One of the first refugee programs that systematically trained large numbers of CHWs as the very basis of health service delivery was that in Somalia in the early 1980s. At that time, almost 1 million refugees from Ethiopia were housed in 35 camps scattered throughout three regions of the country. The Ministry of Health's Refugee Health Unit coordinated the training of approximately 2,000 CHWs and 1,000 traditional birth attendants with the help of NGOs working in the country. The training curriculum was standardized, as were treatment protocols, essential drugs, and salaries and conditions. As NGOs gradually withdrew from the country, health services were largely provided by CHWs and traditional birth attendants, supervised by Somali Ministry of Health trainers, nurses, and doctors.

Despite the range of potential advantages to developing and working with a cadre of refugee health workers, there are also numerous problems. It may be difficult to recruit health workers, especially in unstable settings or if potential workers have other pressing priorities, and they will require training and ongoing supervision. Their selection may be highly political, and identifying the affiliations of potential health workers may be difficult for agencies with limited knowledge of the area in which they are working. There is potential to stimulate rivalry and exacerbate perceptions of inequity if an inappropriate mix of workers from different areas and different backgrounds is selected. In the presence of adequately resourced host-country services, especially those that have sufficient numbers of trained staff, establishing

a cadre of CHWs with more limited skills may not be seen as a priority.

Among the prerequisites for effective CHW training programs are a clear description of the tasks to be performed, an adequate level of logistic and supervisory support, a transparent system of selection and remuneration, and the consent and involvement of the affected and, where relevant, host communities.

Women's and Children's Health Care Services

Children and women, especially pregnant women, have been repeatedly shown to be the most vulnerable members of refugee and displaced populations, especially during the emergency period. Among Rohingya refugees in Bangladesh (1992–1993), women and girl children were seen less at health facilities than men and boys, but had much higher mortality (Figure 10-6).

In Goma in 1994, households headed by women were found to have substantially less food and nonfood commodities that had been issued at general distribution points by international relief officials than those in which an adult male was present. For these reasons, health services oriented to the specific needs of children and women are essential in reducing morbidity and mortality within a population to a minimum level. Women's and children's health (WCH) care should begin within the community, at the household level, and not depend entirely on established health facilities. Often, as discussed earlier, community members, such as traditional birth attendants or others previously trained as CHWs, can be recruited

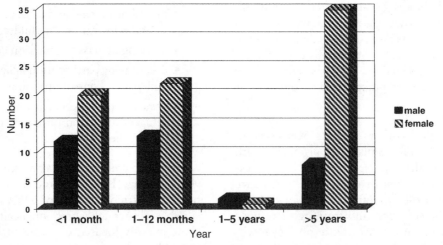

Figure 10-6 Number of Deaths Among Burmese Refugees in the Gundhum II Camp, Bangladesh, May 6 to June 26, 1992, by Age and Sex. *Source:* Data from Centers for Disease Control and Prevention, "Famine Affected, Refugee, and Displaced Populations: Recommendations for Public Health Issues," 1992, *Morbidity and Mortality Weekly Report,* *41*(RR-13).

from within the affected population itself to provide basic services.

For children, routine screening and preventive services are important. Growth monitoring, and the referral of children whose growth is faltering to supplementary feeding programs, is an essential function of WCH services. A WCH program will also ensure that all children are vaccinated on schedule and are receiving regular supplements of vitamin A. When curative care is required, as for diarrhea and acute respiratory infection, it can be offered at the household by trained CHWs, or the child can be referred to peripheral, first-line health facilities.

Pregnant women (who may constitute 3% of the population) should be regularly monitored. At least three prenatal examinations should be conducted to identify high-risk pregnancies. All women should be vaccinated with tetanus toxoid to prevent neonatal tetanus in their newborns. Iron and folic acid should be distributed (and their ingestion monitored, if possible). Insecticide-treated bed nets for the prevention of malaria should be distributed, and the presumptive treatment of malaria, if appropriate, should also be undertaken in the second and third trimesters. In the postnatal period, counseling services addressing a variety of issues, from family planning to child care, and especially breastfeeding, should be offered. Finally, although many elements of WCH can be instituted in the postemergency phase, a critical service that must be provided during the earliest stages of a relief effort is the establishment of emergency obstetrical care. Caesarian section and transfusion facilities and the ability to give parenteral antibiotics are essential if maternal mortality is to be kept low. Provisions for emergency delivery are part of an overall minimum initial service package, discussed in the next section.

Reproductive Health

UNHCR, WHO, and the UN Population Fund (UNFPA) state that although food, water, and shelter remain priorities in an emergency assistance program, reproductive health care is among the crucial elements that give refugees the basic human welfare and dignity that is their right (UNHCR, 1995a). The response to reproductive health problems during emergencies consists of a constellation of assessment, services, and regular monitoring that addresses the implementation of the following programs:

- a minimum initial service package (MISP)
- safe motherhood
- prevention and treatment of sexual and gender-based violence

- prevention and care for sexually transmitted diseases
- family planning
- reproductive health needs of adolescents

Minimum Initial Service Package

Although resources should not be diverted from attempts to control the diseases that have traditionally been the leading causes of death in CEs, there are five interventions related to reproductive health that should be implemented even in the acute phase. In addition, a reproductive health coordinator should be designated to ensure that these measures are adequately addressed.

Emergency Contraception. Forced migration is frequently accompanied by sexual violence. To prevent unwanted pregnancies resulting from rape, emergency postcoital contraceptive supplies should be available to women who request them. Although the extent of this problem has never been adequately documented, and although it is likely to vary from one situation to the next, the current recommendation is for sufficient supplies for 1% of women of reproductive age to be immediately available. Two methods of emergency contraception are currently available: the combined oral contraceptive (two formulations are used), which must be taken within 3 days of unprotected sexual intercourse, or the copper intrauterine device, which must be implanted within 5 days of unprotected intercourse.

Universal Precautions. To prevent the transmission of HIV, universal precautions must be respected from the very outset of an emergency. Although chaotic conditions are frequently prevalent and although health services are implemented under very stressful conditions, the threat of HIV infection can and must be minimized. Universal precautions include the following:

- washing hands with soap and water after contact with body fluids or wounds
- wearing gloves for procedures involving contact with blood or other body fluids
- using protective clothing when exposure to large amounts of blood is likely
- handling sharps safely
- disposing of waste materials safely (burning and/or burial)
- disinfecting or sterilizing medical equipment
- wearing gloves when handling corpses, and washing with soap and water afterward

Availability of Contraceptives. Little is known about sexual behavior during times of emergency. To prevent unwanted pregnancies and to minimize the transmission of sexually preventable infections, including HIV, an adequate supply of condoms should be available on request to all members of the target population. Several guidelines have been developed for the prevention of HIV in refugee and postemergency settings (Holmes, 2003; Inter-Agency Standing Committee Task Force on HIV/AIDS in Emergency Settings, 2003; Sphere Project, 2004).

Delivery Services. All populations affected by CEs will include women in the later stages of pregnancy or who are at high risk for complicated deliveries. These women need services even during the acute phase of the emergency. In a population of 2,500 with a crude birth rate of about 3%, there will be 5 to 8 births per month. To deal with these deliveries, simple supplies must be made available. Simple delivery kits and midwife kits are both readily available from UNICEF and other suppliers of health supplies. Skilled attendants should be present at every delivery. In addition, although it is not a formal part of the MISP, sites where complicated deliveries can be performed should be established as early during an emergency as possible. Caesarean section for obstructed delivery, transfusion for excessive hemorrhage, and parenteral antibiotics for the treatment of sepsis are the only ways to reduce maternal mortality, and these measures should be available and easily accessible from the onset of a relief operation.

Comprehensive Reproductive Health Services. The last element of the MISP is planning for the provision of comprehensive reproductive health services as rapidly as is feasible. To do this, reproductive health indicators should be included in health information systems to allow for the collection of baseline data on maternal, infant, and child mortality, prevalence of sexually transmitted diseases, and population contraceptive prevalence rates. Suitable sites for the delivery of reproductive health services should be identified, but need not be separate from other health facilities. These should be secure and allow for safe passage of women between their home and the clinic. They should be easily accessible to all who wish to use them, guarantee privacy and confidentiality, and have access to clean water and latrines. In addition, an adequate referral system should be identified or established in order to provide care to women with obstetrical complications or other health emergencies.

Postemergency Reproductive Health Programs

When adequate food, water, sanitation, and shelter have been provided, programs to address the initial emergency health priorities have been implemented (e.g., measles vaccination), and mortality rates have declined, the range of reproductive health services should gradually be expanded. In the postemergency phase, health care would be quite incomplete unless the entire range of programs aimed at maintaining or improving reproductive health was included. The key to successful reproductive health programs is soliciting active participation of as many adolescents and women of reproductive age as possible. Although training female health workers (including traditional birth attendants) is usually the focus of such programs, male health workers should also be trained in the basic principles of reproductive health care. In addition, because adequate reproductive health services are frequently unavailable to the local, nonrefugee population, it is a good idea to try to extend whatever programs are being made available to refugees and displaced persons by expatriate relief workers to women and adolescents in the host population.

Communicable Disease Control

Concern for the potential impact of communicable diseases has dominated the public health response in many emergency settings. As discussed previously, this attention has been frequently warranted. Although many of the technical interventions and public health programs used in emergencies draw heavily from their counterparts in stable settings, a few important differences should be considered. Most important among them include addressing the needs of the local, nondisplaced, population; maintaining respect for national health policies when dealing with refugees (but not necessarily adhering to them); and promoting substantial community involvement as early as is feasible.

Measles

Because of the devastating impact that measles has had in many emergencies, it has become almost universally accepted that mass measles vaccination, regardless of vaccination history or place of provenance of the displaced, should be instituted as early during an emergency as possible. Leading reference publications (CDC, 1992; Médecins sans Frontières, 1997; Sphere Project, 2004) accord measles vaccination the highest priority of all health-specific interventions and recommend that it be undertaken immediately after an initial rapid assessment regardless of the circumstances. If children cannot be vaccinated upon arrival or registration, a mass vaccination campaign should be undertaken. In general, this is a rule that should be followed unless extenuating circumstances exist, such as the cholera epidemic in Goma in 1994 that required the full attention of the health services, although any mass vaccination program must be planned very carefully if it is to be implemented successfully. Sufficient vaccine should be on hand (with a reserve in case of excess wastage) and stored in a functioning cold chain of adequate capacity. Only autodestruct syringes should be used, and safety boxes must be available for their storage and disposal.

The target population for measles vaccination in emergencies is usually children aged 6 months to 15 years. WHO recommends reducing the usual minimum age for measles vaccination from 9 months to 6 months because high attack rates and very high CFRs have occurred in younger children, especially in large displaced populations living in relatively crowded conditions. Still, because vaccine efficacy in children aged 6 to 9 months may be lower than optimal because of the persistence of passively transferred maternal antibodies to measles virus, children in this age group should be vaccinated again at the age of 9 months. The upper age limit for mass vaccination is more flexible and depends, to a large extent, on the amount of measles vaccine, injection equipment, and health personnel available and the pressure of competing health care priorities. Because age and undernutrition are such important risk factors for complicated measles and for high CFRs, all children up to 15 years old who are eligible for selective feeding programs or who are hospitalized with other illnesses should be vaccinated against measles on a priority basis. Then, depending on the factors mentioned earlier, all children younger than 2 years should be considered for vaccination, followed by all children younger than 5 years. Finally, if the circumstances allow, the target population can be expanded. In any case, a mass vaccination campaign should seek to achieve at least 95% coverage of the target population.

Because a mass vaccination campaign can reach such a high proportion of the most vulnerable population, there are frequently demands to attach other services to it. Vitamin A, for example, can be offered to the same target group during the course of the campaign. Insecticide-treated bed nets can be distributed to each household in which a child resides. There have been suggestions to provide polio vaccination along with measles vaccine, although the logistical burden of doing so must be carefully considered. In any case, a routine vaccination program for all children using the standard antigens recommended by WHO should be established during the postemergency period. Other vaccines, such as yellow fever and meningitis, are effective in interrupting transmission after an epidemic has been detected, and should not be offered routinely

at the time of measles vaccine. Cholera vaccination has also been recommended at the time of measles vaccination. However, the most commonly available cholera vaccine, a killed whole-cell/B subunit vaccine, cannot interrupt transmission during an outbreak (unlike measles vaccine), because it requires two doses 1 week apart and does not induce immunity until at least 1 week after the second dose.

The early detection of measles cases when they occur is an important feature of an effective community-based surveillance system. Measles treatment includes the administration of two doses of vitamin A and the appropriate treatment of common complications such as pneumonia, diarrhea, malnutrition, and meningoencephalitis. Children with measles should be closely monitored in regard to their nutritional status and, if indicated, should be enrolled in supplementary feeding programs during their convalescence.

Measles remains an important threat to the health of children in many emergency settings. However, as vaccination programs in many parts of the world have progressed and as vaccination coverage levels increase, measles vaccination should be considered alongside other priority interventions. In northern Iraq and in the Balkans, as in Goma, measles vaccination was delayed in order to address other, more urgent problems. On the other hand, in Afghanistan (2002), in Darfur (2004), and in Aceh province, Indonesia, in the wake of the tsunami (2005), measles vaccination was among the very first interventions organized and implemented. Still, in spite of the clear threat that measles poses to the health of populations in emergency settings, it is always appropriate to weigh the public health needs in light of the available resources and to order priorities accordingly.

Diarrheal Diseases

The importance of diarrhea as a contributor to morbidity and mortality in emergency settings cannot be overstated. The detection and reporting of diarrhea should be part of the routine surveillance system in all emergencies. Both acute watery diarrhea and bloody diarrhea should be reported separately by age (under 5 and over 5 years old are minimum age groups) and by gender.

All health personnel should be sensitized to the potential impact of diarrhea and should be skilled in most aspects of prevention and of treatment. The key to prevention lies in providing adequate sanitation facilities and at least the minimum recommended quantity of water of acceptable quality (see "Water and Sanitation," earlier in this chapter). The mainstay of diarrhea case management is oral rehydration therapy (ORT). Although any fluids can be used to prevent the development of dehydration, oral rehydration salts (ORS) can be used in all cases and are the treatment of choice for all levels of dehydration (see Chapter 4). In fact, the first large field trial of ORS took place in a refugee camp in West Bengal, India, where it was shown that cholera patients treated with what was the standard treatment at the time were 3.8 times as likely to die from dehydration as those treated with ORS.

Rehydration facilities should be available in all health facilities, including health posts and outreach sites within the community. Keys to the success of ORT in emergencies, where the case load can be substantial, include careful organization of ORT centers and the presence of concerned and skilled staff. Mothers or other caretakers are important contributors to ORT and must be instructed as to the quantity of fluid that their children require. Assertive administration of ORT, especially for children who are tired and reluctant to drink, is essential. Breastfeeding should be continued, and the nutritional status of children recovering from diarrhea must be carefully monitored. Rehydration of unaccompanied children should be carefully overseen and appropriate follow-up ensured (see Chapter 4).

Cholera. Early detection of possible cases of cholera is key to the effective management of an epidemic. Although noncholera diarrhea is a far more common cause of morbidity and mortality in children, the death of an adult from dehydration should raise suspicions of cholera. Attack rates can be higher in refugee camps than in noncamp situations. Laboratory confirmation should be obtained as quickly as possible at the start of a suspected epidemic, but need not be continued. Whenever cholera is suspected, aggressive attempts to educate the community should be made in order to limit the panic that frequently accompanies this disease. During the course of an epidemic, cases and deaths should be reported on a daily basis through the institution of an active surveillance mechanism.

The need to establish rehydration facilities at multiple sites within the community has been dramatically highlighted by the occurrence of epidemics of cholera. In an outbreak in Somalia in 1985, a new camp with only a centralized treatment facility and no trained CHWs reported a case fatality rate of 23.3%. In contrast, in seven camps in which peripheral ORT corners with trained CHWs had been established in the framework of a primary health care system, case fatality was limited to 2.4%. Even more dramatically, during the devastating outbreak in Goma in 1994, more than 90% of the approximately 45,000 deaths

that occurred during a 3-week period occurred beyond the reach of the health system. Active case finding and rehydration therapy within the community, rather than reliance on overwhelmed and understaffed health facilities, may have averted a significant fraction of these deaths.

Although as many as 90% of patients during a cholera epidemic can be treated orally, intravenous rehydration will be required for the most severe cases. A referral system must be in place, and cholera treatment sites should be identified and prepared with adequate bed capacity, human resources, water, drugs and other supplies, and disposal facilities. The treatment of cholera is the same as is described in Chapter 4. In emergency settings, however, selective chemoprophylaxis is usually not indicated. Resources can be used more efficiently and effectively in other ways, such as establishing adequate water and sanitation and ensuring that all patients are identified and treated quickly and appropriately.

Dysentery Due to Shigella dysenteriae *Type 1.* The management of epidemics of dysentery in emergency settings is very difficult. As is true of other diarrheal diseases, ensuring adequate water and sanitation facilities is essential, but because of the highly communicable nature of *Shigella dysenteriae* type 1, its role in reducing transmission may be limited, especially in the crowded conditions of refugee camps. Nevertheless, the use of narrow-neck containers for water storage to reduce contamination and the distribution and use of soap for hand washing have been shown to be useful. Early case detection and prompt treatment are the keys to limiting spread. An epidemic of *S. dysenteriae* type 1 should be suspected whenever a case of diarrhea with blood in the stool is reported. Laboratory confirmation and sensitivity to antibiotics should be obtained immediately, with careful attention paid to the transport of stool specimens.

The key to dysentery case management is antibiotic therapy. However, there are severe limitations to effective case management on a large scale. These include the large case loads that may require treatment, the resistance of organisms to first-line and even second-line antibiotics, and the difficulty of ensuring patient compliance with 3- to 5-day courses of treatment. In the relatively sheltered environment of refugee or IDP camps or settlements, where an international relief effort may be instituted, access to more expensive antibiotics and better patient supervision may be possible. However, because outbreaks frequently involve the surrounding local population, careful consideration should be given to the level of care provided. During the Goma epidemic, for example, the U.S. military donated a large quantity of ciprofloxacin, then a relatively expensive antibiotic, for the treatment of refugees. The local population, also severely affected by the epidemic, had recourse only to nalidixic acid, an antibiotic to which many of the isolated strains of *S. dysenteriae* type 1 were resistant. This situation created tension between the local public health authorities and the international organizations working with the refugees.

In general, during epidemics of *S. dysenteriae* type 1, an effective antibiotic should be given to all patients, under close supervision of health staff. If supplies of an effective antibiotic are limited, patients who are severely ill or most vulnerable (children, pregnant women, the elderly) should be given antibiotics, and others given supportive treatment only. This would include nutritional support, rehydration when necessary, and other specific measures.

Malaria

Malaria control in emergencies depends to some extent on knowledge of the local vectors. In any case, site planning and selection should be done with the possibility of malaria in mind, and areas with swamps, marshes, and other characteristics that favor vector breeding should be avoided. Where mosquito density is high and immunity of the population is low, periodic residual spraying of interior walls can be undertaken, although it is less effective where temporary and shoddy shelters are in use and where mosquitoes bite and rest outdoors. Aerial spraying should usually be avoided except in special circumstances. Barrier protection methods can also be useful, and the impregnation of materials, including bed nets, curtains, and even clothing, has been effective. The use of impregnated plastic sheeting on dwelling units has shown promise in reducing the incidence of malaria. In all circumstances, long-lasting impregnated bed nets should be distributed (Bloland & Williams, 2003). In emergencies where people are displaced with their livestock, periodic permethrin sponging of the animals has been shown to reduce vector density and malaria transmission.

The presumptive treatment of pregnant women with pyrimethamine/sulfadoxine in a single dose during the second and third trimesters (especially during their first and second pregnancies) is a potentially effective strategy that requires further evaluation. The presumptive treatment of children attending feeding centers can also be considered, and presumptive treatment of children for malaria at the time of measles vaccination or vaccination in routine pro-

grams may also have a role in malaria control after further investigation. Whenever feasible, the diagnosis of malaria should be confirmed, either microscopically or with one of several available colorimetric rapid diagnostic tests. If facilities are not available to do so, malaria should be treated on the basis of a presumptive diagnosis, although other causes of fever should be suspected as well. In determining who should be treated, with which drugs, and according to what dosage schedule, it is important to consider the national guidelines of the host country, although malaria control policies may also be updated in accordance with the latest information regarding antimalarial drug sensitivities. In most parts of the world, artemesenin combination therapy is currently the most effective, and most recommended, treatment. Supplies of artemesenin-containing drugs may be low, however, and effective planning to ensure their availability is required. Strategies for uncomplicated malaria, for severe malaria, and for treatment failures should be developed and explained to all health service personnel.

Malaria may occur in epidemic form, especially when individuals are forcibly displaced into highly malarious areas from areas of low endemicity. Epidemics in Kenya (2002) and in Burundi (2000) have heightened awareness of this possibility.

Meningitis

The detection of outbreaks of meningococcal meningitis at an early stage is essential. During emergencies, a high level of suspicion should be maintained. All clinically suspicious cases should be diagnosed by either visual inspection of cerebrospinal fluid or, where available, by the appropriate microscopic, serologic, and bacteriologic analyses. Background rates of meningococcal disease vary considerably from one area to another, and the occurrence of disease is highly seasonal. The detection of an epidemic therefore requires a sensitive surveillance system. It has become customary to institute epidemic control measures when a threshold incidence rate of 15 cases per 100,000 population per week has been exceeded for 2 consecutive weeks. In small populations, or where the population has not been accurately determined, a weekly doubling of the number of cases over a 3-week period can also signal the early stages of an epidemic. The WHO has established alert and response thresholds that should be reviewed and adhered to when emergencies occur in meningitis-prone areas.

Meningococcal vaccine (for group A and group C *Neisseriae meningitidis*) is effective in conferring at least short-term protection to all population groups and can also contribute to reducing transmission during the course of an epidemic. More recently, a vaccine protecting against the W135 serogroup, which is becoming a more frequent cause of epidemics in Africa, has also become available. Mass vaccination campaigns are an intervention of choice in areas in which an epidemic is occurring, and have been implemented in Burundi (1992), Guinea (1993), Zaire (1994), the Democratic Republic of Congo (2002), Burundi and Tanzania (2002), and Chad (2005) during CEs, as well as in many other countries in other situations. Vaccination campaigns usually target the entire population aged 1 year and older, although resource limitations may require limiting the age group to be vaccinated. As is the case with *Shigella* dysentery, epidemics of meningitis usually occur in both displaced and local populations simultaneously, and arrangements should be made to provide vaccine to the host population as well.

Neither mass chemoprophylaxis nor prophylaxis of household contacts has proven to be an effective intervention during outbreaks, and neither should be instituted. When epidemics occur in Africa, chloramphenicol in oil is the drug of choice, especially in areas with limited health facilities, because a single dose of this long-acting formulation has been shown to be effective. Penicillin, ampicillin, and ceftriaxone are also effective.

Tuberculosis

Tuberculosis control should be instituted only after mortality rates have fallen below 1 per 10,000 per day or when an emergency situation has stabilized and it is apparent that the displaced population will remain for at least 6 months. From a public health standpoint, the objective of TB control is to treat patients so that they cannot infect others, while helping to restore health in infected individuals. For this reason, only sputum smear–positive individuals are usually included in TB control programs, although individuals who are severely ill with noninfectious forms of TB should also be treated if they are identified. Patients should be treated according to WHO guidelines, which stress directly observed therapy with a short course (6 to 8 months) of a combination of antituberculosis drugs. Because both infection with HIV and malnutrition are associated with TB, the presence of these conditions should be determined and dealt with appropriately.

TB programs are complicated. The decision to implement one should not be made unless there are clear written guidelines that will be followed. Laboratory facilities must be available and the regular provision of supplies ensured. Drugs, also, must be stocked and resupply guaranteed. Finally, a system for tracing those who are unable to adhere to treatment regimens must be in place so that they can be identified and assistance provided to ensure treatment completion. Successful implementation of a TB control program requires a high level of community awareness, education, and involvement. Every element of a tuberculosis control program needs to be carefully and meticulously developed and nurtured over time. Agencies that intend to implement TB control programs in postemergency settings should have a clear commitment to continue for at least 12 to 15 months, have an adequate budget, and have the personnel and material resources necessary to run a successful program.

Role of International, National, and Nongovernmental Organizations

The vast and complex array of organizations involved in the various stages of humanitarian emergency preparedness and response reflects the complexity of the international community itself. It is hard to imagine any other situation that attracts such a range of players: heads of state; diplomats; bilateral foreign assistance agencies; UN political, social, economic, and technical organizations; military forces; and a broad variety of nongovernmental organizations, including an increasing number of commercial interests.

The UN Security Council plays a critical role in determining how and when the world will respond to the conflicts that lead to CEs and how emergency humanitarian assistance programs will be protected from the forces that fuel the conflicts themselves. Security Council decisions are in turn determined by the leaders of its member states, in particular the permanent members, the United States, Russia, France, the United Kingdom, and China. OCHA coordinates emergency preparedness and response within the UN system and is governed by an Inter-Agency Standing Committee of relevant UN agencies, including UNHCR, WHO, UNICEF, the World Food Programme (WFP), and UNFPA. OCHA launches joint appeals for funds to support coordinated UN agency response programs; however, these may sometimes compete with appeals launched by individual agencies.

UNHCR is responsible for the protection and care of all refugees who cross international borders. In some emergency situations, such as the crises in the former Yugoslavia, the UN secretary-general has designated UNHCR as the lead relief agency. At other times, as was the case in Somalia and southern Sudan, UNICEF or WFP has been the designated lead agency in the UN system. In general, UNHCR and other lead relief agencies need to be invited to provide assistance by the government of the affected country. In situations of internal conflict, the Security Council may authorize involvement by a UN agency without the approval of the host government, as was the case concerning the displaced Kurdish population in northern Iraq in 1991. The lead UN agency is mandated to coordinate the activities of other relief agencies, including NGOs, in cooperation with the host government where that is appropriate. However, in certain chaotic emergency settings, individual NGOs have sometimes negotiated involvement directly with government authorities and ignored efforts by the lead agency to coordinate activities.

In many emergencies, especially those involving large refugee populations, the host government has granted temporary asylum to the refugees and has become actively engaged in the relief effort. Many countries have coordinating bodies, such as relief commissions, that take a lead role in mobilizing, organizing, and delivering relief services. For example, in Somalia in the early 1980s, the Ministry of Health formed the Refugee Health Unit (RHU), which coordinated public health and nutrition assistance to the 800,000 Ethiopian refugees scattered in 35 camps throughout the country. NGOs wishing to provide assistance to refugees had to agree to follow technical guidelines developed by the unit and signed a tripartite agreement with the RHU and UNHCR. In areas such as southern Sudan where rebel forces are largely in control, relief programs are implemented with little or no involvement by the national government. During the tsunami relief effort of 2004–2005, the picture was mixed. In India and Thailand, most of the relief effort was run entirely by national authorities. In Indonesia and Sri Lanka, a combination of national and international organizations collaborated on policy development and on the day-to-day implementation of relief services.

The International Committee of the Red Cross (ICRC), based in Geneva, is mandated to carry out the protection and care of civilian populations during armed conflict as outlined in the Geneva Conventions. The ICRC relies on low-key and confidential negotiations with all parties to a conflict to allow it to carry out its humanitarian assistance. The ICRC is committed to carrying out its mission with independence, impartiality, and neutrality. Although it was once the only organization to operate within areas affected by conflict, in recent years many other NGOs have joined the ICRC in taking on this challenge. Some of these

NGOs, while providing relief impartially to all those in need, believe that they should also speak out in the face of gross human rights abuses and have become advocates for more effective international responses. This action may sometimes jeopardize their ability to remain in the affected area and is therefore not taken lightly. One of the most debated issues within NGOs is whether to provide humanitarian relief and remain silent about human rights abuses and the diversion of relief resources or to speak out and risk having to leave the area.

There are many NGOs engaged in providing humanitarian assistance in emergencies; they include national Red Cross and Red Crescent societies, international secular and religious agencies, and local churches and community-based organizations in the affected country. Specialized public health agencies such as the U.S. Centers for Disease Control and Prevention, a government agency, and the Paris-based Epicentre, a private organization closely linked to Médecins Sans Frontières, provide technical advice to a range of bilateral, UN, and nongovernmental operational agencies. The level of technical skills, experience, management, and logistics capacity of NGOs varies enormously. In an effort to promote coordination and the implementation of best practices among NGOs, a number of initiatives have been taken. These include the Code of Conduct for the International Red Cross and Red Crescent Movement and NGOs in Disaster Response and the *Humanitarian Charter and Minimum Standards in Disaster Response* (Sphere Project, 2004), which has been referred to frequently in this chapter. Most professional relief NGOs have signed on to these initiatives, and the impact of these codes is being monitored and evaluated (Van Dyke & Waldman, 2004). In addition to relief NGOs, an increasing number of human rights advocacy NGOs have been active in recent years, including Amnesty International, Human Rights Watch, Physicians for Human Rights, and Africa Watch.

Funding for international humanitarian assistance programs generally comes from the governments of high-income countries, such as the United States, Japan, members of the European Union, and other OECD states. The generosity of such governments varies enormously and often depends more on the perceived geopolitical importance of the conflict than the actual needs of the affected populations. High-profile media, such as CNN, the *New York Times*, and the BBC, often play an influential role in the size of the response to an emergency. For example, the blanket media coverage of emergencies in northern Iraq and Kosovo ensured that relief programs were adequately funded. However, the conflict in Somalia was largely ignored prior to late 1992, when then President George H. W. Bush decided to promote a highly visible humanitarian relief operation in the waning months of his presidency. The outpouring of support for the relief efforts that were implemented in response to the Indian Ocean tsunami in December 2004 from both public and private sectors is perhaps unprecedented. Why natural disasters seem to attract a more generous funding response than the silent tsunamis that plague areas in conflict for years and that usually take a much larger toll in human life is a matter of speculation. What is certain is that until there is a consistent response to conflict-related emergencies around the world, the quality and timeliness of humanitarian responses will be unpredictable.

Rehabilitation, Repatriation, and Recovery

In countries emerging from conflict, the costs of reconstruction may be staggering. In the immediate aftermath of the Gulf War, it was estimated that Iraq would require $110 to $200 billion and Kuwait $60 to $95 billion to repair the war damage from the United States–led coalition (Lee & Haines, 1991). Initial estimates for the reconstruction of Afghanistan were on the order of $1 to 2 billion per year for at least a decade. Within 2 weeks of the 26 December 2004 tsunami in the Indian Ocean, $4 billion had been pledged by donor countries for relief and reconstruction. In comparison, implementing worldwide the goals adopted by the World Summit for Children in 1991 would require $20 billion. Estimates of the cost of rehabilitation and recovery in countries affected by the Kosovo crisis show that many billions of dollars will be required annually for a considerable period of time, not only for Kosovo, but for the entire subregion if ongoing conflict is to be averted. However, it is important to note that the entire annual budget of the UN Authority in postconflict Kosovo was less than 50% of the daily cost of the NATO bombing campaign.

A particularly important issue for those engaged in dealing with the aftermath of conflicts is to determine the extent to which the prior health system will be simply reestablished along the lines of how it previously existed, or whether it will be reformed in an effort to improve efficiency, effectiveness, and equity. The usual response is to seek to reconstruct what has been destroyed in the conflict. This apparently logical response may be deeply flawed, however. One key impediment is that the resource base available for re-

constructing and operating the health system may be vastly inferior to what it was previously. In Uganda, the postconflict resource base was less than 10% of that prior to the civil war, making simple reestablishment of prior services totally unfeasible. Furthermore, much changes during the period of ongoing conflict: the range of providers operating, the role of the state, the attitude and demands of the community that uses services, and the approach of the international community and key donor organizations. The latter, for example, may seek to promote a radically different state, one that facilitates but does not provide services, and which places cost-effectiveness and value for money at its core. During the postconflict phase, international financial institutions and donor governments may greatly influence policy direction, and frequently do so in favor of reducing state expenditures and enhancing the role of the private sector.

In the period between the onset of periods of conflict and their resolution, which may last decades, approaches to the nature of health services and who purchases and provides them have changed. In many conflicts, other providers fill the gap left by retreating and undermined state-provided health services—these include for-profit and not-for-profit providers, as well as the indigenous and traditional sector. There has been little documentation of how and why the private sector emerges to play an important role in these settings. Nor is there any clarity about how best to control and regulate such activities in the interests of ensuring that minimum standards are adhered to and that the medical treatment offered by different providers does not compromise public health goals and objectives. The emergence and changing role of the nonprofit, nongovernmental sector is easier to appreciate. It fills gaps resulting from withering state services and is often supported by donor country funds that ensure that humanitarian relief services are provided in acute emergencies and that development-oriented services are offered where suitable funding and partner organizations, including the government, can be identified.

A major weakness of NGO-provided services is that they are often poorly coordinated, act in parallel with the state systems, have a different vision of the system they are seeking to bolster or reestablish, and compete for partners, resources, and publicity. Failing to support indigenous capacity may increase the risk of little being left behind when humanitarian agencies withdraw; increasingly, there is debate regarding how best such services could interface with host government services and policy and could reinforce the limited capacity often present.

A particularly important and difficult challenge is to establish the policy framework within which health services and the health system will operate. Different stakeholders (politicians, professionals, donors, multilateral organizations, private sector) all have their own agendas. A key role of government, when it functions effectively, is to provide a framework within which the different actors can operate. In many settings, including those countries emerging from major periods of conflict, the policy framework may be lacking or challenged, given its often uncertain legitimacy. In the presence of challenges to a government's legitimacy, as in Cambodia after the overthrow of Pol Pot by a Vietnamese-backed party, international donors may withdraw development funding and assistance or, where they do provide such relief and development support, may choose to channel it outside of government structures (Lanjouw, Macrae, & Zwi, 1999). This may simultaneously undermine local capacity and reinforce fragmentation. At the same time, it is important to recognize that NGO-supported interventions may be extremely effective and may facilitate the emergence of good, or at least better, practice. Moreover, NGOs generally promote more genuine participation by local communities in development activities. An important role for policy makers, both locally and internationally, is to facilitate the development of consensus about broad health system direction and the policy framework within which service provision will be undertaken. Exhibit 10-6 discusses the case of postconflict authority in East Timor.

Key issues to be debated in the aftermath of periods of conflict include the financing of health services, the extent to which they can and should be decentralized, the role of the private sector, and the priority to be accorded to issues of equity. These need to be seen within the broader context of promoting and consolidating the peace, reestablishing the economy, facilitating the demobilization of troops and their absorption into the economy, and facilitating the return of refugees and internally displaced people. Other key priorities include demining and establishing accountable systems of governance.

Ensuring that, to as great an extent as possible, existing inequities in distribution and access to health services are resolved in the aftermath of conflict may assist in lowering tensions between groups. Such inequities are often significant contributors to conflict between communities and different social groups in civil society. In the postconflict period, a fundamental challenge is to understand and seek to address those factors that contributed to the conflict. Promoting the development of a more equitable health and social system may provide an important opportunity for bringing together different groups within affected populations, and may provide early opportunities to stimulate debate, exchange of ideas, and the rekindling of trust. The concept of health as a bridge to peace is, however, relatively untested, and it is apparent that in some circumstances health-related interventions, if insensitively or differentially applied, may reinforce tensions and conflicts within and between communities.

Exhibit 10-6   Transitional Authority in East Timor

The violence following the August 1999 independence referendum was stopped by a United Nations–authorized international force in East Timor (INTERFET). In February 2000, responsibility for the administration of the territory was assumed by the UN Transitional Authority in East Timor (UNTAET), headed by a special representative of the UN secretary-general, for a period of 2 years leading up to elections and full independence for the new nation. Security was maintained by UN peacekeepers from 41 member nations.

The development of public policies and services, including health, was conducted in the framework of a National Consultative Council, which comprised three senior UNTAET officials, seven members of the major East Timorese political coalition (CNRT), and seven non-CNRT East Timorese representatives (churches, human rights organizations, etc.). Given the shortage of skilled local specialists, much of the policy direction was driven by consultants from various specialized technical agencies, such as WHO and UNICEF. Although the United Nations was reluctant to work closely with CNRT, the World Bank promptly consulted with the coalition, and a US$20 million trust fund was established for "community empowerment" projects that were to be implemented through local community structures.

In a country of 800,000 people, 60 international NGOs and 68 locally registered NGOs were active in the postconflict phase; however, very few had a commitment to capacity building and long-term national development. Various sectoral committees (e.g., health, education, police) were formed with representation by the various players mentioned earlier. The role of the National Consultative Council was to consider policy recommendations made by these committees and to provide approval when appropriate and in the longer-term national interest.

Identifying opportunities to increase the availability of funds for responding to basic needs in rural, urban, and periurban poor areas will be important in order to ensure a degree of public health control. Enhancing the quality of both publicly and privately provided services, and identifying new partnerships between state and nonstate actors, will similarly be important to developing more sustainable systems for the future.

Gender inequalities permeate many societies; in the postconflict environment, it may be possible to address these given that the conflict itself may have changed gender relations and modified the traditional roles of men and women. Conflict often leads to women taking on a more important role in relation to making household decisions and controlling household resources, given that even in patriarchal societies, men will often be absent during periods of conflict and women will absorb a multitude of usually male-dominated roles. Certain countries, notably Eritrea, Ethiopia, and South Africa, clearly raised gender issues as part of the postconflict dispensation sought by many. The Palestinian conflict drew extensively on women as a major force within the political struggle. Postconflict development of civil society and good governance may reflect opportunities for positive change; if inadequate support is given to such groups, however, such as in the former Yugoslavia, opportunities to promote a more accountable state that seeks negotiated rather than violent means of resolving conflict may be missed.

The reorganization of services to promote preventive and primary care should receive at least as much attention as physical reconstruction of the infrastructure. In many settings, however, emphasis appears to be mistakenly placed largely upon the rehabilitation and construction of hospitals and clinics, with little attention being devoted to the more difficult tasks of improving the policy process, improving management capacity, consolidating human resources, developing the provision of preventive care, and extending services to the poor. Major international donors play a significant role in undermining more effective policy development; donors typically seek high-visibility inputs, often dominated by infrastructure support, or support tightly controlled vertical programs.

An initiative to focus on the health system challenges facing countries emerging from conflict identified a number of key priorities for intervention (Zwi, Ugalde, & Richards, 2005):

- maximizing the contribution of both government and donors to the formulation and development of health policy

- developing a clear conceptual framework, informed by multidisciplinary approaches, to guide health system development

- establishing inclusive processes that involve a range of stakeholders in a participatory and transparent process of identifying needs and priorities and agreeing on models and approaches to health system development

- appreciating the limitations and constraints operating upon the range of different stakeholders (government at central and local levels, UN agencies, NGOs, traditional public and private sector providers) in financing, providing, and overseeing health services

- promoting evidence-based policy and planning to ensure that more good than harm results from interventions and that resources are used as equitably and efficiently as possible.

Donor Assistance and Coordination

As mentioned earlier, there is considerable confusion regarding the different roles played by donors and implementing agencies in relief and development contexts and little clarity regarding how these roles change in relation to the financing and provision of services during periods of postconflict reconstruction, rehabilitation, and development. The provision of relief is dominated by attempts to secure survival with the input of materials and support, often using NGOs as the key providers. In longer-term development projects, equity and reform are key objectives, human resource and institutional capacity development are key inputs, and partnership with government dominates the form of interaction with government. The transition from one phase to another is uncertain, contested, and marked by competition and self-interest.

Since the end of the Cold War, the funds allocated to emergencies have been increasing, and appear to have peaked around the midpoint of the 1990s. At the same time, development assistance has declined, in part because of budgetary pressure, but also reflecting the changing geopolitical situation in the absence of two clear superpowers.

Improving Donor Coordination

Donor coordination is, at the best of times, highly contentious and disputed. Although enhanced donor coordination is clearly desirable, the mechanisms to achieve this in the highly politicized and contested postconflict settings are unclear. Although postconflict settings have heightened needs for policy coordination, they may be particularly unstable and complex, thus lessening government capacity to manage and direct the process. Innovative approaches and sector-wide approaches based on the identification of a common basket of funds and agreement on the key features of reform and development to be promoted may facilitate coordination, although experience of these mechanisms in weak countries emerging from conflict is poor.

Recognizing the problems outlined previously, a group of donors have launched a Good Humanitarian Donorship initiative. Establishing principles and good practices of humanitarian donorship, this group agreed, among other things:

- to strive to ensure that funding of humanitarian action in new crises does not adversely affect meeting the needs in ongoing crises
- to recognize the necessity of a dynamic and flexible response to changing needs in humanitarian crises
- to allocate humanitarian funding in proportion to needs and on the basis of needs assessments
- to request that humanitarian organizations ensure adequate involvement of beneficiaries in the design and implementation of humanitarian response
- to provide humanitarian assistance in ways that are supportive of recovery and long-term development
- to support the central and unique role of the United Nations in providing leadership and coordination of international humanitarian action

This initiative has the potential to bring order to what has been a chaotic area. Time will tell if the actions of the donors will live up to the lofty principles stated in their first meetings.

Conceptual Framework for Health System Development

Having a clear conceptual framework for how the health system will operate is fundamental. The process of establishing this needs to be inclusive, involving a wide range of stakeholders in an open and transparent policy debate. Inputs to such processes include making available relevant literature, reports, and studies to all parties, sponsoring health-related media work, promoting policy forums in which participants from different institutions and organizations can exchange views and develop trust, and developing the roles of professional organizations to promote peace building and more equitable services.

The definition of a clear policy framework is often contested by different parties and groups; any proposed structure will have winners and losers. In the presence of a functional state, the government at the central and especially at local levels should play a key role in policy formulation and implementation. Analysis to inform the development of appropriate frameworks needs to be conducted by credible groups that can assist the state's capacity to manage the period of negotiation and policy formulation.

Experience from Mozambique highlights the value of early preparation and commitment to postwar health system development. Such plans need to be flexible and adaptable to new conditions, but having in place a broad policy framework for planning was valuable in guiding human resource development and capital and recurrent expenditure decisions in the immediate postwar period.

Decentralization and Participation

Promoting more widespread participation in highlighting needs and influencing policy decisions regarding health matters was discussed previously. In particular, local civil society organizations and local government structures could play a valuable role in contributing to policy debates. Working closely with decentralized systems could help ensure more effective targeting—the directing of resources to what and where they were most needed—and could facilitate intersectoral planning and decision making.

Development of Human Resources

The maintenance and development of human resources is a fundamental challenge in postconflict settings. The lack of staff (numbers and quality), the inability to retain staff, difficulty attracting longer-term funding to support an appropriate human resource strategy, and the lack of skills available due to the lack of continuity and decline in infrastructure are all key impediments. Attention needs to be devoted to both public and private sectors, at local and central levels, and in relation to management and technical functions. Improving standards of care and developing a range of training approaches sensitive to different constraints and capacities, including short courses, distance-based learning, and on-the-job training, may be valuable; facilitating ongoing commitment to local institutions and their development is a key pillar of such interventions.

Promoting Evidence-Based Policy

Key inputs to the promotion of evidence-based policy are information about needs and about the perspectives of different actors, especially affected communities, concerning the nature and form of the future health system. Health policy should be based on evidence not only of effectiveness and efficiency but also of equity, sustainability, satisfaction, and local ownership and leadership.

Information needs include assessments of human, material, and financial resources; donor aid flows and activities; private contributions to health sector activity; the distribution and condition of health facilities and logistic supports; the capacity and quality of available human resources; and the availability of drugs and equipment. Assessing health needs requires examination and analysis of baseline information on mortality, morbidity, and disability. Routine surveys such as the Demographic and Health Surveys or UNICEF's Multiple Indicator Cluster Surveys, conducted regularly in some countries, could provide useful data. Qualitative data on community perceptions and priorities are similarly extremely important although often lacking. Making more data available would help promote accountability, transparency, and democracy. Collected data should routinely be made available in the public domain. Such measures should clearly be undertaken within a framework that seeks to build local capacity to undertake and further develop their applied research and information system management capabilities.

Attention to Particular Disease Burdens

Specific disease burdens may be exacerbated by conflict and demand attention. STIs and HIV/AIDS may be exacerbated, as may other communicable diseases such as malaria, tuberculosis, and a variety of water-related conditions. Psychological distress may be widespread, demanding efforts to reestablish communities and their livelihoods. Injuries, violence, and specifically violence against women may be widespread and require attention and collaboration across and between different sectors.

Current Issues

With each new CE, new problems arise that must be addressed. In addition, the response to each emergency has led to reconsideration of previously encountered problems. Although countless issues can be considered to be at the forefront of contemporary thought in this field, there are three that are consistently debated and are deserving of special attention: the role of new humanitarian actors, improving the quality of NGO programs, and the role of research in developing more effective responses.

The Role of the Military and Other Humanitarian Actors

Traditionally the domain of international agencies and not-for-profit nongovernmental humanitarian organizations, CEs have evolved into major geopolitical theaters in which many diverse and disparate actors have sought to define new roles. Because an increasing number of CEs have been precipitated by armed conflict within and between nations, third-party military forces, especially those of Western nations, have been prominently involved in recent relief operations.

Following the Gulf War of 1991, an extensive international humanitarian effort for the Kurdish population of northern Iraq was coordinated by the U.S. military, which operated under the auspices, but not the command, of the United Nations. For almost the first time, NGOs were to a large degree dependent on Western military forces (including Germany, the United Kingdom, France, and Holland, in addition to the United States) for security, transportation, and logistics. The establishment of a secure operational area and the delegation of the delivery of relief services to the humanitarian community were important elements in bringing about a rapid response to the plight of the internally displaced Kurds. However, many NGOs, including the ICRC, were uncomfortable with working closely with the military and were forced to confront and reassess their notions of political neutrality. In addition, although their presence was positive in a number of ways, the military authorities proved to be novices when it came to humanitarian relief. They were ignorant of its basic principles, unfamiliar with appropriate relief services, and unable to promptly deliver essential supplies, such as measles vaccine, to meet the public health needs of a civilian population where maternal and child health problems were the main priority.

The military intervention in Somalia by Allied armed forces, including those of the United States, in 1992 was launched for humanitarian reasons, with the assent of the UN Security Council. In the chaotic situation of generalized lawlessness, severe factional combat, and the total collapse of governance, compounded by crop failure and ensuing famine, the only way to secure the delivery of essential relief was with the protection of armed forces. From a military standpoint, the intervention was felt to be a fiasco. However, many humanitarian organizations felt that the military operation contributed to decreasing the high mortality rate, at least initially. Prior to this episode, military forces had steadfastly maintained that their role should be limited to providing security for humanitarian supplies; following the Somali experience, they began to review in earnest the broader role of the military in humanitarian relief.

The war over Kosovo, fought between NATO and Serbia, was associated with a CE in which the military forces exercised control over the relief operation. A general lack of coordination between UN organizations, NGOs, and the military commanders resulted in information gaps, confusion regarding roles and responsibilities, and a generally chaotic situation. Fortunately, morbidity and mortality levels among the refugees in Macedonia and Albania remained low, but the potential for a humanitarian disaster in the face of a military victory was clearly present.

Following the invasion of Iraq by the United States in 2003 and the overthrow of the Saddam Hussein regime, much of the relief and reconstruction effort was contracted by the U.S. Department of Defense to private contractors. For the first time, NGOs were for the most part sidelined. This event has been the subject of intense debate in the humanitarian community, and it is not clear whether this episode is an exceptional one or whether the entire nature of humanitarian relief is in the process of tumultuous change.

The role of armed forces in the relief efforts that follow natural disasters may be less controversial. The United States, Germany, Australia, Singapore, and many others had armed forces provide humanitarian services in Aceh province, Indonesia, following the December 2004 tsunami. A large Indonesian Army contingent was also present. These forces provided transport, logistic, and hospital support both within the provincial capital of Banda Aceh and along the west coast of Aceh province, where small groups of people would have been entirely without relief were it not for the ability of military forces to access the area by helicopter and ship.

The increasingly constant presence of armed forces in CEs has raised a number of issues within the relief community. There is a need to reconsider whether the fundamental principles of neutrality and impartiality held so dearly by most humanitarian agencies are compatible with such close involvement with the military, who are trained to wage war. At a time when deaths of civilian relief workers outnumber those of peacekeeping forces, there is a need for increased personal security in areas where conflict is occurring. On the other hand, the aversion of many civilian, NGOs to the presence of the military in humanitarian crises should be considered in light of the assistance that these forces may be able to bring to populations in need. In sum, a serious review of the roles and responsibilities of the military, the United Nations, bilateral governmental agencies, and pri-

vate humanitarian organizations should be undertaken. All of these players should strive to develop a mode of operating in CEs that will work to relieve, and not to prolong, the suffering of those in greatest need of humanitarian relief. If military involvement is going to be useful, then commanders may have to relinquish certain decision-making roles to those more experienced in the effective delivery of public health services.

In addition to the military and other participants listed earlier in this chapter, other important agencies have emerged in recent years. Organizations that specialize in monitoring, detecting, and publicizing human rights abuses and prosecuting their perpetrators have become increasingly active during CEs. These include the Office of the UN High Commissioner for Human Rights; regional organizations such as the Office for Security and Cooperation in Europe; private organizations such as Amnesty International, Human Rights Watch, and Physicians for Human Rights; and national committees supporting the international war crimes tribunals. In some situations, such as Rwanda in 1994 and Kosovo in 1999, where human rights abuses were extremely common, these organizations have helped ensure that public health assistance programs addressed the sequelae of these abuses.

Finally, there has been increasing criticism of existing relief organizations because of their perceived inability to implement relief programs on the scale that is frequently necessary. Some have suggested that the rapid construction, maintenance, and management of large refugee camps, global logistical support, organization of health care services to large populations, and even the provision of security services might be done more effectively, rapidly, and efficiently by commercial companies contracted by governments or the UN. This challenge to the existing relief mechanisms, based as they are on the humanitarian motive, has yet to be resolved. In many ways it could lead to the transformation of humanitarian relief into a business enterprise, one that might inevitably become more closely linked to the donor agencies and used by them as agents of foreign policy. This has been the experience of bilateral development programs.

Professionalization

Partly to stave off this challenge, and partly to correct perceptions of incompetence and amateurism, efforts have been made to establish certain minimum standards of performance for relief workers (see Exhibit 10-7). Due to the transient nature of NGO relief programs and the high personnel turnover both in the

---

Exhibit 10-7   **The Sphere Project**

Perhaps the largest single effort to establish minimum standards of care in emergency settings has been The Sphere Project (www.sphereproject.org). Launched in 1997 by a group of private humanitarian agencies, Sphere recognized that humanitarian relief would be increasingly required for many years and that the existing capacity to respond with high-quality interventions was, for the most part, lacking. To address this situation, a large consortium (more than 228 private humanitarian organizations) from around the world participated in the development of the Sphere *Humanitarian Charter and Minimum Standards in Disaster Response*. First published in 1999, and substantially revised in 2004, these standards are intended to govern the overall conduct of relief NGOs and to provide benchmark levels of performance in the areas of water supply and sanitation, food security, nutrition, food aid, shelter and site management, and health services. The Sphere Project does not intend to establish new standards. Instead, it seeks to consolidate and reach agreement based on existing information. Standards will continue to be developed and existing standards will be modified in accordance with new findings, both from research and from experience gained in the field, following the initial dissemination and pilot testing of the charter.

---

field and at headquarters, experiences are not easily institutionalized and lessons need to be learned repeatedly. Limited field experience, a poor understanding of the public health priorities of emergencies, and inadequate skills to carry out the most essential tasks, such as organizing large-scale vaccination and ORT programs, have been frequently observed problems. After what is widely regarded as an initially ineffective relief effort in Goma in 1994, major efforts were undertaken to improve the technical abilities of relief workers in the public health sector.

A number of short-term training courses have been developed and implemented by schools of public health, government disaster relief agencies, and the NGOs themselves. Master of Public Health programs in humanitarian assistance and public health in CEs have been established in schools of public health in the United States and Europe. Although emergency public health workers are not yet required to have accredited qualifications, the quality of health care may improve as more of these training courses become available.

Research

The acquisition of new knowledge relevant to public health practice in displaced populations has been scant. Although most emergency public health programs rely on the safe and effective interventions that already exist (e.g., vaccines, ORS, water purification, essential drugs, and the like), their implementation in emergency settings may be affected by the size of the populations and the urgency of the circumstances. Little is known about the impact of rapid, forced migration on human behavior, disease transmission, and the delivery of effective services in emergency settings. For many years, it had been considered un-

ethical to conduct research of any kind among emergency-affected populations, who could be characterized as the most vulnerable members of the world's population. However, it is increasingly acknowledged that without applied research studies designed specifically to address operational issues in the context of emergencies, it will be difficult to reduce morbidity and mortality levels from their current, excessively high levels.

Existing standards are largely based on field experience; few are based on rigorously designed and evaluated observational field trials. Although policies in some areas, such as measles vaccination and aspects of food and nutrition, are based on field research, this is not the case in other important public health areas, such as reproductive health and the control of sexually transmitted diseases. Similarly, little reliable information is available on which to base policies and programs to promote psychosocial health, despite its rapid emergence as a consistent major public health problem. However, research is only useful where there is genuine concern for improved performance. Unfortunately, emergency relief has been largely guided by short-term concerns.

Much of what is learned in humanitarian response is rapidly lost from view. Of the many people who have worked in the field, few forge careers in humanitarian assistance. Data that are collected and reported by field workers are often either discarded or filed in internal agency reports and never seen again. There is no professional society for humanitarian public health workers, and no peer-reviewed journal in which the results of high-quality studies can be published. Although the number of people affected by CEs continues to grow, a solid body of research on which to base policy and practice is still sadly lacking. Without this database, relief policies will remain relatively uninformed, and mistakes will continue to be made.

Conclusion

Significant progress has been made during the past two decades toward the provision of effective, focused, needs-based humanitarian assistance to conflict-affected populations. Greater emphasis is now placed on the impact, including health outcomes, of international aid. The quantity of aid delivered is no longer considered a valid indicator of effectiveness; its relevance, quality, coverage, and equitable distribution are now accepted as more pertinent. As public health in emergency settings has developed as a specialized technical field, a number of relief agencies, especially NGOs, have developed technical manuals, field guidelines, and targeted training courses. Ability to meet the standard performance indicators developed recently by the Sphere Project and adherence to the international NGO code of ethics are arguably valid criteria to assess the quality of specific agencies.

Although a considerable body of knowledge has accumulated specifically relating to the health needs of emergency-affected populations, there remain many areas that require further development. Donor agencies should acknowledge the need to support applied health research in emergency settings if more effective interventions are to be developed against old problems, such as cholera, and emerging issues such as HIV/AIDS, TB, mental health, and reproductive health. The recent process of identifying applied health research priorities in emergencies, sponsored by WHO, and the creation of research and ethical advisory committees are steps in the right direction.

In planning for responses to future humanitarian emergencies, we need to recognize that improving the technical and management capacity of operational agencies will not be good enough. Recent experience has dramatically demonstrated that those in need will not benefit unless the international community ensures that there are mechanisms to permit secure access by those agencies. The means by which this access is provided is critical and most likely to be the central focus of international policy dialogue. The varied nature of the responses to emergencies in northern Iraq, Somalia, Bosnia, Rwanda, Kosovo, Sierra Leone, East Timor, and Darfur demonstrates the lack of consistency and predictability.

Finally, there remains the issue of primary prevention. The perceived differences between communities are generally tolerated in prosperous societies; conflict and all its consequences generally arise in times of economic distress and political instability. Although programs in good governance proliferate, the reality is that governments everywhere today are perceived to have failed to provide for the basic needs of their peoples. Unless these root causes of conflict are seriously addressed, all that will be accomplished is the perpetuation of a perennial relief industry that inevitably will experience only patchy success.

• • • Discussion Questions

1. What are the major objectives in the initial management of a refugee emergency?
2. What does the word *complex* as used in the term *complex emergency* imply?
3. What is the best indicator of the general health of a refugee population during an emergency?
4. Why are female-headed households in refugee camps at special risk of food scarcity?
5. What are the minimum standards in emergency relief operations for the provision of water and latrines?
6. What roles do general rations, supplementary feeding programs, and therapeutic feeding programs play in maintaining population nutrition?
7. At what age should children in emergency-affected populations be vaccinated against measles?
8. What are the immediate measures that can be taken in an emergency-affected population to prevent HIV/AIDS?
9. How adequate are the existing international legal statutes in protecting internally displaced persons?
10. What roles may community health workers play in an emergency public health program?
11. What are the immediate interventions that should be in place to address the reproductive health needs of women and men?
12. What population-based interventions have been developed to address the mental health needs of emergency-affected populations?

● ● ● **References**

Amnesty International. (1995). *Women in Afghanistan: A human rights catastrophe.* London: Amnesty International.

Babille, M., de Colombani, P., Guerra, R., Zagaria, N. & Zanetti, C. (1994). Post-emergency epidemiological surveillance in Iraqi-Kurdish refugee camps in Iran. *Disasters, 18,* 58–75.

Barnabas, G. A., & Zwi, A. B. (1997). Health policy development in wartime: Establishing the Baito health system in Tigray, Ethiopia. *Health Policy and Planning, 12*(1), 38–49.

Barudy, J. (1989). A programme of mental health for political refugees: Dealing with the invisible pain of political exile. *Social Science and Medicine, 28,* 715–727.

Bhatia, R., & Woodruff, B. (1999, February 11). Nutrition assessment of adolescents. Posting to Ngonut Internet discussion group, archived at http://www.univ-lille1.fr/pfeda/Ngonut/1999/9902a.htm.

Binet, L. (2003). *Genocide of Rwandan Tutsis 1994.* Paris, France: Médecins sans Frontières.

Bloland, P. B., & Williams, H. A. (Eds.). (2003). *Malaria control during mass population movements and natural disasters.* Washington, DC: National Academies Press.

Boccia, D., Klovstad, H., & Guthmann, J. P. (2004). *Outbreak of hepatitis E in Mornay IDP camp, western Darfur, Sudan.* Paris, France: Epicentre.

Boss, L. P., Toole, M. J., & Yip, R. (1994). Assessments of mortality, morbidity, and nutritional status in Somalia during the 1991–1992 famine. *Journal of the American Medical Association, 272,* 371–376.

Bracken, P. J., Giller, J. E., & Kabaganda, S. (1992). Helping victims of violence in Uganda. *Medicine and War, 8*(3), 155–163.

Bracken, P. J., Giller, J. E., & Summerfield, D. (1995). Psychological responses to war and atrocity: The limitations of current concepts. *Social Science and Medicine, 40*(8), 1073–1082.

Brown, V., Moren, A., & Paquet, C. (1999). *Rapid health assessment of refugee or displaced populations* (Annex 3). Paris: Epicentre and Médecins sans Frontières.

Burkholder, B. T., & Toole, M. J. (1995). Evolution of complex disasters. *Lancet, 346,* 1012–1015.

Center for Defense Information. (2005). *Significant ongoing armed conflicts 2004.* http://www.cdi.org.

Centers for Disease Control and Prevention. (1991a). Outbreak of pellagra among Mozambican refugees—Malawi, 1990. *Morbidity and Mortality Weekly Report, 40,* 209–213.

Centers for Disease Control and Prevention. (1991b). Public health consequences of acute displacement of Iraqi citizens: March–May. *Morbidity and Mortality Weekly Report, 40,* 443–446.

Centers for Disease Control and Prevention. (1992). Famine affected, refugee, and displaced populations: Recommendations for public health issues. *Morbidity and Mortality Weekly Report, 41*(RR-13), 1–76.

Centers for Disease Control and Prevention. (1993a). Status of public health—Bosnia and Herzegovina, August–September 1993. *Morbidity and Mortality Weekly Report, 42,* 973–977.

Centers for Disease Control and Prevention. (1993b). Mortality among newly arrived Mozambican refugees, Zimbabwe and Malawi, 1992. *Morbidity and Mortality Weekly Report, 42,* 468–469, 475–477.

Centers for Disease Control and Prevention. (1993c). Nutrition and mortality assessment—southern Sudan, March 1993. *Morbidity and Mortality Weekly Report, 42,* 304–308.

Centers for Disease Control and Prevention. (1994). Health status of displaced persons following civil war—Burundi, December 1993–January 1994. *Morbidity and Mortality Weekly Report, 43*(38), 701–703.

Cliff, J., & Noormahomed, A. R. (1988). Health as a target: South Africa's destabilization of Mozambique. *Social Science and Medicine, 27*(7), 717–722.

Coghlan, B., Brennan, R., Ngoy, P., Dofara, D., Otto, B., & Stewart, T. (2004). *Mortality in the Democratic Republic of Congo: Results from a nationwide survey conducted April–July 2004.* New York: International Rescue Committee and Burnet Institute.

Collins, S. (1993). The need for adult therapeutic care in emergency feeding programs. *Journal of the American Medical Association, 270*(5), 637–638.

Depoortere, E., Checchi, F., Broillet, F., Gerstl, S., Minetti, A., Gayraud, O., Briet, V., Pahl, J., Defourny, I., Tatay, M., & Brown, V. (2004). Violence and mortality in West Darfur, Sudan (2003–2004): Epidemiological evidence from four surveys. *Lancet, 364,* 1315–1320.

Desenclos, J. C., Berry, A. M., Padt, R., Farah, B., Segala, C., & Nabil, A. M. (1989). Epidemiologic patterns of scurvy among Ethiopian refugees. *Bulletin of the World Health Organization, 67,* 309–316.

Dodge, C. P. (1990). Health implications of war in Uganda and Sudan. *Social Science and Medicine, 31,* 691–698.

European Union, UNICEF, and World Food Programme. (1998). Nutrition survey of the Democratic People's Republic of Korea. New York: UNICEF.

Ferro-Luzzi, A., & James, W. P. (1996). Adult malnutrition: Simple assessment techniques for use in emergencies. *British Journal of Nutrition, 75*(1), 3–10.

Garfield, R. (1999). *Mortality Changes in Iraq, 1990–1996: A Review of Evidence,* Occasional Paper, Fourth Freedom Forum. Goshen, India.

Garfield, R., & Neugat, A. I. (1991). Epidemiologic analysis of warfare: A historical review. *Journal of the American Medical Association, 226,* 688–692.

Garfield, R. M., Prado, E., Gates, J. R., & Vermund, S. H. (1989). Malaria in Nicaragua: Community-based control efforts and the impact of war. *International Journal of Epidemiology, 18,* 434–439.

Golden, M. H. (1996). Severe malnutrition. In D. J. Weatherall, J. G. G. Ledington & D. A. Warrell (Eds.), *Oxford textbook of medicine* (3rd ed., pp. 1278–1296). Oxford, England: Oxford University Press.

Golden, M. H. (1999a, June 22). Indicators for adolescent malnutrition. Posting to Ngonut Internet discussion group, archived at http://www.univ-lille1.fr/pfeda/Ngonut/1999/9902a.htm#10.

Golden, M. H. (1999b). Preventing nutritional deficiency in emergencies. Presented at Enhancing the Nutritional Status of Relief Diets, Washington, DC, April 28–30.

Goma Epidemiology Group. (1995). Public health impact of Rwandan refugee crisis. What happened in Goma, Zaire, in July 1994? *Lancet, 345,* 339–344.

Goodhand, J., & Hulme, D. (1999). From wars to complex political emergencies: Understanding conflict and peace building in the new world disorder. *Third World Quarterly, 20*(1), 13–26.

Guha-Sapir, D., & van Panhuis, W. (2004). Conflict-related mortality: An analysis of 37 datasets. *Disasters, 28*(4), 418–428.

Hampton, J. (Ed.). (1998). *Internally displaced people. A global survey.* London: Earthscan.

Harrell-Bond, B. E., Voutira, E., & Leopold, M. (1992). Counting the refugees: Gifts, givers, patrons and clients. *Journal of Refugee Studies, 5*(3/4), 205–225.

Holmes, W. (2003). *Protecting the future: HIV prevention, care, and support among displaced and war-affected populations.* New York: International Rescue Committee and Kumarian Press.

Iacopino, V., Heisler, M., Pishevar, S., & Kirschner, R. H. (1996). Physician complicity in misrepresentation and omission of evidence of torture in postdetention medical examinations in Turkey. *Journal of the American Medical Association, 276*(5), 396–402.

Inter-Agency Standing Committee Task Force on HIV/AIDS in Emergency Settings. (2003).

Guidelines for HIV/AIDS interventions in emergency settings. Geneva, Switzerland, and New York: Inter-Agency Standing Committee Task Force on HIV/AIDS in Emergency Settings.

Jaspars, S., & Shoham, J. (1999). Targeting the vulnerable: A review of the necessity and feasibility of targeting vulnerable households. *Disasters, 23*(4), 359–372.

Keller, A. S., Eisenman, D. P., Saul, J. M., Kim, G. M., Holtz, T. H., & Connell, J. M. (1997). *Striking hard: Torture in Tibet.* Boston: Physicians for Human Rights.

Kloos, H. (1992). Health impacts of war in Ethiopia. *Disasters, 16,* 347–354.

Lanjouw, S., Macrae, J., & Zwi, A. B. (1999). Cambodia and post-conflict rehabilitation of health services: Coordination in chronic political emergencies. *Health Policy and Planning, 14*(3), 229–242.

Lee, I., & Haines, A. (1991). Health costs of the Gulf War. *British Medical Journal, 303,* 303–306.

Levy, B. S., & Sidel, V. W. (Eds.). (1997). *War and public health.* New York: Oxford University Press.

Macrae, J., & Zwi, A. (Eds.). (1994). *War and hunger: Rethinking international responses to complex emergencies.* London: Zed Books.

Manoncourt, S., Doppler, B., Enten, F., Nur, A., Mohamed, A., Vial, P., & Moren, A. (1992). Public health consequences of civil war in Somalia, April 1992. *Lancet, 340,* 176–177.

Marfin, A. A., Moore, J., Collins, C., Bielik, R., Kattel, U., Toole, M., & Moore, P. (1994). Infectious disease surveillance during emergency relief to Bhutanese refugees in Nepal. *Journal of the American Medical Association, 272,* 377–381.

Mears, C., & Young, H. (1998). *Acceptability and use of cereal-based foods in refugee camps: Case studies from Nepal, Ethiopia, and Tanzania.* Oxford, England: Oxfam.

Médecins sans Frontières. (1995). *Nutrition guidelines.* Paris: Médecins sans Frontières.

Médecins sans Frontières. (1997). *Refugee health: An approach to emergency situations.* London: Macmillan.

Médecins sans Frontières. (2001). *Burundi: Fever, hunger, and war.* http://www.msf.org/.

Médecins sans Frontières & Epicentre. (1999). *Rapid health assessment of refugee or displaced populations.* Paris: Médecins sans Frontières.

Moore, P. S., Marfin, A. A., Quenemoen, L. E., Gessner, B. D., Ayub, X. X., Miller, D. S., Sullivan, K. M., & Toole, M. J. (1993). Mortality rates in displaced and resident populations of Central Somalia during the famine of 1992. *Lancet, 341,* 935–938.

Nieburg, P., Waldman, R. J., Leavell, R., Sommer, A., & DeMaeyer, E. (1988). Vitamin A supplementation for refugees and famine victims. *Bulletin of the World Health Organization, 66,* 689–697.

Norwegian Refugee Council. (1997). *Internally displaced people: A global survey.* London: Earthscan.

Palmer, C. A., Lush, L., & Zwi, A. B. (1999). The emerging international policy agenda for reproductive health services in conflict settings. *Social Science and Medicine, 49,* 1689–1703.

Palmer, C. A., & Zwi, A. B. (1998). Women, health and humanitarian aid in conflict. *Disasters, 22*(3), 236–249.

Perrin, P. (1996). *War and public health.* Geneva: International Committee of the Red Cross.

Peterson, E. A., Roberts, L., Toole, M. J., & Peterson, D. E. (1998). Soap use effect on diarrhea: Nyamithutu refugee camp. *International Journal of Epidemiology, 27,* 520–524.

Project Ploughshares. (2002). http://www.ploughshares.ca/.

Reed, H., Haaga, J., & Keely, C. (Eds.). (1998). *The demography of forced migration: Summary of a workshop.* Washington, DC: National Academies Press.

Reed, H. E., & Keeley, C. B. (Eds.). (2001). *Forced migration and mortality*. Washington, DC: National Academies Press.

Roberts, L., Chartier, Y., Chartier, O., Malenga, G., Toole, M. J., & Rodka, H. (2001). Keeping clean water clean in a Malawi refugee camp: A randomized intervention trial. *Bulletin of the World Health Organization, 79*, 280–287.

Roberts, L., Lafta, R., Garfield, R., Khudairi, J., & Burnham, G. (2004). Mortality before and after the 2003 invasion of Iraq: Cluster sample survey. *Lancet, 364*, 1857–1864.

Roberts, L., & Zantop, M. (2003). Elevated mortality associated with armed conflict—Democratic Republic of Congo, 2002. *Morbidity and Mortality Weekly Report, 52*(20), 469–471.

Salama, P., Buzard, N., & Spiegel, R. (2001). Improving standards in international humanitarian response: The Sphere Project and beyond. *Journal of the American Medical Association, 286*, 531–532.

Salama, P., Spiegel, P., & Brennan, R. (2001). No less vulnerable: The internally displaced in humanitarian emergencies. *Lancet, 357*, 1430–1432.

Shrestha, N. M., Sharma, B., Ommeren, M. V., Regini, S., Makaju, R., Komproe, I., Shrestha, G., & de Jong, J. (1998). Impact of torture on refugees displaced within the developing world: Symptomatology among Bhutanese refugees in Nepal. *Journal of the American Medical Association, 280*(5), 443–448.

Simmonds, S., Cutts, F., & Dick, B. (1985). Training refugees as primary health care workers: Past imperfect, future conditional. *Disasters, 9*(1), 64–69.

Simmonds, S., Vaughan, P., & Gunn, S. W. (Eds.). (1983). *Refugee community health care*. Oxford, England: Oxford University Press.

Sivard, R. L. (1996). *World military and social expenditure 1996* (16th ed.). Washington, DC: World Priority Review.

Sphere Project. (2004). *Humanitarian charter and minimum standards in disaster response*. Geneva, Switzerland: The Sphere Project.

Spirer, H. F., & Spirer, L. (1993). *Data analysis for monitoring human rights*. Washington, DC: American Association for the Advancement of Science.

Stiglmayer, A. (Ed). (1994). *Mass rape: The war against women in Bosnia-Herzegovina*. Lincoln: University of Nebraska Press.

Swiss, S., & Giller, J. E. (1993). Rape as a crime of war. *Journal of the American Medical Association, 270*, 612–615.

Toole, M. J., Galson, S., & Brady, W. (1993). Are war and public health compatible? Report from Bosnia-Herzegovina. *Lancet, 341*, 1193–1196.

Toole, M. J., Rodger, A., Peregrino-Go, E., et al. (1999). *Impact of the Asian financial crisis on health*. Melbourne, Australia: Burnet Institute.

Toole, M. J., & Waldman, R. J. (1990). Prevention of excess mortality in refugee and displaced populations in developing countries. *Journal of the American Medical Association, 263*, 3296–3302.

Toole, M. J., & Waldman, R. J. (1993). Refugees and displaced persons: War, hunger, and public health. *Journal of the American Medical Association, 270*, 600–605.

United Nations Administrative Committee on Coordination, Sub-Committee on Nutrition (ACC/SCN). (1994a, August). *Refugee nutrition information system* (No. 6). Geneva, Switzerland: UN ACC/SCN.

United Nations Administrative Committee on Coordination, Sub-Committee on Nutrition (ACC/SCN). (1994b, October). *Refugee nutrition information system* (No. 7). Geneva, Switzerland: UN ACC/SCN.

United Nations Administrative Committee on Coordination, Sub-Committee on Nutrition (ACC/SCN). (1996, April). *Refugee nutrition information system* (No. 15). Geneva, Switzerland: UN ACC/SCN.

United Nations Administrative Committee on Coordination, Sub-Committee on Nutrition (ACC/SCN). (1998, June). *Refugee nutrition information system* (No. 24). Geneva, Switzerland: UN ACC/SCN.

United Nations Administrative Committee on Coordination, Sub-Committee on Nutrition (ACC/SCN). (1999, March). *Refugee nutrition information system* (No. 26). Geneva, Switzerland: UN ACC/SCN.

United Nations Administrative Committee on Coordination, Sub-Committee on Nutrition (ACC/SCN). (2002a, April). *Refugee nutrition information system* (No. 36/37). Geneva, Switzerland: UN ACC/SCN.

United Nations Administrative Committee on Coordination, Sub-Committee on Nutrition (ACC/SCN). (2002b, October). *Refugee nutrition information system* (No. 39). Geneva, Switzerland: UN ACC/SCN.

United Nations Administrative Committee on Coordination, Sub-Committee on Nutrition (ACC/SCN). (2003, November). *Refugee nutrition information system* (No. 43). Geneva, Switzerland: UN ACC/SCN.

United Nations High Commissioner for Refugees. (1992). *Bangladesh social services mission 22–31 March 1992* (UNHCR Program and Technical Support Section, International Report). Geneva, Switzerland: UNHCR.

United Nations High Commissioner for Refugees. (1993). *Refugee protection and sexual violence* (Executive Committee Conclusion No. 73, Preamble). Geneva, Switzerland: UNHCR.

United Nations High Commissioner for Refugees. (1995a). *Reproductive health in refugee situations: An inter-agency field manual.* Geneva, Switzerland: UNHCR.

United Nations High Commissioner for Refugees. (1995b). *Sexual violence against refugees: Guidelines on prevention and response.* Geneva, Switzerland: UNHCR.

United Nations High Commissioner for Refugees & World Food Programme. (1999). *Guidelines for selective feeding programmes in emergency situations.* Geneva, Switzerland: UNHCR.

United Nations Office for the Coordination of Humanitarian Affairs. (2005). *South Asia: Earthquake and tsunami—December 2004.*

http://www.reliefweb.int/rw/dbc.nsf/doc108?Open Form&emid=TS-2004-000147-LKA&rc=3#show.

United Nations Standing Committee on Nutrition. (2004a, February). *Nutrition information in crisis situations* (Report No. I). Geneva, Switzerland: UN Standing Committee on Nutrition.

United Nations Standing Committee on Nutrition. (2004b, May). *Nutrition information in crisis situations* (Report No. II). Geneva, Switzerland: UN Standing Committee on Nutrition.

United Nations Standing Committee on Nutrition. (2004c, August). *Nutrition information in crisis situations* (Report No. III). Geneva, Switzerland: UN Standing Committee on Nutrition.

United Nations Standing Committee on Nutrition. (2004d, November). *Nutrition information in crisis situations* (Report No. IV). Geneva, Switzerland: UN Standing Committee on Nutrition.

United States Committee for Refugees. (1998). *World refugee survey, 1997.* Washington, DC: U.S. Committee for Refugees.

United States Committee for Refugees. (1999a). *Crisis in Kosovo update, June 21, 1999.* http://www.refugees.org.

United States Committee for Refugees. (1999b). *World refugee survey, 1998.* Washington, DC: U.S. Committee for Refugees.

United States Committee for Refugees. (2005). *World refugee survey, 2004.* Washington, DC: U.S. Committee for Refugees.

United States Committee for Refugees. (2005). *Update on Asian tsunami.* http://www.refugees.org/.

Van Damme, W. (1998). *Medical assistance to self-settled refugees: Guinea 1990–96.* Antwerp, Belgium: ITG Press.

Van Dyke, M., & Waldman, R. (2004). *The Sphere Project evaluation report.* New York: Columbia University, Mailman School of Public Health.

Van Ommerem, M., Saxena, S., & Saraceno, B. (2005). Mental and social health during and after acute emergencies: Emerging consensus? *Bulletin of the World Health Organization, 83,* 71–75.

Walt, G. (1988). CHWs: Are national programs in crisis? *Health Policy and Planning, 3,* 1–21.

Walt, G., & Cliff, J. (1986). The dynamics of health policies in Mozambique 1975–1985. *Health Policy and Planning, 1*(2), 148–157.

Woodruff, B. A., & Duffield, A. (2000). *Adults and adolescents: Assessment of nutritional status in emergency-affected populations.* Geneva, Switzerland: United Nations Standing Committee on Nutrition.

World Food Programme/UNHCR. (1997). *Joint WFP/UNHCR guidelines for estimating food and nutritional needs in emergencies.* Rome and Geneva: World Food Programme/UNHCR.

World Health Organization. (1995). *Physical status: The use and interpretation of anthropometry. Report of a World Health Organization expert committee* (Technical Report No. 854). Geneva, Switzerland: World Health Organization.

World Health Organization. (1997). *Tuberculosis control in refugee situations—an inter-agency field manual* (WHO/TB/97.221). Geneva, Switzerland: World Health Organization.

World Health Organization. (1999a). *Rapid health assessment protocols for emergencies.* Geneva, Switzerland: World Health Organization.

World Health Organization. (1999b). *Scurvy and its prevention and control in major emergencies* (WHO/NHD/99.11). Geneva, Switzerland: World Health Organization.

World Health Organization. (1999c). *Thiamine deficiency and its prevention and control in major emergencies* (WHO/NHD/99.13). Geneva, Switzerland: World Health Organization.

World Health Organization. (1999d). *Management of severe malnutrition: A manual for physicians and other senior health workers.* Geneva, Switzerland: World Health Organization.

World Health Organization. (2000a). *Pellagra and its prevention and control in major emergencies* (WHO/NHD/00.10). Geneva, Switzerland: World Health Organization.

World Health Organization. (2000b). *The management of nutrition in major emergencies.* Geneva, Switzerland: World Health Organization.

World Health Organization. (2003). *Communicable disease control in emergencies: A field manual.* Geneva, Switzerland: World Health Organization.

World Health Organization, Health Information Network for Advanced Planning. (2000a). *Health situation report—West Timor, December 8, 1999.* Geneva, Switzerland: World Health Organization.

World Health Organization, Health Information Network for Advanced Planning. (2000b). *Health situation report—West Timor, January 5, 2000.* Geneva, Switzerland: World Health Organization.

World Health Organization, South-East Asia Regional Office (2005). *Situation reports on South-East Asia earthquake and tsunami.* January 26, 2005. http://w3.whosea.org.

Yamauchi, P. E. (1993). Patterns of death: Descriptions of geographic and temporal patterns of rural state terror in Guatemala, 1978–1985. *PSR Quarterly, 3*(2), 67–78.

Yip, R., & Sharp, T. W. (1993). Acute malnutrition and high childhood mortality related to diarrhea. *Journal of the American Medical Association, 270,* 587–590.

Zwi, A. B., & Cabral, A. J. (1991). Identifying 'high risk situations' for preventing AIDS. *British Medical Journal, 303,* 1527–1529.

Zwi, A., Ugalde, A., & Richards, P. (2005). The effects of war and political violence on health services. In L. Kurtz (Ed.), *Encyclopaedia of violence.* New York: Academic Press.

11

The Design of Health Systems

ANNE J. MILLS AND M. KENT RANSON

Health systems are the means whereby many of the programs and interventions discussed in earlier chapters are planned and delivered. They are a crucial influence on the extent to which countries are able to address their disease burden and improve overall levels of health and the health of particular groups in the population.

A *health system* comprises all organizations, institutions, and resources that produce actions whose primary purpose is to improve health (World Health Organization [WHO], 2000). The health care system consists of those organizations, institutions, and resources that deliver health care to individuals. Health systems vary greatly from country to country. Unlike the study of disease, there is only limited standardized terminology or methodology for studying and understanding health systems. Each country's health system is the product of a complex range of factors, especially its historical patterns of development and the power of different interest groups. Nonetheless, it is possible to identify common features, and knowledge is increasing on what design features are associated with what outcomes, thus facilitating cross-country learning.

It is extremely important to study and understand how health systems function and how they can be changed. Total expenditure on health care has risen from 3% of world gross domestic product (GDP) in 1948 to 7.9% in 1997 (WHO, 2000). Health tends to take a rising share of GDP as income increases: World Bank figures show the percentage of GDP absorbed by health care to be 4.3% in low-income countries, 5.9% in middle-income countries, and 10.2% in high-income countries (World Bank, 2003). Health services are thus both a large and expanding sector of the world economy. However, countries at similar income levels differ greatly in how

effectively they look after the health of their populations. The health-related differences between countries of similar income can be enormous, as shown in Figure 11-1 (World Bank, 1997a). Although a variety of factors affect health, it is clear that the health system is an important determinant.

The recent global attention being given to treatment of AIDS patients has focused attention on the state of the health systems of many low- and middle-income countries. Jong-Wook Lee, the director-general of the WHO, appointed in 2003, emphasized that in countries with a high burden of HIV/AIDS, systems are often degraded and dysfunctional because of a combination of underfunding and weak governance (WHO, 2004). More generally, he has argued that "progress in health . . . depends on viable national and local health systems. . . . In most countries, there will be only small and short-lived advances toward acceptable standards of health without the development of health care systems which are strong enough to respond to current challenges" (WHO, 2003, p. vii).

Understanding health systems and how they can be changed is an endeavor that can benefit from the insights of a number of disciplines, most notably economics, sociology, anthropology, political science, and management science. In recent years, not least because concerns regarding resource scarcity, cost inflation, and efficiency have been uppermost in policy makers' minds, the discipline of economics has had a dominant influence on the study of health systems. This chapter therefore draws primarily on economics to review key features of the design of health systems.

The section that follows provides a conceptual map of the health system and its key elements. The historical development of health systems is then

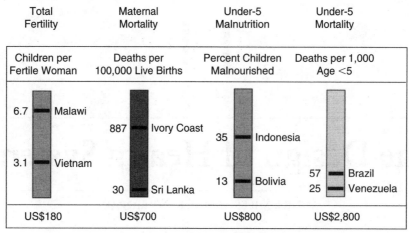

Figure 11-1 Outcomes at Similar Income Levels. *Source:* World Bank, *Sector Strategy: Health, Nutrition and Population* (Washington, DC: World Bank Group, 1997a). Reprinted with permission.

briefly reviewed, followed by a section addressing the fundamental and controversial question of the role of the state. Subsequent sections then consider each of the key functions of health systems in turn: regulation, financing, resource allocation, and provision. Current trends in health system reform and what lessons emerge on reform policies are then reviewed. Throughout, the text is illustrated by country examples, but a core set of illustrations is drawn from Zambia, India, Mexico, and Thailand, which have been chosen to illuminate key differences in health systems across the world.

Conceptual Maps of the Health System

Since the seminal study of Kohn and White in 1976, an expanding body of literature has been attempting to systematize the discussion of the various elements of health systems, categorize health systems into a limited number of different types, and develop performance indicators (e.g., McPake & Machray, 1997; Roemer, 1991; WHO, 2000). These three issues are discussed in turn.

Elements of Health Systems

Roemer (1991) identified five major categories that enable a comprehensive description of a country's health system to be made (Figure 11-2):

- production of resources (trained staff, commodities such as drugs, facilities, knowledge)

- organization of programs (by government ministries, private providers, voluntary agencies)
- economic support mechanisms (sources of funds, such as tax, insurance, and user fees)
- management methods (planning, administration, regulation, legislation)
- delivery of services (preventive and curative personal health services; primary, secondary, and tertiary services; public health services; services for specific population groups, such as children, or for specific conditions, such as mental illness)

More recently, WHO has developed a categorization of health system functions and objectives (WHO, 2000). Health system functions are considered to be as follows:

- service provision
- resource generation (of inputs such as human resources and physical capital)
- financing (revenue collection, pooling of resources, and purchasing health care)
- stewardship (a broader concept than regulation, encompassing the necessary functions of government in safeguarding the health of its people)

These types of categorization are helpful for describing health systems; indeed, Roemer (1991, 1993) applies his approach to a very large number of coun-

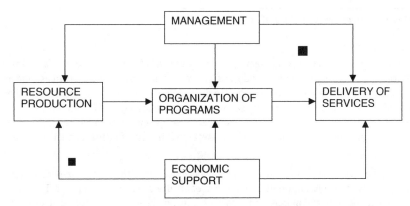

Figure 11-2 The Elements of Health Systems. *Source:* M. I. Roemer, *National Health Systems of the World: Vol. 1. The Countries* (Oxford, England: Oxford University Press, 1991). Copyright 1991 by Oxford University Press, Inc. Reprinted by permission of Oxford University Press, Inc.

tries. However, the categorizations are less helpful for understanding how well health systems perform. This would require much more detailed subcategories and greater elaboration of the relationships, not just within each category but particularly between categories (e.g., between economic support mechanisms and organization of programs).

Typologies of Health Systems

In order to make comparisons of how different types of health systems perform, it is helpful to group countries into a manageable number of types. There have been various attempts to do this. Countries can be classified according to the following:

- the dominant method of financing (e.g., tax, social insurance, private insurance, out-of-pocket payments)
- the underlying political philosophy (e.g., capitalist, socialist)
- the nature of state intervention (e.g., to cover the whole population or only the poor)
- the level of gross national product (GNP) (e.g., low, middle, high)
- historical or cultural attributes (e.g., industrialized, nonindustrialized, transitional)

A key difficulty, however, is that countries do not fit neatly into these categories. Roemer (1991), for example, uses two dimensions:

1. economic level (with four categories: affluent and industrialized, developing and transitional, very poor, resource-rich)

2. health system policies (again with four categories: entrepreneurial and permissive, welfare orientated, universal and comprehensive, socialist and centrally planned)

Although some of these categories are less relevant today than they were at the time of their formulation (e.g., centrally planned), it is also the case that the second dimension does not classify well the health systems of low- and middle-income countries, which tend to be fragmented, with different arrangements for different population groups (McPake & Machray, 1997). For example, Roemer (1991) classifies Thailand as "entrepreneurial and permissive," and Mexico and India as "welfare orientated." Yet, as shown in Exhibit 11-1, which summarizes the structure of the health systems in these three countries plus Zambia, these countries cannot be clearly placed into such neat categories.

The Organization for Economic Cooperation and Development (OECD) has developed a typology that is helpful for categorizing not only the economic dimensions of health systems in OECD countries, but also the directions in which reforms are taking them (OECD, 1992). The key categories are as follows:

- whether the prime funding source consists of payments that are made voluntarily (as in private insurance or payment of user fees) or are compulsory (as in taxation or social insurance)
- whether services are provided by direct ownership (termed the *integrated pattern,* where a ministry of health or social insurance agency provides services itself), by contractual arrangements (where a ministry of health or social

---

Exhibit 11-1   **Illustrations of the Structure of Health Systems**

Zambia (PPP GNI per capita $770)

The health system is made up of a large public sector, covering all levels from primary to tertiary, which until recently has been very centralized. There are networks of industrial services (concentrated in urban areas) and mission (church) services (generally rural) subsidized by the state. Private doctors practice in the main cities, and there is a large informal sector of traditional practitioners and drug sellers. There are relatively few private hospitals (10% of beds are in the private sector and 27% in the mission sector). An executive agency has been created to take over management responsibility from the ministry of health at the national level, and the role of health districts has been strengthened.

India (PPP GNI per capita $2,570)

The public sector is large in absolute terms, providing all levels of care. Health care is in general a state function, with central government involved mainly in overall policy and specific disease control programs. There is a very large formal private sector, providing both ambulatory and inpatient care, and an even larger informal sector consisting of unlicensed and unqualified practitioners and drug sellers. There is very limited formal interaction between public and private sectors. A compulsory state insurance system covers lower paid, formal-sector workers, and another scheme covers government workers. There are numerous community-based health schemes, some with an insurance component.

Mexico (PPP GNI per capita $8,540)

Public and private sectors play an important role in financing and provision. The health sector is highly segmented. Formal sector employees (roughly 60% of the population) are covered by various social insurance institutions (Fundacion Mexicana para la Salud, 1995). The poor receive care through government facilities or private providers (allopathic and traditional). There is very little interaction between public and private sectors, either in the form of regulation or contracting for service delivery. There is much duplication and waste of resources between the three subsystems: social security, other government, and private. Mexico's health sector reform plans are based on decentralization and managed market principles.

Thailand (PPP GNI per capita $6,680)

Both public and private sectors are large, providing all levels of care. There is very widespread use of the private sector, especially for outpatient care. Compulsory social insurance covers those in formal employment and finances care provided by public and private hospitals (chosen by the insured). Civil servants have their own medical benefit scheme which pays for care at public and private hospitals. The remaining part of the population—who formerly could get a low-income card exempting them from fees if they were poor, purchase a voluntary health insurance card, or pay out of pocket for care—are now part of a universal coverage arrangement in which they register at a local facility and can then access a wide range of health care benefits on payment of a nominal fee (waived for the poor, children, and elderly) (Towse, Mills, & Tangcharoensathien, 2004)

Notes: PPP = purchasing power parity. GNI (gross national income) is in 2002 prices (World Bank, 2004)

---

insurance agency contracts with providers to deliver services), or simply by private providers (paid by direct out-of-pocket payments)

- how services are paid for (prospectively, where financial risk is transferred to providers, or retrospectively, where the cost of care is reimbursed)

This framework is most relevant to countries at a relatively advanced stage of development, where the coverage of the health system is universal or consists of a limited number of arrangements. As with the Roemer classification, it does not allow for the diversity of arrangements seen in practice in poorer countries.

Because a typology suitable for low- and middle-income countries has yet to be worked out, the content of this chapter is based on a simple framework

(shown in Figure 11-3) that identifies four key actors and four key functions required in any health system. The actors are as follows:

- the government or professional body that structures and regulates the system
- the population, including patients, who as individuals and households ultimately pay for the health system and receive services
- financing agents, who collect funds and allocate them to providers or purchase services at national or lower levels
- the providers of services, who themselves can be categorized in various ways, such as by level (primary, secondary, tertiary), function (curative, preventive), ownership (public; private,

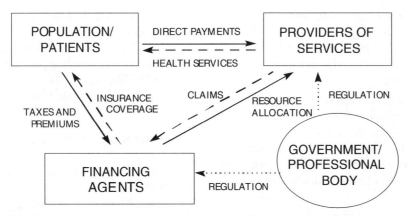

Figure 11-3 A Map of the Health System. *Source:* A. Mills, "Reforming Health Sectors: Fashions, Passions and Common Sense," in A. Mills (Ed.), *Reforming Health Sectors* (London: Kegan Paul International, 2000b), pp. 1–24. Adapted with permission.

for-profit; private, not-for-profit), degree of organization (formal, informal), or medical system (allopathic, ayurvedic)

The functions are as follows:

- regulation
- financing (through taxes, premiums, and direct payments)
- resource allocation
- providing services

Evaluation of Health Systems

WHO (2000) argues that the health system has three main objectives, which are intrinsically valuable:

- good health (both its absolute level and distribution across the population)
- fairness in financial contribution
- responsiveness to peoples' expectations (both level and distribution)

In assessing actual performance of health systems, criteria of efficiency and equity are frequently applied, and it is thus important to understand their various meanings. Efficiency has a number of different dimensions:

- *Macroeconomic efficiency* refers to the total costs of the health system in relation to overall health status; countries differ in how efficiently their health systems convert resources used into health gains.

- *Microeconomic efficiency* refers to the scope for achieving greater efficiency from existing resources. It is of two types:

    Allocative efficiency: devoting resources to that mix of activities that will have the greatest impact on health (i.e., is most cost-effective)

    Technical efficiency: using only the minimum necessary resources to finance, purchase, and deliver a particular activity or set of activities (i.e., avoiding waste).

Equity refers to the fair distribution of the costs of health services and the benefits obtained from their use among different groups in the population. It is inherently a question of values, and views differ as to what constitutes fairness of financing or access to health care. However, indicators of who pays for health services and who receives benefits provide evidence on the basis of which judgments can be made on the degree of equity achieved by particular health systems.

Equity is commonly expressed in two different ways (Donaldson & Gerard, 1993):

1. *Horizontal equity* refers to the equal treatment of equals. With respect to financing and resource allocation, this is taken to imply that the charge levied by all agents or providers for a particular good or service should be the same for households with equal ability to pay (regardless of gender, marital status, and so on). Horizontal equity is therefore assessed by the extent to which contribution levels are

similar between those with similar ability to pay. With respect to provision, horizontal equity means that individuals with the same health condition should have equal access to health services.

2. *Vertical equity* is based on the principle that individuals who are unequal in society should be treated differently. Vertical equity in the financing and purchasing of health services means that consumers should be charged for the same good or service according to their ability to pay.

Table 11-1 demonstrates how equity and efficiency criteria can be used to guide the financing, allocation of resources, and provision of health services and to evaluate performance.

In WHO's *Health Systems: Improving Performance* (WHO 2000), a conceptual framework, based on the goals and functions listed earlier, was applied to country data to assess and understand country health system performance. Countries were ranked in relation to their attainment of the individual goals, in relation to overall goal attainment, and in terms of performance on level of health and the functioning of the overall health system. Although the conceptual framework and new databases have proved useful, the ranking has been extremely controversial (e.g., see Almeida et al., 2001; Coyne & Hilsenrath, 2002) and has not been continued in subsequent *World Health Reports*.

Historical Development of Health Systems

As indicated by archaeological evidence, medicine has had its role in all cultures and civilizations (e.g., in ancient Mesopotamia and Egypt). It has also been a concern of the state: The law code of Hammurabi (1792–1750 BC) specified the fees for an operation to be paid to a healer on a sliding scale, depending on the status of the patient, and also specified penalties for failure. The Romans built hospitals for domestic slaves and soldiers in permanent forts in occupied territories such as England. However, the real development of the hospital derived from the spread of Christianity and of ideas of Christian charity and caring for all who might be in need after the conversion of Constantine (died AD 337) made Christianity an of-

Table 11-1	Equity and Efficiency Criteria Applied to Financing, Resource Allocation, and Provision of Health Care			
	Efficiency		**Equity**	
Functions	**Allocative**	**Technical**	**Horizontal**	**Vertical**
Financing	—	Maximize the proportion of resources raised that are actually available for purchasing health care (e.g., reduce the overhead costs of collecting taxes)	Equal payment by those with equal ability to pay (e.g., same insurance premium for same income group)	Payment in relation to ability to pay (e.g., progressive income tax rates)
Allocating resources	Purchase that mix of interventions that provides the greatest health gains	Maximize the proportion of resources spent by agents that are actually available for providing health care	Services purchased for similar groups (e.g., the elderly) should be the same in different geographic areas	Services purchased should reflect the different needs of different groups (e.g., the elderly versus children)
Providing services	Provide those interventions that return the greatest value for money (e.g., in a poor country, antenatal care should be provided before radiotherapy for cancer)	Make the best use of resources in providing interventions deemed worthwhile (e.g., have nurses as opposed to doctors provide most antenatal care)	Equal access for equal need (e.g., equal waiting time for treatment for patients with similar conditions)	Unequal treatment for unequal need (e.g., unequal treatment of those with trivial versus serious conditions)

Source: C. Donaldson and K. Gerard, *Economics of Health Care Financing: The Visible Hand* (London: Macmillan Press, 1993). Reprinted with permission.

ficial imperial religion (Porter, 1996a). Hospitals developed in the main cities of the Christian world, often associated with churches or monasteries. The Islamic world also developed hospitals, and by the 11th century there were large hospitals in every major Muslim town. Hospitals were for the sick who lacked families or servants to care for them—the poor, travelers, and those working away from home (Abel-Smith, 1994).

In Europe by the Middle Ages, a multiplicity of institutions and organizations had developed with pretensions to authority over medicine: the church, guilds, medical colleges, town councils, and powerful individuals. In Brussels, for example, a board of clergy, doctors, and midwives licensed midwives in the 15th century. The arrival of the plague—the Black Death—which in its first wave killed around 25% of Europe's population, stimulated growing state involvement to protect health through measures such as imposing quarantine and isolating the sick.

From the early 19th century, the scientific basis of medicine was increasingly established, with scientific training becoming essential for the practice of medicine (Porter, 1996b). The 18th and 19th centuries saw a vast expansion of hospitals in Europe and the United States, supported by philanthropy and also by public funds, especially for hospitals for infectious diseases and the mentally ill (Porter, 1996a). The charitable and voluntary basis for the funding of hospitals in many countries faced a crisis as medicine became more elaborate and expensive. The enormous increase in surgery and the development of technology led both to much greater numbers of patients and much higher costs per patient. Voluntary hospitals ran into financial difficulties. In the United States, hospitals developed business strategies based on insurance that could attract the well-off. In the United Kingdom, where insurance was much less well developed, hospitals were eventually brought into public ownership. In Scandinavia, local authorities had had responsibility for providing hospital services since the late 19th century, and so they developed largely as a public service (Abel-Smith, 1994). The strong development of the discipline of public health in the 19th century was a response to the disease hazards of the urban environment. In England and Germany, public health measures focused on safe water supply and drains.

Over the 18th and 19th centuries, modern forms of medical regulation developed. Countries in which medicine was dominated by free markets (such as the United States) converged with countries in Europe with strong state control (such as Germany) to produce the closely regulated medical markets that exist today. However, the degree of state involvement in the provision of health services varied enormously between countries, as it still does.

A key development was the increase in collective arrangements for funding health services. State services developed in all Western countries to provide health services for those who could not afford to purchase them themselves. In addition, mutual insurance schemes developed in Europe and the United States to protect workers against financial losses, and these often included medical care (Abel-Smith, 1994). These schemes were encouraged by the German states and developed into a national program of health insurance. In the United Kingdom, in contrast, they were nationalized as part of the expansion of state welfare. Other European countries also saw the development and expansion of compulsory financial arrangements for health services, whether through the extension of insurance arrangements for medical care (the Bismarck model, named after the German chancellor who introduced the first compulsory insurance scheme) or through general taxation (the Beveridge model, named after the British minister of health who is regarded as the founder of the United Kingdom National Health Service). Since World War II, all high-income countries, with the exception of the United States, have extended mechanisms for protection against the financial risks of ill health to the point where they can be said to have achieved universal coverage.

Another key development in the creation of the modern health system was the development of organized systems of medical care, as opposed to fragmented and competing individual doctors and hospitals. World War I marked a turning point in Europe, when the need to organize medical care on a massive scale highlighted the advantages of a large, coordinated system. In the United Kingdom the Dawson report in 1920 designed a system of district health services based on general practitioners and health centers, with referral upward to hospitals (WHO, 1999). The later development of the philosophy of national economic plans and of a strong government role in many sectors of the economy also supported the development of organized health systems. Even in those countries with less of a tradition of a strong state role in health services, cost escalation in recent decades has forced greater state involvement.

In the late 19th century Western medicine spread around the world, often as part of the process of colonial expansion (Zwi & Mills, 1995). Medicine acted in part as an agency of Western imperialism, and organized health services were a component of British,

French, German, and Belgian colonization. These were initially intended for the military, settler, and civil service communities, but it rapidly became apparent that protecting the health of expatriates required addressing health needs among the colonized. In addition, health services were introduced by commercial interests if they felt economic returns would improve, and by the church as part of missionary activities. To a much greater extent than was the case in the home countries of the colonizers, the provision of health services became associated with the state. This was accentuated in the postcolonial era by the prevalent ideologies of state-led growth and state responsibility for the welfare of all inhabitants. This was seen in its most extreme form in socialist countries such as Tanzania, China, and Vietnam, which banned private practice. However, more generally in Africa and Asia, attention of policy makers focused on publicly financed and provided services, neglecting the often large private sector. The aim was to extend public services to cover the whole population, even if the reality was very different.

Developments in Latin America were somewhat different. As in Africa, the earliest Western health services were developed by the colonists, especially for the armed forces and the police. Major employers provided health services, especially where enterprises were remote from urban centers. Some religious hospitals were built to care for the poor (Abel-Smith, 1994). These hospitals were later supplemented by government hospitals and clinics, especially in areas without charitable hospitals. A key difference with most of Africa and Asia was the early development of compulsory insurance arrangements for workers in the formal sector. Because medical care infrastructure was lacking, the insurance agencies often built and ran their own services, thus contributing to the parallel health systems seen today in many Latin American countries.

The historical development of health services in many countries resulted in a health infrastructure that was biased toward hospitals. Attempts to reorient services culminated in 1978 in the Declaration of Alma Ata, which emphasized the importance of primary health care, involving the delivery of curative and preventive services at the community level. This encouraged strong emphasis on the building up of integrated health services, involving community-based health workers. Nonetheless, a rival approach argued in favor of selective primary health care, to include those interventions that addressed the greatest disease burden and were most cost-effective (Walsh & Warren, 1979). Services for children were a key priority in this

approach, and, together with the emphasis on family planning that resulted from the preoccupation of many donors with world population growth, meant that peripheral health services in many low-income countries were targeted primarily at women and children. Only recently has there been greater emphasis on achieving a more integrated approach to the delivery of health services at peripheral levels.

A marked development in recent years in low- and middle-income countries has been the increasing questioning of the government's role. The most radical changes have occurred in countries formerly under strict communist rule, where a market economy has been introduced and market forces allowed to influence health services (see Saltman & Figueras, 1997, for such developments in eastern and central Europe). Social insurance arrangements are being introduced for those in formal employment, health professionals are permitted to have private practices, private markets are being encouraged in pharmaceuticals, and much greater costs are falling directly on household budgets. In China, for example, in 1981 approximately 71% of the population—including 48% of the rural population—had some insurance protection; by 1993 overall insurance coverage had dropped to 21%, with 7% coverage of the rural population (WHO, 1999). Although changes have been less radical in other parts of the world, governments have been forced by economic crisis to consider how they can best prioritize what they do and ration services to those most in need; many have introduced revenue generation schemes, such as user fees. This reconsideration has also been forced by rapidly growing private markets in medical care.

The Role of the State

This brief historical review indicates that one of the key issues in the design of health systems is the role assigned to the state. This section examines the economic arguments commonly put forward to specify the state's role in health and then considers other explanations for the roles observed in practice.

The first main economic justification lies in explanations of market failure. The efficient outcomes of private markets depend on a number of conditions being met. Because of the particular characteristics of health and health services, this may not be the case in the health sector.

First, the presence of externalities means that the optimal amount would not be produced or consumed. Externalities are costs or benefits that are not taken into account in the transactions of producers or consumers. For example, an individual's decision on whether to be immunized will be related to the value of the protection to that individual, not to the protection that may be accorded to others by reducing the pool of susceptible individuals.

Second, for goods that are public goods, the market may fail to produce them at all. Such goods are those where consumption is nonrival (consumption by one person does not reduce the consumption of another) and nonexcludable (a consumer cannot be prevented from benefiting from the good—for example, through requiring payment). Control of mosquito breeding sites to reduce malaria transmission is an obvious example: All living in the area will benefit regardless of whether they have paid. Information can also be seen to be a public good because it is nonrival; it is not nonexcludable, but the cost of providing information to extra people is often very low. This applies to knowledge gained through research, for example.

Third, monopoly power can lead to market failure, because it enables the provider to charge more than if the market were competitive. Monopoly power may be held by a hospital in a particular geographic area, by a pharmaceutical firm, or even by a profession as a whole (such as the medical profession).

These arguments provide a rather weak justification for state intervention in the entire health system since the range of services they apply to is quite limited. The arguments are most relevant to public health services and preventive care, and less relevant to the bulk of curative services. Moreover, problems such as monopoly are not unique to health and are commonly dealt with by regulation rather than state provision. A more powerful argument for a large state role lies in the asymmetry of information between provider and consumer. Medical consultations are often sought precisely because patients do not know what is wrong with them: They are therefore ill informed, in contrast to the normal assumption in economics of perfectly informed consumers. Hence, in medical care, providers are in an unusually strong position. Although they may act as perfect agents for the consumer, it is also possible, especially when income is related to care provided, that the personal interests of the providers may enter into decisions made on treatment. The poor and less well educated are particularly vulnerable to unscrupulous profit seeking by private providers.

Another characteristic of health care is its uncertain nature, and the potential for very high costs. This makes it an obvious candidate for insurance, but it is generally accepted that private insurance

markets do not work well (World Bank, 1997a). Individuals who purchase insurance may indulge in activities that put their health more at risk than if they were not insured, or once ill may consume more health care. This phenomenon is known as *moral hazard* and will raise the cost of insurance, making it unaffordable for some. Another problem is that those who are at greatest risk of needing care will be more likely to seek insurance, but due to asymmetries of information between insurer and insured, it is often difficult for the insurer to tailor the premium charged to the nature of the risk. This process, known as *adverse selection,* means that the insurer ends up with a more costly risk pool, premiums rise, and the more healthy opt out. In addition, insurance becomes more expensive, excluding many who cannot afford the increased premiums. Although the result is clearly inequitable, it is also inefficient because there will be people unprotected who would be willing and able to purchase insurance if the market worked well.

There are also arguments in favor of state involvement that are distinct from those of market failure. One is the argument that some types of health services are merit goods, that is, goods that society believes should be provided, but that individuals, if left to themselves, might underconsume because they are not the best judge of what is in their own or the public's interest. This argument is strongest for health services for children and the mentally ill.

The other argument is founded on equity principles: that even with perfectly operating private markets for health services and health insurance, there will be individuals too poor to afford to access them. Although it could be argued that this problem could be taken care of by income redistribution policies, equitable access to health services is of concern, and hence it can be argued that providing benefits in kind is appropriate.

Although these are the standard arguments used to explore the appropriate role of the state in health services, the judgment on their significance differs greatly between economists, leading to radically different policy prescriptions. Even though much of this debate has focused on the relative merits of the United States versus the Canadian or British health systems, it has influenced the nature of the debate concerning the reform of health systems in low- and middle-income countries, as noted later in discussion of health reform trends. Underlying this debate are alternative views on the ethical basis of a health system. One view sees access to health services as similar to access to other goods and services, and dependent on an individual's success in gaining or inheriting income.

The other sees access to health services as a right of citizenship that should not depend on individual income or wealth. According to the first view, the state's role in health should be confined to regulation of the market, public health measures, and public welfare for the poor to provide a minimum acceptable level of service, but nothing like the level of service available to those better off. According to the second view, the role of the state should be to ensure equal access to health services that does not differ depending on economic or social status.

It is important to note that although economic arguments provide justification for state involvement, they provide little guidance on the precise nature of intervention, and in particular they do not necessarily imply that the state should itself provide health services (as opposed to contracting others to provide it). A key change in recent decades in thinking about public management has been the recognition that the state need not provide services itself directly, but instead could play an enabling role (Walsh, 1995).

An important influence on this position is a recognition that in many countries the state has failed in its policies to provide public services, including health services, for everyone. These arguments derive from a number of strands of economic thinking, notable among which are public choice theory and property rights theories. The former is concerned with the nature of decision making in government. It argues that government officials are no different from anyone else in pursuing their own interests. Thus, politicians will be concerned to maximize their chances of being reelected, and bureaucrats will serve their own interests (e.g., maximizing their budgets because their own rewards [salary, status] are related to that). The result is that the public sector is wasteful because politicians and bureaucrats have no incentive to promote allocative or technical efficiency.

Property rights theorists argue that the source of inefficiency in the public sector is the weakening of property rights. In the private sector it can be argued that entrepreneurs or shareholders have a strong interest in the efficient use of resources. In the public sector there is little obvious threat to an enterprise if staff perform poorly; hence, incentives for efficient performance are weak.

These theories underlie what has been termed the "new public management," which seeks to expose public services to market pressures, without necessarily privatizing them (Walsh, 1995). Such approaches change the nature of state involvement, with policies of opening up services to competitive tender or putting services out to contract on a competitive basis, introducing internal markets where public providers have to compete for contracts from public purchasers, devolving financial control to organizations such as individual hospitals, and spinning off parts of government into separate public agencies (such as an agency to manage government health services, as in Zambia).

Although theories justifying particular roles of the state feature prominently in writings on health systems, it is clear in practice that the actual role of the state in any particular country is shaped by a wide variety of influences. Most notable are the history of state involvement in health services and the rationale for its involvement over time, the extent to which private providers and insurers developed early in the history of the health system and thus were able to play a prominent role, and the attitude of the medical profession to an increased state role (Mills et al., 2001). One key issue has been the extent to which the state took on itself the responsibility for providing services to the whole population, or instead concerned itself only with the poor and indigent.

Exhibit 11-2 summarizes the role of the state in four countries. In Zambia and India, the state's aims have historically been to provide services free at the point of use to the whole population. In contrast, both Mexico and Thailand have had specific schemes that cater to the poor and indigent, although recently Thailand has extended financial protection to the whole population through its "universal coverage" policy (Towse, Mills, & Tangcharoensathien, 2004).

Regulation

Regulation is the role that all governments must carry out, regardless of their degree of involvement in health service provision. It occurs when government exerts control over the activities of individuals and firms (Roemer, 1993). Its traditional rationale relates to the arguments of market failure outlined previously and also to the desire of governments to meet other social objectives, such as equity. Market failure creates the need either to regulate to make the market work better (e.g., to limit the control any one pharmaceutical firm may have over the market) or to prevent harmful effects (e.g., to ensure minimum quality standards for private clinics). Although regulation is often thought of as action involving control, sanctions, and penalties, it can also take the form of incentives to encourage appropriate behavior. In health services, where outcomes are difficult to observe (i.e., it can be difficult to relate treatment to change in

Exhibit 11-2	Illustrations of the Role of the State

Zambia

Health services for the whole population have traditionally been seen as the responsibility of the state. Government expenditure on health accounts for 3.0% of GDP and 53.1% of total health expenditure (WHO, 2004); 75% of hospital beds are public. Independence brought in a government that was anti-private sector and, until recently, the private health sector was ignored in government policy. Reforms have decentralized public management and introduced fees for public services. Management reforms specify a purchasing role for district authorities. The poor are reliant mainly on state services and the informal private sector.

India

The historical emphasis was on a strong state role, but resources were never provided to make this a reality (public expenditure accounts for 0.9% of GDP and 17.9% of total health expenditure (WHO, 2004); 65% of total hospital beds are public. Public services are often of poor quality and are adversely affected by the private practice of government doctors. People in general distrust the state. The charging policies for public facilities vary by state, but income from fees is very small. There is very widespread use of the private sector by all sections of the population, including the poor.

Mexico

The public health sector makes up 2.7% of GDP, 44.3% of total health expenditure (WHO, 2004), and 80% of hospital beds (Fundacion Mexicana para la Salud, 1995). The government's primary role is as owner of social security institutions, which account for some 67% of general government expenditure on health. The Ministry of Health and municipalities play a residual role in caring for the poor and uninsured. There is dissatisfaction with the quality of both Ministry of Health and social security services, with those who can afford it preferring to use private services.

Thailand

The public health sector is 2.1% of GDP and 57.1% of total health expenditure (WHO, 2004); 74% of total hospital beds are public (Ministry of Public Health, n.d.). There has been a tradition of strong central government and laissez-faire economic policies. Historically, government policies have encouraged the private sector to grow through tax exemptions and public funding for private care for specific groups. With the introduction of the recent universal coverage policy, the government has strengthened its commitment to inclusive social policies. Public services are of generally good quality; their main problem is lack of consumer orientation.

health), it can be argued that incentives are particularly appropriate; they are currently the subject of much interest, with consideration of what is termed "incentive regulation" (Kumaranayake, 1998).

In practice, regulatory action seeks to influence

- market entry and exit
- remuneration of providers
- quality and distribution of services
- standards and quality

Key mechanisms used in the health system to regulate the provision of health services are summarized in Table 11-2. Controls over market entry and exit are not shown separately since they also serve to influence quantities and quality.

Licensing of professionals to provide services is one of the key forms of regulation, with professional councils usually being empowered to carry out this function. As new professions arise or become more important, eventually they are brought within the scope of laws. Although such laws dictate entry into the market, their prime rationale from a government perspective is to maintain quality and protect the consumer. However, actual experience demonstrates that licensing on its own is not adequate to ensure quality.

A second key type of regulation is licensing or registration of facilities, which is required before they can open. Legislation often specifies the requirements particular categories of facility should meet, covering such aspects as trained staff, availability of equipment and supplies, and buildings. Because of the cost-enhancing capabilities of high technology, some countries have an approval process for the purchase of equipment such as computed tomography scanners. Entry to medical school may also be controlled with the same aim: controlling costs by limiting supply. In a normal market such action might be expected to raise costs, but it is considered justified in health because of the power physicians have to generate their own income or to prevail on government to employ greater numbers than the country can really afford.

Often countries are concerned about the geographic distribution of providers, and controls and

Table 11-2	Examples of Regulatory Mechanisms for Health Care Provision	
Variable	**Mechanism**	**Examples from Low- and Middle-Income Countries**
Quantities/ Distribution	• Licensing of providers • Licensing of facilities • Controls on number and size of medical schools • Controls on practicing in overprovided areas • Controls on introduction of high technology • Incentives to practice in underserved areas and specialties • Requiring capitation or case-based payment in order to control supply of services	• Universal for main professional groups • Increasingly common for hospitals and clinics • Common (e.g., Latin America) • South Africa: private hospitals • Being considered by Malaysia and Thailand • Many countries for doctors, often in form of compulsory rural service • Social insurance in Korea (case payment) and Thailand (capitation)
Prices	• Negotiation of salary scales • Fixing of charges (e.g., for lab tests, drug markup) • Negotiation of reimbursement rates	• Zimbabwe, nursing salaries; Argentina, doctors • South Africa: drug markup for reimbursement by medical schemes • Many social insurance schemes (e.g., Chile)
Quality	• Licensing of practitioners • Registration of facilities • Control on nature of services provided • Accessibility • Required complaints procedures • Required provision of information for monitoring quality • Control of training curricula • Requirements for continuing education • Accreditation	• Universal for main professions • Increasingly common; specifies structural standards • Restrictions on drug dispensing by general practitioners (e.g., Zimbabwe); range of procedures (clinical officers, Kenya) • Hospitals legally obliged to provide emergency care irrespective of patient financial status (Thailand, Malaysia) • Consumer laws applicable (India) • Many countries • Many countries • Increasingly being introduced • Increasingly being introduced; existing in Taiwan, and pilot schemes in Brazil and Thailand

Sources: S. Bennett et al., *Public and Private Roles in Health: A Review and Analysis of Experience in Sub-Saharan Africa* (Geneva, Switzerland: World Health Organization, 1994); and L. Kumaranayake, *Economic Aspects of Health Sector Regulation: Strategic Choices for Low and Middle Income Countries* (London: London School of Hygiene and Tropical Medicine, Health Policy Unit, Department of Public Health and Policy, 1998).

incentives are used to influence where new providers can set up. For example, South African provinces can control the creation and expansion of private hospitals, depending on the number of private beds already existing. Certificate of need legislation has been used for many years to control the construction of new buildings and investment in new equipment in the United States (Kumaranayake, 1998).

Control of prices and reimbursement levels may have several purposes: to restrict incomes in the private sector so that remuneration differences between public and private professionals do not get too great; to ensure that health services remain affordable for the not-so-wealthy; and to restrict the financial burden placed on risk-pooling arrangements, such as social insurance or employer medical benefit schemes. However, given the power of the medical profession, there is a risk that price control operates more in the interests of the profession than the public; in addition, it can be difficult to enforce or monitor.

Control of quality is one of the prime concerns of regulation. Licensing and registration have this as an aim, as well as control of quantity. For example, in Kenya a private clinic must be kept in good order and state of repair, not be a residential building, and keep essential drugs and accurate drug records.

Regulations often seek to control the nature of services provided, to ensure that services are within the competence of a particular type of provider and to limit the scope for excessive service provision. Regulations usually lay down what type of health professional can prescribe what type of drug, limiting, for example, the range of drugs that can be given by low-level health workers. It is quite common for private practitioners to be allowed to dispense medicines only if there is no pharmacy nearby. Where this rule does not exist, drug dispensing is often a major source of the income of private doctors, leading to predictable concerns about overprescribing.

Control of training curricula is fundamental to ensuring quality, and is often one of the functions given by law to professional bodies. A trend in high-income countries, which is also becoming apparent elsewhere, is the requirement for professionals to receive regular refresher training if they are to continue to be licensed. Such a provision, however, is demanding on regulatory bodies, since it requires the introduction of monitoring procedures, training programs, and relicensing arrangements.

Accreditation is a process of certifying that a facility meets a certain standard, and is usually applied as a self-regulating procedure that is voluntary and managed by an independent body. However, in practice it may act more as a regulatory device than as a peer review process, especially when accreditation is required for hospitals to be eligible for reimbursement from a social insurance scheme, as in Taiwan.

Governments also regulate other markets with considerable relevance to health services. These include the health insurance and pharmaceutical markets. Both have features unique to themselves. In the case of insurance, regulations may impose a particular approach to risk pooling (e.g., requiring schemes to give lifetime coverage or to use community rather than risk rating). In the case of pharmaceuticals, regulations may establish which drugs can be imported and which can be sold over the counter or require a doctor's prescription, and may specify quality control procedures for imported and locally made drugs.

Separate consideration may also be given in regulatory structures to not-for-profit providers. On the one hand, they may be treated more strictly. For example, their fee structures may be regulated, they may be required to provide a certain amount of free care to the poor, and requirements to provide information may be stricter. On the other hand, they may benefit from their not-for-profit status. For example, tax exemptions are often available to them.

In practice, regulation encounters a number of key problems, as highlighted in Exhibit 11-3 (Mills et al., 2001). One is that laws are frequently out of date and are difficult to change. For example, many low-income countries have laws they inherited from colonial regimes that have not kept pace with the development of the private sector, resulting in whole categories of

Exhibit 11-3	Key Regulatory Problems in Selected Countries
Zambia[a]	

- Laws are antiquated.
- The rapidly increasing private sector is largely self-regulated.
- Private physicians are required to register with government; otherwise, there is really no infrastructure for collection of data on the private sector or for enforcement of laws and regulations.

India

- In 1997, only three states required any registration and inspection of private hospitals.
- Practice by unqualified personnel is widespread.
- Unethical practices (e.g., payments between hospitals and general practitioners to encourage referrals) are widespread.
- No database of private providers exists.
- There is no ability to enforce regulations.
- Regulatory bodies lack resources.

Mexico[b]

- Private hospitals are not subject to a strict process of accreditation that verifies their capacity to provide an acceptable standard of care.
- There is lack of control on pharmacists prescribing and selling most drugs.
- Public facilities are used for treating private patients.
- The private sector resists providing epidemiologic and other information.

Thailand[c]

- Regulatory framework is largely complete, but its application is weak.
- Regulatory bodies lack resources for enforcement.
- There is insufficient information on activity in the private sector.
- It is difficult to control unethical practices (e.g., turning away emergency cases).
- Professional council regulation is largely ineffective.

[a]Sally Lake, personal communication.

[b]Miguel Betancourt, personal communication.

[c]Teerawattananon et al., 2003.

facilities that may be completely unregulated. Private laboratories are often a case in point.

Another problem is that regulation requires substantial knowledge on the part of the regulatory bodies. However, it is common in low- and middle-income countries for even basic information, such as lists of providers and facilities, to be incomplete. Moreover, the poorer the country the greater the proportion of providers who are small and informally organized, making it difficult to require any regular provision of information.

A third problem is that of regulatory capture: The body meant to be doing the regulating in practice operates in the interests of those being regulated, not in the public interest. This is a common problem in the case of regulation of professional groups, which is often done by the profession itself, leading to very slow processing of complaints and considerations of professional negligence. India has had the interesting experience of introducing a consumer rights law, which the courts have ruled applies to government health services as well as those that are privately provided, that is providing an alternative channel for pursuing complaints. However, India is also a country where the overlap of public and private interests makes it extremely difficult to introduce new regulations or change existing laws. In India, as in a number of countries, it is common to find government-employed doctors with private practices—with or without legal sanction—and senior Ministry of Health officials, as well as politicians, having financial interests in private-sector health services (Mills et al., 2001). Thus, a clear distinction between the regulators and those being regulated is absent.

A fourth problem is the inadequacy of the resources provided to the regulatory bodies to apply the laws effectively. Quality monitoring in particular requires regular inspection to ensure laws are being followed. This places great demands on the limited staff capacity of regulatory agencies, especially for drugs and clinics, where outlets are numerous and widely dispersed. It also creates further difficulties when low-paid staff seek illicit payments in place of carrying out their job effectively. An extreme form of this is found in China, where because government subsidies to public health activities have been severely cut, environmental health units are dependent on revenue generation for much of their income and hence may inspect those firms that are more able to pay their fees (Liu & Mills 2002). Those that are less profitable, and hence likely to have worse safety and hygiene practices, go uninspected.

A final problem is a lack of institutional structures to back up the regulatory process. Strong consumer groups, media, professional associations, and insurance agencies all have important roles to play (Kumaranayake, 1998). The consumer role is particularly important since consumers can identify problems through complaint procedures and legal action and also levy pressure more broadly through consumer groups. However, the common imbalance in power and access to resources between consumers and professionals suggests that complementary pressures are also important. One source of these can be the purchasing agencies considered further later in this chapter.

Financing

This section establishes a conceptual model for describing the system for financing health services, defines and evaluates the major sources of health financing in developing countries, describes trends in health financing across countries, and presents the national health account methodology that is increasingly being used to collect health financing data.

Conceptual Model

Financing refers to the raising or collection of revenue to pay for the operation of the system. Financing agents are those entities that collect money to pay providers on behalf of consumers. Financing agents may be publicly or privately owned, and may provide health services directly (e.g., the ministry of health through public hospitals and health centers) or purchase health services from providers (e.g., a private insurer may purchase inpatient care from a variety of hospitals).

There is some disagreement in the literature as to the definition of sources of financing. Sources may be defined as the entities that provide funds to financing agents (Berman, 1997). Individuals and firms can be thought of as the primary sources of funds. Individuals generate income in the form of wages or salaries, while businesses may earn profit on capital investments or rent on properties owned. Resources may pass through several levels of sources before reaching the agents. For example, the ministry of finance can be thought of as a secondary-level source insofar as it generates funds by taxing the incomes of households and businesses and then transfers these resources to other government agencies to purchase health services. A single entity may act both as a source and an agent of financing. For example, households commonly pay for health services both indirectly (through taxation, contributions to social and private insurance, donations to charities, and so on) and directly (through out-of-pocket payments).

More often, however, the term *source* is applied to the method whereby an agent mobilizes or collects resources. For example, the sources of financing to the ministry of health include personal and business taxes, and donations, loans, and grants from domestic and foreign agencies. The sources of financing for private insurance agencies are premiums paid by the enrollees in these schemes. In this chapter, the term *source* is used with this definition in mind unless otherwise indicated.

Description and Evaluation of Predominant Sources

This section defines the most commonly used sources of financing and briefly discusses the efficiency, equity, and revenue-generating ability of each source. Table 11-3 summarizes the relative merits of each source. The relative advantages of differing sources in pooling financial risks are dealt with in detail in Chapter 13, where a more detailed review of evidence on their efficiency and equity implications is also provided.

Efficiency with respect to a source of financing involves a number of elements, including administrative (or technical) efficiency, stability, and flexibility (Zschock, 1979). Administrative efficiency relates to the cost of the management of the system and is the difference between gross yield (all funds that are collected) and net yield (that portion of gross yield that is

actually available for the purposes of health service delivery). This difference results from the costs of revenue collection, allocation, and distribution; advertising and promotion; and funds lost to corruption and fraud as well as the cost of fighting corruption and fraud. The stability of an agent is determined by the degree to which revenue raising varies with changes in economic or political conditions. Finally, for a financing agent to be efficient, there must be flexibility in terms of the allocation of funds to different expenditure categories. Least flexible are those sources of financing pledged to a specific activity. Public-sector sources tend to be less flexible than private-sector sources due to the stringent rules and regulations that are often applied to government spending, as well as the political constraints on reallocation.

The concepts of horizontal and vertical equity of financing were introduced earlier. With respect to vertical equity, a progressive system is one in which lower income groups pay a lower proportion of their income than higher income groups. A regressive system is one in which lower income groups pay a higher share of income than higher income groups. A proportional or neutral system is one in which all income groups pay the same percentage of their income.

Apart from problems of inefficiency and inequity, health systems in many low- and middle-income countries face the difficulty of simply not being able to generate sufficient funds to ensure that the entire population has access to a minimal package of health services. Thus, a goal of the financing function of health systems is to increase the availability of funds

Table 11-3	Evaluation of Health Financing Sources					
	Efficiency			**Equity**		
	Administrative Efficiency	Stability	Flexibility	Horizontal	Vertical	Revenue Generation
Public Sources						
General tax revenues	High	Low	Low	High	Progressive	High
Retail sales taxes	High	High	Low	High	Regressive	Low
Lotteries and betting	Low	High	Low	High	Regressive	Low
Deficit financing	Low	Low	Low	Depends	Depends	Depends
External grants	Low	Low	Low	High	Progressive	Low
Social insurance	Low	High	Low	High	Regressive	Depends on size of formal sector
Private Sources						
Households	Low	High	High	Low	Regressive	High
Employers	Low to medium	High	Variable	Low	Depends	Low
Private insurance	Low	High	High	Low	Regressive	Low
Voluntary organizations	High	Variable	Variable	High	Progressive	Medium

for the purchase and provision of health services. As countries become richer and the demand for high-technology, hospital-based interventions increases, the goal generally shifts from generating funds to constraining the financial flow through the health system (i.e., cost containment).

Public Sources of Financing

Direct taxes are paid directly by individuals or organizations to government and include personal income tax, taxes on domestic business transactions and profits, duties on imports and exports, and property taxes. Some portion of these resources may then be allocated to the annual budget for health services. The best-known examples of general tax financing for health services are in the United Kingdom and other Commonwealth nations (Hsiao, 1995a).

Direct tax revenues should have relatively high net yields, but this will depend on the overhead costs of the government bureaucracy needed to collect, allocate, and disburse them. They may not be a particularly reliable or stable source, because the health sector must compete directly with other social and economic programs for a portion of the government's budget; as such, this source may fluctuate depending on the economic and political climate. Furthermore, this source of financing is likely to be inflexible because it is controlled by public-sector agents that are constrained by rules and regulations and the political feasibility of reallocations.

Direct taxation achieves horizontal equity insofar as taxes on individuals are generally not related to characteristics other than income. Income tax is generally the most progressive form of revenue raising, because income tax rates usually rise as a person's taxable income increases (Doorslaer, Wagstaff, & Rutten, 1993). For example, in Côte d'Ivoire income taxes range from 26% for the lowest income groups to 32% for the highest, and in Peru from 8% for the lowest income groups to 45% for the highest (Baker & van der Gaag, 1993). The ability of taxation to redistribute resources from the rich to the poor is hindered when the wealthy are able to evade the payment of taxes.

Ability to mobilize resources is another strength of direct taxation. Although most developing countries are restricted in their ability to collect income taxes and indirect taxes (due to limited infrastructure and small formal sectors), the government has many other options for generating tax revenue, including property, business, and import and export taxes. As a group, low- and middle-income country governments derive about 30% of their revenue from trade taxes (World Bank, 1997b).

Indirect taxes pass through an intermediary en route to government coffers. Indirect taxes are incorporated into the selling price of a good or service; these include sales and value-added taxes (taxes on a broad variety of items) and excise duties (imposed on the sale of specific items, such as tobacco products, beer, and liquor). Revenues generated in this manner are often allocated to finance specific programs. Taxes that are pledged to a specific sector or activity are termed *hypothecated,* and the practice is known as *earmarking.*

As with direct sales taxes, the net yield of indirect taxes will vary depending on the efficiency of the government agency responsible for collecting them. Indirect taxes are likely to be reliable when they are earmarked for the health sector, or even specific projects within the health sector. The flexibility of this source may be constrained by the government rules and regulations that guide revenue allocation.

Indirect taxation, and excise duties in particular, are generally regressive, because poorer households often spend a higher percentage of their income on the goods being taxed (e.g., alcohol and cigarettes). A study of health care financing in OECD countries, using data from the 1980s and 1990s, found that indirect taxes were regressive in all countries except Spain (Wagstaff et al., 1999).

Lotteries and betting may also serve as sources of earmarked income for health services, although these methods are not often used. They have low net yields because they are costly to administer. As with indirect taxes, the resulting revenues are likely to be reliable because they are earmarked, but inflexible because they are administered by public agents. As with retail sales taxes, lotteries and betting tend to fall particularly heavily on the earnings of the poor (because of their popularity among lower income groups).

National authorities can augment general tax revenues through domestic and international deficit financing (loans) and through grants. Deficit financing means that funds are borrowed for a specific project or activity and have to be paid back to the source over some future period of time. Domestic deficit financing is usually achieved through the issue of debt certificates, or bonds, with guaranteed interest rates. International borrowing is typically in the form of loans from bilateral and multilateral organizations. External grants are transfers to governments made in cash, goods, or services by foreign governments or organizations; they do not have to be repaid.

The largest single international financier of health services in low- and middle-income countries is the World Bank (World Bank, 1999). Two types of loans are provided by the World Bank. The first type is for developing countries that are able to pay near-market interest rates. The second type of loan goes to the poorest countries (GNP per capita below an established threshold, currently US$865). These loans are free of interest, carry a low 0.75% annual administrative charge, and are very long term (35 or 40 years, including 10 years' grace). Loans that bear an interest rate substantially below market interest rates are termed *soft loans*. Major sources of grants include the bilateral donor agencies—such as Britain's Department for International Development (DFID) and the U.S. Agency for International Development (USAID)—the Bill and Melinda Gates Foundation, and the Global Fund to Fight AIDS, Tuberculosis, and Malaria. Progress in expanding coverage to select services—including water and sanitation—has been accelerated through Private Participation in Infrastructure (PPI), a World Bank project that aims to encourage private-sector (domestic and international) investment in infrastructure.

The costs of processing and administering donor assistance in the health sector can be quite high, particularly when the aid to a country is fragmented into a large number of donor projects. Fragmentation is common—according to the World Bank (2004), a typical recipient country in 2000 received aid from about 15 bilateral donor agencies and 10 multilateral agencies—and results in officials spending a large amount of their time meeting donors' requirements. Stability is limited insofar as external funds are typically of short duration, with no guarantee of renewal. The flexibility of loan and grant financing is variable. At one time, it was common for external funds to be made for specific, free-standing health projects; decisions on expenditure were usually made prior to disbursement. Increasingly, donor assistance is being made to sector investment programs (SIPs), whereby government and donors agree to a public-expenditure program that incorporates both domestic and foreign resources. Under SIPs there may be more flexibility over time in the spending of donor funding. On the other hand, the process of shifting funds from one expenditure category to another may be more complicated under SIPs because both government and donors must agree on reforms. Some bilateral donors are increasingly giving direct budgetary support to governments in order to provide predictable, pooled funds under government control.

The equity of deficit financing will depend entirely on how the loan is ultimately paid back. If, for example, funds generated through direct taxation are used to pay back a loan, then their impact may be progressive. External grants should be equitable since they are provided by wealthy nations and are commonly used to establish and run projects in remote or underserved areas. However, the extent to which they actually achieve a progressive redistribution of resources will depend on the extent to which the government shifts spending as the result of the grants. Only limited resources are generated through external loans and grants except in the very poorest countries—donors supply 40% of all public resources (for health and other sectors) in at least 30 poor countries (World Bank, 2004).

Social insurance premiums are mandatory insurance payments made by employers and employees in the formal sector, usually as a percentage of wages, and hence are often termed *payroll taxes*. Social insurance payments can have relatively low net yields due to the cost of processing claims. According to WHO (1993), administrative costs in western European insurance funds amount to approximately 5%, compared with an upper limit of 28% among social insurance schemes in Latin America, and potentially higher costs in Africa. The monies generated are likely to be stable because they are earmarked for the health sector; however, they may not be flexible, again related to government restrictions and requirements.

Social insurance is usually horizontally equitable because the value of premiums is based on income alone, but it tends to be a regressive method of raising revenue. This is because contributions are typically subject to a ceiling, although in some countries the marginal contribution rates themselves decline as earnings rise. Social insurance premiums may be progressive, for example, if ceilings can be eliminated or if low-income groups are exempt from contributions. Occasionally, contributions are levied at a flat rate for administrative simplicity, in which case the scheme is regressive.

Coverage achieved by social insurance schemes in many low- and middle-income countries has been limited, because premiums can only easily be collected from formal-sector employees. This has given rise to much criticism of the equity of social insurance arrangements, since a relatively small proportion of the population has access to better services than much of the rest of the population, and in addition sometimes benefits also from government subsidies to the social insurance program. However, some countries, including Costa Rica, the Republic of Korea, and Taiwan, have achieved universal or near-universal coverage through combining funds from social insurance with general tax revenues, in order to ensure that all population groups have access to similar types and levels of care (Mills, 2000a).

Private Sources

Direct household expenditure includes all out-of-pocket payments or user fees paid by the consumer of health services directly to the provider (including private practitioners, traditional healers, and private pharmacists). Even services provided by the government or an insurance program may include some element of copayment, which may take a variety of different forms. *Coinsurance* means that the consumer is responsible for paying for a certain percentage of all services received. *Limited indemnity* means that the insurer only covers health service costs up to a prespecified absolute amount (or ceiling), above which the consumer is responsible for paying. A *deductible* is a specific amount that must be paid by the consumer, above which reimbursement starts.

The administrative efficiency of direct household expenditure is low, due to the labor-intensive task of collecting fees from individuals. The stability of household spending on health will vary according to household income, but it is likely to be fairly stable unless economic crisis causes widespread poverty. Household spending is extremely flexible and will be allocated to the most pressing health needs as they are perceived by members of the household. Household spending is horizontally inequitable, since it varies according to factors such as distance lived from health facilities and individual preferences. Out-of-pocket payment is the most regressive modality of financing (Doorslaer, Wagstaff, & Rutten, 1993).

Direct employer financing occurs when firms pay for, or directly provide, health services for their employees. Employers as agents are likely to be more efficient than households, though less efficient than compulsory purchasers of care (such as social insurance schemes) due to their fragmentation. Employer financing is likely to be reliable (in the absence of economic crisis) but relatively inflexible because employers are biased toward specific types of health services (e.g., curative care). Direct payment by employers contributes to horizontal inequity in the health system as a whole because employed workers are disproportionately young and healthy. Because the benefits of employer financing are generally restricted to employees of the formal sector, it is likely to have little impact on the redistribution of resources among different income groups. The quantity of resources mobilized by employees is high in some countries; for example, in Zambia, financing provided by parastatal copper mines accounts for roughly 13% of all health resources (Department of Economics, University of Zambia & Swedish Institute for Health Economics, 1996). As governments implement social insurance schemes, these replace employer financing of health services.

Private health insurance premiums are regular, voluntary payments to private insurance companies in return for coverage of prespecified health service costs. Private insurance typically does not cover the costs of frequent, predictable events (such as pregnancies). *Experience rating* means that premiums are based on an individual's actuarially determined likelihood of illness. *Community rating* means that the premium is based on the pooled risk of a defined group of people (e.g., inhabitants of a geographic area or employees of a firm).

Private health insurance tends not to be an efficient method of mobilizing funds for the health sector. Net yield is low because of the costs of assessing risk, setting premiums, designing benefit packages, distributing the insurance, marketing, processing claims, reinsuring, and detecting fraud. The administrative costs of private insurers in OECD countries vary from 5% to almost 30% (Thomson & Mossialos, 2004). In unregulated markets, administrative costs plus profits may account for up to 35% to 45% of the premiums. Private health insurance is a stable agent of financing because it is not subject to political allocation processes, and it must be flexible in order to respond to consumers' needs and to attract clientele.

Private health insurance premiums are a perfect example of a horizontally inequitable source. Experience rating means that premiums will vary according to factors that are considered by the insurer to be related to risk of illness, such as age, sex, and occupation. Private insurance tends to be regressive because rates are adjusted for risk, and the poor are at highest risk of falling ill. The ability to mobilize resources through private insurance is limited in poorer countries because these schemes are targeted at a very small (although well-off) segment of the population—less than 2% of the population in most cases.

Charitable contributions are contributions made in cash or in kind. Examples include cash contributions from wealthy families, business enterprises, or religious organizations; community labor for construction and maintenance of local health facilities, including clinics as well as environmental sanitation projects; and local help in specific disease eradication campaigns. Voluntary organizations or nongovernmental organizations (NGOs) have high net yields, although they may be unpredictable in their ability to generate funds. The flexibility will vary from one voluntary organization to another, but generally they prefer to fund specific types of health services, not necessarily those most suitable for the community being served. Voluntary organization funding should be progressive in that such organizations raise revenue from the better-off, although their ability to mobilize resources is limited.

Mixes of Financing Sources

No one source of financing stands out as being superior in terms of all the outcomes considered. Nor is there an optimal mix of sources that can be prescribed for all countries. Countries vary in terms of the number of different financing agents and methods that are used, and the mix can change over time within a country. The mix of sources used will depend in part on the relative importance that policy makers place on the various objectives described previously and in part on the mix of sources historically used in that country. Most low- and middle-income countries have more pluralistic health financing structures than are found in high-income countries. Low-income countries typically finance the bulk of their health care expenditures from (1) direct household expenditure, (2) taxation, and (3) deficit spending. The most important financing agents are typically the ministry of health (and other government agencies), households, and firms.

Although using a variety of sources may increase the resources available for health care and may allow better adaptation to the diverse social and economic conditions that may exist within a country, it makes the pursuit of health policy goals more complex than in a single-source system (WHO, 1993). The greatest risks in a pluralistic health financing system are those of "duplication and overlap in function and coverage" (WHO, 1993, p. 13). According to Mach and Abel-Smith (1983, p. 13), "in many countries the different financial sectors of the national health effort operate in watertight compartments even when there are monetary flows between them." This adversely affects both efficiency, because of duplication, and equity, because of limited risk pooling and cross subsidies between income groups.

Another complex but important issue relates to the displacement effect that one source of finance may have on others (termed *fungibility*). The introduction or expansion of one source of financing may have an impact on the efficiency, equity, or revenue-generating ability of other sources. This may be especially important when large external grants or loans are introduced into a health sector. For example, it might seem that a large external grant earmarked for

the treatment of tuberculosis among the rural poor would be equitable. However, in response to such a grant, the ministry of health may shift resources that would have been spent on this activity toward high-technology, hospital-based services. Thus, the positive impact that the new source of funding has on equity might be counterbalanced by the negative equity impact of displacement. Fungibility is one of the rationales for SIPs and general budgetary support.

Health Financing Innovations

Certain approaches to raising finance recently have gained popularity as means of improving efficiency, equity, or resource-generating ability. These approaches include community financing, medical savings accounts (MSAs), managed care, and a variety of targeted user fees.

Community financing does not refer to a special source of financing, but rather to programs where the community manages the collection of resources and the purchasing of health services (i.e., the community acts as the financing agent). Resources for community financing may be generated through voluntary contributions, user fees, or insurance premiums. Community management can potentially improve the efficiency, equity, and revenue-generating ability of these sources of financing, although experience is quite varied (McPake, Hanson, & Mills, 1992; Stinson, 1982).

Among the different community financing models, community-based health insurance (CBHI) has received considerable attention as a mechanism for enhancing access to health care services among the poorest and reducing the frequency of medical indebtedness. The *World Health Report 2000*, for example, noted that prepayment schemes represent the most effective way to protect people from the costs of health care, and called for investigation into mechanisms to bring the poor into such schemes (WHO, 2000). CBHI allows for pooling of resources to cover the costs of future, unpredictable health-related events. The communities around which such schemes evolve include people living in the same area (e.g., a town or district, or the area surrounding a missionary hospital), members of a work cooperative (e.g., a dairy cooperative), trade unions, and federations of self-help micro-finance groups. CBHI offers individuals and households protection against the uncertain risk of catastrophic medical expenses in exchange for regular payment of premiums. In contrast to social health insurance, membership is voluntary rather than mandatory.

There is a real shortage of empirical evidence to assess whether CBHI schemes are effective and sustainable. The studies and reviews that have been undertaken suggest that many schemes are short-lived and fail to meet even the goals they set for themselves (Bennett, Creese, & Monasch, 1998). Often, the schemes enroll relatively small populations (of 1,000 people or less), thus limiting the extent to which there can be pooling and resource transfers. Furthermore, CBHIs have tended to exclude the poorest among their target populations, in part because they generally charge a flat (or uniform) premium that is unaffordable to the poorest.

MSAs involve prepayment for health care, but there is no pooling of resources and thus no risk sharing. Generally, individuals are compelled to deposit a fixed portion of their earnings in the MSAs. Withdrawals can only be made to pay for hospital services and selected (typically expensive) outpatient services. Individuals may choose from public and private caregivers. MSAs may be used in combination with a risk-sharing scheme (e.g., social insurance) to cover especially expensive services (as is the case in Singapore). Upon death, any balance left in an MSA becomes part of a person's estate and may be willed to family, friends, or charity (Hsiao, 1995b). Mandatory MSAs were first implemented in Singapore in 1984 and more recently in select cities in China (starting in 1994). They have created widespread interest; by making individuals responsible for managing their health care funds, it was hoped that MSAs would provide incentives for consumers to be more cost-sensitive in their demand for health services. However, evidence from Singapore suggests that MSAs alone do not effectively control cost inflation—even after implementation of MSAs, costs were driven upward by the increased use of expensive technology in private hospitals and rising provider charges (Hsiao, 1995b; Yip & Hsiao, 1997).

Managed care was developed in the United States as a response to escalating health care costs and represents an adaptation of traditional forms of private insurance. The majority of Americans with private health insurance are currently enrolled in managed care plans, and many other countries are incorporating elements of managed care into their health systems. Managed care refers to a broad array of health insurance plans that attempt to control the cost and quality of care by increased coordination between insurance and the provision of services. For example, health maintenance organizations (HMOs, perhaps the most common type of managed care) contract with medical groups to provide a full range of health services for their enrollees for a fixed, prepaid, per-member fee (i.e., a capitated payment). Under managed care organizations, doctors (or provider groups) are made to bear at least some of the financial risk for the volume of services their patients use. There is evidence that managed care has done a better job of controlling costs and improving cost-effectiveness than traditional insurance arrangements (Miller & Luft, 1994). It is unclear how managed care has affected quality and equity. Members of managed care plans often perceive the quality of care to be poor, because they resent the more limited access to specialists and higher-technology diagnostic methods and treatments. Equity of health care delivery may also suffer, because the doctor has a financial incentive to dump elderly or severely ill patients onto other practices.

Abel-Smith (1994) provides examples of how direct spending by households and firms can be made more equitable through targeted user fees:

- Charges can be levied on employers to recoup the full cost of treating accidents at work.

- Fees can be charged to cover the cost of treating motor accident cases and claimed from the insurance policies of the victims.

- Full-cost charges can be levied on patients who bypass the referral system by going directly to hospitals without being referred or being a genuine emergency.

- Charges can be levied for private rooms at government hospitals that cover the full costs.

- Clinics at government facilities can be opened outside normal working hours for those who are willing to pay and want to avoid queues.

Historically, many of these charges have been opposed within the public system, because they acknowledge the existence of two-tier services (different facilities for paying and nonpaying patients). However, economic realities and the need to exploit all possible sources of revenue for public services are changing these attitudes.

Compiling Financing Data: National Health Accounts

The development of improved financing policies is limited by the availability of good information on financial flows. This affects both national analysis and cross-country comparisons, the latter of which is often hampered by the lack of reliable data on out-of-pocket expenditures. Where these exist at all, estimates are often incomplete and prone to measurement errors. Furthermore, private health expenditures are rarely disaggregated into different forms of payments, such as direct fees for service, insurance premiums or other forms of prepayments, and cost-sharing payments (Bos et al., 1998).

Emphasis recently has been placed on creating a national health account (NHA), which is a statement that provides information about the flow of health funds between sources (here referring to the entities that provide funds), agents, and uses in a country (Berman, 1997). The NHA is intended to give a comprehensive picture of both public and private health spending. It requires calculation and presentation of national estimates through a "sources and uses" matrix. Table 11-4 provides such a matrix for national health expenditure in Zambia, and Exhibit 11-4 highlights the findings of NHA studies carried out in Zambia, India, Mexico, and Thailand. (Caution is required in comparing the NHAs in these four countries; despite using similar methodologies, strikingly different categories and data sources were used.)

The main objective of NHAs is to provide the key pieces of information required by decision makers. By systematically bringing together data on sources, agents, and uses of health funds, the NHA can provide answers to many different questions. Data contained in the NHA include the following:

- total health expenditures
- proportion of funds from different sources, including out-of-pocket payments
- health expenditure by level of care

An NHA enables concrete answers to be given to questions such as the extent to which expenditure is biased in favor of hospitals, and the extent to which the burden of paying for care falls on out-of-pocket payment by households. In addition, the NHA provides a framework for modeling reforms and monitoring the effects of changes in financing and provision.

NHAs are becoming increasingly standardized under guidance from the World Health Organization (WHO, World Bank, & USAID, 2003). Establishing an NHA generally involves four steps (Griffiths & Mills, 1983):

1. Define what criteria distinguish "health expenditure" from other expenditures.
2. Define categories of sources, agents, and uses into which the NHA can be divided.
3. Collect the data.
4. Present the results, usually using a sources and uses matrix, and identify policy implications.

Although this four-step process sounds quite simple, complications can arise at almost every step.

It is widely accepted that NHAs should be limited to expenditures that have the primary intention of improving health. This excludes expenditures that have health effects but whose primary goal is not health (e.g., housing, food subsidies, and urban water supply projects). There are, however, many areas of uncertainty. NHAs often fail to capture private expenditures on traditional or nonallopathic providers, such as faith healers, midwives, and practitioners of herbal medicine. Further, it may be difficult to determine when activities performed under the auspices of the education, agriculture, or labor ministries are performed with the primary intention of improving health. Zschock (1979), for example, suggests that the cost of practical training of practitioners be included while the cost of formal medical training (often funded in the education sector) be excluded. Where there is uncertainty, researchers should indicate clearly what has been included in a definition, and, where possible, expenditures should be recorded as separate line items (Berman, 1997).

Defining categories of sources, agents, and uses can also pose difficulties. For example, substantial differences between two health expenditure studies in Thailand were attributed in part to differences in categorizing medical benefits provided by

Table 11-4	Estimated "Sources and Uses" Matrix for Zambian National Health Expenditure in 1998 (as a Percentage of Total Expenditure)					
			Zambia			
Uses	**Public Health System**	**Ministry of Defense**	**Consolidated Copper Mines**	**Households**	**Donors**	**Total**
District	28.4	0.0	0.0	1.0	17.8	47.2
Secondary	8.3	1.0	21.3	2.9	0.0	33.5
Tertiary	15.1	0.0	0.0	1.7	2.6	19.4
Total	51.8	1.0	21.3	5.6	20.4	100.0

Note: Public Health System includes both Ministry of Health and Central Board of Health.

Source: Data from C. N. Mwikisa, L. Mwansa, P. Nankamba, D. Chimfwembe, M. Goma, B. Chitah, and R. Maswenyeho, *Zambia National Health Accounts: 1995–98* (Lusaka: Ministry of Health, n.d.), http://www.afro.who.int/dsd/nha/country-nha/zambia-nha.pdf.

Exhibit 11-4 | **Key Findings of National Health Accounts Studies**

Zambia (1998 data)
- *Sources:* Approximately 53% of health care resources are provided by the government of Zambia. Other major sources include external donors (20%), the semi-autonomous copper mines (21%), and households (6%).
- *Uses:* Primary care delivered at the district level accounts for 47% of health care expenditure. Secondary levels of care account for 33%, and tertiary levels for 19%.

India (1991 data)
- *Sources:* Households are the source of 75% of health care spending. Other major sources include state and local governments (16%) and the central government (6%). External donations are estimated at less than 1%.
- *Uses:* Curative primary care accounts for almost 50% of health care expenditure, and secondary/tertiary inpatient care almost 40%.

Mexico (circa 1994)
- *Sources:* The sources are households (49%), firms (30%), and the federal government (21%). The major financing agents are social security institutes (45%), private funds (firm and household, 40%), and other government agencies (12%).
- *Uses:* Social security services account for 44% of total health expenditures, private services 43%, and services provided by other government agencies roughly 13%.

Thailand (1994 data)
- *Sources:* Households and central government both account for approximately 40% of health care resources. Smaller sources (each accounting for 2% to 4%) include local governments, the social insurance scheme, private firms, and private insurance companies. Donors are estimated to account for only 0.23% of spending.
- *Uses:* Roughly 6% of total expenses are administrative. Public and private providers both account for roughly 40% of total health care spending.

Sources: Data are from C. N. Mwikisa, L. Mwansa, P. Nankamba, D. Chimfwembe, M. Goma, B. Chitah, and R. Maswenyeho, *Zambia National Health Accounts: 1995–98* (Lusaka: Ministry of Health, n.d.), http://www.afro.who.int/dsd/nha/country-nha/zambia-nha.pdf; P. Berman, *Financing of Rural Health Care in India: Estimates of the Resources Available and Their Distribution*, 1995, presented at the International Workshop on Health Insurance in India, Bangalore, India; Fundacion Mexicana para la Salud, *Las Cuentas Nacionales de Salud y el financiamiento de los servicios* (Mexico: Fundacion Mexicana para la Salud, 1994); and V. Tangcharoensathien, A. Laixuthai, J. Vasavit, N. Tantigate, W. Prajuabmoh-Ruffolo, D. Vimolkit, and J. Lertiendumrong, "National Health Accounts Development: Lessons from Thailand," 1999, *Health Policy and Planning, 14*(4), pp. 343–353.

---

state-owned firms. One study considered these benefits to represent income transfers to household members and classified them as private health sector expenditures. The other considered the state-owned firm to be the agent, and classified the expenditures as public (Tangcharoensathien et al., 1999).

Data for NHAs are collected from a great variety of sources, including spending records, records of social and private insurance institutions, sample surveys of firms, national consumer expenditure surveys, and more focused household health utilization and expenditure surveys. In countries where similar data may be collected from more than one source, comparison and triangulation from the different sources helps to improve the accuracy of the results. Perhaps the biggest problem in collecting data on government expenditures is finding data on funds spent as opposed to budgeted. Far more significant problems occur in estimating private health expenditures, specifically, the expenditure size and composition of firms and households. Where secondary data are not available, primary data may need to be collected through firm and household surveys.

Resource Allocation

The significance of processes of resource allocation in a health system has been clearly acknowledged only in the past decade or so. Financing agents, such as government bodies at various levels (ministries of health and provincial offices), social insurance agencies, and private insurers, have always been one of the components of a health system, channeling funds from sources (taxpayers, payers of insurance premiums) to providers. What is new is an emphasis on their role as active purchasers of services rather than passive allocators of funds. For government bodies, such as ministries of health, this has demanded the creation of a clear distinction between their role as purchasers of health services and their role as providers of health services. For other financing agents, this requires them to take a much more active role in decisions on which services should be paid for and how they should be paid for.

The Purchasing Role

An emphasis on the purchasing role has arisen for a number of reasons:

- Integrated systems of purchasing and provision, such as those created in 1948 in the UK's National Health Service and existing in many similar public systems across the world, are thought to operate more in the interests of providers than the general public and to lack incentives to be technically efficient; highlighting purchasing as a separate function helps redress the balance and strengthen the power of managers.

- Patients, who in markets for other goods and services would be the purchasers, are believed—for the reasons laid out earlier—to be in a weak position to be active purchasers.

- In health systems such as the United States, where there is third-party payment (i.e., insurance agencies pay providers), cost escalation has been a major problem because patients choose their health provider, who is then reimbursed by the insurer. Although the insurers fund a large volume of services, traditionally they did not use this power to influence either the quantity or price of services provided. The development of the approach of managed care has led to an emphasis on the role of the purchaser as managing the provision of health services and ensuring that there are incentives for efficiency and cost containment (and also for equity where the purchaser has public respon-

sibilities). "Strategic purchasing" has included, for example, strict control over utilization, especially of specialists and of inpatient care; controlling drug costs by creating drug formularies and using generic medications; and disease prevention and management programs.

Purchasers may be of different types and sizes. The most limited role would be that assumed by an insurance agency whose concerns are solely the patient group it cares for and ensuring it maintains its position in the marketplace. The most extensive role occurs when a purchaser has responsibilities for the health services of the population of a defined geographic area, and hence can plan services on a population basis. This is the position of public purchasers in health systems that were previously integrated but where the roles of purchaser and provider have been distinguished. Table 11-5 sets out the main stages in purchasing for this type of purchaser. In many ways this is no more than a traditional planning cycle; what marks it as different is that the concern of the purchaser is not to maintain a network of services but to purchase services to meet the needs of its population. The contracts that are agreed on with providers may be formal legal contracts (and would need to be where providers are private bodies) or may simply be management agreements. As discussed in "Health System Reform" later in this chapter, contractual relationships have become one of the key features of health reform plans in a number of countries.

An important issue in the design of a purchasing role is whether there should be a single purchaser or a number of purchasers who compete with each other for clients. Private insurance agencies compete for clients, and it can be argued that this ensures that there are pressures for efficiency and services that

Table 11-5	Stages in Purchasing

1. Assess needs of population.
2. Identify cost-effective strategies to meet needs.
3. Relate strategies to existing services to identify scope for change.
4. Consult public, patients, and professionals on their values and priorities.
5. Draw up health service objectives and priorities.
6. Draw up contract specifications.
7. Agree on contracts with providers, including service quantity, quality, and cost.
8. Monitor performance of providers directly and through surveys.
9. Feed back this information into the next round of needs assessment, priority setting, and contracting.

Source: S. Witter, "Purchasing Health Care," in S. Witter and T. Ensor (Eds.), *An Introduction to Health Economics for Eastern Europe and the Former Soviet Union* (Chichester, England: John Wiley & Sons, 1997), p. 83. Adapted with permission.

meet client preferences. It remains an open question for tax-funded and social insurance–funded health systems whether a single purchaser or multiple purchasers is desirable. Reasons for caution about encouraging competition among purchasers include the following:

- If the system of allocating funds does not provide adequate compensation for meeting the costs of the health risks covered, the purchaser will have an incentive to avoid enrolling the more expensive risks; this problem is known as *cream skimming*. In reality, it is difficult to predict the health service needs of a given population and compensate purchasers appropriately.

- It can be difficult for individuals to choose between competing purchasers: The more superficial aspects of the promised package of health services may influence them, rather than technical quality, which is more difficult to judge. This would then lead purchasers to compete on the superficial aspects.

- If there are economies of scale in purchasing, these may be lost.

- Transactions costs—the costs of agreeing on arrangements for purchasing services—may be higher.

Whatever the number of purchasers, information systems are crucial in enabling purchasers to carry out their role. Government health systems traditionally have poor information on cost and quality, and hence new systems have to be developed to underpin the purchasing function. Insurance agencies often have much information since they are paying for services, but commonly do not exploit these data to monitor providers. Purchasers need information in order to act as active purchasers; this includes information on provider performance (e.g., waiting times, specific health outcomes where this can clearly be related to services provided) and adherence to standard treatment protocols (e.g., with respect to use of antibiotics).

Payment Mechanisms

A key influence on the success with which the purchasing role is carried out is the method chosen to pay providers, whether these be bodies responsible for services for specific populations, individual providers, or specific facilities. Although financial remuneration is not the only influence on provider performance, it is a powerful one.

Authorities responsible for the provision of services to a specific population can be provided with a global budget. A key issue is how that budget is determined. There has been increasing interest in using a resource allocation formula to calculate the budget appropriate to the populations of different geographic areas. The most well-known example is that of the United Kingdom, where funds have been allocated from the national level to regions using a formula that reflects the need for health services of each region, as proxied by indicators such as size of population and standardized mortality ratios (Department of Health and Social Security, 1976). Similar formulas are being used in South Africa and Zambia to allocate funds geographically. This approach is combined with various means of paying individual providers and facilities within each geographic area.

Individual providers can be paid by salary, fee for service, or capitation. Salary represents a fixed annual payment unrelated to workload. Salary scales allow an individual's remuneration over time to be increased. Although in theory this can be done on the basis of performance, in practice it is common for years of service alone to determine pay increases and promotions, thus undermining incentives to work hard. Another problem with salary payment that is not inherent in the method is the level of the salary. In low-income countries this is often very low, further weakening the incentive to work hard or to work the required number of hours, and encouraging staff to find additional ways of generating income, such as demanding informal payments from patients.

Additional elements can be added to salary payments to encourage good performance. These can be financial, as when an element of performance-related pay is included (e.g., a pay increase or end-of-year bonus can be based on a performance assessment), or nonfinancial (e.g., award of certificates or other ways of giving recognition to high performers). Salary is the basis for remuneration in public systems, especially in hospitals and in privately owned facilities for nonmedical staff and even for physicians in some high-income countries. Although evidence is scanty, it is probably not uncommon in low- and middle-income countries for at least some of the physicians in private hospitals to be salaried.

Fee for service has traditionally been the payment method for general physicians and specialists in a number of countries in continental Europe and in North America and Japan. It has also been adopted in some new social insurance schemes in Asia and eastern Europe. It is usually the method of payment that physicians prefer since it does not involve an employer/employee relationship, and this explains its persistence despite known problems. Where a financial agent pays the bill, there will be agreement on the fee schedule, which is usually negotiated with the medical association.

From a patient's perspective—particularly a patient covered by insurance—fee for service is attractive. It readily permits free choice of doctors, since payment can follow the patient. It encourages the doctor to be responsive to the patient, and there is no incentive to underprovide. However, from a purchaser's perspective, fee-for-service payment encourages doctors to provide more consultations and more expensive procedures. Visit rates in countries using fee-for-service payment are often double those in countries that use capitation, and more tests and drugs are also prescribed (Ensor, Witter, & Sheiman, 1997). Surgical rates are also often higher (Abel-Smith, 1994). Administrative costs are higher because of the need to monitor claims, and some degree of fraudulent claims is inevitable. When financing agents try to hold down costs by not increasing fee rates, there is good evidence that doctors respond by increasing the volume of service, as in Taiwan.

Some adjustments can be made to fee-for-service methods of payment to address some of these problems. For example, the overall budget can be fixed, as in Germany, so that volume of services in excess of that budgeted for will cause the fee per item of service to fall. Or copayments can be required from patients, although there is little good evidence that these act as a constraint on physicians' behavior, and they may simply render care unaffordable for lower-income groups in the population.

Capitation is most common for primary care services and involves a fixed payment per year per person registered with the provider. It may differ depending on the nature of the patient—for example, the elderly and children may attract a higher payment, reflecting their greater needs for health services. Capitation payment has been the traditional form of payment for general physicians in much of Europe, sometimes supplemented by extra payments to encourage particular aspects of primary care services (such as primary care teams) or priority services (such as preventive care).

This payment system supports continuity of care and an emphasis on preventive services, not just curative care; it makes the general physician a gatekeeper for hospital care, thus encouraging the provision of services at the lowest possible level. It leaves the doctor substantially free to practice medicine and to organize the primary care service with little interference and with minimum administration. From the patient's point of view, capitation can ensure a personal rela-tionship with a doctor and a personal medical record, although changing doctors may be difficult. However, since payment does not depend on the number of times a patient is seen, it can encourage doctors to minimize the volume of services given to patients and to refer patients to the hospital unnecessarily, subject only to the need to keep patients sufficiently satisfied that they do not change doctors. Doctors may also try to avoid registering the more demanding and expensive patients. The extent to which this is a problem will depend on how much of the cost of services is covered by the capitation fee (e.g., whether drugs are paid for separately) and to what degree the capitation fee is risk adjusted.

Hospitals may be paid a fixed annual budget (often called a *global budget*) or in a variety of ways that reflect workload. Fixed budgets have traditionally been paid to public hospitals, but some countries have introduced them even for private hospitals that are paid by an insurance fund. Budgets are a highly effective means of cost containment and can provide a manager with great flexibility if discretion is allowed on line-item expenditure. However, there can be little incentive to have a high turnover of patients (since this increases costs) or to provide good-quality service. These problems can be addressed by good monitoring systems.

Payments to hospitals that reflect workload can be by itemized bill, daily rate (including all recurrent costs), average cost per patient, case adjusted for diagnosis, types of services, or block and volume contracts. These range from the most detailed—and therefore the most demanding and costly to administer—to the least detailed and the simplest to administer. All have their own particular advantages and disadvantages.

Payment by itemized bill has the same inherent problems as fee for service for doctors: It encourages excessive procedures and hospital stays. Per diem rates discourage excessive procedures but encourage unnecessary stays. Average cost per patient discourages long length of stay but does not encourage technical efficiency. Case-based payment, particularly developed in the United States with the diagnosis-related group approach, reimburses hospitals for the "average" case but provides an incentive to classify patients in more expensive groups or to shift patients out of the hospital earlier. Case-based payment is also information intensive and hence costly to administer.

The introduction of contracts into the United Kingdom health system was accompanied in the early years mainly by block and volume contracts. In the former, a provider is contracted to deliver one or more services (e.g., acute hospital services) to a given population for a fixed sum—it is hence, in effect, a capitation payment. It transfers financial risk to the provider and may thus encourage cream skimming and the provision of too few services. This type of payment, often risk adjusted to a certain extent, is increasingly being used in managed care arrangements and between social insurance agencies and providers, as in Thailand. Volume contracts are appropriate where the purchaser wishes to limit the number of procedures paid for (e.g., elective surgery). Purchasers can use these contracts to take advantage of economies of scale that can be achieved by larger units with high volume.

This list of payment methods provides a confusing range of options. The key issues relate to what incentives each payment method creates for providers. These are summarized in Table 11-6. In particular:

- What are the incentives to overprovide or underprovide services to patients within the facility? A key issue is who bears the financial risk—purchaser or provider.

- What are the incentives to be technically efficient?

- What are the incentives to exclude altogether certain types of patients?

- Given these incentives, what are the administrative costs of the payment system together with the monitoring required to prevent abuse?

This provides a rather crude basis for evaluating methods, however, not least because financial remuneration, although important, is not the only factor affecting the behavior of providers. The effects of a method in practice will also depend on the system and context within which it is introduced—for example, the extent to which

- purchasers or patients can change provider

- strict ethical standards are adhered to and monitored by the medical profession (thus limiting cream skimming and both under- and overprovision)

- the media is active in publicizing cases of medical negligence

- consumers are well informed and able to exercise choice effectively

Because each payment approach has its advantages and disadvantages, which depend also on the context in which it is introduced, it is difficult to be prescriptive. In practice, some of the problems with any one method are addressed by combining methods (e.g., using capitation payment but with additional fees for certain procedures). Perhaps the strongest conclusion that can be drawn is that fee-for-service payment should be avoided as the main payment approach. Studies have suggested that providing care on a fee-for-service basis costs one-third more than using capitation, without substantial differences in health outcomes, and that fee-for-service payment for outpatient care is associated with 11% higher expenditures in OECD countries (Ensor, Witter, & Sheiman, 1997). A further conclusion is that no payment method will work well if providers think they are seriously underpaid.

Table 11-6	Key Payment Methods and Their Incentives to Providers	
Payment Method	**Unit of Services Paid For**	**Key Financial Incentives for Providers**
Salary	Usually 1 month's work	Restrict number of patients and services provided
Fee for service	Individual acts or visits	Expand number of cases seen and service intensity; provide more expensive services and drugs
Capitation/block contract	All relevant services (e.g., primary care, hospital care) for a patient in a given time period	Attract more registered patients (especially the more healthy); minimize contacts per patient and service intensity
Fixed budget	All services provided by a facility in a given time period	Reduce number of patients and services provided; keep patients in hospital longer
Daily rate	Patient day	Expand number of bed days (through longer stays or more admissions)
Case payment	Cases of different types	Expand number of cases seen (especially the less serious); decrease service intensity; provide less expensive services

Source: S. Bennett, "Health-Care Markets: Defining Characteristics," in S. Bennett, B. McPake, and A. Mills (Eds.), *Private Health Providers in Developing Countries* (London: Zed Books, 1997), p. 92. Adapted with permission.

Provision of Services

Health service providers in low- and middle-income countries can be categorized into seven main groups:

1. Government-run health services for the general public (these include the services of the ministry of health and those services coming under other government ministries, such as local government and education).

2. Services run by social insurance agencies for the insured and their dependents.

3. NGO services, including those run by church organizations and charitable groups.

4. Occupational health care providers (medical services provided by employers for their employees); this includes services for the armed forces and police, which come under government ministries. Universities may also run services for their own staff.

5. Private, for-profit allopathic providers, both individuals and facilities.

6. Traditional systems of medicine, such as Ayurveda, homeopathy, and Chinese medicine; and traditional healers of various types, including traditional birth attendants.

7. The informal sector of drug peddlers and unqualified practitioners.

In general, the richer a country, the more organized and structured and the less diverse the system of health service provision. For example, over time government-run services may be brought within a single structure, as they were in the United Kingdom under successive rounds of reorganization; services of the ministry of health and social insurance agency may be amalgamated, as they were in Costa Rica. As government services and services for the insured improve, there is less reason for occupational health services to provide general medical care; as regulatory structures strengthen, the informal sector becomes much smaller.

Information on the supply of health services in low- and middle-income countries is sorely lacking, and indeed is much weaker than information on the demand side. Hence it is difficult to summarize the relative significance of these different sources of services. Most studies focus on what is called the *public-private mix*—that is, the relative numbers of providers in public and private sectors. McPake (1997) suggests that there may be at least three different patterns. Among the lowest-income countries, the formal pri-

vate, for-profit sector is small, but especially in Africa there is a rather larger NGO sector. The informal sector is large, consisting of unregistered allopathic providers, drug sellers, and a variety of traditional practitioners. For example, in Zambia 0.2% of beds are in the private, for-profit sector and 25% in the NGO sector, and 73% of private expenditure is on drugs.

However, in some very low-income countries, especially in Asia, the private, for-profit sector plays a much more important role; this constitutes the second pattern. For example, in India 75% of total health expenditure is paid by private households as out-of-pocket expenses (Mills et al., 2001). Large and concentrated populations may be one explanation; another may be a longer history of Western health services and training of professionals, together with government health services that have never extended to provide coverage of the whole population. However, even in these countries, private provision is still concentrated at lower levels of the health system. For example, in India, although 67% of hospitals are private, this amounts to only 35% of beds (1993 data; Mills et al., 2001). Much of the high expenditure on private health services in these countries still goes to informal services, ambulatory care, and drugs: 60% of private expenditure in India is for curative services at the primary level and around 35% for secondary and tertiary services.

McPake (1997) identifies a third pattern of provision, in countries with rather higher per capita GNP, which usually includes a major role for social insurance (funding services either through its own facilities, as is common in Latin America, or through mixed public and private providers, as is more common in Asia) and a private sector that is playing an increasingly important role (certainly at the secondary level and sometimes also at the tertiary level).

Hanson and Berman (1998) assembled what data they could find on private physicians and hospital beds to see if any general patterns emerged. They found extreme variability in both absolute numbers and public/private shares. The supply of both private physicians and for-profit beds is income elastic (i.e., they increase at a rate that is higher than the growth rate of income). In contrast, public beds increase at a much lower rate than the rate of growth of income. Thus, although it is well established that the public role in financing increases with rising income, it seems that the public share of provision (measured in this study as beds and physicians) decreases.

Because the relative roles of public and private sectors have been a key policy question, there has been much interest in whether private providers are more efficient. Those who believe in the virtues of private markets claim this to be the case, but information is scanty, of poor quality, and equivocal. A review by Bennett (1997) finds that private providers are more efficient, but she points out that all the studies refer to not-for-profit providers, suggesting that differences in efficiency are not due to the profit motive. In addition, comparisons are problematic because an increasing number of studies are finding that the nature of the patients seen by private, for-profit hospitals is different from those dealt with by public hospitals. In particular, the illness of patients in the former may be less severe and require only a short length of stay. Moreover, the structure of the payment method for their patients will affect whether they have an incentive to be efficient. For example, in South Africa, medical benefit schemes pay private hospitals a fixed per diem for hotel-type services, which encourages hospitals to organize these as efficiently as possible. However, drugs and supplies are reimbursed with a percentage markup, encouraging use of the most expensive drugs.

Another difficulty in drawing conclusions stems from the fact that there is a tendency to make an overall judgment on all private providers. However, there is ample evidence of highly diverse types of providers. In India, for example, at one end of the spectrum there are private hospitals delivering services of international standard; at the other end are unlicensed and unqualified practitioners using Western prescription drugs. In between are trained physicians and Western-style hospitals whose quality of care can be extremely poor (Bennett, 1997). Private clinics, although in theory run by doctors, in practice often depend on staff with little training; this is because, in many countries, doctors will also have a public post where they spend at least some part of their time, as well as in several clinics. Financial relationships between different types of facilities are also a concern in a number of countries; hospitals, laboratories, and diagnostic centers may pay general practitioners to refer patients to them or may pass them a share of their fee.

Absolute lack of resources can place a limit on the costliness of public facilities. Nevertheless, there is ample evidence of poor resource use, such as very low staff productivity and waste of drugs and supplies (Mills, 1997). However, the evidence is by no means conclusive: It comes from a relatively small number of country-specific studies, and the evidence of greatest inefficiency comes from the lowest-income countries in Africa, making it difficult to know to what extent the conclusions can be generalized. In addi-

tion, there are examples of highly efficient public health centers and hospitals (World Bank, 2003).

As in the case of private facilities, there are a variety of explanations for observed public provider inefficiencies, some of which do not relate to ownership per se (Mills, 1997). In particular, decision making may be centralized and staff at hospital level given little power to control resource use. Very low salaries also contribute to poor performance, because they reduce staff motivation, and staff may need to spend time generating income in other ways to ensure an income adequate for survival.

The clearest area where private facilities outperform public ones is in their acceptability to patients. People commonly complain that the staff of public services are rude and unhelpful, in contrast to private providers. The latter are also open longer hours, especially in the evening, and do not run short of complementary resources, such as drugs. However, people generally make shrewd judgments of the motivations of providers. Patients may use private providers for the convenience and the available resources, but they are aware that it is the profit motive that drives the private providers' behavior and influences the care given, rather than any humanitarian ethic (Mills et al., 2001).

Performance of Different Types of Systems

The previous sections have demonstrated that the design of health systems varies greatly between countries, particularly with respect to the following:

- the sources of funding (e.g., balance between tax, insurance, and out-of-pocket payment)
- the degree of integration of financing agents and providers (are there large numbers of financing agents or one major one, such as a ministry of health or single social insurance agency; are financing agents and providers integrated or separated?)
- the ownership of providers (public; private, not-for-profit; private, for profit)
- the extent to which the whole population of a country has access to the same services, or different groups in the population have different entitlements and use different providers

These marked differences have led not surprisingly to intense debate over whether any one design can be shown to perform better, in terms of criteria such as efficiency and equity, than any other. Attention has particularly focused on differences between the U.S., Canadian, and British systems. The United States relies heavily on voluntary insurance organized largely through employers, plus publicly funded programs for low-income patients and older adults; Canada has a compulsory national insurance system; and the United Kingdom relies largely on general tax revenues. Whereas most services in the United Kingdom are government owned, privately owned services play an important role in Canada and especially the United States. Table 11-7 shows some key comparative indicators for the United States and Canada for 1998 or nearby years (Folland, Goodman, & Stano, 2004). Canada had substantially lower per capita spending on health and GNP share than the United States, despite a bed per population ratio that was greater than that in the United States. The United States spent approximately 82% more per capita than Canada, even though 15% of its population had no health insurance. Health status indicators such as life expectancy were better in Canada. Study of waiting times and physician practice patterns show that in some instances Canadians got less health care or had to wait longer, but there were few observable effects on mortality and other outcome indicators.

Analysis of explanations as to why Canada spent less highlights two key differences. One is that physician fees and hospital costs were significantly lower in Canada, no doubt because these are regulated.

Physician fees are negotiated between physician associations and provinces, and hospital budgets are set by the provinces. Another reason is substantially lower administrative costs. Administration accounted for 24.8% of total hospital costs in the United States in 1990—nearly twice the share in Canada. Studies comparing expenditures in a larger number of rich countries have found that countries in which health services are financed primarily by private payments have the highest expenditures, and that there is no evidence that this is reflected in better health status. Health systems where there is comprehensive risk pooling based on compulsory insurance or tax finance and covering the whole population appear to be more cost-effective (WHO, 1999).

Similar, detailed comparisons have not been done for low- and middle-income countries. They can take two key lessons from richer countries:

1. A significant public share in financing enables greater control of expenditure, meaning that higher population coverage can be achieved at lower cost.

2. The greater the fragmentation of the health system and the greater the reliance on private insurance, the greater the proportion of total health expenditure taken up by administrative costs.

Table 11-7	Comparative Data on U.S. and Canadian Health Systems	
Indicators	**Canada**	**United States**
Population, 2001 (in millions)	31.1	278.0
GDP per capita, 2001 ($1997)	27,350.0	32,928.0
Per capita health expenditure, 1999	2,411.0	4,390.0
Health spending, 1998 (% of GDP)	9.3	12.9
Percentage of health spending, 1998		
Public expenditures	69.9	45.0
Inpatient care	43.1	41.3
Outpatient care	26.7	31.0
Pharmaceuticals	15.0	10.1
Beds per 1,000 population, 1998	4.1	3.7
Average length of stay in days, 1998	8.2	7.1
Percentage of population with no insurance	0.0	15.1
Out-of-pocket payments per capita, 1998	392.0	652.0
Private insurance % expenditure on health, 1998	11.2	33.5
Life expectancy (in years) at birth: females, 1998	81.5	79.5
Life expectancy (in years) at birth: males, 1998	76.1	73.8

Note: Financial data are denoted in U.S. dollars.

Source: S. Folland, A. C. Goodman, and M. Stano, *The Economics of Health and Health Care*, 4th ed. (Upper Saddle River, NJ: Prentice Hall, 2004), p. 494. Reprinted with permission.

However, rich countries demonstrate that there are a variety of ways in which a strong public role and coordinated health system can be achieved, and that the traditional model prevalent in many low- and middle-income countries of an integrated public system financed from general taxation is only one approach.

Health System Reform

Widespread dissatisfaction with the performance of health systems in rich and poor countries alike has encouraged what can be seen as a worldwide movement of health sector reform (Roberts et al., 2004). The term *reform* is used deliberately, in the sense of "a sustained process of fundamental change in policy and institutional arrangements, guided by government, designed to improve the functioning and performance of the health sector, and ultimately the health status of the population" (Sikosana, Dlamini, & Issakov, 1997).

Most recently, vigorous policy debate on reforms has been encouraged by two key events. First, the report of the Commission on Macroeconomics and Health has emphasized the contribution of health to economic growth, and argued that much greater sums of external funding should be made available to the health systems of low-income countries (WHO, 2001). Second, the Millennium Development Goals (MDGs), established at the UN Millennium Summit in 2000, are having an important influence on the focus of external assistance for health. A number of the MDGs concern health—for example, reduced child mortality—and slow progress toward some of the goals, especially in sub-Saharan Africa, is focusing attention on health system deficiencies and what can be done about them (World Bank, 2004).

The key problems that reforms are designed to address have been referred to at various points in this chapter and can be summarized as follows:

- In many low-income countries, resources and funds are grossly inadequate to provide even a basic level of care for the population, with many governments spending less than $10 per capita on health services.
- Levels of health produced by health systems are often lower than what is technically possible.

    Many activities funded by the public sector are not very cost-effective, and coverage of interventions that are highly cost-effective is inadequate (World Bank, 1993); conversely, too high a share of the budget is spent on hospital care, especially higher levels of hospital care.

    Health systems operate with low or very variable levels of technical efficiency: Studies of facility costs invariably show great variation in costs across similar types of services, to an extent that is not easily explained by differences in quality but is more likely to be due to problems of managing resources (Mills, 1997).

- Quality of services is poor in public facilities, especially in the poorer countries where funds are very limited, health service inputs are in short supply, equipment is poorly maintained, and staff are poorly paid and hence poorly motivated; staff are often criticized for their lack of courtesy to patients and lack of responsiveness to their needs. Many private services are also often of very low quality and almost completely unregulated.

- The possibilities for health interventions created by technological developments place ever-increasing demands on limited funds, accentuating the need for governments to consider ways of setting priorities and defining limits to what can be provided.

- New problems, such as HIV/AIDS and the growing importance of chronic diseases are putting even greater pressure on services both in terms of patient needs and, for countries heavily affected by HIV, deaths of health care workers.

- Most low- and middle-income countries fare poorly in terms of both equity of access to health services and equity of payment for services, with a few notable exceptions. Poorer households commonly use health services less frequently, especially in rural areas where access is more difficult and expensive, and spend a much higher proportion of their income on health services, partly because public subsidies do not meet their needs well.

The objectives of health sector reform follow from this list of key problems, namely, increased use of services in the poorest countries and especially improved equity of access, better efficiency, and greater consumer satisfaction. The means of reform are being significantly influenced by shifts in beliefs about the appropriate role of the state and the appropriate means for the delivery of public services. Current ideologies favor a slimmed-down state; increased efficiency in the provision of public services through mechanisms such as decentralization, contracting out, and competition; and an extension in the role of the private sector. While these ideas are being applied to the government's role in general, they are influencing reforms in the health sector. Current thinking emphasizes the following key roles of the state:

- setting and enforcing standards, including minimum quality standards

- monitoring the behavior and performance of providers and insurers (where they exist), including ensuring information is available to do so

- defining an appropriate package of services and benefits

- regulating to encourage efficient and equitable financing and delivery of services and to constrain cost inflation

- ensuring financing of health services through taxation or compulsory insurance arrangements in better-off countries, and targeting public funding at the poorest sections of the population in poorer countries

Table 11-8	The Main Areas of Health Sector Reform
Regulation	
Liberalizing laws regarding the private health sector and introducing incentives for improved efficiency and equity	
Updating regulatory structures	
Financing	
User fees, exemptions, and targeting	
Community financing, including community-based insurance	
Social health insurance	
Resource Allocation	
Creation of purchasing agencies	
Introduction of contractual relationships and management agreements	
Reforming payment systems	
Specification of essential packages	
Provision	
Decentralization of health services and hospital management	
Encouraging competition and diversity of ownership	
Strengthening primary care	
Evidence-based health care	
Quality improvement measures	
Improved accountability to service users and population	

Reforms are considered here following the same headings of the key health system functions used earlier, namely, regulation, financing, resource allocation, and provision. Table 11-8 lists the key reform areas under each heading.

Regulation

As part of health sector reforms, many countries have been amending out-of-date legislation and seeking to ensure that new private activities are brought within the scope of the law. Countries that previously banned or strictly controlled the private sector, such as countries in eastern and central Europe, some countries in Africa, and Vietnam and China, now allow and even in some cases encourage it through tax subsidies. However, much of the expansion of the private sector has taken place without deliberate planning, and often with little regulation.

These changes have increased the need to strengthen regulations, but attempts to tighten regulations are frequently opposed by powerful interest groups. Moreover, regulation of a private sector that consists of numerous small-scale providers is inherently difficult, and few countries have the administrative capacity to do this effectively. Few lessons are yet available on the success of different approaches to strengthening the regulatory role of the state.

Financing

Reform of health financing has been at the top of the policy agenda in many countries, particularly the introduction (or raising) of user fees and compulsory insurance. User fees were at one time argued to offer a significant source of additional revenue, with their harmful effects on access to be countered by exemption policies. Expectations are now less sanguine: Administrative difficulties of fee collection have been significant; ability to pay has been a significant barrier to use, and exemption schemes have not been effective; and even if there is ability to pay, people have been unwilling to pay if service quality does not improve. Interest has therefore developed in other ways of seeking to ensure that public funds are targeted on the poorest. Approaches include geographic targeting through resource allocation formulas, focusing additional funding on specific programs targeted at populations with the least access, and social funds that often involve local communities in decisions on spending (World Bank, 2003, 2004).

Partly because of the increased concern over the equity effects of user fees, attention has also switched to the possibilities for expansion of locally based insurance schemes. Although a number of such schemes exist in various countries, there is as yet little experience of how they can be encouraged to grow in size and scope. Historically, they were an important stage in the development of universal coverage of health services in Europe and Japan, but no low- and middle-income countries have schemes that are yet sufficiently developed to offer this sort of promise in the near future.

The introduction of compulsory insurance has been a component of reform policies in the rapidly industrializing countries of Southeast Asia and in central and eastern Europe. Compulsory insurance has also been of considerable interest in a number of African countries and in the Caribbean, and a number of Latin American countries have sought to reform their existing schemes. According to Mills (2000b), key issues have been the following:

- Should compulsory insurance be introduced when the proportion of the population in formal employment is still rather small?

- Should the insured have a choice of competing schemes or should there be a single fund?

- Is there any role for private insurers?

- What should be the relationship between the insurance agency and providers—what form of contract and what payment method?

- As schemes cover a higher proportion of the population, how can they be integrated with arrangements for other groups of the population in order to remove a two-tier arrangement in which those in the scheme have access to much better services than those outside the scheme?

These questions concern the nature of the purchaser and the provider, rather than of the funding source itself. They are discussed further in subsequent sections.

Resource Allocation

One of the most common features of sectorwide reforms has been the introduction of a purchaser-provider split in public systems that were previously integrated. Planned management reforms in South Africa, Zimbabwe, and Zambia all envisage a purchasing role for local health authorities. In Thailand, the social security office acts as a purchaser on behalf of the insured and accredits and monitors the hospitals that they use. Along with the specification of the purchaser's role has come an emphasis on contractual arrangements between purchasers and providers. At one extreme, these arrangements may be seen as no more than the formalization of a management rela-

tionship, as where annual contracts are agreed upon between the ministry of health and an executive agency (Zambia) or the ministry of health and a regional health authority (Trinidad), or between a province and a district (South Africa, Zambia, Zimbabwe). At the other extreme, the contracts may be awarded on a competitive basis and may be legally binding (as in New Zealand).

A more recent development has been the use of contracts with NGOs to reform or expand service provision in contexts where governments function poorly or have very limited capacity. The experiments with contracting district health services in Cambodia are widely quoted (World Bank, 2003), and similar arrangements are being tried in Afghanistan and Rwanda, for example. Contracting with NGOs is also being increasingly used to expand availability of HIV prevention.

A vital element of the relationship between purchaser and provider is the payment mechanism: the basis on which funds are allocated from purchasers to providers. Health sector reforms commonly involve changes to traditional modes of payment, although the nature of the reforms depends on the starting point and is severely constrained by powerful interest groups; hence, a great variety of reforms are apparent in practice. Although, in general, fee-for-service methods of payment are seen to be undesirable, countries such as those in eastern and central Europe that previously provided salaries to primary care providers have sought to raise remuneration levels and encourage greater productivity by using a mix of salary, fee for service, and capitation. Indeed, capitation appears to be one of the areas where there is most experimentation worldwide. Traditionally an approach for paying primary care providers, capitation has been extended to pay for hospital services as well (e.g., in Thailand) and is the basis for payment in many managed care arrangements.

Global budgets for hospitals have been a feature in Europe under different funding regimes. Concern that they do not provide incentives to efficiency has led to the introduction of mechanisms that relate payment to measures of hospital activity, such as bed days or cases, or even specific services. Some similar reform trends can be seen elsewhere; Thailand, Taiwan, and Korea have all tried case-based payments, with Thailand adopting the approach nationwide.

In those countries introducing compulsory insurance and those engaged in reforming existing systems, a key and controversial issue has been whether to encourage competition between insurance funds and to encourage choice of insurer. In western Europe, countries have proceeded very cautiously. In contrast, there is an active exploration of arrangements that would permit competitive pressures to be felt by financing agents in some countries in Latin America and in central and eastern Europe. A model of reform has been proposed for Latin America that involves the social insurance agencies competing with private insurers to enroll individuals and being compensated by a risk-adjusted capitation payment (Londono & Frenk, 1997). This approach has, for example, been implemented in Colombia and Argentina. However, there is as yet limited evidence of how well it works and whether cream skimming is as much a problem as some fear.

A trend for the future is the increasing prominence of managed care companies anxious to break into low- and middle-income markets. Latin America already has a large number of people enrolled in managed care arrangements, and American companies, keen to expand, are actively exploring markets in Latin America, South Africa, and Asia. Options for involvement include contracting with governments or social insurance agencies to manage health programs for particular population groups, or covering groups allowed to opt out of social insurance arrangements. These possibilities require a strong regulatory framework to be put in place.

The specification of essential packages of health services, which purchasers require providers to make available, has been a key feature of many reform programs. The *World Development Report 1993*, on the basis of analyzing the burden of disease and the cost-effectiveness of interventions, proposed a package of essential health services that governments should ensure are universally available (World Bank, 1993). In low-income countries, this package would comprise the following:

- public health services for children, such as immunization and school health services; tobacco and alcohol control; health, nutrition, and family planning information; vector control; sexually transmitted infection (STI) prevention; and monitoring and surveillance
- clinical services, such as tuberculosis treatment, treatment for sick children, prenatal and delivery care, family planning, STI treatment, treatment of infection and minor trauma, and pain relief

The initial global analysis has been followed by many country studies, to identify country-specific packages. However, ensuring reallocation of public subsidies away from lower-priority services such as tertiary hospital care has proved politically difficult, and there is as yet inadequate evidence of the successful implementation of this approach to priority setting. There is, however, increasing recognition of the need to involve the general public in priority-setting processes in order to ensure acceptability and use of the package.

Provision of Services

Key reform themes affecting providers have been decentralization, competition and diversity of ownership, strengthening primary care services, evidence-based medicine, and quality improvement.

Even in health systems that maintain a strong public role in provision, decentralization has been an almost universal theme. At the national level, decentralization has taken the form of restructuring the role and functions of the ministry of health, with some countries creating executive agencies to take over management responsibility at the national level (e.g., Zambia, Ghana), leaving the ministry to concentrate on regulation, policy, and monitoring. Some form of decentralization to intermediate and local levels is also a common theme, with most countries choosing to decentralize services within a hierarchical structure with the ministry of health at the top, although there are a few notable examples of devolution of health to local government (e.g., the Philippines). Finally, decentralization even further, to hospital level, is a common trend in countries with centrally funded, public systems of health provision (Mills et al., 2001). In the lowest-income countries, because of limits on management capacity, this reform may be confined to teaching hospitals, but in some countries, such as Indonesia, a wider range of hospitals is being made "autonomous" or "corporatized."

Competition between providers is similarly being widely promoted as a means to encourage efficiency, although with rather more caution and doubts about its effects than in the case of decentralization. Diversity of ownership is also promoted as a means to increase competitive pressures, especially on poorly performing public systems of provision. African governments have been urged to give greater emphasis to NGOs. In a number of Southeast Asian countries, tax incentives have been provided for the construction of private hospitals (e.g., India, Philippines, Thailand), although from the perspective of the health sector as a whole there are considerable doubts about the desirability of this policy (Mills et al., 2001).

Strengthening the role of primary care has long been a theme in reforms in many countries, although often without substantial changes in resource allocation patterns. The United Kingdom reforms, which gave funds to primary care doctors to purchase other services, have aroused much interest, although efforts to create high-quality primary care services, with a gatekeeper role for the primary care provider, do not as yet appear to feature strongly in reforms in most low- and middle-income countries.

Included in many reform packages have been measures to improve the quality of the services provided. In rich countries a range of approaches is being used, including evidence-based medicine, technology assessment, clinical guidelines, medical audits, and quality assurance methods. These are beginning to be featured in less wealthy countries, but in the lowest-income countries more basic problems have been addressed, such as availability of drugs and supplies, improvement of staff skills, and maintenance of equipment.

Increasingly, human resources are being highlighted as the key area where reforms are needed. In many of the poorest countries, the number of trained health providers is grossly inadequate to provide even a basic package of services to the whole population. HIV/AIDS is making this far worse in heavily affected countries—for example, in Mozambique, 20% of student nurses died from AIDS in 2000 (World Bank, 2004). The international brain drain is also having a devastating effect on some countries. In Ghana, it is estimated that 31% of trained health personnel left the country between 1993 and 2002. Brain drain is one symptom of a widespread problem in many countries of low financial remuneration of health workers, low motivation, and poor performance, which has to be tackled by action on a number of fronts. Little experience of reforms is yet available, but policy options include greater use of community-based workers; improved remuneration and conditions of service; performance-related pay; and reform of management cultures and systems to put greater emphasis on results and ensure merit-based promotion.

Reforms may also seek to increase the influence of users and communities over health providers—to hold them accountable for good performance—but there are few well-evaluated examples. In many of the poorest countries, local government structures are weak, ruling them out as an immediate means for ensuring local representation. Some reforms include the introduction of health or hospital boards with citizen representation. Often community involvement is seen to occur via NGOs rather than government health services. Little attention has been paid to patient rights, and patients tend to appear as the object of reforms, rather than as the subject.

Conclusion

This chapter has outlined the main components of health systems in low- and middle-income countries. It has focused mainly on the health care system, with little attention, due to lack of space, given to the sectors that supply resources to the health system (such as education and training institutions, and the pharmaceutical, medical supplies, and medical equipment industries) or to broader influences on health, such as government policies on smoking, alcohol consumption, and transport—all of which have major impacts on health.

In terms of the health system, this chapter has identified its key functions as regulation, financing, resource allocation, and provision, and the key actors as the government, populations, financing agents, and providers. Although these core elements can be identified in all systems, the number of bodies involved in each one, and the way they relate to each other, differs enormously in practice, making it difficult to draw clear conclusions on whether any one arrangement of functions and actors is better than any other.

This chapter has also reviewed the most common reforms being proposed and implemented to deal with weaknesses of current health systems. A number of agencies are suggesting that reform policies are converging and include the following features (Mills, 2000b):

- an emphasis on the regulatory and enabling role of the state

- an emphasis on increasing public control over sources of funding and increasing risk pooling (although not necessarily increasing funding from general taxation, except in countries that devote very little public money to health)

- more explicit prioritization of what services can be financed and provided, especially by the public sector (it is often argued that this should be driven by considerations of cost-effectiveness)

- greater targeting of public subsidies to those most in need

- a greater involvement of the private sector, especially in the provision of health services

- greater decentralization of the management of provision within the public sector

- creation of arrangements that encourage competition between providers, in order to improve efficiency and quality

- greater emphasis on the role of consumers, both as informed purchasers and as citizens to whom providers should be accountable

However, there is a tendency for ideology rather than good empirical evidence to drive these reform policies. These types of reforms are much reviewed and discussed, but there is little strong empirical evidence of how well they work and whether systems reformed along these lines will perform better than unreformed ones. Because country health systems differ greatly, so should reform policies, and there is no ideal blueprint for reform (Roberts et al., 2004). Evidence from countries suggests that reform is often more rhetorical than real, not least because it uses the fashionable language of current reform ideology. Reforms affect the position of powerful interest groups, which mobilize to block change. Far greater understanding is needed of the best ways to introduce reforms and manage these various interests.

● ● ● **Discussion Questions**

1. How can the concepts of efficiency and equity be used to assess the performance of a health system?

2. Access to health care can be viewed as similar to access to other goods and services, that is, dependent on an individual's success in gaining or inheriting income, or as a right of citizenship that should not depend on individual income or wealth. Debate the relative merits of these two positions.

3. What should be the respective roles of the government and the private sector in the health systems of low- and middle-income countries?

4. Imagine that you live in a formerly socialist country and that the health system is soon to be opened to private investment. What kind of regulatory mechanisms might be put in place in order to optimize efficiency and equity?

5. What are the relative strengths and weaknesses of the main financing sources in a low- and middle-income country context?

● ● ● **References**

Abel-Smith, B. (1994). *An introduction to health: Policy, planning and financing*. London: Addison Wesley Longman.

Almeida, C., Braveman, P., Gold, M. R., Szwarcwald, C. L, Mendes Ribeiro, J., Miglionico, A., Millar, J. S., Porto, S., do Rosario Costa, N., Ortun Rubio, V., Segall, M., Starfield, B., Travessos, C., Uga, A., Valente, J., Viacava, F. (2001). Methodological concerns and recommendations on policy consequences of the World Health Report 2000. *Lancet, 357*, 1692–1697

Baker, J., & van der Gaag, J. (1993). Equity in health care and health care financing: Evidence from five developing countries. In E. van Doorslaer, A. Wagstaff, & F. Rutten (Eds.), *Equity in the finance and delivery of health care: An international perspective* (pp. 357–394). Oxford, England: Oxford University Press.

Bennett, S. (1997). Health-care markets: Defining characteristics. In S. Bennett, B. McPake, & A. Mills (Eds.), *Private health providers in developing countries* (pp. 85–101). London: Zed Books.

Bennett, S., Creese, A., & Monasch, R. (1998). *Health insurance schemes for people outside formal sector employment*. Geneva: World Health Organization.

Berman, P. (1995). Financing of rural health care in India: Estimates of the resources available and their distribution. Presented at the International Workshop on Health Insurance in India, Bangalore, India.

Berman, P. A. (1997). National health accounts in developing countries: Appropriate methods and recent applications. *Health Economics, 6*, 11–30.

Bos, E., Hon, V., Maeda, A., Chellaraj, G., & Preker, A. (1998). *Health, nutrition, and population indicators: A statistical handbook*. Washington, DC: World Bank.

Coyne, S. C., & Hilsenrath, P. (2002). The World Health Report 2000: Can health care systems be compared using a single measure of performance? *American Journal of Public Health, 92*, 30–33.

Department of Economics, University of Zambia, & Swedish Institute for Health Economics (1996).

Zambia health sector expenditure review, 1995. Lusaka: University of Zambia.

Department of Health and Social Security. (1976). *Sharing resources for health in England. Report of the Resource Allocation Working Party*. London: Her Majesty's Stationery Office.

Donaldson, C., & Gerard, K. (1993). *Economics of health care financing: The visible hand*. London: Macmillan Press.

Doorslaer, E., Wagstaff, A., & Rutten, F. (Eds.). (1993). *Equity in the finance and delivery of health care: An international perspective*. CEC Health Services Research Series. Oxford, England: Oxford University Press.

Ensor, T., Witter, S., & Sheiman, I. (1997). Methods of payment to medical care providers. In S. Witter & T. Ensor (Eds.), *An introduction to health economics for eastern Europe and the former Soviet Union* (pp. 97–114). Chichester, England: John Wiley & Sons.

Folland, S., Goodman, A. C., & Stano, M. (2004). *The economics of health and health care* (4th ed.). Upper Saddle River, NJ: Prentice Hall.

Fundacion Mexicana para la Salud. (1994). *Las Cuentas Nacionales de Salud y el financiamiento de los servicios*. Mexico: Fundacion Mexicana para la Salud.

Fundacion Mexicana para la Salud. (1995). *Health and the economy: Proposals for progress in the Mexican health system*. Mexico: Fundacion Mexicana para la Salud.

Griffiths, A., & Mills, M. (1983). Health sector financing and expenditure surveys. In K. Lee & A. Mills (Eds.), *The economics of health in developing countries* (pp. 43–63). Oxford, England: Oxford University Press.

Hanson, K., & Berman, P. (1998). Private health care provision in developing countries: A preliminary analysis of levels and composition. *Health Policy and Planning, 13*(3): 195–211.

Hsiao, W. C. (1995a). A framework for assessing health financing strategies and the role of health insurance. In D. W. Dunlop & J. M. Martins (Eds.),

An international assessment of health care financing. Washington, DC: World Bank.

Hsiao, W. C. (1995b). Medical savings accounts: Lessons from Singapore. *Health Affairs, 14*(2), 260–266.

Kohn, R., & White, K. L. (1976). *Health care: An international study.* London: Oxford University Press.

Kumaranayake, L. (1998). *Economic aspects of health sector regulation: Strategic choices for low and middle income countries.* London: London School of Hygiene and Tropical Medicine, Health Policy Unit, Department of Public Health and Policy.

Liu, X., & Mills, A. (2002). Financing reforms of public health services in China: Lessons for other nations. *Social Science and Medicine, 54,* 1691–1698.

Londono, J. L., & Frenk, J. (1997). Structured pluralism: Towards an innovative model for health system reform in Latin America. *Health Policy, 41,* 1–36.

Mach, E. P., & Abel-Smith, B. (1983). *Planning the finances of the health sector.* Geneva, Switzerland: World Health Organization.

McPake, B. (1997). The role of the private sector in health service provision. In S. Bennett, B. McPake, & A. Mills (Eds.), *Private health providers in developing countries* (pp. 21–39). London: Zed Books.

McPake, B., Hanson, K., & Mills, A. (1992). *Implementing the Bamako Initiative in Africa.* London: London School of Hygiene and Tropical Medicine, Health Economics and Financing Programme, Health Policy Unit, Department of Public Health and Policy.

McPake, B., & Machray, C. (1997). International comparisons of health sector reform: Towards a comparative framework for developing countries. *Journal of International Development, 9*(4), 621–629.

Miller, R. H., & Luft, H. S. (1994). Managed care plan performance since 1980: A literature analysis. *Journal of the American Medical Association, 271,* 1512–1519.

Mills, A. (1997). Improving the efficiency of public sector health services in developing countries: Bureaucratic versus market approaches. In C. Colclough (Ed.), *Marketizing education and health in developing countries: Miracle or mirage?* (pp. 245–274). Oxford, England: Clarendon Press.

Mills, A. (2000a). The route to universal coverage. In S. Nitayarumphong & A. Mills (Eds.), *Achieving universal coverage of health care: Experiences from middle and upper income countries* (pp. 283–299). Thailand: Ministry of Public Health, Office of Health Care Reform.

Mills, A. (2000b). Reforming health sectors: Fashions, passions and common sense. In A. Mills (Ed.), *Reforming health sectors* (pp. 1–24). London: Kegan Paul International.

Mills, A., Bennett, S., Russell, S., Attanayake, N., Hongoro, C., Muraleedharan, V. R., & Smithson, P. (2001). *The challenge of health sector reform: What must governments do?* Basingstoke, England: Macmillan.

Ministry of Public Health, Thailand. (n.d.). *Thailand health profile 1999–2000* [CD-ROM].

Mwikisa, C. N., Mwansa, L., Nankamba, P., Chimfwembe, D., Goma, M., Chitah, B., & Maswenyeho, R. (n.d.). *Zambia national health accounts: 1995–98.* Lusaka: Ministry of Health. http://www.afro.who.int/dsd/nha/country-nha/zambia-nha.pdf.

Organization for Economic Cooperation and Development. (1992). Sub-systems of financing and delivery of health care. In *The reform of health care* (pp. 19–29). Paris: OECD.

Porter, R. (1996a). Hospitals and surgery. In *The Cambridge illustrated history of medicine* (pp. 202–205). Cambridge, England: Cambridge University Press.

Porter, R. (1996b). Medical science. In *The Cambridge illustrated history of medicine* (pp. 154–201). Cambridge, England: Cambridge University Press.

Roberts, M. J., Hsiao, W., Berman, P., & Reich, M. (2004). *Getting health reform right.* Oxford, England: Oxford University Press.

Roemer, M. I. (1991). *National health systems of the world: Vol. 1. The countries.* Oxford, England: Oxford University Press.

Roemer, M. I. (1993). *National health systems of the world: Vol. 2. The issues.* Oxford, England: Oxford University Press.

Saltman, R. B., & Figueras, J. (1997). *European health care reform: Analysis of current strategies.* Copenhagen, Denmark: WHO Regional Office for Europe.

Sikosana, P. L. N., Dlamini, Q. Q. D., & Issakov, A. (1997). *Health sector reform in sub-Saharan Africa. A review of experiences, information gaps and research needs.* Geneva, Switzerland: World Health Organization.

Stinson, W. (1982). Community financing of primary health care. *Primary Health Care Issues, 1*(4), 1–90.

Tangcharoensathien, V., Laixuthai, A., Vasavit, J., Tantigate, N., Prajuabmoh-Ruffolo, W., Vimolkit, D., & Lertiendumrong, J. (1999). National health accounts development: Lessons from Thailand. *Health Policy and Planning, 14*(4), 343–353.

Teerawattananon, Y., Tangcharoensathien, V., Tantivess, S., & Mills, A. (2003). Health sector regulation in Thailand: Recent progress and the future agenda. *Health Policy, 63,* 323–338.

Thomson, S., & Mossialos, E. (2004). Private health insurance and access to health care in the European Union. *Euro Observer, 6*(1), 1–4.

Towse, A., Mills, A., & Tangcharoensathien, V. (2004). Lessons from the introduction of universal access to subsidised health care in Thailand. *British Medical Journal, 328,* 103–105.

Wagstaff, A., van Doorslaer, E., van der Burg, H., et al. (1999). Equity in the finance of health care: Some further international comparisons. *Journal of Health Economics, 18,* 263–290.

Walsh, J. A., & Warren, K. S. (1979). Selective public health care: An interim disease control strategy in developing countries. *New England Journal of Medicine, 301,* 967–974.

Walsh, K. (1995). *Public services and market mechanisms: Competition, contracting and the new public management.* London: Macmillan Press.

Witter, S. (1997). Purchasing health care. In S. Witter & T. Ensor (Eds.), *An introduction to health economics for eastern Europe and the former Soviet Union* (pp. 81–94). Chichester, England: John Wiley & Sons.

World Bank. (1993). *World development report 1993: Investing in health.* Oxford, England: Oxford University Press.

World Bank. (1997a). *Sector strategy: Health, nutrition and population.* Washington, DC: World Bank Group.

World Bank. (1997b). *World development report 1997: The state in a changing world.* Oxford, England: Oxford University Press.

World Bank. (1999). *What is the World Bank?* http://www.worldbank.org/html/extdr/about.htm.

World Bank. (2003). *World development report 2004: Making services work for poor people.* Oxford, England: Oxford University Press.

World Bank. (2004). *The Millennium Development Goals for health: Rising to the challenges.* Washington, DC: The World Bank.

World Health Organization. (1993). *Evaluation of recent changes in the financing of health services.* Geneva, Switzerland: World Health Organization.

World Health Organization. (1999). *The world health report 1999: Making a difference.* Geneva, Switzerland: World Health Organization.

World Health Organization. (2000). *The world health report 2000: Health systems—improving performance.* Geneva, Switzerland: World Health Organization.

World Health Organization. (2001). *Macroeconomics and health: Investing in health for economic development. Report of the Commission on Macroeconomics and Health.* Geneva, Switzerland: World Health Organization.

World Health Organization. (2003). *The world health report 2003: Shaping the future*. Geneva, Switzerland: World Health Organization.

World Health Organization. (2004). *The world health report 2004: Changing history*. Geneva, Switzerland: World Health Organization.

World Health Organization, World Bank, & USAID. (2003). *Guide to producing national health accounts with special applications for low-income and middle-income countries*. Geneva, Switzerland: World Health Organization.

Yip, W., & Hsiao, W. (1997). Medical savings accounts: Lessons from China. *Health Affairs, 16*(6), 244–251.

Zschock, D. K. (1979). *Health care financing in developing countries*. Washington, DC: American Public Health Association.

Zwi, A., & Mills, A. (1995). Health policy in less developed countries: Past trends and future directions. *Journal of International Development, 7*(3), 299–328.

12

Management and Planning for Public Health

ANDREW GREEN AND CHARLES COLLINS

What Is management?

This chapter focuses on an area essential for all parts of public health—management. Management in the health field has an unfortunate reputation. It is often regarded as an unnecessary activity that at best diverts resources from the real front-line activities of providing health care or preventing ill health. At worst it is seen as interfering in these activities in an unhelpful and bureaucratic manner. When working well, its presence is not noticed; when it is not, it is a likely scapegoat. In this chapter a more balanced perspective on management will be sought. This will begin by asking what management really is.

The key to understanding the meaning of management is the relationship between resources and objectives. Management is a process of making decisions as to how resources will be generated, developed, and used in pursuit of particular organizational objectives.[1] It is hard to deny the need for such decisions, given the fact that resources (both financial and real resources such as professional staff, medical supplies, and transport) are limited.

How these limited resources are deployed is critical. Decisions are needed at a macro level within a health service as to how resources are allocated among different areas of activity, and at a more operational level among different approaches to the delivery of the service. Management is concerned with improving the allocation of such resources. For example, there may be an imbalance between the resources targeted at curative activities versus public health, between

levels of care (primary versus secondary versus tertiary), between disease control programs, between geographic areas, between social or ethnic groups, between spending on different items such as personnel versus drugs, or between allocations of different personnel such as doctors versus nurses.

How such decisions are made is critical, and this in part relates to the question of who manages. Management functions are best carried out by a shared responsibility between staff whose only activity is management and those whose prime function is working as health workers. One critical role of full-time managers is to provide health professionals with the space and resources they require to carry out their roles.

The discussion so far has focused on limited resources and management's key role in responding to this major constraint. However, it is important to recognize other constraints that management has to work with, including political ones (in the widest sense). Managers may respond in different ways to such constraints, including accepting, challenging, or looking for ways of maneuvering around them. Indeed, the success of management is often a function of the creative ability of a manager to work with, rather than accept, constraints. This key attribute of management distinguishes it from administration, which is more related to routine implementation of existing rules and procedures.

The definition of management suggested earlier can give an impression of a technocratic mechanical process. Yet effective management is as much an art as a science. One particular aspect of management often forgotten is its role in dealing with contradictions, a point to be developed later. Indeed we will see that there are no uniform "correct" management approaches.

---

[1]This definition builds on Keeling (1972), as do the differences between management and administration discussed in this chapter.

Management, to be effective, has to recognize the context within which it operates and adapt its approach accordingly. Such contextual factors could include the health situation, degree of political stability, general attitude toward public-sector reforms, and level of economic growth. Solutions that are appropriate in one situation may not work in another. One key message of this chapter is thus to caution against blueprint approaches to management.

The political character of management also needs to be emphasized. It is expressed in two ways. First, although management requires certain technical skills, it inevitably deals with change, which can be threatening to affected groups and thus creates opposition. For management to succeed requires political analysis as well as technical skills. Various techniques have been developed to map attitudes to particular interventions, of which the best known is stakeholder analysis (Brugha & Varvasovszky, 2000). How different groups are involved in management is likely to affect the quality of the management process, speed of decision making, and ownership of resultant decisions and action. For example, consultation may occur at different points in the management process—with different implications. It can be seen as

- seeking views as to priorities and strategies at the beginning of decision making
- seeking views on alternative options once these have been formulated
- seeking views on a formulated plan of action

The later in the process that consultation takes place, the more it may be viewed as a formal and even tokenistic process. The earlier it takes place, the more likely it is to influence the thinking behind the development of management. There are various alternative ways in which consultation can take place, including directly with the stakeholders (e.g., through surveys or focus groups) or indirectly through representative organizations. It can take place through special one-off mechanisms or through ongoing management processes. Each has advantages and disadvantages in terms of the resources and time required and the robustness of the information gathered.

Second, management is not value free. One determinant affecting the particular choice of management approach is the values underpinning the health sector. These could include the following:

- equity
- efficiency
- choice
- gender sensitivity

- transparency and accountability of decision processes
- market values, including the pursuit of profits
- broad participation in decision making
- solidarity

The pursuit and realization of these through management is political in that it affects the interests and views of different groups in society. Furthermore, managers themselves are not value neutral but bring to the job their own political perspectives and positions.

A health sector committed to the pursuit of accountability and transparency is bound to approach its decision-making processes and consultation differently from one that gives less importance to this compared with the pursuit of narrow health care goals or efficiency and cost containment. Closely related to this are differences between approaches to management and planning within the public and private sectors.[2] Although the main difference often suggested is the freedom of maneuver for a manager, we would suggest that the key difference stems from the values and principles that underpin the public and private sectors and in particular their organizational motives. The private (for-profit) sector is aimed at profit maximization and income generation for its owners. This contrasts with the social goals of a public sector whose formal objectives are health promotion and protection, equity and accountability, and, increasingly, efficiency and cost containment. This should suggest different styles of management in the public and private sectors, with the former emphasizing longer-term sustainability, collaborative strategies as opposed to competitive ones, and political debate and negotiation regarding social values. This chapter focuses primarily on public-sector management.

Figure 12-1 sets out a framework for management and the approach taken in this chapter. The chapter follows this schema. It first draws out the important aspects of context, making particular reference to low- and middle-income countries. This is followed by a discussion of the structures within which health care may be organized. We then look at planning as a key activity in management that determines the pattern of activities and services to be developed in order to meet an organization's objectives. The chapter then looks at issues in the management of resources, focusing on finance, staff, transport, and information. It concludes by discussing some

---

[2]Particular aspects of the analysis in this chapter referring to the public sector and its characteristics and contradictions draw on and develop points raised by Stewart and Ranson (1994).

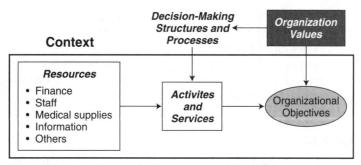

Figure 12-1 Key Elements in Management and Planning.

cross-cutting themes in management. The area of management is very wide, and therefore the analysis in this chapter cannot be exhaustive and is, in parts, necessarily selective.

Health Management and Context

Management is a social process of relations that differs according to the social situation in which it is found. We would not expect the process of management of a public health service in Mali to be the same as management of a multinational corporation based in the United States.

This poses dilemmas for a manager, who needs to recognize that the management process does not occur in a vacuum. The way in which we relate resources to objectives needs to adapt according to the environment in which that management takes place. Yet, there are two difficult issues for the manager. First, the manager has to confront what is called *universalism*—the idea that there is one best way for management to work, irrespective of time, place, or condition (the content of this "one best way" is often similar to an idealized version of how private enterprise is supposed to operate). Second, the relationship between the management process and the context is not easy to understand and respond to. On the one hand, the context has an impact on the management process. Management cannot be simply transplanted from one situation to another. The manager has to read the changing context and assess the most appropriate response. The economic, social, and political context determines the social well-being of communities and the health needs they express, together with the pressures on health care organizations. The context conditions the feasibility and effectiveness of the options available to managers. However, the influences are not just one way. Management can also (and indeed is expected to) have an impact on the environment.

This section analyzes the complex relationship between the management process and the context in which it operates. For organizational purposes, the context is broken down into different areas, such as political, social, and economic. However, one must recognize that these are analytical constructs and do not represent real-life boundaries. The boundaries are overlapping, permeable, and flexible. As Tesch (1990, p. 136) points out, "the entire idea of categorisation as a mental overlay on our world becomes more comfortable when we can think of it as stretchable and soft."

Economic Context

The economic circumstances of a society will condition employment and income and the extent to which individuals and groups can meet their basic needs. These macroeconomic circumstances provide the fundamental backdrop to social well-being, or the lack of it, to which management needs to respond.

The management process is also conditioned by the amount and type of resources available to managers. The flow of resources to, and within, the health sector reflects the country's economic circumstances (e.g., economic growth and amount of government taxation) and resource allocation decisions. The flow of resources has an important impact on the way in which managers are able to work through different options and within constraints.

The economic context does not necessarily change the nature of management in terms of the relationship between resources and objectives. However, the practicalities of management in terms of resource availability and the feasibility and range of management options are affected by the economic context.

Social Context

The broader processes of social change set the scene for the health context in which managers work. For example, unemployment, aging of the population, and migration all raise social and health issues, placing new demands on the health sector. At the same time, social factors condition the feasibility and effectiveness of options. For example, although managers may seek to develop community participation, the feasibility of this will depend on factors such as past experiences of community participation, geographic settlement patterns, and the degree of social homogeneity. Exhibit 12-1 shows two examples from Nepal and Brazil of contextual impact on health management.

Political Context and Public Sector

The political framework in which the public sector operates is also important, with three key issues that are explored in the following subsections.

Public Service Orientation, Corruption, and Patronage

There is an underlying assumption that the management process is concerned with health and health care objectives for the public. To define these is a difficult enough task given the contradictory interests of social and political groups in society. Yet public-sector managers constantly face a contradiction between this public service role and private gain through the public sector in four interrelated ways (Green & Collins, 2003):

- *Corporate gain:* Private companies often profit from the public sector, of which obvious examples are pharmaceutical, construction, and information technology companies. Tax concessions or public-sector training for the private sector may subsidize the private medical industry. The private sector may also be able to capture those public agencies designed to regulate it.

- *Corruption:* Illegal and unethical use of public resources for private gain can take many forms, from bribes to theft, and can have an adverse effect on government activities. It is important to note that corruption is not the preserve of developing countries. As Szeftel (1998) points out, "those looting the African State can only envy the size of the 'pot' available to those in other countries."

- *Patronage:* Public resources may be used to strengthen the political position of a patron or political leader. Complex networks of patronage can emerge and sustain themselves, particularly through the manipulation of employment (Collins, Omar, & Hurst, 2000).

- *Professionalism:* Although its contribution to standards and the quality of care can be a positive attribute, professionalism can also lead to factionalism and the manipulation of public resources to favor the interests of particular professional groups to the detriment of the public interest.

Integrity and Cohesion of the Public Sector

Public-sector management takes place in a system that is not always cohesive. This is particularly an issue in some developing countries. The impact of neocolonial domination, economic crises, political conflict, famine, and national disasters can lead to a disintegration and fragmentation of state authority. These interrelated factors affect the public sector's capacity to generate and use resources to meet health needs.

Exhibit 12-1   Social Context and Health Management

Case 1: Community Involvement and Resource Flows in Nepal
In Nepal, recent legislation stipulated an increased health role for village development committees (VDCs). Research in two rural VDCs showed a correlation between the extent to which lower caste members were represented on the VDCs and community contributions to health centers (Bishai, Niessen, & Shresta, 2002). It would suggest that an option for managers is to look for greater community involvement as a way to increase resources. However, the interaction between management and context also shows that a manager's capacity to increase community involvement is socially conditioned.

Case 2: Local Context and Decentralized Health Management in Brazil
Research analyzed the factors that condition the effectiveness of decentralized health management in three Brazilian municipalities. The study identified various contextual factors, including political patronage, different ethical notions of acceptable practices, and differing commitments of staff to the localities. While showing the impact of context on the management process, the study also raises the role of managers in influencing that context by referring to the "space for the formal health system to influence local social organisation and political culture and offer a potential for change" (Atkinson et al., 2000, p. 632).

Structural Change of the Public Sector

The public sector in many countries is undergoing significant change. Health sector management and planning has been part of that change, as witnessed by the two major waves of international health reform affecting developing countries—the Alma Ata primary health care (PHC) movement and the more recent market-based reforms (discussed in Chapter 11). Table 12-1 identifies potential implications these broader changes have had on the role and operation of health sector management in developing countries.

The management changes outlined in Table 12-1 have been mediated by other factors and have had different impacts both between and within country health systems. First, alternative health sector approaches, drawing their inspiration from the PHC approach, have continued to emphasize, for example, the importance of citizenship, equity, and social justice and focused on community participation in health systems decision making. This can generate contradictions for management (Flynn, 1997). For example, market-based strategies of service delivery emphasizing individual customer choice may contradict more citizen-based strategies based on community participation and collaborative relations within the public sector. Second and quite different to the first point, corruption and patronage frequently maintain a stranglehold on health management and planning. Third, capacity for change in many developing countries is limited in terms of the prevalence of informal arrangements in the economy and public sector and the scarcity of general administrative and managerial skills and systems (Schick, 1998). The result is often a changing blend of different approaches, providing a muddled, confused, and contradictory character to public-sector management. At times, a thin veneer of reform fails to disguise a cumbersome bureaucracy bent on corruption and patronage. At other times, purposive action by dedicated health staff overcomes strong constraints to provide health care to communities.

Table 12-1	Health Sector Change and Management
Management Change	**Examples**
New management responsibilities	The introduction of competitive relations, contracting, voucher systems for service users, and market research to assess customer responses generates new responsibilities for managers.
New management skills	The introduction of the above responsibilities requires new skills in areas such as contracting, customer relations, and quality assurance techniques.
New management boundaries	The introduction of public-private joint ventures, contracting out to the private sector, and the use of competitive markets has led to a blurring of the distinction between the public and private sectors. This suggests new boundaries for public-sector managers, with implications for management values and relations.
Changing management actors	Reforms can lead to greater diversity within the health system as public-sector facilities gain semiautonomous status and private-sector facilities (both nonprofit and for profit) become involved in health care. Managers need to take note of this diversity in developing a range of relations from collaboration to competition.
Changing management objectives and values	Efficiency and health facility financial survival and growth can eclipse objectives and values based more on social justice and equity. For some, the generation of profit or financial surplus becomes an accepted objective of management action.
Changing management structures, systems, and processes	Management structures, processes, and systems associated with the private sector have been introduced into the public sector—for example, performance-based incentives in pay structures and competition between health facilities.
New management options	Reforms in many countries have opened up the option of contracting out service provision to the private sector, as opposed to internal service provision.
Dealing with new challenges and contradictions	Decentralization has been associated in some countries with the requirement that health facilities be financially self-sufficient. Managers face the challenge of simultaneously ensuring the continuity of health care provision, meeting equity objectives, and generating resources for institutional survival.

International Context

The international economic and political context has an important effect on the national and local economic, social, and political processes of a country through, for example, investment, interest rates on debt repayments, and trade. The growth of the international policy presence of the World Bank during the 1980s and 1990s had an important impact on health management reform in developing countries. The powerful financial presence of international donors can leave health ministries in a dependent relationship, although there are cases (such as in Ghana) in which they have developed a relatively autonomous position. The development of budget support, Poverty Reduction Strategy Papers (PRSPs) and sector wide approaches (SWAps) includes changes in the relationship between national governments and international agencies.

The general point raised by this second section is the importance of understanding the interrelationship between context and management action. Managers and management analysts need to interpret the wide range of changing and complex contextual factors that influence the way in which management is actually conducted in the health system. At the same time, managers can be proactive; they are not powerless in affecting the context and taking action to change organizational culture and organizational practice (Atkinson et.al., 2000, Grindle, 1997;). There is a margin of maneuverability in which they can operate, which varies in time but allows purposive action to be developed. Performance can be improved; Grindle (1997), for example, has focused on organizational culture and those aspects of an organization that lead to good performance. These are an organizational mission and a strong sense of attachment to this among staff; good management relations, such as fairness and teamwork; positive expectations concerning staff performance; and institutional autonomy in staff management.

Organizing

An important management function is developing the organizational structure. This refers to the way work is assigned, both vertically and horizontally, together with the formal framework of links with other organizations and groups. In reviewing this organizing function, several points need to be emphasized. First, health managers need to review the full range of structural changes open to the organization. For this purpose, we present a framework setting out the dimensions of a review of the organizational structure. The actual role of managers in structuring an organization will depend on their authority within the organization and the significance of the structural issue to the organization. Second, in deciding on organizational structure, managers need to take into account contextual factors, such as the staff capacity, the health policy, and the overall government structure. Third, there is a need to secure a balance between two factors. On the one hand, managers have to keep the organizational structure under review and implement necessary changes. However, structural changes are not the only component of change. They are just one factor to be considered and balanced against changes in resources, systems, values, and skills. On the other hand, managers need to recognize that structural changes can be both expensive in resource use and disruptive to staff motivation and service delivery. Change should also not be used to mask more difficult and controversial issues of resource availability or health policy content.

Managers usually inherit an established structure. This section therefore takes the form of a review of organizational structure, indicating the key issues and options that managers can take. For illustration, we refer to ministries of health, although the framework could be adapted to decentralized health authorities or health facilities. Three overlapping dimensions of the organizational structure will be reviewed:

- center-periphery relations
- links with other organizations and groups
- internal hierarchy and division of labor

These dimensions relate system-level issues with more microlevel issues, and reference may be made to Chapter 11 on health systems to understand the issues in greater depth.

Center-Periphery Relations

A ministry of health (MOH) is organized according to relations that link the center to the periphery. This raises important dimensions of geographic decentralization, purchaser-provider relations, and delegated semiautonomy.

Decentralization

Authority, resources, and responsibilities may be deconcentrated to lower administrative offices over which the center maintains line management control. In contrast, the same transfer can be made to a devolved level of government over which the center has no line management authority. In this case, the local or regional government is usually multifunctional and will have its own form of appointment or election and its own sources of revenue. One would normally expect devolved governments to have more decision space than local administrative offices, although this is not always the case (Bossert, 1998).

Purchaser-Provider Relations

As explained in Chapter 11, health sector reforms have shifted away from organizationally integrated and hierarchically structured systems to a separation between the purchaser organization, which has the finance and determines the needs, and the provider, responsible for service provision. The separation is intended to increase cost containment, improve efficiency, and remove decisions on service provision from political and professional self-interest. The separation allows the introduction of contracts and quasi-markets into health care—which are supposed to improve effectiveness and efficiency—and the introduction of the private sector through public funding and private-sector provision.

Delegated Semiautonomy

Delegated semiautonomy involves the transfer of semi-autonomous authority to manage an organization. Its most common form is in hospitals organizationally attached to a health ministry. They may be managed by a board that is only partly appointed by the ministry; staff may be hospital (not ministry) employees while the hospital has powers of staff appointment, revenue generation, determination of salaries, and purchasing authority. This delegation can take the form of a purchaser-provider separation and be executed through a contract that formalizes the hospital's responsibilities and the ministry budget allocations to the hospital. Another form of purchaser-provider separation together with delegated semiautonomy occurs when the whole operational side of health care is taken out of the ministry and located in a separate health service structure. This is the case formally in the Ghana Health Service, illustrated in Figure 12-2. The ministry contracts with the provider organization, the Ghana Health Service, which is internally deconcentrated through regional and district levels. Outside this system is the devolved system of elected district assemblies, although these do not have principal provider roles.

On the one hand, managers should have a responsibility for developing the center-periphery relations, or at least be consulted as important stakeholders in the process of organizational change. On the other, these sorts of change are linked to important changes in organizations and the managerial process, as suggested in Exhibit 12-2.

Links with Other Organizations and Groups

Each organizational dimension involves elements of contemporary health policy. Private-sector growth requires organizational links with government such as joint ventures, contracting out, and policy consultation. Community participation raises issues of how the community will be organizationally linked to the MOH. Many developing countries depend on international organizations, both bilateral and multilateral, for significant financing of the health sector and develop important relations around health policy formulation and implementation. The organizational relation can take the form of aid agencies developing links with parts of the health care system when they take responsibility for financing particular disease control programs or particular geographic zones. The more recent development of the SWAp has led to organizational linkages between international donors and the MOH to develop health policy frameworks.

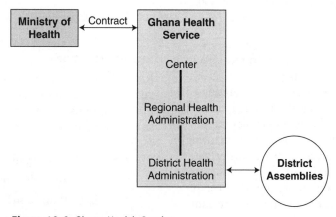

Figure 12-2 Ghana Health Service.

Exhibit 12-2   Center-Periphery Relations and Examples of Management Change

Decentralization and Management

It might be thought that decentralization would lead to improved local health staff motivation through, for example, an improved sense of ownership, greater links with the community, and the general satisfaction from greater authority at the local level. However, a number of studies suggest a more complex situation. A review of health sector decentralization in the Philippines and Zambia by Bossert and Beauvais (2002) noted both positive and negative impact on staff morale. McIntyre and Klugman (2003) have noted problems of staff morale in the area of reproductive health services and decentralization in South Africa; these included the "uncertainty created by the ongoing health sector restructuring" (p. 116), lack of being valued, and the confused lines of accountability. Lakshminarayanan (2003) sees devolution in the Philippines as leading to lower salaries and limited career paths and thereby resulting in staff demotivation, poor morale, and declines in the quality of care.

Purchaser-Provider Separation, Contracting, and Management

The introduction of purchaser-provider separation and contracting requires the development of new skills and systems, such as contract monitoring and evaluation. According to Mather, contracting "strengthens opportunities for quality control and concentration of resources on supervision and compliance" (Mather, 1989, as cited in Walsh, 1995, p. 112). Whether purchasers in developing countries have this capacity is another matter. For example, Abramson's (2001) study of the Costa Rican Social Security Fund's monitoring and evaluation of a contract with a health provider cooperative is informative, showing an unsophisticated system of rating and a deficient relationship between indicators and contract objectives. Mills and Broomberg (1998, p. 25) note "fairly extensive evidence of very weak government capacity to monitor the performance of both for-profit and not-for-profit contractors." Using formal and elaborate contract procedures can lead to greater transaction costs and be considered inappropriate to contracting of primary care activities in developing countries. Not only may purchasers have a low capacity for developing contracts in detail, but also primary care activities are more difficult to specify and monitor (Palmer, 2000).

Delegated Autonomy and Management

Semiautonomy means that the hospital becomes a delegated institution within the organizational scope of the ministry, while having responsibilities in a number of key management areas:

- In human resource management, this might include the hospital determining its own staff establishment, with some measure of autonomy in recruitment, selection, appointment, conditions of service, rewards, and disciplinary system.
- In financial management, one might expect the hospital to possess the right to formulate and submit its own budget to central government for approval, receive a fixed global budget, obtain grants and loans, raise its own income (e.g., through user fees or billing private health insurance, and income from nonhospital ventures, such as the hospital cafeteria), retain surpluses for use in the hospital, and be responsible for its own internal financial management. (Teaching hospitals may also receive additional allocations from the ministry of education or its equivalent.)
- The hospital may also be free to make and submit plans for capital developments, run its own tendering process, and establish its own arrangements for internal management and organization.
- In logistics management, the hospital may be allowed to maintain (service and repair) its own infrastructure internally or through contract.

This is an extensive range of authority. Although direct control by the ministry might well have stifled the practice of management within the hospital, it cannot be assumed that the mere act of delegating authority will automatically generate the skills and systems to make it work.

The MOH also relates to other government agencies; this is typically required as part of the cross-governmental process of management in relating to ministries such as finance, social affairs, and labor. An important aspect of this is the development of a multisectoral approach to health development. Structuring relationships with special interests, such as the private, for-profit health care sector, forms an important part of consultation. At the same time, the MOH is required to exercise regulatory powers over the same special interests.

Internal Structure

Related to the two dimensions of center-periphery and external relations is the organization's own internal relations and assignment of roles. These consist of four factors:

- heirarchy and spans of control
- relations of authority
- horizontal divisions
- internal linking

Hierarchy and Spans of Control

Organizations usually adopt some form of hierarchical shape consisting of different levels of management. These are recognized levels of authority that have a specific depth of authority and span of vision over the organization; the higher up the hierarchy, the greater the authority and the broader the vision. An organization can adopt different hierarchical shapes, although it is often thought that a flatter organizational shape is more appropriate for effective communication and decision making (Child, 1984). Health ministries may suffer from overextended and tall hierarchies. This can result from bloated bureaucracies and the tendency to confuse public service grading systems with management levels (the number of management levels increases to accommodate new grades). Hierarchies can be made flatter by allowing several grades to occupy the same management levels and by widening the average spans of control, leading to a reduction in management levels (Child, 1984). However desirable it may seem to widen the spans of control, this can be difficult. Attention has to be paid, for example, to the capacity of both managers and subordinates in dealing with widened spans of control together with the nature of the work and environment (Child, 1984).

Relations of Authority

Relations of authority are important in binding the organization together. Health care organizations typically exhibit different forms of overlapping authority, such as strategic, main line managerial, technical, professional, and supervisory (Rowbottom & Billis, 1987). Strategic authority is fundamental to a MOH

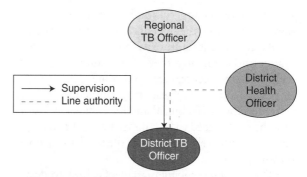

Figure 12-3 Dual Authority Relations. *Source:* R. Rowbottom and D. Billis, *Organisational Design: The Work Level Approach* (Aldershot, England: Gower, 1987), p. 16. Adapted with permission.

and involves decision making with implications for the direction in which the whole or a significant part of the organization is working. One feature of health care organizations is the existence of dual authority relations in which staff are under more than one relation of authority (Rowbottom & Billis, 1987). In Figure 12-3, for example, the district tuberculosis (TB) officer is under the managerial authority of the district health officer but under the technical authority of the TB regional officer.

Dual authority relations can be used to widen spans of control (Rowbottom & Billis, 1987). Figure 12-4 shows how a health manager can increase his or her span of control by appointing a supervisor or support staff to help in the management of staff. The supervisor falls under the main line management control of the health manager, as do the subordinates. Each subordinate, however, is under the joint authority of both the supervisor and main line manager. Since the

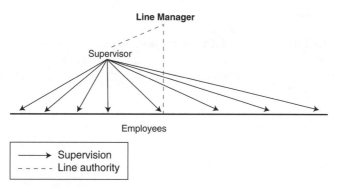

Figure 12-4 Reducing the Burden of Wide Spans of Control on a Main Line Manager Through the Creation of Supervisory Staff. *Source:* R. Rowbottom and D. Billis, *Organisational Design: The Work Level Approach* (Aldershot, England: Gower, 1987), p. 62. Adapted with permission.

pressure of direct supervision has been taken off the main line manager, the span of control can be widened.

Although dual authority relations may appear strange and confusing, they are common. Increasing health system decentralization through devolution to local government is presenting challenges for authority relations. Technical and hierarchical relations with the center need to be balanced with the strengthened horizontal relations within the local government authority.

The challenge facing managers is how to design authority relations in such a way as to avoid potential confusion. There are two ways of clarifying dual authority situations. First, identification of the different forms of authority being used and ensuring that their different meanings are understood by the individuals can help. For example, the relationship in Figure 12-3 between the regional TB officer, district TB officer, and district health officer is clarified by identifying one superior, the district health officer, as possessing main line managerial authority and the other as holding another form of authority, such as technical supervisory, monitoring, coordinating, or prescribing. A second method would be to specify the areas of management for the exercise of authority. Table 12-2 provides a checklist of key areas of authority to be allocated among the authority holders. Both methods require both a clear specification of authority and responsibilities and a culture of understanding between the persons involved.

Horizontal Divisions

At each managerial level, work has to be assigned to staff within different groupings, such as divisions, departments, and units. This division of work may be based on criteria such as geography (e.g., in a decentralized system), functions (as in planning or national disease control programs), or occupational groupings (as in a nursing department) (Child, 1984). The MOH could be based on a simple logic of planning, doing, and supporting, with directorates of planning (including aid coordination and information systems), health services (including primary health care services, national health programs, and hospital services), and support services (including human resources and financial administration) (Collins, 1994). However, this sort of arrangement can lead to a lack of horizontal links between the directorates and to imbalances, with one directorate being the most powerful. Horizontal divisions may also be seen in hospitals, although these offer a wide range of organizational possibilities depending on factors such as size, interprofessional relations, and range of responsibilities (see, for example, Schulz & Johnson, 1990).

Internal Linking

The previous discussion has focused on internal structures dividing work. This runs the danger of fragmenting the organization. The health organization needs to be brought together and act as an integrated whole (Child, 1984). In part this is ensured through the operation of strategic authority. Strategic policy authority and resource allocation flow downward, maintaining vertical integration. At the same time, horizontal collaborative links need to develop between the various divisions, departments, and units in the organization. Typical structural arrangements that may be employed to do this include the following:

- job descriptions to specify lines of authority in the particular job in addition to job liaison responsibilities and membership of teams

Table 12-2	Checklist for Determining the Split of Management Functions in Dual Authority Situations		
		Exercised by	
Management Functions	**District Health Officer**	**Regional TB Officer**	**Others**
Appointment			
Induction and training			
Performance review			
Pay and grading			
Dismissal, suspension, transfer			
Responsibilities and organization			
Methods and standards			
Policies and programs			
Resources and budgets			

Source: R. Rowbottom and D. Billis, *Organisational Design: The Work Level Approach* (Aldershot, England: Gower, 1987), p. 16. Adapted with permission.

- organizational devices, such as interdepartmental committees and task groups, in addition to specific link responsibilities assigned to staff
- matrix systems (e.g., staff may belong to the basic departments in the organization in addition to specific task units and projects)

Planning

Like the more general management function, planning does not have a good reputation in many parts of the health sector.[3] Its record is not good, with plans often not being implemented. The reasons for this are varied but frequently include top-down, rigid, and often bureaucratic centralist processes; a failure to relate planning processes to other decision-making processes such as budgeting; and a failure to involve key groups, including health service managers, professional groups, and users in planning. These criticisms should not, however, be interpreted as an inevitable failure of planning, but rather as a recognition of the need to develop systems appropriate to the particular health care needs and context of a country. This section looks at various background planning issues and then an overview of the planning cycle.

Why Plan?

Planning is an essential element in management and is concerned with making decisions today to influence the future. It is a response to the dilemma that faces organizations, of an inevitable shortfall in resources compared with health needs and hence the need to make choices between competing uses for the resources, that is, to set priorities.

Three other critical issues underpin the importance of planning. First, is the (changing nature of health and health care). Decisions on resource usage need to take account of likely future changes to health needs, resources, and potential health service strategies and technologies. Health need changes include both new diseases, such as HIV/AIDS or, more recently, SARS, and changes in the relative prevalence of particular problems as a result of epidemiologic or demographic transition. Variations on this include the growth of multidrug-resistant strains of, for example, TB. Resource changes that need considering include both financial forecasts and the availability of key resources, in particular, health professionals. For many countries, for example, it would appear likely

that international migration of key staff such as doctors and nurses, may lead to critical future shortages unless appropriate policies are developed now. The last area of forecasting relates to future technology developments and their impact on the health sector.

Second, as we have seen, decisions about priorities take place within a social and political context that will vary between countries and within countries over time.

The third issue is the recognition that the current allocation of resources within the health sector is not optimal, as discussed earlier. Planning is therefore not just concerned with dealing with changes in the future, but also with addressing current problems in a way that will have effects in the future. Shifts in resources will lead to a more effective and efficient use of resources.

What Is Planning?

The discussion so far has assumed a general understanding of what is meant by planning. There are, however, different approaches to, and types of, planning. In particular, we can contrast strategic (or allocative) and operational planning. *Strategic planning* aims to provide an open and formalized process for making these difficult decisions as to which health needs will be met by the limited resources and how. It therefore attempts to provide a broad direction of travel for the health sector. A formal definition is given by Green (1999, p. 3):

> a systematic method of trying to attain explicit objectives for the future through the efficient and appropriate use of resources, available now and in the future.

The important components of this and other similar definitions are as follows:

- where one is going (objectives)
- with what (resources)
- how (efficient and appropriate implementation)
- when (future)
- the degree of formalization (explicitness, systematic, and method) about the process

Operational planning (also known as activity planning) focuses on the detail of implementation by setting out time frames for activities in the short term. In practice the two should be linked, and often there will be elements of both within any particular plan document. A conceptual difference between the two is helpful, however.

---

[3]This section draws on Green (1999).

One criticism of planning is that it is seen as being unfeasible during periods of uncertainty or instability. However, the reverse can also be argued—that it is itself a means of dealing with uncertainty, while retaining a strategic direction. However, it needs to be sufficiently flexible to do this.

There are various common misperceptions about planning that need to be addressed. Table 12-3 sets these out with counter views.

How Would Decisions Be Made Without a Planning System?

In all organizations, decisions are made as to how resources will be used for the future. However, these are not necessarily made in an open, explicit, and *planned* way. There are four potential ways in which decisions may be unsatisfactorily approached. First, they may be avoided, resulting in the status quo prevailing. This failure to face up to the challenge of making decisions is frequently encountered—and unsatisfactory. The second approach is when a small, elite group makes decisions, but in a closed and nonaccessible manner. Such decisions are likely to be suboptimal because they fail to consult widely and obtain the advantages of better information and ownership of resultant decisions. The third approach, common in the health sector, is when the professionals who deliver the services effectively force decisions through their current actions and their power base. The difficulty with this approach is that currently popular specialties may be able to attract funding at the expense of other services. Public health, geriatrics, and mental health are likely to be disadvantaged at the expense of specialties such as surgery, yet this may not reflect the health needs or priorities of a country. The last unsatisfactory alternative is when decisions are made by donor agencies in the absence of adequate national processes.

None of these approaches is satisfactory. As such, planning as an open, formal process is needed, and we turn now to the structures and processes by which this can be ensured.

Planning for Health and the Health Sector

The arguments for a government lead in planning hinge on whether health care is viewed as a special good for which the normal market mechanisms are not appropriate (e.g., because of equity implications or because of their public-good nature). The following discussion takes the widely held position that (1) at a minimum the state has a responsibility to set and regulate policies and (2) will continue to provide certain key health care services for the foreseeable future.

Historically, planning in the public sector has tended to focus on the state's own health care services. It is becoming more widely recognized however, that planning by government needs to recognize the actual and potential inputs (both positive and negative) of other health care agencies, such as the private sector and nongovernmental organizations (NGOs). This calls for the development of new policy and planning tools to implement such strategies (see, for example, Bennett et al., 1994). This is also of increasing importance with the development of strategic plans for SWAps. Second, although we tend to label plans in the health sector as *health* plans, in reality they tend to focus on *health care,* with little recognition of the positive and negative effects of other (non-health-care) agencies on health. Genuine *health* plans need to broaden out and incorporate appropriate actions related to other sectors.

The changes in the structure and roles of government that have been taking place in many health sectors in recent years will often require changes in the government planning approach. In particular, the increasing number of other health care providers that are not directly managed or controlled by one government agency and the decentralization of authority mean that governments need to develop new ways of achieving change in providers other than those that they directly manage. New forms of incentives

Table 12-3	Misperceptions About Planning
Misperception: Planning is. . .	**But. . .**
About the production of plans	Planning is concerned with change, not documents
About capital budgets	Planning should also focus on recurrent budgets
Only concerned with projects	Projects are only one way of achieving change
A highly technical and specialist activity	Much planning is common sense
Carried out by specialist planners	Planning needs to be shared by a wide group of actors
An objective and neutral activity	Planning involves value judgments

Source: A. Green, *An Introduction to Health Planning in Developing Countries,* 2nd ed. (Oxford, England: Oxford University Press, 1999), pp. 300–301. Adapted with permission.

and regulatory powers are needed in contrast with the traditional managerial command-and-control approaches. It also implies that there is a greater onus on the lead government agency to provide overall policy frameworks for the health sector that specify roles for other agencies.

Approaches to Planning and Relationship to the Context Within Which It Occurs

Various different approaches to planning are possible. The following are four contrasting approaches, although it is important to note that they are not mutually exclusive.

1. *Problem-solving reactive approaches versus longer-term needs assessment.* Planning can focus on existing problems and try to identify solutions to these. A well-known example of such an approach was that used in Ghana (Cassels & Janovsky, 1995), and techniques have been developed to assist planners and managers in problem identification and solving, including problem tree and fish-bone analysis (Thunhurst & Barker, 1999). One danger with such an approach is that its focus on current problems may detract from concern about longer-term needs assessment.

2. *Structured logical frameworks versus looser strategic directional approaches.* In recent years a number of organizations, and in particular donor agencies, have adopted an approach to planning (generally projects) using logical frameworks (logframes) that set out in a very structured manner a hierarchy of objectives and activities together with means of identifying whether they have been achieved, and the potential future risks or assumptions. Such an approach can be contrasted with a looser strategic plan.

3. *Geographically focused plans versus organizational plans.* Plans may focus on an organization such as a hospital or take a geographic approach in which an administrative level such as a district develops a plan for the population of that area.

4. *Health plans versus program plans versus project plans.* Plans may be developed at the widest level for all activities and services, or for particular programs (such as reproductive health or TB), or at the most focused level, for specific projects that are time-bound interventions.

The appropriate approach to planning will depend heavily on the context in which the planning occurs. As an extreme example of this, the presence of conflict or an emergency situation will affect planning. For example, in Sierra Leone during the recent civil war, quarterly plans were set recognizing the inability to take a longer-term strategic view during this period.

Planning and Organizational Levels

Planning occurs, or should occur, at all levels in the health system, as illustrated in Figure 12-5. As decentralization policies are implemented, it is important that there is a clear expression of the relative planning responsibilities of the different levels of the health system. Table 12-4 gives an example of the division of responsibilities in a two-level system.

Types of Planning Time Scales

Planning, as we have seen, focuses on actions related to the future. However, decisions have to be made as to the time scale. For many planning systems a period of 5 years has been taken as the standard time frame. However, some health systems are finding this too rigid and are moving toward a rolling process of planning as exemplified in Figure 12-6, where each year the plan period (in this example, 3 years) is rolled on by a year. To maintain an overall set of strategic direction, this is often combined with a long-term perspective plan that sets out a very broad set of policies or direction of strategic travel.

Planning timetables need to take account of both the need for wide consultation at different stages of planning and the fact that planning at each level (e.g., district) needs to link to planning both at higher and lower levels and other parts of the overall system (e.g., local government plans).

Elements of Planning

Figure 12-7 sets out diagrammatically the health planning spiral, which shows the various stages involved in planning. Two general points need to be made. First, conceptually, it is a *spiral* rather than a *cycle*. Second, it refers to a process rather than a chronological sequence. Several activities may be occurring at the same time. Each of these stages in planning will be briefly introduced.

Situational Analysis

The situational analysis step assesses the current situation and projected future changes to it. It also provides a useful mechanism for getting a planning team

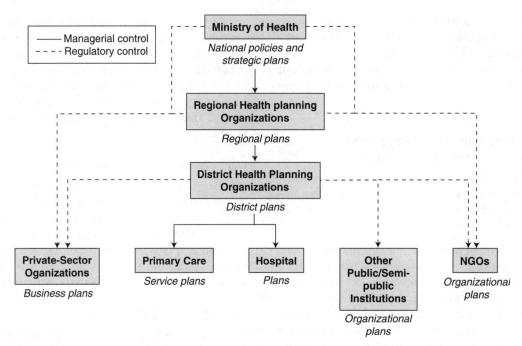

Figure 12-5 Planning at Different Organizational Levels. *Source:* A. Green, *An Introduction to Health Planning in Developing Countries,* 2nd ed. (Oxford, England: Oxford University Press, 1999), p. 36. Adapted with permission.

working well together early in the planning process and for opening up the process to a wider group of agencies and individuals. Table 12-5 sets out key information needs related to both the current situation and likely future trends.

A SWOT (strengths, weaknesses, opportunities, and threats) analysis may also be used (see Figure 12-8). This forces attention on internal and external aspects of institutions and is more suited to assessing an institution such as a commercial firm, but there may be occasions when this provides a useful format.

Priority Setting

The second stage sets priorities for the organization, in the light of competing needs and limited resources. Setting priorities is perhaps the most critical and hardest planning stage and yet cannot be avoided. Priority setting has become one of the areas in which health sector reform has focused through development of essential or minimum packages. For the state providing an overall strategic plan, these need to be sufficiently broad to allow for local variations as a result of differing needs. Underpinning all of the issues

Table 12-4	Example of the Division of Responsibilities Between Center and Periphery	
Central Functions	**Joint Activities**	**Local Functions**
Broad policy leadership	Monitoring and evaluation jointly with central level	Local needs assessment
Resource generation and allocation		Development of local plans
Donor coordination		Implementation of local plans
Liaison with central ministries		
Coordination of local plans		
Planning of central specialist services		
Human resources planning		
Technical planning support		
Legislation		

Source: A. Green, *An Introduction to Health Planning in Developing Countries,* 2nd ed. (Oxford, England: Oxford University Press, 1999), p. 287. Reprinted with permission.

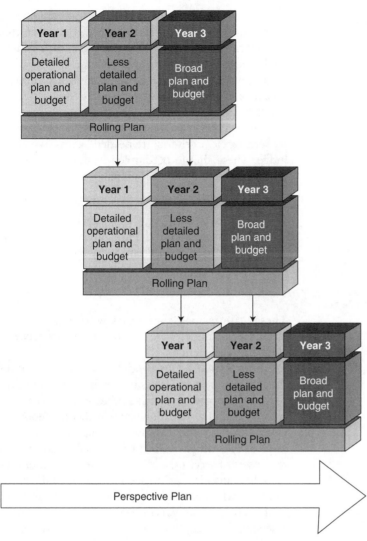

Figure 12-6 Three-Year Rolling Plan and Long-Term Perspective Plan.

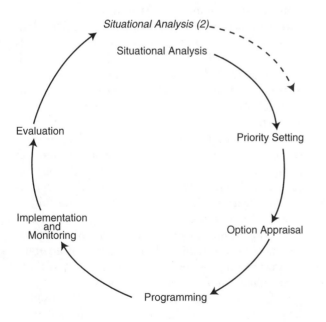

Figure 12-7 The Planning Spiral. *Source:* A. Green, *An Introduction to Health Planning in Developing Countries,* 2nd ed. (Oxford, England: Oxford University Press, 1999), p. 31. Reprinted with permission.

Table 12-5	Key Components of a Situational Analysis
Population Characteristics	
Demographic information Religious, educational, and cultural characteristics	
Area Characteristics and Infrastructure	
Geographic and topographic situation Infrastructure Socioeconomic situation Public- and private-sector structures	
Policy and Political Environment	
Overall national policies Existing health policies Political and ideological environment	
Health Needs	
Medically perceived health needs Community-perceived health needs	
Services Provided by, and Plans of, the Nonhealth Sector	

Health services
    Service facilities
    Service utilization
    Service gaps
    Health service organizational arrangements
Resources
    Financial resources
    Personnel
    Buildings, land, equipment, and vehicles
    Other supplies	

Efficiency, Effectiveness, Equity, and Quality of Current Services	

Source: A. Green, *An Introduction to Health Planning in Developing Countries,* 2nd ed. (Oxford, England: Oxford University Press, 1999), p. 138. Reprinted with permission.

Strengths (internal)	Weaknesses (internal)
Opportunities (external)	Threats (external)

Figure 12-8 SWOT Analysis Framework.

regarding how priorities can be set is a tension between attempts to make decisions on priorities as rigorous as possible and recognition of the essentially political or value-laden nature of such decisions.

What Should Priorities Be Based On? At one level the most obvious answer to the question of the basis for prioritization is that priorities should be set on the basis of greatest health need. However, this in itself raises various further questions, such as how health need is perceived. In particular, is a broad or a narrow view of health taken, how is health need measured, and should priorities focus on health needs or health care needs?

To be as open as possible in the process of priority setting, clear criteria are needed against which to judge. These should be derived from overall policy and could include the following:

- the maximum health gain within available resources (efficiency), which may be expressed as a combination of the magnitude of the potential impact of different interventions
- the equity effects
- public demands

These criteria may sometimes work against each other. For example, there may be a trade-off between equity and efficiency.

Who Should Set Priorities? A critical issue within the planning process relates to who has the right or responsibility to set priorities and at what level in the national health system. For example, there are good arguments for any of the following groups to be involved in priority setting: health professionals, administrators, users of services, and, more widely, communities or politicians. The priorities set will depend significantly on who makes them. Techniques of stakeholder analysis (Brugha & Varvasovszky, 2000) are useful in assessing the strength of different groups in society.

Establishing Priorities Within a Planning Framework. It is important that the planning process makes explicit how priorities are to be set. The planning process needs to satisfy various criteria. It needs to allow a broad view of health, rather than health care alone. Second, it needs to find an appropriate balance between decision making at the national and local levels that reflects the degree of decentralization. Third, the process itself needs to be transparent; stakeholders with an interest in influencing the priorities set need to be able to understand the process and recognize where their legitimate entry into the process can occur. Finally, it needs to end up with objectives that are feasible. A common difficulty with objectives is encountered when everything is viewed as high priority, meaning effectively that no real priorities have been set. Indeed, a good test of a robust priority-setting system is one that makes clear those areas that are not viewed as high priority.

Various processes and techniques can be used to set priorities. These include economic appraisal, multivariable decision matrices, and Delphi techniques. The resource allocation processes from the center to lower health service levels are also an important vehicle for ensuring that broad priorities (and particularly those of equity) are reflected in the budgets allocated for service delivery.

Economic appraisal is frequently suggested as an important technique for setting priorities in that it has the potential for combining consideration of health gain and resources. The 1993 *World Development Report* (World Bank, 1993) suggested that priorities should be set using cost per disability-adjusted life year (DALY). However, arguments against the narrow use of such techniques include the lack of appropriate data and the potentially disempowering nature of economic appraisal (see, for example, Barker & Green, 1996). Furthermore, there is a danger in assuming that economic appraisal is value free, when there are a number of implicit values within it, such as the weighting between disability and life gain (in a DALY), the weighting given to years of life at different ages, and the choice of discount rates.

Multivariable decision matrices provide an alternative approach in which any number of criteria can be incorporated and the information used either quantitatively or qualitatively. Figure 12-9 gives an example. Caution is needed in the use of such tools, however, which can easily mask implicit value judgments such as relative weightings between the criteria.

The end result of a priority-setting process should be a set of clear objectives for an organization. Although different terms are often used by different organizations for objectives (e.g., *goals, purpose, aims, objectives, targets)*, the important feature is that they are structured in a hierarchy with, for example,

- broad overall health goals achieved through x
- Specific health aims related to particular health problems to be achieved by x
- Health sector activity objectives to be monitored by x
- Targets that are milestones

Figure 12-10 sets out an example of a hierarchy of objectives.

The mnemonic SMART is often applied to objectives to suggest that they should be

- specific
- measurable
- attainable
- relevant
- time bound

Option Appraisal

For each priority area, there may be various strategies that can be followed. The third stage in planning appraises each of the alternatives to determine which is most appropriate according to various criteria. These criteria should include those that underpin economic appraisal techniques (cost and effectiveness) but should include others as well, such as equity, feasibility, and acceptability.

It should be borne in mind that there is a variety of options available to any organization, but particularly to the state, which has various carrots and sticks that it can deploy to encourage or require action by other organizations (see, for example, Bennett et al., 1994). Traditionally in command-and-control planning systems, plans were expected

Allocated Score	Criteria			
	Cost per DALY	Public Demands	Mortality Rates	Disability Rates
4	Measles	AIDS	AIDS	Polio
3	TB	Alcoholism	TB	Alcoholism
2	Malaria		Malaria	
1			Gastroenteritis	

Scoring		
	AIDS	8
	Alcoholism	6
	TB	6
	Measles	4
	Malaria	4
	Polio	4
	Gastroenteritis	1

Figure 12-9 Hypothetical Example of a Multivariable Decision Matrix.

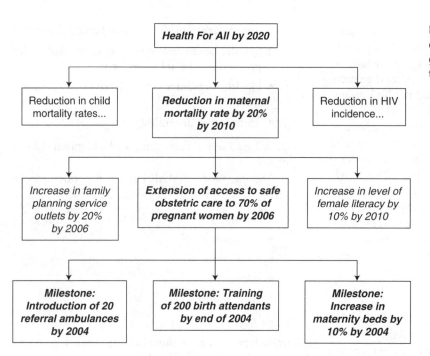

Figure 12-10 Example of the Hierarchy of Objectives. *Note:* Acknowledgment is given to Dr. Nancy Gerein for help with this figure.

to be implemented through managerial commands. With the recognition of the importance of other sectors and providers, a wider range of tools need to be used. Thus, the state may see as one of the options to be appraised the contracting out of services to other, nonstate organizations. Table 12-6 sets out some examples of the tools.

Plans, Programs, Projects, and Services

The next stage is that of programming. The aims and agreed-upon approaches to meeting the organization's objectives are brought together in a document that sets these out with a time frame and financial plan. The level of detail, particularly regarding the budget and time frame, will depend on whether this is primarily

Table 12-6	Examples of Planning Mechanisms and Tools
Resource Related	**Regulation**
Budgeting	Incentives and controls
Resource allocation	Legislation
Health financing flows	Norms and standards of care
Human resource plans	Regulation and licensing of supply of health facilities
Other input planning (e.g., drugs)	Regulation and licensing of health professions
Tax, pricing, subsidy policies	**Public/Private Interface**
External funding support	
Organization and Management	Managed markets
	Contracting of services and outsourcing
Development of health care packages	Privatization of public-sector assets
Organizational restructuring	Nationalization of private-sector assets
Health systems research	
Plan statements	
Projects	
Wider Society	
Policies in health-related sectors	
Development of quasi-public bodies	
Advocacy	
Use of the media	
Source: Based on work done by Jane Shaw.	

strategic or more operational. Table 12-7 sets out the components of a typical plan document.

Logframes (logical frameworks) are often advocated as a means of both ensuring that a logical approach to project design is followed and providing a means of monitoring progress. Figure 12-11 gives an example of a logframe layout.

Implementation and Monitoring

Planning is only useful if it ends up in implementable action. As we have seen, however, planning has a poor implementation record. Reasons cited for poor implementation include the following:

- lack of funds
- lack of relevant resources
- poor timing of inputs
- resistance to change
- neglect of institutional or legal requirements
- unexpected results
- poor coordination
- unforeseen circumstances

Frequently, the *real* cause is poor planning design. Two frequent problems are a failure to recognize the political nature of planning at the design stage and overoptimistic and nonfeasible objectives.

Table 12-7	Possible Outline for a Plan

- Situational analysis, including the health needs or problem being tackled
- Objectives of the plan
- Strategies to meet these objectives
- Resources required, including finance to provide the services, and from where these are to be provided
- Timetable
- Foreseeable constraints or risks

A key activity to improve implementation is monitoring. This requires an explicit time frame for well-specified activities and a clear understanding of who is responsible both for implementation and monitoring of the activities. Techniques such as GANTT charts which set out, in tabular form, activities by expected date of completion. It is also important that monitoring does not end up being viewed as an end in itself but as a means of achieving the set objectives. As such, it is important that only the minimum number of monitoring indicators are chosen and that it is seen as a supportive rather than punitive activity.

This is closely linked to the concept of performance management of an organization, which seeks to identify the progress toward the organization's objectives and any barriers to this.

Objectives	Objectively Verifiable Indicators	Means of Verification	Assumptions/Risks
Goal			
Purpose/Objectives			
Outputs			
Activities	Inputs		

Figure 12-11 Example of a Logframe Layout. *Note:* See Nancholas (1998) for a description of the process.

Evaluation

The final stage of planning involves the evaluation of the plan. Such evaluations may be formative or summative. Evaluations ask questions about outcomes, outputs, and inputs.

Outcomes

- What were the objectives of the activity being evaluated? Were they appropriate?
- Were the objectives set achieved? If not, why not?
- Were any health improvements the direct result of the activity?
- Were there any other effects of the activity?

Outputs

- Were the services provided?
- Were the services appropriate, relevant, and adequate?

Inputs

- Did the resources planned arrive?
- Were they sufficient for the services provided?
- Were the resources turned into services?

The results of the evaluations should be fed into the next round of the situational analysis, hence completing one round of the planning spiral.

Table 12-8	Examples of Political Decisions in Planning
Situational Analysis	
Who chooses the information (e.g., in determining health needs)? Whose view is taken, and what analysis is undertaken (e.g., what groups are taken as the denominator)? What emphasis is placed on the different information?	
Priority Setting	
Whose views are taken? What view of health is chosen and by whom? What criteria for priorities are chosen (e.g., equity versus efficiency)?	
Option Appraisal	
Who chooses, and how, the original options that are appraised? What criteria are chosen, and by whom, for the options?	
Evaluation	
Who is involved in the evaluation? What are the criteria for evaluation?	

Political Aspects of Planning

The preceding has outlined a number of techniques used in developing plans. It is important, however, to recognize that at all of these stages there is a need to consider the political dimension of planning, which is inevitable in a process that is designed to determine who gets what in the health sector (Table 12-8). There are two levels at which planners need to be aware of the political nature of planning as a process. First, planners need to recognize that techniques are rarely completely value free. The *rationalist* model of health care planning tends to downplay this aspect, whereas the *incrementalist* approach emphasizes the political nature of decision making. Second, techniques such as stakeholder analysis and political mapping may be used at different points in the planning cycle to analyze levels of support for different strategies.

Management of Resources

Management, as we have seen, is about resources and how they are generated, combined, and used with a view to achieving objectives. This section looks at how the principal resources—money and staff—are managed. This is followed by some brief general comments on the management of supplies, transport, and information.

Financial Management

A key resource for any organization is, self-evidently, finance, and this section looks at the main elements of good financial management.[4] Finance is, of course, only important in that it allows the hiring of staff and the purchase of goods and services. Good financial management supports the health organization in the achievement of its objectives. As such, it has to be closely linked to other key decision processes and, in particular, planning. Financial management must be viewed as a *means* rather than an *end* in itself.

Resource Generation

Various sources of finance are available to a health service organization; these are explored in Chapter 11.

Resource Allocation

Resource allocation refers to the distribution of resources from a higher level to a lower level in an or-

[4]Acknowledgment is given to Jane Shaw for inputs into this section.

ganization. It is closely related to budgeting but refers to the overall levels of funding rather than specific expenditure plans. Within the public sector, resource allocation from the center is a common feature of the health system, but its importance will depend on the health financing system and the degree of decentralization of resource generation within the health system.

Frequently, resource allocation is based (explicitly or implicitly) on one or more of the following:

- previous allocations
- service or facility patterns and norms
- capital developments and associated recurrent implications
- political profile

These approaches, although potentially non-threatening to existing budget holders, fail to address issues of efficiency and equity. An equity-focused strategy needs to base its resource allocation on an assessment of the needs of particular areas or population groups. Figure 12-12 sets out a conceptual model for such a process. The potential components for allocation are as follows:

- population's size, composition, and health needs
- costs of providing services
- variations in costs between different areas
- costs of activities other than health care, such as research or teaching
- flows of patients across administrative boundaries

Assessment of need is the most significant and hardest to measure, with ingredients including demographic

FAIR: Formula for Allocation of Internal Resources

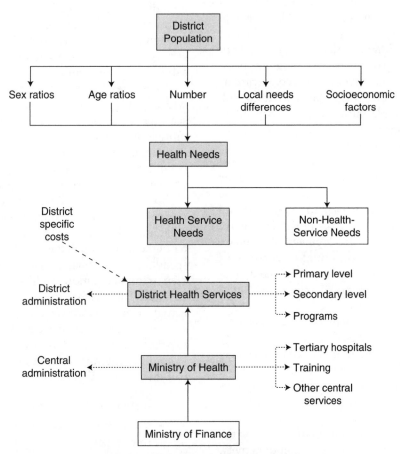

Figure 12-12 Conceptual Model for Needs-Based Resource Allocation. *Source:* Derived from A. Green, *An Introduction to Health Planning in Developing Countries,* 2nd ed. (Oxford, England: Oxford University Press, 1999), p. 221.

factors; morbidity, mortality, and disability; and indicators of deprivation.

There are a number of issues regarding the implementation of such allocation formulas including, most importantly, the availability of information. In some countries it may be necessary to start with very basic allocative formulas based on population before developing more sophisticated formulas.

Budgeting

Budgets are statements of intended expenditure. They should reflect the plans of an institution or service and are vital management tools. There are two main forms of budget:

- *capital/development:* for buildings, large equipment, and vehicles
- *recurrent/revenue:* for running expenses, including salaries and supplies

In addition, there may be separate project budgets, which may combine both of these aspects.

There are two components of a budget: what it is spent on (line items such as personnel, drugs, equipment) and for what purpose (service or institution or geographic area). Within health organizations, budgets may also be set up on the basis of programs (such as maternal health) that cover all aspects of care irrespective of where it takes place. Such program budgets are better for planning because they allow different priorities between programs; however, they are much harder to manage.

Budgets may be set in various ways. The most common is that of historical incrementalism, whereby the previous period budget is increased across the board. Such an approach is easy to administer and nonthreatening; however, it does not reflect major changes in priorities or new developments. A common variant on this involves additional increases to a budget (over and above the historical increment) arising from capital developments such as a new building and its associated service.

A contrasting method is activity-based budgeting, whereby the budget is set based on predicted activity levels. This allows a clear link between the budget and service objectives. An extreme example of this is *zero-based budgeting,* in which no prior assumptions are made, and every item in the budget for each year has to be fully justified.

Such budgeting requires information both on the level of activity and on the costs of a unit of activity. The latter may, of course, change depending on the level of activity and on the relationship between fixed and variable costs.

A possible timetable for budgeting is given in Table 12-9.

Expenditure: Drawing and Disbursing

The next element is that of expenditure against a set budget. Each financial management system will have mechanisms to authorize named officials to incur expenditure, within certain predefined limits and conditions, that reflects the level of decentralized authority.

Expenditure Monitoring and Control

Monitoring of expenditure against the budget throughout the year is an important management function. Critical to this process is a good information system. Each management system will have its own set accounting methods. The system needs to be able to give the manager up-to-date information not only on past expenditure but also on any commitments already made. For managers to understand the real implications of such information, they also need to have an indication of the likely expected profile of expenditure throughout the year so they can discover early enough any variance from the budget to take necessary remedial action. Some resources (such as staff salaries) may be evenly spread; others, however, such as drugs, may be bought in batches and may reflect within-year differences in usage due, for example, to seasonal disease incidence. Capital equipment is even more lumpy in terms of expenditure patterns.

A manager needs to be able to compare actual expenditure against such expected profiles. An example of a simple monitoring tool is given in Table 12-10. It shows a monthly management statement after 9 months of the year. The budget-to-date column shows what might be expected to have been spent one quarter of the way through the year. It is assumed here that spending will be equal each month (which, as we have seen, is unlikely); more sophisticated estimates could be made. The variance columns show the relative (not actual) over- or underspending.

Once managers have identified a projected overexpenditure (or indeed underexpenditure), they need to consider the various options open to them to control this. Potential actions include the following:

- seeking additional funds
- instituting cost-control mechanisms, such as freezing expenditure
- revising service objectives
- reallocating funds from one budget (line item) to another

Table 12-9	Annual Budget Cycle for a Three-Level Deconcentrated Health System
Month	**Activity**
1	Financial year begins.
5	Ministry of health receives provisional annual allocation from central government, together with any special constraints or conditions.
6	Ministry of health issues broad resource allocation guidance to regions on the basis of provisional allocation.
7	Regions issue broad allocations to districts on similar basis.
8	Budget holders develop and return proposals showing the following: • review of service targets in line with plan • estimated expenditure for previous year • estimated expenditure for current year • reasons for under- or overspending • budget proposals for following year, costed and showing how they will meet planned service targets
8	Budgets totaled and reconciled at regional level and then at ministry of health.
9	Adjustments made for the following reasons: • to reflect national policy • to reconcile with other budget proposals • to reflect constraints • to reconcile with central government allocations
9	Discussions with central government.
10	Adjustments with service managers.
11	Informal approval.
12	Government approves budget.
1	Budgets issued to budget holders.

Source: A. Green, *An Introduction to Health Planning in Developing Countries,* 2nd ed. (Oxford, England: Oxford University Press, 1999), Box 11.3. Adapted with permission.

Table 12-10	Monitoring Tool Example

Month: 9	Full-Year Budget ($000)	Expenditure to Date ($000)	Budget to Date ($000)	Variance from Budget to Date (+, underexpenditure; −, overexpenditure) Amount ($000)	Percentage	Projected Year-End Expenditure Projected to Estimated ($000)	Comment
Personnel	600	400	450	+50	+11.1	500	Underspend due to recruitment difficulties
Medical supplies	150	140	112.5	−28	−24.4	160	Earlier epidemic, likely to result in final overspend
Transport	80	75	60	−15	−25.0	95	Earlier epidemic
Utilities	50	10	37.5	+28	+73.3	50	Delays in invoicing
Other	120	100	90	−10	−11.1	100	
Total	1,000	725	750	+25	+3.3	905	Overall underspend projected

To select the appropriate option, the manager needs to have a clear understanding of the reasons for the overspend, since this is likely to give an indication of the best remedial strategy. It is also important that the implications of any remedial actions be viewed against their impact on the organization's objectives. Cost-control mechanisms for example, will have an impact on services in terms of either quantity deliverable, quality, or the efficiency with which they are delivered. The first two of these will be related to the service objectives.

Auditing (Internal and External)

The last element of the financial management process is that of auditing. Internal audit is a process of testing and validating the financial control and accountability systems to ensure they work. This is done by a special department of the organization, which is separate from the normal accountancy group. In external auditing, the accounts of an organization are subjected to independent external scrutiny to confirm that they do not contain errors or hide fraud. For a public-sector organization, such auditing is an important part of the governance of the organization.

Requirements for an Effective and Appropriate Financial Management System

Figure 12-13 sets out a number of critical features of an effective financial management system. Without these aspects there is a real danger that the system will not perform its expected task—that is, to ensure that strategic direction is followed.

Management of Staff

The management of health staff has been a neglected issue in recent years.[5] Attention has tended to focus on reforming health systems through new financing arrangements or organizational changes, such as decentralization. Yet staff costs are a major part of the health budget, and the quality of staff is vital to the effectiveness of health care (Buchan, 2004; Rondeau & Wager, 2001). The development of staff management systems and skills throughout the health system gains greater importance as decentralization and hospital autonomy spread out the management responsibility throughout the health system. It is also becoming increasingly important as international migration and the effects of the HIV/AIDS pandemic

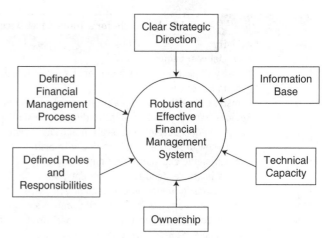

Figure 12-13 Requirements for an Effective Financial Management System.

lead to major staff shortages of key personnel in a number of health systems.

In developing staff management, there are important factors to consider.[6] First, is the problem of the inequitable distribution of health staff. It is often difficult to get health staff to work in the poorer areas, where they lack incentives such as good living conditions and the possibility of private practice. Second, health systems are undergoing important changes, such as decentralization, which has an impact on how health staff are managed (Kolehmainen-Aitken, 2004; Wang et al., 2002). This can mean important changes in civil service arrangements, as set out in Table 12-11. Two further influences on how staff is managed, referred to earlier, are professional authority and power and corruption and patronage.

There are many systems and skills for managing staff, ranging from defining staffing needs and jobs to employing people and developing their performance. The discussion here focuses on a number of key issues and functions.[7]

Staffing Review

Managers need to "a) revise as necessary, the existing personnel structure, b) staff the structure with the most appropriate health workers, and c) keep payroll costs under control" (Kolehmainen-Aitken, 2004, p. 3). These are useful factors for a staffing review. An im-

---

[5]Acknowledgment is given to Tim Martineau for helpful comments on this section.

[6]Useful studies of health human resources are provided by Martineau and Martinez (1997) and Martinez and Martineau (1998).

[7]A more comprehensive and in-depth analysis would cover issues such as employee relations, change management, staff communication, and conflict management.

Table 12-11	Decentralization and Options for Civil Service Structure
Civil Service Option	**Commentary**
Centrally controlled system	Terms for the civil service are centrally controlled and staff are seconded or transferred to local units, as in Papua New Guinea and the Philippines.
Health sector centrally controlled system	Health sector staff are taken out of the national civil service and included in a national system exclusively for health staff, as in Ghana.
A national local government system	All local government units operate under the terms and conditions of a national system that is specifically designed for local government staff.
Local public service commissions	In Uganda, local public service commissions are created, and some form of non-national local service commissions are foreseen in Nepal.
Decentralized unit	The decentralized unit determines the terms and conditions and employs its own staff.
Mixed system	Following decentralization, existing staff are kept as part of the national civil service, while new staff are employed under the new decentralized system, as in Jamaica.

Sources: R.-L. Kolehmainen-Aitken, "Decentralisation's Impact on the Health Workforce: Perspectives of Managers, Workers and National Leaders," 2004, *Human Resources for Health, 2,* p. 5; and C. Collins, *Management and Organisation in Developing Health Systems* (Oxford, England: Oxford University Press, 1994).

portant issue is how the labor force could be used to improve performance in meeting health needs. A review may be undertaken, with key questions about the number of staff employed, possible substitution by technology, and changes in the skill mix and grades currently employed (Strike, 1995). McKee and Healy (2002) and Buchan, Ball, and O'May (2000) refer to this process as reengineering the hospital workforce. A simple technique for defining staffing needs of a health care unit is provided by Kolehmainen-Aitken and Shipp (1990) and involves the definition of job responsibilities and calculation of a standard workload for each person (e.g., number of outpatients attended per day). This is compared with yearly workloads in the health facility to estimate staff required. The possibility of using such planning tools is restricted by the degree of autonomy managers are given, the existence of patronage, the availability of information, the capacity of managers to use the tools, and the willingness of staff to move.

Defining Jobs and Employing

The defining of jobs and staff employment may be viewed as a set of logical steps (Table 12-12). Systematic bias, whether based on gender, family, politics, race, or ethnicity, can stifle the employment process. The definition and use of clear principles and rules and an open and transparent process can make it harder for such bias to occur.

Staff Payment

The issue of payment is related to the staff grading system and form of public service system (see the ear-

lier discussion). Recent health systems changes, such as decentralization, can lead to changes in the source and level of pay. The form of payment may be according to time, physical results produced, individually assessed performance, or a combination of these (Brown & Walsh, 1994). Although payment by time is simple, performance-related pay is both complicated and controversial (Alimo-Metcalfe, 1994; Kessler, 1994). It assumes that staff will work more if their earnings are related to their performance. However, in addition to practical difficulties in measuring performance, this can introduce conflict between staff and counter a teamwork approach. Reliance on material incentives downplays the important motivation staff may derive from the inherent usefulness of their jobs and public service. In fact, the extent to which pay actually acts as a motivator will vary according to the context and the type of staff concerned. For many staff, poor and inequitable pay can be more of a de-motivator than motivator, although low-paid staff may well value more pay. A further controversial area is the extent to which health staff are allowed to earn through practicing privately and how this relates to their public-sector work.

Delegation

Delegation involves transfer, trust, responsibility, tasks, and authority. Delegation is a transfer of authority and tasks between two people or groups of people (Kempner, 1980). It involves entrusting part of your own authority to somebody else (French & Saward, 1984). Although the person receiving the delegation has the responsibility or obligation "to perform tasks

Table 12-12	Steps in the Employing Process
Step	**Commentary**
Job analysis	This is a review of a job to determine the context in which it is performed, relationship with higher-level objectives, job responsibilities, skills required, standards required, and relationship with other jobs. Data are collected, reviewed, and recorded, and managers can use the data for various purposes, including planning staffing need, performance management, writing a job description, recruitment and selection, and defining training and development needs (Schmidt et al., 1992).
Job description	This is a document that sets out the character of a job through a job summary, basic duties, relations with other jobs (accountability, supervision, team membership, and liaison), work conditions (e.g., traveling), background of job holder (e.g., qualifications, experience), training and development in the job, and processes for the review of the job holder's performance (MacMahon, Barton, & Piot, 1992; Schmidt et al., 1992). It is important as a link between staff management functions and in gaining clarity for more effective performance.
Person specification	The person specification links the job analysis and description to the characteristics required of a job holder. This can include physical characteristics (e.g., health history), educational characteristics (e.g., training), skills (e.g., language), and personal characteristics (e.g., motivation). Among its uses are preparing for recruitment and selection and definition of training and promotion exercises.
Recruitment	Through recruitment, managers look to identify candidates for a particular job. Managers need to do such things as decide whether to look inside or outside the organization, ensure employment legislation is respected, conduct initial screening, and draw up a short list.
Selection	The most appropriate person should be selected, although both recruitment and selection can be affected by patronage and corruption. Those involved in selection need to be explicit. Criteria for selection need to be determined, and selection techniques (e.g., interviews, aptitude tests, group tests) defined. The selected candidates need to be informed of the process.
Posting	The new employee needs to be posted to a workplace.
Induction	It is necessary to plan the way in which the new employee is inducted into the post with an understanding of the overall organization, work unit (and particularly the work team), and the particulars of the job (Schmidt et al., 1992).

and account for their satisfactory completion" (Mescon, Albert, & Khedouri, 1985), the person delegating does not lose responsibility for that task (Kempner, 1980). Rather, he or she retains "responsibility for that person's exercise of authority" (French & Saward, 1984, p. 122). The responsibility can also involve authority over resources, and it is important to recognize this in the act of delegation.

The purpose behind the delegation should be clear. It could be used to overcome work overload or underload, to motivate staff, to bring decisions nearer the point of service delivery, or to gain a better understanding of service needs and achieve more timely decisions and increased flexibility and adaptability. Greater ownership among staff may also be achieved with a more participative management style.

Delegation, however, is not easy and has various potential constraints on its effectiveness (see Exhibit 12-3). Limited resources may mean that delegation does not come with authority over resources. Managers may resist losing authority and control;

staff may lack the knowledge, skills, and values to practice delegation. They may also lack motivation where the delegation has no additional incentives and a culture of blame exists in the organization that is not conducive to delegation.

It is important to identify the objectives involved to communicate to staff, monitor the effectiveness of the delegation, and design the means of delegation. There is a concern, however, that managers may delegate because they simply do not like doing a task themselves, they consider the task impossible, or they are displaying favoritism.

The delegation needs to be clearly identifiable in terms of tasks, authority, control over resources, and its limits. A particular issue is the skills, experience, support, and motivation of the person receiving the delegation. Is that person equipped to receive the delegation? A useful concept here is that of staff "maturity" (Hersey, Blanchard, & LaMonica, (1978), which consists of the skills, experience, and willingness to take on new responsibility.

Exhibit 12-3	Staff Interest in Delegated Responsibilities in the Middle East

Research on bureaucracy in Egypt found that "most senior officials did attempt to concentrate as much authority as possible in their own hands; most subordinates did seek to avoid responsibility" (Palmer, Leila, & Yassin, 1989, pp. 149-150). Similar results emerged from interviews conducted in the Ministry of Health in Bahrain (Benjamin, Ahmed, & Al-Darazi, 1997). The research confirmed that lack of delegation was perceived as a key ingredient for efficiency and effectiveness, and its lack as a major problem. Interestingly, the enthusiasm for delegation as a means for improvement was more marked among managers than subordinates.

Performance Management

In the field of staff management, performance management is frequently associated with annual confidential reviews or appraisals that are bureaucratic, routine, and do little to develop performance. Effective performance management requires not only reinvigoration of such yearly events, but also a broader approach of continuous performance management (Table 12-13).

Incentives and Motivation

This is an area in which there has been considerable theoretical debate and which has provided useful indications about possible causes of staff motivation. Theories on motivation, however, often fall short in providing health managers with a comprehensive framework that allows them to understand the wide range of factors that can motivate or de-motivate staff. Furthermore, the list of such factors can be so long that it almost renders itself useless as a managerial guide. Another problem associated with attempts to explain motivation is that different individuals and groups of health staff respond to different factors (Weightman, 1996). Attempts to generalize are not easy, although a general distinction may be made between "satisfiers" and "dissatisfiers" (Herzberg, Mausner, & Snyderman, 1959).[8] The latter are those factors that in themselves do not necessarily motivate but whose

---

[8]For a brief description of Herzberg's approach and its application to a developing country context, see Dieleman et al., (2003).

Table 12-13	Steps in Performance Management	
Steps	**Commentary**	
1. Explain and reinforce the logic of performance management.	Managers explain to staff the organization's performance management and supervision practice.	
2. Understand job context, content, and relations.	Performance management needs to be based on appreciation of the job content and the often complex relations of authority it involves. By understanding job context, managers and staff should recognize the various factors that affect performance.	
3. Agree on performance criteria.	Managers and staff develop a joint understanding about the meaning of "effective work." This agreed standard accompanies an understanding of the conditions that need to be in place (e.g., logistics support, flow of funds, skills) for actual performance to meet these standards.	
4. Compare actual performance with standards.	Managers and staff monitor performance using agreed performance indicators (both quantitative and qualitative).	
5. Discuss and agree on action.	This involves both feedback on performance with dialogue and agreement on the causes of this performance and possible changes required (including agreement on training needs).	
6. Take action and monitor.	Action may need to be taken in areas, such as job context, content, and support. The impact of this action needs to be monitored.	

Sources: R. MacMahon, E. Barton, and M. Piot, *On Being in Charge: A Guide to Management in Primary Health Care* (Geneva, Switzerland: World Health Organization, 1992); R. Bacal, *Performance Management* (New York: McGraw-Hill, 1999); and J. Weightman, *Managing People in the Health Service* (London: Institute of Personnel and Development, 1996).

absence can demotivate and are related primarily to attracting people into jobs and keeping them. Typical examples are pay and security. In contrast, the presence of satisfiers does lead to improved motivation and performance; typical examples are career development and job achievement. The following factors can have a bearing on staff motivation:

- career development
- job characteristics
- working and living conditions
- managerial style and organizational culture
- job rewards

In using such a checklist, managers need to distinguish between the satisfiers and dissatisfiers.

Job characteristics, for example, can be the cause of de-motivation for staff if too many duties are imposed on the job holder or the job lacks variety, scope, and delegated authority and is badly defined and therefore the object of conflict. Job holders may, however, feel that the job is meaningful and contributes to social welfare and solidarity. Staff working in the poorer areas of the country may feel that there are inadequate working conditions (e.g., office accommodation, information technology) and living conditions (e.g., schools). In contrast, transparent and open management, showing an interest in good supervision and communication, staff involvement in policy making and problem solving, good teamwork, and reinforcement of ethical standards can be a positive force. The pattern of rewards and incentives is important and can include the extent to which the basic needs of the health worker are met and are considered equitable, the regularity and security of payment, and nonfinancial rewards such as stability and status of employment. The possibility of career development can also be important.

Supervising

Among the roles of the supervisor are the following (Collins, 1994; Schmidt et al., 1992):

- defining tasks to be carried out and planning their implementation
- providing professional and technical advice
- problem solving and decision making
- ensuring performance standards (technical, ethical, and legal) and providing feedback
- personal counseling and employee motivation
- providing referral, broker, and advocate services

- ensuring appropriate support for the job
- providing training and development support

A distinction may be made between line management authority and supervisory authority. The two may be separated in order to allow the line manager to widen his or her span of control (Rowbottom & Billis, 1987). Depending on the relation between supervisor and line manager, the supervisor can also be involved in disciplinary actions and career development.

Despite its importance, the value of good supervision can be overlooked. Pressures on time and the demoralizing lack of incentives and overall support to managers and health workers can often sideline supervision to a peripheral activity. Yet the importance of effective supervision is well recognized. For example, Trap and associates (2001) recorded the effect of supervision on pharmaceutical management in Zimbabwe and concluded that it had a positive impact, emphasizing the importance of training in supervision. Managers have various options to improve the supervisory process. Individual or group supervisory techniques may be considered (Collins, 1994; Jacobson et al., 1987), and a combination of formal and informal methods (Collins, 1994; MacMahon, Barton, & Piot, 1992). For example, Loevinsohn, Guerrero, and Gregorio (1995) examined the use of systematic supervision schedules in a controlled field trial in the Philippines. A correlation was found between the use of supervision schedules, frequency of supervision, and staff performance. The style of supervision is also important. A distinction can be made between supervision that focuses on the supervisee's performance and supervision that focuses on the more personal relationship factors. This suggests a more contingent style of supervision, and we refer to key factors later in this chapter. Finally, the supervisory process may be formalized. A three-stage scheme is presented by Flahault, Piot, and Franklin (1988): preparation for supervision, supervision, and follow-up.

Teamwork

Teams are widely recognized as a positive influence in the health sector and can improve decision making, problem solving, and innovation; motivate team members; improve communication, collaboration, and support; and allow for training. Teams are used in a variety of health sector settings and for a variety of reasons (Exhibit 12-4).

Although Exhibit 12-4 suggests reasons for developing health teams, they do bring with them potential problems. Accountability within the team may be dispersed and lost, team meetings can put pressure on time, and teams may result in indecision, cover up domination and power (Finlay, 2000), generate conflict, and lead to what has been referred to as *groupthink* (Janis, 1972) whereby diversity and debate are exchanged for the dominant and blinkered ideology of the team.

The effectiveness of teams will depend on factors such as defining the objectives and tasks of the team and modifying the working style to fit, good motivation among team members and leadership, effective team meeting skills, getting team size and members' characteristics right, understanding the changing nature of teams, good team action planning, and achieving a balance between team cohesion and diversity (Noakes, 1992; Pheysey, 1993).

Managing Staff Development

Although training is often associated with off-work courses, there is scope for incorporating staff development into the management process. We have already noted the importance of induction for new recruits. Table 12-14 looks beyond this and suggests informal processes that allow training to be an integral part of the management process. Many of these mechanisms avoid taking workers out of their environment and disrupting service delivery. At the same time, learning in the workplace can be more relevant and realistic. However, interest in these mechanisms may be for the wrong reasons, such as cost cutting or the ineffectiveness of poorly managed training courses. Learning environments are not easily created at work, where there are strong pressures of service delivery. Furthermore, carried out properly, on-the-job training is not a cheap option.

Personnel Administration

Most staff management functions outlined previously may be performed by either line managers (and su-

pervisors) or personnel specialists or administrators. Personnel specialists can take on strategic, advisory, and operational roles (Cole, 1988). In the latter category come the mostly routine administrative and procedural activities associated with functions such as recruitment, selection, pay administration, staff contracts, staff grading, promotion, transfer, staff communication, health, safety, and welfare in addition to maintaining a human resources information system (Strike, 1995).

Supplies Management

Supplies include drugs, other medical supplies, and nonmedical supplies (such as food, fuel, and cleaning materials), although this section focuses mainly on drugs.[9] About one-third of the national budget for health care goes for drugs and, as Reich (1995) shows, this is an area of political interest. It is also a complex area requiring, among other things, international tendering and importation, complex technical specifications, complicated procurement processes, and strict quality control. There are also difficulties in storing and distributing drugs in inhospitable climatic and geographic conditions with limited resources.

Problems with the availability of drugs in many local-level services can be a major source of community complaints and irritation for health staff. In part, this is due to the scarcity of resources and the economic context referred to earlier in this chapter. There are also problems of corruption and stealing in addition to related problems of poor management. The latter include inadequate determination of need and demand, deficient selection, long delays in procurement, poor distribution systems, poor and inefficient systems for drug storage, and improper use.

---

[9]Acknowledgment is given to Mayeh Omar for significant inputs into this section.

Exhibit 12-4	**The Importance of Teams for Health and Health Care**

In the United Kingdom, Noakes (1992) recognizes the importance of teams in primary care, Stead and Leonard (1995) refer to the use of a multidisciplinary team in developing change within a health care unit, Firth-Cozens (1992) analyzes the use of teams in the audit process, and Finlay (2000) looks at the mixed experiences of occupational therapists in multidisciplinary teams. In Zimbabwe, Tumwine (1993) analyzes the use of ward health teams in developing community involvement.

Teams are an essential component of a multisectoral approach to health development (Aminu, 1985). They represent a break from the traditional, bureaucratic, and top-down form of organization that tended to individualize and isolate employees. Teams represent a shift to a more organic, less hierarchical form of organization interested in flexibility, multipurpose roles, and innovation. Although most organizations have a combination of these mechanistic and organic features, the importance of effectively operating teams in shifting organizational balance needs to be recognized.

Table 12-14	Forms of Training Within Management
Form of Training	**Commentary**
Self-development	A learning agreement may be used in which the conditions would be provided for staff to take the initiative in planning their own training. However, this can be isolating, and those less able and in need of training may be less able to achieve self-development. Also, there is no guarantee that the staff view of self-development coincides with the interests of the service.
Shadowing	A worker learns from another through observation. However, the "shadower" may be exploited as a free helper, observation may not be systematically recorded, and the "shadowed" individual may be unconvinced of the usefulness of the procedure. Care needs to be taken that the experience is relevant.
Mentoring	This may involve an experienced colleague (not the worker's manager or supervisor) taking on roles such as providing advice, setting specific learning tasks, and suggesting new work options. Recognizing the problems that can occur, Jackson and Donovan (1999) stress the following: Roles should be clear; mentoring should be voluntary; the relationship should be confidential; and it is not an element in promotion or discipline.
Supervision	Although there is a danger of overloading this important relationship, there are opportunities for supervisor and supervisee to agree upon and implement plans for skills development and problem solving.
Delegation	This may provide an opportunity for developing staff, although the worker receiving the delegated task should have sufficient capacity to perform. Good supervision is necessary to take advantage of delegation.
Secondment	Staff can gain from the experience of temporarily working in another unit or organization. Care needs to be taken to ensure that the secondment experience is relevant to the responsibilities in the original job and that opportunities are given for learning.
Job rotation	Staff may undergo a planned movement about the organization to develop new knowledge and experience.
Action learning	Learning through participation in completing tasks in a challenging environment may be useful. It is important that it is carefully planned and does not disrupt service delivery.
Group-based work	This can involve a range of activities such as study circles, support groups, professional and occupational groups for developing quality standards, and specific group meetings.

Sources: J. Storey, "Management Development," in K. Sisson (Ed.), *Personnel Management: A Comprehensive Guide to Theory and Practice in Britain* (Oxford, England: Blackwell Business, 1994); and J. E. Kerrigan and J. S. Luke, *Management Training Strategies for Developing Countries* (Boulder, CO: Lynne Rienner Publishers, 1987).

Supplies management is sensitive to changes in health systems and health policies. Reorganizations involving, for example, purchaser and provider separation and decentralization require new definitions of responsibilities in supplies management. Economies of scale in central purchasing have to be reconciled with forms of local supplies management. Failure to consider supply systems in the process of decentralization can cause major problems to public health. Bosman (2000), for example, recounts the failure to take into account the supply of TB drugs during the decentralization of the health system in Zambia, resulting in a breakdown of the supply chain, interruption of TB treatment to patients, and the development of drug-resistant TB. The introduction of user fees for drugs and the development of regulatory capacity and rational drug policies are also important national-level policy issues.

The supplies management system for pharmaceuticals can be seen as four basic stages: selection, procurement, distribution, and use. The four stages are linked and cyclical and need to be made operational to ensure that the right quantity and quality of drugs are located and used at the right time and right place. Exhibit 12-5 sets out each of the four stages and identifies some of the key issues and techniques involved.

An important feature of supplies management is that of relating the various resources—supplies, information, money, staff, transport, and equipment. For example, the supplies process has to be linked to budget profiling. Also, efficient supplies management relies on a good management information system for

Exhibit 12-5	Stages of the Supplies System

Selection

Selection should consider the needs of the health units and programs in addition to understanding the health situation of the particular communities concerned, their unmet needs, and how these affect drug requirements. Among the considerations are the drug requirements of the different levels of health care, priorities set, targeting of specific groups (e.g., children under 5 years), the use of an essential drugs list and generic drugs, and the design and implementation of quality assurance specifications.

The quantities required need to be estimated; this can be done through methods that use (1) population-based data on morbidity and mortality complemented by norms, (2) service-based data on diagnoses (and frequency) complemented by standard treatment norms, or (3) historical consumption data. These methods have their pros and cons; for example, method 2 fails to take into account unmet demand, and method 3 may be the easiest but fails to account for changes. Adequate supplies have to be maintained over time; thus, attention needs to be paid to issues such as consumption patterns over time, lead time for procurement, safety stocks, and reconciling drug needs with available resources.

Procurement

Drugs are obtained through a procurement process. This involves actions such as purchase procedures (e.g., tendering, negotiating), choosing the supplier (according to criteria such as price and quality through inspections), setting the terms of supply and supply periods (fixed or variable intervals), monitoring order status, and receiving and checking the drugs.

Distribution

Distribution can be based on a "push" (kits) system or a "pull" (inventory) system. In the former, estimated drugs are sent at regular intervals. The latter system requires the health unit to order drugs according to need. This assumes, for example, a stock control system and good communications for ordering and delivering. Among the issues to be considered are the simplicity, regularity, and reliability of the push system and how it compares with the greater sophistication and adaptability of a pull system.

Use

The use stage involves diagnosis, prescribing, dispensing, and patient compliance. Indicators can be developed to monitor and evaluate drug use, such as percentage of drugs that are prescribed and are on the essential drugs list or formulary, the knowledge of correct dosage shown by the patient, and the availability of key drugs in the health facility.

Source: Courtesy of Mayeh Omar.

data on items such as stocks and treatment. Exhibit 12-6 develops this point by showing the important relationship between effective supplies system, training, and staff supervision in Zimbabwe.

Transport Management

The importance of managing an effective transport system should not be underestimated. Transport is important in ensuring access of patients to health services and the effective working of the referral system through both the emergency ambulance service and the transport of nonemergency patients. Health policies based on improved access and the principle of equity should take full note of the importance of transport systems. For example, Okonofua, Abejide, and Makanjuola (1992) have referred to the impact of transport on equity and maternal mortality in Nigeria. Transportation problems were seen to be "an important cause of delay in the case of maternal deaths" p. 323). Campbell and Sham (1995) drew attention to transport problems in the referral of pregnant women in Sudan. The operation of primary health care units and the implementation of community health programs require transport.

Evidence from a range of countries suggests the importance of good transport systems. MacKenzie and colleagues (1995) mention the importance of good and careful transport for equipment in an otology and audiology study in Kenyan schools, while a study in Tanzania (Ahmed, Mung' Ong' O, & Massawe, 1991) found that poor transport was the second most important health management problem in the urban area, and the first problem in the rural areas. Community work that involves nonresident health workers relies heavily on good transport. In Zimbabwe, poor transport hindered outreach programs in maternal and child health, supplementary food production, and immunization (Woelk, 1994). Mobility and transport are

Exhibit 12-6	Supplies, Training, and Supervision in Zimbabwe

Staff training was conducted in Zimbabwe to improve stock management and rational drug use in the 1980s and 1990s. Although the training led to improvements, these were not sustainable. A new strategy was implemented that involved improving supervision. A randomized controlled trial was conducted in three types of health facilities to assess the impact of supervision on stock management and the level of adherence to standard treatment guidelines. The study showed, in general, improvements in both the variables, although supervisors need to be trained and there are confounding interventions to be taken into account. The authors conclude that "allocating resources to supervision is likely to result in improved performance of health workers with regard to the rational use of drugs, resulting in improved efficiency and effectiveness" (Trap et al., 2001, p. 273).

Table 12-15	Possible Measures for Improving Transport Management

Getting transport into the health policy, planning, and programming process

Determining the organizational arrangements and responsibilities for transport management and planning

Ensuring financial management arrangements for transport

Developing vehicle programming

Developing fleet management, including vehicle maintenance and repair and operational norms for transport use

Managing and developing human resources for transport

Using information for improving transport performance

Clarifying the contribution made by donors to transport management and planning

Sources: C. D. Collins, G. Myers, and N. Nicholson, "A Successful Transport Scenario for the Health Sector in Developing Countries," 1992, *World Hospitals, 28*(3), pp. 9-14; and Transaid, *Transport Management Manual* (London: Transaid Worldwide, 2001).

important for effective management such as supervision and the running of a supplies system. Finally, transport takes up an important part of the health service budget.

Although there are undoubtedly areas of good transport practice, there are also problems in transport management, including lack of management skills and systems. For example, there may be insufficient drivers, inappropriate or poorly maintained vehicles, no supervision, no vehicle scheduling or usage information, or poor maintenance. A tendency to treat transport as a free good may be one cause of a lack of cost consciousness. Donor involvement may lead to a multiplicity of vehicles makes, making it difficult to maintain an effective capacity for spare parts and repairs. There may be corruption and the appropriation of transport for private use. Table 12-15 outlines measures to improve transport management and planning.

Attempts to develop a comprehensive policy for transport management have been made in countries such as Ghana (Ministry of Health, Ghana, 1993) and South Africa (Department of Health and Developmental Social Welfare, 1999). Transaid (a transport international NGO working in the health sector of low- to middle-income countries) has developed a comprehensive framework and guide for developing transport for service delivery organizations (Transaid, 2001). Two elements within this same framework and guide are programming transport use and using information.[10]

Programming assumes that transport in the organization is pooled and that decisions are made on its best use. Programs, health units, and staff identify their transport needs, and subsequent decisions are made based on such criteria as the best vehicle for the job and the health priorities. The use of each vehicle is programmed, every effort being made to meet needs and priorities and to ensure the transparency of the process.

The use of information for improving performance is a theme throughout resource management and is particularly evident in transport. Managers responsible for transport need to pay particular attention to developing the transport inventory; doing needs assessment and comparing this with the inventory; collecting log sheets and checking vehicle kilometers, vehicle availability, vehicle utilization, and fuel consumption; monitoring and controlling expenditure against budget profiles; monitoring fuel use; writing accident and incident reports; writing vehicle maintenance reports; monitoring weekly plan performance; overseeing vehicle expenditure; producing and reviewing corrective action on the basis of weekly performance statistics; and providing a summary of monthly performance statistics to higher levels.

A number of documents are vital for establishing an information base for efficient transport management. These include log sheets, fuel records, job sheets or accounts, accident reports, vehicle maintenance reports, weekly transport plans, and the budget. Key indicators can be drawn from these sources, which managers can use to identify problems and take cor-

---

[10]Points on vehicle programming and information draw on Transaid (2001).

rective action. These indicators include the following (Transaid, 2001):

- kilometers traveled by each vehicle
- fuel utilized by each vehicle
- running cost per kilometer
- availability (the number of days each month the vehicles were available for use)
- utilization (with respect to vehicles available for use, the number of days they were used)
- safety of each vehicle
- satisfaction of transport needs as requested by health units, programs, and workers
- maintenance cost for each vehicle

A particular issue relevant to areas such as facilities, supplies, and transport management is the extent to which these are run on commercial lines and as semiautonomous, self-funding operations within health care organizations and the extent to which the public sector contracts them out to the private sector. Outsourcing through contracts with the private sector is seen as a way of gaining from the economies of scale and the technical expertise of specialist contractors in areas unfamiliar to the central responsibilities of health care organizations. Some would also argue that the private sector's efficiency and the control and accountability of contracts are further advantages. There are, however, concerns such as the transaction costs of contracting out; whether lower costs are merely the result of lower salary costs; the lack of sustainability and management learning in contracts; potential problems with poor quality, collusion, and corruption; and the lack of purchasing skills in purchasing organizations (McPake & Ngalande Banda, 1994; Mills, 1998; Stewart, 1993; Walsh, 1995).

Information for Management and Management of Information

One resource that the manager is both responsible for and relies heavily on is information. The next section discusses issues related to the development of an organizational culture of evidence-based-management. This section looks at issues related to the management of information.

Types of Information

We are all constantly bombarded with, and attempting to make sense of, information. However, we tend to consider information for use in management as that which is explicit, and often the information gold standard is seen as quantified information. However, in practice most managers are continuously using a considerable amount of information without being aware of it—often information derived from their own experience and frequently of a qualitative nature. It is important to recognize and value this, while at the same time being aware that such information may be difficult to validate, in part because of its implicit nature. Managers need to identify where decisions are sensitive to critical information, and, where necessary, triangulate the information. Data collection and analysis also carries substantial costs, and a characteristic of a good manager is someone able to request and use only the minimal amount of information at the minimal level of accuracy required for that decision.

Information, therefore, may be of many types and describe a wide range of issues of importance to a manager. Indeed, we have seen a number of examples of information systems in the preceding sections, including budgetary information, information on transport usage, and personnel information.

Sources of Information

Information may be collected from a number of sources, including the following:

- routine ongoing data collection (such as immunization records)
- specific periodic or one-off surveys (such as community health surveys)
- formal research findings
- comparative information from other health systems

Each source has its strengths and weaknesses in terms of accuracy, costs, and relevance to decision processes. A weakness of some management information systems (MISs) is that too much emphasis is placed on routine data collection systems when less frequent data collection would suffice. There is a temptation to institutionalize all data requirements, which can lead to an unwieldy formal MIS and may lead to a devaluing of the overall system.

Users and Providers of Information

Information systems have a number of components:

- identification of information needs
- collection of relevant data
- analysis of data to provide information
- use of information
- timely feedback to providers of information

Weaknesses can occur in an MIS at any stage. Data collected may not be relevant. For example, a manager seeking to understand why there is low utilization of health care is unlikely to get answers from service-based information. One frequent failing in information systems is a lack of feedback to data providers, which can lead to a downward information spiral in which the accuracy of data collected declines due to poor motivation and, as a result, becomes further unused.

There may be inappropriate amounts and types of information at different levels in the management system. Figure 12-14 illustrates a common failing whereby there is a similar amount of data flowing up all levels of the system, whereas ideally the higher management levels should operate on increasingly selective amounts of key data.

Analysis of data and its transformation into information also raises issues in terms of the level at which this is best done and by whom (a general rule is the closer to the collection of the data, the better).

Finally, the rapid development of information technology provides both opportunities and challenges in this area.

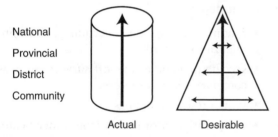

Figure 12-14 Data Flow. *Source:* R. G. Wilson, B. F. Echols, J. H. Bryant, and A. Abrantes (Eds.), *Management Information Systems and Microcomputers in Primary Health Care* (Geneva, Switzerland: Aga Khan Foundation, 1988). Reprinted with permission.

Management Themes

The previous sections have reviewed three key management activities: organizing, planning, and resource management. Permeating these activities are various themes. How these are approached will have an impact on the way management is carried out. This section focuses on

- styles of management
- accountability
- evidence-based management
- systems approach
- linking and working together

- sustainability
- contradictions, tensions, and change

Styles of Management

The various styles of management are outlined in the following subsections.

Proactive

A proactive approach reflects a difference between management and administration and lies at the heart of the pursuit of objectives. Management performance should not be measured by adherence to rules and regulations, as in administration, but by the extent of movement toward objectives. This movement requires a proactive approach and involves predicting constraints and new opportunities, trying to influence the environment, developing coalitions of support, foreseeing future problems and taking early preventive action, and monitoring performance to take corrective action.

There is a potential danger that managers' performance is (perceived to be) judged on their proactive appearance. This can lead to shows of being proactive, such as the appearance of haste, workaholic behavior, and constant change. This is not good management.

Risk Taking

Risk taking reflects another important difference between administration and management and expresses the inventiveness of managers, reflecting an approach that does not accept that existing ways of doing things are the only way. New methods and approaches involve an element of risk, however, and hence danger for managers. There are necessary limits to the extent to which managers should take risks; this is particularly evident in the field of health. The notion of reasonable and acceptable risk needs to be understood.

How staff performance is managed is also related to risk. For example, if staff are routinely criticized for failure and not praised or rewarded for success, then few staff will be willing to take reasonable and acceptable risks. Effective and supportive communication and supervision, together with the existence of clear and agreed-upon ethical and technical work standards, can provide a more conducive environment of acceptable risk taking.

Leadership

Many of the issues related to leadership have been mentioned earlier in connection with supervision. Table 12-16 sets out a view of the functions of a leader.

Table 12-16	Functions of a Leader

- Structuring the situation: making it clear where the group is going and what has to be done
- Controlling group behavior: creating and enforcing appropriate rules for guiding the behavior of group members
- Speaking for the group: sensing and articulating (both internally and externally) the objectives and feelings of the group
- Helping the group achieve its goals and potential: mobilizing and coordinating group resources and decision making

Source: Coleman (1969), as quoted in M. Smith et al., *Introducing Organisational Behaviour* (London: Macmillan Education, 1982).

How managers practice effective leadership will depend on various factors. Personal qualities are important—for example, one would expect a good leader to show personal understanding, confidence, and principled conduct. These personal qualities are difficult to be precise about and measure. Styles of leadership are also important. They can be viewed as varying, for example, from authoritarian to democratic and from technically based to more personal-based leadership. However, leadership style needs to be adapted to the circumstances in which it is practiced. The nature of the task needs to be considered—for example, problems with open-ended solutions may require a more flexible style than more closed or finite problems. Problems requiring immediate solution may lead to a tighter style of leadership.

The category of staff over which leadership is exercised is also important. We have already seen how Hersey, Blanchard, and LaMonica (1978) identified task and relationship behavior as key variables of leadership activities. Four combinations of these variables were identified and related to the maturity of staff: "capacity to set high but attainable goals (achievement-motivation), willingness to take responsibility, and the education and the experience of an individual or group." Managers adapt their style of supervision according to the level of maturity of staff. For example, staff with a low level of maturity need a high level of task leadership exercised over them. As the maturity of the staff increases, the level of task leadership can decrease and relationship behavior increase.

Problem Solving

One function of management is to seek solutions to problems arising from unforeseen changes in circumstances either within the organization or exter-

nally. An attribute of good management is the ability to deal creatively with new issues. One danger of too great an attention to "problems" is a neglect of future emerging issues at the expense of current fire fighting. Problem-solving management needs to be balanced with a more long-term set of considerations.

Accountability

Accountability is about "the means by which individuals and organisations report to a recognised authority, or authorities, and are held responsible for their actions" (Edwards & Hulme, 2002, p. 183). Its importance permeates the health system. It is essential to performance management, underlines the seriousness of health and health care and the concern for people's lives, and is crucial to exercising checks and balances on the use of resources. Networks of different (but overlapping) and changing forms of accountability run through the management of the health system, as illustrated in Table 12-17.

Managers need to recognize and respond to each form of accountability. In some cases they are reporting to authorities: in others, they themselves are the authority. Each form of accountability imposes rights and obligations around the management process. At the same time, those involved in management take part in the design of accountability relations and need to balance the network of complex, changing, and overlapping relations. In so doing they will be influenced by the values in the health system and demands for new forms of accountability. The PHC approach, for example, puts the onus on community-based accountability, whereas the contemporary reform of health systems toward devolution puts an onus on politically devolved forms of accountability. Exhibit 12-7 indicates the thinking of the World Bank's 2004 *World Development Report,* which emphasizes more market-based forms of accountability.

Evidence-Based Management

We have stressed that management differs from administration in that it requires individual initiative rather than reliance on preexisting rules and regulations. The success of a manager in exercising such initiative is a combination of a number of factors, including his or her technical skills and his or her judgment. Both of these rely also on the ability of the manager to draw on existing evidence in making managerial decisions. For this to occur, various preconditions need to be met.

First, there needs to be an organizational culture that seeks, generates, and accepts the use of evidence

Table 12-17	Different and Changing Forms of Accountability
Form of Accountability	**Commentary**
Managerial	Managerial authority sees subordinates as managerially accountable to the hierarchically superior manager. This is typically expressed in the main line managerial relations in the organizational chart.
Professional	Professions are hierarchically structured, so that junior staff are technically accountable to those higher up. Members of the profession may also be accountable to a professional body for their actions and behavior.
Political	Political representatives can hold staff accountable for their actions and behavior—for example, under devolution, where health staff are accountable to an elected local council.
Community	Health staff may be formally accountable to the community through mechanisms that monitor areas such as availability of drugs, personal relations with health staff, and punctuality of staff.
User	This differs from the community form in that health staff are accountable to *users* of a particular service, who could take on similar roles.
Market	Users are viewed as consumers of a particular service, for which they pay. Health staff are accountable to the consumers of the service through the market. Consumers who are dissatisfied with the service may go elsewhere.

Exhibit 12-7	Accountability and the 2004 *World Development Report*

The *World Development Report* of 2004 (World Bank, 2004) recognizes the existence of different forms of accountability and arrangements for service delivery. The most appropriate mix of these arrangements will depend on the nature of politics, the ease of monitoring, and the type of clients. The report identifies "long" accountability routes, such as through pro-poor politics and an accountable public service. However, these features are not always present, and "shorter" routes of accountability based on the power of clients may be appropriate. These could be achieved through such means as increasing choice for clients, introducing co-payments, using voucher schemes, or increasing competition among providers.

The introduction of these shorter routes is controversial. Critics point to the lack of various providers to allow for competition, the impact of payment schemes on access and equity, the asymmetry of information in health care, and the negative impact of competition on collaborative strategies for health.

in its decision making. A major concern of many organizations relates to their failure to use evidence. This may result from either a genuine lack of evidence or a resistance to research-generated evidence that is not perceived as relevant—the "know–do" gap. Some of this resistance may be generated by stakeholders with a vested interest in maintaining a particular position that evidence might challenge. Managers have a responsibility to generate an organizational culture that respects such evidence-based approaches.

Second, a level of accuracy of evidence is needed that is appropriate to the decisions being made. As we have seen, there are clearly costs involved in seeking evidence, and these costs are directly related to the level of validity and accuracy required. A manager needs to request only the minimum level of accuracy necessary for any particular decision. Third, a manager needs to set up, and adequately resource, information systems that will provide the appropriate evidence.

In the end, however, we return to the theme of a manager as a practitioner of an art rather than a science. An undefinable quality of a good manager, which in part results from experience, is the ability to sift information, to select the appropriate information, and act appropriately on it. Judgment is the necessary counterpart to good evidence.

Systems Approach

The advantages of the division of labor lead to organizations and health staff adopting specialized tasks. Although understandable, this approach runs the danger of fragmentation, narrow perspectives, and inflexible working patterns. In the management process, staff need to complement their own specialized responsibilities with a broader, more flexible approach, which we refer to here as a *systems approach*.

First, this means that staff, in addition to their own specialized tasks in management (such as human resources or logistics management), need to adopt a broad range of knowledge, skills, and aptitudes. This is important for the management process because managers need to combine and use different resources. It is also important in that it allows for more flexible working patterns, allowing staff to be more multifunctional to take into account short-term changes in the organization's work.

Second, it means that staff are clear in relating their own position in the organization to the overall organizational objectives. Thus, the TB manager is not just concerned with a reduction in TB morbidity and mortality but also with how overall community morbidity and mortality can be reduced. In this case, staff appreciate how their own actions relate to other parts of the organization. Extra resources for one department or program may be taking resources away from an area of greater priority. Extra staff for a health center in a rich area may mean staff not being assigned to health centers in poorer areas. It means appreciating the opportunity costs of managerial action.

Linking and Working Together

The need for more collaboration is a frequent recommendation in management reports. Collaboration, however, remains an elusive feature of management. The forces behind individualism, exclusive group interests, and group inter- and intraorganizational conflicts are difficult to overcome. Yet the health system, in order to provide improved health care, needs to push collaborative strategies to the front of managerial action. Health staff, in their various organizations, need to work together. This includes the development of integrated management of patient care, team approaches within an organization, interdepartmental cooperation, public-private partnerships, and interorganizational and intersectoral linkages.

The importance of working together through a multisectoral approach has long been advocated. Health depends on a wide range of non-health-care factors. The challenge for management is to devise approaches, actions, mechanisms, structures, and attitudes that can lead to greater ability to work together. The following subsections set out key strategies for this.

Coordination

Coordination involves two or more units agreeing on joint objectives, dedicating resources, and developing a joint organization and program (Rogers & Whetten, 1982). For example, educational and health care organizations could develop a joint program for improving sexual hygiene and the use of condoms in communities. Figure 12-15 delineates the elements of coordination and cooperation between municipal health and education departments.

Cooperation

Cooperation occurs when two or more organizations keep their own separate but compatible objectives and agree to help each other when possible and, at the least, to avoid actions that would hinder the other organization achieving its objectives (Rogers & Whetten, 1982). Health and agricultural organizations could agree to support the cultivation of subsistence crops and to protect fish-bearing rivers to ensure adequate nutrition of rural workers.

Community Supporting

Communities can view needs from a more integrated perspective than that of the public sector. In this case, health and health-related government organizations could support policies designed to strengthen community involvement in decision making and planning. In turn this would lead to more community-based

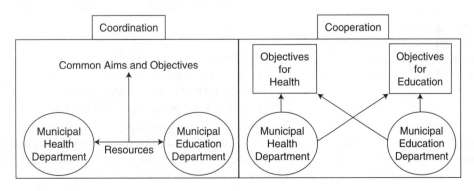

Figure 12-15 Coordination and Cooperation. *Source:* D. L. Rogers and D. A. Whetten, *Interorganizational Coordination: Theory, Research, and Implementation, p. 14* (Ames: Iowa State University, 1982). Adapted with permission.

demands and support for integrated action by the public sector.

Nesting

Nesting involves locating or allocating resources or linking to initiatives in other organizations that support a multisectoral approach. For example, the MOH could strategically support initiatives of a multisectoral character in local governments, community associations, and NGOs by locating or nesting support to strategic points in these locations. In return for action of a multisectoral nature, these bodies would receive resources and technical support.

Advocacy

The MOH takes on the role of advocating for a health perspective to be used across the various sectors of the public sector—for example, through control over tobacco consumption, the use of car seat belts and motorbike helmets, and eliminating fire hazards. This requires, among other things, the MOH to take intellectual policy leadership for health, effectively disseminate research on the causes of ill health and policy analysis on new initiatives, create dialogue concerning health and compatible social, political, and economic objectives, participate in policy forums throughout the different sectors, and develop a wide network of links with policy makers from other sectors.

Regulating

The MOH has authority to ensure compliance from other individuals and organizations. As an extension of the examples given under advocacy, the MOH and other health-related organizations may be invested with legitimate regulatory authority to demand certain behaviors leading to health improvement. This requires the development of legal expertise within the MOH, the focus of regulatory action on health objectives, the creation of regulatory mechanisms to require certain behavior, and the development of a sustainable administrative structure to implement regulations. As in the case of advocacy, it requires a proactive stance in relation to health, developing dialogue and intellectual leadership for health objectives. At the same time, it needs to rest on a political commitment to back up the regulatory authority.

Orientation

Orientation can be given to the wide range of health-related organizations through the strategic health planning system by setting out the health focus of the sector and its openness to developing linkages. Orientation can also be ideological, by backing an ideology of collaboration—a point developed by Bennet and Ferlie (1994) in relation to joint working in HIV/AIDS services.

Shifting Authority Either Upward or Downward

Authority for cross-cutting strategic direction can be shifted upward in the hierarchy of government, moving above the organizational and sectoral divisions. A powerful cross-governmental commission for social development involving related ministries could provide multisectoral decision making and national planning and resource allocation. Authority can also be shifted downward to multifunctional devolved units at the local level. As a form of decentralization, devolution opens up the potential for a multisectoral approach between health care and other departments such as education and social services, although the divisions between departments within local government can still constitute strong constraints.

Developing Collaborative Skills and Techniques

Collaborative skills and techniques need to be fostered among staff in order to develop collaboration.

- Trust is an essential component of effective collaboration, although it is difficult to develop. Hudson and associates (1999) suggest the need to calculate the risk involved in trusting and begin with small ventures to build up confidence; keep to "principled conduct"; and develop personal and more stable relations.

- Support has to be given to the "network and link people" in the organization (Hudson et al., 1999; Hunter, 1990). There are particular skills and tensions involved in occupying these roles, and staff require strong support to carry them out. A particular problem can be that of dual accountability—health staff owing allegiance to their parent organization and also to any new coordinating body (Hudson et al., 1999).

- Effective collaboration has to be based on broad ownership in all the agencies concerned. It cannot be based solely on agreements made by top managers, but requires a more generalized ownership in the agencies concerned.

- Organizational learning (Hardy, Turrell, & Wistow, 1992) is important. Organizations have to learn from the process of collaboration for future ventures.

Management Systems

Collaboration can be built into the management systems of organizations related to how they use resources. Agreements on consultation and use of information could be built into the system of district health planning and other sector planning. Information systems can also take on a multisectoral character (de Kadt, 1988).

Contracting and Agreements

Contracts and legitimate agreements between organizations can be a useful means for developing collaboration.[11] A contract is "an agreement between one or more economic agents through which they undertake to assume or relinquish, do or not do, certain things. A contract is therefore a voluntary alliance of independent parties" (Perrot, Carrin, & Sergent, 1997, p. 17). The existence of a contract assumes some form of separation between the purchaser or commissioner (who has the funds and is the prime agent for determining the needs to be met by the contract) and the provider. The distinction between the two agents is "a contract in which one person (the principal) employs another (the agent) to carry out on his behalf a given task, whereby a degree of decision-making power is delegated to the agent." (Perrot, Carrin, & Sergent, 1997, p. 26). As set out in Figure 12-16, there is a commissioning body or purchaser, the contract, and the provider. The contract itself can include issues relating to services, object, and payment and can take place in a competitive or non-competitive environment.

The elements involved in a contracting process suggest that variations in these can lead to a number of different contractual forms (Table 12-18). Types of contracts have been classified in different ways. Walsh (1995) distinguishes between performance-based contracts and methods-based contracts in addition to sanction-based contracts and cooperative contracts. Flynn (1997, p. 141) distinguishes between an obligational contracting relationship and an adversarial contracting relationship. The former is where "the two parties trust each other, work together for mutual benefit, share risk and do things for each other which go beyond the details of the contract." The latter "is

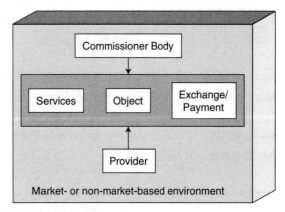

Figure 12-16 Elements in Contracting.

based on low trust, the expectation that each side wishes to gain at the expense of the other and contracts are used to protect each side from the other." Palmer (2000, p. 823) draws on an existing distinction between classical ("discrete transactions between people who will never see each other again"), neoclassical ("less discrete and therefore contain techniques for flexibility within the terms of the contract, such as third party determination of performance"), and relational contracts (the terms of the contract are not the key element; rather, the whole relationship between the parties over time is key, and importance is put on harmony and keeping the relationship). She also suggests that contracting in low- to middle-income countries is often justified in terms of classical and neoclassical contracting, despite the possibility that relational contracting might well be more promising. The different types of contracting allow for the adoption of a contingency approach whereby different types of contracting may be appropriate to different environments.

Sustainability

An important theme in management is that of the sustainability of services. Lafond (1995, p. 63) sees sustainability as "the capacity of the health sector to function effectively over time, with a minimum of external input." The mention of "external input" is of particular relevance to poor countries heavily reliant on funds from international agencies. Olsen's (1998) definition emphasizes the longer term: "A health service is sustainable when operated by an organisational system with the long-term ability to mobilize and allocate sufficient and appropriate resources (manpower, technology, information and finance) for

---

[11]The sections on contracting and sustainability draw on and reproduce parts of a research report (Collins & Green, 2002) written by the authors for a European Union–supported work on contracting and primary care in Central America (Contract ICA4-CT-2001-10011). The European Union holds no responsibility for the content, while the authors take full responsibility for the content reproduced.

Table 12-18	Variables in the Analysis of Contracting Primary Care Services
Variable	**Comment**
Object of the contract	Ranging from type of service to geographic coverage
Type of contracting	Ranging from formal and legalistic to more flexible contracting
Type of commissioner	Could include central or decentralized agencies with different degrees of organizational autonomy and financing (e.g., taxes, insurance systems, fee based)
Type of provider	Public sector, NGO, or private for profit—each with its own variations
Type of exchange or payment	Based on a definition of services and payment system, which could be, for example, performance based
Market or nonmarket based	Contracts can be based on competitive tendering, with services provided in a market environment, or without competitive tendering, with service providers operating in a noncompetitive environment

activities that meet individual or public health needs/demands" (p. 289).

The relevance of sustainability to health management rests on two key points. First, health care is rarely time limited. Disease control, for example, requires continued interventions over time. The continuity of action in TB control is important to limit the spread of disease. In particular, continued drug supply and continued treatment are important to avoid drug-resistant TB (Bosman, 2000). Second, the importance of sustainability draws on four problematic and interrelated features of the public sector, particularly in developing countries (Collins, Omar, & Hurst, 2000):

- The extremely limited resource base of poor societies coupled with the limited authority of national governments leads to intense resource scarcity in the public sector. It is this limitation that underlies the problem of maintaining a secure and constant flow of resources to finance government programs and leads to high levels of dependence on international aid.

- The historical focus of international aid to low-income countries on capital investment and the relatively weak support given to recurrent expenditure leads to difficult problems of maintaining programs of action. This is compounded by the vertical and cyclical nature of foreign aid projects.

- Corruption has a marked impact on the continuity and effectiveness of government given the high level of resource scarcity

- High staff turnover may lead to limited effectiveness of government programs.

Sustainability is, however, not an end in itself, but a means to a wider end. Sustainability is colored by the policy objectives held by the stakeholders. This introduces two possibilities:

- *Appropriate sustainability* is when a particular activity has continuity over time and has outputs that continue to be valued. For example, policy objectives typically may be the achievement of improved and equitable health care, with certain types of action essential to achieve this.

- *Inappropriate sustainability* is when programs and activities need to be stopped at a particular point, but continue. For example, as a particular health problem reduces in incidence, related interventions may need to be reduced. Smallpox vaccination is a classic example.

What is appropriate sustainability to one stakeholder may be viewed as inappropriate to another. Stakeholders in a particular government activity will have different interpretations of a program, largely determined by how it affects their own particular interests. Table 12-19 illustrates the possible interests of different stakeholders in sustainability.

To capture the determining features of sustainability, analysis needs to recognize the broad-ranging character of sustainability and its multiple determinants. The factors influencing sustainability will not only be wide ranging but also will vary between situations.

Contradictions, Tensions, and Change

In the introduction to this chapter, the essentially political character, of health management was raised. In itself, this places the health management process at the center of contradictions, tensions, and change. The importance of context and its impact on management was then examined. Two areas of tension

Table 12-19	Stakeholders and Possible Interests in Sustainability	
Stakeholder	**Possible Interests in Sustainability**
Donors	Shifting resource dependence away from donors and increasing local contributions
Ministry of health	Ensuring regularity of donor resources and/or shifting resource dependence away from donors and increasing local contributions
Staff	Ensuring continuity in employment and career progression
Users	Ensuring continuity of improved service delivery
Nonusers	Expansion of service on a regular basis to cover their needs
Private-sector contractors	Shift to public financing and private provision under favorable conditions

are of particular relevance to the contemporary management process in developing countries (Green & Collins, 2003). First, is the contradiction between public interest and private gain and its manifestations through patronage, corruption, professional self-interest, and corporate gain. Second, many health care systems are undergoing change along pro-market and neoliberal lines. These changes have tended to respond more to an internationally driven ideology than the health needs of poor communities. For the manager, this places an onus on change management and raises issues of using evidence-based decision making to direct change, programming change on the basis of logical sequencing, and consulting and negotiating with affected interests.

The challenge for the management process is how to deal with these contradictions, which is the content of the concluding section.

Conclusion and Challenges for Managers

Management is fundamentally concerned with the relationship between resources and objectives. It deals with scarce resources, operates within constraints, is strongly influenced by values, can operate in a political manner, and has a strong interrelationship with the social, political, economic, and international context. Three interrelated functions of management have been emphasized: planning, organizing and management of resources. Themes permeating these management activities have been referred to: styles of management; accountability; systems approach; linking and working together; sustainability; and contradictions, tensions, and change.

The future of health management in developing countries is far from clear. Certainly, health systems development will require significant improvements in health management and planning. However, such a process cannot be divorced from some challenging questions.

What Is the Future of Public-Sector Management?

Criticisms of the state and public-sector management have ranged from simple market orthodoxy to a more nuanced approach that recognizes its needs and social responsibilities. However, a prevailing sense of corruption, bureaucratic expansion, administrative fragmentation, and patronage has made it easy for many to levy such criticisms. Nevertheless, two points need to be recognized. First, public-sector management operates in a context of low funding, intense need, and unstable environment. We return to this later.

Second, there is a need to recognize the specific characteristics of public-sector management. Public-sector and private-sector management have much to learn from each other. Yet all good learning takes into account specific circumstances and requirements in order to assess appropriateness. The future development of management, and the values that underpin it, need to take into account three factors.[12]

First, the public sector seeks to meet public needs and interests, although different social and political groups have different interpretations of these. This requires open and transparent participation and negotiation regarding the definition of public interest. Public-sector bodies need to define their objectives in relation to those public needs and interests.

Second, the multifaceted nature of public needs means that public-sector organizations can only achieve their objectives through entering into collaborative strategies with other bodies, whether public, NGOs, or private-for-profit organizations. This also requires collaborative strategies between the public sector and communities.

---

[12]These three points draw on Stewart and Ranson (1994).

Finally, social needs are not ephemeral in nature but long term, and require public-sector management to recognize this. Planning, sustainability, continuity of service provision, capacity building, systems development, and career planning are among some of the key features of public management.

Are Managers Being Asked to Manage the Unmanageable?

That managers have to deal with contradictions, tensions, and change is nothing new. The immensity of these challenges is brought out as we consider the paucity of resources available and the scale of the health needs stressed elsewhere in this book. In dealing with these challenges, there is a gap, which varies from one country to another, between the existing capacity of management to meet those challenges and the potential that exists through management strengthening. It is a matter of concern, however, that an already difficult situation is being made worse through sharpening contradictions and weakened means to respond.

First, there is an increasing confusion between public interest and private gain through the growth of public-private partnerships and self-funding public bodies. Second, the importance of the public sector, is under threat through poor rewards for public servants, the downgrading of the role of the public sector, and a hollowing out of its rationale and process. The culture of individualism, internal markets, and self-funding of health units and programs contradict the public sector's perspective of social interests, collaborative strategy, longer-term framework, and public ethos. In the words of Flynn (1997, p. 232):

> What is needed is a change in attitude towards the public sector. If spending could be based on need and a realistic assessment of what is affordable rather than a constant state of crisis and if management arrangements could be based less on distrust and fear and more on cooperation, then public services could make a valuable contribution to the economic health and quality of life of society.

What Are the Challenges Facing Public-Sector Health Managers?

This chapter has given what can only be an overview of the key issues that a manager working in the public health sector needs to consider. Management, we have argued, is a key, but often undervalued, component of a health system. As managers seek to provide the structures, resources, and processes for meeting the Millennium Development Goals, what are the emerging challenges that they face?

First, they will need to grapple with the increasingly diverse structures of the health system and new approaches to funding. The increasingly mixed public and private institutional complexity and changing relations between the center and the local levels, combined with new funding flows through SWAps and public-private partnerships, suggest that managers need to seek new ways to meet these challenges.

Second, although low-income countries continue to face major financial resource constraints, the emerging crisis of the health professional gap must be seen, for many countries, as an even greater constraint. This, coupled with the low morale permeating the staff in many health systems, presents major challenges for managers, who will need to seek new ways to cope.

Third, managers face an increasingly vocal and empowered citizenry, conscious of a rights agenda. This will, rightly, suggest greater demands for accountability on the part of the health system; managers will represent the front line in this.

The nature, and indeed excitement, of management, lies in identifying and responding to such emerging challenges. Management as a scientific art needs continuously to develop new approaches and tools to do this. It is hoped this chapter has provided a platform from which such new approaches can be built.

• • • Discussion Questions

1. Consider what health planning takes place in a country known to you. How successful is it? What major health needs exist that are not met? Can you identify expenditure that is of lower priority than these unmet identified needs? How could health planning be improved?

2. How are health care priorities decided within the health sector of a country known to you? What is the role of the manager in this process?

3. Describe the budgeting system of a country known to you. How are resources allocated to lower levels? How does resource allocation link to the planning process?

4. What system of decentralization exists in your country? What are its strengths and weaknesses for the health sector?

5. What practical steps could be taken to improve intersectoral collaboration for health in your country?

6. Consider the way in which local-level health staff are managed. What steps could be taken to improve the way in which these staff are managed?

● ● ● **References**

Abramson, W. B. (2001). Monitoring and evaluation of contracts for health service delivery in Costa Rica. *Health Policy and Planning, 16*(4), 404–411.

Ahmed, A. M., Mung'Ong'O, E., & Massawe, E. (1991). Tackling obstacles to health care delivery at district level. *World Health Forum, 12*(4), 483–489.

Alimo-Metcalfe, B. (1994, October 20). The poverty of PRP. *Health Services Journal,* pp. 22–23.

Aminu, J. (1985). Teaming up for better health. *Social Science and Medicine, 21*(12), 1349–1353.

Atkinson, S., Medeiros, R. L., Oliveira, P. H., & de Almeida, R. D. (2000). Going down to the local: Incorporating social organisation and political culture into assessments of decentralised health care. *Social Science and Medicine, 51,* 619–636.

Bacal, R. (1999). *Performance management.* New York: McGraw-Hill.

Barker, C., & Green, A. (1996). Opening the debate on DALYs. *Health Policy and Planning, 11*(2), 179–183.

Barker, C., Thunhurst, C., & Ross, D. (1998). An approach to setting priorities in health planning. *Journal of Management in Medicine, 12,* 92–100.

Benjamin, S., Ahmed, A. A., & Al-Darazi, F. (1997). Management in the Ministry of Health: What are the vital signs? *World Hospitals and Health Services, 33*(1), 2–12.

Bennet, C., & Ferlie, E. (1994). *Managing crisis and changes in health care: The organisational response to HIV/AIDS.* Buckingham, England: Open University Press.

Bennett, S., Dakpallah, G., Garner, P., Gilson, L., Nittayaramphong, S., Zurita, B., & Zwi, A. (1994). Carrot and stick: State mechanisms to influence private provider behaviour. *Health Policy and Planning, 9*(1), 1–13.

Bishai, D., Niessen, L. W., & Shrestha, M. (2002). Local governance and community financing of primary care: Evidence from Nepal. *Health Policy and Planning, 17*(2), 202–206.

Bosman, M. C. J. (2000). Health sector reform and tuberculosis control: The case of Zambia. *International Journal of Tuberculosis and Lung Diseases, 4*(7), 606–614.

Bossert, T. (1998). Analysing the decentralisation of health systems in developing countries: Decision space, innovation and performance. *Social Science and Medicine, 47*(10), 1513–1527.

Bossert, T. J., & Beauvais, J. C. (2002). Decentralisation of health systems in Ghana, Zambia, Uganda and the Philippines: A comparative analysis of decision space. *Social Science and Medicine, 17*(1), 14–31.

Brown, W., & Walsh, J. (1994). Managing pay in Britain. In K. Sisson (Ed.), *Personnel management: A comprehensive guide to theory and practice in Britain* (pp. 437–464). Oxford, England: Blackwell Business.

Brugha, R., & Varvasovszky, Z. (2000). Stakeholder analysis: A review. *Health Policy and Planning, 15*(3), 239–246.

Buchan, J. (2004). What difference does ("good") HRM make? *Human Resources for Health, 2,* 6.

Buchan, J., Ball, J., & O'May, F. (2000). *Skill mix in the health workforce* (Issues in Health Services Delivery No. 3). Geneva, Switzerland: World Health Organization.

Campbell, M., & Sham, Z. A. (1995). Sudan: Situational analysis of maternal health in Bara District, North Kordofan. *World Health Statistics Quarterly, 48,* 60–66.

Cassels, A., & Janovsky, K. (1995). *Strengthening health management in districts and provinces.* Geneva, Switzerland: World Health Organization.

Child, J. (1984). *Organization: A guide to problems and practice.* London: Harper and Row.

Cole, G. A. (1988). *Personnel management: Theory and practice.* London: DP Publications.

Collins, C. (1994). *Management and organization in developing health systems.* Oxford, England: Oxford University Press.

Collins, C., & Green, A. (2002). *Public contracting of private providers for primary health care services: Context, sustainability and accountability* CAPUBPRUV, UE ICA4CT-2001-10011.

Collins, C. D., Myers, G., & Nicholson, N. (1992). A successful transport scenario for the health sector in developing countries. *World Hospitals, 28*(3), 9–14.

Collins, C., Omar, M., & Hurst, K. (2000). Staff transfer and management in the government health sector in Balochistan, Pakistan: Problems and context. *Public Administration and Development, 20,* 207–220.

de Kadt, E. (1988). Making health policy management intersectoral: Issues of information analysis and use in less developed countries. *Social Science and Medicine, 29*(4), 503–514.

Department of Health and Developmental Social Welfare (DHDSW). (1999). *Transport management manual.* South Africa: DHDSW, Save the Children (UK), Transaid.

Dieleman, M., Cuong, P. V., Anh, L.V., & Martineau, T. (2003). Identifying factors for job motivation of rural health workers in North Viet Nam. *Human Resources for Health, 1,* 10.

Edwards, M., & Hulme, D. (2002). NGO performance and accountability: Introduction and overview. In M. Edwards & A. Fowler (Eds.), *The Earthscan reader on NGO management* (pp. 187–203). London: Earthscan.

Finlay, L. (2000). Safe haven and battleground: Collaboration and conflict within the treatment team. In C. Davies, L. Finlay, & A. Bullman (Eds.), *Changing practice in health and social care* (pp. 155–162). London: Sage Publications.

Firth-Cozens, J. (1992). Building teams for effective audit. *Quality in Care, 1,* 252–255.

Flahault, D., Piot, M., & Franklin, A. (1988). *Supervision of health personnel at district level.* Geneva, Switzerland: World Health Organization.

Flynn, N. (1997). *Public sector management* (3rd ed.). London: Harvester Wheatsheaf.

French, D., & Saward, H. (1983). *A dictionary of management.* London: Pan.

Green, A. (1999). *An introduction to health planning in developing countries* (2nd ed.). Oxford, England: Oxford University Press.

Green, A., Ali, B., Naeem, A., & Ross, D. (2000). The allocation and budgetary mechanisms for decentralized health systems: Experiences from Balochistan, Pakistan. *Bulletin of the World Health Organization, 78*(8), 1024–1035.

Green, A., & Collins, C. (2003). Health systems in developing countries: public sector managers and the management of contradiction and change. *International Journal of Health Planning and Management, 18,* 67–78.

Grindle, M. S. (1997). Divergent cultures? When public organisations perform well in developing countries. *World Development, 25*(4), 481–495.

Hardy, B., Turrell, A., & Wistow, G. (1992). *Innovation in community care management: Minimising vulnerability.* Aldershot, England: Avebury.

Hersey, P., Blanchard, K. H., & LaMonica, E. L. (1978). A situational response to supervision: Leadership theory and the supervising nurse. In J. S. Rackich & K. Darr (Eds.), *Hospital organization and management: Text and Readings.* New York: Spectrum.

Herzberg, F., Mausner, B., & Snyderman, B. B. (1959). *The motivation to work.* New York: John Wiley & Sons.

Hiscock, J. (1995). Looking a gift horse in the mouth: The shifting power balance between the MoH and donors in Ghana. *Health Policy and Planning, 10*(Suppl.), 28–39.

Hudson, B., Hardy, B., Henwood, M., & Wistow, G. (1999). In pursuit of inter-agency collaboration in the public sector. What is the contribution of theory and research? *Public Management, 1*(2), 235–260.

Hunter, D. (1989, September 28). Changes for the future. *Health Services Journal,* p. 1193.

Hunter, D. (1990). "Managing the cracks": Management development for health care interfaces. *International Journal of Health Care Planning and Management, 5,* 7–14.

Jackson, A. C., & Donovan, F. (1999). *Managing to survive: Managerial practice in not-for-profit organisations.* Buckingham, England: Open University Press.

Jacobson, M. L., Labbok, M. H., Murage, A. N., et al. (1987). Individual and group supervision of community health workers: A comparison. *Journal of Health Administration Education, 5*(1), 83–94.

Janis, I. L. (1972). *Victims of groupthink.* Boston: Houghton-Mifflin.

Keeling, D. (1972). *Management in government.* London: Allen & Unwin.

Kempner, T. (Ed.). (1980). *A handbook of management.* Harmondsworth, England: Penguin.

Kerrigan, J. E., & Luke, J. S. (1987). *Management training strategies for developing countries.* Boulder, CO: Lynne Rienner Publishers.

Kessler, I. (1994). Performance pay. In K. Sisson (Ed.), *Personnel management: A comprehensive guide to theory and practice in Britain* (pp. 465–494). Oxford, England: Blackwell Business.

Kolehmainen-Aitken, R.-L. (2004). Decentralisation's impact on the health workforce: Perspectives of managers, workers and national leaders. *Human Resources for Health, 2,* 5.

Kolehmainen-Aitken, R.-L., & Shipp, P. (1990). "Indicators of staffing need": Assessing health staffing and equity in Papua New Guinea. *Health Policy and Planning, 5*(2), 167–176.

Lafond, A. K. (1995). Improving the quality of investment in health: Lessons on sustainability. *Health Policy and Planning, 10,* 63–76.

Lakshminarayanan, R. (2003). Decentralisation and its implications for reproductive health: The

Philippines experience. *Reproductive Health Matters, 11*(21), 96–107.

Loevinsohn, B. P., Guerrero, E. T., & Gregorio, S. P. (1995). Improving primary health care through systematic supervision: A controlled field trial. *Health Policy and Planning, 10*(2), 144–153.

MacKenzie, I., Thompson, S., Smith, A., Bal, I. S., & Hatcher, J. (1995). Practical advice on field studies into hearing impairment in a developing country. *Tropical Doctor, 25*(1), 25–28.

Martineau, T., & Martinez, J. (1997). *Human resources in the health sector: Guidelines for appraisal and strategic development* (Health and Development Series, Working Paper No. 1). Brussels, Belgium: European Commission.

Martinez, J., & Martineau, T. (1998). Rethinking human resources: An agenda for the millennium. *Health Policy and Planning, 13*(4), 345–358.

McCoy, D., Buch, E., & Palmer, N. (2000). *Protecting efficient, comprehensive and integrated primary health care: Principles for inter-governmental contracts/service agreements.* South Africa: Health Systems Trust.

McIntyre, D., & Klugman, B. (2003). The human face of decentralisation and integration of health services: Experiences from South Africa. *Reproductive Health Matters, 11*(21), 108–119.

McKee, M., & Healy, J. (2002). *Hospitals in a changing Europe.* Buckingham, England: Open University Press.

McMahon, R., Barton, E., & Piot, M. (1992). *On being in charge: A guide to management in primary health care* (2nd ed.). Geneva, Switzerland: World Health Organization.

McPake, B., & Ngalande Banda, E. (1994). Contracting out of health services in developing countries. *Health Policy and Planning, 9*(1), 25–30.

Mescon, M. H., Albert, M., & Khedouri, F. (1985). *Management: Individual and organisational effectiveness.* New York: Harper and Row.

Mills, A. (1998). To contract or not to contract? Issues for low and middle income countries. *Health Policy and Planning, 13*(1), 32–40.

Mills, A., & Broomberg, J. (1998). *Experiences of contracting: An overview of the literature* (Macroeconomics and Health and Development Theory No. 33). Geneva, Switzerland: World Health Organization.

Ministry of Health, Ghana. (1993). *Transport management handbook*. Prepared by Save the Children Fund (UK).

Nancholas, S. (1998). How to do or not to do a logical framework. *Health Policy and Planning, 13*(2), 189–193.

Noakes, J. (1992, June 18). Team spirit. *Health Service Journal*, p. 26.

Okonofua, F. E., Abejide, A., & Makanjuola, R. A. (1992). Maternal mortality in Ile-Ife, Nigeria: A study of risk factors. *Studies in Family Planning, 23*(5), 319–324.

Olsen, I. T. (1998). Sustainability of health care: A framework for analysis. *Health Policy and Planning, 13*(1), 287–295.

Palmer, M., Leila, A., Yassin, E. S. (1989). *The Egyptian bureaucracy*. Cairo, Egypt: American University in Cairo Press.

Palmer, N. (2000). The use of private-sector contracts for primary health care: Theory, evidence and lessons for low-income and middle-income countries. *Bulletin of the World Health Organization, 78*(6), 821–829.

Perrot, J., Carrin, G., & Sergent, F. (1997). *The contractual approach: New partnerships for health in developing countries* (Macroeconomics, Health and Development Series No. 24). Geneva, Switzerland: World Health Organization.

Pheysey, D. C. (1993). *Organizational cultures: Types and transformations*. New York: Routledge.

Reich, M. (1995). The politics of health sector reform in developing countries: Three cases of pharmaceutical policy. *Health Policy, 32,* 47–77.

Rogers, D. L., & Whetten, D. A. (1982). *Interorganizational coordination: Theory, research, and implementation*. Ames: Iowa State University.

Rondeau, K. V., & Wager, T. H. (2001). Impact of human resource management practices on nursing home performance. *Health Service Management Research, 14*(3), 192–202.

Rowbottom, R., & Billis, D. (1987). *Organisational design: The work level approach*. Aldershot, England: Gower.

Schick, A. (1998). Why most developing countries should not try New Zealand's reforms. *World Bank Research Observer, 13*(1), 123–131.

Schmidt, M. J., Riggar, T. F., Crimando, W., & Bordieri, J. E. (1992). *Staffing for success: A guide for health and human service professionals*. London: Sage Publications.

Schulz, R., & Johnson, A. C. (1990). *Management of hospitals and health services: Strategic issues and performance* (3rd ed.). St. Louis, MO: C.V. Mosby.

Smith, M., et al. (1982). *Introducing organisational behaviour*. London: Macmillan Education.

Stead, A., & Leonard, M. C. (1995). Changing to a client-focused quality service through more effective team work. *Health Manpower Management, 21*(4), 23–27.

Stewart, J. (1993). The limitations of government by contract. *Public Money and Management, 13*(3), 7–12.

Stewart, J., & Ranson, S. (1994). Management in the public domain. In A. Lawton & D. McKevitt (Eds.), *Public sector management theory, critique and practice* (pp. 54–70). London: Sage.

Storey, J. (1994). Management development. In K. Sisson (Ed.), *Personnel management: A comprehensive guide to theory and practice in Britain*. Oxford, England: Blackwell Business.

Strike, A. J. (1995). *Human resources in health care: A manager's guide*. Oxford, England: Blackwell Science.

Szeftel, M. (1998). Misunderstanding African politics: Corruption and the governance agenda. *Review of African Political Economy, 25,* 221–240.

Tesch, R. (1990). *Qualitative research: Analysis types and software tools.* New York: The Falmer Press.

Thunhurst, C., & Barker, C. (1999). Using problem structuring methods in strategic planning. *Health Policy and Planning, 14*(2), 127–134.

Transaid. (2001). *Transport management manual.* London: Transaid Worldwide.

Trap, B., Todd, C. H., Moore, H., & Laing, R. (2001). The impact of supervision on stock management and adherence to treatment guidelines: A randomised control trial. *Health Policy and Planning, 16*(3), 273–280.

Tumwine, J. (1993, March–May). Health centres: Involving the community. *Health Action, 4,* 8.

Walsh, K. (1995). *Public services and market mechanisms: Competition, contracting and the new public management.* London: Macmillan.

Wang, Y., Collins, C., Tang, S., & Martineau, T. (2002). Health system decentralisation and human resources management in low and middle income countries. *Public Administration and Development, 22,* 439–453.

Weightman, J. (1996). *Managing people in the health service.* London: Institute of Personnel and Development.

Wilson, R. G., Echols, B. F., Bryant, J. H., & Abrantes, A. (Eds.). (1988). *Management information systems and microcomputers in primary health care.* Geneva, Switzerland: Aga Khan Foundation.

Woelk, G. B. (1994). Primary health care in Zimbabwe: Can it survive? *Social Science and Medicine, 39*(8), 1027–1035.

World Bank. (1993). *World development report 1993: Investing in health.* New York: Oxford University Press.

World Bank. (2004). *World development report 2004: Making services work for poor people.* New York: World Bank and Oxford University Press.

World Health Organization. (2000). *World health report 2000. Health systems: Improving performance.* Geneva, Switzerland: World Health Organization.

World Health Organization. (2001). *World health report 2001. Mental health: New understanding, new hope.* Geneva, Switzerland: World Health Organization.

CHAPTER

13

Health and the Economy

JENNIFER PRAH RUGER, DEAN T. JAMISON, DAVID E. BLOOM, AND DAVID CANNING

Health and health care systems interrelate with the economy in a number of ways, but the multiple causal mechanisms that define this relationship divide naturally into two categories. The first comprises the linkages between health and the growth rate and distribution of income. The second concerns the relationships among health care delivery institutions, health finance policies, and economic outcomes. The two major sections of this chapter follow this division of topics.

Figure 13-1 provides a summary of these linkages and a guide to the structure of the chapter. The first major section deals with relations between the health status of populations and income levels. Health and demography affect income (arrow F) through their impact on labor productivity, savings rates, investments in physical and human capital (education, for example), and age-structure effects. The current literature suggests these effects to be more significant than previously thought, even up to the early 1990s; these issues are addressed in the section titled "Economic Consequences of Ill Health."

The other direction of causality lies in income's impact on health and demography (arrow E). An important part of the literature on the health benefits of higher income assesses the extent to which income operates through improved capacity to purchase food and to have adequate sanitation, housing, and education, and through incentives for fertility limitation. The section titled "Economic Development's Consequences for Health" briefly discusses these points. Further, health systems as a whole play an important role in improving health and are themselves greatly influenced by health finance and related policies (arrows C and D). Other chapters in this volume deal with these issues.

Finally, wealthier countries tend to spend a higher percentage of their income per capita on health and to rely more substantially on public-sector finance than lower-income countries (arrow B). Conversely, health finance and delivery mechanisms affect income level and distribution (arrow A) through their effects on incentives and institutional environments. Some health finance systems are, for example, more progressive than others, favorably affecting the distribution of income, whereas others have detrimental efficiency consequences through their effects on labor markets or on the adequacy with which financial risks are shared. The second major section of the chapter explores these linkages.

Whether the final objective of development policy is economic growth, poverty alleviation, or improved health, these domains are inextricably linked. Better information on the magnitude of the association

Acknowledgments: The original version of this chapter was prepared for the 1998 transition team of the then-incoming World Health Organization (WHO) Director-General Dr. G. H. Brundtland. Preparation of that version was supported by grants from the Royal Norwegian Ministry of Foreign Affairs to WHO and the World Bank. The WHO Commission on Macroeconomics and Health supported extension and revision, and discussions with the commission's chair, Jeffrey Sachs, provided valuable ideas and feedback during preparation of this chapter. Conclusions and opinions are those of the authors and not necessarily those of any of the sponsoring agencies. Felicia Knaul, Lawrence Lau, Pia Malaney, and Anne Mills also made valuable suggestions and comments on earlier drafts. Leslie Evans prepared the tables and graphics.

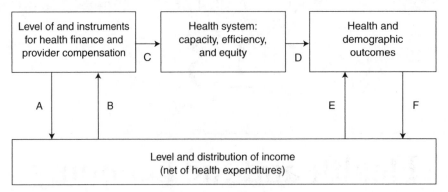

Figure 13-1 Health, Health Policies, and Economic Outcomes.

between health and economic growth and of health systems and economic outcomes can aid academics and policy makers in understanding and devising health and development policies that will improve people's quality of life worldwide. This understanding allows the development of more balanced policy portfolios (Bloom & River Path Associates, 2000).

Health and Economic Development

The evidence presented here suggests that health is closely linked with economic growth and development. Figure 13-2 illustrates the multiple pathways through which illness can have an effect. The top half shows the age-structure effects of demographic transition as seen by a change in the dependency ratio, which has been a significant determinant of growth in East Asia, for example. High levels of fertility and child mortality (both in part a result of child illness), along with reductions in the labor force brought on by mortality and early retirement, can cause an increase in the dependency ratio that ultimately reduces income. A reversal of these effects can cause a decrease in the dependency ratio, which increases per capita income. In addition, childhood health can affect adult health. Recent research points to a strong link between the health of adults and how healthy they were as children (Kuh & Ben-Shlomo, 1997). The relevant arrow in Figure 13-2 represents that additional pathway between child health and economic outcomes. The lower half of Figure 13-2 illustrates the effects of illness and malnutrition, operating through other factors such as reduced investments in human and physical capital, in reducing labor productivity. And finally, reduced labor productivity has a direct impact on reducing per capita income. Economic conditions influence health as well: The relationship be-

tween health and economic development is causal in both directions.

Progress in health and other dimensions of development during the 20th century arguably constitutes one of mankind's greatest achievements. Rates of progress were so high that projecting them back— or forward—in time suggests that never before and, probably, never again will so much be achieved in so short a period. Before turning to the more systematic discussion of health and economic development, it is worth touching on the broader context.

Table 13-1 provides examples of progress in five domains: health itself, fertility rates, physical growth (or nutritional status), cognitive growth, and income, linked in a web of mutual causation. Row 1 takes health using the life expectancy of Chilean females in the period 1909 to 1999 as an example. At the beginning of this period, their life expectancy was 33 years; it then increased at an average rate of 1% per annum over 90 years to a level of 78 years in 1999 (World Health Organization [WHO], 1999). Had this rate been in effect for the preceding 70 years, life expectancy would have been 16 years in 1835, far lower than the actual level. If this rate were to continue, life expectancy would exceed 150 years by 2070—conceivable, but unlikely. For the other indicators, the 20th century also stands out, in some cases more dramatically, in others less so.

The example of cognitive growth may be less familiar than the others. Evidence from an increasing number of studies around the world suggests major improvements in the average level of general, or "fluid," intelligence. The Dutch study cited in the table is particularly suggestive. All Dutch males are screened (including an IQ test) for military service at about age 20. The study matched sons (1982 cohort) with fathers (1952 cohort) and found a 21-point gain. This gain is larger than that found in most studies, but it is indicative of the general pattern. Flynn (1998)

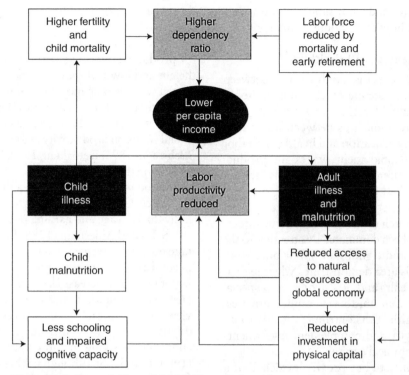

Figure 13-2 Channels Through Which Illness Reduces Income. *Source:* World Health Organization, *World Health Report 1999: Making a Difference* (Geneva, Switzerland: World Health Organization, 1999), p. 11. Reprinted with permission.

Table 13-1	Human Progress in the Twentieth Century: Never Before, Never Again		
Welfare Indicator	**Example**	**Before and After**	**Rate**
Health (proxied by mortality)	Life expectancy, Chilean females (1909–1999)	33 years in 1909 78 years in 1999	1.0% per annum *or* .45 s.d.[a] per generation[b]
Total fertility rate[c]	TFR, Western Pacific Region (1950–1998)	5.9 in 1950 1.9 in 1998	−2.4% per annum *or* −.53 s.d. per generation
Physical growth (height for age or BMI)	Height, 10-year-old Norwegian females (1920–1970)[d]	130.2 cm in 1920 139.6 cm in 1990	1.9 cm/decade *or* .84 s.d. per generation
Cognitive growth (general or "fluid" intelligence)	Dutch males' IQ (1982) relative to that of their own fathers (1952)	IQ = 100 in 1952 IQ = 121 in 1982	7 points per decade *or* 1.4 s.d. per generation
Income	Income per capita, Latin America (1913–1992), in 1990 dollars	$1,440 in 1913 $4,820 in 1992	1.5% per annum

[a]An s.d. refers to an estimate of the standard deviation of the variable's distribution at the initial time.
[b]This defines a generation to equal 30 years.
[c]The total fertility rate (TFR) is the expected number of children a woman would have if she gave birth at the then-current age-specific fertility rates.
[d]Source for 1970: G. H. Brundtland et al., *Acta Paed Scand*, 1975.

summarizes the Dutch and many similar studies (while placing caveats on how they should be interpreted.)

Economic Consequences of Ill Health

Microeconomic analyses that study the link between health and economic outcomes focus on household-, family-, and individual-level data. Such studies typically look at the relationships between human resources, particularly education and health, and labor market outcomes (employment, wages and productivity, and age of retirement). Although it is increasingly well established empirically that a person's health affects his or her labor performance (market and nonmarket), much of the microeconomic literature in the past has been dominated by attention to the role of education and training on labor outcomes. Recent work in this area demonstrates why the relationship between health and productivity is of special interest to low- and middle-income countries. Investments in health both contribute directly to individual productivity and complement investments in education and physical capital.

Macroeconomic studies provide evidence of a different sort by assessing the influence of health on national income in cross-country comparisons. This chapter focuses on such studies from low- and middle-income countries, although a number of examples from high-income countries are included. Thomas and Strauss (1998) provide more extensive coverage of this area, particularly with respect to household studies. Currie and Madrian (1999) cover the research literature concerning health and labor market outcomes in the United States and other high-income countries and provide a careful discussion of problems of causality and statistical specification. This chapter notes those important issues, but does not address them in a substantial way.

Households and Diseases

Health, Nutrition, and Productivity. The growing body of knowledge of the relationship between health and the earnings of individuals can be useful in designing policy interventions aimed at health improvement. These measures have the potential to enhance labor productivity, especially among those in lower-income countries and among lower-income groups within countries.

Much of the work in this area has examined the impact of adult anthropometric measures such as height, weight, body mass index (BMI), and patterns of illness and disability (all measures or indicators of health) on individuals' labor productivity as measured primarily

by wages or earnings. Height and mortality have been found to be inversely related, implying that reductions in height can ultimately reduce an individual's number of productive working years (Schultz, 1997). Short height and low BMI have also been found to be associated with chronic morbidity in midlife (ages 20–50) and with male deaths in late life (Fogel, 1994). A number of other studies have assessed the effects of nutritional status on productivity in lower-income countries (Behrman, 1993; Deolalikar, 1988; Sahn & Alderman, 1988) and the cumulative impact of parental nutrition, childhood nourishment, and health over the course of the life cycle on adult height, which ultimately affects individuals' wage and earning potential.

Sahn and Alderman (1988) found that energy intake influenced wage offers for male and female labor in rural and urban areas of Sri Lanka, suggesting that better nutrition increases labor productivity. Behrman (1993) also found, in a comprehensive literature review, that nutrition has direct effects on the labor productivity of poorer individuals in lower-income countries. Working in rural south India, Deolalikar (1988) found that although neither market wages nor farm output was affected by a worker's daily energy intake, both variables were influenced by weight-for-height ratios, indicating that chronic malnutrition has a significant effect on market wages and farm output. Evidence from Rwanda described in Exhibit 13-1 does, however, show direct effects of energy consumption operating through time allocation.

Thomas and Strauss (1998) have proposed two main reasons why household production studies should focus on health as an important determinant of productivity. First, they argue that the marginal productivity of good health is likely to be higher in lower-income countries than in industrialized societies because of lower absolute levels of health and different patterns of disease. In particular, the predominance of infectious diseases in lower-income countries causes higher rates of infant and child morbidity and mortality. The result can be ill-health consequences that are felt throughout the life cycle and not primarily at older ages, as in the case of higher-income countries. Second, Thomas and Strauss argue that because employment opportunities in lower-income economies tend to depend on physical strength and endurance, the benefits of better health are likely to be greater in these settings. For example, Indonesian men with anemia were found to have 20% lower productivity than men without. In an experiment, men were randomly assigned to one of two groups, receiving either an iron supplement or a placebo. Those who were anemic initially and received the iron treatment increased their productivity to nearly the

Exhibit 13-1	**Nutrient Intake and Time Allocation in Rwanda**

Information on energy (calorie) intake and use can be difficult to obtain in all societies, but it is especially difficult in lower-income countries. Some people are self-sufficient, working primarily on their own land and in their own homes; because they do not receive monetary compensation in the marketplace, measuring the variables necessary to test implications for health is not easy. It can also be difficult to ascertain this relationship when health effects lag behind other changes; for example, simple measures, such as changes in dietary habits through protein intake and micronutrient supplementation for children, can prevent diseases later in the life cycle (Bhargava, 1994). Hence, some scholars analyze time allocation (from time allocation surveys, which document time spent on different activities, such as sleeping, resting or sitting quietly, work involving agriculture or heavy activities, or housework) and evaluate the relationship between time allocation and nutritional status to examine the energy intake, nutritional status, and health nexus.

In a 1982–1983 study of the time allocation patterns of adult men and women in approximately 110 Rwandan households surveyed four times, Bhargava found that low incomes and high food prices reduced households' energy intakes, resulting in more time spent resting and sleeping. The study also gathered statistics on age, consumption, production, protein intake, and weight and height (used to calculate body mass index). The study found that the energy standard for active adult subsistence requires energy intakes of at least twice the basal metabolic rate.

The policy implications of this work are important. Interventions designed to improve nutrient intake and use through better health would enable individuals to carry out the activities necessary for active adult subsistence. Subsistence at higher activity levels will, in turn, enhance people's ability to purchase nutritious food in the marketplace, and dietary guidelines at a broad policy level should reflect the nutritional and energy needs for human activity.

levels of nonanemic workers, and the productivity gains were large when weighed against the costs of treatment. Thus, the effects of improved health are likely to be greatest for the most vulnerable, that is, the lowest income, the sickest, and those with the least education. Further, if there are thresholds of health status below which functioning and productivity are seriously impaired, policies that target those with the poorest health will yield the greatest increases in income. Bhargava and associates (2001) found strong evidence to support the plausible view that the effects of health on growth rates (using adult survival rates as the measure of health) are strongest at low levels of income.

In their earlier work in urban Brazil, Thomas and Strauss (Strauss & Thomas, 1995; Thomas & Strauss, 1997) analyzed the effects on wages of health indicators such as height and BMI, along with energy and protein intake, while controlling for educational variables that also contribute to earnings.[1] Including health variables in their analysis significantly reduced the effects of education on wages. They found that height had a significant effect on wages (taller men and women earned more than shorter men and

women), that higher BMI was associated with higher wages among males, and that this effect was most pronounced for less educated men. In addition, lower levels of energy and protein intake per person were associated with reduced wages for market workers, but not for the self-employed.

In Ghana, Schultz (1996) found that height significantly affected wages; for example, a 1-cm increase resulted in an 8% increase in male hourly wages and a 7% increase in female hourly wages. In Mexico, Knaul (1999b) studied the productivity of investments in health and nutrition for women. The author analyzed the impact of age at menarche, or first menstruation (an indicator of cumulative health and nutritional status), on female labor market productivity and found that investments in health and nutrition had significant effects on productivity. A 1-year decline in age of menarche was associated with a 25% increase in wages.[2] A report by Savedoff and Schultz (2000) contains a number of studies linking health to productivity and income in Latin America.

Human energy intake and nutritional deficiencies significantly affect people's ability to work. A

---

[1]It is important to maintain a sharp distinction, as Strauss and Thomas have done, between nutrient intake and malnutrition. Nutrient intake is one determinant of nutritional status (as measured by anthropometric indicators such as height-for-age ratios, or biochemical indicators such as hematocrit for anemia). In many environments, infectious diseases will also be important determinants of malnutrition. For this reason, prevention or control of infection may often be more cost-effective for controlling malnutrition than attempts to improve diets through food transfers, food subsidies, or social marketing. (See Chapter 5 for more information on nutrition.)

[2]See also Knaul and Parker (1998) on the patterns over time and the determinants of early labor force participation and school dropout in Mexican children and youth.

number of studies (Basta et al., 1979; Gardner et al., 1975; Spurr, 1983) have demonstrated the influence of iron deficiency on oxygen consumption and the positive impact of iron supplementation on labor productivity. The effects of nutritional status on work performance are of interest to policy makers designing food and economic programs to improve energy and nutrient intake.

In summary, the literature indicates a positive relationship among earnings, productivity, and energy intake. Higher earnings give people greater ability to purchase food, improving energy, nutrient intake, and health; improved health ultimately enhances productivity. Leibenstein (1957), Mirrlees (1975), and others have espoused this set of relationships. Fogel (1994) also has done significant historical research in this area, suggesting that improvement in nutritional and health status contributed to the economic growth of England and France from about 1750 onward.

Disability and Income. In a study of the effects of illness on wages and labor supply in Côte d'Ivoire and Ghana, Schultz and Tansel (1997) found that wages were significantly lower for each disabled day; in other words, poor health in the form of disability has negative consequences for labor productivity. In examining the productivity of household investments in health in Colombia, Ribero and Nunez (1999) found that an additional day of disability in a given month decreased male rural earnings hourly by 33% and female earnings by 13%. A disability in a given month was also detrimental to urban workers' wages, decreasing hourly earnings of urban males by 28% and urban females by 14%. Height was also found to affect productivity significantly: a 1-cm increase resulted in a 6.9% increase in urban female earnings and an 8% increase in urban male earnings. Ribero and Nunez (1999) also evaluated the effects of public and private investments in health. They found that an increase in social security coverage in rural areas could result in a lower incidence and duration of illness, whereas increases in urban areas would result in a greater propensity to report illnesses. They also found that, although basic service interventions, such as electricity and sewage or potable water, had very little effect on height and productivity, policies focused on providing adequate housing for those in need did have a positive impact on health and productivity.

Murrugarra and Valdivia (1999) studied the returns to health for Peruvian urban adults. Employing a two-stage process, they first estimated the relationship between education and health; then they examined the effects of health on productivity (measured by wages), looking at different subsamples of the population (e.g., stratified by gender, age, location in the wage distribution, and type of employer, either public or private, small or large, or self-employed). The authors found that schooling's effects on health were positive, strong, and increased with age for urban males. They also found a positive effect of health on wages, controlling for education and income effects, which differed for different subgroups of the population. For example, among older, self-employed males, an additional sick day resulted in a 4.3% reduction in average hourly earnings. These males experienced greater effects due to illness than other groups; for instance, those at the lowest end of the earnings distribution experienced a reduction in average earnings due to an additional sick day of 3.8%, and those in the private sector experienced the weakest effect, with a 1.8% reduction in hourly earnings due to an additional sick day. The results for females were inconclusive.

Finally, disease and disability affect individuals' retirement decisions. For example, in Jamaica, Handa and Neitzert (1998) found that individuals with chronic illness face an increased probability of retirement as compared with healthy individuals. In the United States, Dwyer and Mitchell (1999) studied the impact of mental and physical capacity for work on older men's retirement decisions. They found that health variables were more influential than economic factors on the decision to retire and estimated that men in poor health would retire, on average, 1 to 2 years earlier than those in good health.

In total, these studies suggest that health is related to productivity, both through the direct effects that adult height and chronic morbidity have on adult productivity and through the inverse relationship between height and mortality that can ultimately reduce an individual's number of productive working years. In addition, illness and disability have negative consequences on labor productivity, reducing hourly wages by as much as 33%. The studies summarized in Exhibit 13-2 provide strong evidence that the link from health to productivity is causal in nature. These factors are particularly important in lower-income countries, where a significant proportion of the workforce is involved in agriculture and other forms of manual labor. Also, the negative effects of malnutrition during childhood can have lasting effects on human capacity, and the effects of improved health are probably greatest for the most vulnerable: the lowest income, the sickest, and the least well educated.

Although the causal link between health and productivity levels can usually only be determined by statistical methods based on observation of popula-

Exhibit 13-2	Do Health Changes Cause Income Changes?

In efforts to study the relationships among different variables (such as, for example, health and wages), it is difficult to disentangle mutual causation, that is, the strength of causation in each direction. In some studies, researchers attempt to go beyond standard statistical techniques, such as ordinary least-squares regression, in efforts to deal with both measurement error and the endogeneity of health. These studies require complicated multiple-staged statistical methods and produce results that are suggestive but seldom definitive. Three studies have used data allowing for a simpler, sharper assessment of causality and are illustrative of how data sets including non-income-related determinants of health can resolve the causality problem. Each study confirms a strong causal link from health to economic outcomes.

A British experiment (Moffett et al., 1999) evaluated the effectiveness of an exercise program for patients with lower back pain, through a randomized controlled trial of the program compared with usual primary care management. The results indicated that at 1 year the intervention group showed significantly greater improvement on a scale of back pain, and reported in total only 378 days off work compared with 607 in the control group. The intervention group used fewer health care resources.

Another study, in the United States, traced the consequences for wealth status of a sudden health shock (Smith, 1999), evaluating the impact of the onset of chronic health problems (controlling for demographic factors, health risk behaviors, and preexisting conditions) and mild and severe new health conditions. Researchers found that onsets of even mild health problems may have lowered wealth accumulation by US$3,620. The impact of new, severe health problems on savings was found to be a mean wealth reduction of about US$17,000 or 7% of household wealth (per incident). Finally, among Americans aged 70 and over, a new health condition was found to lower wealth accumulation by about US$10,000, half of which was found to be a reduction in financial assets.

Finally, an experiment involving 6,000 households in Indonesia (Dow et al., 1997) studied the effect of changes in prices of publicly provided health services on labor force participation. By randomly selecting districts where fees were raised, and by holding fees in neighboring control districts constant, the authors found that some health indicators and the use of health care declined in test areas relative to controls. Higher prices were associated with more limitations in daily activities and more days spent in bed, especially among the poor and among women in households with low economic and educational status. Finally, the study found significant declines in labor force participation in the test area among vulnerable groups.

tions, a more direct method is to use either actual or natural experiments to investigate the link. Almond (2003) uses the influenza pandemic of 1918 in the United States as a natural experiment. This pandemic caused health problems later in life for those with in utero exposure. By comparing the life courses of this cohort with those immediately before and after, one can estimate the economic effect of the exposure. More directly, Thomas and colleagues (2003) estimate the effects of a randomized controlled trial that provided iron supplementation and deworming medication to a population in Indonesia with high levels of iron deficiency anemia. They find large effects on productivity levels and earnings for some workers.

Economic Costs of Particular Diseases

The economic effect of specific aspects of health status can be assessed by evaluating the economic burden created by particular diseases. The economic costs of particular diseases typically comprise two elements: (1) the direct costs of prevention and treatment, and (2) the indirect costs of labor time lost due to illness. Although empirical work in this area is limited, this section reviews economic analyses of three diseases—

malaria, tuberculosis, and HIV/AIDS—with additional illustrative examples of the Onchocerciasis Control Program (OCP) and mental illness.

Malaria. Malaria, among the most significant public health problems in lower-income countries, still claims about 1.1 million lives per year. In all WHO member states, the estimated total of disability-adjusted life years (DALYs) lost in 1998 due to malaria is calculated to be 39 million, or 2.8% of the total DALYs lost because of disease (WHO, 1999).[3] The high rates of morbidity and mortality caused by this disease suggest significant economic costs. (See Chapter 4.)

Chima, Goodman, and Mills (2003) and Malaney (1998) have delineated the direct and indirect economic costs of malaria as follows: the direct costs of prevention (mosquito coils, aerosol sprays, bed nets, residual spraying, and mosquito repellents) and treatment (drugs, treatment fees, transport, and costs of

---

[3]The World Bank (1993) introduced disease burden measurements based on DALYs, and the initial full publication of results appears in Murray, Lopez, and Jamison (1994).

subsistence at a health center); and the indirect costs of labor time lost because of illness. Given these two components, malaria directly increases household and public-sector expenditures and reduces labor inputs and can reduce human capital as a result of declines in school attendance, lowered school performance, and increased cognitive impairment. It has also been suggested to cause inefficiencies with respect to land use. Leighton and Foster (1993) estimate the total annual value of malaria-related production loss to be 2% to 6% of gross domestic product (GDP) in Kenya and 1% to 5% of GDP in Nigeria. Malaria-related costs as a percentage of total household costs for small farmers were 0.8% to 5.2% in Kenya and 7.2% to 13.2% in Nigeria.

Microeconomic studies of malaria tend to evaluate the costs of the disease in terms of its impact within a specific economic environment. Potentially more significant, however, is the effect of disease on economic opportunities. If a factory goes unbuilt in a region because of malaria, for example, the consequences for income may be far more substantial than malaria's consequence for productivity in traditional agriculture. Gallup and Sachs (2001) advance this perspective and argue for a macroeconomic approach that uses cross-country time-series data to capture effects that would go unobserved with household data. In particular, they find a significant negative relationship between malaria and GDP growth, with far greater estimated magnitude than reported in the household-level studies. Due to compounding, small changes in the rate of economic growth can have large long-term effects. Gallup and Sachs suggest that the most important ways in which malaria affects long-run economic growth are the effect of the disease on a country's ability to attract foreign direct investment and to create an environment suitable for modern economic growth. Allowing countries to undertake new enterprises, rather than just improving productivity in traditional enterprise, may be the most economically significant consequence of malaria control programs. Although there are shortcomings in the malaria data, the findings remain suggestive, even if not definitive.

Tuberculosis. Tuberculosis is a serious health threat across the globe. In 1998, the number of deaths from tuberculosis in all WHO member states was roughly 1.5 million, or almost 2.5% of all deaths. In 1997, in China alone there were 2.2 million new cases of tuberculosis, with an average case fatality rate of 20% (WHO, 1999). Tuberculosis is estimated to be four times more concentrated in lower-income populations than among the well-off (WHO, 1999). In addition, the considerable barriers to detecting the

disease and to reducing infectiousness exacerbate the impact of tuberculosis and increase the probability of transmitting it to others. It is estimated that only half of all tuberculosis cases are detected. If a patient does receive treatment, the risk of 5-year mortality is reduced to roughly 15%. Tuberculosis is a disease that primarily affects adults, especially those in their most productive years. It is estimated that 77% of tuberculosis DALY cases and deaths occur among adults ranging in age from 15 to 59 years (Murray, Lopez, & Jamison, 1994). (See Chapter 4).

This section discusses two aspects of tuberculosis that have been addressed in the literature: (1) its economic burden, which necessarily compares different treatment options, and (2) the economic benefits and the cost-effectiveness of control, comparing the relative economic merits of different interventions. Exhibit 13-3 discusses the economic benefits of a tuberculosis control program in India.

The economic impact of tuberculosis, like malaria, comprises two components: the direct costs of prevention and treatment, and the indirect costs of earnings lost due to illness or mortality. Because tuberculosis largely affects adults in the most productive stage of their lives, the indirect costs of the disease can be quite high. Ahlburg (2000) provides a cost analysis in various lower-income settings.

In their study of patients presenting to a tuberculosis clinic in northwest Bangladesh, Croft and Croft (1998) found a mean financial loss to the patient of US$245, or 4 months' income (roughly 30% of annual family income based on an average annual income for a Bangladeshi family of US$780). The breakdown of the loss of income was US$115 of US$245, while the direct medical costs totaled roughly US$130, consisting of medicine costs of US$112, doctor's fees of US$9, and laboratory costs of US$8.50. Of the 21 patients studied, 8 were forced to sell land or livestock to pay for necessary treatment. Geography was a significant factor in obtaining treatment: 6 of the 21 patients were able to walk to the clinic, but of the remaining 15 patients, 5 reported that transportation costs (US$0.25–1.25) were a relatively significant amount for their family.

Saunderson (1995) compared the costs and consequences of then-current treatment practices for tuberculosis in Uganda with a program based on treating ambulatory patients at their nearest health unit while they lived at home. He found that the total costs per patient for the current practice was £190 versus £115 for ambulatory care. The breakdown of costs for each program showed a total cost per patient to the health service of £55 for current practice and

Exhibit 13-3	Economic Benefits of Tuberculosis Control in India

Tuberculosis is estimated to be one of the leading causes of ill health and death in India, where, in 1997, there were 4 million tuberculosis sufferers. The health and economic consequences of tuberculosis infection are considerable: prolonged illness and premature mortality, medical costs, and indirect costs due to lost productivity. Although chemotherapy treatment options are available, these programs are often self-administered or are costly in terms of the direct medical costs of treatment in tertiary or hospital settings and in terms of the time necessary to receive care—sometimes as much as 12 months of treatment. These self-administered and long treatment programs in tertiary facilities have limited effectiveness due to high relapse rates, low cure rates, high case fatality rates, and drug resistance.

The World Health Organization developed DOTS (directly observed treatment, short course) to alleviate some of the problems of existing long-course and self-administered chemotherapy. Dholakia and Almeida (1997) attempted to estimate the potential health and economic benefits of successfully implementing the DOTS program in India, based on two primary assumptions: (1) DOTS will succeed in alleviating pulmonary tuberculosis in India, and (2) DOTS will reach 100% of tuberculosis patients with full and instantaneous coverage. They found that, with a relatively high discount rate, a low percentage growth in labor productivity, and use of present value calculations for the future stream of benefits resulting from DOTS, the potential economic benefit to the Indian economy was about 4% of GDP in real terms, or US$8.3 billion in 1993–1994.

Realistically, however, the DOTS strategy will probably not be immediately 100% implementable, involving a phasing-in process in which personnel are trained, the drug supply system is reformed, and organizational and management changes are made. The longer the period of phase-in, the lower the present discounted value of economic benefits associated with DOTS. Dholakia and Almeida (1997) estimated that a phasing in of DOTS coverage in India over 10 years with a conservatively high discount rate of 16% would result in a present value of economic benefits of 2.1% of GDP (1993–1994), or US$4.6 billion, with a 16% rate of return in real terms. This translates into US$750 million per year in tangible economic benefits from a successfully implemented DOTS program that costs US$200 million per year.

£65 for the ambulatory program. In addition, the total costs per patient were £134 for the current practice and £49 for the alternative program. Thus, the largest difference between the two programs was patient costs: The ambulatory care program resulted in roughly one-half of the costs to the patient as compared with the current practice, primarily because of reduced costs before diagnosis (halved in the alternative program due to greater access to the program), the elimination of a hospital stay, and the reduced costs due to work loss.

In a cost-effectiveness analysis between the two programs at different levels of cure rate, the ambulatory program was found to be more cost-effective (at a total cost per cure of £230 for a 50% cure rate, £192 for 60%, and £164 for 70%) than the current practice (at a cost per cure of £380 for a 50% cure rate and £316 for 60%).[4] In comparing the two programs, Saunderson (1995) concluded that savings from the avoidance of loss of work had the greatest effect on cost per cure. Under the current program, the average time spent away from normal activities due to illness was 9.5 months (range: 1 week to 3 years). Interviewing patients revealed that many had spent this time visiting various clinics and hospitals in search of care. The shadow price for time away from work was assumed to be the salary of a nursing aide (approximately £10 per month), for an average loss of £95. Also, 33 of 34 patients interviewed reported that their work and income had been affected by the illness. Eight of 10 patients involved in paid employment or business reported that they had stopped work or closed their business due to illness, and 23 of 24 farmers reported reduced work and lost production as a result of their illness. Five patients noted the need to remove their children from school because they could no longer pay school fees. The assumption was that the time away from work could be reduced by roughly 60% with ambulatory treatment.

In northeastern KwaZulu-Natal (Hlabisa health district) in South Africa, Wilkinson, Floyd, and Gilks (1997) conducted an economic evaluation of the directly observed treatment, short course (DOTS) strategy and the conventionally delivered treatment for managing tuberculosis. They found that the total health system costs per patient in 1996 U.S. dollars were $649 for DOTS and $1,775 for conventional treatment. The total cost per case cured for DOTS was $740 and for conventional treatment $2,047, making DOTS 2.8 times cheaper overall than conventional treatment. In a scenario analysis of the best and worst

---

[4]For another cost-effectiveness analysis of alternative tuberculosis management strategies in South Africa, see Wilkinson, Floyd, and Gilks (1997).

cases, DOTS was 2.4 to 4.2 times more cost-effective, costing $890 per patient cured compared with either $2,095 (best case) or $3,700 (worst case) for conventional treatment. Wilkinson, Floyd, and Gilks attributed the reduced expense of DOTS to reduced hospital stays.

In most of these studies, costs may be underestimated in the sense that they do not always include monetary equivalents of losses in the household's production due to illness (i.e., indirect costs); reduced efficiency of land use; transport, housing, and food costs during treatment; human capital loss (increased absenteeism and reduced performance at school for children of a household with an adult infected with tuberculosis); and the value of pain and suffering. What is clear, though, is that costs are substantial and that cost-effective means of control are available. The case for control efforts will be strong in many contexts.

HIV/AIDS. Most studies find the economic effects of HIV/AIDS on the economy to be relatively small. For example, a study of the impact of HIV/AIDS on the national economy of India (Anand, Pandav, & Nath, 1999) found that the estimated total annual cost of HIV/AIDS in India under low (1.5 million infected), medium (2.5 million), and high (4.5 million) prevalence scenarios was 7 billion, 20 billion, and 59 billion rupees, respectively. AIDS treatment and productivity loss were the two major components of costs. Anand and associates concluded that the estimated annual cost of HIV/AIDS (assuming 4.5 million infected) was roughly 1% of the GDP of India.

Conversely, in a study of 51 developing and industrialized countries, controlling for potentially confounding variables and correcting for simultaneity, Bloom and Mahal (1997) found that the AIDS epidemic—early in its course—had an insignificant effect on the growth of per capita income. Bloom, Rosenfield, and River Path Associates (2000), however, discuss evidence of the economic effects of AIDS on individual businesses. Over, Bertozzi, and Chin (1989) estimated direct and indirect costs attributable to a given HIV infection in the Democratic Republic of the Congo and Tanzania. Estimates of total costs per case of HIV infection ranged from US$940 to US$3,230 (1985 dollars) in the Democratic Republic of the Congo, and from US$2,460 to US$5,320 in Tanzania. Cuddington (1991) and Cuddington and Hancock (1992) estimated that, assuming AIDS treatments are entirely financed from savings and that workers sick with AIDS are 50% as productive as they would be without AIDS, the growth rate of GDP would be reduced by 0.8 percentage point in Tanzania and by 1.5 per-

centage points in Malawi. In 1992, Over estimated that (assuming 50% of AIDS treatment costs come from savings) GDP growth is slowed by 0.9 percentage point per year in the average country (among 34 sub-Saharan countries), and per capita growth by 0.2 point. Ainsworth and Over (1994) find similar results. The International Monetary Fund commissioned assessments of the full range of macroeconomic consequences of the epidemic that document the diversity as well as the magnitude of the effects (Haacker, 2004).

One reason for the small effects found is that economic consequences are usually measured in terms of income per capita. A high death rate reduces both income and the number of people in the economy, causing a sharp reduction in total output but a more modest effect on income per capita. This points to a weakness of using a purely economic measure as the impact of the burden of disease. Jamison, Sachs, and Wang (2001) argue that the main burden of HIV/AIDS is the welfare loss to those with the disease who become ill and die. Using as a metric the income level of the survivors, as is done with income per capita, is inappropriate. When they valued decreases (or increases) in a country's mortality rates using now standard microeconomic estimates and added this to the change in per capita income, Jamison and colleagues found dramatic negative economic consequences of the epidemic in five countries of eastern Africa in the period after 1990. The importance of the direct welfare effects of good health is emphasized by Nordhaus (2003), who argues that the welfare gains from improved health and longevity in the United States in the 20th century were greater than the welfare gains due to rising income levels over the period.

Although to date the economic effects of HIV/AIDS have been relatively small, Bell, Devarajan, and Gersbach (2003) sound a warning note. They argue that the high numbers of orphans in countries with high AIDS mortality rates will lead to a lack of resources for education and the production of successive cohorts with lower levels of schooling and income. In particular, this may plunge sub-Saharan Africa into even greater poverty.

Other Diseases. In a cost-benefit analysis of the OCP in West Africa, which prevents river-blindness, Kim and Benton (1995) estimated OCP's net benefits in terms of net present value (NPV) and economic rate of return (ERR) over two project horizons, 1974 to 2002 and 1974 to 2012. The NPV of labor and land-related benefits together (assuming 85% labor participation and land use) over a 39-year project horizon (1974–2012) ranged between US$3,730 million and

US$485 million, in 1987 constant dollars at discount rates of 3% and 10%, respectively. The estimated ERR under the same assumptions was approximately 20%. Using a project horizon of 29 years yielded an ERR of approximately 18%.

In their study of the impact of mental illness on employment, Ettner, Frank, and Kessler (1997) found that in aggregate, psychiatric disorders reduced the probability of employment by roughly 14% to 15% for both men and women. Robins and Regier (1991), in their analysis of the impact of mental health problems on income, found that 4.5% of women and 3% of men in the United States reported an inability to work or assume normal activities at some point in the past 3 months due to emotional stress. In reviewing a broad range of studies from high-income countries (mostly the United States), Currie and Madrian (1999) pointed to the particular significance of mental illness.

In contrast to the findings of many other condition-specific studies, Svedberg (2000), in a broad assessment of linkages between poverty and undernutrition, concluded that the links from malnutrition to poverty were probably relatively weak. In this he also differs from much of the literature cited earlier in this chapter.

Health and Education

Health and nutritional problems can also have significant consequences for the educational success of many school-aged children. Such problems result not only in direct welfare losses but also in losses of learning opportunities that are essential to the economic, social, and parental success of these individuals and, ultimately, their societies. The close link between health and school attendance and performance raises the question of how educational systems might in-

tervene to improve conditions that undermine both health and educational success.

Figure 13-3 illustrates the different ways in which health, school participation, and learning outcomes are related, and how health and school quality interventions can influence educational outcomes. The evidence examining these relationships is discussed in this section. The figure demonstrates that school quality interventions can affect the learning rate, which, in conjunction with enrollment and attendance rates, can directly affect the distribution of learning in a given age cohort. The figure also illustrates that health-related interventions, through their influence on health and nutrition status, can enhance learning rates and participation, both of which contribute to learning outcomes. School location policies also have direct links to participation rates, which in turn influence learning.

Leslie and Jamison (1990) reviewed the links between health conditions and three important education problems in developing countries: (1) children who are unprepared to begin school at the usual age, (2) the failure of many students to learn adequately in school, and (3) the unequal participation of girls in schooling. Despite data limitations, their study found that several widespread health and nutritional problems clearly have negative consequences for school participation and performance. When children suffer from weakened or lower-than-expected physical capacity (and concomitant problems with cognitive ability, psychological well-being, and social competence), they may be incapable of attending school or be developmentally limited. Lack of school readiness in the form of physical and cognitive abilities and social and communication skills can result in significantly lower than average school performance as compared nationally and internationally. When children are too

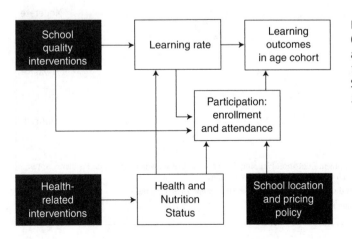

Figure 13-3 Health, School Participation, and Learning Outcomes. *Source:* J. Leslie and D. T. Jamison, "Health and Nutrition Considerations in Education Planning, 1. Educational Consequences of Health Problems Among School-Age Children," 1990, *Food and Nutrition Bulletin, 12*(3). Adapted with permission.

sick to learn in school, they fail to obtain minimal literacy and numeracy skills central not only to educational success but also to later economic and social achievements.

The authors suggest that seven categories of health conditions are likely to affect school participation or learning, and occur frequently in lower-income country contexts. These conditions are (1) nutritional deficiencies, (2) helminthic infections (including intestinal parasites and schistosomiasis), (3) other infections, (4) disabilities, (5) reproductive and sexual problems (including premature fertility, sexual violence, and exposure to sexually transmitted infections), (6) injury and poisoning, and (7) substance abuse. Table 13-2 demonstrates that not all types of childhood illness and malnutrition are important for education, nor are these conditions all easily alleviated through school-based interventions. For example, in dealing with certain health conditions, such as early protein-energy malnutrition, school-based measures offer little help, whereas school is a potentially important venue for intervening against certain other conditions, such as tobacco use, that are important for health but not important for schooling.

In their summary of the relationships between the seven health conditions just mentioned and the three education problems (unpreparedness, failure to learn, and unequal participation by girls), Leslie and Jamison (1990) concluded that nutritional deficiencies have the most significant negative impact on education. Such deficiencies cause reduced cognitive function in both preschool and school-aged children and are directly reflected in poorer school attendance and achievement. Their review suggests that prenatal iodine deficiency causes permanent mental retardation, and chronic iodine deficiency can lead to less severe mental impairment among school-aged children and adults (see also Chapter 5). It also reveals that among infectious diseases, hookworm has a strong negative effect on cognitive function and Guinea worm on school attendance. Finally, although research on the links between education and reproductive health and substance abuse problems is limited, it is believed that the combined effects of early marriage, unwanted pregnancy, and concerns about sexual vulnerability at least partially influence the lower school participation rates of young females compared with those of males.

The question then arises as to how educational systems might intervene to improve the health and nutrition status of school-aged children. In a companion paper reviewing the costs and effectiveness of school-based interventions, Jamison and Leslie (1990) have concluded that, given the current state of research on the health and education relationship, and the relatively low costs of well-designed and targeted programs, increased investment in child health and nutrition will benefit education. School-based interventions with the

Table 13-2 Health Conditions and the Schools			
		Potential for Intervention[b]	
Condition	**Important for Education**[a]	**School-Based**	**Other**
Schistosomiasis (moderate to severe)	Yes	Yes	Yes
Iodine deficiency disorders			
Anemia			
Short-term hunger			
Intestinal helminths (moderate to severe)			
Early protein-energy malnutrition	Yes	Low	Moderate
Diarrheal disease			
Acute respiratory illness			
Ill health of the parents of school-aged children			
Risk behaviors for chronic diseases (e.g., tobacco use)	No	Yes	Yes
Some immunizable diseases			
Mild schistosomiasis or intestinal helminthiasis			
Serious but infrequently occurring childhood diseases	No	No	Limited
Cataract			
Most cancers			

Source: J. Leslie and D. T. Jamison, "Health and Nutrition Considerations in Education Planning: Educational Consequences of Health Problems Among School-Age Children," 1990, *Food and Nutrition Bulletin, 12*(3), pp. 204-214. Adapted with permission.

[a]Conditions that are likely to affect school participation or learning and to occur relatively frequently in some environments.

[b]Conditions for which school-based interventions are likely to offer significant help.

potential to improve both learning and attendance and to improve the participation of girls include improvements in school location and facilities; a school health worker or teacher trained to screen for easily recognized health and nutrition problems and the ability to make referrals to local health facilities and to provide minimum first aid and basic medication; mobile health teams to deal with more extensive clinical problems such as vitamin A and iodine deficiencies and intestinal helminthic infections; school feeding to provide incentives for attendance and to address micronutrient deficiencies; and health, nutrition, and family planning education. School feeding has been the most frequently evaluated program and has had a significantly positive effect on school attendance despite limited evidence of its effects on height or weight. School feeding also was by far the most costly of school-based programs, and benefits would need to be weighed carefully against the high costs. Using evidence of a very different sort on determinants of school attendance, Knaul and Parker (1998) found school participation in Mexico to be adversely affected by indicators of fertility in the child's household.

It is clear that health and nutrition from the earliest age, including influences in utero, can affect subsequent school performance. Glewwe and King (2001) use data from the Philippines to argue that nutritional status up to the age of 2 can have significant effects on school outcomes. Miguel and Kremer (2004) find significant effects on schooling outcomes from a randomized school-based deworming intervention. They find large-scale externalities to the program (due to the lower disease prevalence and transmission rates to those who did not receive the treatment) and an unwillingness to pay for the intervention despite its cost-effectiveness, indicating that public provision may be required for such programs.

In efforts to confront the health and nutrition problems that negatively affect girls' school participation rates, education planners can enhance sexual safety through the location and gender basis of schools, by increasing the number of female teachers, and by improving school security. Other measures include the establishment of a sex, rape-prevention, and family-planning curriculum, and the dissemination of contraceptives and abortion referrals to reduce premature fertility and the onset of sexually transmitted infections. Evaluation of a school feeding program in India found greater positive effects on girls' enrollment as opposed to that of boys. Finally, experience from Bolivia suggests that programs to provide iodine and iron to micronutrient-deficient girls can enhance their cognitive function and school

achievement. In particular, the Bolivia study found that a reduction in goiter was associated with improvements in IQ scores and that this relationship was stronger for school-aged girls than for boys. From the time of puberty, the incidence and severity of both anemia and iodine deficiency in girls substantially exceeds that in boys; hence, the greater intervention impact on girls is not surprising. Perhaps not coincidentally, female enrollment relative to males drops at puberty. In addition to seeking cultural explanations, low-cost nutritional intervention will, in many cases, prove relevant and more amenable to policy.

In an illustrative cost-benefit analysis, Jamison and Leslie suggested that "potential exists for benefits greatly to exceed costs for health and nutrition interventions in schools" (1990, p. 212).

Health and the Wealth of Nations

One of the main empirical tools used to understand variation in income levels and growth rates of countries is cross-country regression of economic growth (typically measured in terms of the growth rate of per capita GDP) on the variables believed to explain that growth.[5] Among the factors that are usually explored in such analyses are levels and patterns of educational attainment (schooling); health status (life expectancy, mortality rates, disease prevalence); population growth, density, and age structure; natural resource abundance; personal and government saving (investment rates); physical capital stock; trade policy, such as the degree of trade openness; quality of public institutions; and geography, such as the location and climate of a country (Bloom & Canning, 2000).

Research focused on the links between several specific variables and economic growth includes both variables that directly link economic performance and health variables, such as life expectancy and mortality rates, and variables that indirectly link health with economic growth, such as geography and demography. Geography, particularly tropical location, is highly correlated with disease burden, which in turn affects economic performance. Demography, on the other hand, which is determined in part by health status, has a direct effect on economic growth through age-structure effects. This section focuses on the avail-

---

[5]Conceptually quite distinct is an attempt by Cutler and Richardson (1998) to assess the value of health in the U.S. economy between 1970 and 1990. Assuming a value for a year in perfect health, one can estimate "health capital." This has increased over time in the United States, but more so for older adults than the young.

able empirical evidence that estimates the influence of these various factors on a nation's overall level and rate of growth of income (see Figure 13-2).

Life Expectancy and Economic Outcomes. Life expectancy has been shown to be a powerful predictor of income levels and subsequent economic growth. Studies (Barro & Lee, 1994; Bloom & Williamson, 1998; Jamison, Lau, & Wang, 2005; Radelet, Sachs, & Lee, 1997) have revealed that lower levels of mortality and higher levels of life expectancy have a statistically and quantitatively significant effect on income levels and growth rates. In a study of determinants across countries of 5-year economic growth rates, Bhargava and colleagues (2001) concluded that health's favorable impact on growth declined with a country's initial income level. The mechanisms through which this effect works are believed to be (1) the improvements in productivity that arise from a healthier workforce and less morbidity-related absenteeism, (2) the increased incentive that higher life expectancy gives individuals and firms to invest in physical and human capital, and (3) the increase in savings rates as working-age individuals save for their retirement years.

Jamison, Lau, and Wang (2005) combined their empirical estimates of the effects of adult survival rates on national income with country-specific estimates of improvements in survival rates to generate estimates of the contribution of health to economic growth. In the sample of 53 countries included in their study, their calculations suggest that on average 11% of total growth rate in per capita income was due to health improvements, though there is substantial variation across countries.

Bloom, Canning, and Sevilla (2004) provide a survey of the results of regression analyses that use life expectancy or other measures of mortality rates to explain economic growth. This survey indicates that findings in the literature of a large and significant impact of initial health status on subsequent economic growth rates are robust.

Historical studies reached similar conclusions using very different types of data. In a study of the determinants of the economic progress in Great Britain between 1780 and 1979, for example, Fogel (1997) estimated that 30% of the per capita growth rate can be explained by health and nutritional improvements.

Although the evidence of a large effect of health on economic growth is robust, there is still an issue of how to interpret this result. One possible explanation is that we are seeing the macroeconomic counterpart of the link between health and worker productivity. Shastry and Weil (2002) take the wage gains predicted by the microeconomic literature and calibrate how large an effect on output we would expect to see across countries due to health differences. They find that health differences, differences in physical capital, and differences in education are roughly equal in their importance in producing cross-country differences in income levels, supporting the view that health has a large macroeconomic effect.

It is also possible that other mechanisms lie behind the link between population health and macroeconomic performance. Improvements in longevity are linked to changes in age structure, and it may be the composition of the population, rather than the productivity of individual workers, that lies behind the health effect. This issue is discussed in the next section; the general finding is that the health effect of aggregate outcome persists even when age-structure effects are included in the model. For example, Bloom, Canning, and Sevilla (2004) find that higher life expectancies go hand in hand with an older, more experienced workforce, but it is the health effect, not the experience level of the workforce, that is important for economic growth.

An alternative reason that life expectancy is important for economic growth is that rising longevity increases the incentive to invest in education and to save for retirement (Kalemli-Ozcan, 2002). Bloom, Canning, and Graham (2003) find empirical evidence that life expectancy is linked to national savings rates. Alsan, Bloom, and Canning (2004) find that health conditions have a significant impact on inward foreign direct investment, perhaps due to availability of a productive labor force or to attractive conditions for expatriate workers.

Another interpretation of the link has been proposed by Acemoglu, Johnson, and Robinson (2003). They argue that health is linked to economic growth because the disease burden in developing countries had an impact on the pattern of European settlement and the subsequent transference and development of institutions. This hypothesis indicates a historic link between health conditions and development but suggests that current improvements in health may have little effect on economic outcomes. This indicates that for policy purposes future macroeconomic research must go further than establishing the link between health and economic performance; it must show that improvements in health are linked to increases in income levels.

One way of investigating such effects is through case studies of public health interventions that lead to dramatic health improvements. For example, Bleakley

(2003) shows that hookworm eradication in the southern states of the United States led to large increases in schooling levels in counties that previously had the highest infection rates, and that this had long-term consequences for earnings.

Demography and Growth. Health improvements also play a role in economic growth through their impact on demography. For example, in the 1940s, improvements in health in East Asia provided impetus for a demographic transition. An initial decline in infant and child mortality prompted a fall in fertility rates somewhat later. These changes in mortality and fertility—the first phase of the demographic transition—substantially altered Asia's age distribution because the working-age population began growing much faster than the youth dependent population, temporarily creating a disproportionately high percentage of working-age adults. This bulge in the population's age structure created an opportunity for increased rates of economic growth (Bloom, Canning, & Sevilla, 2002). By introducing demographic variables into an empirical model of economic growth, Bloom and Williamson (1998) suggest that East Asia's changing health and consequent changes in demography can explain one-third to one-half of the economic growth "miracle" experienced between 1965 and 1990.

Although this demographic dividend provides an opportunity for increasing wealth, it does not guarantee such results. East Asia's growth rates were achieved because government and private sectors were able to mobilize this growing workforce by successfully managing other economic opportunities. Adopting new industrial technologies, investing in education and human capital, and exploiting global markets allowed East Asia to realize the economic growth potential created by the demographic transition.

The importance of demographic variables is supported by Jamison, Lau, and Wang (2005), who examined the role of total fertility rates in relation to economic levels using an aggregate-production function approach. They found a statistically significant negative relationship, similar to findings by Bloom and Freeman (1988), which showed that crude birth rates are negatively correlated with economic growth because they are associated with younger age distributions and lower labor force participation.[6] The

---

[6]In an early paper, Myrdal (1952) raised many of the issues dealt with in health economics in the years to come. Among other points, he noted the links between age distribution, fertility, health, and economic growth.

link between mortality reduction and subsequent fertility reduction constitutes an important component of the total effect of health on development. The strength and causal nature of this link have been discussed, but the direction of the evidence is now fairly clear. Schultz (1997, p. 418), for example, concludes in a major review that "Whatever the cause of the mortality decline, the response of parents has been to reduce their births."

Bloom, Canning, and Malaney (2000) further developed this line of research by incorporating demography into a model of endogenous economic growth. They showed that the interaction of exogenous demographic influences with human and physical capital development can lead to a virtuous cycle of growth, enabling a country to break free of a poverty trap (in which poor health perpetuates low income that itself perpetuates poor health).

Geography, Disease Burden, and Economic Growth. In their cross-country growth studies, Gallup and Sachs (1999) introduced a focus on geographic factors as being among the empirical determinants of economic growth. They found that countries in tropical regions develop more slowly than those in temperate zones. In addition to the effects of climate and geography on soil quality, they believe that an intermediate mechanism through which this effect operates is the interaction of tropical climates and disease burdens; this interaction can have a significant cost in terms of economic performance. Both high disease burdens and geographic isolation can separate countries from the global economy, denying them the benefits of trade, foreign direct investments, and technological interchange.

Economic Development's Consequences for Health

Previous sections have discussed how health can lead to greater growth and reduced poverty. In fact, the causal relationship between health and development operates in both directions. Income influences health through a variety of intervening determinants. More distal determinants include housing, education, water, sanitation, nutrition, energy, health services, institutions, and industrial and agricultural policies. Industrial safety programs and environmental regulations, for example, have specific health objectives and are targeted at specific groups, namely, industrial workers and the general public. Housing policies aimed at subsidizing or providing housing for lower-income individuals have broader social and health objectives, but may also have concrete health impacts. Empowering women through better education, among other measures, can enhance their capacity to improve their health and that of their families. Education is strongly correlated with health in many studies in industrialized countries as well, even after controlling for other factors, including income and medical care (Berger & Leigh, 1989; Farrell & Fuchs, 1982; Fuchs, 1993; Grossman, 1975; Kenkel, 1991).

The 1993 *World Development Report* (World Bank, 1993) provides an extensive overview of the determinants of health that are outside the health sector and their attractiveness from a policy perspective. For example, even if there were no benefits to primary education for girls except health benefits, education would still appear highly cost-effective.

Recent work has highlighted the impact of income on health. Case (2004) finds that pensions to the elderly in South Africa have a significant effect on the health status of household members. Pritchett and Summers (1996) find a link leading from income levels and education to health improvements in a macroeconomic study.

There is also a growing body of information on health inequalities and the experience of relative deprivation as a cause of ill health. In Great Britain, for example, the Whitehall Study (a longitudinal study of behaviors and health status of more than 10,000 British civil servants) found that over a 10-year period males aged 40 to 64 in the lower grades (clerical and manual) of the civil service had an age-adjusted mortality rate 3.5 times higher than males in senior administrative grades (Marmot et al., 1991; Marmot & Theorell, 1988; Wilkinson, 1986). There was a gradient in mortality that stretched across all levels of the civil service: Each status group had a higher mortality rate than the group immediately above it, which was not explainable by access to medical care or other primary goods, such as absolute levels of income, shelter, food, or education.

Other research, aimed at confirming the Whitehall Study findings on a cross-national level, revealed a similar correlation between hierarchy and health. In a study of 11 Organization for Economic Cooperation and Development (OECD) countries from 1975 to 1985, using two measures of income inequality, the Gini coefficient and the ratio between the percentage of income flowing to the top and bottom 30% of a country's population, Wilkinson (1990) found an inverse relationship between the level of income in a country and the average national life expectancy. Whereas nations with absolute levels of higher average income per capita will have higher average life expectancy than those with a lower level of average national income (e.g., industrialized versus lower-income countries), these studies suggest that greater income

inequality within a country may also have a negative influence on life expectancy. Nations with a relatively flat income gradient, such as Japan and Sweden, had higher life expectancies than countries such as the United States and West Germany, which had steeper gradients. Moreover, in the United States, the sensitivity of mortality rates to socioeconomic status has increased sharply between 1960 and the early 1980s (Preston & Elo, 1995).

More recent work (Deaton, 2003; Deaton & Paxson, 2001) interprets the apparent effect of income inequality on health as resulting from effects of ranking within a reference group that is much smaller than a country. If, for example, an academic had a low salary relative to others in her discipline, this might have a deleterious effect on health even if her absolute income were relatively high and she lived in a country where income was relatively evenly distributed. Even if individuals' reference groups are unobserved, individual income levels will provide partial information about the individuals' standing in their reference group (the amount of information depending on the relative levels of within-group and across-group inequality). The mechanism of effect can generate the widely documented adverse effect of inequality on average health status even if there is no real effect of either within-group or between-group inequality on health. Deaton and Paxson's (2001) analyses using U.S. data support the conclusion of no effect. More research will be needed to extend the evidence base on how reference group rankings and socioeconomic inequalities influence health.[7]

An important question in assessing the historical determinants of health is the impact of income, in relation to other factors, on health improvements, especially during the second half of the 20th century. Preston's (1980) work provides a broad framework for assessing income's impact, and his study has influenced subsequent work. A WHO analysis (WHO, 1999) examined these relationships. Figure 13-4 shows the results from this work and illustrates the relationship. From 1952 to 1992, mean income increased by about 66%, from roughly US$1,500 to US$2,500. The curves in Figure 13-4 indicate that

---

[7] Note that the literature on inequalities in health is not, for the most part, about inequality in the univariate distribution of health but generally about the strength of the effect of inequality in other variables (e.g., income) on health levels. Le Grand (1987) assessed univariate distribution of health or pure inequalities. Not surprisingly, these inequalities decline steadily with declines in overall mortality rates, even though the socioeconomic gradient may be getting steeper.

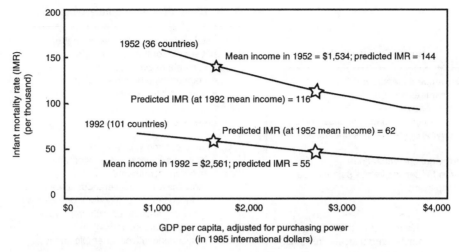

Figure 13-4 The Role of Improvements in Income in Reducing Infant Mortality Rates. *Note:* Results are based on a cross-sectional time-series regression that relates, at 5-year intervals, the natural logarithm of IMR to the natural logarithm of income, the square of the natural logarithm of income, and indicator variables for time. *Source:* World Health Organization, *World Health Report 1999: Making a Difference* (Geneva, Switzerland: World Health Organization, 1999), p. 5. Reprinted with permission.

the infant mortality rate (IMR) declined more than predicted (to 55 per thousand rather than to 116 per thousand) based on the 1952 relationship between income and IMR, suggesting that factors more important than income are influencing health. Historical analyses by Easterlin (1999) point to the same conclusion. The WHO study and related World Bank analyses (Wang et al., 1999) assessed the relative impact of three key areas on health improvements: increases in average income levels, improvements in average education levels, and the generation and application of new knowledge; it found that approximately 50% of health improvements were due to access to better technology, whereas the remaining gains resulted from income improvements and better education. Continued work along these lines (Jamison, Sandbu, & Wang, 2004) finds that country-specific differences in application of new knowledge are large indeed and, when properly accounted for, further reduce the apparent effect of income on health.[8]

Just as health conditions at any time improve with income level, so, too, might adverse income shocks adversely affect health. The major economic crisis of 1998 in Indonesia provides an example. The available evidence is mixed, but Frankenberg and associates (1999) conclude that children's health was no worse after the crisis. (School enrollment rates among the low-income population did, however, decline significantly.) Enduring effects of long-term, income-dependent determinants of health may be countering potential adverse consequences of economic crisis.

Health Systems and Economic Outcomes

An important aspect of the link between health and economic development is how the characteristics of a particular health care system, especially health financing policies, affect economic performance.[9] Health care is one of the largest sectors of the world economy, accounting for 9.9% of total global product in 1998, and has significant potential to affect economic development and growth. This influence can operate at both a macro- and a microeconomic level.

As Figure 13-5 illustrates, health finance policies can have direct economic consequences in one of four ways: the total resources withdrawn by health care

---

[8]Even though income differences may account for only a modest amount of cross-country variations in health outcomes over a period of several decades, the situation can be quite different within a given country at a given time. Important forthcoming work by Wagstaff and colleagues at the World Bank reaches such conclusions.

[9]Chapter 11 provides a description of the main financing mechanisms of health systems; this section has a more detailed presentation of specific aspects of these arrangements in terms of their economic and equity impacts.

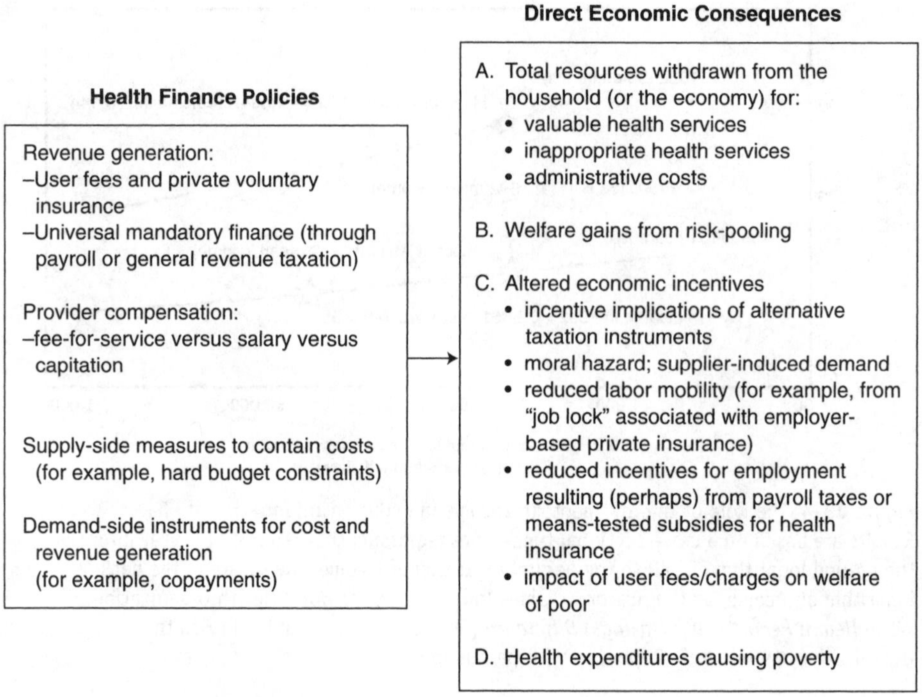

Direct Economic Consequences

Health Finance Policies

Revenue generation:
–User fees and private voluntary
  insurance
–Universal mandatory finance (through
  payroll or general revenue taxation)

Provider compensation:
–fee-for-service versus salary versus
  capitation

Supply-side measures to contain costs
  (for example, hard budget constraints)

Demand-side instruments for cost and
  revenue generation
  (for example, copayments)

A. Total resources withdrawn from the
   household (or the economy) for:
   • valuable health services
   • inappropriate health services
   • administrative costs

B. Welfare gains from risk-pooling

C. Altered economic incentives
   • incentive implications of alternative
     taxation instruments
   • moral hazard; supplier-induced demand
   • reduced labor mobility (for example, from
     "job lock" associated with employer-
     based private insurance)
   • reduced incentives for employment
     resulting (perhaps) from payroll taxes or
     means-tested subsidies for health
     insurance
   • impact of user fees/charges on welfare
     of poor

D. Health expenditures causing poverty

Figure 13-5 Economic Consequences of Health Finance Policies.

systems from the economy (e.g., in terms of health expenditure in relation to GDP); the extent to which these systems provide welfare gains that can be achieved from risk pooling; the incentives that health finance policies can create in terms of the labor market and consumer and provider behavior; and the extent to which health expenditures generate or perpetuate poverty. As introduced in Chapter 11 and as shown in Figure 13-5, financing policies can take a number of different forms (e.g., user fees, private voluntary insurance, universal mandatory finance, public health and social insurance, and supply- and demand-side measures for cost control and revenue generation), depending on the type of health care system. This section reviews the relationship between health care systems and the economy and discusses particular issues within this arena that need to be addressed. Hsiao (2000) addresses many of the same issues from a rather different perspective.

Total Resources Withdrawn from the Economy
Health Expenditures and Gross Domestic Product

Countries tend to devote more resources and increasing shares of their national income to health care as their income increases. Lower-income countries, on average, spend less than wealthier countries on health on a per capita basis, in terms of percentage of GDP and in terms of public spending on health. This leads to a

lower level and a less equitable distribution of health care and public health services—and ultimately of health—in these societies. However, although health care affects health, it is not the only determinant of health. As Table 13-3 illustrates, in the late 1990s, low-income countries spent an average of US$21 per capita as compared with US$116 for middle-income and US$2,736 for high-income countries. South Asia (US$21), East Asia and the Pacific (US$44), and sub-Saharan Africa (US$29) spent the least of low- and middle-income regions, whereas the Middle East and North Africa (US$171) and Latin America and the Caribbean (US$262) spent the most for that group of regions. In the very lowest income countries, annual health spending can be as low as US$2 or $3 per capita, and most of that spending is from private sources (World Bank, 2003).

In terms of percentage of GDP, as shown in Table 13-3, in the late 1990s, low-income countries on average spent 4.3% of GDP on health, whereas middle-income countries spent an average of 5.9% and high-income countries spent an average of 10.2% of GNP on health. By region among low- and middle-income regions, South Asia (4.7% of GDP) spent the least on health, whereas Latin America and the Caribbean spent the most, at approximately 7.0% of GDP (World Bank, 2003).

Both health spending generally and the public share of health spending increase with increases in national

Table 13-3	Health Expenditures by Income Group and Region, Late 1990s					
			Health Expenditures[a,c]		Average Across Countries Spent on Health[a,d]	
Region or Income Group	Population (millions, 2001)[e]	Per Capita GNI (2001 US\$)[b]	Total Health Expenditure Per Capita (1997–2000 US\$)[e]	Total Health Expenditure as % of GNI	Total Expenditure (% of GDP)	Public-Sector Expenditure (% of GDP)	Public Sector (% of total)
World	6,130	5,120	482	9.4	9.3	5.5	59
Low income	2,506	430	21	4.9	4.3	1.2	27
Middle income	2,667	1,860	116	6.2	5.9	3.1	52
High income	957	26,510	2,736	10.3	10.2	6.3	62
Low and middle income by region	5,172	1,160	71	6.1	5.6	2.7	48
East Asia and Pacific	1,823	900	44	4.9	4.7	1.8	39
Europe and Central Asia	475	1,970	108	5.5	5.5	4.0	72
Latin America and the Caribbean	524	3,580	262	7.3	7.0	3.4	48
Middle East and North Africa	301	2,220	171	7.7	4.6	2.9	62
South Asia	1,378	450	21	4.7	4.7	1.0	21
Sub-saharan Africa	674	460	29	6.3	6.0	2.5	42

Source: Data from World Bank, *World Development Indicators* (Washington, DC: World Bank, 2003).

[a]Data are for the most recent year available, which ranges between 1997 and 2000 from *World Development Indicators* 2003.

[b]Gross national income (GNI) is calculated using the *World Bank Atlas* method, *World Development Indicators* 2003.

[c]These figures show the total (that is, public and private) expenditures on health in the indicated regional or country group divided by the total GNI of that group. Countries with high expenditures on health are weighted heavily by this procedure.

[d]For a typical person in the indicated regional or income group, these columns show the expected percentage of GDP spent on health in that person's country. Figures are calculated by averaging across countries, weighted by population (for example, India and China weighted more heavily).

[e]*World Development Indicators*, 2003.

and per capita income. As shown in Table 13-3, the public share of health expenditures (as a percentage of total health spending) was 27% in low-income countries, 52% in middle-income countries, and 62% in high-income countries. Among low- and middle-income countries, regions such as eastern Europe and Central Asia have the largest public share (72%) of health spending, and South Asia has the smallest (21%) (World Bank, 2003). According to Schieber and Maeda (1993), the income elasticity of demand for health services (the percentage change in health expenditures as a result of a 1% change in income) in 1994 was roughly 1.13 worldwide, and in a range of 1.47 for high-income countries, 1.19 for middle-income countries, and 1.00 for low-income countries. This means that for every 1% increase in per capita income, public health expenditures will increase by 1.47% in middle- and high-income countries, by 1.19% in middle-income countries, and by 1.00% in lower-income countries. Thus, the increase in health expenditures in low-income countries is less responsive to increases in income than it is in middle- and high-income countries. Figures 13-6 and 13-7 show the relationships between income and health spending and between income and public health spending, respectively. In addition, these authors found that private health spending (income elasticity of 1.02) is less responsive to increases in per capita income than public health spending (income elasticity of 1.21).

Some of the implications of lower levels of spending in lower-income countries include lower levels of

capital stock, such as clinics, hospitals, and inpatient beds; of human resources, such as physicians and providers; and of service use, such as outpatient and inpatient visits. For example, the number of hospital beds per 1,000 population in the late 1990s was much higher in high-income (7.4) as compared with middle-income (3.3) and low-income (1.7 in 1980, most recent year available) countries (World Bank, 2003). Of the regions worldwide, eastern Europe and Central Asia had the greatest number of hospital beds per 1,000 in the late 1990s, at 9.0, and South Asia (0.7 in 1980) and sub-Saharan Africa (1.1) had the lowest in the mid-1990s. This pattern persists when analyzing physicians per 1,000 population in the late 1990s: High-income countries (3.0) fared better than middle-income (1.9) and low-income (1.0 in the mid-1990s) countries on this indicator of health system infrastructure. Comparing different regions of the world, the number of physicians per 1,000 population in the mid-1990s was highest in eastern Europe and Central Asia (3.1), and lowest in sub-Saharan Africa (0.1 in the mid-1990s) and South Asia (0.4 in the mid-1990s).

Many have taken the evidence regarding the income elasticity of expenditures on health as indicative of the nature of health as a normal consumption good. More recently there has been an upsurge of interest in the nature of health care as an investment good. Expenditures on health care can lead to improvements in health status that, in turn, promote income growth and the efficiency and equity of health systems in both improving health and affecting income, pro-

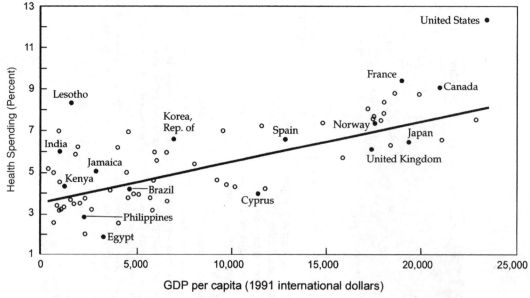

Figure 13-6 Percentage of GDP Spent on Health. *Source:* World Bank, *World Development Report* (Washington, DC: World Bank, 1980). Reprinted with permission.

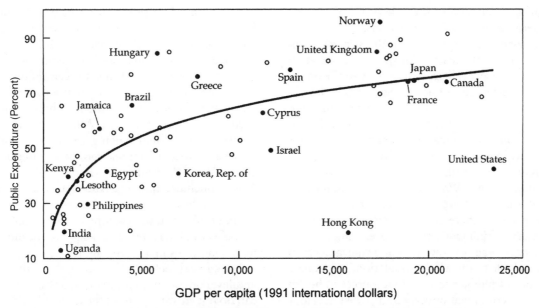

Figure 13-7 Percentage of Total Health Expenditures That Are Public. *Source:* World Bank, *World Development Report* (Washington, DC: World Bank, 1980). Reprinted with permission.

ductivity, and the overall economy. Lower-income countries in particular tend to underinvest in health, leaving their populations vulnerable to disease and disability and ultimately affecting labor productivity and growth. They also have health systems that are often highly inefficient at both macro- and micro-economic levels, and highly inegalitarian in both financing and delivery.

Health System Efficiency and Equity

Macroeconomic Efficiency. Health system efficiency at the macroeconomic level describes the relationship between aggregate health care expenditures and health outcomes. There is considerable variation in both health expenditures and health outcomes by country. For example, in 2001, life expectancy at birth ranged from 37 years in Sierra Leone, 40 in Rwanda, 43 in Uganda, 45 in Guinea-Bissau, 42 in Burundi, and 43 in Afghanistan to 79 in Canada, 78 in Greece, 79 in Israel and Norway, and 81 in Japan (World Bank, 2003). Under-five mortality rates per 1,000 live births in 2001 ranged from 235 in Liberia and 257 in Afghanistan to 5 in Japan, Finland, and Germany and 4 in Norway and Denmark (World Bank, 2003). Many factors influence health outcomes, but some countries appear to be more efficient in the use of health care resources than others.

Expenditures on health systems, however, often correlate poorly with outcomes. For example, in the late 1990s India spent 4.9% of GDP (18% of which

was public spending) to achieve a 2001 IMR of 67 per 1,000 and an average life expectancy at birth in 2001 of 63 years, whereas in the late 1990s China spent 5.2% of GDP (37% from public spending) to achieve a 2001 IMR of 31 per 1,000, and an average life expectancy at birth in 2001 of 70 years (World Bank, 2003). In the same years, Mauritius spent 3.4% of GDP (56% from public spending) to achieve a 2001 IMR of 17 per 1,000 and an average life expectancy at birth in 2001 of 72 years. Among higher-income countries, the patterns are similar. For example, in the late 1990s the United States spent 13% of GDP (44% from public expenditure) to achieve a 2001 IMR of 7 per 1,000 and an average life expectancy in 2001 of 78 years. The United Kingdom spent 7.3% of GDP (81% from public expenditure) and Japan spent 7.8% of GDP (77% from public expenditure) to achieve 2001 IMRs of 6 per 1,000 and 3 per 1,000, respectively, and average life expectancy at birth in 2001 of 77 and 76 years, respectively. Finally, in the same time period, France spent 9.5% of GDP (76% from public expenditure) and Germany spent 10.6% of GDP (75% from public expenditure) to achieve the same 2001 IMR of 4 per 1,000 and an average life expectancy at birth of 79 and 78 years, respectively (World Bank, 2003). Wang and colleagues (1999) present systematic data on 115 countries for the period 1960 to 1991 on country performance relative to income (or income and education) on several health indicators. These performance measures are intended to catalyze discussion of the role of health system characteristics as partial explanations.

This evidence suggests that health systems probably vary in the efficiency with which they produce health. Of course, health care services are only one of multiple determinants of health. Some countries obtain better health for less money; others obtain good health by spending more, and some seem to be in a situation of diminishing marginal returns to increases in health care expenditures. In lower-income countries it is often the case that very little health is obtained for the money spent. When total health spending is as low as it is in some lower-income countries (e.g., 2% to 3% of GDP), there are insufficient resources to cover even the minimum necessary care. Thus, even the most basic package of preventive and clinical services is not available to the whole population. Inadequate allocations of public and private resources to health can lead to continued poverty and stifled development. These countries require increases in money spent (especially equally distributed public resources) on the most basic and cost-effective services. At the other end of the spectrum, countries such as the United States, France, Germany, and Switzerland, which spend more than 9% of GDP on health, have a tripartite health policy focus of increasing access and improving quality with a central emphasis on controlling and decreasing health care costs.

Although there is scant evidence of the economic impact of greater spending on health, some believe that higher health expenditures can reduce a country's relative productivity in the global economy due to the large costs of health benefits for the labor force, and due to resultant reduced investments in other sectors of the economy. Although the labor market effects of certain health policies are addressed later in this section, it is less clear that overall productivity and growth are severely hindered by very high health expenditures. It is not possible to determine the most efficient level or percentage of health spending for any given economy. With this wide range of spending on health care, the challenge is to increase spending among lower-income nations and analyze spending in both higher- and lower-income countries. The aim is to develop methods to enhance the efficient production of health within health care systems.

Microeconomic Efficiency. Microeconomic efficiency focuses on getting the best return on existing resources and reducing the waste and inefficiency that some systems generate. Allocative inefficiency occurs when resources are allocated not to activities that are highly cost-effective but to those that are costly, with a low return in terms of effectiveness. Efficiency means allocating resources to the most cost-effective way of achieving given health objectives (e.g., investing in cost-effective preventive measures, such as immunizations for certain diseases or behavioral modification, rather than spending extensively at later stages of the health cycle through high-cost tertiary services). A health system is allocatively inefficient when greater gains could be achieved with a different pattern of resource use. The 1993 *World Development Report* (World Bank, 1993) concluded that improvements in allocative efficiency of health systems in lower-income countries could be achieved through the introduction of basic cost-effective intervention packages for the most common conditions in a given country.

Technical inefficiencies occur when the pattern and level of resources (human, financial, and physical) do not adequately meet the level of health (or access) outcomes possible with that degree of resource commitment. In lower-income countries, scarcity of providers and basic clinic and hospital resources, in addition to poor quality and accessibility of facilities (ill-equipped and run-down infrastructure) and providers (poorly trained and unqualified), contributes to a failure to meet the health needs of the populations.

In higher-income countries, the focus has been on assessing and improving the efficiency of particular aspects of health systems, including cost and use-control measures on the supply and demand side of the health care market, medical care appropriateness, and health care administration. These topics are addressed in Exhibits 13-4 and 13-5. In addition, some health systems in higher-income countries have begun explicitly to prioritize or ration health services to improve the allocative efficiency and public acceptability of their health systems.

Equity. Equity in health policy should focus on both the financing and the delivery of health care services (Ruger, 1998, 2003b, 2004a). Two important dimensions of equity include vertical and horizontal equity. In terms of financing, vertical equity refers to the requirement that health care be financed by ability to pay; that is, contributions to the cost of health care must be determined by income status. Some mechanisms for raising revenues for health care expenditures are more progressive than others (Van Doorslaer, Wagstaff, & Rutten, 1993). Horizontal financial equity means that individuals with the same ability to pay should contribute the same amount to financing health expenditures regardless of medical need, gender, marital status, geography, age, or employment status. In

Exhibit 13-4	Costs of Health Care Administration

One aspect of health system inefficiency is the perception of some administrative expenditures as wasteful. Comparisons of different health systems suggest that administrative costs can be an important factor in the level and rate of change in health care spending.

Single-payer plans are claimed to be advantageous in that they tend to centralize and therefore reduce the costs of health care administration—a significant issue around the world. International comparisons of international health systems show that administrative costs as a percentage of total costs vary by country and financing mechanism, and these large differences suggest, at first glance, wasteful and inefficient use of resources in some countries. Several national (United States) and cross-national (OECD countries) studies have attempted to estimate such costs (Bovbjerg, 1995; Gauthier et al., 1992; Poullier, 1992; U.S. Congress, 1994; Woolhandler & Himmelstein, 1991, 1997; Woolhandler, Himmelstein, & Lewontin, 1993). One study found that in 1987, U.S. health care administration cost between US$96.8 billion and $120.4 billion ($400 to $497 per capita), equivalent to 19.3% to 24.1% of total health care spending (Woolhandler & Himmelstein, 1991). The same study found that in comparing the United States, Canada, and the United Kingdom, administrative costs in the United States were 60% higher than in Canada and 97% higher than in the United Kingdom.

Another study, employing OECD data from 1991 and 1992, compared costs of health care administration across 20 industrialized countries. With respect to administrative costs, the United States had the highest (and Germany the second highest) per capita spending for health administration. The authors concluded that administrative costs were higher in insurance-based systems than in direct-delivery systems. Insurance-based systems are more complex and involve multiple, decentralized payers, all of which contribute to higher administrative costs (Poullier, 1992).

Illustrating the unusual character of the health sector among sectors of the economy, the available research suggests that single-payer systems (in which a single authority processes claims and pays providers directly for services) have lower administrative costs than multiple-payer systems. Single-payer systems accrue benefits by standardizing, consolidating, and integrating functions. Single-payer systems are well situated to take advantage of efficiency gains from standardization and of technological advances in information systems, especially electronic claims transmission and magnetic card technology. Even without a single-payer system, standardization and reform could reduce costs for multiple payers. For instance, introducing a common electronic administrative system (common formats and standards) that connects multiple systems of insurance and medical information through the use of "smart cards" could improve health system performance. These technologies could bring a number of health administrative functions under common guidelines, thereby improving communication, claims processing, and use review.

Ultimately, the costs and benefits of health administrative reforms must be assessed. Although certain administrative costs might be reduced without the loss of benefits to individuals or to society, others might not. The extent to which the results of administrative reforms are categorized as benefits or costs will also depend on the value that is placed on any given economic or health-related outcome. These values might vary from one community to another. In general, administrative activities that clearly confer benefits to patients and the health system should be prioritized, and in some cases beneficial administrative activities can be provided more efficiently. For example, benefit management costs—including data collection, clinical evaluation, and statistical analysis—confer consumer benefits by improving health care quality, enhancing patients' decision-making autonomy, and reducing inappropriate care. These activities will become an increasingly valuable tool as additional information on effective and cost-effective health service delivery becomes available.

terms of delivery, vertical equity refers to the requirement that individuals with different needs should receive different amounts and levels of health services. Horizontal equity means that individuals with equal needs should receive equal medical treatment (Van Doorslaer, Wagstaff, & Rutten, 1993).

One aspect of health equity involves a concern for the status (health and financial) of the most disadvantaged segments of society (Anand et al., 2001; Ruger, 1998; Ruger, in press a). Improving equity and improving the conditions of the very poor or worse-off may often go together, but sometimes they do not, posing trade-offs (Anand et al., 2001; Ruger, 1998,

2004a) necessitating a comprehensive analysis of health equity (Ruger, in press b).

In the 1990s, many countries in the OECD initiated reforms designed to improve the efficiency and responsiveness of their health systems. Hurst (2000) provides an overview of the achievements of these systems, and of their reforms, while pointing to an essential tension that increasingly confronts public policy in these countries. This tension results from upward pressures on costs (for technological and demographic reasons), core commitments to universal public (or publicly mandated) funding for reasons of efficiency as well as equity, and general reluctance to raise taxes.

Exhibit 13-5	Medical Care Appropriateness and Resource Allocation

While achieving a broad spread of risk, health insurance can, in principle, lead to incentives for too much medical care. When people are insured, they do not individually bear the costs of the medical services they consume, so some individuals will have an incentive to overconsume health care resources. (Countering these financial incentives are other costs of seeking care, such as time, pain, and inconvenience.) This central problem of any insurance plan is called the *moral hazard problem* and has spawned a number of efforts to ensure medical care appropriateness and efficient resource allocation within insurance plans, both public and private. The private insurance markets have developed a number of techniques for assessing and enforcing medical care appropriateness.

The first approach is economic. Health economists endeavor to reduce overuse of health care through the use of various economic incentives on both the supply and demand side of the health care market. On the demand side, copayment plans and health insurance deductibles, which require patients to pay a portion of the price of a given medical procedure, reduce use rates. On the supply side of the health care market, price, budgetary, and salary incentives, such as prospective and capitated payment plans and global budgets, deter physicians and hospitals from providing excess care. These incentives force physicians and hospitals to internalize costs in the process of health service delivery and therefore to provide the most cost-effective services. The rise of health care financing and delivery institutions, such as managed care organizations, is a result of these efforts.

Studies have shown that these economic devices are effective in reducing health care use. For instance, in a randomized controlled health insurance experiment, researchers found that increasing patient copayment on health insurance reduced demand for health care services, in some cases by as much as 40% (RAND Health Insurance Experiment; see Newhouse, 1993). In practice, though, copayments are eliminated for expensive procedures, thereby attenuating the usefulness of copayments in cost containment. In addition, cross-cultural comparisons of national health systems provide evidence for the effectiveness of capitation and global budgeting in reducing health care use (see, for example, Aaron & Schwartz, 1984). However, because these economic approaches are devoid of clinical input, they are blunt instruments in achieving their objective; in most cases, they reduce medically appropriate as well as inappropriate care. Without the ability to discriminate between productive and unproductive care, these tools can have deleterious health consequences and can be highly inegalitarian.

Distinguishing between types of care requires clinical input to create a system of assessing and ranking which treatments are medically appropriate for a given health condition. There is at least one existing model that attempts to do just that: the RAND/UCLA appropriateness method. The method involves multiple stages of collecting and interpreting data about specific procedures from literature and clinicians, with the goal of developing guidelines for appropriate care. Since 1986, more than 30 studies using this method have been conducted to examine the appropriateness of procedures (see accompanying table). This literature suggests that the percentage of inappropriate use across procedures ranges from 2.4% to 75%, whereas the percentage of appropriate care ranges from 35% to 91%, and the percentage of equivocal use ranges from 7% to 32%.*

Ultimately, attempts to achieve the optimal level of health status from any given amount of resources will require a joint economic and clinical solution. Social scientists and clinicians should continue to study the magnitude and determinants of inappropriate care and to harness technological advances to create effective information systems and accessible guidelines for medical care. Economic incentives should follow and complement clinical progress, but not to the exclusion of professional incentives. As the evidence on the magnitude and determinants of inappropriate care accumulates and is widely understood, economists and health policy analysts can create policy instruments that give an incentive for physicians, patients, and planners to provide productive care. Particular attention should be paid to encouraging and training physicians by rewarding the provision of appropriate care and correcting for the provision of inappropriate care.

*See also Bernstein et al. (1993); Brook (1992, 1994, 1995, 1997); Brook & Lohr (1986, 1987, 1990); Brook et al. (1990); Brook, Park, & Chassin (1990); Carlisle et al. (1992); Chassin et al. (1987); Hilborne et al. (1993); Leape et al. (1990, 1993); Kleinman et al. (1994); and Winslow et al. (1988a, 1998b).

Feachem (2000) suggests that in the United Kingdom both radical reform of delivery institutions and increased resources will be required, and Enthoven (2000) reviews the history and lessons from the (incomplete) reforms of the UK National Health Services in the past decade. Preker, Harding, and Travis (2000) review these experiences from the perspective of the "new institutional economics" to reach a number of important conclusions about the evolving roles of the public and private sectors in the health sector. To quote their main findings concerning the public-sector role, "Consequently, in parallel with moving out of the area of production of goods and services, in many low- and middle-income countries it may be desirable

Exhibit 13-5	Medical Care Appropriateness and Resource Allocation (continued)

Medical Appropriateness and Health Care Use

Author(s)	Sample/Procedure	Magnitude of Appropriateness
Winslow, C. M. Solomon, D. H., Chassin, M. R., Kosecoff, J. Merrick, N. J. Brook, R. H. (1988b)	Random sample of 1,302 Medicare patients in three geographic areas who had a carotid endarterectomy in 1981.	Estimated the appropriateness of carotid endarterectomy. Found 35% appropriate, 32% equivocal 32% inappropriate. Concluded that carotid endarterectomy was substantially overused in three geographic areas studied.
Bernstein, S. J., McGlynn, E. A., Siu, A. L., Roth, C. P., Sherwood, M. J., Keesey, J. W., Kosecoff, J. Hicks, N. R., Brook, R. H. (1993)	Retrospective cohort study. Random sample of all nonemergency, nononcological hysterectomies performed in seven managed care organizations, over a 1-year period.	Roughly 16% inappropraite, and only one plan had significantly more hysterectomies rated inappropriate compared with the group mean (27%, unadjusted). Age and race adjustments did not affect percentage appropriate.
Leape, L. L., Hilborne, L. H., Park, R. E., Bernstein, S. J., Kamberg, C. J., Sherwood, M., Brook, R. H. (1993)	Random sample of 1,338 patients from 15 different hospitals undergoing isolated coronary artery bypass graft surgery in New York state in 1990.	Nearly 91% appropriate, 7% equivocal, 2.4% inappropriate. Low inappropriateness rate differs significantly from 14% rate found in 1979, 1980, and 1982 studies. Rates did not vary by hospital, hospital location, volume, or teaching status.
Winslow, C. M., Kosecoff, J. B., Chassin, M., Kanouse, D. E., Brook, R. H. (1988a)	Appropriateness of coronary artery bypass surgeries performed in three randomly selected hospitals in a western state. Data obtained from medical records with 488 indications; 386 cases from years 1979, 1980, and 1982.	Found 56% appropriate, 30% equivocal, 14% inappropriate. Percentage appropriate varied by hospital, from 37% to 78% but did not vary by patient age.
Kleinman, L. C., Kosecoff, J., Dubois, R. W., Brook, R. H. (1994)	Appropriateness of tympanostomy tube surgery for recurrent acute otitis media and/or otitis media with effusion. Random selection of subsample (6,611) of cases deemed appropriate by use review firm methodology. Represented otolaryngologists, practices from 49 states and DC.	Found 41% of proposals appropriate, 32% equivocal, 27% inappropriate. Concluded that roughly 25% of tympanostomy tube insertion for children were proposed to inappropriate indications and 30% for equivocal ones.

Note: All studies cited employed the RAND/UCLA appropriateness method.

to have . . . greater public sector involvement in health care financing, knowledge generation, and the provision of human resources" (p. 877).

Welfare Gains from Risk Pooling

Insurance involves collective risk reduction, reduced financial risks, and increased human welfare. Insurance reduces risks in the aggregate by pooling a large number of people with similar, small, individual risks. This pooling enables insurers to increase aggregate predictability even when given health episodes remain unpredictable. The larger the risk pool, the greater the precision with which insurers can predict the probability of financial loss occurrence. Many health systems in low- and middle-income countries fail to take advantage of the economic and welfare benefits that accrue from collective risk reduction in the form of risk pooling through insurance (Ruger, 2003b).

Risk Aversion

Several aspects of health insurance are rooted in the risk-averse nature of human beings. Individuals do not like, nor can they always financially afford, to pay a large amount of money for what could be an unpredictable adverse health event, such as a heart attack, the onset of AIDS, or a fractured skull. Without insurance, if a person suffers a medical catastrophe, he or she may not have the financial resources to pay the large sums required for treatment of these adverse health events. Instead, a person would prefer, and could better afford, to pay a relatively small amount of money on a regular basis to avoid a large financial loss at one time. This is also known as "smoothing" or "evening out" financial payments for adverse health events.

Risk Pooling

By pooling a large number of people and therefore a large number of adverse health events, insurance companies (which employ statistical experts known as actuaries) are better able to predict the occurrence of these events and to spread the financial risk. Enhancing the predictability of the event reduces the financial risks associated with it. Pooling risks across people is more efficient than pooling risks within individuals but across time. For example, if the risk of an adverse health event that costs $2,000 is 1 in 1,000, and 1,000 people pooled $2 each, then the cost of the health event would be covered should it occur. In this case, each individual would have paid $2, rather than being exposed to the risk of paying $2,000. If the risk-pooling organization, such as an insurance company, has administrative costs to bear or aims to make a profit, the cost per person is increased by the additional administrative costs or profits divided by the number of people in the insurance pool.

There are other ways to pool risks, one of which is to pool risks for a given individual across time—a medical savings account—which can generate potential inefficiency even though there have been some effectively implemented examples (e.g., Singapore). For example, if an individual saved $2 per year to cover a potential cost of $2,000, it would take that person 1,000 years to cover the cost; saving $20 per year would require 100 years; and saving $50 per year would take 40 years. Pooling across individuals is more efficient than pooling within individuals over time, because the same protection against the potential financial loss of $2,000 is achieved through a yearly payment of $2 versus a payment of $2 per year for 1,000 years or perhaps saving $50 per year for 40 years. Because people are risk averse, risk pooling protects people from large financial losses that result from catastrophic health events.

Insurance Versus Direct Purchase

Given its benefits, insurance is a preferred mechanism for financing personal health care services for high-cost, low-probability health events.[10] However, it may not necessarily be the preferred method of payment for low-cost, high-probability health events, because individuals have the ability to plan and save for such occurrences, depending on the relative expense of the event. A low-cost service (relative to income) in a higher-income country may be very costly (relative to income) for individuals in lower-income settings. If the service is relatively inexpensive and highly probable, risk pooling may be of little benefit, especially because administrative costs and expected profits associated with insurance can be high. Attempting to divide services between those who are and those who are not covered entails its own set of problems: Should individuals with different incomes have different cutoffs? Is the incentive for early (usually less costly) care reduced? Will individuals attempt to move to venues (usually hospitals) where care is free but may be less efficiently provided? For all these reasons most national health services do cover routine care, and appear to do so at modest administrative costs.

The financial burden of a direct-purchase system falls disproportionately on the poor, who are more price sensitive than the rich, and who typically have more health problems and higher health costs. As a result, the poor underutilize services (some of which are medically necessary) in such a system. The World Health Organization's *World Health Report 2000* provides a valuable discussion of these issues (WHO, 2000).

---

[10]Public insurance pools health risks through public financing from general taxes or other public revenue sources that are collected through a government mandate (e.g., through a social security program, earmarked taxes, or an employer mandate). Social insurance is also a form of compulsory universal health insurance coverage that is typically implemented under the auspices of a social security–type program and is usually financed by employer and employee contributions to government or nonprofit insurance funds. Social insurance funds usually pool risks through social insurance financed from mandatory earmarked payroll taxes set aside specifically for social programs. Public and social health insurance provision can help alleviate many of the insurance market failures that occur with private insurance markets, and the dominant provision of public insurance obviates the need for health insurance regulation.

Degrees of Risk Sharing. As Figure 13-8 demonstrates, different financing and provider arrangements distribute risks among patients, providers, and third-party insurers in different ways. In this context, it is important to note that government finance is one form of insurance in that it shifts the risk away from the individual. When the patient carries the full financial risk of health care costs, he or she must pay for all services out of pocket and is susceptible to significant financial loss should an expensive adverse health event occur. This type of arrangement represents the majority of health financing plans in low- and middle-income countries and tends to be the least equitable, efficient, and organized form of payment.

Private insurers pool risks to a certain extent, but because they are profit maximizers, their main strategy is risk segmentation, or insuring only the lowest-risk individuals to gain the greatest profit. This practice is known as *cream skimming* or *cherry picking,* and from the perspective of society as a whole is not an efficient or equitable way to spread risk. Risk pooling in private insurance markets can be ensured through regulation. In addition, the existence of private insurance can create a two-tiered system (one in which different groups obtain different sets of benefits) and can exacerbate inequities of access without efforts to enhance the quality and equity of services (typically public) for those in lower income groups. It is also possible to have a system in which providers, such as hospitals, clinics, or practitioners, assume the financial risks of health care costs, a practice that is increasingly common in the United States.

Informal Community Financing and Risk Pooling. Informal community financing can be a useful solution to risk-pooling and health insurance constraints seen in low- and middle-income countries

where neither government risk sharing (that often redistributes wealth through subsidies) nor private or social health insurance exists on a large scale. These plans are typically rural, informal, and nongovernmental in nature, and involve either voluntary or compulsory risk pooling through a community fund to which individuals contribute prepayment of premiums that entitle them to postservice payments of certain health services defined by the community. As Figure 13-8 suggests, these plans can shift risk substantially toward the collective. Some plans obtain contributions from employers and governments. Often, the community fund also manages the organization and provision of care (including immunizations and pharmaceuticals), creating a structure similar to an integrated health maintenance organization.

In their analysis of 82 health insurance plans for people outside formal-sector employment, Bennett, Creese, and Monasch (1998) found that, with the exception of China's rural medical plan, few plans covered very large populations or even high proportions of the eligible population, and many plans faced significant problems of adverse selection. In addition, nearly all the plans depended on external subsidies, but very few served the poorest households, being instead targeted toward the rural middle class. In terms of delivery, plan managers failed to focus sufficiently on efficiently delivering high-quality health care, and the administrative structure and practice of plans varied widely, some focusing on insuring against primary care and others against tertiary or hospital care. Administrative costs for plans ranged from 5% to 17% of total costs, which is low compared with pluralistic systems with multiple insurers (the United States, for example, with administrative costs of 19% to 24%) and compared with Western national health

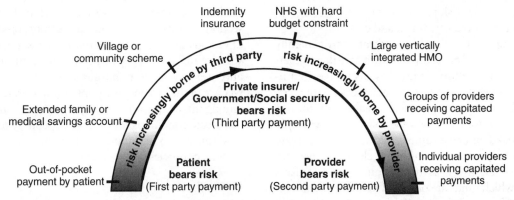

Figure 13-8 Risk-Sharing Arrangements: The Impact of Different Financing Schemes and Provider Payment Systems. *Source:* World Health Organization, *World Health Report 1999: Making a Difference* (Geneva, Switzerland: World Health Organization, 1999), p. 39. Reprinted with permission.

insurance systems (e.g., the Canadian system, with 8% to 11% administrative costs). Many of the plans that were primarily based on tertiary care (e.g., in Nkoranza in Ghana, Masisi in the Democratic Republic of the Congo, Korea, and Taiwan) had problems with overuse of services and cost escalation, whereas plans that were primary care–oriented employed primary care physicians as gatekeepers to control use and costs. Plan managers were found to be highly inefficient in financial planning.

In terms of equity, Bennett, Creese, and Monasch (1998) found that although nearly all of the insurance plans they studied had community-rated insurance premiums (whereby everyone pays the same amount), the premiums were flat rated and therefore regressive in nature. Other taxation or payment measures that associate tax rates with income level (e.g., direct taxes and higher tax rates for higher incomes on a gradient basis) are more progressive than such plans. With the exception of a few plans, there were no exemptions or subsidies for those who had difficulty affording membership in the plan, which amounted to 5% to 10% of an annual household budget in some plans, such as that in Nkoranza district, Ghana. Because the low-income population often could not afford to begin or maintain payments in a plan, they were forced to pay user fees for health services.

The authors also assessed use patterns of different plans and concluded that households located closer to a health facility were more likely to enroll in insurance plans and had higher use rates than those farther away. Thus, geography played an important role in use patterns. This geographic effect could create adverse selection problems, whereby those living farther from a health facility drop out, increasing premiums and leading to further withdrawals. The authors also noted a number of structural features that contributed to poor financial sustainability: small scale, adverse selection leading to smaller risk pools and higher costs, significant administrative structures, and costs.

Although risk pooling and insurance are generally preferred to direct purchase of health care due to their efficiency and welfare gains, they also have significant incentive-altering effects that reduce efficiency and equity in other areas of the health system. For this reason, public and private policy is increasingly shifting risk from government (or third-party private insurers) to providers by moving clockwise around the circle in Figure 13-8. In addition, the mechanisms through which funds are obtained to finance health insurance affect our behavior. Exhibit 13-6 explains two types of health insurance market failures that result from the altered incentives of health insurance, and the

next section addresses many of the incentive effects of various health financing policies.

Health Financing Policies and Their Incentives

The evidence presented earlier suggests that lower-income countries underinvest in health, and their use of already low health investments is often inefficient and inequitable. These factors contribute to lower economic growth and lead to poor health and economic outcomes. To improve these outcomes, lower-income countries face the challenge of raising political support and revenues to sustain greater public investments in health and to improve efficiency in use of both public and private resources. In addition, many health systems in lower-income countries fail to take advantage of the economic and welfare benefits that accrue from collective risk reduction in the form of risk pooling, and from analytical efforts to set priorities through improvements in allocative and technical efficiencies. Constraints that are particular to lower-income countries include low personal income, a large informal or subsistence sector that is exempt from income taxation, and low administrative and tax collection capacity, all of which result in low levels of insurance and risk pooling, health-related capital stock, such as facilities, equipment, beds, and pharmaceutical products, and human resources, such as nurses and providers. Lower-income countries, because of less-targeted and lower levels of public expenditure, are sometimes characterized by greater inequality in the distribution of income compared with more developed economies.

Increasing lower-income countries' overall and public investments in health—and ensuring equitable and efficient use of those resources—is essential to improving health and economic growth and to reducing poverty. However, revenue generation policies have their own economic and equity implications that must be analyzed in order to ensure that efforts to finance health investments do more good than harm. This section assesses the economic and equity consequences of various specific financing mechanisms: taxation; insurance funding, especially as it affects employment; and user fees or user charges and their effect on the welfare of the low-income population. Certain choices among financing and provider compensation options can create conditions for excessive spending on health; this appears to be an emerging problem in middle-income countries.

Taxation

In terms of economic efficiency and revenue generation, most forms of taxation (with the exception of lump sum or poll taxes) distort the consumption and

Exhibit 13-6	Insurance Market Failures: Adverse Selection and Moral Hazard

Insurance market failures, credit shortages, and information asymmetries and insufficiencies can inhibit individuals from realizing the economic benefits of collective risk reduction through risk pooling and efficient insurance systems. Thus, a rationale exists for public financing of health care services or for strong regulation of private health insurance markets. Two commonly noted forms of health insurance market failure are adverse selection and moral hazard.

Adverse Selection

Adverse selection occurs when individuals who are sicker than average self-select into plans that offer better benefits than other plans. This selection increases premiums, making it more likely that average or healthier-than-average individuals will opt out of these plans. If healthier individuals opt out, then spreading risk across the population is no longer possible, because only the sickest are left in the plan. The result is a spiraling effect in which premiums increase and risk pooling disintegrates. In just 3 years in the late 1990s, for example, the indemnity insurance option in the UCLA staff health plan rose from $200 per month to more than $1,000 per month as all but those at highest risk opted for managed care (at less than $50 per month).

Insurance companies attempt to combat adverse selection by screening high-risk individuals through mechanisms such as excluding preexisting conditions from coverage, refusing coverage, requiring medical exams, and having waiting periods. These costly insurance company strategies further add to the instabilities in health insurance markets. Regulating insurers, offering insurance through groups, such as employers, and requiring mandatory public insurance can help alleviate these problems in the private health insurance market.

Moral Hazard

Moral hazard occurs when people are insured and thus do not have to pay the full costs of health care. They have a reduced incentive to avoid certain health care costs, resulting in behavior that may actually increase the probability of occurrence of an event that has been insured against. This feature can be present in either public or private insurance systems. To mitigate moral hazard, insurers create cost sharing, benefit limitation, frequent renewability, and use management features for the health insurance system.

Equity

Ill health and financial ruin resulting from catastrophic illness lead to poverty and income inequality and add to efficiency arguments for government financing of health care services for the low-income population and other vulnerable groups. Equitably financed health systems raise revenues based on people's ability to pay, and equitable delivery systems allocate resources based on people's medical care needs (Ruger, 1998, 2004a). Although often goals can be achieved only at some cost in efficiency, this trade-off is far less acute in health finance precisely because of the insurance market failures just discussed. Private health insurance markets will not ensure equitable revenue generation for health care financing, the equitable distribution of health insurance, or the equitable allocation of health resources. Regulation and public financing are required to achieve equitable as well as efficient outcomes in health finance and delivery.

production decisions made by individuals, households, and firms, resulting in a cost (a deadweight loss) to consider when devising health financing plans involving public taxation. Lump sum and poll taxes, which avoid these burdens, are less desirable on equity grounds and are typically infeasible politically (Schieber & Maeda, 1993).

However, although taxation can be inefficient due to the deadweight loss created by distorting production and consumption decisions, it can also be effective in generating revenue; it serves as a primary mechanism for some types of investment in the economy; and it can be a means for enhancing equity through subsidies and transfers if progressive taxation is employed. A difficulty with general tax revenues in all countries, especially lower-income ones, is that

budget allocations by sector are dependent upon the political support that a given sector generates. In such intersectoral budgetary decisions, health care often loses out to other, more popular, sectors. This fact is especially true when budget projections are overestimated, leaving a shortfall to be made up through budget cuts, as is the case in many lower-income countries. Finally, taxation capacity can be limited in lower-income countries because of underdeveloped and inefficient administrations.

Medical Care Demand Effects of Expanding Private Insurance

The economic impact of expanding private insurance is believed to be the increased demand for private, and the reduced demand for public, insurance among those with the ability to pay the increased insurance rates (higher income groups). Jamaica has experienced such a transition. Gertler and Sturm (1997) studied the demand for public and private medical care with the expansion of private-sector insurance in Jamaica. Jamaica has a universal public health care system in which anyone can use public facilities free of charge, and access to facilities by all groups has been found to be quite good. Jamaica also has a significant private-sector health care market in which higher-quality services are offered at higher prices. Gertler and Sturm (1997) found that insurance did induce individuals to opt out of the public sector in favor of higher-quality private-sector care, and that private insurance coverage was concentrated primarily among the upper income groups, a factor that then freed up public resources for lower-income individuals (see Table 13-4 for results). This stratification also creates a two-tiered system of health care, in which upper-income groups obtain private care through private insurance companies, and lower-income groups obtain publicly financed, and often publicly provided, care.

The work of Gertler and Sturm is especially relevant in the context of low- and middle-income countries because health care financed by governments in these settings often subsidizes the wealthier groups in society. For example, in Indonesia the lowest income quintile consumes less than 14% of public-sector health care expenditure, while the highest income quintile consumes more than 30% (Van de Walle, 1994). Gertler and Sturm (1997) found that introducing mandated private insurance induced covered individuals to opt out of the public sector in favor of perceived higher-quality services in the private sector, and that this shift reduced the total public health expenditure on health care. They also suggested that this policy shift improved the targeting of public health care services toward the low income. Their simulations suggest that "a reduction in total public sector visits from expanding health insurance to the top half of the income distribution implies: (1) a re-duction in public expenditures of about 33%, (2) an increase in the share of public expenditures captured by the poor by about 25%, and (3) a shift in the mix of subsidies away from curative in favor of preventative care" (Gertler and Sturm, 1997, p. 255). This shift could yield significant public-sector cost savings and improved targeting of subsidies to the low income and toward preventive services.

Employer-Related Health Insurance

Some aspects of employer-related health insurance (ERHI) have economic consequences that are worthy of consideration. Securing health insurance through formal employment is typical where the formal employment sector is substantial (higher-income as opposed to lower-income settings) because an individual's income is higher, identifiable, taxed, and subsidized, and because organization is more feasible through formal employment. The extent to which national insurance plans are successful can depend on the size and nature of the formal employment and private insurance sectors and government administrative capacity. Employer-related (or employment-based) health insurance is primarily an American phenomenon. In the United States, approximately 90% of Americans who are covered by private health insurance obtain this coverage through their employment. Of the total compensation package for U.S. workers, health insurance coverage accounts for approximately 34% of benefits expenditures and 7% of the total compensation package (U.S. Bureau of Labor Statistics, 1994).

The link between employment and health insurance in the United States has historical roots in mid-20th century legislation and policies devised to deal with the excess demand for labor in the aftermath of World War II. In particular, two policy efforts confirmed the employment–health insurance link: (1) congressional efforts to restrict wage increases after World War II, which resulted in employer competition for employees on the basis of nonwage benefits such as pensions and health insurance, and (2) tax laws that exempted benefits from taxation,

Table 13-4	The Estimated Effect of Health Insurance on the Demand for Medical Care					
	Preventive Care Visits per Month			Curative Care Visits per Month		
	Public	Private	Total	Public	Private	Total
Insurance	0.138	0.473	0.611	0.022	0.089	0.111
No insurance	0.191	0.221	0.412	0.040	0.065	0.105
Difference	−0.053	0.252	0.199	−0.018	0.024	0.006

Source: P. Gertler and R. Sturm, "Private Health Insurance and Public Expenditures in Jamaica," 1997, *Journal of Econometrics,* 77, pp. 237–257. Reprinted with permission from Elsevier Science.

making them a tax-deductible expenditure of business for employers. Both measures created an incentive for employers to offer health insurance as a benefit of employment (Federal Reserve Bank of San Francisco, 1998). In reality, although employers advertise health insurance as an employer-subsidized benefit, it is the employees who pay for the cost of these services through reduced real wages (except in cases where, like the United States after World War II, core wages have been artificially capped). Given the established employment–health insurance link in the United States, the market for employer-related health insurance has a number of implications for employee decisions regarding job mobility, retirement, and labor supply.

Job Mobility. *Job-lock* is a relatively new term used to describe the situation in which employees are reluctant to change jobs for fear of losing health insurance coverage. It might occur when an individual does not take a better job at a new company because of differences in health insurance coverage between the old job and the new one. Such health insurance differences for this individual might involve requiring a waiting period of several months before health insurance can be obtained, or it might mean that the new employer's coverage excludes health care services that treat one of his or her family's preexisting conditions. Because of the disparities between jobs in the availability and scope of health insurance, and despite potential gains in productivity and income, employees are reluctant to change jobs. Reduction of job mobility not only limits worker freedom, choice, and income, but also has implications for the productivity of the economy if employees are reluctant to take new jobs that will enhance their individual productivity. Although it has long been surmised that job-lock exists, until recently only minimal empirical evidence existed to document the magnitude of this phenomenon in the labor market.

Magnitude of Job-Lock. From 1994 to 1996, at least five studies examined the effects of ERHI on job mobility, productivity, and welfare (e.g., welfare loss from job-lock is the loss in productivity associated with the decline in worker mobility). A review of this literature (Table 13-5) demonstrates that ERHI does deter worker mobility: These studies typically reported a 20% to 40% reduction in mobility rates due to ERHI, depending on workers' marital status, gender, and family size (Buchmueller & Valletta, 1996; Cooper & Monheit, 1993; Holtz-Eakin, 1994; Madrian, 1994; Monheit & Cooper, 1994). One study found that after controlling for pension receipt, job tenure, and spouse job change, there was strong

evidence of job-lock among women, but not among men (Buchmeuller & Valletta, 1996). Another study found that reductions in job mobility due to ERHI were highest for two specific groups: (1) married men with a large family and (2) married men with a pregnant wife (Madrian, 1994).

Fewer studies have been done on the effects of ERHI on worker productivity and macroeconomic efficiencies. However, one such study concluded that in 1987 the economic productivity loss due to job-lock accounted for approximately 0.5% of the total U.S. wage bill ($3.7 billion in annual wages out of $1.262 trillion total, assuming full-time and full-year employment) (Monheit & Cooper, 1994). The authors suggest that this figure can be explained by the fact that these effects are relatively short-lived and affect a relatively small number (1 million of 61 million) of workers. To obtain an estimate of the net effect of ERHI on economic efficiency, these efficiency losses ultimately must be weighed against potential efficiency gains (currently not estimated) that may result from ERHI.

Alleviating or Eliminating Job-Lock. At least three strategies can be employed to mitigate the effects of ERHI on job mobility: (1) Maintain ERHI, but ensure full portability of health insurance coverage across jobs; (2) maintain ERHI, but disallow the exclusion from coverage of preexisting medical conditions; and (3) disassociate health insurance from employment altogether.

There is limited empirical evidence concerning the effectiveness of these policy options, but one study did find that short-term (3 to 20 months) "continuation of coverage" mandates (policies that give individuals the right to purchase health insurance through their former employers for a specific period of time) had a positive effect on worker mobility (Gruber & Madrian, 1994). These results suggest that job-lock may result from short-term (as opposed to long-term) employee concerns over health insurance portability.

Retirement. The decision to retire or continue working is also heavily influenced by ERHI status. This is especially true because the quantity and frequency of medical expenses increase with age, as does the difference between the costs of employer-related health insurance and the insurance policies that can be purchased individually on the open market (Gruber & Madrian, 1995). In some circumstances, older individuals cannot even purchase individual market-based policies.

In their analysis of the impact of continuation-of-coverage laws on retirement decisions, Gruber and Madrian (1995) found that the ability to purchase

Table 13-5	Employment-Related Health Insurance (ERHI) and Job Motility: Estimates of Job-Lock in the United States	
Author(s)	**Sample/Method**	**Magnitude of Job-Lock**
Madrian (1994)	1987 National Medical Expenditure Survey (NMES). Sample of married men aged 20–55. Estimated probit equation of likelihood of job change and examined three experimental groups with difference-in-difference approach.	Estimated that mobility rates decreased by 30% to 31% for those with employment-provided health insurance coverage compared with those without such coverage. Mobility rates reduced by 33% to 37% for those married men with employment-related coverage and large families. Mobility rates decreased by 67% for those with employment-related coverage and a pregnant wife.
Holtz-Eakin (1994)	1984 Panel Study of Income Dynamics (PSID). Full-time workers aged 25–55. Used difference-in-difference approach.	Found no statistically significant results. For job changes during 1984–1985, mobility rates for married men declined by 1.59 percentage points, and rates for single women declined by 1.06 percentage points.
Gruber and Madrian (1994)	Survey of Income and Program Participation (1985, 1986, 1987)	Found that state and federal policy to mandate continuation of coverage increased job mobility of prime-age male workers. Suggested that job-lock may result from short-run (as opposed to long-run) employee concerns over portability.
Monheit and Cooper (1994)	1987 National Medical Expenditure Survey (NMES). Reviewed literature and studied the nature of welfare loss associated with job-lock.	Authors reviewed literature on job-lock and found that studies typically reported a 20% to 40% reduction in mobility rates due to ERHI, depending on worker marital status, gender, and family size. Examined welfare loss due to job-lock and found that the magnitude of welfare loss was $4.8 billion, less than 1% of the wage bill of those affected.
Buchmueller and Valletta (1996)	1984 Survey of Income and Program Participation (SIPP). Included pension receipt, job tenure, spouse job change to estimate ERHI effects on job mobility.	Found, for dual-earner married men and women, strong evidence of job-lock among women, but weak evidence of job-lock among men.

an employment-based plan from a former employer at the same price as if one were employed increases the odds of early retirement (because the individual is no longer working, employees still working will be forced to pay for the subsidy provided to retired workers). The degree to which the likelihood of early retirement increases depends, the authors found, on the duration of the ability to purchase postretirement insurance and the quality of the employer-based post-retirement and publicly offered health insurance options. More specifically, the authors found that among men aged 55 to 64 who are too young for Medicare (which commences at age 65), each additional year of continued coverage increases the likelihood of retiring by 30%.

Labor Supply. Most employers do not offer health benefits to part-time employees. In addition, many low-wage earners in service-sector positions (e.g., fast-food service employees) do not receive health insurance as a benefit of employment (low-wage earners typically do not receive benefits because their earnings are too low to pass on the premium costs). These factors provide an incentive for those who need or value health insurance to choose fulltime over part-time employment. In their analysis of married women's decisions to work full- or part-time, Buchmueller and Valletta (1999) found that wives frequently switched from nonparticipation to work in order to obtain health insurance. Their estimates demonstrate a 15% to 36% increase in married women's labor supply associated with a lack of their husband's health insurance coverage.

Labor Market Effects of Introducing National Health Insurance in Canada

One of the negative economic impacts of introducing national health insurance in a given country is believed to be the deadweight loss and increased unemployment resulting from altered production and consumption decisions due to the necessary increases in payroll taxes.[11] Economic theory predicts that increases in payroll taxes result in economic activity and deadweight losses as a result of altered production and consumption decisions in the economy. At the same time, theory points to efficiency gains from effectively implemented risk-pooling arrangements. From the early 1960s to the early 1970s, Canada moved from a primarily private insurance–based health care system to a national health insurance system financed primarily through lump-sum premiums or general revenue financing, with management decentralized to the provincial level. National health insurance in Canada provides coverage to all citizens.

Gruber and Hanratty (1993) studied the effects of Canada's "natural experiment" of phasing from ERHI (roughly 70% of the population was covered by private health insurance in the mid-1960s) to national health insurance. In examining monthly data on employment, wages, and hours across eight industries and 10 provinces over the period 1961 to 1975, they found that although both employment and wages increased after the introduction of national health insurance, average hours were unchanged. These results were robust to a number of model specifications (different analyses) that controlled for the potential endogeneity of national health insurance and provincial and industry effects. The authors believe that the results might be explained by the notion that the introduction of national health insurance systemati-

cally increases labor demand across all sectors of the economy due, at least in part, to the increases in labor productivity that result from increases in job mobility or health improvements in the labor force. Despite some noted differences in the costs of medical and hospital care, the authors believe that the pre–national health insurance system in Canada is sufficiently similar to that in the United States for this Canadian experiment to offer useful evidence of the effects of a similar transition in the United States.

The Impact of Private User Fees or Public User Charges on the Welfare of the Poor

Private user fees are part of a system in which patients pay directly out of pocket for health care services. These fees can take the form of payment for the whole charge, partial payment for a service, a copayment (a flat amount per visit), or coinsurance (a percentage of the cost of the service). User charges are fees paid by patients for publicly provided services and constitute public revenues. User fee/user charge financing is designed as a demand-side and revenue-generation measure to improve allocative efficiency in the health care system by making patients more cost conscious in health care decision making. In addition to controlling use, user charges have been designed to raise revenues and to decrease the government's financial burden in the health sector, to increase coverage and the quality of care by increasing resources for the health sector, and to increase efficiency in health service delivery.

Higher-income countries promote these types of payments to reduce health care use (by making consumers more conscious of health care costs). Evidence suggests that these mechanisms have been successful in reducing use, regardless of whether reduced health care is medically appropriate (Newhouse, 1993). User fees have a greater health and income impact on the poor and medically indigent because these groups decrease their use of both necessary and unnecessary health care. Rather than employ user fees or user charges, a new system of allocative efficiency, or medical care appropriateness, has emerged to reduce inappropriate care while ensuring that appropriate and necessary care reaches those in need. This system is currently being tested in the United States and is discussed in Exhibit 13-5.

The evidence from a number of in-country experiences with user fees or user charges demonstrates that, for the most part, such fees have not been overwhelmingly successful in raising revenue, enhancing efficiency, or improving equity. With respect to revenue generation, user charges have failed to provide

---

[11]Currie and Madrian (1999) provide an excellent overview and additional references concerning the labor market effects of health insurance, with an emphasis on the situation in the United States. See also Gruber and Hanratty (1993) and Hanratty (1996).

more than 10% of ministry of health recurrent costs in sub-Saharan Africa (Wang'ombe, 1997). Programs in China have been much more successful in cost recovery (24% to 36% of ministry of health recurrent expenditures recovered) than have programs in sub-Saharan Africa, where an average of 5% of operating costs are recouped through user charges. This figure is probably an underestimate of the net yield because the administrative costs of collecting fees must also be considered. In many cases, it is likely that the net yield is near zero or negative for cost recovery. In addition, because systems are not raising enough revenues from user fees or user charges, there is little additional money to channel into improved quality and system reform, especially for public health services targeted at the low income, which are especially hard hit by the lack of additional money. Funding for these efforts still must stem from the ministry of health budget.

A review of the literature on user financing of basic social services by Reddy and Vandemoortele (1996) further supports the conclusion that user fees and user charges generally have had negative effects on use and very little success in raising revenue to cover governmental recurrent costs. As shown in Table 13-6, recent estimates of price elasticity of demand for health care in a number of countries provide compelling evidence that user fees are associated with significant reductions in use rates, especially among the low income and children. The magnitude of revenues raised through health cost recovery in Africa ranges from roughly 0.5% to 20% of the recurrent budget of the ministry of health.

There is additional evidence that user fees or user charges reduce use, but the overall efficiency effects are unclear given that these reductions occur with both necessary and unnecessary care. In his review of the literature on user charges, Creese (1991) found that user fees decrease use, especially among the patients at greatest risk and for whom the most cost-effective preventive and treatment options are appropriate. In the Democratic Republic of the Congo, for instance, relative increases in the cost of health care (as compared with the cost of other consumer products) led to significant decreases in the demand for treatment measures, especially for prenatal care and interventions for children under age 5. The magnitude of the reduction was significant: The overall use rate fell from 37% to 31%, and the coverage rate for prenatal visits fell from 95% to 84% (De Bethune, Alfani, & Lahaye, 1989). As Creese (1991) notes, these study results indicate that the demand for health care is more price elastic among lower-income individuals than in higher income groups. The cost-recovery rate through user charges was insignificant.

Efficiency gains from these mechanisms have also been modest. There is some evidence that the use of graduated user charges (higher fees for hospitals and lower fees for health centers) aimed at improving technical efficiency (delivering primary care at low-level health centers and tertiary care at high-level hospitals) has been successful (Collins et al., 1995). Some countries, namely Côte d'Ivoire, Mali, Namibia, Zambia, and Zimbabwe, have implemented graduated user charges with some successes in technical efficiency (e.g., better use of referrals, and better patterns of use for both primary care received at lower-level facilities such as health centers and tertiary care received at higher-level facilities such as hospitals) (Barnum & Kutzin, 1993; Bennett & Ngalande-Banda, 1994).

In Ghana, Creese (1991) notes, there was a sharp reduction in use as a result of large increases in health care fees. Reduced use was sustained over a 2-year period (Waddington & Enyimayew, 1990). Although the cost-recovery rate of this policy (15%) was fairly high compared with some other projects, the authors believed that the demand shifted from health care sought in government facilities to rural, unlicensed sellers of drugs, which had potentially significant ramifications for health. Finally, Creese (1991) noted a sharp decrease in demand following a policy decision in Swaziland to raise charges at government health units by 300% to 400% (to the same fee levels as mission providers), without raising quality. The resultant decrease in use at government facilities was 32%, but this decrease was coupled with an increase in use of 10% at mission facilities; the overall drop in use was 17%. Use continued to decrease over the course of the year following the policy change, and a disproportionate drop in use (especially for use of government services for sexually transmitted and respiratory infections) occurred among the lower income groups (Yoder, 1989).

The equity effects of user fees and user charges are not favorable. Although some initially argued that equity can be improved through the use of user fees or user charges due to increased service availability and quality (from increased revenues) and better use (from price effects on demand) (De Ferranti, 1985), the subsequent evidence does not necessarily support this argument. For these factors to be equity enhancing, the government would need to ensure that increased revenues are reinvested and targeted toward services that directly affect the low income, and to ensure that low-income and vulnerable groups are ex-

Table 13-6	Estimates of Price Elasticity of Demand for Health Care			
Study	**Location and Year of Data**	**Results**		
Jimenez (1989)	Ethiopia (1985)	Overall	−0.05 to −0.50	
Jimenez (1989)	Sudan (1986)	Overall	−0.37	
Yoder (1989)	Swaziland (1985)	Overall	−0.32	
Gertler and van der Gaag (1988)	Côte d'Ivoire (1985)	**Rural Hospitals**		
		Income Quartile	**Adults**	**Children**
		Lowest	−0.47 to −1.34	−0.65 to −2.32
		Second	−0.44 to −1.27	−0.58 to −1.98
		Third	−0.41 to −1.18	−0.49 to −1.60
		Highest	−0.29 to −0.71	−0.12 to −0.48
Gertler and van der Gaag (1988)	Peru (1985)	**Rural Hospitals**		
		Income Quartile	**Adults**	**Children**
		Lowest	−0.57 to −1.36	−0.57 to −1.72
		Second	−0.38 to −0.91	−0.48 to −1.20
		Third	−0.16 to −0.37	−0.22 to −0.54
		Highest	−0.01 to −0.04	−0.03 to −0.09
Sauerborn et al. (1994)	Burkina Faso (1985)	Overall	−0.79	
		Age Groups		
		<1	−3.64	
		1–14	−1.73	
		15+	−0.27	
		Income Quartile		
		Lowest	−1.44	
		Second	−1.21	
		Third	−1.39	
		Highest	−0.12	

Source: S. Reddy and J. Vandemoortele, *User Financing of Basic Social Services: A Review of Theoretical Arguments and Empirical Evidence* (New York: Office of Evaluation, UNICEF, 1996). Reprinted with permission.

empted from many user fees and charges and offered public subsidies instead. Evidence from sub-Saharan Africa suggests that patients are highly sensitive to user charges and user fees (Bennett & Ngalande-Banda, 1994; Gertler & van der Gaag, 1990; Mwabu and Wang'ombe, 1995; Waddington & Enyimayew, 1990). Although nearly all sub-Saharan African user fee and user charge programs have exemptions for the poor through means testing, this method is hard to implement in many countries and can be exploited by higher-income groups.

Health Expenditures and Poverty

For those without insurance coverage, high health expenditures relative to income either can preclude treatment because of income insufficiencies or, if medical treatment options are pursued, can pose a major

financial burden. Although the evidence on this subject is scant, there are a few studies that demonstrate the implications both of falling ill and of facing catastrophic health expenditure. For example, in their analysis of the post–Cooperative Medical System era in China, Liu and associates (1998) found that high health expenditures were a major cause of poverty in rural areas. Health care costs were found to be high relative to a rural farmer's income: Low-income farmers often had to spend roughly 1.2 years of disposable income to pay for an episode of hospitalization at a county hospital. As Table 13-7 demonstrates, the cost of an outpatient visit as a percentage of weekly income for the lowest-income households varied from 38% in a village facility to 151% at a township provider and 170% in a county facility. In addition, 18% of households using health services incurred health

Table 13-7	The Financial Burden of Health Care Costs for Households with Different Income Levels in China's Poverty Regions	
Level of Facilities	Households with Income/Capita 200 Yuan	Households with Income/Capita 400 Yuan
	Cost of an outpatient visit as % of weekly income	
Village	38%	36%
Township	151%	71%
County	170%	84%
	Cost of an inpatient episode as % of annual income	
Township	28%	22%
County	116%	138%

Source: Y. Liu, S. Hu, W. Fu, and W. C. Hsiao, "Is Community Financing Necessary and Feasible for Rural China?" In M. L. Barer, T. E. Getzen, and G. L. Stoddart (Eds.), *Health, Health Care and Health Economics: Perspectives on Distribution* (New York: John Wiley & Sons, 1998). Copyright 1998 John Wiley & Sons, Ltd. Reprinted with permission.

expenditures exceeding total household income in 1 year (1993), and of the 11,044 rural households surveyed, 24.5% borrowed or became indebted, and 5.5% sold or mortgaged properties to pay for health care. In addition, 72.6% of individuals who did not seek ambulatory care and 89.2% of individuals who did not seek hospital care made this decision based on financial difficulties. In their survey of 30 counties, the authors found that as a result of these burdensome payments, 47% of medically indebted households suffered from hunger.

In a preliminary study of people's ability to cope with catastrophic health shocks in Indonesia, Prescott and Pradhan (1999) found that out-of-pocket health expenditures were highly skewed, suggesting that a proportion of the population faced catastrophic levels of health expenditure relative to income. Social risk management mechanisms, in the form of budget subsidies for publicly provided services and insurance for civil servants, generally benefitted the better-off, whereas lower-income households were forced to reduce demand (especially for inpatient services) and spend less on medical care. In their simulations of the estimated frequency and intensity of catastrophic health shocks, controlling for income, the authors found that the simulated estimate was much higher than the frequency observed from household survey data. With respect to policy measures employed to alleviate the burden on poorer households, the authors believe that efforts to ensure universal coverage through budget subsidies targeting the poor and through insurance options can significantly reduce, but not eliminate, the catastrophic shocks experienced by lower-income households.

Finally, Fabricant, Kamara, and Mills (1999) showed that in Sierra Leone the rural low income were disproportionately disadvantaged by user charges for health care, in that they paid a higher percentage of their incomes for health care than wealthier households. The authors concluded that greater accessibility to basic health facilities and greater reliance on additional resources generated through improved efficiency and cross-subsidization would relieve much of the financial burden placed on these lower-income households. Insurance and prepayment plans also would help reduce the financial burden of health expenditure.

Conclusion

The World Bank's 1980 *World Development Report* on human resources and poverty examined the interrelations between poverty (in terms of low income) and health, education, nutrition, and fertility levels. Table 13-1 points to the enormous progress in this century in several of these domains, progress substantially denied to the world's lowest-income billion. The upper panel of Figure 13-9, reproduced (and modified) from the 1980 report, illustrates both the possible relations among these variables and the entry points for policy operating through them. Although the report indicates the importance of public action in each domain, it concludes that expansion and improvement in primary education, particularly for girls, is the critical priority in most countries. The information presented in this chapter suggests a more central role for health, at least for low-income regions with current high levels of illness. The lower panel of Figure 13-9 places health in this central role.

The consequences of health and health policy for economic development are of major importance to policy makers in the health and development fields.

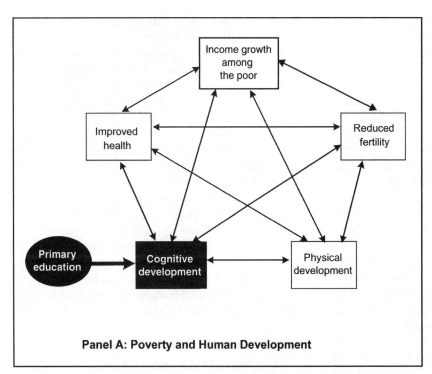

Figure 13-9 Health and Development. *Note:* HFA = height for age; BMI = body mass index. *Source:* World Bank, *World Development Report* (Washington, DC: World Bank, 1980). Adapted with permission.

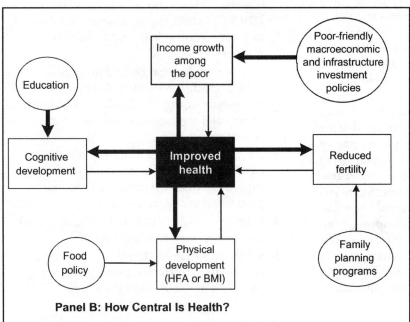

This chapter has provided an assessment of the relevant conclusions from the literature available on this subject, but recognizes that the research base itself is limited. The analysis presented here suggests directions for government policy at several levels. First, it is useful to encourage policies that will accelerate the speed of favorable demographic transitions and incorporate changing age structures into government policies aimed at schooling and job creation. The changing age structure of a population that results from demographic transition provides a window of opportunity that can lead to a transitory boost in economic growth, enabling a country to break free of a poverty trap. Second, a central goal of many countries' health sector development strategies should be to create policies to control infectious diseases, such as malaria, tuberculosis, HIV/AIDS, and sexually transmitted infections, by providing information and resources necessary for avoiding, and in many cases, curing infection. Categorical control policies against the major diseases of the low income probably provide the most efficient means for targeting public expenditures to them. Third, improving the health of the poor is necessary to alleviate poverty. The marginal productivity of health is probably higher in low-income societies, and governments should develop policies to address the health and economic needs of the low-income population.

Efforts also must be made to assess selected health policies based on their effects both on health and economic outcomes (Ruger, 2003a, 2004b). First, practitioners should promote the use of clinical protocols to improve health outcomes and enhance efficient health care spending. Economic incentives to decrease health care use (e.g., copayments, deductibles, capitated payments, and global budgets) do not necessarily distinguish between types of care (appropriate versus inappropriate) and the needs of patients, and can have a disproportionate impact on the poor and medically indigent. Second, governments and policy makers should pursue sustainable health care financing to insure against health-related financial losses and to eliminate distortions in the market for health care. To spread risk and minimize insurance market failure, governments can (1) encourage universal risk pooling through government mandates and taxes, (2) pursue health financing policies that are separate from employment, thereby preempting or reducing labor market distortions that result from ERHI, and (3) discourage the use of user fees to generate revenue and reduce demand for health care services among the poor. Third, efforts should be taken to improve health care systems with inadequate infrastructure and access. In many societies, low levels of health spending and inequitable allocation result in unacceptably low levels of capital stock, human resources, and service use that fail to meet individuals'

health needs. Fourth, health planners should promote efficient health administration policies by avoiding or reducing excessive administrative costs, especially those between hospitals and third-party payers, and by encouraging the efficient use of administrative activities to monitor and reduce the occurrence of costly and medically inappropriate procedures.

Finally, development institutions, nongovernmental organizations, and academic communities should take on a number of activities to investigate further the links between health and economic development. Primarily, they can encourage continued efforts to understand health and development links by helping low- and middle-income countries develop their own capacity to study these connections; by encouraging further generation of relevant primary data; and by ensuring that the appropriate household-level and cross-national databases are maintained, updated, and accessible to all.

● ● ● Discussion Questions

1. In what ways, and to what extent, do major diseases such as tuberculosis, malaria, and HIV/AIDS affect the income and well-being of people living in low- and middle-income countries?

2. What can policy makers and practitioners do in non-health-service-related settings, such as schools, to improve the health and well-being of girls and boys in low- and middle-income countries?

3. How do changes in fertility and mortality patterns work to influence the level and capacity of those contributing to economic production in a given society?

4. Why is the concept of risk pooling in financing health care services so important?

5. What are the health, health care service use, and economic effects of making people pay part of the costs of medical services?

• • • References

Aaron, H., & Schwartz, W. (1984). *The painful prescription: Rationing hospital care*. Washington, DC: Brookings Institution.

Acemoglu, D., Johnson, S., & Robinson, J. A. (2003). Disease and development in historical perspective. *Journal of the European Economic Association, 1*(2), 397–405.

Ahlburg, D. A. (2000). *The economic impacts of tuberculosis* (WHO/CDS/STB/2000.5). Geneva, Switzerland: World Health Organization.

Ainsworth, M., & Over, M. (1994). Aids and African development. *World Bank Research Observer, 9*, 203–240.

Almond, D. (2003). *Is the 1918 influenza pandemic over? Long-term effects of in utero influenza exposure in the post-1940 U.S. population.* Mimeograph, National Bureau of Economic Research, Cambridge, MA.

Alsan, M., Bloom, D. E., & Canning, D. (2004). *The effect of population health on foreign direct investment* (Working Paper No. w10596). Cambridge, MA: National Bureau of Economic Research.

Anand, S., Diderichsen, F., Evans, T., Shkolnikov, V. M., & Wirth, M. (2001). Measuring disparities in health: Methods and indicators. In T. Evans, M. Whitehead, F. Diderichsen, A. Bhuiya, & M. Wirth (Eds.), *Challenging inequities in health: From ethics to action*. London: Oxford University Press.

Anand, K., Pandav, C. S., & Nath, L. M. (1999). Impact of HIV/AIDS on the national economy of India. *Health Policy, 47, 195–205.*

Barnum, H., & Kutzin, J. (1993). *Public hospitals in developing countries: Resource use, cost, financing*. Baltimore: Johns Hopkins University Press for the World Bank.

Barro, R., & Lee, J. W. (1994). Sources of economic growth. *Carnegie-Rochester Conference Series on Public Policy, 40, 1–46.*

Basta, S. S., Soekirman, M. S., Karyadi, D., & Scrimshaw, N. S. (1979). Iron deficiency anemia and the productivity of adult males in Indonesia. *American Journal of Clinical Nutrition, 32,* 916–925.

Behrman, J. (1993). The economic rationale for investing in nutrition in developing countries. *World Development, 21*(11), 1749–1771.

Bell, C., Devarajan, S., & Gersbach, H. (2003). *The long-run economic costs of AIDS: Theory and an application to South Africa* (Policy Research Working Paper No. WPS 3152). Washington, DC: World Bank.

Bennett, S., Creese, A., & Monasch, R. (1998). *Health insurance schemes for people outside formal sector employment.* (Division of Analysis, Research and Assessment Paper No. 16). Geneva, Switzerland: World Health Organization.

Bennett, S., & Ngalande-Banda, E. (1994). *Public and private roles in health: A review and analysis of experience in sub-Saharan Africa* (Strengthening Health Services Paper 6). Geneva, Switzerland: World Health Organization.

Berger, M. C., & Leigh, P. (1989). Schooling, self-selection and health. *Journal of Human Resources, 24, 435–455.*

Bernstein, S. J., McGlynn, E. A., Siu, A. L., Roth, C. P., Sherwood, M. J., Keesey, J. W., Kosecoff, J., Hicks, N. R., & Brook, R. H. (1993). The appropriateness of hysterectomy: A comparison of care in seven health plans. *Journal of the American Medical Association, 269*, 2398–2402.

Bhargava, A. (1994). Modeling the health of Filipino children. *Journal of the Royal Statistical Society, Series A, 157,* 417–432.

Bhargava, A., Jamison, D., Lau, L., & Murray, C. (2001). Modeling the effects of health on economic growth. *Journal of Health Economics, 20*(3), 423–440.

Bleakley, H. (2003). Disease and development: Evidence from the American South. *Journal of the European Economic Association, 1*(2), 376–386.

Bloom, D. E., & Canning, D. (2000). The health and wealth of nations. *Science, 287,* 1207–1209.

Bloom, D. E., Canning, D. & Graham, B. (2003). Longevity and life cycle savings. *Scandinavian Journal of Economics, 105,* 319–338.

Bloom, D. E., Canning, D., & Malaney, P. (2000). Demographic change and economic growth in Asia. *Population and Development Review, 26*(Suppl.), 257–290.

Bloom, D. E., Canning, D., & Sevilla, J. (2002). *The demographic dividend: A new perspective on the economic consequences of population change* (MR-1274). Santa Monica, CA: RAND.

Bloom, D. E., Canning, D., & Sevilla, J. (2004). The effect of health on economic growth: A production function approach. *World Development, 32*(1), 1–13.

Bloom, D. E., & Freeman, R. B. (1988). Economic development and the timing and components of population growth. *Journal of Policy Modeling, 10*(1), 57–82.

Bloom, D. E., & Mahal, A. S. (1997). Does the AIDS epidemic threaten economic growth? *Journal of Econometrics, 77,* 105–124.

Bloom, D. E., & River Path Associates. (2000). Social capitalism and human diversity. In Organization of Economic Cooperation and Development, *The creative society of the 21st century*. Paris: Organization of Economic Cooperation and Development.

Bloom, D. E., Rosenfield, A., & River Path Associates. (2000). A moment in time: AIDS and business. *AIDS Patient Care and STDs, 14*(9), 509–517.

Bloom, D. E., & Williamson, J. G. (1998). Demographic transitions and economic miracles in emerging Asia. *The World Bank Economic Review, 12*(3), 419–455.

Bovbjerg, R. R. (1995). The high cost of administration in health care: Part of the problem or part of the solution? *Journal of Law, Medicine & Ethics, 23,* 186–194.

Brook, R. H. (1992). Improving practice: The clinician's role. *British Journal of Surgery, 79,* 606–607.

Brook, R. H. (1994). The RAND/UCLA appropriateness method. In K. A. McCormick, S. R. Moore, & R. A. Siegel, *Clinical practice guideline development: Methodology perspectives* (AHCPR Publication No. 95-0009). Rockville, MD: Public Health Service.

Brook, R. H. (1995). Medicare quality and getting older: A personal essay. *Health Affairs, 14*(4), 73–81.

Brook, R. H. (1997). Managed care is not the problem. Quality is. *Journal of the American Medical Association, 278,* 1612–1614.

Brook, R. H., Kamberg, C. J., Mayer-Oakes, A., Beers, M. H., Raube, K., & Steiner, A. (1990). Appropriateness of acute medical care for the elderly: An analysis of the literature. *Health Policy, 14,* 225–242.

Brook, R. H., & Lohr, K. N. (1986). Will we need to ration effective health care? *Issues in Science and Technology, 3,* 68–77.

Brook, R. H., & Lohr, K. N. (1987). Monitoring quality of care in the Medicare program: Two proposed systems. *Journal of the American Medical Association, 258,* 3138–3141.

Brook, R. H., & Lohr, K. N. (1990). Efficacy, effectiveness, variations, and quality: Boundary-crossing research. In N. O. Graham (Ed.), *Quality assurance in hospitals: Strategies for assessment and implementation* (2nd ed.). Rockville, MD: Aspen Publishers.

Brook, R. H., Park, R. E., & Chassin, M. R. (1990). Predicting the appropriate use of carotid endarterectomy, upper gastrointestinal endoscopy, and coronary angiography. *New England Journal of Medicine, 323,* 1173–1177.

Buchmueller, T. C., & Valletta, R. G. (1996). The effects of employer-provided health insurance on worker mobility. *Industrial and Labor Relations Review, 49*(3), 439–455.

Buchmueller, T. C., & Valletta, R. G. (1999). The effect of health insurance on married female labor supply. *Journal of Human Resources, 34*(1), 42–70.

Carlisle, D. M., Siu, A. L., Keeler, E. B., McGlynn, E. A., Kahn, K., Rubenstein, L. V., & Brook, R. H. (1992). HMO vs. fee-for-service care of older persons with acute myocardial infraction. *American Journal of Public Health, 82,* 1626–1630.

Case, A. (2004). Does money protect health status? Evidence from South African pensions. In D. Wise (Ed.), *Perspectives on the economics of aging.* Chicago: University of Chicago Press.

Chassin, M. R., Kosecoff, J., Solomon, D. H., & Brook, R. H. (1987). How coronary angiography is used: Clinical determinants of appropriateness. *Journal of the American Medical Association, 258,* 2543–2547.

Chima, R., Goodman, C., & Mills, A. The economic impact of malaria in Africa: A critical review of the evidence. *Health Policy, 63,* 17–36.

Collins, D. H., Quick, J. D., Musau, S. N., & Kraushaar, D. L. (1995). *Health financing reform in Kenya: The fall and rise of cost-sharing, 1989–1994.* Stubbs Monograph Series 1. Boston: Management Sciences for Health.

Cooper, P. F., & Monheit, A. C. (1993). Does employment-related health insurance inhibit job mobility? *Inquiry, 30*(4), 400–416.

Creese, A. L. (1991). User charges for health care: A review of recent experience. *Health Policy and Planning, 6*(4), 309–319.

Croft, R. A., & Croft, R. P. (1998). Expenditure and loss of income incurred by tuberculosis patients before reaching effective treatment in Bangladesh. *International Journal of Tuberculosis and Lung Disease, 2*(3), 252–254.

Cuddington, J. T. (1991). *Modelling the macroeconomic effects of AIDS with an application to Tanzania* (Working Paper No. 91-17). Washington, DC: Georgetown University, Department of Economics.

Cuddington, J. T., & Hancock, J. D. (1992). *Assessing the impact of AIDS on the growth path of the Malawian economy* (Working Paper No. 92-07). Washington, DC: Georgetown University, Department of Economics.

Currie, J., & Madrian, B. C. (1999). Health, health insurance and the labor market. In O. Ashenfelter & D. Card (Eds.). *Handbook of labor economics* (Vol. 3, pp. 3309–3416). New York: Elsevier Science.

Cutler, D. M., & Richardson, E. (1998). The value of health: 1970–1990. *American Economic Review, 88,* 97–100.

Deaton, A. (2003). Health, inequality, and economic development. *Journal of Economic Literature, 41*(1), 113–158.

Deaton, A., & Paxson, C. (2001). Mortality, education, income and inequality among American cohorts. In D. Wise (Ed.), *Themes in the economics of aging.* Chicago: University of Chicago Press.

De Bethune, X., Alfani, S., & Lahaye, J. P. (1989). The influence of an abrupt price increase on health service utilization: Evidence from Zaire. *Health Policy and Planning, 4,* 76–81.

De Ferranti, D. (1985). *Paying for health services in developing countries: An overview* (Staff Working Paper 721). Washington, DC: World Bank.

Deolalikar, A. B. (1988). Nutrition and labor productivity in agriculture: Estimates for rural South India. *Review of Economics and Statistics, 70*(3), 406–413.

Dholakia, R. H., & Almeida, J. (1997). *The potential economic benefits of the DOTS strategy against TB in India.* Geneva, Switzerland: The Global TB Program of the World Health Organization, Research and Surveillance Unit.

Dow, W. H., Gertler, P., Strauss, J., & Thomas, D. (1997). *Health care prices, health and labor outcomes: Experimental evidence.* Unpublished manuscript, RAND, Santa Monica, CA.

Dwyer, D. S., & Mitchell, O. S. (1999). Health problems as determinants of retirement: Are self-rated measures endogenous? *Journal of Health Economics, 18,* 173–193.

Easterlin, R. A. (1999). How beneficent is the market? A look at the modern history of mortality.

European Review of Economic History, 3(3), 257–294.

Enthoven, A. (2000). In pursuit of an improving National Health Service. *Health Affairs, 19,* 102–119.

Ettner, S., Frank, R., & Kessler, R. (1997). The impact of psychiatric disorders on labor market outcomes. *Industrial and Labor Relations Review, 51*(1), 64–81.

Fabricant, S. J., Kamara, C. W., & Mills, A. (1999). Why the poor pay more: Household curative expenditures in rural Sierra Leone. *International Journal of Health Planning and Management, 14*(3), 179–199.

Farrell, P., & Fuchs, V. (1982). Schooling and health: The cigarette connection. *Journal of Health Economics, 1,* 217–230.

Feachem, R. G. A. (2000). The future of NHS: Confronting the big questions. *Health Affairs, 19,* 128–129.

Federal Reserve Bank of San Francisco. (1998). *Economic letter* (No. 98-12). San Francisco: Federal Reserve Bank of San Francisco.

Flynn, J. R. (1998). IQ gains over time: Toward finding the causes. In U. Neisser (Ed.), *The rising curve: Long-term gains in IQ and related measures* (pp. 25–66). Washington, DC: The American Psychological Association.

Fogel, R. W. (1994). Economic growth, population theory and physiology: The bearing of long term processes on the making of economic policy. *American Economic Review, 84*(3), 369–395.

Fogel, R. W. (1997). New findings on secular trends in nutrition and mortality: Some implications for population theory. In M. R. Rosenzweig & O. Stark (Eds.), *Handbook of population and family economics* (Vol. 1A, pp. 433–481). Amsterdam: Elsevier Science.

Frankenberg, E., Beegle, K., Thomas, D., & Suriastini, W. (1999). *Health, education, and the economic crisis in Indonesia.* Paper presented at the 1999 meeting of the Population Association of America.

Fuchs, V. R. (1993). *The future of health policy.* Cambridge, MA: Harvard University Press.

Gallup, J. L., & Sachs, J. (1999). *Geography and economic development* (Consulting Assistance on Economic Return Discussion Paper No. 39). Cambridge, MA: Harvard Institute for International Development.

Gallup, J. L., & Sachs, J. (2001). The economic burden of malaria. *American Journal of Tropical Medicine and Hygiene, 64*(1–2 Suppl.), 85–96.

Gardner, G. W., Edgerton, V. R., Senewiratne, B., Barnard, J. R., & Ohira, Y. (1975). Physical work capacity and metabolic stress in subjects with iron deficiency anemia. *American Journal of Clinical Nutrition, 30,* 910–917.

Gauthier, A. K., Rogal, D. L., Barrand, N. K., & Cohen, A. B. (1992). Administrative costs in the U.S. health care system: The problem or the solution? *Inquiry, 29,* 308–320.

Gertler, P., & Sturm, R. (1997). Private health insurance and public expenditures in Jamaica. *Journal of Econometrics, 77,* 237–257.

Gertler, P., & van der Gaag, J. (1988). *Measuring the willingness to pay for social service in developing countries.* Washington, DC: World Bank.

Gertler, P., & van der Gaag, J. (1990). *The willingness to pay for medical care.* Baltimore: Johns Hopkins University Press.

Glewwe, P., & King, E. M. (2001). The impact of early childhood nutritional status on cognitive development: Does the timing of malnutrition matter? *World Bank Economic Review, 15*(1), 81–113.

Grossman, M. (1975). The correlation between health and schooling. In N. E. Terleckyj (Ed.), *Household production and consumption.* New York: National Bureau of Economic Research, Columbia University Press.

Gruber, J., & Hanratty, M. (1993). *The labor market effects of introducing national health insurance: Evidence from Canada* (Working Paper No. 4589). Cambridge, MA: National Bureau of Economic Research.

Gruber, J., & Madrian, B. C. (1994). Health insurance and job mobility: The effects of public policy on job-lock. *Industrial and Labor Relations Review, 48*(1), 86–102.

Gruber, J., & Madrian, B. C. (1995). Health insurance availability and the retirement decision. *American Economic Review, 85*(4), 938–948.

Haacker M. (2004). *The macroeconomics of HIV/AIDS*. Washington, DC: International Monetary Fund.

Handa, S., & Neitzert, M. (1998). *Chronic illness and retirement in Jamaica* (Living Standards Measurement Study Working Paper No. 131). Washington, DC: The World Bank.

Hanratty, M. (1996). Canadian national health insurance and infant health. *American Economic Review, 86*(91), 276–284.

Hilborne, L. H., Leape, L. L., Bernstein, S. J., Park, R. E., Fiske, M. E., Kamberg, C. J., Roth, C. P., & Brook, R. H. (1993). The appropriateness of use of percutaneous transluminal coronary angioplasty in New York state. *Journal of the American Medical Association, 269*, 761–765.

Holtz-Eakin, D. (1994). Health insurance provision and labor market efficiency in the United States and Germany. In R. M. Blank (Ed.), *Social protection versus economic flexibility* (pp. 157–188). Chicago: University of Chicago Press.

Hsiao, W. (2000). *What should macroeconomists know about health care policy? A primer.* Washington, DC: International Monetary Fund.

Hurst, J. (2000). Challenges for health systems in member countries of the Organisation for Economic Co-operation and Development. *Bulletin of the World Health Organization, 78*, 751–760.

Jamison, D. T., Lau, L. J., & Wang, J. (2005). Health's contribution to economic growth in an environment of partially endogenous technical progress. In G. Lopez-Casasnovas, B. Rivera, & L. Currais (Eds.), *Health and economic growth* (pp 67–91). Cambridge, MA: MIT Press.

Jamison, D. T., & Leslie, J. (1990). Health and nutrition considerations in education planning.

2. The cost and effectiveness of school-based interventions. *Food and Nutrition Bulletin, 12*(3).

Jamison, D. T, Sachs, J., & Wang, J. (2001). *The effect of the AIDS epidemic on economic welfare in sub-Saharan Africa* (Working Paper WG 1). Geneva, Switzerland: WHO Commission on Macroeconomics and Health.

Jamison, D. T., Sandbu, M., & Wang, J. (2004). *Why has infant mortality declined at such different rates in different countries?* (Working Paper No. 14). Bethesda, MD: Disease Control Priorities Project.

Kalemli-Ozcan, S. (2002). Does mortality decline promote economic growth? *Journal of Economic Growth, 7,* 411–439.

Kenkel, D. S. (1991). Health behavior, health knowledge, and schooling. *Journal of Political Economy, 99,* 287–304.

Kim, A., & Benton, B. (1995). *Cost-benefit analysis of the Onchocerciasis Control Program (OCP)* (World Bank Technical Paper No. 282). Washington, DC: World Bank.

Kleinman, L. C., Kosecoff, J., Dubois, R. W., & Brook, R. H. (1994). The medical appropriateness of tympanostomy tubes proposed for children younger than 16 years in the United States. *Journal of the American Medical Association, 271,* 50–55.

Knaul, F. M. (1999a). *The impact of health and health systems on economic growth and development: An overview.* Geneva, Switzerland: World Health Organization.

Knaul, F. M. (1999b). Linking health, nutrition and wages: The evolution of age at menarche and labor earnings among Mexican women (Working Paper Series R-355). Washington, DC: Inter-American Development Bank.

Knaul, F. M., & Parker, S. M. (1998). *Patterns over time and determinants of early labor force participation and school dropout: Evidence from longitudinal and retrospective data on Mexican children and youth.* Paper presented at the 1998 meeting of the Population Association of America.

Kuh, D., & Ben-Shlomo, Y. (Eds.) (1997). *A life course approach to chronic disease epidemiology.* Oxford, England: Oxford University Press.

Leape, L. L., Hilborne, L. H., Park, R. E., Bernstein, S. J., Kamberg, C. J., Sherwood, M., & Brook, R. H. (1993). The appropriateness of use of coronary artery bypass graft surgery in New York state. *Journal of the American Medical Association, 269,* 753–760.

Leape, L., Park, R. E., Solomon, D. H., Chassin, M. R., Kosecoff, J., & Brook, R. H. (1990). Does inappropriate use explain small area variations in the use of health care services? *Journal of the American Medical Association, 263,* 669–672.

Le Grand, J. (1987). Inequalities in health: Some international comparisons. *European Economic Review, 31,* 182–191.

Leibenstein, H. (1957). *Economic backwardness and economic growth.* New York: John Wiley & Sons.

Leighton, C., & Foster, R. (1993). Economic impacts of malaria in Kenya and Nigeria (Major Applied Research Paper No. 6). Bethesda, MD: Abt Associates.

Leslie, J., & Jamison, D. T. (1990, September). Health and nutrition considerations in education planning: Educational consequences of health problems among school-age children. *Food and Nutrition Bulletin, 12,* 204–214.

Liu, Y., Hu, S., Fu, W., & Hsiao, W. C. (1998). Is community financing necessary and feasible for rural China? In M. L. Barer, T. E. Getzen, & G. L. Stoddart (Eds.), *Health, health care and health economics: Perspectives on distribution.* New York: John Wiley & Sons.

Madrian, B. C. (1994). Employment-based health insurance and job mobility: Is there evidence of job-lock? *Quarterly Review of Economics, 109*(1), 27–54.

Malaney, P. (1998). *Benefits of malaria control.* Unpublished manuscript, Harvard Institute for International Development, Cambridge, MA.

Marmot, M. G., Smith, G. D., Stansfeld, S., Patel, C., North, F., Head, L., White, I., Brummer, E., &

Feeney, A. (1991). Health inequalities among British civil servants: The Whitehall II study. *Lancet, 337,* 1387–1393.

Marmot, M. G., & Theorell, T. (1988). Social class and cardiovascular disease: The contribution of work. *International Journal of Health Services, 18,* 659–674.

Miguel, E., & Kremer, M. (2004). Worms: Identifying impacts on education and health in the presence of treatment externalities. *Econometrica, 72*(1), 159–217.

Mirrlees, J. (1975). A pure theory of under-developed economies. In R. Reynolds (Ed.), *Agriculture in development theory.* New Haven, CT: Yale University Press.

Moffett, J. K., Torgerson, D., Bell-Syer, S., Jackson, D., Llewlyn-Phillips, H., Farrin, A., & Barker, J. (1999). Randomized controlled trial of exercise for low back pain: Clinical outcomes, costs, and preferences. *British Medical Journal, 319,* 279–283.

Monheit, A. C., & Cooper, P. F. (1994). Health insurance and job mobility: Theory and evidence. *Industrial and Labor Relations Review, 48*(1), 68–85.

Murray, C. J. L., Lopez, A. D., & Jamison, D. T. (1994). The global burden of disease in 1990: Summary results, sensitivity analysis, and future directions. In C. J. L. Murray and A. Lopez (Eds.), *Global comparative assessments in the health sector: Disease burden, expenditures, and intervention packages* (pp. 97–138). Geneva: World Health Organization.

Murrugarra, E., & Valdivia, M. (1999). *The returns to health for Peruvian urban adults: Differentials across genders, the life-cycle and the wage distribution* (Documento de Trabajo R-352). Washington, DC: Inter-American Development Bank.

Mwabu, G., & Wang'ombe, J. (1995). *User charges in Kenya: Health service pricing reforms in Kenya, 1989–1993. A report on work in progress with support from the International Health Policy Program.* Washington, DC: International Health Policy Program.

Myrdal, G. (1952). Economic aspects of health. *Chronicle of the World Health Organization, 6,* 203–218.

Newhouse, J. P. (1993). *Free for all? Lessons from the RAND health insurance experiment.* Cambridge, MA: Harvard University Press.

Nordhaus, W. (2003). The health of nations: The contribution of improved health to living standards. In K. H. Murphy & R. H. Topel (Eds.), *Measuring the gains from medical research: An economic approach* (pp. 9–40). Chicago: University of Chicago Press.

Over, M. (1992). *The macroeconomic impact of AIDS in sub-Saharan Africa* (Population and Nutrition Technical Working Paper No. 3.). Washington, DC: The World Bank.

Over, M., Bertozzi, S., & Chin, J. (1989). Guidelines for rapid estimation of the direct and indirect costs of HIV infection in a developing country. *Health Policy, 11,* 169–186.

Poullier, J.-P. (1992). Administrative costs in selected industrialized countries. *Health Care Financing Review, 13*(4), 167–172.

Preker, A. S., Harding, A., & Travis, P. (2000). "Make or buy" decisions in the production of health care goods and services: New insights from institutional economics and organizational theory. *Bulletin of the World Health Organization, 78,* 779–790.

Prescott, N., & Pradhan, M. (1999, February). *Coping with catastrophic health shocks.* Revised draft prepared for the Conference on Poverty and Social Protection, Inter-American Development Bank, Washington, DC.

Preston, S. A. (1980). Causes and consequences of mortality decline in less developed countries during the twentieth century. In R. A. Easterlin (Ed.), *Population and economic change in developing countries* (pp. 289–360). Chicago: University of Chicago Press.

Preston, S. H., & Elo, I. T. (1995). Are educational differentials in adult mortality increasing in the United States? *Journal of Aging and Health, 7,* 476–496.

Pritchett, L., & Summers, L. (1996). Wealthier is healthier. *Journal of Human Resources, 31*(4), 844–868.

Radelet, S., Sachs, J. D., & Lee, J.-W. (1997). *Economic growth and transformation* (Development Discussion Paper No. 609). Cambridge, MA: Harvard Institute for International Development.

Reddy, S., & Vandemoortele, J. (1996). *User financing of basic social services: A review of theoretical arguments and empirical evidence.* New York: Office of Evaluation, Policy and Planning, UNICEF.

Ribero, R., & Nunez, J. (1999). *Productivity of household investment in health. The case of Colombia* (Working Paper R-354). Washington, DC: Inter-American Development Bank.

Robins, L. N., & Regier, D. A. (1991). *Psychiatric disorders in America: The epidemiologic catchment area study.* New York: The Free Press.

Ruger, J. P. (1998). *Aristotelian justice and health policy: Capability and incompletely theorized agreements.* Unpublished doctoral dissertation, Harvard University, Cambridge, MA.

Ruger, J. P. (2003a). Health and development. *Lancet, 362,* 678.

Ruger, J. P. (2003b). Catastrophic health expenditure. *Lancet, 362,* 996–997.

Ruger, J. P. (2004a). Health and social justice. *Lancet, 364*(9439), 1075–1080.

Ruger, J. P. (2004b). Ethics of the social determinants of health. *Lancet, 364*(9439), 1092–1097.

Ruger, J. P. (in press a). Health, capability, and justice: Toward a new paradigm of health policy, law and ethics. *Cornell Journal of Law and Public Policy, 2005.*

Ruger, J. P. (in press b). Toward a theory of a right to health: Capability and incompletely theorized agreements. *Yale Journal of Law and Humanities, 2005.*

Sahn, D. E., & Alderman, H. (1988). The effect of human capital on wages, on the determinants of labor supply in a developing country. *Journal of Development Economics, 29*(2), 157–183.

Saunderson, P. R. (1995). An economic evaluation of alternative programme designs for tuberculosis control in rural Uganda. *Social Science Medicine, 40*(9), 1203–1212.

Savedoff, W. D., & Schultz, T. P. (2000). *Wealth from health.* Washington, DC: Inter-American Development Bank.

Schieber, G., & Maeda, A. (1993). A curmudgeon's guide to financing health care in developing countries. In G. J. Schieber (Ed.), *Innovations in health care financing: Proceedings of a World Bank conference, March 10-11, 1997* (World Bank Discussion Paper No. 365). Washington, DC: World Bank.

Schultz, T. P. (1996). *Wage rentals for reproducible human capital: Evidence from two West African countries.* New Haven, CT: Yale University, Economic Growth Center.

Schultz, T. P. (1997). Assessing the productive benefits of nutrition and health: An integrated human capital approach. *Journal of Econometrics, 77,* 144–158.

Schultz, T. P. (1999). Health and schooling investments in Africa. *Journal of Economic Perspectives, 13*(3), 67–88.

Schultz, T. P. (2002). Wage gains associated with height as a form of human capital. *American Economic Review, 92,* 349–353.

Schultz, T. P., & Tansel, A. (1997). Wage and labor supply effects of illness in Cote D'Ivoire and Ghana: Instrumental variable estimates for days disabled. *Journal of Development Economics, 53,* 251–286.

Shastry, G. K., & Weil, D. N. (2002). How much of cross-country income variation is explained by health? *Journal of the European Economic Association, 1,* 387–396.

Smith, J. P. (1999). Healthy bodies and thick wallets: The dual relation between health and economic status. *Journal of Economic Perspectives, 13*(2), 145–166.

Spurr, G. B. (1983). Nutritional status and physical work capacity. *Yearbook of Physical Anthropology, 26,* 1–35.

Strauss, J., & Thomas, D. (1995). Human resources: Empirical modeling of household and family decisions. In J. Behrman & T. N. Srinivasan (Eds.), *Handbook in development economics* (Vol. 3A). Amsterdam: Elsevier Science.

Svedberg, P. (2000). *Poverty and undernutrition.* Oxford, England: Oxford University Press.

Thomas, D., & Strauss, J. (1997). Health and wages: Evidence on men and women in urban Brazil. *Journal of Econometrics, 77,* 159–185.

Thomas, D., & Strauss, J. (1998). The microfoundations of the links between health, nutrition, and development. *Journal of Economic Literature, 36,* 766–817.

Thomas, D., et al. (2003). *Iron deficiency and the well-being of older adults: Preliminary results from a randomized nutrition intervention.* Unpublished manuscript, University of California–Los Angeles.

U.S. Bureau of Labor Statistics. (1994). *Employment cost indexes and levels, 1975–94.* Washington, DC: U.S. Bureau of Labor Statistics.

U.S. Congress. (1994). *International comparisons of administrative costs in health care* (Office of Technology Assessment Publication No. BP-H-135). Washington, DC: U.S. Government Printing Office.

Van de Walle, D. (1994). The benefit-incidence of social sector public expenditures in Indonesia. *World Bank Economic Review, 8,* 115–134.

Van Doorslaer, E., Wagstaff, A., & Rutten, F. (1993). *Equity in the finance and delivery of health care: An international perspective.* Oxford, England: Oxford University Press.

Waddington, C., & Enyimayew, K. (1990). A price to pay, part 2: The impact of user charges in the Volta region of Ghana. *International Journal of Health Planning and Management, 5*(4), 287–312.

Wang, J., Jamison, D. J., Bos, E., Preker, A., & Peabody, J. (1999). *Measuring country perfor-*

mance on health: Selected indicators for 115 countries. Washington, DC: World Bank.

Wang'ombe, J. (1997). Cost recovery strategies in sub-Saharan Africa. In G. J. Schieber (Ed.), *Innovations in health care financing: Proceedings of a World Bank conference, March 10-11, 1997* (World Bank Discussion Paper No. 365, pp. 155–161). Washington, DC: World Bank.

Wilkinson, R. G. (Ed.). (1986). *Class and health: Research and longitudinal data.* New York: Tavistock Publications.

Wilkinson, R. G. (1990). Income distribution and mortality: A natural experiment. *Health and Illness, 12,* 391.

Wilkinson, D., Floyd, K., & Gilks, C. F. (1997). Costs and cost-effectiveness of alternative tuberculosis management strategies in South Africa: Implications for policy. *South African Medical Journal, 87*(4), 451–455.

Winslow, C. M., Kosecoff, J. B., Chassin, M., Kanouse, D. E., & Brook, R. H. (1988a). The appropriateness of performing coronary artery bypass surgery. *Journal of the American Medical Association, 260,* 505–509.

Winslow, C. M., Solomon, D. H., Chassin, M. R., Kosecoff, J., Merrick, N. J., & Brook, R. H. (1988b). The appropriateness of carotid endarterectomy. *New England Journal of Medicine, 318,* 721–727.

Woolhandler, S., & Himmelstein, D. U. (1991). The deteriorating administrative efficiency of the U.S. health care system. *New England Journal of Medicine, 324*(18), 53–57.

Woolhandler, S., & Himmelstein, D. U. (1997). Costs of care and administration at for-profit and other hospitals in the United States. *New England Journal of Medicine, 336*(11), 769–774.

Woolhandler, S., Himmelstein, D. U., & Lewontin, J. P. (1993). Administrative costs in U.S. hospitals. *New England Journal of Medicine, 329*(6), 400–403.

World Bank. (1980). *World bank development report.* Washington, DC: World Bank.

World Bank. (1993). *World development report 1993: Investing in health.* New York: Oxford University Press.

World Bank. (1999). *Health, nutrition and population indicators: A statistical handbook.* Washington, DC: World Bank.

World Bank. (2003). *World development indicators.* Washington, DC: World Bank.

World Health Organization. (1999). *World health report 1999: Making a difference.* Geneva, Switzerland: World Health Organization.

World Health Organization. (2000). *World health report 2000. Health systems: Improving performance.* Geneva, Switzerland: World Health Organization.

Yoder, R. A. (1989). Are people willing and able to pay for health services? *Social Science and Medicine, 29,* 35–42.

Global Cooperation in International Public Health

GILL WALT AND KENT BUSE

Why do countries cooperate in international health? This chapter explores this question, focusing on the cooperation process, the institutions and actors involved in international health cooperation, how they have changed over the past 50 years, and what implications these factors may have for future health policies around the world. A policy approach provides the theoretical framework, drawing on a number of different disciplines and focusing on the interaction among context, actors, and processes (Walt & Gilson, 1994). The chapter suggests that there has been a shift in international cooperation from vertical representation to horizontal participation. Vertical representation describes the relationship between the state and international organizations that make up the United Nations (UN) system, which was established in the mid-1940s to represent the interests of all states and promote cooperation between them. By the end of the century, international cooperation was determined less by formal vertical representation between the state and international organizations than by horizontal partnerships and alliances among many different bodies, including the state, UN agencies, industry, and nongovernmental organizations.

The chapter starts by describing its analytical framework briefly. It goes on to describe the actors (including the state) in international health, to ask why states cooperate, and through what mechanisms. The second half of the chapter analyzes the shifts in international cooperation, demonstrating how vertical representation has been replaced by horizontal participation, and what the implications of these shifts are for international health policy.

The Policy Framework

Many of the earlier chapters in this book have focused on the content of policy: current problems in communicable diseases (e.g., increasing rates of sexually transmitted diseases) or nutrition (e.g., lack of vitamin A leading to blindness), and what sorts of policies are employed to address these problems (e.g., training primary health workers to recognize the signs and symptoms of sexually transmitted infections, or introducing vitamin A into routine immunization programs). Some of the chapters also explore how health systems have been designed and managed to put these policies into practice by emphasizing primary health care (PHC) systems, or decentralization. This chapter provides an understanding of international health policy by focusing on the role of actors and how they are affected by, and influence, the context and processes within which policies are made and implemented.

Actors may be individuals (e.g., a minister of health), or groups (e.g., the National Association of Nurses), but institutions (e.g., a university or the World Bank) and even states (e.g., the United States) also are considered actors. Although actors may be involved in national or global policy, it should not be assumed that all groups, institutions, or states act with one voice, or that there are not quite different, and sometimes contending, groups of actors within institutions. The World Bank, for example, acts according to a particular mission but is made up of individuals who do not necessarily agree with each other or with the World Bank's policy on a particular issue. The extent to which there is space to address differences, how big those differences are, and how they emerge will influence both staff attitudes to work and outputs from the institution. In other words, actors all have their own values and expectations, and these may not always be shared or reflect exactly those of the institutions within which they work.

Because actors are the center of analysis in this chapter, it is helpful to differentiate ways of referring to them. Individuals can be all-important, but alone are not likely to be very effective. Their influence comes because they lead social movements (i.e., bring people together, usually in protest or to promote a particular cause) or are key members of institutions. It was the combination of James Grant, as executive director between 1980 and 1995, and the institution, the United Nations Children's Fund (UNICEF), that gave the organization its high profile and successful reputation in the 1980s. So, understanding institutions and their roles within international health is central. Institutions naturally differ in their reputations: Some are strong, with high levels of influence because of their wealth, knowledge, research, professional expertise, and contribution to the economy. Such institutions (and individuals within them) are likely to have considerable access to other influential individuals in key government departments, corporations, academic institutions, and so on, and be able to influence ideas and policies. However, reputations are not set in stone, and institutions have to adapt and change with time. As will be shown later, one of the struggles that beset the World Health Organization (WHO) in the 1980s and 1990s was to retain its earlier authority and high regard.

In this chapter, then, *actors* refers to individuals and institutions such as UNICEF, WHO, or public-private partnerships at the global level. Ministries of health (MOHs) at the national level, or, more broadly, governments or states also may be actors. The state is an abstract notion, but generally refers to a society within geographic borders. It is made up of all the authoritative decision-making bodies of the society, is legally supreme, and can use force to achieve its ends. The state's lawmaking occurs through government, a narrower concept that includes the public institutions, such as the legislative body, the executive, the bureaucracy, and ministries or departments of state. The judiciary, which is part of government, is responsible for interpreting and applying the law. All governments are organized into different levels, and subnational bodies or local authorities may also be referred to as policy actors. There is a lively contemporary debate about the role of the state, and how trends in globalization are affecting it and reducing its role (Sassen, 1996). However, in this chapter, the state

is assumed to be a central player in international health cooperation, although, as will be shown, its role is changing.

Exhibit 14-1	The Framework Convention on Tobacco Control

Tobacco kills almost 5 million people each year. If current trends continue, it is projected to kill 10 million people a year by 2020, with 70% of those deaths occurring in developing countries. Tobacco also takes an enormous toll in health care costs, lost productivity, and, of course, the intangible costs of the pain and suffering inflicted upon smokers, passive smokers, and their families. In 2003, after 4 years of negotiations, the World Health Assembly unanimously endorsed the Framework Convention on Tobacco Control. This was the first time WHO had used its constitutional authority in global public health to develop an international treaty.

The convention was launched because many perceived that "the tobacco industry's use of international trade agreements, cigarette smuggling, and global marketing techniques" had undermined national control measures and rendered them insufficient to control the tobacco epidemic (Gilmore & Collin, 2002, p. 846). The convention included provision for the enactment of comprehensive bans on tobacco advertising, promotion, and sponsorship; large, rotating health warnings on packaging; and the prohibition of misleading descriptors such as *light* or *mild*.

A large majority of countries backed the convention, and by the closing date for signature (June 29, 2004), 169 of approximately 200 countries had taken steps toward implementing it, by signing the convention. However, of these, very few have taken the next step and ratified it, indicating their agreement to be bound by the provisions after the convention comes into force. Only 5 industrialized countries have ratified the convention, including New Zealand and Norway. Key provisions of the convention, which come into force 40 days after ratification, include bans on advertising and promotion, support for tax increases on tobacco, and protection from passive smoking.

It will take time to assess the prospects of the convention and what its impact has been on tobacco control policies in countries. However, its broader influence was already evident in mid-2004. For example, states have brought together different sectors, such as health and agriculture, to discuss future policy. These efforts have paved the way for further national regulation. A senior vice president for corporate affairs at Philip Morris International said, "the Treaty has had a significant influence on us, simply because it has accelerated the pace of regulation in individual countries" (Davies, 2003, cited in Collins, 2004).

Context refers to a myriad of external factors that affect the way policy is formulated and implemented. Political and economic instability in a country or region may mean that domestic policy makers are prepared to make only short-term, or incremental, changes to policy for fear of losing power; it may mean that internationally agreed-upon policies on immunization campaigns, for example, cannot be executed. A newly elected government may have the legitimacy to introduce major change, as happened in South Africa in 1994 when free health services were introduced for all children under the age of 6 years. Political transformation in eastern Europe led to a host of health reforms being introduced in the countries of the former Soviet Union. Similarly, a new leader in a UN agency may have added legitimacy to initiate new policies; for example, in 1998, after years of taking a very cautious approach on tobacco and its harmful effects on health, a high-level campaign advocating tobacco control was initiated by a new director-general in WHO (Exhibit 14-1). Multiethnicity, linguistic plurality, and the position of women all influence policy at both national and international levels. For example, people may not have the same trust or confidence in a health professional, a scientist, or a consultant from another ethnic or national group or who does not speak their language. Contextual factors may be specific to particular countries or common globally (as with world economic recessions, for example).

The process of policy making will be influenced by the history and role of the different institutions of government. Policy processes can be described in different phases: how issues get onto the policy agenda (is there a role for the media?); who is consulted in the formulation and design of policy (are policies made by a handful of bureaucrats or politicians, or are they discussed with managers and interest groups, such as patients or consumers?); and how policies are communicated, executed, regulated, and assessed (is policy making top down? are policies monitored?). Similar questions affect policy processes at the global level: Do industrialized countries dominate international organizations and decide how and where resources should be allocated?

Who Are the Actors in International Health?

There has been a huge increase in the number and diversity of actors involved in international health since the establishment of the UN system at the end of World War II. The UN was conceived as a system to maintain peace and security in a world that had been torn by strife—"to save succeeding generations from the scourge of war" (Childers & Urquhart, 1994, p. 11). At its center was the sovereign nation-state (able to exercise rule that is supreme, exclusive, and comprehensive over a given territory), which could become a member of the different organs and agencies of the UN. The six principal UN organs, established by charter in 1945, are the General Assembly, the Security Council, the Secretariat, the International Court of Justice, the Trusteeship Council, and the Economic and Social Council (ECOSOC). This last body is entrusted to supervise the work of numerous economic and social commissions and to coordinate the efforts of the specialized agencies associated with the UN. The four largest specialized agencies are the Food and Agriculture Organization (FAO), the International Labor Organization (ILO), the UN Educational, Scientific and Cultural Organization (UNESCO), and WHO. In addition to the specialized agencies, a number of funds and programs have been established (e.g., UNICEF).

The international organizations that made up the UN were established to facilitate exchange and contact between all member states and to coordinate overseas development assistance provided collectively by some nation-states to others, who would use such aid in their exercise of national sovereignty. This was a system of formal, vertical representation, with member states deciding the policies and activities of the international organizations. There was limited interaction between these representative bodies and civil society organizations.

Actors in Health at the Global and Regional Levels

Founded in 1948, WHO is the UN's designated specialized agency in health, expected to play a leading role in coordinating international health activities. It was formed from the amalgamation of two agencies established in 1902 and 1908, respectively: the International Sanitary Bureau, which evolved into the Pan American Health Organization (PAHO), and the Office of Public Hygiene, later incorporated into the League of Nations. With headquarters in Geneva, WHO boasts an unusually decentralized structure of six regional offices plus country offices in some countries. PAHO, representing the Americas, became one of the six WHO regional offices.

Other organizations within the United Nations system also have some responsibilities in health. The more active of these are the first five listed in Table 14-1, although some of the others, such as the World Trade Organization (WTO), have become increasingly important.

Table 14-1	UN Health-Related Organizations

World Health Organization (WHO)

World Bank

UN Children's Fund (UNICEF)

UN Population Fund (UNFPA)

UN Program on HIV/AIDS (UNAIDS)

UN Development Program (UNDP)

UN Educational, Scientific and Cultural Organization
(UNESCO)

Food and Agriculture Organization (FAO)

World Food Program

UN High Commissioner for Refugees (UNHCR)

International Labor Organization (ILO)

UN Environment Program (UNEP)

UN Office on Drugs and Crime (UNODC)

World Trade Organization (WTO)

Source: K. Lee, S. Collinson, G. Walt, and L. Gilson, "Who Should Be Doing What in International Health: A Confusion of Mandates in the United Nations?" 1996, *British Medical Journal, 312*, pp. 302–312. Copyright 1996 BMJ Publishing Group. Reprinted with permission.

Cooperation in health, however, has not been limited to collaboration through the UN and its agencies involved in health. Bilateral organizations, such as the United Kingdom's Department for International Development (DFID), the Swedish International Development Agency (SIDA), or the U.S. Agency for International Development (USAID), among many others, have played important roles at international and regional levels and in many countries. These agencies are often the main contributors to international health programs through UN organizations, but they also provide assistance to lower-income countries through government-to-government agreements known as bilateral aid.

International nongovernmental organizations (NGOs)—increasingly referred to as *civil society organizations* (CSOs)—have also made critical contributions to health development at both the international and domestic level. Although there is no definitive definition of CSOs, there is general agreement that they are typically voluntary, nonformal, and noncommercial associations of individuals who share some common cause or goal (see Exhibits 14-2 and 14-10). NGOs or CSOs make up a broad group of agencies of considerable complexity. They include church missions providing health care to isolated rural communities; agencies such as Oxfam, which may be involved in advocacy on behalf of lower-income countries (e.g., on debt relief) or may be working with local groups (AIDS support groups, for example); and private foundations, such as the Rockefeller, Ford, and the Bill and Melinda Gates Foundations.

The corporate sector has also become more involved in health activities over the last decades, at both the global level (e.g., over 1,000 companies are members of the Global Health Initiative of the World Economic Forum, established to increase the quantity and quality of business programs fighting HIV/AIDS, tuberculosis, and malaria) and the local level (e.g., companies such as Heineken, Anglo-America and Coca-Cola have introduced antiretroviral treatment programs for their workers in Africa).

When the UN was established in the middle of the last century, there were few actors in health, the role of the private sector and CSOs was small, and WHO played the dominant role. By the end of the century there were many more actors interested in health activities, and they were increasingly forming alliances, networks, and partnerships across public

Exhibit 14-2	How Civil Society Groups Affected Access to Medicines in Thailand

In Thailand, civil society groups have been key to challenging the practices of the multinational pharmaceutical industry and governments of industrialized countries in their quest for improved access to medicines. Such groups include the Thai Foundation for Consumers, the Thai NGO Coalition on AIDS, the Thai Network for People Living with HIV/AIDS, and the international NGO Médicins Sans Frontières. Besides lobbying on issues regarding patent protection, providing information, and supporting activities for people living with AIDS, they have also been involved in legal proceedings. For example, in 2001 they filed a lawsuit to try to establish the right to compulsory licensing of a Bristol Myers Squibb antiretroviral drug, didanosine. Compulsory licensing allows governments to overturn patents and produce generic medicines at far lower prices than branded products. Although the final court ruling was complex, the lawsuit set an important precedent, establishing that essential drugs are not just another consumer product but a human right, and that patients are injured by patents. One of the key aspects of the Thai civil society group's activities was to link with like-minded groups across borders. In this particular action, the Thai groups were supported by U.S. AIDS activists who demonstrated in Washington against Bristol Myers Squibb and the U.S. government regarding their repressive trade policies in respect to drugs for HIV (Ford et al., 2004). See also Exhibit 14-10.

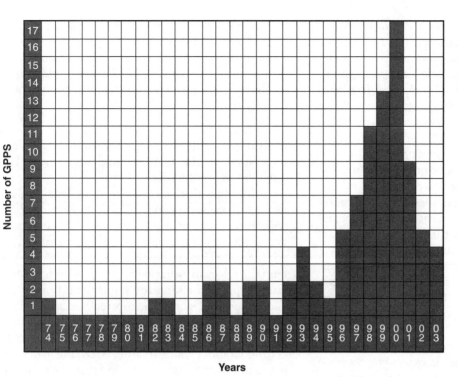

Figure 14-1 The Number of Global Public-Private Partnerships Launched in Health, Up to 2003. *Source:* Based on data from the Initiative on Public-Private Partnerships for Health (http://www.ippph.org).

and private sectors to tackle health issues. Figure 14-1 gives a picture of the increase in the number of global public-private partnerships in health.

Linking Global and Regional Actors with Local Actors

All states take some responsibility for their own health and health services, although the resources they have available differ markedly. On average, public expenditure on health in the higher-income countries is 6% of gross domestic product (GDP), whereas in the low-income countries it is 1.1% (World Bank, 2003). Most resources for health are generated nationally, even in extremely low-income countries, which may also receive significant aid from multilateral, bilateral, or NGO sources.

While states are responsible for health policy within their own borders, they also send representatives to participate in global policy discussions about health at the international level. For example, most states in the world are members of WHO. Every year they send a delegation, usually the minister of health and some officials from the health ministry, to attend the World Health Assembly (WHA) held at WHO's headquarters in Geneva. It is at the WHA that international policies on health are discussed, and ministers of health commit to programs and measures they will introduce or support when they return home. Membership in WHO entitles each state to vote on an

equal basis, although membership contributions are based on population size and wealth. Even though there may be considerable consensus on policies decided at the WHA, all states are sovereign, and if they do not adhere to, or implement, recommendations agreed to at the international level, there is little that WHO can do. Its only sanctions are based on its authority and reputation. Exhibit 14-1 about the Framework Convention on Tobacco Control, illustrates how states may sign up to a particular policy but may be slow to enact it within their own borders.

States may also serve on a rotational basis on the boards of governors of other UN agencies, such as UNICEF or the United Nations Population Fund (UNFPA), and may apply for membership in the international financial institutions (IFIs), such as the World Bank and International Monetary Fund, where membership is subject to financial subscription and other economic criteria, and voting is weighted according to the number of shares held by each member.

States also relate to regional bodies such as the six offices of WHO, participating as members in decision making. For example, the Eastern Mediterranean Regional Office (EMRO) or the Western Pacific Regional Office (WPRO) hold many meetings for countries in their regions, and have considerable power and autonomy to establish regional policies. States may also be involved in other regional bodies that have a strong economic or political focus (or both) and may or may not include health in their jurisdictions. Examples are the European Union (EU); the Organization for Economic Cooperation and Development (OECD), which includes not only all the industrialized nations but also Turkey and Thailand, among others; and the Association of Southeast Asian Nations (ASEAN). All these organizations may provide guidance on a broad set of health-related issues, which may be binding on member states, although adherence to policies will depend on the authority and consensus on which they are based.

The links described so far are vertical and representational: between states (national governments) and multilateral agencies at the global and regional level. States are represented on those bodies and have a say in decision making, although their power to influence those processes will differ. States also retain considerable autonomy in their decision to reject, adopt, and adapt policies proposed by international and regional organizations.

At the national level, however, the state links with a variety of different agencies in expanding horizontal relationships, based more on participation than representation. Not only will the state have dealings with national NGOs or CSOs, but it will also be paying attention to multilateral agencies such as WHO or UNICEF; bilateral agencies such as USAID and SIDA; international NGOs such as Médicins Sans Frontières or Oxfam; and, increasingly, to global initiatives that do not necessarily have a continuing presence in the country but that offer large amounts of aid for specific health interventions. Just in the area of HIV/AIDS there may be several such initiatives. For example, the Clinton Foundation has brokered deals between donors and poor countries such as Mozambique, Rwanda, and Tanzania for AIDS drugs and with pharmaceutical companies to lower the price of antiretroviral drugs; U.S. President Bush's Emergency Plan for Africa (PEPFAR), announced in 2003, has promised $15 billion over 5 years to countries in Africa and the Caribbean. The Global Fund to Fight AIDS, Tuberculosis, and Malaria is providing significant funds to support activities to manage the AIDS epidemic and by March 2004 had disbursed around $260 million to 121 applications (Exhibit 14-3). Reporting on Uganda, Parkhurst (2001, p. 76) observed,

> When one visits Uganda, and sees the actual HIV prevention programs being implemented, it becomes immediately apparent that the government's projects and programs represent only a fraction of the efforts being undertaken in the country. AIDS prevention projects are done by

a myriad of groups and organizations from local level community self-help groups, to religious-based groups, to large donor-financed international NGOs. A 1997 count found over 1020 agencies engaged in HIV/AIDS control activities.

The number of agencies involved in HIV/AIDS is likely to have grown with the advent of global initiatives such as the Global Fund to Fight AIDS, Tuberculosis, and Malaria.

Although all these relationships bring much-needed resources to poor countries and are generally welcomed, they can also have costs. They target particular diseases and conditions and ignore others, are costly to establish and monitor, and may lead to potential neglect of other parts of the health system. Early reports tracking the implementation of the Global Fund to Fight AIDS, Tuberculosis, and Malaria quote national policy makers expressing concern about the amount of time that had to be diverted to getting Country Coordinating Mechanisms established and writing proposals, and then the slowness in getting funds disbursed (Brugha et al., 2004).

Why Do States Cooperate?

Cooperation in health has a long history. Between 1851 and 1909, 10 international meetings were held to discuss quarantine and other measures to deal with epidemics of plague and cholera. Although most of these early meetings were ad hoc and largely limited to epidemic intelligence gathering between scientists or professionals, they led to international agreements on common approaches for the control and treatment of infectious diseases. After two world wars in the first half of the 20th century, such cooperation expanded. The Marshall European Recovery Program of 1948 to 1952, in which the United States gave $13 billion to rebuild the economies of western Europe (Basch, 1999), introduced an era of extensive global aid for many development activities, including support for health services in low-income countries.

The latter half of the 20th century witnessed an increase in trade, travel, and improved communication, some of the factors commonly assumed to have led to the globalization of the world economy. These factors have highlighted risks that states by themselves cannot address adequately within traditional national borders. Such risks include new and emerging infectious diseases, resulting in part from the increased prevalence of drug-resistant pathogens; exposure to dangerous substances, such as contami-

---

Exhibit 14-3 | **The Global Fund to Fight AIDS, Tuberculosis, and Malaria**

The Global Fund to Fight AIDS, Tuberculosis, and Malaria was established in January 2002 to attract, manage, and disburse additional resources to countries to control three diseases that are having a devastating impact in poor countries, especially in sub-Saharan Africa. The Global Fund is an independent organization, governed by a board (18 voting and 5 nonvoting members) and supported by a secretariat of about 70 staff in Geneva. It describes itself as a financing mechanism, with a mandate to "Raise it, Spend it, Prove it."

Countries apply for Fund support by submitting proposals, which are reviewed by a technical review panel of independent experts and considered for approval by the board. By March 2004, US$3.4 billion had been pledged for 2001 to 2004, with further pledges of US$2 billion for 2005 to 2008. Countries applied for Global Fund support in March 2002, September 2002, May 2003, and June 2004. One hundred and seventy one countries were approved to receive about US$2 billion over 2 years for rounds 1 to 4. By March 2004, two-thirds of approved countries had signed grant agreements, and around US$260 million had been disbursed. At that point, sub-Saharan Africa had been approved for over half of committed funds, with about 60% of it earmarked for HIV/AIDS activities.

Given sufficient donations to the Global Fund (and in 2004 there were significant shortfalls in the estimates needed), the achievement of its goal is dependent on the effectiveness of country systems and the structures that recipient countries are required to have in place to manage Fund activities. These include a Country Coordination Mechanism (CCM), Principal Recipients, and a Local Fund Agent.

- The CCM is a partnership tasked with preparing proposals for Global Fund support, selecting Principal Recipient(s), and overseeing and monitoring implementation of successful applications. The Fund requires CCMs to include "broad representation from governments, NGOs, civil society, multilateral and bilateral agencies and the private sector."
- The Principal Recipient (PR) is a country organization that receives funds, implements and monitors programs, and is accountable for how funds are used. The PR enters a grant agreement with the Fund and is legally responsible for program results, monitoring and evaluation, and financial accountability. Ongoing disbursement of funds depends on PRs submitting quarterly reports on performance; where satisfactory, submission can become less frequent.
- The Local Fund Agent (LA) is an independent professional organization, contracted by the Global Fund to be its eyes and ears in-country. The LA assesses the capacity of the PR and provides independent oversight and verification of progress and financial accountability.

The earliest results from studies tracking the Global Fund and implementation at the country level point to one of the major problems being "managing great expectations" (Brugha et al., 2004).

---

nated foodstuffs or banned and toxic substances; environmental exploitation, leading to pollution and such conditions as increased respiratory disorders; and violence, resulting from the huge production and sales of arms as well as chemical and biological weapons.

Although most of the direct health problems are addressed by domestic health policies decided at the national level, some depend on international collaboration. No one state can, by itself, resolve the risks and problems just detailed. Recognizing this concern, many scholars have attempted to identify *international public goods*, defined as activities that countries introduce in collaboration with others, for which national action on its own is ineffective or impossible to organize or encourage. Benefits from an international public good accrue widely, and not just to the entity that pays for it. Many international meetings are held to try to reach agreement among countries on norms and standards regarding pollution levels, the trafficking of illegal drugs, nuclear tests, and other policies from which all will benefit.

However, although states may recognize the benefits of promoting international public goods, cooperation is not always easy to achieve because of conflicting interests. Bad behavior in one country that affects its innocent neighbors may demand interventions that are difficult to implement. For example, excessive and indiscriminate use of antibiotics in both industrialized and low-income countries has created drug resistance, making it more difficult to treat some diseases. Concerted action is needed to combat resistance, but is complex, given that it means changing the behavior of patients who do not complete their antibiotic prescriptions or of doctors who overprescribe antibiotics, or controlling and regulating the production or importation of high-quality antibiotics. Similarly, getting cooperation on issues such as controlling pollution or activities that may lead to global warming is also highly problematic, as was demonstrated in Southeast Asia in 1997. The combination of unfavorable winds, drought, and forest fires in Indonesia in 1997 led to a "poison fog blanket" and an increase in respiratory disorders in several Asian neighbors, who called for closer cooperation to control pollution in the area. Although the situation was partly due to climatic conditions, it was exacerbated by the activities of private companies clearing forests in Indonesia to provide paper and palm oil. Indonesian government policies that had promoted privatization, but employed weak regulatory controls over private-sector actions, created negative externalities.

Even where there is consensus about the value of international public goods produced through international cooperation (cooperation on research to find an AIDS vaccine, for example, or campaigning to eradicate smallpox from the world), achieving international goals can be difficult, and gains may be visible only in the long run. For example, although most countries in the world are committed to the polio eradication program in the hope that future generations will save money on polio vaccines, as well as be rid of a disabling disease, there are many difficulties in reaching that goal. Until the disease is completely eradicated and there is no danger that it will be reimported, all countries have to continue to immunize their children. The United States, for example, has been free of the disease for over 20 years, but still immunizes against polio. Further, the goal of eradication is not guaranteed. In early 2004, government officials in Nigeria boycotted the global polio initiative, citing concerns that it might be part of a Western campaign to spread HIV or infertility. In 2004 a senior WHO official warned that Africa was on the "brink of re-infection" and that the $US3 billion invested over the past 15 years could be jeopardized (Kapp, 2004). There are also challenges regarding long-term biocontainment of both wild and vaccine poliovirus strains and stockpiling of vaccines. See Exhibit 14-4 for a discussion of how neighboring states have collaborated to try to ensure full coverage of polio immunization.

States may also decide to act collectively at the international level because of shortcomings or lack of resources in particular national health systems. Development aid, for example, aims to build and strengthen capacity in low-income countries through technical assistance, grants, or loans. As Howson, Fineberg, and Bloom (1998, p. 586) point out, such engagement has as much relevance for high-income, industrialized countries as for low-income countries:

> All developed countries have a vital and direct stake in the health of people around the world; this stake derives both from enduring traditions of humanitarian concern and from compelling reasons of enlightened self-interest. Considered involvement can serve to protect citizens, improve indigenous economies, and advance national and regional interests on the world stage.

At the extreme, states may cooperate with others because of the threat of force. This scenario is unlikely in international health, but coercion may occur in some situations. Greenough (1995) argues, for example, that at the end of the smallpox campaign in India and Bangladesh, some force was exerted on families who were reluctant (for religious reasons, for example) to have their children vaccinated. Coercion has also sometimes been used in contemporary tuberculosis (and AIDS) programs (see Exhibit 14-5). Some have suggested that the use of policy conditions attached to World Bank loans—forcing countries to introduce changes such as reducing the number of public-sector health workers, charging for health services, or privatizing some health services—is a type of coercion.

Most relations in health are not directly coercive, although states may have little room to maneuver because of pressure from international organizations, the media, or neighboring states. In investigating the use

---

Exhibit 14-4   Eradicating Polio Requires Cross-Border Collaboration

In a paper outlining the lessons from the polio eradication campaign launched in 1998 (Aylward et al., 2003), the authors give an example of how important it is for neighboring countries to collaborate in health activities if they are to avoid transmission across borders. One of the strategies of the eradication campaign was to hold National Immunization Days (NIDs)—the aim of which was to reach, on a few days every year, any children who might not have received a previous immunization against polio. Organizing these days was a huge challenge. In China and India, for example, about 80 million and 150 million children, respectively, were immunized in a few days. The achievement was repeated 1 month later, and then annually for more than 5 years.

Because people crossing borders can transmit poliomyelitis during the interval between NIDs being held in one country and its neighbor, countries have synchronized their NIDs. For example, 18 Asian, European, and Middle Eastern countries immunized 55 million children in April and May 1995, and repeated the activity each year for 3 years. Similar coordination occurred in West Africa and South Asia (Aylward et al., 2003).

| Exhibit 14-5 | Public Health, Civil Liberties, and Tuberculosis |

The New York City epidemic of the late 1980s and early 1990s was halted and reversed through substantial investment, improvements in surveillance and infection control, and the expansion of systems to encourage treatment compliance. Coercion was also used. In 1993 a New York City health code was amended to authorize the City's commissioner of health to detain any non-infectious individual "where there is substantial likelihood . . . that he or she cannot be relied upon to participate in and/or to complete an appropriate prescribed course of medication for tuberculosis." The authority to detain individuals was shifted from depending on an assessment of threat posed to an assessment of treatment compliance. This represented a significant shift in the balance between civil liberties and state authority. Since the amendments were adopted in New York more than 200 non-infectious patients have been detained, many for long periods, some for over two years.

Source: R. Coker, "Public Health, Civil Liberties and Tuberculosis," 1999, *British Medical Journal, 318,* pp. 1434–1435. Reprinted with permission.

---

of policy conditions in structural adjustment programs, for example, Killick (1998, p. 11) distinguishes between "pro forma" and "hard core" conditionality. He argues that the former may well be voluntary, based on consensus, because the recipient essentially agrees with the range of measures suggested by the lender; or agreement may be based on the perceived authority of the international organization. Similarly, in conflict situations, where displaced persons have crossed borders, neighboring states may feel they have to make some response in spite of their own lack of resources or potential conflict with their own populations. Hard-core conditionality, by contrast, consists of "measures that would not otherwise be undertaken or taken within the time frame desired by the lender" (Killick, 1998, p. 11) but that are accepted by recipients because they need the loans.

Another reason for states to cooperate is perceived threats to their security. Several countries, led by the United States, consider global health problems, including HIV/AIDS and other infectious disease epidemics, to be security threats. Feldbaum and associates (2004) compared two security documents before and after September 11, 2001. One published in 1998 discussed public health only as a secondary issue to bioterrorism and environmental degradation, mentioning HIV/AIDS only once. The 2002 document, on the other hand, discussed public health issues in six of the nine chapters, with HIV/AIDS being referred to seven times. This has led to increased support for global health initiatives by the security and foreign policy communities, and more collaboration on issues such as bioterrorism.

How Do States Cooperate?

States come together in many formal and informal ways that result in levels of cooperation. The UN may arrange large international meetings, attended by delegations or representatives from states, international organizations, NGOs, private-sector companies, and others. Specialized meetings may be held, such as the WHA, to which member states send representatives from MOHs, or World Bank meetings, attended by ministers of finance and national and international bankers. Or experts in a particular field may convene in small meetings. WHO, for example, uses expert committees of academics, professionals, and scientists to decide norms and standards, such as what drugs should be included in an essential drugs list or whether hepatitis B vaccine should be included in routine infant immunization schedules. Activities in international health cooperation occur in three areas (Lucas et al., 1997):

1. consensus building and advocacy
2. cross-learning and transfer of knowledge
3. production and sharing of international public goods

Consensus Building and Advocacy

Many of the high-profile UN meetings that take place all over the world are exercises in building consensus on particular themes, with follow-up advocacy. UN conferences are usually agreed to by the General Assembly or the ECOSOC, and arranged outside the regular framework of the UN and its agencies, although they frequently involve inputs in the form of proposals and secretarial provision from those bodies (Taylor, 1993). They are highly formalized and orchestrated, with many groups holding preconference meetings to prepare background papers and recommendations. Originally, UN conferences were attended only by formal delegations representing governments, but over time they have opened to allow the participation of independent groups of NGOs, the media, and others.

In the 1990s, for example, meetings receiving a great deal of media attention were held in Rio de

Janiero, Brazil, and Kobe, Japan (on the environment); in Copenhagen, Denmark (on social-sector support); in Beijing, China (on women); and in Cairo, Egypt (on reproductive health). The 1994 meeting in Cairo, titled the International Conference on Population and Development, followed two earlier meetings, in 1974 in Bucharest and 1984 in Mexico, and is an example of how consensus building, plus other activities, changed attitudes and approaches to population issues over two decades. As Exhibit 14-6 illustrates, in the 40 years of discussions on population growth, ideas changed considerably. In the 1950s and 1960s, discussion largely focused on regulating population growth through family planning programs and was highly contested, partly for religious reasons and partly because of disagreement on the relationship between population growth and development. By the 1990s, family planning programs were universally accepted (with dispute only over the role of abortion), but the increased participation of women's groups in international discussions had broadened the emphasis from contraception to reproductive health. Over four decades considerable energy was expended on advocacy to change public opinion and the views of key policy makers, with Western donors exercising considerable influence on initially reluctant developing countries through policies such as generous funding of family planning programs. See Exhibit 14-7 on

the Millennium Development Goals as a global response to halving poverty by 2015.

Cross-Learning and Transfer of Knowledge

Cooperation in health also occurs through exchange of experience and transfer of knowledge. One of the great strengths of international organizations is that they can ignore political, geographical, or cultural barriers and draw on "epistemic communities," networks of professionals with recognized expertise and competence in a particular domain and an authoritative claim to policy-relevant knowledge within that domain or issue area (Haas, 1992). WHO, for example, can call on a worldwide network of scientist groups, academics, technicians, and practitioners to provide up-to-date assessments and evidence on a range of health matters, from new technologies to emerging problems. From such meetings emerge consensus statements (e.g., what measures health professionals can use to protect themselves when working with infectious diseases), guidelines and manuals (e.g., how to treat childhood diarrheas, appropriate vaccine schedules, how to train community health workers), and various measures of best practice.

Cross-learning may also occur at the regional level, with regional bodies bringing states together in order to transfer information and experience. In the 1980s, PAHO set up interregional coordinating committees to assist in polio eradication in the Americas,

---

| **Exhibit 14-6** | **"Development Is the Best Contraceptive"** |

In the mid-1960s the U.S. government played an active advocacy role, encouraging low- and middle-income countries to adopt policies to reduce population growth, eliciting the participation of other Western donors, and mobilizing UN support for family planning (which until then had taken a cautious approach to population issues). Population activities were largely defined as family planning programs, influenced by the advent of the oral contraceptive. From the mid-1960s, the United States was the largest funder of family planning programs around the world. In 1969 the UN Population Fund (UNFPA) was established to channel additional resources to population activities and was strongly supported by the World Bank, which made its first loans for population activities in the early 1970s.

However, low- and middle-income countries were by no means unanimous about population control or even family planning. At the Bucharest World Population Conference in 1974, Karan Singh, then Minister of Health in India, said, "Development is the best contraceptive" and put population growth in the context of broader political and socioeconomic changes. Even in industrialized countries, birth control was considered a private rather than a public matter, and there was considerable sensitivity in the media not to offend the public. By the 1980s, although family planning programs were more accepted throughout the world, the U.S. government's position changed, as right-wing pro-life interest groups and a powerful antiabortion lobby wrung a series of major concessions on population policy from the Reagan administration. As a result, the debates at the 1984 International Population Conference in Mexico were charged, and the U.S. aid for family planning programs decreased. The balance tipped once again in the 1990s, when President Clinton overturned the Reagan policies, and a meeting held in India to review 40 years of family planning activity was closed by Karan Singh, who reversed his Bucharest aphorism to declare, "Contraception is the best development." By 1994, when the next international conference on population was held in Cairo, a major change had taken place. With more participation in the conference by women's groups than ever before, there was little dissension on the need for family planning. But there was a conceptual change that argued for broader reproductive health policies, which shifted the emphasis from contraception and population control to all aspects of women's health.

Exhibit 14-7	The Eight Millennium Development Goals

The Millennium Development Goals (MDGs) were agreed upon in 2000 by 189 countries of the United Nations, with the support of the International Monetary Fund and the World Bank, the Organization for Economic Cooperation and Development, and the G7 and G20 countries. There are eight goals:

- Eradicate extreme poverty and hunger.
- Achieve universal primary education.
- Promote gender equality and empower women.
- Reduce child mortality.
- Improve maternal health.
- Combat HIV/AIDS, malaria, and other diseases.
- Ensure environmental sustainability.
- Develop a global partnership for development.

Each goal has a number of targets and indicators. In the accompanying table, four of the goals that most directly affect health are enumerated, with their targets and the indicators by which they will be assessed. All these are meant to be achieved by 2015.

Selected Millennium Development Goals (1990–2015)

Goals and Targets	Indicators
Goal: Eradicate extreme poverty and hunger. *Target:* Reduce by half the proportion of people living on less than a dollar a day. *Target:* Reduce by half the proportion of people who suffer from hunger.	1. Proportion of population living on less than US$1/day 2. Poverty gap ratio (incidence and depth of poverty) 3. Share of poorest population quintile in national consumption 4. Prevalence of underweight children ($<$5) 5. Proportion of population below minimum level of dietary energy consumption
Goal: Reduce child mortality. *Target:* Reduce by two-thirds the mortality rate among children under 5.	1. Under-five mortality rate 2. Infant mortality rate 3. Proportion of 1-year-olds immunized against measles
Goal: Improve maternal health. *Target:* Reduce by three-quarters the maternal mortality ratio.	1. Maternal mortality ratio 2. Proportion of births attended by skilled health personnel
Goal: Combat HIV/AIDS, malaria, and other diseases. *Target:* Halt and begin to reverse the spread of HIV/AIDS. *Target:* Halt and begin to reverse the incidence of malaria and other major diseases.	1. HIV prevalence among 15 to 24-year-old pregnant women 2. Contraceptive prevalence rate 3. Number of children orphaned by HIV/AIDS 4. Prevalence and mortality due to malaria 5. Proportion of population in malaria risk areas using malaria prevention and treatment 6. Prevalence and mortality due to tuberculosis (TB) 7. Proportion of TB cases detected and cured

Source: Global Forum for Health Research, *The 10/90 Report on Health Research, 2003–2004* (Geneva: Global Forum for Health Research, 2004). Reprinted with permission.

Although the MDGs have been criticized (e.g., as neglecting noncommunicable diseases and injuries, both of which result in high levels of morbidity and mortality in many low- and middle-income countries), they did represent an unprecedented global agreement to address unacceptable inequalities between rich and poor countries. However, achieving the goals by 2015 is a major challenge. At a meeting in London in 2004, the British Chancellor of the Exchequer, Gordon Brown, reminded the international health community that, according to current forecasts, some of the goals would not be met. Not only would there be a failure to reduce child mortality in sub-Saharan Africa, but in many other continents of the world there would be a failure to halve poverty by 2015. The chancellor made a strong plea to double the aid budget for poor countries, to try to avoid these sorts of failures. He warned, "If we let things slip, the Millennium Goals will become just another dream we once had, and we will indeed be sitting back on our sofas and switching on our TVs and . . . watching people die on our screens for the rest of our lives. We will be the generation that betrayed its own heart" (quoted in Lee, Walt, & Haines 2004, p. 2637).

establishing monitoring systems of immunizable diseases and training nationals in their use. Cooperation was also promoted among these countries by PAHO's establishment of a revolving fund for the purchase of vaccines and related supplies for national immunization programs.

Scholarships, study visits, and training are all mechanisms used by international, regional, and national bodies to stimulate cross-learning.

Producing and Sharing International Public Goods

By producing agreements on international public goods, countries all over the world agree to adopt and use technical standards, norms, and ways of tackling particular issues. Achieving global consensus occurs through the sorts of mechanisms already discussed: meetings of experts and, often, ratification by international, regional, or national bodies. The sorts of activities covered by such international cooperation in health include agreements on technical standards (of vaccines and drugs); the establishment of norms (for the classification and control of diseases); research on questions considered to be high priority (on AIDS, for example); and the setting up of global surveillance systems (e.g., the Global Outbreak and Alert Response Network, which played a critical role in the containment of SARS in 2003). For example, WHO and the FAO together make up the Codex Alimentarius Commission, which sets food safety standards in relation to, among other things, food additives, veterinary drug and pesticide residues, contaminants, and standards of hygienic practice. When there is a failure to produce what would be an international public good, either because it is too costly (e.g., new medicines for malaria) or because industry anticipates negligible returns (e.g., vaccines against diseases that affect few people, or very low-income people), partnerships may be formed between different organizations to overcome market failure (Exhibit 14-8).

The Changing Role of International Cooperation: Vertical Representation To Horizontal Participation

1950s to 1980s: Vertical Tiers of Representation

The high ideals of the UN system, which would bring peace, law, reason, and security to a war-torn world, were short-lived. As domination of membership of the UN by a few industrialized countries was challenged by newly independent nations in the late 1960s and early 1970s, the UN agenda became broader and its decisions less predictable. Growth in nation-state membership of the UN was accompanied by a considerable shift in autonomy between its component parts, and, in contradiction to original hopes, it appeared increasingly competitive and difficult to coordinate. Also, and partly because of dissatisfaction with its performance, the UN suffered financially in the last decades of the century.

In 1993 the UN secretary-general pointed out that halfway through the year arrears stood at $572 million, or half the year's needed resources. Only 47 (of 186) states had fully paid their regular budget assessments—19 industrialized and 28 low- and middle-income countries. However, almost two-thirds of the total $2.2 billion outstanding to the UN was owed by the United States and the Russian Federation (Childers & Urquhart, 1994). By 2004, U.S. arrears were in excess of $1.3 billion.

Similar tensions within the UN in general were reflected in its specialized agencies. Because WHO was designated by the UN as the lead international or-

---

Exhibit 14-8 **The International AIDS Vaccine Initiative**

In 1998 the UK Minister for International Development said that if the development of a vaccine was left to market forces, the strains that were killing people in Africa would not be tackled. To help in the development of a vaccine against AIDS, a number of donors established the International AIDS Vaccine Initiative (IAVI) in 1996 to ensure the development of safe, effective, accessible, preventive HIV vaccines for use throughout the world. The initiative is funded by a number of large foundations, private-sector companies (including Glaxo Wellcome and Levi Strauss), the United Nations Acquired Immune Deficiency Syndrome Program, the World Bank, and the United Kingdom's Department for International Development. By 2004, the Gates Foundation had invested a total of US$16.5 million in IAVI. Partnership is required because a single efficacy trial costs US$25 million, and product development costs up to US$250 million.

In a 1999 article entitled "Bank Woos AIDS Drug Firms," the UK newspaper *The Guardian* reported that the World Bank was exploring ways to end industry's reluctance to invest in vaccines for AIDS in developing countries, by guaranteeing that there would be funds to buy such vaccines, once developed. "Our message is that if a vaccine can be developed, there will be the money to buy it" (Elliott, 1999).

ganization in health, "directing and coordinating international health work," and for many years was so recognized, it is worth understanding how this organization changed between the 1950s and the 1980s. From the outset, WHO was essentially autonomous, accountable to its member states and financing and governing bodies.

WHO: Membership Becomes More Inclusive

Most nations were eager to join WHO when it was established in 1948, and the 55 original members rapidly expanded to 189 in 1998 (Lee, 1998), with most managing to find the resources to make the requisite financial contribution. The real growth of membership occurred in the 1960s, and by the 1970s heterogeneity was evident in the different goals and strategies of different member states. What had been a largely colonized world, dominated by a few industrialized powers, was transformed into a polity of sovereign states, in which members of what was then referred to as the "Third World" formed important groupings such as the Non-Aligned Movement, or the Group of 77. After the breakup of the Soviet Union, 25 more states joined the organization, largely from the newly independent states of central and eastern Europe.

The gradual geopolitical transformation of the world led to confrontation in some specialized agencies, especially in the 1970s, with Third World member states calling for a reordering of the international economic order (in the United Nations Conference on Trade and Development, known as UNCTAD), or a new communications order (in UNESCO), and with the industrialized nations supporting the status quo. The consensual policy environment enjoyed by WHO in the early days (although punctuated by debates over issues such as population growth in the early 1950s) was also challenged by the growth in membership, although the debates were not as polarized as they were in UNCTAD or UNESCO. Health policies shifted from a technological, disease orientation to a more developmental, multisectoral primary health care approach in the late 1970s.

With the change in emphasis, interests and ideas about health diversified, and consensus began to break down. For example, one of the main PHC policies was to introduce the concept of an essential drugs list—a restricted list of only the most common and useful drugs to be used in the public sector, especially at primary health facility levels. Although essential drugs lists represented significant savings for countries that were importing large numbers of nonessential, and sometimes even harmful, drugs, the medical profession and pharmaceutical industry generally were

not in favor of this policy, which WHO promoted strongly. At one point the United States was accused of bending to pressure from its own industry to withhold its contribution to WHO (Kanji et al., 1992). Conflict occurred over the interpretation of PHC policies, too, between UNICEF and WHO, the two agencies that had sponsored the international meeting on PHC at Alma Ata in 1978 (Exhibit 14-9).

As newly independent states joined the organization, new delegations rapidly became more familiar with its workings and more confident about drawing attention to problems in the low-income member states, and they called for greater levels of technical cooperation. By 1966 more than half of WHO's budget was devoted to operational activities in the low- and middle-income countries, in contrast to, say, the ILO's 8%. As technical cooperation grew from the 1960s, differentiation between member states also sharpened: By the 1970s, the industrialized member states were increasingly seen as "donors," supporting middle- and low-income member states. And although all member states had an equal vote at the policy-determining, annual World Health Assembly in Geneva, many felt that the countries that contributed more financially had more influence in decision making.

WHO: Funding Becomes More Exclusive

WHO's funding base changed considerably from its establishment in 1948, when it relied largely on a regular budget (US$6 million in 1950) made up of member states' contributions based on a formula of population size and gross national product (GNP). Beginning in 1960, this regular budget was supplemented by modest voluntary donations that came from other multilateral agencies or donors. For example, by 1971 the regular budget had grown to US$75 million, to which US$25 million were donated as extrabudgetary funds from the United Nations Development Program (UNDP) and UNFPA. Such extrabudgetary funds grew as particular donors (often the higher-income member states, such as the European countries or the United States) gave additional funds to WHO for particular programs—an unprecedented US$100 million toward AIDS in the period from 1989 to 1991, for example. By 2004 about 66% of WHO's budget came from extrabudgetary sources, as opposed to 25% in 1971.

Extrabudgetary funds played an important supplementary role in the last decades of the 20th century because the regular budget was under significant pressure, largely because of member states' decision to adopt a policy of zero growth in real terms of the budgets of all the specialized agencies, but partly be-

| Exhibit 14-9 | Competition Between UNICEF and WHO |

WHO and UNICEF came into conflict in the 1980s over primary health care policy. Some concern about the boundaries of the two organizations had been expressed in the late 1940s: Roscam Abbing (1979) describes the discussion about delineation of responsibilities, saying some feared that UNICEF's activities would not be confined to "medical supply" but would enter the fields that were the responsibility of WHO. A joint health policy committee was set up between the two organizations at the outset, but one observer remarked that coordination was difficult because the terms of reference between the two organizations were different: "UNICEF's approach is a comprehensive and integrated one, revolving around the 'whole' child and programs of assistance are made subject to this objective. Thus for instance, UNICEF is reluctant to assist WHO in its eradication programs, unless these are not complementary to, but part of the development of basic health services."

By the 1980s, it seemed as if the organizations had swapped roles. UNICEF had been a development agency, concerned with general areas that improved health—water and sanitation, women's education, and literacy—with grassroots, participative policies. WHO had been technologically focused and disease-oriented. In the 1980s WHO's concerns were with preventive and multisectoral approaches to health, including nutrition, water supplies, and participation in health care. UNICEF, on the other hand, searching for a role for itself in the launching of primary health care (undertaken jointly with WHO), focused on a few interventions that came to be known as the GOBI interventions: growth monitoring, oral rehydration, breastfeeding, and immunization. In some countries, the way these particular programs were implemented seemed to be contradictory to the integrated approach of primary health care. Often they were run as separate projects, and even if they were incorporated into ministry of health programs, they were managed like vertical programs, with their own staff, vehicles, logos, and accounting systems. The then Director-General, Halfdan Mahler, did not hide his irritability with what he saw as UNICEF's selective, top-down approach to primary health care. In an address to the WHA, and without naming names, he said, "Honorable delegates, while we have been striking ahead with singleness of purpose in WHO based on your collective decision, others appear to have little patience for such systematic efforts . . . I am referring to such initiatives as the selection by people outside the developing countries of a few isolated elements of primary health care" (Mahler, 1983).

The public quarrel between the two agencies was short-lived, but the tensions about policies remained and were resolved by establishing a Task Force on Child Survival and Development in the mid-1980s. The original objective of the Task Force on Child Survival was to accelerate and transform the existing international immunization programs against the main six childhood diseases by getting WHO and UNICEF to work together with other agencies, such as the World Bank and UNDP, with the Rockefeller Foundation acting as a facilitator of the process (Muraskin, 1998). This was one of the early examples of the global partnerships that became a feature of international health cooperation in the late 1990s.

Source: G. Walt, "WHO Under Stress: Implications for Health Policy," 1993, *Health Policy,* 24, pp. 125–144. Reprinted with permission from Elsevier Science.

cause of the nonpayment of contributions. In 2004, the director-general of WHO noted, "I am concerned that US$ 50 million, or 6% of assessed contributions, were not paid. Total unpaid assessed contributions, including amounts due for previous financial periods, is US$ 138 million. Within this figure, long-term arrears stand at US$ 88 million, having increased from US$ 82 million at the end of the biennium 2000–2001" (WHO, 2004).

Although extrabudgetary funds supplemented WHO's budget in the short term, they increased difficulty in coordination and continuity because of changing donor interests and short-term financial commitments, and they led to dependence on a small number of donors. In the 1990s, 10 countries provided 90% of all extrabudgetary funds, and the same countries provided more than half of the regular budget through assessed contributions. "In effect, voluntary contributions increase the risk of placing institutions in the thrall of those who give them the

money " (Taylor, 1993, p. 378). In the 1990s, an investigation of the role of such funds agreed cautiously that there was some truth in the assertion that a small number of donors to WHO were "driving health policy," but concluded that donor involvement had brought many advantages to the organization as a whole (Vaughan et al., 1996).

Changes in membership and funding resulted in two contradictory trajectories. On the one hand, WHO was perceived as a universalist, inclusive membership organization, with a reputation for being neutral in dealing with its member states (in contrast to bilateral organizations, which were seen to be partial for geopolitical or historical reasons). On the other hand, WHO was seen as increasingly dependent on a few donor member states whose interests dominated the activities of the organization. Further, whereas once WHO had escaped much of the criticism levied at other specialized agencies of the UN—most notably UNESCO, FAO, and ILO during the 1970s—by the mid-1980s, dissatisfaction with the organization was apparent.

WHO's Health Policies Come Under Fire

Until the beginning of the 1980s, WHO's leadership in health was unassailable. Its policies were characterized by a relatively cautious, technical approach to health problems, dominated largely by disease-oriented, vertically organized programs tackling major disease burdens—malaria, smallpox, yaws—that could be combated with new technologies (DDT, penicillin, vaccines). Although significant advances were made during this phase, by the mid-1970s it was increasingly evident that the disease approach to health policy was problematic. For example, although malaria had largely been eradicated in southern Europe and a few low- and middle-income country areas, it had become evident that eradication of the disease was unrealistic, and that even controlling malaria was complex. Not only was DDT resistance becoming apparent, but programs were unsustainable without established health infrastructures to continue detection and treatment activities. Attention shifted toward health systems and health planning, and the 1970s were witness to radical rethinking on health policies, culminating in the Alma Ata conference on PHC, sponsored by WHO and UNICEF and forming part of WHO's major policy thrust for the next 20 years: Health For All by the Year 2000.

This second phase of health policies led to a much more politicized era, with WHO and UNICEF not always in accordance over PHC strategies, and with practitioners and academics in fierce debate over how to interpret PHC. On the one side, Walsh and Warren (1979) argued that the PHC approach was too broad and unrealistic, and that developing countries had to select certain diseases that were conducive to cost-effective interventions, a position that UNICEF and other donors supported. On the other side, WHO and others (Rifkin & Walt, 1986; Unger & Killingsworth, 1986) argued that it was health systems that needed to be supported, within context-specific economic and social development, and that PHC was as relevant to industrialized as to developing countries. This debate was played out explicitly as WHO and UNICEF competed to promote their respective interpretations of PHC, as illustrated in Exhibit 14-9.

WHO Challenged by the World Bank

PHC and Health For All were developed in the 1970s but implemented in the resource-constrained 1980s, a period dominated by neoliberal political and economic thinking. The World Bank was playing a major role in indebted countries, introducing structural adjustment programs, and it was increasingly turning its attention to the social sectors, including health. In 1980 the Bank published its *Health Sector Policy Paper* and began direct lending for health services for the first time. At the same time, Western governments, concerned with rising costs of health care, began to review their health systems, and the era of health reforms was introduced, looking toward increased competition in delivery of health services and different forms of financing health systems, among other changes. Health reforms came at a time of considerable financial constraint—world economic recession, indebtedness among many low-income countries, disillusionment with the overextended role of the state—and rapidly became part of a wider program of economic and structural reforms sought by the World Bank and other donors in many low- and middle-income countries. By the late 1980s and 1990s, loans to low- and middle-income countries had conditions attached that called for considerable changes in health systems, especially in financing and service delivery. As the focus on health policies shifted from the delivery of PHC to concerns about financing health systems, WHO lost ground to the World Bank, which was leading the discussion on health reforms.

Some blamed WHO's waning leadership on an organizational mold that did not fit the altered and diverse milieu of the last decades of the century. In more than 50 years the organization had not changed much, and it appeared to critics to be inward-looking, bunkered against external criticism, and disapproving of the movements of other UN organizations into health fields—movements traditionally led by itself. Attempts to reform the organization were initiated in the early 1990s, but the scope, nature, and pace of change were limited and deemed to be slow. Concerns were expressed over WHO's bureaucratic procedures, costs, lack of budget transparency, and inability to decide priorities. Questions were raised openly about its effectiveness as an international organization, as well as its capacity to fulfill its leadership role (Godlee, 1994, 1995). For example, it was argued that WHO was slow in establishing a response to AIDS; that it was UNICEF and other agencies that led the way on polio eradication and universal child immunizations; and that the organization did not identify the serious deficit in health financing during the 1980s, and so allowed the World Bank to define health reform policies for the 1990s.

In 1998 a new director-general, Gro Brundtland, restructured the organization and attempted to reassert WHO's leadership in health policy. She helped to put health on the global policy agenda in several ways: through the initiation of the Commission on Macroeconomics and Health, which demonstrated that ill health was a cause of poverty and that therefore interventions to prevent and treat disease were cost-effective; through the initiation of the Framework Convention on Tobacco Control (see Exhibit 14-1); and through focusing global and UN attention on AIDS. WHO also started to look for increased and more diverse participation in health cooperation. Instead of relying largely on its member states, WHO sought new partnerships (Kickbusch & Quick, 1998), looking beyond the state toward civil society and the market, and leading to a shift in roles from representation to participation. This continued under the leadership of Lee Jong-wook as of 2003, although his focus for WHO was more on what was happening at a country than global level. His stated aims were to shift resources from WHO's Geneva headquarters to the country and regional level (three-quarters of budgetary resources by 2007) and—in WHO's 3 by 5 campaign—to get antiretroviral treatment to 3 million people by 2005. In an interview published in the *Lancet* in 2003, he said "The key question is not whether we can afford to do this, but whether we can afford not to do this" ("AIDS Campaign," 2003, p. 1900).

1990s to 2000s: Horizontal and Expanding Participation

The Role of the State

Although the extent of the state's role in the provision of services—whether health, education, or social security—has differed from country to country, there is no doubt that its size and scope expanded hugely during the 20th century, especially in the industrialized countries. As shown in Figure 14-2, in 1960, OECD industrialized countries' total government expenditure was less than 20% of GDP, and by 1990 it was almost half. Comparable figures for low- and middle-income countries were 15% and 25% (World Bank, 1997).

Until the late 1970s, there was little challenge to the role of the state in its provision of health services, although there were differences among roles in different parts of the world. Most Latin American health systems were segmented between MOHs, which provided health services for the low-income population, and better-endowed institutes of social security, which provided services for workers and their families. In Asia, MOHs functioned within very pluralistic health systems, with a flourishing private sector. In Africa, MOHs were often the main

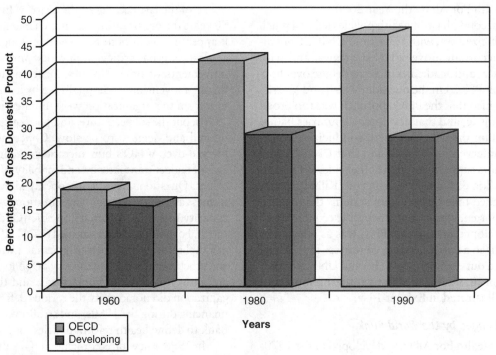

Figure 14-2 The Growth of the State, Measured by Total Government Expenditure as a Percentage of Gross Domestic Product. *Source:* World Bank, *World Development Report: The State in a Changing World* (Oxford, England: Oxford University Press, 1997). Adapted with permission.

providers of health services for urban populations, and with the extension of primary health services in the 1970s and 1980s, for rural populations; however, NGOs, such as missions, were also important providers in rural areas, and the informal private sector (e.g., drug sellers, traditional midwives) provided much first-contact care.

By the 1980s, however, the political and economic environment began to change. Fueled partly by the rise of neoliberal economic policies of the 1980s and partly by disillusionment with what were perceived as overextended, corrupt, inefficient, and nondemocratic states in many low- and middle-income countries, donors began to look beyond the state and MOHs to the private sector and began to promote reforms to health systems that would divest ministries of some of their service roles and extend them to the private sector (see Chapter 11). To achieve such reforms, donors began to attach conditions to their loans and grants to low- and middle-income countries. For example, a donor might agree to provide a grant to support the health system, but only on the condition that the MOH decentralize its authority, introduce user fees for publicly provided services, or pass legislation encouraging private practice. Although the International Monetary Fund had always applied some policy conditionality to countries in search of assistance, the World Bank only moved seriously into policy-related funding in the 1980s. In the 2 years between 1989 and 1991, the average number of policy conditions per World Bank structural adjustment loan was 56 (up from 39 between 1980 and 1988, and minimal before). Although the bilateral organizations always used conditionality to some extent (e.g., by tying aid to purchases of equipment to the donor country), in the 1980s they tended to piggyback on the conditionality of the international financial institutions, with varying degrees of enthusiasm (Killick, 1998).

By the new millennium, a number of changes had resulted from the political and economic reforms started two decades earlier. First, the International Summit on Social Development, held in Copenhagen in 1995, committed world leaders to the eradication of absolute poverty. This was the first-ever UN conference on social development, attended by delegates from 186 countries and 811 NGOs, and nearly 3,000 journalists. This was followed in 2000 by the UN Millennium Summit, at which was agreed a set of eight time-bound and measurable goals (the Millennium Development Goals, or MDGs) and targets for combating poverty, hunger, disease, illiteracy, environmental degradation, and discrimination against women (see Exhibit 14-7). Discussions on how to finance the attainment of the MDGs started formally at the International Conference on Financing for Development in Monterrey in 2002, resulting in a number of different proposals being explored to raise aid levels (see, for example, Lee, Walt, & Haines, 2004). Second, the industrialized countries that made up the G8 spearheaded, with the United Nations, a major initiative to address three particular diseases (HIV/AIDS, tuberculosis, and malaria) that were taking a huge toll in poor countries—especially in Africa. A host of new partnerships were initiated regarding HIV/AIDS in particular as public pressure mounted to do more about the epidemic.

Third, new financial mechanisms for official development aid were devised, following the experiment started by the Global Alliance for Vaccines and Immunization (GAVI) in 1999, and including other global initiatives such as the Global Fund to Fight AIDS, Tuberculosis, and Malaria (see Exhibit 14-3). Countries were expected to submit specific proposals for aid (in the case of GAVI, country applications had to demonstrate levels of immunization coverage, and how they would increase these with new-generation vaccines). Countries were then judged on their performance against their own stated goals. Grants were thus disbursed only in partial payments, and only once results were demonstrated. Increasing emphasis was also made to link aid to notions of "good governance," democracy, and the growth of civil society. These attempts included, for example, promoting increased accountability in the public sector, improving procedures and the rule of law, introducing transparency in financing and other systems, promoting human rights, and encouraging multiparty democratic systems—as well as emphasizing state stewardship of the sector as opposed to a service-delivery role.

These changes put a different emphasis on the role of the state. At the global level, states were more outward looking—having to negotiate their way through a complex web of networks and alliances. At the national level—and especially for those receiving official development assistance—states were held responsible for demonstrating capacity to perform against goals agreed upon in the global networks.

The Rise of Civil Society

Although the notion of "civil society" has a long genesis, it has become common parlance in the development literature only in the past decade or so. The phrase usually refers to all those organizations that are between the state and the household. Some include the private, for-profit sector as part of civil society; others prefer to differentiate between those organizations that form part of the private, corporate sector and those organizations that are essentially nonprofit—most NGOs would fit into this category. Donors have supported the notion of civil society for a number of reasons. By the 1990s, the health sector provided many examples of NGOs that had demonstrated an impact on development, as measured by mortality and morbidity in small communities, through a variety of different interventions. They were perceived to be effective, innovative, and able to reach the grassroots in a way governments and multi- or bilateral donors were not. In the 1990s the focus on NGOs broadened, and donors began funding a wider range of CSOs, whose members often participated in lobbying and other political activities. Support for such groups was seen as a way to build up democracy—by providing outlets for citizens to voice their demands—and to promote social capital, which would lead to improved economic performance. The idea of social capital came from Robert Putnam (1995), who suggested that the difference between the prosperous Italian north and the low-income south was explained by trust, family and civic responsibilities, and sharing a public spirit—all of which represent the cement that holds society together, and which were apparent in the north of Italy but not in the south. Donors saw NGOs and CSOs as ways to build up social capital, as well as to provide antidotes to the supposedly bloated, autocratic, and inefficient state.

Civil society organizations also became far more active in the last decades of the 20th century, moving from largely service-delivery roles to much more active advocacy and lobbying. Transnational advocacy groups were successful in reframing global debates (on debt and trade, for example), arguing for changes in policy, and drawing attention to neglected areas—for example, poor workers' health and safety standards, and access to essential drugs (see Lee, Buse, & Fustukian, 2002, for examples, and Exhibit 14-10).

The Role of the Market

In this chapter, private, for-profit (or market-sector) organizations are considered sufficiently distinct from CSOs to be seen separately. The market sector has grown and, with trade liberalization in global markets, is likely to expand further (Pollock & Price, 2003). In many countries, foreign investment in the health sector, once forbidden or heavily restricted, has opened up. For example, states increasingly allow foreign hospital management companies to invest in local hospitals and in health insurance, often as joint ventures with local, domestic partners. Although some of these moves may be beneficial—for example, the entry of new insurance companies in Brazil is said to have increased coverage of the population by offering improved insurance packages and to have brought down administrative costs—foreign investors may increase inequities within and between countries because it is in their interests to invest in those areas where there is relatively high per capita income, thus improving access and services for those who can pay, but attracting workers from the public sector into the private sector (Zarrilli & Kinnon, 1998).

Exhibit 14-10 | An Expanding Global Role for Civil Society Organizations

Just as the Thai AIDS activists worked in concert with activists in Washington (see Exhibit 14-2), so have other treatment campaigns connected globally. One of the most successful was that of improving access to medicines, spearheaded by Médicins Sans Frontières (MSF) in the 1990s. With groups such as Oxfam and Ralph Nader's Consumer Project on Technology, among others, MSF sought to prevent the multinational pharmaceutical industry from exploiting emerging agreements through the World Trade Organization that attempted to block the production of generic medicines in middle-income countries such as South Africa, Thailand, Brazil, and India. Many national NGOs joined the global campaign and lobbied together on many of the issues. Schneider (2002) reports that in one week in 2001, when a number of pharmaceutical manufacturers took the South African government to court (withdrawing from the court hearing only at the last minute) to prevent regulatory measures to reduce the cost of AIDS drugs, 27 protest activities were reported on the website of the South African NGO Treatment Action Campaign (TAC), involving 12 countries, including the United States, Canada, the United Kingdom, Brazil, and the Philippines.

Lobbying for the Framework Convention on Tobacco Control also took off when the groups supporting the conventions were enhanced by the formation and development of the Framework Convention Alliance (FCA). Initially, civil society groups involved in discussions regarding tobacco control were largely confined to high-income-country NGOs and international health–based NGOs. The FCA was formed as a loose international alliance to support the development and ratification of an effective convention and to engage a larger group of CSOs in the process of drawing up the convention. By 2003 the FCA encompassed more than 180 NGOs from over 70 countries, and had established itself as an important lobbying alliance (Collin, 2004).

Although some private companies clearly are very powerful, with annual turnovers several times larger than the GNP of many lower-income countries, and see as their mandates the pursuit of maximum returns for their shareholders, providing they act within the law, some observers suggest they are taking a broader view of their social responsibilities—if only out of enlightened self-interest—partly because of the actions of CSOs pressuring for particular changes in policies. There are a number of examples of international environmental, human rights, and faith-based groups managing to change companies' policies. Some actions may not be directly health related—for example, one company ceased producing Alar, a chemical agent used on apples, after protests from environmental groups (Wapner, 1995)—but others are. In the United States, Coca-Cola bowed to the lobbying of the Interfaith Center on Corporate Responsibility, among other groups, to agree in 2004 that all their HIV-infected employees in Africa would receive free antiretroviral drugs (Exhibit 14-11). There is little doubt that the prices of the antiretroviral drugs of several pharmaceutical transnational companies were lowered considerably after 2000 largely as a result of pressure and lobbying from CSOs.

There are also increasing examples of pharmaceutical companies offering large donations of drugs to help control or eradicate diseases in low-income countries. Several have followed the example of Merck (Exhibit 14-12). For instance, in 1998 the pharmaceutical company Pfizer announced the establishment of the International Trachoma Initiative, in partnership with the United States' Edna McConnell Clark Foundation and others, to eliminate blinding trachoma. The pharmaceutical company provides the antibiotic Zithromax free of charge in 11 countries, as well as supporting national trachoma control programs. Based on successes achieved during the initial 5 years, the plan is to roll out the initiative to additional countries. Similarly, SmithKline Beecham established a partnership with a number of organizations to undertake a program to eliminate lymphatic filariasis, a disfiguring disease commonly called elephantiasis. About 20% of the world's population live in areas where they are at risk of infection from lymphatic filariasis. The program is based on the free delivery of albendazole, a drug that should help eliminate the disease, and is planned to continue for at least 20 years.

Other pharmaceutical companies have lowered their prices on some antiretroviral drugs to increase access in very poor countries, where the great majority of people cannot afford their high cost. This was achieved over a long decade of painful negotiation (UNAIDS, for example, initiated a dialogue about lowering prices with some pharmaceutical companies in the late 1990s), but it was not until a network of active and vocal CSOs began lobbying that the pharmaceutical industry began to respond to demands for increased access (Exhibit 14-13).

Although strides have been made toward improving access to certain drugs—antiretrovirals being the main example—such moves have been complex, slow, and controversial. As Exhibit 14-2 demonstrates, CSOs have had to go to court to win concessions in Thailand, and Brazil and South Africa have had to fight battles at the global and local level to improve access to drugs. There are also difficult questions about the potential for antiretroviral resistance if drugs are not carefully handled, and concern that too much attention is being paid to treatment in comparison with prevention. Furthermore, suspicions remain about the motives of pharmaceutical companies, fueled by marketing tactics that have not always been

---

| **Exhibit 14-11** | **Coca Cola, AIDS, and Nongovernmental Organizations** |

The Business section of the London *Guardian* newspaper reported in April 2004 on "sisters who stirred the conscience of Coca-Cola" as an illustration of the way in which faith-based organizations have lobbied for greater corporate responsibility among a number of different industries over a number of decades (Pratley, 2004). The Interfaith Center on Corporate Responsibility, which is an organization of 275 faith-based groups, claims an investment portfolio of $110 billion. This strengthens its position in negotiations with industry and enables it to put resolutions to company shareholder and annual meetings. As a result it has been able to influence a number of companies to at least pass resolutions calling on the company to review the economic impact of its operations on the HIV/AIDS pandemic in Africa. Although "not a revolutionary step," the significance of Coca-Cola's resolution lies in the commitments the company has already made to provide antiretroviral drugs to employees. Although ultimately it is in Coca-Cola's self-interest to treat its employees, knowing that the epidemic is also killing its customers and potential customers, there are some companies that have been slow to act or to think more broadly about HIV preventive measures (Pratley, 2004, p. 26).

Exhibit 14-12	Controlling River Blindness: A Win-Win Partnership

Onchocerciasis is a vector-borne disease, often called river blindness because the black flies that transmit the disease survive only within a certain distance of rivers and so infect populations living in the vicinity. It is a serious public health problem, affecting more than 17 million persons in Africa, in 27 countries. Although only a minority of people become blind as a result of the disease (267,000 in 1995, according to WHO), it causes a great deal of misery, including skin changes and itching. One of the ways of controlling the disease is by adding chemicals to rivers to prevent the fly larvae from hatching. Larviciding was used extensively in the Onchocerciasis Control Program (OCP) in West Africa, established in 1974 by a coalition of donors (the World Bank, UNDP, and WHO) with considerable success. However, this method of control is not appropriate to all sites where the disease exists, and in 1987, the drug firm Merck seemed to provide a better answer. Its drug Mectizan (ivermectin) needed to be taken only once a year, in tablet form. In 1987 Merck held a press conference to announce that it would supply as much of the drug as was needed for the treatment of river blindness, at no charge and for as long as necessary. It was able to do this because the drug had been originally developed for veterinary use, and the company had made huge profits from its sale. Although testing its usefulness for humans had generated development costs, the overall cost of production was low, and the drug would be needed for a geographically well-defined population. Further, Foege (1998) has suggested that the drug company had an ethos that allowed it to give the drug free, quoting its founder's son as saying, "We try never to forget that medicine is for the people. It is not for profits and if we have remembered that, they have never failed to appear" (p. S-7).

The Mectizan Donation Program was the largest donation program ever undertaken by a commercial company. It provided free Mectizan not only for the West Africa OCP, but for many other programs in other countries, often through NGOs, but also through governments. In 1997 about 16 million people received Mectizan for the prevention of river blindness. This example of a private-public partnership describes a win-win situation: Many people in Africa formerly vulnerable to the disease were protected from it, and the program served to "enhance Merck's corporate image and increase recognition of Merck's name and helped build relationships and alliances between its key constituents" (Colatrella, 1998, p. S154). It was successful because Merck established a special program—the Mectizan Donation Program—under the auspices of an independent Mectizan Expert Committee, administratively housed at the Task Force for Child Survival and Development and chaired by a respected public health physician. According to Frost and Reich (1998), the success of this institutional arrangement was due to the transparency and open communication between Merck and the Expert Committee; because the roles and functions of each actor were clearly defined and agreed on from the outset; and because, unlike broad-spectrum antibiotics, ivermectin had a specific use and had to be taken only once a year, in an easily ingestible form.

Exhibit 14-13	The Treatment Action Campaign

Three activist groups came together in 1998 in South Africa to form the Treatment Action Campaign (TAC). The first issue on which it campaigned was prevention of mother-to-child transmission of HIV. Scientific studies in Thailand and Uganda had suggested that a single dose of nevirapine (an antiretroviral drug) could reduce the transmission of HIV from mothers to children. Although the drug was being given in many countries, the South African government was reluctant to introduce it in the national health service because of fears of toxicity and emerging drug resistance. The issue was further complicated by President Thabo Mbeki's unorthodox questioning of the relationship between HIV and AIDS, which had been preceded by several local controversies involving the government. One was an accusation that public money had been wasted on a musical aimed to spread a message about AIDS prevention, the other was about government support for a treatment (virodene) that had no benefit (Fassin & Schneider, 2003). As the government wavered on its policy with regard to treatment of mother-to-child-transmission, some provinces ignored national policy and prescribed nevirapine. By 2003 some provinces were claiming very high coverage rates with the drug, but some of the poorest provinces were failing to reach most pregnant women.

One of the other issues TAC campaigned on was to improve access to antiretroviral drugs. A charismatic HIV-positive South African, Zachie Achmat, led a highly publicized AIDS equivalent of a hunger strike—refusing to take antiretroviral drugs until the government reversed its policy and made the drugs available to *all* South Africans. TAC launched spirited campaigns, including civil disobedience protests and the threat of court action against government policy that withheld drugs that could improve lives. In 2003 the government responded to this internal (and external) pressure and announced that it would begin to distribute antiretroviral drugs through public health clinics. A South African pharmaceutical company, Aspen Pharmacare, announced the launch of the first generic antiretroviral drug containing stavudine, developed and manufactured locally—made possible by a voluntary license agreement with Bristol-Myers Squibb ("Hope for South Africa," 2003). The change in both government and pharmaceutical company policy was clearly due to the lively lobbying by civil society organizations, especially within the country.

welcomed. Dayrit (1998), for example, describes one pharmaceutical company's tactics to sell one of its new vaccines against hepatitis B in the Philippines as "unscrupulous and unethical": The company used the media to raise public fears about the disease (so that members of the public would demand the vaccine) and distributed its vaccines to the public health centers, offering special commissions to the health professionals who promoted it. The actions of the company angered public health policy makers, who introduced the vaccine to the public sector's Expanded Program so that it became generally available. However, there were fears that sustaining procurement would not be easy, given the costs of the vaccine and problems with exchange rates.

Although public-sector concerns about the marketing activities of the private sector remain, the 1990s were witness to a concerted effort by the public and private sectors to negotiate ways of working together. For example, in the United States in the early 1990s, the distinguished Institute of Medicine, established in 1970 by the National Academy of Science to advise the government on policy matters pertaining to the public's health, was asked to explore ways of maximizing private- and public-sector participation in programs to advance the immunization of children. This action followed (1) the establishment of the Children's Vaccine Initiative (CVI) in 1990, a partnership between the Rockefeller Foundation, UNDP, UNICEF, WHO, and the World Bank to harness new technologies to enhance immunization and (2) the recognition that there was no overall strategy guiding research, production, procurement, or distribution of vaccines in the United States. There was concern that economic factors that made vaccine research much less profitable than research on drugs were probably also responsible for the fall in vaccine manufacture in the United States: In 1985 there were 10 licensed manufacturers of human vaccines (7 commercial, 2 state laboratories, and a single university), and by 1992 there were only 5 (Lederberg, Shope, & Oaks, 1992).

During the 1990s, a series of meetings between the private and public sectors was held to address concerns about the lack of research and development in vaccines, and the apparent slowness of many countries to include new vaccines in their immunization programs. Such meetings resulted in discussions of a number of new policies (such as removing price controls, or establishing a global targeting strategy and a global fund for vaccines to assist low-income countries in buying vaccines when there were significant shortfalls between what resources they had and what they needed). As a result of some of these discussions,

the International AIDS Vaccine Initiative was established (see Exhibit 14-8), and in late 1999 the Global Alliance for Vaccines and Immunization was set up to "fulfill the right of every child to be protected against vaccine-preventable diseases of public health concern." These public-private vaccine initiatives have been followed by a host of others, including the Children's Vaccine Program at PATH, the Dengue Vaccine Project, the Pediatric Dengue Vaccine Initiative, the Malaria Vaccine Initiative, the European Malaria Vaccine Initiative, the Human Hookworm Vaccine Initiative, the Meningitis Vaccine Project, and the Pneumococcal Vaccines Accelerated Development and Introduction Plan. In addition, a number of cross-cutting public-private partnerships have been established to deal with issues such as safe injection and vaccine vial monitors, and vaccine finance (e.g., the Vaccine Fund).

Vertical Representation to Horizontal Participation: The Implications for Health Policy

This chapter has suggested that states were once able to influence international health policy through their formal representation on the governing bodies or at meetings of the various organizations of the UN. However, this channel of influence has diminished because international health policy is no longer largely decided through the UN or its specialized agency, WHO. Over the past two decades, international cooperation on health has expanded to include a greater diversity of actors, who are cooperating within partnerships that include the UN bodies but do not belong to them and do not necessarily act within their rules and regulations. This shift from representation to participation has some important implications for health policy cooperation in the new century, and raises questions in five arenas: changes in the balance of power, mandates, competition and duplication, coordination, and governance. This final section of the chapter addresses those five arenas.

Shifts in Power

As previously shown, changing trends in international health policies led to shifts in the balance of power among the different organizations involved in international health. Within the UN, WHO led the field until the 1980s, but from 1980 on, the World Bank played a particularly important role, and many perceived it as providing the main leadership, as well as the most funding, for health. At the end of the century one writer suggested that the World Bank was "the new 800 lb gorilla in world health care" (Abbasi, 1999, p. 866).

Although that may have been true for the 1990s, it may be less true for the decades of the new millennium, with the Bill and Melinda Gates Foundation providing significant funds to health programs. The World Bank's yearly lending more than doubled from US$1.1 billion to $2.3 billion in the mid-1990s, but beginning in 2000 the Gates Foundation has spent about $1 billion per annum on global health activities. By comparison, WHO's expenditure was around $900 million a year.

The World Bank's policy stance on health was promoted through its 1993 annual development report, *Investing in Health,* which identified four major problems with international health care systems: the misallocation of funds to less cost-effective interventions; inefficient use of funds; inequity in access to basic health care; and the explosion of health care costs, which were outpacing the growth income. Its policy recommendations included shifting the focus of government investment away from tertiary care toward public health, introducing private or social insurance plans, and fostering competition in the delivery of health services (Abbasi, 1999). Although the World Bank's policies have not gone uncontested, most donors (and industry) supported them in general.

It is not only at the global level that the number of actors in health has diversified and power has shifted. Regional organizations such as the EU have expanded their interests in health. For example, aid disbursed through the European Commission increased from US$1.86 billion in 1987 to US$4.7 billion in 1997, and even WHO's regional offices—particularly PAHO—act as relatively independent institutions in their own right. Bilateral organizations provide funds for health to regional organizations (about one-third of the United Kingdom's overseas development assistance is channeled through the EU) as well as continuing to support WHO and having a significant presence at the country level. Indeed, many bilateral organizations expanded their activities to the country level by channeling funds through NGOs in the health field. External assistance to the health sector through NGOs grew from 13% to 23% between 1982 and 1990 (Michaud & Murray, 1994). Some bilaterals, such as USAID, made a policy decision to provide all their funding through NGOs rather than governments, so that from the 1980s on there was an explosion of NGO activity at both the country level and internationally. The entry of actors from the corporate sector (the pharmaceutical companies,

for example) into health is further changing the landscape of health cooperation.

The power increasingly exercised by global health initiatives and partnerships carries implications not only for the influence exercised by the traditional international organizations (such as WHO and the World Bank) over international health policy but also for national governments, who have different relationships with these new entities than they did with international organizations (Buse & Harmer, 2004). These partnerships are often actively involved in setting technical norms and standards, and their support to countries often takes place within the confines of application criteria and performance results that may be far more restrictive than earlier conditions associated with bilateral support or loans from international finance institutions.

Although this pluralism of activity and partnership has raised the status of health on the policy agenda and changed the balance of power, it has also led to concerns about overlapping mandates, competition and duplication of health activities, poor coordination, and issues of governance.

Overlapping Mandates

Lee and associates (1996) showed that many of the UN organizations' formal mandates (defined as an organization's statement of overall purpose) had evolved over time, and that what the UN organizations were actually doing—their effective mandates—had changed considerably over time. For example, UNICEF's original mandate as "a temporary body to meet the emergency needs of children in postwar Europe" (Koivusalo & Ollila, 1997) graduated from temporary relief and emergency activities to development work with children, and later included the welfare of youth and women. By the 1980s UNICEF's expenditure on health had increased by more than 120% over annual expenses of the previous decade. UNFPA, with a relatively clear formal mandate to promote population programs, did not stray far from activities concerning population issues, including family planning, until after the International Conference on Population and Development in 1994. It was at this conference that population activities were redefined as reproductive health activities, raising debates within UNFPA about its effective mandate. The World Bank, with a mandate to provide financial capital to assist the reconstruction and development of member states, entered the health field through its support for population policies in the late 1960s, and in the 1990s led international health policy, focusing on financing reforms.

It is also not clear that the various partnerships may not end up with a proliferation of arrangements that, far from building comparative advantage, actually lead to duplication and confusion. Just in the field of children's vaccines and immunization programs, there are overlapping interests among several existing organizations: WHO, the partners of the Task Force on Child Survival, GAVI, and the Children's Vaccine Program of the Melinda and Bill Gates Foundation, among others. A 1999 report by Brooks and colleagues that looked at why countries were slow to take advantage of new vaccines suggested that there had been a confusion of priorities and policies at the global and country level, and this confusion had affected vaccine uptake and financing.

Competition and Duplication

One of the recurring concerns of those in international health is the extent to which competition and duplication of health activities occur because there are so many different actors, and the effect this competition and duplication may have on domestic policy environments. MOHs, on the one hand, may experience negative cumulative effects, with multiple donors making demands on officials' time, and each donor wanting its own project presentations, evaluations, accounting systems, and meetings. On the other hand, some have claimed that governments may also use competition for attention to play donors off against each other (Buse & Walt, 1997).

For example, in a few countries where WHO had the lead role among UN agencies in negotiations with the MOH about health care reforms, the World Bank was perceived as a threat and a competitor because of its standing in the country and its access to policy elites beyond the MOH. Case studies of negotiations on health care reforms in Ecuador (Lucas et al., 1997), El Salvador (Homedes et al., 2000), and the Dominican Republic (Glassman et al., 1999) suggest that the World Bank was sometimes seen as competing not only with other international organizations, such as WHO, but also with certain institutions within the government. The effect was to marginalize the MOH, for example, in favor of supporting separately established reform teams. Homedes and associates (2000) suggested that in El Salvador the World Bank preferred negotiating with a health reform group (partly financed by the World Bank and divorced from the MOH) because it saw such a group to be more flexible and able to move more expeditiously than the MOH, which was bound by civil service regulations and bureaucracy. Although all three countries differed to some extent, their reform teams were regarded by those within the health sector with a degree of suspicion, and were perceived as acting secretively and in partnership with the World Bank in competition with other agencies and the public sector.

Concerns are also sometimes expressed about duplication among agencies or between international organizations and governments at the country level. Fryatt (1995) describes the donation of the antituberculosis drug rifampicin from the Japanese government to the Nepalese tuberculosis control program for 3 to 4 years. This generous offer raised a number of questions for managers of programs: about supply difficulties because of the resulting dependence on a single source; about prescribing that was linked to drug availability instead of best prescribing practice; and about sustainability—what would happen after 4 years, when the donor withdrew? Kanji and associates (1992) describe the establishment of a vertical program of essential drugs in Tanzania, where the donors established a drug distribution system parallel to that of the MOH; the system was ultimately not sustainable. Mayhew and colleagues (2005), although observing that the options for alternative delivery systems are limited in countries where donors do not trust the public sector, suggest that a World Bank facility in Kenya designed to ensure the delivery of drugs to PHC facilities specifically for the treatment of sexually transmitted diseases may undermine the MOH system in the longer run.

Poor Coordination

Poor coordination between organizations in health has been a problem long recognized at both the international and country levels. The linkages that exist at the UN, such as the Administrative Committee on Coordination, chaired by the secretary-general, are acknowledged to be very weak. The specialized agencies, funds, and financial institutions act as independent authorities, and although the United Nations Development Program is officially the agency that coordinates UN development aid at the country level, many of the UN agencies tend to act on their own. Coordination through committees, such as the Joint Committee on Health Policy between UNICEF and WHO, for example, has likewise been useful in some instances, but the committees are not generally held in high regard. This does not mean that collaboration between agencies does not occur, both formally and informally. At a global level, it seems to have been most effective when a particular set of agencies (which may include multilateral, bilateral, and private-sector organizations) agreed to work together to achieve a particular goal, as in the case of the Onchocerciasis

Control Program, the Task Force on Child Survival, and the Global Polio Eradication Initiative, among others. The agencies supporting these different partnerships shared a common goal, developed clear objectives, and agreed on complementary roles and responsibilities and the means to assess achievements. These characteristics may be all-important in ensuring their success. Not all of these attempts to improve coordination have been equally effective; an evaluation of the Global Alliance for the Elimination of Leprosy found that partners were concerned that WHO, in its role as Secretariat, was unwilling to relinquish control to other partners (Skolnik et al., 2003).

Poor formal coordination mechanisms may be counterbalanced by informal collaboration through policy communities and networks, although this type of collaboration is difficult to quantify. The professionals who work in international organizations receive postgraduate training in a handful of universities, spend time working in several international organizations, and share professional and technical interests. This network is probably most tangible on the eastern seaboard of the United States, where different nationalities tread well-worn paths between the health, nutrition, and population sectors of the World Bank, UNICEF, USAID, and Johns Hopkins and Harvard Universities, flying to and from WHO in Geneva, and linking up with specific European institutions such as the London School of Hygiene and Tropical Medicine, the Swiss Tropical Institute, the EU, or European bilateral agencies. However, such informal collaborations are also prone to competition between nationalities and institutions, and for funding. One such network, on health care financing reform, has been well documented and described by Lee and Goodman (2002).

At the country level, assistance to the health sector may come from many different donors, and, although the coordination of these donors is agreed by all to be the responsibility of the government, many studies attest to the difficulties governments—in this instance, MOHs—have in coordinating this sometimes "unruly melange" (Buse & Walt, 1997, p. 449). In the late 1990s, many donors at the country level began to promote the idea of a sectorwide approach (SWAp) (Exhibit 14-14) as an instrument through which donors and governments agree on the broad health policy base for the management of domestic and external resources. SWAps have been perceived as the answer to competition and duplication, as well as offering a more effective way of managing resources (Peters & Chao, 1998). Although there was considerable support for the approach, observers noted a number of obstacles to

SWAps achieving their objectives (Cassels, 1997; Walt et al., 1999), among which are weak institutional capacity to coordinate and manage, and continuing competition among donors. Since 2000, increasing numbers of donors have appeared to be favoring a shift toward general budget support (allowing recipient governments to decide their own priorities), which would lessen the need for SWAps.

The growth of global initiatives such as the Global Fund for AIDS, Tuberculosis, and Malaria has further complicated national coordination efforts. Many countries, such as Uganda, now host over 20 global health initiatives. One study (Brugha et al., 2004) suggested that a pervasive impression in Mozambique, Tanzania, Uganda, and Zambia, all countries that had successfully bid for Global Fund resources, was that "their governments and their partners were being overstretched. The Global Fund was just one of several new initiatives that these countries were hosting, which were superimposed on pre-existing funding and partnership processes." A senior government official observed, "The whole thing is a huge juggling act." Another survey of donor practices in 11 recipient countries ranked the five highest burdens for countries as follows: donor-driven priorities and systems, difficulties with donor procedures, uncoordinated donor practices, excessive demands on time, and delays in disbursements (OECD, 2003).

There are many reasons for the problems faced in coordination both among and between governments and donors, including different interests, agendas, and cultures between the different actors; asymmetric power relations; and unique country contexts in which institutional capacities and characteristics play a major role (Walt et al., 1999). Such barriers will continue to affect relationships in the shift from representation to participation, and may require new tools, procedures, and incentives to support partnership processes.

Governance

Concerns about governance arose during the 1980s, when aid was linked with "good governance," human rights, and multiparty democracy. The World Bank initially was concerned with governments that lacked accountability, transparency, and predictability, and countries where the rule of law was weak or absent. However, as Nelson and Eglinton (quoted in Killick, 1998) observe, these concerns led to broader issues:

> Transparency required not only open competition for public contracts, but adequate information on government projects and programs,

Exhibit 14-14	What Is a SWAp?

Sector-wide approaches (SWAps), in the form of program aid, were promoted by the World Bank beginning in the late 1980s, although it was only in the mid-1990s that they were more generally supported by bilateral agencies and some recipient governments. Derived from sector investment programs or sector expenditure programs, SWAps are instruments through which to deliver agreed-on health policies and to manage aid and domestic resources in a rational and optimal way.

What makes SWAps attractive is that they are perceived as being able to strengthen governments' ability to oversee the entire health sector, develop policies and plans, and allocate and manage resources. They are seen in many ways. Although they are primarily a financing or organizational mechanism, because they have been introduced where health system reforms are being developed, many see SWAps as facilitating reforms. For example, some envisage a different and expanded role for ministries of health, in which policy makers will look beyond the public sector to explore the potential role of other stakeholders—whether service deliverers in the private sector or financiers. Peters and Chao (1998) give the example of Ghana, where performance contracts have been developed between mission providers and government and where, like Zambia, public providers are being moved from employment through the civil service to another public agency, with different terms and conditions of employment.

SWAps entail a number of additional implications. For one, they propose that donors will "give up the selection of which projects to finance in exchange for a voice in the process of developing sector policy and allocating resources" (Peters & Chao, 1998, p. 188). Thus, SWAps are seen as being organized around a negotiated program of work, and will only succeed if there is sufficient commitment to shared goals on the part of government and key players in the donor community. Reaching agreement on such goals may be extremely difficult, given the range of motivations driving the different organizations involved in negotiation. Most crucially, they are predicated upon national leadership and ownership, which requires that donors provide recipient authorities with the space and time to think, experiment, fail, and try again, and that recipients are able and willing to assume this risky challenge (Cassels, 1997). In practice, SWAPs have been limited to a few countries and have not been supported by all donors. By the early 2000s, donors were increasingly turning toward a system of budget support, whereby external assistance goes to the government (ministry of finance or the treasury) rather than the health sector (ministry of health), strengthening national ownership by linking aid more closely to local priorities and to parliamentary processes, local commitment, and accountability. Although donors are increasingly giving some budget support to low-income countries (e.g., in 2004, Sweden announced a grant of about US$8 million in budget support to help Nicaragua reduce poverty), not all are convinced of the merits of flexible budget support, and argue that such financing gives inadequate reassurance against funds being misused. What is clear is that traditional ways of providing donor assistance to low-income countries are changing.

Source: G. Walt, E. Pavignani, L. Gilson, and K. Buse, "Managing External Resources: Are There Lessons for SWAps?" 1999, *Health Policy and Planning, 14*(3), pp. 273–284. Copyright 1999 by Oxford University Press, Inc. Reprinted with permission from Oxford University Press, Inc.

and therefore the freedom of the media. Accountability entails not only effective financial accounting and auditing, but penalties for corrupt or inept politicians. That in turn implies some form of elections and freedom of association and speech to make such elections meaningful. A predictable rule of law requires an independent and competent judiciary. (p. 95)

Although notions of governance have been applied largely to government, they are also applicable to global institutions and corporations. Are international organizations characterized by good governance? International organizations differ, but they are all accountable to their member states or governing bodies, which have clear mechanisms for challenging activities. Although budgets and expenditures are not always described as transparent, they are subject to annual audits and are accessible for perusal.

There are clear rules governing the recruitment, selection, and behavior of those employed as international civil servants. In organizations such as WHO, representation of different interests is ensured through the WHA—although in practice, the organization may be dominated by a smaller group of powerful members. Through their ability to draw on worldwide policy communities to provide guidance on issues and reach consensus on policies and best practices, international organizations are vested with significant authority and legitimacy. Although the highest standards are not equally adhered to in all international agencies (UNESCO, for example, was criticized for nepotism, inefficiency, and corruption in the 1980s and again in 1999), the agencies are expected to be publicly accountable.

What is not clear is how the growth in partnerships and alliances at the global level will meet the criteria of good governance, such as transparency and accountability. For example, partnerships have tended to form between powerful UN agencies, large companies, and bilateral organizations, with little representation from low- or middle-income country governments, NGOs, or business groups (Buse, 2004). Not only is representation of recipients or beneficiaries of partnership programs poor, but one review of four large drug donation programs observed that "consultation with recipient countries is often overlooked" (Kale, 1999). A major question for public-private partnerships will, therefore, be in the realm of "representativeness" and accountability. If partnerships are responsible to a myriad of constituencies (shareholders, governing boards, governments, beneficiaries, and consumers), will overall accountability fall between the cracks? Representation is also an issue for national-level mechanisms such as the Country Coordinating Mechanisms (CCMs) established by the Global Fund to Fight AIDS, Tuberculosis, and Malaria. NGOs on such bodies represent themselves and not their constituencies, with whom they have no, or very limited, communication. In 2004, the newsletter of the Global Fund to Fight AIDS, Tuberculosis, and Malaria (available from www.aidspan.org/gfo/archives/newsletter) reported a study suggesting that in only 3 of 13 countries were NGO representatives of people living with HIV/AIDS clearly elected by their communities—in the other countries, they were simply appointed. Further, those representatives often found that "merely having a seat at the table didn't always count for much." On 6 of the 13 CCMs featured, they experienced open bias or paternalism, or had their views discounted (see Exhibit 14-3).

Achieving the governance goal of transparency may also raise difficulties. Differences in public and private ethos may create tensions or conflicts of interest for those involved. For example, sharing information may be difficult: Private industry or research groups may want to protect product leads or early data from trials. There may be debates on risks, such as those involved in public-to-private subsidies (should development agencies be using public money to subsidize the research process of multinational pharmaceutical firms?), or on setting norms and standards (will multinational corporations always set standards at very high levels so that local production of drugs, for example, becomes prohibitive for all but the richest countries?), or on agreement between prices and profitability. In Muraskin's (1995) history of the production of the hepatitis B vaccine, some of these issues are apparent. In one of his examples, he demonstrates the conflict between the public health ethos of Albert Prince and the profit motives of Western pharmaceutical companies. Prince, whose development of a hepatitis B vaccine in the New York Blood Center led to the eventual production of an inexpensive hepatitis B vaccine by a Korean company, suffered subsequent attacks and innuendos from the pharmaceutical companies impugning his motivations, and he ultimately renounced his royalty rights as developer of the vaccine (Exhibit 14-15).

Increasingly, those involved in global health policies are expressing concern about governance issues, and, as partnerships grow, such concerns may take precedence over other issues. Increasingly, good governance criteria are applied not only to governments and international organizations, but also to corporations and NGOs. The OECD has recently promoted a code of practice to raise the standards of private corporations around the world. Key areas include disclosure and transparency, rights and equitable treatment of shareholders, and responsibilities of corporate boards. In a pilot study conducted in 2003, One World Trust, a UK NGO, compared the accountability of a sample of 18 international governmental organizations (IGOs), transnational corporations (TNCs), and international NGOs (Kovach, Neligan, & Burall, 2003). It concluded that international organizations, such as the World Bank, perform worse than international NGOs when it comes to domination by a minority of members—a problem found in the TNCs as well. In contrast, in terms of transparency, the IGOs and TNCs provided more and better information to members. Although the sample was small, this exercise reveals an increasing interest and concern to improve governance within the context of horizontal organizational forms.

Conclusion

The profile of international cooperation in health has changed considerably since the UN was established in the late 1940s to bring peace and security to a world recovering from war. Years of economic growth and relative security (with important exceptions in parts of the world) facilitated a growth in overseas development assistance, and considerable consensus in health cooperation. Since the 1980s, economic growth has faltered, international insecurity has grown, and official development aid has fallen. The pace of globalization trends has changed perceptions and relationships among countries. As these changes have taken place, health cooperation has shifted from systems of formal, vertical representation to forms of

---

Exhibit 14-15   **Vaccines for Developing World Production**

During the 1970s, while the pharmaceutical companies were busy on their hepatitis projects, Albert Prince worked on his own version of the vaccine. His original motivation came directly from his long-standing desire to prevent the disease. However, his research and that of others soon made it clear that hepatitis was more severe and destructive in the Third World than in the West. To fight hepatitis successfully, someone had to develop a technologically simple and cheap vaccine that could be directly transferred to the nations most severely affected. He knew that the drug companies working on the vaccine (e.g., Merck, Sharp & Dohme; Pasteur Vaccins) were using large and costly centrifuges, which made the process prohibitively expensive. The countries of Asia and Africa would not be able to afford such a costly technology. Though Prince worked with both French and German pharmaceutical companies on his project, his goal was the transfer of the new technology from those firms to Third World countries. Prince was committed to a basic egalitarianism that took for granted that Asians and Africans could and should acquire the skills necessary to produce the medical products they consumed. (Muraskin, 1995, p. 20)

Muraskin goes on to describe how Prince's desire to develop his own vaccine became urgent when the Merck hepatitis B vaccine was licensed in the early 1980s at a cost of more than $30 a dose (with three doses required). Prince felt the price was inflated far above what even an expensive technology demanded. Knowing that hepatitis B was a major disease problem in Korea and that the country was already producing some pharmaceuticals and had the potential, and wish, to expand its biotechnology and pharmaceutical production, Prince began a prolonged process of negotiation. With a Korean American professor of genetics in New York, a nonprofit group that provided scientific assistance to the government and academic institutions of Korea, and a Korean company, he and others encouraged the production of a hepatitis B vaccine in Korea, which would some years later be sold at $1 or less a dose. This process was at times unpleasant—for example, when Western pharmaceutical companies attacked Prince for being too closely identified with the Korean company producing the vaccine, impugning his interests in the company. Prince, whose motivation was never one of personal financial gain, renounced his royalty rights as developer of the vaccine.

---

horizontal partnership. The consequences of this transition are not clear, but will serve to focus interest and research in the new millennium. Three concluding points can be made.

First, increasing globalization will lead to different emphases in activities in health. International health cooperation is likely to focus more on issues of governance and regulation at the global level, whether it is on environmental issues, which indirectly affect health, or on transborder trade of health interventions and services, pharmaceuticals, and tobacco products. However, much of the action relating to regulation and governance will center around the WTO rather than the WHO. Juxtaposed against this global-level activity, there is likely to be a continuation, or even growth, in international relief efforts at local levels if internal, ethnic, and secessionist conflicts continue as they have since the end of the Cold War.

Second, it is likely that public-private partnerships and alliances will be an increasing characteristic of cooperation in international health at the global, national, and local levels. There is much yet to be learned about which sorts of partnerships work best, and under what conditions. And although there are clear advantages to this type of cooperation, from the input of new ideas and energy to the harnessing of new financial resources, it is as yet unclear what sorts of problems will be generated through such partnerships. For example, it appears that international

health cooperation is focusing on narrow programs of disease control, which lend themselves to monitoring but neglect other important issues in health, such as developing good-quality and accessible health systems, in which outcomes and impact are more difficult to measure. Partnerships may also raise issues of equity, by choosing to work in some countries with a particular disease rather than all countries. And if aid selectivity becomes a trend, so that aid is given only to those governments that demonstrate they have strong policy environments, what will happen to the people who live in countries considered to have weak policy environments?

Third, cooperation in health will no longer be dominated by the UN or its specialized agencies such as WHO, but will be represented by a much more diverse set of actors. Aside from the private sector, there will be more activity among a range of NGOs, including consumer and professional groups, as well as large and small environmental groups and other CSOs. The revolution in communications technology, which has made it so much easier to communicate electronically across borders, will allow a relatively fluid formation of informal networks and partnerships that may come together to campaign or demonstrate on specific issues.

For all these reasons, horizontal participation is likely to be the key feature of international health cooperation in the new millennium, and although the state will still play a role, it will not be through formal vertical representation as it was in the 20th century.

● ● ● Discussion Questions

1. List the most important actors in international health, differentiating between international organizations, bilateral organizations, NGOs, and public-private partnerships. For each organization, characterize its strengths in terms of financial resources or technical skills. What other factors make organizations influential?

2. Give three reasons why states may cooperate, and the sorts of activities they might undertake together.

3. WHO used to dominate international health policy. Why has its position changed?

4. What are the factors that have led to the shift from vertical to horizontal representation?

5. Name three concerns about increasing public-private partnerships in health.

● ● ● **References**

Abbasi, K. (1999). The World Bank on world health: Under fire. *British Medical Journal, 318,* 1003–1006.

AIDS campaign signals new WHO priorities and approach. (2003). *Lancet, 362,* 1900.

Aylward, B. A., Acharya, A., England, S., Agocs, M., Linkins, J. (2003). Global health goals: Lessons from the worldwide effort to eradicate poliomy-elitis. *Lancet, 362,* 909–914.

Basch, P. (1999). *Textbook of international health* (2nd ed.). Oxford, England: Oxford University Press.

Brooks, A., Cutts, F., Justice, J., & Walt, G. (1999). *Policy study of factors influencing the adoption of new and underutilized vaccines in developing countries.* Unpublished study for Children's Vaccine Initiative, USAID: Geneva, Switzerland, and Washington, DC.

Brugha, R., Donoghue, M., Starling, M., Ndubani, P., Ssengoba, F., Fernandes, B., & Walt, G. (2004). The Global Fund: Managing great expectations. *Lancet, 364,* 95–100.

Buse, K. (2004). Governing public-private infectious disease partnerships. *Brown Journal of World Affairs, 10*(2), 225–242.

Buse, K., & Harmer, A. (2004). Power to the partners? The politics of public-private health partnerships. *Development, 47*(2): 43–48.

Buse, K., & Walt, G. (1997). An unruly melange? Coordinating external resources to the health sector: A review. *Social Science and Medicine, 45,* 449–463.

Buse, K., & Walt, G. (2002). Globalisation and multilateral public-private health partnerships: Issues for health policy. In K. Lee, K. Buse, and S. Fustukian, (Eds.), *Health policy in a globalising world.* Cambridge, England: Cambridge University Press.

Cassels, A. (1997). *A guide to sector-wide approaches to health development: Concepts, issues and working arrangements.* Geneva, Switzerland: World Health Organization.

Childers, E., & Urquhart, B. (1994). *Renewing the United Nations system.* Uppsala, Sweden: Dag Hammarskjold Foundation.

Coker, R. (1999). Public health, civil liberties and tuberculosis. *British Medical Journal, 318,* 1434–1435.

Colatrella, B. D. (1998). Corporate donations. *Annals of Tropical Medicine and Parasitology, 92*(Suppl.), 153–154.

Collin, J. (2004). Tobacco politics. *Development, 47,* 91–96.

Dayrit, E. (1998, April). *Current realities and practices in vaccine introduction and use in the Philippines.* Paper presented to First Asian-Pacific Regional Consultation on Economic and Policy Considerations for the Introduction and Use of New Vaccines, Chiangmai, Thailand.

Elliott, L. (1999, June 21). Bank woos AIDS drug firm. *The Guardian,* p. 21.

Fassin, D., & Schneider, H. (2003). The politics of AIDS in South Africa: Beyond the controversies. *British Medical Journal, 326,* 495–497.

Feldbaum, H., Patel, P., Sondorp, E., & Lee, K. (2004). *Global health and national security: The need for critical engagement.* Unpublished manuscript, Centre on Global Change and Health, London School of Hygiene and Tropical Medicine.

Foege, W. (1998). 10 years of Mectizan. *Annals of Tropical Medicine and Parasitology, 92*(Suppl.), S7–S10.

Ford, N., Wilson, D., Bunjumnong, O., & Van Schoen Angerer, T. (2004). The role of civil society in protecting public health over commercial interests: Lessons from Thailand. *Lancet, 363,* 560–563.

Frost, L., & Reich, M. (1998). *Mectizan donation program: Origins, experiences and relationships with coordinating bodies for onchocerciasis control.* Unpublished report, Harvard School of Public Health, Boston, MA.

Fryatt, B. (1995). Foreign aid and TB control policy in Nepal [Editorial]. *Lancet, 346,* 328.

Gilmore, A., & Collin, J. (2002). The world's first international tobacco control treaty. *British Medical Journal, 325,* 846–847.

Glassman, A., Reich, M., Laserson, K., & Rojas, F. (1999). Applying political analysis to understand health reform: The case of the Dominican Republic. *Health Policy and Planning, 14,* 115–126.

Global Forum for Health Research. (2004). *The 10/90 report on health research, 2003–2004.* Geneva: Global Forum for Health Research.

Godlee, F. (1994). The World Health Organisation. *British Medical Journal, 309,* 1424–1428, 1491–1495, 1566–1570, 1636–1639.

Godlee, F. (1995). The World Health Organisation. *British Medical Journal, 310,* 110–112, 178–182, 389–393, 583–586.

Greenough, P. (1995). Intimidation, coercion and resistance in the final stages of the South Asian smallpox eradication campaign, 1973–1975. *Social Science and Medicine, 41,* 633–645.

Haas, P. M. (1992). Introduction: Epistemic communities and international policy coordination. *International Organization, 46,* 1–35.

Homedes, N., Paz, C., Selva-Sutter, E., Solas, O., & Ugalde, A. (2000). Health reform: Theory and practice. In P. Lloyd Sherlock (Ed.), *Healthcare reform and poverty in Latin America.* London: Institute of Latin American Studies.

Hope for South Africa—at last [Editorial]. (2003). *Lancet, 362,* 501.

Howson, C., Fineberg, H., & Bloom, B. (1998). The pursuit of global health: The relevance of engagement for developed countries. *Lancet, 351,* 586–590.

Kale, O. (1999, October). *Review of disease-specific corporate drug donation programs for the control of communicable diseases.* Paper presented at the Médecins Sans Frontières Foundation–WHO–Rockefeller Foundation meeting, Drugs for Communicable Diseases, Paris, France.

Kanji, N., Hardon, A., Harnmeijer, J. W., Mamdani, M., & Walt, G. (1992). *Drugs policy in developing countries.* London: Zed Books.

Kapp, C. (2004). Nigerian states again boycott polio-vaccination drive. *Lancet, 363,* 709.

Kickbusch, I., & Quick, J. (1998). Partnerships for health in the 21st century. *World Health Statistical Quarterly, 51,* 68–74.

Killick, T., Gunatillaka, R., & Marr, A. (1998). *Aid and the political economy of policy change.* London and New York: Routledge.

Koivusalo, M., & Ollila, E. (1997). *Making a healthy world: Agencies, actors, and policies in international health.* London: Zed Books.

Kovach, H., Neligan, C., & Burall, S. (2003). *Power without accountability? The global accountability report 1.* London: One World Trust.

Lederberg, J., Shope, R., & Oaks, S. (1992). *Emerging infections.* Washington, DC: Institute of Medicine, National Academy Press.

Lee, K. (1998). *Historical dictionary of the World Health Organization.* Lanham, MD: Scarecrow Press.

Lee, K., Buse, K., & Fustukian, S. (Eds.). (2002). *Health policy in a globalising world.* Cambridge, England: Cambridge University Press.

Lee, K., Collinson, S., Walt, G., & Gilson, L. (1996). Who should be doing what in international health: A confusion of mandates in the United Nations? *British Medical Journal, 312,* 302–307.

Lee, K., & Goodman, H. (2002). Global policy networks: The propagation of health care financing reform since the 1980s. In K. Lee, K. Buse, & S. Fustukian, (Eds.). (2002). *Health policy in a globalising world* (pp. 97–119). Cambridge, England: Cambridge University Press.

Lee, K., Walt, G., & Haines, A. (2004). The challenge to improve global health: Financing the Millennium Development Goals. *Journal of the American Medical Association, 291,* 2636–2638.

Lucas, A., Mogedal, S., Walt, G., Hodne-Steen, S., Kruse, S. E., Lee, K., & Hawken, L. (1997). *Cooperation for development: The World Health Organization's support to programs at country level* (Report for the governments of Australia, Canada, Italy, Norway, Sweden, and UK). London: London School of Hygiene and Tropical Medicine.

Mahler, H. (1983, May 3). *The full measure of the strategy for health for all.* Address to the World Health Assembly.

Mayhew, S., Walt, G., Lush, L., & Cleland, J. (2005). Donor involvement in reproductive health: Saying one thing and doing another? *International Journal of Health Services, 35*(3), 579–601.

Michaud, C., & Murray, C. (1994). External assistance to the health sector in developing countries: A detailed analysis 1972–1990. *Bulletin of the World Health Organization, 72,* 161–180.

Muraskin, W. (1995). *The war against hepatitis B.* Philadelphia: University of Pennsylvania Press.

Muraskin, W. (1998). *The politics of international health: The Children's Vaccine Initiative and the struggle to develop vaccines for the third world.* Albany, NY: State University of New York Press.

Organization for Economic Cooperation and Development. (2003). *Harmonizing donor practices for effective aid delivery.* DAC Guidelines and Reference Series. Paris: Organization for Economic Cooperation and Development.

Parkhurst, J. (2001). The crisis of AIDS in Uganda. *International Relations, 15*(6), 69–87.

Peters, C., & Chao, S. (1998). The sector-wide approach in health: What is it? Where is it leading? *International Journal of Health Planning and Management, 13,* 177–190.

Pollock, A. M., & Price, D. (2003). The public health implications of world trade negotiations on the general agreement on trade in services and public services. *Lancet, 363,* 1072–1075.

Pratley, N. (2004, April 10). Sisters who stirred the conscience of Coca-Cola. *The Guardian,* p. 26.

Putnam, R., Leonari, R., & Nanetti, R. (1995). *Making democracy work.* Princeton, NJ: Princeton University Press.

Rifkin, S., & Walt, G. (1986). Why health improves: Defining the issues concerning comprehensive primary health care and selective primary health care. *Social Science and Medicine, 23,* 559–566.

Roscam Abbing, H. (1979). *International organizations in Europe and the right to health care.* Amsterdam: Kluwer-Deventer.

Sassen, S. (1996). *Losing control? Sovereignty in an age of globalization.* New York: Columbia University Press.

Schneider, H. (2002). On the fault-line: The politics of AIDS policy in contemporary South Africa. *African Studies, 61*(1), 145–197.

Skolnik, R., Agueh, F., Justice, J., & Lechat, M. (2003). *Independent evaluation of the Global Alliance for the Elimination of Leprosy.* Geneva, Switzerland: World Health Organization.

Taylor, P. (1993). *International organisation in the modern world.* London: Pinter Publishers.

Unger, J. P., & Killingsworth, J. R. (1986). Selective primary health care: A critical review of methods and results. *Social Science and Medicine, 22,* 1001–1013.

Vaughan, J. P., Mogedal, S., Walt, G., Kruse, S. E., Lee, K., & de Wilde, K. (1996). WHO and the effects of extrabudgetary funds: Is the organization donor driven? *Health Policy and Planning, 11,* 253–264.

Walsh, J., & Warren, K. (1979). Selective primary health care: An interim strategy for disease control in developing countries. *New England Journal of Medicine, 301,* 967–974.

Walt, G., & Gilson, L. (1994). Reforming the health sector in developing countries: The central role of policy analysis. *Health Policy and Planning, 4,* 353–370.

Walt, G., Pavignani, E., Gilson, L., & Buse, K. (1999). Managing external resources: Are there lessons for SWAps? *Health Policy and Planning, 14*(3), 273–284.

Wapner, P. (1995). Environmental activism and world civic politics. *World Politics, 47,* 311–340.

World Bank. (1997). *World development report: The state in a changing world*. Oxford, England: Oxford University Press.

World Bank. (2003). *World development indicators 2003*. Washington, DC: World Bank.

World Health Organization. (2004). *Financial report and audited financial statements presented to 57th World Health Assembly April 2004*. Unpublished document A 57/20, World Health Organization, Geneva, Switzerland.

Zarrilli, S., & Kinnon, C. (1998). *International trade in health services*. Geneva, Switzerland: UNCTAD/WHO.

15

Globalization and Health

KELLEY LEE AND DEREK YACH

Widespread consensus now exists that fundamental changes to human societies around the world are presently under way, broadly referred to as *globalization*. Although historically rooted in how all societies have formed and adapted over millennia, there is a sense that the changes of recent decades are more intense and accelerated. The resulting impacts of globalization potentially affect every individual and community.

The changes arising from globalization extend to the field of public health in three main ways. First, processes of global change are shaping the broad determinants of health. As well as individual lifestyle factors, globalization is influencing such factors as employment, housing, education, water and sanitation, and agriculture and food production. Moreover, general socioeconomic, cultural, and environmental conditions are undergoing change (Dahlgren & Whitehead, 1991). Overall, globalization is restructuring human societies in a diverse range of ways, and hence potentially influencing a broad range of factors that have an impact on individual and population health.

Second, there is growing evidence that health status and outcomes are being influenced by globalization, with different impacts on specific individuals and populations. Many argue that globalization is giving rise to new patterns of health and disease linked to the global restructuring of human societies. This includes the spread of new and emerging diseases, but more profoundly, a reconfiguration of existing health challenges, including health inequalities within and across countries. In short, there are winners and losers in contemporary forms of globalization, and health outcomes are one reflection of this.

Third, as a consequence of the above, societies must adapt their collective responses to changing health determinants and outcomes. Within the broader context of global governance, and specifically global governance for health (see Chapter 14), globalization is influencing health care financing and service provision in a diverse range of countries, and the way in which many products and services that affect health are regulated and marketed. Over the past two decades, there has been a flurry of health sector reforms, with the reforms themselves part of the globalization process as policy ideas have flowed across the world.

This chapter provides an overview of how globalization is affecting health determinants, health status and outcomes, and health care financing and service provision. These impacts can be collectively understood as the transition from *international* to *global* public health. The chapter begins by defining the often-used term *globalization*, which has become so familiar yet is so loosely applied. What precise changes are taking place? What is new and distinct about globalization? What are the key drivers? This is followed by a discussion of the links between globalization and shifting patterns of infectious and chronic diseases. Finally, the impacts on health care financing and service provision begin to be explored through an examination of the migration of health workers, the restructuring of the pharmaceutical industry, and the global spread of health sector reforms. The chapter concludes with potential ways the public health community can promote and protect health in an era of globalization.

What Is Globalization?

Globalization has undoubtedly caught the imagination of many, judging by the enthusiasm with which the term is so frequently used by scholars, policy makers, the business community, mass media, and the general public. Intuitively, the term articulates how the contemporary world is becoming more interdependent, with events in one part of the world having an impact elsewhere. However, if we are to understand the implications of globalization for public health, a more precise understanding of what it means is needed.

It is beyond the scope of this chapter to review the expansive literature on globalization. Moreover, the term remains highly contested, with ongoing debates about whether globalization is really happening or not, what its key drivers are, and perhaps most controversially, whether it is having positive or negative impacts on human societies and the natural world. Beyond the rough and tumble of these debates, it is still possible to define globalization in more precise terms.

First, to assess whether a distinct phenomenon that can be called globalization is really happening or not, it is important to understand more recent developments in their historical context. Although many writers on globalization focus on changes taking place beginning in the late 20th century, it is helpful to see globalization as a longer process of social change over centuries, if not millennia. The early beginnings of globalization might be described as occurring when human beings migrated across continents (as they have done since *Homo erectus* migrated out of Africa 1 million years ago), formed societies, and then interacted with each other across distant territories. This process accelerated and intensified with the development of long-distance modes of transportation (such as ships) that enabled individuals to travel further and in greater numbers. Major developments in social, political, and economic history marked the acceleration of globalization, notably the opening of the Silk Route between Asia and Europe, the arrival of Christopher Columbus in the Americas, the formation of the modern states system, European imperialism, the slave trade, and the Industrial Revolution. Characterizing all of these developments were an increased movement of people (voluntary or otherwise) and other life forms (plants and animals), capital, goods and services, and knowledge and ideas. Thus, what many today refer to as globalization is the contemporary manifestation of the further coming together of human societies across territorial space, albeit to an intensified degree.

Changing patterns of health and disease have been integrally linked to the historical evolution of human societies, including the process of globalization. Perhaps the most familiar example is the bubonic plague pandemic of the 14th century, which killed millions in its path. Spread by travelers along trade routes between Asia and Europe, the Black Death eventually led to the introduction of quarantine practices in 1377, which impeded trade in order to prevent the further importation of the disease. Similarly, the transition of cholera from an endemic disease of South Asia to a pandemic disease from the 1830s onward was caused in large part by the social, political, and economic upheavals inflicted on local communities, economies, and ecosystems by European imperialism (Lee & Dodgson, 2002). The resulting cholera pandemics of the 19th century led to the development of the International Sanitary Conventions, which, in time, became the International Health Regulations.

Yet although globalization can be understood, in the sense just described, as a historical process evolving with human societies, it is still necessary to identify what is distinct about the term *globalization* per se. How is globalization different from *internationalization, liberalization, universalization,* and *Westernization,* terms that are so often used interchangeably? What is "global" about globalization? The work of Scholte (2000) is helpful in this respect. He considers these "redundant concepts of globalization," which he defines in the following way:

- *Internationalization:* The most common usage of the term *globalization* is in reference to the increasing interaction and interdependence of people in different countries. Various measures, such as trade, communication, and migration, certainly confirm that there has been a substantial rise in cross-border exchanges. However, historically there have been many periods of intensified interconnections since the establishment of the modern system of sovereign states some 500 years ago that still defines international relations today. Because these interactions refer to exchanges between nations, or "inter national," the term *internationalization* is an accurate description.

- *Liberalization:* This is a term used especially by advocates of neoliberal ideas, and their critics, whereby a global world is defined as "one without regulatory barriers to transfers of resources between countries." Historically, we can identify periods where statutory constraints on cross-border movements of capital, goods, and services have been reduced. For example, the second half of the 19th century saw a significant expansion of international trade and commerce as a result of widespread liberalization. The rounds of negotiations under the General Agreement on Tariffs and Trade (GATT), now replaced by the World Trade Organization (WTO), from the end of World War II to 1995 also led to successive reductions in trade tariffs. The continuation of this process since the mid-1990s, under multilateral, regional, and bilateral trade agreements, has often been referred to as globalization. However, Scholte (2000, p. 45) argues convincingly that, in this sense, the term *liberalization* is appropriate and there is "little need now to invent a new vocabulary for this old phenomenon." Distinguishing globalization from liberalization addresses criticisms that the former is nothing new.

- *Universalization:* Universalization generally refers to the spread of people and cultures to all corners of the world. Defined in this way, however, we can see that the human species has traveled intercontinentally for a million years or more. Similarly, several world religions have won followers worldwide, and trade has distributed goods and services on a worldwide scale for centuries. In this sense, the term *universalization* is deemed adequate and the new terminology of globalization unnecessary.

- *Westernization:* The term *Westernization* describes the belief that certain cultural values, aspirations, and behaviors characteristic of Western societies, and particularly American society, are being adopted increasingly throughout the world. In this case, globalization is seen as a largely negative process of homogenization, a postindustrial form of colonization through Hollywood films, fast-food diets, and consumerism. Although it is undoubtedly the case that a certain degree of Westernization is taking place, Scholte (2000, p. 45) argues that "intercontinental westernization, too, has unfolded since long before the recent emergence of globe-talk." He suggests that the concepts of modernization and imperialism readily capture ideas of Westernization and "[w]e do not need a new vocabulary of globalization to remake an old analysis."

Strictly speaking, Scholte casts aside these "redundant" terms, and reserves the term *globalization* to describe social interactions that not only *cross* national boundaries, but also *transcend* them. He writes that it is only when territorial boundaries, based on physical geography, are circumvented or become irrelevant that we can speak of globalization. Satellite communications, the Internet, illicit drug trafficking, and undocumented migration are examples of globalization in this strict sense. Thus, it is important to be aware of how the term *globalization* is defined. A looser definition suggests that at least some aspects of what people call globalization today are not novel to the late 20th century. A strict definition of globalization, as the transcendence of territorial boundaries, is distinctive of the transition facing human societies worldwide in recent decades.

A second important definitional question is why globalization is occurring. What are the key drivers of globalization? McMichael (2001) usefully distinguishes between two types of global change. The first type results from the interplay of natural forces—climatic dynamics, continental drift, evolution, and mass extinctions—that occurred during the history of the planet. For example, there have been five great natural extinctions since the advent of vertebrate life half a billion years ago, the last of which marked the end of the dinosaurs 65 million years ago. This was proceeded by a long period of cooling that eventually opened an evolutionary niche 6 million years ago "for an ape able to survive mostly out of the forest." Over the past million years, there have been eight major glaciations, during which *Homo erectus* began to spread throughout Eurasia. It was only during the final interglacial period that *Homo sapiens* began to disperse out of northeast Africa and migrate worldwide. More recently, the rapid postglaciation temperature rise between 15,000 and 10,000 years ago, of around 5° Celsius, caused substantial environmental changes and the extinction of many species of plants and animals.

The second type of global change is human induced, or *anthropomorphic*. These are changes to the world as a result of human actions, individually or collectively, intentional or otherwise. The classic work on this subject is *The Earth as Transformed by Human Action* by W. C. Clark and colleagues (1990), which focuses on anthropomorphic changes to the Earth and its atmosphere. For example, the bulk of existing scientific evidence shows that global warming of recent decades is the result of human activity such as the burning of fossil fuels and deforestation (United Nations Environment Program, 2001).

For the purposes of this chapter, the term *globalization* refers to human-induced rather than naturally occurring change. Globalization is driven, foremost, by the individual or collective actions of human beings—the formation of larger social groupings (e.g., megacities), the mobility of populations, the spread of production and consumption patterns, the intensified use (and, increasingly, overuse) of natural resources, the development and application of new technologies, the creation and application of new knowledge and ideas, and so on.

Some writers describe globalization as driven foremost by technology. It is assumed that communication and transportation technologies, in particular, are enabling people to travel the world more readily, interact with each other across vast distances, and carry out other forms of transactions in ways that circumvent territorial boundaries. Hence, the advent of undersea cables, satellite communications, and the Internet (the so-called Information Revolution), for instance, allows us to engage more quickly, easily, and cheaply in banking, stock market trading, purchasing, advertising and marketing, and all sorts of information gathering (Hundley et al., 2003). The availability of low-cost airlines, bullet trains, and the automobile allows growing millions to travel farther and more frequently. As Lawrence Summers, former Secretary of the U.S. Department of Treasury stated, "Transportation is the industry that connects other industries . . . it is the key to globalization" (quoted in U.S. Department of Transportation, 2000).

Others argue that the key drivers of globalization are largely economic. Fukuyama (1992), for example, sees the emergence of a global economy as reflecting the ultimate triumph of capitalism over socialism. Liberal capitalism is described as "the final form of human government." Fukuyama believes there can be no viable alternative to capitalism and that we have reached the "end of history" as far as ideological development is concerned. It is this assumed economic logic of globalization that lies behind arguments favoring the unleashing of globalization forces in the form of policies favoring trade liberalization, privatization, deregulation, and foreign direct investment. It is argued that all countries must embrace the inevitable and progressive march of globalization, defined in this way, or be left on the economic sidelines (International Chamber of Commerce, 1997).

Although this chapter accepts that technology and economics are key drivers, it does not follow that globalization is somehow inevitable, singular, and logical in its current forms. As a set of change processes driven by human actions, it is vital to recognize that there are powerful interests tied up with current forms of globalization. Global changes are not taking place spontaneously, but are a reflection of the interests of powerful individuals and groups who stand to benefit from how globalization proceeds. This suggests that not only is globalization within

human capacity to shape and direct, but that if adverse social and environmental consequences resulting from globalization are to be minimized, it is imperative that these change processes be actively managed.

This brings us to the final issue of major debate on globalization—whether the resultant changes are having positive or negative impacts on human societies and the natural world. As described, globalization is having effects on a wide range of social spheres, including the economic, political, cultural, technological, and environmental. These effects are creating both positive and negative impacts. Individually, each of us gains and loses from specific aspects of globalization. The Information Revolution has given us 24-hour access to news, entertainment, and personal messages, but at the expense of our ability to switch off and enjoy down time. The globalization of the food industry has diversified our diets and allowed us to have access to off-season fruits and vegetables. Yet the global spread of more intense farming methods, and the transport of more and more products worldwide, is creating adverse environmental consequences.

It is also important to recognize that the distribution of these gains and losses varies considerably across particular individuals and population groups. For the relatively wealthy, educated, gainfully employed, literate (including computer literate), and mobile, globalization offers exciting opportunities for personal growth and material gain. The high-flying business executive, the dot-com entrepreneur, and the global celebrity are the "beautiful people" of globalization. The availablity of an ever-expanding variety of goods and services, declining prices for many of these products, our ability to receive instantaneous news from all corners of the globe, and the possibility of taking package holidays abroad are attractive benefits from globalization to which growing numbers aspire.

For the relatively disadvantaged, however, in terms of socioeconomic status, education, geography, race, and gender, the net balance between gains and losses from globalization is tipped rather more toward the negative. As well as not sharing equitably in benefits, the losers in globalization shoulder a relatively heavier burden of costs. Low wages, insecure employment, poor housing and sanitation, vulnerability to environmental degradation, and greater difficulties of access to health care and education due to costs or availability of services define the experiences of globalization by the world's poor across all countries. Furthermore, it is not only that the losers under globalization are less able to access opportunities and benefits, but that the very nature of current forms of globalization is stacked in favor of some at the expense of others. A good example is the issue of agricultural subsidies. Rich countries spend more than US$311 billion per year on agricultural subsidies, twice the amount of total farm exports by the developing world. American farmers, for example, receive one-fifth of their income from subsidies. In Europe, the Common Agricultural Policy represented US$51 billion in subsidies in 2003, with around 2,000 large farmers (of 4.5 million European farmers) receiving over US$1 billion of this pot. Such heavy subsidies encourage overproduction and export dumping of key commodities such as sugar, cereals, and dairy products, thus depressing world prices and harming producers in the developing world. In low- and middle-income countries, agriculture represents 9% of the gross domestic product (GDP) and accounts for 50% of employed people. In countries with the highest levels of undernutrition, agriculture contributes 30% of GDP and accounts for 70% of those employed. Reform of agricultural subsidies, accompanied by fairer access to markets in rich countries, would lead to clear economic gains for the poor (Food and Agriculture Organization [FAO], 2003).

Another structural inequity of contemporary globalization is the flow of international aid and finance. Few countries have lived up to the agreed commitment to give 0.7% of their gross national income (GNI) as official development assistance (ODA).[1] After a decade of declining aid levels, aid volume rose by 11% during 2002–2003 following the UN Financing for Development Summit held in Monterrey (Manning, 2004), which elicited widespread support for achieving the Millennnium Development Goals (MDGs) by 2015 (see Chapter 14, Exhibit 14–7). Nonetheless, funding of the MDGs remains woefully inadequate (Lee, Walt, & Haines, 2004). Moreover, the developing world now spends US$13 on debt repayment for every US$1 it receives in grants. The cost of servicing debt substantially exceeds the amount received in ODA (4.8% of GDP for debt servicing versus 0.7% for ODA). Even among the least-developed countries, debt constitutes a significant burden at 2.3% of GDP (United Nations Development Program [UNDP], 2004). As described by President Olusegun Obasanjo of Nigeria, "All that we had borrowed up to 1985 or 1986 was around $5 billion and we have paid about $16 billion yet we are still being told that we owe about $28 billion. That $28 billion came about because of

the injustice in the foreign creditors' interest rates. If you ask me what is the worst thing in the world, I will say it is compound interest" (quoted in Jubilee 2000 Coalition, 2000).

This distribution of wealth not only results in rich and poor countries, but also rich and poor people within countries. It is estimated that 75% of the world's wealth is owned by just 25% of the world's population. In Brazil, the wealthiest one-fifth of the population earns 26 times as much as the poorest one-fifth (UNDP, 1999). In the United States, which has enjoyed faster economic growth than any other large industrialized country, since the 1970s virtually all income gains have been enjoyed by the wealthiest 20% of the population. The difference in household income between the poorest and wealthiest one-fifth of Americans narrowed from 1947 to 1973, but increased by more than 50% between 1973 and 1996 (Burtless, 1998).

In terms of health status, other chapters in this book highlight differences that exist between countries and regions in terms of burden of disease and risk. Table 15-1 provides a summary of some of these differences at a rather crude level. It shows that there was a 26.5-year difference in life expectancy between the least-developed countries and the countries in the Organization for Economic Cooperation and Development (OECD) in 2002. Infant mortality in the least-developed countries was 900% higher than in OECD countries. HIV prevalence was 300% higher in the least-developed countries than in OECD countries.

Alongside these inequalities between countries, there are trends in health inequalities within and across countries. These trends are more difficult to observe because of the aggregated nature of available data. There is some evidence, however, that globalization is creating new patterns of health inequalities that do not conform to nationally defined populations. Many lower-income countries now have upper and middle classes whose living conditions are increasingly similar to those in more affluent countries, alongside large populations who remain deeply impoverished. New patterns of winners and losers, in other words, in terms of the global distribution of health and ill-health across countries are emerging.

- Increased impoverishment among the losers of globalization has been accompanied by increasing world hunger, with an estimated 842 million people going to bed hungry every night. Most people suffering from hunger live in Africa and Latin America, but 34 million can

---

[1]Denmark, Norway, and Sweden have achieved the UN target of 0.7% of GNI. By comparison, the United States gives 0.13%.

Table 15-1	Selected Health and Related Measures				
	Developing Countries				
	All	**LDCs**	**Central and Eastern Europe**	**OECD**	**World**
Populations (billions)	4.96	0.76	0.46	1.1	6.26
Life expectancy at birth (yr)	64.6	50.6	69.5	77.1	66.9
Human Development Index*	0.663	0.446	0.796	0.911	0.729
Infant mortality (%)	61.0	99.0	18.0	11.0	56.0
Adult literacy (%)	76.7	52.5	99.3		
Youth literacy (15–24) (%)	88.1	64.3	99.6		
Measles immunization at 1 year (%)	72.0	62.0	96.0	90.0	75.0
HIV prevalence (15–49) (%)	1.2	3.4	0.6	0.3	1.1
Undernourished (%)	17.0	37.0	10.0		
Internet users (per 1,000)	40.9	2.8	71.8	383.1	99.4
Researchers in research (per million)	384.0		2289.0	3483.0	1096.0

Note: LDCs = least-developed countries; OECD = Organization for Economic Cooperation and Development.

*Human Development Index is a measure developed by the UN Development Program based on three indicators: longevity (as measured by life expectancy at birth), educational attainment (as measured by a combination of adult literacy (2/3 weight) and combined gross primary, secondary and tertiary enrollment ratio (1/3 weight), and standard of living (as measured by real GDP per capita (purchasing power parity US$)).

Source: United Nations Development Program, *Human Development Report 2004* (New York: United Nations Development Program, 2004). Reprinted with permission.

now be found in the former Soviet Union and another 10 million in industrialized countries (FAO, 2003).

- There is a rising incidence of type 2 diabetes mellitus reported in children and adolescents in countries as diverse as the United States, Japan, Hong Kong, Singapore, Bangladesh, and Libya. Until recently, most children with diabetes had type 1 disease. The rise is associated with the increase in childhood obesity, linked, in turn, to the globalization of more sedentary lifestyles and diets containing a high fat, sugar, and salt content.

- The increased concentration of ownership in the tobacco industry, and the spread of the industry globally to so-called emerging markets, is expected to lead to a sharp rise in tobacco-related deaths. Today tobacco kills 4.9 million people. This is expected to rise to 10 million by 2030, 70% of deaths to occur in the developing world.

It is these sorts of global health inequalities that led to the work of the Commission on Macroeconomics and Health, formed in 2000 to undertake studies on "how concrete health interventions can lead to economic growth and reduce inequity in developing countries." Among its tasks was to recommend "a set of measures designed to maximize the poverty reduction and economic benefits of health sector investment" (World Health Organization [WHO], 2000).

Within the context just described, it is important to understand how globalization is affecting the broad determinants of health. As defined by Dahlgren and Whitehead (1991), health can be influenced by a broad range of factors (Figure 15-1). As discussed in this chapter, for example, there is growing evidence that human-induced changes to the world's climate (global warming) are affecting the distribution and epidemiology of diseases such as malaria and dengue. Similarly, the globalizing economy of intensified competition for foreign direct investment is said by some to be leading to declining health and safety standards in the workplace. Liberalized trade in food and drink, as well as tobacco products, may be leading to lifestyle changes that will increase the risk of many chronic diseases. What will be critical for the public health community to understand better, if we are to address the existing health gaps and prevent globalization from widening them further, is how the diverse changes taking place around us are influencing each type of determinant.

In summary, the shift from international to global health can be defined in the following ways:

- Globalization must be understood within a historical context over centuries, with contemporary forms of globalization distinguished by the intensity of cross-border (and in some cases transborder) activities taking place and the geographic extent of their reach.

- A strict definition of globalization focuses on the transcendence of geography, whereas looser definitions often use the term to describe related phenomena such as liberalization, Westernization, and universalization.

- Globalization is affecting a broad range of social spheres.

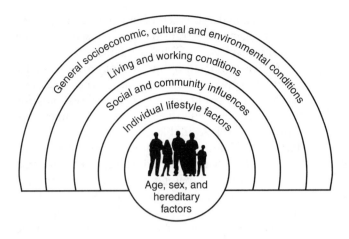

Figure 15-1 The Broad Determinants of Health. *Source:* G. Dahlgren and M. Whitehead, *Policies and Strategies to Promote Social Equity in Health.* (Stockholm, Sweden: Institute for Futures Studies, 1991). Reprinted with permission.

- Globalization is affecting different individuals and population groups in different ways.
- Contemporary forms of globalization appear to be widening inequalities in health for certain individuals and population groups.
- The capacity to address inequalities requires that we understand globalization in relation to the broad determinants of health.

The Global Dimensions of Infectious Disease

The Risks from Infectious Diseases in a Globalizing World

Globalization potentially affects a broad range of biological, environmental, and social factors that influence human infections. Indeed, the implications of globalization on infectious diseases have received considerable attention in recent years. Most importantly, the interaction between human populations and pathogens must be seen in evolutionary terms, within a long history of the development, adaptation, and interaction of human societies. As human societies have formed and interacted with local environments and with other human societies, so too have patterns of infection. Agrarian societies, for instance, where populations live in close proximity to domesticated animals, demonstrate a greater susceptibility to zoonotic infections. Similarly, urbanization, characterized by larger numbers of people living in relatively close proximity, demonstrates greater susceptibility to so-called crowd diseases, including infections spread by close human contact (e.g., plague, influenza). Greater mobility of individuals within and between societies raises the risk of infections spreading further afield.

In this context, we can see how globalization might shape patterns of human settlement and, in turn, the susceptibility of specific populations to certain infections. A good example is the association of meningococcal disease with the centuries-old pilgrimage of Muslims to Mecca (in Saudi Arabia), known as the Haj. Over the past 50 years, the scale of this annual event has grown markedly, with a 100% increase in numbers every decade since 1949. By 2001 almost 2 million people from over 140 countries participated in the event, with 75% of travelers coming from abroad. This growth has been due to the expansion of facilities at the site, greater wealth among potential travelers, and increased accessibility of transportation (88% travel by air). Because the event brings large numbers of people together from widely dispersed communities to interact in close proximity and then to disburse once again, the setting poses an opportunity for the spread of infectious disease. The most well-known health consequence is regular epidemics of meningococcal disease that occur during and after the event. Cases linked to the pilgrimage have been reported in most parts of the world, with secondary epidemics occurring up to 2 years later in destination countries. Universal availability of conjugated quadrivalent meningococcal vaccine is expected to significantly reduce the risk of such outbreaks in the future (Saker et al., 2004).

Although there is growing recognition of the increased risk from infectious diseases posed by globalization, the initial attention by the general public largely focused on frighteningly acute, yet relatively rare, diseases such as Ebola, Marburg, and Lassa fever. Images of masked medics in biohazard suits conjured up primeval fears of plague and pestilence spreading from the developing world through increasingly mobile populations. Since September 11, 2001, the added fear of epidemics being deliberately spread by terrorists wielding biological weapons has intensified public attention to diseases such as anthrax and smallpox.

Another association between global change and infectious disease is the impact of global environmental change (see Chapter 9). The environment consists of not only the natural world but also built and social environments. The natural environment can be modified by local influences, such as weather patterns and physical disasters, as well as global forces, such as changes in the biophysical systems of the world that can alter the world's climate. Environmental changes can either be natural or human induced, and all can play an important role in shaping human health (Saker et al., 2004).

There is a growing body of evidence that links global climate change and the epidemiology of certain infectious diseases, including malaria, yellow fever, and dengue fever. Current concerns about global climate change focus on rising global average land and sea surface temperatures (global warming) and the increasing frequency of extreme weather conditions in many parts of the world. There is now substantial evidence that average temperatures have risen by 0.6°C since the mid-19th century, with most of this change occurring since 1976. Fourteen of the warmest years on record have occurred since 1980. The UN Intergovernmental Panel on Climate Change (IPCC) predicts that average global temperatures will rise by 1.4 to 5.8°C by 2100. Although there remains some controversy over the causes, the IPCC concludes that much of the global warming during the last 50 years can be attributed to human activity (Albritton et al., 2001).

Detecting the influence of observed and predicted changes in global climate on infectious disease transmission is not straightforward. An irrefutable case would require standardized monitoring of exposure (climate), the outcome (incidence of a particular infectious disease), and other determinants of disease (e.g., immunity, treatment, socioeconomic factors) over many years. Such data sets are rare. Nonetheless, best estimates of the likely current and future impacts of climate change come from theoretical consideration of the known effects of climate on disease transmission, and from indirect assessment based on reported effects of climate on infectious diseases in the present or recent past. This tells us that, in general, climate constrains the range of infectious disease, while weather affects the timing and intensity of outbreaks (Dobson & Carper, 1993). Higher ambient air temperatures, along with changes in precipitation and humidity, appear to be affecting the biology and ecology of certain disease vectors and intermediate hosts, the pathogens they transmit, and consequently the risk of transmission (Githeko et al., 2000).

Diseases carried by mosquitoes are especially sensitive to meteorological conditions because these insects have fastidious temperature thresholds for survival and changes in average ambient temperature (Epstein, 2001). Available evidence suggests that in parts of the United States, for example, small outbreaks of locally transmitted malaria have occurred during unseasonably hot weather spells. Malaria is now prevalent in elevated regions where it did not previously exist, such as the rural highlands of Papua New Guinea (Githeko et al., 2000). Climate change may also be a factor contributing to the dramatic advance of dengue fever over the past 30 years, a disease of the tropics transmitted by the *Aedes aegypti* mosquito. In Mexico, higher median temperatures during the rainy season were a strong predictor of dengue prevalence, while in the South Pacific region, outbreaks of dengue from 1970 to 1995 on the fringe of the endemic zone correlated with El Niño events (Hales et al., 2002). Similarly, the first appearance of West Nile virus in the United States (which subsequently spread to Canada and, more recently, southern Europe) is believed to be a consequence of mosquito proliferation following extreme summer drought conditions in the New York area (Githeko et al., 2000).

Although the increased risk from acute and "exotic" diseases, bioterrorism, and climate change are clearly worrying developments, in terms of health impact, they are dwarfed by the challenge posed by the global spread of tuberculosis (TB). *Mycobacterium tuberculosis* has been present in the human population since antiquity, but it was not until 1944 that effective treatments, beginning with streptomycin, were developed. This was followed by the development of a rapid succession of anti-TB drugs, leading public health experts to predict the long-awaited end to this ancient scourge. However, in an age of globalization, we face a very different scenario. Today, one-third of the world's population is infected with TB, causing around 2 million deaths in 2002. The highest number of deaths occurs in Southeast Asia, but the highest mortality per capita is in Africa, where HIV/AIDS has led to rapid increases in the incidence of TB and the likelihood of dying from the disease. Transmission of the disease across borders has increased as a result of population mobility, inadequate health care delivery, and ineffective coordination of control strategies. For example, between 1990 and 1999, TB cases reported in the United States declined from 25,701 to 17,531.

However, the proportion of cases occurring among foreign-born persons rose from 24% to 43%, of which most originated from Mexico and Central America. In 1999, Mexico was the country of origin for 23% of all foreign-born persons with TB in the United States (Centers for Disease Control and Prevention [CDC], 2001). Similarly, along the Thailand-Myanmar border, WHO established a border health program in 2001 for the area's highly mobile population, including migrant workers, refugees, and undocumented migrants.

Of particular concern is the spread of drug-resistant forms of TB, which have arisen from the incorrect or incomplete use of existing regimens (see Chapter 4). Drug-resistant TB is now found in all regions of the world. The prevalence of multidrug-resistant TB (MDR-TB) is especially high in the former Soviet Union, China, Ecuador, and Israel. Russia has the world's highest incidence of MDR-TB, with 13.7% of all TB cases in that country. As Mario Raviglione, director of WHO's Stop TB Department, states, "It is in the interest of every country to support rapid scale-up of TB control if we are to overcome MDR-TB. Passport control will not halt drug resistance; investment in global TB prevention will" (quoted in WHO, 2004a).

Perhaps the most serious infectious disease threat of all, in an era of intensifying globalization, comes from "democratic" infections that are relatively indiscriminate in the populations they can infect. The common cold, for example, is probably the most common illness known. Caused by over 200 different viruses (notably rhinoviruses) and readily transmitted by air and close contact, colds affect adults with an average two to four episodes annually. Fortunately, colds are usually mild and rarely life threatening. The prospect of an infection emerging with the transmissibility of a cold but with more lethal consequences is the public health community's worst-case scenario. It was fears of this scenario that spurred the global response to the SARS outbreak of 2002–2003 (Exhibit 15-1).

Although the number of SARS cases and deaths was eventually less than feared, the experience focused attention on the likely capacity of public health systems to cope with the anticipated pandemic to come with the next major shift in the influenza A virus. Minor changes to the influenza virus (antigenic drift) happen continually over time, which explains its ability to reinfect populations. The change is usually so minimal that the previous year's influenza or vaccine offers some protection. Occasionally (every 10 to 12 years or so), there is an abrupt, major change in the virus (antigenic shift) against which most people have little or no protection. The Spanish influenza pandemic of 1918–1919, for example, killed an estimated 40 million people worldwide. Influenza A viruses are found in many different animals, including ducks, chickens, pigs, whales, horses, and seals. Although it is unusual for people to get influenza infections directly from animals, sporadic human infections and outbreaks caused by certain avian influenza A viruses have been reported.

The danger arising from an antigenic shift in the influenza virus is magnified by globalization. In East Asia, where new strains of influenza more frequently originate, population pressures combined with intense farming methods and close contact with domesticated animals may increase the likelihood of mutations emerging. Once the virus emerges, population mobility means that the outbreak is likely to spread worldwide with great speed. After World War I, influenza spread globally within a month, facilitated by large-scale movements of civilians and armed forces. With the advent of modern transport systems, a new strain of influenza can reach anywhere in the world in a matter of hours. Every day there are about 800 sailings, 100 flights, 20 train connections, and 27,000 vehicle crossings between Hong Kong and mainland China (Hong Kong Trade Development Council, 2000). Hong Kong (Chek Lap Kok) International Airport can handle 49 flights per hour (Hong Kong International Airport, 2002). It was from Hong Kong that SARS spread to Vietnam, Canada, and other countries.

Enhancing Global Governance for Communicable Disease Prevention, Control, and Treatment

Of foremost importance to enabling the public health community to detect and respond to a communicable disease outbreak are epidemiologic and clinical data. The challenges posed by globalization have reinvigorated efforts to strengthen how a global public health community might respond to infectious disease outbreaks. Historically, the pillar of international cooperation on infectious disease control for over a century has been the International Health Regulations (IHR). The regulations, originating in the nineteenth century, were adopted by member states of the World Health Organization (WHO) in 1951, and revised in 1973 and 1981. From the mid-1990s, efforts were made to revise the IHR, given their limited scope (covering cholera, plague and yellow fever only); dependence on country notification; and lack of mechanisms for collaboration, incentives for compliance, and risk-specific measures (WHO, 2002).

The present limitations of the IHR highlight the need to enhance global governance for communicable disease prevention, control, and treatment. For com-

Exhibit 15-1	The Global Warning from Severe Acute Respiratory Syndrome

The outbreak of severe acute respiratory syndrome (SARS) in 2002–2003 demonstrated how a globalizing world can be more vulnerable to infectious disease. SARS is a respiratory illness caused by a previously unknown type of coronavirus (SARS-CoV). Normally, corona viruses cause mild to moderate upper respiratory symptoms. People with SARS develop a high fever (over 38°C), cough, shortness of breath, difficulty breathing, and other, more severe symptoms. Some develop severe pneumonia or respiratory failure that can be fatal. Between November 1, 2002, and July 31, 2003, there were 8,096 cumulative cases and 774 deaths in 27 countries (WHO, 2004b).

Although the eventual disease burden from SARS was relatively low (by comparison, influenza causes 250,000 to 500,000 deaths each year worldwide), the outbreak was seen as an important lesson concerning the global management of such a public health emergency. The outbreak was described as unprecedented in the speed and extent of its global spread. Its airborne transmission, lack of diagnostic technologies, absence of effective vaccine, and, perhaps most importantly, rapid spread via a globally mobile population made it "the first infectious disease epidemic since HIV/AIDS to pose a truly global threat" (Fidler, 2004). As described in a report by the University of Toronto, "In the Middle Ages, it took three years for the plague to spread from Asia to the western reaches of Europe. The SARS virus crossed from Hong Kong to Toronto in about 15 hours" (Joint Centre on Bioethics, 2003). It is believed that air travelers eventually spread SARS to 16 countries (Bonn, 2003).

The economic cost of the outbreak was huge, estimated at between US$30 to $100 billion (Smith & Sommers, 2003). These costs were distributed across a wide range of countries, illustrating the vulnerability of a globalizing economy to public health emergencies of international concern. Had the outbreak been more serious, the economic impact on the global economy is likely to have been substantial. As McKibbin (quoted in Nesmith, 2003) states, "Had it been a larger epidemic, the cost would have been astronomical. It would have produced a major disruption of the international trading system." As such, the outbreak demonstrates the shared interest by all countries in ensuring effective management of such emergencies.

SARS served as an important opportunity to test existing systems of international health cooperation. The initial refusal by the Chinese government to report cases confirmed inherent weaknesses in the International Health Regulations, which required member states to report on only three diseases (yellow fever, plague, and cholera). WHO thus lacks the formal authority to command information that is potentially vital to the world's health, and action comes down to the willingness of the Director-General to challenge the mettle of sovereign states.

Once the outbreak was confirmed, the international community began to mobilize. Within 2 weeks of the Hong Kong outbreak, WHO declared SARS a global health emergency on March 12, 2003. On March 17, a WHO collaborative multicenter research project on SARS diagnosis was established to identify the causative agent and develop a diagnostic test.

For many, WHO's handling of the SARS outbreak reaffirmed the organization's vital and unique role in global health. No other organization had the legitimacy to pull together the international health community. At the same time, the outbreak highlighted the inherent weaknesses in the International Health Regulations, as well as the national public health systems of affected countries. SARS also demonstrated how infectious diseases can provoke public fears, fueled both by the unknown nature of the disease and by the mass media. Fortunately, SARS proved less serious than anticipated, providing a timely opportunity for the global public health community to prepare itself for the next emergency outbreak.

municable disease outbreaks, surveillance data constitute the front line. The sources of such data have traditionally been national public health authorities, reporting to WHO, which are responsible for collating and disseminating this information. Once an outbreak is reported, mechanisms for coordinating clinical data on diagnosis and treatment are needed. Importantly, governments are not legally obliged to report other disease outbreaks, and may indeed choose not to do so when there are risks of economic or political fallout. In May 2005 the revised IHR was adopted to govern a broader range of public health emergencies of international concern including emerging diseases. Countries have broader obligations to build national capacity, and to detect and respond to such emergencies.

There have been efforts to diversify the sources of outbreak information to include both governmental and nongovernmental sources, given the limitations of relying solely on the voluntary cooperation of governments. Some of these sources are listed in Table 15-2, with those involving nongovernmental institutions highlighted in bold. An example is the Global Outbreak Alert and Response Network (GOARN), a technical collaboration created in 2000 from existing institutions and networks that pool human and technical resources for the rapid identification, confirmation, and response to outbreaks of international importance. The rationale for the network is based on "the need for a global network, building on new and existing partnerships, to deal with the global threats of epidemic-prone and emerging diseases" (WHO, 2003).

As well as strengthened disease surveillance, there is a clear need to create appropriate incentive systems that reward compliance and penalize inappropriate actions. Perhaps the key reason why the Chinese gov-

Table 15-2	Broadening Data Sources for Communicable Disease Surveillance
Level	**Data Source**
National	U.S. Centers for Disease Control and Prevention
	Pasteur Institutes, Sentiweb
	UK Public Health Laboratory Service
	Health Canada
	WHO country offices
Regional	WHO regional offices
	EC Rapid Alert System for Non-Food Products (RAPEX)
	European Network for Diagnostics of "Imported" Viral Diseases (ENIVD)
	Pacific Public Health Surveillance Network (PACNET)
International	WHO
	UN Global Program on HIV/AIDS
	UN High Commissioner for Refugees
	UN Development Program
	UN Children's Fund
Global	Global Public Health Intelligence Network (GPHIN–Health Canada)
	PROMED (Federation of American Scientists)
	TravelMed
	Red Cross/Red Crescent
	Médicins Sans Frontières (MSF)
	Merlin
	International Rescue Committee

ernment failed to immediately report the SARS outbreak (see Exhibit 15-1) was the risk of losing trade and investment and tourist revenues. As McKibbin (quoted in Nesmith, 2003) writes, in relation to SARS, "In a world in which news coverage is intense and international trade is vital to most economies, the impact of the disease was magnified." At the same time, it may be difficult to suppress such information in a world of global communications. WHO Director-General Jong-Wook Lee observed, "You have to be very open about it, you have to report it. You have to also inform the WHO because the covering up will not really help resolve the problem—it was a very important lesson we learned" (quoted in Kataria, 2003).

At present, there is no system of governance to regulate the economic impact on countries of disease outbreaks. As a result, countries can suffer losses disproportionate to the actual health risk posed. Outbreaks can also serve as an opportunity for countries to practice a disguised form of trade protectionism. A good example is the food trade. Serious outbreaks of foodborne diseases have been documented on every continent in the past decade. Foodborne diseases are a major source of illness, affecting up to one-third of populations in industrialized countries annually, and are likely to be more widespread in the developing world. As WHO (2002) reports,

Trends in global food production, processing, distribution and preparation present new challenges to food safety. Food grown in one country can now be transported and consumed halfway across the world. People demand a wider variety of foods than in the past; they want foods that are not in season and often eat away from home.

The outbreak of variant Creutzfeldt-Jakob disease in the United Kingdom in the 1990s, arising from the human consumption of cattle infected with bovine spongiform encephalopathy, represented a loss to British taxpayers of around US$7 billion (£4 billion). When the EU eventually lifted the ban on British beef in 1999, the French government continued to impose its own ban, leading to accusations of trade protectionism.

In conclusion, it is perhaps tempting to overplay the increased threat from infectious disease being created by globalization. In some cases, stigmatization of certain population groups (e.g., migrant populations, ethnic minorities) can follow, resulting in politically motivated, rather than evidence-based, public health interventions (e.g., screening). It is important to remember that human populations and infectious diseases have coexisted and coevolved over time. Changes in patterns of human settlement and structures of human societies have led to corresponding changes in infectious disease susceptibility. It is necessary, in this context, to ask how contemporary forms of globalization are changing how human populations live together and in relation to the natural world. There is growing evidence that the epidemiology of some infectious diseases is changing as a result of global change, and that corresponding adaptation by societies around the world is needed to respond to them.

The Globalization of Chronic Diseases

Chapter 6 highlights the impact of chronic diseases and risks on health and economies. It mentions that important processes in globalization—trade, foreign investment, marketing, and the spread of technologies—have implications for the spread and alleviation of chronic diseases. These issues are expanded upon here. The flows of certain commodities that are possible risks for chronic diseases are highlighted. Flows of tobacco are always negative; flows concerning food, alcohol, and goods and services related to physical activity can be both positive and negative.

Trade Liberalization and Chronic Diseases

Searching for new markets across the world, tobacco, alcohol, and food products are flowing on an unprecedented scale from transnational corporations (TNCs), largely headquartered in high-income countries, to the developing world. In the case of tobacco, trade liberalization has facilitated this flow to new markets. Bilateral trade relations, notably between the United States and low- and middle-income countries, have been effectively used as a means of pressuring countries such as Thailand, Taiwan, and South Korea to open up domestic markets to cigarette imports. The Uruguay Round of the GATT, concluded in 1994, liberalized trade in unmanufactured tobacco. Since 1995, multilateral trade agreements under the World Trade Organization have significantly reduced tariff and nontariff barriers to tobacco trade (Bettcher et al., 2003). There have been pressures to include tobacco in regional and multilateral negotiations to liberalize the agricultural sector. This has resulted in greater tobacco trade between countries, leading to increased supply, more extensive marketing of all forms, and lower prices.

More research is needed to understand the implications of changing trends in food trade for chronic diseases. For example, the trade of oilseeds and corn for livestock feed may be associated with the dramatic increase of livestock production in many developing countries and associated increases in meat consump-

tion. Another trend that may have implications for dietary patterns is the increased trade of high-value processed agricultural products (e.g., meats, dairy items, cakes, and frozen foods). Exports of these products from the United States are growing faster than any other category of agricultural exports (Bolling, 1998; Whitton, 2004). The global health implications of increased marketing of processed and fast foods are discussed later in this chapter.

The Impact of Foreign Direct Investment

Foreign direct investment (FDI) has played an unprecedented role in recent decades as a source of capital for economic development in low- and middle-income countries. FDI is an investment by an enterprise from one country into an entity or affiliate in another, in which the parent firm owns a substantial but not necessarily majority interest. The foreign enterprise becomes an affiliate of a parent company, thus creating or joining a TNC. FDI is one of the mechanisms through which TNCs enter new markets, and reflects an intention to remain invested over the long term.

FDI has risen dramatically over the past 25 years. In 2002 alone, US$162 billion flowed into the developing world, mainly from TNCs based in high-income countries (UN Conference on Trade and Development, 2003). Trends in FDI have important implications for chronic diseases because investment in tobacco, food, and alcohol products is high. TNCs have specific incentives to invest in tobacco, food, and alcohol because they favor investments in concentrated markets where there is high brand recognition (Walkenhorst, 2001), of which cigarette, beer, soft drinks, and confectionery products are prime examples. The privatization of tobacco manufacturers in emerging markets provided new opportunities for investment by American and European companies. Soft drinks, processed foods, and alcoholic drinks are also expensive to handle and ship, thus encouraging local production by subsidiaries or licensed manufacturers (Bolling, 2002; Walkenhorst, 2001).

The precise implications of FDI trends for chronic diseases are as yet still unclear, but several trends warrant closer scrutiny (Exhibit 15-2). Of note, 10 of the 100 largest TNCs, ranked by foreign assets, manufacture tobacco, food, or alcohol, as do a high proportion of the largest affiliates of foreign TNCs in developing economies. The FDI provided by these companies exceeds that provided by bilateral agencies to address chronic diseases. As such, FDI provides great economic potential, and developing country governments have thus liberalized investment rules and introduced incentives in order to benefit from the much-needed capital, skills, technology, and goods

Exhibit 15-2	The Food Industry, Foreign Direct Investment, and Chronic Disease Risks

Foreign direct investment (FDI) has so far been overlooked as an important driver of the diet transition. FDI into food processing, service, and retail has become particularly significant since the mid-1980s. Food companies, based mainly (but not exclusively) in western Europe and the United States, have a significant international presence.* In 2001, 12 transnational food companies (TFCs) were among the top 100 holders of foreign assets globally, double the number in 1990. The foreign assets of these companies amounted to US$257.7 billion in 2002, an increase (658%) from US$34 billion in 1990. During the same period, foreign sales increased from US$88.8 to US$234.1 billion (164%). A high proportion of foreign assets and sales are in high-income countries, but foreign affiliates of TFCs are frequently among the largest companies in the tertiary sector in the developing world. In 2001, 8 of the top 40 transnational corporations by sales in Latin America and the Caribbean were food companies. Furthermore, the amount of assets directed to developing countries is rising.

Globally, food processing is the most important recipient of FDI relative to other parts of the food system, including the farm sector. American FDI into foreign food processing companies grew from US$9 billion in 1980 to US$36 billion in 2000, with sales increasing from US$39.2 in 1982 to US$150 billion in 2000. As FDI has risen, the allocation of investment has shifted toward highly processed foods for sale in the host market, and away from products for export to the home market and those produced by primary processing (although they may remain important in certain cases). The tendency to allocate investment into highly processed foods is illustrated by the economies of central and eastern Europe and the Baltic states, which attracted soaring rates of FDI in the food sector in the 1990s. Investment has concentrated on soft drinks and confectionery. The confectionery sector in Poland, for example, attracted FDI of US$963 million between 1990 and 1999, more than the FDI in meat, fish, flour, pasta, bread, sugar, potato products, fruits, vegetables, vegetable oils, and fats put together. On a global scale, this trend has led to the dominance of foreign investors in the highly processed food sector. In China and Mexico, foreign investors dominate packaged foods, such as instant noodles, soft drinks, snacks, sweet biscuits, and fast foods.

Processed food sales in developing countries are lower than in developed countries (one-quarter or less of all food expenditures, compared with almost half). Yet wider availability, lower prices, and new purchasing channels are driving rapid sales growth. Annual sales growth of processed foods is around 29% in low-middle-income countries, compared with 7% in upper-middle-income countries. The market for highly processed foods is expanding fast. Future sales growth for TFCs lies in developing countries. Vietnam, China, and Indonesia are expected to be the fastest-growing markets for packaged food retail sales over the coming years, with growth rates forecasted at 11%, 10%, and 8% respectively. Korea, Thailand, India, and the Philippines rank among the top 10 growing markets, with total packaged food retail sales expected to grow 5% to 7% annually. It is still not clear how the consumption of highly processed foods has affected the diets and nutrition of different households and individuals, but it is likely to fuel increases in diet-related chronic diseases unless effective policies are implemented.

There are two potential approaches to influence FDI and redirect the diet transition toward better health. One would be to impose health-oriented conditions on FDI by TFCs. These policy options (and others) are contained in the WHO Global Strategy on Diet, Physical Activity and Health, and many countries have the structures in place to implement them. Through its position upstream, FDI would be a single entry point at which to implement a multiple range of public health policies.

A second option would be to look directly to TFCs for a solution. An alternative to the regulatory option would be to encourage TFCs to invest in healthier products, such as less salty snacks and baked goods and more low-fat products, nutrient-rich foods, or even foods with functional benefits. At the same time, this would ensure that they did not market unhealthy products and lifestyles to children. These two different approaches reflect one of the fundamental tensions in policy development today: how to balance the role of government and transnational corporations. A mixed approach will probably evolve over time.

Food company refers to a company that is involved in the processing, service, or sale of highly processed food. It includes diversified companies that manufacture, serve, or sell products other than food, such as personal care products or tobacco. It excludes companies concerned solely with agricultural production, processing, or research.

Source: C. Hawkes, *The Global Regulatory Environment Around Nutrition Labels and Health Claims* (Geneva, Switzerland: World Health Organization, 2004).

and services promised by FDI (OECD, 2000). At the same time, the more liberal investment regimes put into place by governments to attract FDI can preclude the introduction of regulations or the raising of standards concerning the good or service in which the investment has been made to bring them into line with what has been shown to be effective in developed countries. For example, FDI may bring with it pressures for tax competition, creating disincentives for a tobacco tax in countries wishing to attract FDI. In the case of FDI in the food sector, there may be pressures exerted by TNCs to avoid effective food labeling or controls on advertising to children when negotiating new contracts. These contracts would usually be decided between TNCs and the ministries of trade and finance, and usually without health aspects being considered.

Gilmore and McKee (2004) offer a case study of how British American Tobacco and Philip Morris, the world's two largest transnational tobacco companies, are among the largest foreign investors in Russia and Moldova. Given their importance to new governments as a source of investment, these companies have been able to negotiate advantageous conditions that benefit their businesses, such as tax breaks, exemption from monopoly regulation, and even a role in drafting health legislation. The International Monetary Fund (IMF) has traditionally supported the privatization of state-owned enterprises in emerging markets, including the tobacco industry. Although this may make sense from a macroeconomic perspective (which is debatable), it ignores the impact that privatization without appropriate government regulation and tax policies can have on a major risk factor in health. Importantly, if the IMF were to draw on the World Bank's more recent policy prescriptions for tobacco control, and support governments prior to privatization, macroeconomic and health goals could be met together.

The Globalization of Marketing, Advertising, and Promotion

The flow of products around the world is accompanied by a flow of marketing and advertising images designed to encourage higher consumption. These images, such as brands, logos, and promotional initiatives, influence behavior through their emotional appeal, having the ability to shift cultural and social norms to a situation in which tobacco, alcohol, and foods high in fats, sugars, and salt are consumed more regularly and frequently (Hawkes, 2002).

TNCs invest heavily in marketing and advertising of these products, spreading so-called global brands all over the world, while tailoring campaigns to local settings. In particular, children or young adults (seen as more malleable to behavior change) are targeted directly via strategies such as advertisements and the sponsorship of sports and music events. Evidence shows that marketing promotes use of tobacco and alcohol (Babor, 2003) and influences dietary habits (Jackson et al., 2002). In developing countries, companies take advantage of weaker regulatory environments to use a wide range of techniques to target specific populations such as young adults and women (Hawkes, 2002; Hawkes, 2004a). In these emerging

markets, companies are highly strategic in attempting to reach lower-income populations. In China, for example, South African Breweries became profitable by targeting the mass market with locally brewed beer (Dawar & Chattopadhyay, 2002). Others take a more targeted approach. In Asian countries, tobacco companies use glamorous images to advertise "light" and "mild" cigarettes specifically to women (Mackay & Eriksen, 2002). Throughout the developing world, transnational food companies attempt to take "stomach share" away from other foods and drinks with techniques specifically designed to attract children into fast food restaurants and toward soft drinks and snacks (Hawkes, 2002). The poor and less well educated are particularly vulnerable to the adverse effects of mass marketing of tobacco, alcohol products, and unhealthy foods.

Globalization, Politics, and Chronic Disease Prevention

In recent years, greater efforts have been made to address these global risks to health through transnational actions. The experiences of developing the Framework Convention on Tobacco Control (FCTC) and the Global Strategy on Diet and Physical Activity, especially health issues related to sugar, provide valuable lessons for public health. These are summarized in Exhibit 15-3.

Both tobacco and sugar were regarded as highly valuable commodities until the 1950s. They were both highly subsidized and protected in developed countries, and seen as earning much-needed trade income for developing countries. When the evidence that they could be harmful to health first appeared, the response by producers and manufacturers was similar: consistent denial of the evidence, creation of front groups to oppose public health action, and intense and sustained lobbying of policy makers over decades to thwart regulatory progress at national and especially international levels.

A growing number of governments eventually took action when the evidence of health and economic harm became evident. Two different approaches have been used by governments, depending on the intensity of industry pressure and the degree of acceptance by the public of the need for government intervention in social policy. Nordic countries led the way, with Canada, in acknowledging that for "healthy choices to be the easy choices," social, environmental, and commercial influences on health need to be addressed through government regulation, fiscal policy, and intersectoral action, combined with educational measures. In contrast, the United States has given primacy

Exhibit 15-3	Building Policy Coherence for Global Tobacco Control

In recent years, policy coherence has improved among UN organizations in the following ways.

- The Policy Strategy Advisory Committee (PSAC) was established by WHO to improve policy coherence on tobacco control, solidify support for WHO activities, and expand the base of advocacy and action. The PSAC included representatives from the World Bank, United Nations Children's Fund (UNICEF), World Self Medication Industry (WSMI), International Nongovernmental Coalition Against Tobacco (INGCAT), Campaign for Tobacco Free Kids, and U.S. Centers for Disease Control and Prevention (CDC).
- WHO was asked by the UN secretary-general to convene the Ad Hoc Inter-Agency Task Force on Tobacco Control. The Task Force replaced the former UN tobacco focal point, which had been situated within the UN Conference on Trade and Development (UNCTAD) and, in doing so, shifted the tobacco debate within the UN from one of addressing issues relating to supply of tobacco as a first order priority (i.e., protection of tobacco farming) to one of putting the protection and promotion of health first. Fifteen UN organizations, as well as the World Bank, the IMF, and the WTO, participate in the work of the Task Force.

Among nongovernmental organizations, policy coherence has been improved in the following ways.

- In 1999 WHO obtained funding from the UN Foundation to develop partnerships with civil society organizations to raise awareness and counter the global marketing practices of the tobacco industry. Based on the successful California counteradvertising campaign, which had pioneered the strategy of exposing the tobacco industry's behavior, the Don't Be Duped campaign sought a new language, a new idiom, and a new sense of purpose and direction for tobacco control. One particularly effective campaign, aimed at countering the rise of the Marlboro man as the 20th century's most successful global advertising icon, was to replace the traditional No Smoking sign with an image of two Marlboro cowboys riding into the sunset with one confiding to the other that he has cancer. The campaign engaged and supported nationally based tobacco control champions and became an important avenue for accessing nongovernmental partners to support and advocate for the FCTC.
- WHO ensured early civil society participation in the FCTC process when it held its first-ever public hearings in October 2000. All interested parties, including the tobacco industry, were invited to present their views on the FCTC. During two days of testimony, over 90 public heath groups took the floor, along with representatives from all four leading tobacco companies (Philip Morris, British American Tobacco, Japan Tobacco International, and Imperial Tobacco). The hearings were widely reported on by the world's media and helped to intensify the emerging global tobacco control debate. Although some tobacco industry representatives challenged the evidence base linking passive smoking to disease, the public hearings did provide the first truly global forum in which tobacco companies admitted the addictive and deadly effects of active smoking.

to the importance of individual responsibility and has thus stressed the importance of health education as the focus of policy and action. These approaches have been debated at every WHO session that addresses behavioral change. Generally, industry has supported the American approach, whereas many nongovernmental organizations (NGOs) have supported the Nordic approach. Increasingly, as evidence of harmful health effects accumulate, it is the latter approach that is gaining support among developing countries. This is illustrated by incorporation of the approach into the adopted texts of the FCTC and Global Strategy.

In estimating the future impact of chronic diseases on disability-adjusted life years (DALYs) and deaths, WHO states that the underlying risks will remain constant. Extrapolations were based on "more of the same" policies. Although helpful, this does not motivate change or give an indication as to the desired future. In the United Kingdom, Derek Wanless led a

process within the Treasury aimed at taking a radically different approach. Rather than "more of the same," three potential scenarios for the next 20 years were described: solid progress, slow uptake, and fully engaged. The fully engaged model was shown to cost the government less over the long term and yielded the best health outcomes. This model is now being used as a basis for the redesign and prioritization of interventions and policies for health across all departments in the United Kingdom. Developing countries, supported by academic institutions and research groups from developed countries, should generate what the fully engaged model would yield for health and the economy by the 2030s. The process would galvanize all who should be engaged in chronic disease control, draw upon work initiated or planned in relation to national commissions on macroeconomics and health following from WHO's commission, stimulate the development of country-specific targets and indicators of progress, and define actual costs and actions required to meet these targets and, through this, generate political and societal commitment for change.

Enhancing Global Governance for Chronic Disease Control

WHO, ministers of health, and other public health advocates need to globally advocate visibly and regularly for a few key components of chronic disease control: tobacco control within the context of the FCTC; healthier diets (with three or four specific messages developed to be used often); increased physical activity; secondary prevention of ischemic heart disease, stroke, diabetes, and cervical cancer; and investment in infrastructure and human resources for chronic disease control. Repeated high-level advocacy would ensure that chronic diseases are maintained high on the health policy agenda and in the mass media. This will lead to more substantial donor support, galvanize civil society organizations, including health professionals, and encourage positive private-sector interaction.

There is also need to strengthen global surveillance of key health risks in adults and children. The WHO stepwise approach to surveillance (STEPS) is the recommended noncommunicable disease (NCD) surveillance tool. The STEPS framework offers an entry point for low- and middle-income countries to begin NCD activities. The stepwise approach is based on the concept that surveillance systems require standardized data collection, as well as sufficient flexibility, in order to be appropriate in a variety of country situations and settings. The aim of this approach is to increase a country's capacity to achieve data comparability over time and between countries, and to ensure that appropriate and relevant information is available to inform country NCD policy. The stepwise approach allows for the development of an increasingly comprehensive and complex surveillance system based on local needs and resources.

The key feature of the STEPS framework is the distinction between different levels of risk factor assessment. STEPS is a sequential process, starting with collecting information on key risk factors by the use of questionnaires (step 1), then moving to simple physical measurements (step 2), and only then recommending the collection of blood samples for biochemical assessment (step 3). Within each step, core, expanded, and optional information can be collected. At a minimum, core information provides the basic, comparable variables to describe prevalence and trends in the most common risk factors.

The key premise is that by using the same standardized questions and protocols, all countries can use the information for assessing both within-country trends and between-country comparisons. Therefore, the questionnaires and methods recommended are relatively simple. The use of the data in developing interventions and policies is an integral part of the STEPS approach, which in turn increases capacity to influence policy. It provides the basic information from which to formulate policy that effectively reduces the burden of disease. STEPS is an integral component of NCD surveillance, prevention, and control strategies developing in the four WHO regions in which it is currently operating. At the country level, data are already being used to inform policy in the western Pacific.

Another good example of strengthening global surveillance is the Global Youth Tobacco Surveillance (GYTS) System, which is the largest assessment of tobacco use among youth, and the single most important database for monitoring country-level progress in adhering to the principles of the FCTC. GYTS was developed by WHO and the CDC to enhance the capacity of countries to design, monitor, implement, and evaluate their comprehensive tobacco control programs. GYTS monitors youth tobacco use, attitudes, exposure to environmental tobacco smoke, and other critical measures by collecting, analyzing, and disseminating representative and reliable data that can be compared across countries. GYTS data allows countries to compare themselves with other countries, to monitor their own tobacco control efforts over time, and, because GYTS uses a common methodology and questionnaire, to use the program successes of other countries as examples that may be useful in their own program efforts. GYTS is the largest global public health surveillance system ever developed and maintained. Of the 192 countries recognized as member states of WHO, 153 are currently active in GYTS. Training was planned for 19 additional countries during 2004, bringing the total to 172. In addition, 17 countries have repeated their GYTS, and 18 others were planning to repeat during 2004. Two complementary surveillance systems are being developed and implemented to monitor tobacco use among school personnel and health professionals. In addition, a "global multi-risk factor surveillance system" is being initiated by WHO and CDC, expanding the methodology of the GYTS to address other major chronic disease risks that affect youth.

There are many global health players currently active in chronic disease control, with some yet to become fully engaged and committed to action. These include the World Bank, IMF, CDC, World Heart

Federation, International Union Against Cancer (UICC), World Medical Association, representative(s) of WHO collaborating centers, the International Federation of Pharmaceutical Manufacturers Association (IFPMA), UNICEF, and the FAO. Each has some impact on the course of the chronic disease epidemics. Not all, however, see their work as playing a key role in influencing incidence and mortality. The FAO, for example, sees its main focus as being to ensure that basic food needs are met and that commercial opportunities for cash crops are created. That often brings it into conflict with WHO's goals of reducing tobacco and sugar consumption and sometimes leads to fractious debates at UN meetings. WHO leadership, through establishment of a policy advisory committee for chronic disease control, could lead to improved policy coherence among players, identification of institutional strengths and weaknesses, development of actions based on comparative advantages, and definition of new partnerships and interactions. The experience of the ad hoc Task Force on Tobacco Control suggests that considerable progress can be made by having the FAO, World Bank, IMF, and others develop one approach to a public health problem and use their different channels of influence to effect change at the country level (see Exhibit 15-3). Reports of meetings should be disseminated to key stakeholders, such as through WHO to the Economic and Social Council (ECOSOC) and the UN. Comparable models of governance could be developed at the country level.

Three key areas require intensive global policy research and action. First, work on "making markets work for chronic disease control" would engage those in selected industries whose products or services have an impact on chronic disease risks and outcomes, as well as the investment community, in a search for incentives that would move industries faster toward products and services that were profitable to them and would advance public health goals. This would require, among other things, careful consideration of the regulatory environment and financial systems in place in relation to new products and services. It is likely that what would emerge would lead to major progressive companies becoming more supportive of health goals, and laggard companies requiring regulation to move faster.

Second, there is a need to identify incentives to encourage prevention within chronic care systems. Some work on this has been under way within Kaiser-Permanente, for example. A useful starting point for this work is to systemically document the extent of unmet opportunities for primary and secondary prevention of chronic disease that exists within current health care systems. Simple surveys adapted from the EURASPIRE model and recently developed WHO work would stimulate the search for solutions, as similar work on measles immunization did in the 1980s. Third, the importance of the promotion of intersectoral action for chronic disease control requires a more sustained and rigorous effort that should include deeper involvement with those responsible for agriculture, transport, urban design, and education policy at international and national levels as starting points.

The above requires capacity building for chronic diseases, which has already been discussed in Chapter 6. Without significant investment in capacity building within academic and research settings in low- and middle-income countries, progress in chronic disease control will be limited and unsustainable. Considerable expertise is already available within academic centers in high-income countries and could, with modest increased support, be made more widely available to the developing world. Twinning arrangements between rich and poor countries, such as supported by the U.S. National Institutes of Health's Fogarty International Center, could be pursued with urgency. A mixture of short-course and longer degree programs in chronic disease control for developing countries could be stimulated though exchanges with major donor agencies.

Finally, there is need for active support of the implementation and monitoring of global norms and standards to enhance health promotion. As discussed, considerable progress has already been made in three important areas: surveillance, the FCTC, and development of a global strategy for diet, physical activity, and health. All three are still in their infancy with regard to impact on public health policy and outcomes, and therefore require intensified support. Yet they are examples of how global norms and standards can establish goals, mobilize resources, and motivate policy action for health promotion. Two areas requiring urgent attention, in terms of the adoption and implementation of global norms and standards, are marketing and advertising targeted at children, and technology foresight and policy development. Increased concern about the marketing of food, tobacco, and alcohol products to children has been expressed by WHO member states and NGOs over the last 5 years. WHO needs to take a comprehensive view with respect to what is needed and, in doing so, critically review where self-regulation has failed. The challenge lies in determining how best to regulate areas with likely marked influence on future consumption patterns.

Impacts on Health Care Financing and Service Provision

As well as having varied impacts on health status and outcomes, globalization is believed to be leading to changes in health care provision and financing (Smith, 2004). In providing an introduction to some of these changes, this section examines three areas: the migration of health workers, the globalization of the pharmaceutical industry, and the global spread of health sector reform.

Migration of Health Workers

It is estimated that almost 175 million people (2.9% of the world's population) were living outside their country of birth in 2000, an increase from 100 million (1.8% of the world's population) in 1995, and a more than doubling since 1965. Population mobility is a core feature of contemporary forms of globalization, encompassing many types of migration, including temporary visitors (e.g., tourists, students), permanent settlers, documented and undocumented migrant laborers, asylum seekers, refugees, and internally displaced persons (Stilwell et al., 2003). Data on these varied types of population movements are notoriously incomplete across countries. Nonetheless, it is clear that globalization is marked by an increase in the number of people moving across national borders, the frequency of such movements, and the distances traveled. As Martin (2001) writes,

> Few countries remain untouched by migration. Nations as varied as Haiti, India, and the former Yugoslavia feed international flows. The United States receives by far the most international migrants, but migrants also pour into Germany, France, Canada, Saudi Arabia, and Iran. Some countries, such as Mexico, send emigrants to other lands, but also receive immigrants—both those planning to settle and those on their way elsewhere.

Given the intensified scale and global reach of migration, countries have sought to develop improved means of regulating and managing population flows. These can be aimed at easing the movements of certain populations (e.g., the recruitment of skilled workers to fill labor shortages) through such measures as harmonizing accreditation and licensing requirements, or reciprocal agreements between countries on workforce migration. Conversely, migration policies can seek to restrict population flows where governments wish to deter mobility.

Trends in the migration of health care workers suggest an emerging global marketplace for such labor. Health workers still represent only a small proportion of highly skilled workers who migrate, given national licensing, language, and other requirements. Nonetheless, there is a clear trend toward the increased migration of doctors and nurses, along with pharmacists, physiotherapists, dentists, laboratory technicians, and other health workers. Historically, health workers have long migrated to greener pastures, enticed by differentials in wages and working conditions. This might occur between two industrialized countries, such as between Canada and the United States, or from poorer to richer countries.

The latter has attracted growing attention in recent years. The so-called brain drain of health workers from the developing world has raised concern for many decades. During the 1960s and 1970s, large number of doctors and nurses from the Commonwealth migrated to the United Kingdom to meet staffing shortages. It was estimated that 35% of all hospital physicians in the United Kingdom were trained overseas, 60% of these in low-income countries (Abel-Smith, 1986, cited in Martineau, Decker, & Bundred, 2002). During the 1970s, at least 140,000 physicians (6% of the world total, excluding China) were based outside their country of birth or training in 1971. Similarly, around 135,000 nurses (4% of the world total) worked outside their country of birth or training (Mejia, 1978).

Since the 1990s, there has been a steep rise in the number of health workers migrating from the developing world, with a wider range of countries involved in the outflow and inflow of health workers. One of the drivers of this change, according to Martineau, Decker, and Bundred (2002), has been "the globalization of markets and the development of free trade agreements [that] have also facilitated international migration and reduced barriers to trade and mobility of services, products and people, including the skills of health professionals." Harmonization of qualifications among member states of the European Union, for example, has enabled a greater flow of health workers. In addition, demand has increased, and is expected to grow further, because of aging populations. Furthermore, worsened economic conditions in many low- and middle-income countries have encouraged health workers to seek better job prospects elsewhere. The data on why health workers migrate are limited, and there are clearly complex push and pull factors at play. Nonetheless, the opportunity to secure better working conditions, salaries, and quality of life has been important.

The brain drain out of Africa is especially worrisome because of the shortage of staff and the decimation of health worker numbers by the HIV/AIDS epidemic. At a time when additional external funds have been made available to provide antiretroviral therapy, there is a declining availability of qualified staff to provide this treatment (Padarath et al., 2003). In Malawi, two-thirds of nursing jobs in the public health system remain vacant. More registered nurses have left to work abroad from 2000 to 2004 than the 330 or so who remain in the public hospitals and clinics that serve the country's 11.6 million people (Dugger, 2004). In Zimbabwe, around 340 nurses graduated each year between 1998 and 2000. In the United Kingdom, the annual number of nurses registering from Zimbabwe totaled 382 (Stilwell et al., 2003). In 2000, more than 500 nurses left Ghana, more than twice the number graduating from nursing programs that year (Buchan & Sochalski, 2004). The Philippines has also been a historically important source of migrant health workers to the world. Given the value of overseas remittances to the national economy, the government has even supported a policy of intentionally training health workers for export. An estimated 85% of Filipino nurses (more than 150,000) are working internationally, while there are more than 30,000 unfilled nursing posts in the country (Aitken et al., 2004).

The United Kingdom remains a key destination for migrating health workers from Commonwealth countries. Between 1999 and 2002, the number of foreign-trained nurses based in the United Kingdom and eligible to practice doubled to around 42,000 (Buchan, 2003). The predicted collective demand for health workers by the United States, Canada, Ireland, Australia, New Zealand, and the United Kingdom is substantial, described as "large enough to deplete the supply of qualified nurses throughout the developing world" (Aitken et al., 2004). It is projected that shortfalls in nurses in the United States will reach 800,000 by 2020 (Dugger, 2004).

The movement of health workers from already resource-poor countries raises serious concerns about the weakening capacity of local health systems. Health inequities lie at the heart of the issue: inequities in available resources for health care between countries, driving individuals to seek employment elsewhere, and inequities in the impact of such an exodus on the health of the populations left behind. Host countries already have at least twice as many nurses per capita as source countries (Aitken et al., 2004).

The issue of migration of health workers must be considered as part of wider efforts to develop a global migration regime. Martin (2001) identifies three issues to be addressed in the creation of such a regime. First, states need to reach consensus that harmonizing policies will make migration "more orderly, safe and manageable." The problems of people smuggling and trafficking, in particular, require international attention. Second, a global migration regime requires standards, policies, and new legal frameworks. Some efforts have been made in host countries to adopt ethical guidelines and standards for the recruitment of health workers from overseas, especially from low- and middle-income countries. In November 1999 the UK Department of Health, for example, introduced such guidelines, which seemed to have resulted in a decline in new registrants from South Africa and the West Indies soon after. However, more recent figures suggest that this decline has been transitory, with increased registrants from countries such as Ghana, India, Nigeria, and Zimbabwe. The exclusion of private recruitment agencies and employers from the UK guidelines is seen as a major limitation (Stilwell et al., 2003).

Third, a global migration regime requires organizational responsibilities to be clarified. The mandate of the most prominent international body responsible for such issues, the International Migration Organization (IMO), includes the migration of health workers. However, it is not part of the United Nations system and is limited by resources and number of member states. As individual countries begin to develop ethical guidelines, a system of assessing the effectiveness of those guidelines in addressing the concerns raised in this chapter and of monitoring adherence to those guidelines is needed.

Globalization and the Pharmaceutical Industry

In recent decades, the pharmaceutical industry has grown in total size and in the size of the largest companies within it. In 2003 the industry earned US$492 billion in sales worldwide, an increase of 9% in 1 year (Chawla, Diwan, & Joshi, 2003). The industry is dominated by large multinational corporations. In 2002, the 10 largest earned almost half of the total revenues (US$184.2 billion) from the world pharmaceuticals market (Table 15-3). Together they marketed 23 products that earned more than US$1 billion each in sales.

Analysis of data collected by the OECD in 1996 by Taribusi and Vickery (1998) found that the industry has been indeed undergoing major restructuring. This has been the result of a flurry of mergers and acquisitions as companies have sought to increase economies of scale (and with it cost savings, market access, and portfolios of products). More recently,

Table 15-3	World's Ten Largest Pharmaceutical Companies, 2002			
Rank	**Headquarters**	**Company**	**Sales (US$ billion)**	**Top-Selling Products**
1	USA	Pfizer	28.28	Lipitor, Novarsc, Zoloft
2	UK	GlaxoSmithKline	28.20	Paxil, Advair, Augmentin
3	USA	Merck	21.63	Zocor, Vioxx, Fosamax
4	UK	AstraZeneca	17.84	Prilosec, Nexium, Seroquel
5	France	Aventis	17.25	Allegra, Lovenox, Taxotere
6	USA	Johnson & Johnson	17.20	Procrit, Risperdal, Remicade
7	Switzerland	Novartis	15.36	Diovan, Sandimmune, Lamisil
8	USA	Bristol-Myers Squibb	14.70	Pravachol, Plavix, Taxol
9	USA	Pharmacia	12.03	Celebrex, Xalatan, Detrol
10	USA	Wyeth	11.70	Effexor, Premarin, Protonix

Source: L. J. Sellers, "Fourth Annual Pharm Exec 50," *Pharmaceutical Executive*, May 2003. Reprinted with permission.

Busfield (2003) updated the OECD data and looked more carefully at the extent to which the term *globalization* can be strictly applied to describe the industry. She confirms that the consolidation of the industry has continued into the early 21st century, with no signs of abatement. The percentage of the world market held by the top 10 companies has continued to increase to almost half, up from around a third in 1995. For example, in 2003 Pfizer acquired Pharmacia for US$60 billion, thus widening its lead over GlaxoSmithKline for top position (McKenna, 2003).

Although it is clear that the industry has become larger in scale and more concentrated in ownership, the extent to which production has become globalized remains subject to debate. Busfield (2003) concludes that it is more accurate to describe the industry as becoming highly internationalized and perhaps globalizing, but not yet globalized. She writes that the industry as yet does not have companies without clear national identities, nor internationalized management or willingness to relocate across the world. So far production and consumption remains concentrated in high-income countries, with signs of richer developing countries playing a more prominent role.

Setting aside these debates, the increased economic might and reach of the industry does raise important policy issues. Pharmaceutical companies, and notably the industry leaders, argue that there is an economic logic to expanding their size because of the increasing need to compete in the global marketplace. It is argued that it is their size, in turn, which enables them to access sufficient resources needed to develop and market new products. As private-sector (profit-seeking) companies, global pharmaceutical companies argue that the demands of the marketplace must invariably drive product development. This means ensuring that pricing and ultimately profits are sufficient to give a sufficient return on investment to share-holders and for future research and development (R&D). Without such returns, companies cannot be viable economic concerns.

Public health advocates, however, have raised a number of concerns about the increasing dominance of the industry by a small number of large firms and, more specifically, their ability to determine the products and prices available to consumers. One important issue is what products are being produced and for what purposes. Critics argue that by pursuing a market-driven approach, drug companies compete for the lucrative customers of the rich world or focus almost exclusively on conditions where there are sufficient buyers, at the expense of those less able to pay for drugs or rarer conditions without a sufficient "customer base." This explains, for example, the proliferation of so-called me-too drugs or the huge investments in drugs to treat obesity and impotence, while investment in serious conditions more common to the developing world is less forthcoming.

Another key issue that has arisen is access to medicines. In 1977, WHO published the first *Model List of Essential Drugs*, which identified some 220 essential drugs that a country could use to meet the majority of its people's health problems calling for drug solutions. The list serves as a model for countries in developing their own national lists. Since that time, the list has been updated to include the most effective and cost-effective drugs. If a pharmaceutical company successfully brings a new product to market, after spending an average of US$500 million on R&D, it will rely on patent protection under intellectual property rights (IPR), which allows it to recoup costs and earn profits. For the world's poor, this means higher drug prices—often, prices that put important medicines beyond their reach.

This clear tension between meeting important public health needs and the practical workings of the market came into intense focus in 2001 with the dispute over access to antiretroviral treatment for HIV/AIDS (Exhibit 15-4). The case highlighted the challenge of reconciling the interests of two very different communities, increasingly brought together by globalization. As a follow-up to the dispute, the British government initiated a Commission on Intellectual Property Rights in 2001 to look at how IPR might work better for poor people and developing countries. The commission was asked to consider the following:

- How national IPR regimes could best be designed to benefit developing countries within the context of international agreements, in-

cluding the Agreement on Trade Related Property Rights (TRIPS).

- How the international framework of rules and agreements might be improved and developed (for instance, in the area of traditional knowledge) and the relationship between IPR rules and regimes covering access to genetic resources.

- The broader policy framework needed to complement intellectual property regimes.

In its final report published in 2002, the commission put forth a series of recommendations to integrate development objectives into the protection of IPR in

---

Exhibit 15-4	The Implications of the TRIPS Agreement for Pharmaceuticals

The Agreement on Trade Related Property Rights (TRIPS) was adopted at the end of the Uruguay Round of international trade negotiations in 1994. The agreement establishes minimum standards for protecting and enforcing nearly all forms of intellectual property rights (i.e., patents, trademarks, and copyright) for WTO member states, with standards derived from legislation in industrialized countries. All member states must comply with these standards, where necessary modifying their national legislation. Importantly, the agreement explicitly acknowledges in Article 8 that, in framing national laws, members "may . . . adopt measures necessary to protect public health and nutrition, and to promote the public interest."

In an important departure from previous conventions, pharmaceutical products are accorded full intellectual property rights under TRIPS. Pharmaceutical companies are granted the legal means, as patent owners of new drug products, to prevent others from making, using, or selling the new invention for a limited period of time. This provision led to concerns within the public health community over its potential implications for access to medicines. TRIPS specifies that patents must be available for all discoveries that "are new, involve an inventive step and are capable of industrial application" (Article 27). Patent protection can thus be obtained for new drug products, which enables the patent holder to have exclusive rights to produce and sell the product. Pharmaceutical companies argue that such rights, and the consequent ability to charge a higher price for a drug under patent, are necessary to recoup the many millions of dollars spent to research and develop the drug and bring it to market. Without the prospect of earning such prices, the incentive to invest in research and development would be seriously undermined. As Sidney Taurel (2003), CEO of Eli Lilly, argued, the "whole process of pharmaceutical innovation is made possible—viable—by two important features of our economic system: one is market-based pricing . . . the other is intellectual property protection."

Within the public health community, however, the increased prices charged for drugs under patent protection raise concerns about access to medicines. For drugs unprotected by patent rights—because such rights were not granted, asserted, or have expired—other producers can manufacture generic versions that can be sold at more competitive prices. This leads to lower drug prices for consumers, especially important for low-income communities and countries. Where a drug is needed for an important public health condition, the high cost of patented drugs becomes a particularly acute issue.

The tension between market economics and public health need came to a head in 2001 when the South African government sought an amendment to the South African Medicines and Related Substances Control Amendment Act that would allow the import and use of cheaper generic versions of prescription drugs. The key clause states that the government could find and "parallel import" the cheapest drug available and grant "compulsory licensing" to other companies allowing them to make copies of patented drugs. It was argued that the prevalence of HIV/AIDS in the country warranted it as a public health emergency and thus exempted it from TRIPS requirements as set forth in Article 8. Thirty-nine pharmaceutical companies, including GlaxoSmithKline, Merck, and Roche, launched legal action to protect their patents, seeing South Africa as a test case for preventing other countries, such as Brazil and India, from following suit.

However, supported by the campaigning of NGOs such as Health Action International and Médicin sans Frontières, the case generated huge public pressure. Faced with negative publicity and strong criticism, the pharmaceutical companies withdrew the case in April 2001.

Source: World Health Organization, *Globalization, TRIPS and Access to Pharmaceuticals,* WHO Policy Perspectives on Medicine No. 3 (Geneva, Switzerland: World Health Organization, 2001); and World Trade Organization, *TRIPS and Pharmaceutical Patents* (Geneva, Switzerland: World Trade Organization, 2003).

developing countries (Commission on Intellectual Property Rights, 2002).

Internationally, the need to balance the creation of new medicines and access to medicines led to the Doha Declaration on TRIPS and Public Health in November 2001. The declaration stated that WTO members had the right to grant compulsory licenses and engage in parallel importing where "public health crises" made this necessary. The declaration also extended exemptions on pharmaceutical patent protection for the least-developed countries until 2016. It remains to be seen under what circumstances and for which conditions the Doha Declaration will be applied in practice. Debate continues over what constitutes a "crisis" and which countries are eligible to be exempted from TRIPS accordingly.

In conclusion, it is more accurate to describe the pharmaceutical industry as a globalizing, rather than globalized, sector. Efforts to standardize products, regulation, and intellectual property rights worldwide can be seen as steps toward the creation of a global market for pharmaceuticals. However, concerns about access to medicines and product development, for example, have led to debates about the costs and benefits to public health of such trends. The term *internationalization*, rather than *globalization*, can perhaps more accurately describe the sector so far given the continued concentration of ownership, staff, R&D, and markets in high-income countries. Globalization would evolve the industry so that production and consumption become distributed more broadly across the world so that companies no longer have clear national identities and have truly internationalized management.

Globalization and Health Sector Reform

One of the key aspects of globalization concerns changes to how we see ourselves and the world around us. Globalization is affecting a wide range of thought processes, including values and beliefs, cultural identities and products, scientific research, and policy decisions (Lee, 2003). Health sector reform over the past two decades is an example of the global power of ideas. Around the world, countries have grappled with the challenge of improving the financing and provision of health care. At their root are shifts in thinking about health care—for example, how better health can best be achieved, how health systems should be restructured, whose needs should get priority, and who should pay for it. The reforms put forth to address these questions have been underpinned by values, beliefs, ideologies, research, and other cognitive processes about what needs to be changed.

The thinking that has driven health sector reform over the past two decades can be described as globalizing, in the sense that ideas about reform have flowed across a diverse range of countries, involving both public- and private-sector actors. The origins of this wave of reform are complex, but stem foremost from pressures on governments to address rising health costs and improve the quality of health services. As Dixon and Preker (1999) describe,

> [I]t would be too easy to blame ideology and economic crises alone for exposing public services to competitive market forces and increasing private sector participation. In reality, the welfare state approach has not always met the health needs of populations. Although state involvement is clearly needed, it has been dogged with the failure of the public sector to provide the services well.

Although there has been considerable debate about how best to meet these challenges, a clear set of ideas emerged from the early 1980s focused on rethinking (and in many cases reducing) the role of the state and introducing market mechanisms to manage and deliver health services. Initially introduced in the United States and United Kingdom, where enthusiasm for health reforms was perhaps most pronounced, these ideas began to be taken up in a wide variety of settings, including many parts of the developing world. Publication of the *World Development Report 1993: Investing in Health* by the World Bank (1993) marked an important point in the emerging discourse of health sector reform. Based on the innovative yet controversial findings of the Global Burden of Disease project, carried out by the Harvard School of Public Health, the report ignited fierce debates about setting priorities and financing health care in the developing world. The *World Development Report 1993* set out a new approach to priority setting that sought to target those conditions inflicting the heaviest disease or disability burden (measured by DALYs) for which there are cost-effective interventions. In addition, a new language of reform known broadly as the "new public management" began to permeate health policy at the national and global levels—internal markets, contracting out, public-private mix, decentralization, cost-effectiveness, rationing, autonomous hospitals, managed care—all bent on making health systems worldwide leaner and meaner.

The content of these reforms, and assessments of their relative merits and demerits at achieving their declared intentions, has been dealt with extensively elsewhere (see, for example, Berman & Bossert, 2000;

Mills, 2001). What is interesting here, in the context of globalization, is the way in which such policy ideas flowed across territorial boundaries more readily than ever before. This might be explained by the inherent "rightness" of the policies themselves, which claim to offer proven and effective measures to deal with practical problems in public-sector management common across countries. However, the adoption of reforms in so many countries prior to the availability of supporting evidence of their effectiveness directly challenges this view. So do the sometimes heated debates surrounding specific reforms—the appropriateness of reforms to local settings, the inequitable effects imposed on certain population groups (especially the poor), the quality of the evidence base and methodology, and the underlying assumptions and values. The debate over WHO's efforts in 2001 to comparatively assess the world's health systems is a good example (Exhibit 15-5).

This suggests that the flow of ideas about health sector reform over the past decade or so cannot be solely explained by the quality of their content. Rather, it is important to recognize that the messengers have been as important as the messages themselves. At the national level, successive conservative-thinking governments favored the adoption of policies based on neoliberal economic principles such as downsizing of the state, deregulation and privatization, and strengthening the market. At the global level, organizations such as the World Bank, IMF, and U.S. Agency for International Development (USAID) advocated similar policies, including structural adjustment programs, which became known as the "Washington Consensus." Together with increased opportunities for policy makers to interact with counterparts across the world, it is perhaps unsurprising that we have seen a considerable degree of policy convergence. Much more needs to be understood about how this takes place, what key individuals and institutions are involved, and which policy issues have been most affected. New areas of research such as policy transfer, policy learning, and network analysis seek to grapple with these questions.

In short, health sector reforms in recent decades illustrate well how transborder flows of thought processes are a key aspect of globalization. Ideas today move across national borders in a variety of forms via the mass media, the advertising industry, research institutions, consultancy firms, governments, civil society, corporations, international organizations, and

---

Exhibit 15-5   **The Global Debate over the *World Health Report 2000***

In 2001 the World Health Organization published its *World Health Report 2000—Health Systems: Improving Performance* (WHO, 2001b) as "the first ever analysis of the world's health systems." Using five performance indicators (overall level of population health, health inequalities within the population, health system responsiveness, distribution of responsiveness, and distribution of the health system's financial burden within the population) to measure health systems in 191 member states, the report was intended "to stimulate a vigorous debate about better ways of measuring health system performance and thus finding a successful new direction for health systems to follow." The report stated that "[b]y shedding new light on what makes health systems behave in certain ways, WHO also hopes to help policy-makers weigh the many complex issues involved, examine their options, and make wise choices." The results found France to be providing the best overall health care, followed by Italy, Spain, Oman, Austria, and Japan. The U.S. health system, which consumes a higher portion of gross domestic product than any other country's system, ranked 37th (WHO, 2001a).

The analysis immediately met with strong criticism on methodological grounds. Many objected to countries being ranked on the basis of untested methods that they felt were also based on ethically unacceptable assumptions. For example, Almeida and associates (2001) wrote that the "measures of health inequalities and fair financing do not seem conceptually sound or useful to guide policy; of particular concern are some ethical aspects of the methodology for both these measures, whose implications for social policy are cause for concern." Similarly, Nolte and McKee (2003) challenged the report's assessment of overall performance of health systems as a composite measure and, in particular, the attribution of health attainment to health systems. Many determinants of health lie outside of health care, and the method used by the *World Health Report* has been criticized for inadequately allowing for them. Applying a measure known as "avoidable mortality" to 19 countries, Nolte and McKee found that "no country retained the same rank with both methods." Even the editor-in-chief of the report subsequently called the data "spurious" and "of no use for judging how well a health system performs" (Musgrove, 2003).

Although a second report with methodological refinements and new rankings never appeared, and criticisms continue about WHO's political judgment in undertaking such an exercise, the report was successful in drawing attention to the importance of better understanding health systems. The exercise spurred efforts to develop better methods and then to use them to unravel the black box of health systems' performance.

individuals (e.g., via the Internet). The health sector is one in which ever-changing knowledge and ideas are at the core of practice. We can thus speak of health sector reforms as being "globalized" to the extent that these ideas driving reform have become universally debated and, in many cases, adopted by diverse health systems around the world.

Although knowledge and ideas have flowed across societies throughout history, the technological advances that characterize contemporary forms of globalization have intensified this flow to an unprecedented degree. Global policy networks of influential individuals and institutions in turn shape which ideas are put into practice in health care financing and service delivery.

Conclusions: Health Protection and Promotion Amidst Globalization

This chapter has presented an introduction to an emerging field in global health. Globalization is a wide-ranging subject that cannot be dealt with in any depth within the scope of this book. The subject is plagued by definitional ambiguity, heated debate, and a limited, albeit growing, evidence base. Despite this, it is clear that the public health community is faced with fundamentally critical and, in some cases, unprecedented challenges. It is increasingly accepted that a transition from international to global public health is taking place, as evident in shifting patterns of health and disease within and across countries. More complex is the need to better understand, and respond effectively to, the causes of these health impacts. Coming to terms with globalization requires us to tackle its implications for the broad determinants of health, which quickly takes the public health community beyond its usual comfort zone. Such issues as trade and finance, agricultural subsidies, corporate restructuring, and international law are unavoidably bumping up against more familiar public health agendas. This requires the acquisition of new sets of knowledge, new skills to deploy them, and a seat at unfamiliar decision-making tables to voice public health concerns.

On some issues, there are signs that the public health community is rising to the challenge. High-profile efforts to globalize tobacco control and to strengthen global responses to infectious disease outbreaks have received deserved attention. Away from the spotlight, there have been efforts to globalize many essential public health functions. For example, the tenth revision of the *International Classification of Diseases* represents the ongoing development of common definitions of diseases and deaths carried out since 1893. Such initiatives represent an important example of how globalization of standards has led to better decision making and improved prospects for global surveillance of major risks and diseases, and smoothed the way toward standardized approaches to prevent and treat conditions. Similarly, common standards for surveillance have been developed for infectious diseases and for chronic disease risks and outcomes.

More controversial will be when public health advocates seek to tackle the causes of global health inequalities that are imbedded within the structures of globalization itself. As well as drawing much-needed attention to unacceptable gaps in health status and outcomes amidst a world of unprecedented economic wealth, political courage will be needed to point fingers at their wider causes. This may mean deeper forays into new areas for the public health community, notably international trade and finance, Third World debt, and corporate regulation and governance.

● ● ● **Discussion Questions**

1. Can you think of examples of how globalization might be affecting each of the broad determinants of health?

2. Can you name goods and services that could benefit or harm health if traded more readily?

3. How do you think your own specific field of work or interest within public health is being influenced by globalization? Are new policy initiatives needed to tackle the issues raised?

• • • **References**

Abel-Smith, B. (1986). The patterns of medical practice in England and the Third World. In S. J. Kingma (Ed.), *The principles and practice of primary health care*. Geneva, Switzerland: Christian Medical Commission and World Council of Churches.

Aitken, L., Buchan, J., Sochalski, J., Nichols, B., & Powell, M. (2004). Trends in international nurse migration. *Health Affairs, 23*(3), 69–77.

Albritton, D. I., et al. (2001). Technical summary. In J. T. Houghton, Y. Ding, D. J. Griggs, et al. (Eds.), *Climate change 2001: The scientific basis—Contribution of Working Group I to the Intergovernmental Panel on Climate Change third assessment report*. Cambridge, England: Cambridge University Press.

Almeida, C., Braveman, P., Gold, M., et al. (2001). Methodological concerns and recommendations on policy consequences of the World Health Report 2000. *Lancet, 357,* 1692–1697.

Babor, T. (2003). *Alcohol: No ordinary commodity. Research and public policy*. Oxford, England: Oxford University Press.

Berman, P., & Bossert, T. (2000). *A decade of health sector reform in developing countries: What have we learned?* Cambridge, MA: Harvard School of Public Health.

Bettcher, D., Subramaniam, C., Guindon, E., Perucic, A.-M., et al. (2003). *Confronting the tobacco epidemic in an era of trade liberalization*. Geneva, Switzerland: World Health Organization.

Bolling, C. (1998). U.S. foreign direct investment in the global processed food industries. In M. E. Burfisher & E. A. Jones, *Regional trade agreements and U.S. agriculture*. Washington, DC: U.S. Department of Agriculture.

Bolling, C. (2002). Globalization of the soft drink industry. *Agricultural Outlook, 297,* 25–27.

Bonn, D. (2003). Closing in on the cause of SARS. *Lancet Infectious Diseases, 3*(5), 268.

Buchan, J. (2003). *Here to stay? International nurses in the UK*. London: Royal College of Nursing.

Buchan, J., & Sochalski, J. (2004). The migration of nurses: Trends and policies. *Bulletin of the World Health Organization, 82*(8), 587–594.

Burtless, G. (1998), Technological change and international trade: How well do they explain the rise in U.S. income inequality? In J. Auerbach & R. Beleous (Eds.), *The inequality paradox: Growth of income disparity* (pp. 60–91). Washington, DC: National Planning Association.

Busfield, J. (2003). Globalization and the pharmaceutical industry revisited. *International Journal of Health Services, 33*(3), 581–605.

Centers for Disease Control and Prevention. (2001). Preventing and controlling tuberculosis along the U.S.-Mexico border: Work group report. *Pan American Journal of Public Health, 9*(3), 196–201.

Chawla, H., Diwan, N., & Joshi, K. (2003). Emerging trends in the world pharmaceutical market—a review. *Business Briefing: North American Pharmacotherapy*. http://www .bbriefings.com/pdf/790/8-chawla.pdf.

Clark, W. C., Kates, R. W., Richards, J. F., Mathews, J. T., Meyer, W. B., & Turner, B. L. (Eds.) (1990). *The Earth as transformed by human action*. Cambridge, England: Cambridge University Press.

Commission on Intellectual Property Rights. (2002, September). *Integrating intellectual property rights and development policy*. London: Commission on Intellectual Property Rights.

Dahlgren, G., & Whitehead, M. (1991). *Policies and strategies to promote social equity in health*. Stockholm, Sweden: Institute for Futures Studies.

Dawar, N., & Chattopadhyay, A. (2002). Rethinking marketing programs for emerging markets. *Long Range Planning, 35*(5), 457–474.

Dixon, J., & Preker, A. (1999). Learning from the NHS. *British Medical Journal, 319,* 1449–1450.

Dobson, A., & Carper, R. (1993). Biodiversity. *Lancet, 342,* 1096–1099.

Dugger, C. (2004, July 12). An exodus of African nurses puts infants and the ill in peril. *New York Times*.

Epstein, P. (2001). Climate change and emerging infectious diseases. *Microbes and Infection, 3,* 747–754.

Fidler, D. (2004). *SARS, governance, and the globalization of disease.* London: Palgrave Macmillan.

Food and Agriculture Organization. (2003). *The state of food insecurity in the world.* Rome: Food and Agriculture Organization.

Fukuyama, F. (1992). *The end of history and the last man.* New York: Free Press.

Gilmore, A. B., & McKee, M. (2004). Moving east: How the transnational tobacco industry gained entry to the emerging markets of the former Soviet Union. Part I: Establishing cigarette imports. *Tobacco Control, 13,* 143–150.

Githeko, A., Lindsay, S., Confalonieri, U., & Patz, J. (2000). Climate change and vector-borne diseases: A regional analysis. *Bulletin of the World Health Organization, 78*(9), 1136–1147.

Hales, S., de Wet, N., Maindonald, J., & Woodward, A. (2002). Potential effect of population and climate changes on global distribution of dengue fever: An empirical model. *Lancet, 360,* 830–834.

Hawkes, C. (2002). Marketing activities of global soft drink and fast food companies in emerging markets: A review. In World Health Organization, *Globalization, diets and noncommunicable diseases.* Geneva, Switzerland: World Health Organization.

Hawkes, C. (2004a). *The global regulatory environment around marketing food to children.* Geneva, Switzerland: World Health Organization.

Hawkes, C. (2004b). *The global regulatory environment around nutrition labels and health claims.* Geneva, Switzerland: World Health Organization.

Hong Kong International Airport. (2002). *Interesting facts and figures.* http://www .hongkongairport.com/eng/aboutus/facts.html.

Hong Kong Trade Development Council. (2000). *Practical tips for doing business with Hong Kong.* http://www.tdctrade.com/visitor/hkgate98.htm.

Hundley, R. O., Anderson, R. H., Bikson, T. K., & Neu, C. R. (2003). *The global course of the information revolution, recurring themes and regional variations.* Washington, DC: RAND Corporation.

International Chamber of Commerce. (1997). *Business and the global economy.* Statement on behalf of world business to the heads of state and government attending the Denver summit, 20–22 June 1997, Paris, 23 May 1997. http://www .iccwbo.org/home/shared_pages/gloecon.asp.

Jackson, M. C., Hastings, G., Wheeler, C., Eadie, D., & Mackintosh, A. M. (2002). Marketing alcohol to young people: Implications for industry regulation and research policy. *Addiction, 95*(Suppl. 4), S597–S608.

Joint Centre for Bioethics. (2003, August 13). *Ethics and SARS: Learning lessons from the Toronto experience.* Working paper, University of Toronto. http://www.utoronto.ca/jcb/SARS_ workingpaper.asp.

Jubilee 2000 Coalition. (2000, 18 August). *Leaders of indebted nations hold London debt summit.* http://www.jubilee2000uk.org/jubilee2000/ news/london180800.html.

Kataria, S. (2003, September 12). WHO chief: More SARS-like diseases likely. *Reuters Health.*

Lee, K. (2003). *Globalization and health: An introduction.* London: Palgrave Macmillan.

Lee, K., & Dodgson, R. (2002). Globalization and cholera: Implications for global governance. In K. Lee (Ed.), *Health impacts of globalization: Towards global governance* (pp. 123–143). London: Palgrave Macmillan.

Lee, K., Walt, G., & Haines, A. (2004). The challenge to improve global health: Financing the Millennium Development Goals. *Journal of the American Medical Association, 291*(21), 2636–2638.

Mackay, J., & Eriksen, M. (2002). *The tobacco atlas.* Geneva, Switzerland: World Health Organization.

Manning R. (2004). Development challenge. *OECD Observer, 243,* 36–37.

Martin, S. (2001). Heavy traffic: International migration in an era of globalization. *Brookings Review, 19*(4), 41–44.

Martineau, T., Decker, K., & Bundred, P. (2002). *Briefing note on international migration of health professionals: Levelling the playing field for developing country health systems.* Briefing paper, Liverpool School of Tropical Medicine, Liverpool, England.

McKenna, C. (2003). Pfizer buys Pharmacia for US$60 bn. *British Medical Journal, 325,* 123.

McMichael, A. J. (2001). *Human frontiers, environments and disease.* Cambridge, England: Cambridge University Press.

Mejia, A. (1978). Migration of physicians and nurses: A world wide picture. *International Journal of Epidemiology, 7*(3), 207–215.

Mills, A. (2001). *The challenge of health sector reform: What must governments do?* London: Palgrave Macmillan.

Musgrove, P. (2003). Judging health systems: Reflections on WHO's methods. *Lancet, 361,* 1817–1820.

Nesmith, J. (2003, October 1). SARS economic impact soared above health costs. *Atlanta Journal-Constitution.*

Nolte, E., & McKee, M. (2003). Measuring the health of nations: Analysis of mortality amenable to health care. *British Medical Journal, 327,* 1129–1133.

Organization for Economic Cooperation and Development. (2000). *Foreign direct investment, development and corporate responsibility.* Paris: Organization for Economic Cooperation and Development.

Padarath, A., Chamberlain, C., McCoy, D., Ntuli, A., Rowson, M., & Loewenson, R. (2003). *Health personnel in southern Africa: Confronting maldistribution and braindrain* (EQUINET Discussion Paper No. 3). Harari, South Africa: Health Systems Trust and Medact.

Saker, L., Lee, K., Cannito, B., Gilmore, A., & Campbell-Lendrum, D. (2004). *Globalization and infectious diseases: A review of the linkages.* Geneva, Switzerland: UNICEF/UNDP/World Bank/WHO Special Programme for Research and Training in Tropical Diseases.

Scholte, J. A. (2000). *Globalization: A critical introduction.* London: Macmillan.

Sellers, L. J. (2003, May). Fourth annual Pharm Exec 50. *Pharmaceutical Executive.*

Smith, R. (2004). Foreign direct investment and trade in health services: A review of the literature. *Social Science and Medicine, 59,* 2313–2323.

Smith, R., & Sommers, T. (2003). *Assessing the Economic Impact of Communicable Disease Outbreaks: The case of SARS.* Report prepared for the Strategy Unit, World Health Organization, Geneva, July.

Stilwell, B., Diallo, K., Zurn, P., Dal Poz, M, Adams, O., & Buchan, J. (2003). Developing evidence-based ethical policies on the migration of health workers: Conceptual and practical challenges. *Human Resources for Health, 1*(8). http://www.human-resources-health.com/content/1/1/8.

Taribusi, C., & Vickery, G. (1998). Globalization in the pharmaceutical industry, part 1. *International Journal of Health Services, 28*(1), 67–105.

Taurel, S. (2003, November 4). *Where drugs come from: The facts of life about pharmaceutical innovation.* Remarks to Hudson Institute Forum, National Press Club, Washington, DC.

United Nations Conference on Trade and Development. (2003). *World investment report 2003. FDI policies for development: National and international perspectives.* Geneva, Switzerland: UN Conference on Trade and Development.

United Nations Development Program. (1999). *Human development report 1999.* New York: UN Development Program.

United Nations Development Program. (2004). *Human development report 2004.* New York: UN Development Program.

United Nations Environment Program. (2001). *IPCC third assessment report. Climate change*

2001: The scientific basis. New York: UN Environment Program, Intergovernmental Panel on Climate Change.

U.S. Department of Transportation. (2000). *The changing face of transportation.* Washington, DC: Bureau of Transportation Statistics.

Walkenhorst, P. (2001). The geography of foreign direct investment in Poland's food industry. *Journal of Agricultural Economics, 52,* 71–86.

Whitton, C. (2004). *Processed agricultural exports led gains in U.S. agricultural exports between 1976 and 2002* (Electronic Output Report FAU-85-01). Washington, DC: U.S. Department of Agriculture, Economic Research Service.

World Health Organization. (2000, January 18). WHO, internationally-renowned economists launch commission on macroeconomics and health [Press release].

World Health Organization. (2001a, July 21). World Health Organization assesses the world's health systems [Press release].

World Health Organization. (2001b). *World health report 2000: Health systems—Improving perform-ance.* Geneva, Switzerland: World Health Organization.

World Health Organization. (2001c). *Globalization, TRIPS and access to pharma-ceuticals* (WHO Policy Perspectives on Medicines No. 3). Geneva, Switzerland: World Health Organization.

World Health Organization. (2002). *Global crises—global solutions: Managing public health emergencies of international concern through the revised International Health Regulations.* Geneva, Switzerland: International Health Regulations Revision Project.

World Health Organization. (2003). *Global Outbreak Alert and Response Network.* http://www.who.int/csr/outbreaknetwork/en/.

World Health Organization. (2004a, March 16). Drug resistant tuberculosis levels ten times higher in eastern Europe and Central Asia [Press release].

World Health Organization. (2004b). *Summary of probable SARS cases with onset of illness between 1 November 2002 to 31 July 2003.* http://www.who.int/csr/sars/country/table2004_04_21/en.

World Bank. (1993). *World development report 1993: Investing in health.* Washington, DC: International Bank for Reconstruction and Development.

World Trade Organization. (2003). *TRIPS and pharmaceutical patents.* Geneva, Switzerland: World Trade Organization.

Acronyms

ACC/SCN Administrative Committee on Coordination/Subcommittee on Nutrition (United Nations)

ACF Action Contre la Faim

AIDS acquired immunodeficiency syndrome

ALRI acute lower respiratory infection

ARI acute respiratory infection

ARV antiretroviral therapy

ASEAN Association of Southeast Asian Nations

AZT zidovudine

BBC British Broadcasting Corporation

BCG bacillus Calmette-Guérin (vaccine)

BMI body mass index

CBH community-based health

CBHI community-based health insurance

CCM country coordination mechanism

CCMD Chinese Classification of Mental Disorders

CDC Centers for Disease Control and Prevention

CDR case disability ratio

CE complex emergency

CFR case fatality ratio

CHD coronary artery disease

CHE complex humanitarian emergency

CHW community health worker

CMD common mental disorder

CMR crude mortality rate

COPD chronic obstructive pulmonary disease

CRA comparative risk assessment

CSO civil society organization

CSR corporate social responsibility

CVD cardiovascular disease

CVI Childhood Vaccine Initiative

DALE disability-adjusted life expectancy

DALY disability-adjusted life year

DDT dichlorodiphenyltrichloroethane

DFID Department for International Development (United Kingdom)

DFLE disability-free life expectancy

DHS demographic and health survey

DOTS directly observed treatment, short course

DPSEEA driving force-pressure-state-exposure-effect-action

DPT diptheria, pertussis, tetanus vaccine

DRC Democratic Republic of Congo

DSM-IV *Diagnostic Statistical Manual of the American Psychiatric Association, Fourth Edition*

ECOSOC Economic and Social Council

EHRA environmental health risk assessment

EIA environmental impact assessment

EMRO Eastern Mediterranean Regional Office (WHO)

EPI Expanded Program on Immunization

EPIDOS European Patent Information and Documentation Systems

ERA environmental risk assessment

ERAP Epilepsy Rapid Assessment Procedures

ERHI employment-related health insurance

ERR economic rate of return

ETEC enterotoxigenic *Escherichia coli*

ETS environmental tobacco smoke

EU European Union

FAO Food and Agriculture Organization

FCTC Framework Convention on Tobacco Control

FDI foreign direct investment

GAVI Global Alliance for Vaccines and Immunizations

GBD Global Burden of Disease

GBS Global Burden of Disease Studies

GDP gross domestic product

GNI gross national income

GNP gross national product

GOARN Global Outbreak Alert and Response Network

GYTS Global Youth Tobacco Survey

HALE health-adjusted life expectancy

HeaLY healthy life years

HIV human immunodeficiency virus

HIV/AIDS human immunodeficiency virus/acquired immunodeficiency syndrome

HMO health maintenance organization

IARC International Agency for Research on Cancer

ICCC Innovative Care for Chronic Conditions

ICD *International Classification of Diseases*

ICD-10 *International Classification of Diseases-Tenth Revision*

ICF International Classification of Functioning, Disability and Health

ICIDH International Classification of Impairments, Disabilities, and Handicaps

ICPD International Conference on Population Development

ICRC International Committee of the Red Cross

IDD iodine deficiency disorders

IDP internally displaced person

IFI international financial institutions

IFPMA International Federation of Pharmaceutical Manufacturers Association

IGO international governmental organization

IHR International Health Regulations

IMCI Integrated Management of Childhood Illness

IMF International Monetary Fund

IMR infant mortality rates

INCAP Instituto Nutricional de Central America y Panama

INGCAT International Nongovernmental Coalition Against Tobacco

INTERFET International Force in East Timor

IPV injectable polio vaccine

IVACG International Vitamin A Consultative Group

LFA local fund agent

MAC *Mycobacterium avium* complex

MDGs Millennium Development Goals

MDR-TB multi-drug resistant tuberculosis

MISP minimum initial service package

MOH Ministry of Health

MSAs medical savings accounts

MSF Médecins sans Frontières

MUAC middle upper arm circumference

NCD noncommunicable disease

NGO nongovernmental organization

NID National Immunization Day

NPV net present value

OCHA Office for the Coordination of Humanitarian Affairs

OCP Onchocerciasis Control Program

OECD Organization for Economic Cooperation and Development

OPV oral polio vaccine

ORS oral rehydration solution

ORT oral rehydration therapy

PAHO Pan American Health Organization

PCBs polychlorinated biphenyls

PEM protein-energy malnutrition

PEPFAR President Bush's Emergency Plan for AIDS Relief

PEV Expanded Program on Immigration (French)

PHC primary health care

PPI Private Participation in Infrastructure

PPYL productive years of life lost

PR Principal Recipient

PSAC Policy Strategy Advisory Committee

PSR pressure-state-response

QALY quality-adjusted life year

QWB quality of well-being

RAP Rapid Assessment Procedures

RARE Rapid Assessment, Response and Evaluation

RBM Roll Back Malaria Partnership

RCT randomized controlled trial

RDA Recommended Dietary Allowance

RENAMO Resistência Nacional Moçambicana

RHU refugee health unit

SARS severe acute respiratory syndrome

SDR social discount rate

SFP supplementary feeding program

SIDA Swedish International Development Agency

SIPs sector investment programs

STEPS stepwise approach to surveillance

SWAp sectorwide approach program

SWOT strengths, weaknesses, opportunities, and threats

TAC Treatment Action Campaign

TB tuberculosis

TEA total exposure assessment

TFC transnational food companies

TFP therapeutic feeding programs

TFR total fertility rate

TGR total goiter rate

TNCs transnational corporations

TRIPS Trade Related Aspects of Intellectual Property Rights

TRL Transport Research Laboratory

TT tetanus toxoid

UCHA United Nations Office for Coordination of Humanitarian Affairs

UICC International Union Against Cancer (French)

UN United Nations

UNAIDS United Nations Programme on HIV/AIDS

UNCHR United Nations Commission on Human Rights

UNCTAD United Nations Conference on Trade and Development

UNDP United Nations Development Program

UNFPA United Nations Population Fund

UNICEF United Nations Children's Fund

USAID United States Agency for International Development

USI universal salt iodization

UVR ultraviolet radiation

VAC vitamin A capsule

WCH women's and children's health

WDR *World Development Report*

WHA World Health Assembly

WHO World Health Organization

WHR *World Health Report*

WPRO Western Pacific Regional Office (WHO)

WSMI World Self Medication Industry

WTO World Trade Organization

YLD years lived with disability

YLL years of life lost

Index

e denotes exhibits; *f* denotes figures; *t* denotes tables